EVIDENCE-BASED
SURGERY

EVIDENCE-BASED
SURGERY

Toby A. Gordon, ScD

Associate Professor, Surgery, Health Policy and Management,
Johns Hopkins University
Vice-President, Planning and Marketing,
The Johns Hopkins Hospital
Baltimore, Maryland

John L. Cameron, MD, FACS

Alfred Blalock Professor and Chairman
Department of Surgery
Johns Hopkins University School of Medicine
Surgeon-in-Chief
The Johns Hopkins Hospital
Baltimore, Maryland

2000
B.C. Decker Inc.
Hamilton • London

B.C. Decker Inc.
4 Hughson Street South
P.O. Box 620, L.C.D. 1
Hamilton, Ontario L8N 3K7
Tel: 905-522-7017; 1-800-568-7281
Fax: 905-522-7839
E-mail: info@bcdecker.com
Website: http://www.bcdecker.com

00 01 02 03 PC 6 5 4 3 2 1

ISBN 1–55009–116–6

Printed in Canada

Sales and Distribution

United States
B.C. Decker Inc.
P.O. Box 785
Lewiston, NY U.S.A. 14092-0785
Tel: 905-522-7017/1-800-568-7281
Fax: 905-522-7839
E-mail: info@bcdecker.com
Website: http://www.bcdecker.com

Canada
B.C. Decker Inc.
4 Hughson Street South
P.O. Box 620, L.C.D. 1
Hamilton, Ontario L8N 3K7
Tel: 905-522-7017/1-800-568-7281
Fax: 905-522-7839
E-mail: info@bcdecker.com
Website: http://www.bcdecker.com

Japan
Igaku-Shoin Ltd.
Foreign Publications Department
3-24-17 Hongo, Bunkyo-ku,
Tokyo 113-8719, Japan
Tel: 3-3817-5676
Fax: 3-3815-6776
E-mail: fd@igaku.shoin.co.jp

U.K., Europe, Scandinavia, Middle East
Blackwell Science Ltd.
Osney Mead
Oxford OX2 0EL
United Kingdom
Tel: 44-1865-206206
Fax: 44-1865-721205
E-mail: info@blackwell-science.com

Australia, New Zealand
Blackwell Science Asia Pty, Ltd.
54 University Street
Carlton, Victoria 3053
Australia
Tel: 03-9347-0300
Fax: 03-9349-3016
E-mail: info@blacksci.asia.com.au

South Korea
Seoul Medical Scientific Books Co.
C.P.O. Box 9794
Seoul 100-697
Seoul, Korea
Tel: 82-2925-5800
Fax: 82-2927-7283

South America
Ernesto Reichmann, Distribuidora
  de Livros Ltda.
Rua Coronel Marques
335-Tatuape, 03440-000
Sao Paulo-SP-Brazil
Tel/Fax: 011-218-2122

Foreign Rights
John Scott & Co.
International Publishers' Agency
P.O. Box 878
Kimberton, PA 19442
Tel: 610-827-1640
Fax: 610-827-1671

Notice: The authors and publisher have made every effort to ensure that the patient care recommended herein, including choice of drugs and drug dosages, is in accord with the accepted standard and practice at the time of publication. However, since research and regulation constantly change clinical standards, the reader is urged to check the product information sheet included in the package of each drug, which includes recommended doses, warnings, and contraindications. This is particularly important with new or infrequently used drugs.

Contributors

Eric B. Bass, MD, MPH
Associate Professor of Medicine and Health
    Policy and Management
Johns Hopkins University
Baltimore, Maryland
Critical Evaluation of Evidence

William A. Baumgartner, MD, FACS
Professor of Surgery
Johns Hopkins University School
    of Medicine
Cardiac Surgeon in Charge
The Johns Hopkins Hospital
Baltimore, Maryland
Cardiac Surgery

Henry Brem, MD
Professor of Neurosurgery, Ophthalmology,
    and Oncology
Johns Hopkins University
Director, Neurosurgical Oncology
Director, Hunterian Neurosurgical Research
    Center
Vice Chairman, Department of
    Neurosurgery
The Johns Hopkins Hospital
Baltimore, Maryland
Neurosurgery

James F. Burdick, MD, FACS
Professor of Surgery
Johns Hopkins University School
    of Medicine
Baltimore, Maryland
Transplantation

Gregg P. Burleyson, RN, MHS
Project Leader, Casemix Information
    Management Department
The Johns Hopkins Hospital
Baltimore, Maryland
Key Economic Outcomes Measures

John L. Cameron, MD, FACS
Alfred Blalock Professor and Chairman
Department of Surgery
Johns Hopkins University School of Medicine
Surgeon-in-Chief
The Johns Hopkins Hospital
Baltimore, Maryland
*Evolution of Modern Surgery; Origins of
    Evidence-Based Surgery*

Kurtis A. Campbell, MD
Assistant Professor of Surgery
Johns Hopkins University School of Medicine
Baltimore, Maryland
Trauma

H. Ballentine Carter, MD
Professor of Urology and Oncology
Johns Hopkins University School of Medicine
Director, Adult Oncology
The Johns Hopkins Hospital
Baltimore, Maryland
Urology

Michael A. Choti, MD, FACS
Associate Professor of Surgery and Oncology
Johns Hopkins University School of Medicine
The Johns Hopkins Hospital
Baltimore, Maryland
Rectal Carcinoma; Hepatobiliary Surgery

Paul M. Colombani, MD, FACS
Professor of Pediatric Surgery
Johns Hopkins University
Pediatric Surgeon-in-Charge
The Johns Hopkins Hospital
Baltimore, Maryland
Pediatric Surgery

Edward E. Cornwell III, MD, FACS, FCCM
Associate Professor of Surgery
Johns Hopkins University
Chief, Adult Trauma Services
Johns Hopkins Medical Institutions
Baltimore, Maryland
Trauma

Mohammed Benn Debba, MD
Assistant Professor, Neurosurgery
Johns Hopkins University School of Medicine
Baltimore, Maryland
Neurosurgery

William C. Dooley, MD
Associate Professor of Surgery
Johns Hopkins University School of Medicine
Director, Breast Center
The Johns Hopkins Hospital
Baltimore, Maryland
Breast Surgery

Dennis Dunn, PhD
Sachs Group
Evanston, Illinois
Administrative Data and Evidence-Based Surgery

Thomas Elkins, MD
Professor of Gynecology and Obstetrics
Johns Hopkins School of Medicine
Director, Gynecological Specialties
The Johns Hopkins Hospital and Medical
    Institutions
Baltimore, Maryland
Gynecologic Surgery

Jonathan I. Epstein, MD
Professor of Pathology, Urology, and Oncology
Johns Hopkins University Medical Institutions
Assistant Director of Surgical Pathology
Director of Consult Services
The Johns Hopkins Hospital
Baltimore, Maryland
Surgical Pathology

Harold E. Fox, MD, MSc
Professor, Johns Hopkins University School
    of Medicine
The Johns Hopkins Hospital
Johns Hopkins Bayview Medical Center
Howard Count General Hospital
Baltimore, Maryland
Gynecologic Surgery

David S. Friedman, MD, MPH
Assistant Professor, Ophthalmology
Johns Hopkins University School of Medicine
Wilmer Eye Institute
The Johns Hopkins Hospital
Baltimore, Maryland
Ophthalmic Surgery

Steven B. Goldin, MD, PhD
Fellow, Surgery
The Johns Hopkins Hospital
Baltimore, Maryland
Colon Surgery

Toby A. Gordon, ScD
Associate Professor, Surgery, Health Policy
    and Management
Johns Hopkins University
Vice-President, Planning and Marketing
The Johns Hopkins Hospital
Baltimore, Maryland
*Evolution of Modern Surgery; Origins of
    Evidence-Based Surgery; Risk Adjustment*

Peter S. Greene, MD, FACS
Associate Professor, Cardiac Surgery and
    Biomedical Information Science
Johns Hopkins University
Division of Cardiac Surgery
Johns Hopkins Medical Institutions
Baltimore, Maryland
*Leveraging Information Technology;
    Cardiac Surgery*

John W. Harmon, MD
Professor, Surgery
Johns Hopkins Bayview Medical Center
Baltimore, Maryland
Colon Surgery

Richard F. Heitmiller, MD, FACS
Associate Professor, Surgery and Oncology
Johns Hopkins University
Chief, Division of Thoracic Surgery
Johns Hopkins Medical Institutions
Esophageal Surgery

Ginny Hsieh, PhD, MPH
Risk Adjustment

John D. Hundt, MHS
Director, Business Development
Planning and Marketing Department
Johns Hopkins Health System
Baltimore, Maryland
*Stakeholder Perspectives; Key Economic
    Outcomes Measures*

David S. Hungerford, MD
Professor, Orthopaedic Surgery
Chief, Arthritis Surgery
Johns Hopkins
Baltimore, Maryland
Orthopaedic Surgery

Lynne C. Jones, PhD
Assistant Professor of Orthopaedic Surgery
Johns Hopkins University School of Medicine
Baltimore, Maryland
Orthopaedic Surgery

Howard S. Kaufman, MD
Assistant Professor, Surgery
The Johns Hopkins Hospital
Baltimore, Maryland
Colon Surgery

Richard P. Kidwell, JD
Managing Attorney, Claims and Litigation
Johns Hopkins Health System and Hospital
Baltimore, Maryland
Legal Issues

Joseph D. Kronz, MD
Chief Resident in Pathology
The Johns Hopkins Hospital
Baltimore, Maryland
Surgical Pathology

David E. Lilienfeld, MD, MPH, MS Engin
Associate Director, Epidemiology
Bristol Myers Squibb Corporation
Princeton, New Jersey
*Health Policy Research: Information Guiding
    Clinical Decision Making at the Population
    Level; Tools and Techniques: Study Design*

Keith D. Lillemoe, MD, FACS
Professor of Surgery
Johns Hopkins University School of Medicine
Active Staff, Surgery
The Johns Hopkins Hospital
Baltimore, Maryland
Stakeholder Perspectives; Gastric Surgery

Pamela A. Lipsett, MD, FACS
Associate Professor, Surgery, Anesthesiology
    and Critical Care Medicine
Johns Hopkins University School of Medicine
The Johns Hopkins Hospital
Baltimore, Maryland
Surgical Critical Care

Donlin M. Long, MD, PhD
Harvey Cushing Professor of Neurosurgery
Director, Department of Neurosurgery
Johns Hopkins University School of Medicine
Neurosurgeon-in-Chief
The Johns Hopkins Hospital
Baltimore, Maryland
Neurosurgery

Alan Lyles, ScD, MPH
Assistant Professor, Health Policy and
    Management
Department of Health and Policy Management
Johns Hopkins School of Public Health
Baltimore, Maryland
Key Economic Outcomes Measures

Steven F. Mandell, MS
Johns Hopkins University
Johns Hopkins Health System
Baltimore, Maryland
Electronic Patient Records

Paul N. Manson, MD, FACS
Professor and Chief, Division of Plastic,
    Reconstructive and Maxillofacial Surgery
The Johns Hopkins Hospital
Baltimore, Maryland
Plastic Surgery

Elizabeth Martinez, MD
Assistant Professor, Anesthesiology and
    Critical Care Medicine
Johns Hopkins Medical Institutions
Baltimore, Maryland
Evidence-Based Anesthesiology

Lord McColl, MS, FRCS, FACS
Professor, University of London
Guy's Hospital
London, United Kingdom
Evidence-Based Surgery in the United Kingdom

Laurence B. McCullough, PhD
Professor of Medicine and Medical Ethics
Baylor College of Medicine
Houston, Texas
Ethical Issues

Helen Bowman Miller, MS
Senior Health Analyst
Life Metrix
McLean, Virginia
Risk Adjustment; Hepatobiliary Surgery

Mehrdad M. Mofid, MD
Fellow, Division of Plastic, Reconstructive and
    Maxillofacial Surgery
The Johns Hopkins Hospital
Baltimore, Maryland
Plastic Surgery

Fredrick J. Montz, MD, KM
Professor in Gynecology and Obstetrics and
   Oncology
Johns Hopkins University School of Medicine
Director, Gynecologic Oncology
The Johns Hopkins Hospital and Medical
   Institutions
Baltimore, Maryland
Gynecologic Surgery

Andrew M. Munster, MD, FRCS, FACS
Professor of Surgery and Plastic Surgery
Johns Hopkins University School of Medicine
Director, Baltimore Regional Burn Center
Baltimore, Maryland
Burns

Mark J. Ott, MD
Instructor, Harvard Medical School
Assistant in Surgery, Massachusetts General
   Hospital
Boston, Massachusetts
Rectal Carcinoma

Carl A. Patow, MD, MPH
Executive Director, Health Partners Institute
   for Medical Education
Clinical Associate Professor, University of
   Minnesota
Minneapolis, Minneapolis
Otolaryngology, Head and Neck Surgery

Bruce A. Perler, MD, FACS
Professor of Surgery
Johns Hopkins University School of Medicine
The Johns Hopkins Hospital
Baltimore, Maryland
Vascular Surgery

Gary Pickens, PhD
Sachs Group
Evanston, Illinois
Administrative Data and Evidence-Based Surgery

Henry A. Pitt, MD, FACS
Professor and Chairman, Surgery
Medical College of Wisconsin
Froedtert Memorial Lutheran Hospital
Milwaukee, Wisconsin
Hepatobiliary Surgery

Joanne E. Pollak, JD
General Counsel
Johns Hopkins Medicine
Baltimore, Maryland
Legal Issues

Neil R. Powe, MD, MPH, MBA
Director, Welch Center for Prevention,
   Epidemiology and Clinical Research
Professor of Medicine, Epidemiology, and
   Health Policy and Management
Johns Hopkins University School of Medicine
Baltimore, Maryland
Practice Guidelines: Evidence and Intuition

Peter Pronovost, MD, PhD
Assistant Professor, Anesthesia and Critical
   Care Medicine, Surgery, Health Policy and
   Management
Johns Hopkins University School of Medicine
Baltimore, Maryland
Evidence-Based Anesthesiology

Stephanie L. Reel, MBA
Chief Information Officer, Clinical
   Information Systems
Johns Hopkins University
Johns Hopkins Health System
Baltimore, Maryland
Electronic Patient Records

Charles Reuland, MHS
Administrator, Department of Medicine
Johns Hopkins University School of Medicine
Baltimore, Maryland
Stakeholder Perspectives

Mark Richardson, MD
Professor and Deputy Director, Otolaryncology,
   Head and Neck Surgery
Johns Hopkins University School of Medicine
Baltimore, Maryland
Otolaryngology, Head and Neck Surgery

Haya R. Rubin, MD, PhD
Associate Professor of Medicine
Johns Hopkins School of Medicine
Director, Quality of Care Research
The Johns Hopkins Hospital
Baltimore, Maryland
Framework for Evidence-Based Surgery

Michael Sachs
Sachs Group
Evanston, Illinois
Administrative Data and Evidence-Based Surgery

Ron Sauder, BA
Former Director of Consumer Health
   Information, Johns Hopkins University
   School of Medicine
Baltimore, Maryland
*Consumer Health Information and Evidence-
   Based Surgery*

Wendy W. Saunders, MA
Research Associate, Biomedical Information
  Sciences
Johns Hopkins University
Baltimore, Maryland
Breast Surgery

Oliver D. Schein, MD, MPH
Professor in Ophthalmology and
  Epidemiology
Johns Hopkins University School of Medicine
Baltimore, Maryland
Ophthalmic Surgery

Lillie Shockney, RN, BS, MAS
Director, Breast Cancer Outreach Education
The Johns Hopkins Hospital
Baltimore, Maryland
Breast Surgery

Julie Ann Sosa, MD
Fellow, Department of Surgery
Johns Hopkins University School of Medicine
Senior Resident, Department of Surgery
The Johns Hopkins Hospital
Baltimore, Maryland
Clinical Outcomes Measures; Endocrine Surgery

Robert J. Spence, MD, FACS
Associate Professor of Surgery
Johns Hopkins University School of Medicine
Chief, Division of Plastic Surgery
Johns Hopkins Bayview Medical Center
Baltimore, Maryland
Plastic Surgery

Mark A. Talamini, MD, FACS
Associate Professor of Surgery
Johns Hopkins University School of Medicine
Baltimore, Maryland
Minimally Invasive Surgery

Sean Tunis, MD, MSc
Assistant Professor of Medicine
Program for Medical Technology and Practice
  Assessment
Johns Hopkins University School of Medicine
Baltimore, Maryland
Practice Guidelines: Evidence and Intuition

Robert Udelsman, MD, FACS
Professor of Surgery and Oncology
Johns Hopkins University School of Medicine
Director, Endocrine and Oncologic Surgery
The Johns Hopkins Hospital
Baltimore, Maryland
Endocrine Surgery

Albert W. Wu, MD, MPH
Associate Professor, Medicine and Health
  Policy and Management
Johns Hopkins University School of Medicine
Baltimore, Maryland
Patient-Reported Outcomes Measures

Suzanne M. Wyatt, MPH
Research Associate
Association of American Medical Colleges
Washington, DC
*Health Policy Research: Information Guiding
  Clinical Decision Making at the Population
  Level*

Stephen C. Yang, MD
Assistant Professor of Surgery and Oncology
Johns Hopkins University School of Medicine
The Johns Hopkins Hospital
Baltimore, Maryland
Thoracic Surgery

Charles J. Yeo, MD, FACS
Professor of Surgery and Oncology
Johns Hopkins University School of Medicine
The Johns Hopkins Hospital
Baltimore, Maryland
Pancreatic Surgery

Howard A. Zacur, MD, PhD
Professor of Reproductive Endocrinology
Theodore and Ingrid Baromki Professor
Johns Hopkins University School of Medicine
Baltimore, Maryland
Gynecologic Surgery

Herbert J. Zeh III, MD
Fellow, Surgery
The Johns Hopkins Hospital
Baltimore, Maryland
Hepatobiliary Surgery

Dedicated to the memory of
Dr. William Stewart Halsted, who contributed greatly to the foundation
upon which evidence-based surgery rests.

Toby A. Gordon
John L. Cameron

Preface

The evidence-based medicine movement has recently experienced exponential growth. The continuous striving of the medical profession to improve health care, the rising demand for health care services, the close scrutiny by government and managed care of health care costs, and the increasingly knowledgeable health care consumer have all contributed to this growth.

Contemporary textbooks on evidence-based medicine focus on the acquisition, evaluation, and application of evidence for the care of the individual patient. This text has a different orientation. The art and science of surgery are dependent on both intuition and evidence, both empirical and experimental. Groundwork must be laid before surgical educators can be called upon to translate the vast body of surgical knowledge into an evidence-based medicine schema. This text focuses on what is required to produce and understand evidence. It reviews the history and evolution of evidence-based surgery, research methods, and study design. For a variety of surgical specialties, seminal works that have influenced surgical practice for the specialty are examined. Case studies of evidence-based surgical research are included to promote an understanding of the many techniques available to produce evidence for surgery.

Surgery as a discipline has perhaps been slower than other specialties to embrace evidence-based principles. Scientific advances in surgery were based on research in anatomy and physiology, and on empiric evidence derived from the laboratory, the operating room, or the patient's bedside. The great progress in surgery in the late nineteenth century and early twentieth centuries in Europe and in the United States took place in a variety of centers where schools of surgery developed. These schools generally were centered around great surgeons who often were technically extraordinarily gifted, had exploring and innovative minds, and had an ability to arrive at intuitive conclusions. The dogma surrounding such schools survived for generations, as one group of surgeons trained and influenced by the great surgeon went out and trained a second generation, which continued the process of educating others. These surgical schools were very disciplined, and it was often difficult for trainees to challenge concepts that had become well established. Thus, for generations surgeons treated patients and carried out operative procedures as they had been taught. The concept of challenging a well-accepted surgical tenet was generally foreign to the discipline. For example, the Halsted radical mastectomy was proposed and promulgated by Dr. William Stewart Halsted, the most influential and productive surgeon that the United States has produced. To surgeons of his day, his operation for cancer of the breast was obviously the perfect operation, providing wide local margins around the tumor and an en bloc removal of the draining nodal basin. It was so clearly the correct operation that for many decades the procedure went unchallenged. Finally, a variety of clinical studies showed that conservative approaches—first the modified radical mastectomy, then lumpectomy, axillary node dissection, and radiotherapy—achieved comparable results. Only after numerous clinical studies, many of which were prospective and randomized, were surgeons willing to accept that what they had learned during their residency training had to be abandoned. Halsted, in the 1904 Annual Address in Medicine at Yale University, summarized well how the lack of evidence-based surgical practice in prior times should be viewed, and his words are as relevant now as they were then: "Tempted to belittle by comparisons the performance of our progenitors, we should remember that the condition of surgery at all times reflected the knowledge and thought of the ablest minds in the profession."[1]

Surgeons today are prepared to challenge the dogma of yesterday. Surgical science, which rests on a strong foundation of laboratory and clinical research, can now be broadened to include the armamentarium of evidence-based medicine to advance surgical knowledge. The value of collecting evidence from sources as varied as population databases and prospective randomized double blind studies is understood and appreciated. In most institutions, such evidence collecting and analysis has supplanted the rote passing down of information by surgeons who, throughout their careers, have practiced in a particular fashion primarily because that was the way they had been trained.

This book has been written for surgeons and others as an introduction to the concept of evidence-based surgery. We hope that they will benefit by reading this introductory text, which focuses on what evidence-based surgery is, how data are collected and evaluated, and how such data are influencing surgical care.

We gratefully acknowledge the contributions from our colleagues at Johns Hopkins and at many other institutions. We are especially appreciative of the thoughtful commentary from Dr. Gert Brieger, MD, PhD, MPH, William H. Welch Professor of the History of Science, Medicine and Technology. We give special thanks for the steadfast efforts of Karen Diesenberg and Tim Zeffiro in all aspects of the editing process, and for the assistance of Andy Harrison of the Alan Mason Chesney Archives in obtaining illustrations to illuminate the text. Last, our heartfelt thanks to Brian Decker, our publisher, whose support, interest and encouragement have enabled an idea to become a reality.

TAG
JLC

March 2000

---

[1] Halsted WS. The training of the surgeon. The Bulletin of The Johns Hopkins Hospital 1904;15(162).

Contents

———⋄———

PRACTICE OF EVIDENCE-BASED SURGERY

PRINCIPLES OF EVIDENCE-BASED SURGERY

CHAPTER 1

Evolution of Modern Surgery

Toby A. Gordon, ScD, and John L. Cameron, MD, FACS

Surgery's origins and history have been extensively documented, revealing the myths, prejudices, and scientific basis of surgical practice. From ancient hieroglyphics and etchings on papyrus to medical textbooks and journals and the World Wide Web, information on the techniques and results of surgery has been written and disseminated to guide and influence the best practices of surgery. From this vast body of historical information, what can be considered the origins of evidence-based surgery?

Narrowly defined, evidence-based surgery can be considered a form of practice in which the surgeon accesses relevant, state-of-the-art research findings to guide the care of the individual patient. More broadly defined, beyond the care of the single patient, evidence-based surgery can also include population-based outcomes research on the interplay of clinical, economic, and patient-reported data. Spanning thousands of years and continually evolving from the mystical beliefs of ancient times to the inception of scientific reasoning, surgical evidence has advanced from anecdote and observation, case studies, and reports of patient series to sophisticated laboratory, clinical, and epidemiologic research. The principles of medicine, mathematics, and public health, convened by the forces of economics, have given rise to evidence-based surgery to educate and influence stakeholders—patients, surgeons, referring physicians, payers, and government regulators. Further, evidence-based surgery has served to guide informed policy relating to the reimbursement of hospitals and physicians, the training of physicians, the licensure of facilities, and the credentialing of physicians and other health care providers.

This chapter describes the origins of evidence-based surgery and examines the progression of the use of evidence in the advancement of the science of surgery. Discussion includes the history of surgical reasoning; the inception of the modern surgical era, including the professionalization of surgery; the growth of the medical literature and specialty societies in the United States, especially the American Surgical Association; and Codman's pioneering efforts to focus on end results. A case study of breast surgery is provided to illustrate the progression of the use of evidence in surgery.

THE HISTORY OF SURGICAL REASONING

The recorded medical history of ancient civilizations reveals, not surprisingly, little of an evidence-based approach to medicine. The oldest medical document from Thebes, dated 1600 BC, makes reference to diseases such as breast abscess, trauma, and infected wounds, based solely on observational data.[1] Anatomic research was first recorded in Alexandria (332 BC), but religious beliefs about supernatural influences on physical ailments prevailed. Hippocrates (circa 460 to 377 BC) challenged these beliefs, advancing the philosophy of humoral interactions with earth, air, water, and fire. This led to the development of a tripartite classification of diseases into those curable by medicine, the knife, and fire (Figure 1–1). Ascribed to Hippocrates are works on fractures, dislocations, and surgical disorders. During Greek and Roman antiquity, surgeons were specialists called upon when diet and drugs failed.[2] Hundreds of years later, Galen (131 to 201 AD) studied anatomy, adding to Hippocrates'

Figure 1–1 Hippocrates, whose place in surgical history was described by Halsted as follows: ". . . distinguished and scholarly men, as well as charlatans and barbers, have practised the art in almost unbroken succession from the time of Hippocrates (460–375 BC) to the present day." *The Works of Hippocrates*, the earliest book on medicine from the Greek school, is thought to have reflected the accumulated knowledge in medicine from the theories, practices, traditions, and legends of the prior 1,500 years. From an 1809 engraving by Chapman, from an ancient intaglio. (Reproduced with permission from Lambert SW, Goodwin GM. Medical leaders: from Hippocrates to Osler. Indianapolis: Bobbs-Merrill Company; 1929.)

concepts of humoral and universal elements the notion of a spirit controlling the whole. These beliefs governed all aspects of medical thinking. Surgery was separated from medicine during or before Galen's time and remained separate for 1500 years until Vesalius (1514 to 1565 AD), whose published text illustrated all that was known about anatomy (Figure 1–2).

In the Middle Ages, monks maintained the medical profession by caring for the sick, teaching, and copying manuscripts, but *materia medica* were less important than prayer and belief in miracles for cure, with one or more saints invoked for nearly every disease. The Council of Rheims (1131 AD) prohibited monks and the clergy from practicing medicine; this, along with the growth of cities and the rise of universities in the eleventh and twelfth centuries, wrested medicine from monastic influence. There is debate today among historians with regard to the Church's stance on surgery; some interpret the Council of Tours (1163) to be a ban on human vivisection while others reject the idea as popular myth. In the thirteenth and fourteenth centuries, medicine was taught in universities whereas surgeons were less educated and were considered a lower class than physicians, as evidenced in England by their union with barbers in a guild. By the fifteenth century, the study of the human body had been approved, and anatomic and pathologic research was advancing the science of surgery. With the advances brought about by the study of anatomy and the growing panoply of surgical interventions came an early intersection of medical science and economics: surgeons treated certain surgical techniques in a proprietary manner, selling this information for "extraordinary amounts."[3]

During the Renaissance (characterized as a time of individual scientific endeavors rather than organized efforts), medical, not surgical problems predominated, and surgeons did not enjoy the status of physicians. Medical teaching flourished in the European universities. Some

Figure 1–2 Frontispiece of *De Humani Corporis Fabrica Libri Septem* of Vesalius, reproduced from the second edition published in 1555. Vesalius is shown with his hand on the abdomen of a cadaver. The *Fabrica*, an anatomy text, was illustrated with numerous woodcuts by John Stephen deCalcar, a pupil of Titian. Not limited to anatomy, it also described surgical and medical treatments. Although the publication of the book was met with more abuse than praise, Vesalius became famous; but his disgust over the attacks on his work caused him to burn his notebooks and the medical books in his library. While anatomic study in Vesalius' time was thought to have advanced surgery, infections prevented the effects of advanced surgical techniques from being immediately apparent. (Reproduced with permission from Lambert SW, Goodwin GM. Medical leaders: from Hippocrates to Osler. Indianapolis: Bobbs-Merrill Company; 1929.)

Figure 1–3 William Hunter (1718 to 1783), noted London surgeon, lecturer, and anatomist in the eighteenth century, a time when clinical advances in medicine came about as the result of enhanced knowledge of separate diseases. William Hunter built up a large practice in obstetrics, established a private school of anatomy, and conducted anatomic research in a private dissecting room on his premises. (Reproduced with permission of the Institute of the History of Medicine, The Johns Hopkins University, from the Historical Collections.)

physicians saw the need to reunite the disciplines of medicine and surgery, and surgeons began to rise in social position, with surgery taught and practiced by respected physicians. Medical textbooks were published, and the end of the seventeenth century saw the appearance of scientific journals.

In the eighteenth century, medical writings grew progressively more concerned with anatomy, pathology, and surgical techniques. Especially notable among surgical writers and educators of the time is William Hunter (1718 to 1783) (Figure 1–3), who built a famous anatomic theater (Figure 1–4) and museum in London where British anatomists and surgeons of the period, including his brother John, were trained. He gave private lectures on dissecting, operative surgery, and bandaging and wrote numerous papers. He was the first to describe arteriovenous aneurysm (1761). John Hunter (1728 to 1793) was the founder of experimental and surgical pathology and a pioneer in comparative physiology and experimental morphology (Figure 1–5). He described shock and studied such things as inflammation, gunshot wounds, and surgical disease of the vascular system.[4]

Events in Great Britain in the eighteenth century offer an interesting chapter in the story of the evolution of evidence-based surgery. Socioeconomic conditions were extremely poor as the country suffered widespread disease, poverty, and crime. The government abdicated control over the education and licensing of physicians. "Surgical charlatans and quacks"[3] flourished in this environment, and little information was available to refute the absurd claims made (Figure 1–6). The growing role of hospitals in caring for the sick and the eventual affiliation of medical schools with hospitals enabled British medicine and surgery to enter a new era as physician education improved and hospitals were able to better serve the sick. British and European universities became the international centers for medical science.

Figure 1–4 "The Dissecting Room," an illustration by Rowlandson, depicting William and John Hunter in attendance. In the eighteenth century, anatomic dissection was a means of teaching surgery and observing the relationship between disease and pathologic anatomy. (Reproduced with permission of the Institute of the History of Medicine, The Johns Hopkins University, from the Historical Collections.)

THE INCEPTION OF THE MODERN SURGICAL ERA

In the early part of the nineteenth century, physicians in Europe, especially those in the Paris School, concentrated their inquisitive and scholarly efforts on trying to correlate postmortem findings with observations of disease in the patient prior to death. During this time, the French surgeon Civiale contributed significantly to the formative growth of surgical practice through his early adherence to lithotrity, or the fragmentation of bladder stones. Though neither the innovator nor the first proponent of lithotrity, Civiale was indeed the first to put the idea into practice with patients. His novel technique for crushing the stones with a drill-like device, developed before the advent of general anesthesia, drastically reduced suffering during the procedure and improved patient outcomes by minimizing collateral injury. Building on the theories of others and aggregating a large series of patients (purportedly over a thousand), Civiale is noted for retiring the "terrors of cutting for the stone."[5]

The active study of anatomy and surgical techniques in France in the early part of the nineteenth century bore great influence in the United States, leading some Americans to pursue surgical research. Samuel D. Gross (1805 to 1884), America's leading general surgeon of the mid-nineteenth century, published the first exhaustive study in the English language on pathologic anatomy in 1839 and was the first to use experimental animals to carry out large-scale surgical studies[5] (Figure 1–7).

American discoveries and innovations in the nineteenth century are described as haphazard and independent of any broad plan, in contrast to the consistent and progressive development of clinical diagnosis and physiology in France and cellular pathology, biochemistry, and physiology in Germany.[6] That little research occurred in America is attributed to several factors. Chief among these was the general aversion to autopsies and human dissection, due in part to the wide acceptance of the theories of Benjamin Rush, who had declared that

Figure 1–5 John Hunter (1728 to 1793), founder of surgical pathology and a pioneer in comparative physiology and morphology. After displaying little interest in formal education, John Hunter came to live with his brother William, assisting him in teaching anatomy and dissection. He was an avid collector of anatomic specimens for study and was legendary for the great lengths to which he went to acquire a specimen. From an engraving by Adock of a painting by Reynolds. (Reproduced with permission of the Institute of the History of Medicine, The Johns Hopkins University, from the Historical Collections.)

illness was due to a single cause and thus, autopsies were unnecessary (Figure 1–8). The lack of research may further be ascribed to a system of training physicians under preceptors rather than with a university-based approach and to the lack of emphasis on scholarly pursuits.

In the nineteenth century, the major obstacles to the progress of surgery were pain, infection, and hemorrhage. The modern surgical era can be considered to have begun in the mid-nineteenth century, when several major events greatly influenced the development of surgery by beginning to remove some of these obstacles: the introduction of anesthesia by Morton (Figure 1–9) in 1846; the development and acceptance of Lister's principles of antisepsis and aseptic surgery in 1867 (Figure 1–10); and the rising use of hospitals as places to care for patients (Figure 1–11). These developments made possible the professionalization of surgery that, along with the advent of totally new operative procedures (including the formulation of William Stewart Halsted's conservative surgical principles [Figure 1–12] and the discovery of x-rays and new principles of hemostasis), brought about considerable advances in surgery from the middle to the end of the nineteenth century, including abdominal, vascular, and orthopedic surgery and increasingly invasive and curative procedures. The increasing professionalism of surgical care also brought about the promulgation of surgical information via texts, articles, and journals as well as the rise of specialty surgical societies and a new model for surgical training in America, developed by Halsted at The Johns Hopkins Hospital.

The establishment of The Johns Hopkins Hospital in 1889, based on the hospital design principles of John Shaw Billings (Figure 1–13), and of the Johns Hopkins University School of Medicine in 1893, based on the educational dictums of Daniel Coit Gilman (Figure 1–14), was a significant turning point for medicine and the movement toward evidence-based medicine. The Hopkins medical school and hospital firmly linked science, research, and graduate education to clinical practice. Many of the leaders of American medicine, who would in turn promulgate this synthesis of science and practice, trained at Johns Hopkins.

THE QUACK DOCTOR'S PRAYER!!

ILLUSTRIOUS ſhade of the renowned *Doctor Rock*, ſtill continue, I beſeech thee, to pour down thy influence on the Endeavours of thy modern Repreſentative, *Doctor Botherem*; thou knoweſt the regular Gradations of the Profeſſion, from a Show Box at a Country Fair, to the luxury of a Chariot rattling down Pall-Mall; it would, therefore, be vain and idle to attempt Diſguiſe before thy penetrating Wiſdom.

I'm the Eyes of the Undiſcerning, my miraculous *cure-all-able* Vegetable Drops, called *Never-faiłibus Infallialibus*, appear the Wonder of the preſent Age, the Ingredients are ſuppoſed to Iſſue from the Laboratory of ESCULAPIUS himſelf beyond the Power of Mortal Analization; but thou well knoweſt how the World is deceived; to thee it appear nothing more than a Decoction of Beet-root, Lump-Sugar, Spring-Water, the beſt Coniac Brandy, and a Daſh of Hollands Gin.—Thou, alſo, knoweſt its great Reputation was firſt aquired by curing *Lady Dun-Dizzle* of Indigeſtion, by throwing her into a temporary State of ſoothing Intoxication, ſince which Time the old Lady reſorts as regularly to her Drops, as her Dram Bottle.

To deceive thee is impoſſible, thou knoweſt we are not infallible, but are all liable to little Accidents in the Exerciſe of our Calling, that are not altogether ſo pleaſing on Reflection; but what grieves me moſt, is the Recollection of the ſudden Demiſe of *Alderman Marrowfat*, even on the firſt Experiment of my *Anti-Gorgean Pills*, and at the very Inſtant he was about to recommend their wonderful Effects to the Mayor, and the whole Body Corporate.

Yet notwithſtanding the Sweets of the Profeſſion amply compenſates for the Bitters, therefore deign to continue to me my Carriages and Equipage, my Town and Country Reſidence, and all other good Things of this Life, and thy humble Petitioner ſhall ever praiſe thee.

PRINTED BY E. SPRAGG, NO. 15, BOW-STREET, COVENT-GARDEN.

Figure 1–6 This illustration depicts a quack praying for continuation of his remunerative practice despite the "sudden demise of Alderman" due to "little accidents in the exercise of our calling." During and after the Renaissance, brilliant achievements in literature, philosophy, astronomy, mathematics, and the conquest of new territories eclipsed studies of medicine and natural history. Quacks and charlatans, astronomers, and alchemists flocked to London. A law was passed to control quackery in 1511, during the reign of Henry VIII, but quacks continued to advertise cures of every and any disease. (Reproduced with permission of the Fry Print Collection, the Yale University Historical Library.)

Figure 1–7 Samuel D. Gross (1805 to 1884), the pre-eminent American professor of surgery in the mid-nineteenth century. Gross published the first exhaustive study in the English language on pathologic anatomy in 1830, was the first to use experimental animals to carry out large-scale studies, and was one of the founders of the American Surgical Association in 1880. (Reproduced with permission of the Institute of the History of Medicine, The Johns Hopkins University, from the Historical Collections.)

Figure 1–8 Benjamin Rush (1745 to 1813), whose precepts and teachings in the late eighteenth and early nineteenth centuries dominated American medical practice, earning him the moniker "Hippocrates of Pennsylvania." This illustration commemorates Rush as physician to the Pennsylvania Hospital (1783 to 1813). (Reproduced with permission of the Alan Mason Chesney Medical Archives, The Johns Hopkins Medical Institutions, from the Howard A. Kelly papers.)

WHO CLAIMED TO HAVE DISCOVERED ANÆSTHESIA BY THE INHALATION
OF SULPHURIC ETHER, AT BOSTON, MASS. SEPT. 30, 1846.

Figure 1–9 William T. G. Morton, the dentist credited with the introduction of ether anesthesia to surgical practice in 1846, seen as one of the major advances in surgery in the nineteenth century. After ether was widely adopted as an anesthetic, surgery was remarkably changed as the importance of the speed of the surgeon gave way to acumen, enabling operations to be developed that were previously impossible. (Reproduced with permission of the Institute of the History of Medicine, The Johns Hopkins University, from the Historical Collections.)

By the end of the nineteenth century, surgeons typically sought hospital appointments for reasons of income, knowledge, and prestige. Specialization was still under attack but became increasingly common during the early twentieth century.[5] William Stewart Halsted encouraged his assistants at Johns Hopkins to develop several fields of surgery, such as neurosurgery (Harvey Cushing) and urology (Hugh Hampton Young). Hospitals were completing their purposive and structural transformation from charitable institutions to medical enterprises described variously as "hotels for the sick," "health factories," and "workshops for physicians." A new association of hospital superintendents in the United States and Canada was formed in 1899 and later became the American Hospital Association.

The Growth of the Medical Literature in the United States

When The Johns Hopkins Hospital opened in 1889, *The Johns Hopkins Hospital Reports* was established as a means of publishing the scientific work from The Johns Hopkins Hospital and Medical School. William Henry Welch, as chief of pathology, founded and edited the *Journal of Experimental Medicine*, the first regularly published American periodical devoted to medical science[5] (Figure 1–15).

Up to the beginning of the Revolutionary War, the American medical literature consisted of one medical book, three reprints, and about twenty pamphlets.[5] The first medical journal in the United States was the *Medical Repository*, published quarterly from 1797 to 1824. After the first 7 years of the *Medical Repository*, medical journals began to appear in increasing numbers, many of them for short periods of time and with little perceived value. From 1797 to 1876, some 195 journals were started. The *New England Journal of Medicine and Surgery*

Figure 1–10 Joseph Lister (1827 to 1912), whose elucidation of the principles of antisepsis and aseptic surgery in the mid-nineteenth century enabled rapid progress in surgery, especially in abdominal surgery. Heretofore, the saturation of wounds with pus, septicemia, pyemia, gangrene, and erysipelas were common postsurgical conditions, and high surgical mortality rates prevailed. Lister's own statistics showed a 45 percent mortality rate for amputations. Noticing the link between healing and lack of putrefaction, and building on the work of Pasteur, Lister successfully set out to prevent the growth of microorganisms in wounds. (Reproduced with permission of the Alan Mason Chesney Medical Archives, The Johns Hopkins Medical Institutions, from the Howard A. Kelly papers.)

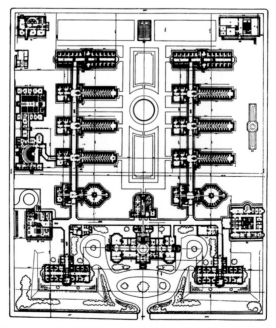

Figure 1–11 The "block plan" devised by John Shaw Billings, MD, in 1875 for The Johns Hopkins Hospital. Then a lieutenant colonel in the US Army, Billings's plan was based on his experiences as an Army officer during and after the Civil War and on his study of the pavilion model for hospitals popular in Europe. (Reproduced with permission of the Alan Mason Chesney Medical Archives, The Johns Hopkins Medical Institutions.)

Figure 1–12 William Stewart Halsted, MD (1852 to 1922), from a photograph by John H. Stocksdale, 1 year before Halsted's death at the end of a long and distinguished career in surgery. Halsted reflected upon the precursor events to the modern era of surgery in his 1904 Yale address: "Pain, hemorrhage, infection, the three great evils which had always embittered the practice of surgery and checked its progress, were, in a moment, in a quarter of a century (1846 to 1873) robbed of their terror." (Published in Halsted WS. The training of the surgeon. Bull Johns Hopkins Hosp 1904 Sept;15[162].) (Reproduced with permission of the Alan Mason Chesney Medical Archives, The Johns Hopkins Medical Institutions, from the William Stewart Halsted papers.)

(Figure 1–16) was established in 1812 and merged with the *Boston Medical Intelligencer* in 1828, adopting the new name *The Boston Medical and Surgical Journal* and later becoming the *New England Journal of Medicine*. In addition to journals and textbooks, the medical literature also contained transactions of state and local medical societies. John Shaw Billings, founder of the Surgeon General's Library in 1880, made great contributions to the advancement of evidence-based surgery; his *Index Catalogue of the Surgeon General's Library* and *Index Medicus* made the ever-expanding medical literature more accessible. Billings reported in 1881 that 655 volumes of journals and transactions had been published worldwide, 156 of which had been produced in the United States.[5]

Significant surgical literature included the *Annals of Surgery*, founded in 1885, the first journal devoted exclusively to surgery. Numerous other articles, books, and monographs on surgery appeared with increasing frequency as well in the nineteenth century. Of note were the many surgical articles by Stephen Smith. The journal *Surgery, Gynecology and Obstetrics*, a highly regarded publication, was founded in 1905.

The Role of Specialty Societies

Paralleling the growth in the medical literature was the rise of specialty medical and surgical societies that, through meetings and publications, disseminated information about patient outcomes from surgery and new surgical procedures. In 1847, the American Medical Association was formed, followed later by societies for pharmaceuticals (1852), ophthalmology (1864), otology (1868), orthopedics (1872), neurology (1875), gynecology (1876), dermatology (1876), and laryngology (1878). Hospital administrative issues were addressed

Figure 1–13 John Shaw Billings, MD (1838 to 1913), not only devised the plan for and oversaw the construction of The Johns Hopkins Hospital but was one of the primary architects of the model for the Johns Hopkins graduate and postgraduate medical education programs. In addition, he was one of the principal founders of the Surgeon General's Library and indexed the entire medical literature of the world, which culminated in the *Index Medicus*. (Reproduced with permission of the Alan Mason Chesney Medical Archives, The Johns Hopkins Medical Institutions.)

initially by the Association of Medical Superintendents of American Institutions for the Insane (1870). The American Surgical Association followed in 1879 (Figure 1–17), and the American College of Surgeons was founded in 1913 (Figure 1–18).

THE PROFESSIONALIZATION OF SURGERY

In the latter decades of the nineteenth century, a number of developments helped support the professionalization of surgery: the establishment of surgical specialty societies such as the American Surgical Association in 1880 and the American College of Surgeons in 1913; the founding of the first journal devoted exclusively to surgery in 1885, the *Annals of Surgery*; the opening of The Johns Hopkins Hospital in 1889, which led to the founding of surgical teaching on the wards, in the clinics, and in the laboratories directed by William Stewart Halsted; the establishment of dedicated journals and textbooks; and the rise of specialization in disciplines within surgery, as encouraged by Halsted.

The surgical training system developed by Halsted during his tenure as the Professor of Surgery at Johns Hopkins from 1889 to his death in 1922 was unique in its primary purpose of establishing a school of surgery that would lead to the dissemination of those principles of surgery and attributes of the surgeon that he considered essential. The main aspects of Halsted's residency training philosophy included increasing responsibility in patient care, culminating in a final period of independent activity; a thorough knowledge of anatomy, physiology, and pathology; time spent in original research; and residence in the hospital so that surgeons became immersed in research activities, teaching responsibilities, and the total clinical care of hospitalized surgical patients. Once the benefits of the long and disciplined period of training in an institution dedicated to teaching and research were demonstrated, the Halsted training system was spread by individuals who had participated in the original program, establishing Halsted-type surgical residencies throughout the country. Halsted described his system

Figure 1–14 Daniel Coit Gilman (1832 to 1908), first president of The Johns Hopkins University and a critic of the educational standards of medical schools of his day. Gilman outlined for The Johns Hopkins University the course of undergraduate premedical study that became the national standard, and he oversaw the organization of the university's medical school, with John Shaw Billings as one of his primary medical advisors. (Reproduced with permission of the Alan Mason Chesney Medical Archives, The Johns Hopkins Medical Institutions.)

in great detail in a Yale commencement address in 1904 (Figure 1–19).[7] Other significant events occurring at this time in American medicine, in addition to the rise of training programs and specialization not only in surgery but in other disciplines, included the increased construction of hospitals and the movement away from "kitchen-table" surgery since hospitals now offered an antiseptic environment and the benefits of anesthesia for surgery.

The professionalization of surgery ultimately enabled and promoted scientific advancement in the field, especially in light of the fact that in prior centuries surgical techniques had been closely guarded "trade secrets."[8] This scientific advancement was based on increasing specialization of the scientific and clinical practice interests of early surgeon-investigators. The need for the American Surgical Association arose during a time when international medical congresses were held every 3 to 4 years (from 1869 until the onset of World War I) and when numerous specialty surgical societies had come into existence.[8] While surgical evidence and theories could be addressed in a number of different forums, the identification of a unifying scope of professional interests laid the groundwork for this professional society.

Efforts to organize a surgical association began at the American Medical Association meeting in 1879, when Dr. Samuel Gross (at age 74) called a meeting of several prominent surgeons to discuss the desirability of organizing the American Surgical Association (ASA). Discussion ensued as to whether this was an attack upon the American Medical Association (AMA), and whether or not the surgical section of the AMA could accomplish the objectives Gross envisioned for the ASA as "a school for mutual instruction and improvement, a court of supreme authority unto which the great questions of surgery should be brought for discussion and judgement, a gathering in social intercourse of the individual workers in surgical

THE JOURNAL OF

EXPERIMENTAL MEDICINE

EDITED BY

WILLIAM H. WELCH, M. D.

Baltimore

ASSOCIATE EDITORS

FOR PHYSIOLOGY	FOR PATHOLOGY
H. P. Bowditch, M. D., Boston	J. George Adami, M. D., Montreal
R. H. Chittenden, Ph. D., New Haven	W. T. Councilman, M. D., Boston
W. H. Howell, M. D., Ph. D., Baltimore	T. Mitchell Prudden, M. D., New York

FOR PHARMACOLOGY	FOR MEDICINE
John J. Abel, M. D., Baltimore	R. H. Fitz, M. D., Boston
Arthur R. Cushny, M. D., Ann Arbor	Wm. Osler, M. D., F. R. C. P., Baltimore
H. C. Wood, M. D., Philadelphia	William Pepper, M. D., Philadelphia

VOLUME SECOND

WITH FIFTY-FOUR PLATES AND THIRTEEN FIGURES IN THE TEXT

NEW YORK

D. APPLETON AND COMPANY

LONDON : 33 BEDFORD STREET, COVENT GARDEN

1897

Figure 1–15 *The Journal of Experimental Medicine*, the first regularly published American periodical devoted to medical science. Edited by William Henry Welch, the chief of pathology at Johns Hopkins and first dean of the School of Medicine from 1896 to 1903, the journal was initially underwritten by The Johns Hopkins University. The voluminous correspondence and overwhelming submission of papers led to Welch's turning over the journal to the Rockefeller Institute, where Simon Flexner and Eugene Opie became its editors. (Reproduced with permission of the Rockefeller University Press.)

science."[8] At the 1880 AMA meeting, Gross's motion for the formation of the American Surgical Association was approved unanimously, and Gross was elected first president.[8]

Ravitch, in *A Century of Surgery, 1880–1980, the History of the American Surgical Association*, extensively reviewed the proceedings of the ASA, describing it as a record of the development of surgery in America.[8] Thus, the origins of evidence-based surgery in the United States can be traced by reviewing these proceedings. The major surgical developments of the nineteenth century were discussed at the ASA meetings: abdominal surgery for appendicitis, gastric cancer, hernia, and diseases of the ovary. The interests of the prominent American surgeons who participated in the ASA are well documented by the early programs, which presumably represented state-of-the-art thinking and formed the basis of early surgical literature. The papers presented indicate the nature of evidence discussed at these professional meetings, ranging from descriptions of new procedures to changes in surgical approaches, results of surgery for a series of patients, and case reports.

Gross's paper in 1881 on "The Influence of Operations upon the Prolongation of Life and Permanent Recovery in Carcinoma of the Breast" perhaps typifies the type of surgical "evidence" in use.[8] Using descriptive analytic techniques, he described cases reported in the literature, by tissue, involved local recurrence rate, and recurrent disease in the nodes. He also reported autopsy data with respect to distant metastases. Meeting discussions are also notable for "widespread distrust of Listerism,"[9] with debate centered on the lack of acceptance of

THE

NEW ENGLAND JOURNAL

OF

MEDICINE AND SURGERY,

AND

THE COLLATERAL BRANCHES OF SCIENCE.

———

CONDUCTED BY A NUMBER OF PHYSICIANS.

———

Homo naturae minister et interpres tantum facit et intelligit, quantum de naturae ordine, re vel mente, observaverit; nec amplius scit aut potest.
Francis Bacon.

VOLUME I.

———

BOSTON.

PUBLISHED BY T. B. WAIT AND CO.
· · · · · ·
1812.

Figure 1–16 The 1812 title page from *The New England Journal of Medicine and Surgery*, the precursor to the present-day *New England Journal of Medicine*. (Reproduced with permission of *The New England Journal of Medicine*.)

Figure 1–17 The original 1880 seal of the American Surgical Association, carrying the association's original name, the American Surgical Society. Although the society's name was changed to the American Surgical Association in 1881, this was never reflected in the seal. (Reproduced with permission of the American Surgical Association, from Ravitch MM. A century of surgery: the history of the American Surgical Association. Philadelphia and Toronto: J. B. Lippincott Company; 1981.)

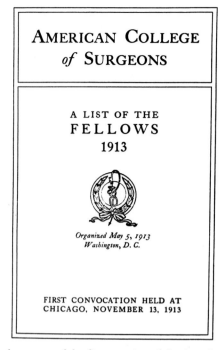

Figure 1-18 Title page from the report of the first meeting of the American College of Surgeons in 1913. Franklin Martin, one of the founders, after organizing the first Clinical Congress of Surgeons of North America in 1910, proposed a national organization of surgeons similar to the Royal College of Surgeons in England. The American College of Surgeons was instrumental in raising the standard of surgical and hospital care in the United States. (Reproduced with permission of the American College of Surgeons.)

Listerian principles of disinfection and the use of carbolic acid to eliminate infection. Nacrede supported Listerism but still defended "cupping and scarification for local blood letting." The early papers of the American Surgical Association also reflect the evolution of surgical subspecialties as seen, for example, by the appearance of papers on thoracic and vascular surgery as early as the 1883 meeting.

Patient lifestyle issues (a precursor to quality-of-life concerns prevalent today) were considered in the 1887 program. Agnew's presidential address, "The Relation of Social Life to Surgical Disease," included his attributions of "catarrh among ladies to the gradually decreasing size of their bonnets, of weak ankles in children to the wearing of high shoes, of small chest and round shoulders to children stooped over their school books . . ."[8] Ashhurst presented "A Contribution to the Study of Excisions of the Larger Joints," discussing the functional result of successful excision of the elbow for destructive arthritis, tuberculosis, compound dislocations, fractures, and simple ankylosis.

In 1890, Bull presented "The Radical Cure of Hernia, with the Results of One Hundred and Thirty-Four Operations."[8] In this paper, he stressed the need for long-term observations before drawing conclusions regarding the efficacy of an operation. Papers presented in following years were increasingly on particular procedures for specific conditions, for example, Willard's "Cholecystectomy for Impacted Gallstones," 1893; Senn's "A New Method of Direct Fixation of Fragments in Compound and Ununited Fractures," 1893; and "The Surgical Treatment of Empyema," by Ashhurst in 1894.[8] Halsted, in his first presentation to the association in 1898, "A Clinical and Histological Study of Certain Adenocarcinomata of the Breast," reported on the long-term survival of his patients (ie, postsurgical mortality for 3 years following surgery) and the incidence rate of local recurrence.[8]

BULLETIN

OF

THE JOHNS HOPKINS HOSPITAL

Entered as Second-Class Matter at the Baltimore, Maryland, Postoffice.

Vol. XV.—No. 162.]　　　　　BALTIMORE, SEPTEMBER, 1904.　　　　　[Price, 25 Cents.

CONTENTS.

THE TRAINING OF THE SURGEON. [1]

By WILLIAM STEWART HALSTED, M. D., Hon. F. R. C. S. (Lond.),

Professor of Surgery, The Johns Hopkins University.

Pain, hemorrhage, infection, the three great evils which had always embittered the practice of surgery and checked its progress, were, in a moment, in a quarter of a century (1846-1873) robbed of their terrors.[2] A new era had dawned; and in the thirty years which have elapsed since the graduation of the class of 1874 from Yale, probably more has been accomplished to place surgery on a truly scientific basis than in all the centuries which had preceded this wondrous period. The *macula levis notæ* clung to surgeons the world over until the beginning of the nineteenth century, although distinguished and scholarly men, as well as charlatans and barbers, have practiced the art in almost unbroken succession from the time of Hippocrates (460-375 B. C.) to the present day. A warning for all time against satisfaction with present achievement and blindness to the possibilities of future development is the imperishable prophecy of the famous French surgeon, Baron Boyer, who over a hundred years ago declared that surgery had then reached almost, if not actually, the highest degree of perfection of which it was capable.[3]

Tempted to belittle by comparisons the performances of our progenitors, we should remember that the condition of surgery has at all times reflected the knowledge and thought of the ablest minds in the profession. We may well recall the admonition so gently given by the highly talented von Volkmann, who was also a popular poet, writing under the pseudonym of Richard Leander,

" Hoch aufhebt Schnee-schimmernd das Haupt in die Wolken
　　die Jungfrau,
　　Aber sie deckt mit dem Fuss ein unendliches Land."

Surgery, like other branches of the healing art, has followed in its progress zigzag paths, often difficult to trace. Now it has seemed to advance by orderly steps or through the influence of some master mind even by bounds; again it has stumbled apparently only from error to error, or has

blessings, is at the same time one of our greatest reproaches, hemorrhage is still awkwardly checked, and of surgical infection once started we have often little control and then mainly by means of the knife. We have reason to hope that the day will come when hemorrhage will be controlled by a quicker procedure than the awkward, time-consuming ligature; when infections will be controlled by specific products of the laboratory; and when pain will be prevented by a drug which will have an affinity only for the definite sensory cells which it is desirable it should affect. The first of these may be last and the last first. Let us trust that it may, as Gross expresses it, "be a long time before the laws of this department of the healing art will be as immutable as those of the Medes and Persians."

"Literature," said Horace Walpole, "has many revolutions: if an author could rise from the dead after a hundred years what would be his surprise at the adventures of his work." Gross recognized, not altogether without regret, that this was particularly true of scientific works however erudite they may be. " Few survive their authors."[4]

[1] The Annual Address in Medicine delivered at Yale University, June 27, 1904.

[2] Verhandlungen der deutschen Ges. f. Chirurgie, 1896, von Esmarch.

[3] Could Boyer, we ask, have been satisfied with the status of surgery when anæsthesia was undiscovered, when hemorrhage was awkwardly and insufficiently controlled, when infection of wounds was not understood and could not be prevented? And yet I might quote from the writings of distinguished men of our time to show that even to-day some think that surgery is almost complete. Anæsthesia, one of the greatest

[4] Gross. Autobiography, Vol. I, p. 140.

Figure 1–19 Halsted gave the Annual Address in Medicine at Yale University in 1904, in which he described the method of surgical training he devised as the chief of surgery at Johns Hopkins. The address, reprinted in the *Bulletin of the Johns Hopkins Hospital*, is a marvelous description of the progress made in surgery both before and during Halsted's time, especially with respect to the promulgation of surgical knowledge via residency training. (Published in Halsted WS. The training of the surgeon. Bull Johns Hopkins Hosp 1904 Sept;15[162]). (Reproduced with permission of the Alan Mason Chesney Medical Archives, The Johns Hopkins Medical Institutions, from the William Stewart Halsted papers.)

An example of early clinical outcomes research relates to the wide debate at the 1899 meeting regarding appendicitis. The clinical diagnosis of appendicitis with surgery for its cure was a dramatic development of the nineteenth century, and appendectomies were performed with increasing frequency. Debate centered on whether every case should be operated upon as soon as the diagnosis was made and whether the appendix should be removed in every case.

In 1925, Ochsner, in his presidential address, "The Surgical Treatment of Habitual Criminals, Imbeciles, Perverts, Paupers, Morons, Epileptics, and Degenerates," argued for castration of such individuals, citing $89 million as the sum per annum for the care of such individuals.[8] Perhaps this can be considered an early example of economics focused research.

Moore, in his 1884 presidential address on the history of medicine, described this time period as the "golden age of inquiry" for surgery.[8] Lund, in his 1930 presidential address, "Fifty Years of the American Surgical Association," reported on the major advances in surgery from 1880 to 1930: technologic developments such as radiation; direct examination of the urinary tract by cystoscopy; blood transfusion; the electric cautery; and improved outcomes via decreased mortality for operations such as thyroidectomy for exophthalmic goiter, gastric resection, and craniotomies.[8]

As reviewed by Barnes,[9] ASA transactions from 1880 to 1942 primarily reflect the results of non-experimental research and practice but contain evidence of interest in "end results," such as an examination of psychologic sequelae of major surgery.[10] To determine the basis for the adoption and subsequent abandonment of commonly performed and widely discussed surgical procedures that ultimately proved nonbeneficial, Barnes analyzed the following:

1. Surgery for ptosis, defined as abnormal placement of abdominal organs, cured by stitching these organs into improved positions (11 papers, 1890 to 1928).
2. Surgery for constipation (18 papers, 1909 to 1933).
3. While successful reports of endocrine surgery abounded, so did false indications, for example, thyroid surgery for dementia praecox, various indications for adrenal gland denervation, and double castration for benign prostatic hypertension (8 papers, 1895 to 1934).
4. Peripheral nervous system surgery for nontraumatic diseases, including "nerve stretching" for various purposes (11 papers, 1888 to 1932).

As Barnes notes, many of the concepts justifying these operations were ultimately proven incorrect. However, due to the poor understanding of disease processes, these surgical approaches endured for considerable spans of time before their demise; for example, ptosis operations extended over a 38-year period. The most significant research flaw for the operations studied was the lack of a control group, but according to Barnes, the major reasons for the prolonged acceptance of ineffectual operations were the following:

- Reports from influential surgeons with limited knowledge of pathology
- Uncritical acceptance of "acceptable" approaches to surgery
- Acceptance of both diagnosis and necessity of surgical treatment
- Absence of ethical constraints in the development and application of new procedures
- Inadequate knowledge of methods for outcome analysis and follow-up

Thus, from 1880 to 1942, new operative approaches often were developed on the basis of intuition and insight and were evaluated primarily on a trial-and-error basis. While the scientific rigor in the accretion of evidence falls short of contemporary approaches, an evidence-based approach nevertheless was one of the contributing factors in the early professionalization of surgery.

THE EARLY TWENTIETH CENTURY: CODMAN'S END-RESULTS SYSTEM

The origins of evidence-based surgery must be considered not only within the context of the evolution of surgical science but also within that of medical education reform and the public

Figure 1–20 Abraham Flexner (1866 to 1959), whose scathing report in 1910 on American medical education brought about significant medical education reform in the United States. The impact of the report was due not only to its findings on the incompetence of the majority of medical schools but also to the detailed descriptions of deficiencies in medical school facilities, equipment, faculty, and curriculum, and state board examinations. (Reproduced with permission of the Alan Mason Chesney Medical Archives, The Johns Hopkins Medical Institutions.)

health movement in the United States. The first two decades of the twentieth century gave rise to several early and significant developments in the evidence-based surgery movement: Flexner's report on medical education; Codman's end-results system; the inception of a system of accreditation of hospitals; and the development of standards for surgical credentials. The ideology of scientific medicine prevailed, that is, the assumption that knowledge can be developed by observation and research and applied to the population by individual practitioners.[10]

The end of the nineteenth century brought applications of industrial approaches to surgery, that is, the use of measurement and analytic techniques to improve efficiencies. These approaches included an examination of surgery statistics, such as the volume of procedures performed, which became standard in hospitals. Devon, in *Surgery, Gynecology and Obstetrics*, reflected the concerns of leading surgeons by recording "an appalling increase" in the number of hysterectomies[10] and estimated in 1906 that 30 percent of gynecologic operations were unnecessary. As a result of the examinations of medical and surgical practice, leading practitioners of medicine, along with the Rockefeller Foundation, pushed for the standardization of the education of physicians.

Flexner's report in 1910 brought about medical education reform and the implementation of full-time faculty appointments in United States medical schools in 1914 (Figure 1–20). The full-time system, financially supported by the Rockefeller Foundation, was designed to encourage medical school faculty to engage predominantly in research and teaching.[11] The industrial approach is typified by the work of Codman and his end-results system for medical reform through use of evidence.

In 1910, Ernest Amory Codman (Figure 1–21) began his efforts to reform clinical medicine and surgery. Discussions of objective criteria for evaluating surgery were part of a wider interest in hospital, industrial, and social efficiency, following Frederick Taylor's 1895

Figure 1–21 Ernest Amory Codman, MD, whose end-results system was the pioneering effort in the measurement of outcomes of care. Codman is viewed by many as the father of evidence-based surgery. (Reproduced with permission of the Massachusetts General Hospital Archives.)

publication on "scientific management," which promoted the analysis of industrial processes to gain optimal efficiency.[6]

After studying at the Massachusetts General Hospital in 1894 and subsequently serving as an assistant surgeon in the outpatient department, Codman developed strong beliefs in medical science. With his surgical mentor, F. B. Harrington, he created a case-monitoring system in 1900, recording cases and their outcomes. The outgrowth of this system was his "end results" idea: a medical records system allowing measurement of surgical and medical outcomes. This system included an end-result card for each patient, which recorded symptoms or conditions, pathologic diagnoses, treatment plans, complications, final diagnoses and the "result and cure afterwards."[6] Codman further proposed that on each card a determination would then be made as to why "perfection" had not been obtained. His nosology of errors included those due to lack of knowledge or technical skill, lack of surgical judgment, lack of adequate equipment, lack of diagnostic skill, incurable disease, refusal of treatment, and incidents, complications, and "calamities of surgery."[6] Codman reasoned that by using his system of comparison surgeons could specialize in operations they did best. To make the end-results system work, each hospital would require an end-results clerk for record keeping, an efficiency committee for monitoring purposes, and publication of the results in a standardized format. Beyond reviewing charts 1 year after discharge and comparing the results in hospitals to find out the best and worst surgeons irrespective of reputation, Codman also proposed that patients should have access to reports of large hospitals to learn if surgery were done well. Codman's approach exemplifies the application of the scientific management principles of industrial efficiency techniques to medicine.

Codman launched a campaign for broad acceptance of the end-results system in 1910. Chicago surgeon Franklin Martin, one of the founders of the American College of Surgeons, launched the first Clinical Congress of Surgeons in 1910, the year in which Flexner published his report on the need for medical education reform and Taylor provided congressional testimony on railroad efficiency, popularizing theories of scientific management. Surgical methods were being standardized due to international meetings and results published in medical journals. The 1911 and 1912 meetings of the Clinical Congress of Surgeons provided the opportunity for surgeons to observe surgical techniques in leading hospitals. When the American College of Surgeons was formed in 1913, it set up the Committee on the Standardization of Hospitals. Codman was appointed chairman and was invited to work with the College to implement the end-results system. However, the American College of Surgeons did not press for a quality assurance system along Codman's lines but instead pushed for standards for hospitals. The surgeons clearly articulated support for turning the hospital into "work shops" to serve professional needs since much surgery was done by "unethical unsafe money grubbing practitioners who saw surgery in the expanding hospitals as wonderful new sources of income."[10]

By 1913, the American College of Surgeons had agreed in principle to the inspection, classification, and standardization of hospitals, thus bringing about hospital accreditation in the United States. At a conference of hospital superintendents in 1917 in which sixty hospitals were represented, the American College of Surgeons' Program of Hospital Standardization was established. The college also established criteria for training programs for surgeons. Fellowship in the college required successful examination following this training. This system of certifying the surgeon's competence emphasized professional authority and was seen as the best way to improve practice.

Codman aggressively pursued acceptance of the end-results system but was frustrated by the difficulty in gaining acceptance of what was seen as a radical idea. Codman publicly challenged the leaders and faculty of the Harvard Medical School and the Massachusetts General Hospital, who ultimately forced him to resign from the Massachusetts Medical Society and the Harvard faculty. Although his audacious efforts brought much attention to his end-results system, the lasting results of Codman's efforts were achieved through the hospital standardization work of the American College of Surgeons.

In 1920, George Gray Ward wrote about the practical application of methods of standardization to the hospital after describing the work of the American College of Surgeons, commenting and expanding upon the basic notion of hospital standards and requirements.[12] He called for the actual results accomplished by each surgeon in the care and treatment of patients to be made public and available for study and described his work toward hospital standardization at Womens' Hospital in New York. To exemplify the application of the standardization approach, Ward reported on the outcomes of 1,166 patients following gynecologic surgery. Ward classified patients as being fully or partially successfully relieved of symptoms or as "failures." Interestingly, he also wrote about the need for standardized orders and treatment plans, perhaps anticipating the work in critical pathways prevalent today. Ward's work represents the application of Codman's ideas in practice, but it was not until several years later that other compelling interests brought attention back to the examination of surgical outcomes. These will be discussed in detail in the next chapter.

CASE STUDY: BREAST CANCER SURGERY

The evolution of evidence-based surgery is typified by the changes in surgical treatment for breast cancer over time. Wagner has extensively reported on the history of breast disease and its treatment as follows:[1] descriptions of diseases of the breast reside in the oldest recorded medical history from ancient Greece, and references to breast disease appear through Babylonian times, the classical Greek period, and the Greco-Roman period. Leonides, a Greek physician in the first century AD, is credited with the first recorded operative treatment for breast cancer, in which repeated incisions and applications of cautery were continued until the entire breast and tumor had been removed. Credit for the first clinical description of cancer is given to Celsus, a Roman in the first century AD who was not a physician but who wrote about medicine: he described four clinical stages of breast cancer. Galen (131 to 201 AD) also described mammary cancer. In the Middle Ages, Rhazes (860 to 932), a highly regarded Arabic physician, condoned excision of the breast for cancer. Albucassis (1013 to 1106), in Spain, agreed that for small tumors removal of the entire breast was advisable, but reported no cures.

During the Renaissance, Paré (1510 to 1590) advocated compassion in surgery by use of vascular ligature and avoidance of cautery and boiling oil. Regarding breast surgery, he observed that breast cancer often caused swelling of the axillary glands. Servitus (1509 to 1553), a Spaniard who studied in Paris, advocated removing the underlying muscle of the breast and also the glands described by Paré; this is considered a forerunner of radical mastectomy.

In the eighteenth century, the anatomist Camper (1722 to 1789) described and illustrated the internal mammary lymph nodes. Death by metastasis from cancer was not yet understood. In France, Petit (1674 to 1750) advocated the removal of the breast, the underlying pectoral muscle, and the axillary lymph nodes—what some consider the first radical mastectomy. Heister (1683 to 1758), a German, favored the use of a guillotine machine for breast removal. Mastectomies were performed in larger numbers at the beginning of the eighteenth century but decreased in the second half of the century because of poor results and indiscriminate mutilation. D'Etiolles's data from France in 1844, based on 1,192 patients, concluded the operation was more harmful than beneficial. At the beginning of the nineteenth century, appropriate treatment for breast cancer was unresolved and may have regressed, with more radical excision without anesthesia.

Sir James Paget (1814 to 1899) questioned in 1856 whether the operation added length of life or comfort to justify its risk. In 1874, he published "Disease of the Mammary Areola Preceding Cancer of the Mammary Gland," reporting an operative mortality of 10 percent, recurrence within 8 years, and longer survival for those without operation.[1] Alfred Armand Louis Marie Velpeau (1795 to 1867), a French surgeon, reported in 1854 on cure rates for over 1,000 breast tumors, benign or malignant. Long-term follow-up until death was unusual, but Velpeau felt he had cured many cases. The 1854 Academie de Medicine discussed whether breast cancer should be treated at all. Charles Moore (1821 to 1879) advanced the belief in wider and more extensive surgery (1867). By the turn of the century, surgical mortality was high due to infection, and there were claims that patients lived longer without surgery.

Surgical treatment in the nineteenth century ultimately benefited from the development of anesthesia and antisepsis, and the modern radical mastectomy was perfected. Halsted's publications in 1894 and 1898 spelled out exact and scientific techniques for breast cancer surgery, and his principles were widely dispersed throughout surgery (Figure 1–22). The Halsted radical mastectomy was established as the ideal treatment method for breast cancer and remained so for approximately 70 years. His technique seemed intuitively and obviously correct, and his results were superior to any previously reported. The Halsted radical mastectomy became the standard of care. Despite this advance in surgical treatment, it became apparent that surgery alone would not be curative. Further developments were based on epidemiologic studies, statistical analyses of surgical results stratified by pathologic stage, and laboratory research.

Following World War II, diverging opinions and reports appeared with respect to radical mastectomy. Cushman Haagensen, who collected, classified, and analyzed breast cancer data for 50 years by studying his private patients, supported the use of the radical mastectomy. Others, including Urban and Wangensteen, advocated "supraradical" mastectomy, with dissection into the mediastinum and neck. Subsequent studies examined simple and modified radical mastectomy with and without radiation, with a striking similarity in survival rates. Since the 1970s, the surgical trend has been toward more-limited surgical procedures, with adjuvant regimens using radiation for local disease and using chemotherapy and hormonal regimens for systemic disease. Current therapy for breast cancer is evidence-based, having been defined on the basis of multiple randomized prospective trials evaluating surgical technique as well as adjuvant therapy.

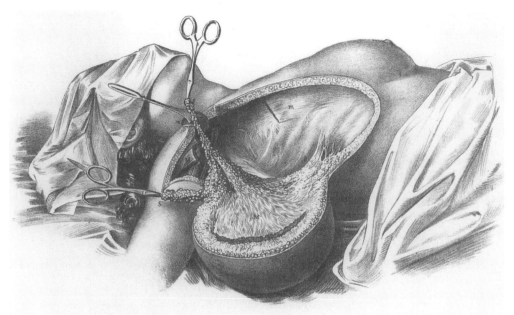

Figure 1–22 The Halsted radical mastectomy. (Reproduced with permission, from an illustration in Halsted WS. The results of operations for the cure of cancer of the breast performed at The Johns Hopkins Hospital from June, 1889 to January, 1894. In: the Surgical Papers by William Stewart Halsted. Baltimore: Lord Baltimore Press; 1924.)

CONCLUSION

The history of breast cancer surgery illustrates the evolution of the use of evidence in surgery. Removal of the breast with no apparent cure was generally the approach for much of recorded medical history, but this approach was eventually abandoned because of poor results with respect to cure and prevention of local recurrence. Not until the application of Lister's principles of antisepsis and Morton's discovery of anesthesia were curative procedures for breast cancer considered again. Halsted's development of the radical mastectomy as a conservative approach with the aim of a cure led to the further development and refinement of this procedure until adjuvant therapies could be used in conjunction with surgery, leading to greatly reduced invasiveness in surgery for the treatment of breast cancer. Today, the physician can provide the patient with information on surgical procedure results and survival statistics for adjuvant regimens. Application of these data, along with patient preferences, promotes an evidence-based approach to the overall treatment and management of breast cancer.

The next chapter reviews the significant events that laid the foundation for the current evidence-based surgery movement: the influences of the public health movement, key learnings from military medicine, the examination of variations in clinical practice, and contemporary trends in evidence-based surgery.

ACKNOWLEDGMENT

We are indebted to Dr. Harry Marks, Associate Professor of the Elizabeth Triede and A. McGehee Harvey Professorship of the History of Medicine and Technology at Johns Hopkins for his invaluable knowledge and guidance in the writing of this chapter.

REFERENCES

1. Wagner FB. History of breast disease and its treatment. In: The breast: comprehensive management of benign and malignant diseases. Philadelphia and London: W.B. Saunders Company, 1991. p. 1–16.

2. Brieger GH. A portrait of surgery: surgery in America, 1875–1889. Surg Clin North Am 1987 Dec;67(6):1181–216.

3. Rutkow IM. Surgery: an illustrated history. St. Louis: Mosby-Year Book, Inc.; 1993.

4. Garrison FH. An introduction to the history of medicine. Philadelphia and London: W. B. Saunders Company; 1929.

5. Bordley J, Harvey AM, editors. Two centuries of American medicine: 1776–1976. Philadelphia: W.B. Saunders Company; 1976.

6. Reverby S. Stealing the golden eggs: Ernest Amory Codman and the science management of medicine. Bull Hist Med 1981;55:156–71.

7. Halsted WS. The training of the surgeon. Bull Johns Hopkins Hosp 1904;15(162).

8. Ravitch MM. A century of surgery: the history of the American Surgical Association. Philadelphia and Toronto: J.B. Lippincott Company; 1981.

9. Bunker JP, Barnes BA, editors. Costs, risks and benefits of surgery. New York: Oxford University Press; 1977. p. 124–69.

10. Stevens R. A national enterprise: setting basic rules. In: In sickness and in wealth. New York: Basic Books, Inc.; 1989. p. 52–79.

11. Heinig SJ, Quon ASW, Meyer RE, Korn D. AAMC paper: the changing landscape for clinical research. Acad Med 1999 Jun;74(6):725–45.

12. Ward GG. The value and need of more attention to end-results and follow-up in hospitals today. Health Matrix 1989; 7:23–9.

CHAPTER 2

Origins of Evidence-Based Surgery

Toby A. Gordon, ScD, and John L. Cameron, MD, FACS

While evidence-based surgery may be viewed as deriving in general from the professionalization of surgery in the nineteenth century and more specifically from Codman's end-results system in the early twentieth century, the origins of contemporary evidence-based surgery have been influenced by several major developments since World War I: the public health movement and the evolution of public policy related to health care delivery; military medicine and key learnings from World War II; and clinical and health services research in practice variations. This chapter will review these influences on the development of evidence-based surgery.

PUBLIC HEALTH AND PUBLIC POLICY

Evidence-based medicine can be thought of as representing the intersection of medicine and public health, closely related disciplines differentiated by the population focus of public health and the individual patient focus of medicine. While the predominant interest of these fields differ, each has addressed different aspects in parallel fashion, namely, infectious disease in the nineteenth century and managed care in the twentieth century.

Public health's beginnings are attributed to John Snow, who in 1850 showed that cholera, an affliction claiming many lives, was spread by contaminated drinking water. In medicine, the pre-eminence of infectious diseases is illustrated by the causes of death during the Civil War: two-thirds of the Union soldiers killed in the Civil War lost their lives to infectious disease rather than to the original injuries they had suffered.[1]

The public health movement in the United States concentrated its attention on the social and health problems of industrialized cities and agricultural workers and was seen as a way to "mitigate the extremes of wealth and poverty, raise levels of productivity and efficiency and conserve human resources, the source of national wealth."[2] During the evolution of the public health movement, early debate focused on social versus biologic approaches to disease prevention and health promotion and the utility of broad public education versus specialized training of public health practitioners. By the early twentieth century, the public health movement had resulted in the municipal control of water and sewage treatment as a method of disease prevention. Graduate schools in public health were established in the first quarter of the century, and the field evolved from one initially focused on epidemiology, pathology, and disease prevention to one inclusive of more broadly defined interests: delivery of medical care, resource allocation, and economic forces in health care (Figure 2–1). The interest of public health practitioners in research examining clinical, economic, and/or patient-reported outcomes, alone or in combination, lies in the potential to improve the health status of a population.

The tremendous social reform following World War I raised many questions about health care delivery in the United States, especially with regard to cost, access, and quality-of-care issues. In the early 1930s, during the Roosevelt administration, two significant studies of American medicine focused on inadequacies in the provision of medical care: the Report of the Commission on Medical Education (1932) and the Report of the Committee on the Cost of Medical Care (1932).[1] Organized medicine found the recommendations radical and deemed them unnecessary, but the seed of health care reform had been planted. A national

Figure 2–1 Simon Flexner looks on as John D. Rockefeller Jr gives a book to Dr. William H. Welch in honor of his 80th birthday. This photograph was taken in 1931 at the Maryland Club in Baltimore, Maryland, and shows three of the major figures in the founding of The Johns Hopkins University School of Hygiene and Public Health. Dr. Welch was the first dean of The Johns Hopkins University School of Medicine, from 1894 to 1898, and the first dean of The Johns Hopkins University School of Hygiene and Public Health, from 1916 to 1927. Rockefeller provided funds for the start-up of the school, and Flexner, the first director of the Rockefeller Institute, was instrumental in supporting the need for such a school. (Reproduced with permission of the Alan Mason Chesney Medical Archives of the Johns Hopkins Medical Institutions, from the William H. Welch papers.)

health survey was ultimately performed to confirm the study findings regarding the lack of adequate medical care, the poorly organized and fragmented health care delivery system, and the limited ability of most patients to pay for treatment.

In 1940, approximately 12 million Americans, less than 10 percent of the population, had some form of health insurance. During World War II, the government freeze on wages brought about the provision of increased benefits to employees, such as health insurance, and this practice continued after the war. By 1950, 77 million Americans had health benefits, enabling more sick people to seek a physician's care. In 1966, much of the nonworking population was given the right to basic health benefits under the federally sponsored Medicare coverage for the elderly and the joint federal and state Medicaid program for the poor. Since its inception in the mid-1960s, the Medicare program, through its support of graduate medical education, teaching hospitals, and medical care for the elderly and disabled, has become a significant and direct supporter of the research and educational aims of academic medical centers.[3] Also, the original Medicare legislation called upon hospitals to guard against inappropriate care by setting up internal peer review committees to review the work of physicians. This peer review process has given way to performance improvement activities under the mandate of the Joint Commission on Accreditation of Healthcare Organizations, which has helped stimulate interest in outcomes research.

Subsequent actions by the Health Care Financing Administration (HCFA), the federal agency responsible for administering the Medicare program, have further supported the growth of evidence-based medicine. These include the implementation of the Medicare Prospective Payment System in 1983, which led to the widespread use of diagnosis related groups (DRGs), and the creation of comprehensive claims databases, used for economic and clinical outcomes research. From this database, the HCFA was subsequently able to provide the public with mortality data by hospital. The agency also promulgated "centers of excellence" (ie, designated cost-effective providers based on economic and clinical outcomes measures) for coronary artery bypass surgery and organ transplantation. In addition, HCFA reimbursement policy has mandated cost-effectiveness research for new surgical technologies such as lung reduction surgery. However, as new surgical procedures are developed, they are often subjected to reimbursement limitations and constraints, and there are only a small number of examples of mandated research to look at surgical procedures. The Health Care Financing Administration has been criticized for insignificant funding of clinical research while continuing to invest in health care of unknown effectiveness.

However, other federal agencies are charged with the responsibility for clinical research, which is differentiated from basic science and animal research through its aims of gaining knowledge useful to the understanding of human disease, preventing and treating illness, promoting health, and health services research.[4] Federally supported clinical research is disproportionately meager relative to basic science and animal research. The National Institutes of Health spend only 10 to 18 percent of its approximately $14 billion budget on clinical research, and the number of physicians applying to the National Institutes of Health for grants for clinical research is dropping.[4]

In the 1980s, the HCFA added another dimension to the development of evidence-based surgery by publicly disseminating mortality data derived from Medicare claims files. This practice continued for several years but was ultimately discontinued when numerous concerns were raised about whether the data had been appropriately risk adjusted.

While the demographic and economic forces at play in the health care arena are beyond the scope of this chapter, it is generally accepted that the ever increasing percent of gross domestic product expended on health care and economic globalization with its concomitant competitive pressures have fueled the cost containment forces in the managed care environment of health care today. These economic forces, coupled with the demographics of aging baby boomers, new medical and surgical technologies and pharmaceuticals, and continual concerns over the uninsured, are the basis for calls for health care reform to contain costs and better allocate health care resources. Evidence-based surgery can play a critical and much needed role in informing these debates by promoting a better understanding of who needs and benefits from surgical care and where and by whom such care should be rendered. Stakeholders in these public policy debates include the government, physicians, hospitals, employers, and consumers.

Since the 1980s, numerous private foundations have also addressed fundamental health policy and outcomes research questions, including the Robert Wood Johnson Foundation and the Commonwealth Foundation. The Department of Health and Human Services established the Agency for Health Care Policy Research (AHCPR) in 1989 as the agency in charge of supporting research aimed at improving the quality of health care, reducing its cost, and broadening access to essential services.

MILITARY MEDICINE AND THE RISE OF MEDICAL RESEARCH

Following World War I, the federal government began to participate in the support of university-based medical research. Toward the end of World War II, massive investments were made to expand the research and training capacity of American medical schools and teaching hospitals. This was further supported by the considerable development of the National Institutes of Health (NIH) following the war; originally founded in 1887 as the one-room Laboratory of Public Hygiene, the NIH would grow to become the largest source of federal support for scientific research in academic settings.

During World War II, a more coordinated approach to medical research and care was required to support military efforts, and several notable surgical advances were derived from military studies of surgery. President Roosevelt formed the Office of Scientific Research and

Figure 2–2 Michael DeBakey, MD, a general surgeon who was assigned to the Army Surgeon General's office as a consultant during World War II, shown with Surgeon General Kirk at the end of the war. During his military service as a surgical consultant, DeBakey provided numerous recommendations to improve military medicine; published articles on cold injuries, vascular surgery, war wounds of the chest and extremities, and experience with streptomycin in Army hospitals; and, given urgent national medical resource requirements shortly after the end of World War II, recruited surgical support for returning servicemen. (Reproduced with permission of the Association of Military Surgeons of the United States, from DeBakey ME. History, the torch that illuminates: lessons from military medicine. Mil Med 1995 Dec;161(12):711–16.

Development (OSRD), which included a Committee on Medical Research. The committee initiated, coordinated, and funded several large projects that resulted in the large-scale production of penicillin as well as in the development of new drugs for malaria. However, no specific surgical projects of this committee are known.

DeBakey[5–7] (Figure 2–2) wrote extensively on "battle injuries of the arteries" and "war wounds of the chest," based on his experiences during World War II, and included incidence rates, morbidity, methods of management, and factors influencing outcomes. Without the benefits of military research, many surgical principles that were established during the war and that later proved applicable to civilian practice might have required many more years of study. These include (a) the concept of phased-wound management; (b) standardization of care, brought about by uniformity of technical procedures, mass instruction of medical personnel, and standardization of basic equipment; (c) definition of the function of each echelon in the chain of evacuation; (d) new treatment approaches for burns and infections, and; (e) the formulation of planning models for acute and rehabilitative services. Surgical specialization was never fully translated into practice during World War I whereas in World War II, consultants in major specialties and subspecialties were eventually appointed in every service command. Surgical consultants were expected to promote the highest standards of medical practice within their areas of responsibilities, including the development of policies and the effective use and continual assessment of specialized surgical personnel.

DeBakey noted that although significant data were available from World War II research studies about shock, hemorrhage, and empyema, the importance of this information was ignored, as the policy early in World War II was to discourage clinical investigations in Army hospitals. Instead, studies were referred to the National Research Council for study by civilians. This military-civilian study methodology did not allow complete integration of ideas between military and civilian research efforts. The barrier between military surgeons and civilian investigators was attributed to security regulations and the belief that problems could not be extracted from the military setting for civilian study.

DeBakey cites the slow development of an optimal method for the treatment of burns as an illustration of the lack of integration of research studies into military surgery. Thus, research efforts were hampered through most of World War II until the ban on military research was lifted, at which time valuable information resulted from the work of small groups of investigators in the field. As the war progressed, the original policy discouraging research in Army installations was modified, with some studies carried out by members of the staff of the Massachusetts General Hospital regarding, for example, physiologic responses to shock, the bacteriology of wounds, and indications for transfusions. In August 1945, the Army Medical Research Board, with proper clinical representation, was set up in the Surgeon General's office.

Some research during the war focused on the process of care, eg, timeliness of postsurgical ambulation. Since few hospitals were built during the Depression and since there were severe bed shortages during and after World War II, especially near factories and shipyards, considerable interest focused on decreasing patients' lengths of stay. Halsted had written in 1889 that following surgery, his patients were not permitted out of bed for 21 days, and lengthy hospital stays were the norm into the 1940s. In an effort to decrease lengths of stay, the National Research Council of the Division of Medical Sciences performed controlled experiments in early activity of postoperative patients, and in 1944, the American Medical Association held a symposium on "The Abuse of Rest in the Treatment of Disease." Powers reported results of a controlled study in which patients with hernia repairs, appendectomies, cholecystectomies, and abdominopelvic operations were grouped by ambulation on the day of or day after surgery versus patients on bed rest for 10 to 15 days.[1] Using matched pairs, all factors analyzed favored earlier ambulation, which was ultimately pursued after the symposium. This study exemplifies the use of outcomes research to influence the care delivery process.

Following World War II, the Veterans Administration (VA) research program was instituted to improve the quality of health care for returning veterans. Since then, VA researchers, often in close concert with academic medical centers, have been active participants in surgical research. The Veterans Administration's current research mandate covers biomedical, mental-illness, rehabilitative, and health care services research. Evidence-based surgical research is supported by the VA primarily in the biomedical and health services research sectors.

Evidence-Based Surgery and Clinical and Health Services Research

Several studies examining variations in clinical practice preceded the well-known work of Wennberg. In the 1920s and 1930s, tonsillectomies came under scrutiny due to the widespread use of this procedure and its concomitant risks such as anesthesia-related mortality. In the late 1920s, tonsillectomies accounted for more than one-fourth of all United States hospital admissions and for one-third of all operations performed under anesthesia.[8] Researchers from the American Child Health Association, concerned about health care for children, studied a sample of 1,000 11-year-olds from the New York City public schools. Sixty-one percent of the children had already had their tonsils removed; the remainder was sent to a group of school doctors who reported that 45 percent of students with tonsils needed tonsillectomies. Students who had been told that their tonsils did not need to be removed were screened again, and 46 percent of that group were advised that tonsillectomy was needed. This process of obtaining additional opinions for children who had been told they did not need their tonsils removed continued, resulting in only 65 of the original 1,000 children not being recommended for tonsillectomy.[8]

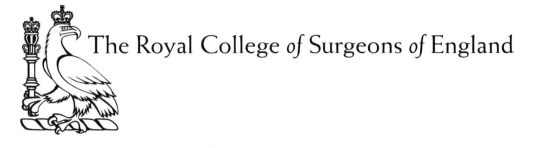

Figure 2–3 The seal of the Royal College of Surgeons of England, to whose members Glover presented the results of his tonsillectomy study. The origins of the Royal College can be traced to the union of barbers and surgeons by Henry VIII in 1540. In 1745, the surgeons formed a separate Company of Surgeons, which was granted a Royal Charter in 1800. (Reproduced with permission of the Royal College of Surgeons.)

Glover, a British physician, analyzed tonsillectomies performed in England and Wales in a related study, noting that at least 85 children under the age of 15 years died from tonsillectomies each year in England and Wales.[8] He reported wide variations in the rate of surgery by geographic area. Since tonsillectomies were thought to be an effective method of reducing ear infections, Glover also examined the correlation between the annual number of tonsillectomies and the rate of ear infections, which was shown to have decreased along with a decreased number of tonsillectomies. Glover presented his results to the 1938 Royal College of Surgeons meeting (Figure 2–3), where his colleagues shared his concerns. However, debate over indications for tonsillectomies persisted into the 1950s, when half of all children in the United States had tonsillectomies although the literature contained no evidence of the procedure's effectiveness. In the 1970s, 50 to 80 percent of tonsillectomies performed were deemed unnecessary, and after this, the frequency began to decline. Insertion of tympanostomy tubes has similarly been called into question as treatment for otitis media, as has the appropriateness of other operations (such as hysterectomies).

In 1960, Dimond evaluated the effectiveness of the surgical therapy for angina pectoris.[9] In this study, patients who received a sham operation (a chest incision only) were compared to patients who had ligation of internal mammary arteries for angina pectoris. Both groups had identical reports of improvements, and the exercise electrocardiograms were not altered by either procedure. Dimond noted that there was not scientific quantification for measurement of angina and that many other factors should be considered in such a study.

A comprehensive review of surgical research methods was conducted by Gilbert for 107 surgical studies from 1964 to 1972 that met the inclusion criteria for his analyses.[10] Approximately one-third were randomized trials; one-half were reports of series of patients without any well-defined comparison group as part of the same study. In the randomized trials that compared innovative therapies to standard treatment, innovative therapies were considered better than standard therapy for 44 percent of patients; for 56 percent, standard therapy was superior.

Contemporary research in surgical practice variation was conducted by Wennberg in 1973: surgical procedure rates in 13 hospital service areas in Vermont were compared[11] (Figure 2–4). Residents of these areas were comparable to each other demographically, and there was little in- or out-migration in the state. Wennberg found that physician preferences were the greatest influence on rates of tonsillectomies, appendectomies, hysterectomies, mastectomies, hemorrhoidectomies, and surgeries for other common conditions, with considerable variation in rates of surgery across service areas. Furthermore, Wennberg was

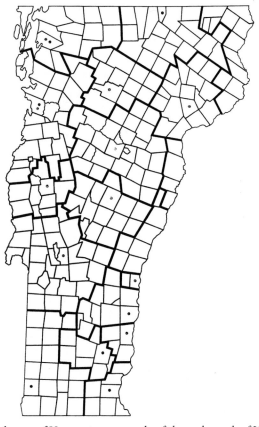

Figure 2–4 Map of the hospital areas of Vermont, an example of the early work of Wennberg, published in 1973. Hospital areas were defined as small areas in which most residents go to a single hospital. On this map, the hospital areas are indicated by heavy lines; boundaries between townships within an area are indicated by light lines, and hospitals are indicated by circles. Wennberg's research, in collaboration with Gittelsohn, revealed that "the amount and cost of hospital treatment in a community have more to do with the number of physicians there, their medical specialties and the procedures they prefer than with the health of the residents." (Reproduced with permission, from Wennberg J, Gittelsohn A. Variations in medical care among small areas. Sci Am 1981;245(4):120–34.)

unable to determine from the literature a consensus on the "right" rates of surgery. Initially, Wennberg's research on practice variations was not received well, and his work was subject to an audit initiated by the medical school in which he worked, but ultimately his findings have been widely accepted and expanded upon in the health services research arena. Further analytic developments were supported by the sophisticated mathematical analysis employed in the 1970s by Eddy, who used breast cancer treatment data to develop the decision analysis methodology for medical care.

In the 1980s and 90s, surgical outcomes research studies were performed with increasing frequency, and have focused on the following:

- The relationship between volume and outcome (eg, open heart surgery, pancreatico-duodenectomies)
- The efficacy and effectiveness of new surgical procedures (eg, laparoscopic cholecystectomies, minimally invasive cardiac surgery)
- Cost-effectiveness research on new versus existing procedures

- Development of validated instruments for clinical and patient-reported outcomes measurements
- Quality-of-life issues in treatment planning (eg, breast cancer)
- Variations in standards of care (eg, Wennberg's small-area-variation research)
- The use and evaluation of critical pathways and practice care
- Patient risk factors in treatment planning (eg, surgery for the elderly)

The 1990s have witnessed the rise of the evidence-based surgery medicine movement. Sackett, one of the leading proponents of evidence-based medicine as a critical component of medicine in general, has published extensively on this subject.[12] He describes evidence-based medicine as the "conscientious, explicit and judicious use of current best evidence in making decisions about the care of individual patients. The practice of evidence-based medicine integrates individual clinical expertise with the best available external clinical evidence from systemic research." Growth in the evidence-based medicine movement, along with the rise in consumer interest in medical care outcomes, has created an imperative for surgeons to understand how to produce and interpret surgical evidence. (This topic is discussed in more detail in the chapter on consumer health information.) The promulgation of surgical evidence requires knowledge of methods to produce and critique evidence.

The present-day focus on evidence-based surgery can be traced to ideals expressed and questions raised over the last century in regard to the health and welfare of the population. Public health concerns frame the resource allocation issues that comprise much of the ultimate use of evidence. These concerns, along with increasingly sophisticated medical treatments and interventions, the growing availability of computer technology, the economic and political forces that brought about managed care and health care reform, and the growing interest of consumers to self-direct their personal care, give rise to current evidence-based surgery. With the growing availability of analytic technology and information, questions can now be adequately considered.

Ultimately, evidence-based surgical research should enable stakeholders in the health care delivery process—patients, physicians, payers, and policymakers—to provide the most clinical and cost-effective care possible. However, as we will see in the next chapter, the perspectives of these stakeholders vary greatly, and given the limited resources available to pursue evidence-based surgery research, competing interests influence what research comes to the fore.

CASE STUDY: PANCREATICODUODENECTOMY

The evolution of evidence-based surgery can be demonstrated by the example of the surgical experience that led to the development, refinement, and ultimate acceptance of pancreaticoduodenectomy for periampullary cancer. Over its 100-year history, the evidence supporting pancreatic resection for periampullary cancer has grown from case reports to extensive series of patients, from observation of the effects of treatment to sophisticated measurement of clinical outcomes, and from findings relevant to advancing the care of the single patient to the improvement of the health status of the population. Most important, the extensive body of clinical experience and research has supported related basic science research, leading to new information on molecular events that lead to the development of pancreatic cancer. This section elucidtaes the development of surgical evidence related to pancreaticoduodenectomy and how this evidence has been used ultimately to improve the public's health.

Pancreatic cancer is the fifth leading cause of cancer death in the United States, with 28,000 new cases diagnosed each year.[13] It is a particularly lethal form of cancer that upon diagnosis is often at a stage precluding any surgical treatment except palliation. However, potentially curative surgical treatment is increasingly being performed. Generally accepted as the biggest and most complex gastrointestinal operation, this procedure is the subject of numerous research reports that have explicated the principles of patient selection, operative technique, and patient management considerations, thus enabling more patients to benefit from potentially curative surgical care.

History of Surgery for Pancreatic Cancer

In 1899, Halsted's case report first established that resection could be successfully performed for a periampullary tumor. In 1898, Codivilla performed an en bloc resection of a portion of the pancreas, part of the duodenum, and the distal stomach in a patient with a tumor involving the duodenum and the head of the pancreas. The patient did not survive. The first successful pancreaticoduodenal resection was performed by Kausch in Berlin in 1912. However, the vast majority of periampullary cancers from 1900 to 1935 were managed by transduodenal incision and local excision of the tumor in the manner described by Halsted.

In 1935, at the American Surgical Association, Whipple and colleagues reported three patients undergoing a two-stage en bloc resection of the head of the pancreas and duodenum for periampullary tumors, which stimulated renewed interest in the radical excision of periampullary tumors.[14] After this, pancreaticoduodenal resection underwent a number of modifications and technical refinements. In 1937, Brunschwig performed the first successful pancreaticoduodenectomy for cancer of the head of the pancreas, and in 1941, Trimble published the first description of a successful one-stage pancreaticoduodenal resection in the United States.

During the 1960s and 1970s, most centers reported operative morality rates for pancreaticoduodenectomy in the 20 to 40 percent range, with postoperative morbidity rates as high as 60 percent. Many physicians and some surgeons believed that pancreaticoduodenectomy should be abandoned for all periampullary carcinomas and particularly for carcinoma of the head of the pancreas, due to excessive operative mortality and few long-term survivors.

In the early 1980s, a dramatic decline in operative morbidity and mortality was realized in a number of centers, with operative mortality rates falling to the range of 2 percent. In one series, 190 consecutive pancreaticoduodenectomies were performed without a mortality. In the most recent Johns Hopkins series, age over 70 years was not associated with an increased operative risk. More than fifty patients aged 80 years or more have undergone a successful Whipple operation at Hopkins, including one 103-year-old woman. Therefore, unless there are major contraindications to general anesthesia and surgery, the option of surgical exploration and resection should be available to all patients with periampullary cancer.[13] (Figure 2–5)

Several factors probably account for the drop in in-hospital mortality: improved surgical management due to better understanding of anatomy, surgical techniques, and management principles; growth in the experience of surgeons and hospitals with this procedure, and; the concomitant development of critical pathways and specialized care teams across all disciplines to support patient care. A number of tertiary care facilities have focused on pancreaticoduodenectomy or Whipple's procedure, resulting in concentrated clinical experience and extensive clinical and basic science research programs at these "centers of excellence."

The experience of one institution, The Johns Hopkins Hospital, illustrates the progression of the surgical study of pancreatic resection for cancer. After Halsted's case report in 1899, surgery for pancreatic resection at Hopkins mirrored the progression of pancreatic surgery as reported in the literature over the next 70 years. In the 1970s, more intensive focus on periampullary tumors by a few surgeons brought about a better understanding of factors effecting mortality for Whipple's operation. Reports followed on improved hospital morbidity, mortality, and survival after Whipple's procedure[15] and on factors influencing survival after pancreaticoduodenectomy for pancreatic cancer.[16] Several large series were next reported: 145 consecutive pancreaticoduodenectomies without mortality in 1993;[17] pancreaticoduodenectomy for cancer of the head of the pancreas for 201 patients in 1995;[18] and later, 650 consecutive pancreaticoduodenectomies in the 1990s.[15,19] Research reports from other centers were similarly encouraging.

Despite the extensive clinical experience and encouraging results, the potential for further surgical advances came under assault when managed care dictums challenged patients' access to The Johns Hopkins Hospital for pancreatic resection for surgery. Due to the inherent costs of teaching and research at an academic medical center, the hospital had been labeled as high cost by many payers, and some patients were denied access to care at Hopkins. As desperate patients sought the best place for care, they demanded payer approval of hospitals with the best outcomes, regardless of cost. This onslaught from managed care stimulated a whole new area of research into the cost-effectiveness of care, initially conducted to determine outcomes of care for the experienced surgical team at the hospital with by far the most extensive experience with the pancreaticoduodenectomy procedure not only in the state but in the geographic region. As a result of outcomes research focused on the relationship between the number of pancreaticoduodenectomy procedures performed at a hospital and in-hospital mortality and cost, the Hopkins team successfully demonstrated the inverse relationship between hospital volume and in-hospital mortality and cost for pancreaticoduodenectomy, as detailed in the later chapter on pancreatic surgery.[20]

Building upon this research in a follow-up study, the Hopkins group next examined the effect of the concentration of pancreaticoduodenectomies at Hopkins as the regional referral center for this procedure in the state.[21] In-hospital mortality and hospital volume were examined for all hospitals in the state over a 12-year period. Over time, regionalization or the aggregation of cases at the high-volume hospital with demonstrably better clinical outcomes was found to significantly reduce statewide in-hospital mortality. Next, the Hopkins team focused on the relationship between volume and outcomes for both curative and palliative treatment of pancreatic cancer, extending the concept of the original pancreaticoduodenectomy research to all surgical care for pancreatic cancer.[22]

The majority of patients with pancreatic cancer referred for surgery do not undergo potentially curative pancreaticoduodenectomy but are instead palliated with biliary stents or surgical bypass procedures. Since the decision to palliate or resect for cure is often not made until the time of laparotomy, the Hopkins group next examined the relationship between hospital surgical volume and clinical and economic outcomes for patients who underwent either palliative or curative surgery for pancreatic cancer. Increased surgical volume was associated with markedly decreased in-hospital mortality with minimal or no increase in hospital charges and lower or similar lengths of stay as compared to lower-volume hospitals for palliative and curative procedures for pancreatic cancer. These findings lend further support to the referral of patients with pancreatic cancer who might benefit from either surgical palliation or more extensive resection to hospitals that perform higher volumes of these procedures. Next, the group examined the volume-outcomes relationship for all high-risk complex gastrointestinal surgical procedures, with similar findings with respect to the relationship between procedure volume and clinical and economic outcomes.[23]

Two theories have been posited regarding the possible explanations for the volume-outcomes relationship observed in the cancer studies: (1) does "practice make perfect" or (2) is there a selective referral process occurring that biases the results?[24,25] In the Hopkins studies, these questions were addressed with careful risk-adjustment techniques, as discussed in a later chapter, with results supporting the "practice makes perfect" explanation rather than the selective referral process explanation. This finding is not unexpected given DeBakey's observation of key learnings from World War II, namely, that concentrated experience can accelerate the determination of methods critical to enhancing patient care.

Basic Science Research

Over the past decade, the Hopkins team's experience with pancreaticoduodenectomy grew, with a doubling of procedure volume from the mid- to late-1990s. As knowledge about the team's interest and experience is disseminated, the volume of referrals to this hospital

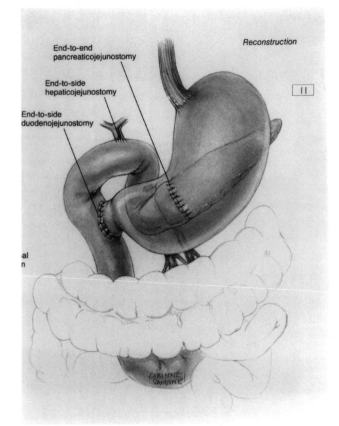

Figure 2–5 The contemporary pancreaticoduodenectomy, showing the various anastomoses. (Reproduced with permission, from an illustration by Corinne Sandone in Cameron JL. Atlas of surgery. Vol 1. Toronto: B.C. Decker; 1990.)

continues to grow. A serendipitous benefit of the extensive surgical volume has been not only the considerable expertise developed in studying the pathology of pancreatic cancer but also the keen interest on the part of pathologists, oncologists, and basic scientists in the molecular events that take place in the pancreas during the development of pancreatic cancer. As a result, the group of molecular biologists at Hopkins has written the largest body of papers to date describing the genetics of pancreatic cancer, and they are working toward a tumor marker that allows the identification of patients with adenocarcinoma of the head of the pancreas at an earlier stage (Figure 2–6).[26,27] One of these scientists has taken the lead in developing a Web site with current information on pancreatic cancer, as described further in the chapter on consumer health information.

Conclusion

By examining the focused clinical experience and research undertaken to improve the surgical management of pancreatic cancer, provide more cost-effective care, and investigate the early molecular events in the development of pancreatic cancer, this case study shows that evidence-based surgery can not only improve patient care but could ultimately help prevent disease. Collaborating investigators in various disciplines, through the complex interplay of their epidemiologic, clinical, and basic science research findings, have advanced the treatment of pancreatic cancer.

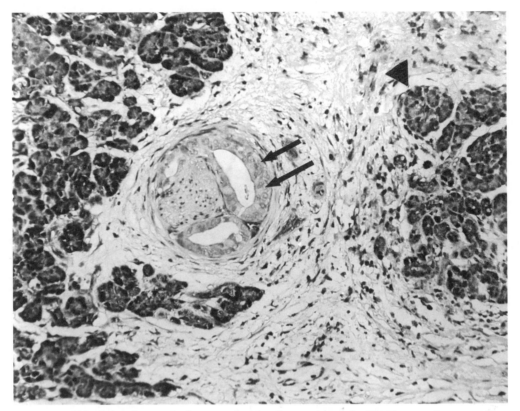

Figure 2–6 This photomicrograph shows a stain of a pancreas cancer for DPC4, a gene important in the development of pancreas cancer, discovered at Hopkins in 1996. This gene is deleted (missing) in over half of pancreatic cancers. The infiltrating cancer (arrows) does not stain for DPC4 whereas the adjacent normal pancreas (arrowhead) strongly stains. The discovery of DPC4 has not only led to the development of useful stains such as this but may also lead to a new rational gene-based treatment for pancreas cancer. (Reproduced with permission, from a photograph provided by Ralph Hruban, MD, The Johns Hopkins Medical Institutions, Department of Pathology.)

Techniques necessary to produce and critique surgical evidence will be explored in later chapters. Ultimately, evidence-based surgical research should enable stakeholders in the health care delivery process—patients, physicians, payers, and policymakers—to provide or benefit from the most clinical and costeffective care possible. However, as we will see in the next chapter, the perspectives of these stakeholders vary greatly, and given the limited resources available for evidence-based surgery research, competing interests influence what research comes to the fore. Beyond stakeholder perspectives are the legal, ethical, and health policy issues, explored in later chapters to provide a perspective on evidence-based surgery in the United States. A perspective on evidence-based surgery in the United Kingdom is also provided.

ACKNOWLEDGMENT

We are indebted to Dr. Harry Marks, Associate Professor of the Elizabeth Triede and A. McGehee Harvey Professor of the History of Medicine and Technology at the William H. Welch Medical Library at Johns Hopkins for his invaluable knowledge and guidance in the writing of this chapter.

REFERENCES

1. Bordley J, Harvey AM, editors. Two centuries of American medicine: 1776–1976. Philadelphia: W.B. Saunders Company; 1976.

2. Fee E. Disease and discovery: a history of the Johns Hopkins School of Hygiene and Public Health. Baltimore: The Johns Hopkins University Press; 1987.

3. Joint Commission on Accreditation of Hospitals. Accreditation manual for hospitals. Chicago: Joint Commission on the Accreditation of Hospitals; 1997.

4. Heinig SJ, Quon ASW, Meyer RE, Korn D. AAMC paper: the changing landscape for clinical research. Acad Med 1999 Jun;74(6):725–45.

5. DeBakey ME, Simeone FA. Battle injuries of the arteries in world war II. Ann Surg 1946 Apr;534–71.

6. DeBakey ME. Military surgery in world war II: a backward glance and a forward look. N Engl Med 1947 Mar;236(10):341–50.

7. DeBakey ME. History, the torch that illuminates: lessons from military medicine. Mil Med 1995 Dec;161(12):711–16.

8. Millenson ML. Demanding medical excellence: doctors and accountability in the information age. Chicago and London: The University of Chicago Press; 1997.

9. Dimond EG, Kittle, CF, Crockett JE. Comparison of internal mammary artery ligation and sham operation for angina pectoris. Am J Cardiol 1960 Apr:483–6.

10. Gilbert JP, McPeek B, Mosteller F. Progress in surgery and anesthesia: benefits and risks of innovative therapy. In: Bunker JP, Barnes BA, editors. Costs, risks and benefits of surgery. New York: Oxford University Press; 1977. p. 124–69.

11. Wennberg J, Gittelsohn A. Variations in medical care among small areas. Sci Am 1981;245(4):120–34.

12. Sackett DL, Richardson WS, Rosenberg W, Haynes RB, editors. Evidence-based medicine: how to practice and teach evidence-based medicine. New York: Churchill Livingstone; 1997.

13. Cameron JL. Long-term survival following pancreaticoduodenectomy for adenocarcinoma of the head of the pancreas. Surg Clin North Am 1995;75(5):939–51.

14. Ratvich MM. A century of surgery: the history of the American Surgical Association. Philadelphia and Toronto: J.B. Lippincott Company; 1981.

15. Crist DW, Sitzmann JV, Cameron JL. Improved hospital morbidity, mortality, and survival after the Whipple procedure. Ann Surg 1987;206(3);358–65.

16. Cameron JL, Crist DW, Sitzmann JV, et al. Factors influencing survival after pancreaticoduodenectomy for pancreatic cancer. Am J Surg 1991;161:120–5.

17. Cameron JL, Pitt HA, Yeo CJ, et al. One hundred and forty-five consecutive pancreaticoduodenectomies without mortality. Ann Surg 1993;217(5):430–8.

18. Yeo CJ, Cameron JL, Lillemoe KD, et al. Pancreaticoduodenectomy for cancer of the head of the pancreas—201 patients. Ann Surg 1995;221(6):721–33.

19. Yeo CJ, Cameron JL, Sohn TA, et al. Six hundred fifty consecutive pancreaticoduodenectomies in the 1990's. Ann Surg 1997;226(3):248–60.

20. Gordon, TA, Burleyson G, Tielsch JM, Cameron JL. The effects of regionalization on cost and outcome for one high-risk general surgical procedure. Ann Surg 1995;221(1):43–9.

21. Gordon TA, Bowman HB, Tielsch JM, et al. Statewide regionalization of pancreaticoduodenectomy and its effect on in-hospital mortality. Ann Surg 1998;228(1):71–8.

22. Sosa JA, Bowman HM, Gordon TA, et al. Importance of hospital volume in the overall management of pancreatic cancer. Ann Surg 1998;22(3):429–38.

23. Gordon TA, Bowman HB, Bass EB, et al. Complex gastrointestinal surgery: impact of provider experience on clinical and economic outcomes. J Am Coll Surg 1999. [In press]

24. Luft HS. The relation between surgical volume and mortality; an exploration of causal factors and alternative models. Med Care 1980;18(9):940–59.

25. Hannan EL, O'Donnell JF, Kilburn H, et al. Investigation of the relationship between volume and mortality for surgical procedures performed in New York State hospitals. JAMA 1989;262(4):503–10.

26. Allison DC, Bose KK, Hruban RH, et al. Pancreatic cancer cell DNA content correlates with long-term survival after pancreaticoduodenectomy. Ann Surg 1991;214(6):648–56.

27. Yeo CJ, Kern SH, Hruban RH, Cameron JL. New aspects of genetics and surgical management in pancreatic cancer: the Johns Hopkins experience. Asian J Surg 1997;20(3):221–8.

CHAPTER 3

Stakeholder Perspectives

John D. Hundt, MHS, Charles Reuland, MHS, and Keith D. Lillemoe, MD

Understanding the perspective from which research information is presented can shed light onto the self-interests, ethical obligations, and economic incentives of those conducting the research. Therefore, one must understand who the stakeholders are in the research and what their perspectives might be. Generally, the stakeholders are thought to be patients; providers, including physicians and hospitals; payers, including managed care organizations, employers and the government; the industrial sectors that support health care delivery, for example, medical supply and device manufacturers; government policymakers, and private nonprofit policy concerns such as research foundations.

The perspectives of these stakeholders range from those of the individual patient to those of society at large. For example, while clinical research is generally from the perspective of the patient, most health policy research attempts to relate to a societal perspective. While such policy research supports resource allocation decisions at the societal level, decisions about one's personal health care are not made at the societal level. Further, conclusions drawn from a societal perspective may not directly influence the delivery of health care since each stakeholder in the health care delivery system has varying degrees of personal and financial risk and responsibility and has different incentives. Ultimately, the authority to organize, coordinate, and improve services rests with providers and payers whereas a patient must decide whether to consent to services offered by a physician.

Outcomes research generally focuses on three dimensions of outcomes: clinical, economic, and patient-reported.[1] Stakeholder perspective may determine which of these dimensions are considered in the research and how they are measured. Much evidence-based medicine is centered around the impact of interventions on patients (eg, biologic measures such as survival; disease or treatment complications; physiologic, anatomic, or laboratory abnormalities; and signs and symptoms). Much of the evidence-based surgery literature describes clinical outcomes, that is, morbidity and mortality. However, purchasers define outcomes principally in economic terms. Measures important to a patient extend beyond clinical and economic outcomes to aspects of physical and social well-being and functional status. (These dimensions of outcome—clinical, patient-reported, and economic—are covered extensively in later chapters.) Cost considerations are of paramount importance in health care today.

The emergence of population-based research coupled with new information technology has created a new literature about outcomes research. Quality, access, and cost are the three traditional parameters of interest to the various stakeholders and must be considered with respect to the role of surgery across the continuum of care including

- early detection and screening,
- diagnostic evaluation,
- primary and adjuvant therapy,
- surveillance and follow-up,
- treatment of recurrence,
- palliative care, and
- end-of-life care.

Significant trends in surgical care technology, including shifts to minimally invasive care and interdisciplinary care, are important considerations along the continuum.

Considerations that might be important to different participants in the health care system are as follows:

- Patients: out-of-pocket costs, lost functionality
- Providers: reimbursement
- Payers: expenses incurred
- Employers: lost productivity, cost of care over time
- Government policymakers: societal costs, use of scarce resources

The health care delivery and financing system in the United States is decentralized and fragmented, and health care information at the patient level across the continuum of care may be scarce. Outcomes analysis may look narrowly at a specific procedure for a specific condition, for example, colectomy for malignant neoplasm of the colon. Outcomes can be analyzed across a surgical specialty, for example, adjusted mortality rates for open heart surgery. Broad measures across patient populations and multiple disciplines may also be used, for example, surgical infection rates for all types of procedures. For a patient or referring physician making a decision about whether to have or perform a specific surgery, broad measures may be less useful. For a payer making a decision about which health systems to include in a health maintenance organization (HMO) network, broad measures may be useful. Whether an analysis is intended to aid in choosing among care options for one specific patient or to help policymakers decide on the adoption of a new technology is an issue of perspective.

SPECIFIC PERSPECTIVES

Patients

Patients are most interested in information that will help them make a decision about treatment they are seeking or that has been recommended. Risk and behavioral factors for a given patient may not be identified in the information on hand. For example, the preferred treatment in the literature may not be recommended to a patient unable to comply with complex postoperative treatment. Patients may require additional help in understanding contraindications to given treatment options. (A separate chapter addresses the topic of consumer health information.)

Patients get information about the value of surgical procedures from a variety of sources, including family and friends, physicians, and the media (as described in a later chapter on consumer health information). Information in the paid media (eg, advertisements) may be aimed at increasing the use of surgical services. For example, in an eight-page supplement to the February 5, 1999, edition of the national newspaper *USA Today*, readers are informed that "recent studies suggest total joint replacement has an increase in the quality of life, relative to cost, to a greater extent than almost any other invention." This supplement was sponsored by the American Association of Hip and Knee Surgeons, with financial support from manufacturers of orthopedic devices and supplies. Thus, evidence-based surgery research can significantly influence the market positions of companies in the medical supply and service sector.

Physicians

A physician's primary obligation is to look out for the welfare of the patient. Historically, this has meant that each patient's care should be personalized with a treatment plan based on individual patient needs, preferences, and risk factors.

Primary issues for physicians with respect to evidence-based surgery relate to planning the most appropriate care for their patients, either as the direct care provider or as the referring physician. Primary care doctors and specialists must also serve as advocates for their patients with managed care organizations.

An increase in the prevalence of risk-based payment and employment models for physicians has had an impact on the perspective of physicians. For example, a surgeon or group of surgeons at financial risk for the cost of services provided to a group of patients has financial incentives to take a more conservative approach to treatment. Again, research on the cost-effectiveness of care, while of interest to all responsible providers of care, may be of even greater interest to those whose economic stake is at risk.

Hospitals

Like other components of the health care system, hospitals are confronted with a complex environment, and this complexity has implications for evidence-based surgery and outcomes research.

Most hospitals in the United States are staffed by voluntary physicians who are not employees of the hospitals. Hospitals are charged with credentialing their medical staffs and documenting that physicians meet the minimum qualifications to perform procedures. While there is a significant amount of variation in practice patterns for treating similar conditions (eg, lumpectomy vs mastectomy for breast cancer), the ability of a hospital to influence the performance of its surgeons is limited. However, hospitals are increasingly using outcomes studies to identify variation among physicians and to pursue the best practices. Hospitals and other credentialing organizations use benchmarks to determine whether a physician is qualified to perform a procedure. Privileges for certain procedures may require that providers have previously completed a certain number of such procedures. Specialty certifications also may have such requirements. This is consistent with the literature, which shows a link between volume and outcomes.

Currently, there are no regulatory requirements for evidence-based surgery unless some aspect of the procedure falls under Food and Drug Administration (FDA) regulations for new devices. The Joint Committee on the Accreditation of Healthcare Organizations (JCAHO) does require an extensive performance improvement process, but the rigor required would not likely meet the requirements of peer-reviewed publications.

Payers

The US health care system is best described as a pluralistic system in terms of its various sources of payment for health care services. As of the end of 1997, 46.4 percent of national health expenditures for US citizens were paid by a government-funded insurance program, 32.9 percent were covered by a private insurance or self-funded employer source, and the remainder was paid directly by individuals.[2] While the United States is extensively supplied with physicians and hospitals and while the United States spends 13.9 percent[3] of its gross national product on health care, approximately 17 percent[4] of the adult population lacks insurance coverage, and there is wide variability in the quality of care available. Yet, economic concerns over health expenditures (rather than concerns about universal access) dominate policy debates. Managed care is the predominant organizing and financing mechanism for health care and has had a dramatic impact on the way services are delivered.

The growth of "managed care" in the 1980s and 1990s has resulted in a variety of different products that incentivize selection only of those providers participating in the patient's insurance plan. These products, including HMOs, point-of-service (POS) products, preferred provider organizations (PPOs), and open access products, are now a significant portion of the governmental and private payer sectors and are referred to as "network products" because they rely on prospectively defined networks of physicians and providers. Table 3–1 shows the size of each major payer sector and the penetration of network products into each major payer sector.

Clearly, there are many products in which network development is a critical function and in which decisions regarding a limited network of providers are made. Because cost, quality,

Table 3–1 Health Care Payers and Stakeholders

Health Care Funding Scenario	Payer	Insurer	Network-Defining Entity
Self-funded employer using a TPA	Employer	Employer	MCO
Employer purchasing an indemnity insurance product	Employer	Insurance company	Insurance company
Employer purchasing an insured managed care product (HMO, POS, PPO) from an MCO	Employer	MCO	MCO
Medicare (traditional)	Federal government	Federal government	Medicare program
Medicare (HMO)	Federal government	MCO	MCO
Medicaid (traditional)	State and federal government	State and federal government	State Medicaid program
Medicaid (HMO)	State and federal government	MCO	MCO

HMO = health maintenance organization; MCO = managed care organization; POS = point of service; PPO = preferred provider organization; TPA = third-party administrator.

and geographic access are all important in the decision to include providers in a network, it is useful to describe the perspectives of the various participants. Most commonly, these participants include the payer (the actual entity that funds the health care services via payments to the insurer), the insurer (the entity that assumes risk for costs above or below expected costs), and the network development entity that defines the network of physicians and hospitals to be used and contracts with the insurer for health care delivery. There are many configurations for payers, insurers, and network developers. Table 3–1 provides examples of the most prevalent funding scenarios and indicates the payer, the insurer, and the network development entity in each scenario. The purpose of this chart is to display the many variants in the decision-making process regarding care delivery options. Those managed care organizations (MCOs) that are responsible for network development set criteria for inclusion in their networks, including cost, access, and quality. Moreover, some MCOs further limit their networks for selected services in "centers of excellence" (COE) networks. These networks identify services believed to be more effectively provided at high-volume centers with demonstrated outcomes. Services frequently identified for COE consideration include organ and bone marrow transplantations and cardiovascular procedures. It is in these MCOs that the value of evidence-based surgery may have the highest potential.

The most recent trends in managed care have shown that individuals and employers are favoring plans that offer a higher level of choice of providers. The ability of a plan to direct enrollees to the highest-quality provider as determined by outcomes analysis may be limited by growth in these types of network product arrangements because enrollees may choose providers by other criteria. Rather than mandating referral to the highest-quality provider, plans may influence selection by publicizing superior outcomes with selected providers while still allowing choice.

To sell network insurance products or to "rent" networks to third-party administrators (TPAs) or self-insured employers, MCOs that perform network development must consider cost, access, and quality. For those products for which the MCO is also the insurer, there may be a greater willingness to limit networks to smaller numbers of providers. The quality indicators most frequently used by such MCOs include licensure and board eligibility or certification. Nonetheless, these organizations may also be interested in evidence-based surgery, particularly to the extent to which costs are either neutral or reduced.

For those MCOs that predominantly do *not* assume insurance risk (PPOs), access and cost are generally more relevant considerations. The National Committee for Quality Assurance (NCQA) is a private, nonprofit organization dedicated to assessing and reporting on the quality of managed care plans. To compare managed care plans, the NCQA maintains the Health Plan Employer Data and Information Set (HEDIS), which is a set of standardized performance measures that enable health plan information to be reliably compared. To a large degree, these measures focus on prevention and screening. The only explicitly surgical measures included in the 1999 HEDIS are the rate of cesarean section and the rate of vaginal birth after cesarean section.

While there are no uniform criteria for determining adequacy of physicians or hospitals, the criteria for selection generally include location of practice, willingness to accept a given reimbursement level, and certain minimum quality measures (eg, training and academic credentials and/or board certification). And in these areas, there is a growing level of standardization, as organizations such as the NCQA become recognized bodies of accreditation for managed care plans. It is only in recent years, however, that the use of demonstrated outcomes has been a key determinant in the selection of some network providers. Indeed, the vast majority of network development is still performed without the use of demonstrated outcomes. Nonetheless, as outcomes data become more readily accessible, differentiating providers on the basis of quality becomes a viable method of network development.

In many respects, the selection of network providers for various products has been critical to the success of managed care products.

Employers

Employers are nearly always payers for their employees regardless of whether they purchase insured products or self-insure. In this regard, employer perspective may be similar to payer perspective. However, employers have several other key concerns that must be addressed. These include the impacts on workforce productivity and employee satisfaction with health insurance benefits.

Those employers that purchase insured products may examine accessibility of the providers in a network product to the employees but probably do not examine the cost of the individual providers. Rather, their cost analysis will be based on the premiums they are likely to pay. Those employers that self-insure may examine the accessibility and cost of a PPO product, and their cost analysis will be based on the costs of the individual providers. To the extent to which there are providers in the vicinity of the employees that are widely believed to be quality providers, it is desirable for the employer to offer its employees health care options that include those providers.

From the employer's perspective, consideration of the quality of providers is likely to depend on whether the employer is purchasing insured products or is self-insured. Employers that purchase insured products may be less likely to consider quality indicators of individual providers and more likely to look for NCQA accreditation as a proxy for quality. The value of evidence-based surgery to these employers is likely to be limited until quality measures of outcomes rather than process of care are reliably available. Employers that self-insure may be more likely to participate in the network development process (and may actually perform it themselves). To these employers, evidence-based surgery has a potentially high value, especially given the inherent employer incentives to maintain and promote the health of its employees.

Government Agencies

State and federal governments have important dual roles in health care. They provide the regulatory oversight for the entire health care industry, and they are the largest payers of health care services. Nationally, Medicaid, Medicare and other governmental spending for health care accounts for approximately 50 percent of total spending.

As part of their roles as regulators, governmental organizations have undertaken the dissemination of outcomes information to improve decision making in health care. A frequently described problem in health care decision making has been the absence of information available for patients to use in decision making. Several programs have been implemented to improve the amount of information available. Although this information is often targeted to patients, it probably has the largest impact on providers (for competitive reasons).

One of the earlier projects in this area included the efforts of the Pennsylvania Health Care Cost Containment Council, which published hospital and surgeon-specific data for coronary artery bypass graft surgery. One of the stated goals of this project was to provide purchasers with information they could use to obtain greater value for their health care dollars when it comes to making health care purchasing decisions.[5] Another goal was to provide hospitals and surgeons with information that could be used to benchmark their performance against others. The outcomes reported included risk-adjusted in-hospital mortality rates, risk-adjusted postsurgical lengths of stay, and average hospital charges.

More recently, efforts have been launched to develop "report cards" to help consumers make decisions. Initial reporting specifically for surgery has been limited, with the rates of cesarean section versus vaginal delivery being the most commonly reported.

The political process can have an impact on perceptions about evidence-based surgery. For example, even though there has been research on the effectiveness of outpatient mastectomies, several state legislatures have passed legislation requiring inpatient stays as an option.

Other Organizations

There are examples of the use of measured outcomes in surgical procedures for network definition purposes. Perhaps the best example is in organ transplantation, where there have been uniform standards for reporting outcomes for many years. The United Network for Organ Sharing (UNOS) requires all transplantation centers to provide certain data elements to a central repository and uses those data to calculate both expected and actual graft and patient survival rates. The expected outcomes are adjusted for various risk factors, including age, sex, race, and diagnosis.

CONCLUSION

Regardless of perspective, a successful outcomes measurement system can be described as[6]
- documenting changes in clinical condition as a result of medical intervention;
- collecting data in a common format;
- maintaining data collected from multiple clinical sites in a single site to facilitate comparison of outcomes;
- incorporating standardized and validated methods of accounting for a health care organization's effect on health and quality;
- enabling physicians to assess and select medical treatments on the basis of the actual results and cost of a treatment, to enable accurate predication of resources needed for care;
- providing data to establish standards or guidelines for treatment;
- providing patients with specific facts to help them make medical decisions, including facts concerning treatments and their cost, efficacy, and impact on quality of life.

As principles of evidence-based surgery become more widely used, the methods used by various stakeholders may converge although differences in perspective will continue to lead to divergent priorities in outcomes research.

REFERENCES

1. Blaiss MS. Outcomes analysis in asthma. JAMA 1997;278(22):1874–80.

2. Health Care Financing Administration. National Health Expenditures, 1998. Table 3a. National health expenditures and average annual percent change, by sources of funds: selected calendar years 1970–2008 [accessed 1999 Dec 16]. Available from: URL: http://www.hcfa.gov/stats/nhe-proj/.

3. Health Care Financing Administration. National Health Expenditures, 1998. Table 1. National health expenditures and selected economic indicators, levels and average annual percent change: selected calendar years 1970–2008 [accessed 1999 Dec 16]. Available from: URL: http://www.hcfa.gov/stats/nhe-proj/.

4. Urban Institute. The uninsured: variations among state and recent trends. John Holahan testimony to Committee Ways and Means, Subcommittee on Health, U.S. House of Representatives. Available from: URL: http://www.urbaninstitute.org/TESTIMON/holahan6-15-99.html.

5. Pennsylvania Health Care Cost Containment Council. Consumer guide to coronary artery bypass graft surgery. 1995 Jun 9 [accessed 1999 Dec 16]. Available from: URL:http://www.phc4.org/reports/pr_cabg.htm.

6. Guice KS, Lipscomb J. Principles of outcomes analysis. Chapter 4. In: Stringer MD, Oldham KT, Mouriquand PDE, Howard ER, editors. Pediatric surgery and urology: long term outcomes. Philadelphia: W.B. Saunders Company; 1998. p. 23–38.

Framework for Evidence-Based Surgery

Haya R. Rubin, MD, PhD

⤬

As health care becomes increasingly accountable for its process and products, purchasers and the public now have the best opportunity ever to become aware of the benefit and value they can derive from high-quality health care and surgery and to find out which health care organizations and providers will deliver that value.

THE BASIC PARADIGM: STRUCTURE, PROCESS, AND OUTCOME

The grandfather of medical quality assessment, Avedis Donabedian, defined a conceptual model in which he described the outcomes of health care as being affected by its structure and its process.[1] Donabedian defined structure as raw materials such as staffing, equipment, and administrative policies and arrangements as well as the characteristics of patients at the start of an episode of care. For example, the type of reimbursement to surgical providers, the type of ventilation system in the operating room, and the patient's severity of illness or risk of specific outcomes prior to surgery would all be structural features, under his definition. Researchers have distinguished between administrative structure, which might include items such as for-profit status and payment arrangements, and clinical structure, which might include items such as the number of patients scheduled in a clinical session. Later authors separated the concept of patient case-mix, or patient risk factors, from the other aspects that Donabedian included in the structure of care, and have included this in a separate category in the conceptual model of what influences outcomes.

Donabedian defined process of care as what was done to and for the patient. Thus, both the antibiotics chosen for prophylaxis and the surgical procedures performed would be examples of the process of care.

Outcomes can be classified as clinical and physiologic measures, patient-reported outcome measures, and economic outcome measures (which will be further described later).

This model of structure, process, and outcome provides a framework for measuring the quality of surgical care and for deriving evidence that specific treatments or procedures are more effective than others.

MAJOR THEMES IN HEALTH CARE: QUALITY, COST, AND ACCESS

Quality of Care

The quality of surgical care can be defined as the degree to which surgical care improves health outcomes compared with the maximum improvement achievable with the best structures (ie, equipment, personnel, and organization) and processes available. Quality can be measured using process criteria, that is, comparing what was actually done to what should have been done according to a set of evidence-based guidelines, or by using "risk-adjusted" outcome measures, comparing observed outcomes to the best achievable outcomes at a given risk level.

Risk adjustment refers to looking at outcomes or processes, adjusting for or looking within specific categories of risk. One important technique for risk adjustment is stratified analysis, that is, examining specific strata or levels of risk, using various scores or indices for

Table 4–1 Examples of Structure, Process, and Outcome Indicators used to Assess Quality of Care

Structure: attributes of the settings in which care occurs*	Process: what is actually done in giving and receiving care*	Outcomes: the effects of care on the health status of patients and populations
Material resources* Facilities Capacity, eg, number of operating rooms	Patient's activities in seeking care and carrying it out*	Severity adjusted mortality* Severity adjusted morbidity*
Equipment, technology Capital	Provider's activities in making a diagnosis and recommending or implementing treatment*	Re-admission rates*

Human resources*
  Number and qualifications of personnel
  Physician specialty mix
  Health personnel per patient
	Practice parameters
	Specialty referrals
	
	Guidelines and critical pathways
	
	Quality assurance methodologies*
		Patient satisfaction*
		
		Patient knowledge of condition, treatment options, prevention, and healthy living

Organizational structure*
  Medical staff organization
  Methods of peer review
  Methods of reimbursement
  Systems characteristics**
  Provider characteristics**
	Provider credentialing process
	
	Treatment decision making
	Patient education about condition and treatment options
		Clinical endpoints**
		
		Functional health status**
		
		General well-being**
		
		Total charges/costs

Patient characteristics**	Lifestyle decisions based on patient education about factors promoting or detrimental to good health	

*Donabedian A. The quality of care: how can it be assessed? JAMA September 23-30, 1988: 1743–48.

**Tarlov AR, Ware JE, Jr, Greenfield S, Nelson EC, Perrin E, Zubkoff M. The medical outcomes study: an application of methods for monitoring the results of medical care. JAMA August 18, 1989; 262(7): 925–930.

rating surgical risk. Another important technique is multivariate analysis, in which logistic regression analysis or proportional hazard models are used to calculate a predicted outcome for each patient on the basis of several predictor variables present prior to surgery and in which observed surgical outcomes are compared to average predicted outcomes. (Chapter 11 will cover techniques for risk adjustment in greater detail).

Sometimes, particularly as part of the accreditation process, structural criteria are used as quality measures. An example in the in-patient setting may be the nurse-to-patient ratio, while an example at the health plan level might be the specific services that are covered. In the few instances in which studies have demonstrated that certain structures are important to the delivery of appropriate processes of care known to improve medical outcomes, structural criteria may be acceptable ways to measure quality. For example, if the nurse-to-bed ratio was linked to improved patient monitoring postoperatively and improved patient monitoring was linked to fewer adverse postoperative outcomes, then a structural criterion measuring the nurse-to-bed ratio would be an appropriate quality measure. However, few evidence-based studies have been performed to confirm the importance of most structural criteria. Therefore, at this point in time, most validated measures of quality of care rely on either process criteria or comparisons of risk-adjusted outcomes. Table 4–1 lists examples of quality indicators based on structure, process and outcome.

Cost of Care

As physician groups begin to assume financial risk in capitated payment systems, cost has become paramount not only to purchasers but (more recently) also to providers. This new emphasis provokes providers to study how the same or better results can be achieved at lower cost and to determine at what cost a certain change in outcome is provided. (Studies of cost, cost-effectiveness, and cost-benefit are discussed in Chapter 12.)

When calculating the costs of medical care or lack of medical care, it is important to include both direct costs, that is, provider fees, equipment and supply costs, medication costs, and hospital costs, as well as indirect costs such as those due to days of work lost by patients and caregivers and those costs of household help necessitated by medical treatments.

Access to Care

Capitated care is increasingly dominant in the health care market, giving managed care organizations incentives to cut costs. Moreover, health care providers who contract with managed care organizations now often assume financial risks themselves and are increasingly concerned with cutting health care costs. One way to cut costs is to limit access to care. While it is socially desirable to reduce access to unnecessary procedures, it is undesirable to limit access to potentially beneficial services. Access to care can be viewed as separate from quality of care if one focuses on an acute health care setting. However, when one focuses at the level of a population or community, access to beneficial services can be seen to be one of the most important dimensions of quality of care. Access may include the ability to see a clinician to obtain a referral to a specialist, obtain a referral for a needed surgical procedure, or obtain emergency care. In surgical care, access to a center of excellence or high-volume center with the most skilled surgeons and aftercare is a critical element. The concept of access also includes waiting times for appointments, surgical procedures, or other care. Insurance coverage also contributes to access, as excessive out-of-pocket costs can prevent patients from obtaining beneficial care.

OUTCOMES IN HEALTH CARE

Clinical and Physiologic Measures

Clinical and physiologic measures may include anatomic descriptors and physical signs, and physiologic or functional data as measured or observed by clinicians, at a specific point in time or within a time period. For example, a study of coronary artery bypass graft surgery outcomes might measure the incidence of myocardial infarcts in the year following surgery as one possible outcome. (Chapter 18 reviews current methods used in surgery outcomes research.)

Patient-Reported Outcomes

Patient-reported outcome measures include two types of data usually collected using standardized questionnaires or surveys: (1) patient-reported health status or health-related quality of life, including functioning and well-being as reported by patients, and (2) patient satisfaction with health care, a general phrase used to describe patients' evaluations of or judgments about the health care they have received. Although surgeons inquire about these outcomes postoperatively when following individual patients, the majority of surgical studies before 5 years ago neglected to collect standardized data about patient-reported health status and quality of life. Yet, many surgical procedures aim at improving the quality of life as well as prolonging life. Therefore, these represent an important group of methods to track systematically if we are to practice evidence-based surgery. (Methods of measurement of these outcomes are reviewed in Chapter 18.)

Economic Outcomes

Costs can be viewed as one way of describing the process of care but are often included as an outcomes measure. In our current health care environment, costs and various resource use units, such as length of stay or number of visits, are ever-present indicators of performance and are critical in determining what must be charged for a procedure, if the health care provider can afford to offer a capitated contract at a particular cost per person, and what it costs to achieve a certain improvement in outcome. Many health care institutions do not track their actual costs carefully, and improving the documentation of resource use will be increasingly necessary to document costs. (Economic outcomes measures are reviewed in Chapter 12.)

TYPES OF EVIDENCE

To practice evidence-based surgery, providers must continually gather and disseminate at least three types of evidence: (1) evidence of process-outcome linkages; (2) data about adherence to evidence-based process criteria; and (3) information about risk-adjusted outcomes. Data about structure-process and structure-outcome linkages may also be useful, and eventually, when more evidence-based structural criteria are derived, it will become useful to monitor health care organizations' adherence to them.

Process-Outcome Linkages: Efficacy and Effectiveness

Surgical investigators must continually acquire evidence about which surgical procedures and techniques and structural arrangements result in the best outcomes and the fewest complications by conducting clinical trials and observational studies, synthesizing this information into evidence-based guidelines or recommendations, and disseminating these recommendations. This type of evidence represents the classic kind used in medicine to advance knowledge and are referred to as studies of efficacy or safety, depending on whether the focus is on beneficial outcomes or adverse events. However, when clinicians and health care organizations continuously document processes and outcomes of care in a standardized way, a much broader range of studies can be done to explore possible links between process and outcomes. Such studies can examine achieved outcomes using different procedures among the entire group of patients to which those procedures are applied, rather than among the carefully limited populations usually enrolled in randomized controlled trials. Such broader studies of process-outcome linkages have been termed effectiveness studies.

Adherence to Evidence-Based Criteria

Surgical providers must monitor the quality of their care by determining how frequently patients receive surgical care that meets recommendations. This second type of evidence indicates where performance improvement efforts are needed in delivery systems and may be focused at the level of individual surgeons, surgical centers, provider groups, health plans, or populations of patients. Comparisons among different groups allow the identification of outstanding surgeons and centers of excellence that can demonstrate how they achieve the highest rates of evidence-based practice and can teach these strategies to others.

Risk-Adjusted Outcomes

Third, surgical providers must measure outcomes, adjusting as best they can for how ill patients are when they enter the episode of care being examined. This is referred to as "risk-adjustment" or "case-mix adjustment." Examining outcome variations among providers allows the identification of opportunities to improve outcomes that may go beyond currently available evidence-based guidelines. For example, Table 4–2 compares coronary artery bypass graft surgery mortality rates and lengths of stay for Maryland hospitals, from public use data for 1995 through the first quarter of 1999. Mortality rates are stratified by risk of mortality using a comorbidity measure included in Maryland's public data set, based on secondary diagnosis codes in hospital discharge data. Hospital 5 has lower lengths of stay in each category, suggesting more efficient management than the others, but has the highest mortality rate for high-risk patients.

Whenever risk-adjusted outcomes differ, a possible explanation is that there are unmeasured differences in severity of illness among hospitals that are not measured by the risk adjustment measure employed. However a closer look at several specific comorbidities indicates there are no differences that would appear to account for hospital 5's lower length of stay or higher mortality rate. The Quality of Care Research Group at Johns Hopkins is using a more detailed comorbidity measure, including age, gender, source of admission, and comorbid diagnoses to provide a better risk adjustment than that available in the public data set used for Table 4–1.

Outcome assessments of this type, comparing time periods or different centers or providers, are critical in identifying unexplained variations in outcomes and thus in generating new hypotheses about why outcomes may vary that can be tested in more-formal studies of process-outcome linkages. However, inferences about the quality or costs of care should be made with great caution from these types of studies because differences in outcomes may also result from differences in the patient population hitherto unrecognized and unmeasured using a particular way of adjusting for risk or comorbidity. Instead, evidence on risk-adjusted outcomes should be used as a screen to point out areas for further study where differences in the process of care might be profitably examined.

Structure-Process or Structure-Outcome Links

More evidence about how various administrative and organizational structures affect the process of care is needed. How can the health care environment, personnel, equipment and supplies, and organizational policies and procedures be optimized to promote the delivery of the most appropriate and effective care? Many more studies of this type are needed to set guidelines or criteria for administrative and organizational aspects of surgical care. Do operating-room policies and procedures influence the efficient and effective delivery of surgical care? Are there minimal staffing criteria for postoperative care? Can specific information system flags and algorithms provide fail-safe prompting to improve drug dosing, avoid medication order errors, and prevent prescription of contraindicated drugs? Is better care delivered if intensivists staff surgical intensive care units? Can the built health care environment, (eg, the design of operating-room ventilation systems) influence the quality of care delivered and affect patient outcomes? Once such studies are completed, they can be used to help set standards for health care organizations and as quality criteria. Quality monitoring will then appropriately include whether organizations are complying with these criteria.

QUALITY OF EVIDENCE

To act on evidence, surgical providers should be convinced that it is valid, or accurate. Several aspects of study methods should influence whether a study is likely to be valid, including the study design, the sampling, the completeness of the conceptual model and the confounding variables that are measured and accounted for, and measurement reliability and validity.

Study Design

When the quality of evidence is evaluated, an important consideration is the strength of the study design. Table 4–3 lists various study designs that can be used in gathering evidence (see also Chapter 8). The strongest study designs for providing causal links between two variables, such as are needed for establishing which procedures are most effective, are randomized clinical trials and matched-pair experimental studies, with blinding. The key issues are whether there is a control group and how well the design guards against there being other differences among patients in control and intervention groups.

Table 4-2 Volume, In-Hospital Mortality Rate and Length of Stay (days) for Isolated Coronary Artery Bypass Graft Surgery by Risk Level for Eight Cardiac Surgery Centers in Maryland and D.C., 1996–1999

Hospital:

	1			2			3			4			5		
	N	% Died	LOS(d)	N	% Died	LOS(d)	N	% Died	LOS(d)	N	% Died	LOS(d)	N	% Died	LOS(d)
Risk Level															
1	248	0	6.2	192	1.0	7.2	8	0	8.0	754	0.1	6.5	213	0	3.9
2	1020	0.8	7.1	572	0.5	8.4	55	0	8.8	1441	0.8	7.7	581	1.0	5.1
3	848	1.8	9.1	444	1.0	10.9	99	1.0	12.4	819	2.9	10.0	360	3.0	7.0
4	201	15.9	16.3	106	16.4	15.8	36	11.1	20.1	290	12.8	18.9	117	17.0	11.8
All	2317	2.4	8.6	1324	2.1	9.7	198	2.5	12.6	3304	2.7	9.0	1271	2.9	6.1

Hospital (continued)

	6			7			8			All		
	N	% Died	LOS(d)	N	% Died	LOS(d)	N	% Died	LOS(d)	N	% Died	LOS(d)
Risk Level												
1	192	0	5.2	318	0.3	5.9	200	1.5	4.9	2124	0.3	5.9
2	747	1.3	6.3	761	1.0	7.2	926	0.8	6.0	6103	0.9	6.9
3	760	1.4	8.1	543	2.4	9.3	741	1.8	8.6	4614	2.0	9.1
4	277	7.6	12.4	187	11.2	16.5	232	16.7	14.6	1456	14.0	15.5
All	1976	2.1	7.8	1809	2.4	8.1	2099	2.8	7.8	4228	2.5	8.4

Derived from the State of Maryland's public data sets.

N = number of cases; LOS = length of stay in days.

Table 4–3 Research Study Designs

Study Design	Description, Strengths and Weaknesses, Similar Alternatives
Randomized controlled trial	*Description:* Patients are assigned in random order to two treatments, types of procedures, or environments. *Strength:* Excellent for drawing conclusions about whether different treatments or procedures matter. *Weakness:* It is often difficult to assign treatment or environmental conditions randomly. *Similar alternative:* Consecutive or apparently unbiased systematic assignment of subjects to different treatments, procedures or environments. Random assignment is always preferable to avoid unintended bias.
Experimental trial with paired data	*Description:* The same patients are *assigned* to different treatments or conditions at different times, *under the direction of investigators.* Each patient serves as his or her own control for comparisons. *Strength:* Excellent for concluding if different treatments, procedures or environmental conditions matter. Conclusions are stronger if patients are randomly assigned to receive one or the other treatment first. *Weakness:* It is often impossible to treat the same patient under different conditions or with more than one treatment or procedure. *Similar alternative:* Experimental trial using the same group of patients with unpaired data analysis. The same patients are assigned to different treatments or conditions at different times, but only the average results for the entire group are compared for the two treatment groups, rather than examining each subject as his own control. *Paired data analysis is always both possible and preferable.*
Observational study with paired data	*Description:* The same patients are observed under different treatments, procedures, or environmental conditions *in the course of routine care. Assignment to treatments or conditions is not controlled but rather occurs naturally.* Each patient serves as his own control. *Strength:* A sound study design for drawing conclusions, although weaker than an experimental trial with paired data. *Weakness:* Because the study does not assign and control the treatments or conditions, other aspects of the setting could differ besides the environmental feature of interest. *Similar alternative:* Observational study using the same patients but with unpaired data analysis. The same patients are assigned to different treatments at different times, but average results for each entire group are compared rather than using each subject as his own control. *Paired data analysis is always possible and preferable.*

Table 4–3 Research Study Designs — *(continued)*

Study Design	*Description, Strengths and Weaknesses, Similar Alternatives*
Observational study of different groups	*Description:* Groups of patients are compared in different treatments, procedures or environments in the course of routine care. If performed in sequential time periods, perhaps before and after adoption of a new surgical procedure or an administrative change, such studies are referred to as "natural history" studies.
	Strength: Easiest to organize. Study can be made stronger by measuring all differences among groups that influence patient outcomes and analyzing possible effects on results.
	Weakness: Because there may be too many differences among groups of patients to account for them accurately and comprehensively, this is the weakest study design.
	Similar alternative: Experimental trial assigning different patients nonrandomly and in a possibly biased fashion to different treatments, procedures, or environmental conditions.

To establish links between a particular surgical procedure or technique and improved outcomes, experimental studies can be performed in many cases. In other cases, however, they are impractical because the pace of the introduction of a new surgical technology or technique outstrips the ability of surgical investigators to arrange a randomized controlled trial to evaluate its effectiveness; for example, surgical techniques that were never tested in randomized or experimental trials include various types of laparoscopic surgery. When trials are impractical or unavailable, quasi-experimental or observational studies can be valuable but must be interpreted with greater caution.

In the medical and surgical literature, it is not uncommon that enthusiastic anecdotal reports and favorable observational studies are followed by randomized controlled trials showing no benefit of a particular therapy or procedure. For example, hormone replacement therapy was thought to reduce cardiac disease for women with existing cardiovascular disease. Observational studies indicated about a 50 percent reduction in risk, and most practitioners prescribed these drugs for patients. But a recent randomized trial indicated no benefit of hormone therapy in this group and, in fact, indicated an increase in deep venous thrombosis.

What accounts for this discrepancy between observational studies and randomized trials? Case reports and observational studies are subject to increased bias, as important initial differences between intervention and control group patients, unrelated to the treatment employed, may be overlooked. Differences among patients are more likely to even out between groups if patients are randomized to a new treatment than if they receive it because of patient or provider interest or provider or investigator convenience.

Risk-adjusted outcomes measurement, comparing providers or time periods, is always observational data and is thus always subject to the pitfalls of weaker study designs. Therefore, until a risk-adjustment system has been demonstrated to be highly predictive of a particular outcome in a particular population and has been accepted by the relevant clinical specialists as providing a comprehensive measure of risk, risk-adjusted outcome studies should be used to generate hypotheses rather than viewed as definitive studies of quality of care.

Random Sampling

Often, patients recruited for a clinical study are dissimilar to the patients for whom investigators wish to generalize results. First, participating centers may have profound differences from nonparticipating centers. For example, centers studying the efficacy of a new surgical procedure may have surgeons more skilled in that procedure. Case series from these centers may thus report inaccurately lower complication rates than will be true as the procedure is more widely adopted. Patient populations being studied at referral centers to determine outcomes of surgery also may differ substantially from patients who are treated at community hospitals. On the one hand, elective and ambulatory patients referred for surgery from elsewhere, who by definition can travel and who often have the resources and social support to go to a distant center, are generally less ill than those who go to a hospital in their geographic area for the same problem.[2] On the other hand, patients transferred from other in-patient facilities are more severely ill on average than patients coming from within the same hospital, and referral hospitals that receive a larger proportion of transferred patients from other facilities may have worse outcomes than other centers for this reason.[3]

Second, even if participating centers are carefully selected to be representative, patients may be included in the study based on a convenience factor also related to the outcome being measured. For example, if patient satisfaction with postoperative care is measured by asking surgical nurses to distribute questionnaires on days when they have the time, only those patients who are in the hospital on these less-busy days will be selected. Such patients might receive better service than those present on busier days, thus biasing the results to appear more positive than the true values.

Even if recruited randomly, patients may fail to enroll or respond, due to factors that may be related to outcomes. For example, sicker patients may not return for follow-up assessments or may fail to complete interviews or questionnaires, thus making health outcomes look better, and nonrespondents to satisfaction studies are usually less satisfied than those who do respond. If such factors vary among control and intervention groups or among centers being compared, they may bias study results.

Investigators must be careful that the patient population included in a study represents the population they wish to generalize about. If this is not the case, likely biases should be measured or estimated so that systematic variations can be taken into account in interpreting the study results.

Completeness of Conceptual Models and Confounding Variables

A valid study must be based on a complete framework of factors that influence outcomes. This becomes particularly important for observational study designs since patient groups being compared are not randomly allocated to interventions and therefore may differ in other ways. If investigators do not determine whether groups are different along all the important dimensions that matter, we cannot judge if there are likely to be other reasons why groups may differ. Ensuring appropriate risk adjustment, as discussed above, is a specific example of this challenge.

A valid study must measure all the important confounding factors, including major patient characteristics or risks that affect the outcomes in question and all important differences in care and environment besides the intervention that may differ among the two groups and that may affect their outcomes.

Measurement Reliability and Validity

The quality of measurement is another important factor that can affect the quality of evidence.

Reliability

Reliability refers to a measure's consistency; that is, does it give the same result over and over when the same thing is measured? For clinical research and quality assessment, reliability is often measured by test-retest reliability, inter-rater reliability, and/or internal consistency reliability.

Test-Retest Reliability

In clinical research, it is particularly important to determine test-retest reliability, that is, to use a measure on the same person twice to see if the same value results, when the property measured is something that should be stable over the time between the two measurements. For a measure for which a specific patient is the only relevant judge, such as a self-rating or self-report about pain, functioning, or mood, this is the best way of determining whether the measure is reliable.

Inter-rater Reliability

For most clinical measures, an important way to determine if a measurement method yields consistent results is to have several observers or judges obtain the information or make judgments and to compare their responses. For example, for interpretation of radiologic or other noninvasive tests, we can examine how different radiologists or surgeons read the same test result. Such studies often find that where human judgment is involved, there is considerable inter-rater variation, and evidence that requires human judgment is subject to these constraints.[4]

Internal Consistency Reliability

Investigators often check internal consistency reliability, or how closely two ways of measuring the same thing at the same time agree with each other. One popular measure of consistency for psychologic measurements (also known as psychometrics) such as patient-reported health status is Cronbach's alpha.[5] This statistic examines the relationships among various questions, or items, that make up a psychometric scale. Cronbach's alpha is valuable only when the items within a scale are hypothesized to be closely related or identical. It is not appropriate for summary indices that add items that are theoretically different to create a global score for a specific category. For example, imagine a pain scale with these two questions that ask about pain globally: (1) Please rate the amount of pain you have had in the last four weeks (none at all, a little, some, a moderate amount, a lot); (2) Please indicate how often you have had pain in the last 4 weeks (never, occasionally, some of the time, a good bit of the time, a lot of the time, constantly). These items are expected to be highly related to each other, and Cronbach's alpha would be a useful statistic to determine whether people answered the pain scale reliably. However, an index may ask about pain in each different part of the body: Please rate the amount of pain in the head, neck, chest, abdomen, legs, back, etc. These items are then summed into a total body pain score. In this case, we would not expect these answers to relate highly to each other, and Cronbach's alpha would be an inappropriate way to find out if a measure obtains reliable results.

What could cause an unbiased measure to be unreliable? Even if not systematically biased or erroneous, a measure may be too sensitive to factors unrelated to what is being measured and therefore have too much "noise" or random measurement error.

Validity

Validity refers to accuracy, that is, whether or not a measure reflects what investigators want to be measuring. While an unreliable or inconsistent measure certainly is not valid, a consistent measure sometimes is also inaccurate because it has built-in sources of bias that always skew it in a particular direction away from the true value. Looking under the light for the quarter lost down the street will consistently fail to turn up a quarter, but this does not mean that the quarter is not down the street. In clinical research, investigators frequently substitute more conveniently measured outcomes for those of greater value that are less convenient to obtain. Such substitutions lower the credibility of the study by adding various biases that cause a result to differ systematically from the true value.

Tests of Validity

There are several ways to test the validity of measures used to collect evidence about the effectiveness or quality of surgical care. These tests assess face validity, content validity, predictive validity, criterion validity, and convergent-discriminant validity.

Face Validity.   This test asks members of various intended audiences and stakeholders whether the measurement used seems likely to obtain accurate results. This basic test represents a necessary minimum when other, more formal ways of measuring validity are absent. For example, many systems comparing mortality rates for surgical centers or individual surgeons performing coronary artery bypass graft surgery are thought to be invalid by surgeons because they do not adequately capture patients' severity of illness.[6] Because such systems are not "face-valid" for the surgeons who are affected by them, many policymakers are more skeptical of them than if they seemed valid to the surgical community.

Content Validity.   Depending on how it is measured, this could be considered a subset of face validity or something more formal. It refers to whether all the important content that is part of a measure is included. For example, if a measure of effectiveness of a surgical procedure examined in-hospital mortality but did not examine 30-day mortality or mortality during any subsequent period, most clinicians considering whether they should refer patients for surgery would consider such a measure to have inadequate content validity. To obtain the best content validity, investigators collecting evidence about effectiveness of treatments or quality of care should base the content of outcomes measured on formal studies of what aspects of health and outcomes are important to patients. Similarly, investigators can know whether a list of process criteria is likely to be comprehensive only if they perform a thorough literature review of evidence-based criteria as well as ask clinicians what aspects of care are likely to be important.

Predictive Validity.   A valid (or evidence-based) process criterion must be demonstrated to predict future events or outcomes. For example, a quality-of-care criterion that patients with symptomatic left main coronary artery stenosis have coronary artery bypass graft surgery must be based on the demonstration that such patients are more likely to survive a year if they have surgery than if they do not. Predictive validity is a general way of describing whether a criterion is supported by evidence linking it to the outcome of interest.

Criterion Validity.   This type of validation is similar to predictive validity. However, it attempts to relate a criterion not to future outcomes but rather to some type of "gold standard" finding already proven or known to be related to subsequent outcomes. For example, investigators may determine if magnetic resonance imaging (MRI) of the knee can accurately detect a medial collateral ligament tear as measured against arthroscopic findings at the time of surgery. The arthroscopic findings are the criterion or gold standard, as they are widely believed or demonstrated to relate to future medical outcomes for the patient.

Convergent-Discriminant Validity.   While carrying out effectiveness research or quality assessment, investigators sometimes wish to measure an outcome or property for which there is no gold standard and no future event against which it can be validated. For example, they may wish to measure a patient's pain 24 hours postoperatively. Most psychologically experienced outcomes do not have gold standard measures; rather, to validate measures of these psychologic states, investigators determine whether the measures agree with (or are "convergent" with) other similar measures and disagree with (or can be discriminated from) measures of states that theoretically should not be related to them. Measures that pass these tests are said to have convergent-discriminant validity. As an example, investigators may theorize that, if valid, people's ratings of their own physical functioning should be somewhat related to a measure of psychologic well-being and mood but much more highly related to responses to a scale asking how well they can perform various physical activities. If the self-ratings of physical functioning were more highly correlated with answers to questions about mood but the responses about mood were only moderately related to the performance of physical activities as theorized, then the responses to the questions rating physical functioning would be suspect and likely to be invalid.

Measurement Causes of Bias

What causes measurement invalidity? As already noted, random noise that causes wide variation around a true value (or unreliability) as well as biases that can cause systematic variations from true values can make a measure invalid. Some common causes of measurement bias in studies include investigator hypotheses and beliefs, rater tendencies, recall bias, and others beyond the scope of this discussion.[7]

Investigator Hypotheses and Beliefs.   If data are collected by an individual who has a certain hypothesis, that person may unwittingly be influenced by his or her beliefs. For example, a physician reviewing a case for errors in care is more likely to find an error if he or she knows the patient died than if otherwise, even if everything else about the case is exactly the same.[8] Therefore, data should be collected by individuals who are "blinded" to which patients are in which of two groups being compared, whether by outcome or type of treatment. If this is not possible, then data collectors should be blinded to the study hypotheses. Investigators with vested interests should commission independent investigators and analysts to determine the results of the study.

Rater Tendencies.   Some people tend to be more lenient, others tend to be harsher. If a study requires human judgment and has only one rater for every event, it must be understood to be subject to bias. This can be minimized by averaging results from several experienced raters.

Recall Bias.   When people participating in a study are asked for information retrospectively about risk factors, they may be more sensitized to reporting risk factors if they have outcomes known to be linked to those factors. For example, a patient with a tumor he has been told was caused by asbestos exposure may be more likely to recall asbestos exposure than a patient who has not had such an adverse outcome and who has never given asbestos exposure a second thought.

CONCLUSION

Patient outcomes are influenced by the structures and processes of surgical care as well as by patient factors and risks. For accountable surgical care, access to health care, and the quality and cost of health care are important aspects to measure. Studies that gather evidence about the effectiveness and quality of surgical care should include clinical and physiologic outcomes, patient-reported outcomes, and economic outcomes. Several kinds of evidence are critical for the practice of evidence-based surgery: process-outcome linkages (what works?), adherence to evidence-based criteria (are we doing what works?), and tracking and comparing risk-adjusted outcomes (how are the patients doing?). This chapter has also reviewed what makes good evidence and how to avoid common pitfalls that invalidate results and evidence.

REFERENCES

1. Donabedian A. The definition of quality and approaches to its assessment. Vol. I. Ann Arbor, MI: Health Administration Press; 1980.

2. Ballard DJ, Bryant SC, O'Brien PC, et al. Referral selection bias in the medicard hospital mortality prediction model: are centers of referral for medicare beneficiaries necessarily centers of excellence? HSR 1994;28(6):771–84.

3. Escarce J. Admission source to the medical intensive care unit predicts hospital death independent of APACHE II score. JAMA 1990;264(18):2389–94.

4. Feinstein AR. A bibliography of publications on observer variability. J Chron Dis 1985;39(8): 619–32.

5. Cronbach LJ. Coefficient alpha and the internal structure of tests. Psychometrika 1951;16:297.

6. Schneider EC, Epstein AM. Influences of cardiac-surgery performance reports on referral practices and access to care. JGIM 1996;335:251–6.

7. Feinstein AR. Clinimetrics. New Haven, CT: Yale University Press; 1987.

8. Caplan RA, Posner KL, Cheney FW. Effect of outcome on physician judgments of appropriateness of care. JAMA 1991;265(15):1957–60.

CHAPTER 5

Legal Issues

Richard P. Kidwell, JD, and Joanne E. Pollak, JD

Evidence-based surgery has yet to have an impact on health care law. In the coming years, however, the legal profession will most likely incorporate concepts of data-driven patient care management into medical malpractice litigation and regulatory issues such as licensure and physician credentialing. Some examples of this type of information are publicly available data, comparative data, peer review materials, critical pathways, and guidelines recommended by professional societies. The levels of this type of information vary from traditional publications of findings in medical literature to procedural experience of institutions or individual practitioners.[1]

SOURCES OF LAW

The "law" is formulated in different ways. Congress or state legislatures enact statutes that become law when signed by the president or governor (statutory law). Administrative agencies (on the federal level—Department of Health and Human Services, Health Care Financing Administration, etc; on the state level in Maryland—Department of Health and Mental Hygiene, Health Services Cost Review Commission, etc) issue regulations to set forth policies and procedures to which health care providers must conform (regulatory law). Courts, too, make law through reported decisions of federal and state courts deciding specific cases (case law). These decisions may interpret statutes or regulations or establish rules of conduct in areas not subject to a specific statute or regulation. Issues concerning licensure and physician credentialing typically fall into the realm of statutory or regulatory law. Expected norms of physician practice have been established by the courts in medical malpractice litigation.

The law always lags behind science in making use of new breakthroughs or approaches and accepting them as evidence. As set forth below, evidence-based surgery will impact both legislators and litigants as measurement processes improve and become more commonplace.

MEDICAL MALPRACTICE

Overview

Although determining if a surgeon has committed malpractice in an evidence-based surgery setting will not differ from the analysis in a traditional surgical setting, evidence-based surgery will offer the opportunity to expand the presentation of evidence to prove surgical malpractice. "The health care provider is not liable for payment of damages unless it is established that the care given by the health care provider is not in accordance with the standards of practice among members of the same health care profession with similar training and experience situated in the same or similar communities."[2] Thus, a plaintiff/patient must prove that his or her injury was caused by a surgeon who failed to act as a prudent surgeon would have in similar circumstances.

Such proof is presented by expert witnesses, usually other surgeons experienced in performing the procedure in question. Through use of their experience and medical literature, these experts tell the jury what the standard of care expected of the defendant doctor was and how that defendant doctor failed to adhere to the standard, causing injury to the patient.

Use of Outcome Data

Widespread use of outcome data by multiple individuals or institutions would permit "comparison shopping" by patients and provide their attorneys in malpractice litigation with the ability to present juries with such information. In evidence-based surgery, the significance of a particular surgeon's or institution's complication rates could be bandied back and forth by the respective parties' experts. The court could become bogged down on collateral issues and could restrict the use of outcome data if case-mix and population adjustments prevented an "apples-to-apples" comparison.[3–6]

Another problem sure to arise from the attempted use of outcome data is the difficulty of applying population-based research to the case-specific matter of the care rendered to a single patient. Comprehending the significance of outcome data will be difficult for a jury already trying to understand medical terms and procedures. As with any expert testimony, the manner in which it is presented will determine its impact on the jury. A persuasive expert is one who not only can present the outcome data because of his or her familiarity with them but who can also explain their relevance and application to the facts being considered by the jury. Without such a cogent explanation, the jury will be left befuddled by outcome data and will disregard it.

Informed Consent

Case law has established the doctrine of informed consent, which mandates that a patient's consent to undergo an operation be an informed choice.

> Simply stated, the doctrine of informed consent imposes on a physician, before he subjects his patient to medical treatment, the duty to explain the procedure to the patient and to warn him of any material risks or dangers inherent in or collateral to the therapy, so as to enable the patient to make an intelligent or informed choice about whether or not to undergo such treatment. . . . The physician is not allowed to substitute his or her judgment for that of the patient with respect to consent for treatment.[7]

A material risk is defined as any risk an ordinarily prudent person would want to know before deciding to undergo a procedure.[7] Courts have not delineated a particular probability or percentage that constitutes a material risk, but a court could look at the statistical evidence of a particular procedure to draw such a line. Although such certainty may be welcomed, it would mean that judges would dictate specific rules for physician-patient interaction, rather than permitting the physician to use his or her discretion in interactions with the patient.

As evidence-based surgery becomes more the norm, courts will be more likely to permit a plaintiff's attorney the opportunity to persuade a jury that outcome data should be presented to a patient. Any failure to do so arguably prevents an informed decision on the patient's part and would give rise to a cause of action for any adverse outcome suffered by the patient.[8] In a case from Wisconsin, the court permitted admission of evidence that the defendant surgeon did not obtain appropriate informed consent (before operating to clip an aneurysm) by failing to (1) divulge the extent of his experience, (2) compare the morbidity and mortality rates among experienced and inexperienced surgeons such as himself, and (3) refer the plaintiff to a tertiary care center staffed by more experienced surgeons.[8]

An institutional defendant may be sued for failing to disclose to its patient the comparative data regarding its surgical staff, thus precluding the patient from making an informed choice about which surgeon should perform the operation. An institution's failure to disclose its outcome data comparing it to other competing institutions could also be used by a patient to demonstrate lack of informed consent where that institution's morbidity and mortality rates substantially exceed those of its competitors.

In any informed consent, surgeons must also include discussion of any other treatments the patient may choose. Failure to present the comparative data (if it exists) among alternative therapies may thus afford another basis for a claim. Of course, a plain-English explanation of scientific studies and findings would be required to characterize the surgeon-patient discussion as one of true informed consent.

Referrals

Referring physicians and managed care organizations (MCOs) would not be immune from expanded patient allegations in litigation involving evidence-based surgery. A referral to a surgeon whose complication rate exceeds the norm or acceptable range may afford a basis for including the primary care physician as a defendant in a lawsuit. Either failure to obtain outcome data from surgeons and institutions or failure to share such data with patients would provide potential grounds for referring physicians or MCOs to be joined as defendants. For example, such information could demonstrate that hospital mortality, length of stay, and cost were significantly less at a high-volume regional medical center compared with all other state hospitals performing pancreatic duodenectomies.[9,10]

Referral of a patient to a hospital with a higher mortality rate could be attacked by counsel for the patient if an adverse outcome results for that patient. In current medical malpractice litigation, all that is necessary for a case to be placed before a jury is testimony from a doctor that the defendant physician owed a duty to the patient and caused injury to the patient by breaching that duty. As in a 1996 Wisconsin case,[8] an expert physician's testimony that a defendant failed to disclose morbidity and mortality rates and personal experience with the procedure would get the case to a jury.

The willingness of courts to permit inventive plaintiffs' attorneys to plead additional allegations and broaden the proof against the surgeon in evidence-based surgery settings will make the defense of malpractice cases even more problematic. It is difficult enough to educate a jury about the medical nuances in a case. Adding the explanation, meaning, and significance of statistical data increases an already heavy burden for defense counsel. Defendants may be judged by a standard of care of disclosure of the favorable outcomes and higher referrals to large academic centers and other centers with good statistical outcomes.

PRACTICE PARAMETERS

The use of outcome data to determine care maps for surgical patients presents its share of potential legal problems as well. First, the nomenclature of the planned care may well make a difference. Labeling such care as a standard, protocol, critical pathway, or practice guideline may make a difference if a particular patient's care deviates from the expected. Counsel for patients would want to hold a surgeon to a standard; any failure by the surgeon to comply would be enough evidence to prove negligence. Defense counsel, on the other hand, would argue that the care maps are merely guidelines for surgeons to follow that do not mandate rigid adherence. Rather, the guidelines would explain why a particular patient's care did not progress as anticipated and why such lack of progress is not indicative of negligence. Attorneys for each side would try to cast the other titles (critical pathway or protocol) as synonyms for either a standard or a guideline, depending, of course, on what would advance their respective clients' cases.

A pitfall associated with any practice guideline or critical pathway is that documenting is done by exception; that is, there is minimal or no documentation in the patient's chart as long as the patient remains on the pathway. If a patient's condition veers from the pathway, health care providers return to more traditional documentation of detailed progress notes and specific laboratory results and vital signs. The note should also contain an explanation of why the pathway is not being followed. Defense counsel faces the task of convincing a jury that the dearth of precomplication documentation does not demonstrate a lack of attentiveness on a surgeon's part. Testimony about the routine care of a patient on a critical pathway and how the complication was timely recognized and treated must substitute for more conventional chart notations. Plaintiffs' attorneys will counter that such testimony does not carry the credibility or weight of contemporaneously made notations in the chart. From a defense standpoint, cases are much easier to defend if there is a note concerning any interaction between a physician and a patient.

Use of Practice Parameters as Evidence

The use of practice parameters in medical malpractice litigation can take two forms: inculpatory or exculpatory. A patient/plaintiff would use the parameters to prove that the surgeon did not meet the standard of care (inculpatory), while a surgeon/defendant would use the parameters to prove that he or she did follow the standard of care (exculpatory). Most of the few states that have addressed this issue by statute permit use of the practice parameters only by the defendant as proof that the standard of care was met.[11] In a survey of attorneys involved in medical malpractice litigation, more than 25 percent of plaintiffs' attorneys claimed that a factor in their decision not to take a case was the existence of a guideline favorable to the defendant. A similar amount, 30.9 percent, claimed that guidelines unfavorable to a defendant influenced them to take a case. More than 25 percent of attorneys responding to the survey were involved in a case that settled because of the use of guidelines applicable to their clients' cases.[12]

State and Federal Efforts

In the state of Maryland, House Bill 1359 was enacted in 1994 as Sections 19-1601 through 19-1606 of the Health General Article, Annotated Code of Maryland. This statute called for the development of practice parameters and prohibited the introduction of such parameters for use in a malpractice case. There has yet to be a single practice parameter adopted under the statute although many providers have adopted their own protocols or practice parameters.

On August 4, 1994, a report on recommendations for implementing the practice parameter provisions of House Bill 1359 was prepared for the Maryland Health Care Access and Cost Commission.[13] The report recommended that Maryland establish a 5-year demonstration project that would permit the use of a limited number of practice parameters as an affirmative defense.[13] This, too, has lain dormant.

Other states that have dealt with this issue include Maine, Florida, Minnesota, and Vermont. There are no reported cases in those jurisdictions on practice parameters or standards. Maine established a 5-year demonstration project beginning in 1991 in which physicians specializing in anesthesiology, emergency medicine, obstetrics and gynecology, and radiology would be permitted to use twenty practice parameters as an affirmative defense in malpractice suits.[14] Florida established a similar demonstration project in 1994, allowing physicians to use practice parameters as an affirmative defense in the areas of cesarean sections, coronary artery bypass grafts, and hip and knee surgeries.[15] Minnesota went further in its 1992 law, which makes adherence to an approved practice parameter an absolute defense against an allegation that a provider did not comply with accepted community standards of practice. No guidelines were developed, and the statute was repealed in 1995.[16] In 1992, Vermont legislation made practice guidelines adopted by the health care authority admissible as evidence of a standard of care in medical malpractice cases.[17]

There have been a few attempts on the federal level to provide for the use of guidelines as defenses but they have failed to pass Congressional scrutiny. It is likely that evidence-based surgery will provide an impetus for the development and adoption of guidelines in those states that have addressed this issue and could provide the basis for Congressional action in the future as well.

PEER REVIEW DATA

The applicability of the peer review process is an area of conflict between widespread use of outcome data and malpractice actions. In Maryland, the proceedings, records, and files of a medical review committee are not discoverable and are not admissible in evidence in any civil action.[18] In Maryland, a medical review committee is defined as including a committee of the medical staff, which (1) evaluates and seeks to improve the quality of health care; (2) evaluates the need for and level of performance of health care provided; and (3) evaluates the qualifications, competence, and performance of health care providers.[19] This includes morbidity and mortality conferences where a particular surgeon's or institution's outcome data would be discussed and complication rates generated. The use of outcome data by an individual or an institution as a marketing tool could jeopardize the peer review privilege. However, the defense should still be successful in preventing disclosure of the findings of the peer review committee with respect to a particular patient's outcome when only overall statistical data is released by a surgeon or institution.

CREDENTIALING

Evidence-based surgery will impact credentialing from the standpoint of both the surgeon (applicant) and the institution (reviewer). The institution's reviewer may use outcome research to establish a required minimum number of times a surgeon must perform a particular procedure before granting a delineated privilege to the surgeon. A hospital or other credentialing facility may also require a surgeon to perform a certain number of particular procedures at the hospital or facility to ensure the surgeon meets quality assurance standards. The institution would then have abundant peer review information directly from its staff rather than relying on others to provide such feedback. By mandating the performance of a minimum number of procedures at its facility, a hospital can ensure that it is receiving some quality benefit in return for credentialing a surgeon, especially in those instances in which the surgeon will make use of his or her privileges at the hospital as a marketing tool.

A credentialing organization could also institute threshold morbidity and mortality rates for each requested privilege. Applicants could be compared to national or local norms. Economic credentialing issues such as length of stay and equivalent in-patient admission (EIPA) could also be considered.

ACCESS TO CARE

In an environment increasingly dominated by managed care, the issue of access to certain types of care will be paramount. Managed care organizations (MCOs) make use of cost analysis studies to contract with low-cost providers. Providers make use of such studies to prove their worth to MCOs by demonstrating cost-effectiveness, quality of care, shorter lengths of stay, or better outcomes. Denying patient referrals to certain surgeons or institutions based on cost studies or denying certain "expensive" procedures and steering patients into less costly alternatives, particularly when better outcome data argues against such steerage, will most certainly lead to increased litigation against MCOs. This is true even though many MCOs act only as plan administrators under the Employee Retirement Income Security Act (ERISA) and even though ERISA law has been used by MCOs to prevent patients from suing them for negligence in administration of the plan as well as for malpractice. To promote uniform interpretation of the Act, Congress included a provision in the statute that has been interpreted to prohibit patients from bringing actions against MCOs for negligent administration (ie, not giving the comparative data) or malpractice (ie, using physicians who do not meet the standard of care). However, courts have recently permitted such actions in certain circumstances, and several states, including Texas, have passed legislation that permits such actions against MCOs. A U.S. District Court in Texas has upheld the constitutionality of this "right to sue" statute but this decision has been appealed.[20] Ultimately, the Supreme Court likely will determine the scope of pre-emption for MCOs under ERISA.

CONCLUSION

As the health care profession conducts more outcomes research and makes increased use of the results of that research, the legal profession will find ways to make use of the data. Courts will probably look favorably on the introduction of such evidence. When it suits them, patients' attorneys or counsel for health care providers and institutions will seek to use such evidence to influence the decisions of judges and juries. Regulators and institutions, too, will incorporate outcomes research in granting, withholding, or modifying licenses and privileges. The one area where evidence-based surgery has had its greatest impact, the managed care setting, will continue to see increased use of outcome data to determine where and to whom patients are referred. Oddly enough, it is this area which also will be likely to generate litigation about the lack of access to care or the denial of care, which will bring evidence-based surgery to the legal forefront and hasten its acceptance and use by the legal profession.

REFERENCES

1. See, eg, the report cards at <www.healthcarereportcards>, issued by Healthcare Report Cards, Inc., purporting to compare the performances of different hospitals in various procedures.

2. Courts and Judicial Proceedings Article § 3-2A-02(c), Annotated Code of Maryland.

3. Twerski A, Cohen N. Comparing medical providers: a first look at the new era of medical statistics. Brookings Law Review 1992;58:5.

4. Green J. Problems in the use of outcome statistics to compare health care providers. Brookings Law Review 1992;58:55.

5. Rheingold PD. The admissibility of evidence in malpractice cases: the performance records of practitioners. Brookings Law Review 1992;58:75.

6. Sharrott D. Provider-specific quality-of-care-data: a proposal for limited mandatory disclosure. Brookings Law Review 1992;59:85.

7. Sard v Hardy, 379 A.2d 1014, 1020 (Md. 1977).

8. Johnson v Kokemoor, 546 N.W.2d 495 (Wis. 1996).

9. Gordon TA, Bowman HM, Tielsch JM, et al. Statewide regionalization of pancreatic duodenectomy and its effect on in-hospital mortality. Ann Surg 1998;228:71–8.

10. Gordon TA, Burleyson GP, Tielsch JM, Cameron JL. The effects of regionalization on cost and outcome for one general high risk surgical procedure. Ann Surg 1995;221:43–9.

11. Noble AA, Hyams AL, Brennan TA. Practice guidelines and medical malpractice litigation: a legal update. Med Pract Management 1997 Jan/Feb:203–7.

12. Hyams AI, Brandenburg BA, Lipsitz SR, et al. Practice guidelines and malpractice litigation: a two-way street. Ann Intern Med 1995;122:450–5.

13. Richardson W. Recommendations on implementing the practice parameters provisions of House Bill 1359. Report to the Maryland Health Care Access and Cost Commission; 1994 Aug 4.

14. Maine Revised Statutes Annotated Title 24, §§ 2971–2979.

15. Florida Statutes Annotated, § 408-02.

16. State of Minnesota, Minnesota Care Act of 1992, Chapter 549 (HF No. 2800) 1992 Legislation Session, Article 7. 1995 Minnesota Chapter 234.

17. 12 Vermont Statutes Annotated § 7003.

18. Health Occupations Article, Annotated Code of Maryland, § 14-501 (d)(8)/. See also, the Health Care Quality Improvement Act of 1986, 41 U.S.C.§§1101, et. seq.

19. Annotated Code of Maryland, §14-501(b)(5), Health Occupations Article.

20. Corporate Health Insurance, Inc. v Texas Department of Insurance, S.D. Texas, H-97-2072, decided 9/18/98.

The authors acknowledge the assistance of Frederick Levy, M.D., J.D.

CHAPTER 6

Ethical Issues

Laurence B. McCullough, PhD

The development, implementation, and evaluation of evidence-based surgery should be understood as part of the larger phenomenon of the managed practice of medicine and surgery.[1-3] This chapter provides a brief account of the emergence during the past two decades of the managed practice of surgery that has replaced the older, fee-for-service cottage industry model of medicine; describes the three major business tools of managed practice; and addresses the ethical challenges of managed practice for surgeons and institutional managers responsible for surgical services. The chapter emphasizes a preventive-ethics approach to these ethical challenges, namely, the development of institutional policies and practices designed to anticipate ethical challenges so that ethical conflicts can be avoided or effectively managed in ways that protect the health interests of patients and the intellectual and moral integrity of the medical profession.[4]

THE COTTAGE INDUSTRY FEE-FOR-SERVICE MODEL OF SURGERY

The medical profession is now well into the era of the managed practice of medicine, and surgery and other specialties that use surgical intervention, such as obstetrics and gynecology, are no exception. The use of evidence-based techniques to develop and evaluate practice guidelines and disease management strategies by institutions such as hospitals, surgical groups, and managed care organizations (MCOs) as well as by both private and public payers is rapidly becoming more commonplace. Surgeons need to place these changes in context so that the ethical challenges presented to surgical practice can be clearly identified and addressed.

The managed practice of medicine and surgery has replaced the older, now rapidly disappearing organizational model of medicine that prevailed in the United States from the colonial period through the early 1980s.[5,6] This older model involved physicians practicing alone or in small groups and can be called a cottage industry model of medical and surgical practice. Even though surgery was, until very recently, mostly performed in the hospital setting, surgeons themselves were organized in practice as solo practitioners or small groups, as were physicians in other medical specialties. In the cottage industry model, the focus of clinical judgment, decision making, and behavior was on the protection and promotion of the health needs of the individual patient. The goal of surgical management was to meet the needs of each individual patient to the greatest extent possible with the least risk of iatrogenic morbidity and mortality. The surgeon and surgical team focused their energies on the patient in the operating room until the procedures were completed and then went on to the next patient, again with the goal of meeting his or her individual health needs.

Medical ethics reflected and re-inforced this approach to the surgical management of patients. The surgeon's moral responsibilities were owed to one patient at a time. Population-based data from the few clinical trials that were undertaken might influence the surgeon's diagnostic or prognostic judgment and might alter surgical technique, but the goal of doing so was to benefit the individual patient undergoing surgery.

Organized into solo practices or small groups (large clinics such as the Scott and White Clinic in Texas or the Cleveland Clinic were the exception), surgeons experienced little accountability to each other for the quality of their surgical practices. The idea that a surgeon could be accountable to a lay manager of a hospital for the quality of surgery was utterly alien to the culture of surgical practice and training. Indeed, the only purpose of institutional managers was to procure and deliver to the surgical suites and recovery areas the resources that surgeons determined that their patients needed, a concept of hospital ethics that goes back at least to the late eighteenth century and the first charity hospitals in the English-speaking world, the Royal Infirmaries of Britain.[7]

In this cottage industry model of surgery, there naturally arose a surgical ethics that can be summarized as "my patient comes first." The surgeon was obligated to do all in his or her power to effect a cure and, short of that, to do the best possible for the patient on the operating table, without regard for other patients. In addition, surgeons enjoyed an extraordinary level of autonomy over their own practices and thus over their ethics (which were the ethics of "my patient comes first").

Instead of plunging back into an economic depression after World War II (which many feared at the time), the United States experienced unprecedented average annual economic growth (about 4%, compared to the previous historical norm of 2.5 to 3%) for more than two decades. This economics of abundance fueled the my-patient-comes-first ethics and reinforced the autonomy of surgeons by making available in hospitals enormous sums of money to support surgical practice, innovation, and education. Indeed, the postwar period witnessed unprecedented innovation and advances in surgery, for example, in cardiovascular surgery with the advent of coronary artery bypass grafting, and in the transplantation of solid organs.

Physicians and surgeons were paid on a fee-for-service basis. This form of payment involved built-in conflicts of interest, that is, conflicts between the surgeon's fiduciary obligation to provide appropriate clinical management of the patient's diagnosis or condition and the surgeon's self-interest in remuneration and job security.[8,9] In an economics of abundance that richly rewarded procedure-oriented specialties, the pressures created by the built-in conflicts of interest of fee-for-service were considerable. Surgeons confronted nontrivial ethical challenges of managing their conflicts of interest such as self-referral and ownership of hospitals in which they practiced. Unfortunately, the inherent ethical instability of fee-for-service payment was not managed uniformly with integrity by all physicians and surgeons. The simple proof of this is that while every physician and surgeon knows that it should not matter to which emergency department a loved one is taken after a myocardial infarction or automobile accident, every physician and surgeon also knows that this is not the case and that they have colleagues into whose hands they would never place the health or life of a loved one. Such colleagues have put personal and financial self-interest ahead of the primary commitment that physicians and surgeons should have to excellence in patient care.

THE MANAGED PRACTICE OF SURGERY AND ITS THREE BUSINESS TOOLS

All of this has changed in the past 15 years, mainly because in the mid-1970s, the American economy, buffeted by international competition in heavy industry, returned to its historically normal average economic growth rates. In the private sector, global competition meant that two strategies for maintaining and increasing profitability that had prevailed in the postwar period—raising prices and increasing market share—produced smaller and smaller yields. This left only control of all the costs of doing business as the only way to maintain and grow corporate profits. Costs were indeed cut, in the form of massive layoffs and relentless control of all other business costs, especially the costs of employee benefits. Because medical costs had been rising faster than the consumer price index for years, they became a prime target of cost control. Business needed medical costs to rise more slowly and predictably; business leaders therefore acted vigorously to achieve these goals.

By the early 1980s, the need to control costs was also affecting the public sector, principally Medicare. Starting in the 1970s, the Health Care Financing Administration (HCFA), which is responsible for Medicare, began to work with physicians to control the rapidly rising costs of Medicare. These efforts did not succeed, and by the early 1980s, the Medicare Trust Fund was projected for serious shortfalls within a decade.

Also by this time, the work of John Wennberg and others had been appearing in the medical literature regularly.[10,11] Wennberg reported on area variations in the use of medical and surgical services and showed that these variations did not result in improved outcomes.[10] "Geography is destiny" summarized these findings: what level of medical or surgical services a patient received was more a function of where he or she lived and went for medical care than of other factors such as severity of illness or the effect of clinical management on improving outcomes.[10,11] It was plain that medicine lacked the scientific rigor that for decades it had claimed for itself and was therefore of variable quality and not economically efficient. The lack of accountability that is a built-in feature of the cottage industry model of medicine and surgery and the fee-for-service payment system contributed to the lack of uniform quality and the resultant economic inefficiency.

It took only standard economic skill and analysis to identify the problem of the early 1980s: fee-for-service encouraged economic inefficiency and was therefore economically irrational. Clinical analysis showed that surgery, along with the rest of medicine, exhibited scientifically unjustified and therefore economically inefficient variation. Patients were paying with their health and even with their lives, for example, when unnecessary carotid endarterectomy was performed. The Health Care Financing Administration had responsibility not only for the actuarial soundness of Medicare but also for Medicare beneficiaries, and costs were out of control, running at a multiple of the consumer price index. Its solution, endorsed by Congress (on behalf of the public), was elegant and powerful: pay hospitals in ways that reward them economically for controlling unnecessary variation in the use of resources and that punish them economically for being inefficient; that is, end fee-for-service payment of hospitals. By the end of the 1980s, the rate of inflation in Medicare had slowed, and the crisis for the Medicare Trust Fund was postponed into the new millennium.

Medicare, in effect, undertook a large social experiment to test a business tool that was known to work in the private sector: paying institutions in ways that gave them economic incentives to perform as desired and that punished them economically when they failed to perform as desired, such as is done with suppliers of automobile parts to automobile manufacturers. The result for hospitals was the imposition on them of economic conflicts of interest in the prospective payment system based on diagnosis-related groups. Medicare thus invented the first business tool of the managed practice of surgery: paying institutions in ways that imposes on them economic conflicts of interest.[1–3]

Hospitals that succeeded in the new Medicare environment changed the average length of stay into a target length of stay and learned how to manage resources and health care professionals in ways that reduced the previous uncontrolled variation in length of stay. In doing so, hospitals began to adapt to the practice of medicine and surgery the techniques of W. Edwards Deming for reducing uncontrolled variation, which is the engine of uncontrolled costs in service and production processes.[12] Hospitals thus began to manage the practice of medicine and other health care professions by developing and implementing the second business tool of the managed practice of surgery: regulating the clinical judgment, decision making, and behavior of surgeons.[1–3] Failure to do so meant economic ruin for hospitals.

These two business tools of the managed practice of surgery were not invented by MCOs. These health care institutions, which rapidly proliferated, picked up where HCFA and hospitals had already started and further developed and refined these two business tools by applying them directly to surgeons. Surgeons had economic conflicts of interest directly imposed on them, for example, in the form of capitated payment for surgical services for a defined population of "covered lives." In this way, MCOs share risk with surgeons, who then make rational economic calculations and adapt their surgical practices in response to that shared risk or face economic ruin and loss of job security. Using evidence-based techniques, MCOs also work with surgeons on practice guidelines and disease management strategies, moving surgery into the outpatient setting, controlling the choice of materials used (eg, using hip replacement hardware with less than a maximum expected life if the patient is in his or her eighties), monitoring the time surgery requires, defining with the greatest possible precision the criteria for conversion from laparoscopic to open surgery, selecting the least expensive but still effective prophylactic antibiotic, and, of course, going Medicare[11] "one better" and discharging patients from the hospital after surgery as rapidly as possible.

If hospitals and physicians change their behavior when their autonomy is restricted, then patients will too. Managed care organizations have taken the next logical step and added a third management tool: *restricting the autonomy of patients*.[1–3] This can be accomplished directly, as when a closed-panel health maintenance organization (HMO) controls referrals to selected surgeons and will not pay for out-of-network surgical services and as when an MCO requires a primary care physician to authorize referral to a surgeon, thus stopping the scientifically irrational and economically inefficient self-referrals by patients directly to surgeons. This can also be accomplished indirectly, as when an employer provides a "hidden" preferred provider organization (PPO) within indemnity insurance that allows the patient to go to any physician but negotiates lower rates with selected surgeons and hospitals, resulting in lower shared payments by the patient—an indirect but powerful economic incentive (especially for hourly wage earners, ie, most Americans) for the patient to go to a less expensive alternative rather than the out-of-network surgeon of the patient's choice.

The old cottage industry fee-for-service model of surgery involved serious ethical challenges, especially concerning the intellectual and moral integrity of the medical profession under the pressure of the built-in economic conflicts of interest. This integrity was not uniform, and the result was the over-, under-, and mistreatment of patients. Surgeons should therefore not address the ethical challenges of the managed practice of surgery on the assumption that the old way of practicing surgery was free of serious ethical challenges, that those ethical challenges were always managed with integrity, and that only the new managed practice of surgery is ethically worrisome.[13–15] Let us turn now to a consideration of ethical challenges in the managed practice of surgery.

ETHICAL CHALLENGES IN THE MANAGED PRACTICE OF SURGERY: A PREVENTIVE-ETHICS APPROACH

Ethical challenges arise in the managed practice of surgery depending on how its three business tools—paying surgeons in ways that impose conflicts of interest on them; regulating the clinical judgment, decision making, and behavior of surgeons; and restricting the autonomy of their patients—are used by surgeons and institutional managers (including physicians and surgeons who are themselves institutional managers such as medical directors of MCOs and vice presidents for medical affairs of hospitals). These challenges become especially demanding when economic incentives are disconnected from the quality of patient care. Evidence-based surgery should be understood and embraced by surgeons as an antidote to the tendency of some MCOs and hospitals to think that the least expensive medical and surgical care is the least amount of such care and to use the first business tool with the primary aim of cost-control, usually short-term cost control. Evidence-based surgery constitutes a key intellectual component of the second business tool when it is aimed at improving quality and thus controlling costs over the long term as the effect of improving quality. (Still to be addressed in the managed practice movement is how to provide access to medical and surgical services for those currently without such access, especially those who lack health insurance and whose medical conditions are not emergent.)

Surgeons should respond to the ethical challenges posed by evidence-based surgery in particular and the managed practice of surgery in general with a preventive-ethics approach. For some who work in the field of bioethics, it is exciting and intellectually engaging to address ethical conflicts and to argue for how they should be resolved. Clinical experience teaches those of us who do bioethics in the clinical setting, however, that the occurrence of preventable ethical conflicts (between surgeons and their patients, within the surgical team, between surgeons and institutional managers, or between surgeons and payers) exacts a moral and personal toll that becomes deleterious when ethical conflicts recur because no one is thinking about prevention. This chapter is based on the author's conviction, developed from more than two decades of teaching in the clinical setting, that the prevention of ethical conflict is far better for everyone, especially for patients and for the intellectual and moral integrity of medical professionals and health care institutions committed to improving the quality of patient care. Preventive ethics identifies strategies for anticipating the potential for ethical conflicts and preventing them from occurring. The three tools of the managed practice of surgery surely have the potential to generate ethical conflicts, making urgent the development of a preventive-ethics approach. Preventive ethics calls for surgeons to assume accountability for the intellectual and moral integrity of the managed practice of surgery and to lead change in surgery, not to follow it.

Assuming Accountability for Intellectual Integrity

The managed practice of surgery will not be worthy of patients' trust unless surgeons take and maintain a central role in ensuring its intellectual and moral integrity. Intellectual integrity requires that practice guidelines and disease management protocols be developed and continuously improved, consistent with the scientific standards that have been articulated by leading authorities. These standards call for surgeons to hold themselves accountable for both the processes and outcomes of the surgical management of their patients, so that over-, under-, and mistreatment of patients are replaced with a level of care consistent with the biologic variability of disease and injury and the biologic variability of the response of disease and injury to surgical management. Evidence-based surgery plays a central role in providing such accountability.

The first step in being accountable is giving up the autonomy to practice surgery in ways that are inconsistent with scientific excellence. In the old cottage industry model of surgery, surgeons enjoyed considerable autonomy over their practice. One result was the scientifically unjustified variation in practice patterns and use documented by the Wennbergs.[10,11] Patients did not benefit from unnecessary coronary bypass grafts, carotid endarterectomies, or tonsillectomies. Indeed, some patients died unnecessarily, and many were injured by these procedures, especially by the long-term effects of these unnecessary surgeries on their health in subsequent years. From the perspective of medical ethics, something odd had occurred: surgeons claimed and were granted the autonomy to practice in ways inconsistent with scientific excellence, as were physicians in other specialties. Yet, the argument of the American Medical Association (AMA) from its founding in the mid-nineteenth century was that university-trained physicians and surgeons, unlike the many "unorthodox" practitioners of that time, could be counted on to bring patients the benefits of scientific medicine.[16] The lack of accountability built into the cottage industry model of medical and surgical practice, ironically, undermined this promise, which requires accountability through the open processes of science, formulating and testing hypotheses in ways accessible to anyone with appropriate scientific training. Scientifically rigorous surgeons and physicians recognize that they should have the autonomy to practice only according to standards of scientific excellence, not in the widely (perhaps even wildly) varying ways that characterized the cottage industry era. Restricting the autonomy of surgeons (to make them practice in ways consistent with evidence-based strategies) is thus at least ethically permissible, if not required. Surgeons, as professionals committed to the well-being of their patients, should claim only the autonomy to practice according to standards of scientific excellence.

The second step in being accountable is setting realistic goals for measuring the quality of the managed practice of surgery. The goal should be to progressively minimize defects in the processes of surgery and thus progressively reduce the mortality and morbidity of disease and injury when such reduction can be achieved at reasonable iatrogenic and economic cost. The most scientific surgery cannot guarantee processes of care to be perfect and thus always effect cures as outcomes. This is because surgery is the managing of human biology, because disease and injury display biologic variability, and because the response of disease and injury to surgical intervention displays biologic variability.

These realistic goals for evidence-based surgery will necessarily be set for a population of patients defined in terms of both diagnosis and surgical intervention, because variation in processes and outcomes of surgery can only be measured in a population.[17] Here, evidence-based surgery in particular, and the managed practice of surgery generally, mark a sharp departure from the single-patient focus and the my-patient-comes-first ethics of the cottage industry era. Surgeons become accountable for the well-being of a population of patients served by an institution, not for one patient at a time. Reduction of mortality and morbidity in a population of patients does not mean that every patient benefits; some will not. This will still count as scientifically excellent surgery.

The third step in being accountable is playing not only an active but also a leading role in the development of evidence-based surgery. High-quality evidence-based surgery worthy of the trust of patients will develop only if surgeons take an active and leading role in developing the hypotheses to be tested and the means of testing them with scientific rigor. Patients should not rationally trust a managed surgical practice in which surgeons themselves do not have intellectual confidence. To be sure, surgeons need to "buy into" evidence-based surgery if quality is to improve. The point here goes beyond buying in, to underscore the central role that surgeons must play in the development of evidence-based surgery to win back the trust of patients.[18] To be sure, there are challenges in surgical research, such as study design to manage variability among operators, but these can be effectively addressed.[19]

The fourth step in being accountable is developing defensible rationing strategies in pursuit of evidence-based surgery. Deming teaches that the keys to continuous quality improvement are (a) to define expected outcomes clearly; (b) to break the process of each surgical procedure down into its component steps, and then to use evidence-based outcomes; (c) to identify which steps do not contribute to the expected outcomes and eliminate those steps; and (d) to constantly improve all remaining steps, to become ever more economically efficient in achieving and improving the expected outcomes.[12] The effect of the last three steps is to ration surgical management down in an evidence-based fashion from the highly intensive resource-use rates that characterized the old cottage industry model of surgery during the economics of abundance in the postwar period. The "best" surgical care of a population of patients is not the "most" that can be done for each patient. We now can be confident that this older way of thinking did not benefit populations of patients with defined diagnoses and indeed probably caused more harm than good in many cases. Moreover, in an era of economic stringency, MCOs, hospitals, and other health care institutions all operate with finite budgets. If these institutions allow surgeons to continue to practice in the old way, in which "best" equals "most," the institution will experience unmanageable fiscal instability and crisis, putting its entire patient population at risk. In other words, the old "my-patient-comes-first" ethics are self-defeating for an institution and thus for individual surgeons, because as institutional budgets go into crisis, it will be those surgeons' individual patients who will pay the iatrogenic price for poor resource management.

If the previous three steps of accountability are in place, surgeons and their patients should have confidence that rationing involves avoiding both over- and undertreatment, because rationing will be progressively more scientifically rigorous and therefore economically efficient. Rationing below an acceptable standard of care, which the Council on Ethical and

Judicial Affairs of the AMA rightly condemns,[20] will become unnecessary. Moreover, such radical, ethically unacceptable rationing will in many (perhaps most) cases fail a cost-benefit test because it will be more expensive as a result of subsequent medical and surgical management that will likely be more extensive and therefore more costly. Economic and moral arguments re-inforce each other here, and surgeons should not hesitate to defend the intellectual integrity of the rationing required to make evidence-based surgery work.

Assuming Accountability for Moral Integrity

Recent commentators have noted that patients appear to be withdrawing trust from the medical profession and health care institutions.[18] This growing distrust has led to the introduction of legislation, at both state and federal levels, to regulate MCOs. Some of the proposed federal legislation is called the patient bill of rights. In the American political lexicon, this phrase is used when the people believe that they cannot trust large institutions that have begun to gather and exercise great power. Surgeons in the new managed practice model of surgery now act as the agents of these powerful institutions; that is, although their autonomy may be decreasing (justifiably, if the above steps for the intellectual accountability of the managed practice of surgery are implemented), their power over their patients is increasing. In the author's view, the current withdrawal of trust can be interpreted as an altogether typical and predictable American response to increasing power that has not explained itself and that may be exercised in the interest of the individuals and institutions that wield such power rather than in the interests of patients. The preventive-ethics approach to the current crisis of trust calls for surgeons to assume accountability for the moral integrity of the managed practice of surgery.

The first step in being accountable is responsibly managing economic conflicts of interest in how surgeons and institutions are paid. The first business tool of the managed practice of surgery involves paying surgeons and institutions in ways that impose conflicts of interest on them and thus jeopardize what should be the primary moral commitment of both (as fiduciaries of their patients) to the protection and promotion of patients' health-related interests. Capitation in its various forms constitutes a powerful and pervasive form of the first business tool of managed practice. In poorly managed MCOs, hospitals, and surgical groups, the first business tool of the managed practice of surgery is used to provide incentives for surgeons simply to control costs. This primary economic emphasis usually focuses on the short term.

A focus on cost control without a concomitant focus on quality imposes severe and probably morally unmanageable conflicts of interests on surgeons and institutions.[21] The preventive-ethics approach to these versions of the first business tool of managed practice is to resist them and negotiate instead for economic incentives tied to quality rather than (merely) cost. The American Medical Association's Council on Ethical and Judicial Affairs rightly has emphasized the importance of an incentive for quality,[20] known as fee-for-performance. Fee-for-performance, which must be evidence-based, does not eliminate ethical challenges associated with conflicts of interest but does make them more manageable by making the patient's well-being the central focus of the business tools of the managed practice. The development of evidence-based surgery becomes urgent in this context because fee-for-performance will not work, nor will it displace incentives for (mere) cost control, without the compelling intellectual foundation that evidence-based surgery will provide. In other words, accountability for the moral integrity of the managed practice of surgery requires successful accountability for its intellectual integrity.

The second step in being accountable is obtaining adequately informed consent from patients to be cared for in the context of the managed practice of surgery. In the old cottage-industry model of surgery, the surgeon had the ethical obligation to obtain adequately informed consent for surgical intervention; institutions played little or no role in the consent process. In the managed practice of surgery, institutions play a major role in patient care because the three business tools of the managed practice of surgery have direct and indirect effects on the well-being of all patients served by an institution. A staple of all ethical theories is that both individuals and institutions are morally responsible and accountable for the consequences of their decisions and actions.

Because they are morally responsible for the consequences of their management policies and practices, it has been argued that physicians and health care institutions are the moral cofiduciaries of a population of patients.[17] The obligation to obtain adequately informed consent is thus a shared obligation. The ethical challenge to be addressed is that many MCOs and other health care institutions still rely on the cottage industry model of informed consent. Surgeons should play an active role in changing this outdated and ineffective approach to informed consent and should implement the concept of shared fiduciary responsibility for the informed consent process in institutional policy and practice.[17]

It is well understood in the ethics and law of informed consent that the surgeon has an affirmative obligation to provide the patient (without waiting to be asked) with information about the patient's diagnosis or condition, the medically and surgically reasonable alternatives for managing that diagnosis or condition, the alternative of nonintervention, and the benefits and risks of each alternative.[22] The standard that should guide this disclosure is called the "reasonable-person standard," the most common legal standard and the uniform ethical standard.[23] One helpful interpretation of this standard is that the surgeon should provide the patient considering surgery the information that is salient in the surgeon's clinical judgment, so that the patient can replicate the surgeon's judgment and assess the surgeon's recommendation(s).[24] The business tools of the managed practice are surely salient in surgical judgment; indeed, evidence-based surgery is intended to scientifically and economically discipline the surgeon's clinical judgment, decision making, and behavior. Thus, the nature and effects of the business tools of the managed practice of surgery count as clinically salient and should therefore be explained to the patient.

In addition to making this disclosure, the surgeon is obligated to do at least two more things. First, the surgeon should make a reasonable effort to ensure that the patient understands the information with which he or she has been provided. Second, the surgeon should make a reasonable effort to ensure that the patient's decision is not coerced (ie, not substantially controlled by others).[22,23]

As surgeons already know, routinely fulfilling these ethical obligations helps achieve another important moral dimension of the informed consent process, namely, moral authority for power. Of all physicians, surgeons wield enormous power over patients (especially after anesthesia, at which point the patient's very life is in the hands of the surgical team), and the patient is most vulnerable to the abuse of the surgeon's power. Moral authority, via the informed consent process, for such power is essential for maintaining the moral integrity of surgery.[22]

One of the central ethical challenges of the managed practice of surgery is that most MCOs, hospitals, and surgical groups have not made the transition from the cottage industry approach to informed consent to the shared-fiduciary approach. Surgeons and institutions both must meet their ethical obligations of informed consent to patients. These obligations have become urgent; most patients have no knowledge or awareness of the three business tools of the managed practice of surgery. It should therefore come as no surprise to those in health care that patients are withdrawing their trust as they confront the growing, unexplained, and therefore unjustified power of health care institutions such as MCOs and of surgeons as the agents of these increasingly powerful institutions.

The preventive-ethics approach to this problem is for institutions and surgeons to work together to ensure that patients are adequately informed and not to follow the current practice of surgeons explaining what patients need to know in the least ideal circumstances (ie, the fractured, disjointed process of consent for surgery that can begin in the outpatient setting with one surgeon and continue the next day in the in-patient setting with another surgeon), or worse still, of no disclosure by anyone to the patient about the business tools of the managed practice of surgery. (It was just such a pattern of nondisclosure in the clinical setting that led courts to establish the reasonable-person standard.[23] Preventive ethics teaches that we should not have to repeat such history to learn from it.)

Because most institutions have not done so, surgeons, especially surgeons in management positions, should take the lead in implementing the shared-responsibility model for informed consent. Institutions should inform patients, when they enroll in their insurance plan, about how that institution and its surgeons use and evaluate the effects of the three business tools of managed practice. Patients should not be discovering these matters when they come for surgery, when their minds are focused, perhaps emergently, on serious threats to their health status. After all, as lay persons of average sophistication, patients should not ethically or legally be expected to know already what the business tools of managed practice are or how those tools will apply in their medical and surgical care.

The following concepts (which are not complex) should be conveyed to patients: (1) The surgeon is paid in a way that creates economic incentives to perform as the plan desires. If those incentives are tied to quality, this should be explained, as well as the basic techniques of evidence-based surgery, which patients should find reassuring. If those incentives are tied merely to cost control, patients should indeed be distrustful of that institution and its surgeons. (2) The surgeon is not a free agent in decisions about matters of resource use, such as whether to perform surgery, whether surgery should be performed on an in-patient or outpatient basis, and how long patients will be hospitalized after in-patient surgery. The plan works with the surgeon to manage and control such matters, using evidence-based and other techniques. (3) Patients will be restricted in their access to surgeons, either directly, by required referral by their primary care physicians (as in a closed-panel HMO), or indirectly, by financial incentives for patients to go to surgeons whom the plan has chosen (as in a PPO). A reasonable effort must be made by the plan to ensure that patients understand this information, that it will indeed apply to them, and that their decision to enroll is not coerced.

If a plan already has in place accountability for the intellectual integrity of the managed practice of medicine and surgery and explains that this is the case, patients should be willing to consent to being cared for under these conditions, thus giving moral authority to the institution's and the surgeon's power over patients. In the author's view, these matters are morally urgent. The longer surgeons and physicians fail to take the lead in forcing institutional change, the more patients will withdraw trust, until it is irreversibly completely withdrawn. This outcome will be a moral catastrophe inasmuch as it will return medicine, patients, and society to the purely commercial model of medical practice that existed 200 years ago in the English-speaking world.[7]

Once patients have been informed in these general terms about how the managed practice of medicine and surgery works in their plan, surgeons can explain to the individual patient the particulars of how the business tools of managed practice will affect the clinical management of his or her diagnosis or condition, including the application of evidence-based surgery in his or her care. The systematic failure of institutions to make adequate disclosure puts surgeons in the unenviable position of having to explain both the business tools of managed practice and their clinical implications to patients who have no idea that these tools exist or apply to them. The preventive-ethics approach to the shared responsibility of informed consent will begin effectively to address this problem.

Consider the following case. A 45-year-old man awakes early one Saturday morning with what he takes to be a stomachache or perhaps gas and for which he takes an antacid tablet. Not only does his discomfort not decrease, it increases and begins to localize to the lower right side of his abdomen. Recalling his high-school biology course and suspecting appendicitis, he calls his family physician's answering service and relays his history to the person who answers. His physician calls back within 5 minutes and, upon listening to the patient's history, advises him that his symptoms are indeed consistent with acute appendicitis and that he should go to the emergency department of Urban Hospital (a fictitious name) immediately. The patient arrives in the emergency department by automobile 10 minutes later and is rapidly worked up by the emergency physician, who arranges for appropriate tests and images and calls for a surgery consult. The on-call surgeon arrives, explains that she thinks that the most likely explanation for the patient's now much worse pain is acute appendicitis, takes the patient through the consent process, and transfers the patient to a surgical suite, where the patient's somewhat inflamed appendix is removed laparoscopically at midmorning without complication.

On Sunday afternoon, the surgeon informs the patient that everything is going well, and that the patient is scheduled for discharge home about 30 hours after surgery. The surgeon provides the patient with information on where to call if problems arise, and a follow-up appointment is scheduled for 3 days later.

Within 2 weeks, the patient receives a copy of his bill from Urban Hospital, the original of which has been sent to his insurance plan. This bill amounts to over $10,000, with $2,500 discounted for the patient's insurance plan. The patient calls the plan administrator and learns that this is a discount negotiated by the plan with the hospital and also that the surgeon and the anesthesiologist have discounted rates with the plan. The patient then begins to wonder whether he was discharged quickly because he was medically and surgically ready to go home or because the surgeon and hospital were not being paid their full fees. In the language of medical ethics, this patient is concerned about how well his surgeon and the hospital managed the economic conflicts of interest created by discounted fee-for-service.

This is not an uncommon story, and it illustrates how the current dominant practice of nondisclosure can raise serious ethical questions in patients' minds that, in the absence of a preventive-ethics approach, can logically lead to the erosion of trust. Imagine how different the patient's experience would have been if (a) his insurance plan had informed him, when he enrolled, about the business tools of managed practice, and (b) the surgeon had taken time after the surgery to explain to the patient how those business tools of managed practice would affect the patient's subsequent clinical management. (Before surgery, there probably was not sufficient time for anything but an abbreviated informed consent process for the surgery itself.) Taking this preventive-ethics approach would have put the surgeon in a position to explain to the patient how her decision for rapid discharge was based on evidence in which the surgeon had a high level of confidence, thus assuring the patient about the intellectual integrity of the discharge plan. Lacking such evidence, the surgeon would be unable to justify her discharge plan intellectually and morally. Moreover, if the patient had learned that the primary goal of such a discharge plan was to protect the patient's health (eg, from nosocomial infections), not to save money for the hospital (which was discounting its charges) and not to save time for the surgeon (who was accepting less than her fee for patients with traditional indemnity insurance), the patient could have been assured of the intellectual and moral integrity of the discharge plan.

CONCLUSION

The managed practice of surgery confronts surgeons, other physicians, health care institutions (MCOs and hospitals), and patients with serious and urgent ethical challenges. The purpose of this chapter has been to identify such ethical challenges in the managed practice of surgery and to identify preventive-ethics strategies for responding to these challenges proactively rather than reactively. In the author's view, the stakes of the social experiment currently under way in medicine and health care—namely, to change from the scientifically less-than-excellent, unmanaged, cottage industry fee-for-service model to a managed-practice model—are very high. If too many surgeons, physicians, and health care institutions fail to respond to these ethical challenges by becoming accountable for the intellectual and moral integrity of the managed practice of medicine and surgery, then the profession of medicine as a fiduciary profession may cease to exist, mainly, in the author's view, as a result of the free decisions of those physicians and institutions. The development and implementation of evidence-based surgery (which, if done well, will be very expensive) constitutes a key step in creating this accountability. To this scientific step, ethics adds the moral steps, especially those concerning the reliable management of conflicts of interest and the need for a shared-responsibility approach to informed consent.

Surgeons and other physicians need to teach their patients what it will take to be a patient in the new managed practice of medicine and surgery. First, surgeons and physicians need to teach that what can be expected from medicine and surgery is always limited by iatrogenic and economic costs. Second, they need to teach that the best medical and surgical care is not the most care possible and that insisting that the best equals the most is a surefire method of breaking institutional budgets and thus putting all patients at unnecessary risk. Third, patients need to school themselves in ordinary courage, to live with and accept the fact that even the most scientifically rigorous evidence-based surgery cannot eliminate mortality and morbidity altogether. Patients need to learn (from their surgeons and physicians, who should be role models) the discipline of managing their diseases and injuries well, not curing them. That a patient is still sick, sicker, or even dead as a result of evidence-based surgery does not mean that such surgery was defective, if the process followed is supported by scientifically rigorous justification, in which evidence-based research plays a fundamental role. The common law will therefore have to change its present concept of negligence (individual mortality or morbidity resulting from a surgeon doing something below the standard of care) into a concept of negligent processes. The standard of care, understood in population-based terms, will always include unavoidable death, disease, injury, and disability. Fourth, patients and both private and public payers must appreciate that the well-managed managed practice of surgery will be expensive. The scientific excellence of evidence-based surgery will not come cheaply.

ACKNOWLEDGMENT

The author would like to thank his esteemed colleague, K. Danner Clouser, PhD, for the opportunity to prepare this chapter. Dr. Clouser was originally to prepare such a chapter, but personal matters made it impossible for him to do so. Hopefully, the present work measures up to his high standards.

REFERENCES

1. Chervenak FA, McCullough LB. The threat of the new managed practice of medicine to patients' autonomy. J Clin Ethics 1995;6:20–3.

2. Chervenak FA, McCullough LB, Chez R. Responding to the ethical challenges posed by the business tools of managed care in the practice of obstetrics and gynecology. Am J Obstet Gynecol 1996; 175:523–7.

3. McCullough LB, Chervenak FA. Ethical challenges in the managed practice of obstetrics and gynecology. Obstet Gynecol 1999;93:304–7.

4. McCullough LB, Chervenak FA. Ethics in obstetrics and gynecology. New York: Oxford University Press; 1994.

5. Starr P. The transformation of American medicine. New York: Basic Books; 1982.

6. Morreim EH. Balancing act: the new medical ethics of medicine's new economics. Washington (DC): Georgetown University Press; 1995.

7. McCullough LB. John Gregory and the invention of professional medical ethics and the profession of medicine. Dordrecht (Netherlands): Kluwer Academic Publishers; 1998.

8. Morreim EH. Conflicts of interest. In: Reich WT, editor. Encyclopedia of bioethics. 2nd ed. New York: Macmillan; 1995. p. 459–65.

9. Speece R, Shimm D, Buchanan A, editors. Conflicts of interest in clinical practice and research. New York: Oxford University Press; 1996.

10. Wennberg J, Gittelsohn A. Small area variations in health care delivery. Science 1973;182:1102–8.

11. Wennberg DE. Variation in the delivery of care: the stakes are high. Ann Intern Med 1998; 128:866–8.

12. Teichholz LE. Quality, Deming's principles and physicians. Mt Sinai J Med 1993;60:350–8.

13. Iserson KV, Jarrell BE. Financial relationships with patients. In: McCullough LB, Jones JW, Brody BA, editors. Surgical ethics. New York: Oxford University Press; 1998. p. 322–41.

14. Khushf G, Gifford R. Understanding, assessing, and managing conflicts of interest. In: McCullough LB, Jones JW, Brody BA, editors. Surgical ethics. New York: Oxford University Press; 1998. p. 342–66.

15. Wildes KW, Wallace RB. Relationships with payers and institutions that manage and deliver patient services. In: McCullough LB, Jones JW, Brody BA, editors. Surgical ethics. New York: Oxford University Press; 1998. p. 367–83.

16. Baker RB, editor. The codification of medical morality. Volume two: Anglo-American medical ethics and jurisprudence in the nineteenth century. Dordrecht (Netherlands): Kluwer Academic Publishers; 1995.

17. McCullough LB. A basic concept in the clinical ethics of managed care: physicians and institutions as economically disciplined moral co-fiduciaries of populations of patients. J Med Philos 1999; 24:77–97.

18. Mechanic D. The impact of managed care on patients' trust in medical care and their physicians. JAMA 1996;275:1693–7.

19. Frader JE, Caniano DA. Research and innovation in surgery. In: McCullough LB, Jones JW, Brody BA, editors. Surgical ethics. New York: Oxford University Press; 1998. p. 216–41.

20. American Medical Association, Council on Ethical and Judicial Affairs. Ethical issues in managed care. JAMA 1995;273:330–5.

21. Khushf G. A radical rupture in the paradigm of modern medicine: conflicts of interest, fiduciary obligations, and the scientific ideal. J Med Philos 1998;23:98–122.

22. McCullough LB, Jones JW, Brody BA. Informed consent: autonomous decision making of the surgical patient. In: McCullough LB, Jones JW, Brody BA, editors. Surgical ethics. New York: Oxford University Press; 1998. p. 15–37.

23. Faden RR, Beauchamp TL. A history and theory of informed consent. New York: Oxford University Press; 1986.

24. Wear S. Informed consent: patient and autonomy and physician beneficence within clinical medicine. Dordrecht (Netherlands): Kluwer Academic Publishers; 1994.

CHAPTER 7

Health Policy Research: Information Guiding Clinical Decision Making at the Population Level

David Lilienfeld, MD, MPH, MS Engin, and Suzanne M. Wyatt, MPH

—⋅—

Public policy, and health policy in particular, is often thought of in terms of complex legislation and lengthy administrative proposals. A clearer and more general view of policy defines it as a method by which a system is administered. Seen in this light, health policy is made not only by lawmakers and the leaders of state and federal health agencies but also by planners and administrators at hospitals and other institutions that provide health services, by leaders at managed care organizations (MCOs) and other third-party payers, by large purchasers of health care, by provider groups, and by the patients themselves.

At its best, policy is created to increase the efficiency with which a system is administered. Health policymakers devise laws and regulations to more efficiently deliver quality care to a population; issues of access, delivery, reimbursement, and financing are all contained within this broader mission of efficient delivery of quality care.

As with any branch of policy, regulations concerning health care are not static; they instead must undergo revision to remain in line with an evolving health care system. In the 1990s, forces ranging from the increasing numbers of the uninsured to developments in biomedical technology have influenced the development of health policy in the United States. Chief among the forces defining the direction of health care in the last decade is the emergence of managed care, and with it, the growing demand for greater fiscal and clinical accountability among providers of health services.

In this new managed health care environment, the need for information that evaluates efficacy and costs associated with particular therapies and modes of delivery of care have never been greater. Increasingly, patterns of care and delivery are not explicitly regulated but are directed instead by market forces. The shift to a market approach in the organization of health care delivery presupposes what economists term "perfect information," that is, valid and readily available comparisons of service. Such information is unavailable for most health services, however, and this information is needed by consumers of health care—purchasers and patients—as well as by the providers themselves, who need it to justify clinical practice patterns as well as to explain the source of costs to third-party payers.

For providers of surgical services (both hospitals and the surgeons themselves) information that enables such negotiations with third-party payers is produced by the application of evidence-based techniques to the practice of surgery. As costs and outcomes of surgical procedures are examined, optimum pathways of care are identified, as are preferred modalities of treatment, optimal loci of care, and methods to contain surgical costs. The application of evidence-based techniques enables surgeons to derive this knowledge, which in turn can be used to create information that influences surgical practice and the delivery of surgical services. Ultimately, the application of evidence-based techniques to analyze information concerning surgical procedures can enable policy researchers and policymakers to establish practice guidelines that optimize the quality of surgical care while restraining resource consumption.

In this chapter, the authors will address the application of evidence-based analytic techniques to the development of health policy at the institutional, local, regional, and national levels. Emphasis will be placed on the national health policy arena, particularly on issues of quality, locus of care, manpower, and education of future health professionals.

HEALTH CARE QUALITY AND HEALTH POLICY

With the emergence of managed care and an increasingly market-driven system of health care delivery, the formation of health policy has shifted from a focus on explicit regulation to a focus on greater clinical and fiscal accountability of health services providers. In such an evolving health care system, policymakers (third-party payers and managed care entities, purchasers of care, and lawmakers) need information that enables valid comparisons of health care professionals, hospitals and other health care institutions, and the services they provide. The use of evidence-based techniques to examine the existing body of literature concerning surgical services delivery can enable health policy researchers to make these comparisons and inform policy that bears on surgical issues.

Under the current cost-driven system, many of the comparisons among providers of surgical services have centered on differences in charges. Another dimension of health services delivery that should be compared among providers is health care quality. Unfortunately, quality in health care is defined in a wide variety of ways, depending on the particular services under scrutiny. Moreover, methods of measuring quality, while simultaneously taking into account such issues as regional differences in incidence and prevalence of disease, institutional case mix, and severity of illness of specific patient cohorts, have yet to be perfected. Lack of standardized techniques of quality measurement, as well as competing efforts and methodologies for assessing health care quality, challenge the application of evidence-based techniques to policy decisions concerning surgical care and are confusing to policymakers who struggle to optimize surgical outcomes while simultaneously restraining costs.

Health policy researchers can influence policy development by applying evidence-based analysis to existing surgical literature and other data that allow for the comparison of surgical techniques, delivery methods, and outcomes. In this way, these researchers can provide the kind of information needed by decision makers who represent competing interests in the formation of health policy. Such decision-making entities—federal agencies (such as the Health Care Financing Administration, the Physician Prospective Payment Commission, or the Health Resources and Services Administration), interest groups, industry representatives, and provider groups and systems of care—may often have competing interests. With the provision of evidence-based analysis, these potentially competing players in health policy formation may be guided by evidence and so may ultimately make more cost-effective decisions that simultaneously improve patient outcomes.

LOCUS OF CARE

Inpatient versus Outpatient Care

In recent years, the provision of surgical care has witnessed a dramatic movement from an inpatient focus to one of outpatient care. With this shift in the surgical setting has come the need for evidence to guide decisions as to which surgeries are best reserved for the inpatient setting, both in terms of cost-effectiveness and patient outcome. Surgeons, health services researchers, policy researchers, and others involved in the use of evidence-based analytic techniques can influence decisions concerning the site of surgical care through the assessment of existing data and literature that addresses this issue.

Case in Safety: Outpatient Surgery and the Higher-Risk Patient

Of special concern to those making decisions about the appropriate site of care is the safety of patients treated in the outpatient setting. A surgeon or researcher, employing an evidence-based analysis of the literature of, for example, laparoscopic cholecystectomy, may find several published articles that address the issue of safety and the higher-risk patient in the outpatient setting. Evidence-based analysis of these articles points to a heavy emphasis on preoperative observation and assessment to determine the likelihood of the need for open cholecystectomy.[1,2] The articles, nonetheless, do not rule out provision of care in the outpatient setting for higher-risk patients. Such an analysis may then be used by health policymakers to develop practice guidelines that promote the provision of this procedure in the outpatient setting provided appropriate preoperative assessment (eg, ultrasound, perioperative observation, etc) is conducted. In this way, evidence-based analysis influences policy that achieves the desired cost savings of a shift to outpatient surgery while simultaneously promoting surgical care that seeks to preserve patient safety.

Certificate of Need and Regionalization

Before the emergence of managed care as a major force in the delivery of health care in the United States, the provision of health services, particularly surgical services, was guided by a largely regulatory approach. In many states, policymakers prevented excessive market competition among health service providers by requiring that a hospital file a certificate of need (CON) prior to providing certain diagnostic or surgical services. This legislation had the effect of concentrating some services into a few hospitals. In some cases, patient outcomes improved, a finding some attributed to the "practice-makes-perfect" phenomenon.

In the managed care era, requirements for certificates of need have given way to a more market-driven approach. The application of evidence-based techniques to the analysis of hospital claims data has led many in policy research to conclude that for a number of health services, concentration of services at one or a few institutions yields improved outcomes at reduced costs. This policy of concentration of services (also called regionalization) has been considered for a wide range of health services, particularly for surgical procedures.

Unlike the regulatory approach, regionalization of services is largely market-based; the use of evidence-based information that argues for concentration of some services could be of great use in encouraging policymakers at the state or institutional level to require regionalization of those services that prove to be most responsive to the effect of such concentration.

The relationship between higher volume and improved outcomes has been demonstrated for a broad range of surgical procedures, from cardiac transplantation to knee replacement to breast cancer surgery.[3–5] A number of studies in the literature have shown that this relationship between higher procedural volume and improved outcomes holds true both when "higher volume" is defined by a surgeon's annual volume for a given procedure and when procedural volume is defined in terms of a hospital's annual caseload.[6,7] Furthermore, while no work has yet been done to characterize procedures that are particularly responsive to the effect of concentration at a limited number of providers, the existing body of literature has shown that the positive volume-outcomes relationship exists for procedures that are rare, common, high-risk, or routine.[6,8,9]

The procedure that has been perhaps the most extensively studied with respect to the volume-outcomes relationship is coronary artery bypass graft (CABG). This common, complex, cardiac procedure carries a relatively low mortality rate (typically under 5%).[10,11] Although other cardiac procedures like percutaneous transluminal coronary angioplasties (PTCAs) now outnumber CABGs, the number of CABGs performed annually in the United States continues to grow; analysis performed at the Association of American Medical Colleges (AAMC) has shown that the annual number of CABGs performed in the United States rose from 136,000 to 360,000 (an increase of 165%) between 1980 and 1995. A number of studies have examined the volume-outcomes relationship for CABG and have found an inverse relationship between surgical volume and inpatient mortality.[7,9,12–15] Reductions in lengths of stay and in the numbers of patients with extremely long lengths of stay were found with an increase in CABG volume in some studies.[9,4,16] In light of the large numbers of this procedure being performed, as well as the sharp increase in these numbers, those interested in making policy that optimizes surgical outcomes and restrains surgical resource use will be interested in monitoring the impact of regionalization on the demand for CABG surgery and on its outcomes.

Much of the research that has examined the volume-outcomes relationship for CABG surgery has focused on a single institution or state. While such analyses are useful to policy researchers and policymakers, decision makers at the national level require analyses that can be generalized to the nation as a whole. Recent work at the AAMC has examined the issue of the volume-outcomes relationship for CABG surgery, using a nationally representative claims data set. Analysis of the Nationwide Inpatient Sample (NIS), a product of the Agency for Health Care Policy and Research, has shown that, nationwide, inpatient mortality rate and length of stay decline as hospital CABG volume increases. Examination of total patient charges, a proxy for patient resource consumption, reveals that these charges tend to be lower in higher-volume hospitals. Analysis of the NIS, along with data from the AAMC's Council of Teaching Hospitals (COTH) database, further reveals that high-volume hospitals tend to also be teaching hospitals.

Taken as a whole, the body of literature that examines the relationship of hospital volume to postsurgical outcomes for CABG surgery points to an inverse relationship between higher surgical volume and negative postsurgical outcomes. Given that the majority of published articles on this subject demonstrate the relationship between higher volumes and improved outcomes, shorter lengths of stay, and reduced resource use, a critical evaluation of the existing literature using evidence-based techniques would direct the health policy researcher to support a regionalized approach to CABG surgery.

Under a regulatory model, policy researchers and health policymakers concerned with the issue of improving outcomes and reducing resource use for CABG surgery would use the knowledge derived from an evidence-based evaluation of the literature to drive development of a regionalization policy. Under such a policy, federal or state lawmakers would restrict the number of institutions that are permitted to perform non-emergent CABG; lower-volume providers would be required to refer or transfer patients in need of CABG to higher-volume institutions. Such a policy would result in the closing of lower-volume surgical units and might well lead to the development of regional "centers of excellence," large units that receive referrals for a particular procedure or class of procedures over a large referral area. Such centers gain experience and efficiency in the delivery of the regionalized service, improvements in outcomes, and reductions of resource use, all as a result of such high volume and specialization.

At the state level, policymakers with a regulatory orientation have attempted to limit the provision of certain services to a few sites by regulating hospital acquisition of medical technology and other capital. Until recently, many states required certificates of need (CONs) to be issued to hospitals before these institutions acquired costly medical technologies. The issuance of CONs was intended to reduce increases in health care costs through reducing the duplication of certain technologies (and thus, certain health services) within a given catchment area.[17] State CON programs declined during the 1980s; under the market-driven reforms of the 1990s, these programs have declined still further.

In the increasingly market-driven health care system that has emerged in the 1990s, a regulatory approach to directing the locus of the provision of surgical care has grown less relevant. More and more, health policy that directs patients to particular sites of care is made by third-party payers, such as managed care entities, rather than by state or federal lawmakers. Under such an evolving system, the need for objective, risk-adjusted comparisons of quality of care is greater than ever. So too is the need for a risk-adjustment system (or other methodology that enables valid comparisons among hospital and patient types) that is accepted by those in the research and policy communities with a stake in this kind of analysis. Under the current system, third party payers may compare cost information alone to determine to what providers of surgical services they will direct their patients. Such cost-based analyses fail to account for differences in case mix, in the severity of conditions treated at different types of hospitals, and in the quality and efficiency of care. Thus, comparisons of institutional providers of surgical services are difficult for payers and purchasers of care. Analyses of claims information and evidence-based analyses of literature on postsurgical costs and outcomes can assist purchasers and payers to select loci of care that provide efficient, high-quality surgical services. However, yet another difficulty encountered in this type of analysis is the limited availability of hospital claims information. (Only a minority of states require full reporting of inpatient claims data.) Moreover, in published literature which examines claims data, this information may be derived from state data tapes, individual institutions' discharge information, or from nationally representative samples. The disparity in claims information makes the application of evidence-based meta-analysis of the literature in this area particularly difficult and so may negatively influence the acceptance of its conclusions by policymakers.

Policy researchers can provide evidence-based analyses of existing literature that can help payers and purchasers select surgical provider sites on the basis of optimum quality and resource use. In evidence-based policy research that evaluates the literature on the locus of care, high-volume surgical providers and teaching hospitals appear to be the logical and preferred sites of care for CABG surgery. It is important to point out here that teaching hospitals have been regarded as excessively costly providers of health services. An evidence-based style review of the literature shows that these institutions are often the most cost-effective providers of CABG surgery, as most high-volume providers are also teaching hospitals.

WORKFORCE ISSUES

Health policymakers must consider issues of the quality and cost-effectiveness of care as well as the provision of appropriate care in the appropriate setting. In addition to procedural and service delivery issues, however, these decision makers must also be concerned with the presence of appropriate health service providers in numbers sufficient for the timely and efficient delivery of care. Once again, the application of evidence-based analysis of existing literature and other data can guide those involved in policy formation.

Perhaps the issue of greatest concern to policymakers concerned with physician workforce issues is that of a potential oversupply of physicians.[18] The perception that medical schools and teaching hospitals are churning out too many high-cost providers of health care is a matter of grave importance to physicians, for such a perception can lead policymakers to divert public dollars from training programs and the institutions that house them.

Once again, the application of evidence-based analysis of published literature and existing data can guide policymakers to decisions that meet the need for cost-effective approaches while simultaneously encouraging the delivery of high-quality care. For example, a policymaker interested in a potential oversupply of surgeons would find, upon application of an evidence-based analysis of the published literature, that post-trauma death rates have declined upon an increase in the number of surgeons in a given region.[19] Mortality from other causes has also been shown to be lower in regions with higher concentrations of medical providers.[20]

A particularly thorny issue in the discussion of physician supply is that of rural health care providers. Rural regions have long been known to suffer physician shortages, a problem that has proved resistant to programmatic solutions at the federal and state level. A body of literature concerning rural physician supply exists, and an analysis of this literature could provide policymakers with the kind of evidence needed to guide decision making in such a way that would meet the needs of rural communities for health services providers. Of note, a disproportionate number of international medical graduates serve rural areas in the United States. Such information could be of use to those forming policy designed to discourage the entrance of these professionals into the United States.[21]

Policy concerning human resources in surgery must address not only the sheer volume of surgeons in a given region but also the distribution of surgeons trained in various specialties. While the explicit legislative regulation of the distribution of surgical specialists is unlikely, policymakers at the level of health institutions can encourage an appropriate volume of particular specialists to cope with the surgical care needs of the surrounding community. While general surgeons may be sufficient to meet many of those needs, a body of the published literature suggests that for some procedures cost of care is lower and postsurgical outcomes are better when a surgical specialist is involved in the surgery. An evidence-based analysis of this literature could guide officials at the hospital and health-system level in terms of staffing decisions.

In addition to staffing issues, the application of evidence-based techniques to the existing literature may also yield information that can effectively guide decision makers within specialty societies, state medical associations, and hospitals and health systems in limiting the credentialing of surgeons to those most likely to provide the highest quality of surgical care. The research literature speaks to the issue of the quality of providers themselves in terms of both training and the volume of cases seen. Analysis of this literature can guide policy that addresses the education of physicians as well as their credentialing.

EDUCATION

Providing high-quality surgical care requires not only an adequate number of surgeons but also that those surgeons be adequately trained. Policymakers, educators, researchers, and others concerned with this issue can once again derive the evidence necessary to guide the making of rational health education policy through the application of evidence-based analysis of the literature.

Perhaps the most obvious application of evidence-based analysis to educational issues is in the determination of the sites and providers of care who produce the best outcomes and maintain the lowest costs. If trainees are exposed to efficiently delivered, high-quality care in their formative years, the practices that they saw should positively impact their future surgical outcomes. Thus, the literature that points to high-volume hospitals and high-volume surgeons as the providers of high-quality surgical care also points to these providers as excellent training sites and potential mentors for future surgeons.

More generally, an evidence-based literature review of medical education literature can be used to develop best-practices guidelines for training at the undergraduate, graduate, and continuing medical education levels. Such guidelines could be developed by policy researchers and educators and then disseminated to policymakers involved in curricular decisions, such as deans, program directors, accreditation bodies, and specialty societies.

In addition to the use of evidence-based techniques to develop better curricula and, ultimately, better surgeons, undergraduate and graduate medical curricula need to incorporate some training in the policy applications of evidence-based surgery. In this way, future surgeons will be better equipped to make decisions concerning the structural delivery of cost-effective, high-quality surgical care. Moreover, such a skills base will empower future surgeons to effectively advocate on their own behalf to state and federal policymakers.

CONCLUSION

Ultimately, evidence-based analysis has not yet been used to its fullest potential in the formation of policy concerning the delivery of surgical care or the training of surgeons. At the regional and institutional levels, evidence-based analysis has been of great use in identifying the need for regionalization of at least some surgical procedures. This has implications both for the delivery of surgical care and for surgical training opportunities. Many more health policy issues of concern to surgeons have not yet fully benefited from the fruits of evidence-based analysis, however. Much more work is needed to inform these areas, and appropriate evidence-based training of surgeons and others involved in health policy formation is clearly warranted.

REFERENCES

1. Votik AJ, Ignatius S, Schouten BD, Mustard RA. Is outpatient surgery safe for the higher risk patient? J Gastrointest Surg 1998;2(2):156–8.

2. Brothers TE, Robison JG, Eliott BM. Relevance of quality improvement methods to surgical practice: prospective assessment of carotid endarterectomy. Am Surg 1997;63(3):213–19.

3. Hosenpud JD, Breen TJ, Edwards EB, et al. The effect of transplant center volume on cardiac transplant outcome. A report of the United Network for Organ Sharing Scientific registry. JAMA 1994;271:1844–9.

4. Gutierrez B, Culler SD, Freund DA. Does hospital procedure-specific volume affect treatment costs? A national study of knee replacement surgery. Health Serv Res 1998;33:489–511.

5. Roohan PJ, Bickell NA, Baptiste MS, et al. Hospital volume differences and five-year survival from breast cancer. Am J Pub Health 1998;88:454–7.

6. Hannan EL, O'Donnell JF, Kilburn H Jr, et al. Investigation of the relationship between volume and mortality for surgical procedures performed in New York state hospitals. JAMA 1989;262:503–10.

7. Luft HS, Garnick DW, Mark DH, McPhee SJ. Hospital volume, physician volume, and patient outcomes. Ann Arbor (MI): Health Administration Press; 1990.

8. Gordon TA, Burleyson GP, Tielsch JM, Cameron JL. The effects of regionalization on costs and outcomes for one general high-risk surgical procedure. Ann Surg 1995;221:43–9.

9. Showstack JA, Rosenfeld KE, Garnick DW, et al. Association of volume with outcomes of coronary artery bypass graft surgery: scheduled vs nonscheduled operations. JAMA 1987;257:785–9.

10. Ghali WA, Ash AS, Hall RE, Moskowitz MA. Statewide quality improvement initiatives and mortality after cardiac surgery. JAMA 1997;277:379–82.

11. Marshall G, Shroyer LW, Grover FL, Hammermeister KE. Time series monitors of outcomes: a new dimension for measuring quality of care. Med Care 1998;36:348–56.

12. Hannan EL, Kilburn H, Bernard H, et al. Coronary artery bypass surgery: the relationship between inhospital mortality rate and surgical volume after controlling for clinical risk factors. Med Care 1991;29:1094–1107.

13. Crawford FA, Anderson RP, Clark RE, et al. Volume requirements for cardiac surgery credentialing: a critical examination. Ann Thorac Surg 1996;61:12–16.

14. Shroyer ALW, Marshall G, Warer BA, et al. No continuous relationship between veterans affairs hospital coronary artery bypas grafting surgical volume and operative mortality. Ann Thorac Surg 1996;61:17–20.

15. Clark RE, Ad Hoc Committee on Cardiac Surgery Credentialing of The Society of Thoracic Surgeons. Outcome as a function of annual coronary artery bypass graft volume. Ann Thorac Surg 1996;61:21–6.

16. Luft HS, Roman PS. Chance, continuity, and change in hospital mortality rates: coronary artery bypass graft patients in California hospitals, 1983 to 1989. JAMA 1993;270:331–7.

17. Thorpe KE. Health care cost containment: reflections and future directions. In: Kovner AR, Jonas S, editors. Health care delivery in the United States. 5th edition. New York: Springer Publishing Company; 1995.

18. Mosberg WH. Medical manpower needs at home and abroad. Neurosurgery 1992;30(4):639–48.

19. Rutledge R, Fakhry SM, Baker CC, et al. A population-based study of the association of medical manpower with county trauma death rates in the United States. Ann Surg 1994;219(5):547–63.

20. Armstrong D, Barnett E, Casper M, Wing S. Community occupational structure, medical and economic resources, and coronary mortality among U.S. blacks and whites, 1980-1988. Ann Epidemiol 1998;8(3):184–91.

21. Baer LD, Risketts TC, Konrad TR, Mick SS. Do international medical graduates reduce rural physician shortages? Med Care 1998;36(11):1534–44.

CHAPTER 8

Evidence-Based Surgery in the United Kingdom

Lord McColl, MS, FRCS, FACS

The practice of evidence-based medicine is the molding of a clinician's expertise by the most reliable published evidence, with consideration for the quality of life of the patients and the cost of their management.[1] Surgeons have additional technical skills in operating and are responsible in many ways for incurring greater health care costs. The aim of evidence-based surgery is to encourage sound research to improve diagnosis, treatment, and the skills of the individual clinician while emphasizing the importance of listening to the patient, taking an excellent history, performing a thorough physical examination, and coming to the best and most sensible conclusions, from the patient's point of view. The need to keep up-to-date

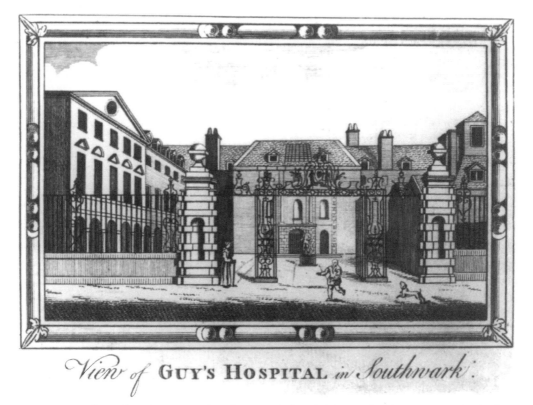

Figure 8–1 Eighteenth-century view of Guy's Hospital, founded in 1724 by Thomas Guy, a bookseller who ultimately realized a vast fortune in publishing and other investments. Guy's Hospital, which received the bulk of his estate, was intended to house 400 sick people who were thought incurable or curable only by extensive treatment, and up to 20 lunatics. From the National Library of Medicine, Bethesda, MD, published in Rutkow IM. American surgery: an illustrated history. St. Louis: Mosby-Year Book, Inc., 1993. (Reproduced with the permission of the publisher.)

Figure 8–2 The old operating theater of Guy's and St. Thomas's Hospitals, London, the only surviving operating theater in England from the nineteenth century. From Rutkow IM. American Surgery: an illustrated history. St. Louis: Mosby-Year Book, Inc., 1993. (Reproduced with the permission of the publisher.)

must be tempered by resistance to the temptation to adopt the latest diagnosis-and-treatment scheme.

For too long, anecdotes have had too much influence on surgical practice ("anecdote" is derived from a Greek word meaning unpublished). The search for evidence-based surgery should not, of course, lead to the wholesale abandonment of operations or treatments that have been hallowed by time yet have no scientific basis. Instead, such operations and treatments should be discarded only when indicated by evidence-based surgery.

Evidence-based surgery has had the important effect of encouraging oncologists, radio-therapists, internists, interventional radiologists, and surgeons to work in teams employing controlled clinical trials or protocols, which means that in the United Kingdom today, the majority of oncology patients under the age of 65 years are in controlled trials. This situation has arisen with the increasing influence of the cooperative spirit among the Royal Colleges, which are working hand in hand, coupled with a surprisingly cost-effective National Health Service. In the United Kingdom, controlled clinical trials and standardized treatments are increasingly drawing attention to the fact that there are far too few clinicians in many specialties.

HISTORICAL ORIGINS: COCHRANE'S CONTRIBUTIONS

A. L. Cochrane made a great contribution to evidence-based medicine and surgery with his enthusiasm for controlled clinical trials in the 1960s. Not surprisingly, his efforts were met with a great deal of opposition, but he took great pains to show that it was, in fact, both ethically acceptable and practical to randomize place of treatment (among home and hospital, outpatient clinic and home, and hospital and outpatient clinic) and length of stay in

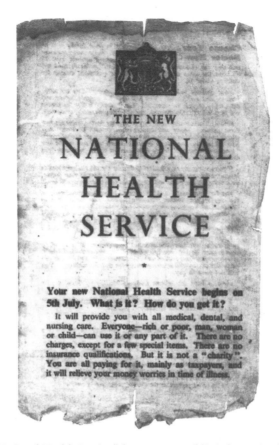

THE NEW

NATIONAL
HEALTH
SERVICE

Your new National Health Service begins on
5th July. What is it? How do you get it?

It will provide you with all medical, dental, and
nursing care. Everyone—rich or poor, man, woman
or child—can use it or any part of it. There are no
charges, except for a few special items. There are no
insurance qualifications. But it is not a "charity".
You are all paying for it, mainly as taxpayers, and
it will relieve your money worries in time of illness.

Figure 8–3 "The New National Health Service," from a 1948 public information leaflet. The National Health Service was founded after World War II to ensure access to health care for all in Great Britain. (From a 1997 report to Parliament.)

hospitals.[2] Cochrane determined that all the patients undergoing cataract operations in one teaching hospital stayed for 13 days. As most of the possible complications occurred in the first 2 days, he tried to persuade the ophthalmologists to have a controlled clinical trial, which they at first refused. When he teased them by stating that this practice stemmed from a director of nursing in 1940 who wanted to change the sheets once every 2 weeks, they finally agreed to randomize five- and ten-day lengths of stay but insisted on carrying out the trial themselves, without his help. Although the trial was not conducted very well, it showed conclusively that the shorter stay was just as effective. Cochrane's next project was a trial to see whether varicose-vein patients should be injected as outpatients or treated surgically as inpatients. He also decided to cost the two sides of the controlled trial, an early venture into health economics.[3–5]

He had much more trouble setting up a controlled clinical trial to determine whether treating myocardial infarctions at home was safer than treating them in coronary care units. A national committee was established to examine the ethics of this study. After 6 months of the trial, there was a slight numerical advantage for those who had been treated at home, but this was statistically insignificant. Because he had encountered so much opposition and trouble in setting up this trial, Cochrane compiled two reports, one reversing the numbers of the deaths on the two sides of the trial. When he presented the "revised" report, his antagonists denounced him and demanded that the trial be stopped immediately. He then apologized and gave them the true results and challenged them to demand that the coronary care unit work be stopped immediately.[6]

It is difficult now to imagine how great the opposition was in those days to scientific trials. In memory of the late Dr. Cochrane, the Cochrane Libraries and Centers have been set up in many parts of the world to propagate up-to-date results of systematic reviews in all branches of medicine and health care. The Cochrane Library publishes CD-ROMs listing an increasing number of these reviews, many of which are surgical reviews.

In the United Kingdom, there is a long tradition of controlled clinical trials, which have been readily carried out within the National Health Service (Figure 8–3). The problem has always been to separate the wheat from the chaff and produce information on evidence-based surgery in a more digestible form. The databases in the Cochrane Library and the Cochrane Collaboration enable the dissemination of systematic reviews on randomized trials of all kinds of health care interventions. The journal *Evidence-Based Medicine* was born in 1995 as a joint venture of the American College of Physicians Journal Club and the British Medical Journal Publications Group.[1] The *British Journal of Surgery* publishes a monthly index of randomized trials and meta-analyses including similar information from the *British Medical Journal*. In 1998, The Royal College of Surgeons set up an evidence-based surgery Web site allowing access to respectable publications on evidence-based surgery, and an increasing number of journals are now available in this form. All these approaches will make it easier for surgeons to practice evidence-based surgery even as quality assurance programs will help to ensure that theory is put into practice.

One of the problems of evidence-based surgery is the enormity of resources and time required to perform a controlled clinical trial on some topics. If an operation has a success rate of 99 percent, it would take a very long trial to demonstrate that any other techniques were superior in terms of recurrence. For example, as far as the induction of pneumoperitoneum is concerned for minimally invasive surgery, the blind insertion of a Verris needle produces damage in approximately 1 in 300 cases to structures such as the aorta, inferior vena cava, and small and large bowels. Hence, the alternative—the insertion of a blunt tapered port through a small incision over the rectus muscle under direct vision—is clearly safer.[7] Is there any point to having such a trial, especially since the direct approach avoids the use of disposable equipment that is much more expensive and that avoids the need for catheterization of the bladder?

In the following section, several case studies are presented to illustrate the application of evidence-based surgery to various aspects of clinical care: diagnosis (of appendicitis); use of clinical trials to evaluate a new procedure (laparoscopic cholecystectomy); use of evidence to improve treatment; pain control treatment planning; risk reductions; and evaluation of standard practices (nasogastric compression).

CASE STUDY: USE OF EVIDENCE IN DIAGNOSIS (APPENDICITIS)

The diagnosis of acute appendicitis continues to present clinicians with problems, as evidenced by the fact that 47 percent of clinical diagnoses of acute appendicitis prove to be wrong.[8] The assessment of pain is notoriously difficult; some patients hardly seem to notice pain, while others are extremely sensitive to it. To complicate matters even further, there are probably very few patients who have not at some time simulated pain of the abdomen to avoid some obligation. It is also necessary to consider the possibility of Munchausen syndrome or even Munchausen syndrome by proxy.[9]

In 20 percent of patients with appendicitis, the diagnosis is missed initially, and in 15 to 40 percent of those who undergo emergency operations for suspected appendicitis, the appendix is normal.[8] Clearly, more precision in the diagnosis is needed. Such precision can be achieved with laparoscopy, which has the advantage of direct visualization of the appendix although it is not entirely free of risk. Among 60 women with signs of appendicitis who were randomly assigned to undergo emergency appendectomy or diagnostic laparoscopy, 37 percent of the appendectomy group had unnecessary appendectomies as compared with 7 percent of the laparoscopy group.[10]

Of the noninvasive diagnostic aids, ultrasonography (US) was for some time the most promising technique, but appendiceal computed tomography (CT) has proved more precise, yielding the correct diagnosis in more than 90 percent of cases.[11] When 100 consecutive patients were examined with both CT and US, the respective results were as follows: sensitivity, 96 percent versus 76 percent; specificity, 89 percent versus 91 percent; accuracy, 94 percent versus 83 percent; positive predictive value, 96 percent versus 95 percent; and negative predictive value, 95 percent versus 76 percent.[12] Similar data have been reported by other investigators.[13] Rao and co-workers have extended their previous studies of CT for the diagnosis of appendicitis,[14–16] demonstrating in a prospective study its high sensitivity, specificity, positive and negative predictive values, and overall accuracy in confirming or ruling out appendicitis.

Appendiceal CT takes 15 minutes to perform; the results are available within an hour, and the dose of radiation is less than that for pelvic CT. Despite these facts and the results noted above, doubts continue. It is worth remembering, however, that not long ago, CT scanning for head injuries was regarded as unnecessary and expensive, but no one now doubts its value and cost-effectiveness. The same is true of the use of CT to detect ureteric stones. Doubts will also be expressed about whether expertise in appendiceal CT will be widely available, but with a sufficient volume of procedures and an adequate audit of their performance, this should not present too great a problem. The main snag is the potential danger of an over-reliance on one technique. At some institutions, experience with appendiceal CT has grown at the expense of the development of accurate ultrasonographic technique.[17] Appendiceal US ought to be developed further, especially for the diagnosis of acute appendicitis in children. Not only is it quicker, simpler, and less expensive than CT, but there is also no radiation involved, and radiation should be avoided for children, however low the dose. In view of the potential disaster of a ruptured appendix in a child, normal ultrasonographic findings should not deter the surgeon from performing an appendectomy if the history is indicative of appendicitis and if unequivocal tenderness is present in the right lower quadrant.

The diagnostic accuracy of CT and US should act as a stimulus to improve, not replace, bedside diagnosis. Skills in history taking and physical examination should be improved to better determine which patients need such scanning. There is always a danger that clinical skills will decrease as more and more patients are subjected to scanning, leading to even more indiscriminate scanning.

When it comes to the claim that appendiceal CT will reduce costs, a note of caution is required. It will certainly reduce the cost per patient suspected of having appendicitis. However, the overall cost to the hospital service will tend to increase as a result of the widespread use of this technique. In the National Health Service, where there is a great demand for hospital beds, any savings in terms of beds occupied by patients with one disease are quickly lost because of the demand for beds for patients with other diseases.

The diagnosis of appendicitis will no doubt continue to present difficulties for clinicians. These difficulties should diminish as appendiceal CT becomes more widely available and as expertise in performing the procedure and interpreting the results increases. These advances should provide another stimulus for clinicians to improve their clinical acumen and thus find fewer surprises within the abdomen.

CASE STUDY: USE OF CLINICAL TRIALS IN EVALUATION OF A NEW PROCEDURE (LAPAROSCOPIC CHOLECYSTECTOMY)

When laparoscopic cholecystectomy was introduced in 1989, there was an enormous wave of enthusiasm for this procedure, a technique that was clearly less traumatic than the orthodox open technique and that was presumed to be much better in all respects. It was a most exciting development; but novelty and enthusiasm, good though they are, must be tempered by science. Therefore, it was salutary to have a randomized prospective, single blind comparison of laparoscopic versus small-incision cholecystectomy in 200 patients.[18] The study was designed to eliminate bias for or against either technique. Previous trials did not take into account the effect of beliefs of patients and surgeons, which may have biased the results. Bias was minimized in this trial by standardizing the two procedures and blinding patients and their surgeons during the preoperative and early postoperative period. The protocol was as follows:

- Preoperative protocol and elective cases were referred to one surgical unit between January 1992 and June 1995.
- Symptomatic gallstones were confirmed by ultrasonography.
- In the outpatient clinic, the nature and purpose of the trials were explained.
- Consent for cholecystectomy for either operation was obtained, and the names were put on the waiting list.

Exclusion criteria were the following:

- Obstructive jaundice/suspected or proven common duct calculi
- Extreme morbid obesity (body mass index > 45)
- Inflammatory mass in the right hypochondrium associated with fever
- Pregnancy
- Cirrhosis of the liver
- Suspected/proven cancer
- Unfitness for general anesthetic

There were four participating surgeons, all of whom had been trained on simulators and had experience of at least 40 laparoscopic cholecystectomies. Randomization was by sealed envelope in the operating room after anesthesia was commenced. Neither the nurses nor the patients knew which kind of operation had been done. Operative cholangiography was attempted in all cases. Nasogastric intubation was used for all patients but was removed immediately after the operation. Deeper tissues were sutured with No. 1 Ethilon, skin closed with 3/0 prolene sutures in all cases.

Indications for Conversion to Open Cholecystectomy

- Common duct calculi found on cholangiograph
- Unsafe or uncertain anatomy
- Bleeding
- Equipment failure

The high transverse subxiphoid incision was kept to a minimum length, compatible with safety. The rectus muscle was cut with diathermy. Hands were not inserted into peritoneal cavity unless absolutely necessary. The common bile duct was explored if common bile duct stones were found. Cholangiography was attempted in all cases, and T-tube drainage was instituted if the common bile duct was explored.

Anesthesia and Pain Relief

- Premedication with 20 mg temazepam 1 hour before induction.
- Thiopentone, fentanyl, vecuronium, nitrous oxide, and ethane.
- All wounds were infiltrated with 0.5 percent bupivicaine. Patient-controlled analgesia, 1 mg bolus of morphine with 5-minute lockout.

Postoperative Protocol

Pain relief was provided with a patient-controlled analgesic system delivering morphine. No restrictions were placed on oral intake of fluids or solids. Patients could get out of bed and go home as soon as they felt fit enough. The family doctor was asked not to try to influence time off work or time back to full activity. No advice was given on how long patients should expect to remain convalescent.

Identical opaque dressings were used for both operations, and each stained with blood-stained fluid or iodide solution. Dressings were not disturbed unless there was definite indication to do so.

Random checks were made to ensure that all protocols were adhered to. Total postoperative stay included any additional hospital stay. Outpatient review occurred in the outpatient clinics 3 weeks after discharge by a research nurse unaware of which operation was performed.

Forty-two patients were excluded because of obstructive jaundice and common bile duct calculus, and seven patients were excluded with (?) carcinoma of the gallbladder. None were excluded due to extreme obesity or pregnancy.

Two patients refused randomization, and 3 patients were withdrawn (1 with hepatic metastases, 1 with hepatic cirrhosis, and the third was operated on by a nonparticipating surgeon). Two hundred patients were randomized, and there were no significant differences between the two groups.

Overall Comparisons

Laparoscopic cholecystectomy took longer than the small-incision operation, and subjects took slightly longer to start eating (Table 8–1). There were no significant differences in the other indices. There was no difference in the proportion of patients in each group with complications (Table 8–2). Conversions of laparoscopic cholecystectomy amounted to 20 percent. In small-incision operations, the median length of incision was 7 cm (range 4 to 18 cm). The authors chose 8 cm or less as indicating that a small-incision cholecystectomy had been successfully completed, and then compared this number (78 out of the original 100 patients) with the 80 patients who had laparoscopic cholecystectomy. Patients in the laparoscopic group had a significantly longer operation time ($p < .001$) and resumed feeding a little later, but there were no significant differences between the two groups in hospital length of stay, time back to work, or time back to full activity.

This controlled trial showed intriguing results but would have been of even greater interest had the authors included in their analysis *all* open cholecystectomies in the trial and not excluded those with incisions longer than 8 cm. If a similar trial were to be conducted on very obese patients above a certain weight, taking into account their height, it could be argued that a laparoscopic operation would be much preferred in terms of the speed of postoperative recovery.

In a separate publication, the authors reported that the laparoscopic cholecystectomy group had significantly less pain but that this did not influence length of stay, possibly due to increased instances of postoperative nausea.[19] Independent of the type of operation, the length of hospital stay was related to the magnitude of both the cortisol (neuroendocrine) and C-reactive protein (inflammatory/immunologic) responses. This may explain why laparoscopic cholecystectomy was associated with less tissue disruption and pain but not with a reduced length of stay.

CASE STUDY: USE OF EVIDENCE IN TREATMENT PLANNING AND RISK REDUCTION

The identification of risk factors that predispose patients to complications of surgical disease provides the patient and the doctor with much more accurate information to help them come to sensible conclusions about the management of the patient's condition and the ways of preventing complications. For instance, it has been found that smoking is associated with an increased risk of complications in patients with diverticular disease.[20] This study was carried out in the Department of Surgery at King's College Hospital in London to try to identify epidemiologic factors that might represent a predisposition to complications in patients with diverticular disease of the colon. It was argued that the identification of such factors might

Table 8–1 Comparative Data by Procedure Type

	Laparoscopic N = 100	Small-incision N = 100	Mann-Whitney U-test (Wilcoxon's test)
Operating time			
Mean (SD)	69.2 (24.6) min	45.4 (19.8) min	p < .001
Median (range)	65.0 (27–140) min	40.0 (18–142) min	
Time to first solid/semi-solid feed			
Mean (SD)	24.7 (8.0) h	22.4 (7–6) h	p = .03
Median (range)	24.0 (6–48) h	24.0 (6–48) h	
Hospital stay (postoperative nights)			
Mean (SD)	3–6 (2.3) nights	3.5 (2–1) nights	p = .74
Median (range)	3.0 (1–17) nights	3.0 (1–14) nights	
Time off work (employed, including self-employed)			
Mean (SD)	5.0 (2–6) weeks	4.6 (2–5) weeks	p = .39
Median (range)	5.0 (1–12) weeks	4.0 (1–10) weeks	
Return to full activity (non-employed)			
Mean (SD)	4.3 (3–8) weeks	3.6 (1–9) weeks	p = .15
Median (range)	3.0 (1–26) weeks	3.0 (1–12) weeks	

SD = standard deviation.

Table 8–2 Cholecystectomy Complications by Procedure Group

	No. of Patients	
Complication	Laparoscopic Group (all) n =100	Small-incision Group (all) n =100
Bile duct injury	1	0
Subphrenic collection	1	1
Wound infection	2	2
Urinary retention	6	10
Chest infection	2	1
Small-bowel injury	1	0

lead to earlier surgery for those at risk and/or to the opportunity to reduce the risk factors, thus avoiding complications.

Eighty patients were studied in two groups: one of 45 with complications who required hospitalization or surgery and another group of 35 with asymptomatic diverticular disease or only minor symptoms. Logistic regression analysis was carried out. The following parameters were examined: age, sex, race, body build, occupation, smoking habits, alcohol intake, past medical history, previous abdominal operations, previous anal disease, constipation, chronic medication, and location of diverticula. No differences in epidemiologic factors were found.

Concurrent and past medical and surgical conditions on chronic medication were detected between the two groups. Smoking seemed to be an independent factor predisposing to complications. The proportions of smokers in group 1 was 10 out of 35 (odds ratio 2:9,

$p = .028$). This result is not supported by a previous prospective study,[21] although there was a positive association between smoking and possibly more advanced diverticular disease. The question, then, becomes, Is this evidence enough for clinicians now to advise abstinence from smoking to decrease the risk of complications in those with this disease? From a practical point of view, patients should be strongly advised to stop smoking.

The problem of generating scientific evidence for preoperative risk assessment has been emphasized.[22] Since bad surgical outcomes are infrequent, they demand large expensive prospective studies to obtain significant differences between groups. Also, selection bias is a problem because only patients who have been operated on are studied whereas those who have the disease but have not been operated on are needed to complete the picture. The definition of a certain complication could vary tenfold. As these decisions are made increasingly by teams rather than by individual clinicians, this problem is magnified.

In the Alder Hey Children's Hospital in Liverpool, a study was carried out to determine the percentage of pediatric surgical interventions that are evidence-based.[23] All consecutive pediatric general surgical patients who were admitted in 1 month were studied. The interventions were categorized by three classifications: (1) those based on randomized controlled trial evidence, (2) those with convincing non-experimental evidence, and (3) those that lacked substantial supportive evidence. The conclusions of this study were that the majority of interventions were based on sound evidence but only 11 percent were based on randomized controlled trial data. This contrasts with work demonstrating that 82 percent of acute in-patient general surgical medicine is evidence-based, either by randomized clinical trial (53 percent) or convincing non-experimental evidence (29 percent).

Three hundred twenty-six consecutive pediatric general surgical admissions for 1 month were prospectively studied. Any patients with definite diagnoses were included, which excluded 14 percent. Of the 281 remaining cases, 77 percent were deemed by a five-doctor team to be evidence-based: 11 percent were considered to be based on randomized controlled clinical trial evidence and 66 percent were determined with convincing non-experimental evidence or were cases where the intervention was so obviously justified that a trial would have been unethical. The remaining 23 percent of those cases lacking supportive evidence were a "mixed bag" of cases, including chronic constipation (which is multifactorial) and bleeding granulation tissue or anal fissure. Only 2 out of the 12 staff members were aware that this study was being carried out.

CASE STUDY: USE OF EVIDENCE IN PAIN CONTROL

Boggia[24] drew attention to the benefits of warming local anesthetics, and for many years, some used this practice before injection, to reduce the pain. Although there was no convincing scientific evidence that this worked, no harm was reported. Subscription to evidence-based surgery would support continuing this practice until the evidence was forthcoming. Recently, blinded controlled clinical trials have indicated that this practice does indeed reduce pain.[25,26]

Adjusting the pH of the local anesthetic solution has also been recorded as reducing pain on injection.[27–29] But this is a more complicated procedure, and it increases the risk that the wrong solution or too much solution might be added to the local anesthetic before injection. It is all very well to establish evidence-based surgery; the problem is to persuade clinicians to adopt it. Most general surgeons and maxillofacial surgeons in the United Kingdom in 1998 did not warm the solution; out of the survey of 400 surgeons described below, only one altered the pH.[30]

Questionnaires were sent to 200 general surgeons drawn at random from the Association of Day Surgeons of England and to 200 maxillofacial surgeons drawn at random from the British Association of Oral and Maxillofacial Surgeons. The questionnaire contained fifteen questions detailing the local anesthetic, the method of warming or buffering the delivery, and (where appropriate) reasons for not warming the local anesthetic. The statistical analysis used the chi-squared test. The findings were as follows: only 8 percent of the general surgeons warmed the solution, compared with 34 percent of maxillofacial surgeons ($p < .001$). Seventy-four percent of the group aimed to heat the solution to 37° centigrade, but 26 percent were ignorant of the temperature required. The benefits of this procedure were known to 81 percent of the maxillofacial surgeons but to just 29 percent of the general surgeons ($p < .001$).

As only half of the surgeons completed the questionnaire, it could well be that an even smaller percentage of surgeons warm local anesthetic prior to injection. Lignocaine and adrenaline solutions should be stored at below room temperature because raising the temperature or making the solution alkaline leads to oxidation of the adrenaline over a number of days. In terms of evidence-based surgery, it seems reasonable to recommend that local anesthetic solutions be warmed to body temperature just before injection, but the evidence that supports altering the pH is less convincing and simply adds a further complication to the procedure.

No responsible discussion about evidence-based surgery can omit the question, Is good practice based on scientific evidence actually implemented? A prospective audit of a hundred emergency admissions was carried out in the Nine Wells Hospital and Medical School in Dundee, United Kingdom, to determine whether patients being admitted with acute abdominal pain were receiving timely analgesia. The main outcome measures investigated were the waiting time for analgesia and the influences of severity of pain, clinical diagnosis, and clinical setting.

Forty percent of patients received analgesia within 1 hour, 17 percent between 1 and 2 hours, and 43 percent from 2 to 22 hours after admission.[31] The conclusion was that 43 percent of patients with acute abdominal pain waited too long for analgesia. Delays were due to the omission of analgesia in the Accident and Emergency Department, as well as the reluctance of junior staff to administer analgesia for fear of masking physical signs. There is a necessity for adherence to guidelines, and constant vigilance is required to ensure that this takes place.

CASE STUDY: USE OF EVIDENCE IN EVALUATION OF STANDARD PRACTICES (POSTOPERATIVE NASOGASTRIC DECOMPRESSION)

As stated previously, another problem with evidence-based surgery is getting surgeons to adopt it. For instance, routine postoperative nasogastric decompression has been standard practice for over 50 years, but doubts about its necessity were voiced in the 1960s,[32] and complications such as pulmonary infections[33] and even strictures of the esophagus occur. Gradually, British clinicians began to polarize; some would always use this technique, others would never use it routinely. As is so often the case, a middle way is usually the answer. It is necessary to devise the right kind of controlled clinical trial, one that would indicate when it is reasonable not to use this technique routinely and when it is necessary. Such a prospective randomized trial was carried out in 1996 and provided good evidence-based practice.[34] Over a 3-year period, 88 patients undergoing major abdominal surgical procedures were prospectively randomized into two groups. One group was treated routinely with postoperative nasogastric decompression and the other group was so treated only when required. Patients with intra-abdominal infections or peritonitis were excluded from the study, as were those with emergency operations or routine cholecystectomies. At the beginning of each operation, a nasogastric tube was inserted, and its position was checked intraoperatively. At the completion of the operation, patients were randomized and assigned blindly to either group at a site remote from the operating room.

In the selective group, the tubes were removed before the patient was transferred to the recovery room, and the tube was re-inserted only when a single large emesis (150 mL) occurred or when significant abdominal distension had taken place. The tubes were removed at the

Table 8–3 Perioperative Complications in Patients Receiving Nasogastric Decompression Routinely or Selectively

Complication	Number of Patients	
	Routine NGD	Selective NGD
Pneumonia	1	0
Ileus	2	3
Anastomotic leak	1	0
Wound infection	2	1
Upper gastrointestinal bleeding	2	0
Seizure	0	1
Delirium tremens	0	1
Death	1	0
Total	9 (23 %)	6 (27%)

NGD = nasogastric decompression.

discretion of the chief surgical resident when gastrointestinal function had returned. The relevant information about perioperative complications was recorded and analyzed using chi-squared analysis for contingency tables. The results showed that of the 88 patients, 12 were excluded: 6 of these required a gastrostomy tube, 4 in the selected group had a tube continued postoperatively at the discretion of the attending surgeon, and 2 in the routine group had their tubes discontinued. Of the remainder 39 were in the routine group and 37 in the selective group. All the patients were men. The selective group consisted of patients who never received a tube postoperatively (N = 18) and patients who ultimately required one (N = 19). Perioperative complications were not significantly different between the two groups (Table 8–3). Analysis of intravenous fluid requirements and nasogastric aspirate revealed no significant differences between the groups. More patients had postoperative fever in the routine group (77%) than in the selective group (60%), but this was not statistically or clinically significant.

Nineteen of 37 patients (51%) in the selective group ultimately required nasogastric intubation, either for large emesis (84%) or significant abdominal distensions (16%). Conversely, only 1 of the 39 patients (2.5%) from the routine group had emesis. In both groups, the mean time period for intubation was 4.7 days. In the selective group, intubation was ultimately necessary within the first 3 days after operation in 11 of the 19 patients. Of those patients who required intubation in the selective group, 11 (58%) had had procedures that involved significant retroperitoneal dissection or vascular procedures such as Whipple's operation or aorto-bifemoral bypass ($p < .001$); in contrast, only 5 (27%) of the patients who never required intubation in the selective group had undergone such procedures. The majority of patients in the selective group who had had intraperitoneal procedures never required intubation (62%); however, of the 16 patients in the selective group who had had vascular or retroperitoneal procedures, 11 required a nasogastric tube. Return of bowel function was not statistically different between the groups, regardless of which procedure was involved. Patients in the selective group returned to a regular diet later than patients in the routine group (mean 8.4 days and 6.6 days, respectively).

Overall, however, patients in the selective group who ultimately required intubation had the longest delay ($p < .05$) of return to a regular diet (mean 9.6 days). The postoperative length of stay was the same (mean 13 days) for the patients in the routine tube group as for those in the selective tube group who ultimately required intubation. However, those patients from the selective group who had never received an epigastric tube had a shorter length of stay in hospital (mean 9 days), and 58 percent of those patients from the selective group who ultimately required intubation had undergone procedures that required major retroperitoneal resections (abdominal aneurysm, aortobifemoral bypass, pancreatic resection, or procedures requiring extensive manipulation of the superior mesenteric root). Of the selective tube patients who did not require intubation, only 27 percent had had such procedures performed. In contrast, only 42 percent of patients in the selective group who required intubation had had intraperitoneal procedures (eg, particle colectomy, gastric procedures), whereas 73 percent of patients who were never intubated had had intraperitoneal procedures. The authors concluded that manipulation of the superior mesenteric root may have played a role in retroperitoneal procedures, due to techniques used to gain adequate exposure in cases involving aortic and other abdominal surgery. They concluded also that manipulative trauma to the autonomic nerve plexuses within the mesentery, accompanied by edema formation and third-space fluid accumulation, may also have been related to the need for nasogastric decompression.

Patients in the selective nasogastric tube group who did not require intubation did have a shorter hospital stay when compared with the routine group and the group with failed selective decompression. These differences in length of stay were not significant, however, and hospital stays were longer overall than those supported in other studies.

The authors' conclusion was that selective management of postoperative nasogastric decompression is a viable alternative to routine intubation and does not appear to be significant in the complication rate when selective management is employed. Avoidance of nasogastric intubation does not lengthen hospital stay and (when successfully employed) may even shorten it. Surgical procedures associated with major retroperitoneal dissections or extensive manipulation of the superior mesenteric root were most likely to be associated with postoperative ileus, abdominal distension, and significant emesis. The authors conclude that their findings support (1) the selective use of intubation in general surgical patients, and (2) the routine use of nasogastric decompression of patients who have retroperitoneal dissections or who require significant superior mesenteric root manipulation.

MEDICAL LEGAL ASPECTS OF EVIDENCE-BASED SURGERY

The legal profession should be encouraged to adopt principles of evidence-based surgery in medical legal cases. For instance, in a recent case in the United Kingdom, a hospital was sued because their cervical screening for incipient squamous cell carcinoma failed to detect three cases of incipient adenocarcinoma of the body of the uterus. The hospital lost the case in spite of three of the five expert witnesses alleging that there had been no negligence. Familiarity with evidence-based surgery and medicine should lead the courts to adopt their own principle of staging identity parades (identification lineups) when identifying suspects. Just as a suspect is paraded with nine other similarly dressed people of the same sex and the witness is asked to identify the suspect, so cervical smears in question should be presented to each of the expert witnesses along with nine other cervical smears, all mounted in the same way.[35] Each expert witness would be given the average time that cervical screeners are given in the Health Service to inspect two sets of ten slides each and to write down their report. Only one set would contain the suspect slide. This would exclude the outcome bias that exists when an expert witness is given a suspect slide and told that it had been taken from a patient who did, in fact, develop a cancer several years later. It would also exclude the context bias that comes to bear when one looks at a smear knowing that it is not a routine smear but that it is involved in litigation, especially if the slide is marked (?) abnormality. The medical profession should demand that the legal profession have more objective procedures in trying to reach a just solution.

Acknowledgment

We are grateful to our colleague, Lord McColl, for offering his perspectives on evidence-based surgery in the United Kingdom.

References

1. Sackett DL, Richardson WS, Rosenberg W, Haynes RB. Evidence-based medicine. Churchill Livingstone; 1997.

2. Cochrane AL, Blythe M. One man's medicine. London (UK): The Memoir Club; 1989.

3. Chant ADB, Jones HO, Weddell JM. Varicose veins: a comparison of surgery and injection/compression sclerotherapy. Lancet 1972;2:1188–91.

4. Piachaud D, Weddell JM. The economics of treating varicose veins. Int J Epidemiol 1972;1:287–91.

5. Piachaud D, Weddell JM. Cost of treating varicose veins. Lancet 1972;2:1191–2.

6. Mather HG, Pearson NG, Read KLQ, et al. Acute myocardial infarction: home and hospital treatment. Br Med J 1971;3:334–8.

7. McColl I, Houghton A, Wickham JEA. Safety, economy and a better view in laparoscopy. Min Invas Ther 1994;3:239–40.

8. Rao PM, Rhea JT, Novelline RA, et al. Effect of computed tomography of the appendix on treatment of patients and use of hospital resources. N Engl J Med 1998;338:141–6.

9. Meadow R. Munchausen syndrome by proxy; the hinterland of child abuse. Lancet 1977; 2:343–5.

10. Olsen JB, Myren CJ, Haahr PE. Randomized study of the value of laparoscopy before appendicectomy Br J Surg 1993;80:922–3.

11. Balthazar EJ, Megibow AJ, Siegel SE, Birnbaum BA. Appendicitis: prospective evaluation with high-resolution CT. Radiology 1991;1980:21–4.

12. Balthazar EJ, Birnbaum BA, Yee J, et al. Acute appendicitis: CT and US correlation in 100 patients. Radiology 1994;190:31–5.

13. Malone AJ Jr, Wolf CR, Malmed AS, Melliere BF. Diagnosis of acute appendicitis: value of unenhanced CT. AJR Am J Roentgenol 1993;160:763–6.

14. Rao PM, Rhea JT, Novelline RA. Sensitivity and specificity of the individual CT signs of appendicitis: experience with 200 helical appendiceal CT examinations. J Comput Assist Tomogr 1997;21:686–92.

15. Rao PM, Rhea JT, Novelline RA, et al. Helical CT technique for the diagnosis of appendicitis: prospective evaluation of a focus appendix CT examination. Radiology 1997;202:363–6.

16. Rao PM, Wittenberg J, McDowell RK, et al. Appendicitis: use of arrowhead sign for diagnosis at CT. Radiology 1997;202:363–6.

17. McColl I. More precision in diagnosing appendicitis. N Engl J Med 1998;338:190–1.

18. Majeed AW, Troy G, Nicholl JP, et al. Randomized prospective single blind comparison of laparoscopic versus small incision cholecystectomy. Lancet 1996;347:989–94.

19. Squirrel DN, Majeed EW, Troy G, et al. A randomized, prospective, blinded comparison of postoperative pain, metabolic response, and perceived health after laparoscopic and small incision cholecystectomy. Surgery 1998;123:485–95.

20. Papagrigoridis S, Macey L, Bourantas N, Rennie JA. Smoking may be associated with complications in diverticular disease. Br J Surg 1999;86:923–6.

21. Aldoori WH, Giovannucci EL, Rimm EB, et al. A prospective study of alcohol, smoking, caffeine and the risk of symptomatic diverticular disease in men. Ann Epidemiol 1995;5:221–8.

22. Lawrence VA. ACP J Club 1993 Sep/Oct 199A–16.

23. Kenny SE, Shankar KR, Rintala R, et al. Evidence-based surgery: interventions in a regional paediatric surgical unit. Arch Dis Child 1997;76(1) 50–3.

24. Boggia R. Heating local anaesthetic cartridges. Br Dent J 1967;122:287.

25. Davidson JAH, Bloom SJ. Warming Lignocaine to reduce pain associated with injection. BMJ 1992;305:617–18.

26. Bainbridge LC. Comparison of room temperature and body temperature—local anaesthetic solutions. Br J Plast Surg 1991;44:147–8.

27. Christoph RA, Buchanan L, Begalla K, Schwartz S. Pain reduction in local anaesthetic administration pH offerings. Ann Emerg Med 1988;17:117–20.

28. Martin AJ. pH adjustment and discomfort caused by the intradermal injection of Lignocaine. Anaesthesia 1990;45:975–8.

29. Strichartz GR, Sanchez V, Arthur G, et al. Fundamental properties of local anesthetics. II. Measured octano: buffer partition coefficients and pKa values of clinically used drugs. Anesth Analg 1990;71:158–70.

30. Courtney DJ, Agrawal S, Revington PJ. Local anaesthesia: to warm or alter the pH? A survey of current practice. J R Coll Surg Edinb 1999;44:167–71.

31. Tait IS, Ionescu NV, Cuschiere A. Do patients with acute abdominal pain wait unduly long for analgesia. J R Coll Surg Edinb 1999;44:3:181–4.

32. Gerber A. An appraisal of paralytic ileus and necessity of post-operative gastrointestinal suction. Surg Gynecol Obstet 1963;117:294–6.

33. Ghahreman IGG, Turner MA, Port RV. Iatrogenic intubation injuries of the upper gastrointestinal tract in adults. Gastrointest Radiol 1980;5:1–10.

34. Montgomery RC, Bar-Natan MF, Thomas SE, Cheadle WG. Post-operative naso-gastric decompression: a prospective randomized trial. South Med J 1996;89:1063–6.

35. McColl I. Cervical cancer screening. House of Lords Hansard 1999;597:1783–5.

CHAPTER 9

Tools and Techniques:
Study Design

David E. Lilienfeld, MD, MPH, MS Engin

A variety of tools and techniques have been developed for the collection and analysis of data needed to assess the efficacy and effectiveness of different surgical and nonsurgical approaches to a myriad of diseases. These tools and techniques derive from sociology and epidemiology, in which they were developed and refined during the past century. For the better part of the last century, the method generally used to evaluate a new procedure in surgery was to assemble a series of cases in which the procedure was used. The problems with this approach will be considered first. This chapter will then consider the evaluation of surgical therapies in the context of the epidemiologic study, a method that counters the problems with case series as evidence of efficacy and effectiveness. Experimental studies will be discussed initially, followed by observational studies. A discussion of the assembling of data from such studies into a meta-analysis and the use of such data in developing decision tools will complete the chapter.

PRE-EXPERIMENTAL DESIGN: THE CASE SERIES

A major component of clinical research for the past one and one-half centuries has been the case report or the case series. In such instances, the clinician examines the response of a well-characterized disease to a new treatment. The information presented in a case report or series thereby provides further data for other clinicians to consider in formulating treatment plans for their own patients.

Case reports present a variety of advantages, including the speed and ease with which the data may be compiled, the facility with which most clinicians can relate to the information in a given report, and the opportunity for all clinicians to contribute to the corpus of medical therapeutics without intensive research training. There are also disadvantages to case reports, including: the lack of a comparison group and the small number of patients usually incorporated in them. The former is a major weakness of this approach to clinical research, as the nature of scientific inference is essentially comparative. The simple act of observation provides little information about what would have happened in the absence of the treatment. In instances in which the disease or injury is always accompanied by death, the comparison group may not contribute much more information;[1] rather, one can infer what the effect of the treatment is simply by observing the case group. Such occurrences are rare, but the treatment of abdominal aortic aneurysm illustrates this point well. In 1950, Estes reported on a series of 102 cases with abdominal aortic aneurysm.[2] The mortality rate from this condition in this case series was greater than 60 percent. Other similar case series also suggested that mortality from rupture was high.[3] Since Laplace's law suggests that all aortic aneurysms will inevitably expand until they rupture, the repair of all abdominal aortic aneurysms, regardless of size, became the standard of care. Hence, Estes' case series represented an advance in the evidence suggesting that abdominal aortic aneurysm repairs should be undertaken in all instances. On the other hand, in the absence of a comparison group, the interpretation of Estes' report was problematic. In 1989, workers at the Mayo Clinic reported that in the population of Olmsted County,

Minnesota, all abdominal aortic aneurysms did not inevitably expand, and the investigators concluded that repair could be delayed until the aneurysm had reached a size necessitating intervention.[4]

THE EPIDEMIOLOGIC STUDY

The epidemiologic study provides the scientific framework within which comparative inferences about clinical phenomena may be made. In such a study, one or more samples of a population are compared with regard to their exposure to factors of interest (which may include personal characteristics) and changes in their health status. If an association between the factors and changes in health status is found, then inferences can be made with regard to the relationship between exposure and those changes. This model was originally developed for investigations of etiologic factors in the development of disease, but it may be easily applied to examining the effects of interventions such as surgical procedures on the natural history of disease. If one considers an outcome of care (such as health status, patient satisfaction, or the cost of care provided) rather than the natural history of disease, then the investigation is termed an "outcome study."

There are two major types of epidemiologic studies: experimental studies and observational studies (Figure 9–1). In an experimental study, the investigator controls the exposure of the population to the factor of interest. The factor of interest can be a certain surgical procedure, a specific pharmaceutical, or a type of behavior, such as a change in diet to consume foods with lower fat content. The two variations of experimental studies are randomized clinical trials and community trials. In a randomized clinical trial, the investigator assigns individuals in a homogeneous population to be exposed or not exposed to the factor of interest. The assignment is made randomly. The individuals are then followed to determine what changes have taken place in their health status as a result of the factor. In a community trial, one of two populations is exposed en masse to a factor of interest such as fluoridation of the water supply or advertisements against cigarette smoking.[1,5] The changes in health status in those populations are then observed after the exposure. It is more difficult to cull a causal association from such a design, but it is feasible. However, this design is not applicable to surgical interventions and will not be considered further.

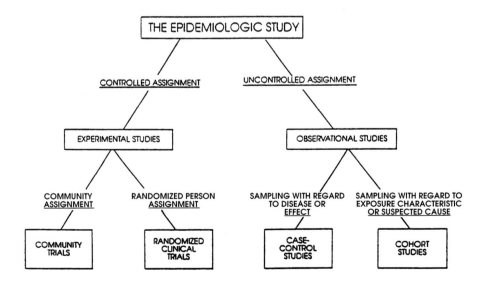

Figure 9–1 The anatomy of the epidemiologic study (Reproduced with permission from Lilienfeld DE, Stolley PD. Foundations of epidemiology. 4th ed. New York: Oxford University Press; 1994, 152.)

The second major type of epidemiologic study is the observational study (see Figure 9–1). In this study form, the investigator does not control the exposure of individuals in the population; rather, the investigator observes the exposure and the changes in health status associated with it. If the members of the population are identified on the basis of their exposure, then the design is termed a "cohort study." For example, an investigator might observe the effect of bilateral oophorectomy on the risk of breast cancer by following patients who underwent the procedure and a comparable group who did not for the subsequent development of breast cancer.[6] If the individuals are identified on the basis of their health status, then the study is termed a "case-control study." For example, the investigator might recruit a group of women with breast cancer (the "cases") and a similar group in the population who do not have breast cancer (the "controls"). The investigator would then ascertain whether the cases and the controls had undergone bilateral oophorectomy prior to developing breast cancer to determine if there was an association between the procedure and the disease. The study design in which the investigator samples the population without regard to either exposure or disease status and then examines the association between the two is termed a "cross-sectional study" or a "morbidity survey." Such studies are analyzed as though they were case-control investigations.

There are a variety of design perturbations possible in epidemiologic observational studies as investigators seek a situation as close as possible to an experimental one. These designs are hybrids and are often referred to as "quasi-experimental designs."[7,8] Although the discussion in this chapter will present the basic concepts in study design sufficiently for a foundation for the chapters that follow, the interested reader may find useful information in Campbell and Stanley and other similar publications.[7,9] The discussion will begin with randomized clinical trials, followed by observational studies, specifically, cohort and case-control designs.

Experimental Studies: the Randomized Clinical Trial

The randomized controlled trial is a design for conducting experiments in a clinical setting. As previously described, in a randomized clinical trial, the investigator assigns individuals to one of two groups. One group receives the treatment of interest (the experimental group) and the other receives the current standard treatment (the comparison group or control group). If no standard treatment exists, the latter group may receive a placebo to minimize the potential effect of any treatment on the results of the investigation. Alternatively, a sham procedure may be used instead of a placebo. For example, in a recent trial testing the efficacy of fetal cell placement in the brain of a patient with Parkinson's disease, the comparison group was treated with a sham procedure in which burr holes were made in the cranium although the dura mater was not exposed.[10,11] Patients in the comparison group were given the same amounts of cyclosporine as the treatment group. This particular design has raised many objections from ethicists regarding the need for the sham procedure and subsequent immunosuppression.[10]

Many investigators try to finesse the issue of controls in a trial by using "historical controls." There are many reasons given for doing so, including the impracticality of a randomized clinical trial and the ethical concerns of not offering a new potentially curative treatment to patients with a disease. Sacks and colleagues addressed this situation with a comparison of the results of studies for six different therapies.[12] The comparison focused on the findings from randomized clinical trials and trials using historical controls. Table 9–1 shows the results of this comparison. In every instance, the studies using historical controls found the therapy examined to be effective whereas the randomized clinical trials on the same questions were at best equivocal with regard to therapy effectiveness. Sacks and colleagues concluded that biases in patient selection "irretrievably weight the outcome" of trials using historical controls in favor of new therapies.

Table 9–1 Comparison of Randomized Clinical Trials and Historical Control Trials of Six Therapeutic Questions

Question Studied	Randomized Clinical Trials		All Historical Control Trials		Historical Control Trials Matched or Adjusted for Prognostic Factors	
	Effective	Ineffective	Effective	Ineffective	Effective	Ineffective
Cirrhosis with varices	6	14	12	6	2	1
Coronary artery surgery	1	7	16	5	9	1
Anticoagulants for acute myocardial infarction	1	9	5	1	3	1
5-FYU adjuvant for colon cancer	0	5	2	0	2	0
BCG adjuvant for melanoma	2	2	4	0	4	0
DES for habitual abortion	0	3	5	0	1	0
Total	10	40	44	12	21	3

5-FYU=5-fluorouracil; BCG=bacille Calmette-Guérin; DES=diethylstilbestrol.

Reprinted with permission from Sacks H, Chalmers TC, Smith H Jr. Randomized versus historical controls for clinical trials. Am J Med 1982;72:233–40.

One of the sentinel features of a randomized clinical trial is that every participant in the trial is treated according to a predetermined protocol that must be strictly followed. Some options may be available to the treating physician for specific instances, but generally the treatments used in the trial are specified and adhered to. In some trials involving a surgical treatment, there may be a requirement that the mortality rate or wound infection rate associated with the procedure at a participating medical center be at or below a specified level. Such a specification would be part of the protocol for the trial.

Randomization

A key concept in the design of randomized clinical trials is randomization. Randomization requires that the chance of any particular individual in the study population receiving a given treatment is the same as that of any other individual; the treatment assignment is made randomly.

It is inherent in the concept of randomization that the comparison group of patients will not receive a new treatment for their disease. One may wonder if a practitioner who has developed a new treatment is not obligated to use it on all persons with the disease. It is possible that the new treatment will be found to be efficacious. It is equally possible that the new treatment will not be efficacious and will be found to be detrimental to those receiving it. In that case, the allocation of an individual to the comparison group would be better for that person than would allocation to the experimental group.

At the start of the trial, the investigator does not know if the treatment is efficacious or if it has side effects harmful enough to outweigh any benefits from the treatment. Hence, there is equal risk of benefit and of harm in the allocation made at the beginning of the trial. It is only through randomization that such allocation can be carried out impartially. Moreover, there are likely myriad factors, many as yet unidentified, that affect the chance of altering the natural history of a disease in an individual. Randomization also assures that the prevalence of such factors is evenly distributed among the treatment and comparison groups, minimizing their impact on the results of the trial.

Once a participant has been randomized to receive one of the treatments, the results for that participant are recorded and attributed to that treatment regardless of whether the individual actually receives it. This analytic approach is termed "intention to treat." It has been used increasingly during the past two decades and is now the standard approach to analyzing data in a randomized clinical trial.

Ethics

The assumption of the individual enrolling in a randomized clinical trial is that in exchange for that individual's assuming the risk of harm from the new treatment, the investigator will defer decisions about the continuation of the trial to an external group without an interest in the specific outcome of the study. This external group is the data safety and monitoring committee (DSMC), which meets regularly (perhaps as often as monthly) to review the conduct of the trial. It determines whether there have been sufficient recorded reports of adverse experiences apparently related to the treatment to merit stopping the trial. The group also determines whether the treatment is so clearly efficacious that the study should be stopped. This level of oversight is key to providing the ethical basis for randomized clinical trials.

Trial Size and Statistical Power

An important parameter in the design of a randomized clinical trial is the number of participants who need to be recruited.[13,14] This sample size is determined by the statistical power of the trial, which in turn is determined by three factors: (1) the risk of incorrectly concluding that the new treatment is no better (or no worse) than the existing one, (2) the risk of incorrectly concluding that the new treatment is better (or worse) than the existing one, and (3) the minimal amount of difference (known as "delta") in the effect of the new treatment in comparison with the existing one that would lead the investigator to conclude that the treatments do in fact differ.[14] The size of delta determines what is considered a clinically important difference in the effects of the treatments. If the treatment effects differ by more than delta, then the treatments are said to differ. If the effects differ by less than delta, then the difference is attributed to chance, and the treatments are said to be equivalent.

The relationship between the risk of incorrectly concluding that the new treatment has the same effect as the existing one and the risk of incorrectly concluding that the new treatment is different from the existing one is shown in Table 9–2 , in which the four possible outcomes of a trial are organized by what is true in reality and by what the results are of the trial. If the trial concludes that the new treatment and the existing one have the same effect, and this accords with reality, the investigator has made no error in inference. However, if the treatments are found in the trial to be different, but the reality is that they are not different, the result is a Type I error (also known as an α error). The probability or chance of committing a Type I error is termed α or the "significance level." Usually, an investigator will use an α of 0.05; α may be set at 0.01 or even lower if the investigator is very conservative. Statistical tests of significance provide estimates of α. If the significance level is less than 0.05, the result is considered statistically significant, and the investigator may conclude that the treatments are truly different from each other. It is also possible that the results of the trial will indicate that the treatments do not differ in their effect. In that case, the result either reflects reality or it is erroneous. In the former, no error has taken place; in the latter, the result is a Type II error (also known as a β error). The power of a trial is 1-β or the chance of correctly concluding that the treatments do not differ by more than delta in their effects. The minimum power considered acceptable in a trial is usually 0.80; an investigator may decide that the trial needs to be of a higher power, perhaps 0.90 or even 0.95. For a given number of participants in the trial and a given delta, the more powerful the trial (and the lower the β), the greater the α. Alternatively, the less powerful the trial, the smaller the β and the greater the α. The only ways to simultaneously reduce both α and β are to increase the number of participants in the trial or to increase the delta.

The importance of an adequate trial (or sample) size in a randomized clinical trial may be appreciated when the consequences of a trial that was too small are considered. At one Middle Atlantic medical center in the early 1980s, an outbreak of median sternotomy wound infections developed after surgeons began using clindamycin for prophylaxis in patients who were allergic to penicillin (and therefore could not receive cefamandole, which was usually used for prophylaxis).[15] The epidemic was traced back to the inability of the clindamycin to provide the needed prophylaxis. The surgeons at that medical center cited a randomized clinical trial demonstrating the equivalence of clindamycin and cefamandole as prophylactic antibiotics as the basis for their practice. However, that particular study had too few participants to show such equivalence and was therefore of insufficient statistical power.

Design Issues

The number of participants needed in a randomized controlled trial is often greater than can be recruited at any one center. The multicenter randomized clinical trial was developed as the

Table 9–2 Outcomes of a Randomized Clinical Trial

	Actual Result	
Conclusion from Trial	Treatment Effective	Treatment Ineffective
Treatment effective	Correct conclusion	Type I error (α error)
Treatment ineffective	Type II error (β error)	Correct conclusion

means to deal with such a circumstance.[1,16] In this study design, the same randomized clinical trial is conducted simultaneously at several different clinical centers. Although the clinical centers recruit the participants, collect the data, and administer the treatments, they do not conduct the randomization of assignment nor the data analysis from the trial; those functions are performed by a coordinating center. Randomization takes place within each clinical center, and the treatments are distributed at each clinical center.

There may be a factor, such as patient age, which interacts with the treatment. If all the persons with the factor were randomized to receive the experimental treatment and persons without it were randomized to receive the usual treatment, then interpreting the results of the trial (whatever they are) would be difficult. For example, in a trial of the use of radiation seeds versus radical prostatectomy for the treatment of prostate cancer, age might be a key factor determining clinical course. A 75-year-old man may respond differently to the radiation seeds than would a 50-year-old man with the same stage of disease. Suppose that all men aged 50 years were randomized to receive the radiation seeds and died within 5 years. Also, all the men aged 75 years were randomized to receive the radical prostatectomy and survived past 5 years. In this trial, one would not be able to attribute the differences in survivorship to the treatments; the differences in survivorship may reflect differences in age between the two groups. To guard against this possibility when designing studies in which such factors can impact the outcome of the trial, the process of "blocking" or "stratification" was developed. In blocking, one determines the various levels of the factor of interest and conducts randomization within each level or "block." In the prostate cancer example, age might be blocked, with men 45 to 54 years of age in one block, those 55 to 64 years of age in another block, and those 65 or more years of age in a third block.

Strengths and Weaknesses

In contrast with other study designs considered in this chapter, randomized clinical trials have both strengths and weaknesses. There are two major strengths. First, randomized clinical trials are generally accepted as the definitive approach for assessing the efficacy of a new treatment. When properly implemented, the process of randomization provides the means by which the myriad factors that may influence the results of a trial are equally distributed between the experimental-treatment group and the usual-care group. Second, randomized clinical trials have the ability to provide information on the natural history of a disease during both usual care and experimental treatment.

There are also several weaknesses in the randomized clinical trial. The costs of such studies are generally considerable. It is impossible to subject all new therapies to a randomized clinical trial evaluation, in part because of those costs. Such studies also require considerable time, both for recruitment and, frequently, to obtain the outcomes of interest. There are also instances in which undertaking a randomized trial is simply not ethical. For instance, it would be unethical to withhold appendectomy after a ruptured appendicitis to determine if antibiotic treatment alone (with a new "wondercillin") was efficacious. Also, randomized clinical trials are not based on random samples of the population of patients. The investigators in a given trial may seek to exclude all but a very specific subset of patients with a particular disease. It is therefore often difficult for the results of a randomized clinical trial to be generalized to the population of patients with that particular disease. These weaknesses must often be carefully weighed against the considerable strengths of this type of study.

There are instances in which a randomized clinical trial cannot be conducted. However, there are still legitimate questions of treatment efficacy and effectiveness that must be resolved even though a randomized trial design is not available. In such circumstances, the investigator will conduct an epidemiologic observational study.

Observational Studies

The second major type of epidemiologic study is the observational study (see Figure 9–1). As noted previously, observational studies differ from randomized clinical trials in that exposure to the factor(s) of interest is determined by the study subject (the exposure is not assigned by the investigator), and the investigator merely observes the result of the exposure. There are two varieties of observational studies: cohort studies and case-control studies. In cohort studies, cohorts of individuals exposed to the factor of interest and those not so exposed are recruited and followed by the investigator for the development of the outcomes of interest. In a case-control study, persons with the outcomes of interest (the cases) are recruited, as are persons who do not have that outcome (the controls). Both groups are queried about their past exposure to the factor(s) of interest. The investigator then determines if an association exists between the exposure and the subsequent outcomes. Each of these designs will be discussed, followed by a consideration of their strengths and weaknesses.

The Cohort Study

In a cohort study, individuals with a specific disease are identified and recruited into the study based upon whether or not they have had a given procedure. These individuals are then followed for the occurrence of the conditions of interest. Cohort studies have been part of the evaluation of surgical procedures for much of the past century. For example, the widespread adoption of the Halsted radical mastectomy as the treatment for breast cancer was based on a cohort study undertaken by Halsted in the 1890s.[17] Specifically, Halsted reported that 6 percent of his patients who underwent the procedure experienced a local recurrence of the cancer. In contrast, 51 to 82 percent of patients who did not undergo the procedure had such recurrences. This sizable reduction in the rate of recurrence was a key reason surgeons quickly adopted the Halsted radical mastectomy as the method of treating breast cancer.

In a cohort study, the incidence rates for the conditions of interest are calculated among those who underwent the procedure ("exposed") and those who did not("not exposed"). (Figure 9–2). These rates are then compared with each other. The ratio of these rates is known as the relative risk. If the relative risk is > 3.0 or < 0.3, an association is said to exist between the procedure and the conditions of interest.[1] A relative risk between 2.0 and 3.0 (or 0.3 and 0.5) is indicative of a weaker, though present, association. Relative risks of < 2.0 are indicative of weak associations.

One of the major issues for the investigator to consider in collecting and analyzing data from cohort studies is the potential presence of a confounding factor. A confounding factor is a factor related to both the surgical procedure and (by that association alone) the outcome of interest. Consider, for example, the outcome for prostatectomy as a treatment of prostate cancer. The patient's age is associated with different outcomes of the procedure. In and of itself, however, age is not a factor in those outcomes. Hence, in an analysis of those outcomes, age

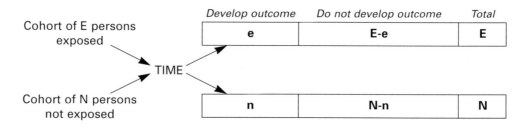

Relative risk for those exposed compared with those not exposed is (e/E) / (n/N).

Figure 9–2 Design of a Cohort Study with E Exposed Persons and N Persons Not Exposed

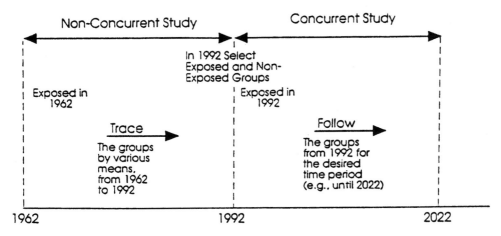

Figure 9–3 The time course of concurrent and noncurrent cohort studies. (Reproduced with permission from Lilienfeld DE and Stolley PD. Foundations of epidemiology. 4th ed. New York: Oxford University Press; 1994, 152.)

would be a confounding factor, and its presence would need to be adjusted for in any statistical analysis of the data. (See Schlesselman for further information about the process of adjustment for a confounding factor.)[18] Logistic regression and log-linear models are two of the techniques used to adjust for confounding.[8,18,19] Direct adjustment is also used for this purpose.[1]

A major challenge in analyzing any data set is to minimize the impact of confounding factors on the strength of the association between the surgical procedure and the outcome. Generally, if the relative risk between the surgical procedure and the factor is > 3.0, it is unlikely that a confounding factor can be identified whose presence would account for that strong an association. One guideline developed by epidemiologists is that the relative risk between the confounding factor and the outcome of interest would need to be twice that for the relationship between the surgical procedure and the outcome for the confounding factor to explain the observed relationship.

The cohort study design, in which the experience of patients who have a surgical procedure done is compared with those who have not, can be used either concurrently or nonconcurrently. In the concurrent study design, the patients are identified at the same time the study data are collected (Figure 9–3). For example, many of the studies of institutional factors related to mortality after a surgical procedure are concurrent cohort studies. The patients who undergo one surgical procedure with one characteristic are compared with regard to their subsequent mortality with those who undergo the procedure with a different characteristic. An example of this type of study would be one of the investigations of total hip replacement with different prostheses. In the nonconcurrent study design, the patients are identified at some time in the past, and their subsequent experience is reconstructed by the investigators. In a nonconcurrent cohort study, the patients may be identified from a surgical logbook, for example. In the previously described 1960s study of bilateral oophorectomy and subsequent breast cancer, Feinleib identified 6,908 women from surgical logbooks who had had surgery during the period from 1920 to 1940 and followed them for the development of breast cancer into the 1960s.[6] Their breast cancer experience was compared with that of 1,479 similar women who underwent a natural menopause. The women who underwent artificial menopause had a lower (< 60%) subsequent risk of breast cancer than did the women who underwent natural menopause.

The Case-Control Study

The case-control study design provides the investigator with a comparison group for the cases that might be described in a case series report. As such, it provides the basis for the derivation

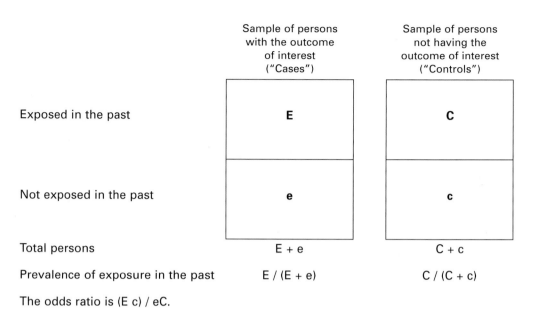

Figure 9–4 Design of a Case-Control Study with E + e Cases and C + c Controls

of inferences. In a case-control study, the investigator assembles a group of cases, such as individuals with a particular type of wound infection, and a group of similar persons who have not developed the outcome of interest. The investigator then compares the prevalence of a prior exposure to a factor, such as a particular surgical procedure or a type of prophylaxis, among the controls (Figure 9–4). If the prevalence among the cases is different than that among the controls, a relationship is deemed to exist between the factor and the outcome. An example of a case-control study is the investigation of median sternotomy wound infections referred to earlier.[15] In this study, the cases were patients who had infections of their median sternotomy wounds, and the controls were similar patients (who had also undergone cardiac surgery with a median sternotomy) who did not develop such infections. The type of antibiotic prophylaxis for each patient was determined from the medical record and the prevalence for each type among cases and controls calculated. A strong association was identified between the use of clindamycin as a prophylactic antibiotic and wound infection.

The "odds ratio" is the measure of association between the factor and the outcome used in the analysis of case-control data; its calculation is shown in Figure 9–4. Under certain conditions, this ratio is an estimate of the relative risk for a given factor and a specific outcome.[1] Whether or not those conditions are present, investigators use the magnitude of the odds ratio to assess the strength of the relationship between the factor and outcome. The scale used is similar to that for relative risk. An odds ratio of 3 or more is considered indicative of a strong association, a ratio between 2 and 3 indicates a moderate association, and an odds ratio of less than 2 shows a weak association.

Comparison of Cohort and Case-Control Study Designs

There are a number of strengths and weaknesses to cohort studies as compared to case-control studies. The strengths of cohort studies include the ability to investigate different outcomes associated with a given surgical procedure and the ability to estimate the specific rate of specific outcomes. Cohort studies can be undertaken concurrently or nonconcurrently. However, when a concurrent design is used, the study may require considerable time and expense before sufficient data have been collected to answer the questions it sought to address.

By contrast, case-control studies are quickly undertaken and relatively inexpensive. The analysis of data from both study designs is straightforward although only cohort studies provide estimates of relative risk. Last, cohort studies are not subject to the potential biases of recall and survivorship inherent in case-control studies. Indeed, it is to avoid such biases that an investigator will chose a cohort design even though a case-control design would be a quicker, less-expensive design to use.

THE META-ANALYSIS

In contrast to the previously discussed study designs, which the investigator uses to collect data to answer a question regarding the outcomes associated with a specific surgical procedure or a related aspect of that procedure (such as prophylaxis), the investigator uses meta-analysis to assemble existing data to provide an aggregate view of them.[1,20] In doing so, the investigator is able to maximize the amount of data available to provide insights into the question of interest.

In a meta-analysis, the investigator reviews the literature for all relevant studies regarding a given surgical procedure and a specific outcome.[20] The number of subjects and the strength of the association between the procedure and the outcome are recorded for each study. An aggregate strength of the association is then calculated, using one of the statistical techniques developed for this purpose. Conceptually, the estimates are weighted by the number of subjects in each study; the larger the study, the more weight is given to that estimate in the calculation.

An example of a meta-analysis is the report by Boyages and colleagues concerning treatment of ductal carcinoma in situ.[21] The issue addressed by these investigators was to determine which factors are predictive of local recurrence of ductal carcinoma in situ after management by mastectomy, conservative surgery alone, or conservative surgery and radiation therapy. The overall recurrence rates by type of treatment are shown in Table 9–3. There were clear differences in recurrence rates among the treatments. Further analysis found that the differences in recurrence between those who underwent conservative surgery and those who underwent both conservative surgery and radiation therapy were in those cases with high-grade tumor or necrosis, those of the comedo subtype, and those with close or positive surgical margins. The investigators concluded that in such cases, when the patient has undergone conservative surgery, radiation therapy should be added to the treatment plan.

Meta-analysis is based on many assumptions,[20,22,23] including the assumptions that the quality of the individual studies are the same, that the factors examined in the studies are the same, that the data missing for any one study will not be prejudicial for the outcomes of interest, that the populations from which the study subjects were drawn are similar, and that the definitions used among the studies are the same. There is also the assumption that all studies involving the factor and the outcome are known to the investigators.[24] This frequently means that the investigator must know about all the studies conducted regarding a given factor and

Table 9–3 Overall Local Recurrence Rate of Ductal Carcinoma In Situ

Type of Treatment	Overall Local Recurrence Rate (%)	
Conservative surgery	22.5	(16.9-28.2)*
Conservative surgery and radiation therapy	8.9	(6.8-11.0)*
Mastectomy	1.4	(0.7-2.1)*

*95 percent confidence interval.

Reprinted with permission from Boyages J, Delaney G, Taylor R. Predictors of local recurrence after treatment of ductal carcinoma in situ: a meta-analysis. Cancer 1999; 85:616–28.

a given outcome.[24] Since studies that do not attain statistical significance are not published as frequently as those that do, some bias (called "publication bias") may attend the results of the meta-analysis. Even when the investigator is aware of such studies and is able to include them in the meta-analysis, it is often difficult to be certain that all such studies have been included.[25] Since all of these assumptions may not be satisfied, one must consider the degree to which they were violated, when interpreting the results of any meta-analysis.

THE DECISION ANALYSIS

Decision analysis is a methodological approach to studying the manner in which decisions are made and improving the underlying decision-making process.[26] It is also the first step in a variety of economic analyses of different treatments.[27] These include cost-benefit, cost-effectiveness, and cost-utility analyses. In undertaking a decision analysis, one is seeking to provide structure to the seemingly myriad issues that confront the clinician and policymaker when assessing the possible results of a choice in action. Decision analysis may therefore be seen as a clinical approach to risk management.[28]

The basis for decision analysis is the development of a description of thought process that the clinician entertains in appraising the status of a given patient.[1] Such a description is usually recorded in the form of a decision tree (Figure 9–5). In a decision tree, the issues are arrayed in the sequence in which they would be considered by the clinician. Hence, the reasoning process is structured, and the decision points at which the clinician must evaluate existing data to render a decision regarding the care of a patient are identified. The final outcomes are then assigned weights that reflect the relative value of those outcomes for the clinician. The probability of making a given decision is then estimated from existing data. From the values of the outcomes and the probability of choosing any of the different paths branching from a decision point, the average outcome for each branch can be calculated. In this manner, the results of a decision or a sequence of decisions can be assessed and compared. If the

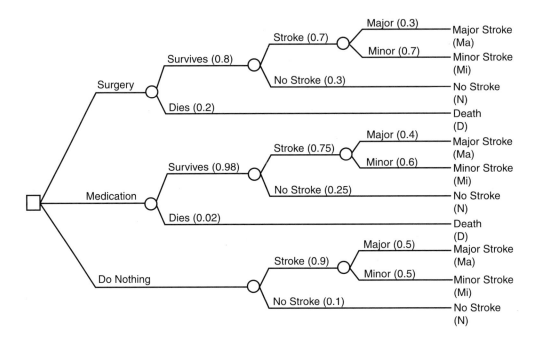

Figure 9–5 An example of a decision tree for very ill patients with a threatened stroke, including the probabilities of occurrence for each branch. (Reproduced with permission from Weinstein MC, Fineberg HV. Clinical decision analysis. Philadelphia: WB Saunders; 1980.)

results of a given decision are not desirable, one need only change the probability of making a given decision in order to change the relative occurrence of the outcomes.

Into this framework for examining the results of a given decision, we can place tools designed to assist the clinician in making that decision. For example, suppose that one desired to determine whether a woman in labor presenting to the hospital for delivery should undergo a cesarean section. There are a number of reasons why cesarean sections are performed, often related to the occurrence of outcomes in the clinician's own experience as well as to results reported in the clinical literature. However, it is difficult for the clinician to incorporate all of the outcomes resulting from cesarean sections in a given population into the decision-making process. To address this situation, Krakauer and colleagues developed a decision support tool for a scheduled cesarean section, based upon the outcomes seen in a national managed care organization.[28] Although the use of the tool (and an associated tool for unscheduled cesarean section) would have increased the rate of cesarean sections in the population from 16 percent to 21 percent, it would have lowered the cost of care for all labor and delivery services in this population by $16 million, chiefly by converting many of the unscheduled cesarean sections into scheduled ones. Both maternal and infant outcomes would have been better on average. This is an example of the power that decision support tools can give physicians.

REFERENCES

1. Lilienfeld DE, Stolley PD. Foundations of epidemiology. 4th ed. New York: Oxford University Press; 1994, 152.

2. Estes JE. Abdominal aortic aneurysm: study of one hundred and two cases. Circulation 1998;2:258–64.

3. Gore I, Hirst AE Jr. Arteriosclerotic aneurysms of the abdominal aorta: a review. Prog Cardiovasc Dis 1973;16:113–50.

4. Nevitt MP, Ballard DJ, Hallett JW Jr. Prognosis of abdominal aortic aneurysms. A population-based study. N Engl J Med 1989;321:1009–14.

5. Murray DM. Design and analysis of group-randomized trials. New York: Oxford University Press; 1998.

6. Feinleib M. Breast cancer and artificial menopause: a cohort study. J Natl Cancer Inst 1968; 41:315–29.

7. Campbell DT, Stanley JC. Experimental and quasi-experimental designs for research. Boston: Houghton Mifflin; 1963.

8. Kelsey JL, Thompson DW, Evans AS. Methods in observational epidemiology. 2nd ed. New York: Oxford University Press; 1996.

9. Elwood JM. Critical appraisal of epidemiological studies and clinical trials. 2nd ed. New York: Oxford University Press; 1998.

10. Stolberg SG. Decisive moment in Parkinson's fetal-cell transplant. The New York Times 1999 Apr 20; F2.

11. Stolberg SG. Sham surgery returns as a research tool. The New York Times 1999 Apr 25; WK3.

12. Sacks H, Chalmers TC, Smith H Jr. Randomized versus historical controls for clinical trials. Am J Med 1982;72:233–40.

13. Fleiss JL. The design and analysis of clinical experiments. New York: John Wiley & Sons; 1986.

14. Fleiss JL. Statistical methods for rates and proportions. New York: J Wiley and Sons; 1981.

15. Lilienfeld DE, Vlahov D, Tenney JH, McLaughlin JS. On antibiotic prophylaxis in cardiac surgery: a risk factor for wound infection. Ann Thorac Surg 1986;42:670–4.

16. Meinert CL. Clinical trials: design, conduct and analysis. New York: Oxford University Press; 1986.

17. Ravitch MM. Carcinoma of the breast: the place of the Halsted radical mastectomy. Johns Hopkins Med J 1971;129:202–11.

18. Schlesselman JJ. Case control studies. New York: Oxford University Press; 1982.

19. Breslow NE, Day NE. Statistical methods in cancer research. New York: Oxford University Press; 1980.

20. Sacks HS, Berrier J, Reitman D, et al. Meta-analysis of randomized controlled trials. N Engl J Med 1987;316:450–5.

21. Boyages J, Delaney G, Taylor R. Predictors of local recurrence after treatment of ductal carcinoma in situ: a meta-analysis. Cancer 1999; 85:616–28.

22. Spector TD, Thompson SG. The potential and limitations of meta-analysis. J Epidemiol Community Health 1991;45:89–92.

23. Meinert CL. Meta-analysis: science or religion? Control Clin Trials 1989;10:257S–63S.

24. Dickersin K, Berlin JA. Meta-analysis: state-of-the-science. Epidemiol Rev 1992;14:154–76.

25. Simes RJ. Publication bias: the case for an international registry of clinical trials. J Clin Oncol 1986;4:1529–41.

26. Weinstein MC, Fineberg HV. Clinical decision analysis. Philadelphia: WB Saunders; 1980.

27. Drummond MF, Stoddart GL, Torrance GW. Methods for the economic evaluation of health care programmes. New York: Oxford University Press; 1987.

28. Krakauer H, Lin MJ, Schone EM, et al.Best clinical practice: assessment of processes of care and of outcomes in the US Military Health Services System. J Eval Clin Pract 1998 Feb;4(1):11–29.

CHAPTER 10

Clinical Outcomes Measures

Julie Ann Sosa, MD

———

In 1988, Ellwood discussed outcomes analysis as a "technology of patient experience."[1] Health status measures have regularly addressed the four Ds—death, disease, disability, and discomfort—identified by Kerr White more than 30 years ago.[2] Today, however, there are many more ways to define the term "outcomes," and perhaps the best way to categorize these definitions is by the perspective of the users of the data. For clinicians, outcomes measures include survival; disease or treatment complications; physiologic, anatomic, or laboratory abnormalities; and signs and symptoms. For health care purchasers, outcomes are defined primarily in economic terms, such as the use of resources, costs, and productivity or disability. The patient's main outcomes measures involve physical and social role functioning and mental health and well-being, or "health-related quality of life." Clinical measures, the focus of this chapter, conventionally include mortality, disease or treatment complications, persistence of pathology, physiologic or laboratory abnormalities, deformity, clinical signs and symptoms, and adverse clinical events such as re-admission to the hospital. Because clinical disagreement is ubiquitous in medicine, and because one's judgment about the usefulness of an intervention or procedure can depend in a crucial way on the clinical outcomes chosen for comparison, *all* clinically relevant outcomes must be reported.

Until recently, outcomes research in the surgical sciences has focused almost exclusively on clinical outcomes. More often than not, patient outcomes have been conveyed in the form of clinical series reported by individual surgeons or institutions.

DATA SOURCES

The most common clinical measures (mortality, morbidity, and utilization) are frequently used because they are the measures most accessible from medical records, health departments, and hospital charts. Detailed clinical information can be collected unobtrusively by retrospective review of medical records. To maximize reliability, abstraction must be performed by trained reviewers with a clinical background. Patient confidentiality must be assured, and institutional review board (IRB) approval must be secured prior to embarking on such a review.

Morbidity surveys on population samples, such as the National Health Survey and National Cancer Surveys, are helpful because they provide population-based descriptions of frequency of death and complications and can be followed to monitor trends over time. Statistical power is obtained with relative ease, and data assembly and analysis is relatively inexpensive. Disease reporting (for communicable diseases and cancer registries) also is helpful for these reasons.

Claims data analysis uses data files, such as those maintained by the Medicare program or accumulated as a by-product of insurance and prepaid medical care plans, to explore patterns of clinical outcomes on a population basis. Several problems limit the value of claims data for assessing medical effectiveness or evaluating the quality of care, however. Since claims data are intended primarily for financial analysis, they may not contain enough detail about clinical features thought to affect prognosis, such as the stage of breast or colon cancer. Chart audits should be performed to confirm accuracy of coded information. The description of diagnoses and complications are often constrained by the International Classification of Diseases (ICD) coding system, and clinical events out of hospital, in the ambulatory setting, and at freestanding surgical centers are frequently excluded from analysis.[3] For reasons of confidentiality, patient records often are not linked over time and across different settings. As a result, these analyses are often cross-sectional rather than longitudinal. Overall, it is often difficult to identify clinically relevant patient groups and to control for clinical factors likely to affect outcomes using claims data.

MEASURES OF CLINICAL BENEFIT

There are at least four clinically useful measures of the consequences of surgical therapy: relative-risk reduction, odds ratio, absolute-risk reduction, and number needed to be treated. Unfortunately, none is a perfect measure of clinical benefit and harm.

Relative-risk reduction is the reduction of adverse events (ie, adverse clinical outcomes due to the progression of disease) achieved by a treatment, expressed as a proportion of the control rate. In other words, it is the difference in event rates between the control and treatment groups, divided by the event rate in the control group. The main disadvantage of using relative-risk reduction in clinical decision making is that it does not reflect the magnitude of the risk without therapy, and it will therefore overestimate or underestimate the absolute impact of therapy when adverse events in untreated patients are very rare or very common, respectively.

The odds ratio is the traditional epidemiologic expression of the relative likelihood of an outcome. Whereas the relative risk is the ratio of the probabilities of adverse outcomes in two treatments being compared, the odds ratio is the ratio of the odds of these adverse outcomes. A probability (p) of .50 (one chance in two) represents odds of 1:2, or $\frac{1}{2}$. The probability of an event's occurrence generally corresponds to odds of $p/(1-p)$. The odds ratio is often used as an approximation of relative risk in case-control studies, but it is also a valid measure of treatment effect in randomized trials. It has distinct statistical advantages over relative risk in terms of its sampling distribution and suitability for modeling and is now the preferred statistic for reporting results from meta-analysis. Like relative risk, however, it is insensitive to differences in the magnitude of risk without therapy.

Absolute-risk reduction (also known as the attributable-risk reduction) is the difference in event rates between the control and treatment groups. Its advantage is that it is an expression of the consequences of giving no treatment and therefore provides an additional measure of clinical effect. However, because the expression of absolute-risk reduction is a decimal fraction, it might not seem sensible to practicing surgeons and so may be difficult to remember and incorporate into daily practice.

Last, the number needed to be treated is the number of patients who must be treated in order to prevent one adverse event. Mathematically, it is equivalent to the reciprocal of the absolute-risk reduction, and it has the same advantage as absolute-risk reduction in that it expresses efficacy in a manner that incorporates both the baseline risk without therapy and the risk reduction with therapy. Moreover, the resulting number needed to be treated is useful because it tells clinicians in more concrete terms how much effort they must expend to prevent one event, thus allowing comparisons with the amounts of effort that must be expended to prevent the same or other events in patients with other medical or surgical problems.

The shortcomings of the foregoing measures of clinical benefit result from the properties of the measures themselves as well as the data used. When estimating the likely benefit of a treatment to their own patients, surgeons must also consider the likelihood that their patients will comply with the intervention. Often trials incorporate compliance-improving strategies that are not applied in routine clinical practice. In addition, any measure of the benefit of treatment may vary considerably in different trials of the same or similar therapy because of different patient populations, trial designs, or chance. In other words, the applicability of the results of a study must be evaluated carefully with a review of the methodology section.

Finally, since trials are of finite duration, they can provide only hints about the consequences (clinical or otherwise) of continuing therapy beyond the period of the trial. Some treatments are not effective until long after they have been started, and there needs to be an adequate duration of follow-up.[4] For example, with coronary bypass surgery, the short-term mortality may be greater than that associated with medical therapy, but longer follow-up reveals an overall benefit of surgery.

GENERIC VERSUS CONDITION-SPECIFIC MEASURES

Outcomes measures can be both generic and specific to a given problem ("condition-specific"). Generic and specific measures can complement each other.

Generic measures, that is, morbidity and mortality, are useful for looking at policy issues or reflecting the bottom-line effects of care on health status or even aspects of quality of life. Generic measures address larger constructs, and their causal links to specific treatment events may be difficult to trace. The more global the outcome measured, the more distant it is from the specific effects of the immediate treatment and the more sensitive it is to the effects of other intervening forces. Isolating the role of treatment in the causal pathway will require controlling for many other variables (see Chapter 11, Risk Adjustment). Alternatively, the analysis will rely on large numbers of observations, with the intent of detecting a relationship despite the "statistical noise" the other factors may create.[5] The simplest ways to assess outcomes across populations have been generic measures of mortality or health services use. Mortality and morbidity measures are generic measures that assess the quantity of health in a given population or across populations. Utility is sometimes used as a proxy for morbidity although other factors beyond illness can influence use.

In contrast, condition-specific measures vary with the condition being treated and are more closely linked to specific interventions, drugs, procedures, or devices. They can detect small treatment effects and can be clinical (using signs, symptoms, and tests) or experiential (capturing the impact of a disease or problem on a patient).[6] Condition-specific measures are especially appealing to clinicians because the measures are practice-based.

LIFE EXPECTANCY

A gain in life expectancy is an important outcome of many surgical interventions, but its interpretation requires that it be placed in context. For example, it has been shown that appendectomy in patients with probable acute appendicitis will lead to a gain in life expectancy of 9 to 31 months; in patients with possible acute appendicitis, the gain is only 2 to 5 months (because there are more negative appendectomies performed).[7]

The interpretation of gains in life expectancy is particularly problematic for preventive interventions for which the gains are often just weeks or even days when averaged across the entire target population.[8] Frequently, only a small fraction of the recipients of the intervention actually realize any benefit, driving down the average gain. Overall, strategies aimed at preventing life-threatening diseases such as colon cancer may appear ineffective alongside treatments for patients who are already ill (eg, with appendicitis). For example, annual fecal occult blood tests (plus barium enema or colonoscopy) every 5 years for 25 years in a target population of 50-year-olds will result in a gain in life expectancy of only 2.5 months for men and just 2.2 months for women. If the surveillance tests are performed every 3 years for 25 years, there will be a slightly larger gain in life expectancy (2.8 months for men and 2.5 months for women).[9]

MORTALITY

Death is clearly an index of the severity of a problem, from both clinical and public health standpoints. It is a useful endpoint when there is a reasonable expectation that the problem being studied has a chance of leading to premature death. In addition, it can be used as an index of the risk of disease. Mortality is the most reliably measured clinical outcome. Ideally, cause of death should be obtained from a death certificate. Remember, however, that countries and regions vary greatly in the quality of the data on their death certificates. Studies of validity of death certificates compared to hospital and autopsy records generally find higher validity for certain diseases, such as cancers, than for others.

Precision should be used when reporting death rates. Mortality is most meaningful if expressed as the proportion of deaths from a particular cause over a defined time interval. For a rate to make sense, anyone in the group represented by the denominator must have the potential to enter the group represented by the numerator. In mortality rates, the denominator represents the entire population at risk of dying from the disease, including both those who have the disease and those who do not have the disease (but who are at risk for developing the disease). In putting a restriction on diagnosis, for example, the same restriction must apply to both the numerator and denominator, so that every person in the denominator group will be at risk for entering the numerator group. This kind of restriction results in a disease-specific or a cause-specific mortality rate. In the oncologic literature, especially, it is important to separately report all-cause mortality and disease-specific (eg, breast cancer) mortality. All-cause mortality is certainly higher than disease-specific mortality, especially in an elderly patient population.

In the clinical literature, the number of deaths is often reported as a mortality rate when in fact it is really a case-fatality rate. While this practice might be an accepted convention in the clinical literature, it is important to understand the difference in definitions. A case-fatality rate (in percent) is calculated by dividing the number of individuals who die during a specified period of time after disease onset or diagnosis by the number of individuals with the disease, then multiplying this quotient by 100. The numerator should ideally be restricted to deaths from that disease;[10] however, it is not always possible to distinguish between deaths from that disease and deaths from other causes. The denominator is limited to those who already have the disease. For this reason, case-fatality is a measure of the severity of the disease. It can also be used to measure any benefits of a new therapy for a disease. As therapy improves, case-fatality would be expected to decline.

When a disease is not fatal, mortality is not a good index of incidence. A mortality rate is a good reflection of incidence rate under two conditions: (1) when the case-fatality rate is high, and (2) when the duration of disease (survival) is short. Under these conditions, mortality is a good measure of incidence and thus a measure of the risk of disease. For example, pancreatic cancer is a highly lethal disease: less than 20 percent of all patients diagnosed with the disease survive 1 year, and the overall 5-year survival is less than 5 percent.[11] Thus, mortality from pancreatic cancer is a good surrogate for incidence of the disease.

The rationale is similar for why mortality is not always a meaningful clinical outcome. While the number of postoperative deaths should always be reported for clinical series, this measure has less meaning in the setting of surgical procedures such as thyroidectomy, where death is an extremely rare event. In the setting of thyroid surgery, therefore, it is more meaningful to report complication rates; collectively, the overall rate of in-hospital complications such as recurrent laryngeal nerve injury, wound infection, or hematoma following thyroidectomy is 7 percent.[12] In such a setting, there would have to be a prohibitively large number of subjects to have sufficient statistical power to compare mortality rates, which are very low. In addition, special statistical tests such as Poisson regression modeling would have to be employed. In contrast to thyroidectomy, death after pancreaticoduodenectomy can be as high as 19 percent, and it is much easier to detect clinically and statistically significant differences in rates of postoperative death.[13]

Postoperative mortality conventionally includes death within 30 days after a procedure. However, patients today commonly have hospital stays that are far shorter than a month, and care must be taken to report mortality culled from the medical record or from a hospital discharge data base as in-hospital, not postoperative, mortality. Death rates among hospital-ized patients have increasingly been used to compare hospitals and to set policy. Some authors have used them to argue for regionalization of procedures, citing data indicating that hospi-tals performing a large number of a specified procedure have lower death rates after the pro-cedures than do hospitals performing a smaller number.[14,15] Others have suggested that hospital death rates may be a useful screening tool for identifying hospitals that provide inad-equate care.[16,17]

MORBIDITY

Morbidity measures the presence of illness and the degree of dysfunction. It can be assessed in several ways. It may reflect the incidence or prevalence of a disease, or it may be assessed as days of work missed or bed disability days. Evaluations relying solely on morbidity measures may exclude important extremes in outcomes, such as death or excellent health. Morbidity usually focuses only on physical health, but it also can capture the consequences of mental health and work-related limitations. If a broader range of dysfunction and other domains of health are relevant, then morbidity is not as useful as other, more comprehensive measures.[18]

In settings where mortality is rare, it is especially important to report complication rates. Complications can range in severity from simple wound infection to life-threatening myocar-dial infarction or pulmonary embolism, so they should be presented separately. In addition, generic surgical complications such as wound infection, pneumonia, urinary tract infection, and bleeding requiring blood transfusion should be examined in addition to disease- or pro-cedure-specific complications. For example, rates of delayed gastric emptying and pancreatic fistula should be reported following pancreaticoduodenectomy,[19] while rates of vocal cord paralysis/recurrent laryngeal nerve injury should be reported after thyroidectomy.[20,21] It is also important to clarify whether reported rates of postoperative events include all complica-tions acquired during the hospitalization or only those that were directly related to the surgi-cal procedure performed. For example, allergic or idiosyncratic drug reactions would be included in the former, but not in the latter.

Complications are coded according to the ICD, now in its tenth revision. Because coding categories and regulations change from one revision to another, any study of time trends in morbidity that spans more than one revision must examine the possibility that observed changes could be due entirely or in part to changes in the ICD. Changes in disease definition can also have a significant effect on the number of cases of the disease that are reported or that are reported and subsequently classified as meeting the diagnostic criteria for the disease.

SIGNS AND SYMPTOMS

A sign is a result reported by a medical professional after a direct examination of a patient. Signs are opinions expressed by medical professionals. Signs are generally considered more valid than symptoms although this assumption may be a result of professional prejudice rather than empirical truth. The validity and reliability of a professional opinion are depen-dent on such factors as the training of the professional, the focus and quality of the instru-ment, and the level of ambiguity of the topic.[22]

A symptom is something reported by the patient but unconfirmed by scientific means. Symptoms are typically the easiest and lowest-cost type of clinical event to measure; investi-gators simply need to ask the patient. However, there are some domains, such as pain, that are notoriously difficult to measure. In addition, symptoms are inherently subjective. As a result, there is a prejudice against using subjective patient opinions, as they are not considered to be as scientific as opinions rendered by trained medical professionals. The major difficulty with symptoms is establishing validity. For example, many different health questionnaires ask patients to rate their own level of pain. What does this measure? Is the pain compared to the worst pain imaginable or to the worst pain the individual has ever felt? Self-reported health measures are strongly influenced by such factors as ethnicity and social class.[23,24] Symptoms do have inherent face validity, and studies of self-reported health have found that it is one of the best available predictors of mortality.[25]

Many clinical signs and symptoms are subtle, and care always must be taken to standardize definitions. For example, the phenomenon of "asymptomatic" primary hyperparathyroidism is only now well understood, and recent data suggest that many of these asymptomatic patients actually have subtle neuropsychiatric impairments (eg, depression, lethargy, and muscle weakness)[26,27] as well as progressive cardiovascular disease resulting in premature death.[28,29] Recent research examining health-related quality of life has shown that parathyroidectomy is associated with marked increases in bone mass and with improvement of many symptoms associated with the disease, arguing in favor of performing early surgery for optimal disease management.[30–32]

When reporting a test value as a clinical outcome, it is essential to define the normal range for the test, since definitions might vary among laboratories or institutions. For example, to say that 90 percent of patients were "normocalcemic" 6 months after parathyroidectomy is imprecise; rather, it would be better to report that the serum calcium for 90 percent of patients returned to less than 10.5 mg/dL 6 months after their surgery. In addition, it is important to clearly define the clinical context in which the test was ordered, so that interpretation of the result is appropriate. For example, preoperatively, an elevated CA-125 level is used as an indication for a cancer operation. Postoperatively, however, trends in the test results are as important as their absolute values, since increases over time represent return of disease and poor clinical outcome.

LONG-TERM FOLLOW-UP OF OUTCOMES

Measuring long-term clinical outcomes requires careful follow-up using patient interviews face-to-face or via telephone or mail. For example, patients often travel a distance to have surgery at a transplantation center or some other tertiary care center but have their routine medical follow-up locally. Therefore, it is especially important not to rely just on the hospital and clinic records at the transplantation center for measuring rates of re-admissions and complications, for such reliance might result in an underestimation of untoward clinical events. Also, many postoperative complications can be managed in the outpatient setting, so access to clinic notes is essential for documentation of less severe postoperative complications such as wound infections. Examining lengths of stay can be an effective way to gauge the severity of complications requiring re-admission to hospital. In oncology, especially, long-term follow-up is essential when reporting rates of recurrence of disease. Cancer registries and pathology databases can be used for this kind of long-term follow-up.

Frequently, intermediate clinical outcomes in the form of laboratory tests or radiographic results are reported as a proxy for longer-term outcomes when they have been shown to be associated with each other in a significant fashion. For example, poorly controlled hypertension has been associated with a significant increase in the eventual risk of cardiac death. Therefore, a study showing that the use of a new drug results in a reduction in blood pressure supports the conclusion that the new drug will also reduce the long-term risk of death from myocardial infarction.

In a similar fashion, new surgical devices or procedures, such as laparoscopic cholecystectomy or laparoscopic nephrectomy, that result in shorter operating-room time and lower estimated blood loss might also be assumed to result in shorter recuperative time and a faster return to work in the long term. In this way, an easily measurable short-term clinical outcome can be used as a proxy for a long-term patient-reported outcome. This is frequently done in the surgical literature, since clinical outcomes are less expensive to measure than long-term patient-reported outcomes. Optimally, however, both sets of outcomes should be reported.

CONCLUSION

In summary, clinical outcomes remain the mainstay of outcomes research in the surgical sciences. However, as more surgeons and surgical residents obtain formal training in health services research, these clinical outcomes must be combined with economic and patient-reported outcomes to present patients, health care providers, and payers with a better understanding of cost-effective surgical care.

REFERENCES

1. Ellwood PM. Shattuck lecture—outcomes management: a technology of patient experience. N Engl J Med 1988;318:1549–56.

2. White KL, Williams TI, Greenberg BG. The ecology of medical care. N Engl J Med 1961;265:885–92.

3. International classification of diseases—clinical modification. 9th rev. Salt Lake City: Med-Index Publications; 1993.

4. Laupacis A, Sackett DL, Roberts RS. An assessment of clinically useful measures of the consequences of treatment. N Engl J Med 1988;318(26):1728–33.

5. Maciejewski M. Generic measures. In: Kane RL, editor. Understanding health care outcomes research. Gaithersburg (MD): Aspen Publishers; 1997.

6. Atherly A. Condition-specific measures. In: Kane RL, editor. Understanding health care outcomes research. Gaithersberg (MD): Aspen Publishers; 1997.

7. Neutra R. Indications for the surgical treatment of suspected acute appendicitis: a cost-effectiveness approach. In: Bunker JP, Barnes BA, Mosteller R, editors. Costs, risks, and benefits of surgery. New York: Oxford University Press; 1977. p. 277–307.

8. Wright JC, Weinstein MC. Gains in life expectancy from medical interventions—standardizing data on outcomes. N Engl J Med 1998;339:380–6.

9. Eddy DM. Screening for colorectal cancer. Ann Intern Med 1990;113:373–84.

10. Gordis L. Epidemiology. Philadelphia: WB Saunders Co.; 1996.

11. National Cancer Institute. Annual cancer statistics review 2987–88. Bethesda (MD): US Department of Health and Human Services; 1991. NIH Pub. No.: 91–2789.

12. Sosa JA, Bowman HM, Tielsch JM, et al. The importance of surgeon experience for clinical and economic outcomes from thyroidectomy. Ann Surg 1998;228(3):320–9.

13. Sosa JA, Bowman HM, Gordon TA, et al. Importance of hospital volume in the overall management of pancreatic cancer. Ann Surg 1998;228(3):429–38.

14. Flood AB, Scott WR, Ewy W. Does practice make perfect? Part 1: the relation between hospital volume and outcomes for selected diagnostic categories. Med Care 1984;22:98–114.

15. Luft HS. The relation beween surgical volume and mortality: an exploration of causal factors and alternative models. Med Care 1980;18:940–59.

16. Duckett SJ, Kristofferson SM. An index of hospital performance. Med Care 1978;16:400–7.

17. Wennberg JE, Roos N, Sola L, et al. Use of claims data systems to evaluate health care outcomes: mortality and reoperation following prostatectomy. JAMA 1987;257:933–6.

18. Kaplan RM, Anderson JP, Wu AW, et al. The quality of well-being scale: applications in AIDS, cystic fibrosis, and arthritis. Med Care 1989;27(3):S27–43.

19. Yeo CJ, Cameron JL, Sohn TA, et al. Six hundred fifty consecutive pancreaticoduodenectomies in the 1990s: pathology, complications, and outcomes. Ann Surg 1997;226(3):248–57.

20. Farrar WB. Complications of thyroidectomy. Surg Clin North Am 1983;63(6);1353–61.

21. Edis AJ. Prevention and management of complications associated with thyroid and parathyroid surgery. Surg Clin North Am 1979;59(1):83–92.

22. Feinstein AR. Clinical biostatistics. St Louis: Mosby; 1977.

23. Meredith LS, Siu AL. Variation and quality of self-report health data: Asian and Pacific Islanders compared with other ethnic groups. Med Care 1995;33(11):1, 120–1, 131.

24. Koos EL. The health of Regionville. New York: Columbia University Press; 1954.

25. Idler EL, Kasl S. Health perceptions and survival: do global evaluations of health status really predict mortality? J Gerontol 1991;46(2):S55–65.

26. Pasieka JL, Parsons L. A prospective surgical outcome study of the relief of symptoms following surgery in patients with primary hyperparathyroidism. World J Surg 1998;22:513–9.

27. Clark OH, Wilkes W, Siperstein AE, Duh Q-Y. Diagnosis and management of asymptomatic hyperparathyroidism: safety, efficacy, and deficiencies in our knowledge. J Bone Miner Res 1991; 6:S135–S142.

28. Hedback G, Tisell L-E, Bengtsson B-A, et al. Premature death in patients operated on for primary hyperparathyroidism. World J Surg 1990;14:829–36.

29. Stefenelli T, Abela C, Frank H, et al. Cardiac abnormalities in patients with primary hyperparathyroidism: implications for follow-up. J Clin Endocrinol Metab 1997;82:106–12.

30. Silverberg S, Locker FG, Bilezikian J. Vertebral osteopenia: a new indication for surgery in primary hyperparathyroidism. J Clin Endocrinol Metab 1998;81:4007–12.

31. Ronnie-Sivula H, Sivula A. Long-term effect of surgical treatment on the symptoms of primary hyperparathyroidism. Ann Clin Res 1985;17:141–7.

32. Solomon BL, Schaaf M, Smallridge RC. Psychologic symptoms before and after parathyroid surgery. Am J Med 1994;96:101–6.

CHAPTER 11

Risk Adjustment

Ginny Hsieh, PhD, MPH, Helen Bowman Miller, MS, and Toby A. Gordon, ScD

Outcomes research studies are often retrospective and population-based, evaluating events that occurred in the past to groups of patients outside of a controlled environment. In such cases, adjustment for risk is essential in comparing patient outcomes since patient-specific risk factors can mask or confound the relationship between interventions or treatments and outcomes.[1] It is well documented in the research literature that patient-specific characteristics and many aspects of patient health status, especially disease comorbidities (ie, coexisting diagnoses and severity of illness), are causally related to the outcomes of care.[2–7] Therefore, risk adjustment (or specifically, adjustment for disease comorbidity and severity of illness) is a way to remove the effects of confounding factors by accounting for pertinent patient characteristics before making inferences about the outcomes of care. These adjustments are particularly relevant to surgical studies in which the effectiveness of different procedures or approaches to care are evaluated to guide evidence-based practice.

COMORBIDITY AND SEVERITY OF ILLNESS

The concept of risk defines the likelihood of a poor outcome, and the dimensions of risk are multi-fold. A broad set of patient risk factors can include age, sex, race, and ethnicity; clinical stability, principal diagnosis, severity of principal diagnosis; extent and severity of comorbidities; physical functional status; psychologic, cognitive, and psychosocial functioning; cultural and socioeconomic attributes and behaviors; health status and quality of life; and patient attitudes and preferences for outcomes.[7]

Comorbidities, or coexisting diagnoses, are usually coded in medical records as secondary diagnoses, diseases unrelated in etiology to the principal diagnosis. Often, comorbidities appear to be chronic conditions such as diabetes mellitus, chronic obstructive pulmonary disease, or chronic ischemic heart disease. Patients with comorbidities often differ significantly from those without these conditions. Besides having a higher risk of death and complications, patients with comorbidities are less able to tolerate treatment and are slower to respond to therapy. In the case of surgery, operative risks often increase due to the presence of comorbidities.[6,7]

Adjustment for severity of illness differs from that for comorbidities. The definition of severity of illness is related to disease prognosis, meaning that expectations about patients' clinical outcomes are evaluated against the extent and nature of disease. For many diagnoses in which death is not an immediate event, defining severity will involve a more subjective standard. Similarly, comparing severity among different diseases or conditions is more of a challenge. However, differentiating patients by severity levels within a single diagnostic category is important to describe the illness burden in general, and distinguishing patients by the severity of their principal diagnoses is a necessary first step. Important considerations beyond severity of the primary diagnosis are the number and severity of comorbid diagnoses, acute physiologic stability, functional status, and resource needs[5] secondary to the illness.

APPLICATION OF RISK ADJUSTMENT IN SURGICAL OUTCOMES STUDIES

Risk Factors

Relating severity and comorbidities to outcomes is complicated. It involves translating different stages of clinical conditions into an overall risk score, which requires sophisticated analysis of very large databases to obtain empirical evidence. It also requires both clinical judgment and an understanding of the limits of empirical analyses.[8] To begin applying adjustments to surgical outcomes, one must first determine which risk factors are important to account for in the study. These could be patient-specific characteristics such as age, sex, race, and medical conditions. In addition, risk factors relating to the patient's condition (such as comorbidities, severity, or other disease-specific conditions) or to the procedure should be adjusted for when examining the relationship between interventions and outcomes of care. These factors are generally determined by literature review and data analysis, examining the correlation between the outcome of interest and each risk factor.

Comorbidity and Severity Indices

The next step in the risk-adjustment process is to determine whether an existing comorbidity and severity index has been validated for the purpose of one's particular surgical study. Researchers over the years have developed several scales or indices to assess different dimensions of the risks.[5,6,9] The decision to use an index developed by others versus developing one's own can depend on many factors, including whether the existing risk-adjustment instrument fits the purpose of the study, whether sufficient data are in the study data set for application of the instrument, and whether the instrument was developed on a similar population.[3,10–12] Thus, the choice of a risk-adjustment strategy is often tied to data availability, as data sources dictate how various dimensions of risk are to be measured and quantified by risk-adjustment methods. Thus, the content and quality of the data determine the validity and accuracy of risk adjustment as well as the scope and strength of inferences that can be drawn from the risk-adjusted outcomes measures.

There are three major sources of databases for most medical and surgical effectiveness research: administrative databases, medical records, and patient-based surveys. Some studies use one data source exclusively while others combine two or three different data sources to capture necessary information to include in the risk-adjustment models. One should be aware of both the strengths and weaknesses of the three data sources, since data quality has a direct influence on the conclusions which can be drawn from the outcomes studies.[13]

Administrative databases, large claims files collected for billing purposes, are very useful for outcomes study of a descriptive nature, such as exploring variations in treatment patterns.[14] Payers, providers, and governmental regulatory agencies collect these types of data. Usually, administrative data sets contain fields describing in-patient, outpatient, and ancillary services provided; primary and secondary diagnosis; primary and secondary procedure codes; patient demographic information; and costs, in the form of charges and reimbursements. Both diagnoses and procedures are coded using the ICD-9-CM coding system. The advantages of administrative databases are their ready availability, their large sample sizes, and their multi-institutional scope. However, there are also drawbacks, including coding errors, incompleteness, and variations in coding.[15]

Medical records, on the other hand, offer a rich source of information about patients and their care. Generally, medical charts document patients' histories, chief complaints, present symptoms, physical examinations, clinical assessments and diagnoses, diagnostic laboratory results, procedures, medications, in-hospital responses to therapy, clinical courses, and discharge plans. For studies relying on medical records, investigators need to have explicit review criteria; otherwise, the study could be biased from interobserver variation and subjectivity. Risk-adjustment methods that rely on clinical measures obtained from medical records, such as vital signs or laboratory findings, can measure risks that are not measurable with administrative data systems. However, the costs of primary data collection from medical records may be prohibitively expensive.[16]

Patient surveys can obtain information unavailable in either administrative files or medical records. Survey instruments can be designed to capture subjective information, such as the perception of quality, satisfaction, personal preferences, or utility. There are many survey scales currently available to measure health behavior and psychosocial characteristics. However, surveying patients for outcomes studies may be expensive. It requires much effort to develop an appropriate instrument and to validate the survey instrument. One needs to be aware of numerous logistic concerns about how the information is obtained from patients. Besides the cost of conducting a survey, there are potential biases relating to data collection. Survey-based information should be tested for its reliability and validity.[17]

Examples of Indices

A variety of severity measures were developed over the past two decades, and some of them have already been through several revisions. The following measures represent a spectrum of instruments available. Each of these indices emphasizes different aspects of severity measurement.

The Charlson Comorbidity Index

This weighted index takes into account the number and the severity of several common comorbid diseases. Weights for each condition are derived from the adjusted relative risk of mortality associated with each disease.[4] In other words, the weight is equivalent to the 1-year relative risk of death for that condition. There are 19 conditions used in the weighted scale. Diseases are assigned a point from 1 to 6, with 1 indicating the least severe condition. The scores for each disease are then summed up to create an index for each patient. The index represents a measure of the burden of comorbid diseases and is more effective in explaining outcomes than models that adjust for each clinical condition individually.[5,6] The instrument has been refined by including age information and has been adapted for use with claims data by matching clinical diseases to specific ICD-9-CM codes. In this case, weights are attributed to secondary diagnosis codes, which correspond to the conditions in the original index.[3]

The Comorbidity Index

The Comorbidity Index (CI) predicts risk of mortality for hospitalized patients. The instrument is validated for older adult patients with breast, prostate, and colorectal cancers. It combines scores from three subscales—initial severity of the comorbid conditions at admission, complications around the time of admission, and functional status into a single index. Then it assigns patients into one of four stages, ranging from a nondiseased state to a life-threatening condition.[18]

The Duke Severity of Illness Checklist

This index was created to measure overall severity of illness but can be adapted as a measure of comorbidity by omitting the primary diagnoses in scoring the instrument. The index calculates a severity score for each disease by summing across four subscales measuring symptom level, complications, prognosis without treatment, and expected response to treatment. The clinical information is collected from a checklist completed by physicians during each patient encounter as well as from medical charts. The most severe diagnoses are assigned the highest weights, which are then summed to obtain the overall score for individual illnesses.[19]

Ambulatory Care Groups

The Ambulatory Care Group system (version 4.1) is a population-oriented measure of health status, designed to predict consumption of health care resources. It is a case-mix methodology, which combines both demographic and morbidity information to adjust for the differences in the "illness burden" of a group of patients. Each ICD-9-CM code is assigned to 1 of 32 ambulatory diagnostic groups (ADGs), based on the similarity of both clinical criteria and expected service use associated with the diagnosis. The ADGs are further collapsed into intermediate groupings that are eventually partitioned into mutually exclusive categories called ambulatory care groups (ACGs). Each patient is assigned a unique ACG category, based on both in-patient and outpatient episodes of care over 1 year.[20]

Diagnosis-Related Groups

Diagnosis-related groups (DRGs) were originally developed to characterize in-patient case mix for cost-profiling purposes. Diagnosis-related groups bundled together cases with similar clinical attributes and resource consumption.[21] Initially, there were 383 DRG categories based on primary diagnosis and length of stay. The categories were refined using information on surgical procedures and patient age. In 1983, DRGs expanded into a set of 467 categories and became the payment mechanism for Medicare known as the Prospective Payment System (PPS). Recently, DRGs were refined with the incorporation of secondary diagnostic information.[22] However, DRGs are limited as a risk-adjustment system because the categories are based on a combination of resource use during intervention and the underlying severity of illness.

Acute Physiology and Chronic Health Evaluation (APACHE)

The original APACHE scoring system was developed to predict the risk of death in patients in intensive care units (ICUs) within the first 32 hours. It consisted of two parts: an acute physiology score (APS) and a chronic health evaluation (CHE) score. Patients were categorized according to their combined scores based on these two measures. The revised APACHE II was based on statistical modeling of in-hospital mortality within the first 24 hours. The revised index incorporated information regarding surgical procedures and age. The chronic health score was modified to discriminate only for severe organ system insufficiency and for the immunocompromised. The patient score summed up values from three parts: APS, age, and CHE scores. The third version, developed in 1991, further refined the instrument to incorporate information on ICU organization and management, which affect hospital care.[23]

MedisGroups

MedisGroups categorizes patients by the cause for admission and by the key clinical findings (KCFs) abstracted from medical records, which indicate abnormal physiology.[24] It rates severity by relative degrees of organ failure. Each KCF is scored from 1 to 4 based on the level of severity, with the most severe KCF as the patient's severity grouping.[25,26]

Summary

Risk adjustment is a critical component of any outcomes research study, whether based on administrative data in cross-sectional analyses or in prospective study designs with original data collected. Investigators are cautioned to use and publish findings based on validated peer-reviewed risk-adjustment methodologies rather than proprietary "black box" methodologies in which risk-adjustment parameters are unknown.

CASE STUDY: RISK ADJUSTMENT IN COST-EFFECTIVENESS RESEARCH

Examination of outcomes of complex, high-risk surgical procedures is important to understand where patients can be most effectively treated, critical knowledge for both patients and policymakers. Many factors influence where patients receive care, including referring-physician practices, patient preferences, and payer rules, which are generally not outcomes based. Given demographic variations across geographic locales, one may not assume that patients cared for in one hospital are comparable to patients cared for in another. To ascertain meaningful clinical differences, outcomes across provider settings can be compared as long as appropriate risk adjustment occurs. Age, gender, race and socioeconomic status are known to be potential confounders in any clinical outcomes analysis and should be considered routine components of risk adjustment in such studies. Similarly, comorbidity and disease severity should be considered and adjusted for.

The first step in risk adjustment for any clinical outcomes study is a review of the literature to determine factors associated with the outcomes of interest in the study. For example, to determine the impact of provider experience on complex gastrointestinal surgery, as was done in a study by Gordon and colleagues, risk-adjustment factors were patient age, gender, and race (Caucasian, African American, or other); admission status (elective, urgent or emergent, or other); diagnosis (benign or malignant); time period; payment source (commercial insurance, Medicare, Medicaid, or other); and place of residence.[4] In addition, the Dartmouth-Manitoba adaptation of the Charlson Comorbidity Index was used to calculate a comorbidity score for each patient. The comorbidity indexing system is an additive model, with each complication scored as one point.

Once the variables of interest for risk adjustment are identified, exploratory data analysis is the next step. Using tabular analysis of the dependent variable (eg, in-hospital mortality) with categorical independent variables such as gender, and by examining the distribution of continuous independent variables (such as age) in comparison to the outcome of interest (the dependent variable), causal associations between risk factors and outcomes can be determined for the study population. Using the chi-squared statistic for categorical variables and the Student's *t*-test or analysis of variance (ANOVA) for continuous variables, statistical significance testing can be performed. Similarly, the distribution of the independent variables can be compared between the study groups. Statistical significance on these analyses identifies factors appropriate for risk adjustment. In the examination of complex gastrointestinal surgery outcomes, the distributions of patient characteristics among provider groups was examined, using ANOVA for continuous variables (age) and the chi-squared statistic for categorical variables (gender, race, comorbidity score, admission status, procedure, diagnosis, time period, payment source, and place of residence). Bivariate analyses were used to assess which independent variables were associated with the outcomes of interest. From these analyses, the authors determined which variables could be confounding factors and for which variables adjustment should be made in each multivariate regression model.

The third step in the risk-adjustment process occurs as part of the main statistical analysis, generally multivariate regression analysis. In this method, multivariate regression accounts for the effects of the risk variables of interest (the independent variables) on the outcome of interest (the dependent variable). In the complex gastrointestinal surgery outcomes paper, Poisson regression was used to assess the relationship between in-hospital mortality and hospital volume, after adjustment for age, procedure, admission status, payment source, place of residence, and comorbidity score. Poisson regression models are commonly used in analyses of mortality data when events (eg, mortality) are rare. (Poisson regression logarithmically converts the value of the variables to enable the analysis to be computed.) Multiple linear regression models were used to assess differences in average length of stay, with adjustments for age, race, procedure, admission status, payment source, place of residence, comorbidity score, and time period. In this study, a regression model for total charges was adjusted for the same variables as in the length-of-stay model, with the addition of gender and diagnosis because of the association of these factors with total charges. In the models, *p*-values were based on two-tailed tests of significance, and reported *p*-values and inferences about statistical significance from the multiple regression models were based on the log-transformed data. Adjusted-log lengths of stay and total charge values calculated from the Poisson regression models were transformed back to their original scales for ease of reporting.

Table 11–1 Distribution of Patient Characteristics and Other Variables by Provider Volume Group*

| | | Provider Volume Groups | | | | |
	Statewide	High	Medium	Low	Minimal	p-Value
Mean age (years)	61.6	58.4	62.1	62.2	65.1	< .01
(standard deviation)	(15.4)	(15.4)	(15.6)	(15.7)	(14.4)	—
Gender (% male)	54.9	55.1	54.6	54.4	55.3	Ns
Race						
% Caucasian	78.5	87.3	74.9	77.6	69.7	< .01
% African American	18.3	9.2	23.6	19.6	26.2	—
Comorbidity score						
% None	47.1	48.0	53.2	47.9	41.9	< .01
% 1	13.8	14.4	10.9	13.7	14.8	—
% 2	6.6	5.6	7.2	4.9	8.4	—
% ≥ 3	32.5	32.0	28.7	33.5	34.9	—
Admission status						
% Elective	51.4	57.6	61.3	43.9	42.2	< .01
% Urgent/emergent	48.6	42.4	38.7	56.1	57.8	—
Procedure						
% Excision of esophagus	11.4	13.2	11.3	10.8	9.4	< .01
% Total gastrectomy	15.5	7.5	15.9	20.0	22.9	—
% Total abdominal colectomy	22.3	14.7	22.8	28.1	28.3	—
% Hepatic lobectomy	6.4	6.4	12.5	4.8	3.9	—
% Biliary tract anastomosis	20.6	17.0	19.8	22.1	24.7	—
% Radical pancreaticoduodenectomy	23.9	41.2	17.7	14.1	10.9	—
Diagnosis						
% Benign	35.3	31.5	35.3	38.8	38.0	< .01
% Malignant	64.7	68.5	64.7	61.2	62.0	—
Case volume distribution by time period†						
% FY 1990–92	35.5	30.3	34.9	38.0	41.0	< .01
% FY 1993–95	36.5	36.1	36.6	37.5	36.3	—
% FY 1996–97	28.0	33.6	28.5	24.5	22.7	—
Payment source						
% Commercial	42.5	50.1	40.9	42.0	34.1	< .01
% Medicare	47.0	39.3	49.1	48.8	54.7	—
% Medicaid	6.4	5.3	7.5	5.9	7.4	—
% Other	4.1	5.3	2.5	3.3	3.8	—
Place of residence						
	9.8	5.8	16.1	5.2	13.9	< .01
% Central Maryland	40.0	27.3	69.2	49.5	34.4	—
% DC suburbs	15.8	10.8	1.7	24.7	25.3	—
% Out of state	20.5	45.4	2.6	8.8	5.5	—

*Chi-squared for categorical variables, analysis of variance (ANOVA) for continuous variable (age) for the comparison between volume groups.

†Row totals for hospital volume groups.

Table 11–2 Unadjusted and Adjusted Outcomes by Provider Volume Group

Outcome	Statewide	Provider Volume Group			
		High	*Medium*	*Low*	*Minimal*
Mortality					
Unadjusted	8.7	2.9%	8.4%	12.7%	14.2%
Unadjusted relative risk	Na	1.0	2.9***	4.4***	5.0***
Adjusted relative risk	Na	1.0	2.1***	3.3***	3.2***
Average length of stay (days)					
Unadjusted	18.8	16.4	19.4**	20.9***	20.5***
Adjusted	Na	14.0	16.1***	15.7***	15.5***
Average total charges ($)					
Unadjusted	29.932	25,727	31,962***	32,852*	32,516***
Adjusted†	Na	21,393	24,982***	23,818***	24,049***

$p < .01$; **$p = .001$; ***$p < .001$. High-volume provider is the comparison.

† Poisson regression model adjusts for age, admission status, payment source, place of residence, comorbidity score, and procedure. Multivariate linear regression model for length of stay adjusts for age, race, admission status, payment source, place of residence, comorbidity score, time period, and procedure. Total hospital charges model adjusts for age, gender, race, admission status, payment source, place of residence, comorbidity score, time period, procedure, and diagnosis.

na = not available.

As shown in Table 11–1, this study found significant differences in demographic and clinical characteristics between patients who underwent complex gastrointestinal surgical procedures at the high-volume provider and patients who underwent the same procedures at medium-, low-, and minimal-volume providers.[27] Patients at the high-volume provider were on average younger and more often Caucasian. There were no significant differences in the gender composition of the groups. Patients at the high-volume provider were more likely to have commercial insurance and more often came from outside of the state. With respect to comorbidity, patients with minimal-volume providers tended to have higher comorbidity scores on average than the other groups. The low- and minimal-volume groups had more patients who were admitted on urgent or emergent bases than the other two groups. The data indicate that the low-volume providers in this study did tend to have patients with higher surgical risk (eg, higher age, greater comorbidity, and a greater proportion of patients presenting urgently and emergently), but after adjustment for differences in patient case mix, there still remained significant mortality differences among the providers. Statewide in-hospital mortality for patients undergoing complex gastrointestinal procedures was 8.7 percent. The high-volume provider had a markedly lower unadjusted in-hospital mortality rate of 2.9 percent as compared to the medium-, low-, and minimal-volume provider groups; after risk adjustment, these groups had a 2.1, 3.3, and 3.2 times greater adjusted risk of in-hospital death, respectively, than patients at the high-volume provider ($p < .001$ for all comparisons) (Table 11–2). Without the adequate risk adjustment, such comparisons could not have been made because of differences in the patient populations across provider sites.

There are many techniques of multivariate regression, a far superior method to another observed analytic approach, (ie, multiple chi-squared or ANOVA analyses), that are fraught with the potential to lead investigators to erroneous conclusions, primarily because the variables are studied singularly and not simultaneously with these approaches. Simultaneous adjustment of potential confounding variables is critical for comparing "apples to apples." Thus, risk adjustment is a critical component but not the sole component in enhancing a study's validity. Other well-documented study design considerations include sample size and statistical power, the distribution of data (normal or otherwise), and the effect of outliers.

REFERENCES

1. Iezzoni, LI. Chapter 1: Risk and Outcomes. In: Iezzoni LI, editor. Risk Adjustment for Measuring Healthcare Outcomes. Chicago: Health Administration Press; 1997: 2-3.

2. Blumberg, MS. Risk Adjusting Health Care Outcomes: A Methodologic Review. Medical Care Review 1986;43(2):351-93.

3. D'Hoore W, Sicotte C, Tilquin C. Risk adjustment in outcome assessment: the Charlson comorbidity index. Methods Inf Med 1993;32(5):382–7.

4. Charlson M. A new method of classifying prognostic comorbidity in longitudinal studies: development and validation. J Chron Dis 1987;40(5):373–83.

5. Romano PG. Adapting a clinical comorbidity index for use with ICD-9-CM administrative data: differing perspectives. J Clin Epidemiol 1993;46(10):1075–9.

6. Deyo R, Cherkin DC, Ciol M. Adapting a clinical comorbidity index for use with ICD-9-CM administrative databases. J Clin Epidemiol 1992;46(6):613–19.

7. Iezzoni, LI. Chapter 2: Dimension of Risk. In: Iezzoni, LI, editor. Risk Adjustment for Measuring Healthcare Outcomes. Chicago: Health Administration Press; 1997.

8. Schwartz, M, Ash A. Chapter 8: Evaluating the Performance of Risk-Adjustment Methods: Continuous Outcomes. In: Iezzoni, LI, editor. Risk Adjustment for Measuring Healthcare Outcomes. Chicago: Health Administration Press; 1997.

9. Charlson, M. A New Method of Classifying Prognostic Comorbidity in Longitudinal Studies: Development and Validation. J Chron Dis 1987;40(5): 373-83.

10. Iezzoni, LI Chapter 3: Data Sources and Implications: Administrative Databases. In: Iezzoni LI, editor. Risk Adjustment for Measuring Healthcare Outcomes. Chicago: Health Administration Press

11. Roos, LL, Sharp SM, Cohen MM. Comparing Clinical Information with Claims Data: Some similarities and differences. J Clin Epidemiol 1989;42:1193-1206.

12. Smith, M. Chapter 6: Severity. In: Kane RL, editor. Understanding Health Care Outcomes Research. Gaithersburg (MD): Aspen Publishers; 1997.

13. Kane RL. Chapter 1: Approaching the outcomes question. In: Kane RL, editor. Understanding health care outcomes research. Gaithersburg (MD): Aspen Publishers; 1997.

14. Anderson G, Steinberg EP, Whittle J, et al. Development of clinical and economic prognoses from Medicare claims data. JAMA 1990;7(263):967–72.

15. Prospective Payment Assessment Commission (ProPAC), Medicare, and the American Health Care System. Report to Congress. Washington (DC): Prospective Payment Assessment Commission; 1996.

16. Roberts RO, Bergstrahl EJ, Schimdt L, Jacobsen SJ. Comparison of self-reported and medical record health care utilization measures. J Clin Epidemiol 1996;9:989–95.

17. Maciejewski M, Kawiecki J, Rockwood T. Chapter 14: Satisfaction. In: Kane RL, editor. Understanding health care outcomes research. Gaithersburg (MD): Aspen Publishers; 1997.

18. Greenfield S, Aronow HU, Elashoff RM, Watanabe D. Flaws in mortality data: the hazards of ignoring comorbid disease. JAMA 1988;260:2253–6.

19. Parkerson GR, Broadhead WE, Tse CJ. The Duke Severity of Illness Checklist (DUSOI) for measurement of severity and comorbidity. J Clin Epidemiol 1993;4:379–93.

20. Weiner JP, Tucker AM, Collins AM, et al. The development of risk-adjusted capitation payment system for medical MCOs: the Maryland model. J Ambulatory Care Management 1998.

21. Fetter RB, Shin Y, Freeman JL, et al. Case mix definition by diagnosis-related groups. Med Care 1980;18:1–53.

22. Freeman JL, Fetter RB, Park H, et al. Diagnosis-related group refinement with diagnosis- and procedure-specific comorbidities and complications. Med Care 1995;33:806–27.

23. Knaus WA, Wagner DP, Draper EA, et al. The APACHE III prognosis system: risk prediction of hospital mortality for critically ill hospitalized adults. Chest 1991;100:1619–36.

24. Brewster AC, Karlin BG, Hyde AA, et al. MEDISGROUPS. A clinically cased approach to classifying hospital patients at admission. Inquiry 1985;22:377–87.

25. Iezzoni L. (Ed.) Risk adjustment for measuring health outcomes. Ann Arbor (MI): Health Administrative Press; 1994.

26. Steen PM, Brewster AC, Bradbury RC, et al. Predicting probabilities of hospital death as a measure of admission severity of illness. Inquiry 1993;2:128–41.

27. Gordon TA, Bowman HM, Bass EB, et al. Complex gastrointestinal surgery: impact of provider experience on clinical and economic outcomes. J Am Coll Surg 1999 Jul;189(1):46–56.

CHAPTER 12

Key Economic Outcomes Measures

John D. Hundt, MHS, Gregg P. Burleyson, RN, MHS, and Alan Lyles, ScD, MPH

As concerns about the cost of health care have risen over the last two decades, the demand for economic outcomes measures that quantify the cost and/or benefit of medical and surgical care has increased dramatically. A review of the literature on evidence-based surgery shows that clinical measures of outcomes (such as mortality or treatment complications) alone are reported much more frequently than economic measures alone or combined with clinical measures. This is probably due in large part to the interests of investigators but also to the difficulties in measuring economic outcomes.

On the surface, economic measures of the cost of health care seem to be rather straightforward. Most health care services result in the production of billing information, which may be aggregated to describe the economic value of the services provided. As will be seen, the definitions of cost from the perspectives of stakeholders within the health care system may differ significantly. In addition, the fragmented nature of health care financing and delivery in the United States and the resultant decentralization of decision making complicate economic analysis. This chapter reviews the basic frame of reference from which economic analyses are performed, describes the components of health care costs, and summarizes methods used for comparing economic costs.

PERSPECTIVES FOR ECONOMIC ANALYSIS

The ideal economic measure of cost from the societal perspective is the social opportunity cost of the inputs to the health care process, that is, the highest value the inputs could earn if used for other purposes.[1] Analyses that compare the utility of additional spending for health care services with the utility of other societal needs are infrequently reported. Such economic research is generally performed for purposes of making policy. An example of this is the effort of the Oregon Medicaid program in 1994 to rationalize service delivery by prioritizing all services provided to beneficiaries, based on cost and utility analysis.[2]

Key parameters for economic analysis include the time period for analysis, the breadth of services included, and the perspective from which costs are defined (for example, the patient, the provider, or the payer). Ideally, analysis would include long-term comparisons of the cost of all services from the perspective of stakeholders. In practicality, the scope of analysis is much narrower, for example, an examination of the perioperative mortality for high-risk surgical procedures may limit the cost analysis to in-patient length of stay as a proxy for cost.[3] Since the benefits and ultimate cost of a surgical intervention may not be realized until years later, studies of only hospitalization do not reflect all societal costs. Thus, a longer time frame of analysis is desirable, such as an episode of illness or 1-year or longer time periods.

Defining Health Care Costs

Accounting for the cost of health care services is a complex process. Reimbursement methodologies may provide incentives to classify and allocate costs differently than would be desirable for outcomes research. In addition, much of the data available for analysis relates to what providers are paid for services rather than to the true economic costs of the services. Depending on the perspective from which costs are analyzed, costs can be defined quite differently. The cost to a health maintenance organization (HMO) is what is paid to a provider whereas the cost to a provider is the cost of the inputs required to produce the service (eg, the provider's time and related expenses, such as office staff, rent, etc). This distinction is important for properly understanding cost analyses. Table 12–1 illustrates possible components of costs for lower back disorders, a common health care problem that can be treated surgically. The following section describes the major components of health care costs and several methods by which costs are classified for analysis.

Major Components of Health Care Costs

Providers

Most health care providers classify costs as labor, supplies, purchased services, uncompensated care, and capital. Labor costs include the costs of providing people to care for patients, clean the rooms, and provide other required services. Supply costs include the costs of providing the supplies needed to provide services. Cost for purchased services are the costs for services purchased from third parties who are not employed by the provider. Uncompensated care and bad debt are the expenses the provider incurs for services to patients for whom no payment is made; these costs are generally spread across all provided services. Capital costs include the costs of providing the buildings and equipment needed to care for patients, such as rental expense, depreciation expense, and interest expense on loans for capital acquisitions.

Each of these types of costs can be classified as fixed, variable, or semivariable to describe how total costs vary as the health care provider's level of activity (ie, services provided) changes. Figure 12–1 illustrates the relationship between total costs and activity levels for these types of costs. Fixed costs remain constant and are unaffected by the volume of services provided. For example, an existing in-patient nursing unit that is minimally staffed has costs associated with the building, equipment, and staff even if there are no patients at any given time. Variable costs are proportionate to the volume of services provided. For example, the cost of preparing surgical instrumentation packs is directly related to the number of procedures performed. Semivariable costs increase in a stepwise fashion as the activity level increases. For example, a clinical laboratory may add new equipment to accommodate higher demand. The equipment cost is fixed within the range of activity accommodated by existing equipment but will increase each time new equipment must be added.

Table 12–1 Possible Cost Components for Lower Back Disorders

Cost Component	Bearer of Cost	Inclusion in Economic Analysis
Diminished productivity due to time lost from work	Employers, society	Infrequently
Reduced wages	Individual	Infrequently
Alternative therapies	Individual	Infrequently
Over-the-counter remedies	Individual	Infrequently
Physician services	Payers (including employers and government)	Usually
Hospital services	Payers (including employers and government)	Usually
Reduced enjoyment of life	Individual	Occasionally

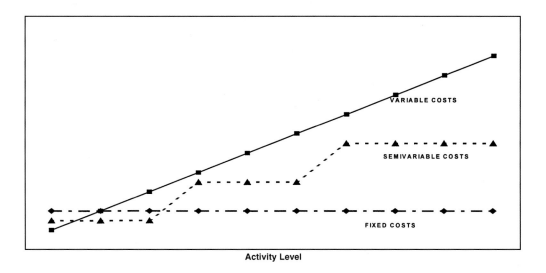

Figure 12–1 Types of Cost Behavior

Understanding the behavior of costs as the level of activity varies is important to users and producers of cost analyses for several reasons. Because of changing activity levels, detailed costs measured at one point in time may not reflect the ongoing costs of providing a service. Furthermore, the marginal cost of adding a new surgical service at a hospital that did not previously offer that service would likely be greater than would be the corresponding cost at another hospital that is expanding the volume of an existing service.

In addition, all types of costs can be classified as direct or indirect. Direct costs can be attributed directly to the service provided; for example, the cost of an operating-room nurse can be directly attributed to surgical patients. Indirect costs (also called overhead costs) are incurred in support operations but are generally not directly related to the care of patients (for example, the cost of a billing clerk). In order to determine the complete cost of providing a service, indirect costs must be allocated to individual services. Some providers may consider the costs of medical equipment as direct and allocate these costs to specific services in the institutions while other providers may consider all equipment costs as indirect and use an allocation method, such as square footage, to distribute all capital costs. This allocation of indirect expenses is a source of great variation in cost accounting.

The health care provider's charges to payers include both the direct costs of services plus a markup, which includes indirect costs and profit or surplus. The markup may also include an adjustment for bad debt, the percentage of total charges that are not paid by patients because they do not have the necessary financial resources. Because many contractual arrangements with payers are based on discounted charges, providers often use a high markup to create charges that are not fully reimbursed by payers. That portion of the charge not paid because of contractual arrangements with payers is classified as a contractual allowance and a reduction in reported revenue in providers' financial statements. Additional costs that may be reflected in health care providers' charges include the cost of medical education, which has both direct components (eg, salaries of medical residents) and indirect components (eg, additional use of diagnostic procedures as part of a resident's learning experience). Because of widely varying markups among different providers and also among billed items from the same provider, the charge on a patient's bill is generally not a good indicator of the actual costs of either provider or payer.

Costs for a particular service may change significantly over time.[4] For example, in the early phase of the use of a new technique such as minimally invasive heart surgery, longer operating-room time will be required as surgeons and other staff become more familiar with the technique. Because of the learning curve and the resultant gains in efficiency over time, it is difficult to predict what the cost of a procedure will be when it reaches maturity. Often, the purchase prices for supplies and instrumentation are very high for new procedures but come down substantially over time. A recent example is the cost of stents used in coronary angioplasty: as more vendors have entered the market to provide these stents, the cost has come down significantly. Economic analyses based on an initial cost may be considerably different than analyses at a later time.

Payers

Further complicating cost analysis is the fragmented reimbursement system in the United States. Although labor, capital, and supply costs are associated with the administrative functions of providing health care coverage to enrollees, the major costs for payers are payments to health care providers. These payments are made under a bewildering array of contractual arrangements. The most common arrangements are fee-for-service contracts, fee schedules, fixed-rate agreements, and capitation. These are not mutually exclusive categories, as payers and providers use varying combinations of payment methods to contract for services.

Fee-for-service or discounted fee-for-service contracts specify a certain amount to be paid for each service, based on a provider's specific rates. In the past, providers developed their own charges, and payers paid what was considered "usual and customary" for each service. Over time, standardized fee schedules have been developed, using common terminology for procedures. Under a discounted fee-for-service arrangement, a payer will negotiate a reduction from a provider's established rates or an established common fee schedule. Because of the high degree of variation in charges among health care providers, comparable discounts across provider charges may not result in comparable costs across providers.

Fixed rate contracts specify payment amounts for specific services, ignoring the provider's charges. For in-patient hospital services the most common examples of fixed-rate payments include diagnosis-related group (DRG) payments and per diems. The DRG system uses diagnosis and procedure data to classify in-patient stays into one of more than 500 specific categories, each with a fixed reimbursement rate. The system was originally adopted by the Health Care Financing Administration (HCFA) in 1983 for the Medicare program but has been used widely by other payers. Per diem rates specify a fixed amount to be paid to providers for each day a patient is an in-patient. These rates may be adjusted for the level of care provided, such as general, acute, intensive, skilled nursing, subacute and other categories of care. Many fixed-rate arrangements allow additional payments for patients who are statistical outliers.

Capitated contracts specify payments to providers for specified services delivered to a certain group of enrollees. For example, a general surgeon or group of surgeons may be paid a certain rate per month to provide surgical care to a group of enrollees, or a multispecialty medical group could be paid a capitated rate for all physician services. Sometimes a payer may contract with a provider group for all health care services at a capitated rate. Generally, the payments are made on a per-member-per-month (PMPM) basis. Because there is no specific payment rendered for the provision of a service, information on the costs of a specific service may be harder to obtain under capitation. Payers have developed alternatives such as encounter reporting to compensate for the loss of episodic billing data under capitation. Encounter reporting requires the submission of the same types of data required under fee-for-service arrangements but does not constitute an actual bill for services.

Payments to physicians are generally made by applying a fee schedule or by using capitated rates. Because the federal government is the largest individual payer of health care services, practices adopted by the federal government are often adopted by other payers. The fee schedule used by Medicare to pay physicians has been widely used in the private sector. Payers negotiate rates indexed to a certain percentage of the Medicare fee schedule, which uses a common coding methodology and assigns a relative weight to each designated code. The relative weights are based on extensive analysis of the costs of delivering services. While much has been done to improve the accuracy of the Medicare fee schedule, comparisons of costs based on this fee schedule must be made with care. Historically, reimbursement for surgical services has been higher than that for evaluation and management services. These differences may be important to consider when comparing surgical treatments to medical treatments.

Patients

Patients must pay providers for health care services not covered by third-party payers. These noncovered services generally include over-the-counter remedies, alternative treatments, and other services that vary by health plan. Analyses that do not adjust for these costs may not present an accurate assessment. For example, an analysis comparing the costs of a chronic but medically manageable condition with high out-of-pocket costs for the patient to the costs of a surgical treatment for the same condition may not capture the impact of the out-of-pocket expenses on patients because these data are not always collected. As an additional example, if chiropractic care is not a covered benefit, the use of health plan claims data to compare surgical and nonsurgical treatment options for back problems may not present the true costs of the treatment options.

In addition to costs for uninsured services, patients may also pay significant deductibles, copayments, and co-insurance for services that are covered. Health plans apply different methodologies for these payments, based on the provider type and setting. In-patient care may have no copayments while copayments for outpatient services such as psychotherapy may be substantial. These payment requirements have been designed to discourage patients from overusing services and to control costs. Because of the lack of consistency in these amounts paid by patients, treatments with identical total costs but delivered in different settings or by different types of providers may have very different out-of-pocket cost profiles for patients.

Patients may be faced with other costs that are indirectly related to health care, such as travel costs or lost wages as a result of missing work due to illness and recovery. These costs may merit consideration in specific circumstances.

Employers

Employers in the United States providing health care coverage for their work force and dependents generally are self-insured, or they contract with HMOs or other insurance companies to provide coverage. Self-insured employers bear the direct cost of health care services provided to beneficiaries. The cost for these services would be the same as for any other payer as discussed above. The cost for employers contracting with HMOs or other insurance companies is in the form of a premium. Under some arrangements, the premium is directly related to the HMO's experience for the covered group. In others, the insurer charges the same rate to all employers in a community regardless of the varying actual claims costs for each employer. The type of plan each employer has in place (whether self-insured or insured or whether an insured plan is experience- or community-rated) will determine whether an employer's cost for health care is sensitive to varying treatment options. In addition to traditional health benefits plans, an employer's costs for health care may include the costs of workers' compensation programs or wellness programs. Some employers are also direct providers of care with in-house physicians and nurses.

Employers may need to pay for replacement workers when employees miss work due to illness and recovery. When replacement workers are not hired, employers may lose revenue from being short-staffed. For health care conditions that have variable recovery times under different treatments, the indirect economic costs to employers may be considerable.

Measuring Costs for Outcomes Studies

Economic measures for clinical outcomes studies may be developed in several ways. Cost analysis can be completed prospectively as part of a clinical trial. Retrospective cost data can be analyzed, typically based on secondary or administrative databases. In other instances, standardized or estimated costs may be applied to models of clinical outcomes.

COST ACCOUNTING

The accurate measurement of the costs to health care providers of providing specific patient care services is extremely complex. Traditionally, costs have been tracked by location (the operating room) or expense type (float nurse) but have not been linked to specific services (heart transplantation). Patient billing systems track charges for the specific services provided but are not linked to cost data. As the pressure for cost containment and accountability has increased, health care providers have implemented cost accounting and decision support information systems that combine cost data from general ledger accounting systems with service utilization data from billing systems.

Cost accounting in the health care field has lagged significantly behind cost accounting in other industries. As competitive pressures from managed care and other forces have increased, health care providers have begun to implement the types of systems needed to capture reliable cost information. Several methods are used to determine the costs of care by providers, including the use of relative value units (RVUs) and cost-to-charge ratios.

Costing Based on Relative Value Units

The basic methodology of costing services using RVUs is as follows:

Assign an RVU value to each billed product or service within a direct patient care department. The unit of measure for the RVU must be predictive of resources used and may be different between departments. For example, minutes may be the units for RVUs in the operating room, patient days in the intensive care unit (ICU), College of American Pathology (CAP) units in the laboratory department, and Medicare resource-based relative value scale units for physician services. The RVU value assigned to a product should indicate the relative amount of department resources (cost) used to deliver each product. In the case of the operating room, if an operating-room minute is the billed product, it will have an RVU value of one. If blocks of operating-room time are the billed products, 1 to 10 minutes may have an RVU value of 5, and 11 to 20 minutes may have a value of 15.

Multiply the RVU value for each product by the number of units provided in a given time period to obtain the total weighted RVUs for the department.

Divide the total department cost for the time period (direct and indirect costs) by the total weighted RVUs to obtain the standard cost per RVU.

A major issue is how to allocate the indirect (overhead) costs to each patient care department.

Multiply the standard cost per RVU by each product's assigned RVU value to determine the standard cost for each product.

Multiply the standard cost for each product by the number of times it was provided to a patient, and sum the results to determine the cost of care for the patient.

Cost-to-Charge Ratios

The RVU methodology described above may be beyond the scope of many clinical investigators. In practice, a cost-to-charge ratio is often used to derive costs from charges. The ratio may be obtained at a departmental or total provider level by dividing total costs by total charges. The ratio can then be multiplied by the appropriate departmental or total charge on a patient's bill to estimate the cost of care for the patient. Investigators can also limit their detailed cost finding to a single department and use cost-to-charge ratios for other costs.

Virtually all hospitals in the United States complete cost reports annually. These cost reports are publicly available and are a source of cost-to-charge ratios for hospitals. Additional information in cost reports allow researchers to adjust for the costs of graduate medical education, uncompensated care, regional wage rate variations, and other factors that may explain differences in costs. Similar data can be developed for physician services although there is no equivalent publicly available data as there is with hospitals.

Other Considerations for Measuring Economic Costs

Unless clinicians have access to payer claims data or contractual arrangements for all patients in a study, they will not be able to determine the payer's cost of payments to health care providers. Payment could be estimated using a percentage of charges (assume discounted fee-for-service) or modeled using a national standard such as the Medicare Prospective Payment System, the contractual rates of which are public information. "In-patient days" can be used as a proxy for cost, under the assumption that there is a direct relationship between patient days and cost of care. Investigators should not use a 1:1 ratio between decreased days and cost savings, since some of the services delivered on the eliminated days will be shifted to the remaining days.

Days of work missed can be used as a proxy to measure the cost of missed work to patients and employers. When patient income is also included, monetary estimates of costs can be made. Measuring the costs of diminished productivity and lost wages may introduce bias in favor of treatments for conditions more prevalent in higher-income populations.

When studies extend over multiple years, cost estimates should be indexed or inflation-adjusted. The Medical Care Component of the Consumer Price Index is a readily obtainable national number that can be used for this purpose. Medical inflation may vary significantly by regions or within the various components of health care costs such as wages or supplies. Additionally, studies that analyze events over a long period of time may need to consider using a discount factor to adjust for the timing of costs and benefits.

A final word of caution about making cost estimates in clinical trials: the random assignment of patients to treatment protocols may help overcome biased clinical results, but unless patients are also randomly assigned to providers, cost findings may be biased if the providers have different cost structures. There are additional reasons that cost data collected in clinical trials may not be the best indicators of cost-effectiveness. Costs under well-organized, protocol directed clinical trials may vary significantly from the less-scrutinized environments where most care will be delivered. Further, estimated cost savings derived from clinical trials may not be realizable in practice. For example, a clinical trial of a gastric ulcer treatment used endoscopy to identify lesions that would have likely gone unnoticed by the patient and physician. The costs and benefits associated with diagnostic and therapeutic protocols of clinical trials may not be indicative of achievable results in the field.[5]

COST-EFFECTIVENESS AND COST-BENEFIT ANALYSES

Purposes and Features

Cost-effectiveness and cost-benefit analyses (CEA and CBA, respectively) are attempts to simultaneously assess the cost of a service, device, product or procedure, and the outcome(s) associated with it. The intent is that these assessments might then be compared to a benchmark or to each other to guide efficient use of constrained resources. While cost-benefit analysis reduces all measurements to dollars, cost-effectiveness analysis compares alternative ways of achieving the same endpoint such as additional years of life, reduced heart attacks, or low-ered serum cholesterol. A key feature of each approach is the use of incremental costs and incremental benefits since average costs do not provide sufficient guidance for decisions on which intervention to use or how much of it to use.

During the mid-1970s, formal technical assessment was adopted by the Office of Technology Assessment (OTA) as an instrument to assist clinical and policy decision makers regarding new technologies.[6] Cost-effectiveness analysis, as a component of medical technol-ogy assessment, arose from many disciplines and consequently contains a diversity of approaches and language. The imprecision in what is intended by "cost-effective" is also a con-sequence of the term's use by different groups for different ends: purchasers use it to focus on assessment of value, producers use it in marketing, and patient groups use it to justify resource needs.[7] These diverse users also influence the cost-effectiveness measure itself; the relevant costs for an insurer and a patient will differ since each user experiences a different set of finan-cial obligations. Similarly, an employer may see a reduction in days lost from work as an off-set to costs whereas the employee who still receives pay while undergoing surgery or rehabilitation may not perceive this as relevant. The impact of perspective on cost-effective-ness studies renders some analyses suspect, others incapable of being compared, and a few capable of providing comparative information. This issue is so important that the editorial policy of a leading academic medical journal precludes consideration of cost-effectiveness studies if the relationship between the research(ers) and the industry or firm producing the research is not sufficiently distant or independent.[8]

Cost-effectiveness studies often rely on published data from clinical trials or on secondary data analysis rather than on trials that explicitly include economic endpoints. This is due in part to the larger variance in financial data compared with physiologic endpoints and the attendant larger sample sizes required to establish statistically significant differences.[9]

Starting almost 30 years ago, a consistent finding of variations in medical practices not associated with detectable differences in health status or need has been reported for many spe-cialties and across geographic regions. From coronary artery bypass grafting to hysterectomy, the differences between contiguous small areas can be substantial.[10] Given this variation, those who pay for medical services have sought to identify inefficiencies and opportunities to elim-inate unnecessary or less-effective services as the cost and proportion of the gross domestic product (GDP) devoted to health care has increased. Similarly, surgeons attacked the issue of cost-effectiveness[11] even before the dominance of managed care. A systematic review of pub-lished CEA/CBA studies compared the 3,206 studies from the 12 years from 1979 to 1990 to the 3,539 studies for the 6 years from 1991 to 1996 alone.[12] These data suggest that CEA analy-ses are increasingly being reported and that the growth in surgical treatments is more pro-nounced for the recent period.

Methodology

The fundamental equation for calculating a cost-effectiveness ratio relates the incremental costs (the numerator) to incremental effectiveness (the denominator) to produce a point esti-mate of cost-effectiveness. Decisions concerning which costs to include (or exclude) among direct and indirect costs, how to treat them (do they belong in the numerator or denomina-tor?), which consequences to include, what time period and what discount rate can produce quite different cost-effectiveness ratios for the same data. A pragmatic approach to resolving these issues and enhancing comparability of CEA results is the recommendation of an expert panel appointed by the US Public Health Service that a reference case analysis be performed for every CEA in addition to whatever additional variant may be more suitable to the ana-lyst.[13] The reference case analysis would conform with explicit recommendations concerning options for components of the analysis. The following is a sample of the recommendations:

- The societal perspective is used for the reference case analysis and will influence what resources to include and at what estimated costs.
- All components of the intervention that influence cost or effectiveness, including the target population, must be identified.
- The intervention being analyzed must be compared to current practice or the best alternative.
- Time horizon, costs, health effect and outcomes, and study boundaries must be specified.
- The numerator should include direct costs for resources consumed as part of the intervention and for non–health care resources required by the intervention.

The time perspective for an intervention is significant in two respects: how subsequent expenses for adverse outcomes are treated and what discount will be applied to costs (and outcomes) in future periods. A significant related consideration is the impact of the learning curve; that is, that the efficiency, cost, and outcome of a program or procedure are often different after considerable experience has been achieved than when it was initially applied. This impact may be substantial when the calculation is the marginal cost, as in CEA, rather than the cumulative or average cost. Learning-curve effects have been demonstrated in heart transplantation by improvements in case fatality rates[14] and by reductions in cost.[15] A more recent study supports the association among surgical volume, improved outcomes, and lower costs for pancreaticoduodenectomies.[16]

Conclusion

Economic measures for outcomes research are not standardized in the health care industry. The lack of common definitions, cost accounting methods, and perspectives for cost analysis makes it of paramount importance that producers and users of economic outcomes studies be explicit about the methodologies used. Perspective, scope, and methods of measurement must be tailored to the subject at hand, with interpretation and generalization of study results tempered by the assumptions made for each analysis.

References

1. Davidoff AJ, Powe NR. The role of perspective in defining economic measures for the evaluation of medical technology. Int J Technol Assess Health Care 1996;12(1):9–21.

2. Health Care Financing Administration. Oregon statewide health reform demonstration fact sheet. [accessed 1999 Nov 22] Available at: URL: http://www.hcfa.gov/medicaid/orfact.htm.

3. Gordon TA, Burleyson GP, Shahrokh S, et al. Cost and outcome for complex high-risk gastrointestinal surgical procedures. Surgical Forum 1996;47:618–20.

4. Cuschieri A, Ferreira E, Goh P, et al. Guidelines for conducting economic outcomes studies for endoscopic procedures. Surg Endosc 1997;11:308–14.

5. Hillman AL, Bloom BS. Economic effects of prophylactic use of misoprostol to prevent gastric ulcer in patients taking nonsteroidal anti-inflammatory drugs. Arch Intern Med 1989;149:2061–5.

6. Luce BR. Pharmacoeconomics and managed care: methodologic and policy issues. Med Decis Making 1998;18(2):S4–S11.

7. Gold MR, Russell LB, Siegel JE, Weinstein MC, editors. Cost-effectiveness in health and medicine. New York: Oxford University Press; 1996. p. 3–22.

8. Kassirer JP, Angell M. The journal's policy on cost-effectiveness analysis. N Engl J Med 1994;331(10):669–70.

9. Powe NR, Griffiths RI. The clinical-economic trial: promises, problems and challenges. Control Clin Trials 1995;16(6):377–94.

10. The Dartmouth atlas of health care in United States 1998. [accessed 1998 Jul 1] Available at: URL: http://www.dartmouth.edu/~atlas/index.html.

11. Meyers AD, Eiseman B, editors. Cost-effective otolaryngology. Philadelphia: B.C. Decker, Inc.; 1990.

12. Elixhauser A, Halerin M, Schmier J, Luce BR. Health Care CBA and CEA from 1991 to 1996: an updated bibliography. Med Care 1998;36:MS1–MS9.

13. Gold MR, Russell LB, Siegel JE, Weinstein MC, editors. Cost-effectiveness in health and medicine. New York: Oxford University Press; 1996. p. 98–101.

14. Smith DB, Larsson JL. The impact of learning on cost: the case of heart transplantation. Hosp Health Serv Adm 1989;34(1):85–97.

15. Saywell RM Jr, Woods JR, Halvrook HG, et al. Cost analysis of heart transplantation from the day of operation to the day of discharge. J Heart Transplant 1989;8(3):244–52.

16. Gordon TA, Burleyson GP, Tielsch JM, Cameron JL. The effects of regionalization on cost outcome for one general high-risk surgical procedure. Ann Surg 1996;221(1):43–9.

CHAPTER 13

Critical Evaluation of Evidence

Eric B. Bass, MD, MPH

BASIC SKILLS

Critical evaluation of evidence requires certain basic skills. One must be able to define the clinical question as clearly as possible, translate the question into a statement that can be used to search the literature, conduct the search, and select the best articles before applying appropriate rules of evidence to evaluate the articles. Although these basic skills often receive inadequate attention during medical school and residency training, they have an important role in the critical evaluation of evidence and in continuing medical education. Without these basic skills, it is nearly impossible to appropriately and efficiently evaluate the evidence concerning a clinical question. Previous work has demonstrated that clinicians can easily acquire these skills,[1,2] and modern electronic methods for searching the medical literature have made it even easier.[3]

First, it is important to define the clinical question of interest, ideally in specific measurable terms: What type(s) of patients are involved? Are they men or women, young or old, with a specific diagnosis or multiple diagnoses? What aspect of surgical management is in question? Does it relate to a therapeutic choice, a diagnostic dilemma, or another issue such as prognosis? What is the time frame for the patient's problem? Is it a short-term or long-term management issue? Defining the question as specifically as possible will make it easier to search for relevant evidence and will increase the likelihood of finding a useful answer to the question.

Once the clinical question is clearly defined, it is necessary to translate it into a statement that can be used to search the literature.[4] It is usually most efficient to search the literature electronically, and the premier electronic database of medical literature, MEDLINE, is available on the Internet free of charge, courtesy of the U.S. National Library of Medicine (NLM). In some locations, such as academic medical centers, other electronic databases of medical literature may be available, but MEDLINE should meet the needs of almost all clinicians. To create a search statement, one identifies the important key words or phrases in the clinical question. One then finds an appropriate NLM medical subject heading (MeSH) for each key word or phrase, using the available search software or the NLM's published list of MeSH terms.[5] Most search software give the user the option of expanding an MeSH term to include all related terms or narrowing it to a specific subset of terms. Most also give the option of limiting the search to articles that have a selected MeSH term as a major topic. A well-defined clinical question helps one decide which options to choose. Sometimes, there is no MeSH term for a particular key word or phrase, in which case it is necessary to use the key word in the final search. Once the best search terms are identified, they should be assembled into a search statement, using the Boolean operator "and" to link two or more terms if searching for articles that contain all terms as an MeSH (or key word), and using the Boolean operator "or" to link terms if searching for articles that contain any one of the terms as an MeSH (or key word).

For most common clinical questions, the initial search will yield far more articles than a busy clinician could ever read. Thus, it usually is necessary to limit the search by applying certain filters. This can be done by limiting the search to articles that have been published recently, that are in the clinician's native language, and that refer to human subjects. When there are too many articles to consider even after applying such filters, it may help to limit the search to recent review articles (see Evaluation of Integrative Articles, for how to evaluate review articles). Alternatively, it can be useful to limit the search to articles that have the strongest study design for the type of question being addressed (see Other Types of Original Studies). For example, when searching for articles relevant to a therapeutic question, the search could be limited to randomized clinical trials.[6] When searching for articles on the prognosis of a condition, the search can be limited to cohort studies.[7] For other questions, it may be impossible to limit the search to a particular study design, but there are terms that can be used to narrow the literature search. When searching for articles relevant to a diagnostic question, the search should be limited to articles that have MeSH subheadings that deal with diagnosis or that have "sensitivity" as a textword.[8] When searching for articles on the etiology of a condition, the search should be limited to articles that have "risk" as a key word.[9] By using such filters, a clinician generally should be able to identify a manageable number of articles pertinent to the clinical question.

APPLICATION OF RULES OF EVIDENCE TO EVALUATE LITERATURE

To properly interpret articles relevant to patient care, it is necessary to understand and apply certain rules of evidence.[10] Whether a clinician is reading an article derived from a targeted search of the literature or simply reading an article in a journal to which he or she subscribes, a systematic yet efficient approach to applying rules of evidence should be used when evaluating an article. Fortunately, such an approach has been developed and disseminated by the international Evidence-Based Medicine Working Group, which has published a series of articles on how to translate the results of medical research into clinical practice.[11–29] These "Users' Guides to the Medical Literature" provide a practical framework for evaluating articles relevant to clinical questions. They were written to help busy clinicians who want to provide effective up-to-date medical care but who have very limited time for reading.[11]

The Users' Guides to the Medical Literature are built around three fundamental questions:[11]

1. Are the results of the study valid?
2. What are the results?
3. Will the results help me in caring for my patients?

The first question emphasizes the need to consider the methodologic strengths and weaknesses of each study, recognizing that no study is perfect. The second question highlights the need to clearly articulate the main findings of a study. The third question points to the need to make decisions for patients with particular characteristics and problems. Unfortunately, the answers to these fundamental questions may not be simple because the evidence is rarely black-and-white. By answering these questions, however, a clinician can better understand the nature of the evidence supporting particular management strategies and can thereby make sound clinical decisions based on the best available evidence.

To answer the fundamental questions, it helps to first consider the type of study being evaluated. Is it an *original study* that refers to therapy, diagnosis, prognosis, etiology, health care utilization, outcome variation, quality of life, or costs? Or is it an *integrative study* that provides a systematic review of a topic or that presents a practice guideline or decision analysis? For each type of study, the Users' Guides to the Medical Literature provide more specific questions for each of the fundamental questions. These more specific questions are discussed in the following two sections.

Evaluation of Original Studies

In many cases, a literature search will reveal a number of original studies that address the clinical question. Often the clinician will want to be familiar with the classic studies as well

Table 13–1 Users' Guides for Selecting Articles Most Likely to Provide Valid Results

Subject	Screening Criteria
	Original Studies
Therapy	Was the assignment of patients to treatments randomized?
	Were all of the patients who entered the trial properly accounted for and attributed at its conclusion?
Diagnosis	Was there an independent, blind comparison with a reference standard?
	Did the patient sample include an appropriate spectrum of the sort of patients to whom the diagnostic test will be applied in clinical practice?
Harm	Were there clearly identified comparison groups that were similar with respect to important determinants of outcome (other than the ones of interest)?
	Were outcomes and exposures measured in the same way in the groups being compared?
Prognosis	Was there a representative patient sample at a well defined point in the course of disease?
	Was follow-up sufficiently long and complete?
	Integrative Studies
Overview	Did the review address a clearly focused question?
	Were appropriate criteria used to select articles for inclusion?*
Practice guidelines	Were options and outcomes clearly specified?
	Did the guideline use an explicit process to identify, select and combine evidence?*
Decision analysis	Did the analysis faithfully model a clinically important decision?
	Was valid evidence used to develop the baseline probabilities and utilities?*

Modified and printed with permission from American Medical Association. JAMA 1993;270(17):2094.

* Each of these guides makes implicit or explicit reference to investigators' need to evaluate the validity of the original studies. The criteria used for evaluation depend on the subject (therapy, diagnosis, prognosis, or harm) and are presented in the table under Original Studies.

as the most recent studies on the topic. However, when time for reading and evaluating studies is limited, the clinician must choose which studies to examine first. It may be best to start with the most recent study because it is most likely to reflect any changes in management that have occurred over the years, and it is likely to refer to previous studies in its discussion section. However, the most recent study is not necessarily the strongest study. For that reason, it is wise to have some simple screening criteria for limiting in-depth reading to articles that at least pass basic tests of validity. Simple guides for selecting such articles are shown in Table 13–1.[11]

As Table 13–1 shows, the key questions about validity vary according to the type of study; indeed, there are specific questions to consider for each type of study. The questions that pertain to the most common types of studies are described below.

Studies about Treatment

Especially in surgical practice, the questions that arise most often relate to choice of treatment. For studies of treatment, the gold standard study design is the randomized controlled trial. Although many high-quality randomized controlled trials have been performed to assess surgical procedures and practices,[30–35] it is unrealistic to expect there will ever be enough randomized controlled trials to address all the important questions encountered in surgical practice.[36] Notably, one study on whether surgical practice is evidence-based found that 95 percent of surgical patients received treatment based on satisfactory evidence, but only 24 percent of patients received treatments based on evidence, from a randomized controlled trial.[37] This compares to a study of general medical treatments that found that only 82 percent of treatments were evidence-based but 53 percent were based on randomized controlled trials.[38] The difference in the percentage of treatment decisions supported by randomized controlled trials can be explained by the fact that the practical difficulties of conducting a randomized controlled trial of a surgical procedure are greater than those encountered with most medical treatments.[36,37,39] Conducting surgical trials can be difficult because standardizing a complex operation can be challenging, performance of surgeons may vary widely, surgical technique may need to be modified for particular patients, and both patients and surgeons may have strong preferences when given a treatment choice for a surgical problem. In addition, difficulties arise from the need to account for rapidly changing technology and the learning curves associated with new procedures. Thus, evidence-based surgery requires attention to different types of study designs and not just to randomized controlled trials. Even case series, such as the Southern Surgeons Club's analysis of 1,518 laparoscopic cholecystectomies,[40] can provide valuable observational information that can lead to better clinical decisions.[41]

The first screening criterion shown in Table 13–1 for articles on therapy, then, should thus apply only to the small percentage of therapeutic questions addressed by randomized controlled trials. For all other therapeutic questions, it will be necessary to examine other types of study designs such as nonrandomized controlled studies, cohort studies with historical controls, and even case series.

In these study designs, the first screening criterion cannot be met, but the second screening criterion can be met. Patients who entered the study should be properly accounted for at the conclusion of the study regardless of the study design. This means that the article should provide information about the completeness of follow-up and the status of all enrolled patients at the end of the study. The more patients that are lost to follow-up, the greater is the concern that not all adverse events have been captured. If the main adverse events are relatively rare, even a small number of patients lost to follow-up could significantly influence the results. Indeed, adverse events such as death may even lead to loss from follow-up if systematic methods for achieving complete follow-up are not used. Proper accounting of all patients enrolled in a study also calls for analyzing patients in the groups to which they were assigned upon enrollment, in a so-called "intention-to-treat" analysis. It is expected in many surgical trials that some patients will need to cross over from the treatment they were originally assigned to another treatment. The presence of many crossovers does not necessarily invalidate the study but may introduce a degree of bias into the study if high-risk patients tend to cross over from one treatment to the other. A large number of crossovers also may make it more difficult to find differences between treatments. The most thorough way to analyze data in such cases is to report the results using both an intention-to-treat analysis and an analysis by treatment actually received.

If neither of the first two key guides is met, there is reason to be concerned about the validity of the study results. That does not mean the study has no useful results. Depending on whether stronger studies are available, the clinician may still want to examine the study to see if there are results that would provide guidance in the care of patients.

Table 13–2 Users' Guides for an Article about Therapy

Are the results of the study valid?

Primary guides

> Was the assignment of patients to treatments randomized?

> Were all patients who entered the trial properly accounted for and attributed at its conclusion?

> Was follow-up complete?

> Were patients analyzed in the groups to which they were assigned?

Secondary guides

> Were patients, health workers, and study personnel blind to treatment?

> Were the groups similar at the start of the trial?

> Aside from experimental intervention, were the groups treated equally?

What were the results?

> How large was the treatment effect?

> How precise was the estimate of the treatment effect?

Will the results help me in caring for my patients?

> Can the results be applied to my patient care?

> Were all clinically important outcomes considered?

> Are the likely treatment benefits worth the potential harms and costs?

Modified and printed with permission from American Medical Association. JAMA 1994;271(1):60 (Table 1).

If the clinician wishes to learn more about the study after considering the two key guides about validity, there are additional questions about the validity of the study which are listed in Table 13–2.[12,13] The question about blinding patients, health workers, and study personnel is important because the absence of blinding at any one of these levels can introduce bias into a study. In medical studies, patients may behave and report symptoms differently depending on whether they do or do not know what treatment they have been given. Also, health workers may give more or less attention to one study group than another if they know what treatment each has been given. Practically speaking, it usually is not possible to blind patients and health workers in studies that compare a surgical procedure to nonsurgical treatment or no treatment although sham procedures have been occasionally performed to keep patients blind to their assigned treatment. In one study comparing laparoscopic and small-incision chole-cystectomy, the nurses providing postoperative care were kept blinded to treatment assignment through the use of identical wound dressings.[31] When blinding of patients and health workers is not possible, the reader should look for evidence that the investigators blinded the study personnel responsible for assessing and analyzing the outcomes in the study groups. For example, in the above-mentioned trial of laparoscopic versus small-incision cholecystectomy, postoperative interview data were collected by a research nurse who was unaware of which operation was performed.[31] Blinding of the study personnel helps assure equal efforts ascertaining the outcomes in all study groups. This is particularly important for subjective outcomes, such as ratings of symptoms, that could be susceptible to bias on the part of the evaluators. However, even an objective outcome such as myocardial infarction can be susceptible to bias if the evaluators do not make equal efforts to look for evidence of the outcome in each study group. In most cases, the absence of blinding will not invalidate the study, but the reader should be aware of the possibility that some degree of bias was introduced thereby.

The next question to consider is whether the study groups being compared were similar at the start of the study. This requires consideration of the demographic and clinical characteristics expected to influence the outcomes of interest. In general, studies should report how the study groups compare in age, gender, severity of the main disease, and comorbidity. The American Society of Anesthesiologists' physical status classification, for example, provides a convenient measure of comorbidity and severity of illness that can be used to compare groups in a surgical study.[42] Randomization does not guarantee that study groups will be similar, so this question applies to randomized as well as nonrandomized controlled clinical trials. The question is particularly important for surgical studies that use a historical control group or a control group drawn from a different population of patients. If the groups are not similar, the reader should consider how the differences would be expected to influence the results when making a final judgment about the overall validity of the study.

The last question about the study's validity is whether the groups were treated equally with respect to all potential co-interventions other than the main intervention of interest. For surgical studies, this requires considering all aspects of pre-, intra-, and postoperative care that could influence patient outcomes. If two surgical procedures are being compared, did patients in both groups receive a comparable preoperative evaluation? Did they receive the same intraoperative anesthesia care? Was their postoperative care similar? The answers to such questions will help the reader determine whether any reported differences in outcomes between study groups are likely to be due to the main intervention of interest or to some combination of factors in the patients' overall care.

If the answers to the questions about the validity of a study indicate that the results are reasonably valid, the next task is to review the results. In reviewing the results, it is helpful to consider the two specific questions shown in Table 13–2 concerning the magnitude and precision of the treatment effect. The magnitude of the treatment effect obviously is important and requires consideration of both the absolute and relative differences in outcomes between study groups. For adverse outcomes that occur infrequently, there may be only a small absolute difference between treatment groups even when there is a large relative difference. The precision of the estimate of the treatment effect also is important because it enables the clinician to estimate the percentage of patients that may achieve a given degree of benefit from one treatment over another. The best way to determine the precision of an estimated treatment effect is to examine the 95 percent confidence interval associated with each outcome measure. Unfortunately, many studies report the statistical significance of study results in terms of a p-value without providing the corresponding confidence intervals. This makes it more difficult for clinicians to understand the range of effect likely to be derived from a given treatment. On the other hand, a narrow confidence interval should increase the clinician's confidence that a given treatment will produce a given degree of benefit whereas a wide confidence interval decreases that confidence. Careful consideration of both precision and magnitude of treatment effects should enable the clinician to inform patients about the potential benefits of one treatment approach versus another.

If the study is valid, and the results indicate a reasonable treatment effect, the last task is to determine whether the results should be applied to the care of individual patients. To determine this, it is helpful to consider the last three questions in Table 13–2. The first of these questions requires examination of the study's eligibility criteria and the characteristics of the study population compared to the characteristics of the clinician's patients, considering factors such as age, gender, race, education, and clinical features of their disease. In some cases, the clinician should be cautious in applying the results because his or her patients are very different from the study population. It is important also to determine whether the study reported on all clinically important outcomes, which generally should include surgical complications and mortality from all causes in addition to other outcomes of interest. If information on relevant outcomes is missing, the clinician must rely on clinical judgment to estimate the effect of treatment on the missing outcome measures before applying the results to the care of patients. The last question emphasizes explicitly considering the trade-offs among benefits, risks, and costs inherent to most treatment decisions. Although studies may not report on all the risks and costs of alternative treatments, the clinician should at least consider whether the magnitude of the benefits justify the expected risks and costs of treatment.

Studies about Diagnosis

An evidence-based approach to surgical practice depends not only on knowledge of studies about treatment choices but also on knowledge of studies about the diagnosis of problems that may require surgery. An understanding of how to evaluate and apply the results of studies on diagnostic tests can be gained by considering the questions in Table 13–3.[14,15]

The first task is to determine whether the results of a study about a diagnostic test or diagnostic strategy are valid. The two most important considerations in this regard are whether there is an independent, blind comparison to an appropriate reference standard and whether the patient sample includes an appropriate spectrum of patients in whom the diagnostic test(s) might be used.

In studies of a diagnostic test for a surgical problem, surgical pathology results can provide an ideal gold standard. In many cases, however, other reference standards need to be used, such as long-term follow-up results. The reader must decide whether the chosen reference standard is reasonable. If the standard is not reasonable, it is unlikely that the study will provide useful information. If the standard is reasonable, then the reader must consider how the diagnostic test was compared to the reference standard. A rigorous study of a diagnostic test should ensure that the test is interpreted independently by clinicians or technicians who do not know the status of the reference standard so that they are not biased in their use of the test. An independent, blinded assessment of the test helps avoid overestimating the test's accuracy.

The second question is important because a test is only useful to clinicians if they know how it performs in an appropriate spectrum of patients. Thus, the reader should consider whether the test has been evaluated in a group of patients that represents the full spectrum of patients seen in clinical practice. Ideally, this should include patients with varying manifestations and severity of disease as well as patients with conditions that are often confused with the disease of interest. For example, investigators eventually determined that carcinoembryonic antigen (CEA) levels were not useful in diagnosing colorectal cancer because CEA levels often were elevated in patients with other types of cancer and gastrointestinal disorders but were not elevated in many patients with less advanced stages of colorectal cancer.[14]

If the answers to these first two questions indicate that the study is likely to be valid and useful, the reader should consider two additional questions. To avoid introducing verification bias,[43] the results of the test being evaluated should not influence the decision to perform the reference standard because this would confound the comparison of the test to the standard. In order to be able to use the test, the clinician must also determine whether the study provided enough detail about the methods for performing the test. Without this information, there is reason to question the usefulness and validity of the study.

For studies that seem valid, the next task according to Table 13–3 is to review the results to determine how well the diagnostic test identifies the target disorder. One of the best ways to assess the accuracy of a diagnostic test is to determine whether a likelihood ratio is presented for each possible test result. Likelihood ratios are helpful because they indicate how much a given test result would raise or lower the pre-test probability of a disorder and because they can be derived for tests that have more than two possible results. Likelihood ratios greater

---

Table 13–3 Users' Guides for Evaluating and Applying Results of Studies of Diagnostic Tests

---

Are the results of the study valid?

Primary guides

    Was there an independent, blind comparison with a reference standard?

    Did the patient sample include an appropriate spectrum of patients to whom the diagnostic test will be applied in clinical practice?

Secondary guides

    Did the results of the test being evaluated influence the decision to perform the reference standard?

    Were the methods for performing the test described in sufficient detail to permit replication?

What were the results?

    Are likelihood ratios for the test results presented or are data necessary for calculation of likelihood ratios provided?

Will the results help me in caring for my patients?

    Will the reproducibility of the test result and its interpretation be satisfactory in my setting?

    Are the results applicable to my patients?

    Will the results change my management?

    Will patients be better off as a result of the test?

Modified and printed with permission from American Medical Association. JAMA 1994;271(5):390 (Table 1).

---

than one increase the probability that the target disorder is present, while likelihood ratios less than one decrease the probability of the disorder. The nomogram shown in Figure 13–1 provides a simple way to estimate the post-test probability of disease from the likelihood ratio and pre-test probability of disease. This nomogram is easier to use than performing the calculations in your head, which requires converting the pre-test probability (p) to odds (defined as $p/[1\text{-}p]$), multiplying by the likelihood ratio, and then converting the post-test odds back to a probability [odds/odds + 1]).[15]

To determine whether the results of a study about a test will help a surgeon care for his/her patients, there are four questions to consider (see Table 13–3). The question about the reproducibility of a test depends partly on whether there are important variations in technical aspects of the test or whether the test requires a skilled interpreter. If either situation applies, the surgeon may find that a test will not perform as well as reported in the study. The question about applicability of a study to a surgeon's own patients requires determining whether the surgeon's patients are similar enough to the patients described in the study. The question about whether the results will change patient management calls for the clinician to think about his or her threshold for treatment or further testing or both and to determine whether test results may change the clinical suspicion of disease enough to cross a threshold for treatment or further testing. A related issue is whether the patient will be better off as a result of using the test. This requires consideration of any risks and costs associated with the test in addition to treatment benefits that may result from establishing a diagnosis.

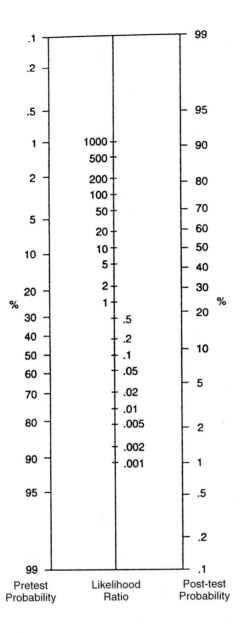

Figure 13–1 Nomogram for interpreting diagnostic test results. Printed with permission from JAMA 1994;271(9):705. Copyright 1994, American Medical Association.

Other Types of Original Studies

A similar approach can be applied to other types of original studies, for which key questions are listed in Table 13–1.

Studies about the prognosis of a disease have an important role in an evidence-based approach to surgical practice because treatment decisions often depend on what a patient's prognosis would be without surgical treatment. For example, decisions about lung volume reduction surgery depend on knowledge of the prognosis of patients with severe emphysema.[44] For studies about the prognosis of a disease, the first key question is whether the sample of patients included in the study is representative of all patients with the disease, including those who are at different points in the course of the disease. In a trial of intermittent positive pressure breathing that provided valuable information about the prognosis of patients with chronic obstructive pulmonary disease, a wide spectrum of patients with the disease were enrolled that excluded only patients with chronic hypoxemia.[45,46] This study therefore provides reasonably representative information on the prognosis of patients with chronic obstructive pulmonary disease and could help guide decisions about the use of lung volume reduction surgery. The second key question for studies about prognosis is whether follow-up was long enough and thorough enough to capture all important outcomes.[17] The trial of intermittent positive pressure breathing mentioned above met this criterion by following 985 patients for nearly 3 years.[45]

When interpreting studies that focus on short- or long-term complications associated with surgical procedures, it can help to refer to guides for appraising studies about the harmful potential of an exposure.[16] For these studies, the first key question is whether there were clearly identified comparison groups that were similar in respect to other important determinants of outcome. In one study of risk factors for permanent hypoparathyroidism after thyroidectomy, investigators found that the incidence of persistent postoperative hypoparathyroidism differed by surgeon's specialty.[47] To interpret this finding, it is necessary to assess how the patients treated by different types of surgeons differed in other important determinants of outcome, such as principal diagnosis and comorbidity. Another question is whether outcomes and exposures were measured in the same way in each group.[16]

There are many studies in the surgical literature that use an observational design to examine sources of variation in patients' outcomes. In evaluating these studies, there are three key questions to ask: (1) Are the outcome measures accurate and comprehensive? (2) Are there clearly identified, sensible comparison groups? and (3) Are the comparison groups similar in respect to important determinants of outcome other than the one of interest?[24] The reader should look for evidence that the outcome measures are reasonably accurate and should consider whether important outcome measures are missing. The reader also should determine whether the study used appropriate comparison groups and whether these groups are similar in respect to important determinants of outcome. If these criteria are not met, the results of the study should be interpreted with caution. These questions can be helpful in understanding the limitations of studies that examine how surgical treatment outcomes differ according to the characteristics of providers.[48–51]

For studies that seek to assess the quality of care, including the use of health care services, a few key tasks are outlined in the Users' Guide on how to use an article about a clinical utilization review.[25] The first task is to determine whether the study used valid criteria in assessing the quality of care and/or the utilization of services. This requires consideration of whether the study used an explicit and sensible process to identify, select, and combine evidence for the criteria.[25] Another task is to determine whether the study applied the review criteria appropriately. This requires an assessment of whether the study demonstrated that the criteria were applied in a reliable and unbiased manner. The last task is to determine whether the review criteria could be applied in the clinician's own practice setting. This is most likely if the review criteria have been shown to be feasible in diverse practice settings.

Studies about health-related quality of life can be important in surgical decision making whenever quality of life is a major consideration in choosing among treatment options. There are two key questions that can be used to judge the validity of these studies.[26] The first is whether the study measured the aspects of life that patients consider most important. The second question is whether the instruments used to measure quality of life actually worked in the way they were supposed to. The answer to the latter question depends on whatever information the study presents about the reproducibility, responsiveness, and validity of the instruments.

Studies about the costs of surgical treatment have increased with the increasing demand for information about how to control health care costs. To interpret articles with economic analyses, begin by considering whether the results are likely to be valid. This can be determined by asking a few key questions.[27] The first question is whether the analysis provided a full comparison of both the costs and outcomes of all relevant health care strategies. The second question to ask is whether the costs and outcomes were properly measured and valued, keeping in mind that there are many ways to estimate costs. In such studies, it is critical to define the economic perspective of the analysis so that the reader knows whether the results refer to costs borne by patients, providers, insurers, or the society at large.

Additional questions about these and other types of original studies are discussed in the Users' Guides to the Medical Literature,[16,17,24–28] but the key questions usually suffice for identifying the studies most likely to provide valid and useful information for clinicians.

Evaluation of Integrative Articles

Although the practice of evidence-based surgery depends on critical evaluation of original studies, it is unrealistic to expect clinicians to keep up with the tremendous volume of original studies that appear in the literature. One way to deal with this problem is to read articles that integrate results from multiple studies. Integrative articles such as reviews, practice guidelines, and decision analyses can be valuable to a busy clinician because they provide efficient access to a large amount of information on a particular topic, particularly when there are a lot of original studies on the topic or when there are conflicting studies. Integrative articles are limited: they rapidly become out-of-date, they depend on the quality of the original studies, and they depend on the quality of the integration. Therefore, clinicians must be able to critically evaluate integrative articles to use the information contained in them appropriately.

Review Articles and Meta-analyses

In the last 10 to 20 years, review articles have evolved considerably as new methods have been developed for conducting reviews and as clinicians have gained more understanding of the biases that can be introduced when a systematic approach to literature reviewing is not used. The most rigorous review article is the meta-analysis, which combines a systematic identification of pertinent studies with a quantitative synthesis of the information contained in the studies.

In identifying review articles most likely to provide unbiased information, there are two key questions to consider:[18] (1) Did the review address a clearly focused question? (2) Were appropriate criteria used to select articles for inclusion? The first question is important because a review is unlikely to provide the specific information that a clinician needs if the author has not clearly defined the questions that are the subject of the review. In addition, the lack of clearly defined questions makes it difficult for the author to ensure that all pertinent literature has been identified and reviewed. Since the literature often includes multiple reviews on a topic, the reader's time is best spent with a review that starts with a clear definition of the questions being addressed. The second question is important because the review's validity and usefulness depend on inclusion of all pertinent studies. The reader should look for a description of the criteria used to select articles for inclusion and should consider whether the criteria fit the questions being addressed. Many journals now require review articles to have a systematic approach to identifying relevant studies because it helps minimize the biases that can be introduced by a selective review of the literature. An example of a review article that meets these two criteria is a review that focused on the effects of pharmacologic therapy, percutaneous transluminal angioplasty, and coronary artery bypass graft surgery in patients with chronic stable angina.[52] In this review, studies were identified by a systematic search of the MEDLINE database supplemented by a review of abstracts from meetings of the American Heart Association and the American College of Cardiology and a review of bibliographies of relevant studies. Studies were selected for inclusion if they were randomized controlled trials or meta-analyses that addressed the question of interest.

Other questions to consider in assessing the validity of a review article are as follows:[18] (1) Is it likely that important, relevant studies were missed? (2) Was the validity of the included studies assessed? (3) Were assessments of the studies reproducible? (4) Were the results similar from study to study?

If the review article has met most of these criteria, the results are likely to be unbiased, and the next task is to review the results and to determine whether they can provide guidance in the care of patients. This requires consideration of whether the information in the review applies to the types of patients seen by the clinician, whether all relevant outcomes were reviewed, and whether the conclusions about reported benefits account for potential harm and costs.

Practice Guidelines

One type of integrative article that has grown greatly in the last 10 years is the practice guideline. Although guidelines often elicit negative reactions from clinicians, there is increasing recognition of their value in surgical practice.[53] Most practice guidelines include a review of pertinent evidence derived from original studies and expert opinions. However, methods for preparing practice guidelines vary dramatically. Thus, it is important for clinicians to be able to critically evaluate the practice guidelines that apply to their area of practice.

When determining whether the recommendations in a guideline are valid, there are several questions to consider.[21,22] The first question to ask is whether all relevant management options and outcomes were clearly specified. For example, in evaluating guidelines for the management of early breast cancer, it is important to identify the specific surgical procedures and adjuvant therapies that were considered and to determine the specific outcomes that were considered, such as disease-free survival, overall survival, and procedure complications. The second question to ask is whether there was an explicit process for identifying, selecting, and combining the evidence on which the recommendations were based. This requires consideration of not only how pertinent literature was identified and synthesized but also how expert opinions were obtained and incorporated into the process.

If the answers to these two key questions indicate that the guideline is likely to be valid, there are still other questions to consider:[21,22] Was an explicit process used to consider the relative value of different outcomes? Can the guideline account for important recent developments? Has the guideline been subject to peer review and testing?

If the answers to all these questions indicate that the guideline is valid, the next step is to review the recommendations, keeping in mind three questions:[21,22] Are practical, clinically important recommendations made? (2) How strong are the recommendations? (3) What is the impact of uncertainty associated with the evidence and values used in the guideline?

The last task in evaluating a guideline is to determine whether it will help clinicians care for their own patients. Here, the clinicians must ask whether the primary objective of the guideline is consistent with their own objectives. This requires an assessment of how much the guideline is intended to reduce health care costs or improve quality of care. It also is important to determine whether the recommendations are applicable to all patients with the problem of interest or only a subset of these patients.

Decision Analyses

One other type of integrative article that is also increasing in frequency is based on decision analysis. Decision analysis generally includes a systematic review of evidence pertinent to a clinical decision and incorporates that evidence into a decision tree or model that projects outcomes expected to be associated with alternative management strategies. Like any other integrative study, a decision analysis depends on the availability and quality of information from original studies and experts as well as the skill of the decision analyst. A major strength of decision analysis is that it provides an explicit way to synthesize information from a variety of sources and formulate recommendations that can guide clinical decision making when the decisions involve complex trade-offs among benefits, risks, and costs. However, to use the information in a decision analysis most effectively, the clinician must be able to critically evaluate the analytic methods used.

The first consideration when evaluating a decision analysis is whether the analysis faithfully modeled a clinically important question.[19,20] This requires determining whether the analysis defined the question appropriately and whether the analysis included all relevant management strategies and all relevant outcomes. The second consideration is whether valid evidence was used to develop the input for the decision analysis. This requires consideration of the source of all parameter estimates included in the decision model, including the probabilities of specific outcomes associated with each management strategy, the utility values associated with the outcomes of different management strategies, and the costs of alternative management strategies. Other questions to consider in assessing the validity of a decision analysis are whether the utility values were obtained in an explicit and sensible way and whether a sensitivity analysis was performed to estimate the potential impact of uncertainty in the parameter estimates.

Proper interpretation of the results of a decision analysis requires examining the baseline analysis and determining whether one strategy is projected to yield clinically important benefits for patients. The clinician should then ask about the strength of the evidence used in the analysis and whether uncertainty in the evidence could change the results.

To decide whether the results of the decision analysis could help in the care of patients, the clinician should ask whether the probability estimates used in the analysis are consistent with the characteristics of his or her patients. The clinician also should consider whether the utility values used in the analysis are consistent with how these patients would view the potential outcomes.

REFERENCES

1. Haynes RB, McKibbon KA, Fitzgerald D, et al. How to keep up with the medical literature. V: Access by personal computer to the medical literature. Ann Intern Med 1986;105:810–14.

2. Haynes RB, McKibbon KA, Walker CJ, et al. Online access to MEDLINE in clinical settings: a study of use and usefulness. Ann Intern Med 1990;112:78–84.

3. McKibbon KA. Beyond ACP Journal Club: how to harness MEDLINE to solve clinical problems. ACP Journal Club 1994;120(Suppl 2):A10–12.

4. Dwyer C. Pointers for making the most of your Medline searches. ACP Observer 1997 Oct:9.

5. National Library of Medicine, National Institutes of Health. Medical Subject Headings—Annotated Alphabetic List. Bethesda (MD): National Technical Information Service, U.S. Department of Commerce; 1998.

6. McKibbon KA, Walker-Dilks CJ. Beyond ACP Journal Club: how to harness MEDLINE for therapy problems. ACP Journal Club 1994;121(Suppl 1):A10–12.

7. McKibbon KA, Walker-Dilks CJ, Haynes RB, Wilczynski N. Beyond ACP Journal Club: how to harness MEDLINE for prognosis problems. ACP Journal Club 1995 123(1): A12–A14.

8. McKibbon KA, Walker-Dilks CJ. Beyond ACP Journal Club: how to harness MEDLINE for diagnostic problems. ACP Journal Club 1994;121(Suppl 2):A10–12.

9. Walker-Dilks CJ, McKibbon KA, Haynes RB. Beyond ACP Journal Club: how to harness MEDLINE for etiology problems. ACP Journal Club 1994;121(Suppl 3):A10–11.

10. Evidence-Based Medicine Working Group. Evidence-based medicine. A new approach to teaching the practice of medicine. JAMA 1992;268:2420–5.

11. Oxman AD, Sackett DL, Guyatt GH, for the Evidence-Based Medicine Working Group. Users' guides to the medical literature. I. How to get started. JAMA 1993;270:2093–5.

12. Guyatt GH, Sackett DL, Cook DJ, for the Evidence-Based Medicine Working Group. Users' guides to the medical literature. II. How to use an article about therapy or prevention. A. Are the results of the study valid? JAMA 1993;270:2598–2601.

13. Guyatt GH, Sackett DL, Cook DJ, for the Evidence-Based Medicine Working Group. Users' guides to the medical literature. II. How to use an article about therapy or prevention. B. What were the results and will they help me in caring for my patients? JAMA 1994;271:59–63.

14. Jaeschke R, Guyatt GH, Sackett DL, for the Evidence-Based Medicine Working Group. Users' guides to the medical literature. III. How to use an article about a diagnostic test. A. Are the results of the study valid? JAMA 1994;271:389–91.

15. Jaeschke R, Guyatt GH, Sackett DL, for the Evidence-Based Medicine Working Group. Users' guides to the medical literature. III. How to use an article about a diagnostic test. B. What are the results and will they help me in caring for my patients? JAMA 1994;271:703–7.

16. Levine M, Walter S, Lee H, et al., for the Evidence-Based Medicine Working Group. Users' guides to the medical literature. IV. How to use an article about harm. JAMA 1994;271:1615–19.

17. Laupacis A, Wells G, Richardson WS, Tugwell P, for the Evidence-Based Medicine Working Group. Users' guides to the medical literature. V. How to use an article about prognosis. JAMA 1994;272:234–7.

18. Oxman AD, Cook DJ, Guyatt GH, for the Evidence-Based Medicine Working Group. Users' guides to the medical literature. VI. How to use an overview. JAMA 1994;272:1367–71.

19. Richardson WS, Detsky AS, for the Evidence-Based Medicine Working Group. Users' guides to the medical literature. VII. How to use a clinical decision analysis. A. Are the results of the study valid? JAMA 1995;273:1292–5.

20. Richardson WS, Detsky AS, for the Evidence-Based Medicine Working Group. Users' guides to the medical literature. VII. How to use a clinical decision analysis. B. What are the results and will they help me in caring for my patients? JAMA 1995;273:1610–13.

21. Hayward R, Wilson M, Tunis S, et al, for the Evidence-Based Medicine Working Group. Users' guides to the medical literature: VIII. How to use clinical practice guidelines. A. Are the recommendations valid? JAMA 1995;274:570–4.

22. Hayward R, Wilson M, Tunis S, et al, for the Evidence-Based Medicine Working Group. Users' guides to the medical literature: VIII. How to use clinical practice guidelines. B. What are the recommendations, and will they help you in caring for your patients? JAMA 1995;274:1630–2.

23. Guyatt GH, Sackett DL, Sinclair JC, et al, for the Evidence-Based Medicine Working Group. Users' guides to the medical literature. IX. A method for grading health care recommendations. JAMA 1995;274:1800–4.

24. Naylor CD, Guyatt GH, for the Evidence-Based Medicine Working Group. Users' guides to the medical literature. X. How to use an article reporting variations in the outcomes of health services. JAMA 1996;275:554–8.

25. Naylor CD, Guyatt GH, for the Evidence-Based Medicine Working Group. Users' guides to the medical literature. XI. How to use an article about a clinical utilization review. JAMA 1996;275:1435–9.

26. Guyatt GH, Naylor CD, Juniper E, et al, for the Evidence-Based Medicine Working Group. Users' guides to the medical literature. XII. How to use articles about health-related quality of life. JAMA 1997;277:1232–7.

27. Drummond MF, Richardson WS, O'Brien BJ, et al, for the Evidence-Based Medicine Working Group. Users' guides to the medical literature. XIII. How to use an article on economic analysis of clinical practice. A. Are the results of the study valid? JAMA 1997;277:1552–7.

28. O'Brien BJ, Heyland D, Richardson WS, et al, for the Evidence-Based Medicine Working Group. Users' guides to the medical literature. XIII. How to use an article on economic analysis of clinical practice. B. What are the results and will they help me in caring for my patients? JAMA 1997;277:1802–6.

29. Dans AL, Dans LF, Guyatt GH, Richardson S, for the Evidence-Based Medicine Working Group. Users' guides to the medical literature. XIV. How to decide on the applicability of clinical trial results to your patients. JAMA 1998;279:545–9.

30. Executive Committee for the Asymptomatic Carotid Atherosclerosis Study. Endarterectomy for asymptomatic carotid artery stenosis. JAMA 1995;273:1421–8.

31. Majeed AW, Troy G, Nicholl JP, et al. Randomized, prospective, single-blind comparison of laparoscopic versus small-incision cholecystectomy. Lancet 1996;347:989–94.

32. Fagevik Olsen M, Hahn I, Nordgren S, et al. Randomized controlled trial of prophylactic chest physiotherapy in major abdominal surgery. Br J Surg 1997;84:1535–8.

33. Merad F, Hay JM, Fingerhut A, et al. Omentoplasty in the prevention of anastomotic leakage after colonic or rectal resection. A prospective randomized study in 712 patients. Ann Surg 1998;227:179–86.

34. AbuRahma AF, Robinson PA, Saiedy S, et al. Prospective randomized trial of carotid endarterectomy with primary closure and patch angioplasty with saphenous vein, jugular vein, and polytetrafluoroethylene: long-term follow-up. J Vasc Surg 1998;27:222–34.

35. Ouriel K, Veith FJ, Sasahara AA, for the Thrombolysis or Peripheral Arterial Surgery (TOPAS) Investigators. A comparison of recombinant urokinase with vascular surgery as initial treatment for acute arterial occlusion of the legs. N Engl J Med 1998;338:1105–11.

36. Clagett GP. Presidential address: trials of the Southern Association for Vascular Surgery. J Vasc Surg 1998;28:391–6.

37. Howes N, Chagla L, Thorpe M, McCulloch P. Surgical practice is evidence based. Br J Surg 1997;84:1220–3.

38. Ellis J, Mulligan I, Rowe J, Sackett DL. Inpatient general medicine is evidence based. Lancet 1995;346:407–10.

39. Solomon MJ, McLeod RS. Should we be performing more randomized controlled trials evaluating surgical operations? Surgery 1995;118:459–67.

40. The Southern Surgeons Club. A prospective analysis of 1518 laparoscopic cholecystectomies. N Engl J Med 1991;324:1073–8.

41. Horton R. Surgical research or comic opera: questions, but few answers. Lancet 1996;347:984–5.

42. Owen WD, Felts JA, Spitznagel EL Jr, et al. ASA physical status classification: a study of consistency ratings. Anaesthesiology 1978;49:239–43.

43. Begg CB, Greenes RA. Assessment of diagnostic tests when disease verification is subject to selection bias. Biometrics 1983;39:207–15.

44. Rodarte JR. Evidence-based surgery. Mayo Clin Proc 1998;73:603–4.

45. IPPB Trial Group. Intermittent positive pressure breathing therapy of chronic obstructive pulmonary disease. Ann Intern Med 1983;99:612–20.

46. Anthonisen NR. Prognosis in chronic obstructive pulmonary disease: results from multicenter clinical trials. Am Rev Respir Dis 1989;140:S95–S99.

47. Burge MR, Zeise T, Johnsen MW, et al. Risks of complications following thyroidectomy: a retrospective study. J Gen Intern Med 1998;13:24–31.

48. Begg CB, Cramer LD, Hoskins WJ, Brennan MF. Impact of hospital volume on operative mortality for major cancer surgery. JAMA 1998;280:1747–51.

49. Hughes RG, Hunt SS, Luft HS. Effects of surgeon volume and hospital volume on quality of care in hospitals. Med Care 1987;25:489–503.

50. Gordon TA, Burleyson GP, Tielsch JM, Cameron JL. The effects of regionalization on cost and outcome for one general high-risk surgical procedure. Ann Surg 1995;221:43–9.

51. Choti MA, Bowman NM, Pitt HA, et al. Should hepatic resections be performed at high volume referral centers? J Gastrointest Surg 1998;2:11–20.

52. Solomon AJ, Gersh BJ. Management of chronic stable angina: medical therapy, percutaneous transluminal coronary angioplasty, and coronary artery bypass graft surgery. Lessons from the randomized trials. Ann Intern Med 1998;128:216–23.

53. Barraclough B. The value of surgical practice guidelines. Aust N Z J Surg 1998;68:6–9.

CHAPTER 14

Leveraging Information Technology

Peter S. Greene, MD, FACS

———⊹⊱•⊰⊹———

Widespread adoption of the World Wide Web (WWW) has raised the hope that clinicians and patients alike might have instantaneous access to high quality medical information. Desktop computers, previously limited to an information storage capacity that would fit on disks or CD-ROMs, can now be connected via the Internet to an expanding global network of databases and information repositories. This has breathed new life into the long-held hope that the clinician's job would be enhanced by the ready availability of on-line information.

There is little doubt that the Internet and other new information technologies will revolutionize the way evidence-based studies are conducted, reported, and implemented. What is less clear is how long it will take to fulfill these promises and to what extent these new resources will replace the more traditional modes of communication such as meetings of medical societies and print publishing in scholarly journals. Leveraging the full potential of information technology will require new skills and practices for investigators and publishers before clinicians can make full use of evidence-based information.

Fortunately, this information revolution is well underway. For evidence-based investigators and practitioners, major changes are occurring in three areas: (1) information gathering, (2) information dissemination, and (3) collaboration in on-line "communities."

INFORMATION GATHERING: SEARCHING THE INTERNET

Gathering information from the Internet has been compared to "trying to get a sip of water from a fire-hose, and you don't even know the quality of the water."[1] It is difficult enough for evidence-based investigators to search the entire peer-reviewed journal literature without having to expand the scope of possible evidence to all of cyberspace. Even in the pre-Web era (ie, prior to 1989), locating information on the Internet was a challenge, and a number of programs and repositories were developed to simplify the task (Table 14–1).

The Web has put a friendlier face on these resources (allowing wide area information server [WAIS] programs to run behind Web pages instead of from a command line), and new

Table 14–1 Internet-Searching Programs

Service	Function
Wide area information server (WAIS)	To locate and retrieve documents containing specified phrases
Veronica (very easy rodent-oriented net-wide index of computerized archives)	To locate Internet resources by keyword
Archie	To locate downloadable software or information in file transfer protocol (FTP) archives
Web search engines (AltaVista, Excite, InfoSeek, HotBot)	To create searchable indices by automated roaming of the Web

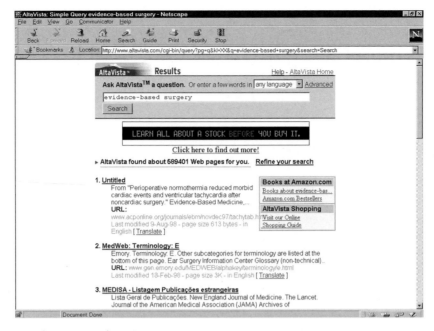

Figure 14–1 AltaVista Search Engine

search engines have been developed to address the growth of information.[2] These engines (known as "robots," "spiders," or "crawlers" for the way they automate the indexing process) require massive hardware platforms to hold and search millions of citations. The AltaVista search engine, for example, hosted by Digital Equipment Corporation, searches an archive of nearly 200 million documents (Figure 14–1).

A quick test of AltaVista demonstrates some of the problems with using Internet search engines for focused investigation of clinical problems. A search for "evidence-based surgery" returns links to 589,401 Web pages in a few seconds. Even the top-ranked pages are a heterogeneous collection of academic, commercial, and personal publications of varying quality and relevance. Many pages are out-of-date (or undated), and some appear to be disconnected from the originating Web site. Because it is often more troublesome to dismantle a Web site than to leave it accessible, there are "ghost town" sites that have been abandoned by their original developers due to lack of interest or funding.

Even if Internet search engines overcome the hardware and software challenges of hosting massive citation indices, they become dysfunctional for the user because of information overload. Search engines such as Yahoo (http://www.yahoo.com), from Santa Clara, California, are somewhat better in that there is more human input to classify, organize, and evaluate individual sites. But for busy clinicians trying to answer specific clinical questions, more focused search strategies are essential.

The MEDLINE Database

For many years, the best place to begin a hunt for clinical evidence has been medical bibliographic indices such as MEDLINE from the National Library of Medicine (NLM). This database contains citations and abstracts from approximately 3,900 current biomedical journals published in the United States and 70 foreign countries, and there are now more than 9 million records dating back to 1966. Over the past decade, the personal computing revolution has led to a desire for better personal searching, and additional interfaces such as Paper Chase and Grateful Med were introduced as tools for all researchers, not just librarians and search experts.

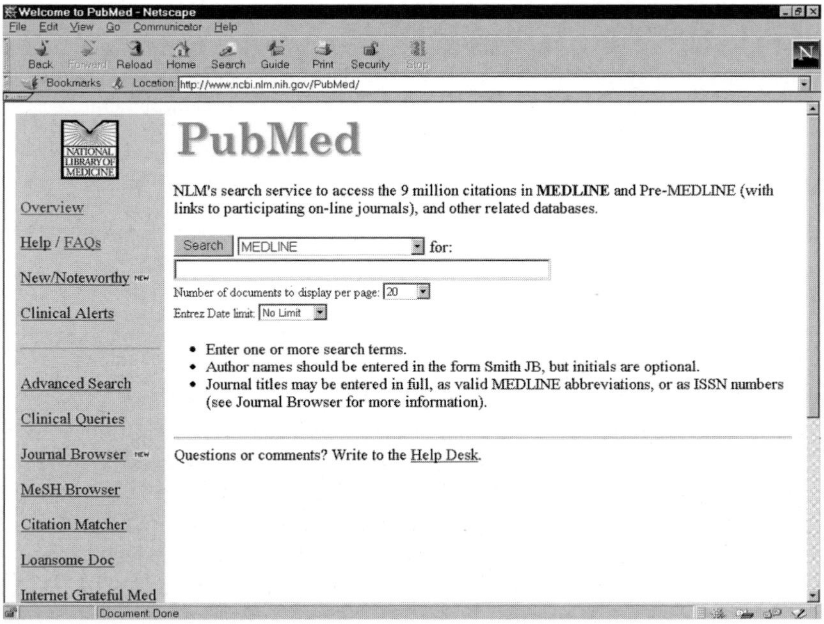

Figure 14–2 PubMed Search Engine

The latest addition to these new tools is PubMed (Figure 14–2), a free Web-based interface to MEDLINE that breaks the final barrier of the cost of on-line searching. PubMed is a project of the National Center for Biotechnology Information at the National Institutes of Health (NIH). Journal publishers supply the NLM with formatted citations prior to publication, and the NLM adds them to the PubMed search system. On-line journal publishers can also use an electronic Citation Matching service, which allows Web programs to locate electronic citations by journal, volume, and page number. This has led to widespread linking to PubMed from the reference citations in electronic journals.

However, even the friendliest Web interface does not overcome all of the difficulties faced by evidence-based researchers.[3] Full-text searching often delivers too many citations, and keyword searches miss valuable citations. Accurate and complete searches often require information-retrieval experts; even the best-delivered articles are of mixed methodology and quality and would benefit from an expert critique prior to application in a real clinical setting.

The Cochrane Library

One attempt to overcome these problems with the vast MEDLINE repository is the Cochrane Library. Named for British epidemiologist Archie Cochrane, the Cochrane Collaboration attempts to provide health care professionals with selected, organized, critiqued reviews of the available evidence for specific clinical problems.[4] This vision has been implemented by more than a dozen centers around the world that create Collaborative Review Groups (CRGs). Using specially developed software tools, systematic reviews of the literature are created and then submitted to a central database. The reviews are then distilled for electronic publication in what is called the Cochrane Library, which is available on both CD-ROM and the Internet.

The Cochrane Library's main component databases are listed in Table 14–2. Access to full-text reviews is limited to subscribers, but review abstracts are open to the general public. To reduce bias, evidence is included or excluded based upon explicit criteria developed by the Cochrane Collaboration. In many cases, data are combined into meta-analyses to increase the power of smaller studies.

Table 14–2 Resources Available in the Cochrane Library

The Cochrane Database of Systematic Reviews	Core collection of randomized trials found by searching the world's medical literature
The Database of Abstracts of Reviews of Effectiveness (DARE)	Abstracts and reviews of more than 1,200 critical articles
The Cochrane Controlled Trial Register	Registry of nearly 200,000 randomized clinical trials
Cochrane Review Methodology Database	Nearly 800 reports and critiques of methods relevant to clinical trials

The National Guideline Clearinghouse (NGC)

Another promising resource has recently become available through a joint public and private sector sponsored project called the National Guideline Clearinghouse (http://www.guideline.gov), (Figure 14–3).[5] Launched in January 1999, this Web site provides evidence-based clinical practice guidelines and related documents from a variety of sources. The project was initiated by the Agency for Health Care Policy and Research (AHCPR) in partnership with the American Medical Association (AMA) and the American Association of Health Plans (AAHP). The National Guideline Clearinghouse (NGC) includes structured summaries of guidelines with details about their authors and development, a utility for visually comparing the attributes of two or more guidelines, syntheses of guidelines covering similar topics, links to full-text guidelines, and annotated bibliographies on guideline development methodology and implementation. If properly supported, this collaborative project will likely become an important centralized repository of clinical guideline information.

INFORMATION DISSEMINATION

One postulate of evidence-based clinical care is that good data must be a part of every medical decision. But busy clinicians need assistance accessing information on a timely basis. One of the great challenges of the evidence-based movement is to have influence beyond academic

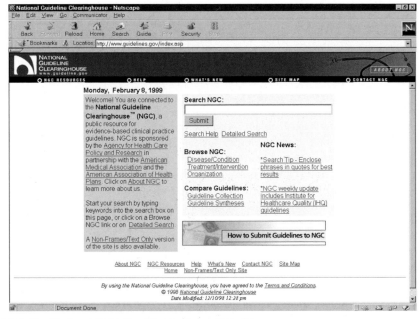

Figure 14–3 The National Guideline Clearinghouse Web Site

Table 14–3 Requirements for Getting Clinicians to Adopt Information Technology (IT) Resources

1. Make IT resources accessible to the clinician.

2. Integrate IT tools into the process of patient care.

3. Create user-friendly interfaces.

4. Overcome the "generation gap" and other sources of clinician reluctance.

5. Teach clinicians to ask clinical questions that can be answered by information systems.

6. Teach clinicians to appraise strength of evidence.

7. Overcome clinician fear of well-informed patients and publicly available resources.

medical centers. "Real-world" relevance requires putting resources in the hands of frontline health professionals where they work, or at least making resources immediately accessible to clinical wards and operating rooms.

Computer Access

Because vast bodies of information may have bearing on specific decisions, computers are necessary intermediaries for culling through large repositories. But are clinicians willing to take the time to consult computer resources? This question was studied by Sackett and Straus[6] who placed what they called "evidence carts," (computers loaded with the Cochrane Library and an array of other electronic resources) onto a busy medical ward and then studied usage patterns by clinicians. Evidence gathered from these computer consultations confirmed the appropriateness of decisions 52 percent of the time, suggested suboptimal diagnostic investigation or management 23 percent of the time, and found additional investigation or treatment necessary 25 percent of the time.

As further studies of this kind are conducted, usage and efficacy statistics will likely vary widely depending upon the complexity of clinical problems, the experience and time constraints of clinicians, the usefulness of the resources, and the usability of the software. Publishers and educators are still new to creating truly useful electronic resources, and there are many challenging requirements. (Table 14–3). One of the biggest difficulties for both resource developers and users is that it is often difficult to define the right question.[7] It is not simply a matter of teaching clinicians to use proper MEDLINE syntax but rather of training them to quickly pose questions that can be addressed by evidence in the literature so that evidence can be incorporated immediately and routinely into clinical decisions.

Electronic Libraries

Once the clinician has located useful information in abstract or review form, there is often an additional hurdle in acquiring original articles. The costs of production and distribution of print journals are typically passed on to readers in the form of subscription fees. Research libraries have served as redistribution points for papers in a rather inefficient system,[3] but even in large institutions, libraries have incomplete or relatively inaccessible journal collections. In addition to distribution costs and accessibility, the print medium is cumbersome for duplicating, archiving, and searching. The advantages of electronic journals (Table 14–4) have not been unnoticed, and in spite of many obstacles, the notion of a "library on a desktop" has begun to become a reality.[1]

Reader demand for full-text and graphics access to electronic journals has fueled rapid innovation. Several companies have become on-line journal "aggregators," intermediaries that typically re-key journal articles and then bundle them as electronic collections for libraries

Table 14–4 Advantages of Electronic Journals

Lower production cost

Minimal distribution cost

Instant accessibility

Fully searchable

Linkage to other articles

Linkage of correspondence and original articles

Linkage of electronic databases

Instant reader comments and discussions

Minimal constraint on space

Multimedia and interactivity enhancements

and other institutions. The leader in this area for biomedical journals has been Ovid Technologies (New York), which offers advanced searching packages for several core journal collections. Acquisition of a number of high-impact biomedical journals has made these collections quite useful, and Ovid has recently been expanding its journal portfolio by as many as 30 titles per month.

Another successful strategy, adopted by Stanford University Library's HighWire Press, has been to work with print publishers as Web copublisher (Figure 14–4). HighWire Press led the way in early 1995; *The Journal of Biological Chemistry*, the most highly cited peer-reviewed journal in the biomedical literature, was the first journal to be displayed, and *Science* and the *Proceedings of the National Academy of Science* were soon added. As of February 1999,

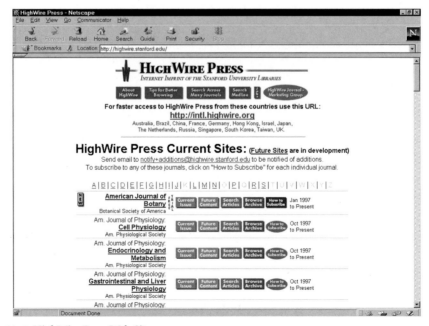

Figure 14–4 HighWire Press Web Site

HighWire electronically copublished more than 100 journals and had plans to add another 100 titles the next year. Most journals require some type of electronic subscription; in most cases, however, single full-text views are allowed for readers following links from another HighWire reference list, even if the reader does not subscribe to the linked journal. This kind of "cross-journal surfing"[3] has been an enormously popular feature and becomes all the more valuable as an electronic collection grows.

Print publishers, anxious not to have their role eroded by these new services, have also begun to create sophisticated electronic products. Elsevier Science offers electronic access to more than 1,200 journals through a new product called Science Direct. The Science Direct collection now includes more than 300,000 scientific journal articles published by Elsevier Science, and an effort is being made to pull in titles from other publishers. The aim is to provide institutional subscriptions to this massive electronic collection to research libraries, universities, and corporations. Elsevier Science is also marketing a related product, ScienceServer, that can run on an institution's local network and provides Web-based search and delivery services for locally stored journals.

Although new in medicine, vast electronic repositories have proved valuable in other sciences such as physics and astronomy. The Los Alamos "E-print" archive has served physicists as a primary means of communication especially for areas of investigation that are evolving rapidly. An analogous "E-biomed" project has been proposed by Harold E. Varmus, Director of the National Institutes of Health, but has been sharply criticized by many traditional journals.[8,9] Biomedical publications may evolve more slowly, but change has already begun with publishers trying to maintain revenues, libraries trying to negotiate better deals on smaller budgets, and readers demanding better access and availability. Print journals are not yet endangered, but ultimately readers will clamor for the full range of electronic features and for new products that will bear little resemblance to traditional paper publications.

On-line Peer Review

The evidence-based movement in medicine relies heavily on the selection and criticism of information prior to incorporation into clinical decision making, yet the traditional peer review process has been criticized for delaying publication, interjecting reviewer or editor bias, and stifling new ideas. Can this process be improved with the new electronic tools of the information age?

Experimentation has begun with more open methods of review. Once again, the physics community has been the most progressive. Scientists place electronic "pre-prints" on the Los Alamos archive, where they are accessible to and open to discussion by the entire community. Most articles subsequently become incorporated into journals, but much of the impact occurs while the article is in the pre-print archive. Most major medical journals expressly prohibit this kind of pre-publishing, but it is expected within the physics community.

The Lancet has experimented with placing unaccepted articles on its Web site and inviting comments by readers and reviewers. However, the medical community has mostly been reluctant to abandon the peer review process, perhaps because there is greater potential for unreviewed information to cause harm. Evidence-based medicine, with its insistence on rigorous methodology and data to support clinical recommendations, raises the review bar even higher. However, it also affirms the value of expert study critique, and this may prompt journal editors to evolve a more open process.

On-line Patient Education

An important movement evolving parallel to evidence-based medicine has been the effort to make patients better-informed participants in their own care. Their combination in an "evidence-based patient choice" movement ensures that patients are empowered to make the best possible decisions. This might involve incorporation of patient values into decision formulas or provision of key information and evidence to patients so they can make their own decisions. Supporting this approach have been studies showing that patients are able to take central roles in discussions and can reproducibly generate their own assessments of the relative values of different treatment outcomes.[10]

Few patients have access to the journal literature, so patients typically consult what is most accessible, whether newspapers, television, or (more recently) Web sites. The potential for misinformation from any of these sources is substantial, but the Web is particularly hazardous because Web publishing is cheap and easy. There is often little to distinguish established, reliable resources from fly-by-night projects. Even a well-intentioned and reliable health care organization may have conceived and constructed a Web site poorly in a wave of enthusiasm, funding the development but not the ongoing maintenance of the site.

One attempt to address the problem of the reliability of health care information on the Internet is Health On the Net (HON), a nonprofit organization headquartered in Geneva, Switzerland, dedicated to advancing new information technologies in the field of health care delivery. One of its most important projects has been the establishment of an eight-principle "code of conduct" for Web sites related to health care. The code is self-governed, but display of the HON Code logo on participating Web sites indicates at least the intention to provide high-quality information (Table 14–5).

COLLABORATION IN ON-LINE "COMMUNITIES"

The birth of the Web in 1989 at CERN, the European Particle Physics Laboratory in Switzerland, can be attributed to the desire of the particle physics community to organize itself

---

Table 14–5 Health On the Net Code of Conduct

1. Any medical/health advice provided and hosted on this site will be given only by medically/health trained and qualified professionals unless a clear statement is made that a piece of advice offered is from a non medically qualified individual or organization.

2. The information provided on this site is designed to support, not replace, the relationship between a patient/site visitor and his/her current physician.

3. Confidentiality of data relating to individual patients and visitors to a medical/health Web site (including their identity) is respected by this Web site. The Web site owners undertake to honor or exceed the legal requirements of medical/health information privacy that apply in the country and state where the Web site and mirror sites are located.

4. Where appropriate, information contained on this site will be supported by clear references to source data and, where possible, will have specific HTML links to that data. The date when a clinical page was last modified will be clearly displayed (eg, at the bottom of the page).

5. Any claims relating to the benefits/performance of a specific treatment, commercial product, or service will be supported by appropriate, balanced evidence in the manner outlined above in Principle 4.

6. The designers of this Web site will seek to provide information in the clearest possible manner and provide contact addresses for visitors who seek further information or support. The Webmaster will display his/her E-mail address clearly throughout the Web site.

7. Support for this Web site, including the identitites of commercial and noncommercial organizations that have contributed funding, services, or material for the site, will be clearly identified.

8. If advertising is a source of funding, it will be clearly stated. A brief description of the advertising policy adopted by the Web site owners will be displayed on the site. Advertising and other promotional material will be presented to viewers in a manner and context that facilitate differentiation between it and the original material created by the institution operating the site.

into a global on-line community for sharing information. The distributed publishing paradigm off the Web expanded enormously what was already possible on the Internet with e-mail and transfer of files. The Web triggered not only the exponential growth in Internet usage, but also what many have called the most significant change in publishing since the invention of the printing press. The wave of interest in on-line communities, begun in physics and other hard sciences, is now beginning to propagate through medical disciplines.

Multi-Center Studies

Evidence-based researchers are likely to be important advocates of the communication and community-building capabilities of the Web. Large multi-center trials, especially those that are prospective and randomized, make invaluable contributions to clinical evidence, yet only a tiny minority of surgical procedures are included in such trials. Even when there are ongoing studies, few patients have the opportunity to participate. If collaboration amongst investigators could be enhanced through Internet communications, it might be more feasible to accrue sufficient numbers of patients in the time frame required to obtain meaningful results from clinical trials.

To date, limitations in Internet access and valid concerns about the privacy of clinical information have held back medical investigators. But these constraints are being addressed as industry ensures adequate access to the Internet and as effective security and encryption technology is put into common use. In order to leverage the full potential of information and Internet technologies, clinical investigators will look for ways to foster links between trial centers, to increase awareness of ongoing investigations, and to facilitate the process of data submission and collection.

Coalescing Organizations into Virtual Communities

As professional organizations and scientists gather on the Web, there has been an important trend toward developing umbrella sites that tailor information to specific scientific communities and span gaps between governments, professional societies, and industry. Because of the ease of providing information over the Web, publishing on these sites extends beyond the scholarly literature and includes news and other less formal informational materials.

Again it was the hard sciences that pioneered these collaborative sites, and the Los Alamos archive, created in 1991, now serves as a primary means of communication for tens of thousands of theoretical physicists around the world. Other scientific community Web sites have begun to mature including ChemWeb (http://www.chemweb.com) in chemistry and BioMedNet (http://www.biomednet.com) in biology. Adoption may occur more slowly in the medical communities less fluent in computer skills, but eventually the convenience and cost savings of these collaborative projects will be compelling advantages.

An example of an on-line surgical community is the Cardiothoracic Surgery Network (CTSNet, http://www.ctsnet.org), a collaborative project sponsored by the three major multinational organizations within the field of cardiothoracic surgery to create a shared Web-based information repository (Figure 14–5). More than 20 organizations participate sharing a common database of information and common Web communication software. All Web pages are saved in a custom document management system that controls access and editorial privileges for individual pages. Content from the leading journals in the field are included in the massive information database, as are data about each surgeon, organization, committee, residency programs, industrial vendors, products, and dozens of other entities.[11]

The Cardiothoracic Surgery Network (CTSNet) is an example of "knowledge environment,"[1] a site that brings together a critical mass of resources and services in a certain area of interest. Scholarly journal articles remain critical building blocks, but the aim is to organize references into useful collections and to provide a wide range of additional resources in a fully integrated fashion. The objectives of these knowledge environments dovetail perfectly with

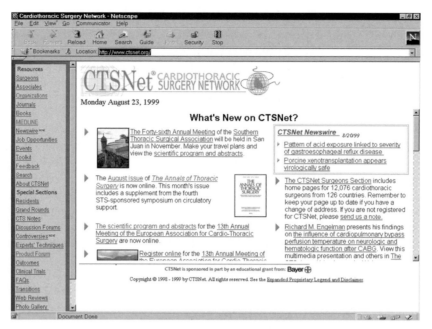

Figure 14–5 The Cardiothoracic Surgery Network (CTSNet)

the aims of evidence-based educators. The best supported clinical evidence can be described succinctly and displayed most prominently, and Web hyperlinks can be used to "drill down" to specific details and to access additional lower quality information.

Conclusion

The Internet revolution presents some exciting opportunities to create widespread access to vast electronic repositories of medical information. There is also a new challenge to avoid "information overload." Publishers and educators are quickly learning how to use technology effectively, and the pace of change has been staggering. The ultimate impact of these innovations, which are still in their infancy, is hard to predict. But for the clinician in need of immediate access to evidence-based information, high-quality information technology will be increasingly essential.

References

1. Butler D. The writing is on the web for science journals in print. Nature 1999; 397: 195–200.

2. Wallace M. Information resources and reference guides. Lancet 1998;351(Suppl I):7.

3. Delamothe T. The electronic future of scientific articles. Lancet 1998;351(Suppl I):5–6.

4. Chalmers I, Dickersin K, Chalmers TC. Getting to grips with Archie Cochrane's agenda. BMJ 1992;305:786–8.

5. Mitka M. Renewed efforts to improve the quality of health care. JAMA 1999; 281(5):404.

6. Sackett DL, Straus SE. Finding and applying evidence during clinical rounds: the "evidence cart". JAMA 1998;280(15):1336–8.

7. Stevens L. Evidence-based medicine: applying new rules to medical problem solving. In: Wayne-Doppke J, editor. Medical Internet Toolkit. Santa Barbara (CA): Cor Healthcare Resources; 1998. p.24–9.

8. Delamothe T, Smith R. Moving beyond journals: the future arrives with a crash. BMJ 1999; 318:1637–9.

9. Relman AS. The NIH "E-BIOMED" proposal; a potential threat to the evaluation and orderly dissemination of new clinical studies. N Engl J Med 1999;340:1793–4.

10. Holmes-Rovner M, Kroll J, Rovner DR, et al. Patient decision support intervention: increased consistency with decision analytic models. Med Care 1999;37(3):270–84.

11. Greene PS. Introducing the cardiothoracic surgery network (CTSNet). Ann Thorac Surg 1997; 63:1824.

CHAPTER 15

Administrative Data and Evidence-Based Surgery

Dennis Dunn, PhD, Gary Pickens, PhD, and Michael Sachs

Evidence-based medicine involves "integrating individual clinical expertise with the best available external clinical evidence from systematic research."[1] From the perspective of payers and policymakers, the practice of evidence-based medicine should reduce adverse outcomes and unnecessary cost.[2]

Administrative databases discussed in this chapter yield information of a different type than that derived from randomized clinical trials: they reflect what happens in the real world of surgical practice. The strength of administrative data is the ability to link patient outcomes to the cost of producing these outcomes. Administrative databases are used to measure the following:

- Outcomes
    Mortality
    Complications
    Hospital re-admission
- Resource use
    Charges and costs
    In-patients' length of stay
    Units of service
- Patient characteristics
    Demographics
    Morbidity and chronic disease

Health care administrative data is used not only by health services researchers. It is also the foundation of many reports found in the media and available to the public in conventional publications or on the Internet. For example:

- U.S. News and World Report produces an annual guide, *America's Best Hospitals*, which identifies where to find the best care in 17 medical and surgical specialties.[3] One criterion used to determine top hospitals is the risk-adjusted mortality rate, computed from hospital administrative data.
- Anyone faced with choosing a health plan can access information about that plan from the National Committee for Quality Assurance (NCQA). A list of health-plan accreditation reports can be viewed on the Internet at http://www.ncqa.org. Included in the accreditation reports are measures of each plan's performance in preventive health services such as mammography. These measures are derived from an analysis of the plan's administrative data (claims).
- Several state organizations publish reports on coronary artery bypass graft (CABG) surgery. For example, a recent report posted on the Internet by the Pennsylvania Health Care Cost Containment Council (http://www.phc4.org/cabg9495) provides information on risk-adjusted mortality rates by surgeon, hospital, and health plan. Portions of this report are based on the analysis of hospital administrative data.

The objective of this chapter is to provide a guide to the use of health care administrative databases for evidence-based surgery studies. We believe that informed use of administrative data by researchers will improve the quality of data that reaches academics, policymakers, and consumers. We discuss

- the production of health care administrative databases,
- the accuracy of administrative databases,
- sources for administrative databases, and
- data analysis issues and examples.

Production of Health Care Administrative Databases

Iezzoni[4] identifies three major data sources used to study patient outcomes:

- Administrative data (computerized data files primarily used for billing or operations)
- Medical record data (data abstracted from provider medical records)
- Patient response data (information collected directly from patients)

In practice, administrative data are obtained from three sources:

- Hospital discharge abstracts derived from internal hospital information systems and by manual abstraction of hospital records
- Claims databases maintained by health insurance companies and health plans
- Encounter forms collected by health plans and other organizations

The vast majority of research work has relied on hospital discharge abstracts from state data organizations and claims databases obtained from the Health Care Financing Administration (HCFA). Encounter data are cited rarely (however, see the National Ambulatory Medical Care Survey).[5] Encounter information is sometimes collected by health plans to track provision of services and quality in capitated payment arrangements, where the submission of bills is not central to provider reimbursement.

Administrative databases are almost always extracted from the internal operational systems of hospitals and health insurance organizations. We will outline how they are produced.

Data Collection Standards

Data entered into administrative databases rely on protocols and data formats to achieve standardization. The most important coding standards are ICD9-CM and HCPCS/CPT. Data format protocols are often based on insurance claim forms, the most important of which are the UB-92 and HCFA 1500 forms. A standardized discharge abstract format is the Uniform Hospital Discharge Dataset (UHDDS).

The ICD9-CM Coding System

The ICD9-CM coding system is the foundation for diagnoses recorded in discharge abstract and claims databases. Hospital discharge abstract data contain procedure codes based on ICD9-CM as well. Iezzoni[4] provides a review of the evolution of ICD9-CM, with an analysis of the system's suitability for specifying clinical conditions. References such as *St. Anthony's Illustrated ICD9-CM Code Book*[6] may be consulted for reference and coding guidelines.

Since the implementation of diagnosis-related groups (DRGs) in 1983, the ICD9-CM system used in the United States has been revised annually. Diagnosis and procedure codes may be downloaded from the HCFA web site (http://www.hcfa.gov) after October 1 of each year.

The HCPCS/CPT Coding Systems

Physician and other professional bills rely on the HCPCS/CPT coding systems. The reference guide, *St. Anthony's HCPCS Level II Code Book*,[7] provides an overview of the relationships among HCPCS, CPT, and local carrier coding schemes.

HCPCS (HCFA Common Procedure Coding System) has three levels:

- CPT (current procedural terminology): a five-digit system maintained by the American Medical Association that describes the procedures and services physicians provide to patients.
- National codes: these codes were devised by HCFA to account for nonphysician services, such as ambulance service or durable medical equipment.
- Local codes: these are codes devised by Medicare carriers to describe services for which there is no defined code. Prior approval of HCFA is required.

The Uniform Bill 92 form

The Uniform Bill 92 (UB-92), known also as the HCFA 1450, has been in use since 1993, and was developed under the auspices of the National Uniform Billing Committee (NUBC).

The UB-92 form is used for bills generated by institutions providing care, such as hospitals, skilled nursing facilities, and home health providers. The UB-92 form superseded form UB-82 and corrected many deficiencies in the previous form. It contains coding standards for the following categories of information:

- Condition, occurrence, and value codes
- Revenue descriptions, codes, and charges
- Payer, insured, and employer information
- Diagnosis, procedure coding, and physician information

A reference such as *St. Anthony's UB-92 Editor: A Guide to Medicare Billing*[8] may be consulted for specific coding standards. Also, the NUBC web site (http://www.nubc.org) contains information on periodic updates to UB-92.

Form HCFA 1500

The HCFA 1500 form is the de facto standard for professional services claims. The HCFA web site (http://www.hcfa.gov) describes the 1500 as ". . . the basic form prescribed by HCFA for the Medicare program for claims from physicians and suppliers, except for ambulance services. It has also been adopted by the Office of Civilian Health and Medical Program of the Uniformed Services (OCHAMPUS) and has received the approval of the American Medical Association (AMA) Council on Medical Services." The HCFA 1500 contains information on (1) the patient and patient insurance and (2) the service provider or supplier. The coding standard for procedures is HCPCS, described above.

The Uniform Hospital Discharge Dataset

The Uniform Hospital Discharge Dataset (UHDDS) defines a set of basic data to be collected for an inpatient's stay. This standard, developed by the National Committee on Vital and Health Statistics, is widely regarded as the minimum information which should be collected during an in-patient's stay. Hospital discharge abstract databases maintained by most organizations are generalizations of the UHDDS model, which provides guidelines for reporting

- patient demographics (date of birth, sex, race, ethnicity, and residence),
- admission and discharge dates,
- provider identification (hospital and physicians),
- diagnoses,
- procedures and dates,
- discharge disposition, and
- expected payment source.

Electronic Submission of Claims

The discussion of UB-92 and HCFA 1500 has used paper forms as the physical model for data collection. However, HCFA reports that, as of January 1998, 96 percent of all Part A claims and

80 percent of all Part B claims were submitted electronically. The HCFA web site (http://www.hcfa.gov/medicare/edi) provides documentation regarding electronic data interchange (EDI) standards for Medicare claims.

Hospital Discharge Abstracts

The National Center for Health Statistics (NCHS) has collected hospital discharge abstract data as part of the National Hospital Discharge Survey (NHDS) from 1979 to present. This survey, which is focused on acute care hospitals, profiles in-patient activity in the United States. Originally, all survey data were collected by completion of manual discharge abstract forms in sampled hospitals. In 1995, more than 34 percent of NHDS discharge abstracts were obtained from commercial abstracting services, state data systems, or a hospital's own hospital information system (HIS).[9] The data model for the abstracts is the Uniform Hospital Discharge Data Set (UHDDS), described above.

Data submitted to NCHS, state data organizations, and commercial vendors will rely more and more on hospital information systems. How do these work?

In the 1980s, internal systems of hospitals were becoming computerized but were not integrated. A hospital information system is information technology which integrates disparate systems, such as the following:

- *Admission and discharge systems.* These systems collect information on the patient's demographics, source of payment, and admitting and discharging physician.
- *Order entry system.* This system contains information about resources used during the hospital stay. Typically, all available hospital resources are inventoried in a charge master. This list of resources is diverse, ranging from surgical supplies to OR time to daily routine accommodation. Order entry systems contain records of service units by charge master code.
- *Medical records systems.* Medical records systems capture data abstracted from the patient's chart as a sequence of diagnoses and procedures performed. All diagnoses and procedures are coded using the ICD9-CM coding system.
- *Billing systems.* Billing systems work with the order entry system to generate a bill for a specific payer. The charge master is used to generate charges for hospital services rendered, and contractual discounts and allowances may be resolved. (See the discussion of facility claims below for a detailed description of the submission process for HCFA).

The ICD9-CM diagnosis and procedure codes are probably the most important aspect of the discharge record from the viewpoint of outcomes studies. The process by which these data are generated starts with the medical records department of the hospital. Most medical records departments abstract diagnoses and procedures from the patient's chart at discharge although some facilities use the practice of "concurrent coding," in which interim diagnosis and procedure codes are generated before the patient is discharged. Questions that require input from physicians can be answered before discharge in the case of concurrent coding, which improves the quality of the medical record data produced.

The medical records department often uses two systems to generate diagnosis and procedure data. The first is an encoding system, which is a computerized ICD9-CM coding manual. The coder uses this to find the appropriate codes when abstracting information from the patient's chart. The second system is an abstracting module which is actually part of the hospital billing system. The coder uses the abstracting module to enter diagnosis and procedure data needed to complete the UB-92 bill submitted by the hospital to the payer.

By the 1990s, it was possible to satisfy a request for a discharge abstract by exporting data from a provider's hospital information system or associated data warehouse into a target format such as UHDDS. Because a discharge abstract is an extraction from hospital operational systems, its content may change if it is generated at a different point in time. This is especially true for charge data, which may change through the process of claims adjudication.

It is important to mention what hospital discharge abstracts do not contain. Much important data generated by the hospital laboratory, radiology, and pharmacy systems are absent, except for that picked up in diagnosis and procedure codes. In particular, detailed laboratory results and radiographic findings, which may provide evidence about the severity of a clinical condition, are not present. Also absent are specific data from the pharmacy systems, which provide not only detailed drug information (usually classified by the National Drug Code [NDC]) but also information on dosage and route of administration. The pharmacy, radiology, and laboratory systems can support studies of protocol compliance or adverse drug effects. Such data distinguishes hospital-discharge abstract databases from "clinical" databases.

Health Insurance Claims

Data stored in health plan claims databases may be logically divided into four major types: facility bills, professional bills, enrollment records, and pharmacy bills. These claims are submitted independently to the payer and may provide duplicate records of a single clinical event. Our discussion of the billing process below concentrates on Medicare claims, the most commonly available research database.

Facility Bills

Facility claims are submitted by institutional providers such as hospitals, hospital outpatient departments, and skilled nursing facilities. These are for the nonprofessional components of medical care, such as room and board expenses for in-patient stays and operating-room costs. In the case of claims submitted to Medicare, all providers must adhere to the UB-92 standard.

Claims are first entered into hospital systems by professional nonmedical coders, who refer to medical charts for clinical information. This process involves abstracting diagnoses and surgical procedures from a medical chart and entering a fixed number of codes into the fields provided by the abstracting system. Coders often consult with physicians concerning the selection and priority of diagnoses. Note that the number (and quality) of diagnoses included at this stage may be limited by accepted practice within each hospital and by the computer systems used by the coder. (See Iezzoni[4] for studies of patterns of coding).

In some institutions, bills are passed through a claims editing system before submission, to ensure compliance with payer regulations and to order diagnosis codes to optimize reimbursement. These alterations may cause the electronic record to differ from the chart in emphasis.

Facility bills are then sent to a Medicare Fiscal Intermediary (FI) or directly to a health plan for non-Medicare claims. Over 99 percent of such bills are submitted electronically. The FI enters the claim into a system to assign a payment amount and to run consistency and utilization checks. The provider may be asked to resubmit the bill if any problems are detected.

Medicare facility bills are not paid immediately by the FI but are forwarded to one of nine regional "host sites" run by HCFA. These sites maintain a comprehensive database of Common Working File Health Insurance Master Records (CWF HIMRs) for each Medicare enrollee in the region. The claim is checked against this record for remaining benefits, deductible status, entitlement, and consistency. Claims may be recycled, rejected, or paid. If the claim is paid, the host site updates the CWF HIMR and transmits the information to a central repository maintained by HCFA. This bill, the "final-action" record, is the last of a sequence of bills which may include interim bills and correction records.

The records which finally appear in a research discharge database (such as Medicare Provider Analysis and Review [MEDPAR]) are generally not identical to the records which are stored internally in the master claims database. The raw claims are abstracted into a single "discharge record." Unedited facility claims streams often contain multiple records per discharge. A researcher may be forced to make certain arbitrary choices in creating a single discharge record from such a sequence. This can contribute additional variation from the original discharge summary in the patient's chart.

Professional Bills

Physicians and other medical professionals usually submit claims for services independently of the facility claims. A major inpatient stay may be represented in a claims database by several facility records and hundreds of physician claims from different physicians. Thus, the professional claims stream provides an independent view of clinical treatment. The submission sequence is similar to that of facility bills, with the following differences:

1. Medicare professional claims are created and submitted from a physician's office. Usually the claim is entered into a medical-office billing system by a nonprofessional assistant whose only reference is a summary list sometimes called a charge master. (This list should not be confused with the facility charge master mentioned previously.) The charge master is usually a single page containing a list of diagnosis and procedure codes commonly used in the practice. The physician can quickly check all relevant codes to be submitted by the coder. The limitations of a particular form can bias the distribution of codes submitted by a practice.

2. Although about 80 percent of physician billing is entered and submitted electronically, there is little standardization in data-entry software. Some medical-office billing systems severely limit the number of diagnosis and procedure codes that can be entered. Other systems may automatically include default secondary diagnoses for a given patient. Although the format of electronic submission to Medicare is standardized (the form 1500), the process of entry can introduce serious biases.

3. Recent changes in Medicare guidelines for evaluation and management billing codes require that physicians justify the use of certain visit codes with appropriate diagnosis codes. Adherence to these new rules is likely to increase the number and severity of diagnoses submitted by physicians, particularly specialists.

4. Since individual physician practices are less likely than facilities to have claim-editing software, correction and adjudication sequences are often present in professional claims databases. However, the research databases released by HCFA have resolved all these duplicates into a single final record. Raw claims data available from private carriers may contain large numbers of such sequences.

5. For complex surgical procedures, many physicians may be present for a single event. A surgeon and an assistant surgeon may each submit the same procedure code for a given surgery. The assistant's claim is distinguishable only by referring to a second code called a modifier. Claims submitted by the anesthesiologist may be coded with a specific anesthesia code or may be coded with the surgical procedure, accompanied with a modifier. In counting units of major surgeries, it is particularly important to detect such duplicates to avoid overcounting.

6. Physicians often submit claims in a batch. Several procedure bills may be submitted in a single claim encoded with the same list of diagnoses. When these claims are reformatted for statistical analysis, it may appear as if many treatments were performed for a single diagnosis. This may emphasize a single code which is actually entered only once.

7. Special contractual arrangements may affect how physician claims are submitted. For example, an oncology group practice may accept a single reimbursement for a course of chemotherapy rather than submit individual bills for each session. A researcher must be aware of these special billing arrangements to count the units of service properly.

Enrollment Data

Enrollment information is proprietary to each health plan and is not stored in any standard format. However, certain information is needed to compute total at-risk member months: (1) member and family identifier, (2) date of enrollment, (3) date of termination, (4) date of birth, and (5) sex.

Researchers working with Medicare data use a file called the Denominator Beneficiary Encrypted File. Although the format of this file is not a standard, it serves as a good example of information available on enrollment records. The file contains one record for each selected beneficiary eligible during a given calendar year. Fields include the following:

- *Encrypted beneficiary account number.* This is a nine-digit number that identifies the primary account for a household. The encryption is consistent across enrollment and all claims files to allow linking.
- *Beneficiary identification.* This two-digit code describes the relationship of the claimant to the primary claimant in the household. These first two fields are usually joined to create an 11-digit code that identifies each beneficiary.
- *State and county of residence.* The state code (two digits) and the county code (three digits) can be combined to form a five-digit code unique to each county. Note that HCFA does not use the standard Federal Information Processing Standard (FIPS) codes of the U.S. Census. A crosswalk may be obtained from the HCFA web site.
- *Blank ZIP code and date of birth.* It is common in enrollment files to blank out or omit any fields which might compromise the confidentiality of the individual beneficiary. Exact address information is rarely provided to researchers.
- *Sex and race.* Although race information is provided, HCFA does not follow the census practice of distinguishing race and ethnicity. Thus, it is impossible to separate black Hispanics from nonblack Hispanics.
- *Entitlement information.* Several fields separate beneficiaries into end-stage renal disease (ESRD), old age, or disability as reasons for entitlement. Since these groups have different health care needs, it is useful to be able to profile utilization and outcomes separately.
- *Reason for termination.* This field can be used to determine if a beneficiary died during the observation period. This is the only reliable indicator of death as an outcome. Physician claims do not generally contain any indication that a patient died. Facility claims may contain a field called discharge disposition but it is not considered reliable and cannot indicate death occurring outside of an institutional stay.
- *Monthly entitlement indicators.* The denominator file includes information for 1 year of coverage. These fields indicate, for each of 12 months, whether a beneficiary was Part A-entitled or Part B-entitled and whether claims were processed through HCFA or through a group health organization (Medicare HMO). These indicators are essential to determine if claims streams are subject to censoring and to determine the at-risk observation period for each individual.

In calculating use rates or rates of complications, the enrollment information is used to calculate at-risk months. The total number of records in the file represents the number of people enrolled during the observation period and can greatly overestimate the number of individuals at risk at a given time. The true denominator for any rate file is determined by adding all months for which an individual was eligible and had claims processed by HCFA. In calculating yearly rates, this number is divided by twelve.

ACCURACY OF ADMINISTRATIVE DATABASES

Claims and hospital discharge abstract databases provide abundant and inexpensive information on encounters with health care providers. How accurate is outcome and other information extracted from administrative databases? This has been addressed by a number of investigators, and we will review the main findings in this section. Most of these studies have found inaccuracies or inadequacies in administrative data and provide cautions about specific uses.

In spite of the limitations outlined below, administrative databases are likely to be used for evaluating provider performance until electronic clinical data become available at reasonable cost. At that point, administrative data may well be used as a screening tool for outcomes research.[10]

Diagnosis and Procedure Coding

The definitive reference on the role of coding in administrative data is Iezzoni, *Risk Adjustment for Measuring Healthcare Outcomes*, chapter 3,[4] which outlines the evolution of the ICD9-CM coding system. Weaknesses in the coding system for outcomes research are summarized, including the lack of operational definitions for codes and the inability of codes to track disease progression. The main sources of error in coding are misspecification, miscoding, and incorrect sequencing.

The strategy used by most researchers investigating accuracy of administrative data is to compare the claims or discharge abstract data with equivalent information from a primary source (eg, reabstracted hospital chart or physician office records).

Incentives to sequence codes for reimbursement purposes are created by DRG assignments. This sequencing can present problems for researchers. Romano and Mark[11] studied hospital discharge abstract and reabstracted data from California. They concluded that comorbid conditions are underestimated among patients who die when the diagnosis list is truncated at five positions. Apparently, coders tend to give precedence to acute complications, causing the comorbid diagnoses to be dropped when the list is truncated. As a result of this and other research, HCFA and many state data organizations supply at least nine diagnosis fields as part of a discharge abstract database. In particular, the UB-92 format provides for nine diagnosis fields.

Fowles and colleagues[12] studied the agreement of Medicare Part B claims with physician office visit records. Using physician records as a gold standard, they concluded that claims underestimate disease prevalence for a number of important diseases. Treating claims as a standard for laboratory tests and procedures, they found that office records also provide poor estimates of tests and procedures use.

Several studies have focused on the use of administrative data compared to clinical data for risk-adjustment models. Hannan and colleagues constructed risk-adjusted mortality models for CABG mortality, using New York (state) discharge abstract data (SPARCS) and records from the Cardiac Surgery Reporting System (CSRS), a clinical database.[13] Risk-adjustment models using CSRS had better predictive power and confirmed expectations of risk factors better than SPARCS information (however, the receiver operating characteristic [ROC] curve statistics are not that different). Hospital-level risk-adjusted mortality rates under the two models had only moderate correlations (0.8). The CSRS variables, ejection fraction, reoperation, and >90 percent narrowing of left main trunk account for much of the difference in performance of the models. In a similar study, Hannan and colleagues found that part of the predictive power of the administrative data models resulted from miscoding postoperative complications as comorbidities used in the risk-adjustment process.[14] Romano and Mark compared administrative and clinical data when measuring risks of mortality due to ischemic heart disease. They concluded that certain comorbidities known to be mortality risk factors are far less prevalent in administrative data than clinical data, causing selective bias in relative-risk models.[11]

Quam and colleagues studied a sample of 2,079 patients with medical and pharmaceutical claims indicating essential hypertension.[15] Essential hypertension was confirmed in a subset of patients, using a survey and review of medical records. The use of medical and pharmaceutical claims gave 96 percent agreement with either the medical record or survey. Baron and colleagues conducted an internal validation study of Medicare claims for hip fracture and prostatectomy.[16] They concluded that agreement between physician and hospital claims on the site of fracture and type of prostatectomy was excellent (89 to 99%).

Iezzoni and colleagues have studied the validity of a computerized complications screening program (CSP) that uses hospital discharge abstract data. They used a sample of 100 cases processed by the CSP, along with physician reviews of complete discharge abstracts for the same cases. They found that the CSP identified 28 of 30 cases targeted by the physicians as having a quality problem (sensitivity of 93%). Conversely, of the 70 cases not targeted by the physicians, the CSP agreed in 45 of the cases (specificity of 64%).[17] In a more extensive validation study focused on Medicare patients, a similar CSP algorithm was used to identify complications in a group of major surgery and medical patients. Patient charts were collected and reabstracted. The investigators found variable confirmation rates, depending on the complication.[18] However, they concluded that cases not flagged by the CSP were unlikely to have complications.

Patient Characteristics

Coding patient characteristics in administrative databases accurately is important for two reasons. First, comparison of demographic characteristics of samples to reference statistics is an important first step in any research project. Second, patient demographics such as age, sex, or ethnicity are often used as adjusters in comparative studies of patient outcomes or resource utilization using administrative data.

Fowles and colleagues studied agreement of patient characteristics in the Medicare health insurance skeleton write-off (HISKEW) file and physician medical records.[12] Other than for name and gender, there is a striking lack of agreement between the sources (ZIP code, 40.3%; date of birth, 58.5%). However, this disagreement is probably due to the inadequacies in the visit section of the physician medical record. Steinwachs and colleagues illustrated the importance of caution when analyzing Medicaid claims in subpopulations.[19] They compared Medicaid claims to records kept by physicians and community health centers. Claims are relatively accurate for measuring ambulatory use but show bias when applied to selected groups of patients, for example, those having low-cost providers or low utilization.

Racial and ethnicity codes in Medicare enrollment data were analyzed by Lauderdale and colleagues.[20] They linked a sample of Medicare enrollees with the Social Security Administration Numerical Identification File, which contains data on country of birth, and demonstrated that race and ethnicity codes disagreed significantly with the actual country of origin.

SOURCES FOR ADMINISTRATIVE DATABASES

Hospital Discharge Abstract Data

The sources for hospital discharge abstract databases are state data organizations, federal surveys and samples, and HCFA.

State Data Organizations

The National Association of Health Data Organizations (NAHDO), a nonprofit organization dedicated to promoting the collection, dissemination, and use of health data, reports that 36 states have mandated the collection, analysis, and dissemination of health care data.[21] Most of this information pertains to in-patient care. States differ in their methods of collecting in-patient data although most make use of the UHDDS and UB-92 formats. We have maintained an inventory of data available by state. Excluding Alaska and Hawaii, only three states have no in-patient data collection activity underway. However, there is considerable variability in the data which is generally available. Release restrictions ordinarily are designed to protect patient and (in some cases) provider confidentiality.

When working with a database from a state data organization, we have found it useful to ask the following questions:

- Is hospital reporting mandatory or voluntary? What hospitals are not included in the database?
- Is there any attempt by the state data organization to collect discharge records of residents migrating out of state for hospital care?
- What type of facilities are included in the database? Are psychiatric and rehabilitation hospitals in the database?
- Is data available at a discharge level? If the data is aggregated, what rules are used to suppress cells with small samples?
- Are data suppressed for any patient types (eg, diagnoses of AIDS)?
- How many diagnosis and procedure codes are available? Are procedure dates included?
- Is there good documentation on the identification of hospital providers? Is a Medicare provider number included? Is there documentation of provider mergers and closures?
- Is patient origin included (ZIP code or county identifier)?
- Are hospital charges reported? Is there a breakdown of charges by departments?
- Are physician identifiers available? Is there documentation on physician specialty, subspecialty, and practice location?

Hospital discharge abstract data provide an excellent cross-sectional view of hospital use by a population when data are present for all hospitals. A weakness of hospital discharge abstract databases is their inability to track a patient over time and across sites of care. (The Agency for Health Care Policy and Research [AHCPR] web site, http://www.ahcpr.gov/data/hcupstat.htm, contains a list of contact persons for information on databases for 19 states. See also Table 15–1.)

Federal Surveys and Samples

There are two federal databases which provide hospital discharge abstract data. The National Hospital Discharge Survey (NHDS) is a sample of discharge abstracts collected from short-stay, nonfederal hospitals. The methodology and availability of data from the survey is well documented.[9] The NHDS relies on the UHDDS as a data model. Patient origin, provider identification, and charge data are not available. The database can be used to produce national estimates of in-patient care. Due to the sample size (276,533 discharge abstracts in 1994), reliable estimates of rare diagnoses and procedure volumes cannot be produced, but the NHDS is generally considered the gold standard for estimates of in-patient volumes and discharge and day rates in the United States.

The Agency for Health Care Policy and Research (AHCPR) sponsors the Health Care Cost and Utilization Project (HCUP). This has supported creation of the National Inpatient Sample (NIS) using discharge abstract data from state data organizations. In addition, AHCPR maintains a State Inpatient Database (SID) where data elements have been combined in a single database for 19 states. The internet address, http://www.ahcpr.gov/data/hcup-pkt.htm, provides additional information about NIS and SID. A big advantage of NIS and SID is standardization of the data across states. The AHCPR web site states: "The uniform data in HCUP make possible comparative studies of health care services and the use and cost of hospital care, including the effects of market forces on hospitals and the care they provide, variations in medical practice, the effectiveness of medical technology and treatments, and use of services by special populations." A weakness of NID and SID is the currency of the data; when this chapter was written, information was available for the years 1988 to 1995.

Table 15–1

State	Source	Internet Site	Public/Private
Alabama	Alabama Department of Health State Health Planning and Development Agency	None	Public
Alaska	Alaska State Hospital and Nursing Home Association	www.ptialaska/net/~ashnha	Unknown
Arizona	Arizona Bureau of Health Statistics	www.hs.state.az.us	Public
Arkansas	Arkansas Department of Health Center for Health Statistics	health.state.ar.us/stats/htm/statshp.htm	Private
California	CA Office of Statewide Health Planning & Development	www.oshpd.cahwnet.gov	Public
Colorado	Colorado Hospital Association	www.cha.com	Public
Connecticut	Connecticut Department of Health Office of Healthcare Access	www.state.ct.us/ohca	Public
Delaware	Deleware Health Statistics Center	None	Public
Florida	Florida Agency for Health Care Administration	www.fdhc.stat.fl.us	Public
Georgia	Georgia State Health Planning Agency	None	Public
Hawaii	Hawaii Health Information Council	www.hhic.org	Private
Idaho	Idaho Department of Health and Welfare	None	Public
Illinois	Illinois Health and Hospital Association	www.ihha.org	Private
Indiana	Indiana State Department of Health Hospital Disclosure & Long Term Care Data Program	www.state.in.us/isdh	Public
Iowa	Iowa Hospitals and Health Systems	www.mdsqmw.ac.uk/rt/ihhs.htm	Public

Table 15–1 *(continued)*

State	Source	Internet Site	Public/Private
Kansas	Kansas Department of Health & Environment Office of Health Care Information	None	Public
Kentucky	Kentucky Cabinet for Human Services Health Policy and Data Analysis Branch	www.state.ky.us	Public
Louisiana	Louisiana Department of Health and Hospitals	www.dhh.state.la.us	Unknown
Maine	Maine Health Data Organization	None	Public
Maryland	MD Health Services Cost Review Commission	www.op.state.md.us	Public
Massachusetts	MA Health Data Consortium	www.mahealthdata.org	Public
Michigan	Michigan Health and Hospital Association	www.mha.org	Private
Minnesota	Minnesota Hospital and Healthcare Partnership	www.mhhp.com	Private
Mississippi	Mississippi State Department of Health	www.msdh.state.ms.us	Unknown
Missouri	Missouri Department of Health Bureau of Health Resources	www.health.state.mo.us	Private
Montana	Montana Hospital Association	www.mtha.org	Private
Nebraska	Nebraska Association of Hospitals and Health Systems	www.nahhsnet.org	Private
Nevada	Division of Health Care Financing Policy	www.state.nv.us/hr/dhcfp/hcfpdopa.htm	Public
New Hampshire	NH Dept of Health and Human Services	www.dhhs.state.nh.us	Public
New Jersey	New Solutions	none	Public

Table 15–1 *(continued)*

State	Source	Internet Site	Public/Private
New Mexico	New Mexico Health Policy Commission	hpc.state.nm.us	Private
New York	NY Department of Health	www.health.state.ny.us	Public
North Carolina	HCIA	www.hcia.com	Public
North Dakota	North Dakota Department of Health	www.health.state.nd.us/ndhd	Public
Ohio	Ohio Hospital Association	www.ohanet.org	Private
Oklahoma	Oklahoma Health Care Authority Division of Health Care Information	www.health.state.ok.us	Private
Oregon	Oregon Association of Hospitals	www.aracnet.com	Public
Pennsylvania	PA Health Care Cost Containment Council	www.phc4.org	Public
Rhode Island	RI Department of Health	www.state.ri.us	Public
South Carolina	South Carolina Budget and Control Board Office of Research and Statistics	www.orss.state.sc.us	Public
South Dakota	South Dakota Department of Health	www.state.sd.us/doh	Public
Tennessee	Tennessee Department of Health Health Statistics & Information Section	www.state.tn.us/health/statistics	Public
Texas	Texas Healthcare Information Council	www.thic.state.tx.us	Public
Utah	UT Department of Health	www.hlunix.hll.state.ut.us/html/utah_doh.html	Public

Table 15–1 *(continued)*

State	Source	Internet Site	Public/Private
Vermont	VT Department of Health	www.state.vt.us/health	Public
Virginia	Virginia Health Information	www.vhi.org	Public
Washington	WA Department of Health	www.doh.wa.gov	Public
West Virginia	West Virginia Health Care Authority	www.hcawv.org	Public
Wisconsin	WI Office of Health Care Information	www.state.wi.us	Public
Wyoming	Wyoming Department of Health	www.wdhfs.state.wy.us/wdh	Public

Health Care Financing Administration

The Health Care Financing Administration (HCFA) maintains a hospital discharge abstract database for Medicare beneficiaries that is assembled from in-patient claims records. The Medicare Provider Analysis and Review (MEDPAR) file contains data from 1983 to the present. This file is available in several formats, depending on whether beneficiary identifiable information is included, and is available for acute care hospitals and skilled nursing facilities.

The Medicare Provider Analysis and Review file contains several useful fields for outcomes and resource use analysis. In-patient claims have been aggregated into revenue centers based on UB-92 charge codes, providing a charge profile for MEDPAR discharges. A common technique is to merge the charge profile with cost and charge data found in the Hospital Cost Report Information System (HCRIS) database to estimate costs of care, based on ratios of cost to charge found in HCRIS.

Another useful field for some studies is admission to date of death. This field is calculated using the HCFA Enrollment Database (EDB). The EDB contains a date of death field, which is obtained through periodic merges against the Social Security Administration Master Beneficiary Record File. We suggest that the contents of this field be evaluated and discharges excluded when illogical data is encountered.

While MEDPAR is the best known in-patient file available from HCFA, there are other databases worth mentioning. The same agency produces Medicare Standard Analytic Files (SAFs) containing final-action records for in-patient and skilled nursing facilities. These files are available in 5 percent and 100 percent versions.

Also available through HCFA are State Medicaid Research Files (SMRFs), which include data from 34 states that participate in the Medicaid Statistical Information System. Using the Personal Summary File and the Inpatient Claims File (described in the following section), it is possible to construct a discharge record resembling the abstracts found in state databases or in MEDPAR.

Sources of Claims Data

The Health Care Financing Administration is the main source of claims information used in outcomes research. Claims-level information is available for both the Medicare and Medicaid populations. Since any information at the individual level is considered restricted use data, the user must submit a data request which includes a study plan or protocol, evidence of funding, and a signed data use agreement. Agreement forms and guidelines for the proposal format are available from HCFA or from the Research Data Assistance Center (RESDAC http://www.hcfa.gov/ord/resdac0.htm).

Medicare claims are available as part of a set of databases called the Standard Analytical Files. Although data is available for 100 percent of the Medicare population, the size of these files is prohibitive; thus, most researchers work with the 5 percent sample files.

The HCFA creates the 5 percent sample by selecting all claims for any beneficiary whose Health Insurance Claim (HIC) number ends with 05, 20, 45, 70, or 95. Claims are available as separate files corresponding to type of provider: physicians, outpatient facilities, in-patient facilities, home health agencies, hospices, and skilled nursing facilities. Beneficiary identification is encrypted on all claims. The encryption is consistent across years and across claims sources; thus, it is possible to collect, sequence, and track all claims submitted for any sampled individual.

The physician file is the largest of the databases, consisting of more than 50 million claims annually. The version of this data for public use contains only final-action claims. Adjudication sequences should not be present. Each record contains all the information submitted on the standard HCFA claim, the Form 1500. Patient demographic fields have been cleaned and updated from HCFA's Common Working File and are quite reliable. Physician specialty is provided, but physician identification numbers have been encrypted. Only the county of residence of the beneficiary is available for small-area analysis. Facility provider numbers are not encrypted and can be linked with HCFA provider files.

Physician claims are stored in a variable-length record format with each record representing a batch of claims submitted at one time. Records can contain between 1 and 13 individual procedures. In reading such data for analysis, it is necessary to generate several single fixed-length records for each variable record. These records each contain all the demographic and diagnostic information of the original variable record plus all information for just one of the batched procedures. Note that this process can create redundant diagnosis information.

Medicaid information available from HCFA is collected in a central claims repository called the Medicaid Statistical Information System (MSIS). As of 1995, research files can be extracted from MSIS for 28 states. These State Medicaid Research Files are divided into five parts:

1. Personal Summary file consists of a single record for each individual eligible for Medicaid. Only summary-level information for eligibility and claims history is contained in this file.
2. In-patient file contains one record for each complete stay.
3. Long Term Care file contains individual claims for nursing facilities and intermediate care facilities.
4. Drug file contains final-action paid claims listed by NDC code.
5. Other Claims file contains all physician, laboratory, and clinic claims.

These files are considered restricted access. They are available to qualified researchers by application.

ANALYSES OF OUTCOMES USING ADMINISTRATIVE DATA

In this section, we outline some steps used in a study documenting variation in the incidence and reporting of venous thromboemboli (VTE) in the Medicare populations over the 2-year period from 1994 to 1995. This provides a good example of the care needed in using claims administrative data for outcomes research.

Data Analysis Issues

The analysis of outcomes based on physician claims is preceded by data preparation, which may well be the most time-consuming phase of the research. The preparation process always involves removing duplicate records that result from adjudication. Although such sequences are removed by HCFA from Medicare research databases, privately available claims streams usually contain such duplicates. Typically, these can be detected by searching for multiple claims for a single beneficiary for the same CPT code on the same day by the same provider. Exceptions to this rule include selected tests and therapies (such as physical therapy) which may legitimately occur many times the same day. Since it is generally the practice to bill these services in batches, the procedure mentioned above is usually reliable.

If research objectives require it, removal of duplicate records is followed by correction of obvious coding inconsistencies and statistical outliers. This assumes that the procedure code is the most reliable field on the claims record, and research supports this assumption.[12] The process, field-by-field, is as follows:

Primary diagnosis

Some claims-editing systems assume that certain procedures must be justified by an appropriate diagnosis code. If a completely inappropriate diagnosis code is present, the record is flagged as suspect. Analysts usually omit these records in later research phases.

Units of service

On most claims, this field is either not coded or coded with 1. Certain services such as physical therapy or chemotherapy are often billed with a single claim for a course of treatment, using the units of service field to indicate multiple billable procedures. However, the coding of this field is inconsistent, for example, units may refer to sessions or minutes. To assure consistency, it is common to determine the distribution of values for each CPT code. Reported units more than 3 standard deviations above the mean for that CPT code are flagged. Further research usually reveals that such outliers are limited to a single carrier or a single provider type. These groups are then excluded.

Place of service

Since reimbursement does not depend on the coding of this field, accuracy is suspect. The most obvious inconsistencies can be detected and corrected by noting that certain procedures can occur only in certain settings. Claims for emergency department visits should always be coded with ER as the place of service. Major surgeries known to be in-patient only should not be coded with physician office or outpatient place of service. Assigning an RVU to each surgical claim can provide a useful definition of in-patient only procedures. Any surgical claim coded *outpatient* that has a total relative value unit (RVU) above some arbitrary threshold can be flagged for further study.

Patient demographics

Patient characteristics such as age and sex are known to be poorly coded on unedited claims. Sex and date of birth should be available on the patient enrollment record. Age can be imputed on the claim by subtracting date of birth from the date of service. This is unnecessary with research databases from HCFA.

Physician specialty

This field may be blank, absent, or miscoded on submitted claims. Where possible, physician specialty should be obtained independently from a physician roster database and substituted for the self-reported specialty.

Total charges

In an adjudication process, several bills may be present for the same service. If such duplicates are detected, total charges are usually calculated as the sum of these records. Care should be taken to detect incomplete sequences, which are common at the beginning of the observation period. This process is not necessary with databases consisting of final-action claims only, such as Medicare claims.

VTE Example

The purpose of this study was to document variation in the incidence and reporting of venous thromboemboli in the Medicare populations over the 2-year period from 1994 to 1995. Since surgical cases are at high risk for this complication, another objective was to document the relative risk associated with several classes of major surgery. A third objective was to determine the proportion of cases that were not diagnosed until after discharge home or to some other facility. The data source used was the Medicare Standard Analytic 5 percent database. Both physician claims and hospital discharges were followed to detect complications.

The primary source of data was physician claims submitted to Medicare for a sample of 5 percent of all Medicare beneficiaries. The database is a systematic sample of 1 in every 20 enrollees in the standard Medicare fee-for-service program. The same individuals are sampled from one year to the next to permit longitudinal studies such as this. The sample population represents approximately 1.7 million insured clients. For each sampled individual, HCFA collects all claims (professional and institutional) for each year. Although all beneficiary ID numbers are encrypted, they are consistently encrypted to allow linkage across sample files.

The physician portion of this database contains over 50 million claims annually. Each claim contains (among other fields) an encrypted beneficiary ID number; an HCPCS procedure code; codes for date of service, place of service, and total submitted charges; and at least one ICD9-CM diagnosis code. Because these were final-action claims which had been through the HCFA review process, some of the initial data-cleaning steps outlined above were unnecessary: removal of duplicate records, and cleaning of patient demographics and physician specialty fields. Place of service, however, was corrected where possible. Since the fill rate for secondary diagnoses is poor, we relied on only the first diagnosis on each physician claim.

The hospital discharge portion contains over 550,000 discharge records annually. Each record contains all standard hospital discharge database fields. For this study, we have used the following: the encrypted beneficiary ID number, DRG, primary diagnosis, secondary diagnoses 1 and 2, date of service, length of stay, and total charges.

To study the incidence of deep vein thromboses and pulmonary emboli (DVT/PE), we first created a subset dataset that consisted of all claims and discharge records which were DVT/PE-related. These records contained diagnoses (either primary or secondary) contained in the following ICD9 codes:

'4151' – '41519' pulmonary embolism
'6738' – '67384' pulmonary embolism
'451' – '45199' deep vein thrombosis
'4538' – '45389' deep vein thrombosis
'4539' – '45399' deep vein thrombosis
'6713' – '67139' deep vein thrombosis
'6714' – '67149' deep vein thrombosis
'6719' – '67199' deep vein thrombosis

We also included any physician claims for any of the following CPT codes:

'75820' – '75822' deep vein thrombosis diagnostic procedures
'93922' – '93931' deep vein thrombosis diagnostic procedures
'93965' – '93990' deep vein thrombosis diagnostic procedures
'78580' – '78599' pulmonary embolism diagnostic procedures
'75741' – '75746' pulmonary embolism diagnostic procedures

The resulting database contained 705,020 physician claims and 14,020 discharge records. We then summarized all physician activity and discharge records for each individual, resulting in a database of 195,043 suspected cases. Many of these cases contained only passing mention of DVT or PE (perhaps a single physician claim). Since DVT and PE are serious conditions that are likely to result in intensive medical treatment, most of the minor cases probably represent either "rule-out" work-ups, individual diagnostic tests, or miscodes—not true cases of DVT or PE. Therefore, our next task was to classify all cases according to source and extent of reporting of the disease. From this information, we developed operational criteria for identifying likely instances of the diseases.

Table 15–2 summarizes the sample sizes grouped by type and source. *Source* indicates which database(s) contain mention of DVT/PE for a given case. It was coded as follows:

- If we found a discharge record containing a DVT or PE diagnosis but no physician claims, the case was classified as Source='DISCH ONLY'. There were a total of 4,218

Table 15–2 Summary of Sample Sizes for Type and Source of DVT/PE Case*

Source	Type				Total
	Major	*One Day*	*Other*	*Rule Out*	*Total*
MD AND DISCH BOTH	**6,072**	1,537	**3,962**	908	12,479
MD CLAIM ONLY	**9,747**	123,715	15,094	34,008	182,564
Grand Total	**15,819**	125,252	19,056	34,916	195,043

*Bold figures represent verified DVT/PE cases.

such cases. Since it is unlikely that a true case of DVT or PE would generate no physician claims, these cases were not regarded as verified cases.

- If we found both discharge records and physician claims with DVT or PE diagnoses (or procedure codes), the case was coded Source='MD AND DISCH BOTH'. There were a total of 12,479 of these cases over the 2 years. Not all of these cases may actually be DVT or PE; many may be only diagnostic work-ups. Total physician claims (see below) would be used to separate actual cases from work-ups.
- If physician claims were found but no discharge record contained a diagnosis, the case was classified as Source='MD CLAIM ONLY'. There were 182,564 such cases, the majority of which would prove to be miscodes or work-ups. If a sufficient number of significant physician claims were present over an extended period, then we concluded that this was a true case of DVT/PE for which the discharge record failed to mention these conditions.

The extent of physician activity was coded as a second variable, *Type*. This variable reflects the number of separate physician claims that either include a DVT or PE diagnosis or one of the CPT codes indicating a DVT or PE diagnostic test. The variable was coded as follows:

- Cases for which all physician claims were for a single day were coded as Type='ONE DAY'. There were a total of 125,252 such cases. These are not likely to be true DVT/PE cases.
- If the only claims found were for diagnostic tests, then the case was coded as Type='RULE OUT'. There were 34,916 such cases.
- Of the remaining cases, those with more than 10 separate claims or more than $1000 in physician claims (over more than 1 day) were coded as 'MAJOR'. There were 15,819 cases in this cell, all taken to be verified cases of DVT or PE.
- All remaining cases contained, by definition, between two and ten physician claims totaling less than $1000. These cases were coded as Type='OTHER'. This group of 19,056 cases were regarded as verified DVT or PE cases only if a DVT/PE discharge record was also present (ie, if Source='MD AND DISCH BOTH').

Table 15–3 summarizes the first identification of DVT/PE by site. The total number of verified DVT and PE cases is 19,781. Thus, almost 90 percent of the 195,043 cases originally identified with some evidence of DVT or PE were ruled out when more exact criteria were used. Furthermore, one of the primary findings of the study was altered by more careful identification of complications.

When the original 195,043 cases were used, the conclusion was that DVT and PE were most often identified after the initial hospital stay. This conclusion changes in the more tightly defined dataset, since 46 percent of the cases were identified in the hospital, and only 28 percent were identified in the office following hospital stay.

Table 15–3 All Cases by Site of First Identification of DVT/PE

Site	All Cases		Final Cases	
	Count	Percentage	Count	Percentage
Office	68,558	35.15	5,587	28.24
In-patient hospital	62,850	32.22	9,060	45.80
Outpatient hospital	48,764	25.00	2,156	10.90
Emergency room	6,728	3.45	1,496	7.56
Other	8,143	4.17	1,482	7.49
Total	195,043	100.00	19,781	100.00

ACKNOWLEDGMENT

We wish to thank David Siegel and Pauline Reisner of Sachs Group for supplying reference information for this article. We are grateful to Nelly Leon-Chisen, Director, Central Office of ICD9-CM, for clarifying the relationship between encoding and hospital billing systems.

REFERENCES

1. Sackett D. Evidence-based medicine. Semin Perinatol 1997;21(1):3–5.

2. Clancy C, Kameron D. Evidence-based medicine meets cost-effectiveness analysis. JAMA 1996;276(4):329–30.

3. U.S. News and World Report: America's best hospitals: where to find top medical care in 17 specialties. U.S. News and World Report 1997 July 28:58–102.

4. Iezzoni L. Risk adjustment for measuring healthcare outcomes. 2nd edition. Chicago: Health Administration Press: 1997.

5. National Center for Health Statistics National ambulatory medical care survey, 1993 data tape documentation. Hyattsville (MD): National Center for Health Statistics: 1995.

6. St. Anthony's illustrated ICD9-CM code book, Reston (VA): St. Anthony's Publishing: 1997.

7. St. Anthony's HCPCS level II code book. Reston (VA): St. Anthony's Publishing: 1996.

8. St. Anthony's UB-92 editor: a guide to Medicare billing. Reston (VA): St. Anthony's Publishing: 1996.

9. National Center for Health Statistics National hospital discharge survey public use data tape documentation, 1994. Hyattsville (MD): National Center for Health Statistics; 1996.

10. Iezzoni L. Assessing quality using administrative data. J Eval Clin Pract 1998;4(1):11–29.

11. Romano P, Mark D. Bias in the coding of hospital discharge data and its implications for quality assessment. Med Care 1994;32(1):81–90.

12. Fowles JB, Lawthers A, Weiner J, et al. Agreement between physicians' office records and Medicare Part B claims data. Health Care Financing Rev 1995;16(4)189–99.

13. Hannan E, Kilburn H, Lindsey M, Lewis R. Clinical versus administrative data bases for CABG surgery. Does it matter? Med Care 1992;30(10):892–907.

14. Hannan E, Petersen E, Jollis J, Racz M. Using Medicare claims data to assess provider quality for CABG surgery: does it work well enough? Cathet Cardiovasc Diagn 1997;40(1):21–32.

15. Quam L, Ellis L, Venus P, et al. Using claims data for epidemiologic research. The concordance of claims-based criteria with the medical record and patient survey for identifying a hypertensive population. Med Care 1993;31(6):498–507.

16. Baron J, Lu-Yao G, Barrett J, et al. Internal validation of Medicare claims data. Epidemiology 1994;5(50):541–4.

17. Iezzoni L, Foley S, Heeren T, et al. A method for screening the quality of hospital care using administrative data: preliminary validation results. Qual Rev Bull 1992 Nov;361–71.

18. Iezzoni L, Lawthers A, Davis R, et al. Project to validate the complications screening program. Final report. Boston (MA): Beth Israel Deaconess Medical Center; 1998.

19. Steinwachs D, Stuart M, Scholle S, et al. A comparison of ambulatory Medicaid claims to medical records: a reliability assessment. Am J Med Qual 1998;13(2):63–9.

20. Lauderdale D, Goldberg J. The expanded racial and ethnic codes in the Medicare data files: their completeness of coverage and accuracy. Am Public Health 1996;86(5):712–16.

21. National Association of Health Data Organizations. 1993: State Health Data Resource Manual: hospital discharge data systems. Falls Church (VA): National Association of Health Data Organizations; 1993.

CHAPTER 16

Electronic Patient Records

Stephanie L. Reel, MBA, and Steven F. Mandell, MS

As noted in a recent article, evidence-based surgery depends upon the "integration of individual clinical expertise with the best available external clinical evidence from systematic research."[1] Today, the best available external clinical evidence is obtainable in electronic format via on-line databases. Clinical and research data are now being published electronically on the World Wide Web (WWW) and are available to clinicians simultaneously around the world the moment they are put on-line. Similarly, health care organizations are moving away from paper-based systems and are providing clinical data in electronic formats to be shared by providers across the enterprise. Other clinical and research data from organizations such as professional societies, pharmaceutical manufacturers, for-profit medical information sources, and so forth, are also now disseminated to the physician's desktop workstation and/or made available as "electronic literature." Thus, the quantity of data available for physicians to review is growing, the dissemination of data is faster, and the communication vehicle is now computer-based rather than paper-based. This chapter will define the electronic patient record (EPR), describe its history, provide a review of medical information systems design, present a case study of the development of one such system, and describe technologic developments and related technologic barriers.

HISTORY OF THE ELECTRONIC PATIENT RECORD

The use of a computer to record a medical history was first described in 1966 at the University of Wisconsin. This early attempt was foiled by the massive machinery required and the limited capability of the software, but the university's medical leaders optimistically predicted that computers would someday be used to capture the patient's entire medical history.[2] As the machinery, the software, and the application of medical informatics to content evolved over the following decades, the ability to delineate, capture, store, and retrieve relevant medical data has dramatically improved. Table 16–1 identifies the major EPR systems developed as first-generation clinical tools that have been a significant source of clinical data for evidence-based medicine.[3–8]

In 1991, the Institute of Medicine (IOM) of the National Academy of Sciences completed a study on improving patient records using improved information management strategies and the latest technology platforms. The study examined the medical record and delineated policies and strategies to overcome impediments and achieve improvements. The institute cited the advantages of a computerized patient record as the ability to maintain longitudinal records, the availability of real-time access to information, the capability of decision support, the vastly greater research opportunities, the potential integration of triggers and reminders for clinical care, and improved legibility.[9] Consequently, EPR has become the "gold standard" for collecting, storing, and using clinical data in support of patient care, medical education, and research.

The Institute of Medicine's 1991 report "The Computer-Based Patient Record: An Essential Technology for Health Care"[10] describes the EPR as "the set of components that form the mechanism by which patient records are created, used, stored and retrieved. It includes people, data, rules and procedures, processing and storage devices, and communication and support facilities. It is designed to support clinicians through the availability of complete and accurate data, practitioner reminders and alerts, clinical decision support systems, links to bodies of medical knowledge, and other aids." The Computer-Based Patient Record Institute (CPRI) has expanded on this work, defining the EPR as a full electronic record of an individual's lifetime health status and health care. It is viewed as a replacement for the paper medical record as the primary record of care, meeting all clinical, legal, and administrative regulations. Thus, the EPR can be a compilation of "facts, observations, interpretations, plans, actions, and outcomes. Health data include information on allergies, history of illness and injury, functional status, diagnostic studies, assessments, orders, consultation reports, treatment records, and so forth."[11] This definition naturally leads to parsing the data in ways that support evidence-based medicine.

Considering the volume of data collected during a hospitalization, the potential for the EPR to improve quality of care and efficiency is significant and has been widely acknowledged.[12] A single hospital stay can generate thousands of separate observations when one includes laboratory results, physiologic monitor output, diagnostic imaging, and so on. The clinical data set is so massive that in one study physicians could not find 10 percent of these data elements stored in their normal place on a paper chart.[13] Given the geographic distribution of components of health care delivery systems in today's managed care environment, the need for the storage and management of these data in electronic format accelerates. When one factors in the burgeoning health care policy-making requirements for evidence-based assessment of clinical practice, the demand for EPRs becomes even more provocative. It has even been noted that technologic terms such as medical informatics, teleradiology, and internet-based hosting of the EPR are now common in the vocabulary of the national debate on health care policy-making.[14]

Today's EPR has emerged from the recognition that improved quality of care and cost savings will be the ultimate outcomes if care processes and outcomes information can be linked together in a meaningful and reliable way. Standardized forms of measurement to determine uniform approaches to clinical problems and to ensure data reliability and validity are needed to provide information for consumers, purchasers, and providers.

DECISION SUPPORT SYSTEMS

Physicians have sought to use computers to aid them in clinical care for several decades. Early decision support systems such as Mycin and Internist were designed at academic medical institutions to assist physicians in the diagnosis and treatment of complex problems. However, these early systems were limited in scope and capabilities. As the clinical community learned more about how computers could play a role in communications and decision making, as programming tools became more robust, and as the prices of hardware systems dropped, more broad-based applications were developed. Some of the most significant products were developed at Latter Day Saints Hospital (LDS) under Reed Gardner, at Regenstrief Institute under Clement McDonald, at Brigham & Women's Hospital under Jonathan Teich, and at Vanderbilt University Medical Center under William Stead and Randolph Miller.

In general, these products were developed to integrate the computer and its power to instantaneously execute millions of complex algorithms directly into the health care process. The goal was to move the computer from its traditional role as a reporter of facts to a role as an active partner in improving the quality of care for the patient.

Desired system attributes include

- Data storage (ie, warehousing) with rapid access to as much relevant clinical information as possible;
- Logical display of all the relevant available information that the caregiver requires, with simple computerized navigational processes to access auxiliary data;
- Screen design and information flow that closely matches clinical practice;

- Focus on the use of encoded data so that relationships between data elements can be linked, clinical rules related to these data can be established, and messages or actions are triggered when rules are met or broken;
- Support of clinical pathways and identification of variance from pathways; and
- Guidance and alerts to physicians regarding duplicate order checking for medications and labs, drug-drug interactions, allergy checking, checking of dose range limits, and so on.

MEDICAL INFORMATION SYSTEMS DESIGN

To better understand the development of the EPR it is useful to comprehend the underlying design of medical information systems. Medical information systems have evolved into three major categories: transactional systems, data repositories, and data warehouses. Transactional systems capture real-time activity and satisfy the specific needs of a defined area of practice. Most of these transactions can be initiated directly by a clinician or through an electronic interface with instruments, analyzers, or physiologic monitors. Transactional data are stored in database structures that can be queried as needed by an array of reporting tools. These niche systems are the foundation for the construction of a comprehensive database of clinical information. Standardized data collection methods among these systems are important, but the general recognition that each of these systems is designed to satisfy a particular need often overshadows cross-platform data integrity. Interfaces and integration tools are often used to mitigate the differences between and among these systems.

Data repositories are often created as a result of several transactional systems interacting together to complete a patient-centered view for a provider. Each transactional system must transmit data in a standard format to a repository where the data can be aggregated and used for decision support. Repositories typically allow for real-time on-line access to this information, often allowing for complex queries to be generated through analytic software programs. These systems can provide views of the data that cut across the transactional systems and can be displayed as text, graphics, or tables.

Warehouses and "data marts" are more often large, complex repositories used for retrospective analyses. These warehouses are designed to ensure accurate and complete data collection and contain vast amounts of information that is refreshed at regular intervals (eg, weekly, monthly, etc). These systems often consist of archived data that may not be available on-line and that lend themselves to complex longitudinal queries. This form of repository is often most valuable when large populations of patients are aggregated to perform comparative studies or to determine the presence or absence of trends.[15] Warehouses also provide a mechanism for queries that might otherwise adversely affect the performance of transactional systems used for direct patient care.

In spite of the obvious value of data warehouses, there are risks associated with their construction. Due to the absence of data standards, including standard data definitions, these warehouses often fall victim to the problems inherent in all poorly managed data. To minimize the impact of this weakness, "data-scrubbing" techniques (ie, editing algorithms) are used to reduce redundant records and correct obvious errors. This effort is often the most complex and time-consuming aspect of creating a comprehensive clinical repository.

The ultimate EPR is typically a combination of the three architectural solutions described above, with a focus on data accuracy and reliability. Designed properly, the EPR will provide the clinician with access to current medical literature as well as all related medical knowledge derived from patient experiences. Other attributes of the ideal EPR include immediate decision support feedback (appropriate to the case) whenever clinical interventions are suggested or ordered. It must be programmed to provide recommendations derived from comprehensive captured information, and it must assist decision making by providing continuous, spontaneous feedback based upon accumulated data. Last, the EPR must provide the needed information in a format that can be easily and readily appreciated and understood. It must capture relevant data from other electronic sources with minimal human intervention, performing required data validation to ensure accuracy and reliability. This data must then be aggregated and assimilated so that it has meaning between and among the various components of the EPR.

CLINICAL DECISION SUPPORT

Computer-assisted rules-based medicine is intended to guide the behavior of clinicians and other members of the health care team. In general, clinicians know the "rules" but are often deprived of the knowledge of the occurrence of a clinical event that might necessitate the application of a rule. A caregiver can react only to facts that are known and can base decisions only on requirements that are understood. Therefore, the first rules to be defined and implemented must focus on the need to notify appropriate staff of the occurrence of an event or the failure of an event to occur; only then can interventions be planned. The challenges associated with providing clinical alerts are not trivial, however, as the magnitude of data input is staggering.

There is a recognition that computers can enhance the ability of a caregiver to manage information, assess inputs, and make informed decisions. This is often different, however, from compliance with automated guidelines. Adherence to computerized pathways or practice guidelines, at least in some disciplines, has been embraced slowly because of the failure of these guidelines to incorporate the inherent decision making that many physicians perform as part of care delivery. There are thought processes that emerge from past experiences or "lessons learned" and from the "art" of medicine. It is often difficult for systems to emulate these processes or to allow for deviations or variations in practice that might result from them.

Within each electronic record available today, there are some expected sets of functionality that will support the physician in all aspects of patient care. Although not every software product provides every component, most are clearly migrating toward a full-service system that can support a patient across the continuum of care. Examples of this functionality include problem lists that can be linked to encounters, providers, diagnoses, orders, and results; health status metrics; input data that led to an intervention; access to knowledge bases; cost metrics and compliance data elements; controlled vocabulary and coding mechanisms; and a data dictionary that allows for varying degrees of granularity. It must be patient-centered when needed, provider-specific in its presentation format, and disease-aware when guiding decisions. To build all of this in an easy-to-use format is a challenge for even the most gifted software developers.

Computerized decision support and pathway development has also evolved over the past decade. The delineation of a medical taxonomy has hastened the growth of pathway development. Now widely acknowledged as a standard, the Arden Syntax is an accepted language for the definition of clinical rules that drive alerts, reminders, clinical guidelines, and data interpretations. (The standard was defined in 1989 at the Arden Homestead Conference in Harriman, New York). It has become the standard language for the definition of rules-based EPRs, particularly when integrated with order management systems. It is within these rule sets that standard pathways and guidelines can be defined.

The Arden Syntax is one important step in a long process of defining and deploying standards to support computer-assisted care delivery. Other important steps are also being taken by the United States government in the establishment of an EPR that will join patient information from the Department of Defense, the Veterans Administration, Indian Health Services, and the Louisiana State University Medical Center. If the United States government is successful with this initiative, the endorsement of standards and the acceptance of definitions will result.

CASE STUDY: THE JOHNS HOPKINS ELECTRONIC PATIENT RECORD

What must a computerized patient record include? What must it contribute to the process of delivering care for it to be worth the investment? In fact, there are many opinions and

Table 16–1 Major Electronic Patient Record Systems

System	Facility	Year
COSTAR	Harvard Medical School	1968
PROMIS (Problem Oriented Medical Record)	Medical Center of Vermont	1969
TMR (The Medical Record)	Duke University Medical Center	1970
The Regenstrief Medical Record System	Indiana University	1972
HELP	Latter Day Saints Hospital of Salt Lake City	1975
STOR (Summary Time-Oriented Record)	University of California Medical Center, San Francisco	1978

components, and nearly all of them must at least be considered when defining, designing, constructing or deploying systems.

A computerized patient record must allow for the inclusion of relevant factors and the exclusion of those not pertinent. It must know if a pertinent relative factor is missing or is likely to be missing. It must know when data are expected to be present or when data are likely to arrive. It must be able to be easily modified or adjusted to react to the subtle differences within and among various patient populations. It must be able to assist the provider, as he or she attempts to assist referring or consulting physicians, when interventions are being considered. It must provide the vehicle for informing all members of the care team when specifications have occurred. This record must present a longitudinal view of the patient for all the practitioners. It must become the gold standard and be used by all members of the care delivery team as only by its use will it provide value. It must serve as the "book of truth" or the single source of knowledge about a patient, and there must be a well-understood, very good reason for using it. The incentives must be apparent and quickly realized. For this computerized record to evolve, it must be responsive to the "law of unpredictable outcomes," remaining flexible in its architecture and presentation format. Although it must be shareable, it must be capable of being customized and personalized. Above all, it must be able to "learn" from all of its past experiences.

As with most large academic medical institutions, the history of the development of the EPR at The Johns Hopkins Hospital has been one of evolution rather than revolution. In the mid-1980s, it became apparent to a number of clinical and technical leaders that automated medical information systems would have to play a major role in improving the continuity of care issues demanded by the new Diagnostic Related Groups (DRG) system, which emphasized shorter hospital stays and maximized the use of outpatient and home care.[16] One such initiative at Johns Hopkins was the development of AUTRES, the automated discharge resume. Designed as the first major computer-generated report to provide complete discharge information for a referring physician or other health care provider, it was piloted in 1984 and went into full production serving the department of medicine in 1988. It was seen as the first part of an automated record that would provide data for future treatment and research.[16] An important component of the AUTRES project was the development of a technical infrastructure that included connectivity among diverse platforms including an IBM mainframe, Digital Equipment Company (DEC) mini computers, and personal computers. In addition, it relied on heterogeneous data sources accessed in part through a middle tier of Remote Procedure Calls (RPC), software designed to transparently deliver data to the user regardless of where it is stored.

The AUTRES technical foundation led to the development of the first version of the Johns Hopkins Electronic Patient Record, conceived in 1989 to provide a patient-centered view of the patient's health care experience, focusing on the in-patient component. Using the hospital's mainframe as the main repository, the application provided the physician with the ability to select and view all of the patient's laboratory values, radiology reports, discharge summaries, and operative notes. Written in a computer language known as CSP and displayed on dumb terminals or personal computers in terminal emulation mode, the application also allowed for on-line editing and signature of summaries and notes from personal computers using specially written scripts. Laboratory results and radiology reports were also available for outpatient episodes of care. Even though it was a text-based non-Windows system, the EPR provided physicians at Johns Hopkins a significant set of data in an electronic format. Although it became the standard for electronic information and initiated considerable interest among the faculty for use in patient care, teaching, and research, it was clear that a more robust version needed to be developed that would provide fast and efficient access to every patient's record across the entire continuum of care at Johns Hopkins.

The second version of this electronic record (EPR95, developed in 1995) was created by a select group of Johns Hopkins' clinical faculty and the Johns Hopkins Medicine Center for Information Systems (JHMCIS) programming staff, using a client-server architecture. The physician workstation has a graphical user interface (GUI) that provides an elegant interaction to an array of functions seamlessly tied to servers across the enterprise from microcomputers to an Amdahl mainframe. The data are "served" from the mainframe database and from databases of other, smaller computer servers. At present, there are about 2,000 client workstations connected to the EPR.

The latest version of the product, EPR98, is being used by over 3,000 clinicians in clinics, nursing units, physicians' offices, and in the medical records department. This version is available at the Johns Hopkins Hospital, the Bayview Medical Center, the Howard County General Hospital, and at ten ambulatory sites in the greater Baltimore metropolitan area. The Johns Hopkins Health System is a large complex academic medical institution with tens of thousands of in-patient visits and over a million outpatient visits per year. Its physical plant is dispersed throughout the state of Maryland. There is no single place where a patient's medical record is stored; even within the main East Baltimore campus, there is no single unified patient record. Therefore, EPR98 has become the primary source for fast, reliable, and complete information. Givers of primary care and consultants are both using the system to access the data, information, and text documents delineated above to enhance patient care. The global access allows caregivers in both in-patient and outpatient settings to see visit histories, laboratory results, and so forth, instantly. Many details of the patient encounter are not yet available at this time, but as more information sources are linked, the goal of an enterprise-wide EPR will be achieved.

Any health care provider (with appropriate security rights) using EPR98 can make use of the following features:

- Selection from over 3 million patient records by patient's identification number, patient's name, provider, in-patient census by nursing unit, or outpatient census by clinic.
- View of the patient's problems, medications, and allergies, with on-line capability to add, modify, and change.
- View of all in-patient and outpatient visits, with "drill-down" to associated information.
- View of over 60 million laboratory results, with stoplight highlighting of out-of-range panic values and all associated pathology comments, searchable by department (pathology, hematology, microbiology, etc) and date range.
- View of 3.5 million radiology reports posted over the past 7 years, searchable by department and date range.
- Ability to create, modify, print, and electronically sign and/or view an array of documents including clinic notes, operative notes, discharge summaries, and so on.

- Ability to dictate into a central dictating service, have those notes electronically posted to the EPR, and then view, edit, print, and electronically sign them. (These are being posted at a rate of about 40,000 per month.)
- Ability to create, modify, and print a health maintenance record including immunizations.
- View of an array of other patient documentation including echocardiograms, EEGs, ECGs, progress notes, sonograms, and so on.
- Ability to access the Central Physician Directory of 80,000 referring physicians and to cut and paste relevant data into notes and other documents.
- Web access to an array of knowledge bases, including Micromedex, MEDLINE, OVID, and so on.

In addition, a Web-enabled read-only version of EPR98 has also been developed using Java Script and is being used widely across the Johns Hopkins' continuum of care for remote access. This version is expected to grow in functionality as the security and patient confidentiality issues associated with Web-based electronic records are resolved.[17]

The electronic patient record at Johns Hopkins is an evolving product with many attributes that support evidence-based medicine, but a number of its important features are still under development.[18] It is expected that the clinical leadership will continue to lead the effort to improve EPR98 continually and to employ the newest technologies available. It is clear that sophisticated decision support services, telemedicine, telesurgery, radiologic imaging, and full-motion video technologies must be fully incorporated into the EPR of the future to ensure that the full value of evidence-based medicine can be realized.

TECHNOLOGIC DEVELOPMENTS IN DECISION SUPPORT

In his seminal work, *The Science of Decision Making*,[19] Nobel laureate Herbert Simon posits the proposition that decision making is composed of three parts: collecting the data, considering all the options, and then selecting the best option. The first task, collecting the data, is remarkably complex when one considers the amount of data published in any one given field in today's global medical marketplace. Medical professionals are facing an information explosion, and medical knowledge is expanding at an unprecedented rate. More than 360,000 articles are published in medical journals each year. The diffusion of knowledge to practitioners is so slow that one study found that 2 years after wide publication, fewer than 50 percent of general practitioners knew that laser surgery could save the sight of some of their diabetic patients.[20] Each day, more and more of that data is available almost as soon as the results are known, via publishing on the Internet and the World Wide Web (WWW). It is estimated that over 800 million documents will be on the Web by the year 2000. A recent keyword search of the Web revealed that more than 930,000 documents contained the word "cancer," 110,000 contained the term "skin cancer," and over 34,000 contained the word "melanoma." Recent estimates indicate there are nearly 100 million users now connected to the Web via 20 million host computers.[21] These numbers grow at a phenomenal rate each year, which is remarkable considering that Tim Berners-Lee "invented" the World Wide Web in 1989 and that the first multi-computer browser, Mosaic, only became available in late 1993.[22]

There is general agreement that the problems clinicians face are lack of robust tools to access data quickly and effectively; lack of time for inquiry; poor organization of the available material; lack of rapid universal access to data sources, and lack of "content-aware" search engines.[23–25] It is believed that the Web is a powerful new tool for delivering on-line clinical information. However, many have pointed out that its value to health care professionals is limited because its information is highly distributed and difficult to locate, its retrieval tools are primitive, and its indexing methodologies are suspect. The result is the development of suboptimal and "fuzzy" searches that interweave clinical content, consumer-oriented clinical information, and nonrelevant information. Medical informaticians are developing tools and methods to resolve this conundrum.

One application, CliniWeb, is an index to clinical information on the Web, providing a browsing and searching interface to clinical content at the level of the health care provider or student. Its database contains a list of clinical information resources on the Web that are indexed in terms from the Medical Subject Headings (MeSH) disease tree and is assisted by the concept-mapping engine of the SAPHIRE system. The CliniWeb database includes links to over 5,000 fully indexed Uniform Resource Locators (URLs) but admittedly suffers from its inability to maintain the database in the dynamic Web environment and provide more sophisticated indexing and retrieval capabilities.[25]

WebMedline, developed at Stanford University, facilitates searching of the medical literature using a standard Web browser. The application authenticates the user, allows input of search criteria, and then composes a legal MEDLINE search statement by removing stopwords from the input, qualifying input terms with appropriate field descriptors, and then joining these qualified input terms with Boolean operators. In addition, it attempts to map keywords to controlled indexing terms and returns MeSH terms to assist in choosing more precise query variables. The results are then output in MEDLINE format, creating links to full-text documents when it finds a corresponding full-text URL. WebMedline is in daily use at the University of California Medical Center in San Francisco, and over 500,000 sessions have been logged to date.[26]

DXplain is a Web-based diagnostic decision support program, designed as an educational tool to assist physicians and medical students in formulating a differential diagnosis based on one or more clinical findings. Developed at the Massachusetts General Hospital with grant support for the Web version from the National Library of Medicine (producer of the MEDLINE database) and Hewlett-Packard,[27] DXplain covers more than 2,000 diseases, more than 5,000 clinical manifestations, and 65,000 interrelationships including laboratory, x-ray, and EKG abnormalities. In addition to suggesting possible diagnoses, DXplain can provide brief descriptions of every disease in the database. This program generates a list of possible diagnoses, using a pseudoprobabilistic algorithm. It first evaluates the term importance and term-evoking strength of each finding diagnosis pair and then calculates a summary score for each disease. A disease score is most influenced by positive findings that have high term-evoking strength. After DXplain evaluates each clinical finding, it displays the highest ranked diagnoses divided into "common diseases" and "rare or very rare diseases." Not all diseases are included, nor does DXplain take into account pre-existing conditions or the chronologic sequence of clinical manifestations. Despite these limitations, it is considered to be a useful educational tool, particularly for medical students in clinical rotations as it fills a niche not adequately covered by the MEDLINE database or the standard medical texts. Entries are continually updated and revised, with input from users strongly encouraged.

In each of the above examples, medical informaticians have tried to join an array of technologies to solve the problems of decision making and information overload. By providing newer and more efficient ways of classifying data, developing more sophisticated matching tools based on "universal" medical syntax, and designing "expert" rules and algorithms, informaticians have made the modern clinical decision support tools more powerful than ever. Yet, these systems still require a large amount of effort to maintain, generally require clinicians to distill what they need from a plethora of relevant and irrelevant information, and require active involvement by clinicians to launch and refine searches.

The Brigham Integrated Computing System (BICS), introduced by Brigham and Women's Hospital in 1989, now includes a full ambulatory medical record, an in-patient order entry system, an event engine, and a lifetime record of a wide variety of tests, clinical summaries, and procedures.[28] It is used 24 hours a day throughout the facility and has had a substantial positive impact on the way medicine is practiced. Orders can be placed for any patient from any workstation, including remote workstations from offices and homes, greatly improving order accuracy, legibility, and timeliness while reducing the number of verbal orders. By inserting practice guidelines, rules, and reminders at the point where the physician places the order, the BICS is able to intervene and reduce 20 percent or more of adverse in-hospital events.[29] It is currently estimated that the system provides alerts for about 30 potential adverse reactions from 4,000 daily medication orders, with almost 50 percent of those warnings resulting in changes to the order. Significant numbers of redundant lab and medication orders are similarly flagged, with nearly 35 percent of those orders being canceled. Thus, not only is patient care enhanced, but it is estimated that the clinical decision support system saves Brigham and Women's Hospital nearly $5 million per year.

The development of WizOrder at Vanderbilt University Medical Center (VUMC), begun in 1994, was an effort to implement a medical decision support system by understanding that such a system could gain widespread acceptance when a "critical mass" of functionality was delivered to the clinical community through an easy-to-use interface on a readily available platform. Randy Miller, quoting Hippocrates' *Aphorisms*, reflected that the basis for decision support systems in medicine has been understood for more than two millennia: "Life is short, art is long, opportunity fleeting, experience treacherous, judgment difficult." The core of the WizOrder application is the assumption that the system enables clinicians to convert their decisions into actions at the time of order writing so that patient-specific decision support is implemented optimally through the order entry process. The design specifications include:

- a single-screen layout that remains stable during the session and has as few dialog boxes as possible
- a list of current active orders visible at all times and displayed in a clinically relevant sequence
- a mechanism to enter orders in a manner similar to handwritten orders
- problem-driven sets of orders that resemble familiar preprinted order sheets
- seamless access to decision support tools

WizOrder is used in nearly every unit of VUMC, and 92 percent of all hospital orders at VUMC are placed in the system, including orders placed by intensive care units, step-down units, the bone marrow transplant unit, and the dialysis unit. Decision support tools currently available include the following: drug monographs; drug-drug and drug-lab interaction warnings; allergy warnings; patient-specific dose range checking; decision trees for selecting empirical antibiotherapies; diagnosis- and procedure-based order sets; an automated link to relevant biomedical literature citations; and various tightly integrated Web-based resources such as extensive drug references, patient education sheets, radiology reference manuals, and so forth.[30] This is supported by importing data and knowledge from other systems known to WizOrder. For instance, a set of about 25,000 references from MEDLINE is downloaded with the VUMC OVID search engine and matched with patient-specific data to provide literature references relevant to each case. Tables from the Unified Medical Language System (UMLS) Metathesaurus are then used to translate drug names and diagnoses into MeSH terms. This process is also used to assist the encoding of diagnoses and procedures in ICD-9.[31]

The ability to notify users and applications of new events is an essential part of the decision support function within the EPR. Most traditional systems rely on the request-reply model to query databases for new data. The systems noted above, for the most part, are synchronous, event-based, clinical systems developed to notify physicians and nurses of critical interactions and results at the time of order entry. Thus, the machine and the clinician must be coupled and in direct communication to complete the transaction. However, the ubiquitous presence of asynchronous events in clinical experience argues for the delineation of a general notification engine as a new component of an extended decision-making tool. Asynchronous processes are now being deployed to track all new patient-centered data, relate that data to known data on the patient, apply rules and understand significant relationships, and provide appropriate alerts .[32] In this manner, the machine and the clinician are decoupled, but the asynchronous event launches processes that facilitate communication in a way that permits the clinician to respond appropriately. For example, if a laboratory value is posted to the patient's record and the system recognizes that there are negative implications for a drug the patient is on, a notice to the clinician in the form of a page, E-mail, or some other alert can be facilitated. Clinical outcomes may thus be improved by proactive patient management or by averting adverse reactions.

TECHNOLOGIC BARRIERS IN DECISION SUPPORT

The medical information systems architecture of transactional systems, data repositories, and data warehouses are coming to fruition due to technologic developments that enable massive data warehousing and analytic query capabilities. Sophisticated and powerful database systems, huge and efficient disk storage systems, and increasingly powerful symmetric parallel processing capabilities are all available today at ever decreasing costs. However, there is a paucity of rigorous standards that would facilitate the exchange of health care data across disparate systems, and the development of a naturally intuitive human-machine interface remains a major challenge despite such advances as GUIs and voice input. Current medical informatics literature is rich with details of projects that try to solve this dilemma with techniques such as speech recognition, digital dictation, structured data entry, content-to-speech generation, and new graphical interaction models.[33,34] Data entry is not typically a strength of the physician, and all of these systems require some form of data entry. Given the frenetic pace of academic medicine and the demand for more and more documentation, there is even greater pressure to create an input methodology that closely emulates the time frame of documenting with pen and paper. Most activity in this area attempts to do two things: reduce the time for data input to "near-paper-and-pen time" and provide value to the health care provider in exchange for the extra time required for electronic input. Until the time difference between paper-and-pen entry and electronic data entry nears zero, and/or continuous speech voice recognition is error-free and speaker-independent, interface issues will remain a significant impediment to making the EPR ubiquitous.

Another barrier that continues to hamper the development of the EPR is the lack of standards that would facilitate the collection and exchange of health care data so that it may be aggregated and analyzed to support clinical decision making. If this data can someday be pooled in regional, national, and global data bases and then made available through reliable, secure networks, evidence-based medicine will be more easily supported. As previously noted, clinical data are stored in an array of systems across the health care continuum. International protocols established by the Institute of Electrical and Electronic Engineers (IEEE), the American National Standards Institute (ANSI), and so forth, set message standards for computer-to-computer communications and define the structure and content that can be exchanged between systems. Given the variety of clinical data formats (eg, text, image, voice), the numbers and maturity of standards make messaging and connectivity a complex problem. The development of interfaces between disparate systems has been a medical informatics topic for nearly 20 years,[35,36] leading to the creation of a number of groups within international standards organizations. The American College of Radiology (ACR) and the National Electrical Manufacturers Association (NEMA) developed the first Digital Imaging and Communications in Medicine (DICOM) standard in 1983 while the ANSI accredited the Health Level Seven (HL7) standard for patient admissions, clinical observations, pharmaceutical and dietary issues, appointment scheduling, and so on, in 1994.[37] Importantly, the United States Health Insurance Portability and Accountability Act of 1996 (HIPAA) requires that standards for electronic exchange of administrative, financial, and clinical data be established. Work is in progress on all fronts in this area, but it will take time for standards to be selected, adopted, and proliferated. In addition to clinicians seeking more robust data, major beneficiaries will be health care policymakers, clinical researchers focusing on the effectiveness and appropriateness of care, regulatory agencies, and third-party payers.

Clearly, the goals posited by the Institute of Medicine (IOM) for a robust EPR are coming to fruition. With new technology, powerful computers, programming tool sets, and medical informatics skills, the deployment of fully functioning EPRs is moving forward in many medical centers. Although there are many difficulties in deploying a system of such breadth and depth,[38] the rewards for patient care, education, and research appear to be rich. However, it should be noted that these systems only scratch the surface in terms of providing the decision support that will be commonplace in the next decade. The examples cited above demonstrate that intelligent systems can be built that notify a clinician of a drug interaction with the drug the patient is currently on or that choose "gentamicin 80 mg intravenous" when a clinician enters the order "gen 80 IV," by matching the order against a known formulary. Although there is great complexity in the system design, these are relatively simple processes that take known data, compare it to certain sets of rules coded in the application, and then trigger events based on the testing of those rules. The new millennium will see far more sophisticated processes and tools incorporated into the decision support function, such as intelligent "medical agents" and nanomedicine technology.

Recent Related Technologic Developments

As the medical community is able to delineate practice as a set of protocols or critical paths, the ability to provide decision support becomes more intriguing. Current systems can support the development of "order sets" or decision rules that mirror protocols in many disciplines.[9,39,40] In these models, the order sets are coded in the system to require the clinician to follow a defined clinical pathway, with branching logic as patient-specific variables require variance from the clinical path or within the decision model. The order sets or protocols are rigid in the sense that they are typically based on some clinical committee's recommendation as to best practice. Thus, these guidelines are changed only when new findings require changes in practice. One limitation of this approach is that the source of advice is limited to a small group of clinicians who craft the rules and who are limited in their ability to constantly survey the global medical environment and entertain new evidence as it is made available.

Intelligent Medical Agents

It is proposed that with the advent of new search engines, a class of intelligent medical agents will arise that will be able to provide continual content-specific, highly correlated medical evidence to take decision support to a new level of sophistication. These medically aware software agents will work much like current "Web crawlers," continually and dynamically searching Web sites globally for relevant medical knowledge and data. For example, acceptable published evidence could be made available to a surgeon when it is needed for clinical care or research.

At present, Carnegie Mellon University's School of Computer Science is developing a collection of intelligent software agents that access, filter, and integrate information in support of the user's needs. This initiative, along with dozens of others, is laying the foundation for the types of intelligent medical agents delineated above. As the demand for decision support increases and as the availability of new evidence in a globally accessible electronic format grows, the development of intelligent medical agents will become crucial to success. Such an approach will further contribute to the evidence available for analysis.

Telemedicine

Telemedicine is the use of modern telecommunications and information technologies to provide health care to individuals when the clinician and patient are physically separated. Instead of transporting the patient to the site of the health care expert, expert knowledge is transported to the health care provider closest to the patient. Telemedicine includes the diagnosis, treatment, and monitoring of patients, using systems that allow ready access to patient information, vital signs, and expert advice. An array of technologies may be used, including real-time physiologic data acquisition, still imaging, full-motion imaging, clinical text, medical data transmission, and audio. To facilitate this movement of image, text, and voice, a rich telecommunications infrastructure must be available to support the transmissions. Participating sites are typically linked through complex networks including satellites, microwave links, and fiber-optic terrestrial and submarine lines.

Until recently, many patients had to travel significant distances to see a specialist for medical consultation. Similarly, medical documents and films were stored in one location and had to be physically transported to the specialist so that the complete medical record was on hand. Medical practice now has powerful tool sets called telemedicine, which enable it to operate in a more distance-independent manner. Telemedicine has obvious applications in the rural United States where specialist care is scarce. In its broadest application, it has the ability to serve the global community, providing resources to patients in the developing countries.

Telemedicine continues to gain importance in both ordinary and extraordinary applications. A recent study addressed the effect of a telecardiology system on the intensive care length of stay of very low birth-weight (VLBW) newborn infants. With telecardiology, the shorter turnaround time for neonatal echocardiography interpretation resulted in a 17 percent reduction of intensive care length of stay. By reducing the time to diagnosis, inappropriate therapies were avoided and critical therapies were initiated more rapidly.[41] Initiatives in home-based asthma telemonitoring,[39] nationwide telecare for diabetics,[40] and neonatal home telemedicine[42] are under way. In a more broad-based application, Cedars-Sinai Medical Center has agreed to provide expert remote care to passengers aboard the new 2,600 passenger, $450 million *Grand Princess* cruise ship. Using the Seamed system, the physicians aboard ship will be able to establish a two-way live video link to obtain assistance in the treatment of cardiac and pulmonary emergencies by sending radiographs and electrocardiograms via satellite to specialists at Cedars-Sinai.[43] Other examples of telemedicine's application in manned space efforts and military operations, where distance and time place heavy restrictions on patient transport to remote medical expertise, are abundant. In fact, the basic telemedicine framework was derived from deliberate engineering and technology transfer, much of it from the field of space and aviation.[44]

The National Aeronautics and Space Administration (NASA) has long used telemedicine for its astronauts and continues to rely on this mode of in-flight medical consultation.[45] Since its very beginning, space medicine has used communications and information processing technologies that mimic those used in earthbound remoteness: telemedicine, telediagnostics, and biotelemetry. In the 1960s, the United States and Russia fostered space telemedicine when they developed capabilities for remote medical monitoring and care for astronauts in their human space-flight programs from Project Mercury to the space shuttle and from *Vostok* to *Mir*. Essentially, medical conferences were held between the crew surgeon and crew members, and during extra-vehicular activity, astronauts were constantly monitored via telemetry. For example, during the Apollo lunar excursions, EKG, heart rate, oxygen consumption, heat production, suit carbon dioxide levels, and other physiologic and environmental variables were monitored by a biomedical team at the NASA Mission Control Center at the Johnson Space Center, Houston, Texas. Flight surgeons were on alert to catch potentially dangerous physiologic events and intervene at the earliest possible moment.[46] As must be noted, this description reprises the goals of the decision support products discussed earlier. The same medical philosophy applies: provide evidence as to best practice, protocolize it, and then apply it universally.

Recently, NASA has established telemedicine links with former Soviet republics for disaster relief.[47] Specifically, the Space Bridge to Armenia/Ufa project provided assistance to persons involved in the 1989 earthquake in Armenia and a major gas explosion in Ufa. The project was the longest-running disaster relief effort by telemedicine on record, and it paved the way for using satellite uplinks and efficiently planned protocols to provide medical care regardless of distance. The Space Bridge project provided medical consultation to several Armenian regional hospitals, linking them via satellite with four American medical centers. The program used two-way interactive audio with one-way full-motion video transmitted from Armenia to the United States. Consultations were provided in neurology, orthopedics, psychiatry, infectious disease, and general surgery. In a separate link, consultation was also provided to the Russian town of Ufa, where a gas explosion during this same period of time caused many casualties. Telemedicine had been used on many occasions; however, it had never before been deployed and tested on such a large scale as it was in the Space Bridge project.[48]

Telesurgery

In the future, telemedicine capability will be an important component in health care aboard the international space station, especially in the prevention and early intervention aspects of disease and injury. In addition, during a medical emergency, telemedicine capability can play an important "lifeline" role in the rapid exchange of patient information and access to special medical expertise and crucial instruction. However, if an emergency is life threatening and requires medical treatment, the combined resources of telemedicine and onboard medical capability may be limited, requiring evacuation to Earth. For missions beyond Earth's orbit, evacuation may not be an option, and onboard medical capability, including expert computer systems and telemedicine capability as well as the crew's medical expertise, will need to be enhanced. Protocol-driven, evidence-based solutions for medical and surgical procedures will be imperative. Intelligent surgical devices with real-time tactile feedback to earthbound surgeons could provide successful solutions to many difficult problems. Current work in this field, telesurgery, describes the application of existing and developing technologies in remote manipulation applied to surgical procedures.[49]

The fundamental principle of a telesurgery system is to make available a surgeon's psychomotor skills and problem-solving abilities to a remote environment. The goal is for a surgeon to operate on a patient in a remote location via real-time tactile and visual feedback from the patient's location to the surgeon. Unlike telerobotic surgery, in which a robotic manipulator is directed by a clinician or preprogrammed computer instructions,[50] or surgical virtual reality, in which manipulations are performed in a simulated environment, telepresence is a unique human-machine technology that directly and transparently projects real-time motion to a remote location. Using this technology, it would be possible to operate at an inaccessible, distant, or dangerous place, such as a space station or a battlefield.

A prototype system that permits precise and accurate remote surgery with all the illusion of being at the actual site consists of a remote work site and a surgeon's console, similar to a computer workstation.[51] This system brings together 3-dimensional vision, enhanced dexterity, and the sense of touch (through feedback sensory information), which provide the realism of actually operating at the remote site. The current version is a one-handed 5-degrees-of-freedom system with paired CCD cameras for stereo vision; the next generation will have two 6-DOF (degrees of freedom) surgical hands and a stereoscopic laparoscope to replace the fixed cameras. In the near future, full remote surgery, relying on evidence-based practice as the guideline, will be commonplace.

CONCLUSION

Over the past 20 years, there have been dramatic changes in the practice of surgery, many due to sophisticated techniques made possible by high-technology surgical tools. As noted, there have been concomitant improvements in medical information systems as well. The EPR, once considered nothing more than a lofty goal, is now a reality in a wide array of iterations. These EPRs now incorporate both asynchronous and synchronous decision support algorithms and Web-based knowledge, storing data in warehouses that can support dynamic queries to enhance patient care and research. The data and outcomes research required to support evidence-based surgery is now available.

Advances in medical informatics will further strengthen evidence-based surgery by enchancing access to the hundreds of millions of documents on the Web to provide data, citations, and practice guidelines on a case-specific basis directly to the surgeon. A new communications framework will emerge, enabled by an even more powerful digital communication infrastructure. It is expected that there will be extremely sophisticated digital connectivity between the surgeon's operating tools and the global information infrastructure providing better data collection and analysis of patient interventions and outcomes than is presently possible. For example, eletronic storage of intraoperative data, such as physiologic readings during invasive procedures, could allow analyses of biologic evidence not presently analyzed. Today's EPR represents only a small fraction of information likely to be available someday to guide and shape practice.

The ability of science to continue to create newer, faster, more compact medical and computing machinery is not doubted, nor is the ability of medical informaticians to develop computer programs to take advantage of these technologies. It appears that the only limitation we will face is that of our own imagination.

REFERENCES

1. Sacket, D. Evidence based medicine. Semin Perinatol 1997:21(1):3–5.

2. Slack WV, Hicks GP, Reed CE, Van Cura LJ. A computer based medical history. N Engl J Med 1966;274:194–8.

3. Barnett GO. The application of computer-based medical records systems in ambulatory practice. N Engl J Med 1984;310:1643–50.

4. Weed LL. Medical records that guide and teach. N Engl J Med 1968;278:593–600.

5. Stead WW, Hammond WE. Computer based medical records: the centerpiece of TMR. MD Comput 1988;5:48–62.

6. McDonald CJ, Blevins L, Tierney WM, Martin DK. The Regenstrief medical records. MD Comput 1988;5:34–47.

7. Pryor TA. The HELP medical record system. MD Comput 1988;5:22–33.

8. Whiting O'Keefe QE, Whiting A, Henke J. The STOR clinical information system. MD Comput 1988;5:8–21.

9. Dick RS, Steen EB. The computer-based patient record: an essential technology for health care. Washington (DC): National Academy Press; 1991.

10. Institute of Medicine. The computer based patient record: an essential technology for health care. Washington (DC): National Academy Press; 1991.

11. CPRI Work Group on CPR Description. Description of the computer based patient record (CPR) and computer based patient record system. 1995. Available from: URL: http://www.cpri.org/docs/hldd.html.

12. McDonald CJ. Need for standards in health information health affairs. 1998;6(17):44–6.

13. Fries J. Alternatives in medical record formats. Med Care 1974:10(12):871–81.

14. Moran DW. Health information: on preparing for the next war. Health Aff 1998;6(17):9–22.

15. Teich JM. Clinical systems for integrated healthcare networks. J Am Med Inform Assoc 1998; 4(1):19–28.

16. Lenhard RE, Buchman JP, Achuff SC, et al. The Johns Hopkins Hospital automated resume. J Med Sys 1991;15:3.

17. Wang DJ, Harkness KB, Allshouse C, et al. Development of a web based electronic patient record extending accessibility to clinical information and integrating ancillary applications. J Am Inform Assoc 1998;131–4.

18. Mandell SF, Szekalski S. The use of an enterprise wide electronic patient record. Proc Am Med Inform Assoc 1997;1029.

19. Simon H. The new science of decision making. New York: Prentice Hall; 1977. p.14.

20. Detmer WM, Shortliffe EH. Using the Internet to improve knowledge diffusion in medicine. Communication of ACM 1997:101–8.

21. Li YC. Finding medical resources on the Internet. Yearbook of medical informatics 1998: Health informatics and the Internet. New York: Schattaver; 1998. p. 108–12.

22. Berners-Lee T. A little history of the World Wide Web. Available from:URL:http://www.org/history.html, Nov, 1998.

23. Tarczy-Hornoch P, Kwann-Gett TS, Fouchel HJ, et al. Meeting clinician information needs by integrating access to the medical record and knowledge resources via the Web. Proc AMIA New York: Prentice Hall; 1997. p. 809.

24. Smith R. What clinical information doctors need? BMJ 1996;313:1062–8.

25. Hersh WR, Brown KE. Cliniweb: managing clinical information on the World Wide Web. J Am Med Inform Assoc 1994;3(4):273–80.

26. Detmer WM, Shortliffe EH. A model of clinical query management that supports integration of biomedical information over the World Wide Web. Proc Annu Symp Comput Appl Med Care 1995;898–902.

27. Barnett GO, Cimino JJ, Hupp JA, Hoffer EP. DXplain: an evolving diagnostic decision support system. JAMA. 1987;258(1):67–74.

28. Teich JM, Glaser JP, Beckley RF, Aranow M. Brigham and Women's Hospital information system. Davies recognition submission. Computer Based Patient Record Institute. 1996.

29. Bates DW, O'Neil AC, Boyle D, Teich JM. Potential identifiablity and preventability of adverse events using information systems. J Am Med Inform Assoc 1994;1:404–41.

30. Guissbuhler A. WizOrder: a physician order management system developed by Vanderbilt University Medical Center. Available from:URL.http://www.mc.Vanderbilt.Edu/dbmi/antoine/wizdemo. Dec, 1998.

31. Guissbuhler AG, Miller RA. A new approach to the implementation of direct care-provider order entry. J Am Med Inform Assoc 1996; 2(3): 689–93.

32. Sullivan SJ. White paper: clinical decision support—why does it matter? Eclipsys Corporation; 1997.

33. Bierner G. TraumaTalk: content to speech generation for decision support at point of care. J Am Med Inform Assoc 1998;4(2):698–702.

34. Sittig DF, Yungton JA, Kuperman GJ, Teich JM. A graphical user interaction model for integrating complex clinical applications: a pilot study. J Am Med Inform Assoc 1998;4(2):708–12.

35. Simborg DW. Networking and medical information systems. J Med Sys 1984;8:43–7.

36. McDonald CJ. The search for national standards for medical data exchange [editorial] MD Comput 1984;1:3–4.

37. Huff SM. Clinical data exchange standards and vocabularies for messages. J Am Med Inform Assoc 1998;62–7.

38. Dolan C, Kissamore L. Untying the Gordian knot. In: Nursing administration. 2nd ed. Managing patient care. New York: Appleton & Lange; 1998.

39. Finkelstein J, Hripcsak G, Cabrera MR. Patients' acceptance of Internet-based home asthma tele-monitoring. J Am Med Inform Assoc 1998;4(1):336–40.

40. Jones PC, Silverman BG, Athanasoulis M, et al. Nationwide telecare for diabetics: a pilot implementation of the HOLON architecture. J Am Med Inform Assoc 1998:4(1):346–50.

41. Rendina MC. The effect of telemedicine on neonatal intensive care unit length of stay in very low birthweight infants. J Am Med Inform Assoc 1998:111–15.

42. Gray J, Pompilio-Weitzner G, Jones PC, et al. Baby CareLink: development and implementation of a WWW-based system for neonatal home telemedicine. J Am Med Inform Assoc 1998;4(1):351–5.

43. ER at sea. Mod Healthcare 1998 June 29;28(26).

44. Garshnek V, Hasseff LH, Davis HQ. Telemedicine—breaking the distance barrier in health care delivery. June 1998. http://AKAMAI.TAMC.AMEDD.ARMY.MIL/TELEMEDICINE.

45. Pool SL, Stonsifer JC, Belasco N. Application of telemedicine systems in future manned space flight. Proceedings of the 2nd Telemedicine Workshop; 1975 Dec; Tucson (AZ).

46. Johnston RS, Dietlein LF, Berry CA, editors. Biomedical results of Apollo. Washington (DC): US Government Printing Office; NASA SP-368.

47. Houtchens BA, Clemmer TP, Holloway HC. Telemedicine and international disaster response: medical consultation to Armenia and Russia via a telemedicine spacebridge. Prehosp Disaster Med 1993;8:57-66.

48. Thring MW. Robots and telechirs. New York: John Wiley & Sons; 1983. p. 275-8.

49. Green P, Satava R, Hill J, Simon I. Telepresence: advanced teleoperator technology for minimally invasive surgery. Surg Endosc 1992;6:62–7.

50. Durlach NT, Mavor AS, editors. Virtual reality: scientific and technical challenges. Washington (DC): National Academy Press; 1995.

51. Simon B. Surgery 2001: concepts of telepresence surgery. Surg Endosc 1993;7:462–3.

CHAPTER 17

Practice Guidelines: Evidence and Intuition

Neil R. Powe, MD, MPH, MBA, and Sean Tunis, MD, MSc

HISTORICAL PERSPECTIVE

Clinical practice guidelines have been present for perhaps centuries, having been introduced in rudimentary form by the ancient Greeks and Egyptians and by the Bible. The first clinical practice guideline of the modern era of surgery and medicine is usually acknowledged to be a guideline on pediatric vaccinations from 1938.[1] However, the recent exponential growth in the number of guidelines being produced began in the 1980s.[2] In part, the recent surge of interest in practice guidelines has stemmed from the pioneering work of Wennberg and others performed in the 1970s. This work showed variations of up to sixfold in the rates of surgical procedures among small geographic areas in New England, areas where rates of underlying disease are not thought to vary substantially. This provocative work suggested that variations in the use of such procedures as prostatectomy, tonsillectomy, and hysterectomy are related to the practice style of physicians and to the number of surgeons in a geographic area, with higher rates in areas where there are more surgeons.[3] Such differences in practice style could stem from lack of awareness of the benefits of surgery, disagreement or uncertainty about the best way to manage a condition, lack of skills to implement new approaches, or differences in patient preferences. Because variation in medical practice has potential quality of care and cost implications, these studies led to a substantial interest among physicians, providers, and health policy makers in finding strategies to decrease this variability in surgery and other specialty practices in the hope of lowering costs and improving outcomes of care.[4] Some pejoratively call this standardizing practice; others call it assuring a uniformly high quality of care in surgical practice. The modern era of clinical practice guidelines is based upon these premises, which often evoke strong emotions among physicians.

On the other hand, surgeons today face intimidating tasks of managing information as they attempt to keep up with the burgeoning biomedical and clinical literature. The lack of awareness, agreement, and implementation skills that may cause physicians to practice in different ways may originate in part from the inability to keep up with the literature to synthesize information for clinical practice. A few relatively new journals have provided some assistance through structured abstracts of published papers that meet basic methodological standards (eg, American College of Physicians (ACP) Journal Club, 1999). Review articles that use systematic methods can help by gathering and combining evidence that relates to common clinical decisions. While useful, these approaches do not always synthesize information in a way that directly supports specific clinical recommendations and that is easy to assimilate for busy clinicians; hence the need for comprehensive, authoritative (but brief) guides for clinical practice. In this chapter, we review the definitions of practice guidelines and related terms, outline the steps in producing practice guidelines, discuss the types of guidelines currently available, and consider whether guidelines will measure up to their promise to improve the quality and cost of care.

DEFINING A PRACTICE GUIDELINE

Clinical practice guidelines represent an attempt to distill a large body of medical knowledge into a convenient, readily usable format.[5] They have been defined as "systematically developed statements to assist practitioner and patient decisions about appropriate health care for specific clinical circumstances."[6] Guidelines go beyond most systematic literature reviews (see Chapter 16), addressing one or more specific questions by attempting to address all the issues relevant to a clinical decision and all the judgments and preferences that might influence a clinical recommendation.

Clinical practice guidelines have been developed for every aspect of clinical decision making: prevention (eg, screening for hypertension), diagnosis (eg, appropriate work-up of a carotid bruit), and treatment (eg, indications for carotid endarterectomy). They can be developed by a variety of interested parties: local hospitals and provider groups, regional managed care organizations, and state legislatures, national agencies (eg, the Agency for Health Care Policy and Research [AHCPR] and the Centers for Disease Control and Prevention), and professional specialty organizations. Estimates of the number of practice guidelines in the United States range from 1,800 to > 26,000.[7]

A number of terms related to practice guidelines have become more commonplace in the past several years. These include the terms "clinical pathways" and "clinical algorithms." Clinical pathways (also known as critical pathways or carepaths) generally are standardized protocols of interventions for particular diagnoses or procedures. These pathways focus on delivering clinical services as efficiently as possible once the decision has been made to provide the service. Clinical guidelines, on the other hand, may focus on the risks and benefits of the initial decision to provide a surgical technology, in addition to a way to apply the technology. Clinical algorithms are chart sequences of clinical decisions in the form of sequential branching flow diagrams. These algorithms may depict a series of recommendations from a single guideline document or from multiple guidelines.[8]

CREATING A PRACTICE GUIDELINE

Guideline development methods include unstructured consensus development (eg, the consensus development program of the National Institutes of Health), formal consensus development (eg, the RAND appropriateness guidelines), and evidence-based methods that explicitly link recommendations with supporting science (eg, guidelines produced by the AHCPR and the American College of Physicians). One important aspect of these different approaches is the role of clinical intuition versus evidence. Guidelines can be developed based on clinical intuition alone, evidence alone, or a combination of the two (ie, clinical intuition as a substitute when evidence is lacking).

While an increasing number of guidelines follow a structured process and attempt to be evidence-based, there is still considerable variability in the quality of guidelines being produced. Guidelines make explicit recommendations, often on behalf of health organizations, with a definite intent of influencing what clinicians do. They reflect value judgments on the relative importance of various health and economic outcomes in specific clinical situations. As a result, they must be evaluated critically in regard to how matters of evidence, clinical intuition, and judgment are handled. Guidelines for appraising clinical practice guidelines have recently been published.[9,10] These Users' Guides help a guideline reader determine what the specific recommendations are, whether they are valid, and whether they will be helpful in caring for a particular group of patients.

Many of the current efforts to develop guidelines use a modified version of the framework developed by the AHCPR.[11] The basic methods for developing evidence-based practice guidelines include the following steps:[11–13]

Step 1: Formation of an Expert Panel

Guideline development usually starts off with the selection of an expert panel whose role is to guide the entire development, including the framing of specific questions, the search for and interpretation of evidence, and the writing of recommendations. Panel members usually include not only clinical experts familiar with the disease or procedure but also methodology experts skilled in evidence synthesis and health system experts who may be involved in implementation. Consumer or patient advocates, members of other specialty societies, and industry experts might also be part of the expert panel. With the addition of these latter groups, enhanced acceptance of the completed guidelines must be weighed with the possible political pressure during the development process.

Step 2: Definition of Topic and Process

The most critical step in developing a clinical practice guideline is defining its topic and scope. The topic and scope should be defined in precise terms, clearly identifying the target condition, management of options (including both surgical and medical approaches), patient population, and potential health outcomes to be addressed. Whether the guideline addresses prevention, diagnosis, therapy, or rehabilitation, it should specify both the interventions of interest and the sensible alternative practices. Without explicit decisions about these aspects of the scope of the guideline, evidence gathering and synthesis cannot proceed efficiently. Many guideline efforts fail to adequately narrow their scope, producing a final document that covers a broad topic with inadequate attention to the critical details of the evidence.

Step 3: Assessment of Clinical Benefits and Harms

Prior to collecting scientific evidence, guideline panels should identify the potential health benefits and risks associated with available interventions. These risks and benefits are identified through informal review of published studies as well as the clinical experience of experts. Doing this will ensure that no critical areas are overlooked in the search for evidence. A diagram outlining the potential benefits, harms, and other influential factors can help the guideline development process.

Step 4: Systematic Review of Scientific Evidence

Relevant literature is retrieved by comprehensively searching the literature to identify all studies within the scope defined by the panel.[14] Appropriate and explicit inclusion and exclusion criteria need to be defined and used to conduct a comprehensive search. Individual studies are then evaluated, using systematic methods to judge the quality of the evidence and to extract the results. The evidence is then displayed in evidence tables and summarized qualitatively, using narrative reviews, evidence tables, and various analytic techniques to combine data (eg, meta-analysis).[15–18]

A quality-of-evidence scale can be used to rate different categories of evidence (eg, expert opinion or clinical investigation) and methods for producing it (eg, blinded or nonblinded outcomes assessment), according to how likely it is that the source or design will yield biased results.[19] It is important to prospectively develop and apply a systematic approach to appraising and classifying evidence so that the strength of evidence supporting the recommendations can be reported.

Step 5: Consideration of Expert Opinion

Many areas of surgical practice unfortunately lack peer-reviewed scientific evidence. In such cases, expert opinion based on clinical intuition and experience is often substituted. Expert opinion is usually gathered from the expert panel itself or by seeking extensive review from outside experts. Expert consensus may be obtained informally (ie, by unstructured discussion) or by more formal techniques (eg, the RAND modified Delphi process) that provide a quantitative basis for analyzing the strength and agreement of opinions.[20] The use of expert opinion should not supersede the search for and use of strong evidence. Even with the best intentions, guidelines based only on expert opinions will be questioned, especially if they go in a direction that economically favors the expert's constituency.

Step 6: Consideration of Resource and Feasibility Issues

Practice guidelines will sometimes consider economic and resource issues through cost-effectiveness and cost-utility analyses. This may require supplemental analysis of economic data and surveys of practitioners or patients to identify barriers to implementation. Practical issues must also be considered, such as whether clinicians have the time, training, and staff support to implement the interventions. Patients must also have the resources that enable them to follow physician prescriptions.

Step 7: Development of Recommendations

The evidence and judgments about the benefits and harms of alternatives provide the basis for recommendations. Evidence and recommendations are often graded to indicate the quality of evidence and the strength of the recommendations. The strength of a recommendation should be formed by multiple considerations: the quality of the investigations that provide the evidence for the recommendations, the magnitude and consistency of positive outcomes relative to negative outcomes (adverse effects, burdens to the patient and the health care system, and costs), and the relative value placed on different outcomes. Even in the presence of strong evidence from randomized clinical trials, the effect benefit of an intervention may be marginal. The intervention may be associated with costs, discomforts, or impracticalities that downgrade the strength of a summary recommendation. These factors are keys to understanding conflicts among guidelines on similar topics from different organizations.[21]

Formal taxonomies of "levels of evidence" and "grades of recommendations" were first popularized by the Canadian Task Force on the Periodic Health Examination[22] and later revised in cooperation with the United States Preventive Services Task Force.[23] These guideline developers emphasized that the strongest evidence comes from rigorous randomized controlled trials and that weaker evidence comes from observational studies using cohort or case control designs. Inferring strength of evidence from study design alone, however, may overlook other determinants of the quality of evidence, such as sample size, recruitment bias, losses to follow-up, unmasked outcome assessment, atypical patient groups, unreproducible interventions, impractical clinical settings, and other threats to internal and external validity. Moreover, results from a single randomized controlled trial with a small sample are not necessarily more convincing than consistent results with high precision from a large number of high-quality trials of nonrandomized design conducted at a variety of places and times. Recent proposals for summarizing strength of evidence have emphasized the need for overviews to filter out studies with major design flaws and for meta-analyses to consider the precision, magnitude, and heterogeneity of study results.[15] The United States Preventive Services Task Force now supplements its "study design categories" with descriptions of flaws in the published evidence.[24]

Step 8: Writing the Guideline

Guideline documents are often the product of a committee or a commissioned author. Wording of recommendations is critical and must be crafted carefully by the panel. The best guidelines report how options and outcomes were chosen, define admissible evidence, report how evidence was found and selected, report how evidence was synthesized, make key data available for review, and report how value judgments were handled.[25] Balance sheets are sometimes used to summarize the likely benefits and harms of available options, which the patient and clinician can review together to determine what best suits the individual.[26] Without this information, the proposed guideline carries the same weight as any other review article or textbook chapter. Because guideline developers often must deal with inadequate evidence, they should be explicit about the type and quantity of evidence on which each recommendation contained in the guideline is based. This means that statements based on intuition rather than judgment should be clearly identified as such.

Linking treatment options to outcomes is a matter of science. In contrast, assigning preferences to outcomes is a matter of values. Consequently, it is important that guideline developers report the sources of their value judgments and the method by which consensus was sought. Panels that include a balance of research methodologists, practicing generalists and specialists, and public representatives are more likely to have considered diverse views in their deliberations. It is particularly important to know how patient preferences were considered. Health interventions have beneficial and harmful effects along with associated costs, and recommendations may differ depending on their relative emphasis on specific benefits, harms, and costs.

Step 9: Peer Review by Experts and Users

As with all complex scientific documents, it is important to have the draft guidelines reviewed by additional content experts, methodologists, and health system managers not involved with the development process. Using health system managers is critical because they may identify potential problems with implementation. Acceptance of a proposed guideline may also be enhanced by input from specialty societies, patient advocacy groups, affected industries, and other groups of experts and stakeholders.

UPDATING PRACTICE GUIDELINES

It is often difficult for guidelines to account for important recent developments. Guidelines often concern controversial health problems about which new knowledge is actively being sought in ongoing studies. Because of the time required to assemble and review evidence and to achieve consensus on recommendations, a guideline may actually be out-of-date by the time it is published. Guideline documents should be examined for two important dates: the publication date of the most recent evidence considered and the date on which the final recommendations were made. Some guidelines also identify important studies in progress and new information that could change the guideline.

Organizations seeking to update guidelines will find the process less intensive than that associated with new development. This is because (a) the key questions will have been defined in the original review, (b) the search for evidence will be guided by the previous process, and (c) clinical intuition and judgement will often be replaceable with evidence. Literature searches are aided by services such as the Science Citation Index, Current Contents and by computer databases from which related articles can be retrieved.

TYPES AND SOURCES OF PRACTICE GUIDELINES

There are now several thousand clinical guidelines that have developed in many aspects of medicine and surgery. The Agency for Health Care Policy and Research (AHCPR), established in 1989, was given the mandate to stimulate and coordinate the development of clinical practice guidelines. From 1992 to 1995, AHCPR produced nearly 20 guidelines.[27] Some of these (benign prostatic hypertrophy, low back pain, and cataract management) deal with surgical issues, particularly regarding indications for surgery. These guidelines and their release dates are listed in Table 17–1.

While the clinical guidelines program at AHCPR was highly successful at producing comprehensive evidence-based guidelines, the agency stopped producing guidelines in 1995. A number of factors prompted this decision, including the fact that the guidelines produced significant controversy in a few instances. In particular, several guidelines that addressed conditions for which surgical intervention was considered an option drew strong objections from parts of the physician community (eg, A group of back surgeons strongly objected to the AHCPR guideline on the management of low back pain). During 1996, AHCPR abandoned its guidelines effort and instead substituted an Evidence-Based Practice Center initiative to assist other organizations such as specialty societies in reviewing the evidence underpinning guideline recommendations. Twelve Evidence-Based Practice Centers, comprising of academic

Table 17–1 Clinical Practice Guidelines Developed by the Agency for Health Care Policy and Research

Guideline Topic	Date Issued
Acute pain management	February 1992
Urinary incontinence in adults	March 1992
Prevention of pressure ulcers	May 1992
Cataract in adults	February 1993
Depression in primary care	April 1993
Sickle cell disease in infants	April 1993
Early HIV infection	January 1994
Benign prostatic hyperplasia	February 1994
Management of cancer pain	March 1994
Unstable angina	March 1994
Heart failure	June 1994
Otitis media with effusion in children	July 1994
Quality determinants of mammography	October 1994
Acute low back problems in adults	December 1994
Treatment of pressure ulcers	December 1994
Post-stroke rehabilitation	May 1995
Cardiac rehabilitation	October 1995

and other organizations, were selected to participate in this effort. Nominations of topics are solicited routinely through notices in the Federal Register. Specific information that accompanies nominations includes the potential questions to be answered by the report or assessment and gives information on the availability of scientific data, disease prevalence and/or severity, practice variation patterns, and plans for using the evidence report or technology assessment to improve quality of care. Some of the projects in the Evidence-Based Practice Center initiative deal with surgical treatment options, including management of stable and unstable angina and management of otitis media, as well as with issues in surgical care such as anesthesia management for cataract surgery.

In addition, AHCPR set up a National Guideline Clearinghouse (NGC), a comprehensive database of evidence-based clinical practice guidelines and related documents produced by AHCPR in partnership with the American Medical Association (AMA) and the American Association of Health Plans (AAHP).[26] The mission of NGC is to give health care providers, health plans, integrated delivery systems, purchasers, physicians, nurses, and other health professionals an accessible way to obtain objective, detailed information on clinical practice guidelines and to further their dissemination, implementation, and use.

Key components of NGC include structured abstracts (summaries) of the guidelines and their development; a utility for comparing the attributes of two or more guidelines in a side-by-side comparison; syntheses of guidelines covering similar topics, highlighting similarities and differences; links to full-text guidelines (where available) and/or information for ordering printed copies; an electronic forum for exchanging information on clinical practice guidelines and their development, implementation, and use; and annotated bibliographies on guideline development methodology, implementation, and use.

Not every guideline is eligible for inclusion into the NGC; there are criteria that a clinical practice guideline must meet to be included. First, the guideline must contain systematically developed statements including information, strategies, or recommendations that assist physicians and/or other health care practitioners and patients to make decisions about appropriate health care for specific clinical circumstances. Second, the guideline must be produced under the auspices of medical specialty associations, relevant professional societies, public or private organizations, government agencies (at the federal, state, or local level), or health care organizations or plans. Third, corroborating documentation must verify that a systematic literature search and review of existing scientific evidence published in peer-reviewed journals was performed during the guideline development process. Last, the guideline must be in English and must be the current and most recent version (ie, developed, reviewed, or revised within the past 5 years).

The National Guideline Clearinghouse should serve as a useful start for cataloging and critiquing clinical practice guidelines. Currently, the NGC contains several guidelines that pertain to surgical patients. These are guidelines on the management of gallstones, neurogenic bowel management in adults with spinal cord injury, total hip replacement, cochlear implants in adults and children, and perioperative cardiac evaluation in patients undergoing noncardiac surgery. Also, there are organizations that produce critical pathways for purchase by providers of health care (eg, Milliman & Robertson, Inc., which produces clinical pathways for surgical care). These carepaths contain activities and milestones that should be completed on each postoperative day.

MEASURING THE IMPACT OF PRACTICE GUIDELINES

It is often assumed that clinical practice guidelines will produce better clinical outcomes; many believe that they will also lead to lower costs of care. However, because most guidelines are based on evidence as well as on intuition and judgment, their intended effects may not be realized. If the underlying evidence is weak, the scientific validity of the guideline will be limited no matter what the degree of consensus or peer review. The weaker the underlying evidence, the greater the argument for actually testing the guideline to determine whether its application improves patient outcomes. Table 17–2 shows a scheme for evaluating the outcomes of a guideline.

The questions for evaluation are whether patient outcomes are better, the same, or worse, and whether costs are higher, the same, or lower. A guideline that leads to better outcomes and lower costs will be ideal from the perspective of physicians, patients, and policymakers. A guideline that leads to worse clinical and economic outcomes will be a failure from anyone's

Table 17–2 Possible Results of Adherence vs Nonadherence to a Clinical Practice Guideline

Economic Outcome of Guideline	Clinical Outcome of Guideline		
	Better	Same	Worse
Higher cost			
Same cost			
Lower cost			

perspective. A guideline that leads to better outcomes and higher costs will spark debate over whether the better outcomes are worth the higher costs. Some examples of evaluations may help to illustrate this.

Weingarten and colleagues examined the implementation of a practice guideline suggesting that low-risk patients in coronary care units should receive early discharge.[28] In a prospective study, the investigators demonstrated that the guideline reminder reduced hospital stays and their associated costs without adversely affecting measured patient outcomes. A study of this type helps to validate the predicted consequences of guideline implementation for defined outcomes.

The initial enthusiasm for guidelines was fueled partly by the belief that authoritative, evidence-based statements about effective care would inevitably influence health care decision making. It is now clear that this was optimistic; the measurable impact of guidelines on clinical practice may be undetectable even for high quality guidelines issued by credible organizations. Lomas and colleagues studied the effects of a national guideline on cesarean section, that, if implemented, would have decreased rates of this procedure. Despite widespread knowledge of and agreement with the guideline, clinical practices were apparently unaffected.[29] Similarly National Institutes of Health (NIH) guidelines developed through consensus conferences have generally not been associated with detectable changes in clinical practice,[30] possibly because physicians were not aware of, did not agree with, or did not adhere to the guidelines. Even intensive implementation efforts involving direct contact with physicians, frequent re-inforcement, or specific recommendations on individual patient charts have been associated with limited changes in practice.[31–33]

More recent studies and reviews have shown that carefully designed intensive efforts to implement clinical guidelines can be successful, and some of the interventions, strategies, and factors have been identified.[34,35] A recent review addresses the issues of why physicians do not comply with guidelines and a framework for interventions.[36] A substantial increase in research for evaluating guidelines is important to translate evidence-based surgery into real changes in patients' health status.

SUMMARY AND CONCLUSION

Practice guidelines have emerged as a possible way to reduce clinical practice variations that result in poor outcomes and high costs. Guidelines are now addressing whether surgery is appropriate in particular clinical circumstances and how to manage surgical patients postoperatively. The creation of practice guidelines is both a science and an art. Systematic synthesis of scientific evidence should be the cornerstone of the development process. Expert judgment is needed to guide the process. Scanty evidence often requires that guideline developers rely on clinical intuition in making recommendations but users often may not know when the boundary between evidence and intuition is crossed. For this reason, surgeons should understand the steps in the creation of practice guidelines as well as what good practice guidelines include and how they should be evaluated. Guidelines will continue to be challenged because of the often necessary reliance on clinical intuition and because of the skepticism of physicians who believe guidelines are being used only to reduce costs. If it can be proved that guidelines do indeed change practice to improve health outcomes, their acceptance and use in surgical practice will increase.

REFERENCES

1. Kelly JT, Swartwout JE. Development of practice parameters by physician organizations. QRB 1990;16:54–57.

2. Sasako M, Sano T, Katai H [Practice guidelines in western countries] [Japanese] Gan To Kaguku Ryoho 1999;26(5):602–8.

3. Wennberg JE, Gittelsohn A. Variations in medical care among small areas. Sci Am 1982;246:120–34.

4. Epstein A. The outcomes movement–will it get us where we want to go. N Engl J Med 1990; 323(4):266–9.

5. Eddy DM. The challenge. JAMA 1990;263:287–90.

6. Institute of Medicine. Clinical practice guidelines: directions for a new program. Washington (DC): National Academy Press; 1990.

7. Woolf SH. Do clinical practice guidelines define good medical care?: the need for good science and the disclosure of uncertainty when defining 'best practices.' Chest 1998;113:166S–171S.

8. Henning J. The role of clinical practice guidelines in disease management. Am J Managed Care 1998;4(12):1715–22.

9. Hayward RSA, Wilson MC, Tunis SR, et al., for the Evidence-Based Medicine Working Group. Users' guides to the medical literature. VIII: How to use clinical practice guidelines. A: Are the recommendations valid? JAMA 1995;274:570–4.

10. Wilson MC, Hayward RSA, Tunis SR, et al., for the Evidence-Based Medicine Working Group. Users' guides to the medical literature. VIII: How to use clinical practice guidelines. B: What are the recommendations and will they help you in caring for your patients? JAMA 1995;274:1630–2.

11. Woolf SH. Manual for clinical practice guideline development. Rockville (MD): Agency for Health Care Policy and Research; 1991. AHCPR Publication No. 91-0007.

12. Eddy DM. A manual for assessing health practices and designing practice policies: the explicit approach. Philadelphia: American College of Physicians; 1992.

13. Woolf SH. Practice guidelines: a new reality in medicine. II: Methods of developing guidelines. Arch Intern Med 1992;152:946–52.

14. Dickersin K, Scherer E, Lefebvre C. Identification of relevant studies for systematic reviews. BMJ 1994;309:1286–91.

15. Cook DJ, Guyatt GH, Laupacis A, et al. Rules of evidence and clinical recommendations on the use of thrombotic agents. Antithrombotic Therapy Consensus Conference. Chest 1992;102 Suppl 4:305S–11S.

16. Cook DJ, Mulrow CD, Haynes RB. Systematic reviews: synthesis of best evidence for clinical decisions. Ann Intern Med 1997;126:376–80.

17. Hadorn DC, Baker D, Hodges JS, et al. Rating the quality of evidence for clinical practice guidelines. J Clin Epidemiol 1996;49:749–54.

18. Oxman AD, Cook DJ, Guyatt GH, for the Evidence-Based Medicine Working Group. Users' guides to the medical literature. VI: how to use an overview. JAMA 1994;272:1367–71.

19. Braunwald E, Mark DB, Jones RH, et al. Unstable angina: diagnosis and management. Clinical Practice Guideline Number 10. Rockville (MD): Dept. of Health and Human Services (US); 1994.

20. Brook RH, Chassin M, Fink A, et al. A method for the detailed assessment of the appropriateness of medical technologies. Santa Monica (CA) RAND Corp.; 1991. RAND note: N-3376-HHS.

21. Eddy DM. Resolving conflicts in practice policies. JAMA 1990;264:389–91.

22. Canadian Task Force on the Periodic Health Examination. The periodic health examination. Can Med Assoc J 1979;121:1193–1254.

23. Woolf SH, Battista RN, Anderson GM, et al. Assessing the clinical effectiveness of preventive maneuvers: analytic principles and systematic methods in reviewing evidence and developing clinical practice recommendations. J Clin Epidemiol 1990;43:891–905.

24. Battista RN, Fletcher SW. Making recommendations on preventive practices: methodological issues. Am J Prev Med 1988;4S:53–67.

25. Hayward RSA, Tunis SR, Wilson MC, et al. More informative abstracts of articles describing clinical practice guidelines. Ann Intern Med 1993;118:731–7.

26. Eddy DM. Comparing benefits and harms: the balance sheet. JAMA 1990;263:2493.

27. Development and implementation of the National Guideline Clearinghouse. Fact sheet, 1998 May 19. Rockville (MD): Agency for Health Care Policy and Research. [accessed 1999 Mar 15] [5 screens] Available from: URL: HYPERLINK http://www.ahcpr.gov/clinic/ngc.

28. Weingarten SR, Reidinger MS, Conner L, et al. Practice guidelines and reminders to reduce duration of hospital stay for patients with chest pain. Ann Intern Med 1994;120:257–63.

29. Lomas J, Anderson GM, Domnick-Pierre K, et al. Do practice guidelines guide practice? The effect of a consensus statement on the practice of physicians. N Engl J Med 1989;321:1306–11.

30. Kosecoff J, Kanouse DE, Rogers WH, et al. Effects of the National Institutes of Health consensus development program on physician practice. JAMA 1987;258:2708–13.

31. Davis DA, Thomson MA, Oxman AD, Haynes RB. Evidence for the effectiveness of CME: a review of 50 randomized controlled trials. JAMA 1992;268:1111–17.

32. Headrick LA, Speroff T, Pelecanos HI, Cebul RD. Efforts to improve compliance with the National Cholesterol Education Program guidelines. Arch Intern Med 1992;152:2490–6.

33. Pilote L, Thomas RJ, Dennis C, et al. Return to work after uncomplicated myocardial infarction: a trial of practice guidelines in the community. Ann Intern Med 1992;117:383–9.

34. Grimshaw JM, Russel IT. Effect of clinical guidelines on medical practice: a systematic review of rigorous evaluations. Lancet 1993;342:1317–22.

35. Davis DA, Thomson MA, Oxman AD, Haynes RB. Changing physician performance: a systematic review of the effect of continuing medical education strategies. JAMA 1995; 274:700–705.

36. Cabana MD, Rand CS, Powe NR, et al. Why don't physicians follow clinical practice guidelines? A framework for improvement. JAMA 1999;282:1458–65.

CHAPTER 18

Patient-Reported Outcomes Measures

Albert W. Wu, MD, MPH

Surgeons treat patients to improve or preserve their health. How do we recognize an excellent surgeon, and how do we know when surgical treatment has been successful? Traditionally, treatment has been directed at modifying the anatomic or physiologic mechanisms underlying the disease process; technical skills and the development of new operative techniques have been highly valued. Reflecting this, surgeons have relied on technical, largely objective endpoints. Thus, operative mortality, complications, laboratory test results and achievement of goals (such as complete resection or correction of deformity) form the basis of treatment evaluation.

At the same time, patients seek medical care in search of relief from symptoms that diminish their quality of life. The successes of modern medicine, paralleled by development of the consumer movement, have led to growth of patient expectations with respect to medical treatment. Conventional measures do not fully capture patients' perceptions of their health and treatment. Recently developed approaches use questionnaires to assess patient-reported outcomes, including functional status, quality of life, and patient satisfaction.

The methods employed to examine patient-reported outcomes originate from the social sciences and health services research and are unfamiliar to most clinical researchers. Many surgeons are skeptical of the validity of quality of life measures because of the subjectivity and susceptibility to bias of these methods but are interested in knowing about the results they achieve. In addition, as issues of cost control, cost-effectiveness, and quality assessment are debated, comprehensive outcome assessment becomes increasingly important.

PATIENT-REPORTED OUTCOMES ASSESSMENT

Outcomes research can be defined as a comprehensive approach to determining the effects of treatment, using a variety of data sources and measurement methods.[1] Outcomes research includes the rigorous determination of what does and does not work in medical care and how different providers compare with regard to their effects on patient outcomes.[2] Emphasis is placed on the evaluation of a comprehensive range of outcomes and the use of multiple assessment tools.

Several factors have led the current emphasis on patient-reported outcomes. These include aging of the population, rising health care costs, changes in the organization and financing of care, unexplained variations in physicians' practice patterns, limitations of available information about the effects of practice, and increased adoption of a model of shared decision making between patient and physician. Technologic advances and procedural innovations such as laparoscopic procedures and minimally invasive coronary bypass surgery hold considerable theoretical appeal but are not certain to deliver benefits over existing options. Novel procedures such as lung volume reduction surgery for emphysema offer hope for previously untreatable conditions but are costly and unproven.

Increases in longevity in industrialized countries has shifted the emphasis in medicine from delivering acute care only to also treating chronic diseases where the goal of treatment may be support and palliation rather than cure. For example, in patients over 75 years of age, the goal of coronary bypass surgery is not necessarily to prolong life (although in many patients this probably occurs) but to decrease or eliminate angina and to return the patient to more normal activity and a better quality of life.[3]

The rising cost of medical care in the United States has led payers and employers to demand evidence for the value and cost-effectiveness of medical and surgical procedures. The growth of prepaid care and prospective payment for hospital care has promoted increased competition among health care providers. Although most of the competition is on the basis of cost, "report cards" detailing performance of health plans, institutions, and even individual physicians are being developed as mechanisms to demonstrate value and improve consumer choice.[4–6] While the appropriateness of medical care is increasingly questioned, the growing dominance of managed care has also led to a clamor about an eroded quality of care.

Studies have documented substantial geographic differences in the practice of medicine and surgery. For example, in some communities in Maine, the rate of hysterectomy for women 70 years of age is less than 20 percent, whereas in nearby towns the rate is over 70 percent.[7] These differences appear to be related to uncertainty about indication rather than differences in patient populations. For example, across the United States, there are large variations in rates of back surgery[8] (Figure 18–1). For some procedures, there are also striking differences in outcomes, depending upon who is operating. For example, as many as 5 additional deaths per 100 can be attributed to which cardiac surgeon performs coronary bypass surgery.[9]

Although much is known about the safety and efficacy of new drugs, much less is known about the efficacy of different approaches to treatment, such as medical versus surgical treatment for chronic sinusitis. There have been few comparisons of different diagnostic approaches to specific problems. Even less is known about the efficacy of using diagnostic tests in combination or repeatedly, for example, repeated magnetic resonance scans for patients with back pain. Nearly nothing is known about the efficacy of cognitive and interpersonal services such as listening to or reassuring patients. Recognition of the considerable uncertainty facing practicing physicians has led to calls for the practice of "evidence-based" medicine and surgery as demonstrated by the existence of this textbook. Such an approach combines pathophysiologic rationale, clinical experience, and patient preferences with valid and current evidence from clinical research.[10]

The traditional model of clinical decision making, in which patients delegate choice to the physician, is being replaced by a model of shared decision making in which patients play an active role in the choice of treatment.[11] This model requires increased emphasis on patient preferences for risks and outcomes and on increased understanding by the patient of the likely outcomes of treatment. The importance of this approach is shown by one study of preferences for treatment of benign prostatic hypertrophy.[12] Since medical and surgical treatments each had different advantages and disadvantages, the "best" treatment for a patient depended on the relative preferences held for different postoperative states of health.

For all of these reasons, interest in patient-reported outcome assessment has grown rapidly.[13] In 1989, Congress established the Agency for Health Care Policy and Research (AHCPR) to promote research on medical outcomes and to develop guidelines for clinical practice. The National Committee on Quality Assurance, an independent accrediting body for managed care organizations, has worked since 1989 to develop measures of plan performance.[14] The Foundation for Accountability (FACCT), another independent organization, is particularly interested in the patient's perspective on the quality of care.[15] It is hoped that better information about the outcomes of various treatments will lead to improved clinical decision making, rational health policy at the local and national levels, and fairness in coverage and payment rules.

Types of Health Outcomes

Outcomes research considers a broad range of indicators, including conventional clinical measures such as survival, complications of disease or treatment, persistence of pathology,

Back Surgery per 1,000 Medicare Enrollees

By Hospital Referral Region (1992–93)

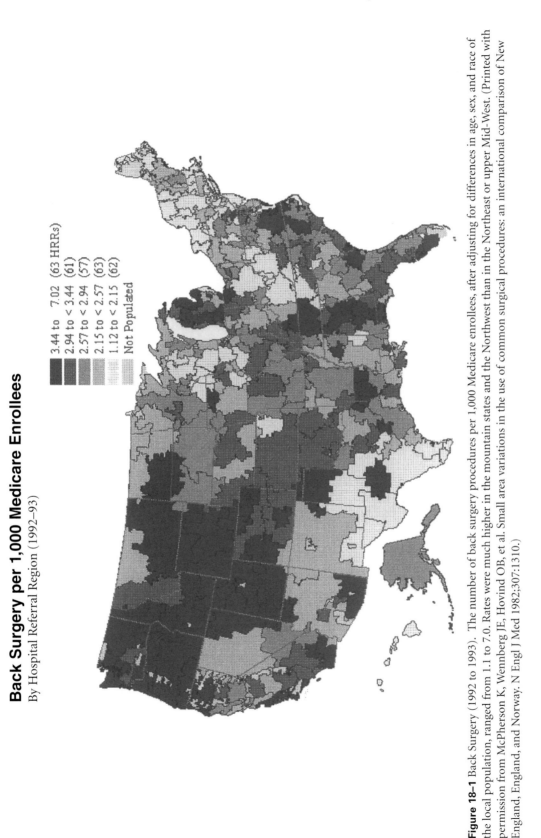

3.44 to 7.02	(63 HRRs)
2.94 to < 3.44	(61)
2.57 to < 2.94	(57)
2.15 to < 2.57	(63)
1.12 to < 2.15	(62)
Not Populated	

Figure 18–1 Back Surgery (1992 to 1993). The number of back surgery procedures per 1,000 Medicare enrollees, after adjusting for differences in age, sex, and race of the local population, ranged from 1.1 to 7.0. Rates were much higher in the mountain states and the Northwest than in the Northeast or upper Mid-West. (Printed with permission from McPherson K, Wennberg JE, Hovind OB, et al. Small area variations in the use of common surgical procedures: an international comparison of New England, England, and Norway. N Engl J Med 1982;307:1310.)

physiologic and laboratory abnormalities, deformity, and other signs of disease. In addition, outcomes research considers patient-reported symptoms, functional status, quality of life, and satisfaction with treatment. Still other types of outcomes are important from a societal perspective. These include the allocation of health care resources and their associated costs and economic losses due to disability or death (Table 18–1).

Measurement Standards

To be useful, a measurement tool must meet standards for reliability, validity, responsiveness, and interpretability (Table 18–2). Reliability refers to the extent to which a measuring procedure yields consistent results on repeated use or for similar subjects. Reliability can be estimated using different methods. For a scale consisting of several items intended to measure the same phenomenon, internal consistency can be estimated using Cronbach's alpha $= N\rho/[1 + \rho (N\text{-}1)]$ where ρ is the mean interitem correlation and N is the number of items.[16] Cronbach's alpha ranges from 0 to 1, with a coefficient of 0.5–0.7 generally considered to be adequate for group comparisons.[17,18] Reliability is also the extent to which a given score will be observed at two different points in time when no change has occurred. Test-retest reliability can be estimated by using the correlation between repeated administrations of an instrument to stable patients.[19] Validity is the extent to which a tool measures what it is intended to measure, for example, that a pain questionnaire actually measures pain rather than the patient's anxiety. For a given application, a measure must cover the breadth

Table 18–1 Types of Health Outcomes

Outcome	Example for Coronary Artery Disease Patient
Clinical	
Mortality	Death in hospital
Pathology	Coronary artery narrowing
Nonfatal clinical event	Stroke
Hospital re-admission	Re-admission within 30 days of hospital discharge
Complication of disease or treatment	Sternal wound infection after coronary artery bypass grafting
Physiologic test	Ejection fraction
Laboratory test	CPK-MB isoenzyme
Symptom	Angina pectoris
Patient-reported	
Health-related quality of life	Ability to perform usual physical activities
Satisfaction with care	Patient ratings of overall quality of care
Cost	
Utilization of health services	Number of physician visits
Direct cost	Cost of physician visits and prescription medications
Indirect cost	Loss of income due to missed days of work

Table 18–2 Measurement Standards

Standard	Definition	Example
Reliability	Does the instrument produce the same results if re-applied to the same situation?	Physical functioning scores are the same at two different points in time for a stable patient
Validity	Does the instrument measure what it purports to measure?	Scores on a pain questionnaire are highly correlated with scores on established pain measures
Responsiveness	Is the instrument capable of identifying small but clinically significant changes?	The mean score on a functional status questionnaire increases significantly 6 months after successful coronary revascularization

and severity of problems likely to be encountered. A common misnomer is to refer to a measure as "valid." There is no specific point at which a measure is considered valid; validity needs to be evaluated separately for each purpose. Validation is the process of accumulating different kinds of evidence to determine the most appropriate interpretation of a score.[20] There are several kinds of validity to consider. Content validity is the extent to which a measure represents a specified domain or universe of content. Construct validity is the extent to which a measure performs in relation to a conceptual model of hypothesized relationships between a scale score and other measures. Criterion validity is the extent to which a measure relates to an accepted gold standard. Since it is difficult to identify a gold standard for most dimensions of health-related quality of life and patient satisfaction, criterion validity is rarely tested. Responsiveness is the ability of a test to detect small but clinically meaningful changes over time.[21,22] For example, if a procedure results in an important improvement in quality of life, a questionnaire should be able to detect that difference. For results to be useful, measurements must also be expressed in terms that clinicians understand. Existing tools vary in reliability, validity, and responsiveness. For a given instrument, these parameters may also vary for populations that differ in demographic characteristics or severity of illness.

PATIENT-ASSESSED OUTCOMES

Several terms are used almost interchangeably to refer to the concept of patients' reports of their own health, including health status, subjective health status, functional status, quality of life, and health-related quality of life. In 1948, the World Health Organization defined "health" as "a state of complete physical, mental, and social well-being, and not merely the absence of disease and infirmity." This definition reflects the multidimensional nature of health with both positive and negative aspects.

Bergner identified five dimensions of health status: (1) genetic and inherited characteristics; (2) the biochemical, physiologic, and anatomic conditions, including the impairment of these systems, disease, signs, and symptoms; (3) functional status, including performance of the usual activities of daily living such as self-care, physical activities, cognition, and work; (4) mental condition, which includes positive and negative emotions; and (5) health potential, including prognosis for longevity and future functioning.[23]

Quality of life is a broad concept that encompasses a person's experience and assessment of aspects of life. Because quality of life includes important domains that are not uniformly responsive to surgical treatment (eg, life satisfaction and aesthetic enjoyment), it is more common to focus on those aspects of quality of life that may be affected by therapeutic measures. "Health-related" quality of life encompasses several dimensions of health directly experienced by the person, including physical functioning, psychological well-being, cognitive functioning, social and role functioning, and general health perceptions. The patient's symptoms are also often included under this definition (Table 18–3).

Measuring Health and the Structure of Measures

Measurement is the process of applying a standard scale to something that varies in the dimension of interest. Measuring health-related quality of life usually relies on the assembling of indicators to create a scale for each dimension of interest. Some measures consist of a single global indicator such as the question, "Would you say your health is excellent, very good, good, fair, or poor?" However, most instruments consist of a series of individual questions or items. Patients respond by selecting from among predetermined graded responses. Responses to these items are numbered, often so that a higher score indicates better health, and the numbers corresponding to the patient's response are summed to yield a score. Thus, these measures are sometimes referred to as summated rating scales.

Responses can also be obtained using a visual analog scale, which is classically a line of fixed length (usually 10 cm) with anchors like "no pain" and "worst imaginable pain" at the extreme ends. Respondents are asked to place a mark, usually an ✕ or a vertical line, on the line at a point corresponding to their perceived states. This method is frequently used to assess pain.[24]

The format of measures may be single indices, health profiles, or utility measures. Single indices attempt to reduce several concepts to a unidimensional scale. For example, the Karnofsky Performance Status score,[25] which is commonly used in cancer trials, combines information about the ability to work, carry out normal activities without assistance, and care for personal needs. Single indices are brief but are less reliable than multi-item scales and generally yield limited information.

Health profiles attempt to measure multiple important dimensions of health-related quality of life. For example, the Sickness Impact Profile[26] assesses a physical dimension (including ambulation, mobility, body care, and movement), a psychosocial dimension (including social interaction, alertness behavior, communication, and emotional behavior), and additional domains, including eating, work, home management, sleep and rest, and recreation. The SF-36 health survey is a brief (36 items), widely used questionnaire that assesses general health perceptions, physical functioning, role limitations due to physical health, role limitations due to mental health, social functioning, pain, mental health, and energy (Figure 18–2).[27]

The measures above can be termed descriptive psychometric measures and are based on the patient's report or rating of their health on a continuum. Utility measures are derived from economic and decision theory.[28] The term "utility" refers to the value placed by the individual on a particular health state. Utility is summarized as a score ranging from 0.0, representing death, to 1.0, representing perfect health. In economic analyses, utilities are used to justify devoting resources to a treatment. Since they weight the duration of life according to its quality, they can be used to generate quality-adjusted life-years. However, because they are expressed as a single score, they do not provide details of how specific aspects of patients' lives are affected. The Quality of Well-Being scale[29] is a widely used instrument that generates a score by combining questions about various dimensions of functional status with community-derived preferences for these states.

Modes of Administration

Questionnaires can be self-administered or given by trained interviewers. Interviews are labor-intensive but assure completeness of response and minimize misinterpretations. Interviews may be conducted in person or by phone. Computer-assisted modes of administration via conventional and touch screen PCs and computer-assisted interviews are also being developed. Sometimes, a surrogate respondent is used to estimate results from a patient, such

3. The following items are about activities you might do during a typical day. Does **your health now limit you** in these activities? If so, how much?

	Yes, limited a lot	Yes, limited a little	No, not limited at all
a) **Vigorous activities**, such as running, lifting heavy objects, participating in strenuous sports	O	O	O
b) **Moderate activities**, such as moving a table, pushing a vacuum cleaner, bowling, or playing golf	O	O	O
c) Lifting or carrying groceries	O	O	O
d) Climbing **several** flights of stairs	O	O	O
e) Climbing **one** flight of stairs	O	O	O
f) Bending, kneeling, or stooping	O	O	O
g) Walking more than a mile	O	O	O
h) Walking **several blocks**	O	O	O
i) Walking **one block**	O	O	O
j) Bathing or dressing yourself	O	O	O

Figure 18–2 Sample questions assessing physical functioning from the SF-36 health survey. (Printed with permission from Ware JE, Snow KK, Kosinski M, et al. SF-36 health survey: manual and interpretation guide. Boston: The Health Institute; 1993.)

as a parent who reports on a child's health or an adult who provides answers for a parent who is unable to respond directly.

Types of Quality-of-Life Measures

There are two basic approaches to quality-of-life assessment: generic and disease-specific.[30] Generic instruments are designed for use across different diseases, treatments, settings, and patient groups. Their major advantage is that they can be used in any population and that they allow comparisons of the relative impacts of various health interventions. However, they may be unresponsive to changes in specific conditions and may be too general to guide clinical decision making. Disease-specific measures focus on dimensions of health related to a particular disease, population, symptom, or problem and may be more responsive to a change in the patient's condition than a generic instrument. For example, the widely used American Urological Association Symptom Scale[31] includes questions about urination. Disease-specific measures are more easily understood by clinicians but are frequently less well tested than generic instruments.

Patient Satisfaction

Patient satisfaction refers to patients' subjective evaluations of their health care.[32] Patient ratings of care reflect what they think is important about the quality of care, including the doctor-patient relationship and their perception of the adequacy of diagnosis and therapy. These care ratings predict patients' subsequent behavior, including how well they comply

Table 18–3 Dimensions of Health-Related Quality of Life

Dimension	Description
Physical functioning	Activities of daily living, strenuous activities
Mental health	Anxiety, depression, happiness
Social functioning	Quantity and quality of social contacts
Role functioning	Ability to perform work or usual activities
Cognitive functioning	Attention, memory, concentration
Energy	Energy and fatigue
General health perceptions	Global self-assessment of health
Pain	Severity and frequency of pain
Symptoms	Nausea, headache, dizziness, etc.
Sexual functioning	Performance and satisfaction
Sleep	Quantity and quality of sleep

with prescribed medications, whether they return to that locale for treatment or go elsewhere, and whether they recommend a particular physician to others.[33] The method used to elicit a patient's judgments about care can affect the results dramatically. For example, when the response choices use the word "satisfied," most patients choose the best possible answer. Rating scales (eg, excellent to poor) result in a better distribution of responses. The Patient Satisfaction Questionnaire (PSQ)[34] and the Medical Outcomes Study 9-item Visit Rating Form[35] are examples of carefully constructed instruments for assessing general medical care and specific physician visits. The Consumer Assessment of Health Plans (CAHPS™) surveys are intended to assess health plans and services and to help consumers select among them.[36] There are few if any established measures of patient satisfaction with surgical care.

Data Sources

Outcomes research frequently relies on questionnaires to assess patient outcomes (Table 18–4). Patients are commonly asked about their ability to function, their well-being, and their satisfaction with their care. Subjective data from patients can sometimes provide valuable information that may not be evident from physiologic measurements. Research has shown that in some situations, patient-reported measures can be at least as reliable as conventional biochemical or physiologic indices.[37] However, although patient reports provide a unique perspective, measures must be chosen with care. Data collection requires cooperation of patients and providers, and selective nonparticipation can threaten generalizability. Study designs must recognize the limitations of patients' recall and the fact that patients' evaluations of outcomes may be affected by their expectations.

Other sources of data, such as medical records and claims and administrative data files, can be used to improve the efficiency of survey-based methods. Claims data files, such as those maintained by the Health Care Financing Administration for all Medicare beneficiaries, can be used to identify the patient population to be surveyed. When linked to clinical and survey data, they can also be used to identify the performance of therapeutic procedures, the utilization of health care, and the frequency of death associated with treatment.

Table 18–4 Data Sources for Outcome Assessments

Data Source	Advantages	Disadvantages
Patient surveys	Provides patient's perspective	Labor intensive
	Provides reliable data	Requires cooperation of patient and providers
		Selective nonparticipation
		Patient's assessment may be affected by expectations
Chart abstraction	Unobtrusive	Costly
	Detailed clinical information	Labor intensive
		May be unreliable
	Can be performed retrospectively	Variables may not be recorded consistently
Claims data	Unobtrusive	Data lack clinical detail for identifying patient groups or risk adjustment
	Low cost	
	Large number	
	Broad cross section of patients	May be inaccurate

IMPORTANT AREAS TO STUDY IN SURGERY

Quality-of-life assessments can be relevant to surgical research and practice for defining indications for surgery, for monitoring the patient, and for evaluating the impact of treatment.[38] Deteriorating quality of life when medical therapy fails can be the major indication for surgery for gastrointestinal disorders such as Crohn's disease.[39,40] Repeated assessment of quality of life has been useful for monitoring patients and to direct treatment changes such as transplantation in end-stage renal disease.[41] Therapeutic evaluation is necessary (1) to compare different treatment strategies for a specific indication, such as alternative revascularization procedures for coronary artery disease;[42–45] (2) to determine the effectiveness of a specific procedure in populations different from those initially studied, for example, the effectiveness of valve replacement surgery for patients over 80 years old;[46] and (3) to determine the effectiveness of surgical approaches for disease entities different than those initially studied, for example, laparoscopic colectomy for oncologic rather than benign conditions.[47]

Quality-of-life assessment in surgery is important when different treatment alternatives might impact differentially on quality of life; when there is a new intervention, a scarcity of resources, or a need to determine the timing of an operative intervention; and when improving quality of life is the goal of intervention. In conditions for which surgery is clearly life saving or is the only treatment choice, quality-of-life assessment may be less important. For example, there are no alternatives to heart transplantation, so quality-of-life assessment plays little role. On the other hand, the main purpose of pancreas transplantation is to improve quality of life. In thoracic surgery, esophageal surgery for benign disease is symptom-based, making quality-of-life assessment a high priority.[48,49] For esophageal malignancies, surgery is primarily palliative, so quality-of-life assessment may be less important. Lung volume reduction surgery for chronic obstructive pulmonary disease is promising but expensive and as yet unproven, making quality-of-life assessment mandatory for research.[50] For cardiovascular surgery of coronary artery disease, there are a number of treatment alternatives that may have different effects on quality of life.[51,42–45] On the other hand, formal quality-of-life assessment has not been a priority for aortic aneurysm repair because treatment is life saving and there is hardly an alternative to operating. In trauma surgery, there is little or no time to perform a quality-of-life assessment before treatment begins. However, treatment has important implications for long-term quality of life, making formal assessment important in evaluating amputation versus limb-sparing surgery for severe lower-extremity injuries.[52,53] In abdominal surgery, quality-of-life assessment is important in chronic states that impair quality of life, such as inflammatory bowel disease[39,40] and chronic pancreatitis.[54] For potentially curable cancers such as rectal cancer, quality-of-life assessment may be important as there are treatment alternatives that might impact differently on quality of life (eg, abdominal perineal resection, anterior resection, local excision).[55]

Since early clinical trials that examined the impact of surgical treatment on quality of life,[52,56–60] studies have helped to identify treatments that are preferable, based on decreased morbidity[61–70] and improved cost-effectiveness.[71–74] Quality-of-life assessment has evolved into a crucial component of clinical trials of new and existing treatments[75–86] as well as cohort studies.[81–84]

Selecting a Quality-of-Life Measure

Selecting an appropriate quality-of-life measure for a specific surgical problem requires a clear formulation of the question to be answered, a consideration of the concepts that must be assessed, a review of available instruments, a review of the evidence for usefulness of instruments in a comparable population, and an examination of practical considerations (Table 18–5). Since most clinical studies are not focused primarily on quality of life, the first step is usually to decide on the research question concerning quality of life. This question may involve the relative impact of two surgical procedures within a specific time frame on patient-reported outcomes. The next step is to determine the domains that should be included. This should be based a priori on clinical experience and knowledge of how patients can be affected by both the condition and the treatment. Important sources of data include patients with the condition, their caregivers, clinicians experienced at treating these patients, and published literature describing the condition. Even if quality of life is not examined specifically, tables on symptoms and side effects from published papers may be helpful. Both generic instruments and an increasing number of specific instruments are becoming available for use.[85–88] When reviewing a candidate instrument, the main concern is the appropriateness of the measure to the question or issue of concern. How well does the content of the measure correspond to the goals of the study? It is crucial to examine the questionnaire itself rather than just to rely on its name or label. Is the model of health broad enough, and do the scales go into sufficient depth? How sick or dysfunctional is the intended study sample and is the measure designed to assess a congruent range of health? The next step is to review the evidence for the reliability, validity, and responsiveness of the questionnaire, ideally in populations similar to that being studied. Finally, a number of practical considerations must be taken into account. Is the reading level of the questionnaire appropriate for your patient population? Is it available in the languages they speak? How is the questionnaire administered, and how long does it take to complete? Is an interview required? How does this correspond to the resources available to the project? How are the questions scored? Is special software required, and are supporting materials available?

Inevitably, in some situations there will not be an "off-the-shelf" measure that is appropriate for a specific application. In this case, it may be necessary to develop, modify, or supplement an existing measure. A measurement strategy that combines an existing generic measure with a newly developed disease-specific measure is often the best approach. Development should be done in collaboration with an investigator experienced in the development and testing of quality-of-life measures in the clinical setting.

Table 18–5 Selection of a Health-Related Quality-of-Life Measure

Question	Example
1. What is the research question concerning quality of life?	What is the relative impact on HRQOL of minimally invasive coronary bypass surgery vs coronary artery bypass surgery in patients with new triple-vessel coronary disease?
a. Specify the time frame	Within the first year of treatment
b. Specify the age group	Ages 45–65 years
2. What concepts are important to assess? a. What aspects of HRQOL are likely to be affected by the condition?	Review of the literature, discussion with cardiologist, and semi-structured interview with patient suggest that general health perceptions, pain, limitations in physical activity, role functioning, and mental health are crucial to assess
b. What aspects of HRQOL are likely to be affected by treatment?	Cognitive functioning, pain, return to work, and worry may differ between treatment options
3. What instruments have been used in this population?	SF-36 Specific Activity Scale, Sickness Impact Profile
a. Do the instruments include the relevant dimension?	The SF-36 measures general health perceptions, pain, limitations in physical activity, role functioning, and mental health
b. Do the scales correspond to the extent of problems present in the study population?	Yes
4. What is the evidence of the usefulness of the instruments in populations similar to the study population?	
a. Reliability	Cronbach's alphas are consistently >0.70 for subscales of the SF-36
b. Validity	Subscales of the SF-36 were related as hypothesized to patients with different New York Health Association classifications
c. Responsiveness	Subscales scores improved over time in patients undergoing PTCA and CABG. Improvement was less for patients with more comorbid conditions and greater for patients without subsequent cardiac events
5. Practical considerations	
a. How is the questionnaire administered?	Self-administered or by interview
b. What is the patient's burden?	Grade level = 8th grade; takes 5–7 minutes to complete
c. Are appropriate language versions available?	Available in American English and Spanish, corresponding to the study population
d. Are scoring and supporting materials available?	User manual and scoring software available

HRQOL=health-related quality of life; CABG=coronary artery bypass graft; PTCA = percutaneous transluminal coronary angioplasty.

Challenges of Patient-Reported Outcomes Assessment in Surgery

Several challenges remain before patient-reported outcomes assessment can be applied to full advantage in surgery. There are large gaps in our understanding of how the structure and process of surgical care influence patient outcomes. Clinical trials are needed to examine the effectiveness of existing and newly developed treatments and procedures. Studies that measure the effectiveness of treatments need to examine both short- and longer-term outcomes.[89] To adequately examine the effectiveness of services, to disseminate information, and to evaluate the quality of surgical care, data systems are required that can characterize variation in the use of treatments and patient outcomes. Surgical researchers and practitioners need to become more familiar with these methods. At the same time, the science of quality-of-life assessment is not mature and will not be uniformly understood or appreciated in the immediate future. Better research tools and measurement techniques are needed, including more reliable, valid, and understandable measures of patient-reported outcomes tested in more diverse populations.[90] Better risk-adjustment models are needed to obtain valid reports and to facilitate comparisons of patient outcomes.[91] To improve decision making in the care of individual patients, students and clinicians must learn to understand and integrate evidence on effective practices with clinical expertise, pathophysiologic knowledge, and patient preferences.[92]

CONCLUSION

The value of health care can be determined only by a systematic examination of patient outcomes. To accomplish this, methods are required that are unfamiliar to many clinical researchers. Clinical research that previously would have focused on physiologic or anatomic outcomes should incorporate patient-reported outcomes measures. This information will be essential in determining which surgical treatment strategies should be abandoned and which should be adopted in the future.

REFERENCES

1. Tarlov AR, Ware JE Jr, Greenfield S, et al. The Medical Outcomes Study: an application of methods for monitoring the results of medical care. JAMA 1989;262:925–30.

2. Brook RH, Kamberg CJ, McGlynn EA. Health system reform and quality. JAMA 1996;276:476–80.

3. Cheitlin MD. Coronary bypass surgery in the elderly. Clin Geriatr Med 1996;12(1):195–205.

4. Schoenbaum SC, Coltin KL. Competition on quality in managed care. Int J Qual Health Care 1998; 10(5):421–6.

5. Hanlon CR. Quality assessment and tracking results of cardiac surgery. Ann Thorac Surg 1997; 64(5):1569–73.

6. Hannan EL, Kumar D, Racz M, et al. New York State's cardiac surgery reporting system: four years later. Ann Thorac Surg 1994;58:1852–7.

7. Wennberg J, Gittelsohn A. Small area variations in health care delivery. Science 1973;14;182(117): 1102–8.

8. McPherson K, Wennberg JE, Hovind OB, Clifford P. Small-area variations in the use of common surgical procedures: an international comparison of New England, England and Norway. N Engl J Med 1982;307:1310–4.

9. Brook RM. Managed care is not the problem, quality is. JAMA 1997;278:1612–4.

10. Evidence-Based Medicine Working Group. Evidence-based medicine: a new approach to teaching the practice of medicine. JAMA 1992;268:2420–5.

11. Laine C, Davidoff F. Patient-centered medicine. A professional evolution. JAMA 1996;275:152–6.

12. Barry MJ, Mulley AG, Fowler FJ, Wennberg JE. Watchful waiting vs immediate transurethral resection for symptomatic prostatism. JAMA 1988;25:3010–7.

13. Ellwood PM. Shattuck Lecture—outcomes management, a technology of patient experience. N Engl J Med 1988;318(23):1549–56.

14. Thompson JW, Bost J, Ahmed F, et al. The NCQA's quality compass: evaluating managed care in the United States. Health Aff (Millwood) 1998;17(1):152–8.

15. Lansky D. Measuring what matters to the public. Health Aff (Millwood) 1998;17(4):40–1.

16. Cronbach LJ. Coefficient alpha and the internal structure of tests. Psychometrika 1951;16:297.

17. Nunnally JC. Psychometric theory. 2nd ed. New York: McGraw-Hill; 1978.

18. Helmstater GC. Principles of psychological measurement. New York: Appleton-Century-Crofts; 1964.

19. Carmines EG, Zeller RA. Quantitative applications in the social sciences: reliability and validity assessment. Newbury Park (CA): Sage Publications; 1979. p. 9–51.

20. Ware JE. Standards for validating health measures: definition and content. J Chron Dis 1987; 40:473–80.

21. Deyo RA, Diehr P, Patrick DL. Reproducibility and responsiveness of health status measures. Statistics and strategies for evaluation. Control Clin Trials 1991;12:142S–158S.

22. Kazis LE, Anderson JJ, Meenan RF. Effect sizes for interpreting changes in health status. Med Care 1989;27(3):S178–S189.

23. Bergner M. Measurement of health status. Med Care 1985;23:696–704.

24. McDowell I, Newell C. Pain measurement. In: Measuring health: a guide to rating scales and questionnaires. New York, Oxford: Oxford University Press; 1995. p. 335–52.

25. Karnofsky DA, Abelman WH, Craver LF, Burcheneal JH. The use of nitrogen mustards in the palliative treatment of carcinoma. Cancer 1948;1:634–56.

26. Bergner M, Bobbitt RA, Carter WB, Gilson BS. The Sickness Impact Profile: development and final revision of a health status measure. Med Care 1981;19:787–805.

27. Ware JE, Snow KK, Kosinski M, et al. SF-36 health survey: manual and interpretation guide. Boston: The Health Institute; 1993.

28. Torrance GW, Feeny D. Utilities and quality adjusted life years. Int J Technol Assess Health Care 1989;5:559–75.

29. Kaplan RM, Anderson JP. The quality of well-being scale: rationale for a single quality of life index. In: Walker CS, editor. Quality of life: assessment and application. London: MTP Press; 1988. p. 51–77.

30. Patrick DL, Deyo RA. Generic and disease-specific measures in assessing health status and quality of life. Med Care 1989;27(3):S217–33.

31. Barry MJ, Fowler FJ Jr, O'Leary MP, et al. The American Urological Association symptom index for benign prostatic hyperplasia. J Urol 1992;148(5):1549–57.

32. Ware JE, Snyder MK, Wright WR, Davies AR. Defining and measuring patient satisfaction with medical care. Evaluation and Program Planning 1983;6:247–63.

33. Rubin HR, Wu AW. Patient satisfaction: its importance and how to measure it. In: Gitnick G, editor. The business of medicine: a physician's guide. New York: Elsevier Science Publishing Company; 1991. p. 397–409.

34. Ware JE, Hays RD. Methods for measuring patient satisfaction with specific medical encounters. Med Care 1988;26:393.

35. Rubin HR, Gandek B, Rogers WH, et al. Patients' ratings of outpatient visits in different practice settings. JAMA 1993;270:835.

36. Consumer Assessment of Health Plans (CAHPS): http://www.ahcpr.gov/qual/cahps.

37. Deyo RA, Andersson G, Bombardier C, et al. Outcome measures for studying patients with low back pain. Spine 1994;15;19(18 Suppl):2032S–2036S.

38. Neugebauer E, Troidl H, Wood-Dauphinee S, et al. Quality-of-life assessment in surgery: results of the Meran Consensus Development Conference. J Theor Surg 1991;6:123–37.

39. Thirlby RC, Land JC, Fenster LF, Lonborg R. Effect of surgery on health-related quality of life in patients with inflammatory bowel disease: a prospective study. Arch Surg 1998;133(8):826–32.

40. Maunder RG, Cohen Z, McLeod RS, Greenberg GR. Effect of intervention in inflammatory bowel disease on health-related quality of life: a critical review. Dis Colon Rectum 1995;38(11):1147–61.

41. Rettig RA, Sadler JH, Meyer KB, et al. Assessing health and quality of life outcomes in dialysis: a report on an Institute of Medicine workshop. Am J Kidney Dis 1997;30(1):140–55.

42. Peduzzi P, Hultgren H, Thomsen J, Detre K. Ten-year effect of medical and surgical therapy on quality of life: Veterans Administration Cooperative Study of Coronary Artery Surgery. Am J Cardiol 1987;59(12):1017–23.

43. Rogers WJ, Coggin CJ, Gersh BJ, et al. Ten-year follow-up of quality of life in patients randomized to receive medical therapy or coronary artery bypass graft surgery. The Coronary Artery Surgery Study (CASS). Circulation 1990;82(5):1647–58.

44. Pocock SJ, Henderson RA, Seed P, et al. Quality of life, employment status, and anginal symptoms after coronary angioplasty or bypass surgery. 3-year follow-up in the Randomized Intervention Treatment of Angina (RITA) trial circulation 1996;94(2):135–42.

45. Hlatky MA, Rogers WJ, Johnstone I, et al. Medical care costs and quality of life after randomization to coronary angioplasty or coronary bypass surgery. N Engl J Med 1997;9:336(2):92–9.

46. Khan JH, McElhinney DB, Hall TS, Merrick SH. Cardiac valve surgery in octogenarians: improving quality of life and functional status. Arch Surg 1998;133(8):887–93.

47. Stocchi L, Nelson H. Laparoscopic colectomy for colon cancer: trial update. J Surg Oncol 1998; 68(4):255–67.

48. Patti MG, Pellegrini CA, Arcerito M, et al. Comparison of medical and minimally invasive surgical therapy for primary esophageal motility disorders. Arch Surg 1995;130(6):609–15.

49. Viljakka M, Nevalainen J, Isolauri J. Lifetime costs of surgical versus medical treatment of severe gastro-oesophageal reflux disease in Finland. Scand J Gastroenterol 1997;32(8):766–72.

50. Fein AM. Lung volume reduction surgery: answering the crucial questions. Chest 1998;113 (4 Suppl):277S–282S.

51. Oz MC, Argenziano M, Rose EA. What is 'minimally invasive' coronary bypass surgery? Experience with a variety of surgical revascularization procedures for single-vessel disease. Chest 1997;5; 112(5):1409–16.

52. Sugarbaker PH, Barofsky I, Rosenberg SA, Gianola FJ. Quality of life assessment of patients in extremity sarcoma clinical trials. Surgery 1982;91(1):17–23.

53. Chang AE, Steinberg SM, Culnane M, et al. Functional and psychosocial effects of multimodality limb-sparing therapy in patients with soft tissue sarcomas. J Clin Oncol 1989;7(9):1217–28.

54. Buchler MW, Friess H, Muller MW, et al. Randomized trial of duodenum-preserving pancreatic head resection versus pylorus-preserving Whipple in chronic pancreatitis. Am J Surg 1995; 169(1):65–9.

55. Reilly WT, Pemberton JH, Wolff BG, et al. Randomized prospective trial comparing ileal pouch-anal anastomosis performed by excising the anal mucosa to ileal pouch-anal anastomosis performed by preserving the anal mucosa. Ann Surg 1997;225(6):666–76.

56. Troidl H, Kusche J, Vestweber KH, et al. Quality of life: an important endpoint both in surgical practice and research. J Chronic Dis 1987;40(6):523–8.

57. Kemeny MM, Wellisch DK, Schain WS. Psychosocial outcome in a randomized surgical trial for treatment of primary breast cancer. Cancer 1988;15;62(6):1231–7.

58. Mommsen S, Jakobsen A, Sell A. Quality of life in patients with advanced bladder cancer. A randomized study comparing cystectomy and irradiation—the Danish Bladder Cancer Study Group (DAVECA protocol 8201). Scand J Urol Nephrol Suppl 1989;125:115–20.

59. Barr H, Krasner N, Raouf A, Walker RJ. Prospective randomised trial of laser therapy only and laser therapy followed by endoscopic intubation for the palliation of malignant dysphagia. Gut 1990; 31(3):252–8.

60. Patchell RA, Tibbs PA, Walsh JW, et al. A randomized trial of surgery in the treatment of single metastases to the brain. N Engl J Med 1990;22:322(8):494–500.

61. Mintz AH, Kestle J, Rathbone MP, et al. A randomized trial to assess the efficacy of surgery in addition to radiotherapy in patients with a single cerebral metastasis. Cancer 1996;1:78(7):1470–6.

62. Irwig L, Bennetts A. Quality of life after breast conservation or mastectomy: a systematic review. Aust N Z J Surg 1997;67:750–4.

63. Lawrence K, McWhinnie D, Goodwin A, et al. Randomised controlled trial of laparoscopic versus open repair of inguinal hernia: early results. BMJ 1995;14;311(7011):981–5.

64. Lim AJ, Brandon AH, Fiedler J, et al. Quality of life: radical prostatectomy versus radiation therapy for prostate cancer. J Urol 1995;154(4):1420–5.

65. Barkun JS, Wexler MJ, Hinchey EJ, et al. Laparoscopic versus open inguinal herniorrhaphy: preliminary results of a randomized controlled trial. Surgery 1995;118(4):703–9.

66. Quint U, Pingsmann A. Surgical treatment of enchondroma in long tubular bones. Preservation of function versus extensive excision in the humerus. Arch Orthop Trauma Surg 1995;114(6):352–6.

67. Wilt TJ, Brawer MK. The Prostate Cancer Intervention Versus Observation Trial: a randomized trial comparing radical prostatectomy versus expectant management for the treatment of clinically localized prostate cancer. J Urol 1994;152(5 Pt 2):1910–4.

68. Ganz PA. Long-range effect of clinical trial interventions on quality of life. Cancer 1994;1:74 (9 Suppl):2620–4.

69. Crosignani PG, Vercellini P, Apolone G, et al. Endometrial resection versus vaginal hysterectomy for menorrhagia: long-term clinical and quality-of-life outcomes. Am J Obstet Gynecol 1997; 177(1):95–101.

70. Furnary AP, Jessup FM, Moreira LP. Multicenter trial of dynamic cardiomyoplasty for chronic heart failure. The American Cardiomyoplasty Group. J Am Coll Cardiol 1996;1:28(5):1175–80.

71. Rorabeck CH, Bourne RB, Laupacis A, et al. A double-blind study of 250 cases comparing cemented with cementless total hip arthroplasty. Cost-effectiveness and its impact on health-related quality of life. Clin Orthop 1994;(298):156–64.

72. Ko CY, Waters PF. Lung volume reduction surgery: a cost and outcomes comparison of sternotomy versus thoracoscopy. Am Surg 1998;64(10):1010–3.

73. Ellstrom M, Ferraz-Nunes J, Hahlin M, Olsson JH. A randomized trial with a cost-consequence analysis after laparoscopic and abdominal hysterectomy. Obstet Gynecol 1998;91(1):30–4.

74. Chung KC, Walters MR, Greenfield ML, Chernew ME. Endoscopic versus open carpal tunnel release: a cost-effectiveness analysis. Plast Reconstr Surg 1998;102(4):1089–99.

75. Finizia C, Hammerlid E, Westin T, Lindstrom J. Quality of life and voice in patients with laryngeal carcinoma: a posttreatment comparison of laryngectomy (salvage surgery) versus radiotherapy. Laryngoscope 1998;108(10):1566–73.

76. Beduschi MC, Oesterling JE. Transurethral needle ablation of the prostate: a minimally invasive treatment for symptomatic benign prostatic hyperplasia. Mayo Clin Proc 1998;73(7):696–701.

77. Curran D, van Dongen JP, Aaronson NK, et al. Quality of life of early-stage breast cancer patients treated with radical mastectomy or breast-conserving procedures: results of EORTC Trial 10801. The European Organization for Research and Treatment of Cancer (EORTC), Breast Cancer Co-operative Group (BCCG). Eur J Cancer 1998;34(3):307–14.

78. Bruskewitz R, Issa MM, Roehrborn CG, et al. A prospective, randomized 1-year clinical trial comparing transurethral needle ablation to transurethral resection of the prostate for the treatment of symptomatic benign prostatic hyperplasia. J Urol 1998;159(5):1588–93.

79. Tyrrell CJ, Kaisary AV, Iversen P, et al. A randomised comparison of 'Casodex' (bicalutamide) 150 mg monotherapy versus castration in the treatment of metastatic and locally advanced prostate cancer. Eur Urol 1998;33(5):447–56.

80. Hammadeh MY, Madaan S, Singh M, Philp T. Two-year follow-up of a prospective randomised trial of electrovaporization versus resection of prostate. Eur Urol 1998;34(3):188–92.

81. Karlsson J, Sjostrom L, Sullivan M. Swedish obese subjects (SOS)—an intervention study of obesity. Two-year follow-up of health-related quality of life (HRQL) and eating behavior after gastric surgery for severe obesity. Int J Obes Relat Metab Disord 1998;22(2):113–26.

82. Metson R, Gliklich RE. Clinical outcome of endoscopic surgery for frontal sinusitis. Arch Otolaryngol Head Neck Surg 1998;124(10):1090–6.

83. Terrell JE, Fisher SG, Wolf GT. Long-term quality of life after treatment of laryngeal cancer. The Veterans Affairs Laryngeal Cancer Study Group. Arch Otolaryngol Head Neck Surg 1998;124(9):964–71.

84. Vickrey BG, Hays RD, Rausch R, et al. Outcomes in 248 patients who had diagnostic evaluations for epilepsy surgery. Lancet 1995;2:346(8988):1445–9.

85. Jenkinson C, Gray A, Doll H, et al. Evaluation of index and profile measures of health status in a randomized controlled trial. Comparison of the Medical Outcomes Study 36-Item Short Form Health Survey, EuroQol, and disease specific measures. Med Care 1997;35:1109–18.

86. McKenna SP, Doward LC, Whalley D. The development and testing of the well-being index for surgical patients (WISP). Qual Life Res 1998;7:167–73.

87. Borstlap M, Zant JL, van Soesbergen RM, van der Korst JK. Quality of life assessment: a comparison of four questionnaires: for measuring improvements after total hip replacement. Clin Rheumatol 1995;14(1):15–20.

88. Klassen A, Jenkinson C, Fitzpatrick R, Goodacre T. Measuring quality of life in cosmetic surgery patients with a condition-specific instrument: the Derriford Scale. Br J Plast Surg 1998;51(5):380–4.

89. Mangione CM, Goldman L, Orav EJ, et al. Health-related quality of life after elective surgery: measurement of longitudinal changes. J Gen Intern Med 1997;12(11):686–97.

90. Deyo RA, Patrick DL. Barriers to the use of health status measures in clinical investigation, patient care, and policy research. Med Care 1989;27(3):S254–68.

91. Iezzoni LI. The risks of risk adjustment. JAMA 1997;19:278(19):1600–7.

92. Guyatt GH, Naylor CD, Juniper E, et al. Users' guides to the medical literature. XII. How to use articles about health-related quality of life. JAMA 1997;277:1232–7.

CHAPTER 19

Consumer Health Information and Evidence-Based Surgery

Ron Sauder, BA

The empowerment of health care consumers through access to an ever more sophisticated body of information about disease treatment and prevention is one of the fundamental forces acting on the health care system today. As is also the case in many other arenas, the consumer revolution is being fanned by accelerating access to an enormous body of on-line information via the Internet. An article in *Business Week* on October 19, 1998, described health care as "the next big thing" on the World Wide Web. "Armed with data they've found online in medical journals, databases, and consumer health sites, patients are walking into doctors' offices and asking about treatments and diseases some physicians may never have heard of or considered. 'It's a fundamental shift of knowledge, and therefore power, from physicians to patients,' says Jim Hudak, global managing partner for health at Andersen Consulting."[1] While on one level the increased access to consumer health information is already contributing to changes in the traditional physician-patient relationship, on another level there is abundant evidence that this access to information may contribute to superior outcomes. A recent report by a panel convened by the (federal) Office of Disease Prevention and Health Promotion lists "empowerment" as one of the central features of health communication and cites research showing that a feeling of empowerment "is closely related to health outcomes in that powerlessness has been shown to be a broad-based risk factor for disease. Studies demonstrate that people who feel 'in control' in a health situation have better outcomes than those who feel 'powerless.' "[2]

So-called consumer health information can encompass a wide range of products, from health-related books and brochures written for a lay audience to "new media" electronic applications such as World Wide Web sites, on-line support groups, and e-mail news bulletins in areas of individual interest. On the advanced end of the spectrum, consumer health information can embrace shared decision support systems between patients and physicians, although some might classify this as patient information (ie, information for persons who are currently being treated in the health care system) rather than consumer health information (ie, information for the mass audience without specific reference to patient status). The goals of consumer health information can include, variously, achieving general disease prevention and promoting wellness; maximizing the efficiency of patient-physician office encounters; increasing the ability of patients to understand and self-manage chronic illness; and reducing inappropriate use of the health care system. A good consensus definition of consumer health information is given in a white paper of the Department of Health and Human Services, Information Infrastructure Task Force: "any information that enables individuals to understand their health and make health related decisions for themselves or their families. This includes information supporting individual and community-based health promotion and enhancement, self-care, shared (professional-patient) decision making, patient education and rehabilitation, using the health care system and selecting insurance or a provider, and peer-group support."[3]

Similarly, a 1995 report by the Office of Technology Assessment defines consumer health informatics as "the study, development, and implementation of computer and telecommunications applications designed to be used by health consumers" and "any information that enables individuals to understand their health and make health-related decisions for themselves or their families."[4]

Academic medical centers such as Johns Hopkins and the Mayo Clinic have profited from and served the mass interest in consumer health information for more than a decade, with commercial newsletters, home encyclopedias, and on-line consumer health information Web sites. The Mayo Clinic has been a major publisher of consumer health information in both print and electronic form. The *Mayo Clinic Family Health Book*, a single-volume health encyclopedia, sold about 700,000 copies in its first edition, published in 1990, and a revised edition appeared in 1996. The Mayo Clinic publishes a nationally circulated subscription newsletter, the *Mayo Clinic Health Letter*, launched in 1983. Mayo Health *O@sis*, a popular Web site, reportedly had 800,000 visitors in August 1998, according to *Business Week*.[1] Harvard University is well established in consumer health information print publishing, with the *Harvard Women's Health Book* and five nationally circulated subscription newsletters, including the *Harvard Health Letter* and the *Harvard Women's Health Watch*. In 1996, Harvard University Medical School entered an alliance with Simon & Schuster calling for publication of a family health book and a related CD-ROM along with a number of other books, newsletters, World Wide Web products, videos, audiobooks, and other publications and products.

The Johns Hopkins University School of Medicine is 10 years into its publication of the best-selling commercial health newsletter branded with the name of a medical school, *Johns Hopkins Health After 50*, published by Rebus, Inc., with a paid subscription base of about 500,000. In 1998, Rebus launched a specialty publication covering advances in prostate cancer and treatment, the *Johns Hopkins Prostate Bulletin*, with an annual subscription price of $195, and reported impressive sales despite the rather steep cost, illustrating the potential market for high-end information for those with a compelling need to know. Rebus also publishes a growing series of consumer monographs known as the *Johns Hopkins White Papers* and a small number of hardcover Johns Hopkins books (the *Medical Handbook, Symptoms and Remedies*, and the *Complete Home Encyclopedia of Drugs*, which are distributed primarily through direct mail). In early 1999, Johns Hopkins and HarperCollins published the 1,650-page *Johns Hopkins Family Health Book*. With a first printing of 140,000, this home encyclopedia was the March 1999 main selection of the Book-of-the-Month Club. In February 1996, Johns Hopkins launched a joint venture with U.S. Healthcare (soon thereafter to become Aetna U.S. Healthcare) to name-brand a leading consumer health information site on the World Wide Web, InteliHealth.com. By the spring of 1999, InteliHealth was logging over 1 million unique visitors per month, putting it in the top echelon of consumer health Web sites, and had been recognized with a Webby award for best health site on the Internet by the International Academy of Digital Arts and Sciences.

For Mayo, Harvard, and Johns Hopkins, which perennially run neck and neck in national hospital and medical school rankings, these print and electronic publishing programs have become major business ventures as well as unprecedented efforts to project their institutional names and expertise on a national and international scale.

At the same time, the federal government has provided a vast and growing amount of information through extensive print and on-line publication programs by such agencies as the Agency for Health Care Policy and Research, the Centers for Disease Control and Prevention, the Food and Drug Administration, and the National Institutes of Health. The federal government's expenditure on health information is enormous. According to a Department of Health and Human Services white paper on consumer health, the department alone spent about $2 billion on health information programs and clearinghouses in 1991. (Presumably, the amount has increased in the years since.)[3]

In addition, major voluntary health agencies such as the American Cancer Society and the American Heart Association, professional associations and societies, hospitals and health systems, and health insurers and managed care organizations have formed Web sites that provide referral information and consumer health information. The 40 largest voluntary health agencies alone spent $623 million on consumer health information in 1991, according to the National Health Council.[3]

Propelled by market competition, health reform, and consumer interests, the rising tide of consumer health information shows no slackening but rather the opposite, as the growing popularity of personal computers and the Internet has created unprecedented ease in information retrieval. Since 1997, consumer access to even the most sophisticated medical literature has accelerated with the initiation of free public MEDLINE searches by the National Library of Medicine (NLM), allowing free access on the World Wide Web to 9 million citations from 3,900 medical journals, as well as to a series of specialty databases. Vice President Albert Gore conducted the first such free search in 1997. By late 1998, "the number of MEDLINE searches ... increased amazingly, from 7 million a year to 120 million," noted Donald A. B. Lindberg, MD, director of the NLM. "And about one-third of them are being done by consumers—indicative of the increasing public appetite for health information."[5]

Other data confirm that enormous numbers of Americans are going on-line in search of health information. According to one recent estimate, there are 15,000 to 25,000 health-related World Wide Web sites.[6] And those sites are attracting viewers. A Louis Harris & Associates poll found that up to 60 million Americans used the Internet last year for searches related to health care.[7] A more conservative estimate, from Cyber Dialogue, Inc., based on a semiannual survey of 2,000 American adults, is that nearly 18 million used the World Wide Web for health searches in 1998, comparable to the number seeking financial investment information, and that the figure will reach 30 million by the end of the century.[8] The 1998 survey showed that slightly more than half of these information seekers (52% of both men and women) were performing searches related to diseases and conditions; about one-third (34% of men and 32% of women) were seeking information on prescription drugs; and about one-fourth of those who search for disease information joined on-line support groups.[9] Moreover, these on-line support networks, usually in the chronic or serious diseases categories, become important sources of health information as well as social support for their members: a 1998 survey of members of the Sapient Health Network found that the 191 respondents rated their fellow members more highly than either specialists or primary doctors in 10 of 12 areas of care, including "best in-depth information" (by a three-to-one margin over specialist and primary doctors, combined) and "best practical knowledge." (The only categories in which specialist doctors were rated more highly than both support groups and primary doctors were "help to diagnose correctly" and "management after diagnosis.")[10] However, other surveys suggest that the mass consumer audience's desire for information branded with known and trustworthy names is as strong in this arena as it is in other sectors. A survey of adult Internet users by MSB Associates found that 81 percent view the information they get from a national medical center as the most trustworthy while 77 percent place on-line information from their own doctor in the same category. Slightly less than half (48%) in this survey said they viewed information from on-line support groups as the most trustworthy.[11]

REVIEW OF THE LITERATURE: USES OF CONSUMER HEALTH INFORMATION

Given this large and growing volume of consumer health information, several questions suggest themselves in the context of evidence-based medicine in general and evidence-based surgery in particular. Is there any evidence that consumers are making use of the growing body of data that are being created to guide their health care choices, including the increasing number of "quality report cards" that distinguish, for example, between various hospitals' and even particular surgeons' outcomes for various procedures? What factors are working for and against consumers' use of such data? Given the growing tendency of consumers to access health information on the World Wide Web, what is known about the quality of the information they find there? Finally, what, if anything, is being done to improve the quality, comprehensibility, and ease of access of this information for consumers? The answers to these questions may well be important to the success of health reform and quality initiatives generally, as well as to providers' ability to respond to increasing cost pressures with better outcomes.

First, while countless individual consumers, many consumer groups, and most health care reform initiatives have featured publicly accessible quality report cards as one of their central objectives, there is, as yet, only mixed evidence that many consumers understand or seek out these report cards or act on the basis of them. A 1996 survey (conducted by the Princeton Survey Research Associates for the Kaiser Family Foundation and the Agency for Health Care Policy and Research) of 2,006 adults showed that while quality of care is what people say they care about most in choosing a health plan (42%), recommendations from their doctors (59%) and friends (57%) are in fact more important to their decisions.[12] Astonishingly (at least from the standpoint of evidence-based medicine), three-quarters of the respondents (76%) said they would choose a surgeon they knew personally rather than a surgeon they did not know, even if the latter had much higher quality ratings. This may be a case where lack of familiarity with quality reporting breeds disinterest; while more than 4 out of 5 respondents said quality comparisons would be useful for people trying to choose doctors, hospitals, or health plans, only 2 out of 5 reported having seen such information in the past year, and only about one-third of respondents had ever used such quality comparisons in their own health care decision making.

This attitude survey is borne out in consumers' actions in the marketplace as well. In a January 1998 editorial in the *Joint Commission Journal on Quality Improvement*, J. William Thomas concluded that "Research indicates that consumers' hospital choices are not affected by public release of such report card data as those of California and Pennsylvania. For example, Mennemeyer and colleagues recently calculated that for the 9-year period during which [the Health Care Financing Administration] was releasing its annual hospital mortality data, a facility having a mortality rate twice as high as HCFA's expected rate would have suffered a reduction in patient demand of fewer than 120 patients."[13]

The referenced study of the 9-year experiment of the Health Care Financing Administration (HCFA) with publicizing hospital death rates concluded that HCFA was justified in dropping the program, because the public overreacted to statistically insignificant reports of patient deaths. At the same time, there was no evidence that the pattern of discharges corresponded to genuinely important data revealed by the study. In a 1997 *Inquiry* report, Mennemeyer, Morrisey, and Howard concluded that "the release of HCFA mortality data, at best, had only a small impact on hospital discharges... However, press results of easily understood, bad outcomes did influence hospital volume. A newspaper account of an unusual hospital death was associated with a 9% reduction in hospital use, for the average hospital."[14]

A major postoperative survey of how heart patients respond to outcomes data in choosing surgeons found that patients seemed to know and care little about the information available to them. The study of 474 persons who had undergone coronary artery bypass graft (CABG) procedures in Pennsylvania between July 1995 and March 1996 found that fewer than 1 percent (4 patients) knew how their surgeon or hospital had been rated in the state's widely publicized *Consumer Guide* to CABG mortality rates or had used that information to guide their choice of surgeon or hospital.[15] Moreover, only 12 percent of the respondents said they had even known of the existence of the *Consumer Guide* prior to their surgery. In a report in the *Journal of the American Medical Association* on the consumer study, Schneider and Epstein noted that since 1992, the Pennsylvania Health Care Cost Containment Council has been issuing risk-adjusted mortality rates for every surgeon, surgical group, and hospital that performs CABGs. The Council distributes 15,000 copies of the *Consumer Guide* to a variety of recipients

hospitals and long-term care facilities and to measure relative performance in those systems both between institutions and within a given institution over time. However, Epstein notes that there are large remaining areas of debate as to what kinds of reports are most useful. For instance, does reporting outcomes for individual physicians, while failing to adjust accurately for relative risk, actually pose the danger of "decreased access for the severely ill"? (For example, would some cardiac surgeons be less willing to operate on high-risk patients, knowing they would be judged through the public release of their outcomes?[16,17,18]) While most current efforts are focused on measuring relative performances of hospitals and health plans, Epstein notes that for consumers, the choice of medical groups or individual physicians may be more important. Yet, "unfortunately almost all of the potential problems with performance reports—risk adjustment, small numbers, political sensitivity, patient confidentiality, and data reliability—become more difficult to manage as we move our focus toward the individual practitioner."[17] While the search for what Epstein calls a "common path" of performance reporting continues, major forces are being brought to bear on the problem of assessing and improving the quality of consumer health information available on the World Wide Web.

CONSUMER HEALTH INFORMATION ON THE WORLD WIDE WEB

That there are significant quality concerns associated with information on the World Wide Web is almost universally acknowledged, although some contrarians have argued for the superiority of the Internet to print. ("In my experience, the quality of information that patients glean from the internet has, in general, been superior to that derived from newspaper articles," wrote rheumatologist P. V. Gardiner in a recent letter to the *British Medical Journal.* "There is plenty of rubbish on the internet, but patients should be given some credit for being able to sort out the wheat from the chaff. People who use the internet are accustomed to accessing several sources of information on a particular subject and comparing the quality of information provided. As large health charities such as the Arthritis Foundation have come online with comprehensive and trustworthy information resources for patients, the professional design of their sites ensures that they will feature at the top of most search lists.")[20] A broader consensus of specialists, however, seems to agree that the Internet presents a unique opportunity for the propagation of false and fallacious claims, especially in the area of alternative medicine and unproven herbal medicines and supplements. As the *Journal of the American Medical Association* put it in an influential 1997 editorial, "At first glance, science and snake oil may not always look all that different on the Net."[21] The *British Medical Journal,* in a 1998 editorial calling for the creation of higher-quality, evidence-based patient information, said that the Internet "will greatly increase access to health information," but much of it is "inaccurate or misleading...."[22] The journal called for the development of a "national public health information strategy" that would include investment in better materials, training for clinicians, "and the development of an accreditation system to help users to judge the quality of health information." In a similar spirit, the *Journal of the American Medical Association* recommended a series of voluntary standards to be adopted by Web site developers, who would systematically disclose authorship, attribution of sources, Web site ownership (including sponsorship, advertising, and underwriting support), and currency, specifying dates of content creation and review. There is no lack of third-party quality-rating services or groups, as noted by A. R. Jadad and A. Gagliardi in a 1998 article in the *Journal of the American Medical Association.* They found no fewer than 47 health-rating services on the World Wide Web, 13 of which specified their criteria for review and 34 of which did not. "In summary, a large number of incompletely developed instruments to evaluate health information on the Internet exist," they wrote. "It is unclear, however, whether they should exist in the first place, whether they should measure what they claim to measure, or whether they lead to more good than harm."[23]

Even when health Web sites appear to be authored by reputable individuals or organizations, however, there can still be significant problems with the information they present, as was documented in a study by Italian researcher Piero Impicciatore and colleagues. Working with 41 Web sites pulled up by two leading search engines, Yahoo® and Excite®, they analyzed recommendations given for the home management of children with fever. In comparing the Web sites' advice with that of medical consensus, the authors concluded that "only four [ie, ten percent] adhered closely to published guidelines for home management of childhood fever." And understandably, they concluded that "Information on the internet should not be a substitute for routine care by family doctors."[24]

The question, of course, is to what degree consumer health information in general, and electronic health information in particular, can be integrated with standard medical recommendations and the needs of doctors to serve some of the objectives for health information outlined at the outset of this chapter: disease treatment and health promotion, consumer empowerment and better patient outcomes, more effective use of physician time in particular and the health care system in general, and shared decision support between physicians and patients. There is clearly a growing need for evidence-based patient information, as noted by the *British Medical Journal*: "If patients are to be active participants in decisions about their care the information they are given must accord with available evidence and be presented in a form that is acceptable and useful. Information materials are no substitute for good verbal discussions, but consultations are usually short and plenty of evidence exists that patients do not receive the information they want and need. Leaflets and other materials can therefore play an important part in supplementing and reinforcing information provided by clinicians, but the information they contain must conform to the highest standards of scientific accuracy and must be tested for comprehensibility and relevance."[22]

In a similar spirit, a recent major report of the Science Panel on Interactive Communication and Health, chartered by the Office of Disease Prevention and Health Promotion of the US Department of Health and Human Services, called for more emphasis on quality control and evaluation measures in the development of interactive health care applications. The panel defined interactive health care communication as "the interaction of an individual consumer, patient, caregiver, or professional—with or through an electronic device or communication technology to access or transmit health information, or to receive or provide guidance and support on a health-related issue. IHC [Interactive Health Communication] applications include health information and support Web sites and other technology-mediated applications that relay information, enable informed decision-making, promote healthy behaviors, promote information exchange and support, promote self-care, or manage demand for health services."[25] The report suggests that these evaluation measures should include a requirement that "developers integrate evaluation methods into product development and implementation as a condition of purchase;" that the results of these evaluations as well as the identities of all developers and sponsors and sources of content should be publicly disclosed; that developers should adopt voluntary quality standards; and that Web sites should be rated on criteria that include their effectiveness.[26]

There is little doubt that health information meeting these exacting standards—written to be comprehensible to its user (and perhaps selected and filtered by so-called intelligent agents, with the precise needs of the user in mind); evaluated for effectiveness; reviewed for medical and scientific accuracy as carefully as if for publication in a professional journal; and prepared in conformance with evidence-based standards—can substantially change the practice of medicine and patient outcomes, including those in many surgical procedures. (Intelligent agents are computer programs that could act on a user's behalf, sifting through vast quantities of information on the World Wide Web and in databases to find information that is precisely relevant to an individual consumer's or patient's needs. Such agents could evolve into "expert systems" that could assist consumers in self-diagnosis and the assessment of treatment options.)[27] In a 1996 study, researchers from Dartmouth Medical School found that viewing an educational videotape about the areas of uncertainty with regard to prostate-specific antigen (PSA) testing and the treatment of early-stage prostate cancer produced substantially different choices among two groups of men over the age of 50 years. Men who viewed the videotape were deemed "better informed" and less likely to choose to have a PSA test, as opposed to men who viewed another videotape or no videotape at all. In addition, they were more likely to choose no active treatment if an early-stage prostate cancer was found. "Preference regarding cancer screening and treatment is greatly affected by information about medical uncertainties," the researchers concluded.[28]

Case Study: Pancreatic Cancer Web Site

Obviously, who develops, reviews, and controls such information, along with who is able to present it in the most accessible and user-friendly form as an integral part of the physician-patient interaction, is the key question that will determine the usefulness of health information in the health care system of the twenty-first century. A case study for what might be a paradigm of academically generated on-line health information at the century's turn is provided by the Pancreatic Cancer Web site of the Department of Pathology at Johns Hopkins (*http://pathology.jhu.edu/pancreas*). Founded in 1995, the site provides a mixture of clinical information on pancreatic cancer, news of recent advances, and a popular unmoderated message board where pancreatic cancer patients, family members, and others interested in the subject can post messages. "Between September 1996 and March 1998, the discussion board received 16,065 messages and 521,624 accesses," Hopkins researchers reported in a letter to the *Journal of the American Medical Association.* "These numbers are remarkable considering that only 27,000 patients are diagnosed annually with pancreatic cancer in the United States and that most patients live only a few months. Clearly, there are considerable needs not being met by the traditional delivery of medical care."[29]

An analysis of user data found that three-quarters of users posting messages to the message board were women (a striking percentage at a time when the majority of Web users were men), that 86 percent of the users were relatives of patients, and that 10 percent were from outside the United States. According to the letter to the *Journal of the American Medical Association*, there were multiple benefits from the Web site, including the provision of high-quality Web-based information for consumers and patients in an area of special expertise at Johns Hopkins; the generation of hospital referrals leading to the performance of a record number of Whipple's operations (167) at Johns Hopkins in 1997; and the identification of many new participants in the National Familial Pancreas Tumor Registry, which is maintained at Johns Hopkins and advertised prominently on the Web site. This registry has grown rapidly and is now the largest pancreatic cancer familial registry in the world, thanks largely to the Web site, says Ralph Hruban, MD, professor of pathology and oncology at Johns Hopkins and the site's developer (personal communication, May 17, 1999). Moreover, the community of users spawned by the Web site has turned into a major boon for pancreatic cancer research at Johns Hopkins, spontaneously organizing a fund-raising event in Los Angeles in November 1998 that netted about $100,000 in gifts (personal communication, May 17, 1999.) A second fund-raiser has been planned for November 1999 by the same group. Dr. Hruban and his colleagues conclude, in their letter to the *Journal of the American Medical Association*, "The tremendous growth in the use of the Johns Hopkins Pancreatic Cancer Web site was unanticipated and underscores a well-recognized Web phenomenon, namely, that Web sites can 'take on a life of their own,' often with unexpected consequences and benefits."

Case Study: InteliHealth Web Site

An equally open-ended experiment at Johns Hopkins, the InteliHealth for-profit joint venture between Johns Hopkins and Aetna U.S. Healthcare (described briefly above) illustrates other facets of the complex and rapidly changing character of consumer health publishing programs on the World Wide Web. With more than 1 million unique visitors per month, InteliHealth had gained a reputation as one of the leading consumer health destinations on the Web, available as an anchor health tenant on America Online, on the Pointcast Network health channel, and on the Web sites of many newspapers around the country, from the *Richmond Times-Dispatch* in Virginia to the *Houston Chronicle* in Texas. While not confining itself to evidence-based protocols per se, Johns Hopkins consumer health information produced for the InteliHealth joint venture was based on a strict principle of direct review of draft copy by faculty members of the Johns Hopkins Schools of Medicine, Nursing, and Public Health. This information (the creation of which is managed administratively by the Johns Hopkins Office of Consumer Health Information, of which the author was the founding director from February 1996 to May 1999) includes written responses by the Johns Hopkins faculty to "Ask-the-Doc" e-mails (six per week); Johns Hopkins faculty commentaries on topical health issues and news developments (four per week); the *Johns Hopkins Health Insider*, a monthly eight-page newsletter available in World Wide Web and print format; special editions of the *Insider* on subjects ranging from arthritis to migraine; a series of four advertising-supported print supplements published on the World Wide Web and in the magazine *Better Homes & Gardens*; large quantities of encyclopedic information on diseases and conditions ranging from childhood illnesses to cancer; and many other projects, including live "Webcasts" of interviews with Johns Hopkins health faculty members, beginning with the November 1998 "Woman's Journey" health conference in Baltimore. By mid-1999, 3 years into the InteliHealth joint venture, the range and number of such on-line consumer health projects was continuing to grow exponentially, having involved more than 200 faculty members since the project's inception. Despite the increasingly lucrative arena of Web-based health information in all its forms, the purpose of the InteliHealth joint venture remained the same as it had been from the beginning: to serve as the "trusted source" for health information on the World Wide Web by continuing to follow rigorous procedures of faculty review.

FUTURE DIRECTIONS

The explosion of the Internet into all aspects of daily life makes it clear that public access to consumer health information will play an increasingly prominent role in the patient-surgeon relationship. (That it will increasingly have major business implications as well is illustrated by the announced $7.9 billion merger in May 1999 of Healtheon, Inc., with WebMD, in a potent combination of medical data, professional health information, and consumer health information companies.) The ability of consumers to identify and retrieve scientific research findings will be greatly enhanced, while proprietary (ie, commercial) and non-peer-reviewed claims will compete for the consumer's attention. The implications for evidence-based surgery are manifold. Surgeons will need to be aware of the panoply of information available to patients on the Web and to be prepared to direct them to preferred sources. Questions about outcomes are likely to become more common as consumers become more aware of, and begin to act upon, comparative data and report cards posted on the Web. Surgeons must be facile in accessing Web sites and interpreting research results in an evidence-based fashion, specific to individual patients, as the proliferation of consumer health information will likely serve to better educate the patient and provide yet more fuel for the consumer movement in health care. In the end, the World Wide Web may become the most powerful engine yet for achieving one of the central goals outlined by the Ottawa Charter for Health Promotion, co-sponsored by the World Health Organization, in 1986: "Enabling people to learn, throughout life, to prepare themselves for all of its stages and to cope with chronic illness and injuries is essential. This has to be facilitated in school, home, work and community settings. Action is required through educational, professional, commercial and voluntary bodies, and within the institutions themselves."[30]

REFERENCES

1. Green H, Himelstein L. A cyber revolt in health care: patients are finding new power through the web. Business Week 1998 Oct 19:154–6.

2. Eng TR, Gustafson DH, editors. Wired for health and well-being: the emergence of interactive health communication. Washington (DC): Science Panel on Interactive Communication and Health, US Dept. of Health and Human Services, US Government Printing Office; 1999 Apr. p. 29.

3. Patrick K, Koss S. Consumer health information white paper. Consumer Health Information Subgroup, Health Information and Application Working Group, Committee on Applications and Technology, Information Infrastructure Task Force. 1995 May 15. *http://nii.nist.gov/pubs/chi.html.*

4. US Congress, Office of Technology Assessment. Bringing health care online: the role of information technologies. Washington (DC): US Government Printing Office; 1995 Sept. OTA-ITC-624 p. 24.

5. National Library of Medicine to work with public libraries to help consumers find answers to medical questions. [cited 1998 Oct 22]. Available from: URL: *http://nlm.nih.gov/news/press_releases/ medplus.html.*

6. Foreman J. Promises and pitfalls of cyber medicine. The Boston Globe 1999 Jan 4; E1.

7. Kaufman M. The Internet: a reliable source? The Washington Post 1999 Feb 16;Z17.

8. Cyber Dialogue, Inc. [press release] 1998 Oct 27 [accessed 1999 Apr 12]. Available from: URL: *http://www.cyberdialogue.com/press/releases/intel_health_day.html.*

9. Cyber Dialogue, Inc. October 1998 survey [accessed 1999 Apr 12]. Available from: URL: http://www.cyberdialogue.com/press/releases/intel_health_day.html.

10. Ferguson T, Kelly WJ. E-patients prefer e-groups to doctors for ten to twelve aspects of health care. The Ferguson Report: The Newsletter of Consumer Health Informatics and Online Health 1999;1(1):1–3.

11. Cavey AR, Lyan G. USA Snapshots. USA Today 1999 Feb 15;1D.

12. Agency for Health Care Policy and Research. Americans as health care consumers: the role of quality information [accessed 1999 Apr 12]. Available from: URL: *http://www.ahcpr.gov/qual/kffhigh.html.*

13. Thomas JW. Report cards—useful to whom and for what? The Joint Commission Journal on Quality Improvement 1998;24(1):50–1.

14. Mennemeyer ST, Morrisey MA, Howard LZ. Death and reputation: how consumers acted upon HCFA mortality information. Inquiry 1997;34:117–28.

15. Schneider EC, Epstein AM. Use of public performance reports: a survey of patients undergoing cardiac surgery. JAMA 1998;279:1638–42.

16. Chassin MR, Hannan EL, DeBuono BA. Benefits and hazards of reporting medical outcomes publicly. N Engl J Med 1996;334:394–8.

17. Epstein AM. Rolling down the runway: the challenges ahead for quality report cards. JAMA 1998;279:1691–6.

18. Mukamel DB, Mushlin AI. Quality of care information makes a difference: an analysis of market share and price changes after publication of the New York State cardiac surgery mortality rates. Med Care 1998;36:945–54.

19. Hannan EL, Stone CC, Biddle TL, DeBuono BA. Public release of cardiac surgery outcomes data in New York: what do New York state cardiologists think of it? Am Heart J 1997;134:1120–7.

20. Gardiner PV. Doctors should be encouraged to develop information resources on the internet [letter]. BMJ 1999;318:461.

21. Silberg WM, Lundberg GD, Musacchio RA. Assessing, controlling, and assuring the quality of medical information on the Internet. JAMA 1997;277:1244–5.

22. Coulter A. Evidence based patient information. BMJ 1998;317:225–6.

23. Jadad AR, Gagliardi A. Rating health information on the Internet: navigating to knowledge or to Babel? JAMA 1998;279:611–14.

24. Impicciatore P, Pandolfini C, Casella N, Bonati M. Reliability of health information on the world wide web: systematic survey of advice on managing fever in children at home. BMJ 1997;314:1875.

25. Eng TR, Gustafson DH, editors. Wired for health and well-being: the emergence of interactive health communication. Washington (DC): Science Panel on Interactive Communication and Health, US Dept. of Health and Human Services, US Government Printing Office; 1999 Apr. p. 1.

26. Eng TR, Gustafson DH, editors. Wired for health and well-being: the emergence of interactive health communication. Washington (DC): Science Panel on Interactive Communication and Health, US Dept. of Health and Human Services, US Government Printing Office; 1999 Apr. p. 100–3.

27. Eng TR, Gustafson DH, editors. Wired for health and well-being: the emergence of interactive health communication. Washington (DC): Science Panel on Interactive Communication and Health, US Dept. of Health and Human Services, US Government Printing Office; 1999 Apr. p. 26.

28. Flood AB, Wennberg JE, Nease RF Jr, et al. The importance of patient preference in the decision to screen for prostate cancer. J Gen Intern Med 1996;11(6):342–9.

29. Goggins M, Leitman A, Miller RE, Yeo CJ, Jaffee E, Coleman J, et al. Use and benefits of a web site for pancreatic cancer. JAMA 1998;280:1309–10.

30. First International Conference on Health Promotion, Ottawa Charter for Health Promotion, 1986. [accessed 1999 Jun 7]. Available from: URL: *http://www.who.int/hpr/documents/ottawa.html*. Co-sponsored by the Canadian Public Health Association, Health and Welfare Canada, and the World Health Organization.

CHAPTER 20

Esophageal Surgery

Richard F. Heitmiller, MD, FACS

Esophageal surgery is uncommon, complex, and frequently associated with significant morbidity, mortality, and potential impact on a patient's quality of life. Professional fees associated with studies to evaluate esophageal diseases and for esophageal surgical procedures reflect this complexity. Esophageal surgery is performed by both general and thoracic surgeons. The distribution of cases between the specialties depends on local training, interest, expertise, and referral patterns. Indications for surgery include carcinoma, benign stricture, motility disorders (including gastroesophageal reflux), diverticular disease, trauma, and perforation. The reason esophageal surgery is uncommon is the low prevalence of most of these disorders. Esophageal cancer accounts for only 1.5 percent of gastrointestinal malignancies, achalasia occurs in 1 to 6 per 100,000 patients,[1] diverticular disease occurs in 1 of 1,500 patients,[2] and perforation complicates esophagoscopy and esophageal dilatation in approximately 1 percent and 0.3 percent of cases, respectively.[3] The exception is gastroesophageal reflux disease (GERD), which although extremely common, is successfully managed medically in the majority of cases. In the author's practice, the most common esophageal operations are esophagogastrectomies, and the second are anti-reflux procedures. This chapter will focus on the most complex esophageal operations, esophagectomy.

LITERATURE REVIEW

Evidence-based surgery uses treatment outcomes to help physicians, health care administrators, and hospitals determine the most appropriate treatment and setting for patient care. Treatment outcomes include cost, morbidity and mortality, and quality of life. Evidence-based surgical reports consistently have shown that increased provider experience improves patient outcome and lowers cost. The important components of provider experience include a systematic multidisciplinary approach to patient care, high-volume experience, and appropriate equipment and treatment facilities (regionalizations). The evidence supporting each of these components will be reviewed below. The beneficial effects are most easily demonstrated for patients requiring complex surgeries. In terms of difficulty, cost, length of stay, morbidity, and mortality, esophageal surgery is considered complex gastrointestinal surgery. Therefore, it would be anticipated that regionalization would favorably affect the care of patients undergoing esophageal surgery; the reported data confirms this speculation.

Systematic Patient Care Plan

Roy and DeMeester,[4] over a decade ago and well before the concept of patient care pathways, stressed the importance of a systematic approach to the surgical management of patients with esophageal carcinoma. It was their premise that such a planned approach would result in lower operative mortality and improved post-therapy quality of life: "Proper perioperative management of the patient with carcinoma of the esophagus is as important to the reduction of operative mortality as technical expertise." Based on their experience, they identified specific surgical risk factors for esophageal cancer patients, including age, tumor stage, nutritional status, respiratory, and cardiovascular function. Treatment algorithms were proposed to assess and optimize each of these risk factors. (Cost issues were not evaluated in this early study.) More recently, planned patient care pathways have been shown to reduce hospital stay and cost while maintaining quality of care for a wide range of surgeries including cardiac,[5,6] general thoracic,[7] pancreatic,[8] esophageal, hepatic, and urologic surgeries. The author's experience with a patient care pathway for patients undergoing esophagectomy will be reviewed later in this chapter.

Surgical Volume

The relationship between surgical volume and operative mortality is well established for some but not all surgical procedures. Luft and colleagues[9] demonstrated a 25 to 41 percent reduction in annual death rates in high-volume hospitals (ie, where individual procedures were performed 200 or more times per year) compared to low-volume hospitals for open heart surgery, vascular surgery, and transurethral resection of the prostate. On the other hand, surgical volume did not correlate with mortality for cholecystectomy. Hannan and co-workers[10] found a significant surgical volume-mortality relationship for coronary bypass surgery, resection of abdominal aortic aneurysm, partial gastrectomy, and colectomy.

Little has been reported on the relationship between surgical volume and outcome for esophageal surgery. Miller and co-workers[11] evaluated the effect of surgical experience (ie, surgical volume) on outcome of esophagectomy for esophageal cancer. In their series, surgeons were classified as "frequent" or "occasional" based on whether the yearly volume of esophagectomies exceeded 6 or was 5 or less, respectively. Although the study was retrospective and involved small patient numbers, the authors reported 7 percent anastomotic leak rates and no mortality for frequent surgeons, and 22 percent anastomotic leak rates and 22 percent mortality rates for occasional surgeons. The difference in operative mortality between the two groups was significant. The authors concluded that esophagectomy for carcinoma should be performed by experienced surgeons who maintain sufficient yearly volumes to maintain competency.

Ellis and co-workers[12] recently reported their experience with 454 patients who underwent esophagectomy for carcinoma of the esophagus and cardia over a 24-year period. In order to assess possible trends, the authors divided the group into three 8-year time intervals. For each successive time interval, the number of esophagectomies performed increased from 64 to 187 to 203. As surgical volume increased, the hospital mortality decreased from 1.9 percent to 1.8 percent to 0.5 percent for the three time intervals respectively. The differences in mortality between time intervals did not reach statistical significance; however, the trend supports the claim that surgical experience and operative mortality for esophagectomy are inversely related.

Gordon and co-workers[13] demonstrated reduced in-house mortality, shorter average length of stay, and lower cost for esophagectomy, total gastrectomy, hepatic lobectomy, subtotal abdominal colectomy, and pancreaticoduodenectomy when these procedures were performed in high-volume centers as opposed to low-volume centers.

Multidisciplinary Approach

Given a wide range of disease processes, specialized preoperative diagnostic tests, technically complex surgery, the need for postoperative intensive care support, and the impact on the patient's nutrition and quality of life, esophageal surgery is ideally suited for a multidisciplinary patient care plan.

A collaboration of surgery and pathology led Heitmiller and co-workers[14] to conclude that prophylactic esophagectomy was indicated for patients with Barrett's esophagus with high-grade epithelial dysplasia, given the safety of the surgery, a reasonable length of hospital stay, and a high prevalence of occult adenocarcinoma (43% in their series).

Forastiere and co-workers[15] (including surgeons, radiation therapists, and medical oncologists) developed a treatment plan for patients with esophageal carcinoma which used synchronous chemoradiation therapy followed by surgery. They looked at outcomes of treatment safety and survival to determine treatment efficacy. They concluded that this aggressive therapy could be administered with acceptable morbidity and mortality and that the survival rate with combination therapy seemed to be higher than with surgery alone.

Respiratory complications following esophagectomies occur in up to 50 percent of patients. Postoperative pneumonia is reported to occur in 5 to 20 percent of patients and is the most common cause of postsurgical mortality. Gillinov and Heitmiller[16] began with the assumption that the majority of postesophagectomy pneumonia resulted from aspiration. They therefore developed a patient management strategy that included the specialties of anesthesiology, critical care medicine, and dietary medicine. It was designed to maximize airway protection in the postoperative period, and it looked at outcome in terms of mortality, incidence of respiratory complications, and length of hospital stay. Using this strategy, the authors reported a 10 percent incidence of major pulmonary complications and a 3 percent incidence of pneumonia (Table 20–1). They also identified patient age and a past history of chronic obstructive pulmonary disease (COPD) as risk factors for postesophagectomy pulmonary complications (Table 20–2).

Post-thoracotomy pain following Ivor-Lewis, left thoracoabdominal, or three-incision esophagectomy may decrease patient mobility and increase postoperative complications, especially respiratory complications, thus increasing intensive care time, length of hospital stay, and overall treatment cost. Brodner and colleagues[17] developed a multimodal approach (surgery, anesthesiology, and critical care medicine) to control postoperative pain in patients undergoing Ivor-Lewis (abdominothoracic) esophagectomy and to see how this would affect early hospital recovery. Their treatment plan called for epidural catheter analgesia, early tracheal extubation and early mobilization. Compared to a retrospective analysis of patients managed by traditional therapy, patients treated with this new regimen showed earlier extubation, earlier mobilization, and shorter stays in intensive and intermediate care units. The authors concluded that their study results should translate to reduced costs for esophagectomy.

Appropriate Equipment and Treatment Facilities

There are no data reporting specifically on the impact the availability of equipment and treatment facilities have on outcome for esophagectomy patients. However, for uncommon and complex surgeries such as esophagectomy, institutional support in terms of personnel,

Table 20–1 Pulmonary Complications after Transhiatal Esophagectomy

Pulmonary Complication	Number	Percent
Major pulmonary complication	11*	10
Pneumonia	3	3
Pleural effusion-drainage required	4	4
Exacerbation of COPD	2	2
Mucus plug	2	2
Minor pulmonary complications	100	99
Atelectasis	97	97
Pleural effusion	85	85
Pneumothorax	3	3

*11 major pulmonary complications occurred in 10 patients.

COPD=chronic obstructive pulmonary disease.

Reprinted with permission from Gillinov AM, Heitmiller RF. Strategies to reduce pulmonary complications after transhiatal esophagectomy. Dis Esophagus 1998;11:43–7.

Table 20–2 Risk Factors for Respiratory Complications after Transhiatal Esophagectomy

Risk Factor	Major Pulmonary Complication N=10	No Major Pulmonary Complication N=91	p-Value
Age	69.3 ± 3.1	59.2 ± 1.3	.012
Tobacco use	9	73	.68
COPD	7	19	.003
Asthma	1	8	.59
Coronary artery disease	2	19	.68
ASA risk score 3 or 4	7	58	.49
Esophageal cancer	7	73	.43

COPD=chronic obstructive pulmonary disease; ASA=American Society of Anesthesiology.
Reprinted with permission from Gillinov AM, Heitmiller RF. Strategies to reduce pulmonary complications after transhiatal esophagectomy. Dis Esophagus 1998;11:43–7.

conference and care facilities, and specialized equipment is related invariably to the volume of patients treated. Specialized services for esophagectomy patients include endoscopic ultrasonography staging, critical care anesthesia, patient-controlled analgesia, and esophagographic video techniques.

CASE STUDY: PATIENT CARE PATHWAYS FOR ESOPHAGECTOMY

The evolution of the evidence-based patient care pathways for esophagectomy at Johns Hopkins medical institutions typifies the development of these pathways in general. Interest in Barrett's esophagus with high-grade dysplasia[14] and esophageal carcinoma,[15] both indications for esophagectomy, increased institutional esophagectomy volume. The increased volume led to the establishment of a formal multidisciplinary collaboration of surgery, anesthesiology, gastroenterology, radiology, oncology, pathology, and dietary medicine to manage these complex patients and to optimize surgical results. Institutional support in terms of personnel, facilities, and specialized equipment increased with increasing patient volume and physician interest. The experience and the results ultimately led to the establishment of specific patient care pathways that are now in routine use for esophagectomy patients at the institution.

The operative procedure of esophagectomy is technically termed a *partial esophagogastrectomy* because a cuff of gastric cardia is included along with the resected esophagus. Rarely is the entire esophagus removed. A portion of proximal esophagus is retained for anastomosis. A number of incisional strategies have been developed to perform a partial esophagogastrectomy. These include transhiatal, left thoracoabdominal, abdominothoracic (Ivor-Lewis), and three-incision techniques (Figure 20–1).[18] All of these approaches have similar morbidity, mortality, and survival. Selection of one approach over another depend primarily on the location of esophageal disease and on the options for esophageal replacement. It has become the author's preference to use the transhiatal approach whenever possible. Potential advantages of the transhiatal technique over thoracotomy include less incisional pain, reduced morbidity with anastomotic leaks, and reduced postsurgical reflux. Davis and Heitmiller[19] showed that for patients who underwent esophagectomy for benign disease, greater use of the transhiatal technique was associated with reduced length of hospital stay (Figures 20–2, 20–3).

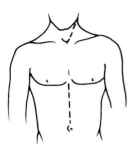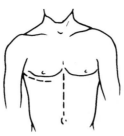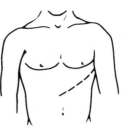

Transhiatal approach   Ivor-Lewis approach   Left thoracoabdominal
                                               approach

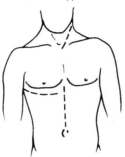

Three-incision approach

Figure 20–1 Incisions for the most common esophagectomy techniques are illustrated. (Printed with permission from Reichle RL, Fishman EK, Nixon MS, et al. Evaluation of the postsurgical esophagus after partial esophagogastrectomy for esophageal cancer. Invest Radiol 1993;28:247–57.)

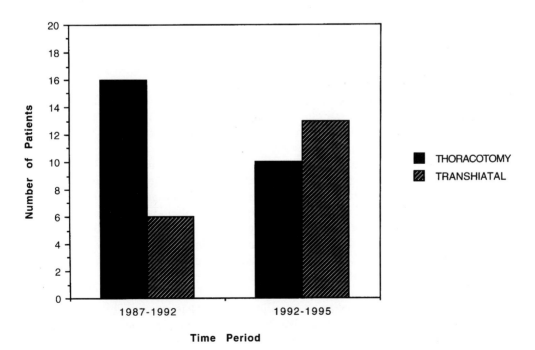

Figure 20–2 The frequency of surgical approach is illustrated for the two time intervals for patients undergoing esophagectomy for benign disease. (Printed with permission from Davis EA, Heitmiller RF. Esophagectomy for benign disease: trends in surgical results and management. Ann Thorac Surg 1996;62:369–72.)

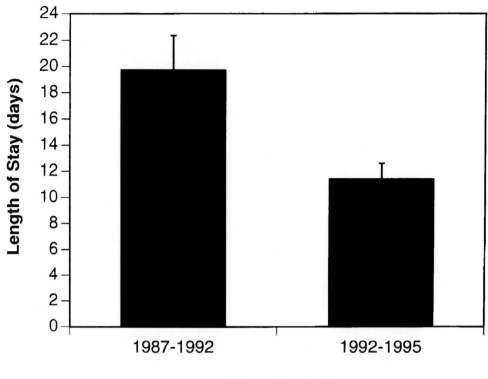

Figure 20–3 Length of hospital stay is illustrated for patients undergoing esophagectomy for benign disease. (Printed with permission from Davis EA, Heitmiller RF. Esophagectomy for benign disease: trends in surgical results and management. Ann Thorac Surg 1996;62:369–72.)

After standardizing the esophagectomy technique, complications unique to this surgery were addressed. The working hypothesis was that by minimizing major complications, safer surgery with shorter hospital stay and reduced cost would be achieved. The following parameters were identified: (1) anastomotic complications, (2) swallowing function, and (3) respiratory complications.

Stone and Heitmiller[20] developed a technique designed to set up a cervical esophagogastric anastomosis to optimize exposure. The authors believed that the resulting enhanced exposure minimized the risk of anastomotic leakage and recurrent laryngeal nerve injury and that it facilitated the teaching of the anastomotic method to residents and fellows. The authors also advocated the use of a two-layer, hand-sewn anastomosis originally described by Sweet[21] and which is now generally referred to as the Massachusetts General Hospital (MGH) anastomosis. The authors' early results with both the anastomotic set-up and the MGH anastomosis demonstrated the safety and effectiveness of these techniques.

Heitmiller and Jones[22] evaluated pre- and postsurgical swallowing function for patients who underwent transhiatal esophagectomy using cine-esophagography. They found that at least some swallowing abnormality was identified in 67 percent of patients (Table 20–3). The most common postsurgical findings were laryngeal aspiration or penetration (47%) and incomplete laryngeal elevation (33%). These postsurgical swallowing changes resolved or significantly improved within 1 month. The authors concluded that cineradiography is a reliable method for monitoring postesophagectomy pharyngeal function, and that the risk of aspiration may be greater in the first month following surgery.

Table 20–3 Summary of Postoperative Cineradiographic Swallowing Studies in Transhiatal Esophagectomy Patients

Radiologic Abnormality	1 Week	1 Month
Postop swallowing abnormality	10/15 (67%)	8/2
Laryngeal penetration or aspiration	7/15 (47%)	4/3
Incomplete laryngeal elevation	5/15 (33%)	4/1
Abnormal epiglottic tilt	2/15 (13%)	2/0
Incomplete pharyngeal stripping	0/15 (0%)	—
Cricopharyngeal obstruction	0/15 (0%)	—

Adapted and printed with permission from Heitmiller RF, Jones B. Transient diminished airway protection after transhiatal esophagectomy. Am J Surg 1991;162:442–6.

Attempting to reduce the incidence of respiratory complications following esophagectomy, Gillinov and Heitmiller[16] made the assumption that most major respiratory problems develop as a result of aspiration. They also postulated that the risk of aspiration was highest in the early postoperative period when patients are sedated and supine and later when oral feedings are resumed. They then developed safeguards to protect against aspiration. To prevent early aspiration, patients are kept intubated and mechanically ventilated through the night of surgery. The following morning, if patients are stable with a clear chest film, they are weaned from the ventilator and extubated when they are fully alert and satisfy standard criteria for oxygenation and ventilation. Chest physiotherapy is introduced post extubation. Prior to starting oral feedings, a video-esophagograph is obtained, followed by the introduction of a graduated postesophagectomy diet that controls quantity, consistency, and calories of meals. If significant aspiration is identified on videographed swallow, oral feedings are withheld, patients are fed enterally via jejunostomy, and video-esophagography is repeated 1 month later. Using this strategy, Gillinov and Heitmiller reported major respiratory complications and pneumonia incidences of 10 percent and 3 percent, respectively, following transhiatal esophagectomy (see Table 20–1).

Prospective Patient Care Pathway

Based on their experience with esophageal surgery, physicians at Johns Hopkins instituted a prospective, standardized, clinical care pathway for patients undergoing partial esophagogastrectomy.[23] The objective was to assess the effect of the patient care pathway on cost, outcome, and length of stay. Two goals were set for pathway development. The first goal was to determine what tests, consultations, and interventions were necessary to treat the *ideal* patient undergoing esophagectomy. These were then incorporated into the postoperative care plan. Because care was standardized, all health care providers were aware of the overall routine for postoperative patient management. Additionally, all nonessential tests secondary to "historical" routine or individual physician variance were eliminated. The second goal was to identify limiting factors in postesophagectomy care that determine length of hospital stay and to manage these factors optimally. The premise was that much of postesophagectomy patient care was based on historic practice guidelines passed down, often unchallenged, through surgical apprenticeship training programs. Challenging these guidelines through dynamic, ongoing modification of the pathway was an essential feature of the practice plan. For esophagectomy, factors which limit hospital stay include pain control, respiratory care, anastomotic healing, and oral alimentation. The hypothesis was that focusing care to optimize the safety of each of these factors would reduce the length of hospital stay and cost without compromising safety.

All partial and complete esophagectomies performed from July 1991 to July 1997 were included in this study. The clinical care pathway was introduced in March 1994. Patients were divided into two groups based on whether their procedure was performed before (Group I) or after (Group II) pathway implementation. The postesophagectomy clinical pathway emphasizes overnight intubation and 24- to 36-hour intensive care unit monitoring. Antibiotics are continued for 24 hours then discontinued. Analgesia is controlled intravenously or by epidural catheter. Enteral feedings via jejunostomy tube are initiated on day 3. On day 5 or 6, video-esophagography is performed, after which a four-stage esophageal diet is commenced. The discharge goal is 10 days. H_2 blockers and analgesics are continued throughout the hospital course. Laboratory tests are performed on days 1, 2, and 4.

The cost for Group I esophagectomies in actual and inflation-adjusted dollars was $21,977 and $29,097, respectively. The cost for Group II esophagectomies in actual and inflation-adjusted dollars was $17,919 and $19 260, respectively. The higher cost for Group I patients compared to Group II patients was statistically significant (Figure 20–4). Significant decreases in charges (Group II compared to Group I) were seen in pharmaceutical, laboratory, radiology, physical therapy, and routine charges. Significant reduction in operating room charges and supplies were not seen (Figure 20–5). There was a continuous reduction in overall charges from 1991 to 1997. Reduction of hospital stay was a significant factor in overall charge reduction. Group I esophagectomy patients had a greater length of stay (LOS) than Group II patients (Figure 20–6). Because routine charges were the highest daily routine costs, reduction of LOS translated to 44 percent of the total savings for Group II versus Group I. Mortality for Group I and II esophagectomies was 3.6 percent and 0 percent, respectively; this difference was not significant.

Conclusions and Clinical Significance

To summarize this experience, establishing a patient care pathway for esophagectomy patients began with the plotting of the course of an *ideal* patient undergoing surgery and having an

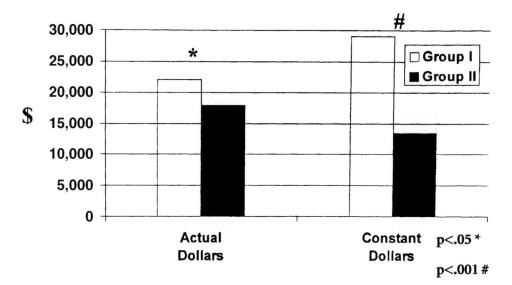

Figure 20–4 Total cost of esophagectomy in actual and constant dollars is shown for patients before the institution of patient care pathway (Group I) and after (Group II). (Printed with permission from Zehr KJ, Dawson P, Yang SC, Heitmiller RF. Standardized clinical care pathways for major thoracic cases reduces hospital costs. Ann Thorac Surg 1998;66:914–9.)

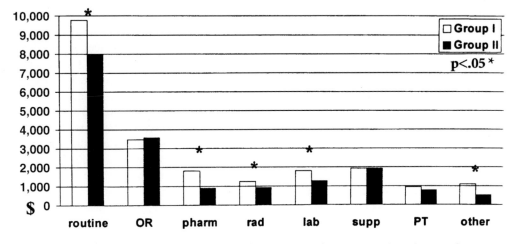

Figure 20–5 Breakdown of esophagectomy cost for Group I and Group II patients into routine, operating room (OR), pharmacology (pharm), radiology (rad), laboratory (lab), supplies (supp), physical therapy (PT), and other. (Printed with permission from Zehr KJ, Dawson P, Yang SC, Heitmiller RF. Standardized clinical care pathways for major thoracic cases reduces hospital costs. Ann Thorac Surg 1998;66:914–9.)

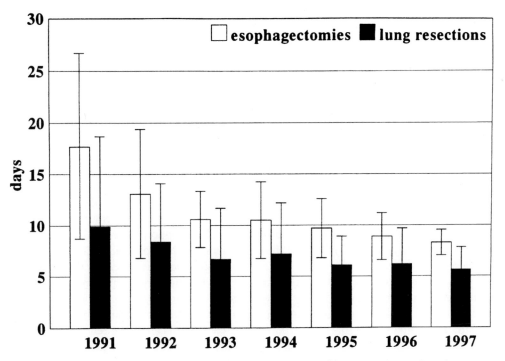

Figure 20–6 Length of hospital stay in days for esophagectomy and lung resection patients by recorded year is illustrated. (Printed with permission from Zehr KJ, Dawson P, Yang SC, Heitmiller RF. Standardized clinical care pathways for major thoracic cases reduces hospital costs. Ann Thorac Surg 1998;66:914–9.)

uncomplicated postoperative course. Only those tests, studies, medications, and consultations that were necessary were ordered as routine. The care for this hypothetical ideal patient was established as the standardized care. The initial target LOS for our ideal patient was 10 days. The physicians then identified complications unique to esophagectomy patients, such as anastomotic and respiratory complications, and developed schemes to minimize them. Pain control was optimized. Finally, historic postesophagectomy patient care guidelines were challenged to determine if LOS could be further reduced safely. All operative procedures have a critical limiting factor which ultimately limits LOS. For esophagectomy patients, that factor is primarily the esophageal anastomotic healing. Historic guidelines for protecting the anastomosis in terms of nasogastric decompression, withholding of oral intake, and techniques for resuming oral feedings have been passed down in our training programs over the years, largely unchallenged. The approach to attempting to reduce LOS and cost was to challenge these historic guidelines. The effect of this has been that Johns Hopkins has reduced the length of nasogastric decompression by 2 days and has instituted oral feeds 1 to 2 days earlier without any change in patient comfort, morbidity, or mortality. It is hoped that the limits of "anastomotic tolerance," as yet undefined, will be determined through laboratory and clinical studies.

Patient care pathways for postesophagectomy patients are particularly important for teaching hospitals, where the resident personnel constantly change and where the level of physician experience varies. Patient care pathways teach residents and fellows a consistent care strategy. It also standardizes individual physician preferences, making postoperative care easier for all care providers to follow and to assess.

In the author's experience, the most significant factor in reducing patient care costs was reduced LOS. Reduction of LOS accounted for 44 percent of the observed cost reduction attributed to our patient care pathway. Operating room, supply, and physical therapy charges were not significantly affected by the pathway system. These areas and charges, which are not under the control of the treating physician, are currently being separately targeted to assess cost-reduction strategies.

Despite the fact that significant changes in postoperative patient care, LOS, and cost have been achieved, the safety of patient care has not been compromised. Morbidity and mortality remain low. The author and his colleagues feel that this comes from a policy of identifying and preventing complications. Their data, and that reported by others, verify the safety and effectiveness of patient care pathways.

THE ROLE FOR EVIDENCE-BASED SURGICAL TECHNIQUES IN OTHER ESOPHAGEAL SURGERIES

All esophageal surgery is considered complex gastrointestinal surgery and would be amenable to evidence-based surgical techniques to improve results and reduce costs. Most indications for esophageal surgery, such as benign obstruction, perforation, or diverticular disease, are infrequent even at centers with a special interest in esophageal surgery, and therefore it has not been practical to apply the techniques to those procedures. The exception is anti-reflux surgery. The prevalence of gastrointestinal reflux and the introduction of laparoscopic anti-reflux surgical techniques have dramatically increased the number of surgeries performed for this disorder.

Many centers now have developed an interest in and large experience with these esophagectomies for carcinoma. Peters and colleagues[24] have reported on an algorithm which standardizes the work-up and selection of patients for anti-reflux surgery. There has been a trend toward standardizing surgical techniques. Surgical results are being reported as a function of the specific technique used.[24,25] Trus and colleagues[26] have documented the safety and effectiveness of laparoscopic anti-reflux surgery in elderly patients (defined as 65 or more years of age).

Data on the cost of anti-reflux surgery are just beginning to be generated. Lundell and colleagues[27] have determined the direct costs (eg, operative and hospital charges) and indirect costs (eg, from loss of production while off work) for patients undergoing open anti-reflux surgery. This cost profile can be used to compare other treatment options for gastrointestinal reflux disease. Gooszen[28] reports the initiation of a prospective randomized trial comparing the effectiveness, cost, and quality of life after open anti-reflux surgery versus laparoscopic anti-reflux surgery in the Netherlands. In a smaller series, Rattner and colleagues[29] compared cost and patient satisfaction after laparoscopic fundoplication versus open Nissen fundoplication. They found less cost and faster recovery using laparoscopic techniques. However, the complication rate and patient satisfaction were the same between the two approaches.

REFERENCES

1. Heitmiller RF. Surgery of achalasia and other motility disorders. In: Kaiser LR, Kron IL, Spray TL, editors. Mastery of cardiothoracic surgery. Philadelphia (PA): Lippincott-Raven Publishers; 1998.p. 151–9.

2. Eypasch E, Barlow A. Surgery for esophageal diverticula. In: Bremner CG, DeMeester TR, Perachia A, editors. Modern approach to benign esophageal disease. St. Louis (MO): Quality Medical Publishing, Inc; 1995.p. 143–53.

3. Handy JR Jr, Reed CE. Esophageal Injury. In: Baue AE, Geha AS, Hammond GL, et al, editors. Glenn's thoracic and cardiovascular surgery. 6th ed. Stamford (CT): Appleton & Lange; 1996.p. 747–59.

4. Roy A, DeMeester TR. Perioperative management of carcinoma of the esophagus: the reduction of operative mortality. In: Delarue NC, Wilkins EW Jr, Wong J, editors. International trends in general thoracic surgery. Vol. 4. C.V. Mosby Company; 1988. p. 101–9.

5. O'Connor GT, Plume SK, Olmstead EM, et al. A regional intervention to improve the hospital mortality associated with coronary artery bypass surgery. JAMA 1996;275:841–6.

6. Engelman RM, Rovsou JA, Flack JE, et al. Fast-track recovery of the coronary bypass patient. Ann Thorac Surg 1994;58:1242–6.

7. Wright CD, Wain JC, Grillo HC, et al. Pulmonary lobectomy patient care pathway: a model to control cost and maintain quality. Ann Thorac Surg 1997;64:299–302.

8. Gordon TA, Bowman HB, Tielsch JM, et al. Statewide regionalization of pancreaticoduodenectomy and its effect on in-hospital mortality. Ann Surg 1998;228:71–80.

9. Luft HS, Bunker JP, Enthoven AC. Should operations be regionalized? The empirical relation between surgical volume and mortality. N Engl J Med 1979;301:1364–9.

10. Hannan EL, Siu AL, Kumar D, et al. The decline in coronary artery bypass graft surgery mortality in New York State. The role of surgeon volume. JAMA 1995;273:209–13.

11. Miller JD, Jain MK, de Gara CJ, et al. Effect of surgical experience on results of esophagectomy for esophageal carcinoma. J Surg Oncol 1997;65:20–1.

12. Ellis FH Jr, Heatley GJ, Krasna MJ, et al. Esophagogastrectomy for carcinoma of the esophagus and cardia: a comparison of findings and results after standard resection in three consecutive eight-year intervals with improved staging criteria. J Thorac Cardiovasc Surg 1997;113:836–48.

13. Gordon TA, Bowman HM, Bass EB, et al. Complex gastrointestinal surgery: Impact of provider team experience on clinical and economic outcomes. J Am Coll Surg 1999; 189:46–56.

14. Heitmiller RF, Redmond M, Hamilton SR. Barrett's esophagus with high grade dysplasia. An indication for prophylactic esophagectomy. Ann Surg 1996;224:66–71.

15. Forastiere AA, Heitmiller RF, Lee DJ, et al. Intensive chemoradiation therapy followed by esophagectomy for squamous cell and adenocarcinoma of the esophagus. Cancer J Sci Am 1997;3:144–52.

16. Gillinov AM, Heitmiller RF. Strategies to reduce pulmonary complications after transhiatal esophagectomy. Dis Esophagus 1998;11:43–7.

17. Brodner G, Pogatzki E, Van Aken H, et al. A multimodal approach to control postoperative patho-physiology and rehabilitation in patients undergoing abdominothoracic esophagectomy. Anesth Analg 1998;86:228–34.

18. Reichle RL, Fishman EK, Nixon MS, et al. Evaluation of the postsurgical esophagus after partial esophagogastrectomy for esophageal cancer. Invest Radiol 1993;28:247–57.

19. Davis EA, Heitmiller RF. Esophagectomy for benign disease: trends in surgical results and management. Ann Thorac Surg 1996;62:369–72.

20. Stone CD, Heitmiller RF. Simplified, standardized technique for cervical esophagogastric anastomosis. Ann Thorac Surg 1994;58:259–61.

21. Sweet RH. Operations on the esophagus (continued). In: Thoracic surgery. 2nd ed. Philadelphia (PA): W.B. Saunders; 1954.p. 285–326.

22. Heitmiller RF, Jones B. Transient diminished airway protection after transhiatal esophagectomy. Am J Surg 1991;162:442–6.

23. Zehr KJ, Dawson P, Yang SC, Heitmiller RF. Standardized clinical care pathways for major thoracic cases reduces hospital costs. Ann Thorac Surg 1998;66:914–9.

24. Peters JH. Gastroesophageal reflux disease. In: Cameron JL, editor. Current surgical therapy. 6th ed. St. Louis: Mosby Publisher; 1998.p. 33–46.

25. Hunter JG, Swanstrom L. Patterns of dysphagia following laparoscopic antireflux surgery. Ann Surg 1996;224:51–7.

26. Trus TL, Laycock WS, Wo JM, et al. Laparoscopic antireflux surgery in the elderly. Am J Gastroenterol 1998;93:351–3.

27. Lundell L, Dalenback J, Janatuinem E, et al. Br J Surg 1998;85:1002–5.

28. Gooszen HG. Is there a place for laparoscopic antireflux surgery in The Netherlands? Scan J Gastroenterol Suppl 1998:225:29–31.

29. Rattner DW, Brooks DC. Patient satisfaction following laparoscopic and open antireflux surgery. Arch Surg 1995;130:289–93.

CHAPTER 21

Gastric Surgery

Keith D. Lillemoe, MD, FACS

Surgery of the stomach was the measure of surgical skill in the late nineteenth century and early twentieth century. The great surgical clinics of Europe and the most prominent surgeons of that time, such as Kocher and Billroth, made many of their major contributions in the field of gastric surgery. Throughout most of the twentieth century, gastric cancer was the leading cause of cancer death in the United States. Furthermore, elective and emergent operations for peptic ulcer disease were also among the most commonly performed surgical procedures.

In the late 1900s, there has been a dramatic decrease in the frequency of gastric surgery in the United States. The incidence of gastric cancer has fallen dramatically since the 1930s. In 1999, gastric cancer is estimated to be only the 10th leading cause of cancer death in both males and females.[1] Only 22,000 estimated new cases of gastric cancer will be diagnosed in 1999, compared to almost 140,000 cases of colorectal cancer and 28,000 cases of pancreatic cancer. Similarly, gastric surgery for benign disease has become increasingly uncommon. Although decreases in peptic ulcer disease were noted prior to the widespread use of the H_2 receptor antagonists and proton pump inhibitors, these agents have almost completely eliminated the need for elective surgery for this condition. More recently, the recognition that the bacterium *Helicobacter pylori* has a fundamental role in both gastric and duodenal ulcer disease as well as gastric carcinoma suggests that the role of surgery for gastric conditions may further decrease in the future. Due to these trends in gastric surgery, this chapter will focus on the surgical management of gastric carcinoma.

ADENOCARCINOMA OF THE STOMACH AND ITS SURGICAL MANAGEMENT

Although gastric lymphoma, gastrointestinal stromal tumors of the stomach, and gastric carcinoid tumors may occur, adenocarcinoma is the predominant malignant tumor of the stomach. Gastric cancer is twice as common in males than in females; however, the major difference is limited to cancers located in the proximal stomach. The gender distribution for antral lesions is equal.

There has been approximately a 65 percent decrease in the incidence of gastric cancer over the last 40 years in the United States.[1] This trend is not worldwide, however, and gastric carcinoma remains a major health care problem throughout the world. Stomach cancer is the second most frequently diagnosed cancer in the world, with 798,000 new cases and 628,000 deaths (12 percent of cancer deaths) per year.[2] Gastric cancer is a major health care problem in Asia, with age-standardized incidence rates highest in Japan (77.9 cases per 100,000 in men and 33.3 cases per 100,000 in women). The problem has become such an important health care issue in Japan that mass screening by photofluoroscopy has been practiced there since the 1960s. This aggressive evaluation has led to a high frequency of diagnoses of early gastric cancer in up to 40 percent of patients in that country.

The clinical presentation of patients with gastric carcinoma depends on the location of the primary tumor, the extent of the tumor, and the presence of ulceration. The most common clinical feature is abdominal pain or dyspeptic symptoms. The pain is usually indistinguishable from that of peptic ulcer disease, and the initial symptoms are commonly attributed to that disorder and are treated accordingly. Lesions of the pylorus or cardia may cause obstructive symptoms. Ulcerative lesions frequently will present with gastrointestinal blood loss, manifested by symptoms of iron deficiency anemia or more acutely by melena or hematemesis. The vagueness of early symptoms is one of the reasons for the typical late diagnosis for gastric cancer. Weight loss generally follows due to decreased oral intake from early satiety, obstruction, or tumor catabolic factors.

The investigation to make the diagnosis of gastric carcinoma begins either with upper gastrointestinal contrast studies or with endoscopy. Almost any abnormality in an upper gastrointestinal contrast study requires endoscopic evaluation. Endoscopy offers the advantage of obtaining a histologic biopsy of any mass or ulcer visualized. Cytologic brushings may also be useful. If initial biopsies are negative, follow-up evaluation after a period of treatment is appropriate in most cases. After the diagnosis of gastric cancer is confirmed by endoscopic biopsies, further preoperative staging with computed tomography (CT) scanning is indicated. Further staging by endoscopic ultrasonography has been advocated in some centers. Exploratory laparotomy, however, remains the essential component of the decision-making process for most patients with gastric carcinoma. Although some advances in chemotherapy and radiation therapy have improved the outlook for certain patient groups, surgical resection offers the only chance for a gastric cancer cure.

The objective of a curative resection is the removal of the primary tumor and regional lymph nodes, keeping the resection margins free of tumor cells. Since the stomach is not vital to a relatively normal life span, the surgical procedure can involve anything up to and including a total gastrectomy. In addition, removal of the omentum, the spleen, the distal pancreas, the lower esophagus, or the proximal portion of the duodenum can be included as necessary. Curative resection should be attempted only on tumors limited to the stomach and neighboring lymph nodes although invasion of surrounding structures does not preclude resection if these structures can be removed en bloc with the primary tumor.

The surgical management of gastric cancer is dictated primarily by the location of the primary tumor. Lesions located in the proximal third of the stomach, including the gastroesophageal junction and fundus, account for approximately one-third of gastric cancers. In recent years, there has been a relative increase in the incidence of tumors in this location. This shift has significant implications in that proximal gastric tumors tend to present later and therefore have a worse prognosis. Furthermore, the operative procedures are associated with higher morbidity and mortality rates. To meet the objectives of curative resection for tumors of the proximal stomach, a total gastrectomy is usually necessary to obtain clear margins and appropriate lymph node resection. A proximal subtotal gastrectomy, with preservation of the pylorus and a small distal gastric remnant, has been advocated by some groups.[3] However, this procedure does not appear to decrease perioperative morbidity and mortality when compared to total gastrectomy.[4,5] Furthermore, it is associated with a higher incidence of local recurrence as well as often poor functional results with a high incidence of alkaline reflux gastritis.[6] A more extensive resection, the extended total gastrectomy including a splenectomy and distal pancreatectomy, has also been advocated but is associated with increased perioperative morbidity and mortality, leading most surgeons to avoid this procedure.[7] A number of surgical approaches are possible for such resections, including a completely transabdominal approach. If the lesion extends up the esophagus, a classic Ivor-Lewis approach, using both an abdominal and right chest incision, may be used, or alternatively, a left thoracoabdominal approach may be used. Finally, a transhiatal approach and total esophagectomy may be appropriate for tumors of the gastrointestinal junction if concern exists as to the upper extent of the tumor.

Lesions of the midstomach account for 15 percent to 30 percent of all gastric cancers. Lesions in this location are often asymptomatic until they have become locally quite extensive, with regional lymph node metastasis. The preferred operation for these lesions is a high radical subtotal gastrectomy. In this procedure, all but a small cuff of the proximal stomach is removed, with the distal stomach and all regional lymph nodes resected. A total gastrectomy, or even extended gastrectomy with pancreatectomy and splenectomy, are also possibilities for extensive tumors.

Finally, lesions of the distal third of the stomach or gastric antrum account for approximately 35 percent of all gastric cancers. It is the incidence of these distal gastric cancers which has diminished in recent years, with a reciprocal rise in the relative incidence of proximal cancers. To achieve the goals of complete removal of the primary tumors, as well as lymph nodes at risk, a radical distal subtotal gastrectomy with regional lymphadenectomy is the operation of choice. This involves resection of approximately 75 percent of the stomach, including most of the lesser curvature, where the margin resections will often be the closest. At least 1 cm of the first part of the duodenum is resected. To assure adequate margins, 5 to 7 cm of normal stomach are required, proximal to the tumor. As with all gastric resections, greater and lesser omentectomy and regional lymph node dissection is required in an attempt to remove all microscopic disease.

The extent of resection necessary to treat gastric carcinoma is controversial. Much of this controversy has arisen from comparison of survival results in the United States with those in Japan. In the United States, curative resection results in overall 5-year survival rates of approximately 25 percent.[8] The survival rates are higher in Japan, where the diagnosis of gastric cancer is generally made in an earlier stage than in Western countries. However, stage-per-stage survival comparisons for more advanced cancers generally show an approximate 10 percent survival advantage in Japanese series (Table 21–1).[9] These findings have led some to speculate that improved survival of more advanced cancer patients in Japan can be attributed to more radical resections and lymphadenectomies.

Gastric adenocarcinoma spreads primarily via the lymphatic channels. Due to the wide consensus on the desirability of standardized extensive lymph node dissection in Japan, the Japanese Research Society for Gastric Cancer has numbered each nodal group and has standardized which nodal groups should be removed for tumors at each location of the stomach (Table 21–2 and Figure 21–1).[10]

The impact of positive lymph nodes on the prognosis of patients with gastric cancer has been demonstrated by a number of analyses. Msika and associates studied prognostic factors in 86 curative resections for gastric cancer and showed, by multivariate analysis using the Cox regression proportional hazard model, that lymph node involvement alone was found to be

Table 21–1 Five-Year Survival Rates after Gastrectomy in Japan and the United States

Stage		5-yr Survival Rate (%)	
		Japan	United States
N0	T1	80	90
	T2	60	58
	T3	30	50
	T4	5	20
N1		53	20
N2		26	10
N3		10	—
N4		3	—

Adapted from Nogachi Y, Imada T, Matsumato A, et al. Radical surgery for gastric cancer: a review of the Japanese experience. Cancer 1989;64:2053–62.

Table 21–2 Regional Lymph Nodes of the Stomach

Perigastric	Extraperigastric
Right pericardial	Left gastric artery
Left pericardial	Common hepatic artery
Lesser curvature	Celiac axis
Greater curvature	Splenic hilus
Suprapyloric	Splenic artery
Intrapyloric	Hepatoduodenal ligament
	Retropancreatic
	Root of mesentery
	Middle colic artery
	Periaortic

Adapted from The Japanese Research Society for Gastric Cancer. The general rules for gastric cancer study in surgery and pathology. I: clinical classification. Jpn J Surg 1981;11:127–39.

the only independent prognostic factor for survival.[11] Similarly, Maruyama performed univariate and multivariate analysis against 25 variables on 4,734 resected gastric cancers and showed, using the Cox regression proportional hazard model, that lymph node metastasis was the most significant prognostic factor besides depth of invasion.[12]

The role of radical lymph node dissection has also become a key area of debate over the management of gastric carcinoma. In the 1960s and 1970s, radical lymph node dissection was essentially abandoned in the United States because of the increased morbidity and mortality associated with more extensive operations with no apparent advantage in survival.[13] However, recent enthusiasm based upon both improved perioperative results and survival from Japanese series has rekindled the debate. Yet, there is not total agreement that these retrospective series from Japan actually indicate improved survival results with R2 gastrectomy.[14,15] These studies compared current Japanese series to both the Western experience (using a more limited R1 resection) and to historical controls from Japan prior to the routine use of R2 resection.

One possible explanation for the difference in survival rates between R2 gastrectomy and the more limited procedures may relate to more accurate staging with the extended lymphadenectomy, namely, the so-called stage migration phenomenon. An example of this phenomenon would be a patient with both N1 and N2 involvement. In a standard Western resection, the N2 disease would go undetected. An R2 resection will identify nodal involvement and will therefore upstage the tumor (Stage I to Stage II, or Stage II to Stage III) independent of the T status of the tumor. Thus, for survival analysis, the patient undergoing a limited resection will appear to do poorly when compared to a group of patients who are more accurately staged by the extended resection. This is the crux of the argument against a "curative" benefit of extended lymphadenectomy for gastric cancer.

REVIEW OF THE LITERATURE

Recognizing these controversies, a careful analysis of the available evidence as to the extent of gastric resection and lymphadenectomy appropriate for the surgical management of gastric carcinoma is necessary. In drawing conclusions from the existing data, one must focus on both the short-term outcome with respect to perioperative morbidity and mortality with more aggressive surgery, as well as determine the long-term advantages with respect to survival after extended surgery. The literature is full of retrospective studies that demonstrate advantages of

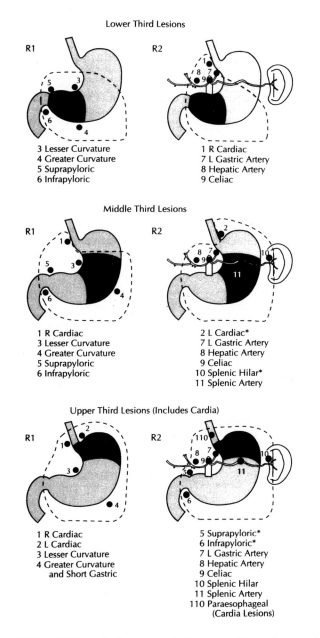

Figure 21–1 Extent of R1 and R2 lymphadenectomy for lower, middle, and upper third gastric cancers. The scope of lymphadenectomy is indicated by the broken line. To qualify as an R2 dissection, all R1-designated lymph nodes must be removed, along with most of the R2-designated nodes (R = right; L = left; * = optional) (Reproduced with permission from Smith JW, Shiu MH, Kelsey L, Brennan MF. Morbidity of radical lymphadenectomy in the curative resection of gastric carcinoma. Arch Surg 1991;126:1469–73.)

both sides of the argument. Western studies tend to demonstrate a higher morbidity and mortality with more aggressive surgery whereas Japanese studies tend to show no difference.

Perioperative Results

In the modern series of gastric cancer resections in Japanese institutions where extended (R2) lymphadenectomy is standard operative therapy, operative mortality rates of 0.9 to 1.9 percent are routinely reported.[16] In a retrospective review of 300 patients who underwent curative gastrectomy with extended lymph node dissection, de Aretxabala and colleagues reported no difference in operative mortalities for patients undergoing R1 versus R2 nodal dissections (3.2% versus 1.6%, respectively).[17] Although results from United States series seldom are as good as Japanese reports, comparable results from a US institution have been reported from Memorial Sloan-Kettering Cancer Center.[5] In this series, no difference was reported in operative mortality in 123 patients undergoing curative gastrectomy with radical ($\geq$ R2) lymphadenectomy when compared to resection with lesser lymphadenectomy in 62 patients (1.6% vs. 0%, respectively).

The most important existing data, however, have come from preliminary reports from prospective randomized trials. The most mature of these trials is the Dutch Gastric Cancer Trial.[18] In 1995, its researchers reported that 1,078 patients were randomized (539 to each group) to receive either a D1 procedure, which included dissection of the perigastric lymph nodes directly attached to the stomach, or resection extended to include regional lymph nodes outside the perigastric area (a D2 procedure). This multicenter trial was initiated in August 1989, with entry of patients until July 1993. Analysis of the data for the patients judged to have curable resections (380-D1, 331-D2 resection) showed that D2 patients had a higher operative mortality rate than D1 patients (10% vs 4%, $p = .004$) and experienced more complications (43% vs 25%, $p < .001$). The length of hospital stay was also significantly longer (D2 median 25 days, range 7 to 277 days vs. D1 median 18 days, range 7 to 143 days, $p < .001$). Analysis of the risk factors in this study showed that age greater than 65 years, male sex, and the extent of nodal dissection and concurrent splenectomy were significant risk factors for death and postoperative complications.

A second large, multicenter prospective randomized trial has been reported from England,[19] in which 200 patients were randomized to receive either a D1 resection (level I lymphadenectomy) or a D2 resection (levels I and II lymphadenectomy). As in the Dutch series, the D2 group had a greater postoperative hospital mortality (13%) than that of the group undergoing the D1 resection (6.5%, $p < .04$). A higher overall postoperative morbidity (46% vs 28%, $p < .001$) and a longer postoperative stay (23 days vs 18 days) were also seen in patients undergoing the more extensive resection. The excess postoperative morbidity and mortality in the radical resection group appeared to be accounted for by the inclusion of a distal pancreatectomy and splenectomy.

A single-institution randomized trial has been reported by Dent and colleagues from South Africa.[20] This small comparison of R1 and R2 gastrectomy for gastric carcinoma included 35 patients randomized to R1 gastrectomy and 31 patients to R2 gastrectomy. The patients were comparable with respect to pathologic stage. There were no postoperative deaths. The R2 group, however, had a longer operative time ($p < .001$) and a greater blood transfusion requirement ($p < .001$). The postoperative stay was also longer ($p < .008$), and more second operations for complications were necessary.

Finally, the only data supporting more radical resection are from a recently reported multicenter Italian trial focusing on extent of resection.[21] In this series, 624 patients with cancer of the distal stomach were randomized to either subtotal gastrectomy (n = 320) or total gastrectomy (n = 304). In both cases, lymphadenectomy was extended to the D2 level. The two groups were similar by all criteria. Nonfatal complications and deaths occurred in 9 percent and 1 percent of subtotal gastrectomy patients versus 13 percent and 2 percent of total gastrectomy patients, respectively (not significant). Splenectomy or resection of adjacent organs was associated with a twofold increased risk of postoperative complications. The mean length of stay, adjusted for extension of surgery, was 13.8 days for subtotal gastrectomy and 15.4 days for total gastrectomy.

Survival Rates

In 1981, Kodama and associates published the first study that showed improved survival for patients undergoing extended lymphadenectomy versus simple resection.[15] In this series, 254 patients underwent a simple resection while 454 patients underwent extensive lymph node dissection, defined as at least R2 lymphadenectomy. Survival analysis demonstrated that patients with advanced gastric carcinoma with involved lymph nodes had a statistically significant improved 5-year survival if they underwent extended lymph node dissection (39%) versus simple resection (18%, $p < .01$). Similarly, a prospective study by Csendes and associates reported 253 cases of stage III gastric carcinoma treated with R1 lymphadenectomy versus extensive lymph node dissection. In this series, the 5-year survival rate with extended lymphadenectomy was 23 percent versus 7.6 percent for R1 resection ($p < .01$).[22] Shiu and colleagues from Memorial Sloan-Kettering Cancer Center reported a multivariate analysis of clinical, pathologic, and treatment factors in a retrospective analysis of 246 patients treated for noncardiac gastric carcinoma[23] and found that insufficient scope of regional lymphadenectomy, relative to the nodal stage, was a significant independent factor predictive of death from gastric cancer. In the only completed prospective randomized trial of R1 versus R2 gastrectomy, Dent and associates reported no difference in the probability of survival between the two groups with a median follow-up of 3.1 years.[20] The study was small (43 patients), and there was likely a lack of statistical power to accurately define who may have benefited from extensive lymphadenectomy.

Although the role of extended lymphadenectomy and more radical surgery has not been clearly defined by prospective studies, there is strong evidence supporting the importance of resection-line clearance in stomach and gastric cancer.[24] These data were obtained from the prospective multicenter British Gastric Cancer Group trial and showed that of 390 patients with resected gastric cancers, 85 (22%) had microscopic disease at the resection margin. When resection margin clearance was achieved, a significantly increased overall survival was found.

In conclusion, results of prospective randomized studies from institutions in Western countries suggest that extended surgery for gastric cancer is associated with significant increases in perioperative morbidity and mortality. To determine the true long-term benefit of this extended surgical procedure, further time will be necessary to allow the survival data from these series to mature.

CASE STUDY: HIGH- AND LOW-VOLUME SURGICAL PROVIDERS

Although questions still remain as to the extent of surgery necessary for gastric cancer, the evidence clearly supports the significant potential risks of perioperative morbidity and mortality in these patients. Recently, considerable evidence has arisen concerning the effects of surgical volume on outcomes in patients undergoing major surgical procedures.[25–28] These studies pursue the theory that for complex surgical procedures associated with potentially high perioperative morbidity and mortality, regionalization (or concentration) of such procedures in or among high-volume hospitals or surgeons offers potential advantages. The most dramatic findings have come from analysis of data reported following pancreatic resection at high-volume centers.[25–28] The performance of total gastrectomy, another procedure with significant potential for morbidity and mortality, has recently been analyzed in a report from this author's institution.[29] In this study, 4,561 patients who underwent complex gastrointestinal surgical procedures in the state of Maryland from July 1990 to June 1997 were analyzed. The data were taken from the Maryland Health Services Cost Review Commission database, a publically available database containing discharge information for all patient encounters at the 52 nonfederal acute care hospitals in the state. The discharge information includes hospital identification, patient demographics, patient disposition at discharge, length of hospital stay, and total hospital charges. The study evaluated a number of complex gastrointestinal procedures that had statewide in-hospital mortality of ≥ 5 percent: esophagectomy, total gastrectomy, total abdominal colectomy, hepatectomy, biliary tract anastomosis, and pancreaticoduodenectomy.

Hospitals were classified into one of four groups, based on the average number of study procedures per year. The results demonstrated that after adjustment for case mix, patients who underwent complex gastrointestinal surgical procedures at medium- , low- , and minimal-volume provider groups had 2.1, 3.3, and 3.2 times greater risk of in-hospital death, respectively, than patients in the state's single high-volume provider ($p < .001$ for all comparisons). In addition, longer lengths of stay were observed at the low- , medium- , and minimal-volume hospitals (16.1, 15.7, and 15.5 days, respectively) than at the high-volume provider (14.0 days, $p \leq .001$ for all comparisons). Finally, adjusted charges at the high-volume provider averaged 14 percent less than those at the low-volume centers, which had the next lowest charges.

With respect to total gastrectomy, specific analysis of the results demonstrated that the statewide mortality was 15.5 percent. The mortality at the high-volume provider was 7.5 percent versus 15.9, 20.0 and 22.9 percent at the medium- , low- , and minimal-volume providers, respectively.

These data suggest that increased hospital volume is associated with a marked decrease in hospital mortality, shorter lengths of stay, and lower hospital charges in the management of complex gastrointestinal disease. These findings were more pronounced for malignant diagnoses than for benign conditions. Provider characteristics, such as the experience level of the physicians and staff, specialized staff, facilities and equipment in the operating rooms and intensive care units, and the use of critical pathways and detailed care management plans, may contribute to these improved results. These results suggest that referral to high-volume centers may improve overall results in the management of gastric cancer, particularly in light of the proposed extended resections necessary for complete eradication of the disease.

FUTURE DIRECTIONS

The results of survival analysis from the already-closed prospective randomized trials of radical versus standard surgery for gastric carcinoma are still anticipated. If, as might be anticipated from the Japanese data, survival is improved, the question that must be faced is whether to propose widespread use of more extended surgery in hopes of improving survival at the expense of documented increased short-term morbidity and mortality. A few bright spots on the horizon do exist with respect to these potential problems. First, prospective results from the Memorial Sloan-Kettering Cancer Center (a high-volume institution specializing in cancer and aggressive cancer therapy) have demonstrated excellent short-term outcomes for extended resections for gastric cancer.[5] Furthermore, extension of the data from the Maryland analysis of complex gastrointestinal surgery[29] as well as the results for other complex surgical procedures from state databases in Maryland, New York and Massachusetts[25–28] also stress the importance of regionalization of surgical care for gastric carcinoma. These results hold the promise that excellent surgical outcomes in the management of gastric cancer can be achieved.

Finally, as with other solid gastrointestinal tumors, new discoveries in the field of antitumor therapies such as chemotherapy and immunotherapy offer the greatest potential for advancing the treatment of this established disease. Furthermore, encouraging results from Japan, based on early detection, also suggest benefit, particularly if newer diagnostic techniques in molecular genetics allow better characterization of the basic abnormalities in the development of gastric cancer. With such advances may come the key to the early detection of gastric tumors by molecular screening techniques.

REFERENCES

1. Landis SH, Murray T, Bolden S, Wingo PA. Cancer statistics, 1999. CA Cancer J Clin 1999;49:8–31.

2. Parkin DM, Pisani P, Ferlay J. Global cancer statistics. CA Cancer J Clin 1999;49:33–64.

3. Ellis FH, Gibb P, Watkins F. Limited esophagogastrectomy for carcinoma of the cardia. Ann Surg 1988;208:354–61.

4. Boddie AW, McBride CM, Balch CM. Gastric cancer. Am J Surg 1989;157:595–605.

5. Smith JW, Shiu MH, Kelsey L, Brennan MF. Morbidity of radical lymphadenectomy in the curative resection of gastric carcinoma. Arch Surg 1991;126:1469–73.

6. Herrington JL. The postgastrectomy syndrome. Contemp Surg 1986;29:13–22.

7. Brady MS, Rogatoko A, Dent L, Shiu MH. Effect of splenectomy on morbidity and survival following curative gastrectomy for carcinoma. Arch Surg 1991;126:359–64.

8. Wanebo HJ, Kennedy BJ, Chmiel J, et al. Cancer of the stomach: a patient care study by the American College of Surgeons. Ann Surg 1993;218:583–92.

9. Noguchi Y, Imada T, Matsumato A, et al. Radical surgery for gastric cancer: a review of the Japanese experience. Cancer 1989;64:2053–62.

10. Japanese Research Society for Gastric Cancer. The general rules for gastric cancer study in surgery and pathology. I: clinical classification. Jpn J Surg 1981;11:127–39.

11. Msika S, Chastang C, Honry S, et al. Lymph node involvement as the only prognostic factor in curative resected gastric carcinoma: a multivariate analysis. World J Surg 1989;13:118–23.

12. Maruyama K. The most important prognostic factors for gastric cancer patients. Scand J Gastroenterol 1987;22(Suppl 133):63–8.

13. Gilbertsen VA. Results of treatment of stomach cancer: an appraisal of efforts for extensive surgery and a report of 1983 cases. Cancer 1969;23:1305–8.

14. Maruyama K, Okabayashi K, Kinoshita T. Progress in gastric cancer surgery in Japan and its limits of radicality. World J Surg 1987;11:418–25.

15. Kodama Y, Sugimachi K, Soehima K, et al. Evaluation of extensive lymph node dissection for carcinoma of the stomach. World J Surg 1981;5:241–8.

16. Nakajima T, Hishi M, Kajitani T. Improvement in treatment results of gastric cancer with surgery and chemotherapy: experience of 9700 cases in the Cancer Institute Hospital, Tokyo. Semin Surg Oncol 1989;7:365–72.

17. de Aretxabala X, Konishi K, Yonemura Y, et al. Node dissection in gastric cancer. Br J Surg 1987;74:770–3.

18. Bonekamp JJ, Songun I, Hermans J. Randomized comparison of morbidity after D1 and D2 surgery for gastric cancer in 996 Dutch patients. Lancet 1995;345:745–8.

19. Cuschieri A, Fayers P, Fielding J, et al. Postoperative morbidity and mortality after D1 and D2 resections for gastric cancer: preliminary results of the MRC randomised controlled surgical trial. Lancet 1996;347:995–9.

20. Dent DM, Madden MV, Price SK. Randomized comparison of R1 and R2 gastrectomy for gastric carcinoma. Br J Surg 1988;75:110–14.

21. Bozzetti F, Marubini E, Bonfati G, et al. Total versus subtotal gastrectomy. Surgical morbidity and mortality rates in a multicenter Italian randomized trial. Ann Surg 1997;226:613–20.

22. Csendes A, Amat J, Alam E, et al. 5-year survival rate of patients with advanced gastric carcinoma submitted to subtotal or total gastrectomy with or without extensive lymph node dissection. Rev Med Chil 1983;111:889–93.

23. Shiu MH, Perrotti M, Brennan MF. Adenocarcinoma of the stomach: a multivariate analysis of clinical, pathologic, and treatment factors. Hepatogastroenterology 1989;36:7–12.

24. British Stomach Cancer Group. Resection line disease in stomach cancer. BMJ 1984;289:601–3.

25. Gordon TA, Burleyson G, Tielsch JM, Cameron JL. The effects of regionalization on cost and outcome for one high-risk general surgical procedure. Ann Surg 1995;221:43–9.

26. Sosa JA, Bowman HM, Gordon TA, et al. The importance of hospital volume in the overall management of pancreatic cancer. Ann Surg 1998;228:429–38.

27. Lieberman MD, Kilburn H, Lindsey M, Brennan MF. Relation of perioperative deaths to hospital volume among patients undergoing pancreatic resection of malignancy. Ann Surg 1995;222(5):638–45.

28. Birkmeyer JD, Finlayson SRG, Tosteson ANA, et al. Effect of hospital volume on in-hospital mortality with Whipple procedures. Surgery 1999;125:250–6.

29. Gordon TA, Bowman HM, Bass EB, et al. Complex gastrointestinal surgery: impact of provider experience on clinical and economic outcomes. J Am Coll Surg 1999;189:46–56.

Since the initial preparation of this chapter, there has been a significant new contribution to the literature with the published results of the long-term survival from the prospective, randomized trial comparing D1 with D2 lymph node dissection in patients undergoing potentially curative resection.* The Dutch Gastric Cancer Group, in a study referred to earlier in this chapter (reference 18), had previously demonstrated that more radical resection (D2) had been associated with increased short-term morbidity, in-hospital mortality, and increased length of hospital stay. This new report now adds the anticipated results on survival: the five-year survival rates were similar in the two groups, 45 percent for the D1 group and 47 percent for the D2 group (95 percent confidence interval for the difference). The authors have concluded that this randomized prospective trial shows that D2 lymph node dissection is not associated with improved survival and therefore its routine use cannot be supported.

---

*Bonenkamp JJ, Hermans J, Sasako M, VanDeveld CGH, The Dutch Gastric Cancer Group. Extended lymph node dissection for gastric cancer. N Engl J Med 1999;340:908–914.

CHAPTER 22

Colon Surgery

Steven B. Goldin, MD, PhD, John W. Harmon, MD, and
Howard S. Kaufman, MD

In the United States, large bowel surgery is most frequently performed for colon cancer. It was estimated that there would be 95,600 new cases of colon cancer in 1998.[1] Colorectal cancer is the second most frequent cause of cancer death in the United States, and 47,700 deaths were expected in 1998. With improvements in treatment modalities, the 5-year survival rate in white Americans increased from approximately 43 percent in 1960 to 63 percent in 1993. The survival rate in African Americans has also improved, from 34 percent to 53 percent over the same time period. The 5-year survival rate for all patients diagnosed with colon and rectal cancer is between 37.5 percent and 62 percent, which increases to between 86 percent and 97.5 percent for those with node-negative disease. Five-year survival rates vary by cancer stage: 95.6 percent for stage I, 76.6 percent for stage II, 30 to 44.5 percent for stage III, and 3.6 percent for stage IV (American Joint Committee on Cancer [AJCC] staging).[2,3] Risk of death attributable to colon cancer is similar to that of the general population 6 years after curative surgery.[4] Poor prognostic factors include advanced tumor (T) stage (depth of penetration), higher grade, and presentation with bowel obstruction or perforation.[5,6] Approximately 20 percent of patients with colon cancer have distant metastases at presentation. Despite the poor prognosis in patients with extrahepatic metastatic disease, palliative colon resection is often recommended to prevent bleeding, obstruction, and symptoms related to local organ invasion.

In patients with a potentially curable colorectal cancer, a properly performed operation is essential for optimal oncologic and functional results. The primary tumor and draining lymph nodes should be resected en bloc without violation and spillage of the tumor into the abdominopelvic cavity. The pre- , intra- , and postoperative management of patients undergoing resection of the large intestine has continued to evolve in recent decades. This chapter discusses selected standard surgical strategies widely used in the management of colorectal cancer and relates their use to patient outcome.

PREOPERATIVE CONSIDERATIONS

Patient Population and Urgency of Operation

Prior to the development of antibiotics, colorectal surgery was associated with prohibitively high mortality rates ranging from 13 to 28 percent for elective procedures.[7,8] Broad-spectrum antibiotics, improved surgical techniques, advances in critical care, and improved perioperative management of patients have resulted in a decline in the mortality rates for elective colorectal surgery into a range of 1.7 to 6 percent.[9–11] Nwiloh and colleagues[12] evaluated the changing patterns in the morbidity and mortality of colorectal surgery over time by retrospectively evaluating complications in 362 patients who underwent colorectal surgery during two different time periods. Patients were divided into two groups consisting of 136 patients treated between 1970 and 1975 (group 1) and 226 patients treated between 1984 and 1987 (group 2). The percentage of patients undergoing elective versus emergent procedures was similar between the groups. Comorbidities and risk were rated according to the American Society of Anesthesiologists (ASA) Physical Status.[13] Although morbidity rates were comparable in both groups (42 percent in group 1 vs 40 percent in group 2), there were significant differences in age and ASA classification between the two groups. The median age of all patients was 65.5 years with a range of 17 to 99 years. The patients in group 2 were older than those in group 1, with 53 percent being over 70 years of age versus 38 percent in group 1 ($p < .05$). Group 2 also had a significantly larger number of higher-risk patients. Of group 1, 76 percent of those being operated upon were rated as ASA I or II while 52 percent of those in group 2 had ASA ratings of III or IV ($p < .05$). The complication rate following elective surgery was similar for group 1 (39%) and group 2 (36%) but was higher following emergency surgery in group 2 (66%) than in group 1 (54%, $p < .05$). There were also differences in the types of complications observed between the two groups. Abdominal complications including wound infection, abdominal abscess, anastomotic leak or fistula, bowel obstruction, or gastrointestinal bleeding decreased from 33 percent in group 1 to 15 percent in group 2. Systemic complications including cardiac, respiratory, renal, or cerebrovascular compromise increased from 26 percent in group 1 to 47 percent in group 2. For elective procedures, the mortality rate decreased from 9 percent in group 1 to 3 percent in group 2 ($p < .05$) and from 19 percent to 6 percent ($p < .001$) following emergent surgery. While the data were not subjected to formal statistical risk adjustment, univariate analysis determined that higher ASA ratings in both groups and advanced age in group 2 were predictors of unfavorable outcomes.

Bokey and colleagues[14] evaluated 1,846 patients who underwent open resection for colorectal cancer. Clinical, operative, and pathologic data were prospectively documented over a 20-year period. Elective procedures were performed in 429 patients with right-sided colon tumors and 542 with left-sided colon tumors. Thirty-day postoperative mortality was 3.6 percent, and there was no significant difference in mortality following right or left colon resection. Postoperative complications are summarized in Table 22–1. At least one complication occurred in 361 patients (37.2%), and pulmonary and cardiac complications as well as wound dehiscence were significantly higher following emergency resection for colon cancer than for elective resection. Scott-Conner and Scher[10] also found significantly higher mortality rates

Table 22–1 Postoperative Morbidity after Urgent and Elective Colon Resection

Complication	Urgent (n = 118)		Elective (n = 971)		p-Value
	No.	%	No.	%	
Respiratory	29	24.6	131	13.5	.002
Wound infection	15	12.7	108	11.1	NS
Abdominal abscess	7	5.9	67	6.9	NS
Cardiac	14	11.9	57	5.9	.017
Wound dehiscence	6	5.1	19	2.0	.040
Pulmonary embolus	5	4.2	20	2.1	NS
Deep vein thrombosis	2	1.7	17	1.8	NS
Urinary tract infection	ND	ND	67	6.9	NA
Renal failure	ND	ND	17	1.8	NA
Postoperative hemorrhage	ND	ND	14	1.4	NA

NS = not significant; NA = not applicable; ND = not determined.
Data from Bokey EL, Chapuis PH, Fung C, et al. Postoperative morbidity and mortality following resection of the colon and rectum for cancer. Dis Colon Rectum 1995;38:480–7.

following emergent procedures in a retrospective review of the records of 137 patients who underwent colorectal surgical procedures. Forty-five (33%) of these patients required emergent operations, and the mortality rates for the emergent and elective procedures were 37.8 percent and 5.1 percent, respectively ($p < .001$). Similarly, Irvin and colleagues[11] found significantly higher mortality following emergency surgery in 691 consecutive patients who underwent colorectal procedures. Operative mortality rates were 28 percent in the urgent group (n = 134) versus 6 percent in the elective group (n = 557).

Bowel Preparation and Antibiotics

The colon is a rich reservoir of bacteria, and mechanical cleansing of the colon before elective colorectal operations is an essential part of preoperative preparation.[15] Oral antibiotic preparations were added to mechanical cleansing in an attempt to further reduce the incidence of septic complications. In 1953, Poth suggested that neomycin was an excellent oral agent because of its low toxicity and poor absorption from the gastrointestinal tract.[16] In 1956, Cohn and Rives[17] demonstrated that the addition of intraluminal neomycin and tetracycline decreased the incidence of septic and anastomotic complications in an experimental model. Nichols and colleagues[18] subsequently documented a reduction in intraluminal bacteria by as much as 10^4- to 10^5-fold by the use of oral antibiotics. Based on these results, Nichols and colleagues[19] prospectively evaluated a combination of neomycin and erythromycin base with mechanical cleansing in 20 patients undergoing elective colon resection. Patients who received oral antibiotics in addition to mechanical cleansing had significantly reduced aerobic and anaerobic bacterial counts (Table 22–2). A prospectively randomized double blind study was then performed to evaluate the role of preoperative oral neomycin and erythromycin combined with mechanical cleansing, with 116 patients entered;[20] however, the study was stopped after interim results from the first 99 patients revealed a clear difference in septic complications between the placebo group (43%) and the antibiotic-treated group (9%, $p < .001$). Furthermore, the rates of wound infection were significantly decreased from 35 percent to 9 percent ($p < .001$) in patients who received oral antibiotics in addition to mechanical cleansing. As a result, the Nichols-Condon prep has become a widely used mechanical and oral antibiotic preoperative regimen for preparation of patients undergoing elective colorectal and rectal procedures in the United States.

Whereas elective preoperative bowel preparation was traditionally performed in the inpatient setting, several recent studies have proven its safety and efficacy as an outpatient procedure. Handelsman and colleagues[21] examined the efficacy of a preoperative mechanical and oral antibiotic bowel preparation (PABP) in 100 patients at The Johns Hopkins Hospital. Patients started a liquid diet 40 hours before surgery. Mechanical cleansing was performed with 45 mL of a buffered oral saline laxative containing 8 g sodium phosphate and 22 g sodium biphosphate as well as bisacodyl tablets and suppositories. Finally, oral erythromycin base and neomycin were administered during a 10-hour schedule as advocated by Clarke and colleagues.[20] Enemas were omitted. Complications attributable to the PABP were minimal. Of the 100 patients in their study, 31 complained of nausea but only 5 vomited. There was no evidence of dehydration. Handelsman and associates concluded that the ambulatory PABP provided both adequate mechanical and antibiotic preparation of the bowel in a manner satisfactory to both surgeons and patients.

Another outpatient bowel preparation was retrospectively evaluated by Le and colleagues[22] who examined the records of 319 patients who underwent elective segmental or total colectomy with primary anastomosis. All patients received 4 L of polyethylene glycol in addition to oral antibiotics. Outpatient bowel preparations were given to 145 patients while 174 patients were admitted for preoperative bowel preparation. The two groups were equally matched for patient characteristics. Complications related to the bowel preparation, including sepsis, anastomotic leak, and wound infection, were identical between those patients who

Table 22–2 Effect of Preoperative Neomycin and Erythromycin after Mechanical Cleansing on Colonic Microflora*

	Mechanical Preparation (n = 10)	Mechanical Preparation and Antibiotics (n = 10)
Aerobes		
Coliforms	6.7±0.4	1.2±0.2‡
Streptococci	5.5±0.5	1.7±0.4‡
Lactobacilli	3.0±0.7	1.3±0.2
Staphylococci	1.1±1.1	1.0±0.0†
Fungi	2.1±0.4	2.7±0.4
Anaerobes		
Bacteroides	8.7±0.2	1.2±0.2‡
Peptostreptococci	5.8±0.9	1.0±0.0‡
Bifidobacteria	3.6±1.1	1.0±0.0
Fusobacteria	3.6±1.1	1.3±0.2
Clostridia	2.4±0.4	1.9±0.4

* (Log_{10} mean ± SEM organisms/mL).
† 1.0 ± 0.0 the value assigned for statistical calculations when no growth is detected.
‡ $p < .001$.
Data from Nichols RL, Broido P, Condon RE, et al. Effect of preoperative neomycin-erythromycin intestinal preparation on the incidence of infectious complications following colon surgery. Ann Surg 1973;178:453–62.

received the in-patient versus outpatient bowel preparations. However, the charges associated with bowel preparation were 10-fold higher in the in-patient setting ($400 vs $40). Finally, Nichols and colleagues[23] recently summarized the preoperative bowel preparation practices of 808 colorectal surgeons who responded to a questionnaire. All surgeons employed mechanical preparations, with 71 percent using polyethylene glycol, 28 percent using oral sodium phosphate solution with or without bisacodyl, and 28 percent using dietary restriction, cathartics, and enemas. Eighty-seven percent also added an oral and parenteral antibiotic to the regimen while 12 percent added only parenteral antibiotics, 1 percent added only oral antibiotics, and 1 percent used no antibiotics.

The use of intravenous broad-spectrum parenteral antibiotics in conjunction with the intraluminal bowel preparation has attracted wide attention. The addition of parenteral antibiotics to mechanical cleansing with oral antibiotics has not consistently reduced the incidence of septic complications associated with elective colorectal surgery. Condon and colleagues[24] performed a prospective controlled trial comparing the addition of parenteral cephalothin or placebo to a mechanical bowel preparation with oral antibiotics. Their final analysis included 1082 patients. Overall septic and wound infection rates were not statistically different between groups. Barber and colleagues[25] performed a prospective double blind randomized trial to study the effect of parenteral antibiotics (gentamicin and clindamycin) in conjunction with oral antibiotics and mechanical bowel preparation. There were no differences in the intra-abdominal infection rates between patients who received parenteral antibiotics and those who received placebos; however, this study has been criticized for its low sample size (n = 59). Schoetz and colleagues[26] performed a prospectively randomized study examining the effect of parenteral cefoxitin on elective colorectal surgery in 197 patients. All patients received mechanical bowel preparation and oral antibiotics. There was no statistical difference between groups with respect to intra-abdominal septic complications (7.3% in the control group vs 5% in the parenteral antibiotics group). However, the incidence of abdominal wound infections was 14.6 percent in the control group versus 5 percent in the cefoxitin-treated group ($p = .02$).

The timing of parenteral antibiotic administration is also important. Burke[27] established that systemic antibiotics prevent wound infection most effectively when present in tissue prior to bacterial inoculation from surgical incision and that they are of no benefit if given 3 hours post incision. Classen and colleagues[28] prospectively evaluated the wound infection rate in 2,847 patients undergoing clean or clean-contaminated surgical procedures. Patients who received antibiotics within 2 hours of starting the procedure had a statistically significant lower risk of infection with a relative risk of 1.0. The relative risk increased to 6.7 if parenteral antibiotics were administered more than 2 hours prior to skin incision ($p < .001$), 2.4 if given after the incision but within 3 hours of starting the procedure ($p = .12$), and 5.8 if given after 3 hours of starting the case ($p < .001$). Most colorectal operations are adequately covered by a single dose of a suitable antibiotic. Pharmacokinetic studies of antibiotic serum and tissue levels in patients undergoing colorectal procedures are not available, but it is advisable to redose antibiotics during longer procedures and if blood loss is greater than 2 L.[29] Twenty-four hours of coverage is also recommended for high-risk patients and if the procedure lasts more than 3 hours.[29] Similarly, patients with intestinal obstruction or serious peritoneal spillage should also receive 24 hours of antibiotic coverage.[29] Antibiotics administered for longer than 24 hours postoperatively may increase costs as well as the risk of superinfection, resistance, and toxicity.

OPERATIVE TECHNIQUE

Extent of Resection

The surgical treatment of colon cancer requires resection of the primary tumor with an adequate amount of normal intestine proximal and distal to the tumor, en bloc resection of contiguously invaded structures, and removal of relevant regional lymph nodes. Pathologic studies indicate that a tumor rarely spreads more than 1.2 cm longitudinally beyond the area of gross involvement.[30] Black and Waugh[30] therefore recommended a distal margin of at least 2 cm while Goligher and colleagues[31] suggested a minimum of 2.5 cm. Enker and colleagues[32] evaluated the oncologic outcomes of 146 patients who underwent colon resection from 1966 to 1970. For stage II cancers, a distal margin of at least 5 cm was associated with a 6.9 percent local recurrence rate, which increased to 20 percent if a lesser margin was obtained. For stage III cancers, a margin of at least 10 cm was needed to reduce the rate of locoregional recurrence seen in stage III lesions (36.8%) to that observed for stage II cancers. Rosi and colleagues[33] advocated 8 to 10 cm because of the possibility of distal spread of tumor via the lymphatics secondary to lymphatic blockage by tumor (retrograde spread); however, this modality of tumor spread is seen only in isolated cases.

The extent of resection for left colon cancer has been controversial. Left hemicolectomy (LHC) has been suggested for descending or proximal sigmoid colon cancers. Complete removal of the rectosigmoid with ligation of the inferior mesenteric artery just distal to the origin of the left colic artery has been suggested for mid- or distal sigmoid colon cancers. Alternatively, left segmental colectomy (LSC), which does not include high ligation of the inferior mesenteric artery (IMA) with corresponding aggressive lymphadenectomy has also been accepted as an adequate cancer operation. However, there are no studies that demonstrate a survival advantage for LHC over LSC.[34] Nonetheless, many authors have stated that

LHC is preferable to LSC for adequately controlling left colon carcinoma and improving survival.[32,33,35–42] Proponents of LHC suggest that lymph nodes at the origin of the IMA are involved in more than 10 percent of cases,[39,40] that skip lesions may be present,[43] and that retrograde lymphatic spread of tumor would be removed only by extended resection. Therefore, proponents of LHC suggest that survival in patients with stage III carcinoma would be improved with wide resection when more than five lymph nodes are involved[44] or when lymph node metastases are distant from the most proximal ligation.[45]

Attempting to answer this question in a prospective randomized trial, Roufett and colleagues[46] of the French Association for Surgical Research enrolled patients at 26 centers between 1980 and 1985. The median and actuarial survival following LHC and LSC were evaluated in 270 consecutive patients with left-sided colon cancer and no evidence of extensive local invasion (T4) or distant metastases (M1). There were numerous exclusion criteria for the trial, including the need for emergent operation as well as a variety of comorbid conditions. Left hemicolectomy was defined by resection of the entire left colon along with the origin of the inferior mesenteric artery and its corresponding lymphatic territory. Left segmental colectomy preserved the origin of the IMA and removed a more restricted segment of colon. Left segmental colectomy was further classified as either left proximal segmental colectomy (LPSC) or left distal segmental colectomy/sigmoidectomy (LDSC). Patients were randomly assigned to LHC or LSC, and proximal and distal margins were required to be at least 15 cm and 5 cm, respectively. Lymph nodes at the origin of the IMA were retrieved for pathology in all cases. After exclusion of 10 patients from the study for protocol violation, data from 131 patients who underwent LHC and 129 who underwent LSC were analyzed. Both groups were similar with respect to preoperative risk factors including age, sex, and other comorbid risk factors. Pathologic findings (tumor size, degree of differentiation, cancer stage, invasion of lymph nodes at the origin of the IMA) were also similar between groups. Lymph node involvement at the origin of the IMA occurred in 2.6 percent of all patients and 10 percent of patients with stage III cancers. Postoperative complications were also similar between groups. The only statistical difference between groups occurred in the lengths of the tumor-free margins of colon removed, which were significantly longer after LHC. No adjuvant radiation or chemotherapy was given to any patient until locally recurrent or distant metastatic disease was documented. There were 11 early postoperative deaths (4%). Eight patients died after LHC with 4 (3%) deaths attributable to peritonitis and/or anastomotic leaks whereas 4 others died of pulmonary embolism, decompensated cirrhosis, heart failure, and stroke. Of the 3 (2%) deaths in the LSC group, 2 were from peritonitis attributable to anastomotic leaks, and 1 was from stroke. The difference in mortality and morbidity between the two groups was not statistically significant, and there were no differences in survival at 12 years (median 10 years) between patients who underwent LHC or those who underwent LSC. Furthermore, there were no differences in survival among the patients with stage III disease, including the 10 patients with positive IMA nodes. The authors noted that the number of patients in this subgroup was too small to provide meaningful conclusions regarding survival and still recommended removing lymph nodes at the origin of the IMA in all patients. These data suggest that the absolute length of colon resected is not a prognostic factor in patients with left-sided colonic carcinoma as long as adequate margins are obtained.

Hand-Sewn versus Stapled Anastomoses

Morbidity and mortality following colorectal surgery are directly related to the integrity of the anastomosis, which may be both surgeon- and patient-dependent. Host factors may include malnutrition, steroid use, or other immunocompromised conditions. Low anastomotic leak rates also reflect attention to operative detail, including the formation of a tension-free anastomosis with good edge-to-edge apposition and adequate luminal patency. Bokey and colleagues[14] prospectively evaluated morbidity and mortality over a 20-year period in 1,846 patients who underwent elective resection for colorectal cancer. All anastomoses were performed using a single layer of interrupted absorbable sutures. Intraperitoneal drains were not used. Clinically significant anastomotic leaks were defined as those that required reoperation. Subclinical leaks were defined as those that could be demonstrated by Gastrografin enema or that formed an abdominal abscess that discharged either spontaneously or following minor surgical drainage. The incidences of clinically significant anastomotic leaks following elective right (0.5%) or left (1.1%) hemicolectomy were not significantly different. The leak rate after elective anterior resection was slightly higher (2.9%) than for colon resection but not significantly different. Clinically significant leaks were statistically higher in emergent versus elective procedures (4.3% vs 0.5%, respectively, $p = .01$). Fielding and colleagues[47] also prospectively evaluated the anastomotic leak rate. They enrolled 2,430 patients with adenocarcinoma of the colon, 2,132 of which underwent colon resection and 1,466 of which had enteric anastomosis performed. Clinical leaks occurred in 77 (18.7%) patients who underwent low anterior resection and 114 patients (10.8%) who underwent other procedures ($p < .001$).

Anastomotic technique (single vs double layered, hand sewn vs stapled) is often based upon personal preference. Evidence suggests that an anastomosis performed by manual suturing and one done by surgical stapling are equivalent in terms of safety. Despite this suggestion, there are minimal scientific data that critically evaluate each technique.[48–53] Proponents of stapled anastomoses cite reduction in tissue manipulation, trauma, bleeding, and edema, as well as a more rapid return of gastrointestinal function and patient recovery as reasons for choosing this technique.[54,55] However, stapling techniques have been criticized for their expense,[51,56] for their potential for stricture formation,[57] and because of reports of local recurrences following rectal resection and reconstruction using circular staplers.[58–61] Convincing conclusions are difficult to draw from any of these prospective studies because of their relatively small sample sizes. Docherty and colleagues[62] performed a multicenter prospective randomized study comparing surgical stapling with manual suturing on 652 patients undergoing any elective or emergent colorectal procedure between 1985 and 1989. Radiologic assessment of anastomotic integrity for left colonic and colorectal anastomoses was made using water-soluble contrast enema performed between 4 and 14 days postoperatively. Radiologic leaks were defined by extravasation of contrast. Clinical leaks were defined by a dehiscence at the anastomosis confirmed by reoperation or at autopsy, the appearance of fecal material from drains, development of a colocutaneous fistula, or the development of systemic sepsis associated with local peritoneal signs in the postoperative period. Among the 652 cases, 29 patients (4.4%) developed clinically evident anastomotic leaks. Hand-sewn and stapled anastomoses had similar leak rates (4.4% and 4.5%, respectively). Of the 224 patients with colorectal anastomoses, 186 had contrast radiology performed. Eighteen patients demonstrated a radiologic leak with no clinical evidence of leak. The leak rate was statistically higher in patients with sutured anastomoses (14.4%) than in patients with stapled anastomoses (5.2%, $p < .05$). However, in the absence of a clinical leak, there was no increase in early morbidity.

Finally, the influence of anastomotic technique on local recurrence and overall survival rates is controversial. In the multicenter trial reported by Docherty,[62] there was a 14 percent reduction (95% confidence interval) in the relative hazard of tumor recurrence and a 28 percent reduction (95% confidence interval) in the relative hazard of cancer-specific mortality in patients with stapled anastomoses when compared to patients with hand-sewn anastomoses. Furthermore, patients with any leak (clinically significant or radiographically demonstrated) had statistically higher recurrence rates (44.7% with anastomotic leak vs 30.2% without leak, $p = .003$) and shorter disease-free survivals. New generations of staplers using improved technology will become available. These include staplers using interlocking disks to secure the two ends of the bowel, which at present have no obvious advantages when compared with conventionally stapled or hand-sewn techniques.[63]

Postoperative Management

Nasogastric Tubes

Traditionally, nasogastric tubes were placed intraoperatively in most patients undergoing intestinal resection and were maintained postoperatively until the passage of flatus or stool. Numerous retrospective and prospective studies investigating the need for postoperative nasogastric decompression following colorectal procedures have been summarized by Sagar and colleagues.[64] These studies have shown that neither the rate of anastomotic complications nor the length of postoperative ileus is affected by the routine use of nasogastric tubes.[65–71] Wolff and colleagues[72] performed a prospective randomized controlled trial of 535 patients undergoing elective colorectal surgery, 274 of whom were randomized to receive postoperative nasogastric tube decompression while 261 patients were not decompressed. Patients who did not receive nasogastric decompression had more abdominal distention (28% vs 16%, $p < .05$), nausea (27% vs 17%, $p < .05$), and vomiting (19% vs 11%, $p < .05$). Thirteen percent of these patients eventually required nasogastric tube decompression. In addition, 5 percent of the patients who had nasogastric tubes postoperatively required tube re-insertion ($p < .05$). There were no significant differences in major complications. The authors concluded that 87 percent of patients did not need routine nasogastric decompression and that it was preferable to selectively place a nasogastric tube if needed postoperatively. Finally, proponents of routine nasogastric decompression have argued that elevated perioperative intra-abdominal pressure would lead to an increased incidence of incisional hernia. Otchy and colleagues[73] performed a prospectively randomized study with 480 patients who underwent elective colorectal surgery, 251 of whom received postoperative nasogastric tube decompression while 229 patients did not. Incisional hernia rates were not significantly different between the groups at a median follow-up of 5.3 years.

Postoperative Feeding

Early postoperative feeding may decrease the average length of stay (ALOS). Binderow and colleagues[74] performed a randomized prospective study comparing traditional feeding at passage of flatus to regular diet on the first postoperative day in 64 patients. No significant differences were seen with respect to vomiting, nasogastric intubation, length of ileus, or ALOS. Reissman and colleagues[75] carried out a prospectively controlled randomized study on 161 patients to assess the safety and efficacy of early feeding after elective abdominal intestinal surgery. Patients either were started on a clear liquid diet on postoperative day 1 and advanced to regular food as tolerated or were fed after resolution of their postoperative ileus. Nasogastric tubes were removed from all patients immediately postoperatively. Of the patients fed early, 79 percent tolerated the diet and were advanced to regular food within 24 to 48 hours. There were no significant differences between patients fed early and those fed after resolution of ileus with respect to vomiting (21% vs 14%), nasogastric tube reinsertion (11% vs 10%), length of ileus (3.8 ± 0.1 days vs 4.1 ± 0.1 days), or overall complications (7.5% vs 6.1%). Patients in the early feeding group tolerated a regular diet before those in the traditionally managed group (2.6 ± 0.1 days vs 5.0 ± 0.1 days, $p < .001$). However, patients were not discharged home prior to the passage of stool, and there was therefore no decrease in ALOS (6.2 ± 0.2 days vs 6.8 ± 0.2 days).

Length of Stay

Health care purchasers are more frequently demanding fiscal restraint in the form of discounted fee-for-service contracts and managed care products. Clinical pathways have been developed to conserve health care dollars and streamline care without sacrificing quality. Coffey and colleagues[76] defined a clinical path as an "optimal sequencing and timing of interventions by physicians, nurses, and other staff for a particular diagnosis or procedure."

Average length of stay (ALOS) has become a major focus of both the health care provider and purchaser. Milliman and Robertson Inc., a frequently quoted managed care consulting firm, has proposed a series of optimum in-patient recovery guidelines for patients undergoing numerous surgical procedures.[77] The proposed lengths of stay, including the day of surgery, for commonly performed abdominal colorectal procedures are summarized in Table 22–3. Although minimal data are available to support these proposed lengths of stay, fear of external imposition of these guidelines has stimulated significant interest in this area. Schoetz and colleagues[78] performed a retrospective analysis of perioperative factors that affect ALOS. The records of 226 patients who underwent open colon resection from 1988 to 1995 were reviewed. The effects of age, type and urgency of the procedure, history of previous abdominal surgery, and postoperative course were investigated. Patients who had ileoanal pouch procedures were excluded from this study. Only patients discharged from the hospital were included in the study, and specific complications were not individually analyzed although none of the patients who underwent anastomosis developed a clinically significant anastomotic leak. Re-admission to the hospital was not studied. The ALOS was 9.9 days with a median length of stay of 8 days (range of 4 to 42 days). There was a trend toward lower ALOS in recent years (11.2 days in 1988 and 8.9 days in 1994). Univariate analysis demonstrated that patients younger than 65 years of age had a statistically shorter ALOS than patients over 65 years of age (8.9 days vs 10.8 days, $p < .0024$). There was no significant difference in ALOS for patients with right- or left-sided anastomoses (8.5 vs 9.1 days); however, the creation of an ostomy was associated with a significantly higher ALOS of 12.1 days ($p < .00001$). The need for postoperative nasogastric intubation (14.9 vs 9.3 days, $p < .00001$) and the need for emergent surgery (12.2 vs 8.5 days, $p < .00001$) were also associated with significantly higher ALOS. A history of prior abdominal surgery was not a significant variable. Resumption of oral feeding and the ability to take medications by mouth were two other important determinants of ALOS. In multivariate analysis, age > 65 years ($p = .0226$), emergent indication for operation ($p = .0004$), ostomy creation ($p = .0021$), and nasogastric tube placement ($p < .00001$) all significantly and independently increased ALOS.

Surgeon and Hospital Volume

Meaningful comparisons of crude rates of morbidity and mortality require some form of risk-adjusted analysis. A simple scoring system for use in general surgery, the physiological and operative severity score for enumeration of mortality and morbidity (POSSUM), has been used in more than 15,000 patients who have undergone vascular, gastrointestinal, and colorectal procedures.[79–81] The POSSUM scoring system measures quality of care and comprehensively reviews a surgeon's performance.[82] The POSSUM scoring system consists of 18 variables divided into two sections. The first group of variables assesses 12 physiologic parameters while

Table 22–3 Ideal Hospital Lengths of Stay*

Procedure	Total Stay (Postoperative Days)
Abdominoperineal resection/total colectomy with proctectomy	5
Colectomy, open without rectal resection	4
Colectomy, laparoscopic without rectal resection	3
Colostomy	4

*According to Milliman and Robertson Inc.
Data from Doyle RL. Inpatient and surgical care. In: Milliman R, editor. Healthcare management guidelines. Vol. I: Radnor; 1995:2:p. 17–18.

the latter 6 variables determine an operative severity score. Each variable receives a score of 1, 2, 4, or 8. The POSSUM scoring system is then used to determine the risk of morbidity and mortality.[83] Sagar and colleagues[84] prospectively compared outcomes among five surgeons using POSSUM in 438 patients who underwent elective and emergent colorectal surgery. Morbidity rates varied among the five surgeons from 13.6 to 30.6 percent, and 30-day mortality rates varied from 4.5 to 6.9 percent. Data adjustment by POSSUM demonstrated that the observed morbidity and mortality rates were nearly equal to those predicated for each surgeon. Therefore, crude morbidity and mortality rates are likely a reflection of case mix rather than surgeon ability.

Sagar and colleagues[81] also used POSSUM to prospectively compare outcomes after colorectal resections between two hospitals. Sixty-six patients who underwent elective or emergent colorectal resection in a university teaching hospital had a mortality rate of 6 percent and a morbidity rate of 9 percent. The mortality and morbidity rates for 182 patients treated in a district general hospital were 9 percent and 26 percent, respectively. While the crude mortality rate was not significantly higher in the district hospital, the morbidity rate was significantly higher ($p < .01$). Analysis of these data by the POSSUM system predicted similar observed-to-expected mortality and morbidity ratios from both institutions, thereby suggesting that the variation in outcomes between the two hospitals was attributable to differences in case mix.

Several studies have evaluated outcome differences between surgeons who specialize in colorectal surgery and general surgeons who perform colorectal surgical procedures. Rosen and colleagues[85] compared mortality rates in 2,805 patients operated on by 6 board-certified colorectal surgeons and 33 other institutional surgeons. Patients who underwent major colorectal procedures between July 1986 and April 1994 were identified by ICD-9-CM codes. Outcomes based on patient comorbidities were also evaluated using a computer program called Atlas, which uses clinical findings obtained from patient records to determine admission severity groups (ASGs), numbered from 0 (correlating with those who had no medical instability) to 4 (which suggested a high risk of death). The mean in-hospital mortality rate for colorectal surgeons was 1.4 percent versus 7.3 percent for other institutional general surgeons ($p = .0001$). There were no differences between colorectal surgeons and surgeons at other institutions in patients with ASG 1 or 4 ($p = .8517$ and $p = .1280$, respectively). However, colorectal surgeons had lower mortality rates than other surgeons for patients in ASG 2 and 3 (0.82% vs 3.8%, $p = .0106$ and 5.7% vs 16.4%, $p = .0021$, respectively).

A positive association between surgeon case volume and outcomes in surgery for colorectal cancer has been described.[86] Study cases (n = 9,739) were taken from the Maryland Health Services Cost Review Commission Non-Confidential Discharge Data collected from 50 hospitals in the state of Maryland between 1992 and 1996. Adult patients with a primary diagnosis of colon or rectal cancer who underwent resection as a primary procedure were identified by ICD-9-CM codes. Surgeons were grouped according to the average number of colorectal resections they performed per year. Short-term hospital outcomes studied included in-hospital mortality, average total cost, and ALOS. Poisson and multiple linear regression analyses were used to adjust for variations between surgeon groups for the type of resection performed, cancer stage, hospital case volume, patient comorbidities, urgency of admissions, and patient demographic variables. The data are reproduced in Table 22–4. Of 812 surgeons who performed resections for colon and rectal cancer, 661 surgeons (81%) performed 5 or less cases per year (representing 35% of cases in this state), 113 surgeons (14%) performed 5 to 10 cases per year, and 38 surgeons (5%) performed more than 10 cases per year. The adjusted relative risk of death was lower in the high-volume group when compared with the low-volume surgeons. Furthermore, adjusted total charges and ALOS were significantly lower in the high-volume group. Tang and colleagues concluded that surgeons performing more than 10 cases per year experienced significantly better outcomes than those performing 5 or fewer cases per year.

Table 22–4 Crude and Case-Mix Adjusted Outcomes by Surgeon Volume Groups

Surgeon volume groups (cases per year)	Low ≤ 5	Medium > 5 and ≤ 10	High > 10	Total
Number of surgeons	661 (81%)	113 (14%)	38 (6%)	812
Number of cases	3,464 (36%)	3,626 (37%)	2,649 (27%)	9,739
Average cases per year	1.8	7.0	14	3.1
Mortality				
Crude mortality (%)	4.5	3.3	2.6	3.5
Adjusted relative risk	1.00	0.80*	0.64†	
Total charges ($)				
Unadjusted	16,884	14,369	13,929	15,142
Adjusted	13,025	11,735†	11,642†	
Length of stay (days)				
Unadjusted	12.6	11.2	10.7	11.5
Adjusted	10.1	9.5†	9.0†‡	

* Comparison with low group, $p = .07$.

† Comparison with low group, $p < .01$.

‡ Comparison with medium group, $p < .01$.

Data from Tang DG, Bowman HM, Gordon TA, et al. Case volume and outcomes in resection for colorectal carcinoma. Surgical Forum Paper 1998;49:559–61.

COLORECTAL SURGERY IN THE GERIATRIC POPULATION

Longer life expectancy will undoubtedly increase the number of major surgical procedures performed for benign and malignant colorectal diseases in older patients. The geriatric population is at high risk for postoperative complications secondary to limited reserve and underlying medical problems. High-risk groups can be identified preoperatively and treated appropriately to decrease morbidity and mortality rates.[87] Although chronologic age may be a risk factor for mortality and morbidity, physiologic factors are more predictive of outcome. Greenburg and colleagues[88] retrospectively analyzed 334 patients aged 70 years and older who underwent elective and emergent colonic surgical procedures. Mortality rates for elective procedures were 0 percent in patients under 49 years of age, 1.6 percent in patients 50 to 69 years of age, and 4.4 percent in those over 70 years of age ($p < .05$ for comparison of groups aged 50 to 69 and > 70 years). Mortality rates for emergent procedures were 0 percent, 9.5 percent, and 19.5 percent, respectively ($p < .05$ for comparison of groups aged < 49 and > 70 years). Ondrula and colleagues[89] retrospectively studied outcomes in 825 patients who underwent 972 colon resections, 276 (33%) of whom were 75 years of age or older. Multivariate analysis found 11 of the 17 preoperative risk factors evaluated (including age > 75 years) to be predictors of surgical outcomes. To isolate the independent effect of age upon outcomes, the authors compared 129 patients aged 75 years or more without significant medical problems to 419 patients younger than 75 years without significant medical problems. No significant differences in major or minor morbidities or mortality were identified when age was selected as the defining risk factor ($p = .074$).

Average length of stay (ALOS) is affected by patient age. Schoetz and colleagues[78] retrospectively evaluated 226 patients who underwent colon resection. Although these data were not adjusted for other comorbidities, patients over 65 years of age had longer hospitalizations than patients 65 and younger (10.8 vs 8.9 days, $p = .0024$). Wise and colleagues[90] also evaluated the effect of age on ALOS in a retrospective review of 56 patients 80 years of age or older who underwent colorectal surgical procedures between 1984 and 1989. Average length of stay was 19 days for the older group as opposed to 10 days for the total patient population.

LAPAROSCOPIC SURGERY

Laparoscopic colon surgery was shown to be technically feasible in the early 1990s,[91–93] and several series have demonstrated excellent results for it in the treatment of benign disease as well as in palliative procedures.[94,95] Advocates of minimally invasive surgical approaches for colorectal disorders suggest that a shortened length of stay, decreased analgesic requirements, shorter periods of ileus, and a more rapid return to full function will offset the associated capital costs.[92,96–98] Laparoscopic surgery can be used to stage patients, perform palliative procedures, and perform curative resections in patients with colorectal carcinoma. Those performing curative procedures state that it is safe and that it fulfills oncologic criteria for cancer surgery.[92,93,96–106] However, enthusiasm for laparoscopic techniques over open resection was blunted by several reports of port site recurrences in patients with early-stage colon cancer.[101,107–111] Several prospective randomized controlled trials are currently under way to address questions of safety and efficacy of the laparoscopic technique when used for curative procedures for colorectal cancer.

Port Site Recurrence in Laparoscopic Surgery

There are currently over 30 case reports in the literature of port site recurrences following curative laparoscopic procedures for colorectal cancer.[101] Although rare, port site recurrence is not unique to laparoscopic colectomy. Port site recurrences have been reported following laparoscopic exploration and resection of an ovarian tumor[112] and after laparoscopic cholecystectomy in patients with unsuspected gallbladder cancer.[94,95] The mechanisms involved in trocar site recurrences remain unclear but may be related to spillage and inoculation of tumor cells, aerosolization of tumor cells, preferential implantation of cancer cells in healing wounds, and exfoliation of viable tumor cells.[113–116] Jones and colleagues[117] have even demonstrated that pneumoperitoneum will triple the occurrence of tumor implantation at trocar sites when free colon cancer cells are injected into the abdominal cavities of hamsters.

Wound recurrences following curative resection for colon cancer are not unique to a laparoscopic approach. Hughes and colleagues[118] attempted curative open resection of colon cancer in 1,603 patients and reported 16 (1%) patients with abdominal wall recurrences of which 11 patients had recurrences in the abdominal wound and 5 patients had recurrences remote from any operative site. Reilly and colleagues[119] evaluated the records of 1,711 patients being prospectively followed with stage II or III colorectal cancer after open resection. Recurrences were reported in 623 patients (36.4%), and 11 patients (0.6%) had wound involvement. Nine of these patients also had other sites of recurrence. Two other studies reporting abdominal wound recurrences are those of Edoute and colleagues[120] and Earls and colleagues.[121]

Wexner and Cohen[101] state that port site recurrences have significance for several reasons. First, recurrences have been observed at ports not used for specimen retrieval. Newman noted a port site metastasis 6 months after resection of a stage III sigmoid carcinoma. The port site of recurrence had not been used for specimen retrieval, and the specimen had been placed in a protective bag before retrieval (Newman, unpublished result). Second, although approximately 30 port site recurrences have been reported, the total number of cases is assumed to be much larger due to lack of reporting. Berends and colleagues[122] noted port site recurrences in 21 percent of the 14 patients they treated laparoscopically. Third, port site recurrences can occur in patients with early-stage disease. Although most reported cases have occurred after curative resection of either stage II or III disease, there have been reports of port site recurrence after resection of stage I colon cancers.[101,123]

Despite a lack of mature data from prospectively randomized controlled clinical trials, there are several recent prospective nonrandomized series that show low rates of port site recurrences. Hoffman and colleagues[124] performed laparoscopic colorectal procedures in 39 patients for carcinoma. No port site recurrences were noted with a mean follow-up of 30 months. Kwok and colleagues[125] prospectively followed 83 patients who underwent laparoscopic colectomy for cancer. The median follow-up was 15.2 months, and only one port site recurrence was noted in a patient with carcinomatosis. Similarly, Lumley and colleagues[98] prospectively evaluated 103 patients who underwent laparoscopic colorectal procedures for cancer and observed only one port site recurrence. Ramos and colleagues[126] evaluated data from a prospective laparoscopic bowel surgery registry on 208 patients. There were 3 port site recurrences (1.44%) in patients with stage III disease, and 2 of these patients also had carcinomatosis. Prasad[127] reported a 4 percent incidence of port site recurrence in 50 laparoscopic colorectal resections for carcinoma. Vukasin and colleagues[128] prospectively followed 504 patients treated for cancer with laparoscopic colectomy. A minimum follow-up of 1 year was obtained for 97.4 percent of their patients. The wound recurrence rate was 1.1 percent, and all recurrences were in patients with stage III disease. Time to recurrence ranged from 2 to 21 months. Two recurrences developed at incisions used for specimen extraction, and three occurred at distant port sites. Fleshman and colleagues[129] retrospectively evaluated the early results of laparoscopic surgery for colorectal cancer in 372 patients treated by the Clinical Outcomes of Surgical Therapy (COST) Study Group. Trocar site or abdominal wall tumor implantation was demonstrated in four patients (1.08%) with the majority having carcinomatosis or multiple sites of recurrence after resection for stage II or III disease. Franklin and colleagues[130] performed 191 laparoscopic procedures for colorectal cancer. There were no port site recurrences observed at a mean follow-up of 37, 35, and 31 months for stage I, II, and III cancers, respectively. In summary, while the incidence of port site recurrence is currently unknown, these data will become available as large multicenter prospective randomized trials mature.

Extent of Resection in Laparoscopic Surgery

Several series have addressed whether a proper oncologic colon resection is feasible with laparoscopic techniques. Franklin and colleagues[130] prospectively but nonrandomly compared open to laparoscopic colon resection for colon carcinoma. Over 65 months, 224 patients underwent open resection while 191 patients were resected with laparoscopic techniques. The pathologic stage of disease and the site of primary tumor were similar in both groups. The number of lymph nodes harvested and the lengths of resected margins were also similar. However, the total length of the specimen was longer in patients undergoing open resection except for the distal margin following low anterior resections, which was longer in the laparoscopic group. Although the study was presented without adequate statistical analysis, the overall recurrence rates appeared lower in the laparoscopically resected group (12 vs 22 percent). Lord and colleagues[96] reviewed their 3-year experience of laparoscopic surgery for colon and rectal carcinoma in 55 patients. There were no significant differences between laparoscopic and open cases in tumor margin length or in the number of nodes resected. Hoffman and colleagues[104] compared results from 80 consecutive laparoscopically assisted colorectal procedures to those of 53 patients who underwent conventional open procedures. Thirty-two procedures were performed with curative intent in patients with cancer. No significant differences were seen between groups with respect to specimen length, margin length, or the number of lymph nodes harvested. Falk and colleagues[93] performed 13 laparoscopic procedures for carcinoma and compared them to 6 patients who required conversion to an open procedure and 41 patients who underwent conventional open colectomy. No significant difference in the number of lymph nodes harvested was observed.

Studies addressing long-term follow-up for patients with colon cancer treated by laparoscopic colectomy are under way. Early outcomes data from a multi-institution retrospective study with mean follow-up of 22.6 months indicates cancer-related death rates of 4 percent for stage I, 17 percent for stage II, 31 percent for stage III, and 70 percent for stage IV.[129] These data are comparable to historical cancer-specific death rates for open resection for colorectal cancer. Hoffman and colleagues[124] published an analysis of the early patterns of recurrence of colon cancer and survival in 39 patients treated by laparoscopy-assisted colectomy. Mean follow-up was 30 months with a range of 24 to 40 months. Six patients had distant metastases at the time of surgery, and three other patients developed recurrences. Recurrence and tumor-related death rates, respectively for each Dukes' stage, were 0/1 and 0/1 for stage A, 0/7 and 0/7 for stage B1, 1/16 and 2/16 for stage B2, 0/1 and 0/1 for stage C1, and 2/8 and 1/8 for stage C2. All six patients with Dukes' stage D disease died of metastatic colorectal cancer between 4 and 14 months following surgery. Although these nonrandomized data are encouraging with respect to oncologic outcomes, at the present time, laparoscopic surgery with curative intent for colorectal cancer should only be performed within a prospective randomized controlled clinical trial.

Morbidity and Mortality: the Learning Curve

Despite minor incisions, laparoscopic colorectal surgery can have major complications. Advanced laparoscopic techniques are needed due to variability in specimen location, the need for optimal port positioning, control of major vascular structures, and resection of bowel with restoration of gastrointestinal continuity. Simons[131] evaluated the learning curve of laparoscopic intestinal surgery by analyzing the operative times of four surgeons beginning to perform laparoscopic colorectal surgery. These surgeons performed 144 procedures with a mean operating time of 130 minutes. It required 11 to 15 cases to reach this mean operating time. Falk and colleagues[93] retrospectively evaluated 66 patients who had undergone laparoscopic procedures and demonstrated that operative times decreased by 50 percent after 12 cases had been performed. Senagore and colleagues[132] prospectively followed all elective colon resections between November 1991 and October 1992, including 38 laparoscopic procedures and 102 open resections. There were no differences in perioperative morbidity between the groups. The conversion rate to an open procedure was 32 percent, and the majority of cases requiring conversion occurred early in the series. Senagore and colleagues[133] later reported on 60 consecutive laparoscopic procedures divided chronologically into 3 groups of 20 patients. Although the complexity of the procedures increased with time, the conversion and complication rates decreased after 40 procedures. Furthermore, significantly fewer complications occurred after 40 procedures had been performed. Wishner and colleagues[134] evaluated 150 consecutive laparoscopically assisted colectomies. The mean operating time decreased from 250 minutes to 140 minutes after surgeons had performed 35 to 50 cases ($p < .001$). Agachan and colleagues[135] prospectively evaluated 167 patients who underwent laparoscopic colectomy for various disease processes including carcinoma and compared results in the early, middle, and late time periods. The overall conversion rate was 22.7 percent. Complication rates decreased from 29 percent to 11 percent and then to 7 percent in the early, middle, and late time periods, respectively. Only 6.5 percent of conversions were related to intraoperative complications, which included enterotomy (5%), bleeding (6%), anastomotic leak (2%) and colotomy (2%). Postoperative complications occurred in 38 patients and consisted of prolonged ileus, anastomotic leaks, high stoma output, pelvic abscess formation, wound infection or cellulitis, bleeding, port site hernias, malrotation of the stoma limb, and stoma outlet obstruction. Other nonoperative complications included atelectasis, pneumonia, urinary tract infection, anemia, cardiac arrhythmia, renal failure, intravenous fluid overload, and catheter line sepsis. The most significant variable affecting the intraoperative complication rate was surgeon experience ($p = .01$), with at least 50 cases being needed to obtain proficiency. In a second report, Agachan and colleagues[136] also noted that despite more procedures on patients with increasing complexity, intraoperative times fell significantly with experience (207 minutes in 1991 to 141 minutes in 1993, $p < .05$).

The learning curve can be related to the open conversion rate if evaluated over time. Conversion rates in the literature vary from 8 percent to 48 percent.[92,137] In a multicenter retrospective analysis, Falk and colleagues[93] reported a conversion rate of 41 percent in 66 laparoscopic colorectal procedures. Conversion was performed most frequently for adhesions and unclear anatomy. Monson and colleagues[138] performed a prospective study on 40 patients with a conversion rate of 17.5 percent. Dean and colleagues[106] prospectively evaluated 122 patients that underwent attempted laparoscopic colectomy with a conversion rate of 48 percent. Intraoperative complications (6%) included small bowel perforation, ureteral transection, bladder injury, bleeding, and the need to resect an additional segment of bowel secondary to a poorly constructed anastomosis recognized during the initial procedure. Postoperative complications (5%) consisted of prolonged ileus, small bowel obstruction, urinary retention, and recurrent rectal prolapse. Wexner and colleagues[139] reported bleeding as the most common reason for conversion in a prospective analysis of their first 140 cases. Lord and colleagues[96] evaluated the conversion rate in 76 laparoscopic procedures and also demonstrated that rates improve with experience. The overall conversion rate was 25 percent, 32 percent in the first 6 months and 8 percent in the last 6 months of a 3-year study. Adhesions were the most common reason for conversion, followed by inability to adequately define the anatomy, excessive operating room time, large tumor size, and bleeding.

Table 22–5 Reasons for Conversion to Celiotomy

Conversion Reasons	Number of Patients
Iatrogenic injuries	
Bleeding	6
Enterotomy	2
Resection of wrong bowel segment	1
Ureteral injury	1
Other technical reasons	
Adhesions	13
Unclear anatomy/obesity	5
Poor mobilization	5
Low tumor	2
Prolonged procedure (proctocolectomy)	1
Infiltration of abdominal wall	1
Pelvic kidney	1
Inability to staple anastomosis	1
Total	39 (20%)

Data from Larach SW, Patankar SK, Ferrara A, et al. Complications of laparoscopic colorectal surgery: analysis and comparison of early vs latter experience. Dis Colon Rectum 1997;40:592–6.

Larach and colleagues[140] analyzed 195 laparoscopic procedures performed between 1991 and 1996, which also included patients from the study by Lord and colleagues. Two consecutive time periods were chosen for comparison: between October 1991 and September 1994 and between October 1994 and July 1996. Data from laparoscopic patients were obtained prospectively and compared to retrospectively obtained data from open controls. Reasons for conversion were categorized as either iatrogenic or secondary to technical reasons and are summarized in Table 22–5. The overall conversion rates were not statistically different between the two time periods; however, there was a qualitative difference between the two groups. Conversion secondary to iatrogenic injuries declined from 7.3 percent in the early group to 1.4 percent in the later group. The incidence of technical problems also fell from 13.8 percent in the early group to 2.8 percent in the later group ($p = .02$). There were 66 complications overall, occurring in 59 patients (30.3%). Complications unique to laparoscopic surgery occurred in 19 patients (9.7%) and are summarized in Table 22–6.

Other studies have examined the relationship between surgeon experience and the complication rate. Reissman and colleagues[141] prospectively assessed the results of their first 100 consecutive patients undergoing laparoscopic or laparoscopically assisted colorectal procedures. Patients were evenly divided into three groups. Complication rates were significantly higher in the early and middle groups (42 percent and 27 percent, respectively) than in the later group (12%, $p < .05$). Total abdominal colectomy was performed more frequently in the early (18) and middle (13) groups than in the late group (5), and the complication rate for this specific procedure was significantly higher (42%) than that for all other procedures (segmental resection 9%, no resection 12%, $p < .01$). After exclusion of patients with total abdominal colectomy from each group, the complication rates were 27 percent, 20 percent, and 10 percent, for the early, middle, and late groups, respectively ($p < .05$).

Effect of Laparoscopic Techniques on Length of Stay

Lord and colleagues[96] reported an ALOS of 5.8 days (range 4 to 22 days) in 91 patients with surgery completed laparoscopically versus 8.2 days (range 4 to 16 days) in 14 patients that had required conversion to open procedures ($p = .02$). Ortega and colleagues[102] compared ALOS in 763 patients who had procedures completed laparoscopically with 293 patients who required conversion to open operations. Average length of stay was significantly reduced in the laparoscopic group, 5.6 days (median, 5 days; range, 0 to 45 days) versus 8.4 days (median, 7 days; range, 0 to 55 days, $p < .001$) for the open group. Wexner and associates[139] were unable

Table 22–6 Intraoperative and Postoperative Complications Specific to Laparoscopic Surgery

Complication	Early (n = 123)	Late (n = 72)
Bleeding	8	1
Enterotomy	2	0
Ureteral injury	1	0
Ureteral stenosis	0	1
Resection of wrong bowel segment	1	0
Port hernias	5	0
Total	17 (13.8%)	2 (2.8%)

Data from Larach K, Patankar SK, Ferrara A, et al. Complications of laparoscopic colorectal surgery: analysis and comparison of early vs latter experience. Dis Colon Rectum 1997;40:592–6.

to demonstrate significant differences in the ALOS for 140 various laparoscopically completed colorectal procedures including total abdominal colectomy (8.4 days), segmental resections (6.5 days), and other procedures (6.3 days).

Cost of Laparoscopic versus Conventional Surgery

Health care cost is a major societal issue. Advocates of laparoscopic colorectal procedures state that despite increased operative time and equipment costs, patients who undergo laparoscopic procedures have shorter hospital stays, less pain, and better cosmetic results when compared to those who undergo standard open procedures.[92,93,138] However, these benefits have not yet been confirmed in randomized controlled clinical trials. Falk and colleagues[93] prospectively evaluated cost in 66 patients who underwent laparoscopic colorectal surgery between 1991 and 1992 by comparing the charges of laparoscopic procedures with open and converted procedures. While hospital stay was shorter in the laparoscopic group, operating room time and charges were significantly higher, offsetting any significant differences in overall hospital charges between the groups. Operating room time, ALOS, and time until return of intestinal function are directly related to hospital charges. Lumley and colleagues[98] evaluated these parameters, which are summarized for various laparoscopic procedures in Table 22–7.

Larach and Ferrara[142] compared charges in 38 laparoscopy-assisted colectomies with 38 patients who underwent open resection between October 1991 and February 1993. Patients were matched for age, sex, hospital, comorbid conditions, resection, and pathology. Charges for operating room time, equipment, and anesthesia were all significantly higher in the laparoscopic group (Table 22–8). Total hospital charges demonstrated a similar trend but were not significantly higher in the laparoscopic group ($26,662 vs $22,938, $p = .3$). Pfeifer and colleagues[143] also failed to demonstrate a significant difference in total hospital charges between 53 patients treated laparoscopically and 53 patients treated with laparotomy.

Effect of Laparoscopic Techniques on Gastrointestinal Motility

Proponents of laparoscopic intestinal resection cite the early return of bowel function as morbidity- and cost-reducing benefits of this technique. Lumley and colleagues[98] prospectively evaluated the return of bowel function in 240 patients undergoing laparoscopic colorectal procedures. While most patients had return of flatus by postoperative day 2 (see Table 22–7), no comparison was made to patients having open procedures. Dean and colleagues[106] prospectively evaluated the return of bowel function in 64 patients undergoing laparoscopy-assisted bowel resections and compared them to 58 patients having conversion to open procedures. Patients who underwent laparoscopic resection tolerated a diet approximately 2 days before those patients who were converted to an open procedure (2.3 vs 4.8 days, $p < .001$). Hoffman and colleagues[104] demonstrated an earlier return of bowel function, as measured by passage of flatus, in 80 consecutive patients resected by laparoscopic techniques when compared to 53 patients who had open procedures. Although no statistical analysis was performed, flatus returned 2 days earlier in the laparoscopic group than in the open group (2 days vs 4 days).

Davies and colleagues[144] studied the effect of laparoscopic colon surgery on postoperative ileus in a dog model. Thirty-nine dogs were divided into three groups: laparoscopic colectomy, laparoscopy-assisted colectomy, and open colectomy. Gastrointestinal function was measured preoperatively (control) and on postoperative days 1, 2, 3, and 5 by radionuclide techniques. The laparoscopic colectomy group had return of normal gastric emptying by 2 days, compared with 3 days for the laparoscopy-assisted colectomy group and 5 days for the open colectomy group. Small bowel transit was similarly affected, with return of small bowel transit to preoperative levels by day 3 in the laparoscopic colectomy and laparoscopy-assisted colectomy groups and by day 5 in the open colectomy group. These data provide further objective evidence for an earlier return of bowel function following laparoscopic procedures.

Table 22-7 Laparoscopic Operating Times, Postoperative Length of Stay, Time until Flatus

Laparoscopic Procedure	Number of Procedures	Operating Time (min) (Median Range [min])	Postoperative Stay (days) (Median Range [days])	Time until Flatus (days) (Median Range [days])
Anterior resection	92	210 (80–420)	6 (2–33)	2 (1–7)
Left hemicolectomy	7	190 (150–300)	6 (5–8)	2 (1–4)
Right hemicolectomy	52	150 (70–270)	5 (3–35)	2 (1–4)
Abdominoperineal resection	27	210 (150–300)	8 (5–80)	2 (1–9)
Colectomy (total/subtotal)	29	285 (100–720)	8 (4–14)	2 (1–6)
Proctocolectomy	6	300 (245–330)	8 (6–37)	2 (1–5)
Ileostomy/colostomy	14	50 (30–150)	6 (4–18)	1 (1–2)
Rectopexy	4	200 (150–240)	4 (2–7)	1 (1–3)
Ileal resection	1	80	4	1

Data from Lumley JW, Fielding GA, Rhodes M, et al. Laparoscopic-assisted colorectal surgery: lessons learned from 240 consecutive patients. Dis Colon Rectum 1996;39:155–9.

Table 22–8 Cost Comparison: Open Resection versus Laparoscopy

	Open Resection	Laparoscopic Resection	p-Value
Charges			
Total cost	$22,938	$26,662	.03
Operating room time	$3,371	$4,227	.011
Operating room equipment	$2,610	$5,478	< .001
Anesthesia	$669	$918	.002
Length of procedure	167 min	196 min	.10
Return of bowel function			
POD bowel sounds	2.87	1.71	< .001
POD flatus	5.11	3.13	< .001
POD bowel movement	6.32	4.45	< .001
POD discharge	8.45	7.05	.075

POD = postoperative day.

Data from Larach SW, Ferrara A. Cost analysis. In: Jager RM, Wexner SD, editors. Laparoscopic colorectal surgery. New York: Churchill-Livingston; 1996. p. 321–3.

CONCLUSION AND FUTURE DIRECTIONS

Colorectal surgical procedures are common and are most frequently performed for cancer. An extensive literature of evidence-based research has guided the evolution of surgery for colon cancer. Outcomes following open resection depend upon preoperative, intraoperative, and postoperative patient care and management. Preoperative care is enhanced by performing necessary procedures electively, maximizing treatment of comorbid conditions, and employing a mechanical bowel preparation with oral antibiotics in addition to parenteral antibiotics at the time of surgery. Intraoperative attention to detail is imperative, especially when constructing the anastomosis. The length of specimen resected can be variable as long as adequate margins are obtained and the draining lymph node basin is resected. Postoperative care demands attention to the fluid electrolyte balance and pulmonary toilet but should not include nasogastric decompression unless indicated. Average lengths of stay, total hospital charges, and mortality rates improve as surgeon case volumes increase. As life expectancy continues to rise, more elderly patients with multiple medical problems will need surgical procedures. Morbidity and mortality are less dependent on age than on the urgency of the procedure underlying comorbid conditions.

The role of laparoscopic surgery in colon cancer is currently being defined. Interestingly, Wexner and colleagues[100] noted that of 425 surgeons surveyed, only 255 (40%) would themselves undergo laparoscopic colorectal surgery for a rectal villous adenoma and only 38 (6%) would have a laparoscopic anterior resection for cancer. The use of laparoscopic technology due to feasibility alone, without supporting outcomes data, must not be condoned. The American Society of Colon and Rectal Surgeons[145,146] and the Society of American Gastrointestinal Endoscopic Surgeons[147] have published guidelines stating that laparoscopic colorectal surgery should be undertaken only in a setting in which proper prospective data retrieval will occur. A surgical consortium entitled Clinical Outcomes of Surgical Therapies (COST) Study Group has initiated a multi-institution prospective randomized controlled trial to compare laparoscopic and open colectomy for curable right, left, and sigmoid colon cancer.[148] Funded by the National Cancer Institute, this study will compare 600 patients in each group. The primary objective of the study is to determine the equivalence of oncologic outcomes among colorectal cancer patients undergoing resection via laparoscopy-based and open techniques. Early and late morbidity and mortality will also be evaluated. Finally, the cost-effectiveness of the laparoscopic approach and its impact on the patient's quality of life relative to the traditional open approach will be evaluated. Given the extensive foundation of evidence on which colon cancer surgery is based as well as the prevalence of colon cancer, this analytic approach will extend over new techniques and adjuvant therapies, with close attention to outcomes for specific risk groups.

REFERENCES

1. Landis SH, Murray T, Bolden S, Wingo PA. Cancer statistics, 1998. CA Cancer J Clin 1998;48:6–29.

2. Bosman FT. Prognostic value of pathological characteristics of colorectal cancer. Eur J Cancer 1995; 31A:1216–21.

3. Roncucci L, Fante R, Losi L, et al. Survival for colon and rectal cancer in a population-based cancer registry. Eur J Cancer 1996;32A:295–302.

4. Sant M, Capocaccia R, Verdecchia A, et al. Comparisons of colon-cancer survival among European countries: The eurocare study. Int J Cancer 1995;63:43–8.

5. Fielding LP, Phillips RKS, Fry JS, Hittinger R. Prediction of outcome after curative resection for large bowel cancer. Lancet 1986;2:904–7.

6. Chapuis PH, Dent OF, Fisher R, et al. A multivariate analysis of clinical and pathological variables in prognosis after resection of large bowel cancer. Br J Surg 1985;72:698–702.

7. Allen AW, Welch CE. Malignant disease of the colon: factors influencing the operability, morbidity and mortality. Am J Surg 1939;46:171–80.

8. Macfee WF. Resection with aseptic end to end anastomosis for carcinoma of the colon. Ann Surg 1937;106:701–13.

9. Localio S, Eng K, Gouge TH, Ranson JH. Abdominosacral resection for carcinoma of the midrectum: ten years experience. Ann Surg 1978;188:475–80.

10. Scott-Conner CE, Scher KS. Implications of emergency operations on the colon. Am J Surg 1987; 153:535–40.

11. Irvin GL, Horsley JS, Caruana JA Jr. The morbidity and mortality of emergent operations for colorectal disease. Ann Surg 1984;199:598–603.

12. Nwiloh J, Dardik H, Dardik M, et al. Changing patterns in the morbidity and mortality of colorectal surgery. Am J Surg 1991;162:83–5.

13. Tinker J, Roberts S. Anesthesia risk. In: Miller RD, editor. Textbook of anesthesia. Vol. 1. New York: Churchill Livingstone; 1986. p. 369–80.

14. Bokey EL, Chapuis PH, Fung C, et al. Postoperative morbidity and mortality following resection of the colon and rectum for cancer. Dis Colon Rectum 1995;38:480–7.

15. Nichols RL, Condon RE. Preoperative preparation of the colon. Surg Gynecol Obstet 1971;132:323–37.

16. Poth EJ. Intestinal antisepsis in surgery. JAMA 1953;153:1516–21.

17. Cohn IJ, Rives JD. Protection of colonic anastomoses with antibiotics. Ann Surg 1956;144:738–52.

18. Nichols RL, Condon RE, Gorbach SL, Nyhus LM. Efficacy of preoperative anti-microbial preparation of the bowel. Ann Surg 1972;176:227–32.

19. Nichols RL, Broido P, Condon RE, et al. Effect of preoperative neomycin-erythromycin intestinal preparation on the incidence of infectious complications following colon surgery. Ann Surg 1973; 178:453–62.

20. Clarke JS, Condon RE, Bartlett JG, et al. Preoperative oral antibiotics reduce septic complications of colon operations: results of prospective, randomized double-blind clinical study. Ann Surg 1977; 186:251–9.

21. Handelsman JC, Zeiler S, Coleman J, et al. Experience with ambulatory preoperative bowel preparation at The Johns Hopkins Hospital. Arch Surg 1993;128:441–4.

22. Le TH, Timmcke AE, Gathright JB, et al. Outpatient bowel preparation for elective colon resection. South Med J 1997;90:526–30.

23. Nichols RL, Smith JW, Garcia RY, et al. Current practices of preoperative bowel preparation among North American colorectal surgeons. Clin Infect Dis 1997;24.

24. Condon RE, Bartlett JG, Greenlee H, et al. Efficacy of oral and systemic antibiotic prophylaxis in colorectal operations. Arch Surg 1983;188:496–502.

25. Barber MS, Hirschberg BC, Rice CL, Atkins CC. Parenteral antibiotics in elective colon surgery? A prospective, controlled clinical study. Surgery 1979;86:23–9.

26. Schoetz DJ, Roberts PL, Murray JJ, et al. Addition of parenteral cefoxitin to regimen of oral antibiotics for elective colorectal operations. Ann Surg 1990;212:209–12.

27. Burke JF. The effective period of preventive antibiotic action in experimental incisions and dermal lesions. Surgery 1961;50:161–8.

28. Classen DC, Evans RS, Pestotnik SL, et al. The timing of prophylactic administration of antibiotics and the risk of surgical wound infection. N Engl J Med 1992;326:281–6.

29. Michalopoulos A, Geroulanos S. Antibiotics for prophylaxis and treatment of intra-abdominal infections. Hepatogastroenterology 1997;44:947–58.

30. Black WA, Waugh JM. The intramural extension of carcinoma of the descending colon, sigmoid and rectosigmoid: a pathologic study. Surg Gynecol Obstet 1948;87:457–64.

31. Goligher JC, Dukes CE, Bussey HJ. Local recurrences after sphincter-saving excisions for carcinoma of the rectum and rectosigmoid. Br J Surg 1951;39:199–211.

32. Enker WE, Laffer V, Block GE. Enhanced survival of patients with colon and rectal cancer is based upon wide anatomic resection. Ann Surg 1979;190:350–60.

33. Rosi PA, Cahill WJ, Carey J. A ten-year study of hemicolectomy in the treatment of carcinoma of the left half of the colon. Surg Gynecol Obstet 1962;114:15–24.

34. Jeekel J. Curative resection of primary colorectal cancer. Br J Surg 1986;73:687–8.

35. Ault GW. A technique for cancer isolation and extended dissection for cancer of the distal colon and rectum. Surg Gynecol Obstet 1958;106:467–77.

36. Bacon EH, McGregor JK. Prevention of recurrent carcinoma of the colon and rectum: report on 236 patients. Dis Colon Rectum 1963;6:209–14.

37. Dwight RW, Higgins GA, Keehn RJ. Factors influencing survival after resection in cancer of the colon and rectum. Am J Surg 1969;117:513–22.

38. Grinnel RS. Results of ligation of inferior mesenteric artery at the aorta in resection of carcinoma of the descending and sigmoid colon and rectum. Surg Gynecol Obstet 1965;120:1031–6.

39. McElwain JW, Bacon HE, Trimpi HD. Lymph node metastases: experience with aortic ligation of inferior mesenteric artery in cancer of the rectum. Surgery 1954;35:513–31.

40. Moynihan BG. The survival treatment of cancer of the sigmoid flexure and rectum. Surg Gynecol Obstet 1908;6:463–6.

41. Polk HCJ. Extended resection for selected adenocarcinoma of the large bowel. Ann Surg 1972; 175:892–9.

42. Surtees P, Ritchie, JK, Phillips RK. High versus low ligation of the inferior mesenteric artery in rectal cancer. Br J Surg 1990;77.

43. Gabriel WB, Dukes C, Bussey HJ. Lymphatic spread in cancer of the rectum. Br J Surg 1935; 23:395–413.

44. Harvey HD, Auchincloss H. Metastases to lymph nodes from carcinomas that were arrested. Cancer 1968;21:684–91.

45. Morgan CN. The comparative results and treatment for cancer of the rectum. Postgrad Med 1959; 26:135–41.

46. Roufett F, Hay J-M, Vacher B, et al. Curative resection for left colonic carcinoma: hemicolectomy vs segmental colectomy. A prospective, controlled, multi-center trial. Dis Colon Rectum 1994; 37:651–9.

47. Fielding LP, Stewart-Brown S, Blesovsky L, Kearney G. Anastomotic integrity after operations for large bowel cancer: a multi-center study. BMJ 1980;281:411–14.

48. Scher KS, Scott-Conner C, Jones CW, Leach M. A comparison of stapled and sutured anastomoses in colonic operations. Surg Gynecol Obstet 1982;155:489–93.

49. Beart RW, Kelly KA. Randomized prospective evaluation of the EEA stapler for colorectal anastomoses. Am J Surg 1981;141.

50. Brennan SS, Pickford IR, Evans M, Pollock AV. Staples or sutures for colonic anastomoses. A controlled clinical trial. Br J Surg 1982;69:722–4.

51. McGinn FP, Gartell PC, Clifford PC, Brunton FJ. Staples or sutures for low colorectal anastomoses: a prospective randomized trial. Br J Surg 1985;72:603–5.

52. Everett WG, Friend PJ, Forty J. Comparison of stapling and hand-sutured for left sided large bowel anastomosis. Br J Surg 1986;73:345–8.

53. Didolkar MS, Reed WP, Elias EG, et al. A prospective randomized study of sutured versus stapled bowel anastomoses in patients with cancer. Cancer 1986;57:456–60.

54. Steichen FM, Ravitch MM. The healing of wounds of the intestines. In: Steichen FM, Ravitch MM, editors. Stapling in surgery. Chicago: Year Book Medical Publisher; 1984. p. 113–37.

55. Gritsman JJ. Mechanical suture by Soviet apparatus in gastric resection: use in 4000 operations. Surgery 1966;59:663–9.

56. Reiling RB, Reiling WA Jr, Bernie WA, et al. Prospective controlled study of gastrointestinal stapled anastomoses. Am J Surg 1980;139:147–52.

57. Dziki AJ, Duncan MD, Harmon JW, et al. Advantages of handsewn over stapled bowel anastomosis. Dis Colon Rectum 1991;34:442–8.

58. Hurst PA, Prout WG, Kelly JM, et al. Local recurrence after low anterior resection using the staple gun. Br J Surg 1982;69:275–6.

59. Anderberg B, Enblad P, Sjodahl R, Wetterfors J. Recurrent rectal carcinoma after anterior resection and rectal stapling. Br J Surg 1994;71:98–100.

60. Reid JDS, Robins RE, Atkinson KG. Pelvic recurrence after anterior resection and EEA stapling anastomosis for potentially curable carcinoma of the rectum. Am J Surg 1984;147:629–32.

61. Bisgaard C, Svanholm H, Jensen AS. Recurrent carcinoma after low anterior resection of the rectum using the EEA staple gun. Acta Chir Scand 1986;152:157–60.

62. Docherty JG, McGregor JR, Akyol M, et al. Comparison of manually constructed and stapled anastomoses in colorectal surgery. Ann Surg 1995;221:176–84.

63. Malthaner RA, Hakki FZ, Saini N, et al. Anastomotic compression button: a new mechanical device for sutureless bowel anastomosis. Dis Colon Rectum 1990;33:291–7.

64. Sagar PM, Kruegener G, Macfie J. Nasogastric intubation and elective abdominal surgery. Br J Surg 1992;79:1127–31.

65. Savassi-Rocha PR, Conceicao SA, Ferreira JT, et al. Evaluation of the routine use of nasogastric tube in digestive operation by a prospective controlled study. Surg Gynecol Obstet 1992;174:317–20.

66. Nathan BN, Pain JA. Nasogastric suction after elective abdominal surgery: a randomized study. Ann R Coll Surg Engl 1991;73:291–4.

67. Michowitz M, Chen J, Waizbard E, Bawnik JB. Abdominal operations without nasogastric tube decompression of the gastrointestinal tract. Am Surg 1988;54:672–5.

68. Cunningham J, Temple WJ, Langevin JM, Kortbeek J. A prospective randomized trial of routine postoperative nasogastric decompression in patients with bowel anastomosis. Can J Surg 1992; 35:629–32.

69. Petrelli NJ, Stulc JP, Rodriguez-Bigas M, Blumenson L. Nasogastric decompression following elective colorectal surgery: a prospective randomized study. Am Surg 1993;59:632–5.

70. Bauer JJ, Gelernet IM, Salky BA, Kreel I. Is routine postoperative nasogastric decompression really necessary? Ann Surg 1985;201:233–6.

71. Jamieson WG, Derose G, Harris KA. Routine nasogastric decompression after abdominal surgery? Can J Surg 1992;35:577–8.

72. Wolff BG, Pemberton JH, van Heerden JA, et al. Elective colon and rectal surgery without nasogastric decompression: a prospective, randomized trial. Ann Surg 1989;209:670–5.

73. Otchy DP, Wolff BG, van Heerden JA, et al. Does the avoidance of nasogastric decompression following elective abdominal colorectal surgery affect the incidence of incisional hernia? Results of a prospective, randomized trial. Dis Colon Rectum 1995;38:604–8.

74. Binderow SR, Cohen SM, Wexner SD, Nogueras JJ. Must early postoperative oral intake be limited to laparoscopy? Dis Colon Rectum 1994;37:584–9.

75. Reissman P, Teoh TA, Cohen SM, et al. Is early oral feeding safe after colorectal surgery? A prospective randomized trial. Ann Surg 1995;222:73–7.

76. Coffey RJ, Richards JS, Remmert CS, et al. An introduction to critical paths. Quality management in health care. Vol. Fall, 1992:45–54.

77. Doyle RL. Inpatient and surgical care. In: Milliman R, editor. Healthcare management guidelines. Vol. I: Radnor; 1995:2:17–18.

78. Schoetz DJJ, Bockler M, Rosenblatt MS, et al. "Ideal" length of stay after colectomy. Whose ideal? Dis Colon Rectum 1997;40:806–10.

79. Copeland GP, Jones D, Wilcox A, Harris PL. Comparative vascular audit using the POSSUM scoring system. Ann R Coll Surg Engl 1993;75:175–7.

80. Copeland GP. The variability of surgical outcome. Colonews 1994;3:1–3.

81. Sagar PM, Hartley MN, Mancey-Jones B, et al. Comparative audit of colorectal resection with the POSSUM scoring system. Br J Surg 1994;81:1492–4.

82. Copeland GP, Sagar PM, Brennan J, et al. Risk-adjusted analysis of surgeon performance: a 1 year study. Br J Surg 1995;82:408–11.

83. Copeland GP, Jones D, Walters M. POSSUM: a scoring system for surgical audit. Br J Surg 1991; 78:355–60.

84. Sagar PM, Hartley MN, MacFie J, et al. Comparison of individual surgeon's performance. Risk-adjusted analysis with POSSUM scoring system. Dis Colon Rectum 1996;39:654–8.

85. Rosen L, Stasik JJ Jr, Reed JF III, et al. Variations in colon and rectal surgical mortality. Comparison of specialties with a state-legislated database. Dis Colon Rectum 1996;39:129–35.

86. Tang DG, Bowman HM, Gordon TA, et al. Case volume and outcomes in resection for colorectal carcinoma. Surgical Forum Paper 1998;49:559–61.

87. Del Guercio LRM, Cohn JD. Monitoring operative risk in the elderly. JAMA 1980;243:1350–5.

88. Greenburg AG, Saik RP, Coyle JJ, Peskin GW. Mortality and gastrointestinal surgery in the aged: elective vs emergency procedures. Arch Surg 1981;116:788–91.

89. Ondrula DP, Nelson RL, Prasad ML, et al. Multi-factorial index of preoperative risk factors in colon resections. Dis Colon Rectum 1992;35:117–22.

90. Wise WEJ, Padmanabhan A, Meesig DM, et al. Abdominal colon and rectal operations in the elderly. Dis Colon Rectum 1991;34:959–63.

91. Soper NJ, Brunt LM, Kerbl K. Laparoscopic general surgery. N Engl J Med 1994;330:409–19.

92. Phillips EH, Franklin M, Carroll BJ, et al. Laparoscopic colectomy. Ann Surg 1992;216:703–7.

93. Falk PM, Beart RW Jr, Wexner SD, et al. Laparoscopic colectomy: a critical appraisal. Dis Colon Rectum 1993;36:28–34.

94. Wade TP, Comitalo JB, Andrus CH, et al. Laparoscopic cancer surgery: lessons from gallbladder cancer. Surg Endosc 1994;8:698–701.

95. Jacobi C, Keller HW, Said S. Implantation metastasis of unsuspected gallbladder carcinoma after laparoscopy [abstract]. Br J Surg 1994;81(Suppl):82.

96. Lord SA, Larach SW, Ferrara A, et al. Laparoscopic resections for colorectal carcinoma: a three-year experience. Dis Colon Rectum 1996;39:148–54.

97. Franklin ME Jr, Ramos R, Rosenthal D, Schuessler W. Laparoscopic colonic procedures. World J Surg 1993;17:51–6.

98. Lumley JW, Fielding GA, Rhodes M, et al. Laparoscopic-assisted colorectal surgery: lessons learned from 240 consecutive patients. Dis Colon Rectum 1996;39:155–9.

99. Cirocco WC, Schwartzman A, Golub RW. Abdominal wall recurrence after laparoscopic colectomy for colon cancer. Surgery 1994;116:842–6.

100. Wexner SD, Cohen SM, Ulrich A, Reissman P. Laparoscopic colorectal surgery—are we being honest with our patients? Dis Colon Rectum 1995;38:723–7.

101. Wexner SD, Cohen SM. Port site metastases after laparoscopic colorectal surgery for cure of malignancy. Br J Surg 1995;82:295–8.

102. Ortega AE, Beart BW Jr, Steele GD Jr, et al. Laparoscopic bowel surgery registry: preliminary results. Dis Colon Rectum 1995;38:681–6.

103. Zucker KA, Pitcher DE, Martin DT, Ford RS. Laparoscopic-assisted colon resection. Surg Endosc 1994;8:12–18.

104. Hoffman G, Baker J, Claiborne F, Vansant J. Laparoscopic-assisted segmental colectomy: initial experience. Ann Surg 1994;219:732–43.

105. Mathis CR, MacFadyn BV. Laparoscopic colorectal resection: a review of the current experience. Int Surg 1994;79:221–5.

106. Dean P, Beart RW, Nelson H, et al. Laparoscopic-assisted segmental colectomy: early Mayo experience. Mayo Clin Proc 1994;69:834–40.

107. Alexander R, Jaques B, Mitchell K. Laparoscopically-assisted colectomy and wound recurrence. Lancet 1993;341:250–94.

108. Walsh D, Wattchow D, Wilson T. Subcutaneous metastases after laparoscopic resection of malignancy. Aust N Z J Surg 1993;63:563–5.

109. O'Rourke N, Price PM, Kelly S, Sikora K. Tumor inoculation during laparoscopy. Lancet 1993;342:368.

110. Guillou PJ, Darzi A, Monson JR. Experience with laparoscopic colorectal surgery for malignant disease. Surg Oncol 1993;2(Suppl 1):43–9.

111. Wexner SD, Cohen S. Laparoscopic colectomy for malignancy: advantages and limitations. Surg Clin North Am 1994;3:637–43.

112. Gleeson NC, Nicosia SV, Mark JE, et al. Abdominal wall metastases from ovarian cancer after laparoscopy. Am J Obstet Gynecol 1993;169:522–3.

113. Pomeranz AA, Garlack JH. Postoperative recurrence of cancer of the colon due to desquamated malignant cells. JAMA 1955;20:1434–46.

114. Skipper D, Jeffrey MJ, Cooper AJ, et al. Enhanced growth of tumor cells in healing colonic anastomoses and laparotomy wounds. Int J Colorect Dis 1989;4:172–7.

115. Thomas CG. Tumor cell contamination of the surgical wound (experimental and clinical observations). Ann Surg 1961;153:697–705.

116. Umpleby HC, Fermor B, Symes MO, Williamson RC. Viability of exfoliated colorectal carcinoma cells. Br J Surg 1984;71:659–63.

117. Jones DB, Guo LW, Reinhard MK, et al. Impact of pneumoperitoneum on trocar site implantation of colon cancer in hamster model. Dis Colon Rectum 1995;38:1182–8.

118. Hughes ES, McDermott FT, Polglase AL, Johnson WR. Tumor recurrence in the abdominal wall scar tissue after large-bowel cancer surgery. Dis Colon Rectum 1983;26:571–2.

119. Reilly WT, Nelson H, Schroeder G, et al. Wound recurrence following conventional treatment of colorectal cancer: a rare but perhaps underestimated problem. Dis Colon Rectum 1996;39:200–7.

120. Edoute Y, Malberger E, Lachter J, Toledano O. Fine needle aspiration cytology of abdominal wall scar lesions for diagnosing recurrent colorectal cancer. J Clin Gastroenterol 1991;13:463–4.

121. Earls JP, Colon-Negron E, Dachman AH. Colorectal carcinoma in young patients: CT detection of an atypical pattern of recurrence. Abdom Imaging 1994;19:441–5.

122. Berends FJ, Kazemier G, Bonjer HJ, Lange JF. Subcutaneous metastases after laparoscopic colectomy [letter]. Lancet 1994;344:58.

123. Lauroy J, Champault G, Risk N, Boutelier P. Metastatic recurrence at the cannula site: should digestive carcinomas still be managed by laparoscopy? [abstract]. Br J Surg 1994;81(Suppl):31.

124. Hoffman GC, Baker JW, Doxey JB, et al. Minimally invasive surgery for colorectal cancer. Initial follow-up. Ann Surg 1996;223:790–8.

125. Kwok SPY, Lau WY, Carey PD, et al. Prospective evaluation of laparoscopic-assisted large bowel excision for cancer. Ann Surg 1996;223:170–6.

126. Ramos JM, Gupta S, Anthone GJ, et al. Laparoscopy and colon cancer. Is the port site at risk? A preliminary report. Arch Surg 1994;129:897–9.

127. Prasad A, Avery C, Foley FJE. Abdominal wall metastases following laparoscopy [letter]. Br J Surg 1994; 81:1697.

128. Vukasin P, Ortega AE, Greene FL, et al. Wound recurrence following laparoscopic colon cancer resection. Results of the American Society of Colon and Rectal Surgeons Laparoscopic Registry. Dis Colon Rectum 1996;39:S20–S23.

129. Fleshman JW, Nelson H, Peters WR, et al. Early results of laparoscopic surgery for colorectal cancer. Retrospective analysis of 372 patients treated by clinical outcomes of surgical therapy (Cost) study group. Dis Colon Rectum 1996;39:S53–S58.

130. Franklin MEJ, Rosenthal D, Abrego-Medina D, et al. Prospective comparison of open vs laparoscopic colon surgery for carcinoma. Five-year results. Dis Colon Rectum 1996;39:S35–S46.

131. Simons AJ, Anthone GJ, Ortega AE, et al. Laparoscopic-assisted colectomy learning curve. Dis Colon Rectum 1995;38:600–3.

132. Senagore AJ, Luchtenfeld MA, MacKeigan JM, Mazier WP. Open colectomy versus laparoscopic colectomy: are there differences? Am Surg 1993;59:549–53.

133. Senagore AJ, Luchtenfeld MA, MacKeigan JM. What is the learning curve for laparoscopic colectomy? Am Surg 1995;61:681–5.

134. Wishner JD, Baker JW Jr, Hoffman GC, et al. Laparoscopic-assisted colectomy: the learning curve. Surg Endosc 1995;9:1179–83.

135. Agachan F, Joo JS, Weiss EG, Wexner SD. Intraoperative laparoscopic complications. Are we getting better? Dis Colon Rectum 1996;39:S14–S19.

136. Agachan F, Gilliland R, Joo JS, et al. The impact of experience on the outcome of laparoscopic colorectal surgery over four years [abstract]. Surg Endosc 1996;10:219.

137. Peters WR, Bartels TL. Minimally invasive colectomy: are the potential benefits realized? Dis Colon Rectum 1993;36:751–6.

138. Monson JRT, Darzi A, Carey PD, Guillou PJ. Prospective evaluation of laparoscopic-assisted colectomy in an unselected group of patients. Lancet 1992;340:831–3.

139. Wexner SD, Reissman P, Pfeifer J, et al. Laparoscopic colorectal surgery: analysis of 140 cases. Surg Endosc 1996;10:133–6.

140. Larach SW, Patankar SK, Ferrara A, et al. Complications of laparoscopic colorectal surgery: analysis and comparison of early vs latter experience. Dis Colon Rectum 1997;40:592–6.

141. Reissman P, Cohen S, Weiss EG, Wexner SD. Laparoscopic colorectal surgery: ascending the learning curve. World J Surg 1996;20:277–82.

142. Larach SW, Ferrara A. Cost analysis. In: Jager RM, Wexner, SD, editors. Laparoscopic colorectal surgery. New York: Churchill-Livingston; 1996. p. 321–3.

143. Pfeifer J, Wexner SD, Reissman P, et al. Laparoscopic vs open colon surgery. Costs and outcome. Surg Endosc 1995;9:1322–6.

144. Davies W, Kollmergen CF, Tu QM, et al. Laparoscopic colectomy shortens postoperative ileus in a canine model. Surgery 1997;121:550–5.

145. Surgeons ASoCaR. Policy Statement. Dis Colon Rectum 1992;35(1):5A.

146. Surgeons SoAGE. The American Society of Colon and Rectal Surgeons. Approved statement on laparoscopic colectomy. Dis Colon Rectum 1994;37:6.

147. Surgeons SoAGE. Granting of privileges for laparoscopic general surgery. Am J Surg 1991;161:324–5.

148. Nelson H, Weeks JC, Wieand HS. Proposed phase III trial comparing laparoscopic-assisted colectomy versus open colectomy for colon cancer. J Natl Cancer Inst Monogr 1995;19:51–6.

CHAPTER 23

Rectal Carcinoma

Mark J. Ott, MD, and Michael A. Choti, MD, FACS

The array of treatment choices facing the clinician managing rectal cancer is greater than that for most surgical diseases. Surgical treatment options can vary from radical transabdominal operations to local excision. Newer techniques are being applied to reduce the necessity for permanent colostomy, improve functional results, and reduce local recurrence. Multimodality treatment strategies, including preoperative neoadjuvant and postoperative adjuvant therapy, are being advocated more commonly. Changing treatment algorithms in this disease make evidence-based management particularly important.

Rectal carcinoma accounts for an annual mortality rate of approximately 77,000 patients worldwide and, combined with colon cancer, is the third most common cause of cancer deaths, behind lung and stomach cancers.[1] In the United States, the incidence rate of colorectal cancer has declined from a high of 53 per 100,000 people in 1985 to 44 per 100,000 in 1994.[2] This decrease has occurred mainly among white people, although rates for African Americans may finally be declining as well. Similarly, mortality from colorectal cancer has declined by 25 percent for women and 13 percent for men in the United States over the past 20 years. Although reasons for the improved statistics in this disease are unclear, changes in lifestyle as well as improved screening and removal of premalignant polyps are likely contributory.

HISTORICAL PERSPECTIVE

The first attempts at surgical treatment of rectal cancer were palliative in nature. Pillore in France performed the first diverting colostomy for an obstructing rectal cancer in 1776.[3] Lisfranc is credited with the first successful resection of a rectal cancer in 1826 via a perineal approach.[4] Kraske in Germany in 1885 championed the removal of the coccyx and portions of the sacrum to improve exposure and perform a primary anastomosis.[5] Using this perineal approach in 1926, Lockhart-Mummery reported a series of 200 patients with an operative mortality of 8.5 percent and a 5-year survival rate of 50 percent.[6] This technique was commonly performed for the treatment of rectal cancer even as late as the 1940s.

In 1908, Sir Ernest Miles was the first to successfully perform a radical resection of rectal cancer using a combined transabdominal and perineal approach.[7] More important than his contribution of the surgical procedure, Miles detailed the route of lymphatic spread and emphasized the importance of a complete resection—removing surrounding tissue distally, laterally, and proximally. There were 5 deaths in his first series of 12 patients. The high mortality seen with this initial report limited the acceptance of the abdominoperineal resection (or "Miles procedure") until improved long-term survival was apparent and further reports demonstrated acceptable perioperative mortality.

The first anterior resection of a rectal tumor with anastomosis was performed in 1897 by Harrison Cripps.[8] Balfour and William Mayo popularized the anterior resection with primary anastomosis for rectosigmoid tumors, using a two-layer anastomosis over a rubber tube that was left in place for 6 days as a stent.[9] It took approximately 30 years before Dixon demonstrated that an end-to-end anastomosis could be safely performed without an internal tube.[10,11] This is one example of how a surgical practice can be propagated solely on the basis of traditional surgical teaching and without any evidence to support its use.

A more recent advance, the end-to-end circular stapling device, was introduced into the United States in 1975.[12] As refinements in the instrumentation occurred and familiarity with the device increased, its role in low rectal surgery became common practice. Many surgeons felt that it facilitated low anastomoses that were otherwise difficult to hand-suture from the anterior approach. A prospective randomized study by Beart and colleagues in 1981 with 35 patients per group demonstrated that the stapled anastomosis was at least equal to the hand-sewn technique.[13] They felt that there were an additional 10 patients (12%) whose anastomoses technically could not have been performed with hand-suturing techniques and that the circular stapler contributed to sphincter preservation. In an analysis of the National Surgical Adjuvant Breast and Bowel Projects (NSABP [R-01]), long-term survival was no different in patients undergoing low anterior resection with hand-sutured versus stapled anastomoses.[14] Although newer hand-sewn colo-anal techniques are being applied to some anastomoses near the dentate line, stapling devices have clearly contributed greatly to the surgical management of rectal cancer.[15,16]

By the early 1980s, the surgical techniques of low anterior resection with primary anastomosis and abdominoperineal resection were the main forms of curative therapy for rectal cancer. The choice of which operation was appropriate was based on the ability to resect the tumor with adequate distal and lateral margins. As early as 1950, it was pointed out by Best and colleagues that mucosal involvement ≥ 2 cm below the distal edge of the lesion was found in < 1 percent of cases.[17] Despite this, the classic teaching of a 5-cm distal rectal mucosal margin beyond the tumor was propagated in most surgical texts for another 35 years. This concept was called into question by several retrospective studies that demonstrated that there was no benefit to be had in metastatic disease or local control from bowel margins > 2 cm.[18,19] There was a further analysis of the NSABP (R-01) trial, showing no difference in recurrence between resections with distal margins > 3 cm versus those within 2 cm.[20]

Similarly, the proximal extent of the lymphatic dissection has historically been a point of contention. While there are no prospective randomized studies, several nonrandomized studies would support including the nodal tissue up to the bifurcation of the left colic from the inferior mesenteric artery. Division of the artery just distal to this bifurcation preserves the left colic blood supply and has not been followed by any survival disadvantage relative to a more extensive proximal lymphadenectomy of periaortic nodes with ligation of the inferior mesenteric artery at its origin. In a retrospective study from St. Mark's Hospital (London, England), 784 patients had ligation distal to the left colic, and 586 patients had resection of the inferior mesenteric artery with accompanying nodal tissue. There were no differences in 5-year survival rates for any Dukes' A, B, or C patients.[21] In a series by Hojo and colleagues, in which they routinely performed more extensive lymphadenectomy, there was only one survivor among 15 patients who had pathologically positive nodes along the inferior mesenteric artery.[22] These uncontrolled studies lend support to the practice of resecting proximal nodal tissue up to and including the origin of the superior hemorrhoidal artery and preserving the inferior mesenteric artery.

THERAPEUTIC CONTROVERSIES

Total Mesorectal Excision

Traditionally, much of the pelvic dissection below the peritoneal reflection for rectal cancer was performed in a blunt fashion. This method of dissection was rapid, and it identified lateral tissue containing vascular, lymphatic, and nervous tissue that was then divided between clamps. In 1982, Heald published his first description of dissection of the mesorectum in a

Table 23–1 Local and Total Recurrence Rates for Total Mesorectal Excision and NCCTG Data[24]

Treatment Group	Local Recurrence (%)	Overall Recurrence (%)
TME	5.0	22.0
Conventional surgery + radiation	25.0	62.7
Conventional surgery + radiation + chemotherapy	13.5	41.5

TME = total mesorectal excision, NCCTG = North Central Cancer Treatment Group.

sharp fashion.[23] This technique, often called total mesorectal excision (TME), involves sharp dissection between the parietal and visceral planes of the endopelvic fascia.

Since his original description, Heald has published several updates of his personal, prospectively collected, consecutive nonrandomized series of patients. His excellent results with local recurrence rates of < 5 percent and overall recurrence at 10 years of 22 percent in curatively operated patients has provoked intense discussions about the true merit of this more time- and labor-intensive technique. In 1993, MacFarlane updated and published an independent analysis of this series of 290 patients, and an evidence-based analysis of that article provides an excellent forum in which to discuss the merits of TME.[24]

The study covered a 13-year period from 1978 to 1991, with a mean follow-up of 7.5 years. Of the 290 patients, 135 "high-risk" patients whose cancers were most likely to recur after curative resection constituted the main group for analysis (Tables 23–1 and 23–2). There were 126 low anterior resections (LARs) and 9 abdominoperineal resections (APRs) in this group. High risk was defined according to Krook's definition from the North Central Cancer Treatment Group (NCCTG).[25] These investigators excluded Dukes' A (Astler Coller A + B1) lesions, those > 12 cm from the anal verge, and those considered "not curative" by the surgeon. The operation was considered curative when, at the end of the procedure, the surgeon believed that all grossly detectable cancer had been removed. Particularly important, none of these patients received adjuvant therapy. This reflected a long-term opinion of Heald's that improved survival and local control could be achieved by optimal surgery alone. This was an obvious divergence from the recommendations of the 1990 National Institutes of Health (NIH) consensus conference, where the combination of radiation therapy and chemotherapy was recommended as the standard of care for stage II and III disease.[26]

In support of Heald's claim that TME alone was superior to standard surgical resection plus adjuvant therapy, the authors then compared their results to the data from the NCCTG study, a prospective randomized study covering the same approximate time period. As can be seen from Table 23–1, Heald's results were superior for both local and overall recurrence. While both studies addressed "high-risk" patients, they are certainly not a good match, as the

Table 23–2 Preoperative Radiation Therapy (Swedish Rectal Cancer Trial)[45]

Study Group	5-year Overall Survival (%)	9-year Disease-Specific Survival (%)	Local Recurrence (%)
Preoperative RT 25 Gy, 5 fractions	58	74	11
Surgery alone	48($p = .004$)	65($p = .002$)	27($p < .001$)

RT = radiation therapy.

NCCTG study had twice as many Dukes' C as Dukes' B patients whereas Heald's group was composed of more Dukes' B than Dukes' C patients. Also, patients in the NCCTG study had a high percentage of nondiploid tumors, and few were well differentiated. Tumor ploidy and differentiation are not included in Heald's study although he comments on their being significant indicators of recurrence. These studies therefore address significantly different patient populations and should not be compared.

The improved local and distant control of selected rectal cancers with TME is not without its costs. The meticulous dissection requires additional operative time of up to 2.5 hours and increased blood transfusion requirements. There is an 11 percent clinical and a 6.4 percent radiologic leak rate with TME. This has lead to Heald's routine use of a temporary diverting colostomy. Due to complications, 5 percent of these colostomies are never reversed. In a group of 350 patients undergoing TME in Norway, the anastomotic leak rate was > 20 percent, leading to emergency surgery, morbidity, and two deaths.[4] Similarly, in a study of 79 unselected consecutive patients at the Queen Elizabeth Hospital (Gateshead, United Kingdom), surgeons who were trained in TME and who preferred to perform it found that only 59 percent of the patients were appropriate for TME.[27] These authors had a 16 percent rate of anastomotic leaks and likewise employed fecal diversion routinely. They had an 11 percent rate of local recurrence, and only 66 percent of their patients underwent potentially curative surgery. Follow-up, still early, has been disappointing, with only 63 percent of the patients still alive.

The functional results of TME have also been put forward, with preservation of autonomic nerve function as one of its major benefits. The standard blunt dissection technique with clamping of the lateral pedicles undoubtedly has resulted in numerous unintended injuries to the pelvic autonomic nerve plexus. This has in turn resulted in alterations of sexual function, urinary, and bowel functions. Unfortunately, Heald emphasized the benefits of sharp dissection with preservation of autonomic nerves, but he provided no objective data in his publications to actually demonstrate a difference.

Based on a variety of retrospective and prospective uncontrolled studies, it appears that surgical technique for rectal cancer resection does have a significant impact on recurrence rates. A survey by Hermanek and colleagues determined rectal cancer outcomes in seven major German cities, showing that local recurrence rates varied among individual surgeons from < 10 percent to > 50 percent.[28,29] A classic study by Quirke and colleagues demonstrated the importance of radial margin clearance.[30] In this prospective series of 52 patients with rectal adenocarcinoma, careful whole-mount sectioning of abdominoperineal resection specimens revealed spread to the lateral margins in 14 patients (27%). Twelve of these patients (85%) developed a local recurrence. Only 1 of 38 patients (3%) with negative radial margins developed a local recurrence. Sharp dissection employed in TME to excise the entire mesorectum reproducibly provides a maximal intact lateral resection margin and may explain the beneficial effects on local control.

This surgical approach remains controversial. Determining true differences in long- and short-term outcomes between TME and a more limited mesorectal resection can only be accomplished with a randomized trial. No such study has been or likely will be done. Most surgeons who practice this procedure would feel it unethical to alter their technique. Others believe that the total mesorectal excision is the technique they have always performed. Even when based on these nonrandomized reported series, it is likely that more meticulous dissection with wide nodal excision leads to a reduction in local recurrence rates. At present, this is the best available data. Future trials evaluating the role of adjuvant therapies will need to account for variations in surgical technique that can impact long-term outcomes.

Local Excision of Rectal Cancer

The surgeon's goal in treating rectal cancer is curative resection of the tumor with minimal morbidity and mortality. Sometimes, the best operation for this is a local excision by a transanal, transcoccygeal, or transsphincteric approach. Proper selection of patients is the key factor. Ideal rectal tumors for this approach are below the peritoneal reflection, < 4 cm in diameter, take up < 40 percent of the rectal circumference, have no palpable or radiologically visible perirectal nodes, are mobile on digital examination, and have a well-differentiated histology.[31,32] It is imperative that the surgical resection achieves a negative margin and a full-thickness excision. Otherwise, therapy is inadequate, and further surgical therapy is indicated. Despite the best preoperative staging presently available, the status of lymphatic involvement is often uncertain. This has important implications as lymph node involvement has the single greatest impact on survival and is present in 40 to 60 percent of patients treated by surgery alone.[33,34] Thus, the decision to pursue local resection (where lymph nodes are generally not removed) versus transabdominal resection (where lymph nodes are resected) can often be problematic. When a patient is a potential candidate for local resectional therapy (tumor confined to mucosa, submucosa, or muscularis propria), tumor biopsy information in terms of tumor grade and evidence of lymphatic or vascular invasion can be very important. Patients with poorly differentiated tumors and evidence of lymphatic or vascular invasion on biopsy have a 36 to 53 percent rate of local recurrence after local resections alone versus a 12 to 15 percent rate of local recurrence after transabdominal resection.[35] Clearly, the histology information should be used in conjunction with pretreatment staging information in deciding on an appropriate therapy. Usually, postoperative radiation and chemotherapy are also given for T2 and T3 lesions. The two prospective series that have looked at this form of therapy indicate a local recurrence rate of 6.5 to 8 percent and a survival rate of 90 percent, which equals the expected results of an abdominoperineal resection.[36,37] Rectal function is reported as good or satisfactory in > 80 percent of the patients.

Adjuvant Therapy

Both randomized and nonrandomized trials have studied the role of radiation therapy with and without chemotherapy, administered either postoperatively or preoperatively. There are certain theoretic advantages to preoperative radiation therapy. Radiation injury to the small bowel may be reduced if radiation is administered before surgery. Long-term bowel function following low anterior resection may be improved when the rectum is irradiated prior to resection. Finally, patients who initially are felt to be candidates only for abdominoperineal resection may achieve a response sufficient to perform sphincter-preserving surgery following treatment. The disadvantages of preoperative therapy include the lack of definitive histologic confirmation of the tumor stage prior to therapy and the potential for overtreatment of patients with early-stage disease.

Postoperative radiation therapy alone has been evaluated in three randomized trials.[38–41] All three demonstrated a decreased rate of pelvic recurrence, but no study demonstrated a statistically significant improvement in overall or disease-free survival. Preoperative radiation therapy alone has been evaluated in four randomized trials, three of which showed a reduction in local but not distant recurrence.[42–45] One trial (the Swedish Rectal Trial[45]) demonstrated an improved survival in the preoperative radiation therapy group (see Table 23–2).

Combination chemoradiation therapy has the advantage of potentially affecting both local and distant recurrence. Moreover, chemotherapy may act as a radiosensitizer, potentially improving the efficacy of radiation therapy. Several large randomized trials examining postoperative combination therapy have demonstrated improvement in both overall and disease-free survival as well as improvement in local control.[38,46,47] Preoperative multimodality therapy has been studied less. In one randomized trial (EORTC) using preoperative 5-fluorouracil with radiation therapy, no benefit was found (Table 23–3).[48]

The preponderance of evidence, primarily based on prospective randomized trials, suggests a benefit of combination radiation and chemotherapy in some patients with rectal cancer. Variability in the type, duration, and sequencing of the regimens in these trials has limited the ability to draw definite conclusions about the optimal therapy. In most of these

Table 23–3 Randomized Trials of Combined Chemoradiation Therapy for Rectal Cancer

Trial	Patients (n)	Study Groups	5-yr Survival (%)	Local Recurrence (%)	Distant Recurrence (%)
Postoperative Therapy					
GITSG(1985)[46]	202	Surg	46	24	34
		Surg + RT	52	20	30
		Surg + Chemo[†]	56	27	27
		Surg + RT + Chemo[†]	58*	11	26
NSABP R-01 (1988)[38]	555	Surg	43	25	26
		Surg + RT	—	16	—
		Surg + RT + Chemo[‡]	53*	21	27
NCCTG (1991)[47]	204	Surg + RT	47	25	46
		Surg + RT + Chemo[†]	58*	14*	29*
Preoperative Therapy					
EORTC (1984)[48]	247	Surg + RT	59	15	—
		Surg + 5-FU	46	15	—

RT = radiation therapy; GITSG = Gastrointestinal Tumor Study Group; EORTC = European Organization for Research and Treatment of Cancer; NCCTG = North Central Cancer Treatment Group; NSABP = National Surgical Adjuvant Breast and Bowel Projects.

* $p < .05$

† 5-FU (5-fluorouracil) and MeCCNU (methyl chlorethyl-cyclohexyl-nitrosourea).

‡ MeCCNU, Oncovin, and 5-FU.

studies, moreover, local recurrence rates in groups treated with surgery alone were 20 to 30 percent, far higher than the 5 to 10 percent rates seen in more recent series employing wide mesorectal excision.

FUTURE AREAS OF INVESTIGATION

Substantial progress in the treatment of rectal cancer has occurred over the past 100 years and especially in the past 2 decades. Excellent surgery is at the heart of any curative regimen. Total mesorectal excision has shown promise in achieving local control and possibly increased survival. However, this premise has not been tested or proved, and it should be the basis of a prospective randomized clinical trial of Dukes' B and C patients. Since these patients are the ones with proven benefit from chemoradiation therapy, chemoradiation therapy should be included for both the standard blunt dissection group and the TME group. There is a small group of investigators who might argue for a surgery-only arm, but this would not be justifiable.

Other areas of ongoing investigation include the proper timing, combination, and amount of chemoradiation therapy. Numerous prospective randomized trials are ongoing, and their results should be available within the next 5 years.

Central to evidence-based research in the area of rectal cancer is the participation of surgeons and their patients in these studies. If surgeons are unwilling to subject their personal beliefs to rigorous investigation, it will be difficult to convince patients to participate in the advancement of their care.

REFERENCES

1. World Health Organization. World Health Report 1997. Available from:URL: http://www.who.ch/whr/1997/factse.html.

2. American Cancer Society. Cancer Facts and Figures. Available from:URL: http://www.cancer.org/statistics/cff98/selectedcancers.html.

3. Dinnick T. The origins and evolution of colostomy. Br J Surg 1934–35;22:142–54.

4. Lisfranc M. Cancer of the lower part of the rectum (E). Lancet 1827;1:10.

5. Rankin FW. How surgery of the colon and rectum developed. Surg Gynecol Obstet 1937;64:705–10.

6. Lockhart-Mummery JP. Two hundred cases of cancer of the rectum treated by perineal excision. Br J Surg 1926;14:110–24.

7. Miles WE. A method of performing abdomino-perineal excision for carcinoma of the rectum and of the terminal portion of the pelvic colon. Lancet 1908;2:1812–3.

8. Cripps WH. On diseases of the rectum and anus. 4th ed. London: Churchill; 1914.

9. Balfour DC. A method of anastomosis between sigmoid and rectum. Ann Surg 1910;51:239–41.

10. Dixon CF. Surgical removal of lesions occurring in the sigmoid and rectosigmoid. Am J Surg 1939;46:12–7.

11. Dixon CF. Anterior resection for carcinoma low in the sigmoid and rectosigmoid. Surgery 1944;15:367–77.

12. Fain SN, Patin CS, Morgenstern L. Use of mechanical suturing apparatus in low colorectal anastomosis. Arch Surg 1975;110:1079–82.

13. Beart RW, Kelly KA. Randomized prospective evaluation of the EEA Stapler for colorectal anastomoses. Am J Surg 1981;141:143–7.

14. Wolmark N, Fisher B. An analysis of survival and treatment failure following abdominoperineal and sphincter-saving resection in Dukes' B and C rectal carcinoma. Ann Surg 1986;204:480–9.

15. Moritz E, Achleitner D, Holbling N, et al. Single vs. double stapling technique in colorectal surgery. Dis Colon Rectum 1991;34:495–7.

16. Griffen FD, Knight CD, Whitaker JM, Knight CD Jr. The double stapling technique for low anterior resection. Ann Surg 1990;211:745–52.

17. Best, RR. Rectosigmoidectomy with anastomosis in carcinoma of rectum and rectosigmoid. J Int Coll Surg 1950;13:203–8.

18. Hojo K. Anastomotic recurrence after sphincter-saving resection for rectal cancer: length of distal clearance of the bowel. Dis Colon Rectum 1986;29:11–4.

19. Pollett WG, Nicholls RJ. The relationship between the extent of distal clearance and survival and local recurrence rates after curative anterior resection for carcinoma of the rectum. Ann Surg 1983;198:159–63.

20. Wolmark N, Fisher B. An analysis of survival and treatment failure following abdominoperineal and sphincter-saving resection in Dukes' B and C rectal carcinoma. Ann Surg 1986;204:480–9.

21. Pezim ME, Nicholls RJ. Survival after high or low ligation of the inferior mesenteric artery during curative surgery for rectal cancer. Ann Surg 1984;200:729–33.

22. Hojo K, Koyama Y, Moriya Y. Lymphatic spread and its prognostic value in patients with rectal cancer. Am J Surg 1982;144:350–4.

23. Heald RJ, Husband EM, Ryall RDH. The mesorectum in rectal cancer surgery—the clue to pelvic recurrence? Br J Surg 1982;69:613–16.

24. MacFarlane JK, Ryall RDH, Heald RJ. Mesorectal excision for rectal cancer. Lancet 1993;341:457–60.

25. Krook JE, Moertel CG, Gunderson LL, et al. Effective surgical adjuvant therapy for high risk rectal carcinoma. N Engl J Med 1991;324:709–15.

26. National Institutes of Health. Consensus Conference. Adjuvant therapy for patients with colon and rectal cancer. JAMA 1990;264:1444–50.

27. Hainsworth PJ, Egan MJ, Cunliffe WJ. Evaluation of a policy of total mesorectal excision for rectal and rectosigmoid cancers. Br J Surg 1997;84:652–6.

28. Hermanek P, Wiebelt H, Staimmer D, Riedl S. Prognostic factors of rectum carcinoma—experience of the German multicenter study SGCRC. German study group colo-rectal carcinoma. Tumori 1995;81:60–4.

29. Hermanek P, Hohenberger W. The importance of volume in colorectal cancer surgery. Eur J Surg Oncol 1996;22:213–5.

30. Quirke P, Durdey P, Dixon MF, Williams NS. Local recurrence of rectal adenocarcinoma due to inadequate surgical resection. Lancet 1986;2:996–9.

31. Breen E, Bleday R. Preservation of the anus in the therapy of distal rectal cancers. Surg Clin North Am 1997;77:71–83.

32. Tanaka S, Yokota T, Saito D, et al. Clinicopathologic features of early rectal carcinoma and indications for endoscopic treatment. Dis Colon Rectum 1995;38:959–63.

33. Dukes C, Bussey H. The spread of rectal cancer and its effect on prognosis. Br J Cancer 1958;12:309–20.

34. Gabriel W, Dukes C, Bussey H. Lymphatic spread in cancer of the rectum. Br J Surg 1935;23:395–413.

35. Willett C, Compton C, Shellito P, Efird J. Selection factors for local excision or abdominoperineal resection of early stage rectal cancer. Cancer 1994;73:2716–20.

36. Bleday R, Breen E, Jessup JM, et al. Prospective evaluation of local excision for small rectal cancers. Dis Colon Rectum 1997;40:388–92.

37. Ota D, Skibber J, Rich T. M. D. Anderson Cancer Center experience with local excision and multi-modality therapy for rectal cancer. Surg Oncol Clin N Am 1992;1:147–52.

38. Fisher B, Wolmark N, Rockette H, et al. Postoperative adjuvant chemotherapy or radiation therapy for rectal cancer: results from NSABP protocol R-01. J Natl Cancer Inst 1988 Mar 2;80(1):21–9.

39. Duttenhaver JR, Hoskins RB, Gunderson LL, Tepper JE. Adjuvant postoperative radiation therapy in the management of adenocarcinoma of the colon. Cancer 1986 Mar 1;57(5):955–63.

40. Treurniet-Donker AD, van Putten WL, Wereldsma JC, et al. Postoperative radiation therapy for rectal cancer. An interim analysis of a prospective, randomized multicenter trial in the Netherlands. Cancer 1991 Apr 15;67(8):2042–8.

41. Rosenthal SA, Trock BJ, Coia LR. Randomized trials of adjuvant radiation therapy for rectal carcinoma: a review. Dis Colon Rectum 1990;33(4):335–43.

42. Goldberg PA, Nicholls RJ, Porter NH, Love S, Grimsey JE. Long-term results of a randomized trial of short-course low-dose adjuvant preoperative radiotherapy for rectal cancer: reduction in local treatment failure. Eur J Cancer 1994;30A(11):1602–6.

43. Cedermark B, Johansson H, Rutqvist LE, Wilking N, for the Stockholm Colorectal Cancer Study Group. The Stockholm I trial of preoperative short term radiotherapy in operable rectal carcinoma. A prospective randomized trial. Cancer 1995 May 1;75(9):2269–75.

44. Gerard A, Buyse M, Nordlinger B, et al. Preoperative radiotherapy as adjuvant treatment in rectal cancer. Final results of a randomized study of the European Organization for Research and Treatment of Cancer (EORTC). Ann Surg 1988;208(5):606–14.

45. Swedish Rectal Cancer Trial. Improved survival with preoperative radiotherapy in resectable rectal cancer. N Eng J Med 1997;336(14):980–7.

46. Gastrointestinal Tumor Study Group. Prolongation of the disease-free interval in surgically treated rectal carcinoma. N Engl J Med 1985 Jun 6;312(23):1465–72.

47. Krook JE, Moertel CG, Gunderson LL, et al. Effective surgical adjuvant therapy for high-risk rectal carcinoma. N Engl J Med 1991 Mar 14;324(11):709–15.

48. Boulis-Wassif S, Gerard A, Loygue J, et al. Final results of a randomized trial on the treatment of rectal cancer with preoperative radiotherapy alone or in combination with 5-fluorouracil, followed by radical surgery. Trial of the European Organization on Research and Treatment of Cancer Gastrointestinal Tract Cancer Cooperative Group. Cancer 1984;53(9):1811–8.

CHAPTER 24

Hepatobiliary Surgery

Herbert J. Zeh III, MD, Michael A. Choti, MD, Helen Bowman Miller, MS
and Henry A. Pitt, MD, FACS

Evidence-based medicine is the conscientious, explicit and judicious use of current best evidence in making decisions about the care of individual patients.[1] The practice of evidence-based surgery entails integrating clinical expertise with the best available external clinical evidence to generate guidelines for the treatment of individual patients. The area of complex hepatobiliary surgery deserves particular attention when applying the practice of evidence-based surgery because these surgical procedures are technically demanding, are frequently associated with significant morbidity and mortality, and have a great impact on the patient's quality of life. The development of evidence-based clinical guidelines in complex hepatobiliary surgery has been impeded by the relatively low volume of these procedures. The inability of many single institutions to achieve population samples of sufficient size to attain statistical validity has led to a paucity of randomized clinical trials. Consequently, many clinical decisions are based on limited retrospective data or small single-institution trials.

A variety of hepatobiliary procedures are performed, including locally ablative procedures such as hepatic arterial pump placement, hepatic artery embolization, cryosurgery, laparoscopic cholecystectomy, and common duct exploration. However, this chapter will focus on two of the more common complex hepatobiliary procedures: (1) liver resections for malignant disease, and (2) hepaticojejunostomy. For both of these procedures, clinically important questions will be identified, and the evidence supporting current clinical practice will be reviewed. Case studies will be provided to illustrate how the literature may be used to improve evidence-based clinical guidelines. Finally, recommendations on directions for future research that would improve evidence-based practice for complex hepatobiliary procedures will be identified.

LIVER RESECTION

A more accurate understanding of liver structure, based on functional/segmental anatomy as well as improvements in operative technique and perioperative care, has resulted in the ability to perform liver resections with low morbidity and mortality. The first successful hepatic resection of metastatic colon carcinoma was reported by Cattell in 1940.[2] Since that time, acceptance of this approach for treating malignant liver tumors has increased. Currently, the two most common tumors of the liver treated by resection are metastatic colon cancer and primary hepatocellular cancer. Metastases from colorectal cancer account for a majority of the elective liver resections performed for malignant disease in the United States today.

Approximately 15 to 20 percent of patients with primary colorectal cancer will have hepatic metastases at the time of presentation.[3] Another 50 percent of those patients, who undergo curative resection of their primary tumors, will subsequently develop metastases to the liver. The natural history of these patients is poor, with few untreated patients surviving beyond 3 years.[4,5] Autopsy studies indicate that approximately one-third of the patients who die from metastatic colorectal cancer have disease isolated to the liver.[6] In some cases in which disease is isolated to the liver, surgical resection has been associated with prolonged survival.[7]

Hepatocellular carcinoma (HCC) accounts for the bulk of the remaining liver resections for malignant disease. Hepatocellular carcinoma is one of the most common gastrointestinal malignancies worldwide, yet its incidence in the United States is considerably lower, with only 6,000 new cases expected annually.[8] Although advances have been made over the past several years in other local and regional therapies for the treatment of HCC, liver resection remains the single most effective treatment when it can be performed safely.[9]

Important Clinical Questions

In developing evidence-based clinical guidelines for the surgical treatment of primary or metastatic liver cancer, three important clinical questions should be answered:

1. What is the evidence to support the long-term efficacy (survival) of surgical resection of colorectal metastases or HCC?
2. What are the short-term costs (morbidity and mortality) associated with liver resection?
3. What prognostic factors exist to predict who will benefit from this procedure?

Review of Clinical Evidence

Prospective randomized clinical trials comparing liver resection to systemic chemotherapy or best supportive therapy for metastatic colorectal cancer have not been performed. Many retrospective reviews and case-control studies have provided compelling evidence that surgery alone is associated with prolonged survival and even cure.[10–18] Wilson and colleagues compared the survival of 60 patients who were resected to 60 patients with comparable disease burden who had only biopsies performed. No patients survived in the biopsy group whereas 25 percent of the resection group survived 5 years.[10] Similarly, Scheele and colleagues compared 183 resected patients with 62 patients who were judged to be resectable but who did not undergo resection; they reported a 38 percent 5-year actuarial survival in the resected group, with no 5-year survivors in the unresected group.[12] In a multi-institution study of 852 patients with liver resection, Hughes and colleagues reported an overall 5-year survival of 32 percent and a disease-free survival of 27 percent.[19] Several other series have reported 30 to 40 percent 5-year survival in carefully selected patients (Table 24–1).[13–18,20] In a single nonrandomized prospective study of patients with colorectal liver metastases, Steele and colleagues observed a statistically significant improvement in survival in those patients undergoing curative resection versus noncurative resection.[21] Retrospective trials of systemic chemotherapy, including 5-fluorouracil and leucovorin, demonstrate response rates of 20 to 35 percent, but

Table 24–1 Results of Hepatic Resection for Colorectal Metastases

Author	No. of Patients	Operative Mortality (%)	5-year Survival (%)
Hughes et al[19] (1988)	607	—	33
Schlag et al[26] (1990)	122	4	30
Doci et al[13] (1991)	100	5	30
Rosen et al[14] (1992)	280	4	25
Scheele et al[15] (1990)	434	4	39
Furhman et al[16] (1995)	107	3	44
Taylor et al[17] (1997)	123	0	34
Fong et al[18] (1997)	456	3	46

the duration of response is limited, and few if any patients survive in the long term.[22–25] Based on these largely retrospective or nonrandomized studies, it is now accepted that hepatic resection is the only potentially curative therapy for patients with hepatic metastases from colorectal cancer.

The perioperative mortality for elective liver resection for metastatic colorectal cancer has been reported to be 3 to 5 percent in most recent series (see Table 24–1). The risk of death is positively correlated with the extent of resection in most of these series. Despite low mortality rates, morbidity following liver resection for metastatic disease remains high, with 20 to 30 percent major complication rates.[13,16, 26] The most common complications include liver failure, bile leak, biliary fistula, and abscess formation.

Surgical resection results in prolonged survival and cure in certain patients with colorectal liver metastases; however, the majority of patients still do not benefit from these procedures. Thus, in developing evidence-based clinical guidelines for the application of hepatectomy to metastatic colorectal cancer, it is important to examine factors that may predict which patients will benefit the most from attempted resection. Several retrospective studies have examined this question.[14,18,19,20,27] Prognostic factors can be divided into four categories: (1) patient-related factors such as performance status and comorbidities; (2) features of the primary tumor, including size and stage; (3) features of the metastatic disease, including size and number of metastases, and; (4) technical factors, such as the ability to obtain adequate margins. Although many of these features have been associated with a worse prognosis, current clinical practice recommendations are that the only contraindications to attempted resection are periportal lymphadenopathy, unresectable extrahepatic disease, or inability to completely resect all of the liver disease.[28]

As with metastatic colorectal cancer to the liver, hepatic resection is currently favored as the most effective therapy for the treatment of HCC, based largely on retrospective data,[9,29–36] yet the efficacy of partial hepatectomy is even more difficult to substantiate, based on these studies. Total hepatectomy with orthotopic liver transplantation has been shown to have comparable survival in select cases.[9] In addition, other locally ablative therapies such as intratumoral ethanol injection can result in prolonged survival in some uncontrolled studies.[37–40] These results vary largely because long-term survival is related as much to associated cirrhosis (present in many of these patients) as to progression of malignant disease. Short-term outcomes following resection for HCC have been examined in several retrospective series.[34,35,41–45] In particular, the presence of cirrhosis is significantly associated with increased perioperative mortality and morbidity.[30] Resection in the presence of even mild cirrhosis increases mortality twofold to threefold.[9,45,46] Patients with more severe cirrhosis are often not considered for partial hepatectomy due to the historically high perioperative mortality rates. Prognostic factors that predict improved long-term survival following resection for HCC are based largely on retrospective series. They include absence of vascular invasion, absence of symptoms, solitary tumor, small tumor size, and favorable histology.[9,31–36]

The evidence supporting short-term and long-term efficacy for liver resection in malignant disease has resulted in a more aggressive surgical approach at many centers and an increased number of liver resections being performed each year.[6,45] However, as discussed above, the majority of the evidence supporting this strategy is based on single-institution series carried out at large tertiary referral centers. The surgical approach, extent of surgery, and presence of comorbid conditions in patients undergoing liver resection can greatly impact on the short- and long-term outcomes. To strengthen the evidence supporting current clinical guidelines for the application of liver resection, it would be important to know if these complex procedures can be performed with comparable safety at low-volume hospitals. Recently, an increasing number of studies have examined the relationship between clinical outcomes and hospital case volume for a variety of other surgical procedures. These studies have demonstrated that high-volume regional providers can deliver improved short-term outcomes at

Table 24–2 Description of Patient Characteristics by Provider Group for Liver Resections (n = 606)

Demographic Variable	High-Volume Provider n = 264	Low-Volume Providers n = 342	p-value
Age (mean years)	54.3	55.4	.45
Gender			
Male	50.4%	54.4%	.33
Female	49.6%	45.6%	
	100.0%	100.0%	
Race			
White	82.2%	67.3%	< .01
African-American	12.1%	27.5%	
Other	5.7%	5.3%	
	100.0%	100.0%	
Number of comorbidities			
0	72.0%	69.6%	.81
1	23.9%	25.7%	
≥ 2	4.2%	4.7%	
	100.1%	100.0%	

Percentages may not add up to 100 due to rounding.

lower costs than community hospitals.[47] Several reports have compared the outcomes of hepatic resections performed in high-volume centers to those performed in low-volume centers.[29,48,49] The majority of these studies have demonstrated overall lower morbidity, mortality, and cost when hepatic resection is performed at centers that perform a greater number of such procedures. The following case study is one example of this type of outcomes research.

Case Study: Should Hepatic Resections Be Performed at High-Volume Referral Centers?[48]

Recent outcomes research explores the hypothesis that patients treated by more experienced surgeons and institutions have better outcomes. In studies using administrative data, surgeon and hospital volume are often used as proxies for experience. Several recent studies have demonstrated a relationship between increased hospital case volume and improved clinical outcomes for a variety of medical and surgical procedures.[47,49–60] The publication detailed herein was the first to examine the relationship between outcomes and provider volume for hepatic resections.

Methods
Study Design
This cross-sectional analysis examined the relationships between provider volume and outcomes for patients who underwent hepatic resection in Maryland from January 1, 1990, through June 30, 1996. Information pertaining to hospital discharges was obtained from the Maryland Health Services Cost Review Commission (HSCRC). Its database includes records for every discharge from all 52 nonfederal acute care hospitals in Maryland. Case selection for the study was based on primary ICD-9 procedure codes 50.22 (partial hepatectomy) and 50.3 (hepatic lobectomy).[61]

Discharges were stratified into high- and low-volume provider groups (high volume was defined as more than 15 resections per year, low volume as 15 or fewer resections per year). The primary outcomes studied were average length of stay, average total hospital charges, and in-hospital mortality. Analysis was performed for the entire study population (606 procedures) and stratified separately by procedure and primary diagnosis. Procedures were grouped into minor (ICD-9 procedure code 50.22 [partial hepatectomy]) and major (ICD-9 code 50.3 [hepatic lobectomy]) liver resections. Primary diagnoses were grouped into primary liver cancer (ICD-9 codes 155.0 and 155.2), metastatic cancer (ICD-9 codes 153.0, 153.9, 154.0, 157.0, 157.4, 197.0, and 197.7), and all other diagnoses, which include liver resection for trauma, benign neoplasms, and infectious processes.

Statistical Analysis

Patient characteristics and comorbidities were examined by provider group to determine potential confounders using the chi-squared statistic for categorical variables and the Student's *t*-test for continuous variables (Table 24–2). The number of comorbidities was analyzed using the Dartmouth-Manitoba adaptation of the Charlson Comorbidity Index,[62,63] a validated index based on secondary diagnoses listed in the discharge abstracts.

Multiple linear regression models were performed to assess the relationship between hospital volume and average length of stay and average total charges, adjusting for age, race, gender, and the number of comorbidities. Since length of stay and total charge variables were not normally distributed, a natural log transformation was performed. All subsequent statistical analyses were performed on the transformed data. Poisson regression was used to examine the relationship between hospital volume and mortality, adjusting for age, race, gender, and the number of comorbidities.

Results

Overall Outcomes

For the 606 total discharges, the aggregate average length of stay was 13.0 days, the average total charges were $20,498, and the in-hospital mortality rate was 5.1 percent. Although the unadjusted average length of stay and hospital charges did not differ between provider groups, the unadjusted hospital mortality was 1.5 percent in the high-volume group compared to a 7.9 percent mortality in the low-volume group (Table 24–3). The adjusted average length of stay was less at the low-volume providers (11.1 vs 9.8 days, $p < .05$), with no difference in total charges. However, relative risk of mortality was 5.2 times higher at the low-volume providers compared to the high-volume provider ($p < .01$). Adjusted outcomes are also shown in Table 24–3.

Outcomes by Procedure and Diagnosis

Of the liver resections, 62 percent were minor resections and 38 percent were major resections. Resource use was significantly higher among patients who underwent major resection; length of stay was nearly 5 days longer on average, while charges were $9,000 higher (see Table 24–3). In-hospital mortality was 3.7 percent for minor resections compared to 7.3 percent for major liver resections ($p = ns$). When outcomes were compared by procedure and provider group, both the average length of stay and total charges for minor resections only were less at the low-volume providers compared to the high-volume provider after case-mix adjustment (see Table 24–3). Differences between provider groups were not statistically significant for major resections. However, the adjusted relative risk of mortality remained higher at the low-volume providers for both minor and major resections (minor: relative risk = 5.3, $p < .05$; major: relative risk = 4.4, $p = .05$) (Figure 24–1).

Eighteen percent of patients underwent resection for primary liver cancer. Resection was performed for metastatic cancer in 47 percent of patients, and 33 percent of resections were performed for other diagnoses, including trauma, benign tumors, and infection. Hepatic resection for primary liver cancer was associated overall with significantly longer length of stay, average total charges, and in-hospital mortality compared to resection for metastatic cancer (Table 24–4). Both unadjusted and adjusted average length of stay and hospital charges did not differ between low- and high-volume providers when examined by primary diagnosis. There was a

Table 24-3 Liver Resection: Unadjusted and Adjusted* Averages for Outcomes of Interest by Procedure and Provider Groups

Procedure	Average Length of Stay			Average Total Charge			Mortality(%)		Relative Risk of Mortality	
	High-Vol	Low-Vol	p-value**	High-Vol	Low-Vol	p-value**	High-Vol	Low-Vol	Low- vs High-Volume	p-value**
Unadjusted										
All procedures	12.7	13.2	0.15	17,923.49	22,485.254	0.49	1.5	7.9	5.21	< 0.01
Minor(partial hepatectomy)	11.7	10.8	< 0.01	16,340.23	17,747.56	0.08	1.1	6.1	5.33	0.03
Major(≤ hepatic lobectomy)	14.9	16.6	0.98	21,090.02	28,999.56	0.02	2.3	10.4	4.58	0.04
Adjusted*										
All procedures	11.1	9.8	0.02	15,434.80	15,326.42	0.90	na	na	5.20	< 0.01
Minor(partial hepatectomy)	10.4	8.4	< 0.01	14,730.56	12,425.31	< 0.01	na	na	5.25	0.03
Major(hepatectomy)	12.8	11.9	0.56	17,127.41	20,318.97	0.08	na	na	4.37	0.05

*Regression models are adjusted for age, gender, race, and number of comorbidities. Linear regression models for average length of stay and average total charge, Poisson regression models for mortality.

**All p-values are from regression models.

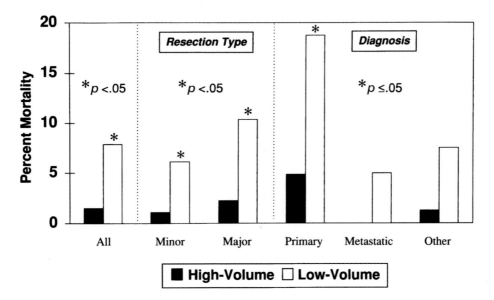

Figure 24–1 Mortality by type of hospital (high volume or low volume), type of procedure (minor or major), and type of disease (primary, metastatic, or other). (Adapted from Choti M, Bowman H, Pitt H, et al. Should hepatic resections be performed at high-volume referral centers? Gastrointest Surg 1998;2:11–19.)

nonstatistical trend toward a higher relative risk of mortality at the low-volume providers compared to the high-volume providers for all three diagnosis categories (see Table 24–4).

Discussion

This study suggests that hepatic resections performed at a high-volume center are associated with improved safety and similar total charges compared to resections performed at low-volume hospitals. The same trend was seen regardless of extent of liver resection or primary diagnosis. The reason for the improved results at the high-volume center is likely multifactorial and may reflect increased expertise associated with larger numbers of procedures performed by experienced surgeons, anesthesia staff, nurses, and other support staff.

Major liver resections were associated with an overall higher resource use and increased mortality risk compared to minor resections. Although one might expect a greater difference in outcomes between high- and low-volume providers with major liver resections than with minor liver resections, this study found significantly decreased mortality at the high-volume provider regardless of extent of resection.

Liver resection for primary hepatic malignancy was associated with overall worse outcomes than resection for metastatic disease. This finding is not unexpected given the often associated cirrhosis and other comorbidities in patients with hepatocellular carcinoma. Although the present study demonstrated improved crude in-hospital mortality at the high-volume center for patients undergoing resection for both primary and metastatic cancer, when adjusted, the mortality trend was toward a greater risk at the low-volume providers but did not differ significantly between provider groups.

This study has several limitations. Because only one hospital was included in the high-volume group, observed differences may not necessarily be related to volume alone but may be associated with variables not analyzed. This single center is a large academic institution with a house staff, facilities, and referral patterns not seen in many community hospitals. However, provider groups were divided in such a way because the greatest difference in volume was seen with this relative distribution of patients and hospitals.

Table 24–4 Liver Resection: Unadjusted and Adjusted* Averages for Outcomes of Interest By Diagnosis and Provider Groups

Diagnoses	Average Length of Stay			Average Total Charge			Mortality(%)		Relative Risk of Mortality	
	High-Vol	Low-Vol	p-value**	High-Vol	Low-Vol	p-value**	High Vol	Low-Vol	Low vs High-Volume	p-value**
Unadjusted										
Primary liver malignancy	14.8	15.4	0.09	20,312.83	26,848.67	0.70	4.9	18.8	3.81	0.05
Metastatic malignancy	11.6	11.4	0.88	17,273.92	17,603.39	0.68	0.0	5.0	> 10.00	0.99
All other diagnoses	13.0	14.6	0.63	17,095.89	26,751.30	0.42	1.3	7.5		
Adjusted										
Primary liver malignancy	13.3	10.9	0.15	18,184.93	18,505.02	0.90	na	na	2.88	0.14
Metastatic malignancy	10.1	9.5	0.31	14,445.41	14,137.53	0.76	na	na	10.00	—
All other diagnoses	10.8	9.8	0.39	14,854.96	15,925.39	0.53	na	na	5.92	0.09

*Regression models are adjusted for age, gender, race, and number of comorbidities. Linear regression models for average length of stay and average total charge, Poisson regression models for mortality.

**All p-values are from regression models.

A second limitation is that only in-hospital clinical outcomes were measured. Clearly, postdischarge deaths, re-admissions, and quality of life could not be examined using this administrative data set. In addition, coding problems with such an administrative data set may oversimplify the complexity of the hepatic resection. Stratification by procedure type (major vs minor) attempted to account for extent of liver resection, but other unknown features of the surgical procedure may significantly impact on outcome variables. In summary, these data lend support for the referral of patients for liver resection to high-volume centers. As with other complex surgical procedures, these operations are costly and carry a relatively high risk of in-hospital death. Studies such as this help to identify those procedures best suited for triage of patients to high-volume centers.

Conclusion and Future Directions

The preponderance of current evidence supports the long-term and short-term efficacy of liver resection for select patients with metastatic colorectal cancer. More recent evidence suggests that these procedures may be delivered most efficaciously at high-volume referral centers. Given the weight of the evidence, randomized trials examining the efficacy of surgery versus systemic chemotherapy or best supportive care are unlikely to gain much support. Another area of active outcomes research is in the use of adjuvant chemotherapy following resection for metastatic colorectal cancer, including regional chemotherapy. Several randomized trials looking at this question are ongoing. Early single-institution trials have suggested some improvement with this strategy; however, more definitive studies will be necessary before firm recommendations can be made. Future trials will also examine the short-term and long-term outcomes of nonsurgical local and regional treatment strategies for the treatment of hepatocellular cancer (eg, the efficacy of ethanol ablation vs surgical resection). The role of ablative procedures such as cryotherapy and radiofrequency also needs further study. Given the low numbers of each of these procedures performed at a single institution, multi-institution randomized trials will most likely be necessary to clearly demonstrate improved efficacy.

COMPLEX BILIARY SURGERY
Bilioenteric Diversion

The introduction of modern anesthetic and antisepsis techniques in the later 1800s led to tremendous advances in the surgical treatment of diseases of the biliary tract. Cholecystostomy, followed quickly by cholecystectomy, rapidly became the mainstay of care of patients with gallstone disease. However, these advances were accompanied by surgical complications. Complications such as biliary fistula and strictures as well as the need to treat malignant biliary obstruction necessitated new surgical techniques to reroute or divert the biliary stream. The first attempt at decompressing the biliary tree consisted of cholecystoenterostomy. Early techniques focused on the suturing of the gallbladder initially to the colon and later to the duodenum or jejunum. The introduction and widespread acceptance of cholecystectomy in the treatment of biliary stone disease stimulated the development of the choledochoenterostomy.[64]

Although Langenbuch first suggested in 1884 that choledochoenterostomy could be performed, high mortality limited its acceptance.[65] Not until 1913, when Franz Sasse described 11 successful operations, was choledochoenterostomy considered an operation with acceptable morbidity and mortality.[66] In 1900, Pendl introduced the retrocolic cholecystojejunostomy. This technique was later modified by Monprofit and Dahl to include the use of a Roux-en-Y segment of jejunum to achieve a tension-free bilioenteric anastomosis.[67–69]

Currently, either choledochojejunostomy-hepaticojejunostomy or cholecystojejunostomy is used for decompression of the obstructed distal biliary system. The most common reason for performing surgical bilioenteric diversion is malignant obstruction of the common bile duct from unresectable tumors of the head of the pancreas, ampulla of Vater, distal common bile duct, or duodenum. Malignant obstructive jaundice results in progressive liver dysfunction and eventually overt liver failure. The symptoms associated with progressive obstructive jaundice (including pruritus, anorexia, nausea, and malnutrition) are unpleasant and particularly difficult to palliate medically.

Important Clinical Questions

Patients presenting with malignant biliary obstruction are extremely diverse and vary greatly in their prognosis, performance status, and overall medical condition. Not all patients may benefit from surgical intervention. Less invasive methods of palliating malignant biliary obstruction include percutaneously or endoscopically placed biliary stents. In developing evidence-based clinical guidelines for the application of surgical bilioenteric bypass, one must consider several important questions:

1.   What are the short-term and long-term outcomes associated with surgical bilioenteric bypass?
2.   What are the short-term and long-term outcomes associated with alternative therapies?
3.   Have any studies directly compared the two approaches?
4.   Which surgical approach (choledochojejunostomy or cholecystojejunostomy) is associated with the best results?

Review of Clinical Evidence

Several retrospective reviews have clearly demonstrated the efficacy of surgical bilioenteric bypass, with successful relief of jaundice in more than 90 percent of patients.[70–73] Overall short-term morbidity and mortality rates have been acceptable yet generally higher than with nonoperative techniques.[74] Nonoperative decompression of the biliary tree in malignant biliary obstruction, by either percutaneous or endoscopic stent placement, is also an extremely effective therapy (> 90% success rate) and is associated with minimal morbidity and mortality.[70,75,76] Several prospective randomized trials comparing nonoperative biliary stenting with surgical decompression for patients with malignant biliary obstruction have been performed (Table 24–5). These studies have shown that surgical and nonoperative approaches are equally effective. However, in each of these trials, the nonoperative approach was associated with significantly lower procedure-related complications and length of hospitalization. In three of the four studies, short-term mortality was also lower for nonoperative techniques[77–80] (11% vs 18%).[71–80] However, surgical decompression in these studies, while associated with slightly higher morbidity and mortality, was found to be significantly better at relieving jaundice in the long term (17% vs 38%). One criticism is that the surgical mortality rates in these trials were considerably higher than those reported from several tertiary care institutions.[71–73]

Other issues to consider when weighing the evidence are the other associated benefits of surgical exploration. Duodenal obstruction can develop in some patients and can be prevented by surgical gastroenterostomy. In several retrospective studies, the rate of duodenal obstruction requiring additional surgical bypass in this patient population has been reported to be from 13 to 17 percent.[70,71,81] Further benefits include the alleviation of severe pain by celiac block at the time of exploration.[82]

As previously described, choledochojejunostomy and cholecystojejunostomy are both currently accepted surgical options for patients with distal biliary obstruction. Some surgeons favor cholecystojejunostomy because of its convenience whereas others believe that the cystic duct and gallbladder are not reliable conduits. Several retrospective trials examining the outcomes of these two alternatives have demonstrated conflicting results.[70,81] In a single-institution trial, Sarfeh and colleagues randomized 50 patients with either malignant or benign distal biliary obstruction to either choledochojejunostomy or cholecystojejunostomy. While overall

Table 24–5 Randomized Trials Comparing Nonoperative versus Operative Palliation of Malignant Biliary Obstruction

Author	Bornman[79]		Shepard[77]		Anderson[78]		Dowsett[80]	
	Stent	*Surgery*	*Stent*	*Surgery*	*Stent*	*Surgery*	*Stent*	*Surgery*
Success (%)	84	76	82	92	96	88	94	94
Complications (%)	28	32	30	56	36	20	23	50
30-day mortality (%)	8	20	9	20	20	24	6	15
Recurrent jaundice/ cholangitis (%)	38	16	30	0	0	0	17	3
Gastric outlet obstruction (%)	14	0	9	4	0	0	14	3

operative time and blood loss was less in the cholecystoenterostomy group, nine bypasses failed after cholecystoenterostomy versus only two after choledochoenterostomy. This difference was statistically significant. Thus, this study and several of the retrospective series support the superiority of choledochoenterostomy in malignant distal biliary obstruction.

As with hepatic resection, the majority of evidence supporting the short- and long-term efficacy of bilioenteric bypass comes from retrospective analysis from tertiary referral centers and a few prospective randomized studies. However, the underlying diagnosis (benign vs malignant) and the type of procedure (hepatico- or choledochojejunostomy vs cholecystojejunostomy) as well as the presence of comorbid conditions can significantly influence short- and long-term outcomes. Again, hospital and surgeon volume may be factors in outcomes such as length of hospital stay, hospital costs, and mortality.

Thus, a recent analysis compared the outcomes at a high-volume academic medical center (AMC) with medium-, low-, and minimal-volume hospitals in the same state.[83] This analysis reviewed three 3-year periods, the first two before and the last after the implementation of a clinical pathway designed to control costs. These same authors further analyzed surgeon-specific data from the AMC for 3 years before and after implementation of the clinical pathway.[84] The results of these complementary case studies are further examples of outcomes research.

Case Study: Can the Cost of Complex Biliary Surgery Be Contained at an Academic Medical Center? [83]

Academic medical centers with special expertise in complex surgery have been considered to be more expensive providers of health care than community hospitals. This study was undertaken to determine whether the development of a clinical pathway for complex biliary anastomotic procedures at an AMC would reduce the length of stay and hospital charges without compromising the high quality of care as measured by hospital mortality.

Methods

Publicly available hospital discharge data were obtained from patients who underwent biliary anastomoses between 1988 and 1996 at the AMC and all other Maryland hospitals. The hospitals were classified according to their annual volume of complex biliary surgery as high- (> 25 procedures), medium- (9 to 25), low- (4 to 8), and minimal-volume (< 4) providers. Patients were included in the study if they underwent a cholecysto-, hepatico-, choledocho-, or "other" enterostomy (ICD-9 codes 51.32, 51.36, 51.37, and 51.39, respectively) as either a

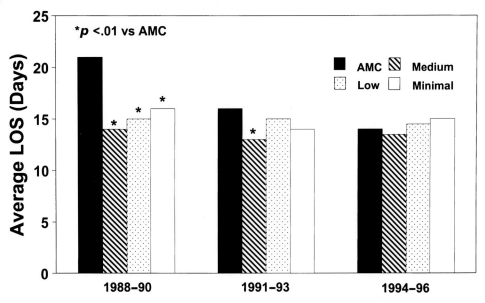

Figure 24–2A Length of hospital stay for three time periods by hospital volume provider. (LOS = length of stay; AMC = academic medical center). (Adapted from Bowman HM, Sosa JA, Pitt HA, et al. The cost of complex biliary surgery can be contained at an academic medical center. Surgery. [In press])

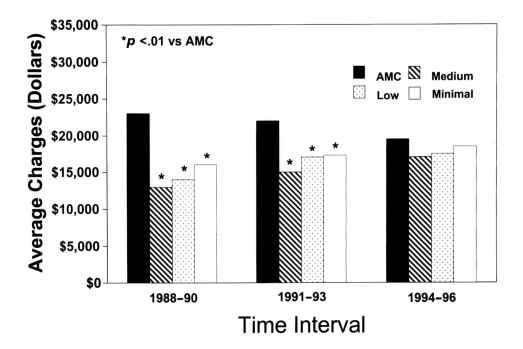

Figure 24–2B Hospital charges for three time periods by hospital volume provider. (AMC = academic medical center). (Adapted from Bowman HM, Sosa JA, Pitt HA, et al. The cost of complex biliary surgery can be contained at an academic medical center. Surgery. [In press])

Methods

Pre- and postoperative length of stay, hospital charges, and mortality were determined for 36 months (period 1) before and for two 18-month periods (periods 2 and 3) after implementation of a clinical pathway for hepaticojejunostomy. Three hundred two of the 339 operations (89%) were performed by four surgeons during this 6-year period. Outcomes data were provided to the surgeons 18 months after pathway implementation to determine whether further clinical practice improvement had occurred. Surgeon A performed 114 operations (34%); surgeon B performed 112 biliary bypass procedures (33%); surgeon C performed 47 operations (14%); and surgeon D performed 29 hepaticojejunostomies (9%).

Results

Total length of stay was 13.3 ± 0.9 days for period 1 compared to 12.5 ± 0.8 days for period 2 ($p =$ ns) and 10.1 ± 0.3 days for period 3 ($p < .03$ vs period 2) (Figure 24–4A). Surgeons A, B, and C each had statistically significant reductions in preoperative, postoperative, or total length of stay in period 3 compared to period 1. Surgeon D had the shortest patient length of stay before pathway implementation and also reduced length of stay (but not significantly) afterward. Hospital charges averaged $24,446 during period 1 compared to $23, 338 during period 2, and $20,240 during period 3 ($p < .01$ vs periods 1 and 2) (Figure 24–4B).

Discussion

The previous case study demonstrated that length of stay and hospital charges at an AMC improved during clinical pathway development. Multiple other clinical pathways had been implemented at the AMC during the 3 years before the pathway for hepaticojejunostomy. Thus, the surgeons involved were attuned to cost savings and excellence in quality of care. Interestingly, length of stay and hospital charges did not improve during the first 18 months

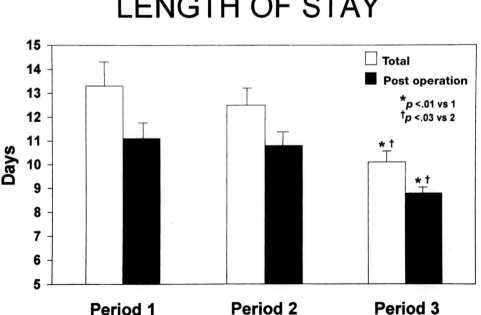

Figure 24–4A Length of hospital stay for periods 1 to 3. (Adapted from Pitt HA, Murray KP, Bowman HM, et al. Clinical pathway implementation improves outcomes for complex biliary surgery. Surgery 1999;126:751–6.

HOSPITAL CHARGES

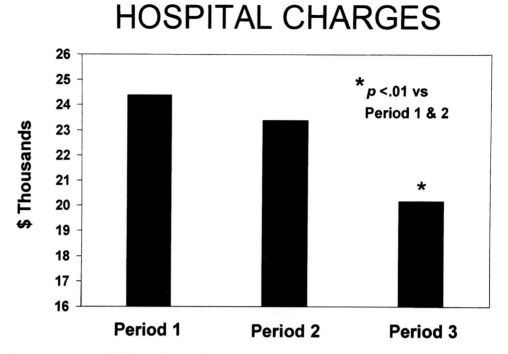

Figure 24–4B Hospital charges for periods 1 to 3. (Adapted from Pitt HA, Murray KP, Bowman HM, et al. Clinical pathway implementation improves outcomes for complex biliary surgery. Surgery. [In press])

after clinical pathway implementation. However, once the data were fed back to the surgeons, hospital stay and charges did decrease significantly ($p < .01$). Thus, the authors concluded that feedback of clinical pathway data was an effective method of controlling costs and achieving further clinical practice improvement at an AMC.

Conclusion and Future Directions

Firm clinical guidelines regarding operative versus nonoperative biliary decompression cannot be established on the basis of the mixed results of the current literature. Although most patients with malignant obstructive jaundice from unresectable tumors of the pancreas, ampulla of Vater, distal bile duct, or duodenum derive benefit from palliative biliary decompression, the best method of achieving this goal remains in question. The clinical approach to each patient must currently be individualized according to the patient's performance status, prognosis, and local institutional expertise. Future trials are necessary to better define those patients likely to benefit from surgical intervention. When surgical decompression is undertaken, current evidence suggests that the best results are achieved by hepatico- or choledochojejunostomy as opposed to cholecystojejunostomy. In addition, recent outcomes studies suggest that the best results for hepaticojejunostomy are achieved by high-volume surgeons at high-volume academic medical centers.

REFERENCES

1. Sackett D, Rosenberg W, Gray J, et al. Evidence based medicine: what it is and what it isn't. BMJ 1996;312:71–2.

2. Cattell R. Successful removal of liver metastasis from a carcinoma of the rectum. Lahey Clin Bull 1940;2:2–11.

3. Parker S, Tong T, Bolden S, Wingo P. Cancer statistics, 1997. Cancer 1997;47:5–6.

4. Bengmark S, Hafstrom L. The natural history of primary and secondary malignant tumors of the liver. I: the prognosis for patients with hepatic metastases from colonic and rectal carcinoma by laparotomy. Cancer 1969;23:198–202.

5. Wood C, Gillis C, Blumgart L. A retrospective study of the natural history of patients with liver metastases from colorectal cancer. Am J Surg 1996;2:285–8.

6. Fong Y, Blumgart L, Cohen A. Surgical treatment of colorectal metastases to the liver. CA Cancer J Clin 1995;45:50–62.

7. Fong Y, Kemeny N, Paty P, et al. Treatment of colorectal cancer: hepatic metastasis. Semin Surg Oncol 1996;12:219–52.

8. Tsai S-L, Liaw Y-F. Etiology and pathogenesis of hepatocellular carcinoma. Dig Surg 1995;12:7–15.

9. Marcos-Alvarez A, Jenkins R, Washburn K, et al. Multimodality treatment of hepatocellular carcinoma in a hepatobiliary specialty center. Arch Surg 1996;131:589–94.

10. Wilson S, Adson M. Surgical treatment of hepatic metastases from colorectal cancers. Arch Surg 1976;111:330–4.

11. Wagner J, Adson M, van Heerden J, et al. The natural history of hepatic metastases from colorectal cancer: a comparison with resection. Ann Surg 1984;199:502–8.

12. Scheele J, Stangle R, Altendorf-Hoffman A, et al. Indicators of prognosis after hepatic resection for colorectal secondaires. Surgery 1991;110:13–29.

13. Doci R, Gennari L, Bignami P, et al. One hundred patients with hepatic metastases from colorectal cancer treated by resection: analysis of prognostic determinants. Br J Surg 1991;77:1241–6.

14. Rosen C, Nagorney D, Taswell H, et al. Perioperative blood transfusion and determinants of survival after liver resection for colorectal metastases. Ann Surg 1992;216:492–505.

15. Scheele J, Stangle R, Altendorf-Hoffman A. Hepatic metastases from colorectal carcinoma: impact of surgical resection on natural history. Br J Surg 1990;77:1241–6.

16. Furhman G, Curley S, Hohn D, Roh M. Improved survival after resection of colorectal liver metastases. Ann Surg Oncol 1995;2:537–41.

17. Taylor M, Forster J, Langer B, et al. A study of prognostic factors for hepatic resection for colorectal metastases. Am J Surg 1997;173:467–71.

18. Fong Y, Cohen A, Fortner J, et al. Liver resection for colorectal metastases. J Clin Oncol 1997;15:938–46.

19. Hughes K, Rosenstein R, Songhorabodi S, et al. Resection of the liver for colorectal carcinoma metastases: a multiinstitutional study of long term survivors. Dis Colon Rectum 1988;31:1–4.

20. Resection of the liver for colorectal carcinoma metastases: a multiinstitutional study of indications for resection. Registry of Hepatic Metastases Surgery 1988;103:278–88.

21. Steele G, Bleday R, Mayer R, et al. A prospective evaluation of hepatic resection for colorectal carcinoma metastases to the liver: Gastrointestinal Tumor Study Group Protocol 6584. J Clin Oncol 1991;9:1105–12.

22. Ansfiels F, Schroeder J, Curreri A. Five years experience with 5-fluorouracil. JAMA 1962;181:295–300.

23. Lokich J, Ahlgren J, Gullo J, et al. A prospective randomized comparison of continuous infusion fluorouracil with a conventional bolus schedule in metastatic colorectal carcinoma: a mid-Atlantic oncology program study. J Clin Oncol 1989;7:425–32.

24. Leichman C, Fleming T, Muggia F, et al. Phase II study of fluorouracil and its modulation in advanced colorectal cancer: a Southwest Oncology Group Study. J Clin Oncol 1995;13:1303–11.

25. Petrelli N, Herrera L, Rustum Y, et al. A prospective randomized trial of 5-fluorouracil versus 5-fluorouracil and high dose leucovorin versus 5-fluorouracil and methotrexate in previously untreated patients with advanced colorectal carcinoma. J Clin Oncol 1987;5:1559–65.

26. Schlag P, Hohenberger P, Herfath C. Resection of liver metastases in colorectal cancer: competitive analysis of treatment results in synchronous vs. metachronous metastases. Eur J Surg 1990;16:360–5.

27. Registry of Hepatic Metastases Resection of the liver for colorectal metastases: a multi-institutional study of patterns of recurrence. Surgery 1986;100:278–84.

28. Choti M, Bulkley G. Management of metastatic disease. In: Schiff E, Sorrell M, Maddrey W, editors. Schiff's diseases of the liver. Philadelphia: Lippincott-Raven Publishers; 1999. p. 1319–33.

29. Nadig D, Wade T, Fairchild R, et al. Major hepatic resection. Arch Surg 1997;132:115–19.

30. Bismuth H, Chiche L, Castaing D. Surgical treatment of hepatocellular carcinomas in noncirrhotic liver: experience with 68 liver resections. World Surg 1995;19:35–41.

31. Kawasaki S, Makuuchi M, Miyagawa S. Resection of hepatocellular carcinoma associated with cirrhosis. Dig Surg 1995;12:40–4.

32. Takenaka K, Kawahara N, Yamaoto K, et al. Results of 280 liver resections for hepatocellular carcinoma. Arch Surg 1996;131:71–6.

33. Fuster J, Garcia-Valdecasas J, Grande L, et al. Hepatocellular carcinoma and cirrhosis: results of surgical treatment in a European series. Ann Surg 1996;223:297–302.

34. Tsao J, Loftus J, Nagorney D, et al. Trends in morbidity and mortality of hepatic resection for malignancy: a matched comparative analysis. Ann Surg 1994;220:199–205.

35. Vauthey JN, Klimstra D, Franceshi D, et al. Factors affecting long term outcome after hepatic resection for hepatocellular carcinoma. Am J Surg 1995;169:28–35.

36. Lee C, Sheu J, Wang M, Hsu H. Long term outcome after surgery for asymptomatic small hepatocellular carcinoma. Br J Surg 1996;83:330–3.

37. Lee M, Mueller P, Dawson S, et al. Percutaneous ethanol injection for the treatment of hepatic tumors: indications, mechanism of action, technique and efficacy. AJR Am J Roentgenol 1995;164:215–20.

38. Shiina S, Tagawa K, Unuma T, et al. Percutaneous ethanol injection therapy of hepatocellular carcinoma: analysis of 77 patients. AJR Am J Roentgenol 1990;155:1221–6.

39. Liveraghi T, Bolondi L, Lazzaroni S. Percutaneous ethanol injection in the treatment of hepatocellular carcinoma in cirrhosis: a study on 207 patients. Cancer 1992;69:925–9.

40. Ebara M, Ohto M, Sugiura N, et al. Percutaneous ethanol injection for the treatment of small hepatocellular carcinoma: study of 95 patients. J Gastroenterol Hepatol 1990;5:616–26.

41. Yamanaka N, Okamoto E, Oriyama T, et al. A prediction scoring system to select the surgical treatment of liver cancer: further refinement based on 10 years of use. Ann Surg 1994;219:342–6.

42. Miyagawa S, Nakuuchi M, Kawasaki S, Kakazu T. Criteria for safe hepatic resection. Am J Surg 1994;169:589–94.

43. Shmada M, Matsumata T, Akazawa K, et al. Estimation of risk of major complications after hepatic resection. Am J Surg 1994;167:399–403.

44. Haratake J, Takeda S, Kasai T. Predictable factors for estimating prognosis of patients after resection of hepatocellular carcinoma. Cancer 1996;72:1178–83.

45. Choi TK, Edward CS, Fan S, et al. Results of surgical resection for hepatocellular carcinoma. Hepatogastroenterology 1990;37:172–5.

46. Schwartz ME, Sung M, Mor E, et al. A multidisciplinary approach to hepatocellular carcinoma in patients with cirrhosis. J Am Coll Surg 1995;180:596–603.

47. Gordon TA, Burleyson G, Tielsch JM, Cameron JL. The effects of regionalization on cost and outcome for one general high risk procedure. Ann Surg 1995;221:43–9.

48. Choti M, Bowman H, Pitt H, et al. Should hepatic resections be performed at high-volume referral centers? Gastrointest Surg 1998;2:11–19.

49. Glasgow R, Showstack J, Katz P, et al. The relationship between hospital volume and outcomes of hepatic resection for hepatocellular carcinoma. Arch Surg 1999;134:30–5.

50. Luft H, Bunker J, Enthoven A. Should operations be regionalized: the empirical relation between surgical volume and mortality. N Engl J Med 1999;301:1364–9.

51. Luft H. The relation between surgical volume and mortality: an exploration of causal factors and alternative models. Med Care 1980;18:940–59.

52. Flood A, Scott W, Ewy W. Does practice make perfect? Part I: the relation between hospital volume and outcomes for selected diagnostic categories. Med Care 1984;22:98–114.

53. Flood A, Scott W, Ewy W. Does practice make perfect? Part II: the relation between volume and outcomes and other hospital characteristics. Med Care 1984;22:115–25.

54. Hannan E, Racz M, Ryan T, et al. Coronary angioplasty volume-outcome relationships for hospitals and cardiologists. JAMA 1997;277(11):892–8.

55. Grumbach K, Anderson G, Luft H, et al. Regionalization of cardiac surgery in the United States and Canada. JAMA 1995;274:1282–8.

56. Lieberman M, Kilburn H, Lindsey M, Brennan M. Relation of perioperative deaths to hospital volume among patients undergoing pancreatic resection for malignancy. Ann Surg 1995;222:638–45.

57. Gordon T, Burleyson G, Shahrokh S, Cameron JL. Cost and outcome for complex high-risk gastrointestinal surgical procedures. Surg Forum 1996;XLVII:618–20.

58. Hannan E, O'Donnell J, Kilburn H, et al. Investigation of the relationship between volume and mortality for surgical procedures performed in New York state hospitals. JAMA 1999;262:503–10.

59. Hannan E, Kilburn J, O'Donnell J, et al. A longitudinal analysis of the relationship between in-hospital mortality in New York state hospitals and the volume of abdominal aortic aneurysm surgeries performed. Health Serv Res 1999;27:518–42.

60. Showstack J, Rosenfeld K, Garnick D, et al. Association of volume with outcome of coronary artery bypass graft surgery: scheduled vs nonscheduled operations. JAMA 1987;257:785–9.

61. Medicode's International Classification of Diseases, Clinical Modification. 4th ed. 1995.

62. Charlson M, Pompei P, Ales K, Mackenzie C. A new method of classifying prognostic co-morbidity in longitudinal studies: development and validation. J Chronic Dis 1987;40:373–83.

63. Romano P, Roos L, Jollis J. Adapting a clinical co-morbidity index for use with ICD-9-CM administrative data: differing perspectives. J Clin Epidemiol 1999;46(10):1075–9.

64. Ahrendt S, Pitt H. A history of the bilioenteric anastomosis. Arch Surg 1990;125:1493–8.

65. Langenbuch C, Janicke T. Einigesüber Operationen am Gallensystem. Zentralbl Chir 1885; 12:515–17.

66. Sasse F, Siegel E, et al. Über Choledochoduodenostomie. Zentralbl Chir 1913;40:942–3.

67. Pendl F. Bietrag zur Casuistik der Choledochotomie und Cholecystenteroanastamose. Wein Klin Wochenschr 1900;13:498–501.

68. Monprofit A. On cholecystoenterostomy in the form of a Y. BMJ 1908;2:991.

69. Dahl R. Eine neue Operation an den Gallenwegen. Zentralbl Chir 1909;36:266–7.

70. Watanapa P, Williamson R. Surgical palliation for pancreatic cancer: developments during the past two decades. Br J Surg 1992;79:8.

71. Singh S, Longmire W, Reber H. Surgical palliation for pancreatic cancer: the UCLA experience. Ann Surg 1990;212:132–6.

72. Lillemoe K, Sauter P, Pitt H, et al. Current status of surgical palliation of periampullary carcinoma. Surg Gynecol Obstet 1993;176:1–6.

73. Potts J, Broughan T, Hermann R. Palliative operations for pancreatic carcinoma. Am J Surg 1990;159:72–8.

74. Lillemoe K. Palliative therapy for pancreatic cancer. Surg Oncol Clin N Am 1998;7:199–216.

75. Neuhaus H, Hagenmuller F, Griebel M, et al. Percutaneous cholangioscopic or transpapillary insertion of self-expanding biliary metal stents. Gastroenterol 1991;37:31–5.

76. Obrien S, Hatfield A, Craig P, et al. A three year follow-up of self expanding metal stents in the endoscopic palliation of long term survivors with malignant biliary obstruction. Gut 1995;36:618–22.

77. Shepard H, Royle G, Ross A, et al. Endoscopic biliary endoprosthesis in the palliation of malignant obstruction of the distal common bile duct: a randomized trial. Br J Surg 1988;75:1166–73.

78. Anderson J, Sorenson S, Kruse A, et al. Randomized trial of endoscopic endoprosthesis versus operative bypass in malignant obstructive jaundice. Gut 1989;30:1132–8.

79. Bornman P, Harries-Jones E, Tobias R, et al. Prospective controlled trial of transhepatic biliary endoprosthesis versus biliary bypass surgery for incurable carcinoma of the head of the pancreas. Lancet 1986;1:69–74.

80. Dowsett J, Russell R, Hatfield A, et al. Malignant obstructive jaundice: a prospective randomized trial of bypass surgery versus endoscopic stenting. Gastroenterol 1989;96:128–34.

81. Sarr M, Cameron JL. Surgical management of unresectable carcinoma of the pancreas. Surgery 1983;91:123.

82. Lillemoe K, Cameron J, Kaufman H, et al. Chemical splanchnicectomy in patients with unresectable pancreatic cancer: a prospective randomized trial. Ann Surg 1993;217:447–52.

83. Bowman HM, Sosa JA, Pitt HA, et al. The cost of complex biliary surgery can be contained at an academic medical center. Surgery. [In press]

84. Pitt HA, Murray KP, Bowman HM, et al. Clinical pathway implementation improves outcomes for complex biliary surgery. Surgery 1999;126:751–6.

CHAPTER 25

Pancreatic Surgery

Charles J. Yeo, MD, FACS

The pancreas occupies a retroperitoneal location in the abdomen, lying posterior to the stomach and gastrohepatic omentum. The gland extends obliquely from the duodenal C-loop toward a more cephalad position near the hilum of the spleen. The normal adult pancreas weighs approximately 100 g and is approximately 15 cm in transverse length and 4 cm in cephalad-to-caudad width. The pancreas has a distinctive multilobulated gross appearance, and it appears yellowish with some elements of tan and pink. Anteriorly, the pancreas is covered by peritoneum and lies posteriorly in proximity to the inferior vena cava, right renal vein, aorta at the level of the first lumbar vertebra, superior mesenteric vessels, and splenic vein. The gland can be divided into four portions: head (which includes the uncinate process), neck, body, and tail.

Two distinct organ systems share a place within the human pancreas. The endocrine portion of pancreatic function is served by the islets of Langerhans. The islets are nearly spherical collections of endocrine cells, scattered throughout the pancreatic parenchyma, which produce humoral substances such as insulin, glucagon, somatostatin, pancreatic polypeptide, and other hormones. The acini and ductal systems constitute the exocrine portion of the pancreas. On a macroscopic level, the exocrine pancreas is analogous to clusters of grapes (acini) on a vine (ducts), terminating in a major trunk termed the main pancreatic duct. Acinar cells are responsible for the synthesis and release of pancreatic enzymes into the ductal system. Ductal cells release bicarbonate into the ductal system.

The pancreas can be affected by both non-neoplastic (inflammatory) and neoplastic processes. Inflammatory conditions such as acute pancreatitis and chronic pancreatitis are most commonly managed nonoperatively, with surgical intervention being limited to specific indications. In regard to neoplastic processes, the pancreas can be the site of various benign tumors (islet cell tumors, cystic neoplasms, etc) or it can harbor malignant tumors such as malignant islet cell tumors, cystadenocarcinoma, or (the most common pancreatic malignancy) pancreatic adenocarcinoma.

This chapter will focus on ductal adenocarcinoma of the pancreas, which is the most common malignancy of the gland. The annual incidence of pancreatic cancer in the United States approaches nine new cases per 100,000 population, ranking pancreatic cancer eleventh among all cancers in the United States. Approximately 28,000 U.S. residents die from pancreatic cancer yearly, making this malignancy the fifth leading cause of cancer death in the U.S. The demographics of pancreatic cancer have been widely investigated, with an increased risk for the tumor being found among older people, African Americans, males, and members of the Jewish religion. There are six genetic syndromes associated with an increased risk of developing pancreatic cancer: hereditary nonpolyposis colorectal cancer (HNPCC), familial breast cancer linked to the *BRCA2* tumor suppressor gene, Peutz-Jeghers syndrome, ataxia-telangiectasia syndrome, familial atypical multiple mole melanoma syndrome (FAMMM), and hereditary pancreatitis.[1] A wealth of sound scientific evidence links cigarette smoking to an increased risk of cancer of the pancreas. Dietary factors that may increase risk include increased total energy intake, carbohydrate intake, cholesterol intake, and meat intake.[2]

Pancreatic adenocarcinoma accounts for over three-fourths of all primary nonendocrine cancers, with 65 percent of these tumors arising in the head, neck, or uncinate process of the pancreas. The majority of patients with pancreatic cancer seek medical attention following the development of obstructive jaundice, which occurs as a result of the cancer obstructing the intrapancreatic portion of the common bile duct. Associated symptoms include weight loss, abdominal pain, pruritus, weakness, alteration of bowel habits, and anorexia. New-onset diabetes may be the first clinical feature in approximately 10 percent of patients. Occasionally, patients present with new-onset pancreatitis, related to partial obstruction of the pancreatic duct by the neoplasm. Routine laboratory studies in pancreatic cancer patients typically reveal elevations of the serum total bilirubin and alkaline phosphatase, with mild elevations of the hepatic aminotransferase. Initial diagnostic imaging is performed with either transabdominal ultrasonography or state-of-the-art computerized tomography (CT), a typical findings being a dilated intra- and extrahepatic biliary tree in association with a mass lesion (or fullness) seen in the head of the pancreas. In general, spiral CT serves as the imaging test of choice for the diagnosis and staging of patients with pancreatic cancer. Spiral CT has the ability to demonstrate liver metastases, to evaluate the primary tumor for size and adjacent organ involvement, to evaluate the major peripancreatic vascular structures for tumor involvement, and thus to provide information regarding resectability. Additional staging procedures can include endoscopic ultrasonography, laparoscopy, and angiography. Following tumor staging, patients are managed via either palliative procedures or via cancer-directed resectional surgery.

REVIEW OF THE LITERATURE

Palliative Intervention

Palliative intervention for patients with pancreatic cancer can be approached either nonoperatively or operatively. Nonoperative management is appropriate in patients who are determined by staging studies to have distant metastases, unresectable local disease, or disseminated intra-abdominal tumor, or in patients with acute or chronic debilitating diseases that prohibit anesthesia and surgery. Palliative surgery for pancreatic cancer is appropriate in patients with unresectable disease discovered only at the time of laparotomy or in low-risk patients whose tumor-related symptoms are poorly alleviated via nonoperative approaches. In both the nonoperative and operative settings, it is the findings of biliary obstruction, potential duodenal obstruction, and tumor-associated pain that merit attention.

In patients to be managed nonoperatively, biliary decompression can be achieved by either endoscopic or percutaneous transhepatic techniques.[3,4] The available data support the use of an endoscopic method as the primary method for nonoperative palliation. One prospective randomized trial[5] and numerous other comparisons[6] have shown a comparable success rate for the endoscopic approach, with a lesser degree of procedure-related morbidity and mortality.

Tumor-associated pain can be a disturbing and incapacitating symptom of pancreatic cancer. In general, pain is not relieved by biliary decompression. Analgesic therapy is guided by the three-step analgesic ladder of the World Health Organization, with pain being best treated with long-acting oral analgesics in appropriate dosages.[7]

Until recently, duodenal obstruction was a symptom poorly managed nonoperatively. The recent application of biliary-type metallic stents with refined delivery systems has allowed endoluminal approaches. The basic approach is to place Wallstents in the native duodenum at the site of tumor infiltration. Progress will likely continue to be made in this area.

The operative approach to palliation of pancreatic cancer symptoms is designed to relieve biliary obstruction, to avoid or treat duodenal obstruction, and to palliate tumor-associated pain, all in an effort to improve quality of life and to prolong survival via one intervention. A review of The Johns Hopkins Hospital experience with surgical palliation reported 118 consecutive patients treated during a 54-month period.[8] Jaundice was the most common presenting symptom, being present in 73 percent of patients. The mean age of the patients was 64.5 years, with 71 percent having abdominal or back pain and 61 percent experiencing weight loss. The patients were found to be unresectable, based upon extensive local involvement (59 patients), hepatic metastases (44 patients), or peritoneal or omental implants (15 patients). The operative procedures performed are listed in Table 25–1. Some form of biliary bypass was performed in 92 patients, with 18 of the remaining 26 patients having had previous biliary decompression via surgical bypass or nonoperative means. A gastrojejunostomy was performed upon 102 of the 118 patients. A combined biliary bypass and gastrojejunostomy was the most common procedure, being performed upon 89 patients (75%). Three deaths occurred during the postoperative period for an in-hospital mortality rate of 2.5 percent. In late follow-up, 20 patients required re-admission to the hospital, 6 for terminal care, 5 for gastric outlet obstruction, 3 each for cholangitis and pain control, 2 for recurrent jaundice and 1 for small bowel obstruction. Survival analyses on these 118 patients undergoing surgical palliation revealed a mean survival time of 7.7 months, with a 6-month actuarial survival rate of 53 percent and a 12-month actuarial survival rate of 30 percent (Figure 25–1).

Table 25–1 Palliative Operations Performed on 118 Patients

Surgical Procedure	No. of Patients	Percentage on 118 Patients
Biliary bypass and gastrojejunostomy	89	75%
Gastrojejunostomy, alone	13	11%
Biliary bypass, alone	3	3%

Adapted with permission from Lillemoe KD, Sauter PK, Pitt HA, et al. Current status of surgical palliation of periampullary carcinoma. Surg Gynecol Obstet 1993;176:1–10.

A number of retrospective reviews have compared both the short-term and long-term results following various types of surgical biliary bypass for palliation of obstructive jaundice. In a review by Sarr and Cameron,[9] the operative mortality and long-term survival rates were similar in hepaticojejunostomy and cholecystojejunostomy, but the incidence of recurrent jaundice was 0 percent after hepaticojejunostomy, compared to 8 percent in patients undergoing cholecystojejunostomy. A more recent meta-analysis[6] found that cholecystojejunostomy carried an 89 percent success rate for alleviating jaundice, compared to a more favorable 97 percent success rate with either choledocho- or hepaticojejunostomy. Based upon these data, it has been recommended that palliative biliary bypass be accomplished by either choledocho- or hepaticojejunostomy in lieu of the use of the gallbladder (cholecystojejunostomy).

At the time of diagnosis, approximately one-third of pancreatic cancer patients have as symptoms nausea, vomiting, or early satiety. Total mechanical obstruction of the duodenum is unusual at presentation. As the malignant disease progresses, however, duodenal obstruction occurs with increasing frequency, at either the duodenal C-loop (by cancer in the head of the pancreas) or the ligament of Treitz (by cancer of the body of the pancreas). Sarr and Cameron[9] reviewed more than 8,000 surgically managed patients and found that 13 percent of patients who did not undergo gastrojejunostomy at their initial operation required gastrojejunostomy before their death, with an additional 20 percent of patients dying with symptoms of duodenal obstruction. A more recent review by Singh and Reber[10] found that 21 percent of patients required a gastrojejunostomy late in the course of their disease. Further, an analysis of more than 1,600 cases found that 17 percent of patients who underwent only biliary bypass

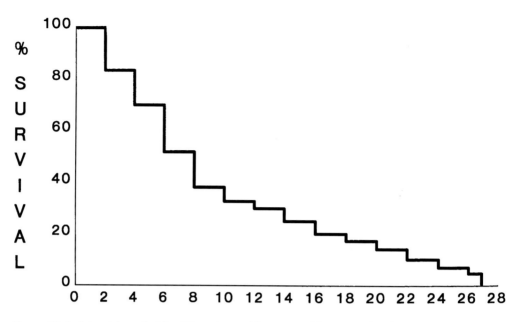

Figure 25–1 Actuarial survival for 118 patients with unresectable pancreatic adenocarcinoma undergoing operative palliation. (Printed with permission from Lillemoe KD, Sauter PK, Pitt HA, et al. Current status of surgical palliation of periampullary carcinoma. Surg Gynecol Obstet 1993;176:1–10.)

developed duodenal obstruction at a mean of 8.6 months following biliary bypass and required subsequent gastric bypass.[6] In spite of these data, there remains some controversy concerning the role of prophylactic gastrojejunostomy in patients with unresectable pancreatic cancer. The author believes the data support a prophylactic gastrojejunostomy, typically performed as a retrocolic isoperistaltic-loop gastrojejunostomy, using the jejunum 20 to 30 cm beyond the ligament of Treitz. The horizontal gastrotomy is placed somewhat posteriorly, in the most dependent portion of the gastric greater curvature. With this technique, the incidence of early delayed gastric emptying is low, and hospital discharge is not delayed. It is important that vagotomy is not performed, as it may contribute to delayed gastric emptying. Instead, routine acid secretory inhibition agents, such as histamine H2 receptor antagonists or proton pump agents (omeprazole or lansoprazole) are used to prevent marginal ulceration.

The abdominal and back pain associated with unresected pancreatic cancer is often a major debilitating symptom for the patient. At the time of palliative surgery, this symptom can be addressed with the use of intraoperative chemical splanchnicectomy. This technique was first introduced by Copping and colleagues in 1969 and was reported as being used in 49 patients in 1978.[11] In 1993, a prospective randomized placebo-controlled study was completed at The Johns Hopkins Hospital, comparing intraoperative chemical splanchnicectomy using 50 percent alcohol to a placebo injection of saline in patients with histologically proven unresectable pancreatic cancer.[12] Using a standard visual analog scale, assessment of pain, mood, and disability was completed preoperatively and at 2-month intervals until death. Chemical splanchnicectomy was performed by the injection of 20 cc of either 50 percent alcohol or saline on either side of the aorta at the level of the celiac axis (Figure 25–2). In this study, 137 patients were evaluable, with 65 patients receiving 50 percent alcohol and 72 patients receiving the saline placebo. The two groups were similar with respect to age, sex, location and stage of tumor, operations performed, the use of postoperative chemoradiation therapy, and the initial assessment scores for pain, mood, and disability. The mean pain scores were significantly lower in the alcohol group at 2, 4, and 6 months of follow-up and at the final

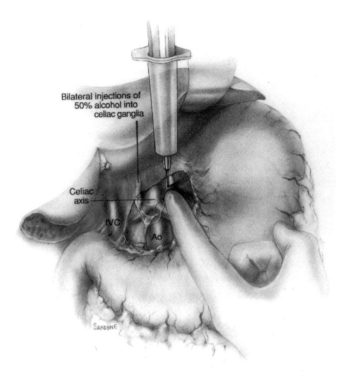

Figure 25–2 Chemical splanchnicectomy was performed using a syringe and a 20- or 22-gauge spinal needle. The solution (50% alcohol or saline placebo) was injected on either side of the aorta (Ao), at the level of the celiac axis. (IVC = inferior vena cava.) (Printed with permission from Lillemoe KD, Cameron JL, Kaufman HS, et al. Chemical splanchnicectomy in patients with unresectable pancreatic cancer: a prospective randomized trial. Ann Surg 1993;217:447–57. [Figure 2])

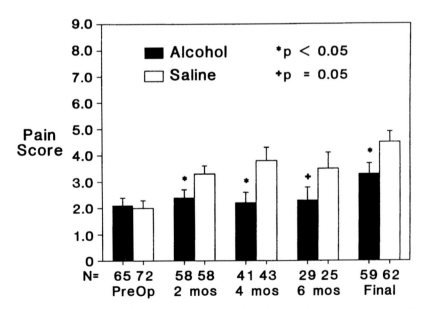

Figure 25–3 Mean pain scores (as measured by a visual analog scale) at the preoperative time point; at 2-, 4-, and 6-months postoperatively; and at final assessment for all randomized patients. (Printed with permission from Lillemoe KD, Cameron JL, Kaufman HS, et al. Chemical splanchnicectomy in patients with unresectable pancreatic cancer: a prospective randomized trial. Ann Surg 1993;217:447–57. [Figure 3])

assessment (Figure 25–3). There were no differences in hospital mortality or morbidity between the two groups. This randomized prospective placebo-controlled double blind study performed with standard quantitative measures of pain assessment clearly demonstrated the usefulness of intraoperative chemical splanchnicectomy in reducing postoperative pain in patients with unresectable pancreatic cancer. The mean pain scores of all randomized patients were significantly lower in the alcohol group, compared to the saline control group. A further finding was a significant improvement in actuarial survival in patients with preoperative pain who received the alcohol chemical splanchnicectomy (Figure 25–4). No reason for this difference could be found with respect to patient characteristics, operative findings, or postoperative treatment. The only difference between the alcohol patients with preoperative pain and the saline patients with preoperative pain appeared to be the use of alcohol for the intraoperative chemical splanchnicectomy. It is likely that the improved pain control provided by chemical splanchnicectomy prolonged life by contributing to an improved quality of life, resulting in improvements in nutrition, mobility, and survival.

Resectional Therapy

Pancreaticoduodenectomy (the Whipple procedure) has been used increasingly in recent years as a safe and appropriate resectional option in appropriately selected patients with malignant and benign disorders of the pancreas and periampullary region. The operative mortality rate after pancreaticoduodenectomy is now less than 4 percent in many high-volume centers.[13] A recent report from The Johns Hopkins Hospital reviewed the experience with pancreaticoduodenectomy from January 1990 through July 1996.[14] The surgical biases at Johns Hopkins have been to perform a standard pancreaticoduodenectomy without use of the extended retroperitoneal lymph node dissection, to perform a pylorus-preserving resection, and to perform partial pancreatectomy, leaving the body and tail of the pancreas in place unless the neoplasm extends into the left side of the pancreas (Figure 25–5). In the 6 years and 7 months of

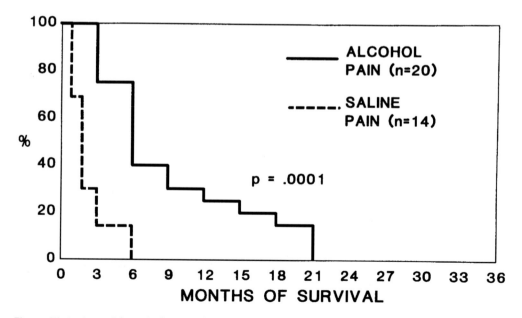

Figure 25–4. Actuarial survival curves from the time of hospital discharge for patients with preoperative pain. Patients receiving alcohol (n = 20) had a significantly longer survival (*p* = .0001) compared to patients receiving the saline placebo (n = 14). (Printed with permission from Lillemoe KD, Cameron JL, Kaufman HS, et al. Chemical splanchnicectomy in patients with unresectable pancreatic cancer: a prospective randomized trial. Ann Surg 1993;217:447–57. [Figure 8])

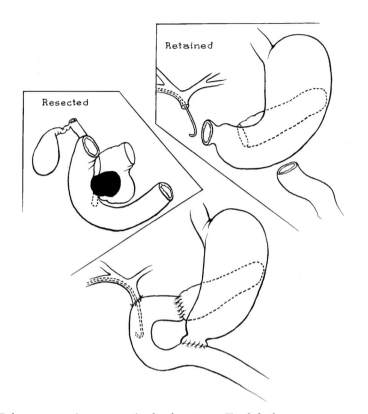

Figure 25–5 Pylorus-preserving pancreaticoduodenectomy. Top left: the structures resected include the duodenum (except for the initial 1 to 2 cm beyond the pylorus); head, neck, and uncinate process of the pancreas, with tumor; gallbladder; and approximately 10 cm of proximal jejunum and distal extrahepatic biliary tree. Top right: the retained structures include the entire stomach, pylorus, proximal 1 to 2 cm of duodenum, body and tail of the pancreas, proximal biliary tree, and the entire jejunoileum distal to the ligament of Treitz. Bottom: the reconstruction is depicted as a proximal end-to-end pancreaticojejunostomy, hepaticojejunostomy decompressed via a percutaneous transhepatic catheter, and a distal duodenojejunostomy. (Reprinted with permission from Yeo CJ, Cameron JC. The pancreas. In: Hardy JD, editor. Hardy's Textbook of Surgery. 2nd ed. Philadelphia: JB Lippincott; 1988.p. 718. [Figure 28–9])

this study, 650 patients underwent pancreaticoduodenectomy. The mean age of the patients was 63 years, ranging from 18 to 89 years. Fifty-four percent of the patients were male and 91 percent were white. The mean intraoperative blood loss was 625 mL, the median number of units of red blood cells transfused was 0, and the median operative time was 7 hours. A pylorus-preserving resection was accomplished in 532 patients (82%), and partial pancreatectomy was accomplished in 620 patients (95%).

Table 25–2 depicts the final pathologic diagnoses in the resected specimens. The majority of patients underwent resection for periampullary carcinoma, with the largest group of patients (n = 282, 43%) having pancreatic adenocarcinoma as the final pathologic diagnosis. Nine deaths occurred in-hospital or within 30 days of operation, for an operative mortality rate of 1.4 percent. Postoperative complications were observed in 266 patients (41%), the most common postoperative complications being early delayed gastric emptying (19%) and pancreatic fistula (14%). The median postoperative length of hospital stay was 13 days.

Two prospective, randomized studies from The Johns Hopkins Hospital have studied the most common complications following pancreaticoduodenectomy, namely, early delayed gastric emptying and pancreatic fistula.

Table 25–2 Diagnoses of 650 Consecutive Pancreaticoduodenectomies*

Pathologic Diagnosis	No. of Patients (n = 650)	Percentage of All Operations
Periampullary adenocarcinoma	443	68%
Pancreatic	282	43%
Ampullary	70	11%
Distal bile duct	65	10%
Duodenal	26	4%
Other	207	32%

*at The Johns Hopkins Hospital from January 1990 to July 1996.
Reprinted with permission from Yeo CJ, Cameron JL, Sohn TA, et al. Six hundred fifty consecutive pancreaticoduodenectomies in the 1990s: pathology, complications, outcomes. Ann Surg 1997;226:248–6.

Early Delayed Gastric Emptying

Early delayed gastric emptying (DGE) can be broadly defined as the need for postoperative nasogastric decompression for more than 10 days following pancreaticoduodenectomy. The condition is often associated with emesis and the need for nasogastric tube reinsertion. Although DGE is generally not life threatening, it can result in a significantly prolonged hospital stay and can contribute to increased hospital cost. One theory regarding the pathogenesis of DGE after pancreaticoduodenectomy suggests that gastric atony results from the reduction in circulating levels of motilin, a hormone primarily localized in enterochromaffin cells of the duodenum and proximal small intestine. Motilin levels fall dramatically after pancreaticoduodenectomy. Erythromycin and related 14-member macrolide compounds act as motilin agonists by binding to motilin receptors and initiating phase 3 activity of the gastric migrating motor complex.

A prospective randomized placebo-controlled double blind study at The Johns Hopkins Hospital tested the hypothesis that erythromycin, a motilin agonist, would improve gastric emptying and reduce the incidence of DGE after pancreaticoduodenectomy.[15] Between November 1990 and January 1993, 128 patients who underwent pancreaticoduodenectomy at The Johns Hopkins Hospital were enrolled in this study and were randomized to either the erythromycin group or the control group. In the erythromycin group (n = 58), intravenous administration of erythromycin lactobionate (200 mg) was commenced on the third postoperative day and was continued every 6 hours intravenously up to and including the tenth postoperative day. Control patients (n = 60) received identical infusions of normal saline for the same time period. For purposes of this study, DGE was defined as either of the following: (1) nasogastric tube left in place for 10 or more days plus (a) emesis after nasogastric tube is removed, or (b) postoperative use of prokinetic agents after postoperative day 10, or (c) reinsertion of nasogastric tube, or (d) failure to progress with diet, or (2) nasogastric tube in place for fewer than 10 days plus two of factors (a) through (d) above. On the tenth postoperative day, a dual-isotope, dual-phase radionuclide gastric-emptying scan was performed to follow the emptying of a combined solid- and liquid-phase meal from the stomach.[16]

The patients who received erythromycin had shorter durations of nasogastric tube drainage and started solid foods earlier (Table 25–3). Other parameters favoring the erythromycin group included the number of patients who required nasogastric tube re-insertion (6 vs 15, $p > .05$) and the number of patients with high-volume gastric residuals after the

Table 25–3 Clinical Measures of Delayed Gastric Emptying*

	Erythromycin Group (n=58)	Control Group (n=60)	p-Value
Postoperative NG tube days	5.5	6.2	.16
Postoperative day solid food begun	11.3	12.8	.18
Re-insertion of NG tube	6	15	< .05
NG residual > 500 mL	5	11	.18
DGE	11 (19%)	18 (30%)	.20

DGE = delayed gastric emptying; NG = nasogastric tube.
*n = 118.
Reprinted with permission from Yeo CJ, Barry MK, Sauter PK, et al. Erythromycin accelerates gastric emptying following pancreaticoduodenectomy: a prospective, randomized placebo controlled trial. Ann Surg 1993;218:229–38.

nasogastric tube was re-inserted. The overall incidence of DGE was 19 percent in the erythromycin group and 30 percent in the control group, indicating a 37 percent reduction in the incidence of DGE with erythromycin administration.

Figure 25–6 illustrates the results of the solid phase radionucleide gastric emptying studies. At all time points, erythromycin was associated with a significant improvement in solid gastric emptying. Similar results were seen for liquid emptying. No major adverse reactions to the erythromycin were observed in any patient.

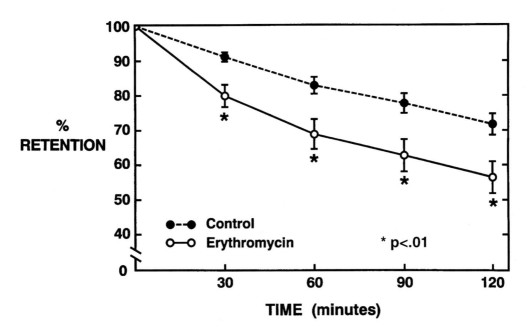

Figure 25–6 The results of the solid phase gastric emptying scans in the control and erythromycin groups 10 days following pancreaticoduodenectomy. At all time points, the erythromycin group had significantly better gastric emptying ($p > .01$). (Printed with permission from Yeo CJ, Barry MK, Sauter PK, et al. Erythromycin accelerates gastric emptying following pancreaticoduodenectomy: a prospective, randomized placebo controlled trial. Ann Surg 1993;218:229–38. [Figure 2])

This prospective, randomized double blind placebo-controlled study suggested that erythromycin lactobionate can significantly accelerate the gastric emptying of both solids and liquids after pancreaticoduodenectomy. This inexpensive drug was associated with quantifiable improvements in gastric emptying as measured by dual phase gastric emptying scans and was associated with a significant reduction in nasogastric tube re-insertion and with an overall 37 percent reduction in the incidence of DGE. These data support the use of erythromycin to decrease early DGE after pancreaticoduodenectomy. Based upon these data, physicians at The Johns Hopkins Hospital routinely administer erythromycin to postpancreaticoduodenectomy patients as part of its critical pathways.

Pancreatic Fistula

Pancreatic fistula in the setting of pancreaticoduodenectomy can be defined as drainage of more than 50 mL of amylase-rich fluid through operatively placed drains on or after postoperative day 10, or pancreatic-enteric anastomotic disruption demonstrated radiographically. This failure of a pancreatic-enteric anastomosis to heal following pancreaticoduodenectomy can cause considerable morbidity and can contribute to mortality. The incidence of pancreatic fistula ranges from 5 to 25 percent in most series, and the pancreatic-enteric anastomosis has been called the Achilles heel of pancreaticoduodenectomy.[17] Although several techniques exist for pancreatic-enteric anastomosis, most surgeons in the past used pancreaticojejunostomy as the preferred method of pancreatic-enteric reconstruction. A recently repopularized option for enteric drainage of the pancreatic remnant is pancreaticogastrostomy, a technique first reported in experiments on dogs in 1934 and used clinically for 50 years.[18–20] At The Johns Hopkins Hospital, a prospective randomized trial was performed to test the hypothesis that pancreaticogastrostomy is safer than pancreaticojejunostomy and less likely to be associated with a postoperative pancreatic fistula.[21] Between May 1993 and January 1995, 145 patients were enrolled and evaluated in this study. Following pancreaticoduodenal resection, the method of pancreatic-enteric reconstruction was randomly assigned. Pancreaticojejunostomy (PJ) was performed in either end-to-side or end-to-end fashion at the surgeon's discretion. Pancreaticogastrostomy (PG) was accomplished by anastomosing the pancreatic remnant to the posterior gastric wall midway between the lesser and greater curvature, at least 7 cm proximal to the pylorus or distal gastric staple line. A schematic illustration of the methods of pancreatic-enteric reconstruction is shown in Figure 25–7. Operatively placed drains left in the vicinity of the pancreatic anastomosis were left undisturbed, and their outputs were recorded daily for at least 5 postoperative days. The presence of a pancreatic fistula was assessed by clinical criteria and radiographic study. The primary study endpoint was pancreatic fistula, with secondary endpoints including assessment of other postoperative complications and length of postoperative stay.

The 145 patients in the study population had a mean age of 62 years. Seventy-three patients were randomized to the PG group and 72 to the PJ group. No differences were observed between the PG and PJ groups when comparing demographics, preoperative parameters, and intraoperative parameters. Table 25–4 depicts the postoperative complications observed. The most common complication was delayed gastric emptying, present in 22 percent in each group. The incidence of pancreatic fistula was 12 percent in the PG group and 11 percent in the PJ group. Overall, there were no significant differences in the complication rates between the PG and PJ groups. In a stepwise multivariate logistic regression model, the strongest predictors of pancreatic fistula were patient volume per surgeon and ampullary or duodenal disease (Table 25–5). The correlation between patient volume per surgeon and pancreatic fistula was associated with a generally increasing odds ratio for pancreatic fistula as the number of patients per surgeon decreased. The associations between pancreatic fistula and ampullary or duodenal disease were also strong, with odds ratios for pancreatic fistula of 5:43 and 12:63 for ampullary or duodenal disease, respectively.

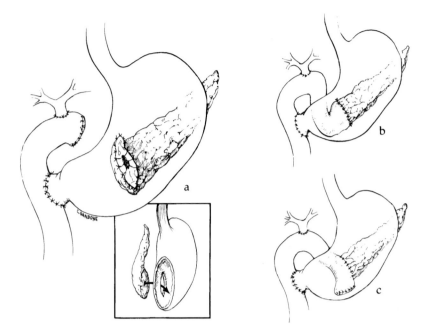

Figure 25–7 Schematic illustration of (A) pancreaticogastrostomy, (B) end-to-end pancreaticojejunostomy, and (C) end-to-side pancreaticojejunostomy. Detail of the pancreaticogastrostomy, indicating the posterior location of the gastrotomy (inset). (Printed with permission from Yeo CJ, Cameron JL, Maher MM, et al. A prospective randomized trial of pancreaticogastrostomy versus pancreaticojejunostomy after pancreaticoduodenectomy. Ann Surg 1995;222:580–92. [Figure 1])

Table 25–4 Postoperative Complications

Complication	PG (%) (n=73)	PJ (%) (n=72)	p-Value
DGE	16 (22)	16 (22)	NS
Wound infection	14 (19)	11 (15)	NS
Pancreatic fistula	9 (12)	8 (11)	NS
Cholangitis	4 (5)	6 (8)	NS
Total patients with complications	36 (49)	31 (43)	NS

PG-pancreaticogastrostomy; PJ-pancreaticojejunostomy; NS = not significant; DGE = early delayed gastric emptying. Reprinted with permission from Yeo CJ, Cameron JL, Maher MM, et al. A prospective randomized trial of pancreaticogastrostomy versus pancreaticojejunostomy after pancreaticoduodenectomy. Ann Surg 1995;222:580–92 (Table 3).

In this series, treatment for the 17 patients who sustained a pancreatic fistula included maintenance of intraoperatively placed drains for 14 patients (82%) and percutaneous drainage for 3 patients (18%). No patient required reoperation for drainage. All pancreatic fistulas closed without the need for completion pancreatectomy or revision of the pancreatic anastomosis. The presence of a pancreatic fistula did, however, lengthen hospital stay, and it was often accompanied by other serious complications such as delayed gastric emptying, cholangitis, and abscess formation. In conclusion, this study demonstrated that pancreatic

Table 25–5 Multivariate Logistic Regression Model for Pancreatic Fistula

Parameter	p-Value	Odds Ratio
Patient volume per surgeon		
76	—	1.00
29	0.120	3.83
17	0.005	12.96
14	0.029	11.62
Pathology		
Pancreas	—	1.00
Bile duct	0.329	3.31
Ampulla	0.024	5.43
Duodenum	0.001	12.63

Reprinted with permission from Yeo CJ, Cameron JL, Maher MM, et al. A prospective randomized trial of pancreaticogastrostomy versus pancreaticojejunostomy after pancreaticoduodenectomy. Ann Surg 1995;222:580–92 (Table 5).

fistula is a common complication after pancreaticoduodenectomy (with an incidence of 11 to 12%) and that it is most strongly associated with a lower patient volume per surgeon and either ampullary or duodenal disease. These data did not support the hypothesis that PG was a safer alternative than PJ nor that PG was associated with a lower incidence of pancreatic fistula.

Survival Following Pancreaticoduodenectomy

The survival of patients undergoing pancreaticoduodenectomy for pathologically verified adenocarcinoma of the pancreas at The Johns Hopkins Hospital has been analyzed.[22] For a group of 201 patients undergoing pancreaticoduodenectomy between April 1970 and April 1994, the postoperative in-hospital mortality rate was 5 percent (0.7% for the last 149 patients), and the actuarial 1-, 3-, and 5-year survival rates were 57 percent, 26 percent, and 21 percent, respectively (Figure 25–8). In evaluating individual patient outcomes, several factors were found to be important predictors of survival by univariate analyses; these factors included tumor diameter, resected lymph node status, resected margin status, and tumor DNA content. An important finding was that patients resected with two favorable parameters (negative resection margins and negative resected lymph nodes, n = 45) had a median survival of 32 months and a 5-year survival of 40 percent, indicating a particularly favorable outcome in this subgroup of patients. A multivariate survival analysis was performed to determine which of the univariate prognostic relationships were independent predictors of outcome. In a cohort of patients with complete histologic and tumor DNA content data, the most powerful predictors of outcome, in descending order, were tumor DNA content, tumor diameter, resected lymph node status, and status of the resection margins (Table 25–6).

A more recent analysis of outcomes in patients with pancreatic cancer resected over 5 years ago via pancreaticoduodenectomy yielded true actual 5-year survival rates.[23] Between April 1970 and May 1992, 242 patients underwent pancreaticoduodenal resection for periampullary adenocarcinoma at The Johns Hopkins Hospital. Of these patients, 149 (62%) were resected for pancreatic adenocarcinoma. In this subgroup of patients with pancreatic primaries, the mean pathologic diameter was 3 cm, with 72 percent of the patients having nodal involvement and 31 percent having positive resection margins (usually at the level of the hepatic or superior mesenteric arteries). The actual 5-year survival rate was 15 percent, with an actuarial 10-year survival rate of 5 percent. Thus, the survival rate for patients with resected pancreatic adenocarcinoma continues to decline between 5 and 10 years post surgery, with

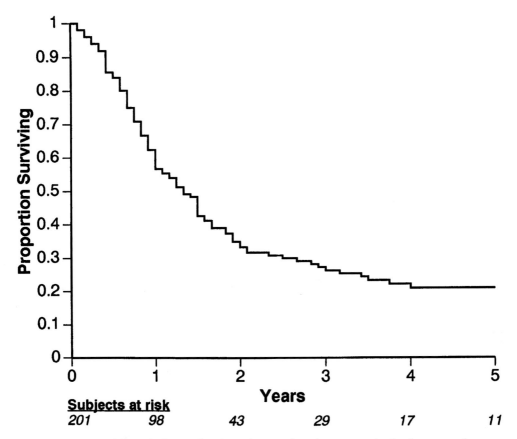

Figure 25–8 Actuarial survival curve for 201 patients undergoing pancreaticoduodenectomy for pancreatic adenocarcinoma. The median survival was 15.5 months and the 1- and 5-year survivals were 57% and 21%, respectively. (Printed with permission from Yeo CJ, Cameron JL, Lillemoe KD, et al. Pancreaticoduodenectomy for cancer of the head of the pancreas: 201 patients. Ann Surg 1995;221:721–33. [Figure 1])

Table 25–6 Multivariate Analysis: 119 Patients with Resected Pancreatic Adenocarcinoma

Parameter	Relative Risk	p-Value
Tumor DNA content (aneuploidy)	2.7	.0001
Tumor diameter ≥ 3 cm	2.2	.003
Positive resected lymph nodes in specimen	1.7	.04
Positive resection margins	1.6	.09

Reprinted with permission from Yeo CJ, Cameron JL, Lillemoe KD, et al. Pancreaticoduodenectomy for cancer of the head of the pancreas: 201 patients. Ann Surg 1995;221:721–33 (Table 5).

most of the late deaths being tumor related. While surgical resection remains the cornerstone of treatment for this malignancy, there is a general belief that progress in adjuvant therapies, perhaps incorporating new combinations of chemotherapy, radiation therapy, and even immunotherapy, may result in improvements in disease-free and overall survival rates.

The Role of Postoperative Adjuvant Chemoradiation Therapy

The goal of postoperative adjuvant chemoradiation following tumor resection is to prolong survival. The rationale for such adjuvant therapy is the high incidence of tumor recurrence both locally and at distant sites after surgical resection. Limited data from two studies of the Gastrointestinal Tumor Study Group (GITSG) in 1985 and 1987 suggested that chemoradiation after pancreatic resection for adenocarcinoma of the pancreas significantly improved both median and long-term survival.[24,25] In the first GITSG study, a prospective, randomized trial evaluated 5-FU-based chemotherapy and external beam radiation therapy after pancreatic resection for pancreatic adenocarcinoma. The 21 patients in the treatment arm had a median survival of 20 months compared to 11 months in the 22 control patients ($p = .03$). The Group confirmed its original findings in a second follow-up study of 30 patients receiving the identical chemoradiation regimen, showing a comparable 18-month median survival in this group. Unfortunately, there was no concurrent control group in the follow-up study, and the small sample sizes, slow patient accrual rates, and inclusion of patients with adenocarcinoma of the body and tail of the pancreas were all considered flaws in these GITSG studies. Data from The Johns Hopkins Hospital provide additional support for using postoperative adjuvant chemoradiation following pancreaticoduodenectomy.[26] A group of patients with pathologically confirmed pancreatic cancer resected between October 1991 and September 1995 were reviewed. During this time, patients were offered two options for postoperative treatment after pancreaticoduodenectomy: standard therapy or intensive therapy. Standard therapy consisted of external beam radiation therapy to the pancreatic bed (4000 to 4500 cGy) given with two 3-day courses of 5-FU at a dose of 500 mg per m^2 per day on days 1 to 3 and 29 to 31, followed by weekly bolus 5-FU for 4 additional months. Intensive therapy consisted of external beam radiation therapy (EBRT) to the pancreatic bed at higher dosages up to 5760 cGy, with prophylactic hepatic irradiation to a dosage of 2700 cGy given with and followed by infusional 5-FU (200 mg per m^2 per day) plus leucovorin (5 mg per m^2 per day) for 5 days a week for 4 months. (Further details of the intensive regimen can be found in the report by Carducci and colleagues).[27] There were 173 patients who survived the postoperative period, with 57 percent electing to receive standard adjuvant therapy, 12 percent electing the intensive therapy regimen, and 31 percent electing no therapy. Patients receiving either type of adjuvant therapy (n = 120) had a median survival of 19.5 months and a 2-year survival of 39 percent, significantly higher than the respective rates of the 53 patients who elected to receive no therapy (13.5 months and 30 percent, $p = .003$) (Figure 25–9). The intensive-therapy group had no survival advantage when compared to the standard-therapy group, with median and 2-year survivals of 17.5 months and 22 percent (intensive), compared to 21 months and 44 percent (standard).

Using a Cox proportional hazards model, a multivariate analysis was undertaken to determine which factors were independent predictors of survival. The probability values and hazard ratios for the final multivariate model are listed in Table 25–7. A tumor diameter ≥ 3 cm was a strong independent predictor of decreased survival, as was intraoperative blood loss ≥ 700 mL. The presence of positive resection margins also was a negative prognostic factor. The use of either adjuvant therapy protocol had a significant impact on survival in this multivariate model, with both hazard ratios being < 1, indicating improvement in survival with therapy. Standard therapy appeared to be a stronger independent predictor of survival than was intensive therapy, based on both the smaller probability value and hazard ratio.

Pancreatic Resection in Elderly Patients

Advancing age is a risk factor for the development of pancreatic cancer. Persons aged 65 years and older account for the fastest growing subset of the U.S. population, and there will be increasing numbers of elderly patients who will be considered candidates for pancreaticoduodenal resection. A recent evaluation of patients at The Johns Hopkins Hospital sought to

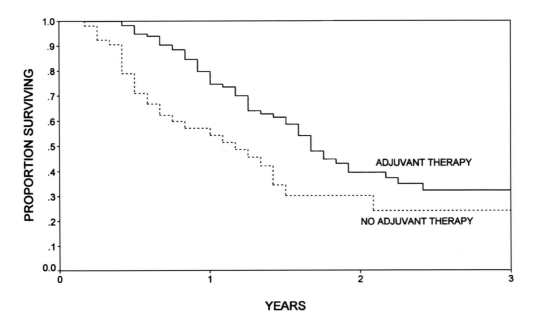

Figure 25–9 Actuarial survival curves for patients undergoing pancreaticoduodenectomy for pancreatic adenocarcinoma, comparing patients receiving adjuvant therapy (n = 120) to those declining therapy (n = 53; *p* = .003). (Printed with permission from Yeo CJ, Abrams RA, Grochow LB, et al. Pancreaticoduodenectomy for pancreatic adenocarcinoma: postoperative adjuvant chemoradiation improves survival. A prospective, single institution experience. Ann Surg 1997;225:621–36. [Figure 2])

Table 25–7 Multivariate Analysis: Survival Following Pancreaticoduodenectomy

Factor	p-*Value*	*Hazard Ratio*
Tumor diameter ≥ 3 cm	> .001	2.28
Intraoperative blood loss ≥ 700 mL	.014	1.75
Positive resection margins	.055	1.59
Intensive therapy	.04	0.50
Standard therapy	> .001	0.35

Reprinted with permission from Yeo CJ, Abrams RA, Grochow LB, et al. Pancreaticoduodenectomy for pancreatic adenocarcinoma: postoperative adjuvant chemoradiation improves survival. A prospective, single institution experience. Ann Surg 1997;225:621–36 (Table 7).

determine whether pancreaticoduodenal resection was justified in patients 80 years of age or older by carefully reviewing morbidity, mortality, and outcomes in this group, as compared to their younger counterparts.[28] During the 9.5 years of this study, 727 patients underwent pancreaticoduodenectomy. Forty-six patients were 80 years of age or older, with a mean age of 83 years and with ages ranging from 80 to 90 years. Of the 46 pancreaticoduodenectomies performed in the older age group, 93 percent were for malignant disease and 25 (54%) were for pancreatic adenocarcinoma. Patients in the elderly group underwent resection with a median operative time of 6 hours and 25 minutes, an average blood loss of 642 mL, and a median of 0.0 units of packed red blood cells transfused. Data on perioperative mortality and morbidity are summarized in Table 25–8. The perioperative mortality rates were 4.3 percent for the older

Table 25-8 Postoperative Course after Pancreaticoduodenectomy

Parameter	> 80 years (n=46)	< 80 years (n=681)	p-Value
Operative mortality	2 (4.3%)	10 (1.6%)	.21
Postoperative complications	26 (57%)	270 (41%)	.05
Median postoperative length of stay	15 days	13 days	.02

Reprinted with permission from Sohn TA, Yeo CJ, Cameron JL, et al. Should pancreaticoduodenectomy be performed in octogenarians? J Gastrointest Surg 1998;2:207–16 (Table IV).

patients and 1.6 percent for the younger patients. Although these mortality rates were not statistically different, the older subgroup experienced a significantly higher incidence of postoperative complications. The most common complications were delayed gastric emptying (33%), pancreatic fistula (15%), wound infection (11%), and cholangitis (11%). The elderly patients also had a significantly longer postoperative length of stay, with a median of 15 days compared to 13 days in the younger cohort. The survival of the older patients with pancreatic adenocarcinoma compared to that of the younger patients is depicted in Figure 25–10. The older group had a median survival of 17 months as compared to 18 months in the younger group. These survival curves are not statistically different and can be used to support the application of pancreaticoduodenectomy to carefully selected octogenarians. Since pancreaticoduodenectomy offers the only hope for long-term survival in patients with pancreatic cancer, healthy patients 80 years of age and older clearly should be considered for potentially curative resection. Age alone is not a contraindication to pancreaticoduodenectomy.

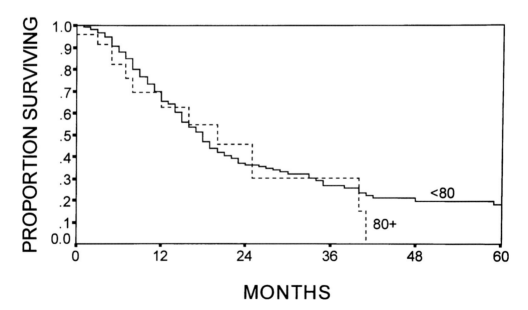

Figure 25–10 Actuarial survival curves comparing patients 80 years of age or older undergoing pancreaticoduodenectomy for pancreatic adenocarcinoma (n = 25; median survival, 18 months; 2-year survival, 46%) to those younger than 80 years (n = 282; median survival, 17 months; 2-year survival, 36%; p = .57). (Printed with permission from Sohn TA, Yeo CJ, Cameron JL, et al. Should pancreaticoduodenectomy be performed in octogenarians? J Gastrointest Surg 1998;2:207–16. [Figure 4])

Case Study

The current management of pancreatic cancer has evolved over the past 2 decades as outlined in the literature review, guided largely by evidence-based data. A variety of prospective randomized clinical studies have produced information that has been incorporated in the management algorithms for patients with both resectable and unresectable pancreatic cancer. These studies have been performed at academic medical centers that serve as high-volume regional referral centers. Promulgation of the study results has led to more of these operations being performed at less experienced centers. The case study presented here exemplifies a relatively new area of evidence-based research: population-based studies that examine cost and outcome. The focus of this case study is the effect of hospital volume on the cost and outcome of patients undergoing pancreatic surgery. There are reports from three statewide databases that have addressed this issue.

Maryland

The first such analysis to be published came from the state of Maryland and used data reported to the Maryland Health Services Cost Review Commission and was designed to evaluate hospital cost and patient outcomes from pancreaticoduodenectomies.[29] Analysis of the data compared cost and outcome between one high-volume regional provider (The Johns Hopkins Hospital) and 38 other Maryland hospitals where at least one pancreaticoduodenectomy had been performed during the study period. (The study period was from 1988 to the first half of 1993.) The primary outcome of interest was in-hospital mortality, and rates were compared using a relative-risk measure. In-hospital costs were estimated for each discharge from the total hospital charges reported. Because hospital charges are regulated strictly in Maryland, charges are a good approximation of real cost.

In this analysis, 501 cases were available. More than half of all patients (54.1%) were treated via pancreaticoduodenectomy performed at The Johns Hopkins Hospital, termed the high-volume regional provider. The remaining 45.9 percent underwent operations at 38 other hospitals in the state, with a minimum of one case and a maximum of 20 cases at any one facility during the 5.5-year study period. There were a number of differences between the patients treated at the high-volume regional provider and those treated by the low-volume providers. Patients treated at the high-volume provider were more likely to have been transferred from another hospital, to have commercial insurance, to have diabetes or hypertension listed as secondary discharge diagnoses, and to be white. Age distributions were similar. Cost and outcome were significantly different for these two hospital groups (Table 25–9). Hospital mortality was six times higher for patients treated at low-volume providers as compared with the high-volume provider. This excess mortality remained after adjustment for age, gender, race, source of payment, source of admission, and comorbidity. Mortality rates increased with decreasing volume, from 2.2 percent at the high-volume regional provider to 19.1 percent among those hospitals with five or fewer cases over the study period (Table 25–10). The high-volume regional center was also associated with a significantly shorter length of stay and a significantly lower total hospital charge (see Table 25–9).

This was the first demonstration that a high-volume regional medical center could achieve superior outcomes at a lower cost for the high-risk surgical procedure of pancreaticoduodenectomy. The most likely explanation for this is that the regional medical center has a group of health care providers with special expertise because of the large number of procedures performed. Other possible explanations include experience-driven early detection and treatment of complications, the use of dedicated attending physicians in the intensive care unit, and the availability of specialty support services. The findings suggested that regionalization of care could have a substantial impact on both cost and outcome for patients undergoing this procedure.

Table 25–9 Maryland Data: In-Hospital Mortality and Costs*

Parameter	Regional Provider (n=1)	Other Maryland Hospitals (n=38)	p-Value
In-hospital mortality	2.2%	13.5%	< .001
Mean length of stay for patients discharged (days)	22.5	27.9	< .001
Mean total charges for patients discharged	$24,478	$31,205	< .001

*among patients undergoing pancreaticoduodenectomy.
Reprinted with permission from Gordon TA, Burleyson GP, Tielsch JM, Cameron JL. The effects of regionalization on cost and outcome for one general high-risk surgical procedure. Ann Surg 1995;221:43–9 (Table 2).

Table 25–10 Maryland Data: Hospital Surgical Volume and Mortality*

Hospital Volume (cases)	Number of Hospitals	Total PDs	Mortality Rate	Relative Risk
1–5	20	42	19.1%	8.7
6–10	9	63	14.3%	6.5
11–15	6	69	13.0%	5.9
16–20	3	56	8.9%	4.0
> 20	1	271	2.2%	1.0

*for patients undergoing pancreaticoduodenectomy.
PD = pancreaticoduodenectomy.
Reprinted with permission from Gordon TA, Burleyson GP, Tielsch JM, Cameron JL. The effects of regionalization on cost and outcome for one general high-risk surgical procedure. Ann Surg 1995;221:43–9 (Table 3).

New York

The second analysis of outcomes versus hospital volume among patients undergoing pancreatic resection for malignancy was reported by Lieberman and colleagues, using data from individual patient discharge abstracts for the years 1984 to 1991. These data were obtained from the State-Wide Planning and Research Cooperative System maintained by the New York State Department of Health.[30] This particular analysis included patients who underwent total pancreatectomies or pancreaticoduodenectomies during the study years. Data for each of the 8 years studied were pooled, and logistic regression analyses were performed to determine the extent to which hospital and surgeon volume were significant predictors of death while patient characteristics were controlled. The analysis of the New York State data included 1972 patients with peripancreatic malignancies who underwent resection. The mean in-hospital mortality rate for all patients was 12.9 percent. The number of hospitals participating per year ranged from 86 to 108. Hospitals were categorized into groups based upon volume, and data on standardized mortality and mean length of stay are presented in Table 25–11. There was an inverse relationship between hospital volume and in-hospital deaths. For example, there was a 5.5 percent standardized mortality rate in the two hospitals performing more than 81 cases over the 8-year period, compared to an 18.9 percent standardized mortality rate for the 124 hospitals performing fewer than 10 cases over the same period.

The New York State data also compared data on standardized mortality and mean postoperative length of stay to surgeon volume groups for patients treated via pancreatic resection (Table 25–12). Based on the number of patients treated during the study period, surgeons were assigned to volume categories of low (fewer than 9 cases), medium (9 to 41 cases), and high (more than 41 cases). Ninety-six percent of the surgeons performed fewer than nine pancreatectomies over the 8-year period, and these surgeons accounted for 67 percent of the pancreatic resections. The low-volume surgeons had higher standardized mortality rates, and their patients had a longer mean hospital stay, compared to the high-volume surgeons. Using logistic regression analysis to evaluate the influence of hospital and surgeon volume on perioperative mortality rates after pancreatic resection, it was demonstrated that perioperative death was significantly related to *hospital volume* when surgeon volume was controlled, but that the surgeon's experience was not significantly related to perioperative mortality when the hospital volume was controlled. These data appear to support a defined minimum hospital volume for optimal outcomes for elective pancreatic resections, which would require some degree of centralization. Without a doubt, this analysis underscored the association between perioperative death, duration of hospitalization, and hospital volume for pancreatic resection.

Table 25–11 New York State Data: Standardized Mortality and Length of Stay*

Hospital Category (cases/8 years)	No. of Hospitals	Standardized Mortality	Mean Postoperative Length of Stay (days)
Minimal (> 10)	124	18.9%	35
Low (10–50)	57	11.8%	32
Medium (51–80)	1	12.9%	22
High (> 81)	2	5.5%	27

*after pancreatic resection, according to hospital volume.
Reprinted with permission from Lieberman MD, Kilburn H, Lindsey M, Brennan MF. Relation of perioperative deaths to hospital volume among patients undergoing pancreatic resection for malignancy. Ann Surg 1995;222:638–45 (Table 3).

Table 25–12 New York State Data: Standardized Mortality Length of Stay*

Surgeon Category (cases/8 years)	No. of Surgeons	Standardized Mortality	Mean Postoperative Length of Stay (days)
Low (< 9)	687	13.0%	34
Medium (9–41)	57	9.7%	26
High (> 41)	4	6.0%	27

*after pancreatic resection, according to surgeon volume.
Reprinted with permission from Lieberman MD, Kilburn H, Lindsey M, Brennan MF. Relation of perioperative deaths to hospital volume among patients undergoing pancreatic resection for malignancy. Ann Surg 1995;222:638–45 (Table 4).

California

A similar analysis determined the relation between hospital volume and outcome in patients undergoing pancreatic resections for malignancies in California.[31] This was a retrospective review of standardized patient discharge abstracts obtained from the California Office of State-Wide Health Planning and Development. The analysis included patients who underwent total pancreatectomies, pancreaticoduodenectomies and distal pancreatectomies for malignancies. This evaluation yielded a study population of 1,910 patients from 298 hospitals. Most of the operations were pancreaticoduodenectomies (83.5%), and these operations had an overall operative mortality rate of 9.4 percent. Total pancreatectomy was performed in 123 patients, with an operative mortality of 16.3 percent, and distal pancreatectomy was performed in 205 patients, with an operative mortality of 1 percent.

Hospitals were grouped into six volume ranges reflecting the number of resections performed during the study period. More than half of all patients were treated at hospitals where 10 or fewer resections were performed, and these hospitals accounted for 88 percent of all reporting hospitals. Whereas the overall mortality for the entire study population was 9.9 percent, the risk-adjusted mortality rate decreased with increasing hospital experience, from 14.1 percent in the low-volume hospital group to 3.5 percent in the high-volume centers (Table 25–13). Using a logistic regression model, the factors found to be independent predictors of increasing operative mortality were decreasing hospital volume, increasing number of secondary diagnoses, performance of total pancreatectomy versus other resections, increasing patient age, and male sex. Total hospital charges decreased from the lowest volume group ($87,857) to the highest volume group ($71,588), and these differences were significant. California was the third state to report a significant relationship between hospital volume and operative mortality for patients undergoing pancreatic resection. The California study further noted that if the standard of care defined by high-volume hospitals had been applied statewide during their study period from 1990 through 1994, 108 additional patients would have survived their operation, with over $20 million saved in hospital charges. Again, these data support the regionalization of this high-risk general surgical procedure (pancreatic resection), with the goal of providing optimal patient outcome and the most cost-effective care.

Further Studies

Beyond the initial three reports from statewide databases, two additional studies have been published recently regarding patients with pancreatic malignancies treated by either

Table 25–13 California Data: Hospital Volume and Risk-Adjusted Mortality*

Hospital Volume (5 years)	No. of Hospitals	Risk-Adjusted Mortality Rate
1–5	210	14.1%
6–10	53	9.6%
11–20	20	8.7%
21–30	9	6.9%
31–50	4	8.3%
> 50	2	3.5%

*for pancreatic resection.
Adapted and printed with permission from Glasgow RE, Mulvihill SJ. Hospital volume influences outcome in patients undergoing pancreatic resection for cancer. West J Med 1996;165:294–300 (Tables 7,8).

pancreaticoduodenectomy or palliative procedures. The first study dealt with the statewide regionalization of pancreaticoduodenectomy and its effect on in-hospital mortality, and the second study evaluated the importance of hospital volume in the overall management of patients with pancreatic cancer (resectional versus palliative procedures).

A recent report examined the statewide trend in Maryland toward regionalization of pancreaticoduodenectomy over a 12-year period and its effect on statewide in-hospital mortality rates.[32] Using hospital discharge data collected by the Maryland Health Services Cost Review Commission, this study examined discharges with the primary procedure being pancreaticoduodenectomy. Hospitals were classified as high-volume or low-volume providers based on the number of pancreaticoduodenectomies performed both annually and in total. The criteria to qualify as a high-volume provider were a minimum of 20 pancreaticoduodenectomies per year for 6 of the 12 years and an average volume during the 12-year study period of ≥ 20 pancreaticoduodenectomies per year. According to these criteria, there was only one high-volume provider, The Johns Hopkins Hospital. This analysis included only patients who resided in the state of Maryland, so that the effects of regionalization on the state population could be studied. Inclusion of out-of-state patients skewed the interpretation of volume trends, and such patients were therefore eliminated from the analysis.

During the 12-year period, 795 pancreaticoduodenectomies were performed on Maryland residents in 43 Maryland hospitals. During the study period, there was a fourfold increase in annual state volume from 29 in 1984 to 123 in 1995, and the high-volume provider increased its yearly share of pancreaticoduodenectomies from 20.7 to 58.5 percent. Further, the statewide in-hospital mortality rate for the procedure decreased from 17.2 to 4.9 percent. After adjustment for patient characteristics and study year, hospital share remained a significant predictor of mortality. An estimated 61 percent of the decline in the statewide in-hospital mortality rate for pancreaticoduodenectomy was attributable to the increase in share of discharges at the high volume provider. The remaining decrease (39%) was caused by the overall improvement in the mortality rate for pancreaticoduodenectomy in the study period across both high- and low-volume provider groups.

These data underscore that regionalization for pancreaticoduodenectomy occurred during the study period, without intervention from providers, payers, or the government. The regional high-volume provider developed a major interest in pancreaticoduodenectomy, organized a team of health care providers dedicated to these patients, formulated treatment protocols and critical pathways for the procedure, standardized diagnostic work-ups, put into place appropriate technical operative details, and disseminated information on provider capabilities and surgical results locally, regionally, and nationally. The increase in referrals to the regional provider benefited the state's population through fewer in-hospital deaths for this procedure; there also was an increase in the volume of pancreaticoduodenal resections performed in the community hospitals. This growth may be attributed to the proliferation of knowledge in the community about the procedure's effectiveness as well as to greater interest in the procedure among surgeons in community hospitals. Not only has regionalization of care at high-volume centers provided outcome and cost benefits for patients undergoing pancreatic resection but recently published data indicate that patients undergoing palliative procedures for pancreatic malignancies have also benefited from it.

The second study was designed to determine whether hospital volume was associated with clinical and economic outcomes for patients with pancreatic cancer undergoing pancreatic resection, palliative surgical bypass, or nonoperative biliary decompression in Maryland between 1990 and 1995.[33] Information was again collected from the Maryland Health Services Cost Review Commission, targeting patients discharged with a diagnosis of pancreatic cancer. The main independent variable in this study was hospital volume. Hospitals were characterized according to their volume of pancreatic cancer procedures performed during the 6-year study period: the high-volume provider performed 20 or more procedures per year, the medium-volume providers performed 5 to 19 procedures per year, and the low-volume providers performed fewer than 5 procedures per year (Figure 25–11). The outcomes of interest included in-hospital mortality rates, mean total hospital length of stay, and mean total hospital charges. The study population included 1,236 patients with pancreatic cancer. Of that population, 36 percent underwent pancreaticoduodenectomy, 4 percent had a total pancreatectomy, 23 percent had a double bypass (hepaticojejunostomy and gastrojejunostomy), 21 percent had a single bypass, and 16 percent had an endoscopic or percutaneous biliary stent placed. The frequency distribution of procedures performed for pancreatic cancer by hospital was highly skewed, with one institution (The Johns Hopkins Hospital) having 528 cases over the 6-year study period (being the high-volume provider) and accounting for 43 percent of the cases. Seven hospitals were medium-volume providers accounting for 22 percent of the pancreatic cancer cases. The remaining low-volume providers accounted for 35 percent of all cases. After adjustment for differences in age, gender, race, comorbidity score, and urgency of admission between the groups, the relative risk of in-hospital mortality was lower at the high-volume provider than at the medium- and low-volume providers across all three procedures (Table 25–14). Patients who underwent resections had a 19.3 times greater risk of in-hospital death at the low-volume providers and an 8.0 times greater risk of death at medium-volume providers when compared to the high-volume provider. Adjusted mean length of hospital stay was consistently the lowest at the high-volume provider across procedure categories (Figure 25–12), with significant differences noted for several comparisons. Differences in mean total hospital charges by hospital volume were less consistent although hospital charges for pancreatic resections were significantly lower at the high-volume provider than at the low-volume provider (Figure 25–13).

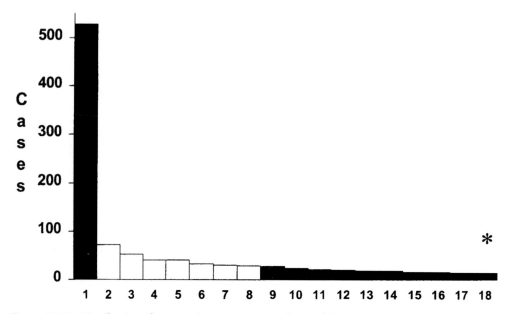

Figure 25–11 Distribution of pancreatic cancer cases per hospital from 1990 to 1995. There was one high-volume provider (at left) and seven medium-volume providers (white bars). The remainder of the hospitals (at right) were classified as low-volume providers. The * indicates that 30 hospitals had fewer than 5 cases per year. (Printed with permission from Sosa JA, Bowman HM, Gordon TA, et al. Importance of hospital volume in the overall management of pancreatic cancer. Ann Surg 1998;228:429–38. [Figure 1])

Table 25–14 Relative Risk of In-Hospital Mortality

Procedure	High-Volume Hospital RR	Medium-Volume Hospital RR	Low-Volume Hospital RR
Pancreatic resection (n=496)	1.0	8.0*	19.3*
Operative bypass (n=542)	1.0	1.9	2.7*
Stent (n=198)	1.0	4.8	4.3

RR = relative risk (defined as 1.0 for the high-volume hospital group).
*$p < .05$, compared to high-volume hospital.
Reprinted with permission from Sosa JA, Bowman HM, Gordon TA, et al. Importance of hospital volume in the overall management of pancreatic cancer. Ann Surg 1998;228:429–38 (Table 2).

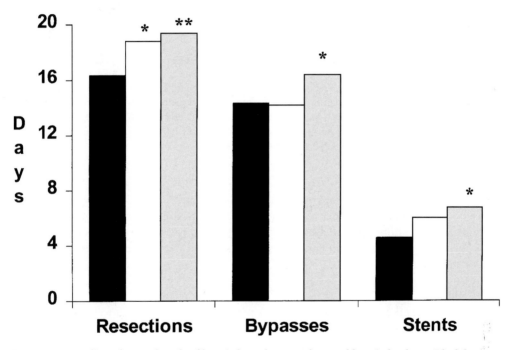

Figure 25–12 Adjusted mean length of hospital stay by procedure and hospital volume. Black bars at left are high-volume provider, white middle bars are medium-volume providers, and gray bars at right are low-volume providers. * $p > .05$; ** $p > .01$ vs the high-volume group. (Printed with permission from Sosa JA, Bowman HM, Gordon TA, et al. Importance of hospital volume in the overall management of pancreatic cancer. Ann Surg 1998;228:429–38. [Figure 3])

The results of this second study support earlier studies linking better outcomes with a greater volume of cases not only for type of procedure performed but also for similar type of diseases, that is, pancreatic cancer. By including not only patients who underwent pancreatic resection but also those treated via palliative procedures for advanced disease, this analysis extends previous work dealing with pancreatic resection alone. These data can be interpreted as indicating that the use of a team of pancreatic cancer care providers at one institution may be more important than the number of operations performed by a particular surgeon. Of the variables included in the data analysis, hospital volume had the strongest and most consistent association with outcomes. It is possible to interpret these data as

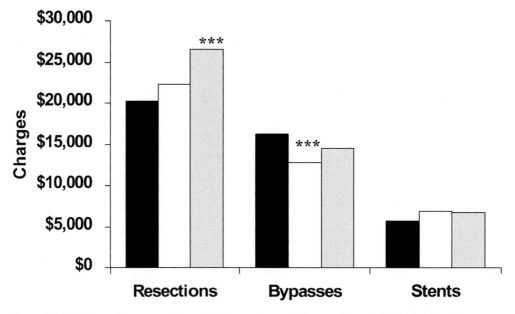

Figure 25–13 Adjusted mean total hospital charges by procedure and hospital volume. Black bars at left are high-volume provider, white middle bars are medium-volume providers, and gray bars at right are low-volume providers. *** $p > .001$ vs the high-volume group. (Printed with permission from Sosa JA, Bowman HM, Gordon TA, et al. Importance of hospital volume in the overall management of pancreatic cancer. Ann Surg 1998;228:429–38. [Figure 4])

suggesting that patients with pancreatic cancer who require procedures may benefit from referral to a high-volume provider regardless of whether they require curative resection, palliative bypass, or a nonoperative stenting procedure. Such referrals would probably help to decrease the substantial morbidity and mortality associated with current patterns of surgical care for these patients.

THE FUTURE

There remain several possibilities for the future treatment of pancreatic cancer. (1) New developments in molecular genetics will allow better characterization of the basic molecular abnormalities within cancer cells. Such advances may provide the key to the detection of early pancreatic tumors by molecular screening techniques. (2) Advances in radiographic imaging techniques may allow for improved determination of tumor staging. Such advances may help improve resectability rates and allow prompt, appropriate choices between operative and nonoperative management. (3) Improvements in surgical techniques and greater surgical experience should result in safer surgery and fewer procedure-related complications. Some improvements should also be anticipated in the field of minimally invasive (laparoscopic) surgery, which may further contribute to improved outcomes, shortened hospital stays, and reduced costs. (4) Discoveries in the field of antitumor therapies (chemotherapy, radiotherapy, immunotherapy, etc) can be anticipated, resulting in safer, more efficacious treatments for patients with resected or unresected neoplasms. (5) Widespread dissemination of the data showing the association of high hospital volumes with improved outcomes and reduced costs may lead to increased regionalization of the care of patients with pancreatic cancer in various "centers of excellence." This has already been documented in Maryland and is undoubtedly occurring in other locations. The apparent shift of patients to such centers of excellence is probably driven by multiple factors: physician referrals, patient referrals, the Internet,[34] and insurers who have reviewed the data and have begun to direct patients to these centers of excellence to take advantage of both improved patient outcomes and reduced charges.

The further accrual of data may well result in major changes in the detection, imaging, and management of patients with pancreatic cancer over the next decade.

REFERENCES

1. Hruban RH, Petersen GM, Ha PK, Kern SE. Genetics of pancreatic cancer: from genes to families. Surg Oncol Clin North Am 1998;7:1–23.

2. Gold EB, Goldin SB. Epidemiology of and risk factors for pancreatic cancer. Surg Oncol Clin North Am 1998;7:67–91.

3. Lichtenstein DR, Carr-Locke DL. Endoscopic palliation for unresectable pancreatic cancer. Surg Clin North Am 1995;75:969–88.

4. Kaufman SL. Percutaneous palliation of unresectable pancreatic cancer. Surg Clin North Am 1995;75:989–99.

5. Speer AG, Cotton PB, Russell RCG, et al. Randomized trial of endoscopic versus percutaneous stent insertion in malignant obstructive jaundice. Lancet 1987;2:57–62.

6. Watanapa P, Williamson RCN. Surgical palliation for pancreatic cancer: developments during the past two decades. Br J Surg 1992;79:8–20.

7. Levy MH. Pharmacologic treatment of cancer pain. N Engl J Med 1996;335:1124–32.

8. Lillemoe KD, Sauter PK, Pitt HA, et al. Current status of surgical palliation of periampullary carcinoma. Surg Gynecol Obstet 1993;176:1–10.

9. Sarr MG, Cameron JL. Surgical management of unresectable carcinoma of the pancreas. Surgery 1983;91:123–33.

10. Singh SM, Reber HA. Surgical palliation for pancreatic cancer. Surg Clin North Am 1989;69:599–611.

11. Copping J, Willix R, Kraft R. Palliative chemical splanchnicectomy. Arch Surg 1978;113:509–11.

12. Lillemoe KD, Cameron JL, Kaufman HS, et al. Chemical splanchnicectomy in patients with unresectable pancreatic cancer: a prospective randomized trial. Ann Surg 1993;217:447–57.

13. Yeo CJ. Pylorus preserving pancreaticoduodenectomy. Surg Oncol Clin North Am 1998;7:143–56.

14. Yeo CJ, Cameron JL, Sohn TA, et al. Six hundred fifty consecutive pancreaticoduodenectomies in the 1990s: pathology, complications, outcomes. Ann Surg 1997;226:248–60.

15. Yeo CJ, Barry MK, Sauter PK, et al. Erythromycin accelerates gastric emptying following pancreaticoduodenectomy: a prospective, randomized placebo controlled trial. Ann Surg 1993;218:229–38.

16. Yung BC-K, Sostre S, Yeo CJ, et al. Comparison of left anterior oblique, anterior, and geometric mean methods in gastric emptying assessment of postpancreaticoduodenectomy patients. Clin Nucl Med 1993;18:776–81.

17. Yeo CJ. Management of complications following pancreaticoduodenectomy. Surg Clin North Am 1995;75:913–24.

18. Tripodi AM, Sherwin CF. Experimental transplantation of the pancreas into the stomach. Arch Surg 1934;28:345–56.

19. Waugh JM, Clagett OT. Resection of the duodenum and head of the pancreas for carcinoma. Surgery 1946;20:224–32.

20. Park CD, Mackie JA, Rhoads JE. Pancreaticogastrostomy. Am J Surg 1967;113:85–90.

21. Yeo CJ, Cameron JL, Maher MM, et al. A prospective randomized trial of pancreaticogastrostomy versus pancreaticojejunostomy after pancreaticoduodenectomy. Ann Surg 1995;222:580–92.

22. Yeo CJ, Cameron JL, Lillemoe KD, et al. Pancreaticoduodenectomy for cancer of the head of the pancreas: 201 patients. Ann Surg 1995;221:721–33.

23. Yeo CJ, Sohn TA, Cameron JL, et al. Periampullary adenocarcinoma: analysis of 5-year survivors. Ann Surg 1998;227:821–31.

24. Kalser MH, Ellenberg SS. Pancreatic cancer. Adjuvant combined radiation and chemotherapy following curative resection. Arch Surg 1985;120:899–903.

25. Gastrointestinal Tumor Study Group. Further evidence of effective adjuvant combined radiation and chemotherapy following curative resection of pancreatic cancer. Cancer 1987;59:2006–10.

26. Yeo CJ, Abrams RA, Grochow LB, et al. Pancreaticoduodenectomy for pancreatic adenocarcinoma: postoperative adjuvant chemoradiation improves survival. A prospective, single institution experience. Ann Surg 1997;225:621–36.

27. Carducci MA, Abrams RA, Yeo CJ, et al. Early evaluation of abdominal/hepatic irradiation and 5-FU/leucovorin infusion after pancreaticoduodenectomy. Int J Radiat Oncol Biol Phys 1996;35:143–50.

28. Sohn TA, Yeo CJ, Cameron JL, et al. Should pancreaticoduodenectomy be performed in octogenarians? J Gastrointest Surg 1998;2:207–16.

29. Gordon TA, Burleyson GP, Tielsch JM, Cameron JL. The effects of regionalization on cost and outcome for one general high-risk surgical procedure. Ann Surg 1995;221:43–9.

30. Lieberman MD, Kilburn H, Lindsey M, Brennan MF. Relation of perioperative deaths to hospital volume among patients undergoing pancreatic resection for malignancy. Ann Surg 1995;222:638–45.

31. Glascow RE, Mulvihill SJ. Hospital volume influences outcome in patients undergoing pancreatic resection for cancer. West J Med 1996;165:294–300.

32. Gordon TA, Bowman HM, Tielsch JM, et al. Statewide regionalization of pancreaticoduodenectomy and its effect on in-hospital mortality. Ann Surg 1998;228:71–8.

33. Sosa JA, Bowman HM, Gordon TA, et al. Importance of hospital volume in the overall management of pancreatic cancer. Ann Surg 1998;228:429–38.

34. Goggins M, Leitman A, Miller RE, et al. Use and benefits of a web site for pancreatic cancer. JAMA 1998;280:1309–10.

CHAPTER 26

Breast Surgery

William C. Dooley, MD, Lillie Shockney, RN, BS, MAS, and
Wendy W. Saunders, MA

Invasive breast cancer is the most prevalent malignancy in women, striking more than 180,000 women a year in the United States. It is the second leading cause of cancer death among American women, accounting for some 43,500 deaths per year. Increased use of mammography to screen for early-stage breast cancer, when it is most curable, detects an additional 20,000 to 60,000 cases of premalignant breast disease a year. Thus, if one combines the number of women diagnosed with premalignant breast disease and noninvasive and invasive breast cancer, the result is that approximately a quarter of a million American women are touched by a diagnosis of breast cancer or a diagnosis that indicates significant risk for breast cancer in the future.[1–5]

The fact that breast cancer affects so many women has overshadowed the fact that the majority (more than 70%) of women diagnosed with breast cancer survive in the long term. The majority of women who survive breast cancer do so because of the relative success of breast cancer therapies, which have changed dramatically over the last 30 years, with profound effects on psychologic as well as physical outcomes. In 1960, for example, women with early-stage breast cancer were usually treated by surgery alone, with moderate success. However, the surgery consisted of breast amputation, a procedure that often left women cosmetically, psychologically, and emotionally devastated.[6–12]

From 1960 to 1980, the role of radiation therapy, hormonal therapies, and chemotherapy began to be explored through a series of multi-institutional prospective trials. These trials were important for two reasons: first, these less disfiguring treatments improved success rates not only in terms of the number of lives saved but also in terms of breast conservation; second, they laid the groundwork for most current evidence-based breast cancer treatment. The consequences of these results were enormous. The first consequence was the recognition of the importance of breast conservation; this was the first step in a long process that continues to evolve and which focuses on the psychologic and emotional devastation that breast cancer often causes. The second consequence—the fact that these trials were the basis for current evidence-based breast cancer treatment—is often overshadowed by the first but is equally important. Today, breast cancer surgery is supported by more evidence than perhaps any other type of surgery.[6–12]

The extent to which both the philosophy and practice of breast cancer surgery have changed over the last several decades is illustrated vividly by a comparison. Today, for example, the majority of breast cancers are identified noninvasively, by routine mammography and clinical breast examination.[13–16] Whereas surgeons previously performed a biopsy by making an open incision in the breast, biopsies are now carried out using noninvasive image-guided methods in over 95 percent of cases.[17–24] The new, nonsurgical methods available for diagnosis and subsequent mapping of the extent of premalignant and malignant breast disease prior to surgery have led to extraordinary increases in breast conservation rates.[1–5,25–28] Specifically, it is now possible to predict with greater than 80 to 85 percent accuracy which patients are the best candidates for breast conservation therapy and to offer the vast majority of these women options for breast preservation.[29–36]

Most women who are diagnosed with early-stage breast cancer can choose among multiple conservation and mastectomy options. Careful consideration of available options is important as differences in outcomes during the follow-up period are associated with different breast conservation and mastectomy therapies.[36–46] During the follow-up period, the main difference in outcomes is in the likelihood of local recurrence; however, numerous large studies show that such a difference does not affect overall long-term survival.[47] The various treatment options and their attendant risks and benefits differ markedly, however, in terms of how they are perceived and accepted by different women; consequently, patients must be actively engaged in the decision-making process. This is in striking contrast to the scenario presented to a comparable patient in the 1960s, when there really was only one therapy for breast cancer. The new role of decision-making in the treatment of breast cancer has made the inclusion of patients and their families (and the provision of appropriate educational material) a hallmark of current breast cancer treatment and a responsibility of the physicians involved.[4,48–56]

The new, more complex role of the surgeons, in collaboration with the rest of the oncologic team, is to develop a treatment plan based on the informed decisions of the patient and family. The ability to develop a treatment plan tailored to the individual patient requires that surgeons and other oncologic physicians have not only the ability to understand and interpret outcomes research but also the ability to communicate complex statistical information in a way that is understandable to patients and their families. The need for effective physician-patient communication in the field of breast cancer surgery is likely to increase as numerous ongoing and future clinical trials are certain to offer increasing choices for therapy.[4,47–56]

However many treatment options ultimately result, one feature they will have in common is that support for their use will derive from evidence-based research. The role of evidence-based research in the development of different breast cancer therapies is a distinguishing feature of this field. The wealth of evidence-based research regarding breast cancer treatment has made it arguably the best-supported surgical field. The fact that breast cancer patients can now choose among different treatment options, as outlined above, is directly attributable to numerous well-designed clinical trials, the results of which have altered both physicians' and patients' perception of standard therapy. The notion that standard therapy is individual, not general, may be the most important legacy of the numerous clinical trials conducted to date, as well as the point of departure for interpreting current and future trials.

REVIEW OF LITERATURE

The majority of breast cancers diagnosed today are early-stage (stages I and II) breast cancers, which are associated with significantly better outcomes than breast cancer diagnosed at later, more advanced stages. Two major factors have achieved earlier diagnosis of breast cancer: the widespread availability of mammographic screening and the population's increased awareness of the prevalence of breast cancer. Despite continuing controversy over the age at which mammographic screening should begin, the confluence of these two factors has resulted in earlier diagnosis of breast cancer, which has been proven through numerous studies to be more likely to result in a successful outcome.

Whereas early diagnosis of breast cancer is known to result in more effective treatment, there remain several treatment options for early-stage breast cancer. The following review and analysis of current treatments of stage I breast cancer illustrate both the advances made in treatment as well as some of the important issues that remain to be resolved.

CURRENT TREATMENTS OF INVASIVE STAGE I BREAST CANCER

Patients who are diagnosed with small breast tumors and who are node negative are frequently cured by initial surgical therapy.[38,57–61] Several clinical trials conducted over the last decade, however, have shown that a subset of patients with small node-negative tumors can achieve substantial survival benefit from the addition of adjuvant chemotherapy and hormone therapy.[62–75] Patients with tumors ranging in size from 10 to 20 mL may still have systemic failure rates and eventual death rates from breast cancer at a rate approaching 20 to 22 percent after 10 to 20 years of follow-up. Among these patients, some carefully selected individuals can achieve a substantial survival benefit from the addition of some form of systemic adjuvant therapy administered in conjunction with their primary surgical procedure.

Clearly, the most important therapy delivered to stage I breast cancer patients is local therapy consisting of either surgery alone or surgery followed by radiation. Numerous well-documented prospective randomized trials have shown that the surgical options of mastectomy (performed with or without reconstruction) or breast conservation surgery followed by radiation therapy are identical in terms of ability to confer long-term survival.[1–3,5,20–31,39–41,64,65,76] The primary difference between the therapies is the incidence of a small but real increased local failure risk observed in the breast conservation options. An important issue that has emerged from these prospective randomized trials but has not yet been addressed is how to identify which patients will benefit from breast conservation versus mastectomy. Indeed, patients who were thought to have absolute contraindications to conservation therapy in the 1980s now commonly undergo conservation procedures. Large prospective studies need to be carried out to determine such important remaining issues as the exact diagnostic work-up needed as well as the relative indications and contraindications for undergoing specific surgical treatment options.

Another important issue that remains unclear in the treatment of invasive stage I breast cancer is the role of axillary lymph node dissection.[77–83] A number of retrospective studies have demonstrated that a certain subset of patients may attain a potential survival benefit from axillary lymph node dissection. However, prospective randomized trials that compared therapy including axillary dissection to therapy without axillary dissection have not demonstrated any statistically significant therapeutic benefit from axillary dissection.[1–3,58–61,84,85] Based on these contradictory findings, axillary dissection tends to be carried out for prognostic purposes only. However, the data sets analyzed in the large prospective randomized trials are flawed on several counts. First, a substantial number of patients included in the "no axillary dissection" arms actually did undergo removal of several axillary nodes. Second, all patients in the trials who subsequently developed any questionable findings in the axilla had therapeutic dissection. Consequently, there are no clear-cut data on which to base decisions regarding axillary node dissection for all breast cancer patients. Nor is the role of limited axillary dissection well understood. A number of investigators have carried out single-institution studies that have demonstrated the value of more-limited axillary dissection using sentinel node technology in patients who were identified with positive axillary nodes.[81–83] These studies were limited, however, in that they required the use of nontraditional pathologic assessment tools, such as mammohistochemistry and DNA technology, to evaluate sentinel nodes. These alternative pathologic studies have not clearly demonstrated a substantial prognostic effect equivalent to that of traditional histologic and epidemiologic studies to detect lymph node metastasis. These unresolved issues raise an important and troubling question: Is there upstaging of a significant number of early-stage breast cancers? And if so, does this artificially inflate the therapeutic efficacy of systemic therapies? In the absence of substantiated data to answer these questions, surgeons at Johns Hopkins, like those in the Canadian Medical Association, have concluded that management of early-stage breast cancer should include an adequate axillary sampling consisting of a minimum of six lymph nodes. Furthermore, it is recommended that substitution of traditional axillary sampling with sentinel node studies should be carried out only as a research tool until prospective survival data become available.

Another modality that has demonstrated efficacy for treating some patients with invasive stage I breast cancer is hormonal therapy or chemotherapy. Whereas certain select patients with small stage I tumors and very favorable histologic subtypes do not demonstrate any added benefit from postadjuvant hormonal therapy or chemotherapy, a possible exception to this rule may be patients with high-grade tumors. The hypothesis that this group of patients may benefit is based on several retrospective studies suggesting that patients with high-grade lesions (independent of lesion size) always derive a survival benefit from undergoing post-operative adjuvant therapies. In particular, three large trials conducted as part of the National Surgical Adjuvant Breast and Bowel Project (NSABP) have demonstrated significant improvement in disease-free survival for estrogen-receptor-negative patients 5 years after treatment.[65–68] Specifically, the NSABP demonstrated disease-free survival improvement for receptor-negative patients treated with adjuvant chemotherapy and in receptor-positive patients treated with tamoxifen therapy. The therapeutic efficacy demonstrated in this trial parallels that shown in the Early Breast Cancer Trialists' Collaborative Group studies.[64,71] Importantly, the toxicities of each of these therapies are well documented in these large prospective randomized trials.[62–75] One particular NSABP trial, B14, evaluated the differences between 5 and 10 years of adjuvant tamoxifen therapy and found no added advantage, in terms of breast cancer recurrence, to continuing tamoxifen therapy beyond 5 years, leading to a National Cancer Institute (NCI) clinical alert to practitioners of this therapy.

Given the increasing number and complexity of breast cancer therapies, an important issue that has arisen and has been the subject of a number of recent randomized trials is the sequencing of therapy.[86–88] Most of these trials have compared the sequence of surgery, chemotherapy, and radiation to the sequence of surgery, radiation, and chemotherapy. While there appear to be no significant effects on rates of local recurrence if radiation therapy is delayed up to 7 months, therapeutic benefits are substantially reduced if adjuvant chemotherapy is delayed beyond 2 to 3 months postsurgery. This finding has led to widespread acceptance of the traditional sequence of surgery, adjuvant chemotherapy, and radiation therapy for stage I breast cancer patients.

RECENT EVIDENCE-BASED WORK: NATIONAL SURGICAL ADJUVANT BREAST AND BOWEL PROJECT B18 TRIAL

The National Surgical Adjuvant Breast and Bowel Project B18 trial was designed to determine whether the administration of intensive chemotherapy prior to surgery would confer a survival advantage as compared to administration following surgery, which has been the traditional practice. The treatment design of the trial is depicted in Figure 26–1. The trial randomized 1,523 patients, of whom 747 received preoperative Adriamycin-Cytoxan and of whom 759 received the traditional course of postoperative Adriamycin-Cytoxan therapy. The clinical size of the breast tumor(s) and axillary nodal disease were determined before each of the cycles of Adriamycin-Cytoxan was initiated; these measurements were also made prior to surgery in those patients who received Adriamycin-Cytoxan preoperatively. Tumor response was classified according to one of four designations: complete clinical response, partial clinical response, stable disease, or progressive disease. Prior to surgery, patients in the neoadjuvant arm who were determined to have a complete clinical response were also evaluated in terms of pathologic response, designated as either partial or complete. The neoadjuvant therapy arm achieved a reduction in breast tumor size in 80 percent of patients. Thirty-six patients had a complete clinical response. These numbers are consistent with a number of previous studies of neoadjuvant therapy in breast cancer and demonstrate a small but dramatic response rate. An additional finding is that the majority of patients had some decrease in tumor size. Other important findings based on this study include the finding that tumor size and clinical nodal status are independent predictors of clinical response rate, with smaller tumors and fewer clinical nodes associated with a more dramatic response. Twenty-six percent of patients who demonstrated a complete clinical response had a complete pathologic response. This means that a total of only 9 percent of patients in the entire group had a complete pathologic response. By contrast, the response in nodes was more dramatic, with 89 percent of node-positive patients showing a clinical response. Specifically, 73 percent of them had a complete clinical response rate, but only 44 percent had a complete pathologic response.

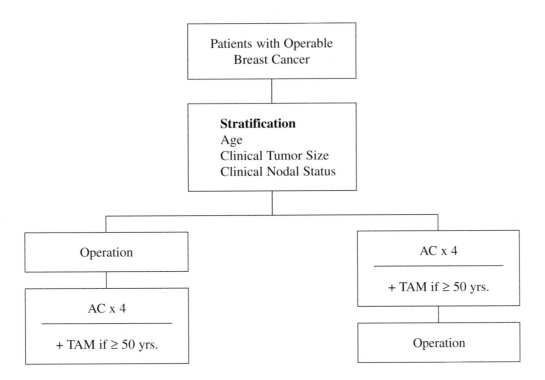

Figure 26–1 Treatment Design of National Surgical Adjuvant Breast and Bowel Project B18 Trial

This resulted in a 37 percent increase in the incidence of pathologically negative nodes in the neoadjuvantly treated patients as compared to the patients who received postoperative adjuvant therapy.

In addition to the specific clinical findings noted above, the data from this large prospective randomized trial are noteworthy in that they demonstrate the power of such trials to ascertain the effectiveness of new disease treatments. This is important in that measures such as clinical response are always subject to significant physician-to-physician variation as well as the bias of investigators. The latter occurs because most investigators feel strongly that they would not submit a patient to a therapy they felt had little or no chance of success. Within this context, it is interesting to evaluate the findings of this trial. Thus, while breast tumor size decreased in a large percentage of patients, only a small percentage of patients showed a complete pathologic response to neoadjuvant therapy; specifically, only 9 percent of tumors were considered pathologically occult at the time of local surgical therapy, and only 37 percent of patients showed an increase in the number of nodes determined to be pathologically negative. Of note, the precise expected increase in the survival rate of the patients who received adjuvant chemotherapy would have been approximately the same as the increased incidence in development of pathologically negative nodes in the patients who received neoadjuvant treatment.

In addition to the strengths noted above, this study had one major weakness, namely, in the evaluation of the likelihood of breast conservation. This important issue was determined as follows: Surgeons had to propose either conservation or mastectomy for their patients prior to the patients' randomization into either the pre- or postoperative adjuvant trial. A major factor in this decision was tumor size. Thus, lumpectomy was proposed for 86 percent of women with tumors smaller than 2 cm in diameter, 70 percent of women with tumors from 2 to 5 cm, and only 3 percent of patients with tumors larger than 5 cm. Interestingly, once the trial was completed, surgeons felt more comfortable with lumpectomy. Lumpectomies were performed 12 percent more often in the patients treated with preoperative chemotherapy; this represents a truly modest increase in the number of lumpectomies performed. However, the designers of this trial did not indicate in their published data whether the criteria used by physician-investigators for determining whether a patient was a suitable candidate for lumpectomy changed significantly following neoadjuvant therapy. Because neoadjuvant therapy appears to shrink the primary tumor, some physicians participating in this study may have felt more comfortable carrying out breast conservation surgery following such therapy. However, it is not possible to address this question as it is not known whether such important criteria as those used to determine acceptable negative margins or acceptable cosmetic results were consistent among participating physicians. What is known is that many patients were encouraged to enroll in this trial with the expectation that they might receive breast conservation surgery if their tumors shrank. Consequently, both physician-investigators and their patients may have been more motivated to pursue conservation in situations in which the results of conservation may not have been equivalent. Follow-up studies published 5 years after surgery showed similar isolateral breast tumor recurrence rates; however, the rate was higher in the patients treated preoperatively than in those treated postoperatively (7.0% and 5.8%, respectively, $p = 2.3$). It is likely that the isolateral breast tumor recurrence rates may continue to diverge over time as the local preventive effects (ie, the ability to inhibit isolateral breast tumor recurrence) of progressive chemotherapy and radiation wear off. Many patients with large tumors have large islands of premalignant breast tumors, such as ductal carcinoma in situ, atypical hyperplasia, and other proliferate abnormalities. Sometimes, many years pass before these proliferate abnormalities, which were present at a margin, cause a second or recurrent isolateral tumor. Although the rates of isolateral breast tumor recurrence have not yet reached statistical significance, it is noteworthy that there is so much divergence this early in the follow-up period.

The more standard measures available, such as disease-free survival, distant disease-free survival, and overall survival, can be measured more accurately and are less subject to bias than such emotionally charged issues as tumor size and whether or not the patient is a good candidate for breast conservation. Each of these more objective criteria showed no difference between the pre- and postoperatively treated patients ($p = .99$ for disease-free survival, $p = .70$ for distant disease-free survival, and $p = .83$ for overall survival). Overall, the preoperatively treated patients had an increase in breast conservation rates of only 8 percent; specifically, this rate rose from 59.8 percent in the postoperatively treated patients to 67.8 percent in the pre-operatively treated patients. Patients with tumors that showed a complete pathologic response had relapse-free survival rates at 5 years of 85.7 percent as compared to 76.9 percent of patients with invasive cancer who had a complete response, 68.1 percent of patients with a partial clinical response, and 63.9 percent of patients who were not considered to have responded clinically. The pathologic response rate measurements are not as prone to observer bias as are clinical response rate measurements. In short, the NSABP B18 study is weakened by the selection bias of the patients who enrolled in the study. In particular, participation in the trial was suggested to patients who were not considered ideal candidates for breast conservation, in the hope that they would be enrolled in the neoadjuvant arm of the trial and would consequently better their chances for breast conservation. The final trial results revealed that only 8 percent more patients in the neoadjuvant arm underwent breast conservation as compared to patients in the postoperative arm. This is a quite modest increase in conservation; what makes this increase troubling is that there is an increased rate of isolateral breast tumor recurrence in the neoadjuvant study arm. This increase, approximately 2.1 percent, is not yet statistically significant. In five years, however, it is likely to become statistically significant as the result of longer periods of follow-up. Furthermore, this figure would have achieved statistical significance had the trial enrolled more patients. This finding suggests a more liberal use of breast conservation techniques in patients who were treated in the neoadjuvant arm. This conclusion would be expected given the fact that physicians were enthusiastic about the effect of neoadjuvant therapy and tumor shrinkage, as demonstrated by high rates of clinical response in spite of very modest rates of pathologic response.

In summary, this study shows that the treatment sequence of surgery and chemotherapy appears to have no effect on survival and only marginal effects on breast conservation rates. In the future, treatment sequencing may be used to determine why the majority of patients seem to achieve no substantial benefit from adjuvant chemotherapy. If it were possible to identify which patients were going to benefit from adjuvant chemotherapy as well as which patients were not, it might become possible to avoid using standard cytotoxic regimens in the majority of patients. This would have important treatment implications in that more than 60 percent of patients appear to derive little or no benefit from adjuvant chemotherapy. Based on this study, it is clear that future investigations are needed to identify radically different approaches for adjuvant systemic therapy; that is, that traditional cytotoxic agents such as Adriamycin, Cytoxan, Methatrycate, and 5-fluorouracil have limited efficacy. Typically, new agents are used only in the management of advanced disease, and their introduction into adjuvant therapy trials for early-stage breast cancer tends to be delayed until such time as dramatic proven benefit is seen over standard treatment in advanced disease. The problem with this approach is that agents such as Receptin, which are immunotherapy based, may exert their most powerful effects as adjuvant therapy in early-stage disease. Neoadjuvant chemotherapy or varying the sequence of chemotherapy relative to surgical intervention are important in that they allow investigators to test which systemic therapies may have the most value. This study clearly demonstrated that the dramatic increase in survival that results from adjuvant therapy is limited to those who demonstrate a significant pathologic response. This is a significant finding as it can be used to gauge the effectiveness of adjuvant therapies, thereby allowing more therapies to be screened rapidly for use in early-stage breast cancer, when the effects may be most dramatic.[89]

FURTHER STUDIES

Future studies will certainly use the principle of variation in therapeutic sequencing to determine the reasons for therapeutic success as well as failure, by increasing the understanding of the basic biology of breast cancer. The provision of pathologic specimens through surgery at various points during the treatment continuum provides the opportunity to investigate and distinguish the characteristics of tumors, which may be more or less sensitive to individual therapies. The hope is that this will allow more precision in future treatment planning. As suggested above, it appears that based on the first attempts at neoadjuvant therapy, as shown by the NSABP trial and other similar but nonprospective randomized trials, the increase in conservation rates is quite modest with neoadjuvant placement of systemic therapies. By changing the sequence of radiation and surgery, however, it may be possible to substantially affect the potential for breast conservation since radiation clearly has a more pronounced effect on local disease than does traditional adjuvant systemic therapy. Innovative methods of interposing different portions of surgical therapy at different points in the sequence of adjuvant systemic therapies may allow sequential surgical therapy instead of the current norm, which is complete surgical therapy carried out as one unit.

To date, no studies have investigated the psychologic and emotional impact of current breast cancer therapies on patients and their families. The option of breast conservation often arouses strong feelings, which can lead patients to choose particular sequences of therapy or treatment courses. The treating physician also has preferences, which can influence the patient's judgment in regard to the choice of treatment. The breast cancer patient community was slow to accept breast conservation, due largely to physician bias and incomplete study data, especially in the early years. Increased awareness of breast cancer and the different treatments available has prompted increasing numbers of patients to request conservation as the treatment of choice. Indeed, the trend toward conservation has reached the point at which it is now often requested even in situations in which it is likely to fail. An area in which considerably more research needs to be carried out is the communication of evidence-based data about management of breast cancer to patients and their families. In particular, it is important to determine how to present such information accurately while also enabling patients to make informed decisions that are in their best medical interests. A critical point is to provide patients and their families with realistic expectations of the risks and benefits of different therapeutic options. This can be a challenge for physicians, who may have devoted many years of their careers to research, including such technically demanding areas as statistical analysis. Such subjects are often difficult for families and their patients to apply to their own situations. For example, the classic statement about statistics made by patients is "If it happens to me, it will be 100 percent." As this statement reflects, it is difficult to extrapolate population data to an individual patient's own case. Many studies have been carried out to determine whether certain aspects of a patient's tumor predict which treatments might be best. In reality, however, treating physicians must often synthesize the results of a number of studies that may not have addressed all the available prognostic factors regarding an individual patient.

New statistical methods may allow physicians to select matching patients from retrospective studies (eg, from the National Cancer Database) and to extrapolate the likelihood of treatment success and failure to a given patient under certain circumstances. Another issue yet to be addressed is how to present such data to patients so that it is valuable yet accurate and, most important, so that it does not inappropriately bias the patient toward one specific treatment as opposed to another.

The wealth of available information has had profound effects on breast cancer patients, who have been particularly vocal in their demands for increased information about their illness. One unfortunate aspect of the information explosion has been that many lay publications give disproportionate information about new discoveries in breast cancer that is often misinterpreted. Increasingly, physicians find themselves in the position of educators—and not just educators who communicate new findings but educators who need to temper sometimes inflated patient expectations with realistic expectations about the likely course of their illness. These complex issues in communication to patients are new and need to be better understood. Another related area that would benefit greatly from research is determination of the methods needed to support patients to make the best treatment decisions possible. Finally, one more relevant issue that requires research is how to help breast cancer patients deal with the psychologic stress and trauma of their therapy. This issue will likely become even more important in the future given the convergence of two facts: (1) survival for stage I breast cancer is high, and (2) the number of women who will be diagnosed with stage I breast cancer is likely to increase over the next decade due to earlier diagnosis and increased public awareness. This group of patients now achieves very high survival; unfortunately, this achievement is tempered by the fact that many of these patients are treated with toxic therapies, such as Adriamycin-Cytoxan, from which many derive no measurable benefit. Thus, an important research goal is to determine which patients are likely to benefit from such toxic therapies and to administer those therapies to this group alone, thereby minimizing the current practice of providing toxic treatment to the breast cancer population as a whole. The reason it is critical to minimize the number of patients who undergo such toxic treatment is that the toxicity is so wide-ranging; it includes not only such well-recognized medical effects as secondary malignancy and bone marrow toxicity but also the psychologic trauma caused by the therapy itself. Other necessary steps in minimizing the psychologic and emotional trauma associated with breast cancer include dealing with issues of false patient expectations, either hopeful or despairing, by providing appropriate educational and psychologic support. Thus, future treatment of breast cancer requires a combination of traditional clinical studies as well as research, education, and communication in areas that are not often associated with standard medical care but that are clearly critical to breast cancer patients.

REFERENCES

1. Fisher B, Anderson S, Redmond CK, et al. Reanalysis and results after 12 years of follow-up in a randomized clinical trial comparing total mastectomy with lumpectomy with or without irradiation in the treatment of breast cancer. N Engl J Med 1995;333(22):1456–61.

2. Early Breast Cancer Trialists' Collaborative Group. Effects of radiotherapy and surgery in early breast cancer. An overview of the randomized trials. N Engl J Med 1995;333(22):1444–55.

3. Jacobson JA, Danforth DN, Cowan KH, et al. Ten-year results of a comparison of conservation with mastectomy in the treatment of stage I and II breast cancer. N Engl J Med 1995;332(14):907–11.

4. Fisher B, Costantino J, Redmond C, et al. Lumpectomy compared with lumpectomy and radiation therapy for the treatment of intraductal breast cancer. N Engl J Med 1993 Jun 3;328(22):1581–6.

5. Veronesi U, Sacozzi R, Del Vecchio M, et al. Comparing radical mastectomy with quadrantectomy, axillary dissection, and radiotherapy in patients with small cancers of the breast. N Engl J Med 1981;305(1):6–11.

6. Heim E, Valach L, Schaffner L. Coping and psychosocial adaptation: longitudinal effects over time and stages in breast cancer. Psychosom Med 1997;59(4):408–18.

7. Carver CS, Pozp-Kaderman C, Price AA, et al. Concern about aspects of body image and adjustment to early stage breast cancer. Psychosom Med 1998;60(2):168–74.

8. Jahkola T. Self-perceptions of women after early breast cancer surgery. Eur J Surg Oncol 1998;24(1):9–14.

9. Lee CO. Quality of life and breast cancer survivors. Psychosocial and treatment issues. Cancer Pract 1997 Sept;5(5):309–16.

10. Wilmoth MC, Ross JA. Women's perception. Breast cancer treatment and sexuality. Cancer Pract 1997 Nov;5(6):353–9.

11. Tjemsland L, Soreide JA, Malt UF. Posttraumatic distress symptoms in operable breast cancer III: status one year after surgery. Breast Cancer Res Treat 1998 Jan;47(2):141–51.

12. Gilbar O, Ungar L, Fried G, et al. Living with mastectomy and breast conservation treatment: who suffers more? Support Care Cancer 1997 Jul;5(4):322–6.

13. Bennington JL, Lagios MD, Margolin FR. Impact of mammographic screening on the size and the relative frequency of invasion in breast cancers seen in a community hospital from 1975–1988. Pathology (Phila) 1992;1(1):11–21.

14. Haffty BG, Lee C, Philpotts L, et al. Prognostic significance of mammographic detection in a cohort of conservatively treated breast cancer patients. Cancer J Sci Am 1998;4(1):35–40.

15. Gail MH, Brinton LA, Byar DP, et al. Projecting individualized probabilities of developing breast cancer for white females who are being examined annually. J Natl Cancer Inst 1989;81(24):1879–86.

16. Ariel IM, Cleary JB, editors. Breast cancer-diagnosis and treatment. New York: McGraw-Hill; 1987.

17. Orel SG, Reynolds C, Schnall MD, et al. Breast carcinoma: MR imaging before re-excisional biopsy. Radiology 1997;205(2):429–36.

18. O'Neil S, Castelli M, Gattuso P, et al. Fine-needle aspiration of 697 palpable breast lesions with histopathologic correlation. Surgery 1997 Oct;122(4):824–8.

19. Pisano ED, Fajardo LL, Tsimikas J, et al. Rate of insufficient samples for fineneedle aspiration for nonpalpable breast lesions in a multicenter clinical trial: the Radiologic Diagnostic Oncology Group 5 study. The RDOG5 investigators. Cancer 1998;82(4):679–88.

20. Meyer JE, Smith DN, Lester SC, et al. Large-needle core biopsy: nonmalignant breast abnormalities evaluate with surgical excision or repeat core biopsy. Radiology 1998;206(3):717–20.

21. Liberman L, Dershaw DD, Rosen PP, et al. Percutaneous removal of malignant mammographic lesions at stereotactic vacuum-assisted biopsy. Radiology 1998;206(3):711–5.

22. Stolier AJ, Rupley DJ. The impact of image-directed core biopsy on the practice of breast surgery: a new algorithm for a changing technology. Am Surg 1997;63(9):827–30.

23. Heywang-Kobrunner SH, Schaumloffel U, Viehweg P, et al. Minimally invasive stereotaxic vacuum core biopsy breast biopsy. Eur Radiol 1998;8(3):337–85.

24. D'Angelo PC, Galliano DE, Rosemurgy AS. Stereotactic excisional breast biopsies utilizing the advanced breast biopsy instrumentation system. Am J Surg 1997;174(3):297–302.

25. Veronesi U, Salvadori B, Luini A, et al. Breast conservation is a safe method in patients with small cancer of the breast: long-term results of three randomised trials on 1,973 patients. Eur J Cancer 1995;31A(10):1574–9.

26. Veronesi U, Luini A, Del Vecchio M, et al. Radiotherapy after breast-preserving surgery in women with localized cancer of the breast. N Engl J Med 1993;328(22):1587–91.

27. Liljegren G, Holmberg L, Adami HO, et al. Sector resection with or without postoperative radiotherapy for stage 1 breast cancer: five-year results of a randomized trial: Uppsala-Orebro Breast Cancer Study Group. J Nat Cancer Inst 1994;86(9):717–22.

28. Clark RM, McCulloch PB, Levine MN, et al. Randomized clinical trial to assess the effectiveness of breast irradiation following lumpectomy and axillary dissection for node-negative breast cancer. J Nat Cancer Inst 1992;84(9):683–9.

29. Bouvet M, Ollila DW, Hunt KK, et al. Role of conservation therapy for invasive lobular carcinoma of the breast. Ann Surg Oncol 1997 Dec;4(8):650–4.

30. Chung MA, Cole B, Wanebo HJ, et al. Optimal surgical treatment of invasive lobular carcinoma of the breast. Ann Surg Oncol 1997 Oct;4(7):545–50.

31. Visser TJ, Haan M, Keidan R, et al. T1a and T1b breast cancer: a twelve-year experience. Am Surg 1997 Jul;63(7):621–6.

32. Mose S, Adamietz IA, Thilmann C, et al. Bilateral breast carcinoma versus unilateral disease. Review of 498 patients. Am J Clin Oncol 1997 Dec;20(6):541–5.

33. Cheng L, Al-Kaisi NK, Gordon NH, et al. Relationship between the size and margin status of ductal carcinoma in situ of the breast and residual disease. J Natl Cancer Inst 1997 Sep 17;89(18)1356–60.

34. Cox CE, Hyacinthe M, Gonzalez RJ, et al. Cytologic evaluation of lumpectomy margins in patients with ductal carcinoma in situ: clinical outcome. Ann Surg Oncol 1997 Dec;4(8):644–9.

35. Holland PA, Gandhi A, Knox WF, et al. The importance of complete excision in the prevention of local recurrence of ductal carcinoma in situ. Br J Cancer 1998;77(1):110–4.

36. Wong JS, Recht A, Beard CJ, et al. Treatment outcome after tangential radiation therapy without axillary dissection in patients with early-stage breast cancer and clinically negative axillary nodes. Int J Radiat Oncol Biol Phys 1997 Nov 1;39(4):915–20.

37. Rutqvist LE, Liedberg A, Hammar N, Dalberg K. Myocardial infarction among women with early stage breast cancer treated with conservative surgery and breast irradiation. Int J Radiat Oncol Biol Phys 1998 Jan 15;40(2):359–63.

38. Nixon AJ, Manola J, Gelman R, et al. No long-term increase in cardiac-related mortality after breast-conserving surgery and radiation therapy using modern techniques. J Clin Oncol 1998 Apr;16(4):1374–9.

39. Arcangeli G, Micheli A, D'Angelo L, et al. Conservative surgery and radiotherapy in early stage breast cancer: a comparison between tumourectomy and quadrantectomy. Radiother Oncol 1998 Jan;46(1):39–45.

40. Hayman JA, Hillner BE, Harris JR, Weeks JC. Cost-effectiveness of routine radiation therapy following conservation surgery for early-stage breast cancer. J Clin Oncol 1998 Mar;16(3):1022–9.

41. Vujovic O, Perea F, Dar AR, et al. Does delay in breast irradiation following conservative breast surgery in node-negative breast cancer patients have an impact on risk of recurrence? Int J Radiat Oncol Biol Phys 1998 Mar 1;40(4):869–74.

42. Strobbe LJ, Peterse HL, Van Tinteren H, et al. Angiosarcoma of the breast after conservation therapy for invasive cancer, the incidence and outcome. An unforeseen sequela. Breast Cancer Res Treat 1998 Jan;47(2):101–9.

43. Hughes LL, Styblo TM, Thomas WW, et al. Cellulitis of the breast as a complication of breast-conserving surgery and irradiation. Am J Clin Oncol 1997 Aug:20(4):338–41.

44. Elkhuizen PH, van de Vijver MJ, Hermans J, et al. Local recurrence after breast-conserving therapy for invasive breast cancer: high incidence in young patients and association with poor survival. Int J Radiat Oncol Biol Phys 1998 Mar 1;40(4):859–67.

45. Marrow M, Bucci C, Rademaker A. Medical contraindications are not a major factor in the under-utilization of breast conserving therapy. J Am Coll Surg 1998 Mar;186(3):269–74.

46. Street RL, Voigt B. Patient participation in deciding breast cancer treatment and subsequent quality of life. Med Decis Making 1997 Jul;17(3):298–306.

47. Ragaz J, Jackson SM, Le N, et al. Adjuvant radiotherapy and chemotherapy in node-positive pre-menopausal women with breast cancer. N Engl J Med 1997 Oct 2;337(14):956–62.

48. Gould SW, Lamb G, Lomax D, et al. Interventional MR-guided excisional biopsy of breast lesions. J Magn Reson Imaging 1998;8(1):26–30.

49. Cleverley JR, Jackson AR, Bateman AC. Pre-operative localization of breast microcalcification using high frequency ultrasound. Clin Radiol 1997;53(12):924–6.

50. More MM, Hargett CW 3rd, Hanks JB, et al. Association of breast cancer with the finding of atypical ductal hyperplasia at core breast biopsy. Ann Surg 1997;225(6):726–31.

51. Casey M, Rosenblatt R, Zimmerman J, Finberg S. Mastectomy without malignancy after carcinoma diagnosed by large-core stereotactic breast biopsy. Mod Pathol 1997;10(12):1209–13.

52. Crippa F, Agresti R, Seregni E, et al. Prospective evaluation of fluorine-18FDG PET in presurgical staging of the axilla in breast cancer. J Nucl Med 1998;39(1):4–8.

53. Mekhmandarov S, Sandbank J, Cohen M, et al. Technetium-99mM1B1 scintimammography in palpable and non-palpable breast lesions. J Nucl Med 1998;39(1):86–91.

54. Piccolo S, Lastoria S, Muto P, et al. Scintimammography with 99mTcMDP in the detection of primary breast cancer. Q J Nucl Med 1997;3:225–30.

55. Tolomos J, Khalkhali I, Vargas H, et al. Detection of axillary lymph node metastasis of breast carcinoma with technetium-99m sestamibi scintimammography. Am Surg 1997; 53(10):850–3.

56. Maini CL, Tofani A, Sciuto R, et al. Technetium-99mMIBI scintigraphy in the assessment of neoadjuvant chemotherapy in breast carcinoma. J Nucl Med 1997, 38(10):1546–51.

57. Winchester DJ, Chang HR, Graves TA, et al. A comparative analysis of lobular and ductal carcinoma of the breast: presentation, treatment, and outcomes. J Am Coll Surg 1998 Apr;186(4):416–22.

58. Rosen PP, Groshen S, Kinne DW. Survival and prognostic factors in node-negative breast cancer: long-term follow-up studies. J Nat Cancer Inst Monogr 1992;11:159–62.

59. Stierer M, Rosen HR, Weber R, et al. Long-term analysis of factors influencing the outcome in carcinoma of the breast smaller than one centimeter. Surg Gynecol Obstet 1992;175(2):151–60.

60. Rosen PP, Groshen S, Kinne DW, et al. Factors influencing prognosis in node-negative breast carcinoma: analysis of 767 T1N0M0/T2N0M0 patients with long-term follow-up. J Clin Oncol 1993;11(11):2090–100.

61. Baum M, Brinkley DM, Dossett JA, et al. Controlled trial of tamoxifen as a single adjuvant agent in the management of early breast cancer: analysis at eight years by Nolvadex Adjuvant Trial Organization. Br J Cancer 1988;57(6):608–11.

62. Bartlett K, Eremin O, Hutcheon A, et al. Adjuvant tamoxifen in the management of operable breast cancer: the Scottish Trial. Lancet 1987;2(8552):171–5.

63. Bonadonna G, Valagussa P, Zambetti M, et al. Milan adjuvant trials for stage I-II breast cancer. In: Salmon SE, editor. Adjuvant therapy of cancer V. New York: Grune and Stratton, Inc.; 1987. p. 211–21.

64. National Institutes of Health Consensus Development Panel. Consensus statement: treatment of early-stage breast cancer. J Nat Cancer Inst Monogr 1992;11:1–5.

65. Fisher B, Redmond C, Dimitrov NV, et al. A randomized clinical trial evaluating sequential methotrexate and fluorouracil in the treatment of patients with node-negative breast cancer who have estrogen-receptor-negative tumors. N Engl J Med 1989;320(8):473–8.

66. Fisher B, Dignam J, Mamounas EP, et al. Sequential methotrexate and fluorouracil for the treatment of node-negative breast cancer patients with estrogen receptor-negative tumors: eight-year results from National Surgical Adjuvant Breast and Bowel Project (NSABP) B-13 and first report of findings from NSABP B-19 comparing methotrexate and fluorouracil with conventional cyclophosphamide, methotrexate, and fluorouracil. J Clin Oncol 1996;14(7):1982–92.

67. Fisher B, Costantino J, Redmond C, et al. A randomized clinical trial evaluating tamoxifen in the treatment of patients with node-negative breast cancer who have estrogen-receptor-positive tumors. N Engl J Med 1989;320(8):479–84.

68. Fisher B, Redmond C. National Surgical Adjuvant Breast and Bowel Project: systemic therapy in node-negative patients: updated findings from NSABP clinical trials. J Nat Cancer Inst Monogr 1992;1:105–16.

69. Mansour EG, Gray R, Shatila AH, et al. Efficacy of adjuvant chemotherapy in high-risk node-negative breast cancer: an intergroup study. N Engl J Med 1989;320(8):485–90.

70. Bianco AR, De Placido S, Gall C, et al. Adjuvant therapy with tamoxifen in operable breast cancer: 10 year results of the Naples (GUN) study. Lancet 1988;2(8620):1095–9.

71. Early Breast Cancer Trialists' Collaborative Group. Systemic treatment of early breast cancer by hormonal, cytotoxic, or immune therapy: 133 randomised trials involving 31,000 recurrences and 24,000 deaths among 75,000 women [review]. Lancet 1992;339(8784):1–15.

72. Goldhirsch A, Gelber RD, Castiglione M. The magnitude of endocrine effects of adjuvant chemotherapy for premenopausal breast cancer patients. Ann Oncol 1990;1(3):183–8.

73. Reyno LM, Levine MN, Skingley P, et al. Chemotherapy induced amenorrhea in a randomised trial of adjuvant chemotherapy duration in breast cancer. Eur J Cancer 1993;29A(1):21–3.

74. Early Breast Cancer Trialists' Collaborative Group. Systemic treatment of early breast cancer by hormonal, cytotoxic, or immune therapy: 133 randomised trials involving 31,000 recurrences and 24,000 deaths among 75,000 women. Lancet 1992;339(8785):71–85.

75. Rivkin SE, Green S, O'Sullivan J, et al. Adjuvant CMFVP versus adjuvant CMFVP plus ovariectomy for premenopausal, node-positive, and estrogen receptor-positive breast cancer patients: a Southwest Oncology Group study. J Clin Oncol 1996;14(1):46–51.

76. Veronesi U, Banfi A, Salvadori B, et al. Breast conservation is the treatment of choice in small breast cancer: long-term results of randomized trial. Eur J Cancer 1990;26(6):668–70.

77. Sosa JA, DienerWest M, Gusev Y, et al. Association between extent of axillary lymph node dissection and survival in patients with stage I breast cancer. Ann Surg Oncol 1998 Mar;5(2):140–9.

78. Giuliano AE, Jones RC, Brennan M, Statman R. Sentinel lymphadenectomy in breast cancer. J Clin Oncol 1997 Jun;15(6):2345–50.

79. The Steering Committee on Clinical Practice Guidelines for the Care and Treatment of Breast Cancer. Practice guideline review. Axillary dissection. Can Med Assoc J 1998 Feb 10;158 Suppl 3:S22–S26.

80. Singhal H, O'Malley FP, Tweedie E, et al. Axillary node dissection in patients with breast cancer diagnosed through the Ontario Breast Screening Program: a need for minimally invasive techniques. Can J Surg 1997 Oct;40(5):377–82.

81. Veronesi U, Paganelli G, Galimberti V, et al. Sentinel-node biopsy to avoid axillary dissection in breast cancer in a community managed care setting. Cancer J Sci Am 1997 Nov;3(6):336–40.

82. Guenther JM, Krishnamoorthy M, Tan LR. Sentinel lymphadenectomy for breast cancer in a community managed care setting. Cancer J Sci Am 1997 Nov;3(6):336–40.

83. Dale PS, Williams JT. Axillary staging utilizing selective sentinel lymphadenectomy for patients with invasive breast carcinoma. Am Surg 1998 Jan;64(1):28–31.

84. Sigurdsoon H, Baldetorp B, Borg A, et al. Indicators of prognosis in node-negative breast cancer. N Engl J Med 1990;322(15):1045–53.

85. Fisher B, Redmond C, Fisher ER, et al. Ten-year results of a randomized clinical trial comparing radical mastectomy and total mastectomy with or without radiation. N Engl J Med 1985; 312(11):674–81.

86. Recht A, Come SE, Henderson IC, et al. The sequencing of chemotherapy and radiation therapy after conservative surgery for early-stage breast cancer. N Engl J Med 1996;334(21):1356–61.

87. Fisher B, Brown AM, Dimitrov NV, et al. Two months of doxorubicincyclophosphamide with and without interval reinduction therapy compared with 5 months of cyclophosphamide, methotrexate, and fluorouracil in positive-node breast cancer patients with tamoxifen-nonresponsive tumors: results from the NSABP B-15. J Clin Oncol 1990;8(9):1483–96.

88. Wallgren A, Bernier J, Gelber RD, et al. Timing of radiotherapy and chemotherapy following breast-conserving surgery for patients with node-positive breast cancer. Int J Radiat Oncol Biol Phys 1996;35(4):646–59.

89. Fisher B, Brown A, Mamounas E, et al. Effect of preoperative chemotherapy on local-regional disease in women with operable breast cancer: findings from National Surgical Adjuvant Breast and Bowel Project B-18. J Clin Oncol 1997;15:2483–93.

CHAPTER 27

Endocrine Surgery

Julie Ann Sosa, MD, and Robert Udelsman, MD, FACS

Outcomes research in endocrinology and endocrine surgery has important public health implications due to the prevalence of endocrine diseases. For example, disorders of the thyroid gland occur in 3 to 5 percent of the population and are the second most prevalent kind of endocrine disease (after diabetes mellitus, which will not be considered in this chapter).[1] Hyperparathyroidism is also a relatively common condition, especially among elderly people. Epidemiologic studies traditionally have found incidence rates in the range of 25 to 28 cases per 100,000 population annually,[2] and average annual incidence rates in white women older than 60 years of age approach 190 cases per 100,000 population per year.[3] Diseases of the adrenal gland are far less common.

REVIEW OF THE LITERATURE

There is a paucity of prospective controlled studies comparing long-term patient outcomes from different management strategies in endocrine surgery. The best population-based studies examining the clinical epidemiology and public health implications of the diagnosis and treatment of endocrine disease have been in the field of primary hyperparathyroidism. Hospitalized patients represent only a fraction of all individuals with the disease, especially when asymptomatic cases are considered, because hospitalization and surgery are generally indicated for the treatment rather than for the diagnosis of hyperparathyroidism. In addition, more endocrine procedures, including parathyroidectomy, are moving into the ambulatory setting.

Therefore, population-based outcomes studies (rather than institutional or clinical series using hospital discharge records) are of particular importance. Because of the unique (and exclusive) relationship between the Mayo Clinic and the community of Rochester, Minnesota, a number of seminal works in the field have come from that institution. One prospective cohort study, performed over 30 months with 401 patients referred to the parathyroid clinic with an elevated serum calcium, compared the clinical results of those who underwent nonoperative management to the results of those who underwent early surgery.[4] In another, all providers of medical care to the population of Rochester, Minnesota, were canvased for cases that met specified criteria for primary hyperparathyroidism.[5] It is striking that the final incidence rate of 27.7 cases per 100,000 persons per year was identical to the incidence of hyperparathyroidism (27.7 per 100,000 persons per year) in a Swedish county after the introduction of automated serum calcium measurements in a central laboratory in 1970 to 1971[6] and that the incidence of hyperparathyroidism in Birmingham, England, in 1979 was similar (26.6 per 100,000 persons per year).[2] A recent update of the Mayo Clinic study, however, suggests that the incidence of hyperparathyroidism has fallen in the last decade perhaps partly as an artifact of the sharp increase in diagnoses resulting from the introduction of automated serum calcium screening in the 1970s and 1980s.[7]

Even among surgeons there is no consensus on appropriate thresholds for operation and optimal preoperative localization studies. Debate also continues over whether lobectomy, total thyroidectomy or near-total thyroidectomy should be performed for patients with well-differentiated thyroid cancer. For example, controversy continues regarding the appropriateness of criteria for medical therapy versus surgical intervention in the management of asymptomatic and minimally symptomatic primary hyperparathyroidism. Operative approaches to adrenalectomy are numerous and largely dependent on the experience of the individual surgeon rather than the optimal technique for the individual patient. Variation in endocrine surgical practice patterns raises concern about increased cost and inconsistent quality of care. Understanding current practice patterns and the reasons for them is the first step in defining indications for new management strategies as well as guiding appropriate and cost-effective management of these patients.

In addition, the practice of endocrine surgery is rapidly changing. In the last decade, Tc-99m-sestamibi scintigraphy for parathyroid localization, outpatient parathyroid and thyroid surgery, minimally invasive or endoscopic parathyroidectomy, intraoperative parathyroid hormone (PTH) measurement, bisphosphonates for the treatment of hyperparathyroidism, and laparoscopic adrenalectomy have entered the mainstream of clinical practice. These important emerging technologies and drug treatments challenge practice patterns. In the current cost-conscious health care environment, it is especially important to incorporate medical costs, patient preferences, and quality-of-life considerations when studying the effectiveness of new technologies.

This chapter will focus on the evaluation of patient outcomes related to the surgical management of thyroid, parathyroid, and adrenal diseases to demonstrate a variety of study designs and methodologies that may be used by endocrine surgeons doing outcomes research.

MANAGEMENT OF THYROID DISEASE

Surgeon Experience and Patient Outcomes

Overall, death from thyroid surgery is rare, and the incidence of recurrent laryngeal nerve injury, neck hematoma, thyroid storm, and hypoparathyroidism is low. Reported complication rates vary dramatically in thyroid surgery, ranging from 0 to 14 percent for permanent recurrent laryngeal nerve injury and from 1.2 to 11 percent for permanent hypoparathyroidism.[8] It has been suggested that these rates are higher after more extensive resections (eg, total thyroidectomy) and redo procedures and when less-experienced surgeons perform thyroid surgery.[9]

Outside of clinical series published by endocrine surgeons, there has been a paucity of objective evidence supporting a consistent association between surgeon experience and patient outcomes. There is no benchmark for comparing the outcomes of thyroid patients operated on by community surgeons. In addition, the evidence is contradictory; some small series suggest that low-volume surgeons, well-supervised trainees, and surgeons at community hospitals can obtain excellent clinical outcomes.[10–12]

To investigate whether surgeon experience affects patient outcomes in thyroid surgery, a cross-sectional analysis of all patients who underwent thyroidectomy in Maryland between 1991 and 1996 was conducted using a computerized statewide hospital discharge database.[13] Surgeons were categorized by volume of thyroidectomies over the 6-year period: A (1 to 9 cases), B (10 to 29 cases), C (30 to 100 cases), and D (> 100 cases). Multivariate regression was used to assess the relation between surgeon caseload and in-hospital complications, length of hospital stay, and total hospital charges, adjusting for case mix and hospital volume.

The highest-volume surgeons (group D) performed the greatest proportion of total thyroidectomies among the 5,860 discharges, and they were more likely to operate on patients with cancer. After adjusting for case mix and hospital volume, highest-volume surgeons had the shortest length of stay and the lowest complication rate. (Table 27–1) Length of stay and complications were determined more by surgeon experience than hospital volume, which had no consistent association with outcomes. This relation was observed in all disease and procedure subgroups, and it remained significant after adjustment for patient case mix and time period.

In brief, this study provides compelling evidence for a significant association between increased surgeon volume and improved patient outcomes after surgical procedures for thyroid disease and supports the referral of patients for thyroidectomy to high-volume surgeons. Although rare overall, postoperative complications such as vocal cord paralysis and airway obstruction can be devastating.[14,15] Therefore, these findings are significant clinically as well as statistically.

Using the rules of evidence, it is impossible to prove causation between higher volumes of thyroidectomies and better clinical and economic outcomes based on this large, population-based study because it is impossible to show a temporal sequence in a cross-sectional analysis. However, the association between surgeon experience and improved outcomes is sensible in thyroid surgery, given the highly technical nature of the procedure. In addition, the consistent association between surgeon volume and outcomes (in spite of adjustment for other factors) and the dose-response gradient make it possible to strongly infer an association.[16]

Extent of Thyroidectomy

Notably, the association between surgeon experience and improved patient outcomes was strongest for more complex thyroid diagnoses and procedures. Although there were not significant differences in complication rates between surgeon volume groups in the management of benign adenomas, highest-volume surgeons (group D) had one-third fewer complications than their lowest-volume colleagues (group A) when operating for other benign conditions (eg, hyperplasia) and nearly two-thirds fewer complications than group A when managing for cancer. For total thyroidectomy, group D had nearly 75 percent fewer postsurgical complications ($p < .001$) and had the lowest charges ($p < .05$ vs group B, $p < .001$ vs group A).

By adjusting separately in regression models for thyroid diagnosis and procedure, the researchers took account of variations in surgeons' choices of procedure within diagnosis categories. Based on this study, the case for referral to high-volume thyroid surgeons is especially compelling for patients with known or suspected thyroid cancer or for patients for whom a near-total or total thyroidectomy is the procedure of choice.

The optimal extent of thyroid gland removal has been widely debated, with opponents of extensive resection arguing that these procedures carry potentially increased complications.[17] Moreover, there is disagreement about the adjuvant use of radioiodine therapy,[18,19] in part because there are no prospective studies evaluating the efficacy of surgical treatment and postoperative iodine therapy.[20] Advocates of total thyroidectomy for cancer maintain that the procedure decreases recurrence, facilitates ^{131}I treatment, improves survival, and is associated with only a slight increase in patient risk. The complexity of this issue was demonstrated in a power-analysis study designed to compare the outcomes of total thyroidectomy versus thyroid lobectomy for well-differentiated thyroid cancer.[21] For example, the predicted complication rates of the two arms of the protocol are similar, based on retrospective data available in the literature. As a result, a prospective trial comparing the complication rates of the two procedures would be prohibitive since it would require a study population of approximately 12,000 randomized patients (assuming a significance level of $\alpha = 0.05$ and a power of 90%).

As a result of conflicting evidence, even surgeons with expertise in endocrine surgery hold considerably varied views on the optimal surgical management of differentiated thyroid cancer.[22]

Thyroidectomy in the Ambulatory Setting

In the current cost-conscious health care environment, there is a mandate to contain costs by shifting surgery to the ambulatory setting. This is already being done in parathyroid surgery. In contrast, postoperative care after total thyroidectomy usually includes close observation in the hospital for 24 hours although 2- to 3-day hospitalizations are still routine in some centers.[23]

Table 27–1 Unadjusted and Adjusted Clinical and Economic Outcomes from Thyroidectomy by Surgeon Volume Group

Outcomes	Surgeon Volume Groups			
	A 1–9 Cases	B 10–29 Cases	C 30–100 Cases	D >100 Cases
Complication rate				
Unadjusted (%)	10.1[**]	6.7[**]	6.9[**]	5.9
Adjusted (%)[†]	8.6[**]	6.1[**]	6.1[**]	5.1
Length of stay				
Unadjusted (days)	2.8[*]	2.1[*]	2.2[*]	1.7
Adjusted (days)[†]	1.9[*]	1.7[*]	1.7[*]	1.4
Hospital charges				
Unadjusted ($)	5,078[**]	4,084[**]	4,016[**]	4,777
Adjusted ($)[†]	3,901	3,693[**]	3,585[**]	3,950

[*]$p < .05$; [**]$p < .001$ for comparisons to group D.
[†]Adjusted for patient age, race, comorbidities, insurance status, diagnosis, procedure, surgeon and hospital volume.
Reprinted with permission from Sosa JA, Bowman HM, Tielsch JM, et al. The importance of surgeon experience for clinical and economic outcomes for thyroidectomy. Ann Surg 1998;228(3):320–30.

A recent focus of research has been the hypothesis that near-total and total thyroidectomy can be done safely and in a cost-effective manner in a short-stay (23 hours, overnight discharge) setting.[24,25] With the creation of a critical pathway whereby patients are admitted the day of operation, observed overnight with serum calcium values obtained at prescribed intervals, and discharged if safety criteria are met, thyroidectomy was performed safely and with apparent savings in costs to the patients as well as to the respective hospitals. It will be important in subsequent studies, however, to assess patient preferences for the rapid-discharge pathway.

MANAGEMENT OF PARATHYROID DISEASE

Epidemiology of Hyperparathyroidism

As a result of the introduction of routine serum calcium screening in the mid-1970s, patients with primary hyperparathyroidism are now diagnosed earlier, and patients commonly present as asymptomatic or minimally symptomatic. The relatively stable clinical course observed in some of these patients has challenged previous beliefs that primary hyperparathyroidism is a progressive disease invariably associated with osseous, renal, gastrointestinal, and neurologic complications.[26] At the same time, surgical cure of these patients is associated with marked increases in bone mass and improvement of many symptoms associated with the disease.[27,28] Recent data suggest that many asymptomatic patients actually have subtle neuropsychiatric impairments[29] as well as progressive cardiovascular disease resulting in premature death.[30] Moreover, surgery in the hands of experienced surgeons is rarely associated with complications.[31] Optimal management of these patients was last addressed in a comprehensive manner in 1991 by a National Institutes of Health (NIH) Consensus Development Conference, which used expert opinion in combination with an unstructured review of the literature to formulate recommendations for optimal management.[32]

When patient-reported measurements of health outcomes after parathyroidectomy for primary hyperparathyroidism were measured, improvement was seen in all aspects of health status and quality of life within 6 months, suggesting that patient preferences in this convenience sample were for early surgery.[33] The 36-question "short form," or SF-36 health status

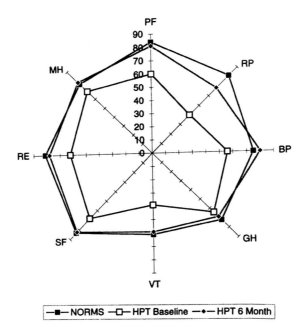

Figure 27–1 Radar plot shows SF-36 scores for patients with hyperparathyroidism at baseline and 6 months postoperation compared with normal population. Scores from normal population (derived from Ware JE. How to score the SF-36 health survey. Boston: Medical Outcomes Trust; 1994). Eight domains of health status are: general health perception (GH), physical function (PF), physical and emotional role limitations (RP, RE), social function (SF), mental health (MH), bodily pain (BP), and energy/fatigue or vitality (VT). (Reproduced with permission from Burney RE, Jones KR, Coon JW, et al. Assessment of patient outcomes after operation for primary hyperparathyroidism. Surgery 1996;120:1013–19.)

questionnaire, was developed at the RAND Corporation under contract to the Health Care Financing Administration (HCFA) for the Medical Outcomes Study. It is a brief validated survey instrument which uses simple questions that define eight domains of health status: (1) general health perception, (2) physical function, (3) physical and (4) emotional role limitations, (5) social function, (6) mental health, (7) bodily pain, and (8) energy/fatigue or vitality.

Patients with hyperparathyroidism had lower SF-36 scores in all health domains at baseline than did healthy patients. By 2 months after parathyroidectomy, however, scale scores for emotional role limitations and bodily pain improved by more than 10 points, and by 6 months, all eight scale scores showed improvement, seven of the eight by 10 points or more. (Figure 27–1) Commensurate improvements in disease-specific measures were also seen. While this study did not have an adequate number of subjects (n = 56) to obtain the statistical power needed to measure statistical significance, the trends in their results are consistent and suggest clinical significance.

Medical Treatment versus Surgery

Controversy surrounds criteria for medical versus surgical treatment in the management of primary hyperparathyroidism. To assess physicians' decision making regarding the surgical management of primary hyperparathyroidism and to measure adherence to the 1991 NIH Consensus Development Conference statement, a national cross-sectional survey of 147 North American endocrine surgeons (response rate, 77%) was conducted.[34] It examined surgeons' thresholds for surgery and the relationship of these criteria to surgeon experience, surgical outcomes (including complication rates and in-hospital mortality) as well as additional physician and patient characteristics that might confound these assessments.

Table 27–2 Laboratory and Clinical Criteria for Surgery on Patients with Primary Hyperparathyroidism: Survey of Endocrine Surgeons

| | Percentage Using Threshold for Surgery in | | | | | |
| | 40-yr-old Patients* | | | 65-yr-old Patients | | |
Lab Test or Symptom	Low	Medium	High	Low	Medium	High
PTH	41.3	43.8	15.0	32.4	46.0	21.6
Serum calcium	45.8	34.4	19.8	38.0	40.2	21.7[†]
Ionized calcium	9.6	62.7	27.7	7.7	62.8	29.5
24-hr urinary calcium	42.7	41.2	16.2	40.6	45.3	14.1[†]
Decrease in creatinine clearance	47.4	33.3	19.3	37.3	40.7	22.0[†]
Nephrolithiasis	—	89.7	6.9	—	85.4[†]	13.4
Bone T-score	45.6	39.2	15.2	35.5	46.1[†]	18.4
6–12-mo bone T-score change	44.2	35.1	20.8	37.0	39.7	23.3
Fracture	—	95.9	4.1	—	95.8[†]	4.2
Gastrointestinal symptoms	58.5	32.1	9.4	46.0	34.0[†]	20.0
Pancreatitis	66.7	33.3	—	65.5	34.5[†]	—
Psychiatric symptoms	55.1	31.9	13.0	53.9	32.3	13.9
Neuromuscular weakness	—	58.3	—	—	52.8[†]	—

PTH=parathyroid hormone.
*1991 NIH Consensus Development Conference statement recommendations are that all patients 50 years of age and younger undergo surgery.
[†]1991 NIH Consensus Development Conference statement recommendation for the 65-year-old patient.
Note: Row totals might not add to 100% due to rounding.
Reprinted with permission from Sosa JA, Powe NR, Levine MA, et al. Thresholds for surgery and surgical outcomes for patients with primary hyperparathyroidism: a national survey of endocrine surgeons. J Clin Endocrinol Metab 1998;83:2658–65.

    The survey found that even among a group of highly experienced surgeons who typically see patients after referrals from endocrinologists, clinical outcomes and criteria for surgery vary widely and appear to be associated with surgeon experience. High-volume surgeons (> 50 cases per year) had significantly lower thresholds for surgery with respect to abnormalities in preoperative creatinine clearance, bone densitometry changes, and levels of intact PTH and urinary calcium, compared to their low-volume colleagues (1 to 15 cases per year).

    In addition, endocrine surgeons' criteria for surgery diverged significantly from NIH guidelines, imploring the endocrine community to examine the evidence base for decisions in the management of primary hyperparathyroidism. Over half of the endocrine surgeons were in agreement with the NIH Consensus Development Conference regarding only 4 of 12 laboratory or clinical findings for patients aged 65 years and older (Table 27–2). They generally reported having higher thresholds than those outlined by the conference for operating on younger patients (< 50 years) but lower thresholds for operating on older patients (> 65 years).

Overall, surgeons who performed more parathyroidectomies had lower thresholds than their colleagues who performed fewer cases.

Compared to high-volume respondents, low-volume endocrine surgeons had significantly higher complication rates after primary operation (1.9% vs 1.0%, respectively; $p < .01$) and reoperation (3.8% vs 1.5%; $p < .001$) as well as higher in-hospital mortality rates (1.0% vs 0.04%; $p < .05$).

Cost Implications of Practice Pattern Variation

A separate cross-sectional analysis of (secondary) administrative data collected by the Health Services Cost Review Commission (HSCRC) in Maryland showed that patients with hyperparathyroidism were increasingly referred to a single endocrine surgery center. This referral pattern resulted in a high cure rate, low morbidity, no mortality, and a significantly shorter length of stay.[35] Based on this in-patient discharge database, length of stay for the 901 parathyroidectomies performed in the state between 1990 and 1994 decreased from 7 to 3.1 days, but length of stay for the high-volume center declined to a mean of 1.3 days over the concurrent period. An important caveat to this finding is that a multivariate regression analysis was not performed to adjust for differences in patient case mix among hospitals.

A break-even analysis performed in 1980 suggested that the cost of early operation for hyperparathyroidism would be exceeded by the cost of 5.5 years of medical follow-up.[5] The economic impact of current practice patterns could be even more substantial, given that the cost of medical surveillance is greater (with the development of new technologies such as bone densitometry) and that the incidence and prevalence of primary hyperparathyroidism have been increasing as a result of routine determination of serum calcium by automated methods. Moreover, medical therapies, such as those using estrogens and bisphosphonates, impose additional costs associated with treatment, follow-up, and management of complications. The charges factored into the break-even analysis also did not include the costs of short- or long-term disability relating to hyperparathyroidism or its treatment. No formal assessment of cost-benefit or cost-effectiveness of any therapeutic modality has been carried out to date.

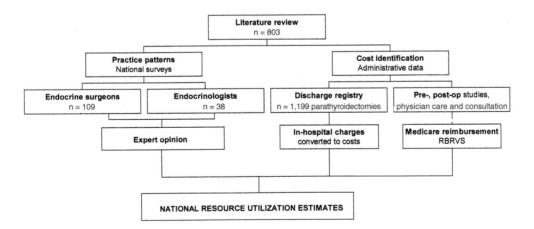

Figure 27–2 Format of cost-identification analysis for the surgical management of primary hyperparathyroidism. Study was conducted with literature review, followed by two surveys of national practice patterns of endocrine surgeons and endocrinologists and analysis of financial data from Maryland discharge abstract registry and Medicare reimbursement fee schedule. Expert opinion was used to ensure reasonable estimates. (RBRVS=Resource-Based Relative Value Scale) (Reproduced with permission from Sosa JA, Powe NR, Levine MA, et al. Thresholds for surgery and surgical outcomes for patients with primary hyperparathyroidism: a national survey of endocrine surgeons. J Clin Endocrinol Metab 1998;83:2658–65.)

Table 27–3 Resource Use by Endocrine Surgeons for Surgical Management of Primary Hyperparathyroidism

Resource Use	Cost per Patient ($)				Total US Cost ($ millions)
	Preop	In-Hospital	Postop	Total	
Average case					
Primary operation	130	7,066	271	7,467	275.0
Reoperation	349	7,312	271	7,932	6.7
Overall					281.7
Low use					
Primary operation	100	6,310	122	6,532	240.6
Reoperation	180	6,547	122	6,849	5.8
Overall					246.4
High use					
Primary operation	141	7,796	508	8,445	311.0
Reoperation	432	8,033	508	8,973	7.5
Overall					318.5

Reprinted with permission from Sosa JA, Powe NR, Levine MA, et al. Cost implications of different surgical management strategies for primary hyperparathyroidism. Surgery 1998;124:1028–36.

An updated cost-identification analysis used information about prevailing practice patterns and associated costs in the surgical management of primary hyperparathyroidism to estimate the cost implications of variation in practice (Figure 27–2).[36] Analysis of practice patterns was based on primary data collected from national surveys of endocrine surgeons and endocrinologists with expertise in bone and mineral metabolism and on a review of the literature. Surgical charge data were obtained from the Maryland HSCRC, and costs of laboratory tests, studies, and professional fees were obtained from Medicare.

This study demonstrated that variation in the management of hyperparathyroidism has important cost implications. Overall, an estimated $282 million is spent annually in the United States on operations for primary hyperparathyroidism. Although there is variation in preoperative and postoperative practice, in-hospital costs have the greatest influence on total cost. National health expenditures could vary by more than $70 million, depending on whether management strategies involving low or high use of resources are employed (Table 27–3).

Localization Studies

The NIH Consensus Development Conference concluded that preoperative localization is not indicated in patients with primary hyperparathyroidism who have not undergone surgical exploration. By contrast, the conference recommended that patients requiring reoperation should undergo localization studies routinely. Despite these recommendations, there continues to be controversy over whether preoperative localization is indicated before initial exploration as well as over the appropriate choice of imaging techniques.

The national survey of endocrine surgeons revealed that 75 percent of patients with primary hyperparathyroidism undergo at least one localization study before initial exploration. Technetium-Tc-99m-sestamibi scan was the study obtained most frequently by endocrine surgeons, followed by ultrasonography and Tc-99m-sestamibi scanning with single photon emission computed tomography (SPECT). Before reoperation, 100 percent of surgeons reported obtaining at least one localization study. The cost of preoperative localization studies varies by more than a factor of six; the cost of an ultrasound examination is $80, a Tc-99m-sestamibi study costs $155, and magnetic resonance imaging (MRI) or venous sampling costs more than $475. Clearly, variation in strategies for obtaining preoperative localization studies has significant cost implications.

Debate about optimal preoperative localization also has important implications for the selection of surgical approach since parathyroidectomy can be performed via a unilateral or bilateral approach. Proponents of the unilateral approach claim that it is associated with less morbidity and shorter operative times. In this approach, preoperative imaging directs the surgeon to the side of the neck with the parathyroid adenoma; the second parathyroid gland on the ipsilateral side can be confirmed by biopsy. A meta-analysis of the literature over the last decade suggested that Tc-99m-sestamibi scanning is specific enough in identifying solitary adenomas to allow unilateral exploration with a failure rate of less than 1 percent and an average saving of $650 per case because of shorter operative time.[37]

New Technologies

Debate about the optimal surgical approach continues because of two other recent innovations: intraoperative PTH measurement and the performance of parathyroidectomy under local anesthesia in the ambulatory setting. An accurate localization study such as a Tc-99m-sestamibi scan, a Tc-99m-sestamibi scan with SPECT, or intraoperative use of a gamma probe after a Tc-99m-sestamibi scan, in combination with an intraoperative PTH concentration that falls to < 50 percent of baseline after removal of a parathyroid adenoma and ipsilateral neck exploration could theoretically negate the need for contralateral neck exploration for a second adenoma or hyperplasia.[38–42]

MANAGEMENT OF ADRENAL DISEASE

Surgical and Laparoscopic Approaches

Surgical approaches to the adrenal gland include anterior transabdominal, flank, thoracoabdominal, supracostal, and posterior approaches and new laparoscopic techniques via a transperitoneal or retroperitoneal approach. Several investigations have compared various anatomic approaches with laparoscopic adrenalectomy. The indications for the laparoscopic procedure have expanded, and this technique, in skilled hands, is appropriate for virtually all nonmalignant adrenal tumors. Most (but not all) endocrine surgeons agree that large tumors and clearly malignant tumors should be excised using an open technique.

It is now clear that laparoscopic adrenalectomy can be performed safely with decreased hospital stays, increased patient comfort, and a shorter interval until resumption of normal activity.[43,44] Recent patient outcomes studies using a case-controlled study design with historical controls to compare the results of laparoscopic and open adrenalectomy have demonstrated a marked reduction in length of stay and time until resumption of normal diet and activity.[45,46] The decreased length of stay has been shown to result in significant savings as measured by hospital charges. It is interesting that savings from decreased length of hospital stay after laparoscopic adrenalectomy for benign disease can offset the additional expense (> 50%, $p < .001$) of disposable laparoscopic equipment, keeping total hospital charges for laparoscopic adrenalectomy ($10,929) lower than the corresponding charges for open adrenalectomy ($13,720). This difference in charges was not statistically significant, however.[47]

It is important that these findings probably underestimate the improvement in economic outcomes observed from the laparoscopic procedure. To date, studies have measured only direct costs (to hospitals and insurers), ignoring indirect cost benefits (eg, minimizing lost salary from work, less pain medication). To estimate these indirect cost benefits in the future, it will be essential to survey patients and their caretakers in the postoperative period. Since laparoscopy is still relatively new in endocrine surgery, long-term differences in patient outcomes are poorly understood.

Adrenal Imaging

Abdominal computed tomography (CT) remains the imaging procedure of choice for most adrenal tumors.[48] The greatest shortcoming of CT is that it relies on size rather than specific tissue characteristics to differentiate among lesions. Adrenal adenomas, carcinomas, and pheochromocytomas can appear similar on CT. Furthermore, false-negatives can result from attempting to image tumors smaller than 1 cm.

Noninvasive imaging methods such as chemical-shift MRI and ^{131}I-6-ß-iodomethyl-19-norcholesterol (NP-59) radionuclide scanning can offer substantial information to distinguish adrenal adenomas from metastatic disease.[49] These new studies might ultimately result in cost saving if they facilitate earlier diagnosis and minimize patient morbidity from invasive diagnostic procedures.

CONCLUSION

The findings from these outcomes studies have important implications for patients, referring physicians, medical educators, and third-party payers responsible for setting medical coverage and reimbursement policies. Clinical trials comparing emerging technologies, drugs, and procedures in endocrine surgery are critical and would be optimal if combined with cost-effectiveness and decision analyses that integrate patient-assessed outcomes. The proliferation of technologic advancements has led to the adoption of techniques in the absence of well-conducted clinical trials. Accordingly, laparoscopic adrenalectomy has already become the technique of choice for adrenal extirpation at many institutions. It also appears that outpatient parathyroidectomy will revolutionize the management of patients with primary hyperparathyroidism. It therefore seems prudent, timely, and clinically important that endocrine surgeons perform appropriate outcomes studies to evaluate these emerging technologies. Many decision analyses have been performed in endocrinology and metabolism, addressing issues ranging from the management of patients with diabetes mellitus to the proper approach for patients with cold thyroid nodules (Table 27–4).[50–54] Such studies are now needed in endocrine surgery. The American College of Surgeons has recently secured funds to address these pressing issues in endocrine surgery via large randomized prospective trials. Such multi-institutional studies are anticipated to have sufficient statistical power to resolve these controversial issues and allow endocrinologists and endocrine surgeons of the next millennium to base their decisions on evidence-based data.

Table 27-4 Selected Decision Analyses in Endocrinology

Study	Clinical Problem and Patient Population	Strategies	Time Horizon	Outcome Measures	Result
Friedman[51]	Diabetic patients aged 30–70 years with asymptomatic gallstones	Elective cholecystectomy vs watchful waiting	Lifetime	Life expectancy	Additional 6.1 months of life with watchful waiting
Midgette[52]	Differential diagnosis of patients with Cushing's disease	Simultaneous bilateral IPSS vs high-dose dexamethasone suppression followed by IPSS if necessary	Short-term (postsurgical)	Lives saved, cost	$1 million per life saved for IPSS
Molitch[53]	Patients with cold thyroid nodules	Immediate subtotal thyroidectomy vs 6-month L-thyroxine therapy followed by surgery if appropriate vs aspiration cytology followed by suppression or surgery as appropriate	Lifetime	Quality-adjusted life expectancy	All options are essentially the same
Stockwell[54]	Adults exposed to upper body irradiation in childhood	Thyroid scan followed by subtotal thyroidectomy with single or multiple scan defects vs no scan with follow-up visits every 2 years	Lifetime	Quality-adjusted life expectancy	Additional 10.2 days of full quality of life for the no-scan strategy

IPSS = inferior petrosal sinus sampling.

Adapted from Powe NR, Danese MD, Ladenson PW. Decision analysis in endocrinology and metabolism. Endocrinol Metab Clin North Am 1997;26(1):89–111.

REFERENCES

1. Tunbridge WMG, Evered DC, Hall R, et al. The spectrum of thyroid disease in a community: the Whickham survey. Clin Endocrinol 1977;7:481–93.

2. Mundy GR, Cove DH, Fisken R. Primary hyperparathyroidism: changes in the pattern of clinical presentation. Lancet 1980;1:1317–20.

3. Heath H. Primary hyperparathyroidism: recent advances in pathogenesis, diagnosis, and management. Adv Intern Med 1991;37:275–93.

4. Purnell DC, Smith LH, Scholz DA, et al. Primary hyperparathyroidism: a prospective clinical study. Am J Med 1971;50:670–8.

5. Heath H III, Hodgson SF, Kennedy MA. Primary hyperparathyroidism: incidence, morbidity, and potential economic impact in a community. N Engl J Med 1980;302:189–93.

6. Stenstrom G, Heedman P-A. Clinical findings in patients with hypercalcaemia. Acta Med Scand 1974;195:473–7.

7. Wermers R, Khosla S, Atkinson E, et al. The rise and fall of primary hyperparathyroidism: a population-based study in Rochester, Minnesota, 1965–92. Ann Intern Med 1997;126:433–40.

8. Harness JK, Fung L, Thompson NW, et al. Total thyroidectomy: complications and technique. World J Surgery 1986;10:781–6.

9. Shaha A, Jaffe BM. Complications of thyroid surgery performed by residents. Surgery 1988;104:1109–14.

10. Martin L, Delbridge L, Martin J, et al. Trainee surgery in teaching hospitals: is there a cost? Aus NZ J Surg 1989;59:257–260.

11. Shindo ML, Sinha UK, Rick DH. Safety of thyroidectomy in residency: a review of 186 consecutive cases. Laryngoscope 1995;105:1173–5.

12. Reeve TS, Curtin A, Fingleton L, et al. Can total thyroidectomy be performed as safely by general surgeons in provincial centers as by surgeons in specialized endocrine surgical units? Arch Surg 1994;129:834–6.

13. Sosa JA, Bowman HM, Tielsch JM, et al. The importance of surgeon experience for clinical and economic outcomes for thyroidectomy. Ann Surg 1998;228(3):320–30.

14. Edis AJ. Prevention and management of complications associated with thyroid and parathyroid surgery. Surg Clin North Am 1979;59(1):83–92.

15. Farrar WB. Complications of thyroidectomy. Surg Clin North Am 1983;63(6):1353–61.

16. Sackett DL, Haynes RB, Buyatt GH, Tugwell P. Clinical epidemiology: a basic science for clinical medicine. 2nd ed. Boston: Little, Brown and Co.; 1991. p. 285.

17. Noguchi M, Katev N, Miyazaki I. Controversies in the surgical management of differentiated thyroid cancer. Int Surg 1996;81:163–7.

18. McHenry C, Jarosz H, Davis M, et al. Selective postoperative radioactive iodine treatment of thyroid carcinoma. Surgery 1989;106:956–9.

19. Varma VM, Beierwaltes WH, Nofal MM, et al. Treatment of thyroid cancer. Death rates after surgery and after surgery followed by sodium iodide [131]I. JAMA 1970;214:1437–42.

20. Cunningham MP, Duda RB, Recant W, et al. Survival discriminant for differentiated thyroid cancer. Am J Surg 1990;160:344–7.

21. Udelsman R, Lakatos E, Ladenson P. Optimal surgery for papillary thyroid carcinoma. World J Surg 1996;20:88–93.

22. Harrison BJ, Wheeler MH. Review of current practice in surgical management of benign thyroid disease. Br J Surg 1993;80:1209.

23. Matthews TW, Lampe HB, LeBlanc S. Same-day admission thyroidectomy programme: quality assurance study. J Otolaryngol 1996;25(5):290–5.

24. Marohn MR, LaCivita KA. Evaluation of total/near-total thyroidectomy in a short-stay hospitalization: safe and cost-effective. Surgery 1995;118:943–8.

25. McHenry CR. "Same-day" thyroid surgery: an analysis of safety, cost savings, and outcome. Am Surg 1997;63:586–90.

26. Al Zahrani A, Levine MA. Primary hyperparathyroidism. Lancet 1997;349:1233–8.

27. Silverberg S, Gartenberg F, Jacobs T, et al. Increased bone mineral density after parathyroidectomy in primary hyperparathyroidism. J Clin Endocrinol Metab 1995;80:729–34.

28. Ronnie-Sivula H, Sivula A. Long-term effect of surgical treatment on the symptoms of primary hyperparathyroidism. Ann Clin Res 1985;17:141–7.

29. Pasieka JL, Parsons L. A prospective surgical outcome study of the relief of symptoms following surgery in patients with primary hyperparathyroidism. World J Surg 1998;22:513–19.

30. Hedback G, Tisell L-E, Bengtsson B-A, et al. Premature death in patients operated on for primary hyperparathyroidism. World J Surg 1990;14:829–36.

31. Malmaeus J, Granberg PO, Halvorsen J, et al. Parathyroid surgery in Scandinavia. Acta Chir Scand 1988;1:54:409–13.

32. Potts JT, editor. Proceedings of the NIH Consensus Development Conference on diagnosis and management of asymptomatic primary hyperparathyroidism. J Bone Miner Res 1991;6 Suppl:9–13.

33. Burney RE, Jones KR, Coon JW, et al. Assessment of patient outcomes after operation for primary hyperparathyroidism. Surgery 1996;120:1013–19.

34. Sosa JA, Powe NR, Levine MA, et al. Thresholds for surgery and surgical outcomes for patients with primary hyperparathyroidism: a national survey of endocrine surgeons. J Clin Endocrinol Metab 1998;83:2658–65.

35. Chen H, Zeiger MA, Gordon TA, Udelsman R. Parathyroidectomy in Maryland: effects of an endocrine center. Surgery 1996;120:948–53.

36. Sosa JA, Powe NR, Levine MA, et al. Cost implications of different surgical management strategies for primary hyperparathyroidism. Surgery 1998;124:1028–36.

37. Denham DW, Norman J. Cost-effectiveness of preoperative sestamibi scan for primary hyperparathyroidism is dependent solely upon the surgeon's choice of operative procedure. J Am Coll Surg 1998;186(3):293–305.

38. Hindi E, Melliere D, Simon D, et al. Primary hyperparathyroidism: is technetium 99m-sestamibi/iodine-123 subtraction scanning the best procedure to locate enlarged glands before surgery? J Clin Endocrinol Metab 1995;80:302–7.

39. Irvin GL, Prudhomme BS, Deriso GT. A new approach to parathyroidectomy. Ann Surg 1994; 219:574–81.

40. Irvin G, Sfakianakis G, Yeung L. Ambulatory parathyroidectomy for primary hyperparathyroidism. Arch Surg 1996;131:1074–8.

41. Norman J, Denham D. Radioguided parathyroidectomy for persistent and recurrent primary hyperparathyroidism. Surgery 1998;124:1088–93.

42. Chen H, Sokoll L, Udelsman R. Outpatient minimally invasive parathyroidectomy: a combination of sestamibi-SPECT localization, cervical block anesthesia, and intraoperative PTH assay. Surgery 1999. [In press]

43. Guazzoni G, Montorsi F, Bergamaschi F, et al. Effectiveness and safety of laparoscopic adrenalectomy. J Urol 1994;152(5 Pt 1):1375–8.

44. Rutherford JC, Stowasser M, Tunny TJ, et al. Laparoscopic adrenalectomy. World J Surg 1996;20(7):758–60.

45. Korman JE, Ho T, Hiatt JR, Phillips EH. Comparison of laparoscopic and open adrenalectomy. Am Surg 1997;63:908–12.

46. Schell SR, Talamini MA, Udelsman R. Laparoscopic adrenalectomy for nonmalignant disease: improved safety, morbidity, and cost-effectiveness. Surg Endosc 1999;13:30–4.

47. Jacobs JK, Goldstein RE, Geer RJ. Laparoscopic adrenalectomy: a new standard of care. Ann Surg 1997;225:495–502.

48. Sosa JA, Udelsman R. Imaging of the adrenal gland. Surg Oncol Clin N Am 1999;8(1):109–27.

49. Thrall JH, Freitas JE, Beierwaltes WH. Adrenal scintigraphy. Semin Nucl Med 1978;8:23–41.

50. Powe NR, Danese MD, Ladenson PW. Decision analysis in endocrinology and metabolism. Endocrinol Metab Clin North Am 1997;26(1):89–111.

51. Friedman LS, Roberts MS, Brett AS, et al. Management of asymptomatic gallstones in the diabetic patient: a decision analysis. Ann Intern Med 1988;109:913–19.

52. Midgette AS, Aron DC. High-dose dexamethasone suppression testing versus inferior petrosal sinus sampling in the differential diagnosis of adrenocorticotropin-dependent Cushing's syndrome: a decision analysis. Am J Med Sci 1995;305:162–70.

53. Molitch MD, Beck JR, Dresman M, et al. The cold nodule: an analysis of diagnostic and therapeutic options. Endocr Rev 1984;5:185–99.

54. Stockwell RM, Barry M, Davidoff F. Managing abnormalities in adults exposed to upper body irradiation in childhood: a decision analysis. Should patients without palpable nodules be scanned and those with scan defects be subjected to subtotal thyroidectomy? J Clin Endocrinol Metab 1984;58:804–12.

CHAPTER 28

Vascular Surgery

Bruce A. Perler, MD, FACS

—————

ECONOMIC BACKGROUND

The Role of the Vascular Surgeon

The specialty of vascular surgery is devoted to the medical and surgical management of disorders of the circulatory system, including arterial, venous, and lymphatic disease. In contemporary practice, most vascular surgeons spend most of their time treating arteriosclerotic, aneurysmal, and occlusive disease of the aorta, iliac, and peripheral arteries. In other words, management of patients with arterial insufficiency due to arteriosclerotic occlusive disease is a central focus of the vascular surgeon in practice today. Over the last three decades, vascular surgery has rapidly evolved and has seen the development of effective techniques to improve the arterial circulation of afflicted individuals, including a variety of endarterectomy and bypass graft procedures.

Demographic Considerations

While economic realities pervade the entire health care system, they are especially relevant for vascular specialists. Arteriosclerosis is unequivocally the most common etiology of peripheral arterial occlusive disease (PAOD) and the most frequent condition treated by vascular surgeons. This pathologic condition predominates among elderly people, the fastest-growing segment of our population. There are currently 25 million individuals in the United States between 65 and 85 years of age, and it is estimated that by 2025 this demographic group will total 58 million, an increase of more than 100 percent. At least 34 million individuals will be older than 75 years of age.[1] In fact, the average life expectancy of a 75-year-old person is currently 10 years, and that of an 80-year-old individual is approximately 7 years.[2] It is estimated that approximately 40 percent of the U.S. population will survive to the age of 80 years.[3] The economic implications of this expansion in our elderly population are obvious. It has been projected, for example, that the fraction of the federal budget devoted to Medicare could increase from 12 percent to 18 percent over the next decade.[4]

These demographic considerations imply that the treatment of PAOD will be an important growth area in medical practice for the foreseeable future. In addition, vascular specialists will have a variety of new technologies to diagnose and treat this patient population. In view of this rapidly expanding patient population, the growing variety of technologically advanced and increasingly expensive management options being developed, and the more limited financial resources available, the vascular surgeon will be expected to exercise sound judgment in the selection of both patients for intervention and the specific intervention itself.

It is now essential that the vascular surgeon become aware of the economic implications of his or her practice and be actively engaged in managing the economic challenges, since one of the most important issues confronting our society today is the financing of quality health care for our citizens. The fraction of our gross domestic product spent on health care was 5 percent in 1950, 7 percent in 1970, 12 percent in 1990, and 14 percent in 1994. In real dollar terms, spending has increased from $20 billion in 1950 to nearly $1 trillion in 1994.[4] This reflects a rate of growth of health care spending roughly 1½ to 2 times the rate of growth of the economy and inflation.[4] It has become quite clear to both payers and providers that this exponential growth in expenditures cannot be sustained indefinitely, and as a result, significant pressure to control health care costs has developed in recent years.

Several factors have contributed to this growth in spending. General economic inflation is responsible for approximately 50 percent of the increase. The rapid aging of the population is another important component. These two factors are clearly beyond the control of the health care provider. On the other hand, defensive medicine, inefficiency in the delivery of care, and increased technology coupled with greater patient demand for that technology are more amenable to practice modification.[4] The latter factor, known as service intensity, may account for as much as 30 percent of the increase in health care spending in recent years.

Since roughly two-thirds of health care expenditures are paid to physicians and hospitals,[5] logical efforts to control health care spending must focus on the providers of that care. Today's medical practitioners are scrutinized to an unprecedented degree by interests such as third-party payers, government health care administrators, quality assurance committees, hospital and managed care executives, and public health leaders. Providers will increasingly be expected to justify diagnostic and therapeutic interventions with sound and credible evidence. Interventions will be judged no longer simply by their effectiveness but by their cost-efficacy as well.[6]

The vascular surgeon should view this economic responsibility as an opportunity or perhaps a privilege. Indeed, in an era in which the demand for clinical services will increasingly exceed the available resources to finance those services, the rationing of health care delivery seems unavoidable to many.[4,6] The only uncertainty is who will make these crucial clinical decisions. This writer would argue that the clinician must continue to play the primary role in directing patient care, that is, in rationing care. However, those decisions can no longer be based on anecdotal experience. Rather, evidence-based decision making will be the new paradigm for medical and surgical practice. This chapter will examine this paradigm within the specific context of the patient presenting with severe, limb-threatening arterial insufficiency or ischemia due to advanced PAOD.

LITERATURE REVIEW: CHRONIC LIMB-THREATENING ISCHEMIA

The most appropriate management of the elderly patient with multiple comorbid medical conditions and a predictably limited life expectancy who presents with severe arterial insufficiency of a lower extremity is an important judgment that has been regularly made by vascular surgeons in this country for decades and one that will be increasingly faced in the future. The fundamental choice is whether to attempt revascularization of the ischemic extremity or to proceed directly with a primary amputation of that limb. What patient would prefer amputation of a leg as opposed to having a bypass operation performed to save it?

Before the evolution of modern vascular surgical techniques, the development of severe ischemic pain, pedal ulcerations, or frank gangrene almost invariably condemned the patient to an above- (AKA) or below-knee amputation (BKA).[7-9] Most patients who present with limb-threatening ischemia require infra-inguinal arterial revascularization, and over the last three decades, improvements in vascular surgical techniques and care have enhanced our ability to successfully perform bypass grafts to the infrapopliteal and pedal level (Table 28-1). This has resulted in a decline in the percentage of patients subjected to primary amputations. For example, in a review of 2,829 patients presenting with limb-threatening ischemia, Veith and colleagues reported that the primary amputation rate declined progressively, from 52 percent in 1974 to 11 percent in 1989.[10] Similarly, in an analysis of diabetic patients presenting with limb-threatening ischemia at the New England Deaconess Hospital, the fraction of patients undergoing an AKA or BKA declined from 40 percent in 1984 to 14 percent in 1990. This decline in the rate of major amputations correlated with a significant increase in distal bypass grafts.[11]

However, bypass operations for limb salvage can be complex and are not without significant risks in the older, medically compromised patient. Furthermore, in some cases the

Table 28–1 Improved Limb Salvage Revascularization: Contributing Factors

Improved noninvasive vascular laboratory testing

Improved arterial imaging modalities
—Digital subtraction angiography
—Magnetic resonance angiography

Technologic improvements
—Surgical instrumentation
—Optical magnification
—Sutures

Multidisciplinary endovascular and surgical revascularization

Improved anesthetic and perioperative management

Postoperative antiplatelet and anticoagulant therapy

Postoperative duplex graft surveillance

bypass is unsuccessful so that the patient must undergo a limb amputation as a secondary procedure, often after protracted hospitalization and considerable cost. In other words, the decision to proceed with revascularization can entail a number of complex interacting considerations, and in the future the treatment elected will have to be supported by credible scientific evidence. The process of gathering this evidence has already begun.

For example, in a recent large retrospective population-based study, it was reported that the cost of treating all patients with PAOD in Maryland rose from approximately $14.7 million in 1979 to $30.5 million in 1989, and that this reflected a significant increase in the number of peripheral bypass operations and percutaneous transluminal angioplasty procedures performed.[12] The authors noted that despite this dramatic increase in service and associated costs, the amputation rate remained stable in the state throughout this decade.[12] The implication was that aggressive revascularization for limb salvage may not be cost-effective. Although the methodology employed in this investigation was fundamentally flawed and its findings were seriously challenged,[13,14] the study nevertheless highlighted some of the important outcomes that must be studied when examining the dichotomous options of revascularization and amputation for critical limb ischemia and also the difficulty of carrying out credible outcomes analyses in this area.

These considerations were succinctly highlighted in a recent editorial entitled "It can be fixed, but should it be?"[15] In this essay, a respected vascular surgeon reported the case of a 75-year-old woman who had developed severe limb ischemia following coronary artery bypass surgery and who subsequently underwent four separate bypass operations, two in each leg, during a continuous 4-month hospitalization. None of the reconstructions remained patent, and the patient finally underwent bilateral above-knee amputations. He noted that although this was hardly an ideal or intended outcome, it was only after the amputations that the patient was finally relieved of pain that had persisted for months. Her depression cleared, and she became engaged again in her family life.[15] This anecdotal report addressed not only the prognostic indicators of a poor surgical outcome of which vascular surgeons have become cognizant through years of clinical experience, but also the issues of the patient's functional activity and quality of life. These outcomes have received little attention to date but clearly will become increasingly important as we move into this era of evidence-based outcomes analysis.

Obviously, the infallible hindsight reflected in this editorial is not available to the practicing surgeon when encountering new patient with severe PAOD. The decision to attempt revascularization is typically a surgical judgment predicated upon previous personal and published clinical experience; in the future, it will be increasingly influenced by data derived from focused outcomes studies. Although traditionally the randomized clinical trial has been the most useful mechanism for defining the superiority of one treatment option over another, not all clinical problems lend themselves to such methodology. Specifically, when a strong bias exists on the part of the clinician or patient in favor of one of the options, randomization may not be possible.[4,16] The choice of revascularization versus amputation for severe arterial insufficiency is a classic example of this limitation. Nevertheless, outcomes analyses still afford an opportunity to develop the necessary evidence upon which the clinician can make rational therapeutic judgments.

In patients with severe limb-threatening ischemia, the traditional outcomes that have been measured include the rates of operative mortality, long-term bypass graft patency, and limb salvage. While these variables continue to be relevant concerns of the vascular surgeon treating a patient with severe limb-threatening ischemia, they provide only part of the information needed to make these clinical decisions today. As noted above, contemporary outcomes analysis requires a measure of the functional outcome experienced by the patient, which is a complicated consideration.[17,18] Furthermore, these outcomes must be achieved in a reasonably cost-effective manner.[5] This chapter will address the issue of revascularization versus primary amputation within this context.

Case Study: Amputation versus Revascularization

The rationale proposed by some in support of primary amputation for elderly patients with severe limb-threatening ischemia includes several components (Table 28–2). While each of these considerations appears logical upon initial reflection, this author would argue that each can be seriously challenged on the basis of credible evidence-based analysis.

Operative Mortality

There is no question that amputation of a limb is a technically uncomplicated procedure that can be rapidly performed in most cases. On the other hand, arterial bypass operations for limb-threatening ischemia are much more time consuming, are technically more difficult, are associated with significant blood loss, and convey a greater risk of relative hypothermia and other pathophysiologic complications. Patients with limb-threatening ischemia invariably suffer from extensive femoropopliteal-femorotibial occlusive disease, and it is well established that infra-inguinal arteriosclerotic disease is a sensitive marker for underlying coronary artery disease. Furthermore, in many patients with PAOD, the underlying coronary disease is clinically silent due to the functional limitations imposed by their peripheral vascular symptoms. It is not surprising, therefore, that cardiac complications represent the most important cause of mortality among patients undergoing arterial revascularization.

In this context it is not unreasonable to assume that the risk of operative mortality must be much higher among patients undergoing limb revascularization than among those in whom a straightforward amputation is performed. However, the available evidence clearly refutes this. For example, in a recent prospective study of patients undergoing infra-inguinal revascularization at The Johns Hopkins Hospital in which 86 percent of the operations were

Table 28–2 Advantages of Primary Amputation for Limb-Threatening Ischemia

• Lower operative mortality

• Shorter length of hospitalization

• Lower cost

• Comparable functional outcome

performed for limb-threatening ischemia, operative mortality was only 2 percent, and nonfatal myocardial infarctions developed in only 4 percent of the survivors.[19] Several other recent reports have documented an operative mortality ranging from 1 to 3 percent among older patients undergoing infra-inguinal revascularization.[20-22] It has been further assumed by some that general anesthesia increases operative risk in this patient population and should be avoided if possible. Yet, in the Hopkins study, in which patients were prospectively randomized to undergo operation under general or epidural anesthesia, no difference in outcome was noted among patients undergoing operation under the two anesthetic techniques.[19] Therefore, it appears that with aggressive preoperative preparation and intra- and postoperative monitoring and management, complex infra-inguinal arterial reconstructive procedures can be performed with a very low operative risk.

Furthermore, limb amputation is not a risk-free intervention. In a review of 1,735 patients who underwent BKA in Veterans Affairs Hospitals in 1991, in-hospital mortality was 12 percent.[23] Several other series have reported operative mortality ranging from 8 to 17 percent among patients undergoing BKA and AKA procedures.[24-27]

While the randomized prospective clinical trial represents the optimal scientific methodology for assessing outcomes (such as operative mortality) of alternative treatment options, such an investigative strategy is not feasible when the alternatives are revascularization versus removal of the ischemic limb. Therefore, much of the evidence on which our judgments in this clinical issue are based has been derived from retrospective clinical studies, which have limitations as noted in Chapter 10. It can be assumed, for example, that patients undergoing primary amputation were older and sicker than those undergoing surgical bypass operations; that is, it may be inappropriate, or even misleading to compare the outcome of limb amputation to that of revascularization through retrospective analyses.

Although the power of evidence reported in retrospective studies is much weaker than what could be derived from prospective trials, credible information has been published. For example, operative mortality was studied among patients who underwent either primary amputation or revascularization for limb salvage at the University of Rochester. Although the study was retrospective, the overall medical comorbidity of two patient populations was objectively characterized using the Goldman cardiac index and the American Society of Anesthesiology (ASA) scoring system.[27] Among the patients at lowest risk (Goldman index <5, and ASA class I or II) there was no operative mortality among patients undergoing primary below-knee amputation or surgical revascularization. Among moderate-risk patients (Goldman index 5 to 9 and ASA class III), operative mortality was 3 percent for primary amputation and 3 percent for surgical revascularization. However, among the sickest patient population (10 or greater on the Goldman scale and ASA class IV and V), operative mortality was 16 percent for primary amputation and 6 percent for surgical reconstruction.[27] Therefore, while it may be inappropriate to conclude that surgical revascularization is associated with less morbidity than limb amputation (based upon this retrospective study), the objective clinical evidence clearly does not support the premise that primary amputation is safer.

Hospital Length of Stay

It has been assumed that patients undergoing a primary amputation require a shorter hospital stay, compared to those undergoing surgical revascularization (see Table 28–2). Inherent in this hypothesis is the presumption that the complication rate should be much greater after a complex surgical reconstructive procedure than after an amputation, which is technically simpler, and that these complications necessarily delay hospital discharge. Furthermore, whereas limb amputation is perceived to be a definitive solution to the severe limb-threatening ischemia, a revascularization patient may require further secondary interventions, such as ischemic wound débridement, or amputations of toes or a portion of the involved foot. However, the assumption that primary amputation is consistently associated with a shorter duration of acute care hospitalization than is surgical revascularization is not supported by the available evidence.

For example, in a retrospective review of 147 patients who presented to the (UCLA) Department of Surgery with limb-threatening ischemia and underwent either uncomplicated primary BKA (n = 53) or infra-inguinal bypass graft (n = 94), the mean length of stay was actually 3 days shorter among those who underwent surgical revascularization (15.4 vs 18.4 days).[28] This study clearly affirmed that surgical complications will prolong the hospital length of stay although the adverse effect of surgical morbidity on length of stay did not change the fundamental findings. For example, the most unfavorable outcome among patients who underwent surgical revascularization for limb salvage was graft thrombosis requiring amputation of the limb as a secondary procedure. This occurred in eight (8.4%) of the patients in this series, and the mean length of stay of these patients was 30.5 days. It is not unreasonable to compare this subset of patients to those who underwent primary BKA and did not heal and thus required revision at the above-knee level. This complication was noted in 12 (22.3%) of the patients undergoing primary BKA; the mean hospital length of stay among this group was 30.8 days.[28] In another review, the hospital courses of 289 patients who underwent surgical revascularization and associated procedures for limb salvage were compared to those of 24 patients who underwent primary amputation. The mean hospital length of stay was significantly shorter among those who underwent revascularization (50 vs 60 days, $p < .05$).[29]

It is not unreasonable to assume that in such retrospective analyses the patient populations undergoing amputation or surgical revascularization are not strictly comparable; that is, the patient population undergoing primary amputation had greater medical comorbidity, which would be expected to adversely influence their length of stay. This confounding influence was addressed in a similar analysis by Ouriel and colleagues in which the comorbidity of each of the patient populations undergoing primary amputation or surgical revascularization were stratified into three groups using the ASA classification system and the Goldman cardiac index.[27] Although these researchers demonstrated a not unexpected progressively longer hospital length of stay associated with greater comorbidity among patients undergoing primary amputation and surgical revascularization, the length of stay at each level of comorbidity was significantly longer among those who underwent primary amputation. Specifically, among ASA class I and II patients, the mean length of stay was 19 days for amputation and 10 days for surgical revascularization ($p < .05$); for ASA class III patients the length of stay was 22 and 12 days, respectively ($p < .01$); and among patients in ASA class IV or V, the length of stay was 31 and 14 days, respectively ($p < .05$).[27] Although our inability to study this issue in randomized prospective fashion is a limitation, there is little support, based upon the available evidence, for the assumption that hospital discharge may be expected earlier after primary amputation than after surgical revascularization.

Early Charges

A definitive analysis of the respective costs of revascularization and primary amputation is limited also by the inability to perform a randomized prospective clinical study. Nevertheless, data derived from retrospective or nonrandomized prospective investigations to date have largely refuted the notion that amputation is a cheaper solution to the problem of severe limb-threatening arterial insufficiency. First, amputation is not inexpensive. In a review of the cost of amputation performed in seven hospitals in Boston in 1993, the mean charge was $22,419 among patients who underwent an uncomplicated BKA. Among patients who developed complications that resulted in mortality, the charge increased to $59,410 per patient.[30] Since a fundamental assumption of the argument favoring primary amputation is that the majority of patients will be successfully rehabilitated (see Table 28–2), an economic analysis of this issue should include the cost of the prosthesis and the associated physical therapy. In the Boston hospitals investigation, the mean outpatient charge accrued during the first year after the amputation was $7,039 per case.[30]

Numerous institutional studies performed over the last two decades have addressed this issue.[28,29,31–37] While the costs of treating patients with severe PAOD have substantially increased, not a single published study indicates that primary amputation is a less costly solution to the problem, and in some studies, the total charges associated with revascularization have actually been lower than those associated with primary amputation (Table 28–3). This is not completely unexpected, since (as noted above) the assumption that primary amputation results in a consistently shorter length of hospital stay has been refuted by several outcomes analyses. These fundamental economic implications have been confirmed in subsequent subset analyses. For example, Panayiotopoulos and colleagues have stratified the outcome among diabetic and nondiabetic patients. Although charges for the care of diabetic patients were higher than those for the care of nondiabetics, this risk factor appeared to influence the costs of revascularization and limb salvage revascularization equally. Specifically, mean charges among diabetic and nondiabetic patients were £9,181 and £6,350 (British) respectively for revascularization, and £15,500 and £12,040 respectively for primary amputation.[38] This investigation also demonstrated that the highly complex surgical bypass operations performed more recently have not altered the economic balance between limb salvage revascularization and primary amputation, since all these patients underwent bypasses to the infra-popliteal or pedal level, which are among the most difficult and time-consuming contemporary surgical revascularization procedures.[38]

Because surgical complications lengthen hospital stay and increase costs, the worst economic scenario is performance of a revascularization procedure which fails early postoperatively, culminating in limb amputation as a secondary procedure. Numerous outcomes studies in recent years have confirmed this. In one report, for example, the mean charges incurred by patients who underwent primary amputation were 30 percent greater than those accrued by patients who underwent successful revascularization for limb salvage (313,000 vs 240,000 Finnish marks). However, charges associated with secondary amputations were nearly 50 percent greater than those associated with primary amputation (402,000 Finnish marks).[35] Gupta and colleagues reported mean charges of $42,000 among patients undergoing secondary amputation, in contrast to $27,225 among those in whom a primary amputation was performed.[33] Similarly, in a report from UCLA, early revision of a limb salvage bypass graft

Table 28–3 Amputation versus Revascularization: Hospital Charges

Study	Total Hospital Charges ($U.S.)	
	Revascularization	Amputation
Heller (1981)	18,950	24,350
Gupta (1982)	19,240	27,770
Auer (1983)	8,395	11,500
Mackey (1986)	27,081	26,142
Gupta (1988)	26,194	27,225
Raviola (1988)	23,946	24,225
Singh (1996)	6,766*	10,162*
Panayiotopoulos (1997)	4,320*	12,730*
Luther (1997)	240,000†	313,000†

* British pounds.
† Finnish marks.

increased mean hospital charges from $20,300 to $28,700 per patient, and the mean charges increased to $42,200 among patients in whom graft failure resulted in secondary limb amputation.[28] However, not all primary amputations result in a completely uneventful postoperative course. For example, nearly 25 percent of the patients in the UCLA study who underwent primary BKA developed significant complications which required revision to an AKA; among these patients, mean hospital charges were $42,600, essentially equivalent to the costs incurred by patients who underwent secondary amputation after a failed arterial bypass graft.[28]

This evidence indicates that the economic rationale in support of limb salvage revascularization over primary amputation depends on achieving successful limb salvage in the majority of patients undergoing arterial bypass operations. Careful surgical judgment is paramount in selecting appropriate candidates for revascularization, and each case must be assessed on its own merits. Numerous outcomes analyses in recent years have identified risk factors for unsuccessful limb salvage revascularization (Table 28–4), and it seems these observations have positively influenced the clinical judgment and practice of contemporary vascular surgeons. For example, in the UCLA experience, early secondary amputation was required in only 8 percent of cases (28), and in the report of Gupta and colleagues, only 13 percent of patients who underwent limb salvage revascularization required a secondary amputation due to early bypass graft failure.[33]

Long-Term Charges

It is well recognized that arteriosclerosis, the primary condition for which the majority of limb salvage surgical revascularization procedures are performed, is an incurable and progressive disease. As a result, patients who undergo successful revascularization for limb salvage remain at risk for disease progression that might predispose to failure of an initially successful arterial revascularization procedure during follow-up, thus jeopardizing limb viability. In other words, the financial costs of achieving limb salvage may continue to accrue longitudinally in many patients as a consequence of the surgeon's efforts to maintain limb viability. An economic outcomes analysis of the financial burden associated with limb salvage should therefore include these long-term costs as well.

This issue was addressed in an important study of long-term outcomes reported by Mackey and colleagues.[34] The longitudinal courses of 78 patients who underwent successful revascularization procedures for limb salvage were compared to those of 28 patients who underwent primary amputation. The patients who underwent revascularization required a mean of 2.4 hospital admissions, spent an additional 67 days as in-patients, and accrued total charges of $40,709 per case, exclusive of the costs of the initial revascularization procedures, during a mean follow-up of 805 days. In view of the natural history of the underlying disease, these observations were not unexpected. What was striking and unexpected was the long-term economic outcome among the primary amputation patient population. These 28 patients required an additional 2.2 hospital admissions, spent an additional 85 days as in-patients, and accrued an additional $40,563 in mean charges per case during a mean follow-up of 663

Table 28–4 Surgical Risk Factors for Unsuccessful Revascularization

- End-stage renal failure
- Previous failed bypass graft
- Poor tibial artery and pedal runoff vessels
- Absent or poor saphenous vein
- Extensive pedal necrotic tissue

days.[34] This investigation extended our understanding of the economic implications of treating limb-threatening ischemia. While numerous reports have indicated that there is no apparent economic advantage to primary amputation in the short-term, the data of Mackey and colleagues emphasized that an economic analysis of only the initial hospitalization and treatment substantially underestimates the financial burden associated with treating this condition. More important, it suggests that there is also no long-term economic benefit of primary amputation when compared to surgical revascularization.

This study further emphasized the importance of careful patient selection for revascularization. Among the 78 patients who underwent successful revascularization for limb salvage, 34 patients experienced bypass graft failure during follow-up, resulting in limb loss. Among these patients, there were 3.1 additional hospitalizations and 97 additional in-patient days, and the mean total charge during follow-up was $56,809 per patient. Conversely, among the 44 patients in whom limb viability was maintained during follow-up, there were only 1.8 additional hospitalizations and 43 additional in-patient days, and the mean total charge per patient was only $28,374.[34] In addition to confirming the importance of carefully selecting patients for revascularization and performing the most durable revascularization procedure during the patient's initial presentation (see Table 28–4), the study demonstrated that although it may be expensive to re-intervene for disease progression and/or failure of the original surgical reconstruction during follow-up of these older patients, such a strategy is cost-effective if intervention maintains limb viability.

Implicit in this analysis is the observation that the longer the limb survives, and (clearly) the longer the patient survives, the greater is the economic benefit of revascularization for limb salvage when compared to primary amputation of the specific extremity. In a recent population-based outcomes analysis, for example, 117 patients who presented with limb-threatening ischemia underwent either primary amputation or surgical revascularization in three hospitals. The costs of all interventions during the initial presentation as well as subsequent revascularization procedures and amputations were captured. The mean total charge was 150,000 Finnish marks (FIM) per survival year among those undergoing a primary amputation but only 47,000 FIM per survival year among those who underwent successful revascularization for limb salvage. Not surprisingly, the long-term costs were highest among those who underwent revascularization for limb salvage and who then experienced ultimate graft failure and secondary limb amputation. However, their costs were 147,000 FIM per survival year, which was equivalent to the costs associated with primary amputation.[35]

Functional Outcome: Ambulation

As noted above, one of the fundamental outcome measures in an analysis of the treatment of limb-threatening ischemia has been the resumption of ambulation. Inherent in the rationale for primary amputation is the assumption that with modern prosthetic technology a high percentage of elderly amputees will be able to walk and achieve a satisfactory functional outcome. While isolated reports from specialized centers have suggested that most elderly amputees can be successfully rehabilitated, these results have been achieved in selected patient populations and may not reflect the rehabilitation potential of this elderly patient population in general.[39] In a recent report from a rehabilitation unit including 101 amputees with a mean age of 69 years, only 87 percent of the patients could be fitted with a prosthesis. Furthermore, only 73 percent of the patients achieved their rehabilitation goals, which most frequently was ambulation with the aid of a walker.[40] Other studies from institutions have documented successful rehabilitation rates ranging from 47 to 66 percent in this patient population.[24,25,27]

In addition, recent population-based studies suggest that reports from individual centers of excellence may overestimate the rehabilitation potential of the elderly amputee population, in part because many elderly amputees may not be candidates for prosthesis fitting or rehabilitation programs. For example, Kald and colleagues studied the outcome of limb amputation among 106 patients who underwent operation in university and community hospitals in Motalo, Sweden, including 47 percent who were 80 years of age or older. Two-thirds of the amputations were performed above the knee. Only 25 percent of the patients received limb prostheses, and just 62 percent of these patients were still ambulatory with their artificial limbs 2 years after amputation. In other words, only 13 percent of the amputees were using their prostheses 2 years after the amputation.[41] These pessimistic results were confirmed in a more recent, larger community-based study in London. Amputations above or below the knee were performed upon 440 individuals in eight hospitals over a 2-year interval. Only 12 percent of these patients resumed bipedal ambulation around the home, including 16 percent of those who underwent BKA and 9 percent of those who underwent AKA.[42] Furthermore, bilateral amputees have a much poorer rehabilitation prognosis than unilateral amputees. Even among successfully rehabilitated amputation patients, therefore, disease progression may adversely affect the long-term functional outcome. Previous work has demonstrated that the unilateral amputee incurs a 15 to 50 percent risk of contralateral amputation; this clearly converts the ambulatory patient to nonambulatory status in many cases.[25,40,43]

The economic implications of limb amputation extend beyond the costs of hospitalization and medical/surgical interventions because amputation may have an economic cost to society as a whole. Currently, 92 percent of individuals 75 years of age in the United States live independently, and in 18 percent of these households, an elderly individual is living alone.[5] If limb amputation is tantamount to a loss of ambulatory status, it will translate into a loss of independence for many of our elderly citizens. The cost of home care or (more likely) institutionalization for a growing population of elderly amputees may represent an enormous financial burden on our society.

Functional Outcome: Quality of Life

While maintaining the patient's ambulatory status has been a fundamental outcome measure among patients who present with limb-threatening ischemia, recent outcomes analyses have attempted to measure more precisely the quality of life experienced by the patient population after amputation or surgical revascularization; maintaining bipedal gait is only one component of the patient's overall sense of well-being. Indeed, maintaining or improving the patient's quality of life is the ultimate goal of the surgeon caring for the patient with limb-threatening ischemia. Outcomes research in this area has been limited by the lack of a validated tool to measure functional status both before and after intervention, specifically among the patient population with severe arterial insufficiency.[44] Nevertheless, recent studies have provided useful information that will serve as the foundation for future research.

Limb-threatening arterial insufficiency clearly has a deleterious impact on the patient's quality of life. In a recent study that used the QL-INDEX of Spitzer and colleagues,[45] it was noted that the QL-INDEX prior to intervention in patients with severe limb ischemia due to infra-inguinal arterial occlusive disease was comparable to that of patients with severe or even terminal cancer.[46] Using components of the Functional Status Questionnaire[47] and the SF-36 Health Survey,[48] a study by Gibbons and colleagues confirmed that patients with severe arterial occlusive disease had a low perception of their overall health.[18]

On the other hand, recovery after even successful arterial reconstruction is not immediate, and may be delayed in many cases. This has two important implications: first, the timing of postintervention functional assessments undoubtedly influences the conclusions derived from those assessments; second, the recovery time associated with the intervention may significantly affect the patient's perception of his or her outcome even when revascularization has been successful. In one recent study, only 45 percent of patients reported feeling "back to normal" 6 months after revascularization.[18] In another recent study, the records of 112 patients with a mean age of 66 years who underwent infra-inguinal surgical revascularization were reviewed 5 to 7 years later.[17] An "ideal" surgical outcome, defined as "elimination of ischemia, uncomplicated wound healing, and rapid return to premorbid functional status without the need for repeat leg operations," was achieved in only 14.3 percent of the cases.[17] Ischemic and operative wounds required a mean of 4.2 (range 0.4 to 48) months to heal completely, and complete healing had not occurred by last follow-up in 22 percent of the patients. Additional surgical interventions were performed in 61 (56%) of the patients during follow-up to maintain graft patency, to manage wound complications, or to treat recurrent or contralateral limb ischemia.[17] The reasonable conclusion is that patients who undergo revascularization for limb salvage are likely to require ongoing or intermittent interventions for the duration of their lives although this observation is not unexpected and is completely consistent with the natural history of the underlying disease.

While it provides a sobering assessment of the medical needs of this patient population, the study in question does not invalidate revascularization for limb salvage for the majority of this patient population. Although the limited number of outcomes studies performed in this area to date have not provided uniform results, the preponderance of evidence continues to support an aggressive policy toward limb salvage. For example, Duggan and colleagues used the RAND 36-Item Health Survey 1.0 to assess functional outcomes among 38 patients aged 65 years or more who presented limb-threatening ischemia.[49] The researchers found no significant difference in overall health perceptions between patients who underwent successful revascularization for limb salvage and those whose grafts failed and resulted in limb amputation. However, this study was severely flawed because there were only four patients in the limb loss group. In addition, the follow-up interval varied from 3 months to 3 years after surgical intervention, which might have significantly influenced the outcomes in view of the natural history of the disease and the frequency of intercurrent problems as noted in other work.[17] The decline in physical function and general health observed in their study subjects is consistent with this phenomenon. In addition, the authors did not analyze the outcomes among a comparable group of patients undergoing primary amputation.

Other studies have directly compared functional outcomes among patients undergoing either revascularization or primary amputation. It has clearly been demonstrated that patient mobility strongly correlates with one's perception of health.[50] In a recent study from the Oregon Health Sciences University, revascularization for limb salvage succeeded in maintaining independent living and ambulation in the majority of patients who survived at least 6 months. Specifically, 96 percent of survivors who were living independently and who were ambulatory prior to operative intervention continued to be ambulatory and living independently 6 months postoperatively.[44] In addition, 29 (21%) patients who were nonambulatory preoperatively became ambulatory following revascularization.[44] On the other hand, only one patient who was living in a nursing home prior to limb revascularization achieved independent living status postoperatively. In another recent investigation, Johnson and colleagues noted that revascularization was associated with more anxiety and depression ($p = .04$) than was major limb amputation although it resulted in greater mobility ($p < .001$), better self-care ($p < .001$), and a better lifestyle ($p < .001$).[51] Similarly, Albers and colleagues reported that the impaired quality of life experienced by patients with severe limb-threatening ischemia could be reversed with limb revascularization (although the benefit may not be apparent during the first 3 months) and sustained during follow-up by maintaining bypass graft patency. However, this improvement in outcome was reversed if limb amputation ultimately had to be performed.[46]

FUTURE DIRECTIONS

The evolution of our approach to the treatment of limb-threatening ischemia over the last three decades is an excellent example of the impact of evidence-based research on the management of clinical problems. Thirty years ago, during the infancy of vascular surgery, infrainguinal occlusive disease was almost a universal prescription for major limb amputation. As methods of surgical revascularization were developed and refined, the pendulum shifted from amputation to attempted revascularization for limb salvage. Early outcomes studies focused on the fundamental endpoints of operative mortality, bypass graft patency, and limb salvage. The generally favorable outcomes reported in these studies stimulated increasingly aggressive attempts at limb salvage. In other words, earlier outcomes analyses helped define the technical limits of the surgical treatment of severe arterial insufficiency.[17]

Over the last decade, with growing awareness of the limited economic resources available and the growing population of potential candidates for revascularization, outcomes studies have increasingly focused on the economic implications of surgical revascularization and have raised new questions about its rationale. While some have recently advocated a more conservative approach to revascularization for limb salvage, the author believes that the aggressive strategy stimulated by early outcomes analyses continues to be supported by more sophisticated contemporary outcomes analyses. Although maintaining ambulation is a fundamental goal of revascularization and a desirable outcome endpoint, it does not provide the entire picture with respect to the quality of life achieved in patients undergoing surgical revascularization and how that quality of life compares to that of the patient cohort undergoing primary amputation. In the future we will need to develop research tools that are specific for measuring quality-of-life outcomes among the patient population presenting with limb-threatening ischemia. Vascular surgeons will also need to develop more sensitive predictors of successful revascularization both acute and long-term. Future outcomes studies will need to address not just how much we can accomplish surgically, but equally important must help us more precisely define when and in whom these surgical reconstructive procedures should be undertaken.[17]

REFERENCES

1. Perler BA. Vascular disease in the elderly patient. Surg Clin North Am 1974;74:199–216.

2. National Center for Health Statistics. Vital Statistics of U.S.A.: Vol.II Sec. 6, life tables. Washington (DC): Public Health Service, U.S. Government Printing Office; 1984. DHHS publication No. (PHS) 84-1104.

3. Treiman RL, Levine KA, Cohen JL, et al. Aneurysmectomy in the octogenarian: a study of morbidity and quality of survival. Am J Surg 1982;144:194–7.

4. Schwartz JS. Clinical economics and noncoronary vascular disease. J Vasc Interven Radiol 1995;6:116S–124S.

5. Perler BA. Cost-efficacy issues in the treatment of peripheral vascular disease: primary amputation or revascularization for limb-threatening ischemia. J Vasc Interven Radiol 1995;6:111S–115S.

6. Wennberg JE. Outcomes research, cost containment, and the fear of health care rationing. N Engl J Med 1990;323:1202–4.

7. O'Donnell JA, Brener BJ, Brief DK, et al. Realistic expectations for patients having lower extremity bypass surgery for limb salvage. Arch Surg 1977;112:1356–63.

8. Stoney RJ, James DR, Wylie EJ. Surgery for femoropopliteal atherosclerosis. Arch Surg 1971;103:548–53.

9. Thompson JE, Garrett WV. The application of distal bypass operations for limb salvage. Surgery 1980;87:717–8.

10. Veith FJ, Gupta SK, Wengerter KR, et al. Changing arteriosclerotic disease patterns and management strategies in lower-limb-threatening ischemia. Ann Surg 1990;212:402–14.

11. LoGerfo FW, Gibbons GW, Pomposelli FB, et al. Trends in the care of the diabetic foot. Expanded role of arterial reconstruction. Arch Surg 1992;127:617–21.

12. Tunis SR, Bass EB, Steinberg EP. The use of angioplasty, bypass surgery, and amputation in the management of peripheral vascular disease. N Engl J Med 1991;325:556–62.

13. Veith FJ, Perler BA, Bakal CW. The use of angioplasty, bypass surgery, and amputation in the management of peripheral vascular disease [letter]. N Engl J Med 1992;326:413.

14. Becker GJ, Ferguson J, Bakal CW, et al. Angioplasty, bypass surgery, and amputation for lower extremity arterial disease in Maryland: a closer look. Radiology 1993;1:118–21.

15. Skillman SJ. It can be fixed, but should it be? Ann Surg 1993;218:713–4.

16. Wennberg J. Some considerations in outcomes research. JVIR 1995;6:102S–103S.

17. Nicoloff AD, Taylor LM Jr, McLafferty RB, et al. Patient recovery after infrainguinal bypass grafting for limb salvage. J Vasc Surg 1998;27:256–66.

18. Gibbons GW, Burgess AM, Guadagnoli E, et al. Return to well-being and function after infrainguinal revascularization. J Vasc Surg 1995;21:35–45.

19. Christopherson R, Beattie C, Gottlieb SO, et al. Major perioperative morbidity in patients randomized to epidural or general anesthesia for lower extremity vascular surgery. Anesthesiology 1993; 79:422–34.

20. Taylor LM, Edwards JM, Porter JM. Present status of reversed vein bypass grafting: five-year results of a modern series. J Vasc Surg 1990;11:193–206.

21. Bergamini TM, Towne JB, Bandyk DF, et al. Experience with in situ saphenous vein bypass during 1981–1989: determinant factors of long-term patency. J Vasc Surg 1991;13:137–49.

22. Donaldson MC, Mannick JA, Whittemore AD. Femoral-distal bypass with in situ greater saphenous vein: long-term results using the Mills valvulotome. Ann Surg 1991;213:457–65.

23. Jacobs LA, Durance PW. Below-the-knee amputation. In: Ernst CB, Stanley JC, editors. Current therapy in vascular surgery. 3rd ed. St. Louis: Mosby; 1995. p. 674–7.

24. High RM, McDowell DE, Savrin RA. A critical review of amputation in vascular patients. J Vasc Surg 1984;1:653–5.

25. Kihn B, Warren R, Beebe GW. The "geriatric" amputee. Ann Surg 1972;176:305–9.

26. Otteman MG, Stahlgren LH. Evaluation of factors which influence mortality and morbidity following major lower extremity amputation for atherosclerosis. Surg Gynecol Obstet 1965; 120:1217–20.

27. Ouriel K, Fiore WM, Geary JE. Limb-threatening ischemia in the medically compromised patient: amputation or revascularization? Surgery 1986;104:667–72.

28. Raviola CA, Nichter LS, Baker JD, et al. Cost of treating advanced leg ischemia. Bypass graft vs primary amputation. Arch Surg 1988;123:495–6.

29. Gupta SK, Veith FJ, Ascer E, et al. Cost factors in limb-threatening ischemia due to infrainguinal arteriosclerosis. Eur J Vasc Surg 1988;2:1223-6.

30. Eckman MH, Greenfield S, Mackey WC, et al. Foot infections in diabetic patients. Decision and cost-effectiveness analyses. JAMA 1995;273:712–20.

31. Auer AI, Hurley JJ, Binnington B, et al. Distal tibial grafts for limb salvage. Arch Surg 1983; 118:597–602.

32. Heller J, Callow A, O'Donnell T, et al. The economic impact of limb salvage. Program and abstracts of the 15th Annual Meeting of the Association for Academic Surgery; 1981 Nov 8–11; Chicago.

33. Gupta SK, Veith FJ, Samson RH, et al. Cost analysis of operations for infrainguinal arteriosclerosis. Circulation 1982;66:2–9.

34. Mackey WC, McCullough JL, Conlon TP, et al. The costs of surgery for limb-threatening ischemia. Surgery 1986;99:26–35.

35. Luther M. Surgical treatment for chronic critical leg ischaemia: a 5 year follow-up of socioeconomic outcome. Eur J Endovasc Surg 1997;13:452–9.

36. Singh S, Evans L, Datta D, et al. The costs of managing lower limb-threatening ischaemia. Eur J Vasc Endovasc Surg 1996;12:359–62.

37. Panayiotopoulos YP, Tyrrell MR, Owen SE, et al. Outcome and cost analysis after femorocrural and femoropedal grafting for critical limb ischaemia. Br J Surg 1997;84:207–12.

38. Panayiotopoulos YP, Tyrrell MR, Arnold FJ, et al. Results and cost analysis of distal (crural/pedal) arterial revascularization for limb salvage in diabetic and non-diabetic patients. Diabet Med 1997;14:214–20.

39. Malone JM, Moore WS, Goldstone J, Malone SJ. Therapeutic and economic impact of a modern amputation program. Ann Surg 1979;189:798–802.

40. Harris KA, van Schie L, Carroll SE, et al. Rehabilitation potential of elderly patients with major amputations. J Cardiovasc Surg 1991;32:463–7.

41. Kald A, Carlson R, Nilsson E. Major amputation in a defined population: incidence, mortality, and results of treatment. Br J Surg 1989;76:308–10.

42. Houghton AD, Taylor FR, Thurlow S, et al. Success rates for rehabilitation of vascular amputees: implications for preoperative assessment and amputation level. Br J Surg 1992;79:753–5.

43. Bodily KC, Burgess EM. Contralateral limb and patient survival after leg amputation. Am J Surg 1983;46:280–2.

44. Abou-Zamzam AM Jr, Lee RW, Moneta GL, et al. Functional outcome after infrainguinal bypass for limb salvage. J Vasc Surg 1997;25:287–97.

45. Spitzer WO, Dobson AJ, Hall AL, et al. Measuring the quality of life of cancer patients: a concise QL-INDEX for use by physicians. J Chron Dis 1981;34:585–97.

46. Albers M, Fratezi AC, De Luccia N. Assessment of quality of life of patients with severe ischemia as a result of infrainguinal arterial occlusive disease. J Vasc Surg 1992;16:54–9.

47. Jette AM, Davies AR, Cleary PV, et al. The functional status questionnaire: its reliability and validity when used in primary care. J Gen Intern Med 1986;1:143–9.

48. Ware JE Jr. SF-36 Health Survey: manual and interpretation guide. Boston: The Health Institute, New England Medical Center; 1993. p. 1–22.

49. Duggan MM, Woodson J, Scott TE, et al. Functional outcome in limb salvage surgery. Am J Surg 1994;168:188–91.

50. Pell JP, Donnan PT, Fowkes FGR, Ruckley CV. Quality of life following lower limb amputation for peripheral arterial disease. Eur J Vasc Surg 1993;7:448–51.

51. Johnson BF, Evans L, Drury R, et al. Surgery for limb threatening ischemia: a reappraisal of the costs and benefits. Eur J Endovasc Surg 1995;9:181–8.

CHAPTER 29

Surgical Critical Care

Pamela A. Lipsett, MD, FACS

The discipline of surgical critical care encompasses the prevention, recognition, and treatment of critically ill and injured patients. Akin to all disciplines, surgical critical care involves patient care, education, and research. Patient care can be divided into two broad areas: (1) intensive monitoring of patients that is intended to allow the early identification and timely treatment of critical illness, and (2) immediate intervention providing life support for acute life-threatening emergencies. Because the specialty is new and dependent on evolving technology and therapy, ongoing evaluation of the treatment alternatives, outcomes, and their risks and benefits is essential to good clinical care. For each clinical decision, one must consider the patient's viewpoint, practical considerations of the treatment alternatives, and the ethical, economic, and societal issues involved.

The intensive care unit (ICU) is an area with high resource utilization. In today's environment of cost containment, ICU care is subject to close examination of efficacy. Interestingly, societal pressures currently focus on new technology, advanced monitoring, and innovative and costly treatment options. This societal tendency to drive utilization upward is not consistent with current budgetary constraints. Moreover, current trends imply that in the future there may be some type of rationing. Under these circumstances, rational decision making based on the best available evidence is mandatory. Evidence-based medicine is founded on the strength and quality of the evidence on which practice is based. Evidence-based medicine focuses on clinical trials as human experiments but also considers the strength and depth of laboratory research and observational studies on humans and animals.[1] Well-designed and executed clinical trials form the ideal cornerstones of therapy while nonhuman and uncontrolled studies should be interpreted with caution. Each study is validated and incorporated based on an assessment of its application to the clinician's practice.

In evidence-based medicine, critical appraisal of a clinical problem involves defining the specific patient problem, searching the available data and information, and appraising and sensibly applying information from the literature. Evidence-based medicine is intended to (1) clarify when information is incomplete or of poor quality; (2) acknowledge when decisions are made under uncertainty, and; (3) prioritize future research questions.[1]

The information explosion in all fields of science and medical practice frequently requires that the clinician depend on reviews of primary research to attain new knowledge. Systematic reviews must therefore include a comprehensive review of the literature (to minimize publication bias), selection criteria that include all relevant studies, critical appraisal of the primary studies, and reproducible decisions regarding evidence, selection, and methodologic rigor of the primary review.[2] In addition to the systematic review, a meta-analysis has been used to clarify results quantitatively of a previously researched topic (see examples). The Cochrane Collaboration coordinates the efforts of health care workers internationally to prepare, maintain, and disseminate systematic reviews of randomized interventions in health care.[3] In addition to individual systematic review, several journals have begun to incorporate evidence-based articles or articles regarding interpretation of the medical literature into the mainstream.[4–7] In addition to reviews, focused symposia and consensus conferences offer the opportunity not only for expert opinion but also for a review of all available literature and an assessment of the quality of that information.

This chapter will review some of the important works in critical care medicine over the past 2 years and will give examples of a subject review, a meta-analysis, and a consensus statement on topics of interest to the practicing intensivist. Because the field of surgical critical care involves the entire fields of medicine and surgery, only specific topics of broad interest to the practicing surgical intensivist will be discussed.

CRITICAL CARE UPDATE

Over the past 2 years there has been an explosion of both the basic science and clinical investigation of critically ill patients. Most articles published on critically ill patients involve a therapeutic intervention. Application of a study requires examination of three global questions: (1) Are the results of the study valid? (2) What were the results (ie, the magnitude of the treatment effect)? (3) Will the results help me in caring for my patients? Treatment or practice is unlikely to change from the results of a single study. Many trials may not apply to all patient groups, and the results may not generalize to additional patient populations. The clinician may decide that the clinical outcome or endpoint may not be important or that the risks, benefits, and costs may not have been studied in the initial study. This section will describe some of the recent literature but will not include studies involving specific surgical topics such as trauma since these are discussed elsewhere.

Pulmonary and Ventilation Studies

In the area of mechanical ventilation there has been ongoing debate about the best strategy for ventilating patients with the adult respiratory distress syndrome (ARDS).[7] A popular but not yet entirely proven strategy for the management of these patients is the use of low tidal volume and pressure-limited ventilation.[7,8] This strategy is intended to prevent additional lung injury and barotrauma. As a consequence of low tidal volume management, permissive hypercapnea occurs. In an indirect examination of whether pressure or volume ventilation used according to conventional strategies caused air leak and pneumothorax, Weg and colleagues examined prospective data from another trial for patients with ARDS secondary to sepsis.[8] The authors specifically questioned whether the conventional volumes and pressures were high and associated with air leaks and pneumothorax. They found that mechanical ventilation with conventional pressures and volumes was not correlated with the development of high pressures and pneumothorax. Moreover, they did not show an association of pneumothorax and mortality. Amato and colleagues and Stewart and colleagues published articles examining the effect of a "protective lung strategy" on patients with or at high risk for ARDS.[9,10] Since these studies incorporate different patient populations, one cannot conclude that the strategy of "protective ventilation" is or is not effective. Moreover, the definition and application of the protective strategies were different in the two studies. In the study by Amato and colleagues, 53 patients with ARDS were randomly assigned to a conventional versus a low tidal volume strategy.[9] The conventional group had the lowest possible positive end expiratory pressure (PEEP) to maintain adequate oxygenation, a tidal volume of 12 mL per kilogram of body weight, and normal levels of arterial blood gases (35 to 38 mm Hg). The protective-ventilation group involved maintaining end-expiratory pressures above the lower inflection point on the static pressure-volume curve, a tidal volume of < 6 mL per kg, driving pressures of < 20 cm of water above PEEP value, permissive hypercapnea, and preferential use of pressure-limited ventilation. The authors demonstrated a mortality difference in the two groups at 28 days, a higher rate of weaning from mechanical ventilation, and a lower rate of barotrauma when patients were managed with a protective strategy.[9] However, there was no difference in survival to hospital discharge between the patient groups. These results are encouraging, especially given the small number of patients randomized in this study. However, one of the major precepts in managing patients in this algorithm is the interpretation of the lower inflection point of the static pressure-volume curve. This measurement is subject to substantial interobserver variation. Thus, the results of this study are questionable. In the study of Stewart and colleagues, patients "at risk" for ARDS were enrolled into one of two arms of mechanical ventilation.[10] The protective-strategy arm limited peak inspiratory pressure to 30 cm or less and tidal volume of 8 mL per kg or less, versus the conventional group where the peak inspiratory pressure was allowed to rise as high as 50 cm of water and the tidal volume ranged from 10 to 15 mL per kg. There was no difference in mortality between the groups, and there was an increase in the need for paralysis and dialysis for acute renal failure in the limited-ventilation group.[10] Clearly, these studies cannot be directly compared because they involved potentially different patient populations and used different management strategies. Current larger randomized controlled trials aimed at answering the question of protective versus conventional ventilation are ongoing.

New interventions for the treatment of ARDS are evolving. A phase II trial of the use of nitric oxide (NO) in the treatment of ARDS has been published.[11] As a phase II trial, it was intended to study the safety and physiologic effects of inhaled nitric oxide in patients with ARDS. This multicenter trial randomized 177 patients within 72 hours of the diagnosis of ARDS to variable concentrations of NO (1.25 to 80 ppm) versus placebo. The NO was well tolerated and was associated with an improvement in oxygenation when compared to placebo over the next 4 hours.[11] Whether this finding will have any effect on patient outcome awaits a phase III study.[11]

Predictors of successful weaning from mechanical ventilation have been frequently reported. In 1991, Yang and Tobin proposed that use of the ratio of frequency (f) to tidal volume(V_T) was the most accurate predictor of successful weaning.[12] Jaeschke and colleagues have published an excellent review of this topic demonstrating the use of diagnostic test articles.[13] The authors specifically review the Yang and Tobin paper and describe the process of appraising the applicability of the previous study to their ICU practice. Incorporated as an important concept in this paper is the use of pretest probability and likelihood ratios and how diagnosis or outcome is affected with incorporation of the test. The f/V_T ratio can be useful in predicting a successful extubation. When the calculated ratio for f/V_T is < 80, then the likelihood ratio (LR) is 7.53 whereas the LR is 0.04 if the calculated ratio is > 100. A gray zone for clinical usefulness exists when the result is between 80 and 100, with an LR of 0.77. The use of this clinical tool, however, must be confined to the circumstances under which it was originally studied. In this study, patients were asked to breathe spontaneously for 1 minute, and the frequency and tidal volume were measured. Success was defined as the ability to maintain spontaneous breathing for > 24 hours after extubation. Failure was defined as the need for re-intubation within 24 hours.[12] When used with clinical judgment, this index appears to be a useful adjunct in bedside decision making.

Nosocomial pneumonia is an important cause of morbidity and mortality in hospitalized patients.[14] The best way to diagnose nosocomial pneumonia in mechanically ventilated patients and the importance of individual risk factors have been debated.[15,16] The use of bronchoscopy to diagnose ventilator-associated pneumonia (VAP) has remained controversial. This is in part due to difficulties in the methodologies of individual studies. Clinicians have questioned the use of quantitative bacterial counts because the accuracy for defining the exact number of bacteria present has not been well established, the method may not be reproducible from hospital to hospital, and bacterial thresholds may affect the detection of an early pneumonia. Moreover, the technique which accrues this information is not standardized, and the use of antibiotics may greatly influence the outcome. Last, the use of invasive methods to diagnose VAP has not been shown to affect mortality.[17] The study by Bregeon and colleagues assessed the effect of recent antibiotic use on the diagnostic accuracy of bronchoscopically obtained samples.[16] Recent introduction of an antibiotic for suspected VAP affected the diagnostic accuracy of the previously established quantitative threshold of 10^3 organisms. The authors suggested that this new threshold should be 10^2 when recent antibiotics have been employed. However, current antibiotic treatment for a previous infectious disease did not affect diagnostic accuracy.[16] This study is small but reminds intensivists that the methods for diagnosing VAP have not been tested or applied in large patient populations. The review of Cook and Kollef reminds us about the risk factors for nosocomial pneumonia in ICU patients.[15] The proportion of ICU patients that acquire pneumonia ranges from 9 to 17 percent when clinical criteria are used for diagnosis. In mechanically ventilated patients, the range for pneumonia in studies is 13 to 38 percent. Patients with neurologic injury (OR 3.9 to 4.2) and patients with mechanical ventilation (OR 1.1 to 3.1) appear to be at increased risk of pneumonia.[15] Manipulation of the airway (OR 3.1 to 5.0) and care of the ventilatory circuit may also predispose to aspiration and VAP. The importance of the gastrointestinal tract and VAP has been postulated in several studies that show that pH alteration of the stomach (OR 2.1 to 2.5), the presence of a nasogastric tube (OR 6.5), and the supine position (OR 2.9) are all associated with an increase in VAP.[16] Understanding the cause of many of these risk factors may lead to future prevention strategies. This has been difficult to study to date because of problems in defining the disease and because of the highly variable patient populations and potential for etiologic differences.

Hemodynamics: Monitoring

Recently, the most significant contributions in surgical critical care and evidence-based medicine has been publication of the report of the consensus conference on the use of the pulmonary artery catheter and the results of the recent meta-analysis on the use of crystalloid or colloids for hypovolemia. Both subjects are discussed in detail in the section on case studies. The routine use of "renal" dose dopamine has been questioned in a review article examining the science or evidence behind what is routine practice in many ICUs.[17]

Outcome Predictors

Many studies have attempted to determine predictors of outcome. One interesting paper published over the past year attempted to determine the ultimate outcome of patients with gastrointestinal bleeding. This paper by Kollef and colleagues examined 465 patients admitted from the emergency departments of two hospitals.[18] The authors developed and validated a clinical prediction tool (BLEED: ongoing Bleeding, Low systolic blood pressure, Elevated prothrombin time, Erratic mental status, unstable comorbid Disease). This current study is an independent validation data set on their previously published work that originally identified these factors. The tool was applied without the knowledge of the physicians who triaged patients in the emergency department. The authors defined outcome as recurrent gastrointestinal hemorrhage, the need for emergent surgery to control the source of hemorrhage, and hospital mortality. Patients with BLEED criteria (high risk) had significantly greater rates of in-hospital complications (RR 2.47 [1.38–4.44, $p < .001$]) than those without these criteria. This study validates the clinical judgment probably already in use because most patients without BLEED criteria were not admitted to an ICU environment at one of the two hospitals.[18] However, the study did point out interesting differences in the triage decisions at the two institutions. Because the institutions may have different resources both in the ICU and on the ward, one cannot simply conclude that patients without BLEED criteria should go to a general ward. Further studies are necessary to define what the level of care and monitoring for these patients require.

Outcome from burn injury has been re-examined in light of the dramatic changes in outcome over the past 20 years.[19] This study is a retrospective logistic regression analysis of data from 1990 to 1994 on clinical predictors of outcome from burn injury.[19] A mortality formula was used to prospectively examine validity of the data set of all patients in 1995 and 1996. Outcomes were also compared with historical controls in 1984. These predictors were based on 1,665 patients with a mean burn size of 14 ± 20 percent of body surface area, with 96 percent survival. Three predictors of mortality were identified: age > 60 years, area burned > 40 percent of body surface, and inhalation injury. The mortality formula developed predicted 0.3 percent, 3 percent, 33 percent, and 90 percent mortality depending on whether 0, 1, 2, 3, or 4 risk factors were present.[19] Again, these easily remembered criteria can help clinicians understand at the time of injury the probability of death given a certain set of risk factors and using modern surgical and critical care of burn-injured patients.

Many institutions have struggled with the notion of antibiotic restriction and management of both drug costs and control of resistant organisms. Evans and colleagues have provided the clinician with a computer-assisted decision support system.[20,21] The authors document improved management of antibiotic use through improved timing of preoperative antibiotics. Antibiotics-associated adverse events decreased by 30 percent, and antimicrobial resistance patterns were unchanged.[20] Moreover, antibiotic costs per treated patient decreased by almost 50 percent (adjusted for inflation), and antibiotic use overall decreased by 22.8 percent.[20] Thus, new methods for assisting clinical decision making may be both helpful and cost-effective. These studies, however, did not include an analysis of the costs of personnel, computer equipment, or maintenance.

Ulcer Prophylaxis

Stress ulcer prophylaxis has been recommended in the prevention of upper gastrointestinal bleeding in critically ill patients but perhaps not universally.[22] One of the most important risk factors for bleeding appears to be respiratory failure and the need for mechanical ventilation.[22] Thus, these patients should receive stress ulcer prophylaxis. Randomized controlled trials have shown that prophylaxis with H_2 receptor antagonists, antacids, and the cytoprotective agent sucralfate has demonstrated efficacy in preventing bleeding. Sucralfate has a trend toward a lower ventilator-associated pneumonia rate when compared to the combined use of H_2 antagonists and antacids. Cook and colleagues performed a multicenter randomized blinded placebo-controlled trial of sucralfate versus H_2 receptor antagonists for preventing upper gastrointestinal bleeding in 1,200 patients who required mechanical ventilation.[22] The authors demonstrated a 1.7 percent incidence of clinically important bleeding with the H_2 receptor group versus a 3.8 percent incidence in the sucralfate group (RR 0.44 [0.21–0.92], $p = .02$). The incidence of ventilator-associated pneumonia was 19.1 percent in the H_2 receptor group versus 16.2 in the sucralfate group (RR 1.18 [0.92–1.51], $p = .19$).[22] There were no differences in mortality in the ICU nor in duration of stay between the two groups. The authors further concluded that 48 critically ill patients undergoing mechanical ventilation for more than 48 hours would need to receive prophylaxis with ranitidine rather than sucralfate to prevent one clinically important gastrointestinal hemorrhage.[22] This is a well-planned and well-conducted study that favors the conclusion of the authors.

Case Studies

Pulmonary Artery Catheters

Pulmonary artery catheterization was introduced into clinical practice in the early 1970s.[23] Today, most clinicians believe that pulmonary artery catheters (PACs) are useful in guiding intravascular volume administration and pharmacologic intervention in selected critically ill patients.[24,25] However, in spite of widespread belief in the effectiveness of PACs, no clear evidence supports this belief. In 1996, Connors and colleagues published a report suggesting that right heart (PA) catheterization was associated with an increase in both mortality and use of health care resources.[26] A corresponding editorial suggested a moratorium on the use of PA catheters.[27] A joint meeting of representatives of the Food and Drug Administration and the National Heart, Lung, and Blood Institute considered but declined a moratorium on the use of these catheters. In response to this controversy, The Pulmonary Artery Consensus Conference was convened, with representatives from the American Association of Critical Care Nurses, the American College of Chest Physicians, The American Thoracic Society, the European Society of Intensive Care Medicine, and the Society of Critical Care Medicine.[28] The conference's goals were to review the use of the PAC in specific patient populations and to make recommendations for clinical practice and future clinical and epidemiologic research. Details of the development of the "raw materials" used in the consensus conference are published in *New Horizons*.[29]

The Problem: Effectiveness of the Pulmonary Artery Catheter

As stated above, the vast majority of clinicians believe that hemodynamic information provided by a PAC is helpful and influences patient care positively. This is primarily because the ability to accurately assess cardiac output and left ventricular filling pressure in critically ill patients is less than optimal in spite of a careful history and physical examination. Thus, the PAC provides information not obtainable from clinical diagnosis alone. However, the effectiveness of the PAC is dependent on proper interpretation of the data. Disturbing data exist suggesting that knowledge of the complications of PAC placement and other basic interpretation is suboptimal.[25, 30–33] Nonetheless, over 2 million PACs are sold annually worldwide.[24] In addition to proper interpretation of the data, the technique of measurement itself must be reliable and accurate. Once the hemodynamic information has been interpreted, the data must be applied in a cohesive manner. Thus, the value of the PAC versus the clinician's skill in using the technology is difficult to determine, and these variables have not been studied in a large clinical trial. A large randomized controlled clinical trial has been difficult to consider since use of the PAC has been considered the standard of care for the past 25 years. Enrollment of patients into a trial for management of patients with or without PACs is subject to enormous selection bias. Specifically, prior to the paper by Connors and colleagues,[26] enrolling patients into the non-PAC arm would have been considered by many to be unethical.

To answer these questions, the Pulmonary Artery Consensus Conference was held in December 1996.[28,29] The conference followed standard protocols with questions presented to the participants prior to the meeting. Presenters had no underlying financial or fixed professional bias. The presenter had 30 minutes to present the answer to a previously researched question; this was followed by 30 minutes of discussion. In the concluding session, each presenter restated the question and defended and summarized the groups' rationale and recommendations.[29] Levels of evidence and graded response to questions were discussed in detail. Finally, the methodology discussed by Sackett was used[34] and modified (Table 29–1 and 29–2). This grading method was expanded beyond Sackett's to better serve the goals of the consensus. Questions were organized as "yes," "no," and "uncertain." The grade and the answer thus determined the level of evidence. For example, an answer of "yes" with a grade of "A" implied that the data consistently supported the answer and were of high quality (at least two large randomized trials with clear-cut results; a low risk of false-positive [α] or false negative [β] error) while the answer "yes" with a grade "E" implied that the supporting data were only at the level of nonrandomized historical controls, case series, uncontrolled studies, or expert opinion.[29]

Table 29–1 Grading of Responses to Questions

A	Supported by at least two Level I investigations
B	Supported by only one Level I investigation
C	Supported by Level II investigations only
D	Supported by at least one Level III investigation
E	Supported by Level IV or Level V evidence

Table 29–2 Levels of Evidence

Level I	Large, randomized trials with clear-cut results; low risk of false-positive (α) error or false-negative (β) error
Level II	Small, randomized trials with uncertain results; moderate to high risk of false-positive (α) and/or false-negative (β) error
Level III	Nonrandomized, contemporaneous controls
Level IV	Nonrandomized, historical controls and expert opinion
Level V	Case series, uncontrolled studies, and expert opinion

The Pulmonary Artery Consensus Conference

The conference divided the questions into the following areas: (1) cardiovascular disease; (2) perioperative use; (3) trauma; (4) sepsis/septic shock; (5) supranormal oxygen delivery; (6) respiratory failure; (7) critically ill pediatric patients; (8) continuous venous oximetry/right ventricular ejection/continuous cardiac output pulmonary catheters; (9) complications/data collection/data interpretation; (10) future investigations, and; (11) the need for a moratorium on PAC use.[28] These findings are discussed below in detail.

For patients with myocardial infarction (right or left ventricle) and shock or mechanical complications of a myocardial infarction, PAC use was supported to improve outcome.[7,29,35–37] This use was supported by conflicting results in case series and retrospective studies but had the weight of expert opinion. For patients with myocardial infarction and refractory congestive heart failure, the benefit of a PAC was considered uncertain (this categorization was used when results were conflicting or studies were too flawed to interpret). Though the American College of Cardiology/American Heart Association guidelines recommend the use of the PAC for these clinical circumstances, the study of Connors and colleagues[26] showed no benefit to the use of the PAC. Similarly, the data for improved outcome in patients with pulmonary hypertension showed that the PAC may help guide diagnosis and may guide vasodilator management, but further studies may show a less invasive modality (such as echocardiography) to be equally useful.

The use of the PAC for surgical patients has been examined mostly in small studies that are at risk of α and β error. This is considered Level II evidence of support for their use. Low-risk patients undergoing cardiac surgery do not appear to have decreased perioperative complications or mortality (Level II) when the PAC is used routinely. On the other hand, the use of the PAC in high-risk patients is uncertain (Level II). Two studies supported the use of the PAC but did not use mortality, morbidity, or complications as the endpoint.[38,39] In larger studies by Pearson and Tuman, no differences were seen in those patients with or without PACs.[40,41] For the same indications and questions in peripheral vascular surgery, support exists for reduced complications (grade D) but not for reduced mortality (uncertain, grade D).[42,43] Similar to cardiac surgical patients, patients undergoing aortic surgery have been divided into low- and high-risk groups. For low-risk patients, the conclusion for PAC use is uncertain because early studies differ in outcome from more recent clinical trials, which show no benefit of the PAC in reducing complications or mortality perioperatively. However, in patients with left ventricular dysfunction and/or significant coronary cardiac disease, little information exists. Expert opinion supported the use of the catheter in these patients.

Many surgeons might consider elderly patients at specific risk of perioperative complications. However, routine use of the PAC to reduce perioperative complications and mortality based on age alone was not supported (grade E). This was based on only two studies:[44,45] the Del Guercio and Cohn study had no control group and enrolled "physiological older" patients;[44] the study by Schrader and colleagues examined 46 nonagenarians in whom a PAC was not used.[45] No deaths occurred in these latter patients, and only one complication may have been prevented by a PAC.[45] Thus, the use of a PAC should not be routine, based on age alone.[28]

Patients having neurosurgery have not been studied in randomized studies perioperatively for either PAC-guided or non-PAC-guided management. One study examined the use of the PAC for the identification and therapy of venous air embolism during neurosurgery.[46] The PAC was less sensitive than Doppler ultrasonography for diagnosis of air embolus. Only a small quantity of air could be aspirated from the PAC. Thus, a Doppler examination is the preferred mode for diagnosing venous embolism during neurosurgery.

For trauma patients, expert opinions felt that PAC-guided therapy could alter diagnosis and improve functional outcome in the trauma patient (grade E).[47,48] However, no clinical trials met the inclusion criteria of the consensus conference. Experts felt that diagnosis and functional outcome of the critically injured patient might be altered by PAC-guided management under specific circumstances, including associated neurologic injury, and with complications such as acute respiratory distress syndrome (ARDS), and progressive oliguria. For trauma patients and mortality as the defining outcome, treating with a PAC and resuscitation protocols yielded conflicting results. No randomized controlled trial has demonstrated that traumatically injured patients unresponsive to standard resuscitation protocols and subjected to a change in therapy based on PAC-derived information experience improved outcomes independent of other variables (grade B). Thus, the PAC may alter therapy but is unproved as a mode of therapy to improve outcome in trauma patients.

Septic shock is common in surgical patients and is initially treated with aggressive fluid resuscitation. Currently, insufficient evidence exists to support the routine use of PACs in all patients with septic shock. Mimoz and colleagues have demonstrated that patient outcomes may be better when a PAC is used in the subgroup of patients if in those patients information obtained from the PAC prompts a change in therapy.[49] However, in Connors' study, the placement of a PAC in the first 24 hours after ICU admission did not show any difference in outcome in a general population of patients with sepsis or sepsis and multiple-organ dysfunction syndrome.[26] Studies designed to investigate the accuracy and effectiveness of the PAC in diagnosis and response to therapeutic intervention have been suggested. However, necessary components of this study must include the construction of management protocols and the assessment of adherence to these protocols along with uniform interpretation and prestudy education.

Many studies involving over 1,300 patients have investigated the use of a PAC to augment oxygen delivery to supranormal levels.[47,50,52–57] With the exception of two studies in trauma patients, no study has demonstrated improved organ-specific or general survival in patients randomized to protocol-guided augmentation of oxygen delivery to supranormal levels when compared with conventional therapy.[47,51] The study by Hayes and colleagues demonstrated increased mortality with attempts at an enhanced oxygen delivery strategy.[53]

In patients with respiratory failure, the PAC appears to alter diagnosis and treatment. This is supported by studies by Connors and colleagues[58] and Eisenberg,[59] which demonstrated that physical examination and radiography were inaccurate in predicting hemodynamic values. In addition, half of all patients had treatment altered based on these findings. However, the data regarding a difference in outcome with PAC-guided therapy and respiratory failure were far less certain (grade E).[59] Smaller studies demonstrated that patients with hypotension or end-organ failure and patients refractory to diuretic therapy benefit from a PAC.[60–63] Once again, the Connors review indicated that patients with ARDS or pneumonia and a PAC had an increased risk of death (relative hazard 1.30; 95% confidence interval 1.05–1.61).[26] Expert opinion at the conference concluded there was insufficient evidence from existing clinical trials and case series to define benefit or harm from PAC use in patients with respiratory failure.[29]

Although data on critically ill pediatric patients are limited, patients with pulmonary hypertension, shock refractory to fluid administration, severe respiratory failure, and multiple-organ dysfunction syndrome appear to benefit from the use of a PAC (grade E).[63–65] These studies show that hemodynamics may be clarified in pediatric patients, but only a limited number of patients benefit from PAC-guided management, and complications of PAC use are present.[66] Unlike in the case of adult patients, there are no studies that demonstrate overall harm or benefit to children from a PAC.

In spite of the lack of well-designed and conducted large clinical trials on PAC use and benefit, the technology of PACs has advanced to include continuous venous oximetry, right ventricular ejection fraction, and continuous cardiac output pulmonary artery catheters.[67,68] Though these catheters appear to be accurate measuring devices (grade D),[67,68] there are no studies that support their use over the use of standard pulmonary catheters. These advanced catheters are considerably more expensive, and it is unclear whether this cost can be recovered by altered personnel time.

Although PAC use is associated with a low incidence of complications and (occasionally) mortality, the common use of catheters mandates consideration of the complication rate and whether clinicians are minimizing complications.[69–72] Further, PAC use in low-risk patients is unlikely to provide benefit but exposes the patient to potential harm. Deciding which patients would benefit from a PAC and using the information to alter therapy is critical to the proper use of the PAC. Because the PAC is a diagnostic modality, ignoring or misinterpreting the data exposes the patient to potential risk without benefit. If PAC data are misinterpreted, incorrect treatment strategies might be employed. Multiple studies[30–33] document an unsatisfactory level of common knowledge of the indications, complications, and interpretation of the PAC extending across all work forces and workplaces; a major educational effort is thus required. Quality improvement programs should consider education in the use of PACs a potentially important issue.[29]

The last two issues the consensus conference addressed relate to the future of PAC use. First, experts agreed that the Food and Drug Administration should not place a moratorium on the use of the PAC.[28,29] Second, participants felt that randomized controlled trials of PAC use could be ethically conducted (grade E).[28,29] Many issues in clinical practice have not been subjected to rigorous clinical trials. Many practitioners have strong clinical preferences regarding the indications for PACs and the resulting therapy. For a clinical trial to occur with valid results, clinicians must be willing to enroll patients without selection biases.[73–75] Clinical equipoise exists when physicians are willing to enroll patients in a randomized trial based on available data with the firm belief that one treatment has no demonstrated proven advantage over another. When more than 70 percent of the clinicians believe one arm of the therapy to be advantageous, equipoise does not exist, and the trial cannot ethically be performed.[76]

The widespread use of the pulmonary artery catheter is an example of applying a new technology as a standard of care without well-designed and conducted clinical trials. A consensus conference allows the reader to review all of the best evidence on the use of the PAC and to see the rationale and recommendations of the experts at the conference. When data are lacking, specific recommendations for further clinical trials are suggested, by a consensus conference.

Fluid Resuscitation: Meta-analysis of Use of Colloids and Crystalloids

Fluid resuscitation is an integral part of the management of the acutely ill hypovolemic patient. For as long as colloidal solutions have been available, there has been debate over the value of colloids over crystalloids. Colloids recently have been recommended in a number of resuscitation guidelines[77,78] but review of their actual use has exceeded the guideline expectations.[79] Moreover, there are significant cost implications because using colloids is considerably more expensive than using crystalloids.[80]

Over the past 30 years, there have been many clinical studies comparing crystalloids to colloids, and these studies in many circumstances have shown different physiologic endpoints.

Thus, the data supporting the use of one type of solution over another depends on the endpoint selected. The final logical physiologic difference in fluid administration is patient mortality. However, there is no universal consensus on the effect of solution choice on mortality. Three meta-analyses have been published regarding the effect of crystalloids versus colloids on mortality in randomized clinical trials of resuscitation.[81–83] The first two of these meta-analyses did not meet the criteria for a systematic review.[4] The more recent meta-analysis by Schierhout and Roberts will be discussed in detail because it incorporates the recently performed unconfounded clinical trials with synthetic colloids and hypertonic crystalloid solutions.[83]

In deciding the value of a systematic review and a meta-analysis, the proper identification and selection of clinical trials is critical and must be fully outlined. In the above study, the selection of trials was based on random or quasi-random allocation of treatment groups.[5] Studies included patients with critical illness resulting from trauma, burn injury, surgery, or sepsis. Trials were considered unconfounded only if one treatment group differed from another by the treatment of interest. Randomized crossover trials were excluded as were studies in which "elective" volume administration to enhance intravascular volume in preparation for cardiopulmonary bypass or for other perioperative use was performed. Patients in such studies were excluded because the endpoint analysis was intended to reflect an effect on mortality. Because the results of the meta-analysis depend on which studies are included, the search for eligible articles must be extensive and complete. This usually includes a computerized search such as the previously mentioned Cochrane Controlled Trials register, and collections such as MEDLINE, Embase, and the BIDS Index to Scientific and Technical Proceedings. However, a computerized search by itself is probably incomplete, especially if geographic limitations or language restrictions are placed on the search. References included in cited articles must be investigated, and authors must be contacted for knowledge of additional studies. These criteria were established in the Schierhout and Roberts study.[83]

Each meta-analysis must include a detailed description of the outcome and data abstraction methodology as well as data analysis and statistical methods employed. In the above trial, the endpoint sought was the mortality at the end of follow-up or at the study's completion. Prospective data included type of patient, type of crystalloid and colloid use, duration of follow-up, mortality at the end of follow-up, and quality of concealment of allocation.[5] Relative risks and 95 percent confidence intervals for mortality in each trial based on intention to treat was calculated by the Mantel-Haenszel Method. Tests for heterogeneity were done and a regression analysis was performed based on the possibility of selective publication of randomized trials with positive findings. The meta-analysis identified 48 trials, of which 37 met the inclusion criteria. Of the 37 trials, allocation concealment was adequate in 10 trials, unclear in 20, and inadequate in 7.

Nineteen of the eligible trials included an assessment of mortality. The authors reported that they contacted each of the trial authors when mortality was not reported but that no additional information was provided. Thus, the analysis included 1,315 patients in 19 trials. Patient type did not influence the effect of specific fluid administration except that the assessment for elective surgical patients was imprecise due to the small numbers of patients and an overall low mortality (4.7%) in that group of patients. Importantly, there was no heterogeneity between trials ($p = .75$). In four trials included in the analysis, the concealment of allocation was adequate. The pooled relative risk of death for all patient groups was 1.19 (95%, confidence interval 0.99 to 1.45). The risk of death for patients given colloids was 24 percent, and the risk of death in patients given crystalloids was 20 percent, giving a 4 percent (0 to 8%) absolute risk of mortality for resuscitation with colloids. If only the trials in which allocation concealment was adequate were considered, the pooled relative risk of death was 1.29 (0.94 to 1.77) with an increase in absolute risk of mortality for resuscitation with colloids of 7 percent (–1 to 15%).[83]

Thus, this meta-analysis concluded that evidence from published randomized controlled trials comparing colloid and crystalloid fluid resuscitation demonstrated across a wide range of patient populations that colloids offered no advantage in mortality.[83] Moreover, when trials with inadequate concealment were excluded, the pooled relative risk shifted to increased mortality for colloids compared with crystalloids. The authors carefully attempted to exclude or document publication bias and could not confirm any statistical evidence of such. Nonetheless, as is true of all meta-analyses, the study may suffer because patients were sufficiently different that summary estimates of the effects of the intervention must be questioned. In addition, patients were subjected to different protocols of resuscitation and also to different types, concentrations, and quantities of fluid. In spite of these considerations, the direction of the effect is unlikely to be different; rather, the magnitude of the effect would be influenced since all patients were hypovolemic and in need of volume replacement. Though intensivists may conclude that their individual patient populations differed substantially from that of the authors, this is not likely since there was little unexplained heterogeneity in the results. Therefore, there is no evidence that supports any survival advantage from colloids. Colloids are expensive, and their use exceeds current guidelines and may be associated with an absolute increased risk of mortality.

The examples from the Pulmonary Artery Consensus Conference and the meta-analysis on fluid administration demonstrate the value of evidence-based medicine in solidifying clinical judgment in areas not clearly defined in clinical trials. In addition, the examples point out areas for future focused research to find solutions to currently undefined important clinical questions.

FUTURE AREAS OF INVESTIGATION

Since critical care medicine is highly dependent on both technology and a disproportionate amount of resources, it is incumbent on intensivists to accumulate evidence that ICUs and their dedicated teams add benefit in either outcome (decreased morbidity and/or mortality) or cost-effectiveness. Outcome studies directed at functional outcome after prolonged ICU stay are needed, and the value of this outcome must be assessed with respect to cost, quality, and allocation of resources.

Current technologies used in the ICU must be systematically assessed for contributions to patient outcome. An example of this is the previous illustration of the Swan-Ganz catheter, a technological advance that has been accepted into routine therapeutic and diagnostic use without documentation of outcome endpoint. Future studies are expected to examine this endpoint more closely. New ventilator therapies and strategies for management such as partial liquid ventilation and permissive hypercapnia are being developed and are under active investigation. Certainly as new agents such as biologic modifiers are developed for therapy, studies must examine the medical benefit to patients across the entire spectrum of care from admission to discharge, including measures of life expectancy and quality of life.

REFERENCES

1. Cook DJ, Sibbald WJ, Vincent J-L, et al. Evidence based critical care medicine: what is it and what can it do for us? Crit Care Med 1996;24:334–7.

2. Cook DJ, Sackett DL, Spitzer WO. Methodologic guidelines for systematic reviews of randomized control trials in health care from the Potsdam Consultation on Meta-Analysis. J Clin Epidemiol 1995;48:167–71.

3. Chalmers I. Doing more good than harm. The evaluation of health care interventions. Ann NY Acad Sci 1993;703:153–63.

4. Oxman AD, Cook DJ, Guyatt GH. Users' guide to the medical literature. VI. How to use an overview. JAMA 1994;272:1367–71.

5. Schulz KF, Chalmers I, Hayes RJ, et al. Dimensions of methodological quality associated with estimates of treatment effects in controlled trials. JAMA 1995;273:408–12.

6. Ellrodt G, Cook DJ, Lee J, et al. Evidence-based disease management. JAMA 1997;278:1687–92.

7. Meade MO, Cook DJ, Kernerman P, et al. How to use articles about harm: the relationship between high tidal volumes, ventilating pressures, and ventilator-induced lung injury. Crit Care Med 1997; 25:1915–22.

8. Weg JG, Anzueto A, Balk RA, et al. The relation of pneumothorax and other air leaks to mortality in the acute respiratory distress syndrome. N Engl J Med 1998;338:341–6.

9. Amato MBP, Barbas CSV, Medeiros DM, et al. Effect of a protective-ventilation strategy on mortality in the acute respiratory distress syndrome. N Engl J Med 1998;338:347–54.

10. Stewart TE, Meade MO, Cook DJ, et al, and the Pressure- and Volume-Limited Ventilation Strategy Group. Evaluation of a ventilation strategy to prevent barotrauma in patients at high risk for acute respiratory distress syndrome. N Engl J Med 1998;338:355–61.

11. Dellinger RP, Zimmerman JL, Taylor RW, et al, and the Inhaled Nitric Oxide in ARDS Study Group. Effects of inhaled nitric oxide in patients with acute respiratory distress syndrome: results of a randomized phase II trial. Crit Care Med 1998;26:15–23.

12. Yang KL, Tobin MJ. A prospective study of indexes predicting the outcome of trials of weaning from mechanical ventilation. N Engl J Med 1991;325:1445–50.

13. Jaeschke RZ, Meade MO, Guyatt GH, et al. How to use diagnostic test articles in the intensive care unit: diagnosing weanability using f/Vt. Crit Care Med 1997;25:1514–21.

14. Vincent JL, Bihari DL, Suter PM, et al. The prevalence of nosocomial infection in intensive care units in Europe. Results of the European Prevalence of Infection in Intensive Care (EPIC) Study. EPIC International Advisory Committee. JAMA 1995;274:639–44.

15. Cook DJ, Kollef MH. Risk factors for ICU-acquired pneumonia. JAMA 1998;279:1605–6.

16. Bregeon F, Papazian L, Visconti A, et al. Relationship of microbiologic diagnostic criteria to morbidity and mortality in patients with ventilator-associated pneumonia. JAMA 1997;277:655–62.

17. Perdue PW, Balser JR, Lipsett PA, et al. "Renal dose" dopamine in surgical patients: dogma or science? Ann Surg 1998;227:470–3.

18. Kollef MH, O'Brien JD, Zuckerman GR, et al. A classification tool to predict outcomes in patients with acute upper and lower gastrointestinal hemorrhage. Crit Care Med 1997;25:1125–32.

19. Ryan CM, Schoenfeld DA, Thorpe WP, et al. Objective estimates of the probability of death from burn injuries. N Engl J Med 1998;338:362–6.

20. Pestotnik SL, Classen DC, Evans RS, et al. Implementing antibiotic practice guidelines through computer-assisted decision support: clinical and financial outcomes. Ann Intern Med 1996;124: 884–90.

21. Evans RS, Pestotnik SL, Classen DC, et al. A computer-assisted management program for antibiotics and other antiinfective agents. N Engl J Med 1998;338:232–8.

22. Cook D, Guyatt G, Marshall J, et al, for the Canadian Critical Care Trials Group. A comparison of sucralfate and ranitidine for the prevention of upper gastrointestinal bleeding in patients requiring mechanical ventilation. N Engl J Med 1998;338:791–7.

23. Swan HJC, Ganz W, Forrester J, et al. Catheterization of the heart in man with use of a flow-directed balloon-tipped catheter. N Engl J Med 1970;283:447–51.

24. Ginosar Y, Sprung CL. The Swan-Ganz catheter: twenty-five years of monitoring. Crit Care Clin 1996;12:771–6.

25. Trottier SJ, Taylor RW. Physician's attitudes towards and knowledge of the pulmonary artery catheter: Society of Critical Care Medicine membership survey. New Horiz 1997;5:201–6.

26. Connors AF Jr, Speroff T, Dawson NV, et al. The effectiveness of right heart catheterization in the initial care of critically ill patients. JAMA 1996;18:889–97.

27. Dalen JE, Bone RC. Is it time to pull the pulmonary artery catheter? JAMA 1996;18:916–18.

28. Pulmonary Artery Consensus Conference Participants. Pulmonary Artery Consensus Conference: New Horiz 1997;5:175–93.

29. Taylor R, editor. Controversies in pulmonary artery catheterization. New Horiz 1997;5:173–296.

30. Iberti TJ, Fischer EP, Leibowitz AB, et al. A multicenter study of physicians' knowledge of the pulmonary artery catheter. JAMA 1990;264:2928–32.

31. Gnaegi A, Feihl F, Perret C. Intensive care physicians' insufficient knowledge of right-heart catheterization at the bedside: time to act? Crit Care Med 1997;25:213–20.

32. Iberti TJ, Daily EK, Leibowitz AB, et al. Assessment of critical care nurses' knowledge of the pulmonary artery catheter. Crit Care Med 1994;22:1674–8.

33. Burns D, Burns D, Shively M. Critical care nurses' knowledge of pulmonary artery catheters. Am J Crit Care 1996;5:49–54.

34. Sackett DL. Rules of evidence and clinical recommendations on the use of antithrombotic agents. Chest 1989;95(2 Suppl):25–45.

35. Dalen JE. Does pulmonary artery catheterization benefit patients with acute myocardial infarction? Chest 1990;98:1313–14.

36. Zion MM, Balkin J, Rosenmann D, et al, and SPRINT Study Group. Use of pulmonary artery catheters in patients with acute myocardial infarction. Analysis of experience in 5,841 patients in the SPRINT registry. Chest 1990;98:1331–5.

37. Berisha S, Kastrati A, Goda A, et al. Optimal value of filling pressure in the right side of the heart in acute right ventricular infarction. Br Heart J 1990;63:98–102.

38. Kaplan JA, Wells PH. Early diagnosis of myocardial ischemia using the pulmonary arterial catheter. Anesth Analg 1981;60:789–93.

39. Davies MJ, Cronin HD, Domaingue CM. Pulmonary artery catheterization. An assessment of risks and benefits in 220 surgical patients. Anesth Intensive Care 1982;10:9–14.

40. Pearson KS, Gomez MN, Moyers JR, et al. A cost/benefit analysis of randomized invasive monitoring for patients undergoing cardiac surgery. Anesth Analg 1989;69:336–41.

41. Tuman KJ, McCarthy RJ, Speiss BD, et al. Effect of pulmonary artery catheterization on outcome in patients undergoing coronary artery surgery. Anesthesiology 1989;70:199–206.

42. Bush HL, LoGerfo FW, Weisel RD, et al. Assessment of myocardial performance and optimal volume loading during elective abdominal aortic aneurysm resection. Arch Surg 1977;112:1301–6.

43. Rice CL, Hobelman CF, John DA, et al. Central venous pressure or pulmonary capillary wedge pressure as the determinant of fluid replacement in aortic surgery. Surgery 1978;84:437–40.

44. Del Guerico LR, Cohn JD. Monitoring operative risk in the elderly. JAMA 1980;243:1350–5.

45. Schrader LL, McMillen MA, Watson CB, et al. Is routine preoperative hemodynamic evaluation of nonagenarians necessary. J Am Geriatr Soc 1991;39:1–5.

46. Bedford RF, Marshall WK, Butler A, et al. Cardiac catheters for diagnosis and treatment of venous air embolism: a prospective study in man. J Neurosurg 1981;55:610–14.

47. Bishop MH, Shoemaker WC, Appel PL, et al. Prospective, randomized trial of survivor values of cardiac index, oxygen delivery, and oxygen consumption as resuscitation endpoints in severe trauma. J Trauma 1995;38:780–7.

48. Moore F, Haenel JB, Moore EE, et al. Incommensurate oxygen consumption in response to maximal oxygen availability predicts post injury multiple organ system failure. J Trauma 1992;3:58–67.

49. Mimoz O, Rauss A, Rekik N, et al. Pulmonary artery catheterization in critically ill patients: a prospective analysis of outcome changes associated with catheter-prompted changes in therapy. Crit Care Med 1994;22:573–9.

50. Durham RM, Neunaber K, Mazuski JE, et al. The use of oxygen consumption and delivery as endpoints for resuscitation in critically ill patients. J Trauma 1996;41:32–40.

51. Fleming A, Bishop M, Shoemaker W, et al. Prospective trial of supranormal values as goals of resuscitation in severe trauma. Arch Surg 1992;127:1175–81.

52. Tuchschmidt J, Fried J, Astiz M, et al. Elevation of cardiac output and oxygen delivery improves outcome in septic shock. Chest 1992;102:216–20.

53. Hayes MA, Timmins AC, Yau EHE, et al. Elevation of systemic oxygen delivery in critically ill patients. N Engl J Med 1994;330:1717–22.

54. Yu M, Levy MM, Smith P, et al. Effect of maximizing oxygen delivery on morbidity and mortality rates in critically ill patients: a prospective, randomized, controlled study. Crit Care Med 1993;21:830–8.

55. Boyd O, Grounds RM, Bennett ED. A randomized clinical trial of the effect of deliberate perioperative increase of oxygen delivery on mortality in high-risk surgical patients. JAMA 1993;270:2699–2707.

56. Shoemaker WC, Kram KB, Appel PL, et al. Prospective trial of supranormal values of survivors as therapeutic goals in high risk surgical patients. Chest 1988;94:1176–86.

57. Yu M, Takanishi D, Myers SA, et al. Frequency of mortality and myocardial infarction during maximizing oxygen delivery: a prospective, randomized trial. Crit Care Med 1995;23:1025–32.

58. Connors AF Jr, McCaffree DR, Gray BA. Evaluation of right heart catheterization in the critically ill patient without acute myocardial infarction. N Engl J Med 1983;308:263–7.

59. Eisenberg PR, Jaffe AS, Schuster DP. Clinical evaluation compared to pulmonary artery catheterization in the hemodynamic assessment of critically ill patients. Crit Care Med 1984;12:549–53.

60. Gattinoni L, Brazzi L, Pelosi P, et al. A trial of goal-oriented hemodynamic therapy in critically ill patients. N Engl J Med 1995;333:1025–32.

61. Fein AM, Goldberg SK, Walkenstein MD, et al. Is pulmonary artery catheterization necessary for the diagnosis of pulmonary edema? Am Rev Respir Dis 1984;129:1006–9.

62. Humphrey H, Hall J, Sznajder I, et al. Improved survival in ARDS patients associated with a reduction in pulmonary capillary wedge pressure. Chest 1990;97:1176–80.

63. Pollack MM, Reed TP, Holbrook PR, et al. Bedside pulmonary artery catheterization in pediatrics. J Pediatr 1980;96:274–6.

64. Stopfkuchen H. Hemodynamic monitoring in childhood. Intensive Care Med 1989;15 Suppl: S27–S31.

65. Carcillo JA, Davis AL, Zaritsky A. Role of early fluid resuscitation in pediatric septic shock. JAMA 1991;266:1242–5.

66. Krafte-Jacobs B, Sivit CJ, Mejia R, et al. Catheter-related thrombosis in critically ill children: comparison of catheters with and without heparin bonding. J Pediatr 1995;126:50–4.

67. Baele PL, McMichan T, Marsh HM, et al. Continuous monitoring of mixed venous oxygen saturation in critically ill patients. Anesth Analg 1982;61:513–17.

68. Nelson LD. Continuous venous oximetry in surgical patients. Ann Surg 1986;203:329–33.

69. Boyd KD, Thomas SJ, Gold J, et al. A prospective study of complications of pulmonary artery catheters in 500 consecutive patients. Chest 1983;84:245–9.

70. Mermel LA, McCormick RD, Springman SR, et al. The pathogenesis and epidemiology of catheter-related infection with pulmonary artery Swan-Ganz catheters: a prospective study utilizing molecular subtyping. Am J Med 1991;91:197S–205S.

71. Connors AF Jr, Castele RJ, Farhat NZ, et al. Complications of right heart catheterization. A prospective autopsy study. Chest 1985;88:567–72.

72. Elliott CG, Zimmerman GA, Clemmer TP. Complications of pulmonary artery catheterization in the care of critically ill patients: a prospective study. Chest 1979;76:647–52.

73. Sackett DL. The competing objectives of randomized trials. N Engl J Med 1980;303:1059–69.

74. Schafer A. The ethics of the randomized clinical trial. N Engl J Med 1982;307:719–24.

75. Freedman B. Equipoise and the ethics of clinical research. N Engl J Med 1987;317:141–5.

76. Johnson N, Lilford RJ, Brazier W. At what level of collective equipoise does a clinical trial become ethical? J Med Ethics 1991;17:30–4.

77. Vermeulen LC, Ratko TA, Erstad BL, et al. A paradigm for consensus. The University Hospital Consortium guidelines for the use of albumin, nonprotein colloid, and crystalloid solutions. Arch Intern Med 1995;155:373–9.

78. Armstrong RF, Bullen C, Cohen SL, et al. Critical algorithms. Oxford: Oxford Medical Publications, Oxford University Press, 1994.

79. Yim JM, Vermeulen LC, Erstad BL, et al. Albumin and nonprotein colloid solution use in US academic health centers. Arch Intern Med 1995;155:2450–5.

80. Subcommittee of the Victorian Drug Usage Advisory Committee. Human albumin solutions: an audit of use in three major metropolitan hospitals. Med J Aust 1991;154(10):657–60.

81. Velanovich V. Crystalloid versus colloid fluid resuscitation: a meta-analysis of mortality. Surgery 1989;105:65–71.

82. Bisonni RS, Holtgrave DR, Lawler F, et al. Colloids versus crystalloids in fluid resuscitation: an analysis of randomized controlled trials. J Fam Pract 1991;32:387–90.

83. Schierhout G, Roberts I. Fluid resuscitation with colloid or crystalloid solutions in critically ill patients: a systematic review of randomized trials. BMJ 1998;316:961–4.

CHAPTER 30

Trauma

Edward E. Cornwell III, MD, FACS, FCCM, and Kurtis A. Campbell, MD

The area of trauma care merits special consideration when attempting to develop clinical practice guidelines based on scientific evidence. On the one hand, variations in mechanism, severity, and patterns of injuries as well as heterogeneity of pre-existing disease among injured patients create challenges in establishing the validity and applicability of the available clinical evidence. On the other hand, the easily identified outcome parameters of mortality, morbidity, length of stay, and return to functional status lend themselves readily to the trauma patient. This perhaps results from the fact that trauma surgery by its very nature (emergent, frequently performed in a physiologically compromised patient and in a contaminated surgical field without the opportunity for preparation) is associated with mortality and morbidity rates that would be unacceptable in elective surgical practice. Clinical studies designed to evaluate the efficacy of treatment modalities aimed at reducing death and complications more easily achieve statistical validity with population sizes that are obtainable by a single institution when the outcome parameter (eg, death from head injuries, or septic complications following colon injuries) is a common one. These advantages and pitfalls of applying evidence-based surgical concepts to trauma care imply that there will be variations in the quality of clinical evidence in the literature, and by necessity, in the strengths of recommendations generated from that literature. Without solid evidence-based clinical guidelines, variations in diagnostics and therapeutics will persist. In 1997, the Agency for Health Care Policy and Research (AHCPR) partly addressed variations in data and recommendations by stating that "guidelines are intended to address documented disparity in healthcare delivery and disparity in medical and surgical procedure use, hospitalization rates, and the use of medications."[1] This chapter will evaluate the development of guidelines in three specific areas of trauma care:

1. The management of severe head injury
2. Antibiotic prophylaxis in penetrating abdominal trauma
3. The surgical management of colon injuries

These three topics provide illustrative examples of evidence-based clinical practice guidelines that (a) contributed to more standardized care protocols and identified questions to be researched (head injuries); (b) are well established but frequently abandoned by clinicians (antibiotics for penetrating abdominal trauma), and; (c) seem well established but deserve re-examination (management of colon injury). The analysis of the generation of clinical practice guidelines in these three areas will consider the questions to be answered; the appraisal of the validity of clinical evidence addressing the questions; the application of that appraisal to clinical practice; and the establishment of recommendations for future research.

Table 30–1 lists the terminology that will be used to denote the quality of clinical data and the strength of recommendations based on that data.[2]

Table 30–1 Classification of Data and Recommendations with Evidence-Based Surgery

	Classification of Data
Class 1	Prospective randomized controlled trials (preferably blinded) of adequate statistical power
Class 2	Other prospective trials, including nonrandomized studies Major retrospective studies with statistically matched controls
Class 3	Retrospective case series Meta-analysis evaluations
	Strength of Recommendations
Level I	A consensus recommendation supported by adequate class 1 data. The recommendation in some cases may be interpreted as the standard of care.
Level II	A recommendation supported by a preponderance of class 2 and 3 data and informed expert opinion. Implementation is optional.
Level III	A recommendation supported by some class 2 or 3 data and informed expert opinion. A recommendation may represent prevalent practice but have little scientific support.

HEAD INJURY

Head injury is responsible for much of the death, disability, and economic impact of trauma in America.[3] By any measure, recovery from a head injury is the most important determinant of the outcome experienced by the multisystem-injured patient.[3,4] This, combined with the fact that the majority of brain-injured patients are managed in the first minutes of care by physicians who are not neurosurgeons (primarily trauma surgeons and emergency medicine physicians), demonstrates the importance of clinical practice guidelines. Yet, until recently, there was much variation in treatment protocols applied to head-injured patients.

Important work was performed by the Brain Trauma Foundation in collaboration with the Joint Section on Neurotrauma in Critical Care of the American Association of Neurological Surgeons (AANS) and the Congress of Neurological Surgeons (CNS) in developing guidelines for managing severe head injury.[5] Recommendations were made regarding the role of the neurosurgeon and concerning 13 specific clinical issues[5–8] (Table 30–2). The committee used the terms "standards" for level I recommendation, "guidelines" for level II recommendations, and "options" for level III recommendations. The quality of the supporting evidence (class 1, class 2, class 3) was clearly and thoroughly described. Only three of the thirteen clinical recommendations achieved the level I (standard) degree of certainty: (1) recommendations against the prophylactic use of antiseizure medications to prevent late post-traumatic seizures; (2) recommendations against the use of glucocorticoids in the treatment of severe head injury, and; (3) recommendations against the use of chronic prolonged hyperventilation in the absence of documentation of increased intracranial pressure (ICP) (See Table 30–2).

There was an early and measurable impact following the development of the head injury guidelines.[9] After receiving comments from experts in various disciplines, countries, and scientific organizations, the committee generated a seventh and final version in 1995. By late 1996, the guidelines were sent to all board-certified neurosurgeons in the United States and Canada. Within 9 months, 93 percent of the 1239 neurosurgeons responding to a questionnaire indicated they were familiar with the guidelines, and 45 percent stated that the guidelines had changed their practice. Indeed, the development and dissemination of head injury clinical practice guidelines was one of the sentinel events in trauma care in 1996 and 1997.[10]

compromised from shock or multiple blood transfusions at the time of surgical intervention. The efficacy of prophylactic antibiotics in penetrating abdominal trauma was established by a retrospective trial reported by Fullen and coworkers.[14] It is important to highlight this as an unusual example of routinely accepted clinical practice that is established on the basis of a retrospective study. There has not been, and probably never will be, a placebo-controlled prospective randomized trial to evaluate the question of *if* patients with penetrating abdominal trauma should receive prophylactic antibiotics. In evaluating 295 patients, Fullen and colleagues noted that roughly equal groups of patients received prophylactic penicillin and doxycycline preoperatively, intraoperatively, or postoperatively. Patients receiving preoperative antibiotics had a 7 percent postoperative infection rate compared with 33 percent for those receiving antibiotics intraoperatively and 30 percent for those receiving antibiotics postoperatively.

If we accept the premise that prophylactic antibiotics should be given to patients with penetrating abdominal trauma as soon as possible after admission, the question arises as to which antibiotics should be used. The need to provide broad-spectrum antimicrobial coverage that is also effective against anaerobic bacteria was suggested by a literature review performed by Dellinger.[15] In analyzing 18 comparative studies between 1973 and 1991 involving 2,679 patients (Table 30–3), he found that antibiotic regimens with poor anaerobic coverage had generally higher postoperative abdominal infection rates than those in patients receiving regimens with good anaerobic coverage.

Caution should be exercised in attempting to draw conclusions from a heterogenous group of studies with variability in the incidences of intestinal injuries. Accordingly, one can point to prospective randomized comparative series that establish that a single beta-lactam antibiotic with activity against gram-negative aerobes and anaerobes (eg, cefoxitin) is as safe and effective as (and usually less expensive than) double or triple antibiotic therapeutic regimens.[16–19] A meta-analysis of 1956 patients by Hooker and colleagues in 1991 further supported the concept that single-drug beta-lactam therapy was as effective as traditional combinations including aminoglycosides in victims of penetrating abdominal trauma.[20]

With the concept of early administration of a broad-spectrum agent with good coverage against gram-negative and anaerobic bacteria seemingly well established and adhered to in the management of patients with penetrating abdominal trauma, attention may be turned to the issue of the duration of antibiotic therapy. This issue represents an interesting example of the difficulty clinicians have in adhering to clinical practice guidelines when the guidelines run

Table 30–3 Abdominal Infection Rates*

Poor Anaerobic Coverage			Good Anaerobic Coverage		
Regimen	No. of pts. with that specific regimen	Infection Rate (%)	Regimen	No. of pts.	Infection Rate (%)
Aminoglycoside/ cephalothin	97	26	Aminoglycoside/ clindamycin	878	14
Cefamandole	229	20	Cefoxitin	578	14
Doxycycline/ penicillin	81	20	Aminoglycoside/ metronidazole	80	13
			Carbenicillin	90	12
			Cefotaxime	368	10
			Moxalactam	278	7

*from 18 collected series of patients with penetrating abdominal trauma (review by Dellinger).

counter to intuition and emotion. Short-duration (24 hours or less) antibiotic therapy in penetrating abdominal trauma has evolved over a 20-year period ending in the early 1990s. None of the controlled studies addressing the issue have shown an advantage of long-term antibiotic therapy over a short-term course.[15,21–26] In fact, the literature would lead one to conclude that the number of organs injured,[19] the specific organs injured (liver, colon, pancreas),[19,26] the Penetrating Abdominal Trauma Index (PATI),[27] the number of units of blood transfused,[28] but *not* the duration of antibiotic therapy, can be used to predict the likelihood of septic postoperative complications in penetrating abdominal trauma patients.

Recommendations from the literature notwithstanding, there is evidence that many trauma patients receive more than 24 hours of antibiotic prophylaxis. A survey of the membership of the American Association for the Surgery of Trauma regarding the management of colon injuries was reported at the 1997 annual meeting.[29] Of the 342 respondents, 88 percent held academic appointments and 10 percent had published on the subject. When questioned about the preferred duration of antibiotic administration for "a patient with an isolated colon injury," only 36 percent stated they would give antibiotics for less than 24 hours. Fifty-four percent said they would give antibiotics for 1 to 3 days, and 9 percent would give antibiotics for more than 4 days. An ancillary study of a multicenter prospective randomized trial of recombinant interferon gamma therapy for severely injured patients observed the antibiotic-prescribing patterns among the 212 enrolled severely injured patients (ISS ≥ 20 [ISS = Injury Severity Score] with contaminated wounds).[30,31] That study, of which 62 percent of enrolled patients were penetrating trauma victims, identified a common practice of prescribing multiple antibiotics for a prolonged period. An average of 15 antibiotic days (number of antibiotics x number of days prescribed) were prescribed for those 115 patients who never developed an infection during their hospital course.

Why do clinicians have difficulty discontinuing antibiotics after 24 hours with their trauma patients? The reasons may include the following: (1) the fact that patients at "high risk" for septic complications represent a small percentage of those subjects enrolled in controlled trials studying antibiotic duration and therefore are not well studied; (2) the difficulty in discontinuing antibiotic therapy after 24 hours in a sick patient with severe injuries; and (3) the difficulty of making the connection between excessively long antibiotic administration and the subsequent emergence of resistant organisms which may appear in the hospital environment weeks, months, or years later.[32] Whatever the reason for these practices, it is clear that controlled clinical trials to study antibiotic duration in exclusively high-risk abdominal trauma patients are necessary. Given the increased expense and the potential for side effects, toxicity, and antibiotic resistance, the practice can be justified only if it results in a reduction in postoperative septic complications. Lacking such a study, clinical practice proceeds without scientific validity.

A prospective randomized trial comparing short-course (1 day) to long-course (5 days) antibiotic therapy exclusively among abdominal trauma patients at high risk for septic complications was performed at the Los Angeles County + University of Southern California Medical Center (LAC + USC). The entry criteria were sufficiently rigid to include only those patients deemed at highest risk for postoperative septic complications using the following inclusion criteria:

> Full thickness injuries to the colon *and* one of the following:
> PATI ≥ 25 *or*
> units packed red blood cells (PRBC) transfused ≥ 6 *or*
> more than 4 hours from injury to operation

All patients were given 2 g cefoxitin intravenously piggyback en route to the operating room, with a second dose at 4 hours in cases lasting that long. After surgical confirmation of eligibility, patients were then randomized to 24 hours versus 5 days total length of cefoxitin therapy (2 g intravenously piggyback every 6 hours).

Power Analysis

A power analysis was performed considering figures derived from a logistic regression analysis by Nichols and colleagues of risk factors for postoperative infections following penetrating abdominal trauma (high risk > 70%, low risk ≤ 40%).[24] Using a 2-sided test with power of 0.80, a *p*-value of .05, and an assumption that one mode of therapy would decrease the infection rate from 65 to 30 percent, 74 patients (37 in each arm) would be necessary to identify such a difference with statistical significance. Differences in morbidity and mortality were analyzed using the Yates corrected chi-square test. Assuming a 20 percent dropout after intention to treat, 93 patients would need to be enrolled initially.

Results

There were 94 patients who had abdominal injuries of sufficient severity to be eligible for inclusion. Of these, 20 patients were excluded on the basis of antibiotic regimens prescribed for associated injuries requiring antibiotic therapy (18 patients with open fractures, 2 patients with prosthetic vascular grafts); 4 patients met the criteria but died within the first 24 hours from associated head or chest injuries; and 7 patients met the criteria but were not enrolled due to violation of the protocol. The remaining 63 patients were enrolled and completely evaluated to death or discharge, and these patients form the study group. The groups were well matched in terms of risk factors for septic complications (Table 30–4).

A longer course of antibiotic therapy was ineffective in reducing the predictably high septic complication intra-abdominal infection rates among this high-risk group of patients (Table 30–5).

The results described here are of interest when compared with the subset of patients described in a well-controlled series by Fabian and colleagues.[26] Theirs is the largest prospective randomized trial on antibiotic duration for penetrating abdominal trauma and has carefully described subgroup analysis. The study included 515 patients: 235 with hollow viscus injuries, 111 with colon injuries, 74 with hollow viscus injuries and a PATI > 25, and 56 with colon injuries and a PATI > 25. In no group did 5 days of cefoxitin or cefotetan therapy decrease morbidity over 1 day of treatment. Because of similar study designs, and in order to

Table 30–4 Risk Factors for Septic Complications in Short- and Long-Course Antibiotic Therapy Groups

Patients	1 Day (n = 31)	5 Days (n = 32)	p-Value
Mean age in years (range)	27.9 (16–62)	29.7 (17–68)	NS
Mean PATI	34.4	32.4	NS
No. with PATI ≥ 25	30 (97%)	26 (82%)	NS
No. with destructive colon wounds requiring resection	14 (45%)	13 (41%)	NS
Mean Injury Severity Score (ISS)	14.5	17.1	NS
No. with ISS > 15	14 (45%)	23 (72%)	NS
No. with multiple blood transfusions	24 (78%)	23 (72%)	NS
No. with 6 units blood transfused	15 (49%)	10 (32%)	NS
No. with SICU stay	19 (61%)	18 (56%)	NS

PATI = Penetrating Abdominal Trauma Index; NS = not significant; SICU = surgical intensive care unit.

Table 30–5 Outcome Parameters in Short- and Long-Course Antibiotic Therapy Groups

Patients	1 Day (n = 31)	5 Days (n = 32)	p-Value
No. with intra-abdominal infection	6 (19%)	12 (38%)	NS
No. with any septic complication	18 (58%)	14 (44%)	NS
Average length of stay (days)	17.8	19.0	NS
Mortality (rate)	1 (3%)	5 (16%)	NS

NS = not significant.

analyze a larger sample size, a mini-meta-analysis of the two studies (including only the most severely injured patients) can be performed (Table 30–6).

If anything, the trend suggests that longer-course therapy is associated with a *higher* abdominal infection rate. Combining the two studies only improves the statistical power (to state that no differences exist) from 0.27 to 0.32. Given the incidence of intra-abdominal infections (1 day, 19%; 5 days, 33%), the sample size required to detect a 14 percent difference in incidence with an 80 percent power and to avoid a Type II statistical error (conclusion of no difference based on insufficient sample size) would be 344 "high-risk" patients (172 in each group). This is three times the number of patients with the highest risk enrolled at two busy trauma centers over 2.5 to 3 years. Although the variability of reporting makes it difficult to ascertain, it appears that no other prospective study has more than 53 patients who would meet the inclusion criteria described herein.[21–25] It is clear from the above that to definitively answer whether extending antibiotic therapy in even the highest-risk trauma patients would decrease the postoperative complication rate, a multi-institutional trial is necessary.

This analysis therefore concludes that despite exhaustive studies regarding antibiotic therapy in patients with penetrating abdominal trauma, there remains a small area where further clinical research (probably a multi-institutional trial) is necessary. Until then, the following statements appear to be supported by the clinical evidence:

1. Systemic antibiotics should be administered as soon as possible after injury for patients with penetrating abdominal trauma requiring surgical intervention.
2. A single broad-spectrum agent is at least as safe and effective as a double- or triple-antibiotic therapeutic regimen.
3. High postoperative septic complication rates can be expected in patients with gunshot injuries to the colon, high PATI scores, major blood loss, and common need for postoperative intensive care. There is no evidence to date that extending anti-

Table 30–6 Combined Intra-abdominal Infection Rates in Two Studies*

Institution	No. of Abdominal Infections (Rate)		
	1 day	5 Days	p-Value
U. of Southern California	6/31 (19%)	12/32 (38%)	—
U. of Tennessee	5/27 (19%)	8/29 (28%)	—
Total	11/58 (19%)	20/61 (33%)	.13

*Prospective randomized trials of 1-day vs 5-days' antibiotic duration (only highest-risk patients).

biotic therapy beyond 24 hours decreases that high risk. A multi-institutional trial is necessary to confirm the statistical validity of all patients, regardless of risk, receiving only a short course of antibiotics following penetrating abdominal trauma.

These are similar to the conclusions of the trauma clinical practice guidelines committee of the Eastern Association for the Surgery of Trauma (EAST).[33]

THE MANAGEMENT OF COLON INJURIES

The evolution of the management of traumatic penetrating colon injuries in the last half of the twentieth century is an interesting example of the need to continually question clinical recommendations as new information becomes available. In 1943, the United States Army, following the guidelines of the Surgeon General of the United States mandated that all colon injuries be managed by colostomy either at or proximal to the site of injury (as opposed to primary repair or resection and anastomosis).[34] The justification for this mandate reportedly was that colon injuries during the Civil War carried an associated 90 percent mortality and those during World War I were associated with a 60 percent mortality.[35] The 30 percent mortality seen during World War II with mandatory colostomies purportedly implied the wisdom of the policy.[36] However, the benefit of many years of perspective allows one to suggest that fluid replacement, plasma preservation, blood-banking techniques, and superior military evacuation probably contributed to the lower mortality rate. As surgeons began to appreciate the difference between high-velocity military injuries and low-velocity injuries seen in the civilian setting, published reports in the 1950s began to challenge the routine use of colostomies.[37,38] A report in 1951 identified a 9 percent mortality rate when primary repair of selected colon injuries was used.[37]

Over the next 3 decades, nearly 60 published reports addressed the issue of primary repair versus diversion for colon injuries in the civilian setting.[39–41] A major breakthrough occurred with the landmark paper published by Stone and Fabian in 1979.[42] They empirically derived criteria for mandatory colostomy: shock, major hemorrhage, multiple organ injury, gross fecal soilage, long delay to repair, destructive colon wounds requiring resection, and major abdominal wall loss. Roughly half of their 269 patients met the criteria for mandatory colostomy. The remaining patients were prospectively randomized to either primary repair or diversion. One of the 67 patients (1.5%) randomized to primary repair developed a fecal fistula, which closed spontaneously. The empirically derived criteria were thus recommended as those that determined whether or not primary repair could be safely performed. Since that report, refinements have been made in the identifying of penetrating trauma patients at high risk for postoperative septic complications. Moore and colleagues devised the PATI (which quantifies trauma on the basis of specific organs injured and the severity of those injuries) and found that there were dramatic differences in complication rates above or below a PATI of 25 (46% for PATI > 25 vs 7% for PATI ≤ 25).[27] Nichols and associates performed logistic regression analysis on series of 145 patients with penetrating abdominal trauma at two hospitals during a period that overlapped that of the study by Moore and co-workers.[19] This analysis identified increased age, colon injuries requiring colostomy, multiple units of transfused blood, and a larger number of organs injured as risk factors for postoperative infection. It appeared to corroborate the findings of Moore and associates although the term "PATI" was not used. As consensus emerges regarding colon injury, multiple blood transfusions, and PATI as predictors of postoperative septic complications, the question arises of whether avoiding a colonic anastomosis decreases the risk.[19,27,28,43,44] This question arises because comparing frequencies of outcome parameters suggests that abdominal septic complication (fascial dehiscence, intra-abdominal abscess, and wound infection) is not necessarily synonymous with suture line disruption.[41–46]

American surgeons trained from the 1950s through the 1980s have developed the ability to identify patients who have extremely severe injuries and pronounced physiologic derangements. Historically, these sicker patients are managed by performing a colostomy. Not

Table 30–7 Prospective Randomized Trials: Colostomy versus Primary Repair

Year	Author	Number with Colostomy, % Compare	Morbidity			Resection and Anastomosis[†] (n)
			Number with Primary Repair	Mean PATI*	Colon Suture Line Disruption (%)	
1979	Stone and Fabian	72, 10%	67, 1%	—	1.5	0/268
1991	Chappuis et al.	28, 17%	28, 21%	26	0	11/56 (20%)
1992	Falcone et al.	11, 22%	11, 9%	40.5	0	9/22 (41%)
1995	Sasaki et al.	28, 36%	43, 19%	25.5	0	12/71 (17%)
1996	Gonzalez et al.	53, 25%	56, 20%	24.3	0	5/109 (5%)

PATI = penetrating abdominal trauma index.
*for pts. with primary repair.
[†]denominator is total number of patients in series.

surprisingly, therefore, virtually every retrospective and prospective nonrandomized study analyzing intra-abdominal septic complications has found that patients who received primary repair had complication rates equal to or less than those who received colostomy.[41,43–48] The question of whether colostomy will reduce the risk of septic complications can be answered only by prospective randomized analyses where patients are equally likely to receive one treatment mode or the other, without regard to the severity of their injuries. There are four such trials in the literature;[49–52] the results of these trials (as well as the 1979 study by Stone and Fabian) are detailed in Table 30–7.

Overall, these prospective randomized trials imply that the added expense and potential morbidity of a second operation for colostomy closure is not justified in most cases. However, the circumstance of destructive colon injuries requiring resection and anastomosis (as compared with suture repair of a through-and-through perforation) in patients with more severe physiologic derangements should be closely inspected.

A question arises of whether there are enough patients in the prospective randomized trials who require resection and anastomosis under physiologically compromised situations to routinely recommend primary repair in this circumstance. A 1994 report by Stewart and associates, for example, demonstrated a 14 percent rate of anastomotic leak among 43 patients with colon injuries requiring colon resection and anastomosis.[53] Leaks occurred in 5 of 12 patients (42%) who had a pre-existing medical condition or more than 6 units of blood transfused and in 1 of 31 (3%) patients without those risk factors. A prospective study by Cornwell and colleagues of 56 patients with colon injuries at high risk for septic complications (PATI ≥ 25, ≥ 6 units of blood transfused, or ≥ 6 hours elapsed between injury and surgery) reported anastomotic disruptions in 2 of 25 patients (80%) who underwent resection and anastomosis.[54] Table 30–7 demonstrates that there have been only 37 patients cumulatively described in the prospective randomized studies who underwent resection and anastomosis.[49–52] Three of the four series (1991 to 1996) described after the term "PATI" was coined report mean PATIs of around 25; so it is unclear how many of the 37 patients were at actual high risk for septic complications (destructive colon injuries requiring resection were excluded from primary anastomosis in the first series). None of the 37 patients had identified suture line disruption, but there appears to be an inadequate number of patients with destructive colon injuries and other major risk factors to recommend (as some authors have) that colostomies be abandoned altogether.[51,52,55] Guidelines recently developed by EAST reflect these concerns, reserving colostomy as a level II recommendation for patients with destructive colon injuries that require resection in a setting of shock, underlying disease, or severe associated injury.[33]

In summary, the story of evidence-based clinical guidelines as they relate to the management of colon injuries is one of constant evolution based on increasing information. The cumulative literature to date would support the following evidence-based recommendations:

1. Multiple blood transfusions, shock, and a high PATI reliably identify patients at high risk for septic complications following penetrating colon injuries.
2. The risk is not obviated by colostomy, and intra-abdominal sepsis frequently occurs in the absence of suture line disruption. Accordingly, the majority of colon injuries in civilian practice may be managed with primary repair.
3. Given the small number of patients in high-risk categories with destructive colon injuries requiring resection who were randomized to primary repair (37 total resections in the cumulative prospective randomized studies), there is still room to consider colostomy in the management of these patients.

FUTURE DIRECTIONS AND CONCLUSION

The foregoing sections give a clear indication of future directions in trauma care. Trauma practice guidelines that are being generated by various societies can rely on evidence-based methodologies to address specific questions (for example, the duration of antibiotic use in the highest-risk penetrating abdominal trauma patients, the utility of primary repair in patients with destructive colon injuries and comorbid factors). Even when insufficient data exists to generate level I recommendations, important areas for further research are identified by this process.

In conclusion, clinical guidelines are only as solid as the evidence on which they are based. Evidence-based surgery as it relates to trauma care should be considered an evolving science, with new questions being generated based on the implementation of previous recommendations. The generation of new knowledge should provide the basis for recommendations that will justify the upgrading of options to guidelines and of guidelines to standards.

REFERENCES

1. Chesley FD. The AHCPR clinical practice guideline program: lessons learned and future direction. Society of General Internal Medicine Forum 1997;11:5–8.

2. Barie PS, Fabian TC, Pasquale M, Rogers FB. Symposium: the development of diagnostic and therapeutic practice management guidelines for trauma patients. Contemp Surg 1998;52(6):413–30.

3. Gennarelli TA, Champion HR, Copes WS, Sacco WJ. Comparison of mortality, morbidity, and severity of 59,713 head injured patients with 114,447 patients with extracranial injuries. J Trauma 1994;37(6):962–8.

4. Shackford SR, Mackersie RC, Davis JW, et al. Epidemiology and pathology of traumatic deaths occurring at a level I trauma center in a regionalized system: the importance of secondary brain injury. J Trauma 1989;29(10):1392–7.

5. Brain Trauma Foundation. The integration of brain-specific treatments into the initial resuscitation of the severe head injury patient. J Neurotrauma 1996;13:653–9.

6. Brain Trauma Foundation. Critical pathway for the treatment of established intracranial hypertension. J Neurotrauma 1996;13:719–20.

7. Brain Trauma Foundation. The use of hyperventilation in the acute management of severe traumatic brain injury. J Neurotrauma 1997;13:699–703.

8. Brain Trauma Foundation. Indications for intracranial pressure monitoring. J Neurotrauma 1997;13:667–9.

9. Marion DW, Firlik K. Management of severe traumatic brain injury in 1997: the impact of the guidelines for the management of severe head injuries. Parkridge (IL): American Association for Neurological Surgeons Neurotrauma Newsletter 1997 summer/fall:2–3.

10. Cornwell EE. What's new in trauma and critical care. J Am Coll Surg 1998;186(2):115–21.

11. Miles AA, Miles EM, Burke JF. The value and duration of defence reactions of the skin to the primary lodgement of bacteria. Br J Exp Pathol 1957;38:79–96.

12. Burke JF. The effective period of preventive antibiotic action in experimental incisions and dermal lesions. Surgery 1961;50:161–8.

13. Polk HC Jr, Lopez-Mayor JF. Postoperative wound infection: a prospective study of determinant factors and prevention. Surgery 1969;66:97–103.

14. Fullen WD, Hunt J, Altemeier WA. Prophylactic antibiotics in penetrating wounds of the abdomen. J Trauma 1972;12:282–9.

15. Dellinger EP. Antibiotic prophylaxis in trauma: penetrating abdominal injuries and open fractures. Rev Infect Dis 1991;13:S847–57.

16. Hofsetter SR, Pachter HL, Bailey AA, Coppa GF. A prospective comparison of two regimens of prophylactic antibiotics in abdominal trauma: cefoxitin versus triple drug. J Trauma 1984;24:307–10.

17. Gentry LO, Feliciano DV, Lea AS, et al. Perioperative antibiotic therapy for penetrating injuries of the abdomen. Ann Surg 1984;200:561–6.

18. Jones RC, Thal ED, Johnson NA, Gollihar LN. Evaluation of antibiotic therapy following penetrating abdominal trauma. Ann Surg 1985;201:576–85.

19. Nichols RL, Smith JW, Klein DB, et al. Risk of infection after penetrating abdominal trauma. NEJM 1984;311:1065–70.

20. Hooker KD, DiPiro JT, Wynn JJ. Aminoglycoside combinations versus beta-lactams alone for penetrating abdominal trauma: a meta-analysis. J Trauma 1991;31:1155–60.

21. Oreskovich MR, Dellinger EP, Lennard ES, et al. Duration of preventive antibiotic administration for penetrating abdominal trauma. Arch Surg 1982;117:200–5.

22. Dellinger EP, Wertz MJ, Lennard ES, Oreskovich MR. Efficacy of short-course antibiotic prophylaxis after penetrating intestinal injury. Arch Surg 1986;121:23–30.

23. Demetriades D, Lakhoo M, Pezikis A, et al. Short-course antibiotic prophylaxis in penetrating abdominal injuries: ceftriaxone versus cefoxitin. Injury 1991;22:20–4.

24. Nichols RL, Smith JW, Robertson GD, et al. Prospective alterations in therapy for penetrating abdominal trauma. Arch Surg 1993;128:55–64.

25. Rowlands BJ, Ericsson CD, Fischer RP. Penetrating abdominal trauma: the use of operative findings to determine length of antibiotic therapy. J Trauma 1987;27:250–5.

26. Fabian TC, Croce MA, Payne LW, et al. Duration of antibiotic therapy for penetrating abdominal trauma: a prospective trial. Surgery 1992;112:788–95.

27. Moore EE, Dunn EL, Moore JB, Thompson JS. Penetrating abdominal trauma index. J Trauma 1981;21:439–45.

28. Moore FA, Moore EE, Sauaia A. Blood transfusion: an independent risk factor for post injury multiple organ failure. Arch Surg 1997;132:620–5.

29. Eshraghi N, Mullins RJ, Mayberry JC, et al. Surveyed opinion of American trauma surgeons in management of colon injuries. J Trauma 1998;44(1):93–7.

30. Polk HC Jr, Cheadle WG, Livingston DH, et al. A randomized prospective clinical trial to determine the efficacy of interferon-gamma in severely injured patients. Am J Surg 1992;163:191–6.

31. Hadjiminas D, Cheadle WG, Spain DA, et al. Antibiotic overkill of trauma victims? Am J Surg 1994;168:288–90.

32. Steinberg S, Salomone J, Flint L, et al. Practicing what we preach: do antibiotic (ATB) use patterns alter the risk of nosocomial infection in surgical intensive care unit (SICU) patients? Presented at the Surgical Infection Society; 1997 May 2; Pittsburgh (PA).

33. Eastern Association for the Surgery of Trauma. Trauma practice guidelines; 1998.

34. Office of the Surgeon General of the United States. Washington (DC); 1943 Oct 23. Circular Letter No. 178.

35. Fraser J, Drummond H. A clinical and experimental study of three hundred perforating wounds of the abdomen. Br Med J 1917;1:321–30.

36. Ogilvie WH. Abdominal wounds in western desert. Surg Gynecol Obstet 1944;78:225–38.

37. Woodhall JP, Ochsner A. The management of perforating injuries of the colon and rectum in civilian practice. Surg 1951;29:305–20.

38. Pontius RG, Creech O, DeBakey ME. Management of large bowel injuries in civilian practice. Ann Surg 1957;146:291–5.

39. Bartizal JR, Boyd DR, Folk FR, et al. A critical review of management of 392 colonic and rectal injuries. Dis Colon Rectum 1974;17:313–18.

40. LoCicerro I, Tajima T, Drapanas T. A half-century of experience in the management of colon injuries: changing concepts. J Trauma 1975;15:575–9.

41. Burch JM, Martin R, Richardson RJ, et al. Evolution of the treatment of the injured colon in the 1980s. Arch Surg 1991;126:980–4.

42. Stone HH, Fabian TC. Management of perforating colon trauma: randomization between primary closure and exteriorization. Ann Surg 1979;190:430–5.

43. George SM, Fabian TC, Mangiante EC. Colon trauma: further support for primary repair. Am J Surg 1988;156:16–20.

44. Nelken N, Lewis F. The influence of injury severity on complication rates after primary closure or colostomy for penetrating colon trauma. Ann Surg 1989;209:439–47.

45. Demetriades D, Rabinowitz B, Sofianos C, Prumm E. The management of colon injuries by primary repair or colostomy. Br J Surg 1985;72:881–3.

46. George SM, Fabian TC, Voeller GR, et al. Primary repair of colon wounds: a prospective trial in nonselected patients. Ann Surg 1989;209(6):728–34.

47. Demetriades D, Charalambides D, Pantanowitz D. Gunshot wounds of the colon: role of primary repair. Ann R Coll Surg Engl 1992;74:381–4.

48. Sasaki LS, Mittal V, Allaben RD. Primary repair of colon injuries: a retrospective analysis. Am Surg 1994;60:522–7.

49. Chappuis CW, Frey DJ, Dietzen CD, et al. Management of penetrating colon injuries: a prospective randomized trial. Ann Surg 1991;213:492–8.

50. Falcone RE, Wanamaker SR, Santanello SA, Carey LC. Colorectal trauma: primary repair or anastomosis with intracolonic bypass vs. ostomy. Dis Colon Rectum 1992;35:957–63.

51. Sasaki LS, Allaben RD, Golwala R, Mittal VK. Primary repair of colon injuries: a prospective randomized study. J Trauma 1995;39:895–901.

52. Gonzalez RP, Merlotti GJ, Holevar MR. Colostomy in penetrating colon injury: is it necessary? J Trauma 1996;41:271–5.

53. Stewart RM, Fabian TC, Croce MA, et al. Is resection with primary anastomosis following destructive colon wounds always safe? Am J Surg 1994;168:316–20.

54. Cornwell EE, Velmahos GC, Berne TV, et al. The fate of colonic suture lines in high-risk trauma patients: a prospective analysis. J Am Coll Surg 1998;187(1):58–63.

55. Jacobson LE, Gomez GA, Broadie TA. Primary repair of 58 consecutive penetrating injuries of the colon: should colostomy be abandoned? Am Surg 1997;63:170–7.

CHAPTER 31

Burns

Andrew M. Munster, MD

Modern burn care over the past 50 years has been advanced by a number of pivotal develop-ments. Fortunately, because of the early introduction of burn size (the percentage of total body surface involved) as a measurement of injury severity, improvements in outcome have been easier to track than in many other disciplines of surgery. The first major stimulus to improved treatment was the Coconut Grove nightclub disaster of 1942, after which the concept of intra-venous resuscitation based on scientifically sound animal models was first introduced.[1] The advent of effective topical chemotherapy in the early 1960s had a dramatic impact. The first effective topical agent, mafenide acetate (Sulfamylon), reduced the gross mortality rate range from the 38 to 45 percent to 14 to 24 percent.[2] At about the same time, special burn care units with the primary goals of reducing cross infection and training health care workers in the spe-cial needs of burn patients were introduced around the world and in the United States. The most recent major advance came from the appreciation that early surgical resection of the burned tissue and immediate coverage of the wound made the possibility of survival in patients with hitherto lethal injuries a reality. Improved measures have also been introduced in less dramatic areas, including nutritional support and improved management of inhalation injury.

The national mortality rate in major burn centers today is around 5 percent (Figure 31–1). The emphasis in management is shifting to a consideration of improved quality of life and functional outcome in addition to mere survival. For this approach to be effective, essen-tial rehabilitation and psychosocial issues must be addressed, and outcome considerations in these areas must be scrutinized in a scientific rather than an anecdotal manner.

In this chapter, evidence of the impact of these major strategies will be examined. The current techniques and difficulties of measuring functional outcome will be discussed. Finally, the cost-effectiveness of various therapies will be considered. Included in this last section will be a case study illustrating the important relationship between surgical excision with wound closure and the cost of care from the author's own institution.

LITERATURE REVIEW

Evolution of Outcome Measurements in Burn Surgery

Burn Size

The first formal expression of burn size as a percentage of total body surface was introduced in 1924 and provided a method of assessing outcome before more rigorous techniques were avail-able.[3] This was followed by the development of univariate probit analysis by Bull,[4] a classic methodology which has stood the test of time for 40 years. The advent of computer-assisted programs of data analysis has enabled outcome measurements to become so rapid and sophis-ticated that trends by age and other variables impacting outcome can now be included. Some workers, rather than use crude percent mortality as an outcome index, have preferred the LA50 or lethal average 50, which is the burn size over which 50 percent of patients can be expected to succumb. The LA50 has been steadily rising in most age groups over the past 30 years.[5]

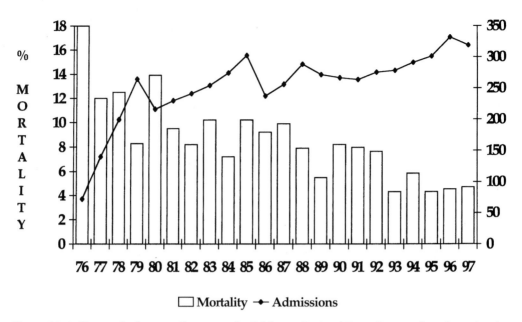

Figure 31–1 Changes in the mortality rate at the Baltimore Regional Burn Center reflect the national trend.

Recognition of comorbidities

In a recent study of 103 consecutive pediatric burn patients with massive burns (over 80 percent total or over 70 percent third degree), it was demonstrated by multivariate logistic regression that the following factors significantly increased mortality rate:[6] lower age, larger burn size, presence of inhalation injury, delayed intravenous access, lower admission hematocrit, lower base deficit, higher serum osmolarity on admission, sepsis, inotropic support requirement, low platelet count, and ventilator dependency. In a study from Ludwigshafen, Germany, alcohol abuse, smoking, and pre-existing neurologic and cardiovascular disease were also found to contribute significantly to mortality.[7] In a large study from the Shriners Burn Institute of Boston, an attempt has recently been made to simplify these formulas to aid families in decision making. In this logistic regression analysis, three risk factors for death were identified: age greater than 60 years, burn size larger than 40 percent, and inhalation injury. However, the authors noted that the increasing amount of "do not resuscitate" requests and orders by patients and families complicates the analysis.[8]

With the advent of these sophisticated techniques of predicting and measuring mortality rates from burns, it should be theoretically easy to demonstrate the effect of any new advance which might affect mortality. However, given that the mortality rate is already so low, this will prove difficult. To demonstrate an impact, the statistical power of any new intervention would have to be so large that participation in a prospective multicenter trial would have to involve all major centers in the United States—hardly a practical proposition.

THE EFFECT OF SPECIFIC INTERVENTIONS

Affecting the Mortality Rate

Surgical Wound Closure

There has never been a prospective randomized trial of excision versus conservative therapy to show the impact of excisional therapy on mortality rate; all data are historic. Nevertheless, surgical excision and coverage of the burn wound, introduced in the 1970s, has now become the gold standard for treating life-threatening burns. In 1974, Burke reported on a series of children whose full-thickness burns were excised and allografted, with allograft rejection being controlled by immunosuppression. In a trial of 32 children with massive burns (average 65 percent of total body surface area), unprecedented survival was accomplished.[9] There have been several major trials of excision and wound closure since that time which, compared with large numbers of historic controls carefully matched for burn size and other variables, have shown substantial reductions in mortality rate. The mortality rate for adult burn patients at the Massachusetts General Hospital fell from 24 percent in 1974 to 7 percent in 1984 after the institution of excision and wound closure.[10] Perhaps the most dramatic reduction in mortality rate from excision and prompt wound closure was reported in a series of children by the Galveston group.[11] When compared with the revised Bull and Fisher formula,[12] significant reductions of mortality rate were noted in all age groups; the LA50 was particularly impressive in the 0 to 14-year age group, where it rose to 98 percent. Only adults with smoke inhalation did not show an improved survival benefit from early excision. Similar studies have been performed in the elderly, in whom early wound closure appears to be particularly beneficial.[13,14]

While the optimal closure of surgically excised burn wounds remains closure with autologous split-thickness donor skin, enough donor sites may not be available in timely fashion to accomplish this goal. For many years, various techniques were used to increase the amount of autologous skin available, including "meshing" skin with various expansion ratios, alternating strips of allograft and autograft, punching square holes into allograft into which autograft could be inserted (the "Chinese method"), and combinations thereof. With the discovery of a clinically acceptable technique of growing cultured epithelial autografts (CEAs),[15] a new era in the surgical closure of burn wounds was introduced. Today, CEAs are commercially available, and many burn units grow their own cells. There are temporary epidermal covers that provide time for donor sites to heal, adherent plastic sheetings to provide pain relief and improved healing, and various biologic skin substitutes. In the near future, composite biodegradable dermis and CEA—the theoretically "ideal" wound cover—will be available.[16] Outcome analysis of these products is extremely difficult. Because each patient is different in the physiology of healing, experimental materials to close wounds and control sites must necessarily be in the same patient. This eliminates mortality as an endpoint, and secondary endpoints such as the speed and quality of healing have to be measured. Evaluation of outcome rests therefore with the thickness of the donor skin necessary to cover the wound, in terms of donor site healing, and the quality of the resultant scar tissue in the grafted areas, which must be evaluated for at least a year after surgery and for which various scales are available. All of the above techniques are expensive, all have their advocates, and at this time of writing no technique has been proved superior to another. In one reported prospective randomized series of cultured epithelial autografts, the mortality rate was significantly reduced over controls;[17] but these results essentially confirm the value of early excision and wound closure rather than prove the value of one technique of closure over another. The late results of grafting with cultured skin versus native skin do not seem markedly different.[18] The author's opinion is that outcome analysis of the different methods of wound coverage is probably not going to demonstrate significant differences between the various available products. Cost will therefore become a determining factor, and autologous split-thickness skin grafts will remain the standard of care for most patients. However, clear-cut data on this subject probably will not be available for several more years.

Topical Therapy

The empirical introduction of effective topical chemotherapy between the 1960s and the 1970s[2] has so reduced the mortality rate that prospective randomized trials are no longer possible for comparing a new topical agent to no topical agent; it is possible only to analyze one topical agent against another. In addition, the establishment of excisional therapy and early wound closure in the surgical armamentarium has reduced the importance of topical chemotherapeutic agents in burn management. The principal need for topical medications in the past had been the need to penetrate large volumes of nonviable, necrotic eschar to prevent fatal burn wound sepsis; with effective early wound closure, this threat is averted. New therapeutic agents for the treatment of partial-thickness wounds and donor sites or for the temporary treatment of full-thickness wounds until excision and closure can be accomplished can now be evaluated using measures based on patient comfort, nursing convenience, and costs. There is still a considerable need to improve the current instruments used to measure these secondary endpoints; for example, although visual analog scales are widely used to measure pain and discomfort, they are frequently unreliable in the postoperative setting.

Other Interventions

Inhalation injury remains one of the last major complications of injury by fire and smoke against which it has been difficult to make inroads. Patients with inhalation injury of some severity frequently develop adult respiratory distress syndrome and/or pneumonia as the final cause of death. The introduction of high-frequency ventilation has reportedly accounted for some decrease in mortality of these patients.[19] This study, however, as well as a more recent one using aerosolized heparin and acetylcystine,[20] used historical controls and did not have a prospective randomized design; the technique has not been widely adopted at this time. There has been some enthusiasm for the use of hyperbaric oxygen therapy in the treatment of patients with inhalation injury. Outcome-based studies have been difficult because most institutions with burn centers do not have a hyperbaric chamber; thus the selection of patients for a prospective randomized trial would fall to the transport workers in the field, which is clearly not only difficult but inappropriate. In one institution that houses both a burn center and a hyperbaric oxygen facility, in a prospective study of 125 matched patients randomized for burn size and inhalation injury, no difference in survival could be demonstrated by the use of hyperbaric oxygen.[21]

Growth hormone has been advocated as a technique of increasing survival following major burns.[22] Again, comparisons were made with reported predictive formulas of outcome and therefore cannot be accepted as totally reliable. We investigated the effect of antiendotoxin therapy on the generation of the cytokine cascade, serum endotoxin levels, and survival[23] in a rigorous prospective randomized trial. Although endotoxin levels were successfully reduced, there was no effect on mortality rate, on induction of the cytokine cascade, or on measured clinical parameters of sepsis. Had this trial not been controlled for the last three variables, that is, if only reduction of endotoxemia had been analyzed, one may have falsely concluded that this was a promising intervention.

As pointed out above, for new interventions to impact the mortality rate of thermally injured patients, massive prospective randomized trials containing several thousand patients would have to be undertaken; this will obviously be difficult.

Affecting Functional Outcome

In the 1960s and 1970s, the emphasis of research was on reduction of the mortality rate, as previously discussed. A controversial paper by Linn in 1977 triggered a widening of focus.[24] This paper examined the outcome of burn therapy in a number of Florida hospitals, both community based and university based, and found no difference in survival outcomes. This paper was criticized widely by the trauma and burn establishment because it appeared to diminish the importance of specialized burn centers. A critical review of the data, however, indicated that the problem lay elsewhere: the mortality rate was already so low that the number of patients entered into the study did not have enough power to produce a significant difference in mortality rate. At that time, many workers in this field began to realize that perhaps it would be appropriate to pay attention to other aspects of burn care, that is, survival and the quality of survival as a measure of outcome in addition to the mortality rate.

This was not, of course, the first time that attempts at measuring functional or psychologic outcome of burn injury had been addressed, but prior work had been sporadic. Early work had included neuropsychiatric observations following the Coconut Grove disaster.[25,26] The role of rehabilitation medicine was addressed in the first issue of *Surgical Clinics of North America* devoted to burns.[27] In the mid-1970s, the team at the Baltimore Regional Burn Center constructed a crude instrument to measure quality of life. This instrument had domains encompassing physical, psychosocial, and general health issues. It quickly produced surprising results indicating that the total burn *size* did not contribute as much to the quality of life as the *distribution* (ie, patients with facial and hand burns did far worse than patients with burns that covered a much larger surface area but that did not affect the face and hands). The survey also indicated that recovery from burn injury was slow and dynamic up to at least 1 year from the time of the accident and that recovery from physical injury proceeded much more rapidly than recovery from psychosocial sequelae. At this point, the work was expanded to develop an extensively constructed and validated outcome scale for burns.[28] This scale was eventually shortened to the Abbreviated Burn Specific Health Scale.[29] The Burn Specific Health Scale has recently been further refined and simplified and now includes work-related outcomes.[30] Currently, this scale is being widely used nationally as well as in Britain, Australia, Denmark, and the Netherlands.

Psychosocial and physical issues have been recently examined in both adults and children.[31–36] At this point, the best single predictor of a patient's ability to return to work is the presence or absence of all the components of post-traumatic stress disorder syndrome (or post-traumatic distress, as it is now termed), which correlates closely with the Burn Specific Health Scale.[37]

The scientific basis for measuring outcome from interventions in burn management has been soundly laid. Both psychologic and psychosocial improvements in rehabilitation can be designed to impact outcome in a measurable form. This development, however, is quite recent, and studies now need to be designed to capitalize on this work.

COST-EFFECTIVENESS OF THERAPIES: CASE STUDY

The Baltimore Regional Burn Center conducted a 14-year review encompassing 3,561 patients between 1978 and 1991. Patients were divided into the first 7 years and the second 7 years of the study and were studied by age, burn size, third degree component, mortality rate, and mortality rate with inhalation injury. The severity of injury was classified according to burn size, third degree component, and diagnosis-related groups (burn DRGs 456 to 460). The length of hospital stay was recorded, and the interval between the first and each subsequent surgical procedure for excision and closure was noted. Charges generated by the medical center were compared with the U.S. Consumer Price Index and the general hospital basket for the same period of time.

Mortality rate declined by over 2 percent (from 9.8 percent in the first 7 years to 7.3 percent in the second 7 years, $p < .001$) during the study period. Multiple regression analysis indicated that the percentage of burn, the presence of inhalation injury, and age had a significant effect on mortality; however, these variables as well as DRGs were statistically evenly distributed over the 14-year study. The length of stay decreased from an average of 23 days in 1979 to 14.2 days in 1990, which correlated significantly with a decrease in the interval between surgical interventions, which fell from 14.7 days to 6.1 days during the same period (Figure 31–2). In addition, the average annual increase of hospital charges for burn care, which grew at 9.6 percent per year, was higher than the U.S. Consumer Price Index during the same time (5.8 percent) but substantially lower than the hospital market as a whole (10.8 percent). This study definitively demonstrated that aggressive surgical management of burned patients could be carried out with good clinical results and effective cost containment and that the decrease in cost was due entirely to shortened length of stay.[38] These findings have been confirmed by a later report involving 222 patients from the Augusta Regional Medical Center.[39]

GUIDELINES AND FUTURE DIRECTIONS

Using all of the currently known interventions which affect mortality and functional outcome, certain guidelines have been developed for the management of burn patients. Perioperative management systems as well as critical pathways have been constructed.[40] The American Burn Association has published a consensus document on optimal goals for the delivery of burn care[41] and has also officially published a document on optimal care of patients.[42] Using the above criteria, the American College of Surgeons and the American Burn Association have developed a verification process for burn centers, a program that began in 1995 based entirely on the guidelines mentioned above.

There are some presumptions derived from the reduction of mortality in severe burns by modern surgical techniques and the expectation of improved functional outcome when care is given by an expert rehabilitation team. One is that the training and talent required to accomplish this goal resides in specialized centers. This has by no means been proved and to a certain extent runs counter to the modern fiscal need for flexibility of beds and staff, particularly in critical care. Previous indications for the need for major burn centers, based on the risk of cross infection and death from sepsis, have been practically eliminated by early excisional surgery. It is therefore incumbent on individuals who are interested in burn care and who work in major burn centers to use outcome-based techniques to prove the continuing need for such specialized care centers. But where are the controls? As opposed to standard surgical operations, which are performed in major academic settings as well as in rural or

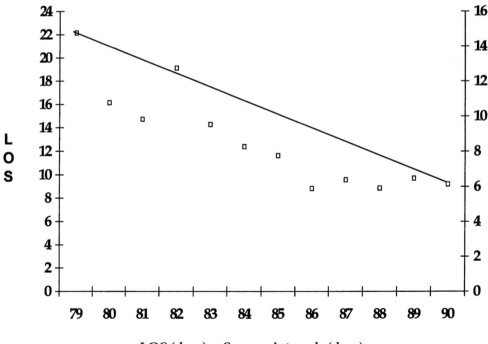

LOS (days) □ Surgery intervals (days)

Figure 31–2 Illustration of the linear correlation between the decrease in length of stay and shortened intervals between surgical interventions for wound coverage over a period of 12 years at the Baltimore Regional Burn Center, $p < .01$.

community settings, almost all major burn care (certainly that of more severely injured individuals) in the United States, today takes place in major burn centers. The need for physical burn units as opposed to well-organized, expert burn services in a hospital, except for the ease and convenience of logistics, remains somewhat open to question.

More important, perhaps, is the concept of impacting the quality of rehabilitation. Few studies have been performed on rates of patients' return to work and return into the community. Major projects for the next 10 to 20 years will have to focus on utilizing outcome measurements to demonstrate that interventions, be they social, psychological or physical, can improve burn survivors' return to society, to work, and (by implication) to the tax base. Then, funding for these activities can be upgraded, and both patients and society at large will benefit.

References

1. Evans EI, Purnell OJ, Robinett PW, et al. Fluid and electrolyte requirements in severe burns. Ann Surg 1952;135:804.

2. Moncrief JA. Topical antibacterial treatment of the burn wound. In: Artz CP, Moncrief JA, Pruitt BA, editors. Burns: a team approach. Philadelphia: WB Saunders; 1979.

3. Berkow SG. Method of estimating extensiveness of lesions (burn and scalds) based on surface area proportions. Arch Surg 1924;8(1):138–48.

4. Bull JB, Squire JR. A study of mortality in a burns unit: standards for the evaluation of alternative methods of treatment. Ann Surg 1949;130(2):160–73.

5. Pruitt BA Jr, Mason AD. Epidemiological, demographic, and outcome characteristics of burn injury. In: Herndon DN, editor. Total burn care. London: WB Saunders; 1996.

6. Wolfe SE, Rose JK, Desai MH, et al. Mortality determinants in massive pediatric burns. Ann Surg 1997;225(5):554–65.

7. Raff T, Germann G, Barthold U. Factors influencing the early prediction of outcome from burns. Acta Chir Plast 1996;38(4):122–7.

8. Ryan CM, Schoenfeld DA, Thorpe WP, et al. Objective estimates of the probability of death from burn injuries. N Engl J Med 1998;338(6):362–6.

9. Burke JF, Bandoc CC, Quimby WZ. Primary burn excision and immediate grafting: a method for shortening illness. J Trauma 1974;14:389–95.

10. Tompkins RG, Burke JF, Schoenfeld DA, et al. Prompt eschar excision: a treatment system contributing to reduce burn mortality. Ann Surg 1986;204(3):272–81.

11. Muller MJ, Herndon DN. The challenge of burns. Lancet 1994;343:216–20.

12. Bow JB, Fisher AJ. A study of mortality in a burns unit: a revised estimate. Ann Surg 1954;139:269–74.

13. Deitch EA, Clothier J. Burns in the elderly: an early surgical approach. J Trauma 1983;23(10):891–4.

14. Saffle JR, Lawson CM, Sullivan J, Shelby J. The continuing challenge of burn care in the elderly. Surgery 1990;108(3):534–43.

15. Green H, Kehinde O, Thomas J. Growth of human epidermal cell into multiple epithelia suitable for grafting. Proc Natl Acad Sci USA 1979;76:5665–8.

16. Munster AM. Whither skin replacement? [editorial] Burns 1997 Feb 23.

17. Munster AM, Weiner S, Spence RB. Cultured epidermis for the coverage of massive burns: a single center experience. Ann Surg 1990;211:676–80.

18. Boyce ST, Garetzski MJ, Greenheld DG, et al. Comparative assessment of cultured skin substitutes and native skin autograft for the treatment of full thickness burn wounds. Ann Surg 1995;222(6):743–52.

19. Rue LW III, Cioffi WG, Mason ED, et al. Improved survival of burn patients with inhalation injury. Arch Surg 1993;128:772–80.

20. Desai MH, Mlcak R, Richardson J, et al. Reduction in mortality in pediatric patients with inhalation injury with aerosolized heparin/acetylcystin therapy. J Burn Care Rehabil 1998;19:210–12.

21. Brannen AL, Still J, Haynes M, et al. A randomized prospective trial of hyperbaric oxygen in a referral burn center population. Am Surg 1997;63(3):205–8.

22. Knox J, Demling R, Wilmore D, et al. Increased survival after major thermal injury: the effect of growth hormone therapy in adults. J Trauma 1995;39(3):526–30.

23. Munster AM, Smith-Meek M, Dickerson C, Winchurch RA. Translocation—incidental phenomenon or true pathology? Ann Surg 1993;218:321–7.

24. Linn BS, Stephenson SS, Smith J. Evaluation of burn care in Florida: the assessment of needs for burn care. N Engl J Med 1977;296:311–15.

25. Adler A. Neuropsychiatric complications in victims of Boston's Coconut Grove disaster. JAMA 1943;123:1098–1101.

26. Cobb S, Lindeman E. Coconut Grove burns: neuropsychiatric observations. Ann Surg 1943;117:814–24.

27. Koepke GH. The rôle of physical medicine in the treatment of burns. Surg Clin North Am 1970;50(6):1385–99.

28. Munster AM, Blades BC, Mannon J, Kaszuba A. Development of an outcome scale for burns: methods, problems and prospects. In: McNeill BJ, Cravelho EG, editors. Proceedings on critical issues in medical technology. Boston: Auburn House; 1982.

29. Munster AM, Horowitz GL, Tudahl LA. The abbreviated burn-specific health scale. J Trauma 1987;27:425–8.

30. Blalock SJ, Bunker BJ, DeVellis RF. Measuring health status among survivors of burn injury: revisions of the burn specific health scale. J Trauma 1994;36:508–15.

31. Staley M, Richard R, Warden GD, et al. Functional outcomes for the patient with burn injuries. JBCR 1996;17:362–8.

32. Saffle JR, Tuohig GM, Sullivan JJ, et al. Return to work as a measure of outcome in adults hospitalized for acute burn treatment. JBCR 1996;17:353–61.

33. Blakeney P, Meyer W, Moore P, et al. Psychosocial sequelae of pediatric burns involving 80% or greater total body surface area. JBCR 1993;14:684–9.

34. Jonsson CE, Schuldt K, Linder J, et al. Rehabilitative, psychiatric, functional and aesthetic problems in patients treated for burn injuries—a preliminary follow-up study. Acta Chir Plast 1997;39:3–8.

35. Blalock SJ, Bunker BJ, DeVellis RF. Psychological distress among survivors of burn injury: the role of outcome expectations and perceptions of importance. JBCR 1994;15:421–7.

36. Bryant RA. Predictors of post traumatic stress disorder following burn injury. Burns 1996;22:89–92.

37. Munster AM, Fauerbach JA, Lawrence J. Development and utilization of a psychometric instrument for measuring quality of life in burn patients, 1976–96. Acta Chir Plast 1996;38(4):128–31.

38. Munster AM, Meek M, Sharkey P. The effect of early surgical intervention on mortality and cost-effectiveness in burn care, 1978–1991. Burns 1994;20:61–4.

39. Still JM Jr, Law EJ, Belcher K, Thiruvaiyarv D. Decreasing length of hospital stay by early excision and grafting of burns. South Med J 1996;89(6):578–82.

40. Mesmer RJ. Patient-focused perioperative documentation: an outcome management approach. Semin Perioper Nurs 1997;6(4):223–32.

41. Helvig EI, Upright J, Bartleson BJ. The development of outcome statements for burn care. Semin Perioper Nurs 1997;6(4):197–200.

42. Guidelines for the operation of burn centers. Chicago, IL: American Burn Association 1994.

CHAPTER 32

Transplantation

James F. Burdick, MD, FACS

THE EVOLUTION OF ABDOMINAL ORGAN TRANSPLANTATION

The history of transplantation has paralleled that of vascular surgery. Early work by Carrel and others on techniques for vascular anastomoses led to the obvious possibility of attaching new organs to patients. This was tried with animal as well as human organs, unsuccessfully early in the twentieth century. As the particular need for the care of patients with end-stage renal disease heightened, renewed efforts at kidney transplantation were undertaken. The typical immunosuppression was not based on specific evidence regarding transplants but rather was adapted from cancer chemotherapy or regimens for other immunosuppressive purposes. The anatomic process as well as the immunosuppression for early kidney transplantation was exploratory, but the kidney transplantation operation has gone relatively unchanged for over three decades. In the early 1980s, an ongoing effort (particularly by Drs. Starzl and Calne with liver transplantation and Dr. Shumway for heart transplantation) established the anatomic approach to these procedures. However, results were relatively poor, and this treatment was not generally adopted initially. In 1984, the remarkable new agent cyclosporine was approved for sale by the FDA, and the modern era of transplantation ensued. The safety and effectiveness of immunosuppression combining cyclosporine and prednisone was such a great improvement that kidney transplantation became routine, and centers doing cardiac and liver transplantation proliferated. As will be described in this chapter, there have been two dominant influences in the evidence-based aspects of this field: the multicenter trials that have established the value of many of the new drugs, and the multicenter data collection that has been accomplished, particularly in the United States, under the aegis of the United Network for Organ Sharing (UNOS).

REVIEW OF LITERATURE

Of the thousands of papers on clinical transplantation, the following are some of historic and recent significance.

Based on the major issue of vascular connections (with less apparent importance of the urinary tract connection) some early transplantations were actually placed in the upper thigh, where access to the femoral vessels was easy. The report by Hume and colleagues[1] delineates some of the early observations about obtaining good flow through the graft and the problems that can occur in the immunosuppressed incision under the old regimen. The operation now has evolved to placement in the lower quadrant retroperitoneally on one side or the other,[2] using the iliac vessels; this allows easy anastomosis to the bladder. This operation has evolved, without particular evidence being developed in the literature, to the use of end-to-side anastomosis of the ends of both the renal artery and renal vein to the sides of the iliac artery and vein. In the earlier era prior to cyclosporine, wound problems with urine leak and infection and occasional vascular rupture were infrequent disasters, somewhat like the problems described by Hume for the leg placement. However, an important advantage of cyclosporine was that the surgical wound in the transplanted patient became of much less concern. The specificity of modern immunosuppression has decreased the impact of common bacterial infections. Thus, the end-to-side anastomosis of the artery is not a concern with regard to a deep wound infection that would lead to rupture, this being very uncommon with modern immunosuppression.

The first long-term successful kidney transplantation avoided immunological problems using an identical twin for the donor.[2,3] This widely hailed operation clearly demonstrated the physiological capacity of the transplanted kidney to function well and the long-term success of revascularization in the lower abdomen. The procedure eventually won a Nobel prize for the lead surgeon, Dr. Joseph Murray.

For much of the early era, there were only two or three surgeons running liver transplantation programs, among them Dr. Roy Calne at Cambridge in England and Dr. James Williams in Tennessee and then Chicago. The most successful long-term effort was the work of Dr. Thomas Starzl, which provided the basis of the modern liver transplantation operation and spread the technique throughout Western medicine. This long-term effort using agents available in the early transplantation era established an operation with a remarkable surgical integrity, notable for the extraordinary anatomic undertaking involved in the replacement of a patient's liver with another. As with the heart, several factors dictate orthotopic placement (Figure 32–1), and this process was successfully developed by Dr. Starzl.[4] The operation has persisted largely as outlined in this early work, with no important improvement needed or found in recent times. One issue that required study was the biliary tract drainage. The convenience of gallbladder drainage recommended it, and many early cases were done this way. At one point in his series, however, Dr. Starzl did a complete review of the process and found that many patients that had done poorly probably failed mainly on the basis of the biliary tract. The option of direct duct-to-duct anastomosis in most cases or anastomosis of the liver graft duct to an intestinal loop became routine as a result of this work.[5] This early experience in developing anatomic technique placed liver transplantation firmly in a position to exploit modern immunosuppression in the mid-1980s.

The secondary nature of the ureteral drainage for the kidney transplantation in Dr. Hume's early work was resolved by retroperitoneal placement and anastomosis of the bladder, typically using a Politano-Ledbetter tunneled intracystic technique to generate an anti-reflux valve. This was the general approach for many years although there was evidence that reflux in kidney transplants was common despite these attempts. Less complex techniques for bladder drainage were described on occasion, and finally came an important report of a new operation. Gibbons in Oregon[6] described the placement of two parallel incisions on the bladder, a tunnel bringing the ureter through under this bridge of bladder muscularis over the mucosa to provide an anti-reflux valve and then anastomosis of the end of the ureter to the mucosa in the more distal incision. This more distal incision is then closed over. A thousand cases were reported with excellent outcomes. The ease and reported success of this operation has led to the adoption of either this tunneled approach or an open approach of creating a flap over the ureter with an extra vesicle, a technique that is more generally used now. The long-term results of this approach cannot provide the 20 years of follow-up that successful kidney transplants enjoy at present but early results seem to warrant the adoption of some such extra-vesicle approach, which is an important improvement in the operation.

Although every program strives to minimize the need for transplant nephrectomy, this need obviously occurs when a patient's kidney fails and produces a complication. This transplant nephrectomy operation often occurs in a setting where there have been multiple problems, such as infection or intercurrent rejection episodes, requiring treatment. The patient may have been returned to dialysis but may not be entirely stable physiologically. An expeditious operation with low morbidity to remove the transplant is critical in these circumstances when the transplant has failed. The obvious option of dissecting out the individual structures at the hilum is complex, and an important improvement was the report of the technique by Sutherland and colleagues.[7] This involved dissection underneath the transplant capsule on the surface of the kidney to circumferentially free it and deliver it up and out of the wound to

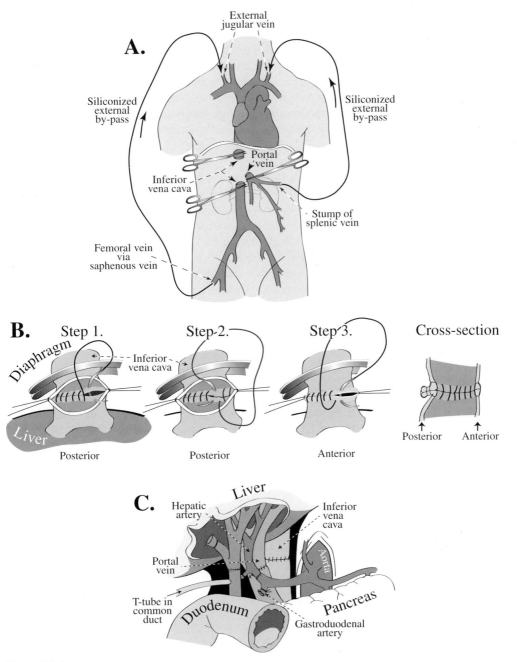

Figure 32–1

some degree. Then, with appropriate retraction, it is possible to place a large clamp on the hilar structures and to remove the transplant. The hilar structures there are oversewn down and back similarly to the way a lung biopsy is done. This often is a simple, expeditious procedure with little blood loss and high reliability in terms of controlling the vascular structures and preventing postoperative complications.

An important corollary of the success of kidney transplantation in the cyclosporine era was the remarkably improved success rate for living-donor transplantations regardless of histocompatibility. It has become apparent from the UNOS database that results with poorly matched living donors are equivalent to results with zero mismatched best-cadaver donors. Furthermore, there has been a major increase in the disparity between the number of patients waiting and the number of donors available so that the waiting time for kidney transplantation has become much longer in many areas of the country. For these reasons, living-donor transplantation has increasingly become the optimal approach. Facilitating this was the development by Kavoussi and Ratner[8] of the laparoscopic approach to living-donor transplant nephrectomy. The entire operation is essentially done transperitoneally through the laparoscope except for a small incision about the width of the kidney just below the umbilicus and through which the kidney can be extracted in a receiver bag (Figure 32–2). Although general anesthesia and dissection result in some early post-transplantation morbidity, patients typically lower requirements for pain medication, earlier discharge, and an earlier return to work and normal daily activities. Residual concerns regarding the venous pressure effect of the pneumoperitoneum are necessary, and the particular problems with the right kidney when the left is anatomically inappropriate continue to be evaluated. However, it seems likely that this laparoscopic approach will become the standard for the majority of living-donor transplantations.

Interestingly, liver transplantation has continued to have biliary tract drainage as its major anatomic or technical concern, somewhat reflective of the ongoing evolution in ureteral implantation for kidneys. The evolution of noninvasive techniques for dealing with strictures and leaks has resulted in a major improvement in the handling of complications of the biliary tract after liver transplantation. An example of the success of this approach is the Hopkins series by Klein and colleagues.[9] The advantage that routine nonoperative management provides, exemplified in this study, has had a major impact on the re-exploration requirement after liver transplantation. There are ongoing explorations of internal stenting without a T tube or, in the absence of stent, the best technique for the anastomosis.

MULTICENTER STUDIES IN TRANSPLANTATION

The relatively few transplantations done at individual centers is dictated by the small number of donors. The relative success of transplantation in recent years has been accompanied by larger waiting lists but relatively small changes in the number of transplantations, because of this paucity of donors. Accordingly, the most powerful studies have been the multicenter efforts in transplantation. Two areas that exemplify this will be discussed in detail. The first involves the trials of modern pharmacologic agents. The transformation that transplantation underwent beginning in the mid-1980s was based totally on advances in selectivity and specificity for allograft rejection of modern immunosuppressive agents. Sequentially, several

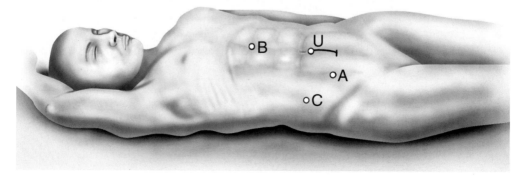

Figure 32–2 Laparoscopic Donor Approach. Ratner et al, 1997. The videoendoscope is placed via the umbilical port (U). Additional ports are at A, B, and C.

of these agents have undergone extensive analysis by clinical trials in transplantation centers, setting the stage for approval by the United States Food and Drug Administration (FDA) and establishing in the transplantation professional community the relevance of these drugs to improved results. The second area in which multicenter data analysis has been critical is in the national database managed by UNOS since 1987, the use of which has provided information for both clinical practice and national policy.

Trials of New Drugs

The seminal agent in the development of modern transplantation was cyclosporine (Neoral). It was clear within a few months of instituting the use of cyclosporine that kidney transplantation had entered a new era. Results improved dramatically. Patients were discharged sooner, and morbidity and mortality were diminished. Although this strong effect might have been sufficient to establish the drug without formal trials, there were, in fact, randomized data from several single centers that supported the use of cyclosporine. These included comparative trials at UCSF[10] and Brigham and Women's Hospital.[11] Interestingly, a similar single-center trial at the University of Minnesota (which had particularly good results in the era before cyclosporine) did not show a significant improvement from this drug[12] in spite of the general benefit found at most centers. However, the face of the future was seen in a multicenter trial carried out in Canada.[13] In this study, kidney transplant recipients were given either cyclosporine and prednisone or the best alternative therapy. Patient and graft survival were determined at 1 year. The results were strongly in favor of the cyclosporine treatment limb.

In the late 1970s and early 1980s, polyclonal lymphocyte serum preparations had been used quite extensively in transplantation as an additional immunosuppressive agent. With the landmark development of monoclonal antibodies, it seemed there would be possibilities for new immunosuppressive agents using this technology to provide high specificity for a given manipulation of immunoresponsiveness. One antibody fulfilled this promise early on: a reagent with specificity for all mature human T cells against what eventually came to be called cluster differentiation 3 or CD3 (at the time, the only generic designation was OKT3). This was an IgG murine immunoglobulin. Initial trials indicated an apparent immunosuppressive quality, and therefore, a multicenter trial was carried out under the aegis of the sponsor, Ortho Pharmaceuticals. A total of 123 patients were entered and randomized to receive either Solumedrol treatment or OKT3 treatment for the first rejection episode after kidney transplantation.[14] Findings of improved rejection reversal and even improved graft survival at 1 year in the patients treated initially with OKT3 (Figure 32–3) established this reagent as an important new immunosuppressive. It also represented the pivotal data that allowed both FDA approval and marketing of the drug. One objection was that treatment with OKT3 was not directed against the best therapy; perhaps a comparison with antithymocyte globulin (ATGAM) or Minnesota antilymphocyte globulin would have been more appropriate. Furthermore, cyclosporine was just beginning to be used in patients, and there was a question as to whether this result would be obtained in the cyclosporine setting. In spite of these questions, the drug has continued to be used by the transplantation community as a first line of treatment, particularly for severe rejection, based on this study. Although the study provided clear evidence favoring OKT3 instead of corticosteroids for the initial treatment of any significant rejection episode, this has not become the rule in most centers.

In spite of the initial hopes, this result was followed in the next decade by no new monoclonal antibodies that could be used for treatment. In the interim, the mechanism of OKT3 was worked out. It became clear that the CD3 site to which the monoclonal antibody attaches is one of the chains that exist on the cell surface in conjunction with the T cell receptor and is involved in the stimulation of the cell produced by interaction of the specific antigen with the T cell receptor. Surrogate triggering of this receptor by the monoclonal antibody apparently

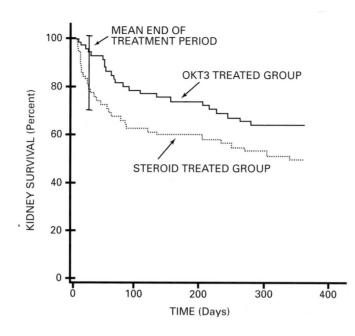

Figure 32–3

causes sterile activation and absence of the T cell receptor on circulating T cells, as well as removal of T cells from the circulation due to other actions of the antibody. (This is a good example of therapeutic success progressing in advance of understanding of the mechanisms.) Other targeted candidates for monoclonal antibody therapy failed in part because of the absence of such a powerful effect.

More recently, evidence has suggested that antibody against the interleukin-2 (IL-2) receptor would be immunosuppressive. This was rendered particularly appealing by concurrent data indicating interference with interleukin-2 secretion as an important action of cyclosporine. Eventually, a murine monoclonal antibody was found to be effective, but it had the drawbacks of all xenoantibodies in therapeutic treatment, namely a short half-life and a tendency to produce sensitization, which limited its usefulness. However, in a remarkable technological development, the murine antibody was "humanized." This involved identifying the specific amino acids responsible for the interaction with the specific antigen and inserting them in a neutral human immunoglobulin, thus leaving a molecule that was nearly human, different only in the specificities for the human CD3 protein, absent in normal human antibodies. This resulted in a modest decrement in affinity to approximately ½ or ¼ of the original murine molecule. However, since the affinity constant is still high, the resulting reagent is still very specific. Initial trials in bone marrow were disappointing, but it is clear that there are mechanisms involved in graft-versus-host reaction that are not as dominantly related to the IL-2 mechanism as the mechanism for graft rejection. Therefore, a multicenter trial in kidney transplantation was performed.[15] Patients given best standard therapy were treated with anti-IL-2 antibody (anti-TAC or Zenapax) or placebo in addition to routine therapy initially after kidney transplantation. Randomization of the 260 patients was easily blinded since patients had very little of the reactivity associated with other monoclonal antibody therapy because of the *humanization*. The major finding (Table 32–1) was that the incidence of biopsy-documented acute rejection during the first 6 months after transplantation was decreased in the IL-2 antibody group (22% vs 35%, $p = .03$). This benefit was not associated with increased side effects, and there was a nonsignificant trend toward better patient and graft survival in the treatment group. The role of this new reagent continues to be studied, but it seems likely that it will be used in at least some settings for initiation of immunosuppressive treatment.

Table 32–1 Results of the Trial of Initial Treatment with Humanized Monoclonal Anti-IL-2 Receptor Antibody

Rejection	Placebo (N = 134)	Daclizumas (N = 125)	p-Value
One or more biopsy-confirmed episodes—no. of patients (%)	47 (35)	28 (22)	.03
One or more biopsy-confirmed or presumptive episodes—no. of patients (%)	52 (39)	32 (25)	.04
Two or more biopsy-confirmed or presumptive episodes—no. of patients (%)	18 (13)	9 (7)	.08
Mean no. of episodes/patient	0.6	0.3	.01
Time to first episode—days*	30±27	73±59	.008
Episode requiring antilymphocyte therapy-no. of patients (%)[†]	19 (14)	10 (8)	.09

*Plus-minus values are means ±SD.
[†]Antilymphocyte therapy consisted of OKT3 or polyclonal antithymocyte globulin.
Vincent et al, 1998.

When the new drug FK506 (Prograf) became available, it was championed by Dr. Starzl and the group at Pittsburgh for liver transplantation. Because it was found to be potent on a per milligram dose basis and nephrotoxic, there was initial concern about its use in kidney transplantation. A multicenter trial was appealing early in the history of the drug because of major advocacy from a single center (which advocacy, however, was based upon poorly controlled data) and because of concerns on the part of other centers about the drug's therapeutic window. It was decided that the initial randomized trial for testing it would be in liver transplants. This was partly due to the particular interest liver transplant surgeons developed in this potentially useful drug. It was also a testimony to the routine to which liver transplantation had evolved in many centers, which allowed a homogenous multicenter trial that would be meaningful. One-year graft survival and patient survival were assessed in a randomized trial. The results showed no difference in the good outcomes at 1 year,[16] but did show some tendencies to less rejection and fewer problems in general for the FK506 group. The experience regarding nephrotoxicity was sufficiently promising that it was soon possible to perform a similar randomized trial for kidney transplantation. This also revealed equivalence if not benefit,[17] and the place of FK506 as an alternative to cyclosporine was firmly established. The findings in the trial of alternative secondary side effects of FK506 versus cyclosporine were that FK506 produces a lesser tendency to hyperlipidemia and gum hypertrophy, but appears to carry an increased risk of immunosuppression-related diabetes, which, although sometimes transient, can represent a serious issue. These contrasts, which are part of the rationale for using one drug or the other in individual circumstances, were best delineated by the comparisons provided in these multicenter randomized trials.

A synthetic approach to a new drug was successful in the development of an antimetabolite called mycophenolate mofetil, an ester of mycophenolic acid, which produces a specific inhibition of the inositol monophosphate dehydrogenase pathway. Because lymphocytes lack a thymidine salvage pathway to overcome the purine synthesis block produced by the drug, it has a specific effect on lymphocytes. It therefore can be used in dosages that are more effective than those of its long-standing alternative, azathioprine, with relative protection from side effects. A multicenter trial of its use in kidney transplantation was performed in the United

States and Europe and was quite clear in its general results. Patients treated with CellCept, an alternative to azathioprine, with otherwise conventional therapy had significantly fewer rejection episodes.[18] Again, patient or graft survival did not improve. The excellent results achieved in control groups in such studies now make it difficult to demonstrate improvements in early outcomes. Studies now are designed also to look at longer-term outcomes. CellCept has thus gained a place through these trials as a useful adjunct to decrease morbidity after transplantation by safely reducing the tendency to rejection episodes.

The United Network for Organ Sharing Database

Transplantation programs have become increasingly tied together over the past 30 years by the common importance to all of the donor organs. The common phenomenon in which an organ cannot be used at one center but might be at another was realized early, and exchanges evolved. This led eventually to the organ procurement transplant network run as a government contract by the United Network for Organ Sharing (UNOS). A major ingredient in this effort was the collection of accurate data on all phases of the treatment. This allows monitoring to provide reassurance that usage is appropriate at each center. More importantly, it provides data that allow the community to shape clinical practices. The data have provided such a basis in terms of treatment alternatives for individual centers. Moreover, it has provided a basis for the continued evolution of appropriate rules for allocation and the process of making the allocation work.

The data are submitted from the time that the recipient's candidacy is registered on the national computerized list. Additional information on the recipient and the donor is collected at the time of transplantation and subsequently at intervals for follow-up. This consists of extensive forms returned at specified intervals. It is likely that there will be increasing opportunity for programs to process the data electronically. Review is performed internally, and the program's information is returned to it for verification. In addition, validation visits are performed on occasion to each center. Individuals from UNOS do on-site reviews of selected data to ensure complete and accurate compliance. This data collection began at the national level in October 1987. The information now available represents a remarkable achievement in accuracy and extent. It is essentially complete for all cases at an individual center, and includes all centers in the country.

The kidney transplant data have been used perhaps most extensively for providing the basis and ongoing review of the impact of histocompatibility matching. In the days when allograft rejection was just beginning to be understood, it was clear that the histocompatibility leukocyte antigen (HLA) system was dominant in terms of potential clinical outcome. This was particularly evident in the case of HLA-identical siblings, for whom graft survival was more easily ensured by even the early immunosuppressive regimens although it was also clear that even with matching, the results were quite different than with the original identical twins between whom the first successful kidney transplant was performed. However, because of the dominance of HLA, it seemed that sharing to ensure the possibility of a kidney transplant that was completely matched by HLA would produce better survival. Several past studies have confirmed this. Some important issues have been raised about the impact of confounding variables, and increasingly sophisticated data have been provided on this score. An example of a recent report addressing this is the extensive multivariate analysis of the UNOS data.[19] This study employed the 1994 release of Center Specific Graft and Patient Survival Rates and reviewed impact of HLA-mismatch level on kidney graft survival, corrected for all of the covariants employed for the center-specific data release. Relative to the overall results, patients receiving a six-antigen match, a zero-ABDR mismatch or a zero-BDR mismatch all had probability of graft failure at 1 and 3 years reduced to essentially half of the risk. This continues to confirm the benefit in outcome for the individual recipient. However, questions remain about the overall impact on the system, and another large review of data has assessed the impact of using both truly matched donors and donors who do not appear to present any mismatches to the recipient. This showed that zero-HLA-mismatched kidneys had a 50 percent higher expectance of graft half-life, that is, 12 years compared to an 8-year half-life for mismatched grafts. Furthermore, the fraction of these particularly good matches increased from 2.5 percent to 15.5 percent but the major improvement afforded by HLA matching persisted. These data, using present highly effective immunosuppressive regimens, continue to support for UNOS policy. These issues are important because there continue to be proposals for changing the HLA matching process due to other related problems. These are practical clinical considerations as well as issues of fairness. The debate, however, is able to focus on the political and practical issues. This is facilitated by the very solid evidence regarding the biologic and clinical facts from the multicenter UNOS database.

Another important approach in renal transplantation to the problem of organ donor shortage is the possibility of using more living donors. When cyclosporine first came into general use, it was presumed that living-donor transplantation would decrease because the results with cadaver donors were becoming so good. A reversal of thought occurred when it became apparent that using non-HLA-identical donors and including cyclosporine in the regimen gave remarkably better results. Thus, it became reasonable to consider using unrelated individuals, and there was sufficient experience within a few years to review this. The UNOS database results reported by Terasaki and colleagues[20] included hundreds of unrelated individuals in addition to living related and cadaveric transplants. It was found that the 3-year survival rate for wife-to-husband grafts was 87 percent and that unrelated living-donor transplants were generally very successful (Figure 32–4). These excellent results were not explained by good HLA matching. Hence, it is clear that the very short preservation time (generally ½ to 1 hour of cold time) between clamping the vessels at retrieval and restoring flow in the graft in the recipient is a major factor that improves outcome when using a living donor. This has been an important influence on the field since the incidence of transplantation from unrelated individuals has expanded considerably and because there is active consideration of the possibilities of kidney exchanges among potential donors who cannot give to the intended recipient.

Another important approach to the donor shortage in kidney transplantation is to consider the possibility of using donors previously considered suboptimal. It has been found that older donors produce a poorer long-term result,[21] with the use of donors over age 55 resulting in a graft survival of 72 percent versus 83 percent from donors under age 50. Although other factors may have played a role, a stepwise multivariate analysis of these

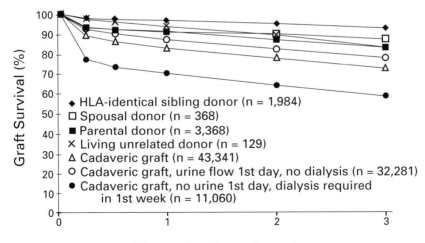

Figure 32–4

extensive UNOS data demonstrated that donor age is one of the most powerful independent predictors (odds ratio = 2.01).

This has been assessed further with the proposal that pulsatile perfusion might be of benefit. Analysis of over 60,000 patients using UNOS data indicated that the disadvantage of older donors decreased by approximately one-half when pulsatile perfusion was used.[22] This even resulted in improved graft survival at 1 year (Table 32–2) and may represent an incentive for expanding the use of pulsatile perfusion for kidneys from compromised donors in the future. Reassurance that other such settings might provide useful organs was provided by analysis of the "not-heartbeating donor" data from UNOS.[23] It was found that the survival rate at 1 year was 83 percent for kidney grafts from donors without heartbeats as opposed to 86 percent (not significant) from heartbeating donors. Subgroups were assessed and other data included in this review will provide guidance for development of the field. The possibility of expanding the donor pool by an increase in the removal of such organs when the appropriate arrangements can be put in place is supported by both of these studies.

Establishing appropriate criteria for membership compliance has also relied on UNOS data. The issue of assessing the differences in outcomes among transplantation programs, the majority of which have relatively small numbers of transplantations per year, is a problem. Interestingly, comparison of center-specific data was attempted for nontransplantation considerations by HCFA but was discontinued because of the level of questioning raised about the relevance of the data based partly on risk-factor differences. There are at least two factors that must be dealt with to produce a successful comparison. One is appropriate risk adjustment so that the centers' outcomes are adjusted for the patient mix. This can produce major differences in transplantation, and the extensive studies done within UNOS with risk-adjusted data allowing center-specific reports for each program at regular intervals, giving the risk-adjusted comparison to the mean for each center, was referred to above. This has provided a basis for comparing centers in determining which centers have sufficiently poor results that they should be reviewed for quality improvement. The other important factor is a concept for comparing levels of importance of data statistically given small numbers. A difference that is quite large and therefore would seem clinically relevant but that is statistically not significant because of the small numbers involved can occur and must be addressed if the use of the data is to be greeted as relevant and fair. This has been done[24] by establishing that a difference of less than 10 percent between a center's results and the average outcome level (the expected result) is not clinically or biologically relevant. Differences that are 10 percent or greater start an iterative review process if they are statistically significant at the level of $p \leq .05$. However, if the numbers are relatively small, a gradually increasing degree of difference versus statistical effect is employed, so that a difference between the center's observed results and the expected results that is 25 percent poorer will be reviewed even if the $p = .4$. The straight line produced by these points on the graph of results versus statistical significance allows easy conceptualization of the importance of a difference and provides a general formula that applies to all programs (making further analysis of the identified centers difficult to criticize).

Liver transplantation has also benefited from the extensive data available at UNOS. In view of the disparity between donors and potential recipients, older-donor livers have been

Table 32–2 Effect of Pulsatile Perfusion on 1-Year Graft Survival

Variables of Interest	Odds Ratio	p-Value
Iced younger donor vs pumped older donor	0.825	.0462
Pumped younger donor vs pumped older donor	0.810	.0389
Iced older donor vs pumped older donor	1.294	.0098

Burdick et al, 1997

evaluated. A review of UNOS data involving gradual progression of increase in donor age on the average (but also improvements in other technology) was assessed.[25] In the most recent era, graft failure from the oldest donors (≥ 50 years of age) was not importantly different than that from the youngest (27.2% vs 26.9%). These data are thus reassuring for the practice of using older donors for liver transplantation. Another important area was the concern that transplantation of very sick patients produces poorer results. The distinction between chronic and acute liver disease was of particular concern with the concept that fulminant hepatic failure patients, whose dominant problem is absence of liver function but who are without other concurrent medical problems, have a relatively good outcome. This was supported by a review of UNOS data in over 8,000 liver transplants.[26] It thus supported the practice of continuing to provide high status for fulminant hepatic failure patients.

With the advent of the special perfusion solution developed by Beltzer and colleagues (Viaspan), it was apparent that longer liver preservation times could be acceptable. There has been considerable experience in liver preservation time beyond 10 hours, and a concern has developed that primary nonfunction may be increasing. A recent study supports the increasing penalty for longer cold times.[27] The outcome after hepatic retransplantation was evaluated to determine a formula that would allow prediction of survival. This is important because, although it is known that retransplantation has a higher chance of failure on the average, it is sufficiently successful that it should be continued in appropriate cases. The ability to determine in which settings it would fail would thereby improve its use by individualizing the choice based on the chance of a good clinical outcome. It was found that, of the five variables, ischemia greater than 12 hours was one of the factors that had an independent prognostic significance in multivariant regression. This model was developed with the center's data at the University of California in Los Angeles (UCLA) but then was validated with a second cohort in the UNOS data registry, of importance because of the potential to improve results with retransplantation. However, the particular concern about increased cold time is likely to be relevant for liver transplantation in general.

Impact of Multicenter Studies on Practices

In less than two decades, several remarkable new drugs have appeared, have been tested in solid multicenter clinical trials, and have been found to provide special advantages. These multicenter trials have provided a strong basis for the choice of immunosuppressive regimens in the modern transplant era.

Because of the variety and multiplicity of new agents, the clinical investigators' meetings have become an important secondary vehicle for exchanging clinical information and data, somewhat like professional society meetings or institutional educational efforts. It is of particular advantage to centers to participate in such trials since transplantation advances have been rapid. To remain current on the value of new agents and their application, it is important to be involved in these trials. Furthermore, patients typically benefit because in most cases there is good preliminary reason to expect that patients will do no worse and perhaps fare better with the new agent. The increased monitoring of patients regardless of treatment randomization may also be helpful.

The advantage of multicenter trials and data collection has other ramifications for clinical decision making. The small numbers of transplantations in an individual program due to the shortage of donors makes it necessary to deal in an anecdotal fashion with local problems or successes that may not be scientifically sound. Availability of multicenter information to assess these local findings (as with the cold preservation study noted above[27] but also in many other settings) greatly improves the ability of each individual program to optimize its treatment protocols.

Finally, because of the special interconnectedness that characterizes programs in transplantation, the large national database at UNOS is a major resource for decisions about national rules in clinical transplantation and allocation. There are many difficult issues regarding this at the national level; the availability of valid complete national data greatly facilitates attempts to improve the national approach to transplantation.

Topics for Further Studies

One of the most remarkable phenomena in recent years is the general improvement in transplant outcomes in the short term, such as at 1 year. This is evident in many of the clinical trials in which new drugs are unable to show an overall benefit in graft or patient survival, for example, because of the good results in the control group. Therefore, it is increasingly important to do longer-term multicenter studies, looking more extensively at 3-, 5-, and 10-year results to determine what can be done early in the patient's course to optimize the chances of long-term success. In many cases, the studies could be continued if appropriate support were obtained, based on the patients already randomized in recent years. Future studies will continue to explicitly include these long-term issues, at least as secondary endpoints.

Continued analysis of national information through the UNOS database is important. This provides reassurance to the public and the government that standards are being met and that the policies employed are consistent with the best use of the scarce supply of donated organs.

Finally, shortage of organ donors may continue to yield slightly from ongoing efforts in evaluation of multicenter data. Expanding the use of living-donor organs and improving the ability to determine which formerly rejected donor organs will have a good likelihood of a successful outcome are important avenues in the continued effort to improve the availability of donor organs. The large-scale multicenter analyses, as illustrated above, will continue to be important in this effort.

References

1. Hume DM, Merrill JP, Miller BF, Thorn GW. Experiences with renal homotransplantation in the human: report of nine cases. J Clin Invest 1955;34:327–82.

2. Merrill JP, Murray JE, Harrison JH, Guild WR. Successful homotransplantation of the human kidney between identical twins. JAMA 1956;160(4):277–82.

3. Murray JE, Harrison JH. Surgical management of 50 patients with kidney transplants including 18 pairs of twins. Am J Surg 1963;105:205.

4. Starzl TE, Marchioro TL, Von Kaulla KN, et al. Homotransplantation of the liver in humans. Surg Gynecol Obstet 1963;117:659–76.

5. Starzl TE, Putnam CW, Hansbrough JF, et al. Biliary complications after liver transplantation: with special reference to the biliary cast syndrome and techniques of secondary duct repair. Surgery 1977;81(2):212–21.

6. Gibbons WS, Barry JM, Hefty TR. Complications following unstented parallel incision extravesical ureteroneocystostomy in 1,000 kidney transplants. J Urol 1992;148:38–40.

7. Sutherland DER, Simmons RL, Howard RJ, et al. Intracapsular technique of transplant nephrectomy. Surg Gynecol Obstet 1978;146:950.

8. Ratner LE, Kavoussi LR, Sroka M, et al. Laparoscopic assisted live donor nephrectomy—a comparison with the open approach. Transplantation 1997;63:229–33.

9. Klein AS, Savader S, Burdick JF, et al. Reduction of morbidity and mortality from biliary complications after liver transplantation. Hepatology 1991;14(5):818–23.

10. Feduska NJ, Melzer J, Amend WJC, et al. Clinical management of immunosuppressive therapy for cyclosporine-treated recipients of cadaver kidney transplants at one to six months. Transplant Proc 1986;18(2 Suppl 1):136–40.

11. Milford EL, Kirkman RL, Tilney NL, et al. Clinical experience with cyclosporine and azathioprine at Brigham and Women's Hospital. Am J Kidney Dis 1985;5:313–17.

12. Najarian JS, Fryd DS, Strand M, et al. A single institution, randomized, prospective trial of cyclosporine versus azathioprine—antilymphocyte globulin for immunosuppression in renal allograft recipients. Ann Surg 1985;201(2):142–57.

13. The Canadian Multicenter Transplant Group. A randomized clinical trial of cyclosporine in cadaveric renal transplantation. Analysis of three years. N Engl J Med 1986;314:1219–25.

14. Ortho Multicenter Transplant Study Group. A randomized clinical trial of OKT3 monoclonal antibody for acute rejection of cadaveric renal transplants. N Engl J Med 1985;313(6):337–42.

15. The Daclizumab Triple Therapy Study Group. Interleukin-2-receptor blockade with Daclizumab to prevent acute rejection in renal transplantation. N Engl J Med 1998;338(3):161–5.

16. The U.S. Multicenter FK506 Liver Study Group. A comparison of tacrolimus (FK506) and cyclosporine for immunosuppression in liver transplantation. N Engl J Med 1994;331:1110–15.

17. Pirsch JD, Miller J, Deirhoi M, Vincenti F. A comparison of Tacrolimus (FK506) and cyclosporine for immunosuppression after cadaveric renal transplantation. Transplantation 1997;63(7):983–97.

18. Sollinger M, for the US Renal Transplant Mycophenolate Mofetil Study Group. Mycophenolate mofetil for the prevention of acute rejection in primary cadaveric renal allograft recipients. Transplantation 1995;60:225–32.

19. Hata Y, Cecka JM, Takemoto S, et al. Effects of changes in the criteria for nationally shared kidney transplants for HLA-matched patients. Transplantation 1998;65:208–12.

20. Terasaki PI, Cecka JM, Gjertson DW, Takemoto S. High survival rates of kidney transplants from spousal and living unrelated donors. N Engl J Med 1995;333(6):333–6.

21. Terasaki PI, Gjertson DW, Cecka JM, et al. Significance of the donor age effect on kidney transplants. Clin Transplant 1997;11(5 Pt 1):366–72.

22. Burdick JF, Rosendale JD, McBride MA, et al. National impact of pulsatile perfusion on cadaveric kidney transplantation. Transplantation 1997;64(12):1730–3.

23. Cho YW, Terasaki PI, Cecka JM, Gjertson DW. Transplantation of kidneys from donors whose hearts have stopped beating. N Engl J Med 1998;338(4):221–5.

24. Burdick JF, Norman DJ, Hunsicker L, et al. Identification of poorly performing transplant centers using the UNOS center specific data. Transplant Proced 1997;29:1495.

25. Detre KM, Lombardero M, Belle S, et al. Influence of donor age on graft survival after liver transplantation—United Network for Organ Sharing registry. Liver Trans Surg 1995;1(5):311–19.

26. Detre KM, Belle S, Beringer K, Daily OP. Liver transplantation for fulminant hepatic failure in the United States: October 1987 through December 1991. Clin Transplant 1994;8:274–80.

27. Markmann JF, Gornbein J, Markowitz JS, et al. A simple model to estimate survival after retransplantation of the liver. Transplantation 1999; 67(3):422–30.

CHAPTER 33

Minimally Invasive Surgery

Mark A. Talamini, MD, FACS

Laparoscopic surgery was not a new field when it revolutionized general surgery over the past decade. Gynecologic surgeons had long been performing laparoscopic tubal ligation, head and neck surgeons had already developed endoscopic sinus surgery, and orthopedic surgeons were already familiar with joint visualization and repair using tiny scopes. The development of laparoscopic techniques in these fields came about out of the necessity to maneuver surgically with reduced pain and disability following surgery. Laparoscopy in general surgery has entered the arena differently. Laparoscopic general surgery became mainstream during the emerging era of cost containment and outcomes evaluation, when improved technology was necessary to maintain patient flow. This has created some differences in general surgery as compared to other specialties with respect to the evolution of laparoscopic cholecystectomy and the general surgical procedures that followed it. The most obvious difference was the close scrutiny of both economic and clinical outcomes of the procedure compared to its counterparts in other surgical specialties prior to widespread acceptance.

The index minimally invasive procedure in general surgery was laparoscopic cholecystectomy, first performed in the United States in 1989. Amazingly, by 1991 over 75 percent of cholecystectomies in the state of Maryland were performed in this manner.[1] Most of the general surgical workforce in Maryland was trained in this procedure in just over 1 year. This training occurred outside the normal controlled academic environment, largely through private courses driven by market forces. This was typical of the experience throughout the country.

A variety of forces impelled the rapid deployment of laparoscopic procedures. The surgeon's desire to provide a better operation for the patient was the most important. Patients desired a less painful operation that would cause less loss of productive time. Industry quickly recognized an opportunity to provide highly profitable disposable equipment essential for these new procedures, thus helping the rapid spread of both equipment and expertise. Payers initially resisted reimbursement for laparoscopic cholecystectomy, fearing an avalanche of procedures. Over time, payers recognized that the widespread use of laparoscopic cholecystectomy was inevitable and therefore dropped their resistance to the new procedure. Media propagation and competition among surgeons also played key roles. Once laparoscopic cholecystectomy appeared on the evening news, patients desired its benefits. If the local surgeon was not capable of performing the procedure, a patient could easily find a nearby surgeon who was. Since cholecystectomy was the most common intra-abdominal procedure performed by general surgeons, there was immense pressure on the surgical workforce to learn the new technology.

Other procedures quickly followed, with variable acceptance; examples include laparoscopic appendectomy, herniorrhaphy, bowel resection, Nissen fundoplication, donor nephrectomy, and lung resection. The avalanche of laparoscopic procedures has made the medical community examine certain questions requiring outcomes investigation: Is the laparoscopic procedure safe? Is it better in some way for the patient? Is it less expensive than the open procedure in terms of hospitalization and other fees? Should hospitals invest in expensive new technology?

This chapter will examine the introduction and evolution of laparoscopic cholecystectomy and some of the key outcomes studies that have influenced current practice. A brief review of key literature will be followed by an investigation of a study of the penetration of laparoscopic cholecystectomy into the surgical community in Maryland and a look into the current trend toward outpatient laparoscopic cholecystectomy. These studies provide examples of the ability of outcomes studies to provide useful guidance to the surgical community. These approaches should provide a template for investigating current and future emerging procedures and technologies.

LITERATURE REVIEW

Rapidly evolving medical technologies raise the question of how and when to assess those technologies. This issue was examined by Mowatt and colleagues.[2] In a careful literature review, they examined several emerging technologies: laparoscopic cholecystectomy, chorionic villus sampling, teleradiology, teledermatology, and genetic screening. They concluded that more early outcomes data regarding side effects and results are needed. They found that product champions and opinion leaders often disseminate information, which leads to rapid diffusion of techniques before adequate evaluation, and that the only way to ensure thorough evaluation would be through regulatory control.

The most substantial early study on the new procedure of laparoscopic cholecystectomy was carried out by the Southern Surgeons Club.[3] In this prospective analysis, about half of the 1,518 laparoscopic cholecystectomies were performed at academic institutions, and half were done in private hospitals. The average hospital stay was 1.2 days (range, 6 hours to 30 days). Even in this early study, the conversion rate to an open operation was quite low (4.7%). The most common reason for conversion was the inability, due to inflammation in the patient, to clearly identify anatomy. The overall complication rate was 5.1 percent, with 7 identified injuries to the common bile duct (0.5%). A "learning-curve" effect was observed. The bile duct injury rate among the aggregate first 13 patients for each surgeon was 2.2 percent, as opposed to 0.1 percent for subsequent patients. There was no difference in bile duct injury rates between academic and private institutions. This was the first large multi-institutional prospective study to show that laparoscopic cholecystectomy was a safe procedure that compared favorably to open cholecystectomy in terms of complications. The authors also clearly demonstrated the now well-documented increased incidence of bile duct injury in laparoscopic cholecystectomy compared to open cholecystectomy even after the learning curve was passed.

Cohen and colleagues reported one of the largest cross-sectional outcomes studies regarding laparoscopic cholecystectomy.[4] In the controlled medical environment of Ontario, this group used hospital discharge data to compare the time periods 1989 to 1990 and 1993 to 1994. The number of cholecystectomy procedures increased by 30.4 percent, while the number of laparoscopic cholecystectomies increased from 1 to 85 percent between the study time periods. The length of stay dropped precipitously (from 7.5 days to 2.6 days). The death rate was not significantly different between the two time periods (0.3% in the earlier period vs 0.2% in the later period). However, the bile duct injury rate tripled in that time (0.3% to 0.9%), and the adjusted risk for having at least one complication was 1.90 in 1993 to 1994 compared with 1989 to 1990. This study clearly demonstrated an increase in cholecystectomy rates, suggesting that the threshold had been lowered. In addition, these researchers demonstrated a clear increase in complications, led by common bile duct injury.

A number of studies have examined whether the threshold has changed for laparoscopic cholecystectomy (ie, operating for less severe symptoms). Comparing the pre-laparoscopic-cholecystectomy era (1989) to the current era (1993), a group from the University of Pennsylvania examined outcomes using a retrospective chart review.[5] Indeed, the volume of cholecystectomies was 26 percent higher in the recent era (1,611 in 1989 vs 2,031 in 1993), suggesting a lowering of the threshold. In addition, the length of stay was lower in the recent era but intra-operative complications (bile duct injury, blood vessel injury, etc) increased.

The increase in overall cholecystectomy rates apparently did not occur in the U.S. Veterans Administration (VA) hospitals.[6] In a multicenter retrospective study, Chen and colleagues found that the overall number of cholecystectomies did not increase between October 1991 and December 1993, nor did the overall complication rate change. Interestingly, laparoscopic cholecystectomy appeared to be implemented more slowly in the VA system than in the private sector. As in other studies, length of stay decreased as laparoscopic cholecystectomy was implemented.

Wu and colleagues from Washington University in St. Louis examined the evolution of laparoscopic cholecystectomy at an academic institution.[7] The total number of patients operated upon laparoscopically was 1,165 over nearly 8 years. The overall conversion rate to open procedure was 2.1 percent, and the mortality rate was 0.1 percent (one death). During the most recent period, the authors noted that the procedures were being performed primarily by residents and that operating-room time had decreased while complication and conversion rates remained the same.

One of the best outcomes studies regarding laparoscopic cholecystectomy analyzed data from the state of Minnesota.[8] Medical records of 3,448 patients undergoing cholecystectomy were analyzed, and questionnaires regarding post-operative functional status were sent to all patients 6 months after their procedure. Laparoscopic cholecystectomy was performed in 2,490 patients (72%), of whom 195 (7.8%) were converted to open surgery. Open cholecystectomy patients returned to work after an average of 31 days compared to 15 days for laparoscopic surgery patients. The study demonstrated no increase in cholecystectomies in those areas where laparoscopic cholecystectomy was available. The researchers did find evidence of a learning curve for surgeons: the more laparoscopic cholecystectomies a surgeon performed, the fewer operative and general complications occurred.

IN-PATIENT LAPAROSCOPIC CHOLECYSTECTOMY

When laparoscopic cholecystectomy was introduced, the hypothesis was put forward that the rate of cholecystectomy increased, suggesting that there might be an element of "unnecessary surgery." This, combined with early reports of increases in dangerous complications (such as bile duct injury), raised serious concerns among surgeons and health care providers. Laparoscopic cholecystectomy was never subjected to the "gold standard" of medical studies, the randomized prospective blinded trial; it simply spread quickly. Who would want their patients to be in the control group and undergoing open surgery when the benefits of the laparoscopic procedure seem so obvious? Thus, the medical community had to rely on retrospective and outcomes studies.

To investigate these questions, a group of surgeons and outcomes researchers at The Johns Hopkins Medical Institutions examined laparoscopic cholecystectomy using a statewide hospital database. Maryland has a confidential detailed discharge database maintained by the Maryland Health Services Cost Review Commission. Data were collected from all hospitalizations at the 54 nonfederal acute care hospitals in Maryland on matters such as age, sex, race, marital status, health insurance, and length of stay. In addition, ICD-9 codes for diagnosis and procedures were collected. (See Table 33–1 for a list of elements extracted from the database regarding laparoscopic cholecystectomy.) Data were examined for the period from January 1985 to December 1992.

The attempt to extract useful information from this database demonstrated the importance of collaboration between outcomes researchers and clinicians. During the early period examined, there was no ICD-9 code for laparoscopic cholecystectomy. To find the laparoscopic procedures, we assumed that a patient underwent a laparoscopic cholecystectomy if the patient had coding for total cholecystectomy and laparoscopy but had no other potential

Table 33–1 Extracted Elements from Laparascopic Cholecystectomy Database

Data captured includes:

       Age
       Gender
       Race
       Marital status
       Residence
       Health insurance
       Type of admission
       Length of hospital stay
       Disposition discharge
       ICD-9 codes
       Comorbidities

disease diagnosis (such as inguinal hernia, appendicitis, or a gynecologic disease) that could have led to another laparoscopic operation. The search included all patients with a diagnosis of gallbladder disease. These fine distinctions would have been difficult without the involvement of clinicians familiar with these procedures.

To test the validity of these assumptions, particularly regarding open versus laparoscopic procedures, we pursued direct observations. Ten of the hospitals surveyed were chosen randomly for direct investigation. Researchers questioned operating-room or department personnel regarding the numbers of open and laparoscopic cholecystectomies in 1990 and 1991. The correlation was surprisingly tight for both laparoscopic (Spearman's rho = 0.87) and open (Spearman's rho = 0.89) cholecystectomy. The algorithm used had slightly underpredicted laparoscopic cholecystectomies in these directly investigated hospitals (1,026 vs 1,118) and had overpredicted open cholecystectomies (1,212 vs 1,178).

Cholecystectomy rates did increase during the investigated time period (See Table 33–2 for rates of cholecystectomy). Rates of cholecystectomy up to 1989 were stable at 1.65 to 1.69 cholecystectomies per 1,000 Maryland residents per year. With the introduction of laparoscopic cholecystectomy, the rate of all cholecystectomies increased by 28 percent, while the

Table 33–2 Numbers and Rates of Cholecystectomy by Type in Maryland, 1985–1992

Year	Number of Procedures (Rate*)		
	Laparoscopic	Open	Both†
1985	0	7,215 (1.65)	7,215 (1.65)
1986	1 (0)	7,268 (1.65)	7,269 (1.65)
1987	1 (0)	7,561 (1.68)	7,562 (1.68)
1988	3 (0)	7,711 (1.68)	7,714 (1.68)
1989	9 (0)	7,917 (1.69)	7,926 (1.69)
1990	1,181 (0.25)	7,606 (1.59)	8,787 (1.84)
1991	5,056 (1.04)	5,437 (1.12)	10,493 (2.16)
1992	8,037 (1.66)	2,534 (0.51)	10,571 (2.17)

*Per 1,000 Maryland residents, after adjustment for age.
†The increase in the rate for both types of cholecystectomy combined was significant over time ($p < .001$ chi-squared for linear trend).

rate of open cholecystectomy fell by 70 percent. Most amazing was the finding that 76 percent of the cholecystectomies in Maryland by 1992 were performed laparoscopically. Thus, within 2 years of the procedure's introduction, it was widespread in this state. These numbers confirmed observers' impressions that this procedure had taken the country by storm. It is not surprising that speculation arose regarding the safety of such a momentous and rapid shift in surgical practice.

During the 3-year period of introduction of the laparoscopic cholecystectomy (from 1990 to 1992), the mortality rate was lower for those undergoing laparoscopic cholecystectomy (Table 33–3), and the overall mortality rate for all cholecystectomies declined. However, the mortality rate for open cholecystectomy increased. Again, surgeon behavior may explain these findings. It makes sense that surgeons would choose their healthiest patients for a new procedure with which they are becoming comfortable and that the sickest patients would have open cholecystectomies. To further investigate this possible effect, multiple logistic regression analyses were performed to identify independent factors associated with an increased likelihood of having a laparoscopic (as opposed to open) cholecystectomy or an increased likelihood of dying (Table 33–4). Even controlling for comorbidities, patients who underwent laparoscopic cholecystectomy were more likely to survive (adjusted odds ratio, 0.22; 95% confidence interval, 0.13 to 0.37). An additional independent predictor was Medicaid insurance. Patients with Medicaid were nearly three times more likely to die following cholecystectomy (open and laparoscopic) than privately insured patients.

A number of conclusions were drawn from this study. First, laparoscopic cholecystectomy had been safely introduced into the surgical community in Maryland in a very short period of time. By 1992, 76 percent of all cholecystectomies in Maryland were being performed with the laparoscope. Second, the overall rate of cholecystectomy did in fact increase

Table 33–3 Operative Mortality Associated with Cholecystectomy, According to Type of Procedure*

	% Who Died in the Hospital, by Type of Cholecystectomy			Unadjusted Odds Ratio (95% Confidence Interval)†
Year	All	Open	Laparoscopic	
1985	1.09	1.09	—	—
1986	0.91	0.91	—	—
1987	1.00	1.00	—	—
1988	1.17	1.17	—	—
1989	0.84	0.84	—	—
1990	0.71	0.80	0.17‡	4.7 (1.1–28.1)
1991	0.65	1.21	0.10§	12.3 (4.8–34.8)
1992	0.56"	2.04#	0.18§	11.8 (6.2–22.6)

* Operative mortality was defined as the percentage of patients with a primary procedure code for either an open or a laparoscopic procedure and who died during the hospitalization.
† Denotes the odds of operative mortality with open as compared with laparoscopic cholecystectomy.
‡ $p < .05$ by the chi-squared test for the comparison with open cholecystectomy.
§ $p < .01$ by the chi-squared test for the comparison with open cholecystectomy.
" $p < .05$ by the chi-squared test for the comparison with the 1989 value.
# $p < .01$ by the chi-squared test for the comparison with the 1990 value.

Table 33–4 Multiple Logistic Regression of Factors Independently Associated with Operative Mortality from Cholecystectomy in Maryland, 1990–1992*

Characteristic	No. of Patients (N = 29,271)	No. of Deaths (N = 180)	Unadjusted Odds Ratio (95% Confidence Interval)†	Adjusted Odds Ratio (95% Confidence Interval)†
Age (yr)	—	—	—	1.008 (1.004–1.011)‡
Males (vs female) sex	7,495	82	2.33 (1.72–3.13)	1.5 (1.06–2.12)
Marital status (vs widowed)				
Married	17,594	78	0.20 (0.14–0.28)	0.57 (0.39–0.84)
Single, separated, or divorced	6,637	22	0.15 (0.09–0.25)	0.43 (0.25–0.74)
Insurance status (vs private)				
Medicare	7,443	140	12.6 (7.73–20.8)	2.2 (1.0–5.0)
Medicaid	2,079	11	3.50 (1.57–7.67)	2.7 (1.6–4.5)
HMO	4,354	7	1.06 (0.41–2.64)	1.07 (0.44–2.6)
Emergency (vs other) admission	9,023	141	10.3 (6.67–16.2)	3.2 (2.0–5.1)
Coexisting conditions				
Hypertension	4,132	11	0.38 (0.19–0.71)	0.37 (0.20–0.69)
Acute myocardial infarction	63	15	50 (25–100)	14.1 (7.0–28.2)
Conduction disease or arrhythmia	1,636	59	8.3 (5.88–70.0)	5.2 (3.2–8.3)
Pneumonia	252	15	11.1 (5.88–70.0)	5.2 (3.2–8.3)
Kidney disease	190	24	25.0 (16.7–50.0)	8.8 (5.2–15.0)
Cancer	420	29	14.3 (9.1–70.0)	5.2 (3.2–8.3)
Cerebrovascular disease	178	10	10.0 (4.8–20.0)	3.0 (1.4–6.3)
Laparoscopic (vs open) cholecystectomy	14,131	21	0.13 (0.08–0.21)	0.22 (0.13–0.37)

* This analysis includes only cholecystectomies that were listed as primary procedures.

† Adjusted odds ratios were derived from a multiple logistic regression analysis in which each odds ratio was adjusted for all other characteristics listed. An odds ratio of less than 1 indicates that patients with the characteristic in question have a lower risk of death than those without the characteristic. An odds ratio higher than 1 indicates that patients with the characteristic have a higher risk of death than those without the characteristic.

‡ Denotes the odds of death per year of increasing age.

in Maryland following the introduction of laparoscopic cholecystectomy. The nature of the disease explains this finding, at least in part. Many cholecystectomies are performed for chronic symptoms. Patients in this category have pain and discomfort with variable frequency and intensity, with symptoms often worsening over time to the point where patients are willing to undergo surgery. Patients make their decisions regarding surgery based on whether 5 days in the hospital, severe abdominal pain, and 6 weeks off work is a reasonable price tag to pay to be rid of their chronic symptoms. When laparoscopic cholecystectomy became available, this risk-benefit analysis changed. Thus, many patients who were frequently experiencing abdominal pain with meals were suddenly willing to undergo an operation that created less pain and required only one night in the hospital. Some might interpret these data as revealing a new outbreak of "unnecessary surgery," but patients who were relieved of their troublesome symptoms probably did not see it that way. It is still not clear today whether the rates of cholecystectomy have remained elevated or have dropped back down to their pre-laparoscopic-cholecystectomy level. Third, laparoscopic cholecystectomy appeared to be safer than open cholecystectomy in terms of overall mortality. During this time period in Maryland, a patient was roughly eight times more likely to die from an open cholecystectomy than a laparoscopic cholecystectomy. While not the result of a prospective randomized trial, this finding in a well-designed outcomes study was important as it confirmed the conclusions of a number of retrospective studies. Finally, there was an increased rate of mortality in the Medicaid patients compared to privately insured patients. This is probably more a sociologic issue than a medical one; however, it points out the power of an outcomes study to uncover important, unexpected information. A related finding was the more complete penetration of this procedure in health management organization (HMO) populations. This may have been due to younger, more aggressive practitioners who gravitated to the HMO environment early in their careers or due to HMO managers who may have realized early the potential savings in hospital stay with laparoscopic cholecystectomy.

OUTPATIENT LAPAROSCOPIC CHOLECYSTECTOMY

Laparoscopic cholecystectomy clearly held huge advantages for patients, reducing pain, disability, cosmetic disfigurement, and hospital stay. Soon, surgeons and administrators wondered if costs could be further reduced and patient comfort further enhanced by performing laparoscopic cholecystectomy as an outpatient procedure. The evolution of outpatient open hernia repair during the previous decade suggested that such an evolution could also occur with cholecystectomy. A number of clear differences existed, however. Cholecystectomy requires general anesthesia whereas hernia repair can be performed with local anesthesia. It would be nearly impossible for an outpatient hernia patient to suffer life threatening bleeding without recognition, because the blood would be obvious in the wound. Cholecystectomy patients could have a clip dislodge from the cystic artery in their sleep (possibly) and lose a great deal of blood before discovery. In addition, patients seemed to vary greatly in their pain response to laparoscopic cholecystectomy; some had little or no pain whereas others continued to have pain for quite a while.

Some groups were retaining patients for 23 hours to fit into advantageous insurance categories. At Johns Hopkins, we considered moving to an outpatient laparoscopic cholecystectomy program, and we decided to ask whether our current patients and the nurses caring for them felt they could have been cared for at home. The outcome we measured was the patients' willingness to return home the day of surgery. The tool we used to measure this outcome was a simple survey of our (then) current laparoscopic cholecystectomy patients to determine their attitudes regarding the possibility of an outpatient laparoscopic cholecystectomy.[9] We also surveyed the nurses who had primary responsibility for these patients the evening following surgery. We were also looking for problems that could impair the development of a successful program of outpatient laparoscopic cholecystectomy.

We surveyed the patients and their nurses the day following laparoscopic cholecystectomy, and asked the questions indicated in Tables 33–5 and 33–6. We then requested a voluntary survey of patients undergoing laparoscopic cholecystectomy over a 10-month period. None of the 32 patients surveyed refused to answer the questions. The results were unexpected. Seventy-one percent of the patients did not favor same-day discharge following laparoscopic cholecystectomy, and their nurses agreed with them. The detailed answers reveal the reasons for their reluctance: 55 percent experienced nausea, 45 percent vomited, and 53 percent said they could not consume a liquid diet. Also important was the nurses' reporting that 61 percent of the time, patients were not receptive to postoperative instructions on the evening following laparoscopic cholecystectomy. Pain was also more intense than expected; 25 percent of patients reported that their pain was 9 or 10 on a scale of 1 to 10.

Table 33–5 Laparoscopic Cholecystectomy Patient Questionnaire*

The evening of your surgery:	Yes	No
Were you able to go to the bathroom by yourself (without assistance from another person?)	55%	45%
Could you have consumed a liquid diet?	53%	47%
Were you able to walk (move about) on your own?	58%	42%
Were you having any pain?	81%	19%
What was the worst pain?		
Did you have any nausea?	55%	45%
Did you have any vomiting?	45%	55%
Do you feel you would have been able to understand discharge instructions if you could have gone home the evening of your surgery?	48%	52%
Would you have had someone (family, friends) to help you at home?	48%	52%
At home the evening of your surgery, would you have been able to:		
Walk to the bathroom?	53%	47%
Give yourself medication?	47%	53%
Walk up stairs?	39%	61%
Get food on your own?	39%	61%
Do you feel you could have gone home?	29%	71%

*N = 32 (all patients).

Table 33–6 Laparoscopic Cholecystectomy Nursing Questionnaire*

In assessing your patient the evening of their surgery:	Yes	No
Was the patient able to go to the bathroom with assistance?	82%	18%
Was the patient able to tolerate a clear liquid diet?	42%	58%
Was the patient able to ambulate without assistance?	41%	58%
Was the patient having any pain (incisional, shoulder, etc)?	70%	30%
Was the patient nauseated?	68%	32%
Did the patient vomit?	33%	67%
Would you have felt comfortable teaching discharge instruction to the patient the evening of their surgery?	39%	61%
Do you feel the patient would have been receptive to discharge teaching the evening of their surgery?	44%	56%
Do you feel the patients could have gone home the evening of surgery?	19%	81%

*N = 32 (all patients).

This study clearly had some drawbacks. The patients were questioned the day after surgery, while they were still experiencing pain; had they been questioned later, the response may have been quite different. The pain measurement was crude: simply a 1-to-10 scale. However, the data were sufficient to guide further efforts. We therefore concluded that a program of outpatient laparoscopic cholecystectomy would succeed only if we minimized nausea, vomiting, and pain. We also needed to teach patients before rather than after their procedure.

With this information, we designed a program of outpatient laparoscopic cholecystectomy and a means of measuring outcomes of this program. In designing the care, we joined with our anesthesiology colleagues to minimize nausea and pain by altering the anesthetic, using propofol rather than inhalation agents. During induction of anesthesia, patients were given ondansetron as an antinausea agent. The maintenance anesthesia regimen was fentanyl (a short-acting narcotic), intravenous propofol, and nitrous oxide (70%). Neuromuscular blockade was initiated and maintained with mivacurium. Surgeons rated each procedure as easy, medium, or difficult from a technical standpoint. For additional pain control, long-acting local anesthetic was injected into the port sites and in the operative field. Ketorolac (a nonsteroidal anti-inflammatory agent) was given during the operation. For purposes of the study, each patient was admitted to an observational unit within the hospital, which was treated as a home setting (ie, nurses provided care only when specifically asked; otherwise, the patients were left on their own to self-administer pain medicines and to advance their own diet). Data were collected regarding pain medicine requirements, patient needs, and complications that would have required re-admission to the hospital. Cost analyses were performed retrospectively.

We studied 99 consecutive patients in this manner between July 1994 and June 1996. In all cases, informed consent was obtained prior to enrollment in the study. Patients were enrolled as long as they were considered not to be at excessive anesthetic risk (ASA catagory I,II, or III). Of the 99 patients, 96 would have met the discharge criteria to go home the same day as their laparoscopic cholecystectomy. The incidence of nausea and vomiting (11 of these patients) was substantially lower than that reflected by our survey of laparoscopic cholecystectomy patients prior to the institution of our protocol.

Our anesthetic regimen was clearly more expensive than the standard inhalation agents due to the use of more expensive agents such as propofol and ondansetron. Our decision analysis suggested that the best strategy would be to send patients home after their laparoscopic cholecystectomy and re-admit directly those who suffered postoperative nausea and vomiting at home. Such a strategy would have saved an average of $742 per patient. Based upon these outcomes studies, we now offer outpatient laparoscopic cholecystectomy to all patients undergoing uncomplicated laparoscopic cholecystectomies of reasonable anesthetic risk. The anesthetic protocol is used for all outpatient cholecystectomies.

To further measure the outcome of our outpatient laparoscopic cholecystectomy program, we retrospectively studied the first 130 patients who had undergone outpatient laparoscopic cholecystectomy, contacting them by telephone to collect the data. The average length of time in the recovery room was 200 minutes (range, 95 to 460 minutes ± 79 minutes). Eight (6.2%) patients required direct admission to the hospital. Of the remaining 122 patients who went home, 6 (4.9%) required rehospitalization. No major complications were encountered. Ninety-eight patients were available for telephone follow-up. The outpatient experience was rated as good by 75.5 percent, fair by 22.5 percent, and poor by 2 percent of patients. Twenty percent of the patients reported that they would have preferred being in the hospital the night following their surgery.

This series of issues and studies illustrates how outcomes investigations can be used to guide the evolution of a procedure as it moves into the minimally invasive arena. In our original survey, 71 percent of patients and their nurses felt that they could not have gone home right after their surgery. We addressed the issues involved and carefully studied our modifications using an inpatient clinical investigation setting. We then measured again (by survey) our degree of success in the real outpatient arena. We found that 80 percent of the patients had gone home and were satisfied with the experience. We believe that similar studies can be applied as additional minimally invasive procedures evolve.

FUTURE DIRECTIONS

As the field of minimally invasive surgery matures and broadens, outcomes studies will be carefully watched by patients, insurance providers, the media, and the government. The widespread media attention this field has attracted has perhaps raised unrealistic expectations in the general public ("Why can't you do my operation with the laser through a pinhole?"). Physicians have a responsibility to determine whether the benefits of these operations truly outweigh the possible increased risks and the likely increased costs. In some situations, it will take long periods of study to make these determinations. Laparoscopic resection of colon cancer is an excellent example. When a patient has a cancer, most feel that the size of the incision should take a back seat to achieving a good cancer operation. On the other hand, if colon cancer resection can be performed with less pain and disability and with the same cancer-curing result, patients will choose that option. Unfortunately, it will take time to make this determination, since cancer outcomes regarding cure are measured in 3-, 5-, and 10-year survival rates. During such long study periods, the technology will continue to change and improve, thus making these determinations more difficult.

Other minimally invasive procedures seem to be showing immediate benefit. Laparoscopic nephrectomy in living donors for kidney transplantation seems to have multiplied willing kidney donors almost overnight.[10] But with such positive early outcomes, longterm study will be important. Who should be doing these potentially dangerous operations? How should such increased willingness change the paradigm for choosing appropriate donors and recipients? These are difficult questions, answerable only in the long term.

Perhaps the most difficult issue over time will be the effect of technology on traditional surgical judgment. As technology advances, there will be ever more amazing things that surgeons can do with minimally invasive surgery. The important questions of who, where and when to perform "telesurgery" are currently being debated.[11] It may soon be possible for a surgeon in one location to perform an operation on a patient at a remote location. It is hard to believe that patients would want their surgeon to be anywhere but right in the room where they are having their operation. However, this could be lifesaving technology for military applications, and would allow the services to increase the effectiveness of their medical personnel.

Clearly, surgery 50 years from now will look very different than surgery now, and minimally invasive surgical technology will drive much of that change. Carefully performed outcomes research must be our guide as we move into this new era of surgery.

REFERENCES

1. Steiner CA, Bass EB, Talamini MA, et al. Surgical rates and operative mortality for open and laparoscopic cholecystectomy in Maryland. N Engl J Med 1994 Feb 10;330:404–8.

2. Mowatt G, Cairns JA, Bower DJ, et al. When and how to assess fast-changing technologies: a comparative study of medical applications of four generic technologies. Health Technol Assess 1997;1(14):i–iv,1–149.

3. The Southern Surgeons Club. A prospective analysis of 1518 laparoscopic cholecystectomies. N Engl J Med 1991 Apr 18;324(16):1073–8.

4. Cohen MM, Young W, Theriault ME, Hernandez R. Has laparoscopic cholecystectomy changed patterns of practice and patient outcome in Ontario? Can Med Assoc J 1996 Jul 15;155(2):161–2.

5. Shea JA, Berlin JA, Bachwich DR, et al. Indications for and outcomes of cholecystectomy: a comparison of the pre and post laparoscopic eras. Ann Surg 1998;227(3):343–50.

6. Chen AY, Daley J, Pappas TN, et al. Growing use of laparoscopic cholecystectomy in the national Veterans Affairs Surgical Risk Study: effects on volume, patient selection, and selected outcomes. Ann Surg 1998;227(1):12–24.

7. Wu JS, Dunnegan DL, Luttmann DR, Soper NJ. The evolution and maturation of laparoscopic cholecystectomy in an academic practice. J Am Coll Surg 1998;186(5):5554–60.

8. Kane RL, Lurie N, Borbas C, et al. The outcomes of elective laparoscopic and open cholecystectomies. J Am Coll Surg 1995;180(2):136–45.

9. Talamini MA, Coleman J, Sauter P, et al. Outpatient laparoscopic cholecystectomy: patient and nursing perspective. Surgical Laparoscopy Endoscopy and Percutaneous Techniques (in press).

10. Rattner LE, Cisek LJ, Moore RG, et al. Laparoscopic live donor nephrectomies. Transportation 1995; 60:1047–9.

11. Cubano M, Poulose BK, Talamini MA, et al. Long distance telementoring: a novel tool for laparoscopy aboard the USS Abraham Lincoln. Surgical Endoscopy 1999; 13:673–8.

CHAPTER 34

Thoracic Surgery

Stephen C. Yang, MD

There is no specific event or exact date that signifies the birth of general thoracic surgery; rather, the specialty has grown over the past century out of a need to address specific pathology. Around World War I, general surgeons were asked to address surgical issues concerning lung abscess and empyema, common conditions at the time. This was followed by the need for pulmonary resection for tuberculosis in the 1940s. Finally, thoracic surgery became an autonomous specialty when interest in coronary artery disease and cardiac surgery led to cardiac surgery as a separate specialty. Hence, the terms "general thoracic surgery" and "noncardiac thoracic surgery" came into existence to describe these areas.

Today, general thoracic surgery encompasses a range of diverse diagnostic and therapeutic procedures to address chest pathology. These include (outlined in Table 34–1): esophageal surgery for benign and malignant diseases (see Chapter 20 Esophageal Surgery); pulmonary surgery for neoplasms and infections; mediastinal surgery for the diagnosis and treatment of pathologic masses and tumors, and pleural and chest wall procedures for infections and neoplasms. Although the number of technical advances and indications for surgery remained relatively stagnant for most of this century, the last decade has brought about new excitement in many areas. While evidence-based practice guidelines have been developed for the more traditional procedures for lung cancer, empyema and lung biopsies, newer indications and techniques are undergoing constant debate not on whether they could be done but on whether they should be done. These innovations included lung transplantation, video-assisted thoracic surgery (VATS), surgery on an outpatient basis rather than on an in-patient basis, and more recently, the debate regarding lung volume reduction surgery (LVRS). This chapter will examine the evidence for many of these traditional procedures, and comment on more recent controversial areas.

LITERATURE REVIEW

Pulmonary Resection for Bronchogenic Carcinoma

Over 175,000 new cases of lung cancer are diagnosed yearly, and lung cancer remains the number one cause of cancer-related deaths in the U.S. adult population, with an associated 160,000 deaths. Surgical resection remains the most effective therapy for early-stage non-small cell lung carcinoma (NSCLC), though appropriate for only less than one-fourth of all new cases. The feasibility of surgical treatment relies upon the ability to resect all tumor while imposing little risk to the patient and leaving adequate pulmonary reserve. Resection en bloc of involved adjacent structures, if technically possible, can be performed with minimal morbidity and mortality. Chemotherapy and radiation therapy used alone or in combination have been effective for palliation but have not achieved the success rates of surgery.

Extent of Surgical Resection

Complete resection of all involved tissue is the primary goal in the surgical management of any cancer. Evarts Graham is credited with having performed the first successful pneumonectomy for bronchogenic carcinoma in 1932,[1] which at that time became standard therapy for

Table 34–1 General Thoracic Surgical Procedures

Organ Systems	Procedures	Disease Processes
Upper airway	Laryngoscopy Bronchoscopy Endoscopic laser ablation Stent insertion	Congenital anomalies Tracheomalacia Stenosis Traumatic tears Airway tumors
Lung	Mediastinoscopy Lung biopsy Pulmonary resections: wedge, segmental, lobectomy, sleeve resection, pneumonectomy Video-assisted thoracic surgery Lung transplantation	Infections: bacterial, tuberculous, mycotic Congenital anomalies Interstitial lung disease Bronchogenic tumors Pulmonary metastasis COPD
Pleura	Pleural stripping Pleurodesis Bleb resection Thoracoplasty Open and closed drainage	Benign and malignant pleural effusions Pleura-based tumors Mesothelioma Spontaneous pneumothorax Chylothorax Fibrothorax Hemothorax
Chest wall	Chest wall resection Cervical/first rib resection	Primary neoplasms Thoracic outlet syndrome
Diaphragm	Plication Phrenic nerve pacing Hernia repair	Eventration Phrenic nerve paralysis Congenital hernias
Mediastinum	Thymectomy Resection of mediastinal masses or cysts Pericardial windows Pericardial stripping	Thymoma/myasthenia gravis Mediastinal cysts Lymphoma Germ cell tumors Neurogenic tumors Pericardial effusions Restrictive pericarditis
Esophagus	Esophagectomy Esophagomyotomy Resection of esophageal diverticula Anti-reflux procedures Esophageal diversion	Primary neoplasms Motor disorders: achalasia, diffuse esophageal spasm Gastroesophageal reflux Perforation Diverticular disease

COPD = chronic obstructive pulmonary disease.

all surgical candidates. When individual ligation of the bronchus and vessels was introduced by Rienhoff,[2] lobectomy could be performed for disease limited to one lobe. Without compromising adequacy of tumor resection, survival rates similar to pneumonectomy were achieved while conserving functional pulmonary tissue. Further advances in surgical technique led to segmental resections by Churchill in 1939, which soon became the preferred option to further preserve adequate lung function.[3] Wedge resection was reserved for older patients, for those with compromised pulmonary function, or for those with significant coexisting medical conditions but was considered inadequate for curative intent.

As with other primary tumors, surgical failure due to local recurrence is a major problem, especially with advanced and incompletely resected disease. As the extent of surgical resection evolved, it became evident that "radical" pneumonectomy, which included intrapericardial dissection and removal of all mediastinal lymph nodes, offered no significant survival advantage over lobectomy for early-stage disease.[4] Lobectomy is now viewed as the procedure of choice for non-small cell lung carcinoma and has become the most commonly performed procedure, followed by segmentectomy, wedge resection, and pneumonectomy. Retrospective and prospective data from the Lung Cancer Study Group (LCSG) support lobectomy over lesser resections (segmentectomy, wedge resection) as standard therapy for patients with resectable disease and good pulmonary function.[5,6] In these same reports, segmental resection is associated with less chance of local recurrence than wedge resection though still greater than lobectomy. Although lesser resections have the benefit of conserving resected lung tissue, the risk of a 25 to 40 percent recurrence should restrict this therapy to those patients with limited lung reserve. The risk of recurrence (but not survival) has been lessened by adding postoperative radiation therapy to the surrounding lung tissue and mediastinum.[7,8] Accepted mortality from pneumonectomy, lobectomy, and lesser resections are 8 percent, 3 percent, and 1 percent, respectively.[9]

Results from lung volume reduction surgery for chronic obstructive pulmonary disease have demonstrated improved pulmonary function in patients with severe disease,[10] and will be discussed later in more detail. These encouraging results, along with improvement in the perioperative management of this high-risk population, have prompted many institutions to apply this concept of lung volume reduction surgery to lung cancer patients whose disease appears resectable but removal of which is precluded by poor pulmonary function. Recent reports show that selected patients with low preoperative forced expiratory volume in 1 second (FEV_1, < 60% of predicted) are less likely to lose ventilatory function after lobectomy and may actually have improved pulmonary function.[11]

Lymph Node Dissection

The controversy of complete mediastinal lymph node resection versus selective sampling has existed since Cahan first introduced complete dissection.[12] This approach was adopted for all tumors, especially those with hilar or mediastinal involvement, in an effort to improve overall survival. Positive results have been observed by some investigators.[13,14] In addition, occult metastasis has been found in 15 percent of patients with clinically negative (size < 1 cm) nodes.[15,16] However, no study has conclusively demonstrated any survival advantage with either complete ipsilateral[17] or bilateral mediastinal lymph node dissection with removal of the supraclavicular lymph nodes as adopted by surgeons in Japan.[18] Currently, regional and mediastinal lymph node sampling should at least be performed at the time of operation for accurate staging. Large randomized trials will be required to answer this controversy.

Staging

It is standard practice to accurately stage all lung cancers clinically and pathologically at the time of surgery, not only to determine the appropriate individual course of therapy but also to provide a prognosis. In 1986, Mountain proposed the international tumor node metastasis (TNM) staging system in response to the need for a unified classification to accurately stage all lung cancers.[19] This system was recently revised[20] to account for several observations that emerged from the 1986 system. Prognosis was significantly affected by tumor size, and thus stages I and II were subgrouped to account for smaller and larger tumors. Chest wall invasion without lymph node metastasis was found to have a better prognosis than originally thought and was subsequently staged down from IIIA to IIB. Finally, metastatic sites to other lobes of the lung were classified as metastatic disease.

Surgical Approach

Posterolateral thoracotomy provides the best exposure for pulmonary resection, but other approaches such as sternotomy, anterior thoracotomy, and transverse thoracosternotomy (clamshell) also provide alternatives in appropriate situations. Muscle-sparing incisions have been used to reduce postoperative pain and improve cosmesis but are done at the expense of limited exposure and usefulness. Despite these theoretical advantages, no randomized study has shown clear benefits to any one of these approaches.

The role of video-assisted thorascopic surgical lobectomy as an option for lung cancer resection remains controversial. Due to its popularity, it has been used extensively for wedge and lobar resections. Although it can be technically accomplished along with improvement in cosmesis, postoperative pain, and hospital stay, two randomized prospective studies ironically did not conclusively show any benefit with this approach[21,22] in length of stay, morbidity, or (most importantly) survival. However, future evidence will need to emphasize long-term survival, disease-free analysis, and assurance that local and port site recurrences will not be a problem before VATS is offered as a reasonable option to open thoracotomy.

Tumors with Chest Wall Invasion

Peripheral tumors involving the chest wall and superior sulcus are still amenable to resection, yielding 5-year survival rates of up to 40 percent, provided there is no nodal or distant metastasis.[7] Extent of invasion, completeness of resection, and nodal involvement affect survival. Adjuvant radiation therapy helps to decrease local recurrence but often does not extend survival beyond 2.5 years.[23]

Solitary Metastasis

Although distant metastasis is often regarded as an absolute contraindication for surgical resection of a primary tumor, patients with non-small cell lung carcinoma who present with synchronous metastasis or develop subsequent distant recurrence following initial pulmonary resection may be candidates for resection of both sites. Both sites must be completely resected and subsequently show no evidence of nodal or other distant systemic involvement.

Brain metastases account for nearly one-third of all recurrences following resection of non-small cell lung carcinoma and are more commonly associated with the adenocarcinoma histology than with squamous or large cell carcinoma. When disease in the lung and in the brain can be completely resected (in either sequence), and when resection can be combined with postoperative cranial irradiation, 1- and 5-year survivals of 50 percent and 20 percent, respectively, can be achieved.[24] The same principles can be applied to solitary adrenal metastases. These lesions are detected earlier because of routine upper abdominal views from preoperative chest CT scans. Long-term results parallel those of resecting solitary brain metastases.

A second pulmonary lesion more often represents a second primary cancer rather than a metastatic lesion. The same principles should be adhered to in completely resecting both lesions as with other distant solitary metastatic deposits. Five-year survivals up to 22 percent are achieved.[25]

Resection for Pulmonary Metastases

Except for regional nodal involvement, the lung is the most common solid organ site of metastasis for a majority of the more common malignancies. Pulmonary metastatic deposits were once thought to connote disseminated disease without surgical options. However, several retrospective series dating back to 1939 have shown improvement in survival with intentional pulmonary metastasectomies. As criteria became more rigid, coming to include control of local primary disease, absence of distant extrapulmonary metastasis, and ability to remove all pulmonary nodules, so too have the indications and recommended aggressiveness for intervention become more stringent.

The aggressiveness of surgical therapy for pulmonary metastasis is dependent upon the histologic cell type of the primary tumor and the tumor's relative responsiveness to chemotherapy and radiation therapy. The overall 5-year survival rate following metastasectomy is approximately 40 percent. Despite having effective chemotherapy, nonseminomatous germ cell tumors are associated with the highest 5-year survival rate of 65 percent following resection of pulmonary metastases.[26] Primary tumors with an intermediate response rate of 40 to 50 percent following surgical resection include head and neck tumors,[27] renal cell carcinoma,[28,29] colorectal tumors,[30,31] and soft-tissue[32] and osteogenic sarcomas.[33] Those primary tumors with the poorest prognosis (5 to 15%) include breast tumors,[34,35] and melanoma.[36]

An aggressive multimodality approach has been adopted in the past several years, including multiple thoracotomies for resection of all recurrent disease.[37] Common factors adversely affecting prognosis for nonsarcomatous pulmonary metastases include a disease-free interval of < 12 months, size of > 3 cm, multiple lesions, and lymphatic or lymph node involvement.

Video-Assisted Thoracic Surgery

Thoracoscopic techniques were originally put into practice during the early 1900s for diagnosing and treating tuberculosis.[38] With the evolution of and refinement in minimally invasive techniques and instrumentation during the 1980s, VATS has assumed a major role in the management of a number of surgical diseases of the chest and has become a powerful tool in the surgical options available to the modern thoracic surgeon. As the need for VATS expanded, so did the indications for its use in the diagnosis and treatment of a variety of thoracic disorders, as listed in Table 34–2.

Basic approach strategies have been developed by many centers throughout the world with broad access to these techniques and skills.[39] Morbidity and mortality is low, with diagnostic and therapeutic results as effective as those of formal open procedures. With the use of conventional instrumentation and the minimization of manipulative incisions, excellent exposure can be attained without compromising the goals of the procedure. Video-assisted thoracic surgery ultimately offers similar advantages over traditional methods in regard to surgical expediency and safety, reduced postoperative pain, better cosmesis, faster functional recovery, shortened hospital stay, and savings in total hospital costs.

Table 34–2 Diagnostic and Therapeutic Indications for Video-Assisted Thoracic Surgery

Area of Disorder	Diagnostic Indications	Therapeutic Indications
Lungs	Evaluation of nodules and infiltrates Cancer staging	Wedge resection for cancer[40,41] Management of blebs and bulla
Esophagus	Cancer staging	Esophagomyotomy[42–44]
Pleura	Evaluation of masses or effusions	Empyemectomy[45] Drainage of effusions Evaluation of hemothorax Treatment of spontaneous pneumothorax Closure of persistent air leak Pleurodesis/pleurectomy Retrieval of retained/foreign bodies
Mediastinum	Diagnosis of masses	Resection of masses or cysts
Pericardium	Evaluation of effusions	Creation of pericardial windows[46, 47]
Autonomic nervous system	Evaluation of masses	Sympathectomy[48] Splanchnicectomy

Thoracoscopic Lung Biopsy

Patients with diffuse pulmonary infiltrates often require biopsy for a diagnosis to guide therapy. Open wedge resection via thoracotomy was traditionally considered as the standard operative approach, but it is associated with known morbidity. Few studies have critically compared video-assisted thoracic surgical lung biopsy with limited thoracotomy, hypothesizing that the former is associated with greater selection of biopsy sites, reduced postoperative pain, and shorter hospital stay. Overall accuracy cited in initial reports has exceeded 90 percent.[49]

Most reports are retrospective but generally conclude that operating time, number of specimens obtained, chest tube output, day of chest tube removal, and amount of analgesics required during the postoperative period did not differ between the open and video-assisted thoracic surgical approaches for lung biopsy. Although VATS was associated with greater operating room and anesthesia-related costs,[50] these were offset by shorter hospital stays, and ultimately lower total costs.[51,52]

Although video-assisted thoracic surgical lung biopsy supplanted open lung biopsy as the most common operative technique for diagnosing diffuse pulmonary abnormalities, its availability for lung biopsy should not alter the current indications for the initial use of bronchoscopic techniques in selected patients. In addition, because of the additional risk carried by thoracoscopic lung biopsy, open lung biopsy should still be used preferentially in patients suffering from acute decompensation, pulmonary hypertension, or coagulation disorders. When compared with the open technique, VATS does have the following advantages: it provides equivalent specimen volume, achieves equal diagnostic accuracy, does not add operative time or complications, reduces the time necessary for pleural drainage, and reduces the length of hospital stay.[53]

Lung Transplantation

Lung transplantation has proven to be successful for many end-stage lung disease processes. The more common indications for transplantation (accounting for over 90% of cases) include chronic obstructive pulmonary disease (COPD), α-1 antitrypsin deficiency, cystic fibrosis, primary pulmonary hypertension, Eisenmenger's physiology (with closure of the cardiac defect), idiopathic pulmonary fibrosis, sarcoidosis, and bronchiectasis. The most common condition requiring transplantation in the adult population is COPD while cystic fibrosis, mandating transplantation of both lungs because of bilateral septic foci, is the leading cause for transplantation in the pediatric age group.

Hardy performed the first successful human lung transplantation in 1963.[54] Subsequent attempts over the next two decades were associated with an unacceptably high mortality rate from infection, rejection, and poor bronchial healing due to high dosages of the only immunosuppressive agents (prednisone and azathioprine) available at the time. Enthusiasm for this procedure was regained with the introduction of cyclosporine, which led to the first successful heart-lung transplantation by Reitz and colleagues in 1981.[55]

The modern era of isolated lung transplantation is credited to Cooper and his colleagues from Toronto when a patient with pulmonary fibrosis underwent single lung transplantation in 1983.[56,57] Over the past 15 years, a number of technical advances have shaped modern operative techniques. Morbidity and mortality from airway complications decreased by lowering prednisone dosages, improving the bronchial anastomotic technique, and wrapping this anastomosis with vascularized tissue like omentum and muscle. However, it soon became apparent that double lung transplantation en bloc involving a single tracheal anastomosis was associated with a high incidence of tracheal anastomotic dehiscence or mainstem bronchial stenosis or ischemia. This was overcome in 1989 by performing sequential bilateral transplantations.[58] Although single lung transplantation is performed via a posterolateral thoracotomy, bilateral sequential implantation is best accomplished via a transverse (clamshell) thoracosternotomy.[59] Cardiopulmonary bypass, once thought necessary for all procedures, can be avoided in most cases due to better anesthetic management and monitoring and the use of vasoactive agents such as dopamine, dobutamine, prostacyclin, and nitric oxide. Although required in nearly all pediatric procedures, cardiopulmonary bypass is needed in approximately 25 percent of adult cases, primarily in patients with pulmonary hypertension, pulmonary fibrosis, and cystic fibrosis.[60]

Over 1,200 single and bilateral lung transplantations are performed yearly at approximately 150 registered centers throughout the world.[61] As the indications for transplantation grew, so too has the waiting list, with over 3,100 patients currently awaiting transplantation in the United States.[62] The problem of the shortage of organ donors is the most severe for lungs compared to other organ systems because the lungs are suitable for transplantation in only 10 to 15 percent of all appropriate cadaveric donors. As a result, the average waiting times for single and bilateral lung transplantation candidates approaches 15 and 18 months, respectively,[63] and the waiting list continues to grow with a relative plateau in the number of transplants (Figure 34–1). Since donor lungs are allocated to patients on the waiting list primarily by the amount of time on the waiting list, an inevitable delay of 1 to 2 years must be incorporated into the strategy of the timing for listing. Mortality on the waiting list ranges from 10 to 75 percent depending upon the underlying disease. Unlike heart and liver transplantation, there is no prioritization for clinical status or severity of illness. Since patients with pulmonary fibrosis historically have a high mortality rate while on the waiting list, in the United States they are currently awarded 90 days of waiting time when they are registered for listing.

Outcomes following lung transplantation can be gauged with several endpoints: survival, complications, physiologic function, quality of life, and cost-effectiveness. With improvements in selection strategies, operative technique, and postoperative management, morbidity and mortality have been dramatically reduced. Operative mortality is 13 percent and 21 percent for single and double lung transplantation, respectively,[64] but is reduced to 10 percent at experienced centers performing more than 35 cases annually.[65] Though mortality in the first

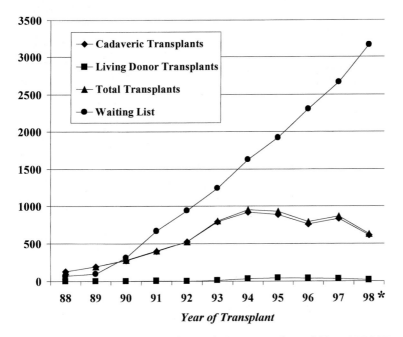

Figure 34–1 Lung transplant waiting list and transplantations performed (from UNOS Lung Transplant Registry).
*through September 30, 1998.

postoperative month is attributed to graft failure (Figure 34–2), infection due to *Cytomegalovirus* or other opportunistic organisms is thereafter the most common cause of death through the first year. However, bronchiolitis obliterans and chronic rejection ultimately preclude long-term survival of the allografts. These data translate into a 1-year 71 percent actuarial survival rate, and 5-year survival rates of 43 percent and 48 percent for single and bilateral transplants, respectively.[52]

Physiologic functional recovery depends on the underlying disease and type of transplant operation. By 2 months after surgery, normal levels of activity are reached without the need for supplemental oxygen.[66] Most patients display marked improvement in their pulmonary function parameters within the first 6 months, reaching 90 percent of improvement by 1 year. Improvement in patients with pulmonary fibrosis lags behind those of other disease groups; this is attributed mainly to steroid myopathy preoperatively and associated generalized debilitation. Controversy exists over performing bilateral lung replacement in younger patients and those with COPD and pulmonary hypertension. Though pulmonary function is better with bilateral transplantation, conflicting results regarding exercise and functional improvement have been reported in comparing single and bilateral recipients.

Several studies have documented significant improvement in quality of life following lung transplantation.[67,68] Although enhancement may not be noticeable during the first few months following surgery, most patients perceive improvement in physical function, social activities, and general and mental health (Table 34–3). Nearly 90 percent of all recipients were satisfied with their decision to pursue transplantation and would encourage others to seek the same assistance; but should complications occur, opinions are adversely affected.

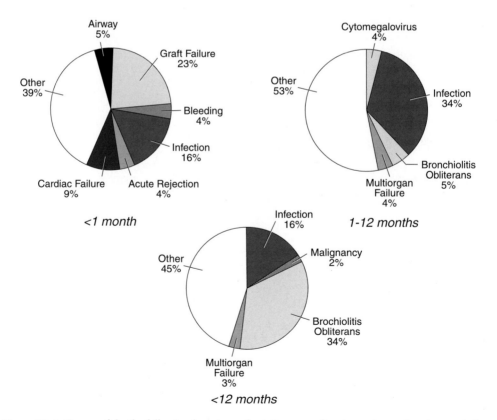

Figure 34–2 Causes of deaths following lung transplantation according to postoperative time period. Data from the International Society for Heart and Lung Transplantation (ISHLT) registry, 15th Annual Report.

Table 34–3 Quality of Life Following Lung Transplantation*

| | Percentage of Patients | |
	1 year	3 years
Activity		
No limitations	82	90
Some assistance needed	14	9
Total assistance	4	1
Work		
Full-time	23.5	29.1
Part-time	9.3	10.5
Not working	59.1	55.8
Retired	8.2	4.7

*Adapted from International Society for Heart and Lung Transplantation data.[52]

Though lung transplantation has had good overall success, one of the major obstacles preventing further growth remains the limited donor pool. Because of the donor shortage, Starnes pioneered the technique of lobar transplantation from living donors in 1993.[69,70] To date, approximately 75 lobar transplant procedures have been performed worldwide. Actuarial 1-year survival is 75 percent, with improvement in lung function and quality of life similar to cadaveric whole-lung transplantation. There have been no donor deaths, and morbidity is similar to that of patients undergoing lobectomy for carcinoma, with an average decrease in pulmonary function by 18 percent.

Surgery for Emphysema

Conservative medical therapy has been the standard approach for patients with advanced emphysema for many decades. In most cases, the pathogenesis is related to smoking, and therapy has been directed toward bronchodilators, steroids, antibiotics, and oxygen therapy for the severely hypoxic patient. Recently, rehabilitation programs and dietary and psychologic counseling have helped to improve quality of life but not survival. Surgical attempts during this century aimed at correcting hypothetical physiologic causes of emphysema have failed;[71] however, when successes were achieved, results were difficult to accept due to the lack of objective data and controlled trials comparing medical and surgical treatments.

Bullectomy

The one procedure that has withstood the test of time is bullectomy. In this situation, overdistention of the bulla causes underlying normal lung compression and mediastinal shifting. Surgery is indicated for those lesions that occupy more than half of the hemithorax or those that become infected and persist despite antibiotic therapy. Surgery is also performed to reduce the risk of spontaneous pneumothorax in patients with a high-risk occupation.[72] Once the indication for surgery has been determined, operative risk factors are weighed into the decision for thoracotomy. Important preoperative factors that correlate with successful surgical outcomes include age (< 40 years), past surgical and medical history, surgical approach and technique, absence of comorbid diseases and chronic bronchitis, weight loss (< 10%), smoking history, and cardiac status.[73,74]

Reported mortality rates varied from 1 to 5 percent. Most deaths were due to respiratory complications. Survival rates clearly correlated with the surgical approach and standardization of patient selection.[75,76] Early results showed that postoperative pulmonary function (FEV_1) improved by 50 to 200 percent. The patients who benefited the most from bullectomy were those who had an apical bulla occupying at least 50 percent of the hemithorax, a moderate degree of underlying lung compression, and a displacement of adjacent mediastinal structures.[77,78] Although early results were excellent, long-term data show that dyspnea gradually returned to preoperative levels by the fifth year.[36,79] Thus, these evidence-based data suggest that surgical bullectomy is associated with short-term relief but that sustained improvement is improbable.

Lung Volume Reduction Surgery

One of the more recent hotly debated topics in thoracic surgery is that of the benefits of lung volume reduction surgery (LVRS) for patients with end-stage emphysema. At least 2 million people in the United States suffer from emphysema, with an estimated death rate of 20,000 per year. Once the FEV_1 drops below 0.75 L, the 2-year survival rate approaches 50 percent.[80] Although emphysema is the most common indication for lung transplantation, many patients are denied consideration as a direct result of scarcity of donors, inappropriate age of patient (> 65 years), expense of transplantation, or a clinical situation not severe enough for listing.

Because of the prevalence of emphysema, the economic burden, and the devastating effects on quality of life, surgical options for emphysema were rekindled earlier this decade. These operations aimed for a 20 to 30 percent reduction in lung volume, with improvement in pulmonary function attributed to enhanced elastic recoil, correction of ventilation-perfusion mismatch, improved efficiency of respiratory musculature, and improved right ventricular filling. The earliest reports by Wakabayashi touted laser ablation of emphysematous lung as definitive therapy.[81] Although some benefit was reported, it was associated with significant operative morbidity. In a randomized prospective trial comparing stapled lung reduction to laser bullectomy, McKenna showed that mean postoperative improvement in FEV_1 at 6 months was significantly greater for the patients who underwent the staple technique (32.9% vs 13.4% , $p = .01$) than for the laser treatment group.[82]

Originally described by Brantigan in 1959,[83] LVRS was revived by Cooper in 1993 as a possible alternative or bridge to transplantation.[84] In his initial series of 20 patients, significant improvement in FEV_1 and forced vital capacity (FVC) with significant reduction in total lung capacity (TLC) and residual volume (RV) were observed. These were associated with marked improvement in perceived dyspnea, exercise tolerance, and quality of life. Since then, over 2,000 lung reduction procedures have been performed worldwide, generating tremendous debate on selection criteria and operative approaches and culminating in variable outcomes. The more commonly accepted patient selection criteria are listed in Table 34–4. The regional distribution of emphysematous disease has been perceived to be the most important criterion for patient selection.[85–89] Computed tomography or quantitative ventilation-perfusion scans are used to provide "target areas" of relatively functionless tissue for surgical resection. Patients with upper-lobe-predominant emphysema are seen as better candidates for LVRS than those with homogeneous distribution of disease.

Results from LVRS focus on improvement in pulmonary function, with short-term improvement in FEV_1 ranging from 30 to 99 percent of baseline, depending upon the operative approach (Table 34–5). Although FEV_1 improves in most patients who undergo LVRS, this parameter alone fails to explain clinical improvement in those without changes in FEV_1. In order to add to the current understanding of the physiologic improvement, recent studies have examined other factors thought to account for the improvement, including decrease in total lung capacity and residual volume, increase in transdiaphragmatic pressure, improvement in lung recoil and respiratory muscle function, and reduction of dynamic hyperinflation.[90]

Table 34–4 Patient Selection Criteria Parameters for Lung Volume Reduction Surgery

Inclusion Criteria	Exclusion Criteria

General
  Age < 80 years
  Severe impact on quality of life
  No prior major thoracic surgery or pleurodesis
  Good rehabilitation potential
	General
	  Any tobacco use in past 3 months
	  Substance abuse in past 12 months
	  Major psychologic illness
	  Severe anxiety disorder
	  Severe bronchitis or asthma

Anatomic parameters
  Presence of emphysema with hyperinflation
  Heterogeneous distribution of disease
	Significant comorbidities
	  Malignancy
	  Organ failure
	  Ventilator dependence
	  Significant coronary artery disease

Physiologic parameters
  FEV_1 < 35% predicted
  RV > 250%
  TLC > 120%
  Normal right and left ventricular function
	Anatomic parameters
	  Homogeneous distribution of disease
	  Large bullous disease
	  Prior major thoracic surgery or pleurodesis

	Physiologic parameters
	  Pulmonary hypertension
	    PA systolic > 50 mm Hg
	    PA mean > 35 mm Hg
	  Hypercapnia: $paCO_2$ > 55 mm Hg
	  DLCO < 10% predicted

FEV_1 = forced expiratory volume in 1 second; RV = residual volume; TLC = total lung capacity; PA = pulmonary artery; $PaCO_2$ = partial pressure of carbon dioxide; DLCO = diffusion capacity of carbon monoxide.

Most series report a 30-day operative mortality of 0 to 10 percent, depending on the operative approach and whether one or both sides are performed (see Table 34–5). Although long-term survival statistics are just maturing, 1-year mortality ranges from 7 to 17 percent,[91] with 5- and 8-year survival rates of 50 percent and 36 percent, respectively, in a cohort of 18 patients.[92] However, published mortality figures from LVRS likely underestimate rates at many centers that fail to report their results. Similarly, morbidity figures are difficult to interpret as established centers tend to overreport complications, while smaller groups report lower, insignificant rates. Surgical complications and associated morbidity rates are shown in Table 34–6.

Common to most reported series, a majority of patients find improvement in subjective dyspnea and objective pulmonary function and exercise tolerance, while oxygen and steroid dependence are reduced or eliminated with acceptable mortality and morbidity. Although bilateral procedures produce a greater improvement, the lung resection and not the operative approach is critical to the success of the operation. Although the sternotomy and VATS approaches lead to similar results, the latter is associated with a lower incidence of complications and decreased mortality. Irrespective of the technique used, the surgical treatment of emphysema remains palliative in nature.

It will take several years to determine the optimal pathway in selecting the proper subset of COPD patients for either LVRS or lung transplantation. The current decision algorithm at the Johns Hopkins Hospital is shown in Figure 34–3. By obviating the need for transplantation, LVRS offers patients more "quality" years of life without immunosuppression, expands the shrinking donor pool, and offers patients too old for transplantation an alternative surgical approach.

Table 34–5 Reported Forced Expiratory Volume 1s Improvement Following Lung Volume Reduction Surgery

Study	No. of Patients	FEV$_1$ Increase (%)	Mean Follow-up (months)	Mortality*
Median sternotomy, bilateral				
Cooper, 1995[84]	20	82	6.4	NA
Cooper, 1996[88]	127	51	6	4/7
Daniel, 1996[93]	26	49	3	NA
Miller, 1996[94]	65	39	3	NA
Kottloff, 1996[95]	80	40	6	4.2/13.8
Hazelrigg, 1998[96]	29	40	NA	0/14
Date, 1998[97]	39	41	3	0/NA
VATS, bilateral simultaneous				
McKenna, 1996[82]	39	33	NA	2.5/NA
Bingisser, 1996[98]	25	42	3	NA
Brenner, 1996[99]	122	46	1–3	NA
Keenan, 1996[100]	17	41	3	NA
Kottloff, 1996[95]	40	40	6	2.5/2.5
Stammberger, 1997[101]	42	43	12	0/0.5
Vigneswaran, 1998[102]	15	51	3	0/NA
VATS, bilateral staged				
Hazelrigg, 1998[96]	50	50	NA	0/0

NA = not available.
*operative mortality/1-year mortality.

Mediastinal Surgery

Within the mediastinum lies an array of pathological processes that require a multidisciplinary approach for diagnosis and treatment. The etiology of these problems can largely be divided into infections and tumors of the mediastinum. A partial list is outlined in Table 34–7. The estimated incidence of significant mediastinal pathology requiring surgical intervention is 1 per 100,000, much lower than that of bronchial and esophageal carcinomas.

The evaluation of primary lesions of the mediastinum begins with appropriate radiographic studies to determine which anatomic compartment is involved. After identification by plain chest films, chest CT is the study of choice to provide superior resolution of the abnormality while clarifying its position and relationship to surrounding structures.[103] Magnetic resonance imaging is not indicated in all cases but has been found to be superior to CT for involvement of the brachial plexus, major vascular structures, neural foramina, diaphragm, and mediastinal tissue.[104]

Table 34–6 Complications Following Lung Reduction Surgery

Complication	Reported Rates (%)	Reference
Prolonged air leak (> 7 days)	30–54	87–89,91,143
Dysrhythmia	7–21	89,143
Pneumonia	4–17	87–89,91,143
Mechanical ventilation	6–17	87–89,143
Reoperation	5–16	87,88,91
Gastrointestinal event	1–15	87–89,91,143
Tracheostomy	3–13	88,89
Empyema	5	143
Cerebrovascular event	2	143
Other neurologic event	19	89
Pleural space problem	2	88
Myocardial infarction or cardiac arrest	2–3	87,88

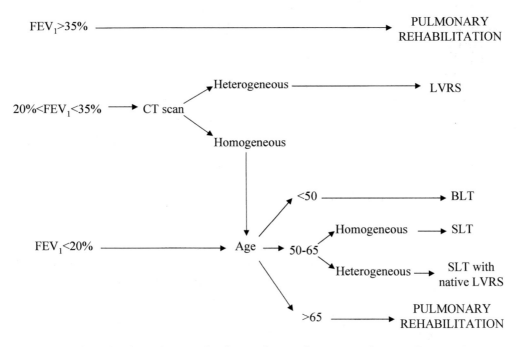

Figure 34–3 Algorithm for evaluation of end-stage chronic obstructive pulmonary disease patients based on percentage of forced expiratory volume in 1 second (FEV_1) predicted and distribution of emphysematous disease on CT scan (LVRS = lung volume reduction surgery; SLT = single lung transplant; BLT = bilateral lung transplant).

Table 34–7 Pathologic Processes of the Mediastinum

Infections

Acute mediastinitis
    Esophageal perforation
    Oral
    Postoperative (cardiac)

Acute descending necrotizing mediastinitis
    Oral
    Bacterial

Subacute mediastinitis
    Fungal
    Mycobacterial
    Actinomycotic

Chronic mediastinitis—granulomatous lymphadenitis
    Mycobacterial
    Fungal
    Sarcoidosis
    Silicosis
    Wegener's granulomatosis
    Lymphoid hamartoma—Castleman's disease

Chronic fibrosis mediastinitis
    Fungal—histoplasmosis
    Mycobacterial
    Bacterial—nocardiosis, actinomycosis
    Autoimmune disease
    Sarcoidosis
    Rheumatic fever
    Neoplasms
    Trauma
    Drugs
    Idiopathic

Masses

Neural tumors
    Neurofibroma
    Ganglioneuroma
    Pheochromocytoma
    Granular cell tumor

Thymic tumors
    Thymoma
    Carcinoid
    Carcinoma
    Hodgkin's disease

Lymphomas
    Hodgkin's disease
    Non-Hodgkin's lymphoma

Table 34–7 Pathologic Processes of the Mediastinum *(Continued)*

Germ cell tumors
   Teratoma/dermoid cyst
   Seminoma
   Embryonal cell carcinoma
   Choriocarcinoma

Cysts
   Thymic
   Bronchogenic
   Pericardial
   Esophageal duplication
   Mesothelial

Vascular lesions

Retrospective evidence has shown that clinical acumen should dictate diagnostic and therapeutic interventions. Surgery plays only a diagnostic role for lymphoproliferative diseases. Combination chemotherapy and radiation therapy are required depending upon the subtype and stage. Germ cell tumors occur primarily in the anterior mediastinum; elevated serum markers such as alphafetoprotein, human chorionic gonadotropin, and carcinoembryonic antigen are helpful in making the diagnosis. Most other solid masses should be managed with surgical resection, usually without biopsy. Mediastinal cysts are best removed if they are causing symptoms, are infected, or show a moderate growth rate. In the posterior compartment, neural tumors are the most common mediastinal masses overall. A dumbbell tumor, formed by both intraspinous and intrathoracic components, should be assessed by MRI; if present, surgical resection will necessitate both a thoracotomy and laminectomy.[105]

Thymic tumors represent 20 percent of all mediastinal masses and are predominantly in the anterior mediastinum. Primary resection should be performed whenever possible with complete removal of all thymic and fatty tissue. Simple enucleation, either by open technique or by VATS, has resulted in an unacceptable incidence of local recurrence.[106] Sternotomy remains the surgical approach of choice. However, several "cosmetic" modifications have been made to include inframammary, transverse sternal, and manubrial split incisions. Radiotherapy and chemotherapy for unresectable or recurrent lesions show early promising results, but there has been insufficient data to date.

The relationship between myasthenia gravis and parathymic syndromes remains unclear. Thymomas are present in 15 percent of myasthenic patients. Since Blalock's original observations in 1939,[107] thymectomy has clearly been shown to benefit those patients with myasthenia gravis. The procedure is usually reserved for patients who have become refractory to medical therapy, including immunosuppression, steroids, anticholinesterase drugs, and plasmapheresis. Preoperative preparation is essential for the success of surgery. High-dosage steroids are avoided, and cholinesterase inhibitors are withheld the night before surgery. Baseline pulmonary function is measured to help guide recovery.

As with resection for thymic tumors, all thymic and fatty tissue is removed in the superior and anterior mediastinum, with wide pleural dissection carefully preserving both phrenic nerves. Although sternotomy is the most commonly used incision for exposure, other techniques have evolved. An upper partial sternal splitting of the manubrium can provide good exposure in thin patients. A transcervical approach introduced in 1969[108] and later popularized by Cooper[109] has a more cosmetic appeal.

It is difficult to interpret the long-term result following thymectomy for myasthenia gravis because the natural history of these parathymic syndromes are so variable and recovery is ill defined. Irrespective of the surgical approach, adult patients without thymomas who undergo thymectomy have a tendency for more complete and persistent remissions than patients who do not undergo the procedure.[110] Reported operative benefits and remission rates vary from 80 to 95 percent and 21 to 52 percent, respectively.[80,90,111,112] One prospective study (by Olanow in 1982) confirmed that 83 percent of 47 patients who underwent thymectomy were free of weakness postoperatively and 61 percent were free of medication at 2 years.[113] Results are not as encouraging for patients with noninvasive thymoma and myasthenia gravis, and patients with the invasive type have the worst prognosis. Overall results and realistic expectations following thymectomy for myasthenia gravis by Kirschner[114] are outlined in Table 34–8.

CASE STUDY

Clinical Care Pathways

One effective way to improve the quality of patient care and surgical outcome is to provide a consistent level of care according to well-established treatment guidelines. Physician-directed diagnostic and therapeutic plans have been shown to be crucial in this area.[115] These have evolved into evidence-based patient care pathways, developed for a variety of disease processes requiring medical and surgical intervention.[116–120] Pathway implementation reduces hospital length of stay and significantly reduces diagnostic testing. Ultimately, this translates into postoperative cost containment in this era of rising health care costs and limited resources. Clear expectations on the part of the caregivers and the patients and their families have decreased the need for defensive medicine.[121]

Table 34–8 General Results of Thymectomy for Myasthenia Gravis

Age—young adults better	
Sex—female better	
Preoperative duration of symptoms—the shorter, the better	

Thymic pathology
  Hyperplasia better than atrophy
  Hyperplasia better than thymoma	

Prior medical therapy—the fewer medications, the better	

Type of thymectomy
  Transcervical—poorest
  Transsternal simple—better
  Transsternal extended—best
  Transcervical+transsternal—debatably best	

Surgical mortality—near 0%	
Surgical morbidity—low	

Remission
  Complete drug-free remission
  Drug-maintained remission
	25–50%
	10–20%
	15–30%

Improvement	35–50%
No change	10%
Worse or recurrence	Few

Based on institutional experience with thoracotomies for pulmonary resections, the author instituted a prospective, standardized clinical care pathway for all patients undergoing anatomic (segmentectomy, lobectomy, and pneumonectomy) lung resections via thoracotomy at the Johns Hopkins Hospital.[122] The creation and maintenance of this pathway has been a dynamic process. There were two goals set for pathway development and ongoing refinement. The first goal was to find out what tests and interventions were necessary to treat the ideal patient undergoing routine anatomical lung resections. Standardizing postoperative care by omitting superfluous tests would explain the observed initial decrease in cost of care. The second goal was to identify limiting factors in postoperative care that dictate the length of hospital stay for a given operative procedure and to see what could be done to optimally manage these factors. The premise was that many of the benchmarks for surgical care of the patient with lung cancer are based on historic clinical practice guidelines passed down, often unchallenged, through an apprenticeship program approach to care of these patients. As previously described in the literature review, acceptable and appropriate surgical approaches and techniques have been addressed in a multitude of studies and reports. The development of clinical care pathways affords an opportunity to apply these findings to the pre-, peri- and postoperative care of the patient. Challenging these guidelines through periodic and dynamic modification of the pathway has been a hallmark of care of these patients at Johns Hopkins. For lung resections, factors that affect length of stay include pain control, air leaks, supplemental oxygen requirements, and respiratory care. Therefore, measures to improve postoperative pain control and respiratory care, techniques to reduce lung air leaks, and better insight into the process of anastomotic healing would all be expected to reduce length of stay without compromising safety of care.

The purpose of this study was to assess the effects of these decision pathways on length of stay, hospital charges, and outcome following major thoracotomy procedures. All anatomic lung resections performed from July 1991 to July 1997 were retrospectively analyzed for these parameters. Although the clinical pathways were introduced in March 1994, the database for this study was developed prospectively. Patients were categorized into two groups depending on whether their procedure was performed before (group I) or after (group II) pathway implementation. Costs were categorized and compared by routine charges, operating room charges, pharmaceuticals, radiologic tests, laboratory tests, supplies, physical therapy charges, and miscellaneous costs.

The thoracotomy clinical pathway emphasizes operating room extubation and 12- to 24-hour intensive care unit monitoring. Patients are on telemetry, and their vital signs are continuously monitored. Postoperative analgesia is patient-controlled via an epidural catheter or intravenously. A postoperative chest film is obtained. Thereafter, one chest film per day is obtained until the chest drains are removed on postoperative day 3 or 4, depending on the presence of an air leak and the amount of drainage. On postoperative day 1, the patient is transferred to the ward. Supplemental oxygen is weaned. Laboratory testing is performed on postoperative day 1 and only when necessary thereafter. Early mobilization is stressed, beginning the night of surgery. The goal for discharge is postoperative day 6. Adjustments for constant dollars was made using inflation rates per year and were compounded yearly.

Results of this study are summarized in Table 34–9. The cost for group I lung resections trended downward compared to group II in actual dollars ($13,113 ± $10,711 vs $12,404 ± $7189, p = NS), but were significantly reduced when adjusted for inflation ($17,103 ± $13,211 vs $13,432 ± 8056, $p < .01$). This represented a savings of $170,628 in actual dollars and $854,029 in dollars adjusted for inflation, a decrease of 5.4 percent and 21 percent, respectively. Significant reductions (Figure 34–4) were observed in charges for pharmaceuticals and supplies as well as for miscellaneous and routine charges. Significant decreases in radiology and laboratory charges were not seen, and operating room charges were unaffected by pathway implementation. Actual costs and costs adjusted for inflation were significantly reduced

Table 34–9 Thoracotomy Clinical Care Pathway Results from The Johns Hopkins Hospital

	Group I	Group II	Significance*
Number	185	214	—
Actual costs	$13,113±$10,711	$12,404±$7,189	NS
Adjusted costs†	$17,103±$13,211	$13,432±$8,056	p < .01
Total savings‡			
Actual		$170,628 (↓5.4%)	
Adjusted		$854,029 (↓21%)	
Length of stay			
Preoperative	0.37±1.84	0.22±1.5	NS
Postoperative	7.6±5.6	6.1±3.4	p < .01
Total	8.0±6.2	6.4±3.8	p < .002
Mortality	0.5%	0.8%	NS

NS = not significant.

* Statistical analysis performed using two-tailed student t-test, significance $p < .05$.

† Adjustment for constant dollars made, using inflation rates per year and compounded yearly.

‡ Total savings comparing Group I and II.

from 1991 to 1997, from $14,553 to $11,980 and from $20,665 to $11,980, respectively (Figure 34–5). Despite the cost savings in most categories, mortality was not significantly affected (group I, 0.5%; group II, 0.8%).

INFLUENCE ON PRACTICE PATTERNS

Clinical Practice Guidelines

Non-Small Cell Lung Cancer

Due to the wide discrepancy in the diagnosis and treatment of non-small cell lung carcinoma (NSCLC) by caregivers from all specialties, the National Comprehensive Cancer Network (NCCN) was created to help standardize the clinical practice guidelines for this cancer and other primary cancers.[123] These guidelines, created from evidence-based historical work, provide step-by-step algorithms for evaluation, surgical and medical treatments, and follow-up surveillance for patients with NSCLC in all stages of disease. Despite a heterogeneous population of patients, these efforts should have the advantages of expediting diagnostic testing, increasing the resectability rate and thus prognosis, while lowering medical costs by the efficient use of current medical and technological resources.

Cardiothoracic Procedures

In 1989, the Council of The Society of Thoracic Surgeons decided to develop practice guidelines for cardiothoracic surgery. These guidelines were developed through extensive discussions, with conclusions reflecting the consensus of the cardiothoracic surgical community based on current clinical evidence and opinions. These guidelines were approved by all four major cardiothoracic surgical societies: The American Association for Thoracic Surgery, The

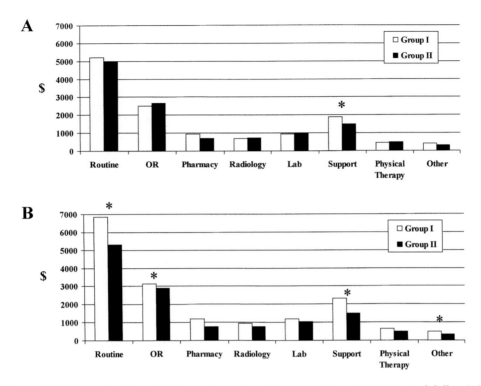

Figure 34–4 Categorized hospital charges for anatomic lung resection patients in actual dollars (A) and in constant dollars adjusted for inflation (B). (OR = operating room charges; Lab = laboratory charges; * = Group I vs Group II, $p < .01$).

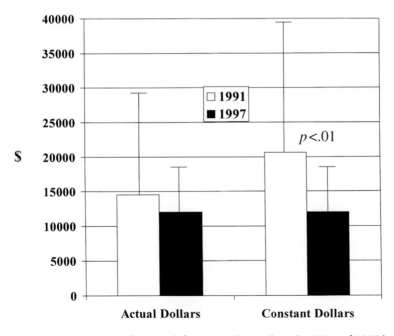

Figure 34–5 Decreasing charges of anatomic lung resection patients in 1991 and 1997 in actual and constant dollars adjusted for inflation.

Society of Thoracic Surgeons, the Southern Thoracic Surgical Association, and the Western Thoracic Surgical Association. The guidelines were procedure-oriented for both cardiac and general thoracic specific diseases, the latter including chest wall, diaphragm, mediastinum, and pericardium diseases;[124] bronchopulmonary disease;[125] VATS;[126] and cardiopulmonary transplantation.[127] These articles outline for each organ-specific procedure the commonly accepted criteria for the following parameters: diagnosis; procedure; indications; contraindications; actions prior to, during, and following the procedure; outcome, and; complications.

Clinical Care Pathways

Clinical care pathways were developed to standardize postoperative patient care. The primary impetus to develop clinical pathways was to improve the quality of care. However, in this day of rising health care costs and capitation, there has been tremendous pressure to reduce costs while maintaining quality of care. These pathways at the Johns Hopkins Hospital were designed to accomplish both goals. These methodologies have already been addressed in other areas of cardiothoracic surgical care, including coronary artery bypass surgery, thoracoscopic procedures, congenital heart surgery, and pulmonary lobectomies. The data suggest the ongoing dynamic nature of the pathways and their effect on costs. Though there has been a continuous decrease in both actual and inflation-adjusted dollars, the most rapid decline occurred in the early 1990s when cost containment became a priority due to changes resulting from pathway caregivers' feedback.

Clinical care pathways are particularly applicable to surgical services in large teaching hospitals where there is a steady stream of residents and fellows-in-training taking care of patients postoperatively. In these situations, there is tremendous variety of opinion regarding necessary tests and interventions for patient care. Costs directly controlled by the physician include the following categories: laboratory, radiologic, pharmaceutical, and operating room. Indirect and routine costs are influenced by length of stay. Reduction in variability of these costs is evidenced by a decrease in the standard deviation in all categories since the introduction of these pathways (see Figure 34–4 and 34–5). Residents and fellows learn a consistent pattern of care as opposed to a trial-and-error approach.

Reduced length of stay was the most significant component in cost reduction. Factors accounting for this include the earlier removal of chest tubes and the elimination of the preoperative day. Indirectly, improved pain management and earlier return to physical activity are associated with improved pulmonary function and earlier self-sufficiency, thus rendering patients for earlier discharge. Finally, morbidity, mortality and the need for early rehospitalization after discharge have remained low despite these substantial changes in clinical practice.

Video-Assisted Thoracic Surgery

A survey was recently conducted of predominantly academic general thoracic surgeons, asking the role of VATS in their practice and their opinions regarding the appropriate applications, advantages, and limitations of the approach.[128] Video-assisted thoracic surgery is considered the preferred procedure in the following conditions: (a) undiagnosed pulmonary infiltrate in the non-ventilator-dependent patient, (b) indeterminate pulmonary nodule, (c) undiagnosed disease of the pleural space, (d) recurrent or persistent pneumothorax, (e) mediastinal or pericardial cystic tumors, (f) conditions requiring thoracic sympathectomy, and (g) selected conditions requiring esophagocardiomyotomy. Unacceptable or investigational indications include thymectomy, lobectomy, and lung volume reduction operations. Video-assisted thoracic surgery still represents only a small portion of the thoracic procedures performed, but its rate of use has gradually increased although 38.1 percent of this group of academic thoracic surgeons expressed concern regarding overuse. The main limitation was thought to be in the management of oncologic disease. It appears that VATS is a valuable addition to the practice of thoracic surgery but significant limitations exist.

FUTURE STUDIES

Lung Cancer

There have been no major advances in the treatment of lung cancer for the past three decades. The overall 5-year survival rate remains 15 percent despite advances in surgical technique, chemotherapeutic agents, and radiotherapy protocols. A number of novel therapies lie on the horizon, including chemoprevention, gene therapy, anti-angiogenesis factor, and immuno-therapy (Table 34–10). However, human trials are still in early development, and any impact on long-term survival will take many years to develop. Currently, there are several areas on which to focus research efforts in improving lung cancer survival. These include (a) prevention by smoking cessation and chemoprevention; (b) early detection in the population at large and in high-risk groups; (c) improvement of preoperative patient selection, by cost-effective

Table 34–10 Future Studies in General Thoracic Surgery

Lung cancer
    Thoracoscopic vs open resection
    Neoadjuvant chemotherapy with or without radiation therapy
    Role of PET scanning in diagnosis and staging
    Early detection studies—population at large and high-risk groups
    Prevention—smoking cessation, chemoprevention
    Improving preoperative patient selection—cost-effective detection of metastasis, risk stratification
        for resection
    Predicting postoperative recurrence—locoregional and distal disease, second primary tumors
    Improving chemotherapy—predicting drug resistance, new more effective drugs
    Optimizing multimodality therapy—neoadjuvant therapy
    Faster clinical trials

Video-assisted thoracic surgery
    Diagnostic work-up for lung and esophageal cancer
    Lobectomy for benign and malignant processes
    Therapy for pulmonary metastases

Lung transplantation
    Best immunosuppressive therapy
    Induction therapy
    Best operation
    Increasing ischemic times
    Living-donor transplantation
    Quality of life
    Bronchiolitis obliterans

Lung volume reduction surgery
    Comparison to medical pulmonary rehabilitation therapy
    Bridge to transplantation
    Medical vs surgical therapy
    Open sternotomy vs closed thoracoscopy
    Unilateral vs bilateral approach
    Simultaneous approach vs two-stage operation
    Stapled vs laser
    Bovine pericardium vs polytetrafluoroethylene
    Management of incidental pulmonary nodules
    Simultaneous procedures: cancer resection, CABG, lung transplantation
    Cost-efficiency

PET = positron emission tomography; CABG = coronary artery bypass graft.

detection of metastasis and risk stratification for resection; (d) improvement in ability to predict postoperative recurrence from locoregional failure, distant metastasis, or second primary tumors; (e) development of better adjuvant chemotherapy and radiation therapy protocols; (f) development of new, more effective drugs; (g) optimization of multimodality therapy by adding neoadjuvant therapy modalities, and; (h) generation of faster clinical trials.

Video-Assisted Thoracic Surgery

Since the introduction of minimally invasive surgical techniques in thoracic surgery in 1990, VATS has become the approach for many thoracic operations. The role of VATS has slowly evolved but has not been clearly defined. The use of VATS for the management of lung cancer is currently undergoing investigation throughout the world, for it remains unknown whether VATS lobectomy provides adequate surgical resection and lymph node staging. Cost factors and the ability to palpate the remaining lung still have to be determined. Many traditional procedures requiring open thoracotomy are now being attempted via VATS to prove the efficacy in these areas. Other controversial areas are listed in Table 34–11. The role of VATS for resection of pulmonary metastases should be limited because of the high incidence of undetected second lesions found by palpation at the time of thoracotomy.[129] As with any new procedure, results from these operations should improve as surgical experience increases. Most of the techniques listed in Table 34–11 should be regarded as investigational, and future studies will critically evaluate these results and define limitations of the procedure with respect to overall cost, efficacy, safety, and clinical outcomes. The challenge in future years is not to determine whether a procedure can be performed via VATS but to determine (after weighing the risks and benefits) whether it should be done.

Lung Transplantation

Lung transplantation is now commonly accepted as a surgical alternative in patients with end-stage pulmonary disease. Though a vast number of registered programs exist, the more successful programs have a dedicated multidisciplinary approach to the evaluation, postoperative management, and long-term care of these complicated patients. However, the issues that continue to plague this area include the limited donor supply, the relative short allograft preservation times, the optimal immunosuppressive regimen, and the management of chronic allograft rejection. These inadequacies translate into a 5-year 50 percent actuarial survival rate in this patient population, the poorest rate of all the solid organs transplanted. Future prospective trials are needed to improve patient care strategies by working out these issues of lung preservation and immunosuppression, improving the management of bronchiolitis obliterans, determining the role of retransplantation, and clarifying the ethical and surgical issues surrounding living-donor lobar transplantation.

Lung Volume Reduction Surgery

Due to its widespread popularity and occasional overuse, lung volume reduction surgery (LVRS) was being billed to Medicare using a variety of current procedural terminology (CPT)

Table 34–11 Controversial Uses for Video-Assisted Thoracic Surgery

Lobectomy for bronchogenic carcinoma

Lung volume reduction surgery

Esophageal resection, reconstruction or fundoplication

Thymectomy for myasthenia gravis

Role for empyema

codes. Eventually, officials from the Health Care Financing Administration (HCFA) released information reporting a 1-year mortality rate of 26 percent in 700 Medicare patients who underwent LVRS in 1995 while many others suffered complications requiring further hospitalization.[130] Since that report, Medicare has refused to reimburse any type of lung volume reduction surgical procedure; many private insurance carriers and health maintenance organizations have followed the same guidelines, excluding it as a covered benefit. As the debate over reimbursement, efficacy, safety, selection criteria, technique, and results intensified, many investigators and patients voiced their strong objections to the HCFA, viewing it as a mistake for Medicare not to include LVRS as a covered benefit.

As a result of the controversial benefits, a unique study has been organized to establish a registry while examining the duration of benefits, safety, and costs of LVRS compared to optimal medical treatment and rehabilitation therapy. The National Emphysema Treatment Trial (NETT) was formed, cosponsored by HCFA and the National Institutes of Health (NIH), in which Medicare patients could be covered for the surgery if randomized to the surgical arm. Results, however, will not be known for 7 years, as 4,700 patients at 18 participating centers will be randomized into 1 of 3 study arms: medical therapy alone with rehabilitation therapy; bilateral LVRS via median sternotomy; or bilateral LVRS via thoracoscopy.

Though the true short- and long-term mortality rates from LVRS may not be known until the NETT is completed, some investigators estimate that late mortality approaches 50 percent. Prior historical controls have shown that certain subsets of patients with COPD managed medically have a 5-year survival rate of 40 to 60 percent. Thus, it remains to be seen how closely these two estimates converge and what impact LVRS has on this subset of patients.

Despite the lack of controlled studies and the cautiously optimistic early results, surgical experience thus far has generated a number of basic principles for evaluating any patient for LVRS which can sometimes be outweighed by the controversies generated (Table 34–12). Both LVRS and lung transplantation procedures are considered palliative. As with any novel therapy, more questions are raised than answered. In addition to the technical surgical debates listed, pulmonary specialists are not totally convinced of the beneficial effects of LVRS over aggressive medical management. To date, there are no consistent physiologic or pulmonary parameters that accurately predict postoperative outcome or duration of improvement. Since other disease states such as lung cancer and cardiac disease coexist with COPD, resection of incidental solitary pulmonary nodules and limited lung cancer[131–134] and coronary artery bypass grafting have been performed simultaneously with LVRS. Up to 40 percent of patients evaluated for LVRS were found to have asymptomatic pulmonary nodules, 6 percent of these being malignant in nature after resection.[135] The introduction of LVRS has thus added a new factor in the algorithm for the evaluation and treatment of lung cancer and coronary artery disease in selected patients previously considered ineligible because of advanced emphysema. Although associated with minimal morbidity and significantly improved pulmonary function and dyspnea, definite conclusions cannot be made based on the small experience in a highly select population. Candidates for LVRS combined with other procedures should be selected cautiously and studied further once LVRS alone is shown to be effective.

Due to cadaveric organ shortages, LVRS initially was thought of as a possible bridge to transplantation for those on the waiting list. In addition, it offered an alternative approach to a subpopulation of COPD patients who did not respond well to medical management but were not sick enough for transplantation, and it provided an option to those too old for transplantation. Since then, a number of small series have shown clearly that LVRS may obviate the need for transplantation, and Bavaria showed that 16 percent of patients failed LVRS, requiring listing for transplantation.[136,137]

Single lung transplantation has been an effective surgical option for COPD. The natural history of emphysema suggests that progression of disease in the native lung may contribute to late deterioration in respiratory function by compressing the contralateral transplant

Table 34–12 Lung Volume Reduction Surgery: Lessons and Controversies

Lessons Learned*	Controversies Created
The operation is palliative.	Medical vs surgical therapy
Adhere to patient selection criteria.	Essential pre- and postoperative testing
Preoperative rehabilitation therapy is essential.	Best surgical procedure
	Open sternotomy vs closed VATS
Don't oversell the procedure.	Uni- vs bilateral approach
Learn to say no to patients.	Stapled vs laser
	Bovine pericardium vs PTFE graft
Patients do not have to die on the operating table.	How much lung should be resected
	Management of incidental pulmonary nodules
Control anxiety preoperatively.	Cost-effectiveness vs that of medical therapy
Emphasize the unknown: complications and results.	Physiologic predictors of outcome
	Patient selection criteria
	Physiologic mechanisms altered by surgery
	A bridge to transplantation or obviates the need?
	Role of LVRS and transplantation: simultaneous or staged procedure
	Resection of localized carcinoma in high-risk patients
	Combined procedures: expanding role to perform simultaneous CABG

VATS = video-assisted thoracic surgery; PTFE = polytetrafluoroethylene; LVRS = lung volume reduction surgery; CABG = coronary artery bypass graft.
*Adapted from Miller JL Jr, Lee RB, Mansour KA. Lung volume reduction surgery: lessons learned. Ann Thorac Surg 1996;61:1464–6[89], and Utz JP, Hubmayr RD, Deschamps C. Lung volume reduction surgery for emphysema: out on a limb without a NETT. Mayo Clin Proc 1998;73:552–66.[144]

allograft. Although this phenomenon is uncommon, LVRS of the native lung in selected patients following transplantation has shown objective improvement in pulmonary function and exercise tolerance.[138,139] This approach has been extended at the time of initial transplantation, with minimal associated morbidity and good functional outcomes.[140] Unilateral LVRS may be considered as an alternative strategy in single lung transplant recipients with emphysema who exhibit clinically significant functional deterioration. However, it is necessary to differentiate between the adverse effects of hyperinflation of the native lung and other more common potential causes of late deterioration following transplantation. Further follow-up is required to assess the long-term results of this approach.

Finally, the cost-effectiveness of LVRS has not been fully assessed. Recently, Huizenga analyzed the cost data generated when Medicare reimbursed an estimated 1,200 procedures from 1994 to 1996.[141] The average Medicare reimbursement per procedure was $31,398, with total expenditures estimated between $30 million and $50 million. Other estimates projected that if only 10 percent of patients in the United States with emphysema were eligible candidates for LVRS, total direct costs would exceed $4.6 billion.[142] It is unknown whether the initial expense of the operation, barring major complications, would result in fewer dollars spent than for medical therapy, including outpatient clinic visits, medication, oxygen use, rehabilitation therapy, and hospitalization. These questions should be answered by the NETT.

The National Emphysema Treatment Trial is unique in that for the first time, a major new surgical therapy is being questioned about its benefits over medical therapy. Sponsored by the NIH but denied for coverage by Medicare, it is financially supported by the HCFA. In many circles, LVRS remains an experimental therapy. In light of continued increasing health care expenditures, LVRS represents a prime example of a procedure that demands proof that expensive therapy is beneficial. If successful, the NETT will provide powerful data for evidence-based surgery and become a benchmark for evaluating other potential advances in surgery.

Internet Resources

One of the more modern ways of efficient and up-to-date communication for evidence-based references is the Internet. A large number of organizations have taken advantage of this development to provide information and services for their members, patients, and other interested parties. These web sites also provide a secure environment for surgeons and organizations to communicate privately and also to share public databases, such as updates in transplantation statistics. They also provide an international forum for educational materials and communication among colleagues, allowing participants to stay abreast of current clinical trials and literature. In addition, full-text editions of major journals including the *Annals of Thoracic Surgery* and the *Journal of Thoracic and Cardiovascular Surgery* are accessible via certain web sites. Web site addresses pertinent to the field of thoracic surgery are listed in Table 34–13.

Conclusion

Innovation remains the building block of surgical progress. Creativity eventually gives way to the need for objective assessments to ensure that no harm is done, that the new is better than the old, and that patients are better off with these novel ideas. Such has been the evolution of general thoracic surgery over the past century. Once an area practiced by all surgeons, general thoracic surgery is now a practice fractionated into different specialties of oncology, transplantation, minimally invasive surgery, and emphysema. With an explosion of innovations in the past 15 years, these areas demand an evidence-based approach for the surgeon to better assimilate the massive amount of data generated and to curtail health care expenditures.

Table 34–13 Useful Thoracic Surgical Web Sites

Organization	Web Site Address	Area of Interest
American Lung Association	www.lungusa.org	Lung cancer, emphysema surgery
American Cancer Society	www.cancer.org	Thoracic oncology, clinical trials
American College of Chest Physicians	www.chestnet.org	Cardiopulmonary diseases, thoracic oncology, LVRS
American Society of Clinical Oncologists	www.asco.org	Thoracic oncology, clinical trials
Cardiothoracic Society Network	www.ctsnet.org	Thoracic surgery, on-line journals, LVRS forum
International Society for Heart and Lung Transplantation	www.ishlt.org	Transplant statistics
National Institutes of Health	www.nhlbi.nih.gov	NETT update
United Network for Organ Sharing	www.unos.org	Transplant statistics

LVRS = lung volume reduction surgery; NETT = National Emphysema Treatment Trial.

REFERENCES

1. Graham EA, Singer JJ. Successful removal of the entire lung for carcinoma of the bronchus. JAMA 1933;101:1371–5.

2. Rienhoff WF. Pneumonectomy. A preliminary report on the operative technique in two successful cases. Bull Hopkins Hosp 1933;55:390.

3. Churchill E, Belsey HR. Segmental pneumonectomy in bronchiectasis. Ann Surg 1939;109:481.

4. Bains M. Surgical treatment of lung cancer. Chest 1991;100:826–37.

5. Ginsberg RJ, Rubinstein LV. Randomized trial of lobectomy versus limited resection for T1N0 non-small cell lung cancer. Ann Thorac Surg 1995;60:615–23.

6. Warren WH, Faber LP. Segmentectomy versus lobectomy in patients with stage I pulmonary carcinoma: five-year survival and patterns of intrathoracic recurrence. J Thorac Cardiovasc Surg 1994;107:1087–94.

7. Errett LE, Wilson J, Chiu RC, Munro DD. Wedge resection as an alternative procedure for peripheral bronchogenic carcinoma in poor-risk patients. J Thorac Cardiovasc Surg 1985;90:656–61.

8. Read RC, Yoder G, Schaeffer RC. Survival after consecutive resection for T1N0M0 non-small cell lung cancer. Ann Thorac Surg 1990;49:391–400.

9. Ginsberg RJ, Hill LD, Eagan RT, et al. Modern thirty-day operative mortality for surgical resections in lung cancer. J Thorac Cardiovasc Surg 1983;86:654–8.

10. Cooper JD, Trulock EY, Triantafillon AN. Bilateral pneumectomy (volume reduction) for chronic obstructive pulmonary disease. J Thorac Cardiovasc Surg 1995;109:106–19.

11. Korst RJ, Ginsberg RJ, Ailawadi M, et al. Lobectomy improves ventilatory function in selected patients with severe COPD. Ann Thor Surg 1998;66:898–902.

12. Cahan WG, Watson WL, Pool JL. Radical pneumonectomy. J Thorac Cardiovasc Surg 1951;22:449–73.

13. Martini N, Flehinger BJ. The role of surgery in N2 lung cancer. Surg Clin North Am 1987;67:1037–49.

14. Naruke T, Suemasu K, Ishikawa S. Lymph node mapping and curability of various levels of metastases in resected lung cancer. J Thorac Cardiovasc Surg 1978;76:832–9.

15. Sagawa M, Saito Y, Takahashi S, et al. Clinical and prognostic assessment of patients with resected small peripheral lung cancer lesions. Cancer 1990;66:2653–7.

16. van Raemdonck DE, Schneider A, Ginsberg RJ. Surgical treatment for higher stage non-small cell lung cancer: a collective review. Ann Thorac Surg 1992;54:999–1013.

17. Izbicki JR, Thetter O, Habekost M, et al. Radical systematic mediastinal lymphadenectomy in non-small cell lung cancer: a randomized trial. Br J Surg 1994;81:229–35.

18. Hata E, Miyamoto H, Kohiyama R. Resection of N2/N3 mediastinal disease. In: Motta G, editor. Lung cancer frontiers in science and treatment. Genoa, Italy: Grafica LP; 1994. p. 431–44.

19. Mountain CF. A new international staging system for lung cancer. Chest 1986;89(Suppl):225S–33S.

20. Mountain CF. Revisions in the international system for staging lung cancer. Chest 1998;111:1710–17.

21. Giudicelli R, Thomas R, Lonjon T, et al. Video-assisted minithoracotomy versus muscle-sparing thoracotomy for performing lobectomy. Ann Thorac Surg 1994;58:712–18.

22. Kirby TJ, Mack MJ, Landreneau RJ, Rice TW. Lobectomy—video-assisted surgery versus muscle sparing thoracotomy. A randomized trial. J Thorac Cardiovasc Surg 1995;109:997–1002.

23. Piehler JM, Pairolero PC, Weiland LH, et al. Bronchogenic carcinoma with chest wall invasion: factors affecting survival following en bloc resection. Ann Thorac Surg 1982;34:684–91.

24. Burt M, Wronski M, Arbit E, Galicich JH. Resection of brain metastases from non-small-cell lung carcinoma. Results of therapy. J Thorac Cardiovasc Surg 1992;103:399–401.

25. Deslauriers J, Brisson J, Cartier R, et al. Carcinoma of the lung. Evaluation of satellite nodules as a factor influencing prognosis after resection. J Thorac Cardiovasc Surg 1989;97:504–12.

26. Callery CD, Holmes EC, Vernon S, et al. Resection of pulmonary metastases from nonseminomatous testicular tumors. Correlation of clinical and histological features with treatment outcome. Cancer 1983;51:1152–8.

27. Mazer TM, Robbins KT, McMurtrey MJ, Byers RM. Resection of pulmonary metastasis from squamous carcinoma of the head and neck. Am J Surg 1988;156:238–42.

28. Jett JR, Hollinger CG, Zinsmiester AR, Pairolero PC. Pulmonary resection of metastatic renal cell carcinoma. Chest 1983;884:442–5.

29. Schott G, Weissmuller J, Vecera E. Methods and prognosis of the extirpation of pulmonary metastases following tumor nephrectomy. Urol Int 1988;43:272–4.

30. Goya T, Miyazawa N, Kondo H, et al. Surgical resection of pulmonary metastases from colorectal cancer. 10-year follow-up. Cancer 1989;64:1418–21.

31. McAfee MK, Allen MS, Trastek VF, et al. Colorectal lung metastases: results of surgical excision. Ann Thorac Surg 1992;53:780–6.

32. Roth JA, Putnam JB, Wesley MN, Rosenberg S. Differing determinants of prognosis following resection of pulmonary metastases from osteogenic and soft-tissue sarcoma patients. Cancer 1985; 155:1361–6.

33. Lanza LA, Miser JS, Pass HI, Roth JA. The role of resection in the treatment of pulmonary metastases from Ewing's sarcoma. J Thorac Cardiovasc Surg 1987;94:181–7.

34. McCormack P. Surgical resection of pulmonary metastases. Semin Surg Oncol 1990;6:297–302.

35. Lanza LA, Natarajan G, Roth JA, Putnam JB. Long-term survival after resection of pulmonary metastases from carcinoma of the breast. Ann Thor Surg 1992;54:244–7.

36. Harpole DH Jr, Johnson CM, Wolf WG, et al. Analysis of 945 cases of pulmonary metastatic melanoma. J Thorac Cardiovasc Surg 1992;103:743–50.

37. Casson AG, Putnam JB, Natarajan G, et al. Efficacy of pulmonary metastasectomy for recurrent soft tissue sarcoma. J Clin Oncol 1991;47:1–4.

38. Jacobaeus HC. The cauterization of adhesions in pneumothorax treatment of tuberculosis. Surg Gynecol Obstet 1921;32:493–5.

39. McKneally MF. Video-assisted thoracic surgery. Standards and guidelines. Chest Surg Clin North Am 1993;3:345–51.

40. Ferson PF, Landreneau RJ. Thoracoscopic lung biopsy or open lung biopsy for interstitial lung disease. Chest Surg Clinic N Am 1998;8:749–62.

41. Hazelrigg SR, Magee MJ, Cetindag IB. Video-assisted thoracic surgery for diagnosis of the solitary lung nodule. Chest Surg Clin N Am 1998;8:763–74.

42. Sugarbaker DJ, Jaklitsch MT, Liptay MJ. Thoracoscopic staging and surgical therapy for esophageal cancer. Chest 1995;107:218S–223S.

43. Pellegrini CA, Leichter R, Patti M, Somberg K, et al. Thoracoscopic esophageal myotomy in the treatment of achalasia. Ann Thorac Surg 1993;56:680–2.

44. Maher JW. Thoracoscopic esophagomyotomy for achalasia. Maximum gain, minimum pain. Surgery 1997;122:836–40.

45. Ronson RS, Miller JI. Video-assisted thoracoscopy for pleural disease. Chest Surg Clin N Am 1998; 8:919–32.

46. Liu HP, Chang CH, Lin PJ, et al. Thoracoscopic management of effusive pericardial disease: indications and technique. Ann Thorac Surg 1994;58:1695–7.

47. Flores RM, Jaklitsch MT, DeCamp MM, Sugarbaker DJ. Video-assisted thoracic surgery pericardial resection for effusive disease. Chest Surg Clin N Am 1998;8:835–51.

48. Hazelrigg SR, Mack JM. Surgery for autonomic disorders. In: Kaiser LR, Daniel RM, editors. Thoracoscopic Surgery. Boston: Little, Brown and Company; 1993. p. 189.

49. Kadokura M, Colby TV, Myers JL, et al. Pathologic comparison of video-assisted thoracic surgical lung biopsy with traditional open lung biopsy. J Thorac Cardiovasc Surg 1995;109:494–8.

50. Molin LJ, Steinberg JB, Lanza LA. VATS increases costs in patients undergoing lung biopsy for interstitial lung disease. Ann Thorac Surg 1994;58:1595–8.

51. Ferguson MK. Thoracoscopy for diagnosis of diffuse lung disease. Ann Thorac Surg 1993;56:694–6.

52. Ferson PF, Landreneau RJ, Dowling RD, et al. Comparison of open versus thoracoscopic lung biopsy for diffuse infiltrative pulmonary disease. J Thorac Cardiovasc Surg 1993;106:194–9.

53. Bensard DD, McIntyre RC Jr, Waring BJ, Simon JS. Comparison of video thoracoscopic lung biopsy to open lung biopsy in the diagnosis of interstitial lung disease. Chest 1993;103:765–70.

54. Hardy JD, Webb WR, Dolton ML Jr. Lung transplantation in man: report of the initial case. JAMA 1963;186:1065–74.

55. Reitz BA, Burton NA, Jamieson SW, et al. Heart and lung transplantation: autotransplantation and allotransplantation in primates with extended survival. J Thorac Cardiovasc Surg 1980;80:360–72.

56. Cooper JD, Pearson FG, Patterson GA, et al. Technique of successful lung transplantation in humans. J Thorac Cardiovasc Surg 1987;93:173–81.

57. Cooper JD, Pearson GA, Grossman R, Maurer J. Double-lung transplant for advanced chronic obstructive lung disease. Am Rev Respir Dis 1989;139:303–7.

58. Pasque MK, Cooper JD, Kaiser LR, et al. An improved technique for bilateral lung transplantation: rationale and initial clinical experience. Ann Thorac Surg 1990;49:785–91.

59. Noirclerc MJ, Metras D, Vaillant A, et al. Bilateral bronchial anastomosis in double lung and heart-lung transplantations. Eur J Cardiothorac Surg 1990;4:314–17.

60. Triantafillou ANMK, Pasque CB, Huddleston CG, et al. Predictors, frequency and indications for cardiopulmonary bypass during lung transplantation in adults. Ann Thorac Surg 1994;57:1248–51.

61. The International Society for Heart and Lung Transplantation (ISHLT) 15th Annual Report. Web site: www.ishlt.org. Update April 1998.

62. United Network for Organ Sharing (UNOS). Web site: www.unos.org. Update 1998 July 31.

63. Division of Transplantation, Bureau of Health Resources Development. Transplant data: 1988–1994. 1995 Annual Report of the U.S. Scientific Registry for Transplant Recipients and the Organ Procurement and Transplantation Network Rockville (MD): Health Resources and Services Administration, U.S. Department of Health and Human Services; 1995.

64. deHoyos AL, Patterson GA, Maurer JR, et al. Pulmonary transplantation: early and late results. J Thorac Cardiovasc Surg 1992;103:295–306.

65. Patterson GA. Adult lung transplantation: introduction. Semin Thorac Cardiovasc Surg 1998; 10:190.

66. Trulock EP. Lung transplantation. Am J Respir Crit Care Med 1997;155:789–818.

67. Gross C, Savik K, Bolman RM, Hertz MI. Long-term health status and quality of life outcomes of lung transplant recipients. Chest 1995;108:1587–93.

68. Squier HC, Ries AL, Kaplan RM, et al. Quality of well-being predicts survival in lung transplantation candidates. Am J Respir Crit Care Med 1995;152:2032–6.

69. Cohen RG, Barr ML, Schenkel FA, et al. Living-related donor lobectomy for bilateral lobar transplantation in patients with cystic fibrosis. Ann Thorac Surg 1994;57:1423–8.

70. Starnes VA, Barr ML, Cohen RG. Lobar transplantation: indications, technique, and outcome. J Thorac Cardiovasc Surg 1994;108:403–11.

71. Deslauriers J. History of surgery for emphysema. Semin Thorac Cardiovasc Surg 1996;8:43–51.

72. Spear HG, Daughty DC, Chesney JG. The surgical management of large pulmonary blebs and bullae. Am Rev Respir Dis 1961;84:186.

73. Gaensler EA, Jederlinic PJ, Fitzgerald MX. Patient workup for bullectomy. J Thorac Imaging 1986; 1:75–93.

74. Hughes JA, MacArthur AM, Hutchinson DSC. Long term changes in lung function after surgical treatment of bullous emphysema in smokers and non-smokers. Thorax 1985;39:140.

75. Witz JP, Roeslin N. Surgery of bullous emphysema in the adult. Long-term results. Rev Fr Mal Respir 1980;8:121–31.

76. Connolly JE, Wilson A. The current status of surgery for bullous emphysema. J Thorac Cardiovasc Surg 1989;97:351–61.

77. Gunstensen J, McCormack RJM. The surgical management of bullous emphysema. J Thorac Cardiovasc Surg 1973;65:920–5.

78. Laros CD, Gelissen HJ, Bergstein PG, et al. Bullectomy for giant bullae in emphysema. J Thorac Cardiovasc Surg 1986;91:63–70.

79. Pearson MG, Ogilvie C. Surgical treatment of emphysematous bullae: late outcome. Thorax 1983; 38:134–7.

80. Diener CV, Burrows B. Further observations on the course and prognosis of chronic obstructive lung disease. Am Rev Resp Dis 1975;111:719–24.

81. Wakabayashi A, Brenner M, Kayaleh RA, et al. Thoracoscopic carbon dioxide laser treatment for bullous emphysema. Lancet 1991;337:881–3.

82. McKenna RJ Jr, Brenner M, Gelb AF, et al. A randomized, prospective trial of stapled lung reduction versus laser bullectomy for diffuse emphysema. J Thorac Cardiovasc Surg 1996;111:317–21.

83. Brantigan OC, Mueller E, Kress MB. A surgical approach to pulmonary emphysema. Am Rev Respir Dis 1959;80:195.

84. Cooper JD, Trulock EP, Triantafillou AN, et al. Bilateral pneumectomy (volume reduction) for chronic obstructive pulmonary disease. J Thorac Cardiovasc Surg 1995;109:106–19.

85. McKenna RJ Jr, Brenner M, Fischel RJ, et al. Patient selection criteria for lung volume reduction surgery. J Thorac Cardiovasc Surg 1997;114:957–64.

86. Slone RM, Glerada DS. Radiology of pulmonary emphysema and lung volume reduction surgery. Semin Thorac Cardiovasc Surg 1996;8:61–82.

87. Naunheim KS, Ferguson MK. The current status of lung volume reduction operations for emphysema. Ann Thorac Surg 1996;62:601–12.

88. Cooper JD, Patterson GA, Sundaresan RS, et al. Results of 150 consecutive bilateral lung volume reduction procedures in patients with severe emphysema. J Thorac Cardiovasc Surg 1996; 112:1319–29.

89. Miller JL Jr, Lee RB, Mansour KA. Lung volume reduction surgery: lessons learned. Ann Thorac Surg 1996;61:1464–8.

90. Martinez FJ, de Oca MM, Whyte RI, et al. Lung-volume reduction improves dyspnea, dynamic hyperinflation, and respiratory muscle function. Am J Respir Crit Care Med 1997;155:1984–90.

91. McKenna RJ Jr, Brenner M, Fischel RJ, Gelb AF. Should lung volume reduction for emphysema be unilateral or bilateral? J Thorac Cardiovasc Surg 1996;112:1331–8.

92. Petureau F, Krempf M, Berjaud J, et al. Long term survival after reduction surgery in eighteen emphysematous patients [abstract]. Am J Respir Crit Care Med 1996;153:A451.

93. Daniel TM, Chan BB, Bhaskar V, et al. Lung volume reduction surgery: case selection, operative technique, and clinical results. Ann Surg 1996;223:526–31.

94. Miller DL, Dowling RD, McConnell JW, Skolnick JL. Effects of lung volume reduction surgery on lung and chest wall mechanics. Presented at the 32nd Annual Meeting of the Society of Thoracic Surgeons; 1996 Jan 30; Orlando (FL).

95. Kotloff RM, Tino G, Bavaria JE, et al. Bilateral lung volume reduction surgery for advanced emphysema: a comparison of median sternotomy and thoracoscopic approaches. Chest 1996;110:1399–1406.

96. Hazelrigg SR, Boley TM, Magee MJ, et al. Comparison of staged thoracoscopy and median sternotomy for lung volume reduction. Ann Thorac Surg 1998;66:1134–9.

97. Date H, Goto K, Souda R, et al. Bilateral lung volume reduction surgery via median sternotomy for severe pulmonary emphysema. Ann Thorac Surg 1998;65:939–42.

98. Bingisser R, Zollinger A, Hause M, et al. Bilateral volume reduction surgery for diffuse pulmonary emphysema by video-assisted thoracoscopy. J Thorac Cardiovasc Surg 1996;112:875–82.

99. Brenner M, McKenna R, Fischel R, et al. Assessment of response in a large prospective trial of bilateral stapled lung volume reduction surgery for emphysema [abstract]. Chest 1996;110(Suppl):49S.

100. Keenan R, Sciurba F, Landreneau R. Superiority of bilateral versus unilateral thoracoscopic approaches to lung reduction surgery [abstract]. Am J Respir Crit Care Med 1996;153:A268.

101. Stammberger U, Thurnheer R, Bloch KE, et al. Thoracoscopic bilateral lung volume reduction for diffuse pulmonary emphysema. Eur J Cardiothorac Surg 1997;11:1005–10.

102. Vigneswaran WT, Podbielski FJ, Halldorsson A, et al. Single-stage, bilateral, video-assisted thoracoscopic lung volume reduction surgery for end-stage emphysema, Worl J Surg 1998;22:799–802.

103. Feigin DS, Padua EM. Mediastinal masses: a system for diagnosis based on computed tomography. J CT 1986;10:11–21.

104. Moore EH. Radiologic evaluation of mediastinal masses. Chest Surg Clin N Am 1992;2:1–22.

105. Grillo HC, Ojemann RG, Scannell JG, Zervas NT. Combined approach to "dumbbell" intrathoracic and intraspinal neurogenic tumors. Ann Thorac Surg 1983;36:402–7.

106. Warren WH, Gould VE. Epithelial neoplasms of the thymus. Chest Surg Clin N Am 1992;2:137–63.

107. Blalock A. Myasthenia gravis and tumors of the thymic region: report of a case in which the tumor was removed. Ann Surg 1939;110:544–6.

108. Kirschner PA, Osserman KE, Kark AE. Studies in myasthenia gravis: transcervical total thymectomy. JAMA 1969;209:906–10.

109. Cooper JD, Al-Jilaihawa AN, Pearson FG, et al. An improved technique to facilitate transcervical thymectomy for myasthenia gravis. Ann Thorac Surg 1988;45:242–7.

110. Monden Y, Nakahara K, Kagotani K, et al. Myasthenia gravis with thymoma: analysis of and postoperative prognosis for 65 patients with thymomatous myasthenia gravis. Ann Thorac Surg 1984; 38:46–52.

111. Jaretzki A III, Penn AS, Younger DS, et al. "Maximal" thymectomy for myasthenia gravis. J Thorac Cardiovasc Surg 1988;95:747–57.

112. Mulder DG, Graves M, Herrmann C. Thymectomy for myasthenia gravis: recent observations and comparisons with past experience. Ann Thorac Surg 1989;48:551–5.

113. Olanow CW, Wechsler AS, Roses AD. A prospective study of thymectomy and serum acetylcholine receptor antibodies in myasthenia gravis. Ann Surg 1982;196:113–21.

114. Kirschner PA. Myasthenia gravis and other parathymic syndromes. Chest Surg Clin N Am 1992; 2:183–99.

115. Hart RI, Musfeldt CM. MD-directed critical pathways: it's time. Hospitals 1992;66:56.

116. Musfeldt C, Hart RI. Physician-directed diagnostic and therapeutic plans: a quality cure for America's health-care crisis. J Soc Health Syst 1993;4:80–8.

117. Patton MD, Scaerf R. Thoracotomy, critical pathway, and clinical outcomes. Cancer Pract 1995; 3:286–94.

118. Wright CD, Wain JC, Grillo HC, et al. Pulmonary lobectomy patient care pathway: a model to control cost and maintain quality. Ann Thorac Surg 1997;6:299–302.

119. Velasco FT, Ko W, Rosengart T, et al. Cost containment in cardiac surgery: results with a critical pathway for coronary bypass surgery at the New York Hospital-Cornell Medical Center. Best Pract Benchmarking Healthcare 1996;1:21–8.

120. Cohen J, Stock M, Anderson P, Everts E. Critical pathways for head and neck surgery. Development and implementation. Arch Otolaryngol Head Neck Surg 1997;123:11–14.

121. Shulkin DJ, Ferniany IW. The effect of developing patient compendiums for critical pathways on patient satisfaction. Am J Med Qual 1996;11:43–5.

122. Zehr KJ, Dawson PB, Yang SC, Heitmiller RF. Standardized clinical care pathways for major thoracic cases reduce hospital costs. Ann Thorac Surg 1998;66:914–19.

123. Ettinger DS, Cox JD, Ginsberg RJ, et al. NCCN Non-Small-Cell Lung Cancer Practice Guidelines. The National Comprehensive Cancer Network. Oncology 1996;10(11 Suppl):81–111.

124. Kaiser GC. Practice guidelines: chest wall, diaphragm, mediastinum, pericardium. Ann Thorac Surg 1992;53:729–37.

125. Kaiser GC. Practice guidelines: bronchopulmonary disease. Ann Thorac Surg 1993;56:1203–13.

126. Kaiser GC. Practice guidelines: video-assisted thoracic surgery. Ann Thorac Surg 1994;58:596–602.

127. Kaiser GC. Practice guidelines: cardiopulmonary transplantation. Ann Thorac Surg 1994; 58:903–10.

128. Mack MJ, Scruggs GR, Kelly KM, et al. Video-assisted thoracic surgery: has technology found its place? Ann Thorac Surg 1997;64:211–15.

129. McCormack PM, Bains MS, Begg CB, et al. Role of video-assisted thoracic surgery in the treatment of pulmonary metastases: results of a prospective trial. Ann Thorac Surg 1996;62:213–16.

130. Vladeck BC. Testimony before the U.S. House of Representatives Ways and Means Subcommittee on Health (April 17, 1997).

131. Ojo TC, Martinez F, Paine R 3rd, et al. Lung volume reduction surgery alters management of pulmonary nodules in patients with severe COPD. Chest 1997;112:1494–1500.

132. Rozenshtein A, White CS, Austin JH, et al. Incidental lung carcinoma detected at CT in patients selected for lung volume reduction surgery to treat severe pulmonary emphysema. Radiology 1998;207:487–90.

133. DeMeester SR, Patterson GA, Sundaresan RS, Cooper JD. Lobectomy combined with volume reduction for patients with lung cancer and advanced emphysema. J Thorac Cardiovasc Surg 1998;115:681–8.

134. DeRose JJ Jr, Argenziano M, El-Amir N, et al. Lung reduction operation and resection of pulmonary nodules in patients with severe emphysema. Ann Thorac Surg 1998;65:314–18.

135. Hazelrigg SR, Boley TM, Weber D, et al. Incidence of lung nodules found in patients undergoing lung volume reduction. Ann Thorac Surg 1997;62:994–9.

136. Zenati M, Keenan RJ, Sciurba FC, et al. Role of lung reduction in lung transplant candidates with pulmonary emphysema. Ann Thorac Surg 1996;62:994–9.

137. Bavaria JE, Pochettino A, Kotloff RM, et al. Effect of volume reduction on lung transplant timing and selection for chronic obstructive pulmonary disease. J Thorac Cardiovasc Surg 1998;115:9–17.

138. Kroshus TJ, Bolman RM III, Kshettry VR. Unilateral volume reduction after single-lung transplantation for emphysema. Ann Thorac Surg 1996;62:363–8.

139. Anderson MB, Kriett JM, Kapelanski DP, et al. Volume reduction surgery in the native lung after single lung transplantation for emphysema. J Heart Lung Transplant 1997;16:752–7.

140. Khaghani A, al-Kattan KM, Tadjkarimi S, et al. Early experience with single lung transplantation for emphysema with simultaneous volume reduction of the contralateral lung. Eur J Cardiothorac Surg 1997;11:604–8.

141. Huizenga HF, Ramsey SD, Albert RK. Estimated growth of lung volume reduction surgery among Medicare enrollees: 1994 to 1996. Chest 1998;114:1583–7.

142. Albert RK, Lewis S, Wood D, Benditt JO. Economic aspects of lung volume reduction surgery. Chest 1996;110:1068–71.

143. Keenan RJ, Landreneau RJ, Sciurba FC, et al. Unilateral thoracoscopic surgical approach for diffuse emphysema. J Thorac Cardiovasc Surg 1996;111:308–15.

144. Utz JP, Hubmayr RD, Deschamps C. Lung volume reduction surgery for emphysema: out on a limb without a NETT. Mayo Clin Proc 1998;73:552–66.

CHAPTER 35

Cardiac Surgery

Peter S. Greene, MD, FACS, and William A. Baumgartner, MD

Perhaps no surgical specialty has been called upon to defend its indications, alternatives, and outcomes so thoroughly as has cardiac surgery. There is good reason for the intense interest: cardiac surgical procedures can be risky, invasive, and expensive. Shortly after its birth, the specialty faced demands for a randomized controlled trial to demonstrate the efficacy of coronary artery bypass grafts (CABGs), and the need for evidence of efficacy has only increased as less-invasive and less-expensive catheter-based procedures have evolved. In 1996, an estimated 598,000 patients had coronary bypass grafts performed in the United States at an estimated cost of $44,820 per person.[1] With this enormous expenditure, analysis of outcomes is no longer left to clinicians and researchers but now involves a plethora of federal and state regulatory agencies, third- party payer organizations, and (most recently) the media.

As interest shifted to measuring individual provider performance, many cardiac surgeons rebelled at the external scrutiny and raised valid objections to the methods and motives of those monitoring their services. But increasingly, there is recognition inside the profession that performance monitoring is an essential part of good care delivery, and most cardiac surgeons have become focused on outcomes measurement.

The quest for risk-adjusted performance metrics distinguishes cardiac surgery from most other surgical specialties and will be the focus of this chapter. Three critical questions need to be addressed:

1. Will risk assessment allow better prediction of patient outcomes?
2. Will risk adjustment enable accurate measurement of surgeon and hospital performance?
3. Will monitoring of risk-adjusted performance lead to better clinical care?

To be meaningful, risk-adjustment endeavors must allow these questions to be answered in the affirmative. Randomized trials have shown that despite carrying the greatest operative risk, the sickest patients with the most damaged hearts often benefit the most from surgical procedures.[2] Auditing performance without appropriately factoring in the severity of illness is unfair to surgeons, who will inevitably respond by denying surgical services to high-risk patients. On the other hand, optimizing the surgeon's understanding of risk and outcomes and delivering useful performance information may improve patient care.

DEFINITION OF TERMS

Outcomes are health-related end products that can be measured after some episode of care. To be meaningful, the outcomes under study must be important to patients or to the health care system as a whole, relatively common, and linked temporally and causally to the care provided.[3]

The term "risk adjustment" can have one of two meanings, depending upon one's purpose: (1) to assess patient-related comorbidities as a first step in monitoring the quality of clinical care, or (2) to predict resource consumption and to modify payments to hospitals or doctors. The former definition is intended in this chapter. Risk adjustment has come into favor over a number of other frequently ill-defined terms and phrases (such as case mix, severity, sickness, intensity, complexity, comorbidity, and health status).[4]

Reliability refers to the degree to which different observers quantify risk in a similar way for each case. As an example of a problematic area, the reliability of hospital coding practices may be low, especially if financial motives vary. As data are abstracted from medical records, reliability is affected by a number of factors including

- the clarity and definition of requested data elements,
- the rules established for interpreting terminology,
- subjective reviewer judgments,
- the preference for physician versus nonphysician data, and
- the legibility, completeness, and timeliness of the medical records.

The greatest threat to reliability is not random error but the potential for data manipulation. The possibility of "gaming" the system has been well documented[5] and has brought into focus the need for the auditing of individual reporting units.[6]

Statistical performance refers to how well a risk-adjustment model actually predicts outcomes. Most biomedical events cannot be modeled perfectly. From a statistical perspective, regression models explain part of the variability in operative mortality, but the residual variability might be explained by uncollected variables or random variation. Assessment of the capability of the model is therefore important. Performance can be further characterized by discrimination (ie, how well the model distinguishes between different outcomes) and calibration (ie, how well a model overestimates or underestimates risk in specified ranges).[7]

REVIEW OF RISK-ASSESSMENT INITIATIVES

By far, the bulk of available experience with risk stratification in cardiac surgery deals with risk factors associated with operative mortality in patients undergoing coronary bypass grafting. Other outcomes, such as quality of life or resource use, have also been studied. For the large reporting initiatives, however, operative mortality is an easily defined and readily measured outcome, and its value to patients is undeniable.

The Northern New England Cardiovascular Disease Study Group

In 1987, a group of medical centers in Maine, New Hampshire, and Vermont began to track clinical outcomes of all cardiovascular procedures to determine whether feedback and training in quality improvement techniques would improve hospital mortality rates.[8] This Northern New England Cardiovascular Disease Study Group (NNECVDSG) has undertaken a number of innovative approaches not only to gathering data but also to making specific interventions based on their analyses.

After collecting a broad range of demographic, historical, and physiologic data, both pre- and post-CABG, the group implemented three interventions: (1) centers were given risk-adjusted feedback on their results, (2) all providers were given training in continuous quality improvement techniques, and (3) site visits were conducted by multidisciplinary teams to one another's institutions. During visits, all aspects of care were examined, including decision making, surgical technique, work environments, and leadership. Borrowing from the Total Quality Management (TQM) approaches used in industry,[9] process control techniques were implemented to correct deficiencies. A critical concern was to give providers simple, graphic displays of results on an ongoing basis.[10] In a 1996 report, the group found that these interventions reduced the in-hospital mortality rate for CABGs in their centers by 24 percent.[8]

The NNECVDSG also focused on "critical pathways," studying two postoperative events in detail: (1) transfer from the cardiothoracic intensive care unit, and (2) discharge from the hospital. Key milestones that had to be achieved before the patient could be advanced were identified. Pathway progress charts were made available at the bedside to all caregivers, and the staff was given extensive instruction. After 12 months, the median length of stay for patients undergoing primary elective CABGs had decreased from 7 to 6 days, with an increase of 20 to 40 percent in the number of patients discharged at 5 days or less.[10]

At the heart of the NNECVDSG effort is a respected risk-adjustment model, which allows examination of differences in results at different institutions. Because the program was comprehensive and credible, the initial findings of "nonrandom" variations in mortality were taken seriously by providers.[10] The program is an outstanding illustration of how outcomes can actually lead to improved results.

New York State

Another important initiative, conducted on a statewide level, is the Cardiac Surgery Reporting System (CSRS) of New York. Beginning in 1989, a Cardiac Advisory Committee, composed of practicing New York cardiac surgeons, cardiologists, and advisors, designed a data collection form for tracking all cardiac surgical cases in the state. All hospitals were required to complete the data collection process at the time of discharge for every patient. A similar collection process was initiated for catheter-based revascularization.

The process was begun with the intention of making data available to hospitals. However, because the process was conducted by the state, the publication *Newsday* was able to sue for public release of the information under a state freedom-of-information act. The suit was successful, and surgeon- and hospital-specific information was released to the public by the lay press.

Both this public reporting and the analysis of the influence of such public reporting were controversial. It has been claimed that there has been a decline in risk-adjusted mortality rates for patients undergoing CABGs in New York. The inference is that the CSRS increased pressure on surgeons and hospitals to perform optimally, leading to improved results. But alternative suggestions have been proposed; namely, that surgeons may have refused to operate on high-risk patients or that providers may have misrepresented preoperative risk factors to improve their risk-adjusted mortality rates.

These claims have been difficult to substantiate. The Cleveland Clinic reported that New York State residency was an independent risk factor in their CABG patient population,[11] and at least one New York hospital admitted to turning down high-risk patients specifically to improve reported CABG outcomes.[12] Recently, a survey of practicing surgeons showed that 62 percent had refused surgery to at least one high-risk CABG patient in the prior year, primarily due to public reporting.[13] Clearly, there has been significant distrust of the process by a large number of New York surgeons and hospitals.

There have been some clearly positive outcomes from the CSRS. Dziuban and colleagues reported that after their hospital was initially identified as a high-mortality outlier, clinician frustration and skepticism was overcome, and a careful investigation led to specific improvements.[14] In this particular case, the excess mortality occurred only in high-risk patients, and the cardiology and cardiac surgical teams modified their care by increasing the use of intra-aortic balloon pumps to stabilize patients prior to surgery.

Society of Thoracic Surgeons Database

In 1987, The Society of Thoracic Surgeons (STS) recognized the need to offer members a way to benchmark their surgical results. A volunteer national database effort was begun, and the first results were reported in 1990. The database has grown into the largest collection of data on coronary artery bypass grafting, and the 1997 report included approximately 1.2 million patients from 500 different sites.[15]

Voluntary data collection projects are challenging, and the STS has faced a number of problems. Several years into the project, the STS recognized that a method of checking completeness and accuracy at the provider level was essential to ensure credibility. An Audit and Validation Subcommittee was formed in 1996 to address these issues, and an Expert Advisory Panel was formed to ensure the high quality of the information collected. Because the data were gathered from many different states and legal jurisdictions, the effort has been hampered by the differing local requirements for tracking identifiers for either patients or surgeons. This inability to track identifiers has proved to be a major impediment to more comprehensive data collection. The complete STS data set encompasses more than 400 elements, and some units are unable to collect this complex data set, a circumstance that reduces the reliability and validity of the project to the lowest common denominator. Nonetheless, the STS project has been a remarkably successful volunteer effort, and its usefulness for improving clinical care has been well described for both individual programs[16] and regional database projects.[17] A summary of the critical variables and odds ratios for predicting operative mortality following CABG is shown in Table 35–1.

Table 35–1 Variables and Odds Ratios of Operative Mortality for Coronary Artery Bypass Grafting*

Variable	Odds Ratio
Age (in 10-year increments)	1.640
Female gender	1.157
Noncaucasian ethnic group	1.249
Ejection fraction	0.988
Diabetes	1.188
Renal failure	1.533
Serum creatinine (if renal failure is present)	1.080
Dialysis dependence (if renal failure is present)	1.381
Pulmonary hypertension	1.185
Cerebrovascular accident timing	1.198
Chronic obstructive pulmonary disease	1.296
Peripheral vascular disease	1.487
Cerebrovascular disease	1.244
Acute evolving, extending myocardial infarction	1.282
Myocardial infarction timing	1.117
Cardiogenic shock	2.211
Use of diuretics	1.122
Hemodynamic instability	1.747
Triple-vessel disease	1.155
Left main disease > 50%	1.119
Preoperative intra-aortic balloon pump	1.480
Urgent or emergent status	1.189
Emergent salvage	3.654

Table 35–1 Variables and Odds Ratios of Operative Mortality for Coronary Artery Bypass Grafting* *(continued)*

Variable	Odds Ratio
First reoperation	2.738
Multiple reoperations	4.282
Arrhythmias	1.099
Body surface area	0.488
Obesity	1.242
New York Heart Association class IV	1.098
Use of steroids	1.214
Congestive heart failure	1.191
Percutaneous transluminal coronary angioplasty within 6 hours of surgery	1.332
Angiographic accident with hemodynamic instability	1.203
Use of digitalis	1.168
Use of intravenous nitrates	1.088

* Society of Thoracic Surgeons logistic regression model.[15]

METHODOLOGICAL DIFFICULTIES

Data Collection

At first glance, it might appear easy to collect data on cardiac operations. The life-or-death outcome is a simple measure, and there seems to be a plethora of hemodynamic and clinical information that is collected in the medical record during patient evaluation.

But standardization of risk factor and event definitions has proved to be a significant challenge. Some variables (such as age, gender, and reoperation status) are easy to define. But the critical factor of left ventricular function, for example, can be measured in many different ways and can vary with the patient's instantaneous hemodynamic condition. Some functional measurements (such as renal function) can vary significantly during the preoperative evaluation period. Other factors, such as urgency of operation, chronic obstructive pulmonary disease, or peripheral vascular disease, suffer from vague definitions. Even mortality, which would seem to be easy to measure, has proved complex due to variations in tracking in-hospital versus 30-day mortality and the difficulty of handling the transfer of patients to rehabilitation facilities.[18]

Comprehensive data collection is also challenging and expensive. Software tools are often cumbersome and poorly integrated with workflow for clinicians, requiring most practices to have separate data collection staff, which adds to the administrative costs of delivering cardiac surgical care. There is an alarming possibility that the hospitals that incur the considerable logistic costs of collecting and analyzing risk data may be more expensive and may therefore become less attractive to payers. Ultimately, improved quality will be cost-efficient, but the start-up costs are daunting.[17]

Data Analysis

The analysis phase also has its pitfalls. The cost of data collection leads to parsimonious models, frequently borrowed from existing data information systems such as administrative and billing databases. But these systems were designed to predict resource consumption, not mortality. Surgeons are rightly suspicious of the clinical accuracy of information derived from billing activities; even for the intended financial purpose of such activities, there are significant concerns about their reliability and completeness. Mistrust of administrative data overwhelms recognition of the important virtue of their ready availability for population-based comparisons.

Mathematical regression models, which underpin most risk-adjustment efforts, can also be problematic. With current software tools, sophisticated analyses such as multiple logistic regression are easy to perform but much more difficult to interpret. The mathematical rigor of these models might tempt one to believe that they can control for all variables and answer all questions, but this is not the case. The complexity of biologic and medical events defies all current modeling approaches, and few physicians have the statistical sophistication to really understand the capabilities and limitations of these approaches.[19] One survey of New York cardiologists showed that only a small fraction were significantly skeptical about the reliability of the analyses.[20]

Given the importance of this endeavor, more attention needs to be paid to model performance. Surprisingly little work has been done in assessing the reliability and validity of risk-adjustment methods used with large cardiac surgical databases. Efforts to create some kind of model can nearly always be made successfully, yet there is no minimum standard for risk adjustment.[19] What sample size is required to distinguish the signal from the noise? What is the reliability? How well must a model perform before it can be said that outcomes are adjusted for risk? Some analyses fail to report any measure of the "goodness-of-fit" for the data being analyzed; those that do report it typically report the area under the Receiver Operator Characteristic (ROC) curve (Figure 35-1), or c-statistic. In most analyses, this statistic never reaches above approximately 0.75, which is midway between a useless (0.5) and perfect (1.0) model.[21] So, in a rough sense, the variables in the model explain only half of the story.

Result Interpretation

The interpretation phase introduces more complexity. Studies from the New York[22] and Pennsylvania[23] database projects show that year-to-year variation in death rates for individual surgeons can be substantial even when fully risk adjusted. Does this represent performance variation or noise in the model? For surgeons, this question can threaten the credibility of an entire project. Many clinicians find themselves intuitively suspicious of the process but feel unqualified to mount a statistical defense of their views. Is the process fair if all programs and surgeons are subjected to the same limited methodology?[24]

There is rarely any solid evidence that differences in risk-adjusted mortalities across providers reflect real differences in the quality of care. Although this connection may seem obvious, it is far from proven. The little information available is inconsistent. Hartz and Kuhn found that differences in mortality rates appeared to correlate with differences in care,[25] but one study from New York suggested that nearly all variations in mortality among hospitals reflected variation in patient characteristics rather than hospital processes.[26] In statistical terms, the residual variability in operative mortality may be explained by risk factors omitted from the regression models. New putative risk factors may improve the validity and precision of the model and change the assessment of the quality of care dramatically.

Even if shown to measure quality of care, outcomes measurement in isolation cannot improve quality of care. There is no direct information on why one center or physician might have superior or inferior results. If poor performance is identified, what is the next step? Constructive use of outcomes information is an enormous challenge, and failure at this stage

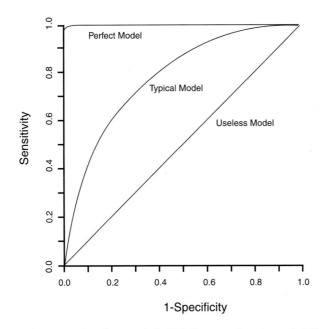

Figure 35–1 A receiver operating characteristic (ROC) curve plots the probability of a true positive result (sensitivity) against the probability of a false positive result (1-specificity) over a range of cut-offs. The c-statistic measures the area under the ROC curve. A perfect model would have an area of 1.0, and a useless model (equal false positive and false negative rates at all cutoffs) would be a diagonal line (area = 0.5). Typically, models fall somewhere in between these values.

undermines even the highest-quality information. The Northern New England Cardiovascular Disease Study Group (NNECVDSG) and the Veteran's Administration Cardiac Surgery Risk Assessment Program teams have begun to address the question of what to do after collecting and analyzing the data. Future reports from these efforts will likely better define what outcomes measures mean for the quality of care.

Patient Counseling

Deficiencies in modeling and result interpretation can become obvious when one is trying to predict risks for individual patients.[26] The best models may have relatively good calibration in most levels except that of high-risk patients, because of problems with modeling unusual but important risk factors and other statistical anomalies that arise when risk factors are highly correlated. Models that break down at the perimeter of the statistical analysis can further contribute to clinician frustration. It is precisely for these high-risk patients that the surgeon would most like to have an accurate assessment of risk for preoperative counseling.

Result Reporting

No issue in cardiac surgery outcomes analysis has stimulated controversy more than the public unveiling of program- and surgeon-specific data. In most of the state and federally funded initiatives, public disclosure has been out of the hands of surgeons. When this information appears in the media, headlines are not always well supported by evidence, and often little attention is paid to the quality of the data or the reliability of the analyses.[27] It is not surprising that patients are interested in seeing whatever information is available, regardless of its quality. Although the process has appalled surgeons, one study from Pennsylvania has shown almost no change in referral patterns as a result of the public release of quality data.[23] Freedom-of-information laws will likely continue to drive the disclosure process, and most surgeons have decided that the best strategy is to improve the quality of the risk-assessment process.

Few would question that the public has a right to know that surgeons are watching themselves to ensure that performance standards are met. The hazards of failing to maintain this surveillance was demonstrated dramatically by the Bristol affair in the United Kingdom. Two pediatric cardiac surgeons were identified as having poor clinical outcomes for several congenital cardiac procedures. Internal auditing systems failed, and eventually there was widespread media exposure of the poor results. The surgeons were found guilty of serious professional misconduct by the General Medical Counsel and were struck from the medical register. When the failure of the surgical community to monitor its own performance was exposed, the tide of public opinion turned rapidly against the entire profession.[28] In the end, the public's confidence in the medical profession was damaged.[29]

FUTURE APPROACHES TO RISK ADJUSTMENT

Advanced Statistical Techniques

One critical weakness of current approaches to risk adjustment is that a variable may contribute significantly to outcomes but occur too infrequently to be useful in a multiple regression analysis. Statistical techniques such as cluster analysis or neural networks may provide a way to incorporate this kind of rare but essential information into the risk-adjustment process.[18] Both techniques involve pattern detection approaches that might be relevant for unusual clinical events. An initial investigation of a neural network approach, however, did not show any enhanced predictive ability;[30] this artificial intelligence technique failed to improve upon the ROC curve of logistic regression. But the investigation did not involve adding any additional, unusual clinical variables and therefore may not have been an optimal test of the technique.

Enhanced Information Management

Risk stratification depends upon complete and accurate clinical data. The fallibility of claims databases is well recognized, and this has led to greater interest in getting more important clinical information out of the medical record. Unfortunately, few patient records are electronic, and even those that are lack standards that would allow risk-adjustment information to be collected in an automated fashion. For the monitoring of patient outcomes to be cost-effective, considerable progress must be made in this area.

Cost of Care Management

Lurking behind the interest in outcomes data is the issue of cost containment and resource use. Generally, newer treatments are unlikely to be less expensive, and the young specialty of cardiac surgery has been closely tied to innovation and new technology. Payers might use outcomes data as a way to manage costs and control medical practice. Such an approach may adversely influence patient care since physicians or hospitals may be less willing to accept difficult cases.

Disease-Based Tracking

One enormous failure of many current efforts is that only data on patients undergoing operations are tracked. Limiting the patient population for outcomes-driven quality assessment to procedures offers no information about underuse of the procedures. Of much greater interest would be the outcomes of all patients with similar presentations of illness, whether or not the patients were operated upon. Surgeons should be measured by the patients whom they turn down for surgery as well as by those upon whom they operate. The current system is bound to penalize surgeons who are willing to tackle difficult cases. No amount of risk adjustment can compensate for this failure to track critical information.

CONCLUSION

The goal of risk adjustment is to determine the contribution of patient-related risk factors so that patient outcomes can be used to measure the performance of providers and so that hospitals can be assessed on the basis of outcomes. This chapter has outlined some of the serious pitfalls in the process as it has been performed with existing data sets and methodologies. Cardiothoracic surgery has found itself at the forefront of these efforts and has often suffered from "bleeding edge" methodology and a lack of sophistication on the part of all interested parties. Despite these shortcomings and recent reports noting the failure of physician profiling,[31] risk analysis needs to become an increasingly important part of clinical care. Refinements in the process will need to occur at many levels of health care delivery and will include the following:

1. Tracking of useful clinical data in electronic information systems as a part of clinical care
2. Broadening of focus from procedures to populations of patients with identified illness or symptoms
3. Interdisciplinary collaboration to transfer outcomes information into common clinical practice
4. Refinement of data analyses to improve and measure the utility of adjustment models
5. Establishment of minimum standards for model reporting so that low-utility reports, which undermine the credibility of the process, can be avoided
6. Acknowledgment of the limitations of these models for detecting some of the points of interest (such as whether they measure quality)
7. Education of the medical community and the public on the proper use of outcomes information

Dr. Paul Ebert, former president of the American College of Surgeons, has noted that we are in a transition stage from the widespread use of clinical judgment to the use of risk-adjusted outcomes data for clinical decision making, with our methods of using data still infantile.[27] At this point, it is best to heed the advice of one of the recognized fathers of outcomes analysis, A. Donabedian: "Outcomes are much more easily used ... only as cues that prompt and motivate the assessment of process and structure in a search for causes that can be remedied."[32]

Beyond improved risk-adjustment analyses, cardiac surgery outcomes research in the future will likely focus on the efficacy and effectiveness of minimally invasive cardiac surgery, alternatives to cardiac surgery, and the application of patient-reported measures. In the decision process of cardiac surgery, locus of care is also likely to be a focus of attention, as community hospital-based programs have proliferated in spite of the well-documented volume-outcome relationship in cardiac surgery. Finally, the principles of evidence-based medicine will no doubt be applied to cardiac surgery for use in treatment planning for the individual patient, based on experimental and observational studies.

REFERENCES

1. American Heart Association Web site [accessed 1999 Sep 1] Available from: URL: http://www.americanheart.org/Heart_and_Stroke_A_Z_Guide/openh.html.

2. Keogh BE, Dussek J, Watson D, et al. Public confidence and cardiac surgical outcome. BMJ 1998; 316:1759–60.

3. Iezzoni LI. Using risk-adjusted outcomes to assess clinical practice: an overview of issues pertaining to risk adjustment. Ann Thorac Surg 1994;58:1822–6.

4. Iezzoni LI. The risks of risk adjustment. JAMA 1997;278:1600–7.

5. Hofer TP, Hayward RA, Greenfield S. The unreliability of individual physician "report cards" for assessing the costs and quality of care of a chronic disease. JAMA 1999 Jun 9;281:2098–105.

6. Shroyer AL, Edwards FH, Grover FL. Updates to the data quality review program: The Society of Thoracic Surgeons Adult Cardiac National Database. Ann Thorac Surg 1998;65:1494–7.

7. Steen PM. Approaches to predictive modeling. Ann Thorac Surg 1994;58:1836–40.

8. O'Connor GT, Plume SK, Olmstead EM, et al. A regional intervention to improve the hospital mortality associated with coronary artery bypass graft surgery. The Northern New England Cardiovascular Disease Study Group. JAMA 1996 Mar 20;275(11):841–6.

9. Wheeler DJ, Chambros DS. Understanding statistical process control. Knoxville (TN): SPC Press; 1992.

10. Nugent WC, Schults WC. Playing by the numbers: how collecting outcomes data changed by life. Ann Thorac Surg 1994 Dec;58(6):1866–70.

11. Omoigui NA, Miller DP, Annan K, et al. Outmigration for coronary bypass surgery in an era of public dissemination of clinical outcomes. Circulation 1996 Jan 1;93(1):27–33.

12. Topol EJ, Califf RM. Score card cardiovascular medicine: its impact and future direction. Ann Intern Med 1994;120:65–70.

13. Burack JH, Impellizzeri P, Homel P, Cunningham JN. Public reporting of surgical mortality: a survey of New York State cardiothoracic surgeons. Ann Thorac Surg 1999;68:1195–200.

14. Dziuban SW, McIlduff JB, Miller SJ, Dal Col RH. How a New York cardiac surgery program uses outcomes data. Ann Thorac Surg 1994;58:1871–6.

15. Shroyer AL, Plomondon ME, Grover FL, Edwards FH. The 1996 coronary artery bypass risk model: the Society of Thoracic Surgeons Adult Cardiac National Database. Ann Thorac Surg 1999 Apr;67:1205–8.

16. Nikas DJ, Freeman JE, Luterman AR, et al. Use of a national database to assess perioperative risk, morbidity, mortality, and cost savings in coronary artery bypass grafting. South Med J 1996 Nov;89(11):1074–7.

17. Arom KV, Petersen RJ, Orszulak TA, et al. Establishing and using a local/regional cardiac surgery database. Ann Thorac Surg 1997 Nov;64(5):1245–9.

18. Hammermeister KE, Daley J, Grover FL. Using outcomes data to improve clinical practice: what we have learned. Ann Thorac Surg 1994 Dec;58(6):1809–11.

19. Krumholz HM. Mathematical models and the assessment of performance in cardiology. Circulation 1999;99:2067–9.

20. Hannan EL, Stone CC, Biddle TL, DeBuono BA. Public release of cardiac surgery outcomes data in New York State. What do New York State cardiologists think of it? Am Heart J 1997;124:1120–8.

21. Ivanov J, Tu JV, Naylor CD. Ready-made, recalibrated, or remodeled? Issues in the use of risk indexes for assessing mortality after coronary artery bypass grafting. Circulation 1999;99:2098–104.

22. Green J, Winfield N. Report cards on cardiac surgeons: assessing New York State's approach. N Engl J Med 1995;332:1229–32.

23. Schneider EC, Epstein AM. Influence of cardiac surgery performance reports on referral practices and access to care. N Engl J Med 1996 Jul 25;335(4):251–6.

24. Iezzoni LI. Using risk-adjusted outcomes to assess clinical practice: an overview of issues pertaining to risk adjustment. Ann Thorac Surg 1994 Dec;58(6):1822–6.

25. Hartz AJ, Kuhn EM. Comparing hospitals that perform coronary artery bypass surgery: the effect of outcome measures and data sources. Am J Public Health 1994 Oct;84(10):1609–14.

26. Weintraub WS, Deaton C, Shaw L, et al. Can cardiovascular clinical characteristics be identified and outcome models be developed from an in-patient claims database? Am J Cardiol 1999 Jul 15;84(2):166–9.

27. Ebert PA. The importance of data in improving practice: effective clinical use of outcomes data. Ann Thorac Surg 1994;58:1812–14.

28. Smith R. All changed, changed utterly. British medicine will be transformed by the Bristol case. BMJ 1998 Jun 27;316(7149):1917–18.

29. Treasure T. Lessons from the Bristol case. BMJ 1998;316:1685–6.

30. Lippmann RP, Shahian DM. Coronary artery bypass risk predictions using neural networks. Ann Thorac Surg 1997;63:1635–43.

31. Hofes TP, Hayward RA, Greenfield S, et al. The unreliability of individual physician "report cards" for assessing the costs and quality of care of a chronic disease. JAMA 281:2098–2105.

32. Donabedian A. Evaluating the quality of medical care. Milbank 1996;44:166–203.

CHAPTER 36

Plastic Surgery

Mehrdad M. Mofid, MD, Robert J. Spence, MD, FACS, and
Paul N. Manson, MD, FACS

Plastic surgery today is a nearly unrecognizable discipline when compared to its origins as a subspecialty 80 years ago. The development of new techniques and technologies have spawned disparate subspecialties and innovations that permit countless reconstructive options limited only by the imagination of the surgeon. Indeed, by its very nature, the question "What is plastic surgery?" is difficult to answer. The essence of plastic surgery is perhaps best described as the repair of injury, the surgical refinement of form, and the restoration of function of the human body. The father of modern plastic surgery, a sixteenth-century Italian surgeon named Gaspare Tagliacozzi, explained that as plastic surgeons "We bring back, refashion and restore to wholeness the features which nature gave but chance destroyed, not that they may charm the eye but that they may be an advantage to the living soul."[1]

As a result of the breadth of plastic surgery and the diversity of procedures that plastic surgeons perform, much information remains to be developed from evidence-based outcomes research. Unlike other surgical disciplines, in which clearly defined endpoints exist to compare procedures on measures such as mortality, morbidity, recurrence, and length of the procedure or hospitalization, outcomes in plastic surgery rely heavily upon the patient's subjective interpretation of the results and perception of improved aesthetics or function. Attempts to compare patient outcomes, both within and between clinical studies, must be done cautiously since the benefits of treatment are often less tangible and more difficult to assess.[2]

Although there are additional challenges in outcomes research for plastic surgery, the field is vulnerable to the same cost-benefit analysis to which the whole of medicine is subjected. Most aesthetic procedures will be exempted from this process since they are rarely covered by third-party payers. In contrast, reconstructive operations will likely require supporting outcomes data that demonstrate clear benefits relative to costs.

Because the definitions of cosmetic and reconstructive surgery are important in distinguishing procedures that will or will not be covered by third-party payers, the American Society of Plastic and Reconstructive Surgeons (ASPRS) wrote accurate and usable definitions that were further modified by the American Medical Association (AMA) in 1989 and jointly approved. The approved definition states that "cosmetic surgery is performed to reshape normal structures of the body in order to improve the patient's appearance and self-esteem. Reconstructive surgery is performed on abnormal structures of the body, caused by congenital defects, developmental abnormalities, trauma, infection, tumors or disease. It is generally performed to improve function, but may also be done to approximate a normal appearance."[3]

Although the plastic surgery literature is replete with publications documenting complication rates, aesthetics, and narrowly defined functional results, the existing literature often lacks more broadly defined, long-term outcomes research that addresses a comprehensive range of parameters. Data that reflect the effects of treatment on physical and psychosocial functioning, quality of life, and well-being are critical to ensuring the continuing availability of reconstructive procedures. A collection of reliable perioperative and long-term financial data is also essential so that the benefits of these operations may be compared with their costs.[4]

To provide an overview of available data on plastic surgery outcomes, selected prototype procedures within each of the major disciplines of plastic surgery have been selected for analysis in this chapter, with a comparison of currently acceptable approaches to the same problem when appropriate. Breast reduction surgery, one of the better-documented topics in the plastic surgery literature in terms of outcomes research, will be discussed with respect to functional, symptomatic, and aesthetic outcomes. Advances in breast reconstructive options will be presented along with a comparison of implants and the use of autogenous tissue (pedicled flaps vs free tissue transfer). Microvascular techniques are relatively new to plastic surgery, having been used for less than 20 years; an examination of the increasing popularity of the free transverse rectus abdominus myocutaneous (TRAM) procedure will be used to highlight the advantages of microvascular surgery in breast reconstruction. In regard to the field of craniofacial surgery, the experience with early surgery for craniosynostosis will be presented by several case studies encompassing 20 years of experience.

Sadly, the field of aesthetic surgery suffers from a dearth of rigorous outcomes-oriented research. Although the lay press is rife with descriptions of new technologies and procedures available for aesthetic surgery, these advances have generally not been subject to the scrutiny of studies documenting their efficacy and appropriateness. There are multiple explanations as to why the academic literature is largely devoid of studies examining the sizable aesthetic surgery market. Among these explanations are that third-party payers are not driving the need to demonstrate an appropriate cost-benefit ratio and that aesthetic surgery offers primarily subjective and less functionally oriented benefits that are difficult to measure and interpret. Nevertheless, several studies that examine psychologic outcomes and quality-of-life changes in aesthetic surgery patients will be presented. As a model for the introduction of a new technology into aesthetic surgery, data comparing ultrasonic to conventional liposuction, (the most common aesthetic procedure performed by plastic surgeons) will be presented.

The field of hand surgery, a subspecialty shared by both plastic and orthopedic surgeons, will be examined with particular attention to open versus endoscopic carpal tunnel release. Burn surgery, a discipline within the field of plastic surgery, is discussed in a separate chapter.

BREAST REDUCTION

In 1997, 65,000 women in the United States underwent reduction mammaplasty.[5] This procedure is usually performed to relieve painful symptoms and physical signs of macromastia, defined as breast hyperplasia or hypertrophy. Macromastia is a relative term describing a breast size too large for a patient's proportions, causing physical or emotional disturbances. Most women who request reduction mammaplasty cite physical symptoms (such as pain) rather than aesthetic or psychologic problems as the main reason for requesting surgery. Therefore, the justification for reduction mammaplasty, which concerns third-party payers, should be based on the probability of relieving the clinical signs and symptoms of macromastia and thereby increasing health and well-being. In response to an increasingly cost-conscious health care environment within the last 10 years, many journal articles have emphasized the significant benefits of reduction mammaplasty for the relief of physical symptoms.

A common complaint among patients seeking breast reduction surgery and among plastic surgeons is that third-party payers restrict access to reduction mammaplasty by using increasingly stringent criteria that vary by payer. Most third-party payers require that patients be within 10 to 20 percent of ideal body weight according to standardized height-weight tables. To validate coverage, most also require previously documented evidence from a primary medical doctor of some of the following symptoms: back, neck, shoulder, or breast pain; significant bra-strap grooves and breast ptosis; intertriginous dermatitis; postural defects; upper extremity paresthesias; and interference of the breasts with normal work or social function. Nearly all insurance companies have specific guidelines for the amount of tissue that must be removed at the time of surgery, usually between 500 and 700 g. As a result of these

results. It is clear, however, that the results are clinically significant in that they show near-universal improvement (albeit self-reported) in the physical symptoms of 543 breast reduction patients, the vast majority of whom were happy with the results of their surgery.

While there are accepted and validated tools to measure satisfaction and quality of life, these have not yet been adopted widely in plastic surgery. However, a well-designed study addressing broadly defined outcomes and a comprehensive range of parameters in reduction mammaplasty patients comes from Britain's outcomes-oriented National Health Service. Shakespeare and Cole prospectively studied by questionnaire 110 patients who presented for breast reduction surgery in 1995, and followed up with questionnaires at 3 and 6 months postoperatively.[10] The response rate was 82 percent at 3 months and 76 percent at 6 months. All data were collected and processed by an independent research analyst and were not seen by medical staff. The assessment packet for patients at each interval included the SF-36 health survey questionnaire and the Rosenberg self-esteem scale, both of which address multiple dimensions of physical and psychologic well-being and from which normative data exist on a large number of subjects in the United States and the United Kingdom. The body mass index for all patients in the study was calculated, classifying 43 patients as normal, 48 patients as overweight, 17 patients as obese, and 2 patients as severely obese. No patients indicated aesthetic concerns as the primary reason for requesting breast reduction surgery. This study documented a decrease in the postoperative physical symptoms (Figure 36–2) similar to previous studies, with complication rates of 37 percent at 3 months and 5 percent at 6 months. Most of the complications were minor wound infections that did not require rehospitalization.

A rigorous statistical analysis was performed on all data from SF-36 and Rosenberg questionnaires, using dependent *t*-tests and matched-pairs Wilcoxon's signed rank tests (when appropriate) to test for differences in means between preoperative and postoperative data. A comparison with age-appropriate female population means showed that preoperative breast

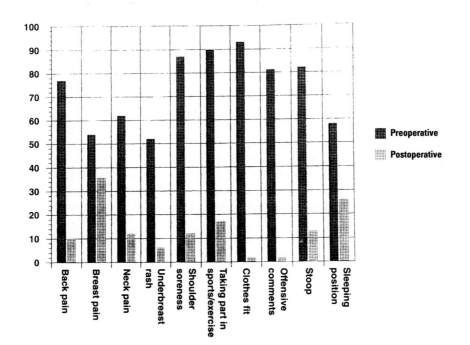

Figure 36–2 Percentage of patients at 3 months after reduction mammaplasty answering "yes" to the question "Do you currently have any of the following problems?" (Reproduced with permission from Shakespeare V, Cole RP. Measuring patient-based outcomes in a plastic surgery service: breast reduction surgical patients. Br J Plast Surg 1997;50:244.)

reduction patients scored significantly below normative values on six out of eight dimensions of health. At 6 months postoperatively, scores in all dimensions were comparable with normative values except for mental health and energy, which were above normal. Significant improvements were seen between preoperative and postoperative states for general health, physical and social function, mental health, self-esteem, pain, and energy. Of the patients enrolled in this study, 98 percent were happy with their decision to have surgery and would recommend reduction mammaplasty to a friend.

Schnur and colleagues have attempted to help third-party payers solve the problem of distinguishing those women who seek reduction mammaplasty for medical reasons versus those who choose surgery for aesthetic reasons.[11] Ninety-two of 220 plastic surgeons responded to a mailed survey asking for information on the height, weight, and amount of breast tissue removed for their last twenty reduction mammaplasty patients, providing information on 591 women. Of the same 220 plastic surgeons, 132 responded to a separately mailed questionnaire asking (based upon the surgeons' professional experience) what percentages of reduction mammaplasties are performed for purely symptomatic reasons, for purely aesthetic reasons, and for mixed reasons. Schnur, averaging the data from the second mailing, found that (in the judgment of plastic surgeons) 78 percent of reduction mammaplasties are performed for purely symptomatic reasons, 5 percent are performed for purely aesthetic reasons, and 17 percent are performed for mixed reasons. Inferring that the volume of breast tissue in macromastia is directly related to symptoms (ie, the larger the breast, the more it hurts), and using the data from the first survey on height, weight, and volume of breast tissue removed, Schnur graphed the logarithm of breast tissue removed from the arbitrarily selected right breast against body surface area (BSA), with relationships showing the 5th and 22nd percentile cutoff lines to reflect women seeking surgery for purely symptomatic reasons, aesthetic reasons, and mixed reasons (Figure 36–3 and Table 36–2). According to the authors, the least squares regression line was calculated and was satisfactorily linear, allowing for percentile lines to be drawn as shown in the figure. The BSA formula used in the study is:

$$\text{BSA (m}^2) = 0.007184 \times \text{height (cm)}^{0.725} \times \text{weight (kg)}^{0.425}$$

The criticism of this methodology is that it must first be proven that breast tissue volume in macromastia is directly related to the severity of physical symptoms, with minimal variance in the relationship, before such an inference can be the basis for the study. Schnur and colleagues responded to this criticism by pointing out that physical complaints are soft data and that third-party payers cannot accept patient history alone since patients can fabricate stories for financial gain. It also would have been valuable for the authors to perform a statistical analysis of variation on the responses from plastic surgeons regarding patient motivation for reduction mammaplasty. Despite these limitations, this study is a valuable contribution to the literature in that it is a surgeon-directed study intended to assist third-party payers in fair payment practices.

The above studies indicate substantial benefits in terms of improvement in physical health and psychologic well-being for women with macromastia who undergo reduction mammaplasty. If health care is to be based on demonstrable need and evidence of health gain by patients, then reduction mammaplasty meets these criteria. Of note, obesity or variance from ideal body weight by more than 10 or 20 percent should not be a factor in denying third-party coverage of breast reduction procedures. This practice by insurance companies is not supported by the existing literature, and in fact, obese women who undergo reduction mammaplasty have outcomes no different from those of thinner women. There are documented improvements in activity levels and regular exercise in reduction mammaplasty patients that should be considered an especially desirable outcome in obese women.

Table 36–2 Body Surface Area and Cutoff Weight of Right Breast Tissue Removed

Body Surface Area (m²)	Right Breast (g)	
	Lower 5%	Lower 22%
1.35	127	199
1.40	139	218
1.45	152	238
1.50	166	260
1.55	181	284
1.60	198	310
1.65	216	338
1.70	236	370
1.75	258	404
1.80	282	441
1.85	308	482
1.90	336	527
1.95	367	575
2.00	401	628
2.05	439	687
2.10	479	750
2.15	523	819
2.20	572	895
2.25	625	978
2.30	682	1,068
2.35	745	1,167
2.40	814	1,275
2.45	890	1,393
2.50	972	1,522
2.55	1,062	1,662

Reprinted with permission from Schnur PL, Hoehn JG, Ilstrup DM, et al. Reduction mammaplasty: cosmetic or reconstructive procedure? Ann Plast Surg 1991;27:237.

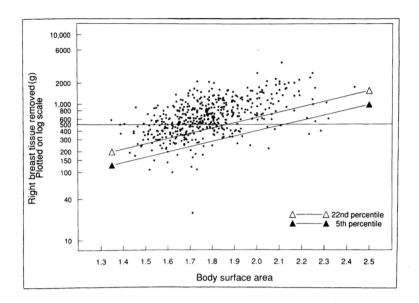

Figure 36–3 Logarithm of weight of right breast tissue removed plotted as a function of body surface area (m2). Included are 5th and 22nd percentile cutoff lines. (Reproduced with permission from Schnur PL, Hoehn JG, Ilstrup DM, et al. Reduction mammaplasty: cosmetic or reconstructive procedure? Ann Plast Surg 1991;27:235.)

Breast Reconstruction and Microvascular Surgery

Reconstruction of the breast after mastectomy has become widely accepted and necessary for the psychologic and emotional well-being of the breast cancer survivor. This realization was highlighted in October 1998 by Congressional approval of a bill in the United States that mandates health insurance companies to cover the cost of reconstructive breast surgery for women who have undergone a mastectomy. Over the last 15 years, there has been significant progress in the reconstructive options offered to women after a mastectomy. The historic reliance on implants and prostheses is giving way to the current trend toward autogenous tissue reconstruction. Enthusiasm for autogenous tissue in breast reconstruction stems from the durability, consistency, and more natural appearance that it offers. Autogenous tissue breast reconstruction also avoids the complications associated with implants, such as infections, capsular contracture, and implant rupture. The most widely used technique of autogenous tissue reconstruction, the TRAM flap, was introduced in 1982 as a superiorly based pedicle transfer using the nondominant superior epigastric blood supply to the rectus muscle and overlying infraumbilical fat and skin.[12] The addition of microvascular techniques that base the TRAM flap on its dominant deep inferior epigastric blood supply with anastomosis to the rich blood supply of the axilla has improved the viability of this flap and has minimized the incidence of abdominal wall weakness and hernias. Since the thoracodorsal vessels are skeletonized and readily available following axillary dissection in immediate reconstructions, no extra work is required to find the donor vessels. First described by Hölmstrom in 1979, the first free TRAM flap reconstruction in the United States was done by Friedman and colleagues in 1985 (Figure 36–4).[13,14]

   In 1997, of the 50,000 breast reconstructions performed in the United States, 26 percent were performed as pedicle TRAM procedures, 2.2 percent were performed as free TRAM procedures, 6 percent were latissimus dorsi flap procedures, and the remainder were implants with or without prior tissue expansion.[5] As the plastic surgery outcomes literature continues

Ipsilateral Pedicle   **Contralateral Pedicle**

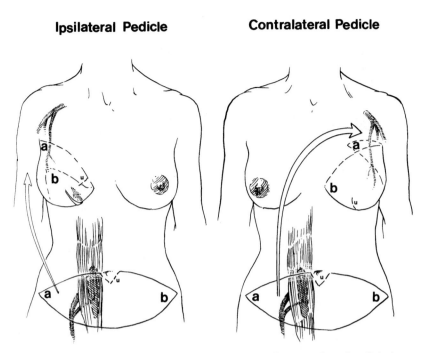

Figure 36–4 Diagram comparing use of the ipsilateral versus the contralateral pedicle for reconstruction of the breast mound. (Reproduced with permission from Elliott L, Eskenazi L, Beegle P, et al. Immediate TRAM flap breast reconstruction: 128 consecutive cases. Plast Reconstr Surg 1993;92:223.)

to demonstrate the superiority of the free flap technique and as more microvascular surgeons are trained, these numbers are likely to change, reflecting the growing enthusiasm for the free TRAM procedure (Figure 36–5). The advantages of the free TRAM over the conventional TRAM procedure are severalfold. By carrying the lower abdominal tissue on the inferior epigastric pedicle, only a small portion of the rectus abdominis muscle is sacrificed rather than the full length or width of the rectus muscle as in the pedicle TRAM procedure, which carries a greater risk of hernias and weakening of the abdominal wall. The greatest aesthetic improvement from the free flap technique lies in maintenance of the medial and inferior inframammary fold. Since it is unnecessary to tunnel the abdominal flap into the breast wound, there is no medial bulge from the rectus muscle as seen with the conventional procedure. Lastly, the flap is healthier, with a lower incidence of partial flap necrosis because of the direct inflow and venous drainage through large donor and recipient vessels that base the flap on its dominant blood supply. Moon and Taylor have performed a detailed anatomic analysis of the abdominal wall and have demonstrated that the blood supply from the superior system drops in a stepwise fashion at each inscription through a series of "choke" vessels and that the most direct blood supply to the lower abdominal skin comes from the deep inferior epigastric system.[15] The enhanced blood supply allows for a larger skin flap and volume for primary contouring and greater freedom of design for breast reconstruction.

In a study of 325 postmastectomy reconstructions in 287 patients between 1986 and 1989, Kroll compared the conventional TRAM procedure to the latissimus dorsi myocutaneous flap and tissue expansion.[16] The mean follow-up interval for all types of reconstruction was greater than 1 year. Results were graded retrospectively on a scale of 1 to 4 (excellent to poor) on the basis of symmetry, shape, ptosis, and scarring, through a review of photographs by four judges independent of the surgical team. This study found that the failure rate (defined as either a failing score from all the judges or a failure to complete the reconstruction) was highest (21%)

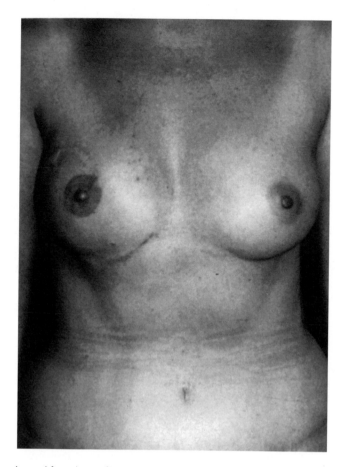

Figure 36–5 A patient with an immediate TRAM flap right breast reconstruction. (Reproduced with permission from Kroll S, Baldwin B. A comparison of outcomes using three different methods of breast reconstruction. Plast Reconstr Surg 1992;90:456.)

in tissue expansion, usually as a result of infection, exposure, or severe capsular contracture that prevented adequate expansion from taking place. (This high failure rate using implants is greater than that found in our published series of 197 patients from The Johns Hopkins Hospital, but we agree that it is much higher than the failure rates for all other types of reconstruction.)[17] In our own experience, there is a significant need for revisions of reconstructions using tissue expansion (57%), and there are significant rates of complication (10%) and failure (3.5%). In Kroll's study, the failure rate for the pedicled TRAM procedure was 3 percent and that for the latissimus dorsi flap procedure was 9 percent. The average overall grade of the completed TRAM flap reconstructions (2.07) was significantly better than tissue expansion (2.57) and latissimus dorsi (2.21) reconstructions ($p < .0001$). The authors commented that regardless of the technique used, the best outcomes were attained in women with bilateral reconstructions, and that the delayed reconstructions were generally inferior to immediate reconstructions because of the shortage of skin and the loss of normal landmarks such as the inframammary fold. The authors found that although the conventional TRAM flap procedure has the disadvantage of being a more complex and technically demanding procedure requiring a longer hospitalization and recovery, its low failure rate, aesthetic success, and long-term freedom from late complications made it an attractive option.

In a more recent study directly comparing the conventional TRAM to free TRAM procedures in 128 patients who underwent breast reconstruction between 1985 and 1990, Elliott and colleagues found that in 86 conventional TRAM procedures there was 1 total flap loss, 5 partial flap losses (loss of 20 to 50% of the flap), and 10 instances of fat necrosis (loss of less than 20% of the flap).[18] The total number of flap-related complications in this group was 19 percent. Among the 42 free TRAM procedures, there was 1 total flap loss, no partial flap losses, and only 2 flaps with fat necrosis, resulting in a flap-related complication rate of 7 percent. These favorable results were obtained in spite of the fact that in this series, the free TRAM flap group was composed of 63 percent high-risk patients (smokers, diabetics, and the obese) while the conventional TRAM flap group was composed of only 28 percent high-risk patients. In a series at the University of Texas M.D. Anderson Cancer Center, 211 free TRAM flap breast reconstructions performed between 1989 and 1992 in 163 patients were followed prospectively.[19] Total flap losses occurred in 3 cases, for a success rate of 99 percent. Partial flap losses or fat necrosis occurred in 15 reconstructions (7%). There was a statistically significant higher incidence of fat necrosis in smokers: 12 of 99 reconstructions with fat necrosis in smokers (12%) compared to 3 of 112 reconstructions with fat necrosis in nonsmokers (3%, $p = .02$). In a multicenter European study of free TRAM flap procedures, obesity was also shown to affect complication rates (partial or total flap loss and abdominal wall weakness).[20] Of patients divided into three groups—slim (n = 12), average to moderately overweight (n = 86), and obese (n = 13)—the respective total complication rates were 0 percent, 22 percent, and 38 percent.

Although some series have published total flap losses as high as 5 percent, failure rates in the most experienced hands are between 1 and 3 percent. There is clearly a learning curve in microsurgery, and as a result, there are fewer overall complications in the more recent published series of free TRAM procedures. Shaw has stated that in his series of 160 free TRAM procedures between 1985 and 1993, he had only one flap loss, for a failure rate of 0.6 percent.[21] Through 1994, Kroll documents only 4 total losses in 347 free TRAM procedures (1.2%) with a 6 percent incidence of fat necrosis.[22] In addition, his incidence of abdominal wall complications decreased from 22 percent prior to 1990 to less than 1 percent since that time in 121 patients using a two-layer fascial repair. The most important factors in successful free tissue transfer are a good anastomosis and a reliable flap monitoring system that enables the salvage of flaps if the anastomosis should fail. In well-monitored situations, salvage rates are typically in the range of 60 to 90 percent.[23]

The experience at The Johns Hopkins Hospital with the free TRAM procedure in 132 breast reconstructions has been favorable.[24] Since 1994, we have had 2 flap losses for a failure rate of 1.5 percent and an overall complication rate of 29.5 percent. Fat necrosis occurred in 14 reconstructions (10.6%), and wound healing complications at either the TRAM or abdominal harvest site occurred in 14 reconstructions (10.6%). Hernias occurred in only 2 patients (1.5%). Smoking and obesity were found to be significant risk factors for complications: 9 of 64 reconstructions with complications in smokers (14.1%) compared with 1 of 64 reconstructions with complications in nonsmokers (1.5%, $p < .05$), and 5 of 37 reconstructions with complications in obese women (13.5%) compared with 5 of 95 reconstructions with complications in nonobese women (5.3%, $p < .1$) The average length of hospitalization in our series was 4.6 days. (While reporting on series of patients is standard in the surgical literature, one of the major limitations of this approach is the lack of risk adjustment. Thus, care should be exercised in comparing results across series.)

Several studies have addressed concerns about abdominal wall competence after the TRAM procedure. This is especially important for younger women, who are better candidates for TRAM reconstruction, who typically lead active lives, and who frequently question the potential effects of this surgery on their sport and work activities. The pedicled TRAM procedure carries a greater theoretical risk of abdominal weakness and hernias due to the more extensive muscle harvest and abdominal wall dissection. Performance of bilateral pedicled TRAM flap procedures to reconstruct both breasts or a bipedicled TRAM procedure (a modification of the pedicled TRAM flap procedure, in which both rectus muscles are harvested to improve flap vascularity in the reconstruction of a single breast) raises important questions about the long-term effects on abdominal wall competence and on strength, posture, and back pain.

In a 5-year follow-up study of abdominal wall strength, Mizgala, Hartrampf, and Bennett followed 150 women who underwent pedicle TRAM reconstruction between 1984 and 1987.[25] Of 150 patients enrolled in the study, 132 responded to a questionnaire and were examined by physicians other than the operating surgeon 5 to 7 years after pedicle TRAM procedures. In 80 patients, a single rectus muscle pedicle was used for unilateral reconstruction. Only one single-pedicle patient required mesh reinforcement of the fascial closure. Double-pedicle single flaps or bilateral flaps harvesting both rectus muscles were raised in 66 patients. Direct repair in this group was performed in 39 patients, with mesh repair required in 27 patients. As expected, performance in activities of daily living and getting up from the prone position differed significantly between the two groups. Fifteen percent of the single-pedicle group and 31 percent of the double-pedicle group reported difficulty lifting heavy objects ($p = .03$). When tested, 97 percent of control (preoperative) patients could get up from a supine position to a full upright stance without using their upper limbs for assistance, but only 34 percent of postoperative patients could do the same ($p = .0005$). Significantly more single-pedicle patients were able to perform this task (44%) compared to the double-pedicle group (21%). About one-quarter of all postoperative patients noted worsened aerobics and tennis performance (Tables 36–3 and 36–4).

Abdominal wall competence was also evaluated, and all patients were examined for evidence of herniation through the fascial harvest site, umbilical hernias, femoral hernias, or generalized abdominal laxity. Of the 132 patients, 16 (12%) had abdominal wall complications. The majority were asymptomatic, and only 5 were repaired. Three of the 4 umbilical hernias were repaired at the time of nipple reconstruction. Of the 8 patients found to have generalized abdominal laxity, 7 were double-pedicle TRAM procedure patients, with equal numbers having had direct and mesh repairs. Only 1 of these patients requested surgical repair.

Table 36–3 Responses to Patient Questionnaire*

Question	Percentage of All Respondents (135)		
	Improved	No Change	Worse
Overall change in abdomen	63.6	20.5	15.9
Abdominal appearance	72.4	15.7	11.9
Abdominal muscle strength	8.2	46.3	45.5
Ability to exercise	3.0	72.0	25.0
Ability to perform housework	2.3	92.4	5.3
Ability to render child care	1.0	93.3	5.8
Performance of regular occupation	1.6	94.4	4.0
Lifting objects	1.5	76.3	22.1
Getting up from prone position	1.5	55.7	42.7
Posture	19.5	76.7	3.8

*Comparison between present status (5 to 7.5 years postoperatively) and preoperative status in women undergoing pedicle TRAM procedures.

Reprinted with permission from Mizgala C, Hartrampf C, Bennett K. Assessment of the abdominal wall after pedicled TRAM flap surgery: 5- to 7-year follow-up of 150 consecutive patients. Plast Reconstr Surg 1994;93:991.

Table 36–4 Impact of Pedicle TRAM Flap Surgery on Sports Activities*

Sport	No. Participants	Percentage of Respondents Participating in Each Sport		
		Improved	*No Change*	*Worse*
Walking	129	8.5	87.6	3.9
Swimming	77	7.8	85.7	6.5
Aerobics	53	9.4	64.2	26.4
Jogging	34	14.7	82.4	2.9
Tennis	33	9.1	66.7	24.2
Snow skiing	19	10.5	78.9	10.5

*Distribution of responses to patient questionnaire at 5 or more years postoperatively.
Reprinted with permission from Mizgala C, Hartrampf C, Bennett K. Assessment of the abdominal wall after pedicled TRAM flap surgery: 5- to 7-year follow-up of 150 consecutive patients. Plast Reconstr Surg 1994;93:988–992.

The vast majority of patients in this study (93%) considered the TRAM procedure worthwhile and would recommend it to others. The same percentage considered the abdominal scars acceptable, and 72 percent felt there was an improvement in the appearance of their abdomens. The generally poor results in abdominal wall strength and competence found in the double-pedicle group should discourage this practice in favor of bilateral free TRAM procedures.

In a study of 25 patients comparing abdominal wall function between single-pedicled TRAM flap patients and free TRAM flap patients over a 1-year period using a machine that measures flexion torque, free TRAM flap patients outperformed the pedicled TRAM flap patients in nearly every test, although numbers were too small to achieve statistical significance.[26] Both groups were evenly matched in age, weight, and preoperative strength. The indications in the series for a free TRAM flap procedure were a reconstructive tissue requirement greater than 60 percent of the abdominal pannus, a history of smoking, obesity, and previous upper abdominal surgery. The greatest differences were found at the 6-week postoperative period, when the maximum isometric flexion torque of the pedicled TRAM flap group decreased to 58 ± 10 percent of baseline, while the unilateral free TRAM flap group average was 87 ± 11 percent of baseline ($p < .004$). At 1 year, there were no statistically significant differences between the two groups, with the pedicled TRAM flap group achieving 77 ± 9 percent of baseline flexion torque and the free TRAM flap group achieving 82 ± 7 percent of baseline. None of the free TRAM flap patients reported abdominal wall weakness at 1 year. In contrast, one-fourth of the pedicled TRAM flap patients in this series reported abdominal wall weakness at 1 year. One of the pedicled TRAM flap patients required surgical repair of an asymptomatic abdominal bulge. Half of the pedicled TRAM flap group of patients underwent a muscle-sparing procedure that leaves a strip of rectus abdominis muscle on either side of the superior pedicle. The authors comment that the muscle dissection is time consuming, causes increased blood loss, and puts the superior vascular pedicle at risk. Although this process may theoretically add support to the abdominal wall, pedicled TRAM flap patients in this study who underwent the muscle-sparing procedure had lower test results than patients in whom the entire rectus abdominis muscle was harvested; therefore, the authors discourage this muscle-sparing procedure.

Serletti and Moran analyzed the total costs associated with the free versus pedicled TRAM flaps in 125 patients who underwent breast reconstruction between 1990 and 1995.[27] During this 5-year period, 72 free flap and 53 pedicle flap procedures were performed. The average operating room time for either procedure was 7 hours. The total cost of a free TRAM flap breast reconstruction was $10,300, and the total cost of a pedicled TRAM flap breast reconstruction was $8,800. However, complications including flap loss, fat necrosis, hernia, and asymmetry requiring revision were greater in pedicled flap patients. Complications occurred in 17 percent of the free flap patients and 28 percent of the pedicled flap patients. Averaging the total cost of the treatment of these complications per patient treated for complications resulted in an excess cost of $5,500 per free TRAM reconstruction and $9,800 per pedicled TRAM reconstruction. Although they found no significant differences in patient reported satisfaction between both groups, the authors felt they had achieved better symmetry with the free TRAM procedure and had thus avoided secondary contouring procedures.

Theoretically, immediate reconstruction after mastectomy, regardless of the reconstructive option, should be less expensive than delayed reconstruction. In immediate reconstruction, the patient is already anesthetized, the defect does not have to be recreated, and the patient recovers from fewer procedures. Several studies show that this cost differential is many thousands of dollars. In a study of 276 subjects at the University of Texas M.D. Anderson Cancer Center who had completed the entire reconstructive process, total resource costs were calculated. On average, delayed reconstructions ($28,843) were found to be 62 percent more expensive than immediate reconstructions ($17,801).[28] Similar differences were found when patients were subgrouped by type of reconstruction, history of preoperative radiation, and plurality (unilateral vs bilateral) (Table 36–5).

Elkowitz and colleagues at three different institutions compared the hospital bills of 287 patients who underwent breast reconstruction from 1988 to 1991.[29] In a rigorous analysis, they extrapolated the final cost of breast reconstruction and compared various methods of reconstruction. When reconstruction was delayed, the extra costs for in-patient hospital stays, anesthesia fees, recovery room time, preoperative testing, and pathology specimens resulted in an enormous cost differential regardless of the reconstruction option used (Table 36–6). They also point out that due to the extra costs associated with secondary procedures, immediate and delayed tissue expander placement is actually more expensive than TRAM reconstructions in the long run. Based on the current literature on breast reconstruction, there is an average of 2.8 procedures per immediate tissue expander reconstruction, which includes insertion, implant exchange with nipple reconstruction, and 0.8 revisions. Using available data from this study, the total cost is $38,012. Using the same approach, a pedicle TRAM flap reconstruction that averages 1.5 procedures per reconstruction costs $36,674. On the basis of available data, the authors recommend performing immediate reconstructions when possible, with subsequent revisions as outpatient procedures. Immediate reconstruction further benefits the patient, who awakens from a mastectomy with the beginnings of a newly formed breast, and thus causes less disruption of body image and results in less total recuperation time.

Table 36–5 Mean Corrected Resource Costs of Immediate and Delayed Breast Reconstruction by Method of Reconstruction

Reconstruction Group	n	Total Resource Cost ($)
Immediate TRAM flap	142	17,957*
Delayed TRAM flap	52	29,173*
Immediate tissue expansion	77	17,514**
Delayed tissue expansion	5	25,411**

*$p < .001$; **$p < .034$.
TRAM = transverse rectus abdominis myocutaneous.
Reprinted with permission from Khoo A, Kroll S, Reece G, et al. A comparison of resource costs of immediate and delayed breast reconstruction. Plast Reconstr Surg 1998;101:966.

Table 36–6 Combinations of Procedures: Difference in Cost Between Immediate and Delayed Breast Reconstructions

Procedure Combination	Cost ($)
Delayed implant with mastectomy	27,961
Immediate implant with mastectomy	21,175
Cost difference	6,786
Delayed latissimus flap with mastectomy	39,745
Immediate latissimus flap with mastectomy	32,544
Cost difference	7,201
Delayed TRAM flap with mastectomy	38,509
Immediate TRAM flap with mastectomy	27,893
Cost difference	10,616
Delayed free gluteal flap with mastectomy	40,198
Immediate free flap with mastectomy	35,106
Cost difference	5,092
Delayed free TRAM flap with mastectomy	42,923
Immediate free TRAM flap with mastectomy	35,106
Cost difference	7,817
Inpatient tissue-expander exchange	10,646
Outpatient tissue-expander exchange	5,187
Cost difference	5,459

Reprinted with permission from Elkowitz A, Colen S, Slavin S, et al. Various methods of breast reconstruction after mastectomy: an economic comparison. Plast Reconstr Surg 1993;92:79.

As a result of this extensive body of outcomes research, and as more microsurgeons are trained, there will likely be a trend toward performing more free TRAM procedures, which cause fewer complications and less abdominal wall morbidity and which achieve better symmetry and aesthetic results. However, the unipedicled TRAM flap, the latissimus dorsi flap, and tissue expansion continue to play a role in breast reconstruction. To summarize the evidence-based findings to date: when considering the TRAM procedure, firm indications for free rather than pedicled TRAM procedures include bilateral reconstructions, the need for more than 60 percent of the abdominal flap volume, and high-risk factors such as smoking and obesity. Even with the free TRAM procedure, however, smokers and obese women carry significantly higher risks of flap and wound healing complications. When possible, reconstructions should be immediate rather than delayed since the aesthetic results are better and the cost is significantly less. Thus, specific practice guidelines can be developed, based on outcomes research findings in support of cost-effective care.

CRANIOFACIAL SURGERY

Craniofacial surgery is a field that has evolved beyond the reduction of maxillofacial fractures and includes the reconstruction of complex congenital craniofacial abnormalities. Since 1967, when Paul Tessier dramatically demonstrated massive en bloc mobilization of segments of the craniofacial skeleton to improve form and facial appearance, craniofacial surgeons all over the world have applied his principles in younger patients and even infants, with considerable success.[30] Several landmark studies from centers in Philadelphia, Paris, and New York representing twenty years of experience have examined the outcomes of early surgery for both syndromic and nonsyndromic craniosynostosis. The following section emphasizes the results of early surgery for craniofacial deformities caused by craniosynostosis (premature closure of the cranial sutures) and summarizes the available data on aesthetic results, complication rates, the timing of surgery, and the need for reoperation.

Craniosynostosis

There are obvious advantages to the surgical correction of craniofacial abnormalities before functional, psychologic, and social limitations have developed in the patient. Although outcomes analyses have not directly compared surgical intervention in younger versus older patients with abnormal craniofacial growth, many authors have described additional theoretic benefits to early surgery. Tessier demonstrated that growth of the cranial vault is directly influenced by the brain and that until 4 years of age, the base, like the cranial vault, follows the rapid growth of the brain.[31] Whitaker, Marchac, and McCarthy postulated that by applying the substantial early growth rates of the brain and ocular globes, the release of constricting forces at an early age (less than 1 year) would beneficially affect craniofacial growth by taking advantage of the rapidly expanding volume and direction of brain growth and would evoke potentially normal development. Persing confirmed this in the rabbit model by showing that early release of prematurely immobilized coronal sutures improves normal growth.[32] Improvements in pediatric anesthesia and postoperative monitoring techniques now permit major surgical intervention in infants with greater safety and success. Over a 20-year period, these authors and many others have documented the results of early craniofacial remodeling in a variety of clinical situations.

Although much has been learned about the developmental biology and genetic associations of craniosynostosis, it remains unclear why the craniosynostoses occur in diverse groups of patients, with variable severity. Accordingly, treatment options range from conservative observation until complete or near-complete craniofacial growth is achieved to radical remodeling during the first few months of life. Whitaker and colleagues have retrospectively reviewed 164 patients who underwent surgical correction for asymmetric coronal synostosis (plagiocephaly, 74 patients) and symmetric synostoses (brachycephaly, Crouzon's syndrome, Apert's syndrome, etc, 90 patients).[33] Patients were subclassified by age group. Of 164 patients operated on between 1972 and 1984, 145 were available for long-term follow-up that ranged from 1 to 12 years. Although there were no deaths, major complications including osteomyelitis, hydrocephalus, and cerebrospinal fluid leakage occurred in 8 percent of patients. Minor complications such as hematoma and delayed wound healing occurred in 11 percent of patients. Aesthetic results were classified into four categories, which have since been designated in the craniofacial literature as Whitaker categories. Category I patients required no refinements or surgical revisions. In category II patients, soft-tissue or lesser bone-contouring revisions were desirable whether performed or not. Category III patients required major osteotomies and bone-grafting procedures that were not as extensive as the original procedure. Category IV patients required a major craniofacial procedure duplicating or exceeding the original procedure. Among patients with plagiocephaly (Figure 36–6), category I results were achieved in 78 percent and category II results were achieved in 15 percent through the surgical technique of unilateral orbital repositioning and forehead remodeling. Of interest, as the age of the patient at surgery increased, the likelihood of secondary surgery being required also increased. Only 3 percent of patients with plagiocephaly operated on before the age of 18 months were category III or IV patients while 27 percent of those operated on after the age of 18 months were category III or IV. Of all patients with symmetric craniosynostosis, including

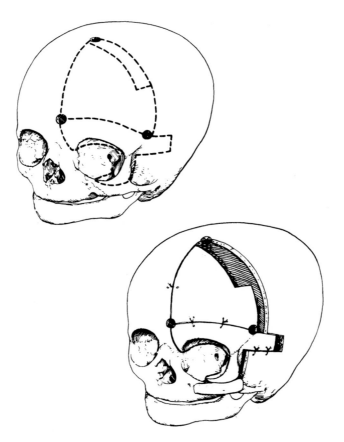

Figure 36–6 Operative approach to the treatment of asymmetric craniosynostosis (plagiocephaly). A unilateral osteotomy of two-thirds of the orbital circumference is performed, the orbit is advanced tongue-in-groove fashion and rigidly positioned with interosseous wires, and an inlay bone strut is placed at the pterion. The frontal bone is then repositioned and shaped, and an onlay cranial bone graft is placed over the zygoma for symmetry as necessary. (Reproduced with permission from Whitaker L, Bartlett S, Schut L, Brucke D. Craniosynostosis: an analysis of the timing, treatment, and complications in 164 consecutive patients. Plast Reconstr Surg 1987;80:196.)

those with moderate and severe deformities, 64 percent were postoperatively categorized as III or IV, reflecting the more extensive deformities associated with craniosynostosis syndromes and bilateral craniosynostosis (Figures 36–7 and 36–8). Within this subgroup, all patients with Apert's syndrome were category III and IV patients postoperatively. Interestingly, the patient's age at surgery did not influence the need for secondary revisions when all patients with symmetric synostosis ranging from mild to severe deformity were considered as one group. Of those with symmetric craniosynostosis operated on prior to 18 months of age, 68 percent required secondary revisions while 63 percent of those operated on after 18 months of age required secondary revisions. Within the subgroup of craniofacial dysostosis or variant symmetric synostosis, including those with Crouzon's disease, 9 of 18 (50%) patients operated on prior to 18 months of age had category I or II results.

Based upon the results of their study of 145 patients, the most extensive series analyzed to date at the time of publication, Whitaker and colleagues concluded that the ideal age for treatment of asymmetric and less severe symmetric synostosis is from 4 to 12 months. In 97 percent of the asymmetric synostosis patients and 50 percent of the less severe symmetric synostosis patients operated on prior to the age of 18 months, category I or II results were

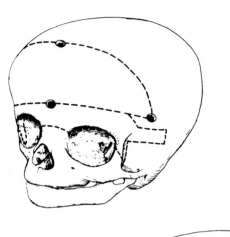

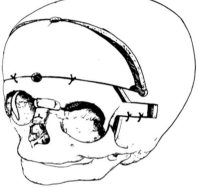

Figure 36–7 Operative approach for mild upper face symmetric synostosis. Osteotomies of superior and lateral orbit completed with tongue-in-groove extension into temporal bone laterally and across nose at nasofrontal suture medially. Following advancement, rigid fixation is performed and nasal onlay bone grafts are placed as necessary in addition to frontal bone repositioning and contouring. (Reproduced with permission from Whitaker L, Bartlett S, Schut L, Brucke D. Craniosynostosis: an analysis of the timing, treatment, and complications in 164 consecutive patients. Plast Reconstr Surg 1987;80:197.)

achieved. For moderate and severe craniofacial deformities, Whitaker recommended that early surgery be confined to craniectomies and that the more extensive calvarial reshaping and mid-face and orbital advancements (with preference for the Le Fort III monoblock advancement procedure) be done at 7 to 14 years of age due to the high likelihood of additional surgery being required with early surgical intervention.

It is important to note that the types of operative procedures employed for given defor-mities vary considerably among craniofacial surgeons. Although simple strip craniectomy was the first method described in the late nineteenth century for treatment of premature synosto-sis,[34,35] poor results have led to the abandonment of this practice in most cases over the last 20 years except for the treatment of scaphocephaly (sagittal synostosis). Two recent studies have documented the long-term improvement in craniofacial form for scaphocephaly when sagittal strip craniectomies are carried out before 1 year of age. Albright has documented normal or near-normal postoperative appearance in 93 percent of 27 patients with sagittal synostosis treated by craniectomy at follow-up of 5 to 10 years.[36] Better cosmetic outcomes and significantly improved cephalometric measurements have been documented when strip craniectomies for scaphocephaly are performed before 1 year of age.[37]

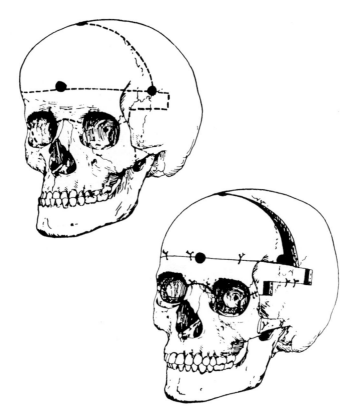

Figure 36–8 Operative approach for moderate to severe symmetric synostosis—extended Le Fort III osteotomy to include the supraorbital ridges. Following midface and supraorbital advancement, bone grafts are placed as shown (including pterygomaxillary fissure), and the segments are rigidly wired into position. Frontal bone repositioning completes the procedure. (Reproduced with permission from Whitaker L, Bartlett S, Schut L, Brucke D. Craniosynostosis: an analysis of the timing, treatment, and complications in 164 consecutive patients. Plast Reconstr Surg 1987;80:197.)

There are several commonly used surgical approaches to the treatment of plagiocephaly, one of the most common craniosynostoses characterized by vertical orbital displacement ipsilaterally, nasal root deviation to the ipsilateral side and tip deviation to the contralateral side, flattening of the zygomatic prominence on the ipsilateral side, and hypoplasia of the ipsilateral malar region. Marchac advocates bilateral frontocranial remodeling using the "floating forehead" technique and leaving a wide coronal gap. McCarthy prefers a bilateral fronto-orbital advancement with tongue-in-groove osteotomy, and Whitaker has found success with unilateral fronto-orbital repositioning. Each author has found success with his own technique. Marchac, who published the results of his 20-year experience with craniosynostosis in 983 patients, achieved 100 percent category I or II results in his series of patients with plagiocephaly, using a bilateral approach, which he feels offers better symmetry (Figure 36–9).[38–41] In addition, he advocates even earlier surgery for craniosynostosis (before the age of 4 months) to take maximal advantage of early brain expansion in cranial growth (termed "brain push"), rapid reossification of cranial defects after advancement, and excellent pliability of cranial bone for molding. In his series of 610 patients with isolated craniosynostoses, less than 3 percent required reoperations for uncorrected deformities. In a retrospective study by Bartlett of 48 children operated on in infancy by either unilateral (32 patients) or bilateral (16 patients) approach with a minimum 3-year follow-up, no statistically significant difference in the aesthetic results was found between the two procedures.[40]

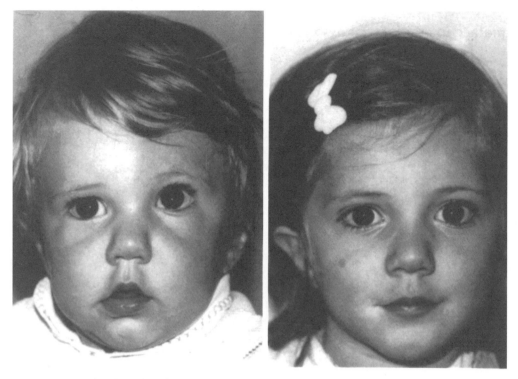

Figure 36–9 (Left) This infant shows a typical plagiocephaly with depressed forehead and orbitonasal deviation. (Right) Same patient at 4 years of age, 3½ years after bilateral frontal remodeling performed at 6 months of age. (Reproduced with permission from Marchac D. Discussion of Whitaker L, Bartlett S, Schut L, et al. Craniosynostosis: an analysis of the timing, treatment, and complications in 164 consecutive patients. Plast Reconstr Surg 1987;80:208.)

McCarthy has also retrospectively reviewed his 20-year experience with early surgery for craniosynostosis in 180 patients.[41] All patients with isolated craniofacial synostosis, which he considered separately from syndromic synostosis and pansynostosis, underwent surgery before the age of 18 months (Table 36–7). In the group with isolated craniofacial synostosis, 13 percent required a secondary cranial vault operation to address residual deficits in craniofacial form, 5 percent experienced perioperative complications, and there was no mortality. At an average 4-year follow-up, 87.5 percent of these patients were found to have Whitaker category I or II results. Among the 57 patients with plagiocephaly, nasal tip deviation to the contralateral side observed in 32 patients preoperatively was completely corrected in 25 patients postoperatively and improved in the remaining 7. Vertical orbital dystopia was seen in 32 of the 57 patients preoperatively, corrected in 12, improved in 14, and unchanged in the remaining 6. Strabismus was seen postoperatively in 18 patients and required extraocular muscle surgery in 14. In total, 86 percent of the postoperative results for plagiocephaly were graded as Whitaker category I or II.

During the 20-year interval of McCarthy's study, 29 patients with metopic suture synostosis (trigonocephaly) underwent surgery and were followed postoperatively, as were 24 patients with mild deformity who were followed with observation alone. Among the 29 patients who underwent surgery, 28 were found to have category I or II results. Of the 24 patients who did not undergo surgery, 15 showed significant improvement in frontoorbital form, and none demonstrated progression of the deformity. As far as we are aware, this is the only study in the craniofacial literature with long-term follow-up of an unoperated control group. Given that more than half the patients in this group with mild deformity showed

Table 36–7 Comparison of Long-Term Results of Early Surgery for Craniosynostosis

Diagnostic Group	No. of Patients	Mean Length of Follow-Up	Latest Evaluation Percentage at Classification*	
			I-II	III-IV
Bilateral coronal synostosis	10	51.6 months	70.0	20.0†
Unilateral coronal synostosis	57	51.7 months	86.0	14.0
Metopic synostosis	29	38.9 months	96.6	3.4
Sagittal synostosis	8	24.6 months	87.5	12.5
Total	104	46.0 months	87.5	11.5†

*Whitaker classification.
†Some rows do not add to 100 percent because of a deceased patient.
Reprinted with permission from McCarthy J, Glasberg S, Cutting C, et al. Twenty-year experience with early surgery for craniosynostosis: I. Isolated craniofacial synostosis II. The craniofacial synostosis syndromes and pansynostosis-results and unsolved problems. Plast Reconstr Surg 1995;96:274.

improvement without surgery, it would be useful to perform longitudinal studies of unoperated controls with mild deformity caused by synostosis of other sutures.

McCarthy's results of surgery for syndromic synostosis and pansynostosis in 76 patients have largely mirrored previous studies documenting the need for more extensive surgery such as a Le Fort III advancement for midface hypoplasia in 65 percent of patients, a higher reoperation rate, more complications, and inferior results. As compared with the isolated craniofacial synostosis group, his incidences of secondary and tertiary procedures (44.7% vs 13.5%), perioperative complications (11.3% vs 5.0%), hydrocephalus (42.1% vs 3.9%), and seizures (11.8 vs 2.9%) were significantly increased. At an average 6-year postoperative follow-up, 73.7 percent of these patients were considered to have at least satisfactory craniofacial form (Whitaker category I or II). Based on this experience, McCarthy advocates staged surgical intervention with fronto-orbital advancement and cranial vault remodeling to be performed at 6 to 9 months, Le Fort III advancement when indicated for midface retrusion at age 4 years, and maxillomandibular osteotomy and genioplasty as needed in adolescence.

In summary, based on optimizing outcome and minimizing reoperation, the craniofacial surgery literature supports early surgical correction of craniofacial abnormalities although the exact timing of intervention remains disputed. In asymmetric and less severe symmetric synostosis, successful outcomes have been reported when surgery is performed at between 4 and 12 months of age. Although frontocranial remodeling has been advocated by Marchac in children as young as 2 months of age, a retrospective study in 22 patients with nonsyndromic bicoronal synostosis showed that there is no evidence for improved results when surgery is performed before the age of 6 months.[42] For the treatment of plagiocephaly, although both bilateral frontocranial remodeling and unilateral fronto-orbital advancement have been shown to produce excellent results in expert hands, most craniofacial surgeons today favor the bilateral approach. Surgical intervention for moderate and severe craniofacial deformities, especially the syndromic synostoses, carries greater risks of perioperative complications, requires more extensive surgery, requires reoperation more commonly, and generally results in inferior outcomes. In these cases, staged surgical intervention is recommended, with early surgery (between 4 and 12 months of age) limited to the upper face and cranial vault and with later surgery (after 4 years of age) for midface advancement. Repeat cranial vault operations in this group are common.

Complex Facial Fractures

Although techniques for the repair of complex maxillofacial trauma and associated complication rates have been well documented by Manson, Gruss, Kawamoto, and others, comprehensive outcomes-oriented studies with long-term follow-up are relatively lacking. This can be attributed partially to significant confounding factors such as recurrent facial trauma, drug and alcohol use, low socioeconomic status, and inadequate follow-up in the large facial-fracture population subset that is assault-related, all of which make standard outcomes parameters difficult to assess and interpret. In the section below, epidemiologic data and complication rates from facial-fracture fixation are presented. In addition, currently unpublished data from The Johns Hopkins Hospital and the University of Maryland Shock Trauma Center on long-term functional outcomes following complex facial fractures are presented.

In the United States, approximately 25,000 people die of assault-related injuries each year and thousands more acquire permanent physical disabilities.[43] Of all assault-related injuries, the face is the most commonly affected body region (83% of all assault-related injuries), and most injuries result from unarmed and nonpenetrating injury (> 70%). In a retrospective study of 802 patients in San Francisco who sustained facial injury from blunt assault, Greene has shown that social variables including tobacco, drug and alcohol use, and low socioeconomic status produce a dramatic worsening of both injury incidence and outcome.[44] In this study, 89 percent of subjects were male, 50 percent were unemployed at the time of injury, 20 percent were homeless, 10 percent had a history of psychiatric illness, 44 percent abused alcohol, 39 percent smoked, and 27 percent used illicit drugs. Twenty-one percent of patients were repeat victims of assault, and 17 percent sustained previous facial trauma from assault.

Girotto has retrospectively reviewed data on 190 patients who underwent repair of complex facial fractures secondary to blunt trauma with a minimal 18-month follow-up by telephone interview and has found significant long-term morbidity.[45] A broad range of functional outcomes and physical impairments were measured in this study, including general physical and mental health, diplopia, facial numbness, difficulty with chewing and breathing, persistent pain, and alterations in smell, taste, and vision. Of study participants who sustained Le Fort fractures, 31 percent reported difficulty with mastication due to pain, malocclusion, or difficulty with opening the mouth; 35 percent complained of alteration in smell or taste; 33 percent reported difficulty with breathing; and 32 percent had residual facial numbness. Fifty-six percent of study participants had visual problems, including epiphora (tearing eyes, 45%) and diplopia (25%). However, in studies of midface fractures and postoperative diplopia, there appears to be a resolution in symptoms with time;[46] Steidler found that diplopia following reduction of midface fractures decreased from 32 to 8 percent over three years.[47]

Facial-fracture reconstruction using plates and screws and rigid fixation is often necessary to provide firm support and to restore the bony framework. Significant complications, including infection, pain, and prominence, exposure, loosening, and migration of hardware, can result from plate-and-screw fixation. In a 5-year study of 507 patients with 1,112 fractures resulting from trauma, 61 patients (12%) required removal of hardware, the major reason for extraction being infection (91%).[48] The most common sites of removal were the mandible and maxillary buttresses, which are also the most contaminated sites due to the presence of bacteria from oral secretions and in the sinuses that are in direct contact with hardware. In a study of 384 patients who underwent reduction of mandible fractures using open reduction (rigid fixation with plates and screws) versus closed reduction (maxillomandibular fixation with wires), the complication rate was 27.6 percent for open reduction versus 11 percent with closed reduction ($p < .001$, chi-squared test).[49]

In summary, there is significant long-term morbidity after facial-fracture reconstruction in complex facial trauma, due to residual visual disturbances, difficulty with chewing and breathing, pain, numbness, and changes in taste and smell. Complications resulting from surgery include infection, prominence and loosening of hardware, and pain, which frequently requires the removal of hardware. In the case of patients with facial fractures, social variables, including tobacco, drug, and alcohol use and low socioeconomic status, produce a dramatic worsening of both injury incidence and outcome. The quantification of these results will enable the measurements of the effectiveness of treatment approaches over time.

AESTHETIC SURGERY

Aesthetic surgery is an increasingly common medical procedure in contemporary society, as shown by the 529,000 aesthetic procedures performed in the United States in 1997, a 50 percent increase in the number of aesthetic procedures performed since 1992 and a tripling in the number of breast augmentation and liposuction procedures.[50] The ultimate objective of aesthetic surgery is to improve psychologic well-being, which is one dimension of health, through surgical modification of the patient's body image. Although surgeons traditionally judge their results objectively on the basis of concrete parameters and complication-free results, outcomes in aesthetic surgery are best judged through quality-of-life indices that incorporate the patient's subjective interpretation of the final results. Given the array of aesthetic procedures available, which include liposuction, breast surgery (augmentation, reduction, and mastopexy), abdominoplasty, and facial surgery (rhinoplasty, blepharoplasty, rhytidectomy, genioplasty, otoplasty, laser resurfacing, collagen injection, implants, etc), assessing outcomes for each is a formidable task. To further complicate matters, with the recent introduction of new technologies such as endoscopic surgery for face-lifts, CO_2 lasers for facial resurfacing and blepharoplasty, and ultrasonic liposuction, outcomes of conventional techniques need to be compared with those of new methods. Since a comprehensive analysis of each procedure is beyond the scope of this chapter, an overview of available psychologic studies will be provided as well as recent data comparing conventional and ultrasonic liposuction, the most commonly performed aesthetic surgical procedure.

Although aesthetic surgery is becoming increasingly common and accepted, various authors have noted a disproportionate representation of certain personality types among patients seeking aesthetic procedures. Several studies have shown that there is predictive value for overall patient satisfaction depending upon patient personality characteristics. For this reason, plastic surgeons should identify warning signals when evaluating patients for aesthetic surgery, to prevent poor outcomes and unnecessary surgery. In a study of 133 patients in a typical private practice who underwent aesthetic surgery over a 1.5-year period beginning in 1987, patients were evaluated by a clinical psychologist and were categorized according to standard psychiatric (Axis I) and personality (Axis II) disorder descriptions found in the *Diagnostic and Statistical Manual of Mental Disorders* of the American Psychiatric Association.[51] Nearly 20 percent of the patients in the study were found to have Axis I psychiatric diagnoses such as anxiety disorder, thought disorder, and depression. According to Axis II criteria, only 29 percent of patients were regarded as "normal" by the author: 25 percent were narcissistic, 12 percent were dependent, 10 percent were histrionic, 9 percent were borderline, 4 percent were obsessive-compulsive, and 11 percent met criteria for other personality disorders. In this study, patients with an Axis I disorder were generally found to be satisfied patients in contradistinction to patients with certain Axis II diagnoses (narcissistic, borderline, and obsessive-compulsive), who were disproportionately dissatisfied. Preoperative expectations among patients were also found to be related to levels of satisfaction, with frequent postoperative disappointment found among those patients who were judged preoperatively to have unrealistic expectations. Given this finding, the author cautions against the marketing style of some cosmetic surgeons who advertise their best results and emphasize dramatic improvements. Lastly, a relationship was found to exist between the number of surgical sites requested and satisfaction. The group of least-satisfied patients, made up of the borderline personality type, requested the highest number of aesthetic surgical procedures, averaging 4.5, at the time of consultation. The author urges careful evaluation of patients who request complete makeovers and cautions against performing multiple procedures during a single operative session. The results of this study demonstrate that cosmetic surgeons can benefit from understanding the psychologic makeup of their patients and should recognize that objective assessments of the surgical outcome are not necessarily predictive of the patient's ultimate satisfaction.

Quality-of-Life Outcomes

Two recent studies have comprehensively evaluated quality-of-life outcomes after aesthetic surgery, using questionnaires that assess many parameters including anxiety, dissatisfaction, loneliness, self-confidence, affect, and social and sexual functions. In a study of 105 patients undergoing seven different aesthetic procedures evaluated preoperatively and over a period of 6 months postoperatively, quality-of-life index scores improved significantly from mean levels of 3.24 to 2.11, and mean scores for depression (using a standardized scale) improved from 11.2 preoperatively to 6.3 at 6 months after surgery.[52] When compared with matched controls, the study subjects were classified in the high normal range preoperatively on the scale for depression. Scores at 6 months after aesthetic surgery placed subjects into the least depressed end of the normal range and below the general average population norms. The results of this study confirmed the authors' hypothesis that surgery to enhance appearance improves the multidimensional domain of health status by improving psychologic affect and self-confidence. Subjects reported positive changes in their social lives, interpersonal relationships, and sexual activity, and reported enjoying more leisure activities.

A British National Health Service (NHS) study evaluated the health-related quality of life among 198 patients in the Oxford region by questionnaire before aesthetic surgery and 6 months after aesthetic surgery.[53] Reflecting the rationing of health care in the NHS for elective surgery through long waiting lists, the average patient in this study seeking aesthetic surgery waited 106 days for an outpatient appointment and 321 days for surgery after the initial appointment. The formal health survey evaluated emotional problems, social function, mental health, self-esteem, and psychologic well-being in all patients. In this study, aesthetic surgery led to health gains in nearly all aspects of social, psychologic, and physical functioning. The majority of patients (55.1%) saw a great deal of change in their appearance, thought the result very good or excellent (75%), and were pleased with the effect of the surgery on their lives (85.3%).

Liposuction: Conventional versus Ultrasonic

In 1997, liposuction was performed on 149,000 people in the United States. Over the 20 years since the introduction of suction-assisted lipectomy, numerous refinements have been made through the introduction of blunt cannulae, tumescent techniques that allow larger volumes of fat removal with less blood loss, and recently, ultrasound technology, which is particularly effective for use in fibrous areas such as the back and the male breast. Many studies have documented that suction-assisted lipoplasty, the most commonly performed aesthetic surgical procedure in the United States, is a safe and effective procedure. The first ultrasound-assisted liposuction machine was introduced in Italy in the late 1980s by Zocchi and consisted of a solid probe that delivered ultrasonic energy into the subcutaneous tissue, followed by evacuation with a traditional liposuction cannula.[54] Ultrasound-assisted liposuction (UAL) removes fat through a fat emulsification process termed "cavitation," which differs from the traditional method that achieves contouring through the mechanical avulsion of fat. In UAL, ultrasonic energy liquefies fat by cellular fragmentation, causing the release of cellular contents into the intercellular space. The fatty emulsion is then suctioned, using standard techniques. Recent advances in UAL include the development of a hollow cannula that allows simultaneous cavitation and aspiration. The risks of superficial burns and seromas that can result from thermal energy released by UAL are reduced through constant motion of the cannula and avoidance of the superficial subdermal fat plane. In the United States, ultrasound technology applied to liposuction was introduced through a unique collaboration in 1995 among the five major plastic surgery organizations, manufacturers, and the US Food and Drug Administration (FDA) to ensure the safety and efficacy of the procedure as well as to develop an instructional curriculum. This effort resulted in several major studies comparing complications and results of UAL with those of traditional liposuction methods.

The results of three large series published to date comparing UAL and standard liposuction techniques have yielded mixed results and differing opinions about the benefits of ultrasound technology. In a series of 250 patients, Maxwell and Gingrass advocate UAL as the preferred method of suction-assisted lipoplasty in many clinical situations.[55] They suggest that benefits such as decreased surgeon fatigue, exceptional control of contour, minimal blood loss and bruising, and the ability to suction large volumes of fat outweigh the risks of a significantly higher complication rate. In this study, 11.2 percent of patients developed seromas greater than 50 cc, requiring one or several aspiration attempts; this is in contrast to the negligible risk of seromas experienced with the conventional method. Furthermore, 1.2 percent of patients, all of whom underwent UAL early in the series, experienced the serious complication of abdominal skin necrosis that the authors attributed to extensive ultrasonic treatment of the superficial subdermal plane.

Fodor and Watson regard UAL with less enthusiasm at the conclusion of their study, which failed to prove most of the benefits attributed to ultrasound technology. In their study of 100 patients, 63 patients underwent ipsilateral traditional lipoplasty and contralateral UAL. Although no complications were noted by the authors, postoperative surgeon and patient ratings of both sides were no different with regard to contouring, bruising, or sensory changes. The authors comment that 90 percent of the patients in this study reported high levels of satisfaction with the procedure. Pointing out the increased expense, the learning curve, the larger incisions, and the 40 percent greater operative time associated with UAL, the authors refute the superiority of UAL over traditional lipoplasty in the typical lipoplasty patient. In a study of 114 patients over 13 months, Rohrich and colleagues also documented increases of 50 to 100 percent in operative times with UAL as compared to conventional methods.[56] Three patients (2.6%) developed seromas in this study, and there was one case of a superficial burn. However, the authors remain optimistic that UAL can serve as an adjunct in the field of body contouring in difficult fibrous areas such as the back and the male breast or in reoperative liposuction.

In summary, there are a vast number of procedures that fall under the umbrella of aesthetic surgery. The ultimate objective of all of these procedures is to improve psychologic well-being, which is one dimension of health, through surgical modification of body image. Outcomes studies have documented significant gains from aesthetic surgery on quality-of-life scales that measure depression, anxiety, self-esteem, and social and sexual functioning. Given the fact that aesthetic surgery is intended to alter the patient's psyche, cosmetic surgeons must be able to evaluate their patients' motives for surgery and identify potential warning signals that portend postoperative dissatisfaction. Lastly, given the rapid introduction of new technologies such as endoscopic surgery, laser surgery, and UAL, more outcomes studies are needed to compare new methods with conventional techniques. The cooperative efforts between industry, the FDA, and plastic surgical organizations for the evaluation of ultrasound in liposuction is a model that should be emulated. Although more study is needed, such as a prospective randomized trial comparing the two techniques, there is no evidence yet that UAL should replace conventional suction-assisted lipoplasty.

HAND SURGERY

Since the hands are functionally integral to nearly all routine daily activities, it is difficult for most of us to imagine the devastating effects of a serious hand injury. The field of hand surgery is a specialty shared by plastic surgeons, orthopedic surgeons, and general surgeons who have completed hand fellowships. The scope of procedures performed include (1) the repair of fractures and injuries to the tendons, ligaments, and soft tissues; (2) microsurgery for limb and digit replantation, free-tissue transfers, and the repair of vessels and nerves; (3) reconstruction of congenital hand defects; (4) decompression of nerves; (5) surgical management of hand and forearm infections and compartment syndromes; and (6) surgical management of certain progressive soft-tissue and joint diseases such as Dupuytren's contracture and rheumatoid arthritis.

In 1997, plastic surgeons performed 137,000 operative hand procedures in the United States, the most common being carpal tunnel releases (39,000 procedures, of which 4,800 were performed endoscopically).[5] Since 1989, advocates for endoscopic carpal tunnel release (ECTR) have promoted this procedure due to its shortened postoperative disability time and decreased early postoperative pain compared to the conventional open method. There has been controversy, however, over the significant complications associated with ECTR even when in experienced hands. Since a comprehensive discussion of outcomes associated with all hand procedures is beyond the scope of this chapter, surgery for carpal tunnel syndrome (CTS), the most common procedure that hand surgeons perform, is evaluated, and a review of the experience with ECTR is presented.

Although CTS is essentially a clinical diagnosis, many surgeons rely upon electrodiagnostic or other studies to confirm the diagnosis. These studies can be of particular value when the physical findings are not altogether clear or when there is the potential for secondary gain to the patient as in cases of workers' compensation. Patients typically present with subjective symptoms of numbness and tingling in the median nerve distribution and on physical exam have a positive result on Phalen's maneuver (complaint of paresthesia in the median nerve distribution with maximum passive wrist flexion for less than 30 seconds) and for Tinel's sign (complaint of hypersensitivity on percussion of the median nerve at the wrist).

The criteria for an abnormal electrodiagnostic study (EDS) are presented in Table 36–8.[57] An alternative to EDS using the pressure specified sensory device (PSSD) (Sensory Management Services, LLC, Lutherville, MD) was developed in 1993 for the diagnosis of upper extremity peripheral nerve disease such as carpal and cubital tunnel syndrome, brachial plexus injury, and thoracic inlet syndrome (Figure 36–10). This device measures the pressure required for moving and static touch and the pressure and distance required for two-point discrimination.[58,59] Unlike EDS, which is expensive (at least $1,000) and painful for the patient, PSSD is not painful, uses no needles, is fun for the patient, and is significantly less expensive than traditional nerve conduction studies (approximately $300 per test). Furthermore, the PSSD is more sensitive and specific than EDS in the diagnosis of carpal tunnel syndrome. In a study of 80 patients, 26 normals and 54 with CTS diagnosed by physical examination alone, the sensitivity for the PSSD was 89 percent versus 78 percent for EDS, and the specificity for PSSD was 82 percent versus 72 percent for EDS.[60]

It is appropriate to offer some patients, especially those with mild or intermittent symptoms, a trial of conservative therapy that consists of steroid injection into the carpal tunnel and a palmar splint to prevent wrist flexion. In a series of 130 hands, Kulick and colleagues reported that 69 percent of patients diagnosed with CTS experienced relief of symptoms from the initial steroid injection and that this relief lasted more than a year in 32 percent of patients.[61] Kulick has also shown value in steroid injections as an indicator of surgical prognosis. In the same series, all 51 hands that benefited from conservative therapy for more than 6 months had complete alleviation of symptoms at an average follow-up of 4.5 years after

Table 36–8 Diagnostic Criteria of the Electromyogram for Carpal Tunnel Syndrome

1. Above the motor latency 4.0 ms

2. Above the sensory latency 3.0 ms

3. Below the sensory amplitude 20μV

4. Above the ratio of median over ulnar motor latency 1.5

5. Above the ratio of median over ulnar sensory latency 1.2

6. Below the ratio of median over ulnar sensory amplitude 0.6

Reprinted with permission from Choi S, Ahn D. Correlation of clinical history and electrodiagnostic abnormalities with outcome after surgery for carpal tunnel syndrome. Plast Reconstr Surg 1998;102:2375.

carpal tunnel release. Conversely, 17 of the 25 hands that were symptomatic more than 4 years after surgery failed to receive any benefit from the initial steroid injection.

Upon review of the literature, the long-term success rate for complete resolution of all symptoms associated with CTS after open carpal tunnel release is greater than 80 percent.[57,62–65] The open technique has been credited as a reliable, simple procedure usually lasting less than 1 hour and having a minimal complication rate. During an open release, the surgeon may inspect the median nerve and flexor tendons and divide the transverse carpal ligament with confidence under full visualization of all neurovascular structures. In most patients, numbness and paresthesias subside within the first few weeks after surgery, and grip strength, which is initially weaker postoperatively, begins to exceed preoperative levels at 3 to 6 months.[66] Even patients who have had symptoms of CTS for more than 10 years will have a high rate of recovery from some symptoms (> 90%) within a year after surgery.[57]

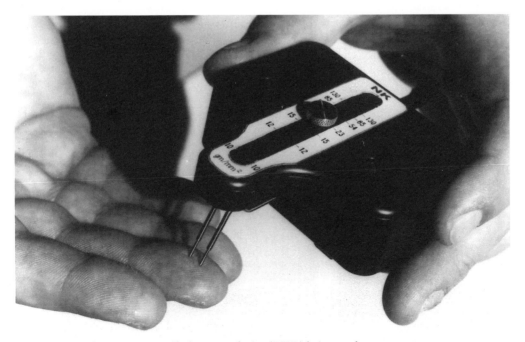

Figure 36–10 The pressure specified sensory device (PSSD) being used to measure cutaneous pressure threshold. (Reproduced with permission from Sensory Management Services, LLC, Lutherville, MD; [410] 583–0200.)

In contrast to other popular applications of endoscopic technology such as cholecystectomy and arthroscopy, the significant advantages of improved visualization and duration of hospitalization do not hold for carpal tunnel release. Regardless of approach used, carpal tunnel release is an outpatient procedure. Furthermore, improved exposure of the carpal canal and its contents is not obtained with endoscopic carpal tunnel instrumentation. Therefore, the benefits of ECTR are based exclusively on patient outcome factors such as postoperative pain, weakness, and length of convalescence.

Endoscopic carpal tunnel release has been credited with less postoperative scar tenderness, less pillar pain (pain over the thenar and hypothenar eminences), and an earlier return to work. Several prospective multicenter randomized studies have confirmed these advantages of ECTR over the open technique, but reports of significant complications, including median and ulnar nerve transections and damage to the superficial palmar arch, have lessened the enthusiasm for this otherwise simple and effective procedure.[67] Endoscopic technology has also advanced, and the single-portal technique has been replaced by a two-portal method that allows visualization of tunnel structures during transection of the carpal tunnel ligament.

In a multicenter prospective randomized trial of 169 hands (85 open method, 84 ECTR) in 145 patients, Brown and colleagues compared two-portal ECTR to the open method, with a follow-up of 12 weeks.[68] Over the duration of the study, there was no difference between the two groups in postoperative carpal tunnel pressure, Semmes-Weinstein monofilament testing, grip strength, two-point discrimination, pillar tenderness, or relief of numbness and paresthesias. However, there were differences in scar tenderness and median time for returning to work. At 12 weeks, 39 percent of open procedure patients had no scar tenderness, and 15 percent had moderate to severe tenderness. Sixty-four percent of ECTR patients had no scar tenderness, 1 percent had moderate tenderness, and none had severe tenderness. The median time for returning to work was 28 days among open procedure patients and 14 days among ECTR patients. There were no complications in patients who underwent the open procedure, while four major complications occurred in ECTR patients: partial transection of the superficial palmar arch, ulnar nerve neurapraxia, digital nerve contusion, and large hematoma. Although surgeons' fees were the same for both groups, the average total cost of ECTR was $3,468 and the cost of the open technique was $2,977. The average procedure time was lengthened by 10 minutes (57 minutes for ECTR vs 67 minutes for the open method). The authors of this study concluded that "the greater rate of complications indicates that intra-operative safety must be improved before ECTR is performed on a widespread basis."

In a prospective study of 147 hands (82 ECTR, 65 open method) in 10 centers, Agee and colleagues found that among patients not drawing workers' compensation, the median time for returning to work among ECTR patients was 16.5 days versus 45.5 days for those undergoing open release.[69] Two patients in this study required conversion from ECTR to the open technique, and two ECTR patients developed a transient ulnar neurapraxia. Although there were no differences in scar tenderness and pillar pain at 26 weeks between groups, there were significant differences through 9 weeks, to which the authors attribute the earlier return to work among ECTR patients.

In summary, carpal tunnel release is the most common procedure of the hands performed by plastic surgeons. As the standard for comparison, open carpal tunnel release is a highly successful procedure with an > 80 percent rate of complete resolution of symptoms. Endoscopic carpal tunnel release, which has been in use since 1989, is credited with decreased early postoperative (< 9 weeks) scar tenderness and an earlier return to work by 2 to 4 weeks. No differences have been found in long-term scar tenderness, grip strength, or recurrence of symptoms. Significant complications have occurred in the early experience with ECTR, which at present do not justify widespread use of this procedure when the open technique is used as the standard for comparison.

REFERENCES

1. Tagliacozzi G. De Curtorum Chirurgia per Insitionem. Venice: Gaspare Bindoni; 1597.

2. Coady MSE. Measuring outcomes in plastic surgery. Br J Plast Surg 1997;50:200–5.

3. Cosmetic and reconstructive procedures in plastic surgery. Arlington Heights (IL): American Society of Plastic and Reconstructive Surgeons; 1989.

4. Wilkins EG, Lowery JC, Smith DJ Jr. Outcomes research: a primer for plastic surgeons. Ann Plast Surg 1996;37:1–11.

5. American Society of Plastic and Reconstructive Surgeons. Procedural statistics. Arlington Heights (IL): American Society of Plastic and Reconstructive Surgeons; 1998.

6. Dabbah A, Lehman JA Jr, Parker MG, et al. Reduction mammaplasty: an outcome analysis. Ann Plast Surg 1995;35:337–41.

7. Raispis T, Zehring RD, Downey DL. Long-term functional results after reduction mammaplasty. Ann Plast Surg 1995;34:113–6.

8. Boschert M, Barone C, Puckett C. Outcome analysis of reduction mammaplasty. Plast Reconstr Surg 1996;98:451–4.

9. Serletti JM, Reading G, Caldwell E, Wray RC. Long-term patient satisfaction following reduction mammaplasty. Ann Plast Surg 1992;28:363–5.

10. Shakespeare V, Cole RP. Measuring patient-based outcomes in a plastic surgery service: breast reduction surgical patients. Br J Plast Surg 1997;50:242–8.

11. Schnur PL, Hoehn JG, Ilstrup DM, et al. Reduction mammaplasty: cosmetic or reconstructive procedure? Ann Plast Surg 1991;27:232–7.

12. Hartrampf C, Scheflan M, Black P. Breast reconstruction with a transverse abdominal island flap. Plast Reconstr Surg 1982;69:216.

13. Hölmstrom H. The free abdominoplasty flap and its use in breast reconstruction. Scand J Plast Reconstr Surg 1979;13:423.

14. Friedman R, Argenta L, Anderson R. Deep inferior epigastric free flap for breast reconstructions after radical mastectomy. Plast Reconstr Surg 1985;76:455–8.

15. Moon H, Taylor G. The vascular anatomy of rectus abdominis musculocutaneous flaps based on the deep superior epigastric system. Plast Reconstr Surg 1988;82:815.

16. Kroll S, Baldwin B. A comparison of outcomes using three different methods of breast reconstruction. Plast Reconstr Surg 1992;90:455–62.

17. Francel T, Ryan J, Manson P. Breast reconstruction utilizing implants: a local experience and comparison of three techniques. Plast Reconstr Surg 1993;92:786–94.

18. Elliott L, Eskenazi L, Beegle P, et al. Immediate TRAM flap breast reconstruction: 128 consecutive cases. Plast Reconstr Surg 1993;92:217–27.

19. Schusterman M, Kroll S, Miller M, et al. The free transverse rectus abdominis musculocutaneous flap for breast reconstruction: one center's experience with 211 consecutive cases. Ann Plast Surg 1994;32:234–42.

20. Banic A, Boeckx W, Greulich M, et al. Late results of breast reconstruction with free TRAM flaps: a prospective multicentric study. Plast Reconstr Surg 1995;95:1195–206.

21. Shaw W. Invited discussion of Schusterman M, Kroll S, Miller M, et al. The free transverse rectus abdominis musculocutaneous flap for breast reconstruction: one center's experience with 211 consecutive cases. Ann Plast Surg 1994;32:241.

22. Kroll S. Discussion of Banic A, Boeckx W, Greulich M, et al. Late results of breast reconstruction with free TRAM flaps: a prospective multicentric study. Plast Reconstr Surg 1995;95:1205.

23. Whitney T, Buncke H, Lineaweaver W, Alpert B. Reconstruction of the upper extremity with multiple microvascular transplants: analysis of method, cost, and complications. Ann Plast Surg 1989;23:396–400.

24. Chang B, Wang B. Personal communication of unpublished data. Division of Plastic and Reconstructive Surgery, The Johns Hopkins Hospital; 1998.

25. Mizgala C, Hartrampf C, Bennett K. Assessment of the abdominal wall after pedicled TRAM flap surgery: 5- to 7-year follow-up of 150 consecutive patients. Plast Reconstr Surg 1994;93:988–1004.

26. Kind G, Rademaker A, Mustoe T. Abdominal-wall recovery following TRAM flap: a functional outcome study. Plast Reconstr Surg 1997;99:417–28.

27. Serletti J, Moran S. Free versus the pedicled TRAM flap: a cost comparison and outcome analysis. Plast Reconstr Surg 1997;100:1418–24.

28. Khoo A, Kroll S, Reece G, et al. A comparison of resource costs of immediate and delayed breast reconstruction. Plast Reconstr Surg 1998;101:964–70.

29. Elkowitz A, Colen S, Slavin S, et al. Various methods of breast reconstruction after mastectomy: an economic comparison. Plast Reconstr Surg 1993;92:77–83.

30. Tessier P. Osteotomies totales de la face. Syndrome de Crouzon. Syndrome d'Apert. Oxycephalies. Turricephalies. Ann Chir Plast 1967;12:273.

31. Tessier P. The definitive plastic surgical treatment of the severe facial deformities of craniofacial dysostoses. Plast Reconstr Surg 1971;48:419.

32. Persing J, Babler W, Winn H, et al. Age as a critical factor in the success of surgical correction of craniosynostosis. J Neurosurg 1981;54:601.

33. Whitaker L, Bartlett S, Schut L, Brucke D. Craniosynostosis: an analysis of the timing, treatment, and complications in 164 consecutive patients. Plast Reconstr Surg 1987;80:195–212.

34. Lane L. Pioneer craniectomy for relief of mental imbecility due to premature sutural closure and microcephalus. JAMA 1892;18:49.

35. Lannelongue M. De la craniectomie dans la microcephalie. Compte Rendu Acad Sci 1890;110:1382.

36. Albright A, Towbin R, Shultz B. Long-term outcome after sagittal synostosis operations. Pediatr Neurosurg 1996;25:78–82.

37. Krasnicanova H, Zemkova D, Skodova I. Longitudinal follow-up of children after surgical treatment of scaphocephaly. Acta Chir Plast 1996;38:50–3.

38. Marchac D. Discussion of Whitaker L, Bartlett S, Schut L, et al. Craniosynostosis: an analysis of the timing, treatment, and complications in 164 consecutive patients. Plast Reconstr Surg 1987;80:207–12.

39. Marchac D, Renier D, Broumand S. Timing and treatment for craniosynostosis and fasciocraniosynostosis: a 20-year experience. Br J Plast Surg 1994;47:211–22.

40. Bartlett S, Whitaker L, Marchac D. The operative treatment of isolated craniofacial dysostosis (plagiocephaly): a comparison of the unilateral and bilateral techniques. Plast Reconstr Surg 1990;85:677–83.

41. McCarthy J, Glasberg S, Cutting C, et al. Twenty-year experience with early surgery for cranio-synostosis: I. Isolated craniofacial synostosis II. The craniofacial synostosis syndromes and pan-synostosis-results and unsolved problems. Plast Reconstr Surg 1995;96:272–98.

42. Wagner J, Cohen S, Maher H, et al. Critical analysis of results of craniofacial surgery for nonsyn-dromic bicoronal synostosis. J Craniofac Surg 1995;6:32–9.

43. Eastman A. Blood in our streets: the status and evolution of trauma care systems. Arch Surg 1992;127:677–81.

44. Greene D, Raven R, Carvalho G, Maas C. Epidemiology of facial injury in blunt assault: determi-nants of incidence and outcome in 802 patients. Arch Otolaryngol Head Neck Surg 1997;123:923–8.

45. Girotto, J, Mackenzie E, Fowler C, et al. Long term physical impairment and functional outcomes following complex facial fractures. Baltimore (MD): The Johns Hopkins Hospital and University of Maryland Shock Trauma Center; 1986–1994. [Unpublished]

46. Al-Qurainy I, Stassen L, Dutton G, et al. Diplopia following midfacial fractures. Br J Oral Maxillofac Surg 1991;29:302.

47. Steidler N, Cook R, Reade P. Residual complications in patients with major middle third facial fractures. Int J Oral Surg 1980;9:259–66.

48. Francel T, Birely B, Ringelman P, Manson P. The fate of plates and screws after facial fracture recon-struction. Plast Reconstr Surg 1992;90:568–73.

49. Greene D, Raven R, Carvalho G, Maas C. Epidemiology of facial injury in blunt assault: determi-nants of incidence and outcome in 802 patients. Arch Otolaryngol Head Neck Surg 1997;123:923–8.

50. American Society of Plastic and Reconstructive Surgeons. Procedural statistics. Arlington Heights (IL): American Society of Plastic and Reconstructive Surgeons; 1996.

51. Napoleon A. The presentation of personalities in plastic surgery. Ann Plast Surg 1993;31:193–208.

52. Rankin M, Borah G, Perry A, Wey P. Quality-of-life outcomes after cosmetic surgery. Plast Reconstr Surg 1998;102:2139–45.

53. Klassen A, Jenkinson C, Fitzpatrick R, Goodacre T. Patients' health related quality of life before and after aesthetic surgery. Br J Plast Surg 1996;49:433–8.

54. Zocchi M. Ultrasound assisted lipoplasty: technical refinements and clinical evaluations. Clin Plast Surg 1996;23:575.

55. Maxwell G, Gingrass M. Ultrasound-assisted lipoplasty: a clinical study of 250 consecutive patients. Plast Reconstr Surg 1998;101:189–204.

56. Rohrich R, Beran S, Kenkel J, et al. Extending the role of liposuction in body contouring with ultra-sound-assisted liposuction. Plast Reconstr Surg 1998;101:1090–102.

57. Choi S, Ahn D. Correlation of clinical history and electrodiagnostic abnormalities with outcome after surgery for carpal tunnel syndrome. Plast Reconstr Surg 1998;102:2374–80.

58. Dellon ES, Keller KM, Moratz VS, Dellon AL. Validation of cutaneous pressure threshold measure-ment with the pressure specifying sensory device. Ann Plast Surg 1997;38:485–92.

59. Dellon AL, Keller KM. Evaluation of carpal and cubital tunnel syndrome utilizing the pressure specifying sensory device for quantitative sensory testing. Ann Plast Surg 1997;38:493–502.

60. Weber R, Schuchmann J, Ortiz J. Comparison of nerve conduction velocity and the pressure specified sensory device in the diagnosis of carpal tunnel syndrome. J Reconstr Microsurg 1998;14:596.

61. Kulick M, Gordillo G, Javidi T, et al. Long-term analysis of patients having surgical treatment for carpal tunnel syndrome. J Hand Surg 1986;11A:59–66.

62. Glowacki K, Breen C, Sachar K. Electrodiagnostic testing and carpal tunnel release outcome. J Hand Surg (Am) 1996;21:117.

63. Graham R. Carpal tunnel syndrome: a statistical analysis of 214 cases. Orthopedics 1983;41:232.

64. Harris C, Tanner E, Goldstein M. The surgical treatment of the carpal-tunnel syndrome correlated with preoperative nerve-conduction studies. J Bone Joint Surg (Am) 1979;61:93.

65. Thurston A, Lam N. Results of open carpal tunnel release: a comprehensive, retrospective study of 188 hands. Aust N Z J Surg 1997;67:283–8.

66. Gellman H, Kan D, Gee V, et al. Analysis of pinch and grip strength after carpal tunnel release. J Hand Surg 1989;14A:863–4.

67. Feinstien P. Endoscopic carpal tunnel release in a community-based series. J Hand Surg 1993;18A:451–4.

68. Brown R, Gelberman R, Seiler J, et al. Carpal tunnel release. J Bone Joint Surg 1993;75A:1265–75.

69. Agee J, McCarroll R, Tortosa R, et al. Endoscopic release of the carpal tunnel: a randomized prospective multicenter study. J Hand Surg 1992;17A:987–95.

CHAPTER 37

Pediatric Surgery

Paul M. Colombani, MD

THE PRACTICE OF PEDIATRIC SURGERY

Pediatric surgery is a subspecialty of general and thoracic surgery that primarily devotes itself to the surgical problems of the pediatric age group, usually children under 18 years of age. Special emphasis is placed on the unique problems of children, with a wide variety of congenital anomalies that require surgical correction. The practice of pediatric surgery is one of the last areas of general surgery in which surgeons remain generalists and routinely perform surgical procedures from multiple subspecialties of general surgery (thoracic, vascular, transplant, colon/rectal, endocrine, oncologic, and trauma). For the most part, however, the general pediatric surgeons practice what is usually considered to be general abdominal surgery although they also perform surgical procedures from other specialties including otolaryngology, urology, minor orthopedics, plastic surgery, and cardiothoracic surgery. In the United States, many common procedures in children are performed by nonpediatric general surgeons, and pediatric surgeons are principally involved in the surgical correction of the more unusual congenital anomalies in a variety of organ systems in newborns and infants. In Europe and Asia, the pediatric surgeon performs most surgeries in children.

As alluded to in other chapters, the randomized controlled clinical trial is the "gold standard" for medical practice.[1] Surgical studies, however, have been mostly empiric applications of surgical techniques to various clinical problems.[2,3] At times, surgeons have been almost evangelical in their enthusiasm for promoting their own (considered best) technique for a particular surgical problem. The practice of general pediatric surgery is no different. Pediatric surgeons have primarily adopted surgeon-initiated empiric techniques for common diagnoses such as appendicitis and tumors in children. Pediatric surgeons have also created new procedures to correct the many unique anomalies found in the pediatric age group, such as esophageal atresia, imperforate anus, and various intestinal atresias.

Many of the techniques used to treat these unique anomalies were forged in a trial-and-error fashion during what may be termed the "heroic age" of pediatric surgery. This period, following World War I, began when a few nonpediatric general surgeons first became affiliated with children's hospitals. These surgeons began to tackle the unique surgical problems in the pediatric age group. After World War II, general surgeons in increasing numbers devoted their careers full-time to the care of children. This period lasted into the 1960s and was characterized by pioneering efforts to surgically correct or treat the wide array of anomalies, tumors, and general surgical conditions in infants and children, with little or rudimentary anesthetic, physiologic, or nutritional support.[4,5]

The modern age of pediatric surgery coincided with the rapid advances made in critical care and anesthesia, especially for neonates and pre-term infants. These advances in care were made with improvements in technical and clinical support with the miniaturization of equipment (intravenous cannulas, endotracheal tubes, ventilators, extracorporeal membrane oxygenation [ECMO], etc) and improvements in clinical practice (chemotherapy, antibiotics, anesthetic agents, paralyzing agents, intravenous nutrition, etc). Any in-depth analysis of the roots of evidence-based pediatric surgical practice needs to examine these elements, namely, the actual procedure-driven evidence for surgical practice, and any advances in technical and medical supportive care.

LITERATURE REVIEW

As previously described, the principle form of evidence for pediatric surgical practice has been empiric and has been based on reports on selected consecutive series of patients or case reports by individual surgeons. This evidence by trial and error forms the framework for the practice of pediatric surgery,[6,7] primarily because the frequency of many of these unique anomalies is quite low. In the clinical careers of most pediatric surgeons, even of those practicing at a large children's hospital, many of these anomalies will not be seen frequently enough to provide the necessary volume for randomized controlled trials or case controlled studies. This has hampered the use of randomization or other study design techniques to assess possibly equivalent operative solutions to a given problem. In addition, most children's hospitals have worked in isolation from each other, often developing and championing unique methods to correct similar surgical problems or provide supportive clinical care. As a result, the number of patients available to any particular institution or group of institutions for clinical trials or scientific study is quite limited. Only recently have professional groups for pediatric surgeons emerged to provide the framework for multicenter clinical trials. These groups include the American Academy of Pediatrics, the American Pediatric Surgical Association, and the specialty groups in areas such as surgical oncology, trauma, and transplantation.

In addition to evidence for the type of surgical procedure done for a given clinical condition, the evidence base for technical and supportive clinical care should be addressed. The basis for mechanical and medical supportive care can be found in both the pediatric surgical and pediatric medical literature. The fields of neonatology, pediatric anesthesia, pediatric critical care, and other pediatric subspecialties overlap heavily with the practice of pediatric surgery.[8]

These advances have allowed the pediatric surgeon to operate on smaller and more critically ill infants. The biggest change has been in neonatal care, with the ability to keep small, preterm infants alive. Many of these infants develop surgical problems that may require treatment. Similarly, advances in fields such as surgical oncology and transplantation have required the pediatric surgeon to develop techniques related to the complicated care of these patients.[9,10,11] With the rapid advance of these changes in practice and the economic pressure of the 1990s to control costs, a number of recent studies have sought to establish the evidence base for pediatric surgical practice.[12–14]

THE SEARCH FOR EVIDENCE-BASED STUDIES IN PEDIATRIC SURGERY

Practicing pediatric surgeons rely on their clinical expertise and on the best available evidence to formulate a clinical plan for a given patient; this is the fundamental basis of evidence-based surgery. Evidence-based surgery helps practitioners organize their practice by allowing them to critically appraise the scientific (or other) origins of their own current practice. As a discipline, evidence-based surgery gives the practitioner the tools to seek the best treatment plan for a patient. With these tools, the surgeon is able to search and then critically appraise the literature available for a particular clinical problem.[1] In addition, evidence-based surgery may also help the surgeon develop more cost-effective care by evolving or changing practice patterns based on current available evidence.[12] For the pediatric surgeon, idiosyncratic clinical experience and facility with various surgical methods may take precedence over externally derived textbook or "cookbook" methods of care. This practice is borne out in the literature in pediatric surgery as well as in an analysis of current practice.[1]

Three methods have been used to seek the evidence base for the best medical practice for the pediatric surgical patient: (1) review of the core pediatric surgical literature, (2) examination of the literature supporting pediatric surgical practice by clinical diagnosis and/or treatment, and (3) development of clinical practice guidelines.[6,7,15]

There have been a number of studies that have examined the pediatric surgical literature and categorized the literature on the basis of the evidence presented in published papers. A variety of methodologies have been used to critically appraise the published literature in medicine and surgery.[15] Table 37–1 describes a common breakdown of the types of journals in the scientific literature.[16] For clinical studies there are three major groups of papers. Observational studies run the gamut from a single case report to prospective noncontrolled studies. Nonrandomized controlled and randomized controlled studies form the other two major categories of clinical papers. Nonclinical scientific studies may be grouped according to the type of paper (animal studies, scientific, technical, educational, editorial, or letter).

The widely applied categorization of the scientific and clinical literature by level of evidence uses a format developed by the US Agency for Health Care Policy and Research (AHCPR).[16] Table 37–2 lists the generally accepted hierarchy of levels of evidence, ranging from level 1a (meta-analysis of multiple randomized clinical trials) down to level 4 (anecdotal evidence or opinions from respected authorities or consensus groups). One recent study examined the type of evidence presented in the literature in a review of the National Library of Medicine MEDLINE database. In examining over 9,000 references in the core pediatric surgical literature, only 0.3 percent and 1.48 percent of papers were classified as randomized controlled trials or prospective studies, respectively. Almost 60 percent of the references were retrospective review series and 34.6 percent were case reports (Table 37–3). This review reflects quite accurately the issues alluded to above that have limited the specialty's ability to perform randomized clinical trials.[15]

The second type of examination of clinical practice looks at the evidence base for a surgeon's practice by the type of admitting diagnoses and procedures performed on a chronologic group of patients. A number of papers have looked at the evidence base supporting various treatments in patients admitted to a children's hospital.[6,7] Studies of internal medicine practices done in this fashion reveal that for the most part, 82 percent of acute in-patient care is evidence-based on either a randomized clinical trial or convincing non-experimental evidence.[17] In reviewing pediatric surgical practice, similar results were obtained in a number of studies which demonstrated that the bulk of pediatric surgical procedures were based on

Table 37–1 Types of Journal Articles

Observational study
    Descriptive
        Case report
        Review articles
    Analytic
        Cross-section design
        Retrospective
        Prospective

Case-controlled study (nonrandomized)

Randomized controlled trial (single, meta-analysis)

Audit

Nonclinical
    Animal studies
    Scientific
    Technical (new instruments and techniques)
    Educational (quiz, historical vignettes, directories)
    Editorials
    Letters

Table 37–2 Levels of Evidence*

1a	Meta-analysis of randomized controlled trials
1b	Randomized controlled trial
2a	Well-designed nonrandomized controlled study
2b	Well-designed quasi-experimental study
3	Well-designed non-experimental descriptive studies
4	Evidence from expert committee reports; opinions and clinical experience of respected authorities

*from US Agency for Health Care Policy and Research (1992).

either controlled trials or convincing non-experimental evidence. In one study, treatments of pediatric surgical patients were categorized into three levels by the evidence base for a particular treatment[6] (Table 37–4). Only 25 percent of patient interventions could be categorized as based on empiric treatment that was not evidence based. A full 75 percent of treatment was based on valid, often controlled, clinical studies.

In reviewing the evidence base for the clinical practice of surgery, another category needs to be examined. That category would include those treatments that are obviously effective and should not be subjected to clinical trials. For example, it is obvious that patients with appendicitis benefit from a timely appendectomy, and this treatment should not need to be subjected to a randomized controlled clinical trial. Another recent study examining the research evidence base for pediatric surgical practice includes this category of evidence.[7] The authors divided the evidence base into five categories (Table 37–5). The authors found that 26 percent of treatments were based on randomized controlled trials while an additional 68 percent were based on other types of prospective, retrospective, or case studies. Three percent were self-evident and efficacious, but 3 percent were empiric with no supporting evidence for efficacy.

Cost control pressures and the pursuit of profit from the health care industry has generated two more aspects of evidence-based medicine: practice guidelines and performance improvement. The need for cost controls has introduced the notion of "best medical practice" to provide medical care with optimal efficacy at the lowest cost. Practice guidelines are being generated for a number of medical specialties, including pediatrics and neonatology; surgical subspecialties are following suit with published practice guidelines.[8] In addition, an increasing number of studies are using clinical performance improvement strategies to examine the

Table 37–3 Core Pediatric Surgical Literature*

Type of Paper	Percentage of Literature
Randomized controlled trials	0.3
Prospective case series	1.5
Retrospective case series	53.4
Case reports	30.6
Laboratory studies	11.8
Review articles	2.1
Miscellaneous	0.3

*Review of the National Library of Medicine MEDLINE database.

Table 37–4 Treatment Classifications

Category	Evidence Base
1	RCT evidence
2	No RCT data but convincing nonexperimental evidence
3	Empiric treatment, no evidence base

RCT = randomized controlled trial.

clinical care of surgical patients. To lower hospital costs, much of this is driven by managed care. An increasing number of these studies, however, are using these techniques to improve care and reduce morbidity and mortality in patient groups.

The next section will examine a few of these evidence-based works to highlight how evidence-based surgery can impact the practice of pediatric surgery.

DETAILED ANALYSIS OF PEDIATRIC SURGICAL LITERATURE

To review the pediatric surgical literature, four published papers were selected. These papers illustrate the evolution of pediatric surgical care with increasing sophistication on the part of the pediatric surgeon.

"Posterior Sagittal Anorectoplasty," by DeVries and Pena, was presented in 1981 at the annual meeting of the Surgical Section of the American Academy of Pediatrics[18] and was a landmark paper in the management of anorectal malformations. The paper reviewed the historical development of operations for imperforate anus and laid out the scientific and anatomical basis for Pena's approach to the repair of imperforate anus. The authors reported the initial experience with 34 cases using this new posterior approach to repair. Critical analysis of the paper reveals that this study, although prospective, fits into a category 2 classification because no randomization or controls were used. The procedure is based on anatomic guidelines. Using a strict application of AHCPR criteria, this paper could be considered as level 4 evidence since it is based on the clinical experience of a respected authority in this area.

This publication prompted a change in practice by many pediatric surgeons, who began using the posterior sagittal anorectoplasty for the repair of imperforate anus in infants. At that time, the authors presented no direct comparison of their procedure to those of other respected authorities in pediatric surgery, and no long-term results were presented for these patients. Since the publication of that paper, a number of other published studies have shown that the postoperative problems of obstruction, scar formation, prolapse, incontinence, and fecal soiling regularly occur in patients undergoing a posterior sagittal anorectoplasty, as was the case with other procedures for this congenital anomaly. Thus, as alluded to earlier in this

Table 37–5 Categories of Evidence Base

I	Evidence based on RCTs
II	Self-evidence: value is obvious; RCT unnecessary
III	Evidence based on prospective ± comparative studies
IV	Evidence based on follow-up or retrospective case studies: value supported by long-term follow-up and case analysis
V	No evidence for or against effectiveness

RCT = randomized controlled trial.

chapter, this type of paper, which uses a prospective series of patients who have undergone a particular surgical procedure for a particular congenital anomaly, has formed the basis for much of the practice of pediatric surgery.

The next paper is more recent and analyzes popular practice with the availability of laparoscopic and thoracoscopic techniques in surgery. This study is a nonrandomized study from Japan, where laparoscopic extramucosal pyloromyotomy was compared to open pyloromyotomy for infants with pyloric stenosis.[14] This paper, by Fujimoto and colleagues, was presented at the annual meeting of the British Association of Pediatric Surgeons in July 1998. This paper was also a prospective paper analyzing 60 patients with pyloric stenosis between 1994 and 1997. The patients, however, were assigned alternately to an open surgery group and a laparoscopic surgery group. There is no documentation that a full randomization was performed for these patients. The patients then underwent either laparoscopic or open pyloromyotomy and were followed prospectively for outcomes. The authors concluded that the laparoscopic pyloromyotomy improved cosmetic results and that there was "decreased surgical stress and shorter hospitalization."

Using controls to compare two techniques, this paper typifies a more strict level of evidence base than the previous paper. This paper falls into the group of case-controlled, possibly nonrandomized studies and would fall into evidence level 2a. If the authors had specified a randomization scheme for enrolling patients into the study, it could have met the criteria for level 1b and would have been more definitive and convincing.

The third paper elevates the pediatric surgical evidence basis to yet another level. This paper from Los Angeles and Denver by Nio and colleagues was presented at the annual meeting of the Pacific Association of Pediatric Surgeons in May 1993.[19] This paper was a prospective randomized trial of delayed versus immediate repair of congenital diaphragmatic hernia. Patients in this study were newborn infants who met strict entry criteria following a diagnosis of diaphragmatic hernia. Patients were randomly assigned to one of two groups. One group received immediate surgical repair of their diaphragmatic hernia after medical stabilization, and the other group received a delayed repair.

This paper documented no difference in outcomes (mortality and frequency of ECMO) between early and delayed repair. Since this paper, it has become standard practice to delay operative repair of congenital diaphragmatic hernia until after a prolonged period of stabilization. Improvements in respiratory care subsequent to this paper have also increased survival and decreased the need for ECMO support in this group of patients. This paper is a single randomized clinical trial paper and fulfills criteria for level 1b.

The final paper to be reviewed in this chapter turns to a more recent phenomenon in medical and surgical literature, namely, the use of clinical pathways both as a method for standardizing postoperative care and as an attempt to decrease hospital stays and resultant hospital costs. This paper, by Warner and colleagues, is from Cincinnati, Ohio, and is entitled "An Evidence-Based Clinical Pathway for Acute Appendicitis Decreases Hospital Duration and Cost."[13] The paper is a prospective study in which children with appendicitis were operated on and enrolled in one of two postoperative clinical pathways. The clinical pathway for patients with nonperforated appendicitis resulted in early discharge from the hospital at 24 hours. The pathway for patients with perforated appendicitis also yielded a shorter hospital stay compared to historical controls. The drawback for this paper was that historical controls for perforated and nonperforated appendicitis were used to demonstrate cost savings. Although this is not an optimal method to truly determine the efficacy of these pathways, it is a frequently used method for achieving clinical performance improvement. The technique entails the alteration of current clinical protocols, and the change in practice is prospectively followed to determine if the desired optimal result will occur. This paper would be described as an analytical prospective type of journal article and would probably fall into the 2b level of evidence. It is a well-designed quasi-experimental study using historical controls.

Alternatively, this could also be a 2a level of evidence since it also could be described as a non-randomized controlled study albeit using historical controls.

CONCLUSION

In general, the practice of pediatric surgery uses both unique and standard surgical techniques to manage congenital anomalies and other problems in the pediatric age group. These surgical procedures are derived primarily from clinical nonrandomized uncontrolled series of patients undergoing particular types of operations. As is shown in this chapter, this type of practice does not easily lend itself to a rigorous analysis of current surgical practice. Much of the difficulty relates to the low frequency of many of these congenital anomalies for which randomized controlled studies would be impractical even for groups of surgical centers. These issues are also present for other surgical specialties. For the more common procedures performed in children, focused randomized trials or clinical performance improvement protocols may be of use in optimizing and fine-tuning the management of these patients.

Historically, the practice of pediatric surgery is relatively young, emerging from general surgery as a distinct specialty in the decade following World War II. There is a slowly increasing body of literature providing an evidence basis for the practice of pediatric surgery. The majority of this evidence is based on noncontrolled studies; very little relies on randomized controlled trials. The practice, however, is based on consecutive series or prospective trials. An increasing number of studies have used performance improvement techniques to develop clinical pathways and potential practice guidelines. Most authors who have evaluated the pediatric surgical literature have concluded that the bulk of the practice of pediatric surgery is based on sound surgical techniques using comparative, prospective, or retrospective studies from authoritative practitioners in the specialty.

REFERENCES

1. Sackett DL, Richardson WS, Rosenberg W, Haynes RB, editors. Evidence-based medicine: how to practice and teach EBM. New York: Churchill Livingston; 1997.

2. Browning GG. Is there an evidence base for the practice of ENT surgery? Clin Otolaryngol 1998;23:1–2.

3. Howes N, Chagla L, Thorpe M, McCulloch P. Surgical practice is evidence based. Br J Surg 1997;84:1220–3.

4. Randolph J. Introduction: North American historical perspective. In: Stringer MD, Mouriquand PDE, Oldham K, Howard ER, editors. Pediatric surgery and urology: long term outcomes. London, England: W.B. Saunders Company; 1999.

5. Introduction: European historical perspective. In: Stringer MD, Mouriquand PDE, Oldham K, Howard ER editors. O'Donnell B. Pediatric surgery and urology: long term outcomes. London, England: W.B. Saunders Company; 1999.

6. Kenny SE, Shankar KR, Rintala R, et al. Evidence-based surgery: interventions in a regional paediatric surgical unit. Arch Dis Child 1997;76:50–3.

7. Baraldini V, Spitz L, Pierro A. Evidence-based operations in paediatric surgery. Pediatr Surg Int 1998;13:331–5.

8. Merritt TA, Palmer D, Bergman DA, Shiono PH. Clinical practice guidelines in pediatric and newborn medicine: implications for their use in practice. Clin Pract Guide Pediatr Newborn Med 1997;100:1114.

9. Rodarte JR. Evidence-based surgery. Mayo Clin Proc 1998;73:603.

10. Sutton C. Minimal access therapy and endoscopic surgery: the evolution of new technologies continues, but surely the time has come to assess the results by standards of evidence-based medicine. Curr Opin Obstet Gynecol 1998;10:293–4.

11. Sondenaa K, Nesvik I, Solhaug JH, Soreide O. Randomization to surgery or observation in patients with symptomatic gallbladder stone disease. Scand J Gastroenterol 1998;32:611–16.

12. Barraclough B. The value of surgical practice guidelines. Aust N Z J Surg 1998;68:6–9.

13. Warner BW, Kulick RM, Stoops MM, et al. An evidence-based clinical pathway for acute appendicitis decreases hospital duration and cost. J Pediatr Surg 1998;33(9):1371–5.

14. Fujimoto T, Lane GJ, Segawa O, et al. Laparoscopic extramucosal pyloromyotomy versus open pyloromyotomy for infantile hypertrophic pyloric stenosis: which is better? J Pediatr Surg 1999;34(2):370–2.

15. Hardin WD Jr, Stylianos S, Lally KP. Evidence-based practice in pediatric surgery: a review of the first fifty years. Accepted for publication J. Pediatr Surg; [In press] 1999.

16. Maran AGD, Molony NC, Armstrong MWJ, Ah-See K. Is there an evidence base for the practice of ENT surgery? Clin Otolaryngol 1997;22:152–7.

17. Ellis J, Mulligan I, Rowe J, et al. Inpatient general medicine is evidence based. Lancet 1995;346:407–10.

18. DeVries PA, Pena A. Posterior sagittal anorectoplasty. J Pediatr Surg 1982;17(5):638–43.

19. Nio M, Haase G, Kennaugh J, et al. A prospective randomized trial of delayed versus immediate repair of congenital diaphragmatic hernia. J Pediatr Surg 1994;(29)5:618–21.

CHAPTER 38

Gynecologic Surgery

Fredrick J. Montz, MD, KM,
Howard A. Zacur, MD, PhD,
Harold E. Fox, MD, MSc, and
Thomas Elkins, MD

Evidence-based medicine has been described as "the conscientious, explicit, and judicious use of the current best evidence in making decisions about the care of individual patients; the integration of individual clinical expertise with the best available external clinical evidence from systemic research."[1] Unquestionably, this latter "clinical evidence from systemic research" can be and is of variable quality. There have been attempts made by numerous groups to quantify the quality of evidence. One of the most widely used and respected classifications is that of the United States Preventive Services Task Force (Table 38–1).[2] A working knowledge of this system of qualification is essential when attempting to make rational evidence-based decisions on patient care.

By reviewing this classification it is evident that much of the clinical decision making performed by the average practicing surgeon (ie, that based upon anecdotal, personal experience, gestalt, etc) falls outside the realm of evidence-based medicine. Though these clinical decisions may be the best in a given setting, such "non-evidence-based" decisions may not be optimal when extrapolated to a large group of similar patients. It is specifically such potentially harmful clinical decisions that evidence-based medicine seeks to avoid.

THE SCOPE OF GYNECOLOGIC SURGERY

It is important for students of both gynecologic surgery and evidence-based medicine to appreciate the diversity of the former discipline and the associated potential pitfalls of attempting to apply the latter's principles to clinical decision making.

Table 38–1 United States Preventive Services Task Force Classification of Levels of Evidence

Level	Quality of Evidence
I	Evidence obtained from at least one properly conducted randomized controlled trial (RCT)
II-1	Evidence obtained from well-designed controlled trials without randomization
II-2	Evidence from well-designed cohort or case controlled analytic studies, preferably from more than one center or research group
II-3	Evidence obtained from several time series (with or without intervention) or dramatic results in uncontrolled experiments
III	Opinions of respected authorities based on clinical experiences, descriptive studies and case reports, or reports of expert committees

To the memory of our friend, colleague, and co-author, Thomas (Tommy) Elkins, MD.

Table 38–2 Subdisciplines of Gynecologic Surgery

Infertility

Benign gynecology

Incontinence and pelvic floor defects

Gynecologic oncology

Breadth of Subspecialties

The discipline of gynecologic surgery includes a broad range of operative interventions and treatments and is divided into four subdisciplines (Table 38–2) with (depending on the individual surgeon and his community of practice) a wide range of crossover among these subdisciplines.

Within each of the subdisciplines, there is a diverse array of surgical procedures performed. Infertility surgery has predominantly focused on the operative management of potentially fertility-impairing conditions (metroplasties for uterine structural abnormalities, myomectomies, resection of endometriosis with associated symptom-controlling surgical adjuvants, etc) or those conditions that have led to documented infertility (distal tubal disease, extensive intraperitoneal adhesions, and prior surgical sterilization).

Benign or "general" gynecologic surgery includes the most commonly completed operations (ovarian cystectomies for management of nonmalignant disease entities; hysterectomies, independent of approach, for symptomatic uterine myomas, etc). In the general community and away from highly structured academic institutions, there is extensive overlap among those procedures that are performed by the general gynecologic surgeon (ie, one who has not completed formal subspecialty training) and those performed by associates who have completed a fellowship or similar training that would allow the granting of a certificate of special competency.

Urogynecology and pelvic floor reconstructive procedures have been performed since the earliest days of pelvic surgery. For over a century, these procedures were considered to be within the general gynecologic surgeon's arena. However, with the concomitant expansion of knowledge and the decrease in the procedures performed-to-surgeon ratio, an increasing and dominant percentage of these procedures (retropubic urethropexies as management of urinary incontinence; paravaginal, sacrocolpopexy, and similar combined complex pelvic floor reconstructions) are performed at centers of excellence by uniquely trained or extensively experienced surgeons.

Gynecologic oncology, due to the complexity and potential risks of the procedures performed and the associated structured credentialing requirements and limitations set by health care organizations, is probably the most strictly controlled of all of the subspecialties of gynecologic surgery. The procedural armamentarium of the gynecologic oncologist includes techniques for debulking of advanced ovarian cancer and pelvic exenterations with neo-vagina construction, continent urinary diversions, and rectosigmoid anastomosis. Also included are the more routine radical hysterectomies for early cervical cancer and the performance of simple hysterectomies and staging for endometrial cancer, the most common gynecologic malignancy. In the case of this latter procedure, there is a significant overlap with those procedures performed by the general gynecologist. In the United States, only a selected, small subset of women with endometrial cancer benefit from thorough surgical staging although the international guidelines set by La Federation Internationale de Gynecologie et d'Obstetrique (FIGO) mandate lymph node sampling in all patients with endometrial cancer to fulfill staging criteria.

REVIEW OF THE LITERATURE

In regard to evidence-based medicine as described above, there is a massive volume of information addressing issues of gynecologic surgery. Most of this evidence would be considered higher level (ie, of lower quality) and therefore not optimal evidence from which critical decisions can be made. However, there is available level I evidence in the form of sentinel research for selected surgical situations for each of the subdisciplines.

Infertility

The use of evidence-based medicine to evaluate the efficacy of surgery in the treatment of infertility has been strongly advocated. The surgical treatment of endometriosis to improve fecundity has provoked both rancor and controversy. Until recently, recommendations for surgery to improve the chances of conception were based mostly upon results of uncontrolled or descriptive studies, that is, level II-3 or level III criteria.

Older clinical studies which described the surgical treatment of endometriosis for treatment of infertility used arbitrary classification schemes to specify the extent of endometriosis. Unfortunately, these classification schemes were never validated. These older studies also used methods of reporting pregnancies post treatment that were statistically flawed. At present, there is no agreement on the validity of current staging methods used to report the extent of endometriosis. For example, the current system of staging endometriosis developed by the American Society of Reproductive Medicine is based upon the size and depth of the endometrial implants and the presence of pelvic adhesions. However, the "extent" of endometriosis does not correlate with the patient's complaints of pelvic pain. No prospective study has been performed for infertility to establish a correlation between extent of endometriosis and the difficulty of conceiving. However, some retrospective studies have been able to correlate severity of disease with likelihood of conceiving following treatment.

A common indication for surgical treatment of endometriosis is infertility, with the most "successful" outcome of surgery being pregnancy. Results from previous studies suggesting improved rates of pregnancy following surgical treatment of endometriosis were uncontrolled and anecdotal. These studies reported results in terms of crude pregnancy rates. (The crude pregnancy rate is the number of patients pregnant divided by the number of patients treated.) Crude pregnancy rates depend upon length of follow-up. The use of only crude pregnancy rates to compare treatment modalities may deliver varying results at different time intervals of patient follow-up. More recent studies rely upon life table or survival analysis. Life table analysis avoids the issue of duration of follow-up by estimating the percentage of study subjects conceiving at any given period.[3,4]

Questions concerning the surgical treatment of endometriosis for infertility have included whether to treat endometrial implants by medical therapy only or by surgery. If surgery is performed, should it consist of laparoscopy only or laparoscopy with cauterization or laser vaporization of implants? Alternatively, should endometriosis be treated only at the time of a laparotomy? Lastly, should infertile patients with endometriosis forgo surgery and utilize assisted reproductive technologies? Answers to these questions have been difficult to obtain using data from studies that have not used level I criteria and have not reported results as cumulative pregnancy rates over time.

Marcoux and colleagues recently gave a more informed answer to one of the questions concerning treatment of endometriosis. They reported on the merits of surgical treatment (fulguration or resection) accompanying diagnostic laparoscopy in infertile women with minimal or mild endometriosis, that is, enhanced fecundity. They noted a fecundity rate of 6.1 percent in 172 women treated by laparoscopic surgery versus a 3.2 percent fecundity rate in 169 women treated by diagnostic laparoscopy without surgical treatment.[5] This was a prospective/randomized trial involving several medical centers. The results of this study differ from results of previous studies, which have shown no difference between operative laparoscopy with surgical management of endometriosis as compared to diagnostic laparoscopy followed by concomitant medical therapy (ie, progesterone, Gn-RH agonists, etc). The failure to appreciate a difference in outcome may have resulted from smaller patient numbers[6] or may truly reflect scientific fact. Both medical and surgical treatment at laparotomy have been shown by meta-analysis to result in lower pregnancy rates than laparoscopic surgery, but a prospective randomized trial to confirm these findings is needed.[7]

The fecundity rate for infertile patients with endometriosis treated[8] by surgery at laparoscopy is still lower than the 20 percent fecundity rate expected for fertile patients. Retrospective studies have shown that pregnancy success per cycle attempted for in vitro fertilization is no different between infertile patients diagnosed with endometriosis and those diagnosed with tubal infertility. A pregnancy rate of 28.9 percent per infertility treatment cycle has been reported for endometriosis patients treated by in vitro fertilization, which approaches the expected fecundity rate for fertile women.[9] Since laparoscopic evaluation of the pelvis is currently considered to be a standard component of the infertility evaluation, it seems reasonable to suggest that for appropriate patients, diagnostic laparoscopy with associated surgical treatment of extant endometriosis followed by efforts to conceive should be undertaken prior to in vitro fertilization. Results from appropriately designed clinical studies are needed to determine whether it is more effective to precede with in vitro fertilization rather than to utilize such diagnostic and therapeutic measures as operative laparoscopy for the treatment of infertility.

Benign Gynecology

It is in this subspecialty of gynecologic surgery that the largest body of Level I evidence exists for the physician to use in his clinical decision making.

Of the evidence that would fulfill the Level I criteria, the largest single block is focused on the use of specific antibiotic regimens as prophylaxis against or treatment of soft-tissue infections occurring as a comorbidity of pelvic surgery. In general, these studies have proved the prophylactic benefit of using a single dose of a broad-spectrum cephalosporin administered in a timely fashion prior to the initial surgical incision.[10–12]

A second large body of Level 1 evidence has arisen from investigations evaluating the benefits of selected forms of anti-deep vein thrombosis (DVT) prophylaxis in recipients of a wide range of gynecologic surgical operations. Women undergoing a pelvic surgical procedure are inherently at higher risk of developing a DVT than males undergoing similar procedures. However, there is a significant difference in the associated potential for developing a DVT or pulmonary embolus (PE) depending on the indication for the procedure (benign vs malignant process) and, within these two general groups, the specific procedure being performed. In general, the more extensive the procedure, particularly if the procedure includes major blood loss or vessel manipulation, the more likely it is that a DVT/PE will occur. The value of some form of prophylaxis has been demonstrated for all but the most minor gynecologic surgical procedures although a sizable percentage of the data demonstrating these benefits does not fulfill Level I evidence criteria. The more thrombogenic the surgery, the more intense is the prophylaxis needed.[13] The National Institutes of Health (NIH) Consensus Development Conference on the Prevention of Venous Thrombosis and Pulmonary Embolism has recommended, based upon data from multiple randomized clinical trials (RCTs), the use of multi-modality prophylaxis (heparin plus pneumatic compression stockings) in women undergoing radical pelvic surgery as therapy for gynecologic malignancy. Select Level I studies have also demonstrated advantages of low molecular weight heparin in DVT/PE prophylaxis.[14,15] The advantages of these newer heparins arise not from an improvement in prevention of clots but from ease of dosing and a decrease in specific heparin-induced morbidities.

In addition to the Level I data that exists for these questions, there is Level I data that supports specific therapeutic choices in a range of other gynecologic surgical settings (optimal management of ectopic pregnancy,[16–18] management of first trimester spontaneous pregnancy loss,[19] optimal methods of performance of elective pregnancy termination,[20] and preferred methods to control postoperative pain,[21,22] among others).

In recent years, a large volume of data has been generated that addresses the issue of the preferred approaches to hysterectomy for a given disease process. Though much of the published information would not qualify as even Level III evidence, data from cases-controlled series have helped illuminate the merits of each approach.[23,24] Interestingly, there is significant controversy as to whether studies that fulfill the Level I criteria are possible and even ethical to complete.[25] There have been recently published studies that despite evident deficiencies do fulfill the Level I evidence criteria.[26,27] Because we will be dissecting an example of these articles in the section below, a summary of this data will be deferred.

Incontinence and Pelvic Floor Defects

For almost a century the choice of which surgical procedure to employ in the management of genuine stress urinary incontinence or pelvic floor defects depended on which school of surgery the treating physician had been trained in, on what geographic region of the United States the surgeon resided in, or on other non-evidence-based variables. Beginning in the late 1970s, there was an increase in efforts to generate evidence from which a physician could make decisions. During the next decade, a large body of data was generated, which improved the quality of evidence even though none of the data fulfilled Level I criteria. Prospective randomized clinical trials were designed and completed in an attempt to sift through the plethora of surgical procedures and answer the question, Which works best? A sentinel investigation that demonstrated the capacity to perform randomized clinical trials (RCTs) in this setting was that of Bergman and colleagues who determined that, in a standardized patient population and when performed by a select group of mature surgeons, transabdominal retropubic urethropexies have preferable success rates and complication profiles.[28] Subsequent trials have validated Bergman's report[29] although assimilation of this information into community practice has been slow.

There is less high-quality evidence supporting a given procedure for the management of complex pelvic floor defects, and even the highest-quality articles are reports on the use of a single type of operation from one institution.[30,31] As the concept of evidence-based medicine has been accepted by younger investigators, attempts have been made to institute prospective clinical trials.[32]

Gynecologic Oncology

There is a large volume of Level I evidence focusing on the management of patients with gynecologic malignancies. Most of these data do not involve issues of surgical care or procedure performance. Instead, the RCTs completed have focused on selected chemotherapeutic regimens with a relative scarcity of data that could be classified as surgically based.[33] There have been RCTs evaluating the merit of antibiotic prophylaxis,[34,35] postoperative adjuvant radiation therapy in the setting of early endometrial or cervical cancer,[36] DVT/PE prophylaxis (as discussed above), primary cytoreductive surgery for advanced ovarian cancer versus a neoadjuvant regimen, and surgical management of early vulvar cancer,[37] as well as others. Only during the 1990s and the revolution in endoscopic surgery has there been the capacity to design an RCT which directly compares two different surgical procedures for the management of one standardized disease process (laparoscopically assisted vaginal hysterectomy with laparoscopically assisted surgical staging [LAVH/LASS] vs traditional total abdominal hysterectomy [TAH] plus lymph node sampling for early endometrial cancer). Prior to the inception of this RCT, which is ongoing under the auspices of the Gynecologic Oncology Group (GOG Protocol LAP 2), there was available lower-quality evidence addressing the use of LAVH/LASS in the management of this disease process.[38,39] None of this evidence would reach the standards of the United States Preventive Services Task Force[40] for Level I evidence. Though it will be years before the results

Table 38–3 Level I Evidence Deficiencies in Gynecologic Surgery Database

Infertility	Relationship between form of surgical management of endometriosis (resection vs ablation) and outcome (fertility, pain, etc)
	Value of distal tubal surgery or aggressive surgery for endometriosis vs in vitro fertilization or other forms of assisted reproductive technology
	Others
Benign gynecology	Laparoscopic myomectomy vs open techniques
	Myomectomy embolization vs surgical removal
	Others
Incontinence and pelvic floor defects	Vaginal vs abdominal vault suspension
	Laparoscopic retropubic urethropexy vs traditional transabdominal urethropexy
	Preferred procedure for management of recurrent disease
	Others
Gynecologic oncology	Surgery vs radiation therapy for stage Ib2 cervical cancer
	Stage IIIc and IV ovarian cancer: neoadjuvant chemotherapy vs initial cytoreduction surgery
	Preferred class of radical hysterectomy for selected early FIGO stages of endometrial and cervical cancer
	Others

FIGO = Federation Internationale de Gynecologie et d'Obstetrique.

of GOG Protocol LAP 2 are available, the simple commitment to performing an RCT that compares two different surgical procedures is a significant advance and change in mind-set.

DEFICIENCIES IN THE KNOWLEDGE BASES

Though much headway has been made in the crusade to improve the quality of available evidence from which to make clinical decisions, there still remain major defects in the knowledge pool of Level I evidence. These deficiencies are outlined in Table 38–3.

Case Study

A Multicenter Randomized Comparison of Laparoscopic Assisted Vaginal Hysterectomy and Abdominal Hysterectomy in Abdominal Hysterectomy Candidates. Robert L. Summitt Jr, Thomas G. Stovall, John F. Steege, and Gary H. Lipscomb. Obstetrics and Gynecology 1998; 92:321-326. Reproduced with permission.

Abstract

Objective: To compare intraoperative and postoperative outcomes between laparoscopically assisted vaginal hysterectomy and abdominal hysterectomy among patients who are not eligible for vaginal hysterectomy.

Methods: Study subjects were randomly assigned to undergo laparoscopically assisted vaginal hysterectomy or standard abdominal hysterectomy. Intraoperative and postoperative management was similar for each group. Surgical characteristics, complications, length of hospital stay, charges, and convalescence was analyzed.

Results: Sixty-five women at three institutions underwent laparoscopically assisted vaginal hysterectomy (n = 34) or abdominal hysterectomy (n = 31). Three patients in the laparoscopy group required conversion to abdominal hysterectomy. Mean operating time was significantly longer for laparoscopically assisted vaginal hysterectomy (179.8 versus 146.0 minutes). There were no differences in blood loss or incidence of intraoperative complications. There was a higher incidence of wound complications in the abdominal hysterectomy group, but no significant difference in the frequency of postoperative complications. Laparoscopically assisted vaginal hysterectomy required a significantly shorter mean hospital stay (2.1 days) and convalescence (28.0 days) than abdominal hysterectomy (4.1 days and 38.0 days, respectively). There were no significant differences in mean hospital charges between the study groups (laparoscopic $8161, abdominal $6974).

Conclusions: Except for operating time, there are no differences between laparoscopically assisted vaginal hysterectomy and abdominal hysterectomy candidates. Postoperatively, laparoscopically assisted vaginal hysterectomy requires a shorter hospital stay and convalescence. Hospital charges are similar between the procedures. A larger number of cases will help determine the indications for laparoscopically assisted vaginal hysterectomy.

We chose this study report for scrutiny for the following reasons:

1. It is the result of a randomized prospective clinical trial comparing two different surgical procedures (one a "gold standard" and the other a developing technique) in the management of allegedly matched patients. Therefore, it demonstrates many of the frailties of attempting to perform RCTs in the surgical setting, a setting that can never be double blind as regards the procedures performed.
2. The question addressed (ie, which of these two procedures is superior?) is clinically important because of the frequency of the performance of each procedure because of the massive number of women affected. This question is therefore commonly addressed in current academic debates; the answer is unknown yet all surgeons have their often strongly held opinions regarding the merits of LAVH.
3. The investigators are prominent gynecologic surgeons who are recognized as modern thought leaders.
4. The article is published as the lead article in the first fall issue of a high-impact journal that also happens to be the official publication of the dominant national professional society (American College of Obstetricians and Gynecologists [ACOG]) to which most U.S. gynecologic surgeons belong. The journal (Obstetrics and Gynecology) is a free benefit of membership in ACOG.

As with any study that attempts to randomize patients to one of two arms, there are three potential variables that should be controlled for: (1) patient characteristics, (2) procedure and how performed, and (3) surgeon skill. These three variables are harder to standardize as one goes from 1 to 3. Though the study by Summitt and colleagues is well designed, there are problems with its execution and interpretation. It suffers in the following ways:

1. The patients are well matched. However, an important group of variables that may be related to a difference in outcome that the authors addressed (wound infections) was not controlled for. It is unknown whether the trend toward a higher rate of wound infections in those individuals who underwent an abdominal hysterectomy was a result of the larger abdominal incision or a result of undescribed confounders such as diabetes, chronic renal or vascular diseases, and so forth. An associated problem is the difference between the two groups of patients as regards an important preoperative variable (the number of prior abdominal surgeries/laparotomies). This may have been a confounding variable, which played a role in the differences in rates of wound infections. Unfortunately, it is unclear from the manuscript whether the patients who underwent laparoscopy or those who underwent laparotomy had a higher rate of prior abdominal surgeries. The text states one fact (higher rate in laparoscopy group, page 323, paragraph 2, line 3) and Table 2 demonstrates the inverse.

2. Though there was an attempt to standardize how the two different surgical procedures were performed, there was allowance for what could have been a wide variance in technique.

3. Surgeon variables are not addressed in the report of this study. There were at least three surgeons guiding the performance of the surgical interventions; the actual number of different primary surgeons was not supplied to the reader. Regardless of the number of surgeons, skill at a given procedure is difficult to quantify. No attempts to do so were made, and what the experience and competence of the senior surgeons were is unknown (ie, where they were on their individual learning curves, an important variable that was not standardized).

An equally important part of any data presentation is a discussion of the "power" of the study, which can be translated simplistically as what the chance is that a difference of predetermined proportion will be detected. The authors did supply information regarding the study's statistical ability to determine significant cost differences although no comment was made regarding the power to appreciate differences not noted but previously reported in similar studies (ie, complication rates and length of operation).

Appreciating the above deficiencies and weaknesses and the associated limitations of any conclusions the authors may have drawn, many of their conclusions are valid. An example of a failure to supply clarifying information supporting a conclusion can be seen in the results set forth in Table 4 of the manuscript. The authors here demonstrate that there was no difference in the changes in hematocrit between the two arms of the trial. Unfortunately, it appears (by inference from the numbers listed at the top of each of the table columns) the authors did not exclude from these data the two patients in the laparotomy group with estimated blood losses (EBL) > 1000 cc who received blood transfusions. Also important, similar patients in the laparoscopy group did not receive blood transfusions. Therefore, the greater number of transfusions in the laparotomy group could mask a potentially important difference, that is, a mean change in hematocrit. It would have been preferable if the authors had used a more accurate measure of blood volume (hemoglobin) than the one they selected (hematocrit) as the latter is much more sensitive to changes in total volume status, another unstratified variable.

What can be concluded from this article and from others similar to it is that women who have LAVHs substituted for TAHs will both recover and return to their normal level of function more quickly. Whether there is a persistent and reproducible cost or complication rate difference between the two techniques remains unknown.

EVIDENCE-BASED GYNECOLOGIC SURGERY: WHAT IS NEEDED?

First, the most glaring deficit that needs to be addressed is the combined lack of application of the merits of evidence-based techniques in assessing data necessary for delivering optimal surgical care and a continued dependence on anecdote and personal experience as the standard for surgical decision making. Second, evidence-based techniques need to be incorporated into the methodology of the assessment of gynecologic surgical procedures. When possible, studies investigating the validity and merit of any given surgical technique should be designed in a way that would fulfill Level I criteria. As illustrated in Table 38–3, there are many important unanswered questions in each of the four subdisciplines of gynecologic surgery.

It is the authors' hope that practicing surgeons will continue to be increasingly aware of the standards for high-quality evidence on which surgical decisions should be based. This awareness will lead not only to a demand by surgeons for the highest level of evidence when assessing published experiences but also to a secondary benefit: an elevation of the standards applied to new surgical trials so that these trials could generate Level I evidence.

REFERENCES

1. Sackett DL, Rosenberg WMC, Gray JAM, et al. Evidenced based medicine: what it is and what it isn't. BMJ 1996;312:71–2.

2. United States Preventative Services Task Force. Guide to clinical preventive services. Baltimore: Williams and Wilkins; 1995.

3. Guzick DS, Rock JA. Estimation of a model of cumulative pregnancy following infertility therapy. Am J Obstet Gynecol 1981;140:573–8.

4. Olive DL. Analysis of clinical fertility trials: a metrologic review. Fertil Steril 1986;45:157–71.

5. Marcoux S, Maheux R, Berube S, and the Canadian Collaborative Group on Endometriosis. N Engl J Med 1997;337:217–22.

6. Adamson GD, Hurd SJ, Pasta DJ, Rodriguez BD. Laparoscopic endometriosis treatment: is it better? Fertil Steril 1993;59:35–44.

7. Adamson GD, Pasta DJ. Surgical treatment of endometriosis-associated infertility: meta-analysis compared with survival analysis. Am J Obstet Gynecol 1994;171:1488–504, discussion 1504–5.

8. Cramer DW, Walker AM, Schiff I. Statistical methods in evaluating the outcome of infertility therapy. Fertil Steril 1979;32:80–6.

9. Olivennes F, Feldberg D, Liu HC, et al. Endometriosis: a stage by stage analysis—the role of in vitro fertilization. Fertil Steril 1995;64:392–8.

10. French JI, McKinney PJ, Milligan K. Comparison of single-dose ceftizoxime with multidose cefoxitin chemoprophylaxis for patients undergoing hysterectomy. Clin Ther 1990;12 Suppl C:45–52.

11. Gerstner GJ. Comparison of ceftriaxine (1 x 1g/day) versus cefotaxime (3 x 1 g/day) for gynecologic and obstetric infections. A randomized clinical trial. Gynecol Obstet Invest 1990;29:273–7.

12. Willems FT, Loriaux SM, Meewis JM. Prophylaxis in gynaecologic surgery: a prospective randomized comparison between single dose prophylaxis with amoxycillin/clavulanate and the combination of cefuroxime and metronidazole. J Antimicrob Chemother 1989 Nov; 24 Suppl B:213–16.

13. Clarke-Pearson DL, DeLong ER, Synan IS, et al. Variables associated with postoperative deep venous thrombosis: a prospective study of 411 gynecologic patients and creation of a prognostic model. Obstet Gynecol 1987;69:146–53.

14. Keller K, Luscher T, Schreiner WE. A prospective randomized trial of low molecular weight heparin-DHE and conventional heparin DHE (with acenocoumarol) in patients undergoing gynaecological surgery. Arch Gynecol Obstet 1989;244:141–50.

15. Doller P, Hermann CP. Prevention of thromboembolism in hysterectomies with low molecular weight heparin Fragmin. Geburtshilfe Frauenheilkd 1988 Mar;48:160–4.

16. Zilber U, Pansky M, Bukovshy I, Golan A. Laparoscopic salpingostomy versus laparoscopic local methotrexate injection in the management of unruptured ectopic gestation. Am J Obstet Gynecol 1996;175:600–2.

17. Vermseh M, Silva PD, Rosen GF, et al. Management of unruptured ectopic gestation by linear salpingostomy: a prospective, randomized clinical trial of laparoscopy versus laparotomy. Obstet Gynecol 1989 Mar;73:400–4.

18. Saraj AJ, Wilcox JG, Najmabadi S, et al. Resolution of hormonal markers of ectopic gestation: a randomized trial comparing single-dose intramuscular methotrexate with salpingostomy. Obstet Gynecol 1998;92:989–94.

19. Forbes K. Management of first trimester spontaneous abortions. BMJ 1995 Jun 3;310(6992):1426.

20. Iverson T, Skjeldestad FE. Intracervical administration of prostaglandin E2 prior to vacuum aspiration. A prospective double blind randomized study. Int J Gynaecol Obstet 1985;23:95–9.

21. Jorgensen BC, Schmidt JF, Risbo A, et al. Regular preventive pain relief compared with on demand treatment after hysterectomy. Pain 1985;21:137–42.

22. Ke RW, Portera G, Bagous W, Lincoln SR. A randomized, double-blinded trial of pre-emptive analgesia in laparoscopy. Obstet Gynecol 1998;92:972–5.

23. Boike GM, Elfstrand EP, DelPriore G, et al. Laparoscopically assisted vaginal hysterectomy in a university hospital: report of 82 cases and comparison with abdominal and vaginal hysterectomy. Am J Obstet Gynecol 1993;168:1690–701.

24. Carter JE, Ryoo J, Katz A. Laparoscopic-assisted vaginal hysterectomy: a case control comparative study with total abdominal hysterectomy. J Am Assoc Gynecol Laparosc 1994;1:116–21.

25. Cosson M, Querleu D, Subtil D, et al. Alternatives and access routes in hysterectomies. Are randomizations dangerous? J Gynecol Obstet Biol Reprod 1996;25:257–63.

26. Summitt RL, Stovall TG, Lipscomb GH, Ling FW. Randomized comparison of laparoscopically-assisted vaginal hysterectomy with standard vaginal hysterectomy in an outpatient setting. Obstet Gynecol 1992;80:895–901.

27. Thakar BR, Ugwumadu AH, Manyonda IT. A randomized prospective trial comparing laparoscopic and abdominal hysterectomy. Br J Obstet Gynaecol 1996;103:1171–3.

28. Bergman A, Koonings PP, Ballard CA. Primary stress urinary incontinence and pelvic relaxation: prospective randomized comparison of three different operations. Am J Obstet Gynecol 1989; 161:97–101.

29. Park GS, Miller EJ. Surgical treatment of stress urinary incontinence: a comparison of the Kelly Plication, Marshall-Marchetti-Krantz, and Pereyra procedure. Obstet Gynecol 1988;71:575–9.

30. Porges RF, Smilen SW. Long term analysis of the surgical management of pelvic support defects. Am J Obstet Gynecol 1994;171:1518–22.

31. Valatis SR, Stanton SL. Sacrocolpopexy: a retrospective study of a clinician's experience. Br J Obstet Gynaecol 1994;101:518–22.

32. Thomas AG, Brodman ML, Dottino PR, et al. Manchester procedure vs. vaginal hysterectomy for uterine prolapse: a comparison. J Reprod Med 1995;40:299–301.

33. Faridi A, Schroder W, Rath W. Current trends in the surgical management of ovarian cancer. Zentralbl Gynakol 1998;120:3–16.

34. Micha JP, Kucera PR, Birkett JP, et al. Prophylactic mezlocillin in radical hysterectomy. Obstet Gynecol 1987;69:251–4.

35. Rosenshein NB, Ruth JC, Villar J, et al. A prospective randomized study of doxycycline as a prophylactic antibiotic in patients undergoing radical hysterectomy. Gynecol Oncol 1983;15:201–6.

36. Bilek K, Ebeling K, Leitsmann H, Seidel G. Radical pelvic surgery versus radical surgery plus radiotherapy for stage Ib carcinoma of the cervix uteri. Preliminary results of a prospective randomized clinical study. Arch Geschwulstforsch 1982;52:223–9.

37. Stehman FB, Bundy BN, Dvoretsky PM, et al. Early stage I carcinoma of the vulva treated with ipsilateral superficial inguinal lymphadenectomy and modified radical hemivulvectomy: prospective study of the Gynecologic Oncology Group. Obstet Gynecol 1992;79:480–97.

38. Childers JM, Brzechffa PR, Hatch KD, et al. Laparoscopic assisted surgical staging of endometrial cancer. Gynecol Oncol 1993;51:33–8.

39. Fowler JM. Laparoscopic staging of endometrial cancer. Clin Obstet Gynecol 1996;39:669–85.

40. United States Preventative Services Task Force. Guide to clinical preventive services. Baltimore: Williams and Wilkins; 1995.

CHAPTER 39

Ophthalmic Surgery

David S. Friedman, MD, MPH, and Oliver D. Schein, MD, MPH

———◆———

Ophthalmic surgery has evolved rapidly over the past few decades. The major eye diseases treated surgically include cataract (the most common surgical procedure performed on Medicare recipients), glaucoma (which affects 2% of whites and 6% of blacks over the age of 40), and diabetic retinopathy (the leading cause of blindness among individuals 20 to 70 years of age). The rapid technological advances in surgical equipment have transformed ophthalmic surgery. For example, cataract operations that used to be done under general anesthesia and required one-week hospital stays can now be done using only eyedrops for anesthesia with the patient able to go home within an hour of the surgery. While many of the incremental changes were made based on surgical experience and innovation, large clinical trials and prospective studies support a significant proportion of what ophthalmologists do today. This chapter will detail the evidence supporting the current approaches to cataract management, glaucoma surgery, and the treatment of diabetic retinopathy. Ophthalmologists perform many other surgeries, but these were selected because they represent the most common blinding eye conditions that are treatable by surgery.

OVERVIEW OF EYE ANATOMY

Figures 39–1 and 39–2 show in simplistic form the basic eye anatomy. Figure 39–3 shows how the cornea and crystalline lens focus light on the retina, which transmits visual information to the brain via the optic nerve. Cataract is an opacification of the lens, causing decreased vision. Damage to the retina (eg, diabetic retinopathy), especially to the center of vision (the macula), can disrupt the normal processing of images (just as damaged film in a camera would lead to poor-quality photographs). Finally, diseases of the ganglion cells that form the optic nerve can prevent the normal transmission of images to the brain, causing vision loss (as is seen in glaucoma).

The most common surgical procedures performed in developed countries are cataract extraction, laser capsulotomy after cataract extraction, laser treatment for diabetic retinopathy, and glaucoma surgery. The following discussion focuses on the evidence in the literature for cataract extraction and the surgical management of diabetic retinopathy and glaucoma.

CATARACT SURGERY

Cataract is defined in epidemiologic studies as an opacification of the crystalline lens whereas clinically it is a lens opacification that leads to decreased visual function. The lens loses clarity as one ages, and virtually all individuals over the age of 60 years have some evidence of lenticular opacification. The vast majority of cataract is age-related although other forms exist (eg, congenital and traumatic). Cataract is the leading cause of blindness in the world, causing close to half of the world's blindness.[1,2] The strongest risk factor for the disease is age; diabetes, smoking, exposure to ultraviolet light, alcohol consumption, and the use of steroid medications are also known associations.[3] The only treatment currently available for vision-impairing cataract is surgical removal of the lens.

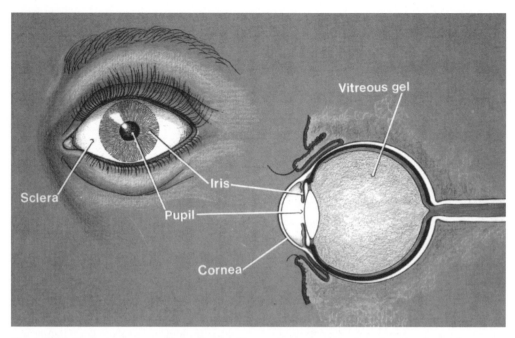

Figure 39–1 Basic eye anatomy. Reproduced with permission from the American Academy of Ophthalmology. Introduction to ophthalmology. San Francisco: 1980; p. 7.

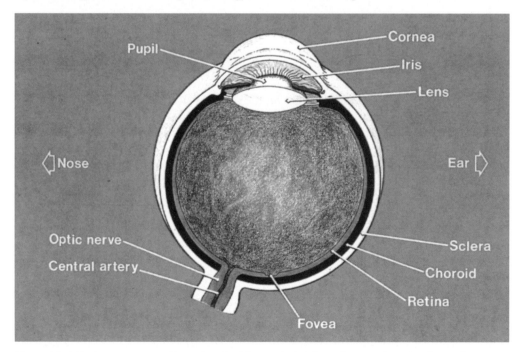

Figure 39–2 Basic eye anatomy. Reproduced with permission from the American Academy of Ophthalmology. Introduction to ophthalmology. San Francisco: 1980; p. 8.

The crystalline lens comprises the lens capsule, a thin cortical layer, and a central nucleus (Figure 39–4). While much of the developing world still removes the entire lens and capsule at the time of surgery (intracapsular cataract extraction or ICCE), virtually 100 percent of cases in the United States are performed using extracapsular cataract extraction (ECCE)

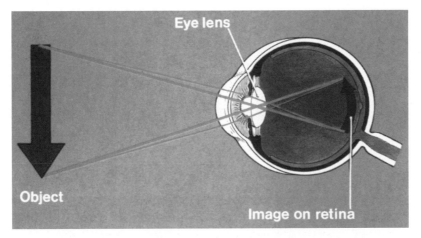

Figure 39–3 The cornea and the lens of the eye bend light to form an image on the retina. Reproduced with permission from the American Academy of Ophthalmology. Introduction to ophthalmology. San Francisco: 1980; p. 10.

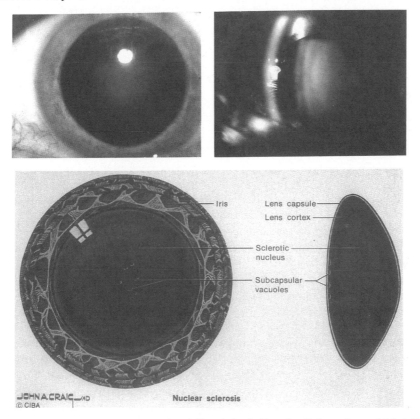

Figure 39–4 Top, nuclear cataract seen with a diffuse light (left) and a slit lamp beam (right). Bottom, schematic of cataract. Reproduced with permission from Basic and Clinical Science Course, 1998–1999. Sec II. Lens and cataract. San Francisco: The American Academy of Ophthalmology; p. 42.

techniques, in which the surgeon removes part of the anterior capsule and then extracts the lens and cortical material, leaving the posterior capsule intact. This approach has fewer complications and allows the surgeon to place a prosthetic intraocular lens (IOL) in the remaining capsular bag (Figure 39–5).

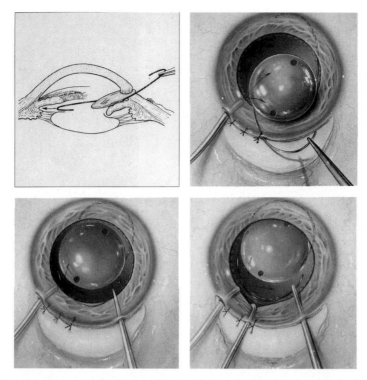

Figure 39–5 Drawing demonstrating how an intraocular lens is placed in the capsular bag during cataract surgery. Reproduced with permission from Heilmann K, Paton D, editors. Atlas of ophthalmic surgery. Volume II. New York: Georg Thieme Verlag Publishers; 1987.

Two approaches to ECCE have evolved over the past two decades; manual ECCE and phacoemulsification (PE). Manual ECCE requires a larger wound to remove the intact nucleus of the lens while PE uses an ultrasonographic device to emulsify the lens and then aspirates the fragments through an instrument inserted through a smaller incision. Phacoemulsification requires a smaller wound and can be performed with a self-sealing wound that often does not require sutures (Figure 39–6).

The rate of cataract surgery in the United States has quadrupled since the early 1980s. In 1995, approximately 1.3 million cataract surgeries were performed on Medicare beneficiaries. This phenomenal increase in cataract surgery can likely be explained by technological improvements developed in the 1970s and 1980s that have appropriately lowered both surgeon and patient thresholds for performing cataract surgery. Prior to the technical revolution of safe IOLs, cataract surgery was not routinely performed until the patient had advanced bilateral cataracts. This was because the surgery necessitated the use of either aphakic spectacles, which cause severe optical image distortion, or contact lenses, which are often difficult for elderly persons to manipulate. Cataracts had to be "ripe" for surgery because vision after surgery was often of such poor quality that only the severely impaired were likely to benefit.

Cataract surgery is now the most commonly performed operation on the Medicare population, costing an estimated $3.4 billion in 1986 to 1987 or 12 percent of Medicare Part B payments.[4] The economic impact of treating cataracts and the increasing rate at which cataract surgery was being performed led the government to fund research aimed at clarifying the benefits of current management practices for cataract. Specific questions addressed included: (1) What are the indications for surgery? (2) How does one define cataract-related disability? (3) Are outcomes different depending on surgical technique?

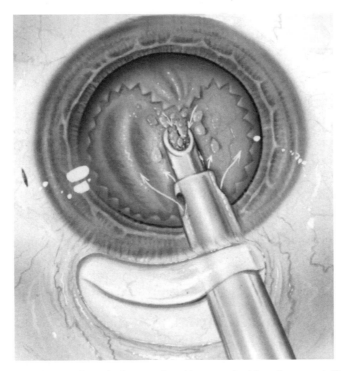

Figure 39–6 Drawing showing how the lens nucleus is removed with a phacoemulsification device through a small incision. Reproduced with permission from Heilmann K, Paton D, editors. Atlas of ophthalmic surgery. Volume II. New York: Georg Thieme Verlag Publishers; 1987.

Measuring Outcomes of Cataract Surgery

Prior to the 1990s, outcomes of cataract surgery were measured by looking at rates of vision-threatening complications and reporting the final best-corrected visual acuity. Major vision-reducing surgical complications include infection (endophthalmitis), retinal detachment, and severe intraocular hemorrhage. These are fortunately rare using modern techniques, with combined rates of around 1 percent.[5] In the 1980s, surgical "success" was based on achieved postoperative best-corrected visual acuity. A synthesis by Johns Hopkins researchers of the available literature in 1991 found that over 95 percent of individuals without pre-existing ocular comorbidity achieved vision of 20/40 or better.[5]

The traditional methods for evaluating surgical success did not fully assess the impact of cataract surgery on patient function. Visual acuity testing is typically performed in a darkened room using high-contrast black letters against a white background. The test itself and the physical environment in which it is performed do not reflect the full range of visual tasks or needs of patients. Documenting that cataract surgery led to improvement in tests of visual acuity did not necessarily indicate that patients were indeed benefiting from surgery in their daily lives.

Scales were developed to assess the effect of cataract on the patient's ability to function. Bernth-Peterson first attempted to quantify the effect of cataract on visual function in the early 1980s.[6–8] He focused on direct visual limitations, mobility limitations due to vision loss, and social limitations due to visual difficulties. He found that close to 75 percent of individuals reported no functional limitations after cataract surgery, a significant improvement over baseline. Brenner enrolled patients prior to cataract surgery and interviewed them about vision symptoms, visual function (using eight items covering near, middle-range, and far-range vision), and perceived quality of vision.[9] To place visual function results in the context of the general health of the patient, subjects were also tested for psychological problems (using the Profile of Mood States, shortened form[10]) and general health and social function. Scores on the visual function questionnaires used correlated with patients' perceptions of their general health.

In 1989, the Agency for Health Care Policy and Research (AHCPR) funded its first Patient Outcome Research Teams (PORTs). Investigators at Johns Hopkins University were awarded a PORT grant to study cataract management. The premise of the research was that cataract surgery outcomes are multifaceted (ie, not limited to visual acuity and complications) and that the "inputs" to cataract surgery management are multidimensional. Figure 39–7 depicts this concept in simplistic form. The investigators developed and validated a new questionnaire, designated VF-14, to measure patient-perceived visual dysfunction related to cataract.[11,12] The VF-14 (Table 39–1) assesses whether vision causes difficulty with near tasks, hobbies, and driving. Subject responses range from "none" to "a great deal." To gain further insight into the effect of cataract on the patient's quality of life, the researchers also asked specifically about symptoms likely to be caused by cataract (such as glare) and asked patients to rate their overall trouble and satisfaction with vision. Finally, the researchers evaluated the impact of cataract surgery on general functional status using the Sickness Impact Profile (SIP), a 136-point questionnaire. A modification to the SIP was also employed to ask if reported difficulties in the SIP were vision-related. Responses were used to calculate a score for a vision-related SIP (VR-SIP).

The VF-14 has high internal consistency, is reproducible, and correlates well with global assessment of trouble or satisfaction with vision.[11–14] Furthermore, VF-14 results improve significantly with cataract surgery and strongly correlate with the subjective grading of satisfaction with vision. The prior gold standard, preoperative visual acuity in the operated eye, did not correlate well with patient-perceived improvement in vision. The effect size (the mean change before and after surgery divided by the standard deviation at baseline) of the VF-14 is over 1.0, meaning that cataract surgery leads to significant changes in the VF-14 results.[12,15] In addition, the effect size is largest among those who report less trouble with vision after surgery. The VF-14 has been applied in Canada, Denmark, and Spain, yielding similar findings and documenting its wide applicability.[15]

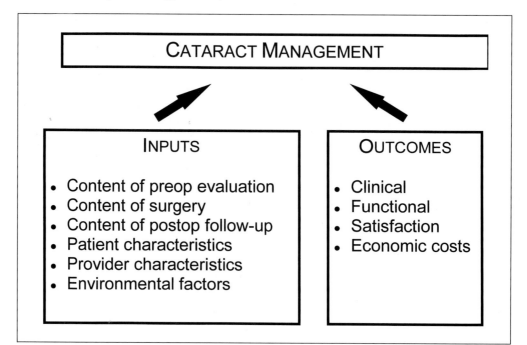

Figure 39–7 Cataract management.

Table 39–1 VF-14 Questions

How much difficulty do you have driving during the day because of your vision?

How much difficulty do you have driving at night because of your vision?

How much difficulty do you have reading small print such as labels on medicine bottles, a telephone book, food labels

How much difficulty do you have reading a newspaper or book

How much difficulty do you have reading a large print book or large print newspaper

How much difficulty do you have recognizing people when they are close to you

How much difficulty do you have seeing steps, stairs, or curbs

How much difficulty do you have reading traffic signs, street signs, store signs

How much difficulty do you have doing fine handwork like sewing, knitting, crocheting, carpentry

How much difficulty do you have writing checks or filling out forms

How much difficulty do you have playing games such as bingo, dominos, card games, mah jong

How much difficulty do you have taking part in sports like bowling, handball, tennis, golf

How much difficulty do you have cooking

How much difficulty do you have watching television

Steinberg EP, Bass EB, Luthra R, et al. Variation in ophthalmic testing before cataract surgery. Results of a national survey of ophthalmologists [comments], Arch Ophthalmol 1994; 112:896–902.

The ability of standardized questionnaires of visual function to predict who will improve with surgery was confirmed with another instrument, the Activities of Daily Vision Scale (ADVS).[16] The authors found that a substantial proportion of visual disability was not captured by measuring visual acuity and that a low score on the ADVS preoperatively was predictive of an improvement on the ADVS 1 year postoperatively. Other instruments to assess visual function in cataract patients include the Cataract Symptom Score,[10] the "Catquest,"[17] the Visual Activities Questionnaire,[18] and the National Eye Institute Visual Function Questionnaire (NEI-VFQ).[19]

Other investigators have attempted to understand the impact of cataract on patients' lives relative to the impact of other health problems. Preference values are one way to quantify the importance of different health states to patients. These studies help to place cataract surgery on a metric of patient values that can be used to compare one procedure to another when attempting cost-benefit analyses. Individuals scheduled for cataract surgery assigned a preference value of 0.33 for complete blindness on a scale where 0 equaled death and 1 equaled perfect health.[20] In comparison, general clinic populations rated blindness 0.39 and rated home dialysis for renal failure 0.54.[21] Patients place a tremendous value on not going blind. The mean preference value that a cohort of patients with mild to moderate cataract awaiting surgery placed on their then present state of vision was 0.68.[22] This contrasts with a preference value of 0.79 for requiring a mechanical device to help with walking.[19]

Cataract Surgery and General Health

Cataract surgery has less impact on general health measures such as the SIP and the SF-36 than on vision-specific questionnaires. Generic health questionnaires are useful for comparing patients across many disease states whereas disease-specific measures are often more useful for assessing the impact of interventions aimed at a specific illness.[23] The cataract PORT found that visual acuity in the better eye preoperatively was strongly associated with limitations in daily activities reported on the SIP.[24] However, trouble and satisfaction with vision were not correlated with the SIP score. This is in contradistinction to the strong correlation between VF-14 score and patient-reported trouble and satisfaction with vision. In addition, while the VF-14 was quite responsive to cataract surgery, the overall SIP score improved minimally after cataract surgery in the PORT study. Others have documented improvements in generic health measures.[9,25] Brenner questioned subjects about physical and mental function and showed improvement in both after cataract surgery.[9] Mangione used the SF-36 and found that it had declined in seven of the eight subscales at 1 year after cataract extraction. Among the 80 percent in whom the ADVS score improved, however, the SF-36 score declined at a slower rate than among those whose ADVS score did not improve.[24] This indicates that those who have improved visual function after cataract surgery might have slower declines in overall health.

Visual Acuity as a Measure of Surgical Need

One irony of recent research is that visual acuity, the standard test used to measure the impact of cataract, has been shown to be one of the worst predictors of surgical success.[14,15,26] Schein and colleagues reported that preoperative visual acuity was not predictive of surgical outcome.[14] The same study showed that there was little correlation between preoperative visual acuity in the operated eye and postoperative self-reported trouble and satisfaction with vision.[11] In contrast, patients with low preoperative VF-14 scores were more likely to improve with cataract surgery than those with high scores. The international cataract PORT reproduced these results in Spain, Denmark, and Canada.[15] Another large, well-designed study using the ADVS also found that preoperative visual acuity in the operated eye was not associated with documented improvement on the ADVS 12 months after surgery.[27] All three of the above studies found higher correlations on tests of functional improvement with vision in the better-seeing eye than with the vision obtained in the operated eye. Finally, a study of patient preference values for their then current visual state showed no correlation between visual acuity in the operated eye and the value assigned.[20] There was a weak correlation with the vision in the better-seeing eye.

Tests to Assess the Need for Surgery

Other "objective" tests of vision have been developed to evaluate the patient with cataract. Potential acuity, glare disability, and contrast sensitivity tests all assess visual acuity in different ways in an attempt to determine whether removing a cataract will improve vision. The potential acuity meter projects the Snellen acuity chart onto the retina through a small aperture, bypassing the adverse effect of cataract on visual acuity. Glare disability tests assess visual acuity in the presence of bright lights. Contrast sensitivity is tested by presenting letters with progressively less contrast with background until the patient can no longer distinguish the letters. In surveys conducted in 1992,[27,28] both ophthalmologists and optometrists reported using these tests routinely on cataract patients in spite of the fact that there was little support for such preoperative testing in the literature. Thirty-three percent of ophthalmologists and 23 percent of optometrists reported frequently or always testing glare disability, and 7 percent of ophthalmologists and 19 percent of optometrists tested contrast sensitivity. Finally, 37 percent of ophthalmologists and 25 percent of optometrists reported using the potential acuity meter frequently or always.

In 1993, the AHCPR funded a guideline development project for several medical or surgical conditions, one of which was cataract. The basis for the guideline was a literature review which found no convincing evidence that glare testing, measuring potential acuity with specially designed instruments, or contrast sensitivity testing provide an increased likelihood of benefit of cataract surgery over that obtained by a routine competent ophthalmologic examination.[29] While abnormal glare testing and contrast sensitivity are associated with cataracts and are likely to improve after cataract surgery, they are not specific for cataracts and do not distinguish those who will improve from those who will not. Potential acuity tests suffer from substantial inaccuracy in patients with significant cataract and/or macular pathology. Unfortunately, these are the situations where such a test is needed. While ocular comorbidity (including age-related macular degeneration and diabetes) is associated with worse surgical outcomes,[14,27] no "objective" tests have been shown to distinguish those who will have a successful outcome following cataract surgery from those who will not. This has led to the recommendation that these tests need not be performed routinely.[29,30] That a high proportion of ophthalmologists and optometrists relied on these tests in the evaluation of cataract patients despite such limited evidence for their usefulness points to the common use of diagnostic technologies to assist surgical decision making even when no proof of a benefit exists. This finding is interesting because there is no direct financial incentive for performing these tests as their costs are not individually reimbursed by payers. No studies have looked at how physician practice has changed since the guidelines were published.

Second-Eye Surgery

The primary cost of cataract surgery is direct payment for surgical services.[4] In the early 1990s, several insurers explored limiting access to second-eye surgery to decrease costs. Three prospective studies demonstrated functional improvements after cataract surgery in the second eye.[31–33] Javitt and colleagues from Johns Hopkins showed that VF-14 scores as well as overall assessment of trouble and satisfaction with vision improved significantly after second-eye surgery.[32] A study by Laidlaw documented decreased patient-reported symptoms, improved stereo vision, and improvement on binocular contrast sensitivity tests after second-eye cataract extraction.[31] A more recent study from England confirmed that second-eye surgery further improves the VF-14 score over and above the improvement found with first-eye surgery. The authors also documented an additional benefit of greater improvement on the SIP for individuals who underwent second-eye surgery than for those operated on in only one eye.[33]

Incorporating Evidence into Practice

The American Academy of Ophthalmology has incorporated the AHCPR findings into its own guidelines for cataract surgery.[34] The Academy recommends against the routine use of glare, contrast sensitivity, and potential acuity testing. It also recognizes the limitations of visual acuity testing and the importance of the patient's perspective by stating, "The primary indication for surgery is when vision impaired by cataract no longer meets the patient's needs and surgery provides a reasonable likelihood of improved visual function." No research has been published documenting the impact of these guidelines on clinical practice. In addition, while some insurers require documentation of functional disability, few surgeons currently collect visual function data in a systematic way using one of the questionnaires described above. This points to the practical difficulties of using scales developed for research in the day-to-day care of patients.

Evaluating Surgical Technique: Manual ECCE versus Phacoemulsification

The evolution from intracapsular cataract extraction (ICCE) to manual extracapsular cataract extraction (ECCE) was hastened by the development of implantable intraocular lenses (IOLs). The current IOLs are designed to sit within the capsular bag. Keeping the capsule intact is a primary goal of modern cataract surgery because capsular rupture is associated with an increased risk of retinal detachment,[35,36] cystoid macular edema,[37] and endophthalmitis.[38] In the late 1980s, PE was adopted widely on the presumed benefits of more rapid rehabilitation and less astigmatism associated with smaller surgical wounds. Studies as of 1990 did not show better surgical results with PE versus ECCE in terms of visual acuity, time to healing, amount of astigmatism, or rates of major surgical complications.[39] A pooled meta-analysis of 90 studies published between 1979 and 1991 found similar postoperative visual acuity and rates of complications when comparing PE to ECCE.[5] There was weak support for an increased rate of expulsive choroidal hemorrhage with ECCE while nuclear fragments were possibly more frequently lost into the vitreous cavity with PE.

A survey of ophthalmologists in 1992 found significant variation in intraoperative techniques, with 46 percent performing PE in over 75 percent of cases while 41 percent used ECCE.[39] Higher-volume surgeons and those recently graduated from medical school tended to use PE in the belief that it decreased astigmatism and healing time. Surgeons using ECCE and PE all felt that the procedure they used had fewer complications and resulted in superior visual acuity. A prospective observational study of outcomes after cataract surgery found no difference in 4-month visual acuity when comparing PE to ECCE. Iris abnormalities were more common in the ECCE-treated group, and posterior capsule opacification was more common after PE. Posterior capsule opacification was attributable to higher rates of laser treatment for this condition among higher-volume surgeons.

This study also found that high-volume cataract surgeons (those performing > 200 surgeries per year) had similar rates of complications to those of moderate-volume surgeons (those performing 51 to 200 surgeries per year). Posterior capsule opacification, a complication requiring a laser procedure with an associated increased risk of macular edema and retinal detachment, was, in fact, reported more commonly by the high-volume surgeons. Because capsular opacification was determined subjectively by the operating surgeon, the differential rate of opacification found may well be due to a higher threshold for documenting this complication among the moderate-volume surgeons or a lower threshold among higher-volume surgeons. The finding of similar outcomes by surgical volume is significant because it does not follow the trend of better outcomes among higher-volume surgeons that has been identified for aortic aneurysm repair[40] and coronary artery bypass grafting.[41] It is notable that low-volume surgeons (< 50 operations per year) were excluded from the study.

Since the AHCPR publication of guidelines, several studies have shown that phacoemulsification is associated with less induced astigmatism in the early postoperative period.[42–44] This early disparity more or less equalizes after 6 months. One of the problems with assessing astigmatism is defining the proportion of postoperative astigmatism that is induced by the surgery. Most authors report both the mean astigmatic correction and the "induced astigmatism," which relies on vector analysis.[45] The only published trial in which individuals were randomly assigned to ECCE or PE found consistently higher rates of induced astigmatism among the ECCE group, with the lowest rates among those undergoing PE with the smallest incisions.[42] Uncorrected vision and best-corrected vision were better among the smallest-incision PE group at 60 to 90 days although this was not statistically significant. In the smallest-incision PE group, 96 percent of eyes had astigmatism ≤ 1.5 diopters at 2 to 3 months versus 69 percent in the ECCE group, and 96 percent of those in the smallest-incision PE group versus 76 percent in the ECCE group achieved a best-corrected visual acuity > 20/40 at that time. Other studies support these findings. One retrospective study found large differences in astigmatism at 6 weeks with almost no difference in induced astigmatism at 1 year.[43] Others have documented that the astigmatic correction stabilizes more rapidly with PE compared to ECCE.[44] Finally, one randomized clinical trial comparing larger wound sizes with smaller ones using PE alone showed less astigmatism in those with smaller wounds, an effect that lasted for at least 3 years.[46]

In summary, ECCE and PE both have high surgical success rates with few complications. Both yield similar visual acuities in the operated eye 4 months after surgery. Recent evidence supports the clinical impression that smaller wound sizes associated with PE result in more rapid healing, less astigmatism, and earlier return of good vision. Whether these benefits are worth the additional instrument-related costs of PE has not been evaluated.

Patient Care: Surgery and Co-management

Cataract surgery changed from an inpatient procedure to an outpatient one due to a 1984 Health Care Financing Administration (HCFA) policy requiring that virtually all cataract surgery on Medicare patients be performed in an outpatient setting. At the time, approximately half of all cataract patients were admitted to hospitals for surgery. Although HCFA acted with little evidence supporting outpatient over inpatient surgery, Javitt and colleagues retrospectively evaluated the Medicare database and found no increase in the rates of retinal detachment or endophthalmitis after the 1984 ruling.[47] While research is limited on the impact of this sea change in patient care, the general consensus is that the decision to move to outpatient management has not diminished quality of care or patient outcomes.

Another marketplace-driven change is the shared postoperative care of patients by optometrists and ophthalmologists. Many patients are co-managed by an ophthalmologist who performs the operation and an optometrist who manages varying aspects of the postoperative course. Whether this alters the quality of surgical care is a subject of debate.[48] One retrospective study documented good results in subjects co-managed after cataract surgery;[49] 86 percent of co-managed cases had 20/40 or better vision at 90 days after surgery, a number similar to those reported in the literature. However, optometrists working outside surgical centers did not recognize 41 percent of all diagnosed complications. This may have been due to onset of complications after the optometrist's examination, lack of documentation by the optometrist, or differences in clinical abilities between outside optometrists and center ophthalmologists.[48] The question remains unanswered and is an area requiring further research.

Conclusion

Cataract surgery has been the subject of extensive research in the last decade. As the procedure has improved, the indications for surgery have changed. Whereas 25 years ago one had to be virtually blind before risking an operation due to the severe optical aberrations associated with aphakic spectacles, the excellent results obtainable today have lowered the threshold for surgery. Cataract surgery has performed well under the scrutiny of outcomes research. Adverse outcomes are rare, the vast majority of individuals undergoing the procedure are more satisfied with their vision than they were prior to surgery, and tests of visual function improve dramatically after surgery. The benefit of second-eye surgery has also been documented. Finally, the research findings have been synthesized and incorporated into guidelines and preferred practice patterns for clinicians to use. The research on cataract extraction illustrates well the use of the patient's perspective in assessing the value of surgical procedures.

SURGICAL MANAGEMENT OF DIABETIC RETINOPATHY

Diabetic retinopathy is the leading cause of new cases of blindness in the United States in individuals between the ages of 20 and 74 years.[50] Since it causes visual impairment among younger Americans, there are tremendous associated economic costs.[51] Diabetes causes damage to the retinal microvasculature causing two vision-threatening conditions—proliferative diabetic retinopathy (PDR) and macular edema. The first occurs when new blood vessels grow on the retina and into the vitreous cavity. These blood vessels are fragile and frequently bleed into the vitreous. In addition, they cause fibrosis, which pulls on the retina, wrinkling and detaching it from its normal position. Untreated PDR results in blindness in close to 50 percent of affected individuals within 5 years. Macular edema (swelling of the central part of the retina) occurs when diabetes damages the microvasculature of the retina, causing blood vessels to leak. The accumulation of fluid blurs vision and progressively damages the retina, which can result in severe visual disability or blindness. A combination of laser and vitreous surgery is currently used to manage PDR while the mainstay for treatment of macular edema is laser photocoagulation.

Evidence for Effectiveness of Current Management

The laser treatment of macular edema differs from that used for PDR. Macular edema is treated with a focal laser to leaking microaneurysms and a grid laser to areas of retinal thickening. The treatment for PDR uses higher energies to destroy the retina in the periphery, a procedure called panretinal photocoagulation (PRP). This heavy laser treatment in the periphery presumably removes the stimulus for the new blood vessel growth that is the hallmark of PDR.

After initially promising case reports of decreased PDR after laser therapy,[52] a large randomized controlled clinical trial of laser surgery versus no treatment established that laser photocoagulation to the retina reduces the rate of severe vision loss from PDR. The Diabetic Retinopathy Study (DRS) confirmed earlier reports that close to half of those with PDR go on to blindness within 3 to 5 years if left untreated.[53] Panretinal photocoagulation reduced the risk by 60 percent.[54] The DRS identified high-risk ocular characteristics associated with a better outcome with treatment.[55] Later analysis of the data identified additional risk factors for a poor outcome.[56]

The vitreous plays an important role in the development of PDR by acting as scaffolding for the growth of new blood vessels. The theoretical benefit of removing the vitreous (vitrectomy) to prevent worsening of PDR was studied in the Diabetic Retinopathy Vitrectomy Study (DRVS).[57] The DRVS had several arms, one of which was an observational natural history study to identify ocular characteristics associated with poor prognosis in eyes with severe PDR and useful vision.[58] The study then compared conventional management (nonsurgical observation until the development of specific findings requiring vitrectomy) with early vitrectomy. The principle outcomes were visual acuity $\geq$ 20/40, < 5/200 vision, and no light perception vision. No effort was made to assess patient perceptions of visual function. While the early intervention group had slightly higher rates of no light perception vision, the percent with vision $\geq$ 20/40 was much higher in the treated group (44% vs 28% at 4 years).[58] A third study conducted by DRVS investigators assessed the role of early vitrectomy in nonclearing vitreous hemorrhage obscuring the view of the fundus.[59] This study identified a clear benefit for Type I diabetics (36% vs 12% with vision $\geq$ 20/40 at 2 years) but showed no improvement with treatment for Type II diabetics. This study also found higher rates of no light perception vision in the treated group for the first 18 months of the study, after which the rates were the same in the two groups.

A third randomized controlled clinical trial, the Early Treatment Diabetic Retinopathy Study (ETDRS) examined two important questions for the management of diabetic retinopathy: when is the most effective time to intervene with PRP for proliferative disease, and does laser treatment decrease the incidence of vision loss due to macular edema.[60] The authors reviewing the literature noted that previous studies using laser photocoagulation to treat macular edema had not been randomized, were subject to bias and confounding, had unclear treatment regimens, and had small sample sizes. The ETDRS showed that laser photocoagulation halves the rate of central vision loss in individuals with a well-defined set of clinical abnormalities called "clinically significant macular edema."

Cost-Benefit and Cost-Effectiveness Analyses

Various researchers[61–63] have attempted to quantify the benefit of treating diabetic retinopathy.[62–64] Ferris looked at how effective diabetic treatment is in preventing severe vision loss (visual acuity < 5/200) using data from the DRS and the ETDRS. He found that only 4 percent of diabetics with PDR, when appropriately treated in the ETDRS, developed severe visual loss at 5 years and only 1 percent had bilateral loss.[63] Rates of blindness (visual acuity < 20/200) with PDR can be reduced from almost 50 percent without treatment down to 5 percent at 5 years (Figure 39–8).

Javitt and colleagues performed a cost-benefit analysis of treating retinopathy in juvenile-onset Type I diabetics.[64] The authors did not include many of the costs of blindness such as rehabilitation expenses and lost productivity in their model. The model used Monte Carlo

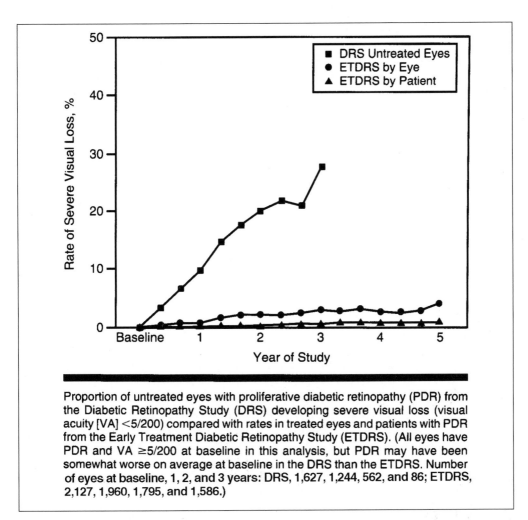

Proportion of untreated eyes with proliferative diabetic retinopathy (PDR) from the Diabetic Retinopathy Study (DRS) developing severe visual loss (visual acuity [VA] <5/200) compared with rates in treated eyes and patients with PDR from the Early Treatment Diabetic Retinopathy Study (ETDRS). (All eyes have PDR and VA ≥5/200 at baseline in this analysis, but PDR may have been somewhat worse on average at baseline in the DRS than the ETDRS. Number of eyes at baseline, 1, 2, and 3 years: DRS, 1,627, 1,244, 562, and 86; ETDRS, 2,127, 1,960, 1,795, and 1,586.)

Figure 39–8 JAMA 1993; 269(10): 1291.

simulation to follow each member of a diseased cohort, applying known annual risks for disease progression, mortality, and vision loss. Annual events were followed concurrently with the costs of treatment and screening. The model's predictions correlated well with population-based data on the incidence of diabetic retinopathy and median survival times. The model predicted that in 1986, it would cost $966 per person-year of sight saved and $1,118 per person-year of reading vision saved with routine screening and surgical treatment by an ophthalmologist. Given that the federal government alone paid an average of $6,900 in disability benefits annually to blind individuals, the cost of screening and treatment was estimated to be one-tenth that of social welfare costs. As noted above, this model did not consider lost productivity or quality of life. A follow-up cost-benefit analysis adding updated data found that screening for and treating diabetic retinopathy would cost an average of $1,757 (in 1990 dollars) per year of vision saved.[64] Lower costs were associated with screening and treating Type I than Type II diabetes. The authors also found that the average cost per quality-adjusted life-year was only $3,190, considerably less than for coronary artery bypass grafting of left main artery disease ($5,100) or liver transplantation ($250,000). Additional cost-benefit analysis from the perspective of the U.S. government using the same model found that screening and treating only 60 percent of Type 1 diabetics saves over $100 million annually.[51]

There is little research on the impact of diabetic retinopathy and its treatment on visual function.[65] One study was unable to show any impact on the SF-36 of best-eye vision, worst-eye vision, Amsler grid score (a test of central vision), or severity of diabetic retinopathy. No visual function questionnaire was administered, however. Nevertheless, most of the treatments prevent blindness, and research and common sense indicate that individuals place a high value on avoiding this outcome.[20]

Conclusion

Large, well-designed randomized controlled clinical trials have documented that laser surgery for diabetic retinopathy is effective in preventing severe vision loss. Vitrectomy is also effective at preserving good central vision in severe PDR. While little is known about the impact of lesser degrees of retinopathy on visual function, it is clear that blinding retinopathy has a significant impact on a patient's ability to live independently. The treatments discussed in this section significantly reduce the likelihood of blindness among diabetics. Cost-benefit and cost-effectiveness analyses have shown that screening and surgical intervention reduce costs in Type I diabetics and that the cost per quality-adjusted life-year of this intervention, even in later-onset Type II diabetes, is extremely low.

MANAGEMENT OF OPEN-ANGLE GLAUCOMA

Glaucoma is a progressive optic neuropathy in which neurons (ganglion cells) die, producing characteristic progressive enlargement of the optic nerve cup, or cupping (Figure 39–9). The loss of neurons also leads to functional impairment, typically starting with loss of peripheral vision and which may progress to loss of central vision. The standard evaluation of functional damage caused by glaucoma is the automated visual field test. This test suffers from significant long- and short-term fluctuation as well as learning effects. These limitations hamper efforts both to diagnose glaucoma and to determine if it has gotten worse over time.

Several distinct disease syndromes make up the glaucomas, including open-angle glaucoma (OAG), the most common form, angle-closure glaucoma, congenital glaucoma, and many secondary forms of the disease. This section will focus on the evidence for the current management of open-angle glaucoma.

Intraocular pressure (IOP) is a strong risk factor for the disease, but glaucoma occurs in individuals with normal pressures as well. The circulation of aqueous humor in the eye maintains IOP. Aqueous is produced by the ciliary body and exits the eye at the filtering angle (Figure 39–10). The fact that IOP is a major risk factor and that all treatments currently used for OAG attempt to lower IOP has led some to mistakenly equate OAG with elevated IOP. Elevated

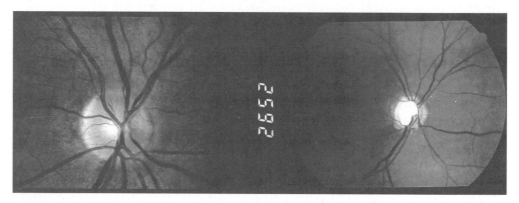

Figure 39–9 Left, normal optic nerve. Right, glaucomatous optic nerve. Reproduced with permission from Basic and Clinical Science Course, 1998–1999. Sec. 10. Glaucoma. San Francisco: The American Academy of Ophthalmology; p. 7.

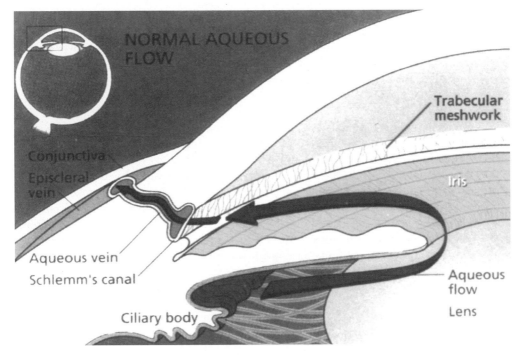

Figure 39–10 Schematic of aqueous flow in the eye.

IOP without optic nerve damage or visual field loss is referred to as ocular hypertension. Whether treating this at-risk population results in better outcomes is the subject of an ongoing randomized clinical trial funded by the National Eye Institute, the Ocular Hypertension Treatment Study. The remainder of this discussion will focus on individuals with OAG.

The definition of OAG has not been uniform in population-based surveys, but it is clear that OAG is more prevalent in black people than in white people. The Baltimore Eye Survey estimated that 1.1 percent of white individuals 40 years of age or older had glaucoma while 4.2 percent of black people of similar age were affected.[66] Higher rates were noted among the black population in Barbados.[67] There is little published in the English literature about the prevalence of OAG in Asian populations, but a small study from Mongolia estimated its rate at 0.70 percent in individuals over 40 years of age.[68]

Age and IOP are the strongest risk factors known for glaucoma. Other risk factors include a positive family history, high myopia, low perfusion pressure to the eye, and possibly diabetes.[69–71]

Limitations of Research in Glaucoma Management

All treatments for OAG lower IOP. No other forms of therapy are available although neuroprotective agents are under investigation. The fundamental assumption of glaucoma management to date is that since IOP is strongly associated with the prevalence of OAG, lowering IOP will slow its progression. While studies indicate that lowering IOP slows the progression of glaucoma,[72,73] only one study to date has conclusively shown that lowering the IOP preserves the visual field in individuals with glaucoma.[74] Another study comparing treatment versus no treatment for early glaucoma, The Early Manifest Glaucoma Trial, is underway in Sweden to look at this question.

One problem in assessing the effectiveness of different approaches to glaucoma management is the slow, chronic course of the disease. One study concluded that given the large variation in the results of visual field testing, a minimum of 5 years of annual visual field testing is needed before it is certain that an individual's visual field has worsened.[75] The large variability in performance on visual field testing led one investigator to require 3 repeat visual field tests documenting progression before accepting that the glaucoma had worsened.[76] Most studies of glaucoma management do not follow patients for sufficient time or perform enough visual field tests to use progression of visual field defects as an endpoint. The majority of glaucoma research has therefore used the outcome of IOP lowering to determine the efficacy of an intervention.

Another limitation of published glaucoma research is that the functional impact of peripheral field loss remains poorly understood. Three studies have documented moderate correlation between visual field score and patient-reported visual function using both the NEI-VFQ and the VF-14.[77–79] One study showed moderate correlations with patient reports of decreased visual function and binocular visual field testing while another looked at correlations with function and the visual field in the better-seeing eye. A glaucoma symptom scale has been developed that has ten questions and is composed of two domains: visual symptoms and visual function.[78] The scale identified differences between normal individuals and those with glaucoma, and the visual function domain was moderately correlated with visual field test scores. The symptom scale will likely be incorporated into future research on the impact of glaucoma treatment. While these three studies have documented a modest correlation between visual field loss and patient-reported function, they did not address how much damage is required for an individual to suffer any functional loss. This is a crucial question for determining which patients require treatment and how aggressively treatment should be pursued. Should the goal be to avoid all field loss, or can some field loss be tolerated before therapy is initiated? This is an important question since treatment has costs and side effects and because OAG is largely a disease of the elderly with slow progression.

Surgery for Glaucoma

There are many ways to lower IOP surgically. The standard operation for glaucoma is trabeculectomy, which involves making an opening in the eye wall that allows fluid to filter out of the eye. The opening is covered by the outermost layer of the eye, the conjunctiva, forming a small blister or filtering bleb (Figure 39–11). An alternative approach is to use a laser to create 80 to 100 small burns in the filtering angle where the fluid normally leaves the eye. This procedure, argon laser trabeculoplasty (ALT), increases the flow of aqueous out of the eye, resulting in a lower IOP. While ALT often lowers IOP initially, its effect deteriorates with time.[80,81]

A third approach to lowering IOP is to use medications. The text of the current American Academy of Ophthalmology Preferred Practice Pattern for Open-Angle Glaucoma illustrates the uncertainty that exists regarding the optimal initial therapy: "in most instances, topical medications are initial therapy. Argon laser trabeculoplasty is an appropriate initial therapy alternative, and filtering surgery may be an appropriate initial therapy for patients with moderate or severe glaucoma."[30] How to define the best approach to the initial management of glaucoma is widely debated and has been the subject of multiple randomized clinical trials.[72,73,81–85] Each of the initial approaches is discussed below.

Argon Laser Trabeculoplasy versus Medicines

The Glaucoma Laser Trial (GLT) randomized individuals to either ALT or medications as initial treatment for glaucoma.[81] Intraocular pressure was consistently lower up to 9 years after randomization in the laser-treated group, and visual fields were slightly better in the laser-treated group at an average follow-up of 42 months.[82] In addition, assessment of the optic nerve showed slightly less evidence of progressive damage in the laser-treated group.[86] The better IOP-lowering effect of initial laser treatment was also seen in a smaller randomized clinical trial.[73] Despite the results and the rarity of complications, many still believe that ALT is too invasive, and the glaucoma community has not adopted it as first-line treatment.[87]

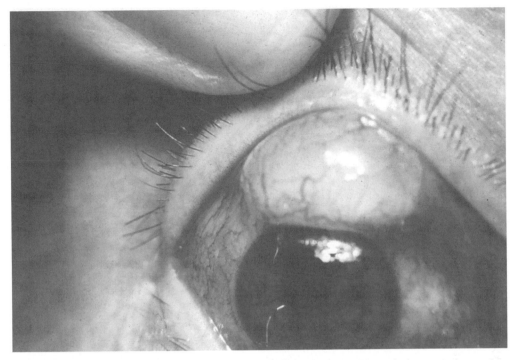

Figure 39–11 Filtering bleb after glaucoma surgery. Fluid leaves the eye through the surgical wound and accumulates under the conjunctiva.

However, others worry about the potential side effects of medications and recommend greater use of ALT.[88]

Trabeculectomy versus Medical Treatment

Several randomized trials have compared trabeculectomy to medical treatment as initial management for glaucoma.[72,85,89] Each of these demonstrated greater IOP lowering with surgery than with medications. In addition, while visual field criteria varied in the studies and no confirmatory fields were obtained, all three studies demonstrated less visual field loss in the group treated surgically from the outset (failure of medical therapy led to trabeculectomy in a significant proportion of the medication-first groups). The study by Migdal also found that some of the differences in visual field results were not attributable to IOP lowering and postulated that some medications may cause worse visual field results through other means. An example of this is the effect of pilocarpine on the size of the pupil, leading to a worse visual field result. These studies only enrolled individuals with high IOPs, thus limiting their generalizability. A large randomized clinical trial (The Collaborative Initial Glaucoma Treatment Study) which will look at the effect of the two different treatments on quality of life, quality of vision, and general health is currently underway.

Trabeculectomy versus Argon Laser Trabeculoplasty

A large randomized clinical trial of surgery versus ALT as initial therapy for individuals using maximally tolerated medical treatment found that black patients had better preservation of visual field and central vision when ALT was used as initial therapy whereas white patients did better with surgery first.[83] No explanation for this was found although black patients had slightly higher rates of success with ALT than did white patients and lower success rates with trabeculectomy. A smaller study in a white population found a trend toward better preservation of visual field in the trabeculectomy-first group and lower IOPs, but the preservation of visual field was not statistically significant.[72]

Trabeculectomy to Lower Intraocular Pressure

The most common incisional surgery for glaucoma is trabeculectomy in which the surgeon creates a full-thickness opening in the scleral wall at the surgical limbus (Figures 39–12 and 39–13). The conjunctiva can be incised in the fornix approximately 8 mm from the surgical limbus, or it can be disinserted directly at the limbus. The potential benefits of the latter procedure include better visualization of the surgical field and faster operating time.[90] One concern, however, is that the latter technique might not be as effective. Several small studies addressing this question showed no difference in surgical results between the two techniques[90–93] while one study found slightly better results with the latter technique.[94] Many surgeons still prefer placing the incision further from the limbus for fear of wound leaks, however.

Glaucoma filtration procedures most frequently fail because the body heals the surgical wound. The use of antimetabolites to modulate wound healing after trabeculectomy is a major improvement in the last decade. Eyes that have had prior conjunctival surgery (eg, cataract extraction or failed trabeculectomy) are at high risk of failing to achieve IOP control after trabeculectomy. A large randomized controlled clinical trial showed that using the antimetabolite 5-fluorouracil (5-FU) in the post-operative period significantly increases the likelihood that a trabeculectomy will continue to lower IOP for up to 5 years in eyes at high risk of surgical failure.[95] Not only was IOP lower, but fewer medications were required by the patients treated with 5-FU. This study found no differences between the two groups in visual field progression over the 5 years of the study, however. Administering 5-FU according to the study protocol was a major undertaking as it had to be injected subconjunctivally twice a day for 2 weeks. An alternative antimetabolite, mitomycin-C (MMC) leads to even lower IOP than 5-FU in these high-risk eyes and requires only one application at the time of surgery.[96] This greater ease of use has led surgeons to select MMC over 5-FU for these high-risk eyes, but its effectiveness comes at a price. A large randomized controlled trial has documented that MMC leads to increased

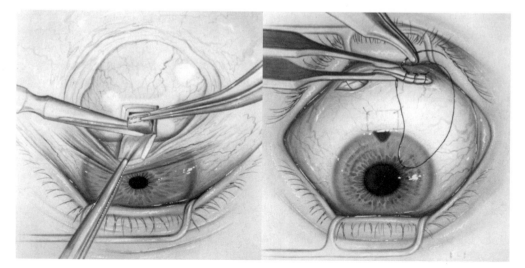

Figure 39–12 and 39–13 The surgeon creates a partial-thickness flap in the sclera. This is reflected and the sclera under the flap is removed. This creates a full-thickness hole with partial-thickness sclera covering it. The hole in the eye wall lowers eye pressure by allowing aqueous to leave the eye through a new pathway. Reproduced with permission from Heilmann K, Paton D, editors. Atlas of ophthalmic surgery. Volume II. New York: Georg Thieme Verlag Publishers; 1987.

cataract formation after trabeculectomy and is associated with a higher risk of low eye pressure that can damage the retina (hypotony maculopathy), especially in younger patients.[97]

While the use of antimetabolites in eyes at high risk for bleb failure has been widely adopted, controversy still exists over the use of 5-FU or MMC for primary trabeculectomies. One randomized controlled multicenter study of 62 patients who underwent primary trabeculectomy found that patients treated with 5-FU (in lower doses than those described above) had lower IOP and required fewer medications at 1 year than the control group patients. Hypotony was more common in the 5-FU group, however. Similar results have been found using MMC in primary trabeculectomies.[97] This study found that the lower doses of MMC can be used without significantly decreasing the success rate. While diluting current MMC doses 10-fold reduces its effectiveness,[98] little information exists regarding the optimal dose.

The decision to use MMC in primary trabeculectomies is further complicated by the likely increase in endophthalmitis in eyes treated with antimetabolites.[99] Whether or not an increase in surgical "success" from 80 to 90 percent associated with lower IOPs and less need for glaucoma medications at 1 year is worth the increased rate of cataract formation, the greater likelihood of hypotony and increased risk of endophthalmitis has not been determined. Most glaucoma specialists weighing the evidence currently use MMC in primary trabeculectomies.

Required Future Research

The effectiveness of glaucoma management is difficult to judge given the limited research in this area; limited data are available to assess the impact of visual field loss on the function and quality of life of glaucoma patients. Although the NEI-VFQ and the VF-14 have been applied to glaucoma patients, more research is needed to clarify the impact of different interventions on these parameters. In addition, research into the functional impact of field loss (eg, increased accidents and falls) is lacking.

Several large clinical trials are underway to answer some of these questions (Table 39–2). While the primary endpoint for these studies is progression of visual field loss, many of them have incorporated instruments to quantify the impact of various interventions on the patient's quality of life and vision. The results will facilitate clinical decision making and future analyses of the costs and benefits of various treatment approaches.

The value patients give to preserving peripheral field vision has not been addressed, and this lack would hamper any attempts at decision analysis. In addition, the cost-effectiveness of alternative glaucoma treatments has not been adequately studied. Are screening efforts

Table 39–2 Ongoing Clinical Trials in Glaucoma Management

Name	Study Design	Recruitment Goal (No. of Patients)	Projected Follow-up (Yrs)
Ocular Hypertension Treatment Study	Ocular hypertensive patients: medicine vs no treatment	1,500	5+
Early Manifest Glaucoma Trial	Newly diagnosed POAG: medicine and laser trabeculoplasty vs. trabeculectomy	300	4+
Collaborative Initial Glaucoma Treatment Study	Newly diagnosed POAG: medicine vs trabeculectomy	600	5+

Adapted from the American Academy of Ophthalmology Preferred Practice Pattern, 1996

American Academy of Ophthalmology. Preferred practice pattern: primary open-angle glaucoma. 1996. San Francisco (CA) AAO; p. 7.

that detect early vision loss and result in medical treatment and surgery worth the effort? How much does it cost to manage a glaucoma patient in the first year? More research in these areas is needed so that better policy decisions can be made regarding effective glaucoma management.

References

1. Thylefors B, Negrel AD, Pararajasegaram R, Dadzie KY. Global data on blindness. Bull World Health Organ 1995;73:115–21.

2. Javitt JC, Wang F, West SK. Blindness due to cataract: epidemiology and prevention. Ann Rev Public Health 1996;17:159–77.

3. West SK, Valmadrid CT. Epidemiology of risk factors for age-related cataract. Surv Ophthalmol 1995;39:323–34.

4. Steinberg EP, Javitt JC, Sharkey PD, et al. The content and cost of cataract surgery. Arch Ophthalmol 1993;111:1041–9.

5. Powe NR, Schein OD, Gieser SC, et al, and the Cataract Patient Outcome Research Team. Synthesis of the literature on visual acuity and complications following cataract extraction with intraocular lens implantation. Arch Ophthalmol 1994;112:239–52.

6. Bernth-Petersen P. Visual functioning in cataract patients. Methods of measuring and results. Acta Ophthalmol 1981;59:198–205.

7. Javitt JC, Brenner MH, Curbow B, et al. Outcomes of cataract surgery. Improvement in visual acuity and subjective visual function after surgery in the first, second, and both eyes. Arch Ophthalmol 1993;111:686–91.

8. Javitt JC, Wang F, Trentacost DJ, et al. Outcomes of cataract extraction with multifocal intraocular lens implantation: functional status and quality of life. Ophthalmology 1997;104:589–99.

9. Brenner MH, Curbow B, Javitt JC, et al. Vision change and quality of life in the elderly. Arch Ophthalmol 1993;111:680–5.

10. Schachau S. A shortened version of the profile of mood states. J Pers Assess 1983;47:305–6.

11. Steinberg EP, Tielsch JM, Schein OD, et al. The VF-14. Arch Ophthalmol 1994;112:630–8.

12. Cassard SD, Patrick DL, Damiano AM, et al. Reproducibility and responsiveness of the VF-14. An index of functional impairment in patients with cataracts. Arch Ophthalmol 1995;113:1508–13.

13. Steinberg EP, Tielsch JM, Schein OD, et al. National study of cataract surgery outcomes. Opthalmology 1994;101:1131–41.

14. Schein OD, Steinberg EP, Cassard SD, et al. Predictors of outcome in patients who underwent cataract surgery. Ophthalmology 1995;102:817–23.

15. Alonso J, Espallargues M, Andersen TF, et al. International applicability of the VF-14. Ophthalmology 1997;104:799–807.

16. Mangione CM, Phillips RS, Seddon JM, et al. Development of the activities of daily vision scale. Med Care 1992;30:1111–26.

17. Lundstrom M, Roos P, Jensen S, Fregell G. Catquest questionnaire for use in cataract surgery care: description, validity, and reliability. J Cataract Refract Surg 1997;23:1226–36.

18. Sloane ME, Ball K, Owsley C, et al. The visual activities questionnaire: developing an instrument for assessing problems in everyday visual tasks. Technical Digest, Noninvasive Assessment of the Visual System 1992;1:26–9.

19. Mangione CM, Berry S, Spritzer K, et al. Identifying the content area for the 51-item National Eye Institute Visual Function Questionnaire: results from focus groups with visually impaired persons. Arch Ophthalmol 1998;116:227–33.

20. Bass EB, Wills S, Scott IU, et al. Preference values for visual states in patients planning to undergo cataract surgery. Med Decis Making 1997;17:324–30.

21. Torrance G, Feeny D. Utilities and quality-adjusted life years. Int J Technol Assess Health Care 1989; 5:559–75.

22. Patrick DL, Deyo RA. Generic and disease-specific measures in assessing health status and quality of life. Med Care 1989;27:S217.

23. Damiano AM, Steinberg EP, Cassard SD, et al. Comparison of generic versus disease-specific measures of functional impairment in patients with cataract. Med Care 1995;33:AS120–AS130.

24. Mangione CM, Phillips RS, Lawrence MG, et al. Improved visual function and attenuation of declines in health-related quality of life after cataract extraction. Arch Ophthalmol 1994;112:1419–25.

25. Mangione CM, Orav EJ, Lawrence MG, et al. Prediction of visual function after cataract surgery. A prospectively validated model. Arch Ophthalmol 1995;113:1305–11.

26. Mangione CM, Orav J, Lawrence MG, et al. Prediction of visual function after cataract surgery. Arch Ophthalmol 1995;113:1305–11.

27. Steinberg EP, Bass EB, Luthra R, et al. Variation in ophthalmic testing before cataract surgery. Results of a national survey of ophthalmologists [comments]. Arch Ophthalmol 1994;112:896–902.

28. Bass EB, Steinberg EP, Luthra R, et al. Variation in ophthalmic testing prior to cataract surgery. Results of a national survey of optometrists. Cataract Patient Outcome Research Team. Arch Ophthalmol 1995;113:27–31.

29. Agency for Health Care Policy and Research. Cataract in adults: management of functional impairment. Rockville (MD): US DHHS; 1993.

30. American Academy of Ophthalmology. Preferred practice pattern: primary open-angle glaucoma. San Francisco (CA): The Academy; 1996.

31. Laidlaw A, Harrad R. Can second eye cataract extraction be justified? Eye 1993;7:680–6.

32. Javitt JC, Steinberg EP, Sharkey P, et al. Cataract surgery in one eye or both. A billion dollar per year issue. Ophthalmology 1995;102:1583–92.

33. Desai P, Reidy A, Minassian DC, et al. Gains from cataract surgery: visual function and quality of life. Br J Ophthalmol 1996;80:868–73.

34. American Academy of Ophthalmology. Preferred practice guidelines: cataract in the adult. San Francisco (CA): The Academy; 1996.

35. Javitt JC, Street DA, Tielsch JM, et al. National outcomes of cataract extraction. Retinal detachment and endophthalmitis after outpatient cataract surgery. Cataract Patient Outcomes Research Team. Ophthalmology 1994;101:100–5.

36. Tielsch JM, Legro MW, Cassard SD, et al. Risk factors for retinal detachment after cataract surgery. A population-based case-control study. Ophthalmology 1996;103:1537–45.

37. Jaffe N, Clyman H, Jaffe M. Cystoid macular edema after intracapsular and extracapsular cataract surgery with and without an intraocular implant. Ophthalmology 1982;80:25–9.

38. Menikoff JA, Speaker MG, Marmor M, Raskin EM. A case-control study of risk factors for postoperative endophthalmitis. Ophthalmology 1991;98:1761–8.

39. Schein OD, Bass EB, Sharkey P, et al. Cataract surgical techniques: preferences and underlying beliefs. Arch Ophthalmol 1995;113:1108–12.

40. Hannan EL, Kilburn HJ, O'Donnell JF, et al. A longitudinal analysis of the relationship between in-hospital mortality in New York State and the volume of abdominal aortic aneurysm surgeries performed. Health Serv Res 1992;27:517–42.

41. Hannan EL, Kilburn HJ, Bernard H, et al. Coronary artery bypass surgery: the relationship between inhospital mortality rate and surgical volume after controlling for clinical risk factors. Med Care 1992;29:1094–1107.

42. Leen MM, Ho CC, Yanoff M. Association between surgically-induced astigmatism and cataract incision size in the early postoperative period. Ophthalmic Surg 1993;24:586–92.

43. Van Den Berkt AC, DeWaard PWT, Pameijer JH. Comparison between postoperative astigmatism after classic extracapsular lens extraction and after phacoemulsification with implantation of a Pearce tripod or Pearce vaulted Y-loop intraocular lens. Doc Ophthalmol 1992;82:1–7.

44. Oshika T, Shunji T. Astigmatic and refractive stabilization after cataract surgery. Ophthalmic Surg 1995;26:309–15.

45. Neumann AC, McCarty GR, Sanders DR, Raanan MG. Small incisions to control astigmatism during cataract surgery. J Cataract Refract Surg 1989;15:78–84.

46. Olson RJ, Crandall AS. Prospective randomized comparison of phacoemulsification cataract surgery with a 3.2-mm vs a 5.5-mm sutureless incision. Am J Ophthalmol 1998;125:612–20.

47. Javitt JC, Street DA, Tielsch JM, et al. National outcomes of cataract extraction. Retinal detachment and endophthalmitis after outpatient cataract surgery. Cataract Patient Outcomes Research Team. Ophthalmology 1994;101:100–5.

48. Steinberg EP. Do optometrists see what ophthalmologists see when they look you in the eye? [editorial]. J Clin Epidemiol 1993;46:3–4.

49. Revicki DA, Brown RE, Adler MA. Patient outcomes with co-managed post-operative care after cataract surgery. J Clin Epidemiol 1993;46:5–15.

50. Klein R, Klein B. Vision disorders in diabetes. In: Diabetes in America. Bethesda (MD): US Department of Health and Human Services; 1985. p. 1–36.

51. Javitt JC, Aiello LP, Bassi LJ, et al. Detecting and treating retinopathy in patients with type I diabetes mellitus. Savings associated with improved implementation of current guidelines. American Academy of Ophthalmology. Ophthalmology 1991;98:1565–73.

52. Beetham WP, Aiello LM, Balodimos MC, Koncz L. Ruby laser photocoagulation of early diabetic neovascular retinopathy. Arch Ophthalmol 1970;88:261–72.

53. Beetham WP. Visual prognosis of proliferating diabetic retinopathy. Br J Ophthalmol 1963;47:611–19.

54. The Diabetic Retinopathy Study Research Group. Photocoagulation treatment of proliferative diabetic retinopathy. Clinical application of Diabetic Retinopathy Study (DRS) findings, DRS Report Number 8. Ophthalmology 1981;88:583–600.

55. The Diabetic Retinopathy Study Research Group. Four risk factors for severe visual loss in diabetic retinopathy. Diabetic Retinopathy Study Report No. 3. Arch Ophthalmol 1979;97:654–5.

56. Rand LI, Prud'homme GJ, Ederer F, Canner PL. Factors influencing the development of visual loss in advanced diabetic retinopathy. Diabetic Retinopathy Study (DRS) Report No. 10. Invest Ophthalmol Vis Sci 1985;26:983–91.

57. The Diabetic Retinopathy Vitrectomy Study Research Group. Two-year course of visual acuity in severe proliferative diabetic retinopathy with conventional management. Diabetic Retinopathy Vitrectomy Study Report No. 1. Ophthalmology 1985;92:492–502.

58. The Diabetic Retinopathy Vitrectomy Study Research Group. Early vitrectomy for severe proliferative diabetic retinopathy in eyes with useful vision. Clinical application of results of a randomized trial. Diabetic Retinopathy Vitrectomy Study Report No. 4. Ophthalmology 1988;95:1321–34.

59. The Diabetic Retinopathy Vitrectomy Study Research Group. Early vitrectomy for severe vitreous hemorrhage in diabetic retinopathy. Two-year results of a randomized trial. Diabetic Retinopathy Vitrectomy Study Report No. 2. Arch Ophthalmol 1985;103:1644–52.

60. Early Treatment Diabetic Retinopathy Study Research Group. Photocoagulation for diabetic macular edema. Early Treatment Diabetic Retinopathy Study Report No. 1. Arch Ophthalmol 1985;103:1796–1806.

61. Javitt JC, Aiello LP, Chiang Y, et al. Preventive eye care in people with diabetes is cost-saving to the federal government. Implications for health-care reform. Diabetes Care 1994;17:909–17.

62. Javitt JC, Aiello LP. Cost-effectiveness of detecting and treating diabetic retinopathy. Ann Intern Med 1996;124:164–9.

63. Ferris FLI. How effective are treatments for diabetic retinopathy? JAMA 1993;269:1290–1.

64. Javitt JC, Canner JK, Frank RG, et al. Detecting and treating retinopathy in patients with type I diabetes mellitus. A health policy model. Ophthalmology 1990;97:483–94.

65. Lee PP, Whitcup SM, Hays RD, et al. The relationship between visual acuity and functioning and well-being among diabetics. Qual Life Res 1995;4:319–23.

66. Tielsch JM, Sommer A, Katz J, et al. Racial variations in the prevalence of primary open-angle glaucoma. The Baltimore Eye Survey. JAMA 1991;266:369–74.

67. Leske M, Connell A, Schachat A, Hyman L. The Barbados eye study. Prevalence of open-angle glaucoma. Arch Ophthalmol 1994;112:821–9.

68. Foster PJ, Baasanhu J, Alsbirk PH, et al. Glaucoma in Mongolia. A population-based survey in Hovsgol province, northern Mongolia. Arch Ophthalmol 1996;114:1235–41.

69. Tielsch JM, Katz J, Quigley HA, et al. Diabetes, intraocular pressure, and primary open-angle glaucoma in the Baltimore Eye Survey. Ophthalmology 1995;102:48–53.

70. Tielsch JM, Katz J, Sommer A, et al. Hypertension, perfusion pressure, and primary open-angle glaucoma. A population-based assessment. Arch Ophthalmol 1995;113:216–21.

71. Dielemans I, Vingerling JR, Wolfs RCW, et al. The prevalence of primary open-angle glaucoma in a population-based study in the Netherlands: the Rotterdam study. Ophthalmology 1994;101:1851–5.

72. Migdal C, Gregory W, Hitchings R. Long-term functional outcome after early surgery compared with laser and medicine in open-angle glaucoma. Ophthalmology 1994;101:1651–6.

73. Jay J, Allan D. The benefit of trabeculectomy versus conventional management in primary open angle glaucoma relative to severity of eye disease. Eye 1989;3:528–35.

74. Collaborative Normal-Tension Glaucoma Study Group. The effectiveness of intraocular pressure reduction in the treatment of normal-tension glaucoma, Am J Ophthalmol 1998;126:498–505.

75. Smith SD, Katz J, Quigley HA. Analysis of progressive change in automated visual fields in glaucoma. Invest Ophthalmol Vis Sci 1996;37:1419–28.

76. Shultzer M. Errors in the diagnosis of visual field progression in normal-tension glaucoma (see comments). Ophthalmology 1994;101:1589–94.

77. Parrish RK, Geddes SJ, Scott IU, et al. Visual function and quality of life among patients with glaucoma. Arch Ophthalmol 1997;115:1447–55.

78. Lee BL, Gutierrez P, Gordon M, et al. The glaucoma symptom scale: a brief index of glaucoma-specific symptoms. Arch Ophthalmol 1998;116:861–6.

79. Guttierrez P, Wilson MR, Johnson C, et al. Influence of glaucomatous visual field as health-related quality of life. Arch Ophthalmol 1997;115:777–84.

80. The Glaucoma Laser Trial Research Group. The glaucoma laser trial (GLT) and glaucoma laser trial follow-up study: 7. Results. Am J Ophthalmol 1995;120:718–31.

81. The Glaucoma Laser Trial Research Group. The Glaucoma Laser Trial (GLT): 2. Results of argon laser trabeculoplasty versus topical medicines. Ophthalmology 1990;97:1403–13.

82. Sharir M, Zimmerman TJ. Initial treatment of glaucoma: medical therapy. Surv Ophthalmol 1993;93:299–303.

83. The advanced glaucoma intervention study (AGIS): 4. Comparison of treatment outcomes within race. Ophthalmology 1998;105:1146–64.

84. Sherwood MB, Migdal CS, Hitchings RA. Initial treatment of glaucoma: filtration surgery. Surv Ophthalmol 1993;37:293–9.

85. Jay JL, Murray SB. Early trabeculectomy versus conventional management in primary open angle glaucoma. Br J Ophthalmol 1988;72:881–9.

86. The Glaucoma Laser Trial Research Group. The Glaucoma Laser Trial (GLT): 6. Treatment group differences in visual field changes. Am J Ophthalmol 1995;120:10–22.

87. Lichter PR. Practice implications of the Glaucoma Laser Trial [editorial]. Ophthalmology 1990;97:1401–2.

88. Jampel HD. Initial treatment for open-angle glaucoma—medical, laser, or surgical? Laser trabeculoplasty is the treatment of choice for chronic open-angle glaucoma [comment]. Arch Ophthalmol 1998;116:240–1.

89. Smith RJH. The enigma of primary open angle glaucoma. Trans Ophthalmol Soc UK 1986;105:618–33.

90. Traverso CE, Tomey KF, Antonios S. Limbal- vs fornix-based conjunctival trabeculectomy flaps. Am J Ophthalmol 1987;104:28–32.

91. Reichert R, Stewart W, Shields MB. Limbus-based versus fornix-based conjunctival flaps in trabeculectomy. Ophthalmic Surg 1987;18:672–6.

92. Shuster JN, Krupin T, Kolker AE, Becker B. Limbus- v fornix-based conjunctival flap in trabeculectomy. A long-term randomized study. Arch Ophthalmol 1984;102:361–2.

93. Grehn F, Mauthe S, Pfeiffer N. Limbus-based versus fornix-based conjunctival flap in filtering surgery. A randomized prospective study. Int Ophthalmol 1989;13:139–43.

94. Brincker P, Kessing SV. Limbus-based versus fornix-based conjunctival flap in glaucoma filtering surgery. Acta Ophthalmol 1992;70:641–4.

95. The Fluorouracil Filtering Surgery Study Group. Five-year follow-up of the Fluorouracil Filtering Surgery Study. Am J Ophthalmol 1996;121:349–66.

96. Kitazawa Y, Kawase K, Matsushita H, Minobe M. Trabeculectomy with mitomycin. A comparative study with fluorouracil. Arch Ophthalmol 1991;109:1693–8.

97. Robin AL, Ramakrishnan R, Krishnadas R, et al. A long-term dose-response study of mitomycin in glaucoma filtration surgery. Arch Ophthalmol 1997;115:969–74.

98. Kitazawa Y, Suemori-Matsushita H, Yamamato T, Kawase K. Low-dose and high-dose mitomycin trabeculectomy as an initial surgery in primary open-angle glaucoma. Ophthalmology 1993;100:1624–8.

99. Jampel HD, Kerrigan LA, Quigley HA. Risk factors for late endophthalmitis following glaucoma filtration surgery (Glaucoma Surgical Outcomes Study) [abstract]. Invest Ophthalmol Vis Sci 1998;39:S879.

CHAPTER 40

Orthopaedic Surgery

David S. Hungerford, MD, and Lynne C. Jones, PhD

Orthopaedic surgery involves the diagnosis and treatment of the diseases of and trauma to the musculoskeletal system and encompasses the treatment of this system from birth to death. Moreover, the implications of such treatment must often be measured in decades, and therefore, many interventions which appear to be successful in the short term may in fact have deleterious long-term outcomes. In the past 30 years, orthopaedic surgery has been subdivided into seven major subspecialties including pediatric orthopaedics, spine surgery, trauma, adult reconstructive orthopaedic surgery, hand and upper extremities, foot surgery, oncology, and sports medicine. Although not every academic orthopaedic department will have separate divisions devoted to each of these subspecialties, each of those mentioned above is sufficiently developed to have its own specialty society. In fact, some subspecialties mentioned above have become so well developed that area-specific societies have been developed, for example, the Hip Society and the Knee Society. While that may appear to the nonorthopaedist (and more importantly, to third-party carriers) that this "fractionalization" of orthopaedics is divisive, there are large numbers of practitioners who restrict their area of practice and expertise to just such subjects. When one considers that there are over 500,000 joint replacements performed in the United States alone and more than 1 million joint replacements done annually in the world,[1] it appears less unreasonable that a highly focused area like this attracts physicians willing to dedicate their professional activities to it.

Therefore, the evidence basis for practice must be considered for each subspecialty area, even though the types of procedures performed have much in common across the areas of subspecialization. The musculoskeletal system is a complex organ system that involves six different kinds of tissues (bone, muscle, ligament, tendon, articular cartilage, and synovial membrane) which are innervated and (with the exception of articular cartilage) vascularized. Orthopaedic disease can be caused by disorders of the blood supply to the tissues of the musculoskeletal system and by diseases and disorders of the aforementioned tissues. The joints of the body consist of a particular interaction among these tissues. Each joint has a unique shape and function; therefore, similar afflictions may result in differing disabilities even though there may be many similarities among the disease processes. For example, the hip joint is a relatively simple ball-and-socket joint. In contrast, the knee joint is extremely complicated, with a complex motion pattern involving trade-offs between ligamentous stability and muscular stability. Therefore, functional instability problems almost never affect the hip but are common at the knee.

During growth, the long bones contain a growth plate called the epiphysis. Injury and infection can cause damage to this growth plate, resulting in deformity of the developing long bones. Treatment consists of correcting the deformity through bracing, splinting, or in many instances, performing a corrective osteotomy. There is also a host of congenital, developmental, and genetic afflictions of the epiphyseal plate.

Once the musculoskeletal system is mature, there are a finite number of afflictions that can affect it. In order to understand orthopaedics, it is necessary to first understand the function of the musculoskeletal system. The musculoskeletal system allows the organism to interface with its environment. The system physically allows the organism to impact the environment and modulate the impact of the environment on the organism. The key feature that makes this possible is the joint, otherwise known as the diarthrodial articulation. The joint has four key components: movement, control, stability, and comfort. The loss of any of these four essential characteristics of the joint produces disease. Most orthopaedic surgery involves either re-establishing the lost characteristic or compensating for that loss. For example, polio produces muscle dysfunction that results in the loss of movement and control of the joint. Because the muscle function cannot be restored, this loss of function must be compensated for either by bracing or fusing the joint. Degenerative joint disease results in the loss of comfort for the joint and, in the end stages, can also result in loss of motion. Articular cartilage is a unique tissue in that it has no nerve supply and no blood supply. Therefore, when it is damaged, it does not heal. When the cartilage is intact, forces applied to the joint are not felt. Once the cartilage has been damaged, the forces that cross the joint can cause pain. One means of restoring the comfort of the joint is to provide a new anesthetic surface made of artificial materials and called a total joint replacement.

Given the multiplicity of conditions treated by orthopaedic surgeons, outcomes of interest range from reduction of disease burden to improved functional status and quality of life: given the array of treatments available, economic considerations have come to the fore in recent years.

LITERATURE REVIEW

The modern era of orthopaedics began in the 1960s with the development of total joint replacement (TJR) for the treatment of osteoarthritis, particularly of the hip and the knee.[2–10] Prior to the development of this technology, osteoarthritis was treated with a variety of pain-reducing medications, protection from the forces of normal activity, and modification mostly in the form of protective weight bearing with external devices and bracing in some cases. There were a few surgical procedures, such as fusion for the knee[11] and resection arthroplasty for the hip,[12,13] that in themselves produced significant disability, often nearly as great as the disease they were designed to treat. They were only applicable to the very last stages of the disease.

During the 1960s, '70s and '80s, three technological advances revolutionized the ability of the orthopaedic surgeon to positively impact the common disorders of the musculoskeletal system. The first was total joint replacement, which gave surgeons an increasingly effective tool for managing severe osteoarthritis of virtually any joint, but was most commonly applied to the hip[2–6] and to the knee.[7–10] The second advance was effective means of open reduction and internal fixation of complex fractures.[14–16] This increased the success rate for re-establishing the integrity of the skeleton after major injury and allowed rapid return to activity and restoration of function. The third technological advance that has impacted orthopaedics is the development of the arthroscope.[17–27] This has allowed minimally invasive treatment of a variety of disorders of joints, particularly of the knee[18–20,22,24–27] and of the shoulder,[23] and has also facilitated ligamentous reconstruction of damage to the unstable knee,[17,24] frequently a consequence of sports injuries.

As a specialty, orthopaedics has enjoyed tremendously increased attention, as success rates in treatment (as measured by clinical outcomes of operations) are now commonly in the upper 80 to upper 90 percent range. Prior to these new treatment technologies success rates were often in the 60 to 70 percent range. Even then, the quality of the good result seldom approached the quality obtainable at present. Because of the success of these treatments, orthopaedics became a highly sought after subspecialty, and the competition for orthopaedic residency positions over the past 15 years has greatly increased.

During the past few decades, a large portion of the orthopaedic literature consisted of reports of the results of applying specific techniques to groups of patients.[28–37] These were often reports of follow-ups of a sequentially treated patient group for a specific disease entity.[30-36] It was considered neither feasible nor ethical to construct placebo-controlled randomization for surgical procedures. However, the results of one surgical approach could be compared with those of another.[38-41] For example, the posterior approach[41] to the total hip replacement could be compared to a transtrochanteric approach.[41] Such studies ocasionally were prospective and randomized.[42,45,48] The other comparison that lent itself to scientific evaluation was the comparison of one prosthetic system to another or one method of reconstruction to another.[43-57] Although a great deal of experience was gained during this period, the resolution of many of the outstanding questions was only infrequently attempted.

Although the aforementioned technologies of TJR, arthroscopy, and open reduction and internal fixation will continue to play a major role in the treatment of disorders of the musculoskeletal system, orthopaedic surgery appears now to be entering a new and exciting phase. The tissues of the musculoskeletal system are extremely complex and particularly difficult to study. The articular chondrocytes are imbedded in a complex gel matrix that traps water in a mesh scaffold of a very specific collagen fiber. Type II collagen is unique to articular cartilage, and other tissues that generate collagen tend not to generate type II collagen. Articular cartilage, once damaged, does not heal.[58-64] Within the past few years, greater understanding of cell biology has led to a major increase in knowledge about the function of all the cellular and subcellular mechanisms of the specific tissues of the musculoskeletal system: synoviocytes, osteocytes, and chondrocytes. New knowledge of cell biology is leading to very innovative treatment considerations, including gene therapy,[65-70] nutritional supplements,[71-75] biologically active substances,[65,76-81] cytokines,[82-86] and even tissue engineering.[87-96] These new modalities are already having an impact on treatment options.

The nature of the musculoskeletal system and its disorders, particularly the long latency period that often exists in the evolution of arthritis, poses significant problems for evidence-based surgery. For example, even though it is well known clinically that once damaged, articular cartilage does not heal, the progression from damaged articular cartilage to the actual disease state of osteoarthritis is extremely variable. Autopsy studies performed by Øwre showed that a significant portion of subjects (even teenagers) had degenerative changes in the articular cartilage of the patella and that the majority of individuals in their forties had significant degenerative patellar articular cartilage lesions.[97] The majority of patients in their twenties, thirties, and forties are completely unaware of any symptoms, yet symptomatic osteoarthritis does progress with age. Furthermore, with the increasing longevity of the population, the treatment of symptomatic osteoarthritis is consuming an ever increasing percentage of health care dollars. During the federally sponsored Patient Outcomes Research Team (PORT) study from 1991 to 1995, total knee replacements (TKRs) increased by 25 percent on a per capita basis. Even if a treatment that could heal damaged articular cartilage were available, how could one measure the outcome when the patient might not experience the clinical consequences of that damage for 10 or 15 years? Obviously evaluation criteria will have to be developed as long-term follow-up studies are constructed.

CLINICAL STUDIES IN ORTHOPAEDICS

The technology relating to orthopaedic surgery has rapidly grown from the late 1970s to the '90s. Abstracts published annually by the Orthopaedic Research Society increased from 235 in 1976 to 1,091 in 1999. As there was no consensus within the medical community on how clinical research should be conducted on technologic advances, the design and quality of clinical studies varied greatly. Most studies conducted during this time were based upon series of patients, were mostly single-institution studies, and were frequently carried out by the physician co-developer of the prosthesis or surgical procedure under study.

Research methods that have been used to evaluate orthopaedic surgical techniques and prostheses include meta-analysis and various experimental case-control study designs.

Meta-analysis is a statistical methodology which is used to combine results from numerous studies reported in the literature. This methodology is more involved than just pooling the results from several studies; rather, it is a fairly sophisticated and systematic approach to the summary of results.[98–102] Meta-analysis is based on a certain set of assumptions. Combining the results of studies requires that the investigators use the same outcomes criteria. For example, in one study, failure may be defined as progression to total joint arthroplasty, while in another study the definition of failure may be expanded to include increased osteolysis surrounding an implant. Although there are methods of analysis for when all the trials reviewed are designed for a fixed sample size, these same methods are not valid when sequentially designed studies are incorporated.[99] Practice variations are common in orthopaedics and are likely to influence outcomes. Examples of this in total joint arthroplasty include differences in surgical approaches, perioperative thrombosis prophylaxis, and postoperative limitations in weightbearing. Different studies may also include different time periods. In these cases, data could be pooled using survival analysis, assuming comparable outcome measures. A major advantage of this type of study is that pooled results across multiple studies can be more rapidly analyzed than data from 3 to 5-year clinical trials. As it includes the findings from several different centers, it is less likely to reflect one study's biases. However, there is no standardized methodology for conducting meta-analyses.[98,99] Therefore, studies called meta-analyses in the literature use widely varying statistical techniques.

Meta-analysis has enjoyed increasing popularity in orthopaedics. A number of studies using various methodologies for meta-analysis have been published.[103–110] However, the primary usefulness of this type of study is for the review of standards of available care and technology. The relatively slow publication rates of orthopaedic journals usually require that an article be submitted over a year prior to the article's proposed publication date. Therefore, experimental study designs are needed to evaluate emerging technologies.

Prospective Studies

Prospective studies in orthopaedics generally compare patient groups subjected to different clinical interventions or treatments. For example, prospective studies have been conducted to evaluate potential differences in outcomes for cemented joint replacements as compared to cementless joint replacements. There are numerous examples of this type of study design in the orthopaedic literature.[42–46]

Outcomes research in orthopaedics has been supported by federal funding for major evidence-based initiatives to study clinically relevant and costly problems in the clinical realm. The agency for Health Care Policy Research initiated the Patient Outcomes Research Team (PORT) studies. One such study in orthopaedics, "Assessing and Improving Outcomes: Total Knee Replacement," was carried out from 1990 to 1995 to estimate cost and effectiveness of total knee replacement through retrospective and prospective surveys of physicians and patients, comparing the United States to the province of Ontario, Canada.[111] At the time this study was initiated (1991), there were approximately 210,000 total knee replacements performed annually in the United States, with a direct medical cost of more than $5 billion. Because of the number of cases and the magnitude of the cost, the Agency for Health Care Policy and Research (AHCPR) of the U.S. Department of Health and Human Services deemed it important to assess the outcomes and effectiveness of this procedure. The goals of this project were to better understand the variation in the rates and outcomes of total knee replacement and to reduce unexpected variations in practice through dissemination of findings to practicing physicians.

There were seven specific aims identified for the PORT study:

1. Identify key areas of controversy concerning total knee replacement.
2. Determine the frequency of important outcomes from total knee replacement and assess the factors impacting outcome.

3. Examine regional variation in outcomes and relationships between total knee replacement rates, patient providers, and system characteristics that emerge from aim #1.
4. Estimate effectiveness of total knee replacement by comparing primary and secondary data from patients having arthritis and undergoing total knee replacement to corresponding data from patients having arthritis but not undergoing total knee replacement.
5. Construct and analyze decision models that incorporate important health states in terms of patient values, to devise guidelines for preferred patient care.
6. Design and implement strategies for summarizing and disseminating the findings of aims #1 through #5 to reduce unnecessary variations in rates of total knee replacement.
7. Determine how dissemination of the findings affects attitudes and practice styles of primary care physicians.

To accomplish these aims, PORT joined with researchers at the University of Toronto, McMaster University, the Research Triangle Institute, and the Pittsburgh Research Institute, calling upon expertise in many disciplines including economics, epidemiology, biostatistics, survey research, claims analysis, decision analysis, utility analysis, and clinical medicine (primary care, rheumatology, radiology, and orthopaedic surgery). The researchers undertook the following specific research efforts:

1. A meta-analysis of the published literature, summarizing findings to understand clinical outcomes following total knee replacement.
2. A survey of practicing orthopaedic surgeons in Indiana and Ontario, Canada, as well as primary care physicians in Indiana.
3. The acquisition and analysis of Medicare claims files for all Medicare patients undergoing knee replacement in the United States over a 6-year period as well as claims from all patients who underwent knee replacement in Ontario for the same time period. This method addressed specific aim #2.
4. The development of a survey instrument to measure outcomes following total knee replacement and to develop a random sample of patients in the United States from the claims file in order to conduct a mail survey.
5. A prospective community cohort study enrolling patients scheduled for total knee replacement and comparing them to patients with arthritis who are not scheduled for total knee replacement, following both groups for 2 years.
6. The development and employment of a new instrument to measure the relative value utility of total knee replacement in the sample of cohort patients (to address patient relative values for outcomes following total knee replacement).
7. A network simulation model incorporating data from the claims surveys and cohort studies, to derive patient-specific guidelines for knee replacement.
8. A reference manual providing patient-specific data regarding outcomes following knee replacement, comparing quality-adjusted life-year (QALY) outcomes for surgical and medical therapy.
9. A randomized controlled clinical trial of the impact of guidelines for total knee replacement on physician satisfaction with the decision-making process in regard to recommending total knee replacement for patients.

Prior to the work of the PORT study on total knee replacement, most of the literature on the subject consisted of series of patients with total knee replacements who were operated on in academic medical centers where much experience had been accumulated. However, 75 percent of total knee replacements in the United States are implanted by physicians who do fewer than 20 cases per year. Therefore, it was uncertain whether the literature was actually representative of the outcomes experienced by the majority of patients. Moreover, the literature was essentially silent on some of the potential associated risk factors such as age, obesity, and other patient-specific factors. Both the retrospective study and the cohort study indicated that total knee replacement is effective in older patients and patients who are significantly overweight, as well as the non-obese patients from 60 to 70 years of age. The PORT study also documented significant differences among various health care providers in their expectations for total knee replacements. Orthopaedic surgeons perform total knee replacement with the expectation of improving the patient's pain level while primary care physicians most value increased mobility for the patients they refer for total knee replacement.

Using Medicare claims data, the PORT study documented a low mortality rate within the 30 days following surgery but also discovered that African American men over the age of 70 years are 10 times more likely to die in the perioperative period than, for example, white women aged 65 years. While claims data show that complications are treatable, are non-life threatening, and occur at low rates, complications (such as infections, anemias and thromboses) are more frequent in hospitals whose physicians do fewer total knee replacements. Again, using Medicare claims data, the likelihood of reoperation following a primary total knee replacement was in the range of 0.5 to 1 percent per year. Bilateral simultaneous total knee replacement was found to be less expensive than two primary total knee replacements 3 months apart. With follow-up of up to 7 years, total knee replacement was found to be a very effective procedure, with significant decrease in pain for all patients and with 60 percent of patients also reporting improvement in mobility. Moreover, there was no significant deterioration of the results up to 7 years of follow-up. Using QALY data over the 7 years of the retrospective portion of the PORT study, the gain for total knee replacement versus medical management of osteoarthritis of the knee was 0.6 QALYs. Using cost data from the Medicare claim forms, this computes to $18,300 per QALY. This compares to similarly invasive surgical procedures such as a coronary artery bypass graft, where the cost is between $50,000 and $100,000 per QALY.

In the later stages of the PORT study, the group developed a decision support tool to provide outcome data for primary care physicians. In the original survey of primary care physicians, 60 percent reported they were dissatisfied with the information available to help them decide whether to refer a patient for total knee replacement. Using a randomized trial format, the PORT study team found that use of a clinical guideline decision support tool increased primary care physicians' satisfaction with their information from 40 percent to 75 percent.

Although there is tremendous variability, on a per capita basis, in the use of total knee replacement, the PORT study indicated that total knee replacement is an underused procedure. The cohort study compared those patients with grade II or higher osteoarthritis who were managed with total knee replacements to a group that was medically managed. Using this information, there were few patients who received total knee replacement who would not have been predicted by the model to benefit from it. However, 45 percent of the patients in the medically managed cohort would have had more improvement in pain and function if they had undergone surgery. In other words, more patients would benefit if primary physicians, rheumatologists, or orthopaedists better targeted potential candidates for primary total knee replacement.

The prospective community cohort study enrolled patients scheduled for total knee replacement and patients with knee arthritis not scheduled for total knee replacement. Total patient enrollment included 485 nonsurgery patients and 291 presurgery patients. The PORT study information has so far resulted in 23 published papers, 17 abstracts, 6 papers in press, and 6 papers in review. The PORT study undoubtedly provides patients, orthopaedists, rheumatologists, internists, and primary care physicians with valuable information with which to better judge the impact of total knee replacements, and it shows that total knee replacement is indeed effective over a broad range of patient demographic characteristics. However, the PORT study is also an enormous investment of time and money. The 5-year study had a budget of $5 million and at one level or another involved 75 individuals, some of whom acted as consultants but several of whom were employed full-time over the 5-year period. Although this investment yielded several significant findings which could affect the majority of total knee replacement patients over 40 years of age, it is unlikely that there will be the research funds and personnel available to resolve all of the important questions involving the effectiveness of orthopaedic surgical procedures across the breadth of the specialty.

Retrospective Studies

Retrospective analysis involves the review of clinical results already collected for each patient. Many clinical studies reported in the orthopaedic literature are of this type. The information from retrospective studies can be used as a first approach to identify problems or areas of interest. For example, when cementless total hip prostheses were first introduced, the medical community was unaware that there might be a problem with thigh pain. A review of charts would answer the question of how frequently thigh pain occurs. This could then be compared to the frequency of thigh pain in patients with cemented total hip prostheses. A prospective study could then be conducted that would look at sequential visits to determine when, if ever, the thigh pain resolved and whether any change in postoperative care affected this outcome.

Surgeons performing large volumes of surgical procedures over significant time periods can develop, at reasonable costs, comprehensive databases that can be analyzed for relevant information. These databases can then be used for performance improvement and outcomes research to evaluate factors affecting the outcome of a specific surgical procedure on specific groups of patients. The Division of Arthritis Surgery (DAS) of the Department of Orthopaedic Surgery at Johns Hopkins University (JHU) has maintained a prospective database on all total knee and total hip replacements since 1980. For the most part, this database has been created and maintained by the personnel active in orthopaedic surgery, supplemented by part-time efforts from study coordinators and a database manager funded by educational grants from industry. From 1980 until the present, we have collected and tabulated data on 3,129 patients who have undergone primary or revision total knee replacement.

Of primary interest has been the different demographic characteristics that may impact outcomes of total knee replacement. These include (but are not limited to) age, weight, date of surgery, pain scores, functional assessment scores, presence or absence of radiolucencies, range of motion, and the necessity and date of the revision (if revision was deemed necessary).

Using this type of retrospective analysis, the impact of obesity,[112] age,[113–115] type of disease,[116] prior surgery,[117–119] osteotomy during surgery[120], and the influence of Workers' Compensation insurance coverages[121] on the outcomes of total knee replacement have been studied. In addition, the occurence of infection,[122,123] the assessment of radiographic loosening,[124] and the natural history of the contralateral joint[125] were also evaluated. Essentially the same methodology was employed for each of these studies. First, a potential factor that might influence the success or failure of a total knee replacement is identified (eg, weight or age). A hypothesis is developed, frequently comparing two groups of patients. For example, patients 40 percent or more above their ideal weight are compared to patients of normal weight, or patients over 50 years of age are compared to patients under 50 years of age. As with prospective studies, the sample number needed to obtain statistical significance, given a minimum expected difference, can be estimated prior to conducting the study. The database can then be searched to collect a number of outcome measures.

Using the technique of comparative analysis, patients with the particular demographic characteristic are compared to a matched control group from the database. Matched control patients are identified by conducting multiple searches using database software (eg, ACCESS®). Patients would be matched for age, sex, diagnosis, type of deformity, degree of deformity, severity of disease, and so on. In general, matching occurred on seven or eight characteristics, obviously with the exception of the characteristic to be studied. Chi-squared analysis is then completed on the control and treated groups to confirm that no significant differences in the frequency of these selection criteria exist. The results of such a study can then be statistically analyzed using a number of statistical methods ranging from simple chi-squared analyses to complex regression modeling. There are numerous available software packages of different levels of sophistication with which to analyze the collected findings (eg, SAS®, SSPS®, PEPI®, Jmp®, Statsoft®).

We found no significant difference with this type of analysis in the outcomes for obese patients as compared to those of non-obese patients.[112] The single variation trend was toward slower healing and increased superficial infections that did not affect the implant. A patient who was over 80 years of age had as good an outcome, with no increased consumption of supplies or increase in complications, as that of a patient who was under 65 years of age; a later study documented the same conclusion for patients over the age of 85 years of age.[113,114] Patients with diabetes also had similar expected outcomes, again with a higher incidence of superficial wound infections that did not affect implant performance.[116] Patients with a prior patellectomy had decidedly inferior outcomes as compared to the group, but a subset of them who had had fewer than three surgical procedures in association with the patellectomy before or after the patellectomy had outcomes similar to those of patients who had not had a patellectomy.[117] On the other hand, patients who had active Workers' Compensation claims pending at the time of their total knee replacements had dramatically inferior results, compared to a matched set of control patients who did not have pending Workers' Compensation actions.[121] The total knee evaluation protocol used was devised by the Knee Society and is extensively used. It has a high weight (50%) for pain in the outcome as do most evaluation instruments since pain is the principal indication for carrying out total knee replacements. Even though the Workers' Compensation cohort were not significantly different from the control group in terms of reoperation, range of motion, or the objective evaluation of stability, the good and excellent results in the study cohort were only 35 percent compared to 92 percent good and excellent results in the control group because the Workers' Compensation cohort had dramatically different outcomes in terms of pain.

Much orthopaedic surgery is elective, which means that the patient needs to choose to have the surgical procedure and so needs reliable information concerning the outcome and the risks. In the case of total knee replacement reported series, outcomes using modern instruments and modern prostheses report good and excellent results as high as the upper 90 percents. However, individual patient and risk characteristics can be assessed for procedures in the database. From both the PORT study and from our own matched control studies at Johns Hopkins, it can be concluded that total knee replacement is generally an effective procedure and that obesity and advanced age are not negative indicators for the procedure when otherwise indicated. However, a patellectomy patient who has had multiple prior surgical procedures is at a much higher risk of having an unsatisfactory outcome. Also, patients with Workers' Compensation claims have a much lower likelihood of success. Therefore, the risk benefit ratio is altered in a negative way.

One significant difference between the PORT study and the retrospective studies reported herein is the scope of the problem each is trying to answer. With the PORT study, the research addressed outcomes of total knee replacement at the population level. In contrast, the matched-control studies were used to clarify specific questions about total knee replacement, for example, the expected outcome for a specific type of patient (eg, old vs young, rheumatoid arthritic vs osteonecrotic, diabetic vs nondiabetic). By finding the answers to specific questions, we are able to get better inclusion and exclusion criteria for the procedure.

For the results of any of the aforementioned studies to be of significant statistical power (ie, to have a high probability of finding an effect when there really is one), sufficient numbers of patients are needed. This is easily attainable in practices with large volumes. However, what about the orthopaedic surgeon with a low patient volume, the "solo" practice physician? Mining of individual physician databases will reflect the experience and outcomes of the surgeon, dependent on how often he performs a specific procedure as well as what type of patient he sees. As the solo private practice physician makes up a majority of the orthopaedic surgeons in practice, outcomes data from this source are important. But no one physician has enough of a patient base to make significant conclusions, which is why it is critical to standardize the collection of specific outcomes data so that the results can be pooled and analyzed across practice sites.

CRITIQUE OF CLINICAL STUDY METHODOLOGIES

There are advantages and disadvantages to each of the methodologies described. However, each may be useful for studying some aspect of outcomes data.

Meta-analysis can be completed more rapidly than most short (3 to 5 year) prospective studies, but its greatest time-saving value may be in compiling large data sets to asess outcomes. Another advantage is that it involves the pooling of results from several centers and is therefore less likely to reflect one individual's bias. However, variations in practice are common and are likely to influence the outcomes. Examples of this in total joint arthroplasty are thrombi prophylaxis, surgical approaches, and the use of passive motion devices and limitations in weight bearing during the postoperative period. Other possible limitations include differences in patient selection, classification of the extent of the disease process, and times of postoperative follow-up visits. Meta-analyses which are dependent on combining the results from small trials may be exposed to sampling errors. However, the most significant disadvantage is that the outcomes data collected may differ between centers. For example, the time to walk fifty feet may be recorded at one center, while the distance walked in one minute may be recorded at another center. A number of articles have been published on the strengths and weaknesses of the interpretation of meta-analysis results, and the reader is encouraged to review these.[98–102]

The prospective multicenter study is the optimum method of controlling confounding variables and ensuring that results from different centers are easily compared. The investigator(s) can set up a standard protocol for all to follow, and the outcomes data of interest can be identified and collected in a uniform manner. This lends itself to an easier statistical analysis. Prospective studies can be costly and can require considerable effort, but their most significant disadvantage is that the results of the study will not be available for some time after the study has been started.

If the investigator has an established routine for data collection and a current database, retrospective studies can be conducted rapidly with minimal cost. Furthermore, the collection of the data will be less biased because it will have been conducted prior to the establishment of a hypothesis. However, a major disadvantage may be that not all of the necessary information may have been collected. Furthermore, in a multicenter study, the same protocol might not be done at all centers. The information would need to be stratified and analyzed accordingly, possibly necessitating the inclusion of more patients.

Regardless of which type of study is conducted, the type of control patients to be included in the study needs to be defined. Should treatment be withheld from a randomly selected group of patients? This would be unethical in many cases. Should the comparison be made to patients receiving standard care? However, "standard" care varies between institutions. Furthermore, biases in patient selection may be introduced. Should a new technology that has been shown experimentally to have superior qualities be compared to a Food and Drug Administration (FDA)–approved technology with known problems? What if, based on their own experience, surgeons truly believe that the alternative treatment will yield inferior results? Different treatments may yield asymmetric outcomes, and the risks of each treatment may differ. With respect to prospective studies, two types of control populations have been used: retrospective controls and concurrent controls. Again, concurrent controls may be optimal but not always feasible. Last, and most important, patients frequently do not like being the controls. Dropout rates may vary, confounding the interpretation of the results.

Optimizing Retrospective Studies

Can one draw valid conclusions from retrospective studies as compared to prospective studies? We believe that there are means of arriving at reasonable conclusions with much less effort and lower cost than with the large, multicenter, prospective study. Information technology may help solve part of this dilemma by providing an uncomplicated way to collect generally accepted data that can be archived, retrieved, and correlated. When properly structured, the routine collection of clinical data (information the physician needs to make a proper diagnosis and to construct a treatment regimen) can be carried out in such a way that both populating a clinical database and preparing a clinical note and letter to the referring physician takes no additional time. Software programs are now available for carrying this out in the normal practice of medicine. It is the widespread development of this kind of information that will allow the important clinical and demographic correlations that can influence the treatment of the individual patient. The goal of the whole movement is to provide effective treatment not only for classes of disease and classes of patients but also for the individual patient. For this to be accomplished, there is need for a consensus on the type of outcomes data to be collected.

Determining Outcomes

The collection of outcomes data is not new to orthopaedic surgeons. However, the type of information and its use in determining cost and benefit to the patient have been recently re-evaluated. Large studies, many of them the result of the FDA-approved Investigational Device Evaluations (IDE), have used assessments of pain and function to evaluate new prostheses. While several scoring systems have been used in the past,[126–128] the most commonly used instrument today is the Knee Society Score.[129] This scoring system, completed by the physician, includes assessments of pain (0 to 50 points), range of motion (up to 25 points), stability (0 to 10 for anterior/posterior, 0 to 15 for medial/lateral), walking (0 to 50), and stair climbing (0 to 50), and deductions for flexion contracture (0 to -15 points), extension lag (0 to -15 points), malalignment (0 to -20), and support (-5 to -20). Although the Knee Society Score is frequently reported as a single value, more information is provided by examining each subsection. Many instruments used commonly in rheumatology have now found widespread use in orthopaedics. One frequently used instrument in the orthopaedic community is the Western Ontario and McMaster Universities (WOMAC) osteoarthritis index.[130] It was also designed to assess pain, stiffness, and physical disability in patients with osteoarthritis of either the hip or the knee joint. Unlike the Knee Society Score, however, this tool was developed to be self-administered.

Quality of life and the patient's opinion on whether surgery was a success have been largely ignored until recently. The mantra of the orthopaedist has always been that the mission of orthopaedic surgery is to restore function and relieve pain. How does that translate into quality of life? As this is influenced by the patients' perceptions and definitions of quality of life, it has been necessary to get the patients more involved in their own outcomes assessment. The SF-36 (Medical Outcomes Trust, Boston, Mass.) was developed to measure health outcomes from the patient's point of view. It incorporates assessments of limitations in physical activities, social activities, activities of daily living, bodily pain, general mental health, energy and fatigue, and general health perceptions.[131]

In conclusion, the evaluation of the results of evidence-based studies requires the inclusion of instruments designed to assess pain, function, and quality of life. Furthermore, many advocate using both the patient's and the physician's global assessments. This information can help normalize data according to patient and physician variability.

FUTURE DIRECTIONS

Orthopaedic surgery has passed from the mechanical age to the biologic age. Improved understanding of cellular and molecular function of chondrocytes, synoviocytes, osteocytes, osteoblasts, and osteoclasts is leading to a revolution in therapy. Recently, cell-based therapies have been introduced and clinically applied as expensive procedures with little documentation of their efficacy and cost-effectiveness.[87–96] Given the aging population in the United States, increasing demands for service, increasing musculoskeletal complaints, and incidences of total hip and total knee replacements that are growing more rapidly than the aging population, it will be important to separate effective procedures from ineffective procedures.

Because of the breadth of orthopaedics and the huge number of questions needing answers, it is more likely that those answers will come from widespread standardization in medical reporting rather than from expensive studies like the PORT study referenced here. This is certainly not to imply that PORT studies on widely done procedures should not be carried out, but to emphasize that creating of a relational database within the standard practice of medicine can yield valid information that impacts the practice of the specialty.

Anyone who has ever tried to do a retrospective chart review realizes that common practice does not usually result in quantifiable data. One the most important things that could be done to provide usable information would be to standardize the kinds of data to be collected at the time of the patient encounter. While it seems normal in a medical record to find a conversational-style descriptor, such as "the patient is doing quite well," this approach does not allow quantification or comparison. Standardized electronic records are just now being introduced into orthopaedic practice, records that by their very nature limit the number of choices the user has for the description of the patient's current state. These choices will often be based on commonly used evaluation scoring systems. While they are certainly better than randomized descriptions such as "pretty good" and "not too bad," many of these scoring systems, even though in widespread use for decades, have never been validated. The widespread use of validated outcomes measures for the entire breadth of procedures used in the specialty will result in a huge increase in available data. The processing of these data will refine the indications and will identify the procedures that are working.

A consensus on what data should be collected by all orthopaedic surgeons would provide a better understanding of the impact of different surgical procedures on the population. It would also lead to a more standardized reporting of results in the literature, which would make cross-analysis easier to achieve. Therefore, orthopaedic surgeons need to agree on what information to collect and which instruments to use. However, there is a balance between too much and too little. There is an unlimited amount of information that can be collected, but at some point, data-gathering that is achievable in a routine clinical setting crosses over into full-blown outcomes research that can be performed only at an academic institution.

Wennberg suggests that the following are needed to determine outcomes research strategies: (1) patient focus groups, (2) physician focus groups, (3) structured review of the literature, (4) large databases, (5) good patient outcomes measures and instruments, and (6) decision models. The PORT study incorporated many of these features. Instead of repeating similar studies for different applications, perhaps the most expedient way to move forward is to build on their conclusions. Many of their findings may hold true for other types of surgical procedures. A change of this magnitude in the way orthopaedists assess their surgical results will only come about with the support of the medical community as defined by the specialty societies, the board-certified surgeons who make up those societies, the insurance industry, the device manufacturers, the government, and the patients. These groups already recognize that the information collected from outcomes-based research is important. Now they need to take the next step forward and agree to be active participants in the process.

The process of deciding who will and will not benefit from these procedures will become very important as pressure from health care providers comes to bear on the cost-effectiveness of the outcomes. It seems reasonable that both the federal government, as a primary health care funder, and the private health care funders would provide the necessary dollars for this essential research to determine which treatment courses are most effective and cost-effective, but there has been little indication so far that these funds will be forth-coming in the near future. In the meantime, maintenance of good clinical records in a rela-tional database will allow practice groups to develop rich data over time to support the effectiveness of current standard treatments or to develop even more effective standards. This will become important as new technology and bioengineering, in particular, lead to new treatments.

REFERENCES

1. Wright TM, Goodman SB. Implant wear: the future of total joint replacement. Rosemont(IL): American Academy of Orthopaedic Surgeons; 1996.

2. Charnley JC. Arthroplasty of the hip: a new operation. Lancet 1961;1:1129.

3. Charnley JC. Total hip replacement. JAMA 1974;230:1025–8.

4. Charnley JC. Low friction arthroplasty of the hip. Theory and practice, New York:Springer-Verlag; 1979.

5. McKee GK. Development of total prosthetic replacement of the hip. Clin Orthop 1970;72:85–103.

6. Amstutz HC. Complications of total hip replacement. Clin Orthop 1970;72:123–37.

7. Gunston. Polycentric knee arthroplasty. Prosthetic simulation of normal knee movement. J Bone Joint Surg 1971;53-B:272–7.

8. Arden GP. Total knee replacement. Clin Orthop 1973;94:92–103.

9. Ewald FC. Metal to plastic total knee replacement. Orthop Clin North Am 1975;6:811–21.

10. Freeman MA, Swanson SA, Zahir A. Total replacement of knee using metal polyethylene two-part prosthesis. Proc R Soc Med 1972;65:374–5.

11. Siller TN, Hadjipavlou A. Knee arthrodesis: long-term results. Can J Surg 1976; 19:217–9.

12. Vatopoulos PK, Diacomopoulos GJ, Demiris CS, et al. Girdlestone's operation: a follow-up study. Acta Orthop Scand 1976;47:324–8.

13. Zabihi T, Kohanim M, Amir-Jahed AK. A modified Girdlestone operation in the treatment of com-plications of fractures of the femoral neck. J Bone Joint Surg 1973;55-A:129–36.

14. Laurence M, Freeman MA, Swanson SA. Engineering considerations in the internal fixation of frac-tures of the tibial shaft. J Bone Joint Surg 1969;51-B:754–68.

15. Perren SM, Russenberger M, Steinemann S, et al. A dynamic compression plate. Acta Orthop Scand Suppl 1969;125:31–41.

16. Perren SM, Huggler A, Russenberger M, et al. The reaction of cortical bone to compression. Acta Orthop Scand Suppl 1969;125:19–29.

17. Curran WP Jr, Woodward EP. Arthroscopy: its role in diagnosis and treatment of athletic knee injuries. Am J Sports Med 1980;8:415–8.

18. Jackson RW. The role of arthroscopy in the management of the arthritic knee. Clin Orthop 1974;101:28–35.

19. Edgar MA, Lowy M. Arthroscopy of the knee: a preliminary review of fifty cases. Proc R Soc Med 1973;66:512–15.

20. Jackson RW, Abe I. The role of arthroscopy in the management of disorders of the knee. An analy-sis of 200 consecutive examinations. J Bone Joint Surg 1972;54-B:310–22.

21. Watanabe M. Present status and future of arthroscopy. Geka Chiryo 1972;26:73–7.

22. Casscells SW. Arthroscopy of the knee joint. A review of 150 cases. J Bone Joint Surg 1971;53-A:287–98.

23. Johnson LL. Arthroscopy of the shoulder. Orthop Clin North Am 1980;11:197–204.

24. Dandy DJ, et al. Arthroscopy and the management of the ruptured anterior cruciate ligament. Clin Orthop 1982;167:43–9.

25. Bartlett EC. Arthroscopic repair and augmentation of the anterior cruciate ligament in cadaver knees. Clin Orthop 1983;172:107–11.

26. Fox JM, Sherman OH, Markolf K. Arthroscopic anterior cruciate ligament repair: preliminary results and instrumented testing for anterior stability. Arthroscopy 1985;1:175–81.

27. Andersson C, Odensten M, Good L, Gillquist J. Surgical or nonsurgical treatment of acute rupture of the anterior cruciate ligament. A randomized study with long-term follow-up. J Bone Joint Surg 1989;71:965–74.

28. Stauffer RN. Ten-year follow-up study of total hip replacement. J Bone Joint Surg 1982;64-A:983–90.

29. Breck LW. Experience with total hip joint replacement without cement. Clin Orthop 1974;103:24–5.

30. Brattstrom H, et al. Long-term results in knee arthrodesis in rheumatoid arthritis. Reconstr Surg Traumatol 1971;12:125–37.

31. Cornell CN, Salvati EA, Pellici PM. Long-term follow-up of total hip replacement in patients with osteonecrosis. Orthop Clin North Am 1985;16:757–69.

32. Ranawat CS, Atkinson RE, Salvati EA, et al. Conventional total hip arthroplasty for degenerative joint disease in patients between the ages of forty and sixty years. J Bone Joint Surg 1984;66-A:745–52.

33. Serna F, Mont MA, Krackow KA, Hungerford DS. Total knee arthroplasty in diabetic patients. Comparison to a matched control group. J Arthroplasty 1994;9:375–9.

34. Amstutz HC, Thomas BJ, Jinnah R, et al. Treatment of primary osteoarthritis of the hip. A comparison of total joint and surface replacement arthroplasty. J Bone Joint Surg 1984;66-A:228–41.

35. Menon TJ, Thjellesen D, Wroblewski BM. Charnley low-friction arthroplasty in diabetic patients. J Bone Joint Surg 1983;65:580–1.

36. Small M, Steven MM, Freeman PA, et al. Total knee arthroplasty in haemophilic arthritis. J Bone Joint Surg 1983;65:163–5.

37. Dorr LD, Takei GK, Conaty JP. Total hip arthroplasties in patients less than forty-five years old. J Bone Joint Surg 1983;65-A:474–9.

38. Vicar AJ, Coleman CR. A comparison of the anterolateral, transtrochanteris, and posterior surgical approaches in primary total hip arthroplasty. Clin Orthop 1984;188:152–9.

39. Roberts JM, Fu FH, McClain EJ, Ferguson AB Jr. A comparison of the posterolateral and anterolateral approaches to total hip arthroplasty. Clin Orthop 1984;187:205–10.

40. Gore DR, Murray MP, Sepic SB, Gardner GM. Anterolateral compared to posterior approach in total hip arthroplasty: differences in component positioning, hip strength, and hip motion. Clin Orthop 1982;165;180–97.

41. Robinson RP, Robinson HJ Jr, Salvati EA. Comparison of the transtrochanteric and posterior approaches for total hip replacement. Clin Orthop 1980;147:143–7.

42. McCaskie AW, Deehan DJ, Green TP, et al. Randomized, prospective study comparing cemented and cementless total knee replacement: results of press-fit condylar total knee replacement at five years. J Bone Joint Surg 1998;80-B:971–5.

43. Duffy GP, Berry DJ, Rand JA. Cement versus cementless fixation in total knee arthroplasty. Clin Orthop 1998;356:66–72.

44. Cracchiolo A III, Benson M, Finerman GA, et al. A prospective comparative clinical analysis of the first-generation knee replacements: polycentric vs. geometric knee arthroplasty. Clin Orthop 1979;145:37–46.

45. Jacobsson SA, Djerf K, Gillquist J, et al. A prospective comparison of Butel and PCA hip arthroplasty. J Bone Joint Surg 1993;75-B:624–9.

46. McArthur PA, Milner RH. A prospective comparison of Sutter and Swanson silastic spacers. J Hand Surg 1998;23-B:574–5.

47. Gibbs AN, Green GA, Taylor JG. A comparison of the Freeman-Swanson (ICLH) and Walldius prostheses in total knee replacement. J Bone Joint Surg 1979;61-B:358–61.

48. Meding JB, Ritter MA, Keating EM, et al. Comparison of collared and collarless femoral components in primary cemented total hip arthroplasty: a randomized clinical trial. J Arthroplasty 1999;14:123–30.

49. Rand JA, Ilstrup DM. Comparison of Charnley and T-28 total hip arthroplasty. Clin Orthop 1983;180:201–5.

50. Kim WC, Grogan T, Amstutz HC, Dorey F. Survivorship comparison of THARIES and conventional hip arthroplasty in patients younger than 40 years old. Clin Orthop 1987;214:269–77.

51. Gallannaugh C. The Attenborough and Gallannaugh knee prostheses for total knee arthroplasty. A comparison and survival analysis. Clin Orthop 1992;281:177–88.

52. Burkart BC, Bourne RB, Rorabeck CH, Kirk PG. Thigh pain in cementless total hip arthroplasty. A comparison of two systems at 2 years' follow-up. Orthop Clin North Am 1993;24:645–53.

53. Moran CG. Total knee arthroplasty in elderly patients: comparison of tibial component designs. J Arthroplasty 1993;8:447–8.

54. Yahiro MA, Gantenberg JB, Nelson R, et al. Comparison of the results of cemented, porous-ingrowth, and threaded acetabular cup fixation. A meta-analysis of the orthopaedic literature. J Arthroplasty 1995;10:339–50.

55. Hearn SL, Bicalho PS, Eng K, et al. Comparison of cemented and cementless total hip arthroplasty in patients with bilateral hip arthroplasties. J Arthroplasty 1995;10:603–8.

56. Schroder J, Saris D, Besselaar PP, Marti RK. Comparison of the results of the Girdlestone pseudoarthrosis with reimplantation of a total hip replacement. Int Orthop 1998;22:215–8.

57. Isobe Y, Okuno M, Otsuki T, Yamamoto K. Clinical Study on arthroplasties for osteoarthritic hip by quantitative gait analysis. Comparison between total hip arthroplasty and bipolar endoprosthetic arthroscopy. Biomed Mater Eng 1998;8:167–75.

58. Hunziker EB, Rosenberg LC. Repair of partial-thickness defects in articular cartilage: cell recruitment from the synovial membrane. J Bone Joint Surg 1996;78:721–33.

59. Campbell CJ. The healing of cartilage defects. Clin Orthop 1969;64:45–63.

60. Fuller JA, Ghadially FN. Ultrastructural observations on surgically produced partial-thickness defects in articular cartilage. Clin Orthop 1972;86:193–205.

61. Bennett GA, Bauer W. A study of the repair of articular cartilage and the reaction of normal joints of adult dogs to surgically created defects of articular cartilage, "Joint Mice" and "Patellar Displacement." Amer J Pathol 1932;8:499–523.

62. Mankin HJ. The reaction of articular cartilage to injury and osteoarthritis. N Eng J Med 1974;291:1285–92.

63. Mankin HJ. The response of articular cartilage to mechanical injury. J Bone Joint Surg 1982; 64-A:460–6.

64. Hunter W. On the structure and diseases of articulating cartilage. Philos Trans R Soc Lond B Biol Sci 1743;42b:514–21.

65. Mageed RA, Adams G, Woodrow D, et al. Prevention of collagen-induced arthritis by gene delivery of soluble p75 tumor necrosis factor receptor. Gene Ther 1998;5:1584–92.

66. Triantaphyllopoulos KA, Williams RO, Tailor H, Chernajovsky Y. Amelioration of collagen-induced arthritis and suppression of interferon-gamma, interleukin-12, and tumor necrosis factor alpha production by interferon-beta gene therapy. Arthritis Rheum 1999;42:90–9.

67. Herndon JH, Robbins PD, Evans CH. Arthritis: is the cure in your genes? J Bone Joint Surg Am 1999;81:152–7.

68. Robbins PD, Evans CH, Chernajovsky Y. Gene therapy for rheumatoid arthritis. Springer Semin Immunopathol 1998;20:197–209.

69. Evans CH, Ghivizzani SC, Robbins PD. Blocking cytokines with genes. J Leukoc Biol 1998;64:55–61.

70. Rediske J, Abramson S. Gene therapy and arthritis. Inflamm Res 1997;46:479–81.

71. Uebelhart D, Thonar EJ, Delmas PD, et al. Effects of oral chondroitin sulfate on the progression of knee osteoarthritis: a pilot study. Osteoarthritis Cartilage 1998;6 Suppl A:39–46.

72. Paroli E. Antonilli L, Biffoni M. A pharmacological approach to glycosaminoglycans. Drugs Exp Clin Res 1991;17:9–19.

73. Conte A, Volpi N, Palmieri L, et al. Biochemical and pharmacokinetic aspects of oral treatment with chondroitin sulfate. Arzneimittlforschung Drug Res 1995;45:918–25.

74. McNamara PS, Barr SC, Erb HN. Hematologic, hemostatic, and biochemical effects in dogs receiving an oral chondroprotective agent for thirty days. Am J Vet Res 1996;57:1390–4.

75. Das AK Jr, Hammad T, Eitel J. Efficacy of a combination of glucosamine hydrochloride, sodium chondroitin sulfate, and manganese ascorbate in the management of knee osteoarthritis: a randomized double-blind placebo-controlled clinical trial. 66th Annual Meeting Proceedings of the American Academy of Orthopaedic Surgeons; 1999.p.50.

76. Felson D, Lafyatis R, Korn J. Rheumatology. Biological agents—is the promise realized? Lancet 1998;352 Suppl 4:SIV25.

77. Snowden JA, Biggs JC, Milliken ST, et al. A randomized, blinded, placebo-controlled, dose escalation study of the tolerability and efficacy of filgrastim for haemopoietic stem cell mobilization in patients with severe active rheumatoid arthritis. Bone Marrow Transplant 1998;22:1035–41.

78. Yoshizaki K, Nishimoto N, Mihara M, Kishimoto T. Therapy of rheumatoid arthritis by blocking IL-6 signal transduction with a humanized anti-IL-6 receptor antibody. Springer Semin Immunopathol 1998;20:247–59.

79. Gabay C, Arend WP. Treatment of rheumatoid arthritis with Il-1 inhibitors. Springer Semin Immunopathol 1998;20:229–46.

80. Houssiau FA, Lauwerys BR. Immunotherapeutic approaches of rheumatic disorders. Acta Clin Belg 1998;53:155–61.

81. Strand V. Future use of biologic agents alone and in combination for the treatment of rheumatoid arthritis. Z Rheumatol 1998;57:41–5.

82. Hermann J, Walmsley M, Brennan FM. Cytokine therapy in rheumatoid arthritis. Springer Semin Immunopathol 1998;20:275–88.

83. Breedveld F. New tumor necrosis factor-alpha biologic therapies for rheumatoid arthritis. Eur Cytokine Netw 1998;9:233–8.

84. Keystone E, Wherry J, Grint P. IL-10 as a therapeutic strategy in the treatment of rheumatoid arthritis. Rheum Dis Clin North Am 1998;24:629–39.

85. Jorgensen C, Apparailly F, Couret I, et al. Interleukin-4 and interleukin-10 are chondroprotective and decrease mononuclear cell recruitment in human rheumatoid synovium in vivo. Immunology 1998;93:518–23.

86. Horsfall AC, Butler DM, Marinova L, et al. 1997. Suppression of collagen-induced arthritis by continuous administration of IL-4. J. Immunol 1997;159:5687–96.

87. Brittberg M, Lindahl A, Nilsson A, et al. Treatment of deep cartilage defects in the knee with autologous chondrocyte implantation. New Eng J Med 1994;331:889–95.

88. Minas T, Peterson L. Chondrocyte transplantation. Operative Techniques in Orthopaedics. 1997;7:323–33.

89. Minas T, Nehres S. Current concepts in the treatment of articular cartilage defects. Orthopaedics 1997;20:525–38.

90. Aigner J. Tegeler J, Hutler P, et al. Cartilage tissue engineering with novel nonwoven structured biomaterial based on hyaluronic acid benzyl ester. J Biomed Mater Res 1998;42:172–81.

91. Frenkl SR, Toolan B, Menchie D, et al. Chondrocyte transplantation using a collagen bilayer matrix for cartilage repair. J Bone Joint Surg 1997;79-B:831–6.

92. Grande DA, Pitman MI, Peterson L, et al. The repair of experimentally produced defects in rabbit articular cartilage by autologous chondrocyte transplantation. J Orthop Res 1989;7:208–18.

93. Wakitani S, Goto T, Young RG, et al. Repair of large full thickness articular cartilage defects with allograft articular chondrocytes embedded in a collagen gel. Tissue Eng 1998;4:429–44.

94. Gillogly SD, Voight M, Blackburn T. Treatment of articular cartilage of the knee with autologous chondrocyte implantation. J Orthop Sports Phys Ther 1998;28:241–51.

95. Toolan BC, Frenkel SR, Pereira DS, Alexander H. Development of a novel osteochondral graft for cartilage repair. J Biomed Mater Res 1998;41:244–50.

96. Rudert M, With CJ. Cartilage cell transplantation. Experimental principles and clinical applications (translation). Orthopade 1997;26:741–7.

97. Øwre AA. Chondromalacia patellae. Acta Chir Scand 1936;77 Suppl: 41.

98. Fagard RH, Staessen JA, Thijs L. Advantages and disadvantages of the meta-analysis approach. J Hypertens Suppl 1996;14:S9–S12.

99. Jadad AR, Cook DJ, Jones A, et al. Methodology and reports of systematic reviews and meta-analyses. A comparison of Cochrane reviews with articles published in paper-based journals. JAMA 1998;280:278–80.

100. Todd S. Incorporation of sequential trials into a fixed effects meta-analysis. Stat Med 1997;16: 2915–25.

101. Flather MD, Farkough ME, Pogue JM, Yusuf S. Strengths and limitations of meta-analysis: larger studies may be more reliable. Control Clin Trials 1997;18:568–79.

102. Beard MT, Curray EL, Edwards K, Adams BN. Advances in meta-analysis as a research tool. ABNF J 1997;8:92–7.

103. Fitzpatrick R, Shortall E, Scupher M, et al. Primary total hip replacement surgery: a systematic review of outcomes and modelling of cost-effectiveness associated with different prostheses. Health Technol Assess 1998;2:1–64.

104. Alho A. Concurrent ipsilateral fractures of the hip and shaft of the femur. A systematic review of 722 cases. Ann Chir Gynaecol 1997;86:326–36.

105. Palmer AJ, Koppenhagen K, Kirchhof B, et al. Efficacy and safety of low molecular weight heparin, unfractionated heparin and warfarin for thrombo-embolism prophylaxis in orthopaedic surgery: a meta-analysis of randomized clinical trials. Haemostasis 1997;27:75–84.

106. Anders RL, Ornellas EM. Acute management of patients with hip fracture, a research literature review. Orthop Nurs 1997;16:31–46.

107. Alho A. Concurrent ipsilateral fractures of the hip and femoral shaft: a meta-analysis of 659 cases. Acta Orthop Scand 1996;67:19–28.

108. Parker MJ, Pryor GA. Gamma versus DHS nailing for extracapsular femoral fractures. Meta-analysis of ten randomized trials. Int Orthop 1996;20:163–8.

109. Haher TR, Merola A, Zipnick RI, et al. Meta-analysis of surgical outcome in adolescent idiopathic scoliosis. A 35-year English literature review of 11,000 patients. Spine 1995;20:1575–84.

110. Mont MA, Carbone JJ, Fairbank AC. Core decompression versus nonoperative management for osteonecrosis of the hip. Clin Orthop 1996;324:169–78.

111. Freund DA, Dittus RS. Final report. Assessing and improving outcomes total knee replacement patient outcomes research team (PORT) 1995.

112. Mont MA, Mathur SK, Krackow KA, et al. Cementless total knee arthroplasty in obese patients. A comparison to a matched control group. J Arthroplasty 1996;11:153–6.

113. Hungerford DS, Krackow KA, Kenna RV. Cementless total knee replacement in patients 50 years old and under. Orthop Clin North Am 1989;20:131–45.

114. Cohn BT, Krackow KA, Hungerford DS, et al. Approaches to senior care #9. Results of total knee arthroplasty in patients 80 years and older. Orthop Rev 1990;19:451–60.

115. Myers T, Mont MA, Hungerford DS. Total knee replacement for osteonecrosis in patients who are less than fifty years old. Association Research Circulation Osseous 1995;7:93.

116. Serna F, Mont MA, Krackow KA, Hungerford DS. Total knee arthroplasty in diabetic patients—a comparison to a matched control group. J Arthroplasty 1994;9:375–79.

117. Lennox DW, Hungerford DS, Krackow KA. Total knee arthroplasty following patellectomy. Clin Orthop 1987;223:220–4.

118. Mont MA, Antonaides S, Krackow KA, Hungerford DS. Total knee replacement following high tibial osteotomy. Clin Orthop 1993;299:125–30.

119. Mont MA, Alexander N, Krackow KA, Hungerford DS. Total knee arthroplasty after failed high tibial osteotomy. Orthop Clin North Am 1994;25:515–25.

120. Wolff AM, Hungerford DS, Krackow KA, Jacobs MA. Osteotomy of the tibial tubercle during total knee replacement. A report of twenty-six cases. J Bone Joint Surg 1989;71-A:848–52.

121. Mont MA, Mayerson JA, Krackow KA, Hungerford DS. Total knee arthroplasty in patients receiving workers' compensation. J Bone Joint Surg 1998;80:1285–90.

122. Mont MA, Waldman B, Banerjee C, et al. Multiple irrigation, debridement, and retention of components in infected total knee arthroplasty. J Arthroplasty 1997;12:426–33.

123. Waldman BJ, Mont MA, Hungerford DS. Total knee arthroplasty infections associated with dental procedures. Clin Orthop 1997;343:164–72.

124. Mont MA, Fairbank AC, Yammamoto V, et al. Radiographic characterization of aseptically loosened cementless total knee replacement. Clin Orthop 1995;321:73–8.

125. Mont MA, Mitzner D, Jones LC, Hungerford DS. History of the contralateral knee after primary knee arthroplasty for osteoarthritis. Clin Orthop 1995;321:145–50.

126. Insall JN, Ranawat CS, Anglietti P, Shine J. A comparison of four models of total knee replacement prostheses. J Bone Joint Surg 1976; 58–A:754–65.

127. Freeman MA, Swanson SA, Todd RC. Total replacement of the knee using the Freeman-Swanson knee prosthesis. Clin Orthop 1973; 94:153–70.

128. Hungerford DS, Kenna RV, Krackow KA. The porous-coated anatomic total knee. Orthop Clin North Am 1982;13:103–22.

129. Insall JN, Dorr LD, Scott RD, Scott WN. Rationale of the Knee Society clinical rating system. Clin Orthop 1989; 248:13–14.

130. Bellamy N, Buchanan WW, Goldsmith CH, et al. Validation study of WOMAC: a health status instrument for measuring clinically important patient relevant outcomes to antirheumatic drug therapy in patients with osteoarthritis of the hip or knee. J Rheumatol 1988;15:1833–40.

131. Ware JE, Sherbourne CD. The MOS 36-item short-form health survey (SF–36). I. Conceptual framework and item selection. Med Care 1992;30:473–83.

CHAPTER 41

Otolaryngology, Head and Neck Surgery

Carl A. Patow, MD, MPH, and Mark Richardson, MD

Otolaryngology is a surgical specialty that includes comprehensive medical and surgical care of patients with diseases and disorders that affect the ears, the respiratory and upper alimentary systems, and related structures—the head and neck, in general. The otolaryngologist/ head and neck surgeon has knowledge, skills, and understanding of the following:

1. The basic medical sciences relevant to the head and neck; the respiratory and upper alimentary systems; the communication sciences, including audiology and speech-language pathology; the chemical senses; and allergology, endocrinology, and neurology as they relate to the head and neck.
2. The clinical aspects of diagnosis and the medical and/or surgical therapy or prevention for diseases, neoplasms, deformities, and disorders and/or injuries of the ears, respiratory and upper alimentary systems, face, jaws, and other head and neck systems. Head-neck oncology and facial plastic and reconstructive surgery are fundamental areas of expertise.[1]

Many otolaryngologists further define their practices in subspecialties including pediatric otolaryngology, facial plastic and reconstructive surgery, otolaryngic allergy, rhinology, laryngology, head and neck surgery, and others.

The practice of otolaryngology includes treatment of the ears, nose, throat, and related structures using medications as well as surgical procedures. Quality improvement efforts, however, frequently focus on the procedures involved because procedures are easily enumerated. It is therefore useful to list some frequently performed or unique procedures for each anatomic area of the head and neck.

Common procedures related to the ear include tympanotomy (creating a small hole in the eardrum) and placement of pressure-equalizing tubes for treatment of middle-ear effusion, mastoidectomy, ossicular reconstruction (rebuilding the bones that conduct sound through the middle ear), and otoplasty (reshaping the outer ear). One of the most technologically sophisticated procedures performed by otolaryngologists is placement of cochlear implants, used in severely and profoundly deaf patients in an attempt to replace the nonfunctional inner ear's hair-cell transducer system by direct electrical stimulation of the cochlear nerve.

Otolaryngologists provide both medical and surgical management of nasal and sinus disease and allergies. Sinus procedures, including examination and removal of tissues from the sinuses, control of epistaxis, and repair of cerebrospinal fluid leak, are most often performed endoscopically. Straightening of the septum to improve nasal airflow is a common nasal procedure.

While otolaryngologists do not perform surgical procedures on the brain parenchyma, they do perform procedures on the skull base. These are often extensive, intricate, and delicate procedures of the vascular, neural, and bony tissues adjacent to the brain that can be affected by neoplasms or vascular conditions.

A change in the quality of the voice may be an indication of upper aero-digestive tract pathology, including such diverse conditions as gastroesophageal reflux disease, vocal cord paralysis, and laryngeal cancer. Diagnostic endoscopy of the larynx and upper respiratory tract is a commonly performed procedure in the office. Surgical procedures for treatment of vocal cord paralysis and laryngeal malignancy have been a major focus of research.

Soft-tissue surgery of salivary glands, thyroid gland, and neck lymphatics usually relates to neoplasms, benign and malignant. Soft-tissue surgical procedures encompass a wide spectrum of complexity, from a simple needle aspirate of a suspicious mass to a major resection of a large malignancy of the oral cavity with dissection of the neck lymphatics and reconstruction with free flaps. In addition to reconstructive procedures, otolaryngologists perform cosmetic facial plastic procedures, such as rhinoplasty (nose shaping), rhytidectomy (face-lifting) and blepharoplasty (eyelid refinement).

Recently, there has been renewed interest by otolaryngologists in the treatment of sleep disorders. New procedures based on technological advances in measuring sleep parameters and shaping pharyngeal tissues have increased the surgical options for treatment.

REVIEW OF THE LITERATURE

Publications by otolaryngologists supporting evidence-based clinical decision making have become more frequent over the past decade.[2] In part, this reflects a major emphasis placed on evidence-based care by the American Academy of Otolaryngology Head and Neck Surgery (AAOHNS), the National Institute on Deafness and Other Communication Disorders (NIDCD), and other specialty societies. Education of otolaryngologists in an evidence-based approach to care has evolved along two lines: (1) development of general awareness of evidence-based methodologies within the specialty, and (2) research in specific clinical areas of concern to otolaryngologists.

In support of the general education of otolaryngologists in evidence-based practice, several major symposia have been presented. In 1992, the NIDCD and the American Speech-Language Hearing Association sponsored a symposium entitled "Models for the Evaluation of Treatment Efficacy."[3] The symposium included presentations on design requirements in efficacy research, selection of appropriate research design, measurement of health outcomes from the patient's point of view, service delivery implications, bioethics, and treatment efficacy. Three years later, the NIDCD, the AAOHNS, and the Virginia Bloedel Hearing Research Center at the University of Washington sponsored a national conference on outcomes research.[4] The topics discussed included instrument design and validation, statistical considerations, meta-analysis, Patient Outcome Research Teams (PORT), analysis of databases, and questions in otolaryngology that have not been adequately addressed by evidence-based research.

These and other conferences have stimulated otolaryngologists to become expert in evidence-based surgery and to contribute to the general understanding of the subject. Examples of general work in the field published by otolaryngologists include: "Outcomes Research Primer,"[5] "How to Systematically Review the Literature,"[6] and "The Seven Habits of Highly Effective Data Users."[7] Other reports have centered on the importance of data collection and the standardization of data sets to improve consistency of reporting across the continuum of care.[8–10] Practice guidelines have also been developed for certain otolaryngologic procedures although their use is not widespread. General experience with practice guidelines in a residency training program[11] and with community-based outcomes research[12] has shown both promise and limitations. All these efforts demonstrate otolaryngologists' increasing awareness of and experience with these principles.

Aside from these general contributions to evidence-based medicine, many advances have been reported for specific organ systems cared for by otolaryngologists. Specifically, there has been a significant amount of research into clinical decision analysis, clinical practice guidelines, outcomes of health services, quality-of-life measurement, and economic analysis of clinical practice.

Otology, the study of care of the ear, has a history of using audiometric measurements to assess treatment progress. Recently, technological advances in cochlear implantation have stimulated interest in reporting patient perceptions of increased ability to hear and patient satisfaction with outcomes of the procedure. Aside from audiologic data, outcomes measures have included standardized scales for quality of life, such as the Center for Epidemiologic Studies Depression Scale and Quality of Well-Being Scale. Using standardized measures of self-assessment of quality of life permits comparison of the outcomes of cochlear implantation to other benchmark procedures. One study concluded that "Clearly cochlear implantation at $31,711 per well year is one of the most efficacious surgical interventions that has been reported and can even be shown to be more cost effective than some widely used and well accepted medical interventions."[13] The study went on to describe personal achievements of some cochlear implant recipients. Social interaction has also been studied as an outcome measure for cochlear implantation.[14]

Because otology is a highly technology-dependent specialty, technology assessment and cost-effectiveness are of interest. A detailed assessment of a controversial technology for assessing loss of balance, computerized dynamic platform posturography, has been performed.[15] Use of an advanced scanning technology, magnetic resonance imaging (MRI), in diagnosing common hearing conditions is also controversial. An evaluation of the cost-effectiveness of MRI for diagnosis of asymmetric sensorineural hearing loss determined that, by eliminating the need for follow-up audiometric or electrophysiologic studies, focused MRI can be a cost-effective modality.[16] The importance of using MRI for this hearing loss condition is in its potential to identify small benign tumors of the acoustic nerve. Once discovered, the tumors may be treated surgically or nonsurgically. A recent abstract[17] compared nonsurgical with surgical management of acoustic schwannomas by measuring tumor characteristics, clinical symptoms and signs, comorbidities, cost of management, and patient responses to a standardized telephone questionnaire. The authors concluded that while patients with nonsurgical management had greater comorbidities, both groups were generally satisfied with their management.

Sinusitis is a prevalent condition that affects an estimated 14 percent of the population. The societal cost in lost work days is great and is reportedly increasing.[18] Efforts are underway to establish a better foundation for evidence-based treatment of this condition as well as rhinitis. One instrument that has been developed is a 20-item Sinonasal Outcome Test (SNOT-20) that asks patients to describe their disease-specific health status and quality of life by indicating both the severity of symptoms and their importance across different domains. The test has been validated and is a sensitive disease-specific measure for patients with nasal symptoms.[19] Other symptom-based surveys have been proposed, including one for chronic sinusitis symptoms.[20] The study of rhinosinusitis has been a major effort of a task force of the American Academy of Otolaryngology. In its published report,[21] the task force defines adult rhinosinusitis and describes its clinical evaluation, laboratory diagnosis, radiologic diagnosis, staging, and management. A summary of many survey instruments for determination of outcomes of care is provided in the report.[22]

Head and neck surgery can involve major resections of functional structures such as the larynx, pharynx, or tongue. Because of the magnitude of the surgical procedures and the functional consequences to the patient, evidence-based research in head and neck surgery has focused on the implementation of guidelines and the determination of patient quality of life after oncologic therapy. One approach to integrating care across the disease continuum is through case management.[23] Nursing case management is defined as a set of logical steps and a process of interaction with service networks that ensures that a client receives needed services in a supportive, effective, efficient, and cost-effective manner.[24] One critical element of the case management model is a standard of care that is continually refined through regular review. The use of a standardized clinical care pathway has been shown by several investigators to reduce cost without compromising quality of care for laryngectomy (removal of the voice box)[25] and other major head and neck surgical procedures.[26] Quality-of-life measures have also been developed specifically for head and neck cancer patients.[27] Mailed questionnaires, including a core questionnaire, a tumor-specific questionnaire, and a psychological distress measure, were sensitive to changes in function and symptoms. There was evidence for a high level of psychiatric distress, reporting 21 percent of patients with probable psychiatric morbidity at the time of diagnosis.

Psychiatric stress is extraordinarily high in patients faced with the prospect of losing their voices due to cancer of the larynx. Laryngectomy is often the recommended treatment for advanced cancers of the larynx, and with laryngectomy the patient loses his or her natural voice. Although mechanical and prosthetic voice substitutes are available, a hypothetical alternative is to replace the excised larynx with a laryngeal transplant. The potential of experimental laryngeal transplantation raises some ethical questions.[28] To quantify the risk of the procedure compared to the potential benefit in the context of the patient's values will require an evidence-based approach in an experimental setting.

Sleep apnea is another condition that is more prevalent than appreciated and that has recently captured the attention of physicians in multiple specialties. An increasing variety of procedures and the application of new technologies have added depth to the surgical armamentarium for treating this condition. Uvulopalatopharyngoplasty, a standard procedure to shorten the palate and contour the pharyngeal tissues, has recently been joined by other procedures attempting to open the pharyngeal airway, including laser procedures, radio frequency cautery, tongue suspension from an anterior mandibular bone screw, and laryngeal suspension. Unfortunately, little evidence-based research is available to support the effectiveness of these modalities in treating sleep apnea. General and disease-specific health status measures have been used to assess the response of a limited number of patients to treatment over a short duration.[29] Until the new therapeutic modalities have been assessed with similar methodologies and repeated studies, determination of which therapies are most appropriate for a patient population will be inexact at best.

CASE STUDY

The most comprehensive attempt to specifically determine care guidelines and a treatment algorithm for an otolaryngologic problem was made by the Agency for Health Care Policy and Research (AHCPR) and the American Academy of Pediatrics, with help from the American Academy of Family Practitioners and the AAOHNS.[30] A review of the successes and failures of this effort provides lessons in developing and evaluating outcomes-based treatment recommendations.

Methodology

The purpose of AHCPR-supported clinical guidelines is to "enhance the quality, appropriateness, and effectiveness of health care."[31] This is accomplished through the use of the best available research and professional judgment. An emphasis is placed on comprehensive evaluation of scientific and empirical evidence of effectiveness, outcomes, benefits, and harm. If evidence is lacking, professional judgment and group consensus are used, and these areas may suggest a research agenda. Steps of the process include:

1. Defining the major questions regarding the clinical problem under consideration
2. A review and analysis of the available scientific research for each question as it relates to the particular clinical problem
3. An assessment of the clinical benefit and harm of each intervention
4. A review of the estimates of important patient outcomes for each intervention being considered
5. A review of the current and potential costs associated with interventions and alternative therapies
6. Inviting information and comments on the guideline topics from interested professionals, consumer organizations, other researchers, and manufacturers
7. Preparing a draft guideline

8. Submitting the guideline for peer review
9. Revising the guideline based on actual use
10. Preparing the guideline for use in different formats for practitioners, educators, and consumers

Topic Selection

The selection of topics is based on many factors:

1. The potential for reducing clinically significant variations in services used in prevention, diagnosis, treatment, management, or outcomes related to the condition
2. The number of patients affected
3. The adequacy of available scientific evidence
4. The amenability of a particular condition to prevention
5. Specific needs of the Medicare and Medicaid population
6. Cost of the condition to all payers, including patients

Why Otitis Media?

The selection of otitis media met the criteria for topic selection in several respects. Otitis media (OM) is one of the most frequently diagnosed early childhood diseases, affecting millions annually. It is treated by a variety of practitioners including pediatricians, otolaryngologists, and family physicians, all of whom have different training and methods of practice. Its incidence may be as high as 61 to 83 percent of all children, and its presence may be diagnosed at 5 to 10 percent of all well-baby visits. Costs cannot be fully calculated but have been estimated at $1 billion to $5 billion annually. Otitis media also has been the focus of research activity throughout the world. Although primarily a childhood disease, it may have a significant role in affecting speech and language development as a child ages.

Scientific Review and Panel Development

The topic was narrowed to "otitis media with effusion in otherwise healthy children ages 1–3 years with no craniofacial, neurologic abnormalities, or sensory deficits." Within this general problem focus, the following subtopics were spotlighted.

Diagnosis and Management

Thirty-two organizations submitted names for nomination to the panel. Based on expertise, geographic location, race, and gender, the final panel consisted of 17 with two panel co-chairs. From the 3,578 bibliographic citations reviewed, 1,362 abstracts were evaluated. Full text articles from 378 references were selected for data extraction, and more than 100 additional references were identified and added for review. The panel was divided into subgroups to facilitate review of the literature, but decisions were brought to the full panel for consensus. If fewer than four panel members disagreed, the decision was carried forward without comments.

Recommendations

The panel graded individual recommendations as follows:

- Strong recommendations were based on high-quality scientific evidence or strong consensus among panel members.
- Moderate recommendations were based on good quality science or expert opinion.
- Recommendations not otherwise specified were based on limited scientific evidence or expert opinion.
- Clinical options were interventions for which the panel failed to find compelling evidence for or against. These are interventions that a practitioner may or may not implement based on his or her own practice.[32]
- No recommendation was made when scientific evidence was lacking and expert opinion lacked consensus.

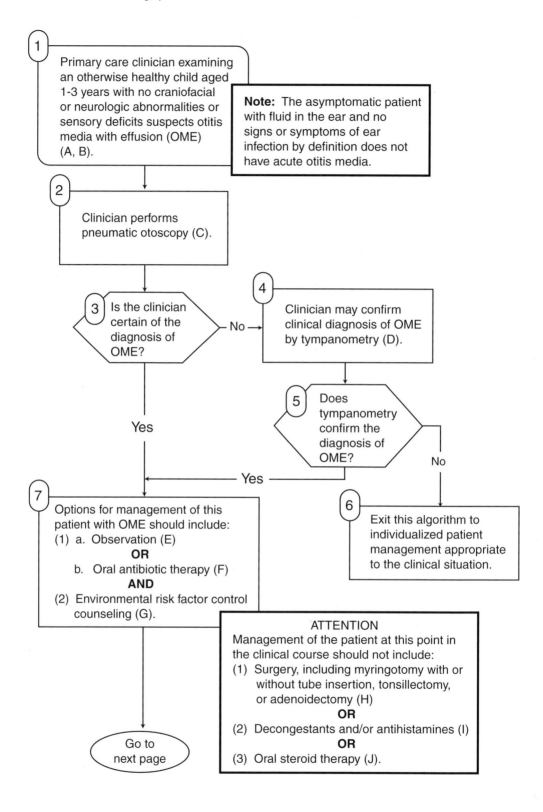

Figure 41–1 Algorithm for managing otitis media with effusion in an otherwise healthy child age 1 through 3 years

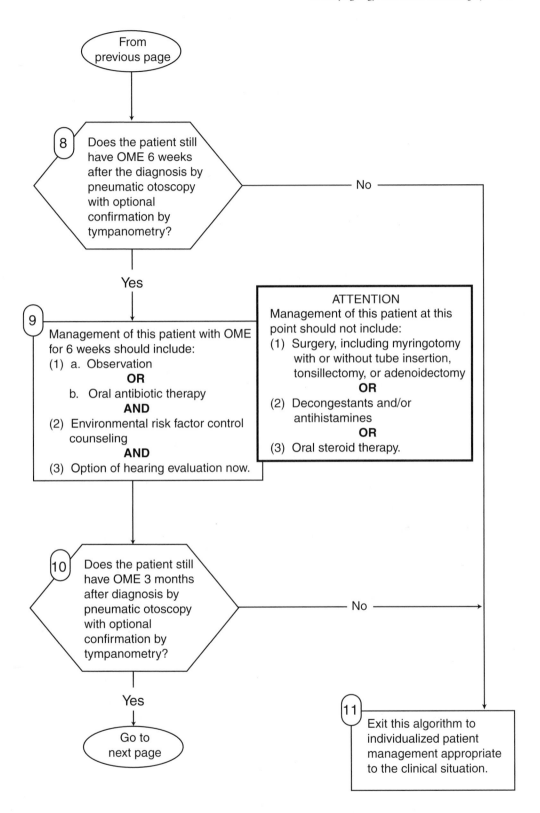

Figure 41–1 *(continued)*

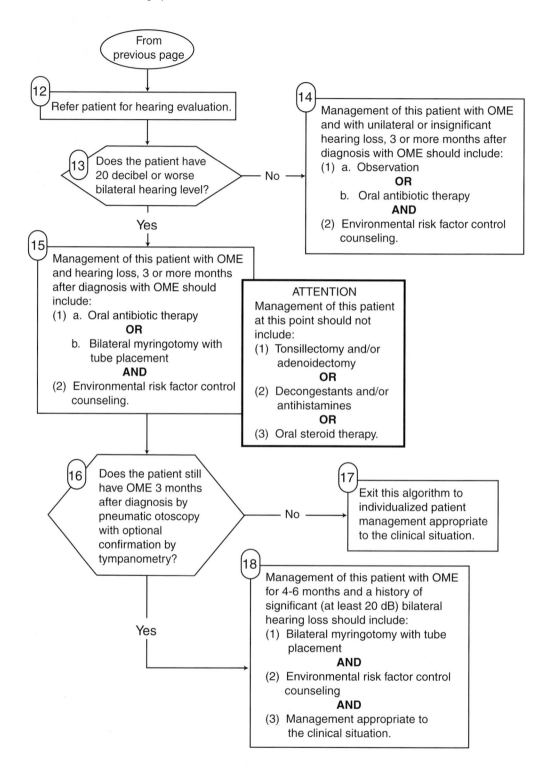

Figure 41–1

Table 41–1 Clinical Areas in Otolaryngology Requiring Additional Investigation

---

Head and Neck Oncology
- Optimal surgery for differentiated thyroid cancer
- Efficacy of organ preservation protocols versus standard therapy for cancer of the head and neck
- Efficacy of elective neck dissection in the management of cancer of the head and neck
- Efficacy of adjuvant radiation in cancer of the head and neck
- Efficacy of chemo-prevention in cancer of the head and neck

Hearing and Balance
- Ménière's disease—outcome of medical versus surgical management
- Perilymphatic fistulas—need for a definitive objective test to determine true incidence, correct diagnosis, and best treatment
- Bell's palsy—better definition and outcome studies on efficacy of different treatment strategies
- Role of gamma knife in treating acoustic neuroma, including long-term effects of treatment
- Estimate of growth rate of acoustic neuromas in the elderly population and its implications for treatment strategy
- Efficacy of vestibular rehabilitation
- Efficacy of diazide in the treatment of endolymphatic hydrops
- Efficacy of particle repositioning for benign positional vertigo
- Optimal therapy for migraine-associated dizziness

Laryngology
- Outcome of treatment in gastroesophageal reflux disease
- Efficacy of phonosurgery and long-term results
- Etiology and management of spasmotic dysphonia
- Outcome of various medical and surgical strategies for sleep apnea

Pediatric Otolaryngology
- Role of adenoidectomy for the treatment and prevention of recurrent acute otitis media and chronic middle-ear effusion
- Outcome of treatment with antimicrobial agents of otitis media with effusion versus no treatment
- Outcome of treatment of recurrent acute otitis media and chronic middle-ear effusion with tympanostomy tubes
- Do children with mild to moderate sleep apnea benefit from tonsillectomy and adenoidectomy, and can they be evaluated in a cost-effective manner?
- Definition of maximal medical therapy for sinusitis, including steroids
- Role of aspirate-directed intravenous antibiotics in the treatment of chronic sinusitis
- Indications and outcomes of functional endoscopic sinus surgery
- Value of functional endoscopic sinus surgery in patient with cystic fibrosis with and without lung transplants

---

The consensus panel developed a clinical guideline, summarized in the management algorithm presented in Figure 41–1.

Weakness of the Project

Baseline assumptions of "an otherwise healthy child" assumed no comorbidities such as noticeable hearing loss, sinusitis, nasal obstruction, sleep apnea, immune deficiency, and so forth. In fact, the majority of children who present with persistent middle-ear effusion do have concomitant medical conditions, which may exclude them from the proposed algorithm.[33] The assessment of hearing was also downplayed, and although there are many children with persistent middle-ear effusion who may have hearing loss of < 20 dB, the hearing loss may fluctuate, depending on the amount of fluid present, and may range as high as

35 dB. A single hearing assessment simply does not answer the question of significant hearing impairment. The panel was unable to come to any recommendation relating to the effect of otitis media with effusion on speech and language development. There was also no recommendation relating to the role of adenoidectomy and its potential effect on otitis media.

Strengths of the Project

The widespread dissemination of information obviously increased the awareness of the medical condition and its associated problems among all individuals involved in the care of that particular condition, including the consumer. Risk factors were identified and recommendations made for their control. Diagnostic methods were outlined, and data were reviewed and presented. There was emphasis on the self-limiting factor of the disease process and on hearing acuity for making management decisions.[34] Antimicrobials were advised only for limited use. The pros and cons of myringotomy and tubes were discussed. Tonsillectomy and antihistamines were dismissed as ineffective in resolving or improving outcome.

Additional Concerns

The development of any guidelines leads to several concerns and questions including the following:

1. Does deviation from the guidelines result in any change of policies regarding payment by third-party payers?
2. Does deviation from the guidelines lead to medical or legal liability?
3. Is there a potential for extending the guidelines to patients outside of the defined patient population?
4. Will the guidelines be implemented uniformly throughout the disciplines involved?
5. To what extent will the guidelines be accepted by all practitioners? (In this particular example, there was disagreement on the part of several of the specialists on the panel.)
6. Once developed through the funding of the AHCPR, how easy will it be to change these guidelines, and under what circumstances will that take place?

Implementation

The guidelines have been generally accepted, but complete adherence has not been the case. One study of 59 children identified an extremely low rate of compliance with the algorithm (around 5%). Lack of compliance occurred from a diagnostic standpoint, with a low use of pneumatic otoscopy, audiometry, and tympanometry. Delayed referral was another deficiency, with over half of the patients developing complications by the time of referral.

Guidelines may represent "best practice." However, guidelines seem likely only to influence practitioners rather than dictate patterns of treatment. Community standards may take precedence over national guidelines.

TOPICS FOR FUTURE STUDIES

Eugene Myers, in a symposium on outcomes research, summarized the important clinical areas in otolaryngology that require additional investigation (Table 41–1).[35] His list includes many fundamental clinical questions that require elucidation before otolaryngology is firmly grounded as an evidence-based surgical discipline. Clearly, many investigators are engaged in acquiring this knowledge, and much of the fundamental work in developing and validating data collection instruments has begun. Perhaps a greater challenge, once we have the evidence on which to base decisions, will be educating both primary care physicians and specialists on best practices and the continual improvement of patient care.

REFERENCES

1. The American Board of Otolaryngology. Booklet of information. Houston, TX. p. 1–8. July 1998.

2. Ah-See KW, Molony NC, Maran AG. Trends in randomized controlled trials in ENT: a 30-year review. J Laryngol Otol 1997;111(7):611–3.

3. NIDCD, American Speech-Language Hearing Association. Models for the evaluation of treatment efficacy. 1992 November 17–18; San Antonio, Texas.

4. 1995 Outcomes research in otolaryngology-head and neck surgery. Virginia Merrill Bloedel Hearing Research Center; 1995 Oct 20–22; University of Washington, Seattle, Washington.

5. Piccirillo JF, Stewart MG, Glicklich RE, Yueh B. Outcomes research primer. Otolaryngol Head Neck Surg 1997;117:380–7.

6. Rosenfeld RM. How to systematically review the medical literature. Otolaryngol Head Neck Surg 1996;115(1):53–63.

7. Rosenfeld RM. The seven habits of highly effective data users. Otolaryngol Head Neck Surg 1998;118:144–58.

8. Klercker T, Trell E, Lundquist PG. Towards an essential data set for ambulatory otorhinolaryngological care in general practice. Med Inf (Lond) 1994;19(3):253–67.

9. Patow CA. Defining and measuring quality in the practice of otolaryngology and head and neck surgery. Curr Opin Otolaryngol Head Neck Surg 1997;5:177–80.

10. Robinson K, Gatehouse S, Browning GG. Measuring patient benefit from otorhinolaryngological surgery and therapy. Ann Otol Rhinol Laryngol 1996;105(6):415–22.

11. Stewart MG, Harril WC, Ohlms LA. The effects of an outpatient practice guideline at a teaching hospital: a prospective pilot study. Otolaryngol Head Neck Surg 1997;117:338–93.

12. Isenberg SF, Rosenfeld RM. Problems and pitfalls in community-based outcomes research. Otolaryngol Head Neck Surg 1997;116:6662–5.

13. Harris JP, Anderson JP, Novak R. An outcomes study of cochlear implants in deaf patients. Arch Otolaryngol Head Neck Surg 1995;121:398–404.

14. Knutson JF, Boyd R, Reid JB, et al. Observational assessments of the interaction of implant recipients with family and peers: preliminary findings. Otolaryngol Head Neck Surg 1997; 117:196–207.

15. Monsell EM, Furiman JM, Herdman SJ, et al. Computerized dynamic platform posturography. Otolaryngol Head Neck Surg 1997;117:394–8.

16. Carrier DA, Arriaga MA. Cost-effective evaluation of asymmetric sensorineural hearing loss with focused magnetic resonance imaging. Otolaryngol Head Neck Surg 1997;116:567–74.

17. Kwiatkowski TJ, Sataloff RT. Operative versus nonoperative management of acoustic schwannoma: cost, comorbidity, and patient satisfaction in a single neurotologist practice. Otolaryngol Head Neck Surg 1998;199(2):188.

18. Kaliner MA, Osguthorpe JD, Fireman P, et al. Bench to bedside. Otolaryngol Head Neck Surg 1997 Jun;116(6 Pt 2) Suppl:S1–S20.

19. Piccirillo JF, Merritt MG, Jones ML. Validity of the 20-item sinonasal outcome test. Otolaryngol Head Neck Surg 1998 Aug;199(2):52–3.

20. Glicklich RE, Metson R. Techniques for outcomes research in chronic sinusitis. Laryngoscope 1995;105:387.

21. Lanza DC, Kennedy DW. Adult rhinosinusitis defined. Otolaryngol Head Neck Surg 1997;117:S1–S7.

22. Leopold D, Ferguson BJ, Piccirillo JF. Outcomes assessment. Otolaryngol Head Neck Surg 1997;117:S58–S68.

23. Hudak M. Implementing case management for a head and neck unit. ORL Head Neck Nursing 1993;11(2):16–19.

24. Weil M, Karls J. Historical origins and recent development. In: Weil M, et al, editors. Case management in human service practice. San Francisco (CA): Jossey-Bass Publishers;2.

25. Hanna E, Schultz S, Doctor D, et al. Development and implementation of a clinical pathway for patients undergoing total laryngectomy: impact on cost and quality of life. 1998 combined program of the American Society for Head and Neck Surgery and the Society of Head and Neck Surgeons; 1998 May 14–16; Palm Beach, Florida.

26. Husbands J, Weber RS, Karpati R, et al. Decreasing length of stay with a head and neck surgical pathway. Otolaryngol Head Neck Surg 1998; Aug 199(2):111.

27. Hammerlid E, Bjordal K, Ahlner-Elmqvist M. Prospective, longitudinal quality-of-life study of patients with head and neck cancer: a feasibility study including the EORTC QLQ-C30. Otolaryngol Head Neck Surg 1997;116:666–73.

28. Strome S, Strome M. Laryngeal transplantation: ethical considerations. Am J Otolaryngol 1992;13(2): 75–7.

29. Piccirillo JF, Gates GA, White DL, Schectman KB. Obstructive sleep apnea treatment outcomes pilot study. Otolaryngol Head Neck Surg 1998;118:833–44.

30. AHCPR program note: clinical practice guideline development. U.S. Department of Health and Human Services, Public Health Service, Agency for Health Care Policy and Research. Washington, DC: 1993 Aug. AHCPR Publication No.: 93-0023.

31. Stool SE, Berg AO, Berman S, et al. Managing otitis media with effusion in young children. Quick reference guide for clinicians. U.S. Department of Health and Human Services, Public Health Service, Agency for Health Care Policy and Research; 1994 July. Washington, DC. AHCPR Publication No.: 94-0623.

32. Stool SE, Berg AO, Berman S, et al. Otitis media with effusion in young children. Clinical practice guideline. U.S. Department of Health and Human Services, Public Health Service, Agency for Health Care Policy and Research. 1994 July. Washington, DC. AHCPR Publication No.: 94-0622.

33. Bluestone CD, Klein JO. Clinical practice guideline on otitis media in young children: strengths and weaknesses. Otolaryngol Head Neck Surg 1995 Apr;112(4):507–11.

34. Hsu GS, Levine SC, Giebink GS. Management of otitis media using Agency for Health Care Policy and Research guidelines. Otolaryngol Head Neck Surg 1998 April;118(4):437–43.

35. Myers EN. Important unanswered clinical research questions. 1995 Outcomes Research in Otolaryngology-Head and Neck Surgery; 1995 Oct 20–22; Seattle, Washington. Virginia Merrill Bloedel Hearing Research Center.

CHAPTER 42

Urology

H. Ballentine Carter, MD

THE SPECIALTY OF UROLOGY

The specialty of urology encompasses the diagnosis and management of diseases of the male genitourinary system and female urinary tract. The most commonly seen problems in adult urologic practice include urinary tract stones (calculi), incontinence (especially female), erectile dysfunction in the male, and diseases of the prostate.

A better understanding of the pathophysiology, etiology, and natural history of urologic disease has led to improvements in patient care and outcomes. For example, the recent availability of an oral medication (with minimal side effects) for the treatment of erectile dysfunction[1] is based on an understanding of the mechanisms that promote smooth-muscle relaxation within the corporal bodies of the penis—a necessary event for achievement and maintenance of an erection. Also, improvements in technology have led to alternative treatments for common urologic problems. For example, shock wave lithotripsy (disintegration of urinary tract stones with focused energy), ureteroscopy (retrieval of stones in the urinary tract with miniature endoscopes), and percutaneous lithotripsy (creation of an access tract through the flank into the kidney for stone removal) have virtually eliminated the need for open surgery to manage urinary tract stones. Despite improvements in patient care, there is a need for well-designed studies that clarify the appropriate selection of patients for a given management option that will result in optimal patient outcomes, especially with respect to quality of life.

Agency for Health Care Policy and Research Guidelines

The Agency for Health Care Policy and Research (AHCPR) was created to improve the quality, appropriateness, and effectiveness of health care (Omnibus Budget Reconciliation Act of 1989). Both the American Urological Association and the AHCPR have published guidelines for the diagnosis and management of the most common urologic problems. These guidelines are designed to assist both physicians and patients in making decisions about appropriate health care and are based on empirical evidence and outcomes derived from the published literature. Guidelines for urologic practice published since 1994 include those dealing with the management of large kidney stones (staghorn calculi),[2] stones located in the ureter,[3] female stress incontinence,[4] male erectile dysfunction,[5] localized prostate cancer,[6] and benign prostatic hyperplasia (BPH).[7]

The published literature does not always contain enough evidence to make valid comparisons among different treatment options. In the case of localized prostate cancer—the most commonly diagnosed male cancer in the United States—a guidelines panel found wide variability in how patient outcomes were characterized, and a lack of randomized trials on which to base management decisions.[6] Thus, the only policy recommendation that could be made, based on the available published literature, was that patients should be informed of all commonly accepted treatment options. Given the lack of comparative outcome data in the literature on the diagnosis and management of localized prostate cancer, some investigators have attempted to use decision analysis as an alternative to randomized studies.

Table 42–1 Utility Values* for Calculation of Quality-Adjusted Life Expectancy

Health Status	Utility Value[†] (physician derived)	Utility Value[‡] (patient derived)
Treatment-related impotence	.95	.69
Treatment-related total incontinence	.70	.57
Treatment-related bowel injury	.85	—
Hormonally responsive metastatic cancer	.90	.42
Hormonally refractory metastatic cancer	.50	.13

*Utility values, with 1.0 equal to full health and 0.0 equal to death.

[†]Adapted with permission from Fleming C, Wasson JH, Albertson PC, et al, for the Prostate Patient Outcomes Research Team. A decision analysis of alternative treatment strategies for clinically localized prostate cancer. JAMA 1993;269:2650–8.

[‡]Adapted with permission from Cowen ME, Cahill D, Kattan MW, Miles BJ. The value or utility of prostate cancer states. J Urol 1996;155:376A.

Decision Analysis in the Evaluation of Prostate Cancer Diagnosis and Management

Krahn and colleagues[8] performed a cost-utility decision analysis of prostate cancer screening. Based on published rates of clinical events, the authors found that screening decreased quality-adjusted life expectancy (QALE) in unselected men between 50 and 70 years of age. This highly publicized study—based on uncontrolled observations—reported that screening for prostate cancer would likely result in poorer health outcomes while increasing costs dramatically.

The model structure in the Krahn study[8] was based on a single episode of screening that was more likely to pick up advanced disease, not on a series of annual or repeated screens more likely to pick up curable disease. Indeed, the authors held the prostate-specific antigen (PSA) test to a higher standard than any other screening test since no screening test used once would be expected to prolong life. In addition, the authors used unrealistically low prostate cancer mortality and progression rates in untreated men based on one study[9] which they concluded was "the single best study of the natural history of untreated prostate cancer." These rates (inputs into the model) have been shown to be grossly underestimated,[10] resulting in an apparent lack of efficacy for any treatment after diagnosis. Finally, the authors assigned similar utility weights (for calculation of QALE) to the development of metastatic disease for which there is no treatment and to incontinence after radical prostatectomy for which there is effective treatment. Thus, the decision analysis did not provide clinically useful information regarding prostate cancer screening.

Fleming and colleagues[11] used decision analysis to evaluate the management of clinically localized prostate cancer. The authors concluded that in most cases, treatment offers less than a 1-year improvement in QALE or decreases the QALE compared with watchful waiting. The utility values used for calculating QALE are shown in Table 42–1 and are based on a consensus of clinicians involved in outcomes research. One can see that to physicians, the development of metastatic prostate cancer was considered preferable to incontinence or bowel injury, similar to impotence. However, when patients assigned preferences,[12] the utility values were quite different and logically reflect what the physicians in the Fleming study[11] chose to ignore—there is no effective treatment for metastatic cancer but incontinence and impotence can be treated.

The core of the study by Fleming and colleagues[11] (as in the study by Krahn[8]) was a model of the natural history of prostate cancer that was based on unrealistically low metastatic rates in the absence of treatment. Based on these low metastatic rates, the estimated benefit of surgery for moderately differentiated prostate cancer was 0.75 years without quality adjustments. When realistic metastatic rates based on more recent data were used in the same model, the estimated benefit of surgery was 3 years.[13] Thus, the authors underestimated the benefit of treatment for prostate cancer by using unrealistic metastatic rates from older studies. These data emphasize the importance of the initial inputs in any decision analysis model.

In contrast to the lack of controlled long-term data to support one management decision over another for men with clinically localized prostate cancer, a number of well-designed trials have changed the management of benign prostatic hyperplasia (BPH). In the field of urology, BPH is a paradigm for evidence-based surgery.

BENIGN PROSTATIC HYPERPLASIA

Definition and Prevalence of Disease

Benign prostatic hyperplasia is a nonmalignant, hyperplastic process involving both the epithelium and stroma (connective tissue and smooth muscle) of the prostate. The etiology of the disease is poorly understood. However, it is known that androgens are necessary for disease development since BPH does not develop in males castrated prior to puberty or when androgen action or production is affected by genetic disease.

Benign prostatic hyperplasia originates in the transition zone of the prostate, a glandular region surrounding the urethra. The transition zone gradually enlarges in the aging male, and nodules of hyperplastic epithelium and stroma develop within this zone in men with BPH. This process can result in pressure to the urethra and associated increased resistance to urine flow manifested by lower urinary tract symptoms, decreased urinary flow (cc per sec), and increased residual urine. Obstructive (weak urinary stream, hesitancy, feeling of incomplete bladder emptying, straining) and irritative (frequency, nocturia, urgency) lower urinary tract symptoms may occur as a result of obstruction-induced changes in bladder muscular function (contractility) and decreased compliance and storage function of the bladder. However, there is only a weak correlation between the severity of lower urinary tract symptoms, the degree of obstruction, and the size of the prostate. This suggests that factors other than transition zone enlargement and increased urethral pressure are involved in the development of lower urinary tract symptoms in the aging male.

The clinical diagnosis of BPH, made on the basis of a history of lower urinary tract symptoms and physical examination, closely approximates by age the histologic prevalence of BPH in the population.[14] More than 50 percent of men have histologic evidence of BPH by age 60 years, and about 90 percent by age 85 years.[15] Macroscopic enlargement of the prostate occurs in about half of the men with microscopic evidence of BPH, and about half of those men develop the lower urinary tract symptoms characteristic of BPH.[16] Thus, it is estimated that 1 in 4 men in the United States will be treated for BPH by age 80 years.[17,18] With a shift in the age distribution of the U.S. population toward older individuals, the percentage of men seeking treatment for BPH will increase.

Prostatectomy for Benign Prostatic Hyperplasia

Surgical removal of hyperplastic tissue by endoscopic resection (transurethral resection of the prostate, or TURP) or open enucleation is the most effective treatment for BPH and was until recently the only accepted intervention for BPH other than expectant management (no treatment). The age-adjusted rate of TURP peaked in 1987, when it was the second most common surgical procedure (cataract surgery being the most common) performed in the Medicare population, with more than 300,000 procedures annually.[19]

The most common indications for TURP were bothersome lower urinary tract symptoms that reduce quality of life. The indications for TURP in men with BPH were poorly defined for a number of reasons including (1) a lack of information regarding the natural history of the disease and treatment outcomes, (2) the nonspecific nature of lower urinary tract symptoms, and (3) the poor correlation between clinical findings (endoscopy, urodynamic measurements, prostate size) and symptoms. Thus, the appropriate timing of and need for surgical treatment were not always clear, leading to a subjective application of treatment. As a result, large variations in prostatectomy rates were documented.

One study demonstrated that men living in the New England states were twice as likely to undergo prostatectomy as men living in England.[20] In addition to international differences in prostatectomy rates, small area variations (as much as fourfold) within the United States were noted.[18] These variations were believed to be the result of differences among urologists regarding management decisions for BPH rather than geographic variation in the prevalence or severity of the disease.

The number of prostatectomies performed for BPH has decreased since 1987,[19] and today there are less than 200,000 TURPs performed yearly in the Medicare population. In 1996, the last year for which there are complete data, 116,000 TURPs were performed in the United States, a 60 percent reduction from 1987. This decrease in the prostatectomy rate may be due to multiple factors including development of alternate treatment strategies (eg, medical therapy), availability of outcomes data from prospective trials, and development of evidence-based guidelines for the diagnosis and management of BPH.[7]

Alternate Treatments: Medical Therapy

The most commonly used medical therapies for BPH are based on two observations. First, the development of BPH is an androgen-dependent process that does not occur in the absence of androgens. Thus, withdrawal of androgens results in regression of BPH tissue, primarily the epithelial component.[21] Second, it is believed that clinical symptoms related to bladder outlet obstruction are partly due to increased smooth-muscle tone within the prostate.[22] Thus, a decrease in smooth-muscle tone with α-blockers can relieve bothersome lower urinary tract symptoms.

Androgen suppression (pharmacologic castration) results in regression of the epithelial components of BPH.[21] Castration (medical or surgical), however, causes numerous side effects (eg, erectile dysfunction) as a result of lowering serum testosterone that would be unacceptable to men with BPH. The most potent intracellular androgen is dihydrotestosterone (DHT), which is derived from the reduction of testosterone by the enzyme 5α-reductase. Inhibition of 5α-reductase reduces androgenic stimuli to the prostate. Because testosterone is still present, however, the androgenic reduction is not complete (ie, at castrate level). The FDA approval in 1992 of a 5α-reductase inhibitor (finasteride) that lowers intracellular DHT without affecting serum testosterone provided an alternate treatment for BPH with minimal side effects.[23]

The discovery that prostatic smooth-muscle tone is primarily mediated by α_1-adrenergic receptors[24,25] led to the study and use of specific α_1-receptor blockers in the treatment of lower urinary tract symptoms. These agents have been shown to relax prostatic smooth-muscle tone and reduce lower urinary tract symptoms in some men.

The availability of alternative management options for BPH led to greater interest in developing accurate measures of symptoms that would reflect the outcomes of treatment.

Symptom Assessment Questionnaire and Other Direct Outcome Measures

Serious health effects from obstructive BPH (eg, renal deterioration) that result in a shorter length of life rarely occur. However, lower urinary tract symptoms resulting from BPH are common and are bothersome to many men, ultimately resulting in a lower quality of life. How much a patient is bothered by lower urinary tract symptoms varies even among men with similar symptom severity.[26] Thus, an assessment of symptom severity and the degree to which symptoms are bothersome is a key element in choosing management for a disease that requires intervention primarily due to a decrease in quality of life.

Table 42–2 Median Probability for Symptom Improvement*

Treatment Modality	Median Probability	90% Confidence Interval
Placebo	45%	26–65%
Watchful waiting	42%	31–55%
α-blocker	74%	59–86%
Finasteride	67%	54–78%
TURP	88%	75–96%

TURP = transurethral resection of the prostate
*Adapted with permission from McConnell JD, Barry MJ, Bruskewitz RC, et al. Benign prostatic hyperplasia: diagnosis and treatment. Clinical Practice Guideline No. 8. Rockville (MD): US Department of Health and Human Services; 1994.

The American Urological Association appointed a measurement committee to develop and validate a symptom index for BPH.[26,27] The primary purpose of the index was to capture changes in symptoms over time so that different treatment strategies could be compared and to differentiate men in terms of symptom bother.[28,29] The validated seven-question index (with five possible scores for each item), together with a quality-of-life question, has been recommended by the U.S. Agency for Health Care Policy and Research (AHCPR),[7] in the initial evaluation of men with BPH. The symptom index is commonly used as a starting point for the discussion of management options in men with mild (score 0 to 7), moderate (score 8 to 19), and severe (score 20 to 35) lower urinary tract symptoms. In addition, the index captures changes in BPH symptoms after treatment and in this regard is a direct outcome measure. However, the index does not discriminate (nor was it designed to discriminate) between the different causes of lower urinary tract symptoms.

In addition to symptom improvement, other outcome measures important to patients include complications (including mortality) of the various treatment options and the need for re-treatment due to recurrence of symptoms. In general, the probability and the magnitude of symptom improvement as well as the risk of complications are greater for surgical than for nonsurgical treatment while the probability of re-treatment is higher for medical and less invasive treatment options than it is for surgery.

Indirect Outcome Measures

While symptom improvement is the most important outcome to patients, peak urinary flow rate (uroflowmetry) measured in cubic centimeters per second and post-void residual urine measurements (retained urine volume) are commonly reported indirect outcome measures. An increase in peak urinary flow rate and a decrease in post-void residual urine is considered desirable in terms of treatment outcome, but it is not possible to define a threshold change in flow rate or residual urine volume that is perceptible to a patient. Like symptom assessment, these measures are not specific for BPH.

Outcome Studies that Have Influenced Management

The natural history of BPH is such that symptoms are not always progressive, and some patients have improvement in symptoms and urinary flow rates without treatment (watchful waiting) or with placebo. Table 42–2 shows both the probability of achieving symptom improvement with various management options and the importance of the placebo effect in men with BPH. Thus, randomized placebo-controlled study designs—or comparisons of new surgical technologies to standard treatment options or "sham"—are necessary to prove treatment effectiveness in BPH.

Urologists have been familiar with the marked improvement in quality of life among their patients who underwent surgery for lower urinary tract symptoms. However, several uncontrolled observations raised concern regarding the use of TURP for the treatment of BPH. First, Roos and colleagues,[30] in a review of insurance claim data, reported that the death rate at 90 days was significantly higher for TURP than for open surgery for BPH. These data raised the alarm that something intrinsic to TURP (one of the most commonly performed procedures in the United States) was responsible for higher postoperative death rates. In fact, subsequent analyses[31] demonstrated that failure to adjust for comorbidity between groups was responsible for the findings of Roos and colleagues.[30] Second, the variation in surgical rates in the United States suggested that surgery was being utilized indiscriminately, and treatment complications such as incontinence and impotence were felt to be significant (although outcomes were not well defined in randomized studies).[32] These concerns regarding TURP prompted further study by investigators who were concerned that improvements in quality of life might be minimal relative to surgical morbidity.

Randomized Study: Surgery versus Watchful Waiting

Wasson and colleagues[33] conducted a multicenter randomized trial comparing surgery and watchful waiting for men with moderate symptoms of BPH, in which 556 men (mean age 66 ± 5 years) were evaluated (280 in the surgery group, 276 in the watchful waiting group) with follow-up to 3 years (average 2.8 years). During the first 30 days after surgery, 91 percent of the surgical patients had no complications, and there were no deaths associated with surgery. After 3 years, mortality rates did not differ between the groups. Treatment failure—defined as death, urinary retention, bladder calculus, incontinence, severe symptoms, and deterioration of renal function—was 50 percent higher in the watchful waiting group (6 per 100 person-years of follow-up) compared to the surgery group (3 per 100 person-years of follow-up, $p = .002$). Of men in the watchful waiting group, 24 percent underwent surgery during the 3-year follow-up period.

With respect to symptoms and quality of life, surgery was associated with statistically significant improvements ($p < .001$) in bother from urinary symptoms and interference with daily activities. Surgery was also associated with statistically significant increases in urinary flow rate ($p < .001$) and reductions in residual urine volume ($p = .015$). Despite previous concerns about urinary incontinence resulting from TURP, the surgery group showed statistically significant improvements in symptoms of urinary incontinence when compared to the watchful waiting group ($p = .002$). Surgery was not, however, associated with changes in general well-being, social activities, or sexual performance.

The two factors that significantly influenced outcomes after surgical treatment of BPH were the management choice (watchful waiting vs surgery) and the baseline bother of urinary difficulties. Men who were most bothered by their symptoms were more likely to have improvement after surgery and were more likely (twofold) to undergo surgery when watched, compared to men who were less bothered by their symptoms.

These data from a prospective randomized trial refuted the uncontrolled observation[32] that TURP frequently leads to incontinence and impotence. Furthermore, the study documented that an assessment of symptom bother was predictive of clinical outcome whereas other assessments such as endoscopic evaluation and uroflowmetry were not. Based upon these data and subsequent studies, it is now well recognized that for men with bothersome symptoms from BPH, TURP is a safe and effective option.

Medical Therapy Controlled Trials: Finasteride

Finasteride is an inhibitor of the intracellular enzyme (5α-reductase) that converts testosterone to DHT, the most potent intracellular androgen within the prostate. Development of finasteride was based on the finding that men with congenital absence of this enzyme had no prostates but were normally virilized at puberty by the action of testosterone.[34,35] Finasteride was initially shown to reduce prostate volume by approximately 30 percent and to increase urinary flow rates.[36]

Two large placebo-controlled trials randomized 533 men to finasteride and 553 men to placebo for 1 year.[23,37] Because of the significant placebo effect with BPH (see Table 42–2), the study design incorporated a placebo run-in phase for the entire study cohort prior to treatment with finasteride. There was a statistically significant improvement in symptom score and urinary flow rate and an average 32 percent reduction in prostate volume in the finasteride arm of the trials. The major side effects (in 3 to 4% of men) were erectile dysfunction and a decrease in ejaculatory volume. Thus, finasteride was shown to be safe and effective in relieving the symptoms of BPH in some men.

There remained the questions of which men with BPH benefit the most from treatment with finasteride, and whether finasteride could prevent progression of BPH. The Veterans Affairs (VA) Cooperative Studies Benign Prostatic Hyperplasia Study Group clarified the first question.[38]

Randomized Study: Finasteride Compared to α_1-Adrenergic Antagonists

In addition to medical treatment of BPH with finasteride, α_1-adrenergic antagonists can relax prostatic smooth muscle and improve lower urinary tract symptoms. The Veterans Affairs Cooperative Studies Benign Prostatic Hyperplasia Study Group addressed the question of which drug is most effective and whether a combination of the two drugs would be more effective than one drug alone.[38] The randomized study arms were placebo (n = 305), finasteride (n = 310), terazosin (an α_1-adrenergic antagonist, n = 305), and a combination of finasteride and terazosin (n = 309). The authors found that treatment with terazosin improved symptoms and urinary flow rate significantly whereas treatment with finasteride reduced the size of the prostate but did not improve symptoms or urinary flow rate significantly. The combination of finasteride and terazosin was no more effective than terazosin alone. Side effects were significantly greater in the terazosin arm and included dizziness, asthenia, and postural hypotension.

These data were in contrast to previous trials demonstrating the efficacy of finasteride in the treatment of BPH. However, the study population in the finasteride and terazosin trial[38] was quite different from the previous finasteride trials[23,37] in one important respect.

In the VA Cooperative trial,[38] in which no threshold prostate size was required for study entry, the average prostate volume was 37 mL. The finasteride trials[23,37] had an entry criteria for prostate size of > 30 mL, and the average prostate volume in these two trials was 47 mL and 60 mL. Because men with larger prostates are more likely to have epithelial hyperplasia, and since androgen withdrawal results primarily in regression of the epithelial components of BPH, one would expect treatment with finasteride to be more effective in men with larger prostates. A subset analysis of men in the finasteride arm of the VA Cooperative trial[38] with prostate volumes > 50 mL demonstrated that these men had a statistically significant improvement in symptoms and urinary flow rate when compared to those in the placebo group, albeit less than men in the terazosin arm. Thus, the VA Cooperative Trial[38] further clarified the choice of medical treatment among men with BPH. Those men with large prostates on digital rectal examination who opt for medical therapy (25% of men aged 60 to 69 years) can be treated with either finasteride or an α_1-adrenergic antagonist like terazosin. If the prostate is not enlarged, these men should be treated with an α_1-adrenergic antagonist if medical therapy is chosen. However, the choice of medical therapy for BPH should take long-term outcomes into consideration.

Finasteride in the Prevention of Disease Progression: Long-Term Outcome

Benign prostatic hyperplasia is a chronic condition with the potential for progression resulting in deterioration of the quality of life due to urinary symptoms, urinary retention, and required surgical relief (ultimately) of symptoms or retention. Treatment for BPH should improve quality of life and prevent the progression of disease. The Finasteride Long-Term Efficacy and Safety Group[39] evaluated the effect of finasteride on the risk of urinary retention and the need for surgery in men with BPH. In a double blind randomized placebo-controlled trial, 3,040 men with moderate to severe symptoms of BPH and enlarged prostates were studied for 4 years. A 55 percent reduction in the risk of surgery and a 57 percent reduction in the risk of urinary retention was noted in the finasteride group when compared to the placebo arm. There was a statistically significant improvement in urinary symptoms and flow rate and a reduction in prostate volume among the men treated with finasteride. Thus, long-term efficacy in symptom improvement and prevention of disease progression was demonstrated with finasteride. This type of outcome data is unavailable for α_1-adrenergic antagonists.

Current Management of Benign Prostatic Hyperplasia Based on Randomized Studies

When the only available treatment for BPH was surgery, diagnosis was based on symptoms and physical examination, and surgery was usually successful by removing obstructing tissue. Physicians usually recommended surgery when symptoms were bothersome, based on uncontrolled observations that symptoms would progress and result in the eventual need for surgery. With the advent of alternative treatments for BPH and controlled studies that document outcomes, men with mild symptoms can safely be watched, and men with moderate and severe bothersome symptoms have a choice between surgical and medical therapy; both of which are safe approaches. Practitioners now have guidelines based on the best available evidence to help their patients with BPH make management decisions.[40]

AREAS FOR FUTURE RESEARCH

There are many areas of urologic practice in which strong evidence is not available to support current beliefs and practices in the evaluation and treatment of urologic disease. Because prostate cancer is the most commonly diagnosed cancer among males in the United States and the second leading cause of male cancer deaths, it is an area for which outcome data are especially important. For example, the routine use of digital rectal examination (DRE) and the PSA test (a blood test used to screen for prostate cancer) in asymptomatic men as a means of reducing prostate cancer mortality by earlier detection and treatment is controversial yet widespread. The American Cancer Society and the American Urological Association recommends the routine use of DRE and PSA tests in asymptomatic men over 50 years of age. The Canadian Task Force on the Periodic Health Examination and the U.S. Preventive Services Task Force do not support routine use of PSA tests for prostate cancer screening. Arguments for prostate cancer screening are based on the belief (not evidence) that early detection will decrease disease mortality as follows: (1) there is no effective treatment for advanced prostate cancer; (2) simple tests (DRE and PSA testing) are available and when used together, result in the increased detection of organ-confined prostate cancer and; (3) effective treatment is available for prostate cancer confined to the prostate. Arguments against prostate cancer screening are based on the belief that early detection could result in more overall harm than improvement of health in large populations as follows: (1) lack of evidence, based on randomized trials, that aggressive treatment for early prostate cancer is beneficial through documentation showing that treated and untreated men with early disease have significantly different outcomes; (2) PSA testing may result in excessive, unnecessary, costly further evaluations without proof that screening will reduce prostate cancer mortality and; (3) the morbidity of treatment is considered excessive. A definitive answer to this controversy, based on a well-designed randomized trial, is not available at present. Two trials are currently recruiting patients to answer these questions regarding detection and treatment of prostate cancer. In a National Cancer Institute trial, patients are being randomized to prostate cancer screening and nonscreening arms, and in another trial, men with localized prostate cancer are being randomized to surgery and no treatment. Because of the long natural history of untreated prostate cancer, it will be more than a decade before definitive answers are available.

CONCLUSION

Urologic surgeons have been active in the development of guidelines based on empirical evidence and outcomes for the management of common urologic diseases. There is a need for well-designed studies that provide the data to support management decisions leading to optimal patient outcomes. Decision analysis models using invalid probability and rate inputs have been substituted for valid trials needed to improve the quality of care for men with prostate cancer. Men with BPH have benefited from evidence provided by prospective trials that clarify the natural history of the disease and the response to alternative treatment strategies.

REFERENCES

1. Goldstein I, Lue TF, Padma-Nathan H, et al. Oral sildenafil in the treatment of erectile dysfunction. N Engl J Med 1998;338:1397–1404.

2. Segura JW, Preminger GM, Assimos DG, et al. Nephrolithiasis clinical guidelines panel summary report on the management of staghorn calculi. J Urol 1994;151:1648–51.

3. Segura JW, Preminger GM, Assimos DG, et al. Ureteral stones clinical guidelines panel summary report on the management of ureteral calculi. J Urol 1997;158:1915–21.

4. Leach GE, Dmochowski RR, Appell RA, et al. Female stress urinary incontinence clinical guidelines panel summary report on surgical management of female stress urinary incontinence. J Urol 1997;158:875–80.

5. Mantague DK, Barada JH, Belker AM, et al. Clinical guidelines panel on erectile dysfunction: summary report on the treatment of organic erectile dysfunction. J Urol 1996;156:2007–11.

6. Middleton RG, Thompson IM, Austenfeld MS, et al. Prostate cancer clinical guidelines panel summary report on the management of clinically localized prostate cancer. J Urol 1995;154:2144–8.

7. McConnell JD, Barry MJ, Bruskewitz RC, et al. Benign prostatic hyperplasia: diagnosis and treatment. Clinical Practice Guideline No. 8. Rockville (MD): US Department of Health and Human Services; 1994.

8. Krahn MD, Mahoney JE, Eckman MH, Trachtenberg J, et al. Screening for prostate cancer: a decision analytic view. JAMA 1994;272:773–80.

9. Johansson JE, Adami HO, Andersson SO, et al. High 10-year survival rate in patients with early, untreated prostatic cancer. JAMA 1992;267:2191–6.

10. Aus G, Hugosson J, Norlen L. Long-term survival and mortality in prostate cancer treated with noncurative intent. J Urol 1995;154:460–5.

11. Fleming C, Wasson JH, Albertsen PC, et al, for the Prostate Patient Outcomes Research Team. A decision analysis of alternative treatment strategies for clinically localized prostate cancer. JAMA 1993;269:2650–8.

12. Cowen ME, Cahill D, Kattan MW, Miles BJ. The value or utility of prostate cancer states. J Urol 1996;155:376A.

13. Beck JR, Kattan MW, Miles BJ. A critique of the decision analysis for clinically localized prostate cancer. J Urol 1994;152:1894–9.

14. Guess HA, Arrighi HM, Metter EJ, Fozard JL. The cumulative prevalence of prostatism matches the autopsy prevalence of benign prostatic hyperplasia. Prostate 1990;17:241–6.

15. Berry SJ, Coffey DS, Walsh PC, Ewing LL. The development of human benign prostatic hyperplasia with age. J Urol 1984;132:474–9.

16. Isaacs JT. Importance of the natural history of benign prostatic hyperplasia in the evaluation of pharmacologic intervention. Prostate Suppl 1990;3:1–7.

17. Barry MJ. Medical outcomes research and benign prostatic hyperplasia. Prostate Suppl 1990;3:61–74.

18. Barry MJ. Physicians: taking the lead. Health Manage Q 1991;13(2):20–3.

19. Lu-Yao GL, Barry MJ, Chang C-H, et al, and the Prostate Outcomes Research Team (PORT). Transurethral resection of the prostate among Medicare beneficiaries in the United States: time trends and outcomes. Urology 1994;44:692–8.

20. McPherson K, Wennberg JE, Hovind OB, Clifford P. Small area variations in the use of common surgical procedures: an international comparison of New England, England and Norway. N Engl J Med 1982;307:1310–14.

21. Peters CA, Walsh PC. The effect of nafarelin acetate, a luteinizing-hormone-releasing hormone agonist, on benign prostatic hyperplasia. N Engl J Med 1987;317:599–604.

22. Caine M. The present role of alpha adrenergic blockers in the treatment of benign prostatic hypertrophy. J Urol 1986;136:1–6.

23. Gormley G, Stoner E, Bruskewitz RC, et al. The effect of finasteride in men with benign prostatic hyperplasia. N Engl J Med 1992;327:1185–91.

24. Hieble JP, Caine M, Zalaznik E. In vitro characterization of the alpha-adrenoceptors in human prostate. Eur J Pharmacol 1985;107:111–17.

25. Lepor H, Shapiro E. Characterization of the alpha-1 adrenergic receptor in human benign prostatic hyperplasia. J Urol 1984;132:1226–9.

26. Barry MJ, Fowler FJ Jr, O'Leary MP, et al, and the Measurement Committee of the American Urological Association. The American Urological Association symptom index for benign prostatic hyperplasia. J Urol 1992;148:1549–57.

27. Barry MJ, Fowler FJ Jr, O'Leary MP, et al, and the Measurement Committee of the American Urological Association. Correlation of the American Urological Association symptom index with self-administered versions of the Madsen-Iversen, Boyarsky and Maine Medical Assessment Program symptom indexes. J Urol 1992;148:1558–63.

28. Cockett ATK, Barry MJ, Holtgrewe HL, et al. Indications for treatment of benign prostatic hyperplasia. Cancer 1992;70:280–3.

29. Holtgrewe HL. An American Urological Association prospective, randomized clinical trial in the treatment of benign prostatic hyperplasia. Cancer 1992;70:351–4.

30. Roos NP, Wennberg JE, Malenka DJ, et al. Mortality and reoperation after open and transurethral resection of the prostate for benign prostatic hyperplasia. N Engl J Med 1989;320:1120–3.

31. Concato J, Horwitz RI, Feinstein AR, et al. Problems of co-morbidity in mortality after prostatectomy. JAMA 1992;267:1077–86.

32. Graverson PH, Gasser TC, Wasson JH, et al. Controversies about indications for transurethral resection of the prostate. J Urol 1989;141:475–81.

33. Wasson JH, Reda DJ, Bruskewitz RC, et al. A comparison of transurethral surgery with watchful waiting for moderate symptoms of benign prostatic hyperplasia. N Engl J Med 1995;332:75–9.

34. Imperato-McGinley J, Guerrero L, Gautier T, Peterson RE. Steroid 5a-reductase deficiency in man: an inherited form of male pseudohermaphroditism. Science 1974;186:1213–15.

35. Walsh PC, Madden JD, Harrod MJ, et al. Familial incomplete male pseudohermaphroditism, type 2: decreased dihydrotestosterone formation in pseudovaginal perineoscrotal hypospadias. N Engl J Med 1974;291:944–9.

36. Stoner E, and the Finasteride Study Group. The clinical effects of a 5a-reductase inhibitor, finasteride, on benign prostatic hyperplasia. J Urol 1992;147:1298–1302.

37. Finasteride Study Group. Finasteride (MK-906) in the treatment of benign prostatic hyperplasia. Prostate 1993;22:291–9.

38. Lepor H, Williford WO, Barry MJ, et al. The efficacy of terazosin, finasteride, or both in benign prostatic hyperplasia. N Engl J Med 1996;335:533–9.

39. McConnell JD, Bruskewitz RC, Walsh PC, et al. The effect of finasteride on the risk of acute urinary retention and the need for surgical treatment among men with benign prostatic hyperplasia. N Engl J Med 1998;338:557–63.

40. Walsh PC. Treatment of benign prostatic hyperplasia. N Engl J Med 1996;335:586–7.

CHAPTER 43

Neurosurgery

Donlin M. Long, MD, PhD, Mohammed Benn Debba, MD,
and Henry Brem, MD

Neurologic surgery comprises a broad spectrum of procedures to treat an equally broad spectrum of diseases that affect the brain, spinal cord, peripheral nerves, and the tissues that surround them as well as their vascular supply. Neurosurgeons treat intra- and extracranial abnormalities of many kinds. The majority of neurosurgical practice relates to the spine. A small number of neurosurgeons specialize in peripheral nerve abnormalities. Relief of pain also is an important neurosurgical consideration. In addition to treating traditional diseases, neurosurgeons are trained to provide relief of symptoms of other neurologic diseases. Examples include the surgical treatment of epilepsy and the relief of tremor or other disorders of movement. In addition, there are still important indications for limited varieties of psychosurgery. Finally, neurosurgeons are required to render nonsurgical supportive care for both brain and spinal cord trauma, tumor, stroke, the effects of intracranial hemorrhage, spinal cord injury, and spinal cord compression. All of these are complex conditions that require detailed understanding of a diverse group of pathophysiologies that include membrane injury, axonal disruption, ischemia, and edema. Brain edema is a unique complicating factor which is unlike any condition found in any other organ system.[1]

Because of the complexity of the organs and the multiplicity of diseases that neurosurgeons treat, concerns for evidence have gone well beyond the need to determine the efficacy of specific operative procedures. Neurosurgeons were among the first to begin longitudinal clinical studies that have profoundly modified practice, and they continue to examine natural history and the results of operative and nonoperative treatments in a broad spectrum of neurosurgical diseases.

One of the earliest neurosurgically based outcome studies was the longitudinal examination of subarachnoid hemorrhage and the results of various therapies including surgery. This aneurysm study first delineated the lethality of subarachnoid hemorrhage, timing of rehemorrhage, and incidence of vasospasm. The results of pioneering surgical approaches were compared, leading to rapid improvement in the technical aspects of surgery and in the management of patients. Early practice dictated late surgery after 3 weeks of conservative care. Studies of the natural history and the outcome of surgery suggested that better results were obtained with urgent operation. Emergency surgery has also been compared with urgent surgery. Detailed analysis of outcomes has set standards by which aneurysm surgery is judged. Examination of patients has demonstrated the deficiencies in current management techniques and the problems that remain to be solved. Virtually the whole standard of practice for the managing of subarachnoid hemorrhage is based upon data from this 4-decade study.[2–4]

Perhaps the most important result of outcomes research in neurosurgery was the introduction of glucocorticoids in large dosages for the treatment of brain edema. Prior to steroid usage, brain edema could be treated only by hyperosmolar agents, which were of limited value. Brain tumor mortalities remained high, and much of the mortality was related to postoperative brain swelling. Amelioration of edema with glucosteroids brought a dramatic decrease in perioperative mortality. Because the decrease in mortality and morbidity was so dramatic, the original placebo-controlled studies were abandoned, and effectiveness studies were relied upon for proof of efficacy. Glucosteroid administration as a brain protectant when brain edema is present or expected is now routine in neurosurgical practice and undoubtedly has saved thousands of lives.[1,5–8]

Glucosteroids were also applied early in the management of spinal cord trauma, but definitive studies were not done for many years. In the recent past, massive doses of glucosteroids administered within 6 hours of cervical spinal cord trauma have shown a benefit of a statistically significant improvement in neurologic function in those patients treated. This was the first evidence that any therapy would benefit patients with severe spinal cord trauma, and the so-called steroid protocol has since become a standard part of neurosurgical management of spinal cord injury.[9–12]

Vasospasm remains a serious postoperative and postsubarachnoid hemorrhage complication in patients harboring intracranial aneurysms. It is responsible for serious adverse consequences in up to 20 percent of these patients. Controlled clinical trials of the β-blocking agent nimodipine demonstrated substantial reduction in the ischemic consequences of spasm. The studies were sufficient to result in Federal Drug Administration approval of nimodipine for this use, and the use of calcium channel blocking agents has become a standard perioperative treatment for patients with or at risk for vasospasm.[13]

Another important study was the examination of the value of the arterial bypass operation for prevention of stroke. Microanastomosis of an extracranial vessel with intracranial vessels, with or without an interposed graft, was devised as a way to provide collateral blood flow to the potentially ischemic brain. The operation was widely taught and employed until a controlled clinical trial of the operation's value for prevention of stroke demonstrated that patients who underwent the surgery fared no better than those who were treated with medical means. The operation was eliminated from neurosurgical practice for ischemic cerebrovascular disease although it remains of value when used to provide blood flow distal to a planned surgical occlusion of a major vessel. The saved medical costs from this modification of practice have been enormous.[14] Carotid endarterectomy was a popular operation for many years after its introduction for the treatment of ischemic events following carotid embolization or thrombosis. Individual surgeons were able to present huge series of patients, and there was a steady reduction in mortality and morbidity of the procedure. The very frequency of the operation led to a more serious review of its potential benefits. The North American Symptomatic Carotid Endarterectomy Trial collaboration study presented the results of the randomized clinical trial carried out at 50 centers in North America. This trial investigated the surgical results for patients with carotid stenosis between 30 percent and 70 percent and between 70 percent and 99 percent. This first study demonstrated substantial reduction in both major and minor stroke rates. A subsequent study, termed the Asymptomatic Carotid Atherosclerosis Study, followed similar lines. This was a prospective randomized clinical trial involving 39 North American clinical sites. It examined the value of endarterectomy for asymptomatic patients with carotid artery stenosis of 60 percent or greater. The study demonstrated that there was a reduced 5-year risk of ipsilateral stroke only if carotid endarterectomy was performed with less than a 3 percent perioperative morbidity. Aggressive management of modifiable risk factors was required as well. In 1998, the North American Symptomatic Carotid Endarterectomy Trial collaborators presented their data from a randomized trial of symptomatic patients with moderate stenosis between 50 percent and 69 percent. In this group of patients, endarterectomy yielded a moderate reduction in risk but only if surgical skill and perioperative management kept mortality and morbidity at an extremely low level. Patients with stenosis of less than 50 percent did not benefit from surgery.[15,16]

EVIDENCE-BASED STUDIES

There are three kinds of studies from which evidence is easily derived that can help modify practice. The best known of these is the clinical trial. In clinical trials, simple questions are asked that usually have dichotomous answers. Generally, these take the form of, "Is therapy A better than therapy B, or no therapy?" Populations compared must be homogenous and comparable, and questions must be simple. Random assignment is required. The controlled clinical trial is an appropriate way to examine the value of a surgical procedure versus medical treatment or no treatment or to examine the utility of a drug in the treatment of some nonsurgical condition.

The second important source of evidence that can influence medical practice is the effectiveness study. These studies are useful for the prospective evaluation of heterogenous groups of patients subjected to one or more forms of treatment for the same complaints or disease. To do an effectiveness study, it is necessary to have fixed entrance criteria and outcome measurements that are applied to all. Exclusion criteria are also required. All suitable patients are admitted to the study, the therapies they receive are recorded, and identical outcome measures are used for all. Thus, the value of each therapy can be assessed. This kind of study does not compare therapies directly; the outcomes measure the value of treatment for specific groups of patients. Comparisons are made only through controlled clinical trials. Nevertheless, the impact of many kinds of therapy on a particular disease can be accurately assessed through the effectiveness study. Outcome measures may be directly related to patients, but the study may also include a variety of socioeconomic measures of interest to those responsible for planning health care. It is also possible to identify homogenous subgroups within a large heterogenous population and to accurately predict outcomes of various therapies for them.

The third important source is the retrospective study. It is important to recognize the limitations of retrospective examination of patient outcomes in neurosurgery. Their greatest use is in examining outcomes from the public health standpoint. Costs, demographics of health care, and major factors such as serious morbidity and mortality are usually discernible from these data if they are sufficiently detailed. Prevalence of treatment in a population may be available although the patient base is often not well defined. It is not possible to compare therapies or outcomes through retrospective reviews because selection criteria for therapies are unknown. Nevertheless, much valuable information, particularly cost and socioeconomic data, can be derived from retrospective reviews.

At Johns Hopkins, we have employed all three types of studies with study outcomes that can substantiate changes in practice. These studies also identify health policy issues which need definition and discussion.

Typical Clinical Studies at Johns Hopkins

A Controlled Clinical Trial: Local Chemotherapy for Glioblastoma Multiforme

In 1985, Henry Brem at Johns Hopkins University, working with Robert S. Langer of the chemical engineering department at the Massachusetts Institute of Technology (M.I.T.), developed a new treatment approach to brain tumors.[17] They recognized that over 90 percent of brain tumor patients die of tumor within a 1- to 2-cm margin of the original tumor site and that most therapies appear to fail locally. They also noted that many therapies which appeared effective in vitro in the laboratory were ineffective when given systemically to patients. Simultaneous with these observations was the discovery by Langer's group at M.I.T. that a class of synthetic polymers, polyanhydrides, could be used to deliver macromolecules over a sustained period of time. These macromolecules were biodegradable and appeared to be biocompatible.[17]

Brem and Langer hypothesized that if chemotherapeutic agents could be delivered directly to a brain tumor in a sustained fashion by a biodegradable polymer, then the survival of these patients could be improved while minimizing the toxicity of the therapeutic agents themselves. To test this hypothesis, they elected to use an FDA-approved drug, carmustine (BCNU), together with the newly developed carboxyphenoxypropane anhydride with sebacic acid. The advantage of these polymers was that they could release BCNU with near zero-order kinetics, avoiding a burst release within the brain. The polymers were noncarcinogenic and could be formulated in such a manner that they could be delivered directly to a brain tumor resection cavity.[17]

Early in their work, they met with representatives of the U.S. Food and Drug Administration (FDA), explained their idea, and reviewed the necessary steps for initiating clinical trials. They agreed with the FDA that three types of experiments would be needed prior to initiating clinical trials. First, biocompatible studies in rats, rabbits, and monkeys were needed to determine that the polymer itself, as well as the polymer plus the chemotherapeutic agent, were safe to the brain and the rest of the body. Second, pharmacokinetic studies were needed to determine the concentrations of the drug to which the brain and the rest of the body would each be exposed as well as the biodistribution of the breakdown products of the biodegradable polymer. Last, a model would need to be developed with which the efficacy of this approach could be demonstrated and shown to be equal to or better than that of systemically administered drugs.[17,18]

Funds for these laboratory projects were obtained from Nova Pharmaceutical Corporation (the company that licensed the patent for the polyanhydrides from M.I.T.) and the National Cancer Institute of the National Institutes of Health. Each of the laboratory studies was carried out in the Johns Hopkins neurosurgery laboratory, and the work was published in peer reviewed journals. They demonstrated that the polymers with various concentrations of BCNU were safe in the brain, that virtually none of the drug was released into the systemic circulation, and that the drugs traveled significant distances within the brain for a period of 2 to 3 weeks. They further demonstrated in rats implanted with an intracerebral brain tumor that the median survival of animals treated with BCNU-impregnated polymers was significantly longer than that of those treated with systemic BCNU. When treated with locally administered chemotherapy delivered by polymer, 25 percent of the animals were cured of their tumors. This was compared to the 100 percent fatality in this tumor model when treated with conventional systemic administration of the same drug. Based on this laboratory information, clinical trials were initiated in 1987.[19]

Prior to starting the first clinical trial, there was considerable debate on whether to utilize BCNU or a different, newer drug. The arguments in favor of BCNU were that it was the only FDA-approved treatment for brain tumors and that it was well known and familiar to the clinical investigators who would participate in the trials. The arguments against BCNU were that it had a poor track record, with only about 30 percent of patients responding in a clinically significant manner, and that it was a relatively small molecule that was lipid soluble and therefore appropriate for systemic delivery. By contrast, water-soluble agents such as Taxol, carboplatin, or 4-hydroperoxycyclophosamide were poorly delivered systemically and were ideal for delivery by the polymer. In the end, however, they decided to introduce only one clinical variable (the new polymer system) rather than multiple variables (a new drug and a new polymer delivery system). Thus, the hypothesis entering the clinical studies was that a standard chemotherapeutic drug with which there was extensive clinical experience, could be administered in a safer and more effective manner by utilizing the newly developed polyanhydride polymer wafer discs.

To test this hypothesis, a phase I clinical trial was carried out at five leading brain tumor centers. There was discussion of whether to try the initial phase I trial for tumor recurrence or at the time of initial presentation. In oncology, all treatments work better at initial presentation rather than at recurrence, and initial presentation would have been the more appropriate time to treat these patients with the BCNU-impregnated polymer. However, a number of medical advisors recommended starting with recurrent brain tumors; since there was no known effective therapy for these patients, it would be appropriate to experiment with a new modality. The study proceeded in a five-institution phase I clinical trial to test the safety of the BCNU-impregnated wafers and to determine the optimal dosage.

Twenty-one patients who had unilateral recurrent malignant gliomas and who had failed standard therapies including surgery, radiation, and/or chemotherapy were entered into the study.[19] After resection of the recurrent brain tumor, the cavity was coated with up to eight BCNU polymer implants. Five patients were treated with 3.85 mg of BCNU in the polymer wafers, 5 patients with 7.7 mg of BCNU wafer, and 11 patients with 12.7 mg of BCNU wafer. This study demonstrated the safety of this approach since there were no untoward events that were attributed to the BCNU polymer wafer implants. With immediate survival of over 60 weeks after recurrence, these studies suggested improved survival and therefore were the basis of proceeding with phase III testing.[20]

Prior to the polymer study, no randomized prospective placebo-controlled study had been undertaken for developing a new therapy for malignant gliomas. However, there were many examples in the literature of phase II studies which failed to yield definitive results. It was therefore decided to follow a pathway similar to what had been done previously in the laboratory. A rigorous phase III prospective randomized placebo-controlled study for patients with recurrent malignant gliomas was designed using 3.85μg-loaded BCNU polymer implants. The study's hypothesis was that these BCNU polymer implants could reduce the 6-month mortality in patients undergoing reoperation for recurrent glioma. This study enrolled 222 patients in 27 medical centers in the United States and Canada. The patients in the treatment group received up to eight polymer implants loaded with 3.85μg of BCNU; the other patients underwent the same operation with empty placebo polymers. The code was broken 6 months after the last patient was entered into the study. The BCNU polymer implants had been given to 110 patients, and 112 patients received the placebo polymers. All of the known prognostic factors were equally randomized between the two groups. Of the patients who were given empty polymers, 47 percent were alive at 6 months in contrast to 60 percent of those treated with BCNU polymer implants. Seventy percent of the patients had the most aggressive type of malignant brain tumor, that is, glioblastoma multiforme. Among these patients, the 6-month survival was 50 percent greater in those with BCNU than in those with the empty polymers. Overall, the median survival of the patients who received BCNU polymers was 31 weeks versus 23 weeks for those who received placebo polymers. Multiple regression analysis was carried out. These findings demonstrated a statistically significant improvement in survival when any of the known prognostic factors for malignant brain tumors were controlled. There were no clinically important local or systemic adverse reactions to BCNU polymers demonstrated in this study.

Once these studies were underway and it became apparent that significant toxicity was not being demonstrated, the use of polymer implants as the initial therapy for brain tumors was evaluated. The first concern was whether the synergy between locally delivered chemotherapy and radiation therapy (which must be used as the initial therapy for brain tumors) would cause increased toxicity. To answer this question, initially monkeys were studied. The results demonstrated no difference between those monkeys receiving radiation without, or simultaneously with, Gliadel implants. Therefore, a phase I study at three institutions was done, demonstrating the safety of the Gliadel implant in conjunction with radiation therapy as the initial therapy.[21]

Valtonen and colleagues[22] in Helsinki, Finland, then carried out a phase III randomized prospective placebo-controlled study designed the same as the previous study in the United States, except that these patients were initially treated with the Gliadel wafer[22] or the placebo wafer. Unlike in the United States, where the clinical trials involved many different treatment modalities in addition to the variable of placebo or chemotherapy polymer, patients in Europe were treated more simply and only received polymer at the time of surgery and radiation therapy, with no further treatments. These different approaches to treating malignant gliomas reflect differing medical philosophies among surgeons and medical oncologists in different countries.

The Valtonen study randomized and entered 32 patients.[22] The study was kept blinded for 2 years. Only 32 patients were entered due to lack of supply of the polymer from Nova Pharmaceutical Corporation. (In the ensuing years, Nova was bought out and was no longer able to produce the polymers. It was not until a few years later that the production of the polymer wafers was resumed by a new company, Guilford Pharmaceuticals Inc., which continued to carry out clinical trials.) Each arm consisted of 16 patients. The median survival was 58 weeks for the group receiving BCNU polymer implants in constrast to 40 weeks in the control arm (p-value = .012). Perhaps of greater significance, 33 percent of the treatment group was alive at 2 years compared to 6 percent of the placebo group. At 3 years, 25 percent of the treatment group was alive as compared to 6 percent of the patients in the placebo polymer treated in the standard manner.

This study was criticized for its small size (32 patients) and for there being a mixture of grade III and grade IV gliomas in the treatment group while the placebo group had all grade IV gliomas. Therefore, a separate analysis was carried out comparing the 11 glioblastoma patients in the Gliadel-treated arm with the 16 patients with glioblastoma on placebo. Again, the improvement in median survival was statistically significant. There was minimal toxicity attributed to the use of the polymer wafers.

A further study was then carried out to look at safety in a large number of patients. This study demonstrated that patients treated with Gliadel wafers needed to be watched for possible increased incidence of seizure, brain swelling, and infection, all of which could be treated in a straightforward manner by medical therapies.

The data from the above studies was presented to the FDA in 1996, 9 years after the first clinical trial was initiated. Based on the large-scale phase III trial, the FDA gave approval to Gliadel for the treatment of recurrent glioblastoma multiforme. The FDA withheld listing on the package insert the use of Gliadel as the initial treatment of brain tumors until a repeat large-scale phase III study could be carried out. This trial is currently underway in Europe with a target of entering 200 patients. The Canadian regulatory agency approved Gliadel both for initial therapy and recurrence, on the basis of these studies. Drug approval has also been granted in Israel, Europe, and South America.

The rigor of the clinical trials for the Gliadel wafer led to the first FDA approval in 23 years of a new treatment for brain tumors. The trials represent a new approach for treating brain tumors that was hypothesis driven and was first evaluated and tested in the laboratory and then brought systematically from phase I to phase III clinical trials. Its role in treating malignant brain tumors was critically analyzed and has withstood the rigorous analysis of the FDA, leading to its introduction as an addition to the treatment armamentarium for brain tumors.

Effectiveness Study: Current Therapies for Low Back Pain

The National Low Back Pain Study was a nationwide, eight-center evaluation of the outcomes of current therapies for patients with back and leg pain referred to expert orthopedic and neurospinal surgeons. Over 4,000 patients were entered according to specific criteria. The surgeons involved were allowed to evaluate and treat patients as they saw fit, and all treatments in and out of the study were recorded in longitudinal follow-up by nonclinical research staff. Outcome criteria included pain, function, psychological status, need for further therapy, and medication use. All therapies were evaluated at 3 months by the institution, and at 6, 12, and 24 months by study personnel unrelated to the patients' clinical care. Three major groups of patients undergoing similar treatments were identified in the database. One large group received no treatment of any kind after admission to the study, and this allowed them to constitute a natural history of the disease group. The largest group received only conservative care. Over thirty kinds of conservative care, alone or in combinations, were examined. One group came to immediate surgery or had surgery done 6 months or more after entering the study, and patients in the third surgical subgroup received operations from surgeons outside the study, against the advice of study physicians. All of these groupings could be examined longitudinally. Demographic data proved the study cohort to be a cross section of the population of the United States. The findings of the study oppose many of the beliefs of experts in the field of spinal disease, most of which are held without valid and generalizable evidence. Detailed examination of the psychologic status of the patients revealed no differences from the normal ill population. Many hold that low back pain is an important psychosomatic complaint and that there is a large psychologic component in the typical patient. No evidence was found to support this contention. Chronicity is thought by many to lead to the consequences of the pain syndrome, that is, pain behavior, psychological deterioration, depression, anxiety, and neurotic fixation upon pain. It is commonly stated in the pain literature that 6 months of chronic pain is enough to produce these symptoms. The study found no evidence of a correlation between chronicity and these psychologic symptoms. Psychopathology was present in 5 percent of patients and bore no relationship to chronicity, nor was there any evidence that unrelieved pain in our patients led to the development of the chronic pain syndrome. The only predictor of the chronic pain syndrome was pre-existing psychologic disturbance. It is generally held that patients with these spinal problems spontaneously improve, and the majority of patients with acute spinal pain do improve. However, the study was able to identify a group of patients in whom spontaneous improvement did not occur and who experienced the "persistent pain syndrome." When pain did not spontaneously relent within the first 3 to 6 months, there was no evidence of remission in the next 2-year follow-up period. The patients were stable, and improvements in all outcome measures were not statistically significant.

The impact of conservative care upon outcome functions was assessed. These nonoperative care programs included physical therapy, exercise, manipulation therapy, drug treatments of many kinds, alternative medical therapies including acupuncture, and intensive rehabilitation programs such as back schools and pain treatment centers. A number of other forms of therapy were also examined, including those sought by the patient as well as those prescribed by physicians. All have been claimed to be effective for complaints of back and leg pain. Most of the evidence is anecdotal or based on the presentation of uncontrolled therapy for groups of patients in whom selection and diagnostic criteria are undefined. No conservative treatment program that could be examined could be differentiated from no treatment in terms of outcome. None had a discernible effect upon patients. This does not imply that any of these therapies might not have an effect on a specific subgroup of patients, but no such subgroups were discerned. For the patient with back and leg pain persisting for more than 3 to 6 months, the effect of such treatments cannot be separated from no treatment. One group receiving a specific therapy was improved. Intensive in-patient/outpatient physical rehabilitation measures were employed at a single clinic with resulting significant improvement in function for patients. This indicates that the study techniques would have determined improvement in subgroups of patients had they occurred with any of the therapies the patients underwent. It cannot be stated from the data that any of these therapies, employed by specialists adept at selecting patients for their treatments, might not have an effect. However, the study concluded that the conservative treatments as currently employed by a broad spectrum of practitioners across the United States have no discernible effect upon the disease they are supposed to treat.

By contrast, the small number of patients who came to surgery were immediately relieved of symptoms and improved in function. Maximum improvement occurred within 3 months for those operated upon promptly. The need for surgery was never prevented by interposition of conservative care. Delayed surgery prolonged the recovery period by an average of 15 months. Patients operated upon outside the study against the advice of study experts generally worsened, and the overall success rate was 10 percent or less. By contrast, 90 percent of patients who underwent a first or second surgical procedure within the study were improved no matter what type of surgery was required.[23–27]

Retrospective Study: Outcome of Craniotomy for Brain Tumor

The third form of study from which evidence can be derived is the retrospective examination of outcomes of current therapies for categories of patients. When performed on the practice of a single individual or within a single institution, outcome is so influenced by selection bias that the study becomes only a description of the practice of that individual or institution. However, when data are available for a sizable region, it is possible to assess the outcomes of current therapies across a broad spectrum of practitioners and institutions. The Maryland Health Services Cost Review Commission database offers an opportunity to examine cost and outcome of specific procedures in specific diagnoses over a substantial period. We recently examined this database for the years 1990 to 1996 to ascertain the theoretical effects of regionalization of tertiary care for brain tumors. All patients undergoing craniotomy in Maryland for that time period could be studied, and 4,723 patients were included. Available outcome measures included mortality, average total charges, and length of hospital stay. Data for all surgeons and hospitals in the state were available for comparison. Hospitals fell into two categories: high volume (> 50 craniotomies per year) and low volume (< 50 craniotomies per year). Nearly 50 percent of the craniotomies were performed at two hospitals in the state. The remaining hospitals fell into the low-volume category. When craniotomies were examined as a group, mortality in community-based low-volume hospitals was 4.9 percent and was 2.5 percent in high-volume centers ($p < .001$). This is true when disease equivalency is assumed; in fact, high-volume centers care for more seriously ill patients. Average length of stay in tertiary care high-volume centers was 9.9 days versus 12.5 days in high-volume community hospitals; however, average cost was $16,997 in low-volume centers and $19,356 in high-volume centers. The obvious conclusion is that lives can be saved (46 patients in this example) but at a somewhat higher cost if regionalization of craniotomies was to take place.

Further analysis of the data provides more information. The discrepancies between low-volume and high-volume hospitals become more apparent. Mortality for craniotomy for metastatic disease was above 10 percent in low-volume hospitals and was 3.8 percent in high-volume centers. For benign neoplasms, the hospital with the highest volume recorded a 1.3 percent mortality rate while the mortality rate in the remainder of the hospitals studied was 2.7 percent. With both diagnoses, costs were less in the high-volume hospitals. For intrinsic malignant neoplasms, mortality and charges were equivalent, but other data demonstrated that patients who underwent craniotomy at one of the regional centers had access to extensive investigational protocols which extended functional life.[28] A similar analysis has demonstrated the advantage of carrying out cerebral aneurysm surgery in large-volume medical centers in New York State.[29]

Development of Guidelines

An important technique used to evaluate and improve outcome is the compilation of current data for analysis by experts, a technique used by the Health Policy Institute to develop guidelines for practice. The guidelines recently developed for the management of acute low back pain serve as an example. In such a study, a group of experts in one institution or in multiple sites assemble to examine the efficacy of current therapies for a particular problem to develop guidelines that will provide a template for recommended management of that health problem. The usual strategy is first to develop arbitrary weighting and ranking criteria by which published material can be judged. Typically, the controlled clinical trial is given the greatest weight. Effectiveness studies have not been given the weight that they deserve. Uncontrolled prospective reviews are better than retrospective analyses, and unsubstantiated reports of treatment are given the least weight. The published opinions of experts are considered but are weighted according to the data that supports them. The articles are then ranked by subgroup, usually treatment type, diagnostic modality, and verification of outcome. The original broad category of patients may also be subdivided into homogenous groups. Literature reviews and meta-analyses are considered, and those that achieve statistical validity are given more credence than those that do not.

These data are collated and used by the experts to create an arbitrary set of rules which if followed, will provide an adequate outcome most of the time. Typically, the suggested consensus rules are published after review by many experts and then discussed for years since they often are at variance with accepted practice or have major implications for one group of practitioners. The acute care guidelines, under continual debate, are a typical example. Following the techniques outlined, those who developed and reviewed the acute care guidelines concluded that most patients with acute back and leg pain require no evaluation and no treatment. Unusually severe or persistent pain, neurologic deficit, or evidence of intercurrent disease might lead to urgent evaluation and treatment, but no therapy was indicated for the majority of patients. All the usual physical modalities were rejected although a minor effect for manipulation therapy applied in a specific period was noted. Thus, the guidelines reject virtually all imaging and therapeutic maneuvers in the first month. Such guidelines might have dramatic effects on practice but their implementation is voluntary. Those whose activities would be most curtailed are the most likely to be critical and the least likely to follow the guidelines no matter how rationally derived they are.[30]

THE IMPACT OF EVIDENCE IN NEUROSURGERY

The examples given illustrate the impact of each type of investigation. There were three clinical trials cited. The first involved use of a drug (glucosteroid) that had such a dramatic effect that placebo-controlled clinical trials could not be continued. This is an important issue as evidence-based studies are implemented. While other concurrent factors also were important, the dramatic decrease in mortality from brain tumors occurred with the introduction of steroids into practice; hence, thousands of lives have been saved over the intervening years. Virtually all patients with brain tumors and brain edema undergoing craniotomy are now treated with steroids. The impact has been enormous and world-wide.[1]

The use of nimodipine to reduce ischemic deficits following vasospasm is an example of a focused therapy applicable to a specific, well-defined group of patients. The study suggested that the incidence of clinically significant ischemia from vasospasm could be reduced from 20 percent of all patients undergoing aneurysm surgery to approximately 7 percent. Calcium channel blocking agents are now used routinely in craniotomy for vascular lesions. Their impact is much less than that of glucosteroids, but these drugs are still an important adjunct, reducing morbidity and improving outcome for many patients.[13]

The clinical trial that demonstrates extended survival in patients with glioblastoma using local chemotherapeutic agents is important for another reason: it is the first evidence for increased longevity attributable to a new therapy in patients with malignant glioma. No other adjunctive treatment employed over the years has demonstrated such an effect.[31] The rigors of the randomized prospective placebo-controlled clinical studies led to achieving FDA approval of a new therapy for patients with brain tumors. It is unlikely this would have been achieved using less rigorous evaluation methods. These studies now set a new standard to judge future therapies. They also demonstrate a "proof of principle" which will permit other new therapies to be evaluated, for example, polymer-releasing steroids[32] or other biological agents.[17–19,28]

The effectiveness study is also an excellent way to change practice. The data from the National Low Back Pain Study (in publication) and the guidelines for acute low back pain management certainly should change the care for one of the major public health problems in the United States. The guidelines developed for acute back pain indicate that evaluation and management should be by symptomatic care without the need for expensive imaging or physical modalities, and early surgery is indicated only for a small number of patients. This effectiveness study first identifies a subgroup of patients who do not improve spontaneously and who can be identified after 1 to 3 months. It also demonstrates that for patients with persistent back pain, the same physical modalities that are unnecessary in the acute situation are ineffective later as well. The popular physical therapy techniques, including manipulation, acupuncture, and many less common similar modalities, produced no discernible effect upon the complaint, pain, or function. These data have enormous implications for current practice since physical therapy, manipulation therapy, acupuncture, and a host of other treatments are routinely employed in these patients at substantial cost.[26,27]

It is important that such an effectiveness study not be generalized at face value and that specific treatment claims are analyzed through additional studies. Clinical trials can follow a well-done effectiveness study to be certain that a therapy should be accepted or rejected. Once these data are available, it is possible to make specific statements restricting the use of treatments known to be ineffective or harmful. Another important use of the effectiveness study is to analyze the success of a particular treatment. The surgeons involved in our study obviously were very adept at choosing those patients who would most benefit from operation. The patients who underwent surgery against the advice of the study surgeons generally worsened. The data can be analyzed to determine the predictors of success and failure, and these predictors at least can be made known to the medical public. The potential use of such data to restrict patient and physician choice is a philosophical issue that remains to be settled in American medicine.

The guideline protocols are useful for synthesizing known information in a field. Unfortunately, those promulgating the guidelines rarely have the capacity to enforce them. Incorporation of guidelines into practice is a matter for individual physicians. When the guidelines conflict with current practice, pluralism usually defeats science. Another problem with the guidelines concept is that lack of proof of efficacy of any modality may only be lack of information. The fact that we do not have data which proves or disproves the value of a particular treatment does not mean that the therapy is not valuable; it means only that the data supporting the treatment are not available. This problem will probably limit the use of guidelines as a tool for serious restructuring of practice. Nevertheless, guidelines play an important role in telling us what we know, what we do not know, and what information is required to prove or disprove the value of a particular treatment.

ISSUES FOR FURTHER STUDIES

The authors believe that virtually all therapeutic aspects of medicine should be evidence-based.[33,34] Neurosurgery is a small specialty that deals with a specific number of circumscribed diseases and is thus an ideal area in which to carry out the studies required to provide evidence for the value of particular treatments. Surgical technique plays such an important role in neurosurgery, and has been so venerated over the years, that neurosurgeons are just beginning to enter the evidence-based paradigm. Much of neurosurgical education remains "how I do it," not what is best to do. There is another important aspect of evidence-based medicine that is not so apparent: the fact that one expert surgeon using a technique achieves specific results does not imply that all surgeons using that technique will achieve the same results.[35–38] Thus, evidence is required not only for the best surgeons at the most famous institutions but for all practitioners wherever they work. Only when the individual data of individual surgeons are known and compared will the practice of evidence-based medicine be truly achieved.[39–43]

Needs for the future fall in three broad categories. First, there is an important need for ongoing studies of the kinds described for important neurosurgical diseases. Second, it is important to develop outcome measures that can be applied across specific geographic areas, across the country, and across the world, to determine the outcome of what neurosurgeons now do. Finally, individual surgeons need a mechanism to continuously monitor their own treatment outcomes to those of other physicians treating similar patients.

An important need is the definition of patients currently undergoing spinal surgery and the analysis of their outcomes. Every new procedure should be assessed before it is made available if it is a departure from standard practice. Minor variations in hardware or surgical technique do not require such proof. However, if a radical new concept like percutaneous discectomy is introduced, the studies proving its value should occur before the technique is popularized among spinal surgeons. Neurosurgeons need much better definitions of who will benefit from a specific treatment and who will not. For example, there are important questions in the field of spinal disease waiting to be addressed: Does spinal decompressive surgery satisfactorily treat patients with spinal stenosis? Who should be fused and who should not? Does instrumentation significantly improve outcomes for patients? Does decompressive surgery play a role in spinal cord trauma and if so, what is the appropriate timing of surgery? Are there specific conservative spinal rehabilitation programs which will benefit the majority of patients with persistent low back pain? Any group claiming that their particular treatment is effective for patients with low back pain should be expected to demonstrate this by appropriately designed controlled clinical trials.

The comparison of focused radiation with traditional surgery for many kinds of benign tumors is important. The use of clinical trials in the field of brain tumors is well established, and the neuro-oncologists have led the neurosurgeons in this regard. The natural histories of many of the benign tumors, particularly those that occur at the base of the skull, need to be studied. The value of the radical techniques of skull-based surgery should be examined through outcome studies.

Management of vasospasm is still an issue, and any new treatment certainly is amenable to clinical trial. The management of arteriovenous malformations is difficult to study because of the number of modalities used; however, claims for the efficacy of radiosurgery, for instance, need to be substantiated as do outcomes of all treatments. The overall outcome for the patient is important to know in addition to the mortality and specific effects of individual treatments.

We need the ability to determine if guidelines have an effect on practice. The questions raised by guidelines (and particularly any negative answers to those questions) should be explored carefully before sweeping changes in practice occur.[44]

After assessment of outcome of what we now do, the most important issue is how new technology is introduced into neurosurgical practice. Endovascular techniques are currently popular, and attempts are being made to substitute endovascular procedures for traditional endarterectomy. It may also be possible to expand these endovascular techniques to previously untreatable intracranial disease by controlled clinical trials to determine their place in the management of vascular disease. The EC/IC study[16,45] and the carotid endarterectomy studies are prototypes for how such questions can be asked and answered with major impact upon the practice of neurosurgery.

REFERENCES

1. Samdani AF, Tamargo RJ, Long DM. Brain tumor edema and the role of the blood-brain barrier. In: Vecht CJ, editor. Handbook of clinical neurology. Vol. 23(67). The Netherlands: Elsevier Science BV; 1997.p. 71–102.

2. Adams HP Jr, Kassell NF, Torner JC, et al. Early management of aneurysmal subarachnoid hemorrhage: a report of the Cooperative Aneurysm Study. J Neurosurg 1981;54:141–5.

3. Kassell NF, Adams HP Jr, Torner JC, Sahs AL. Influence of timing of admission after aneurysmal subarachnoid hemorrhage on overall outcome: report of the Cooperative Aneurysm Study. Stroke 1981;12:620–3.

4. Torner JC, Kassell NF, Wallace RB, Adams HP Jr. Preoperative prognostic factors for rebleeding and survival in aneurysm patients receiving antifibrinolytic therapy: report of the Cooperative Aneurysm Study. Neurosurgery 1981;9:506–13.

(The work described above was partially funded by NIH, NCDDG CA52857 and the National Cancer Institute, CA62474. Dr. Brem is a consultant to Guilford Pharmaceuticals, Inc. and to Rhone-Poulenc Rorer, and Guilford has provided a gift for research in Dr. Brem's laboratory. The Johns Hopkins University and Dr. Brem own Guilford stock, the sale of which is subject to certain restrictions under University policy. The terms of this arrangement are being managed by the University in accordance with its conflict of interest policies.)

5. Long DM. The ultrastructure of cerebral edema and its response to glucosteroid administration. Med Bull U of Minn 1965 May;36(9):339–41.

6. Long DM, Hartmann JF, French LA. The response of human cerebral edema to glucosteroid administration. An electron microscopic study. Neurology 1996 May;16(5):521–8.

7. Long DM, Maxwell RE, French LA. The effect of glucosteroids upon cold induced edema. VI Congress of International Pathology; Aug 31–Sept 4; Paris. 1970:1035–7.

8. Maxwell RE, Long DM, French LA. The clinical effects of a synthetic gluco-corticoid used for brain edema in the practice of neurosurgery. In: Reulen HJ, Schurmann K, editors. Steroids and Brain Edema. Berlin, Heidelberg, New York: Springer-Verlag; 1972.p. 219–32.

9. Bracken MB, Collins WF, Freeman DF, et al. Efficacy of methylprednisolone in acute spinal cord injury. JAMA 1984;251:45–52.

10. Bracken MB, Shepard MJ, Collins WF, et al. A randomized, controlled trial of methylprednisolone or naloxone in the treatment of acute spinal cord injury. Results of the second National Acute Spinal Cord Injury Study. N Engl J Med 1990;322:1405–11.

11. Bracken MB, Shepard MJ, Collins WF, et al. Methylprednisolone or naloxone treatment after acute spinal cord injury: 1-year follow-up data. Results of the second National Acute Spinal Cord Injury Study. J Neurosurg 1992;76:23–31.

12. Bracken MB, Shepard MJ, Hellenbrand KG, et al. Methylprednisolone and neurological function 1 year after spinal cord injury. Results of the National Acute Spinal Cord Injury Study. J Neurosurg 1985;63:704–13.

13. Allen GS, Ahn HS, Preziosi TJ, Battye R, et al. Cerebral arterial spasm—a controlled trial of nimodipine in patients with subarachnoid hemorrhage. N Engl J Med 1983;308(11):619–24.

14. The EC/IC Bypass Study Group. Failure of extracranial-intracranial arterial bypass to reduce the risk of ischemic stroke. Results of an international randomized trial. N Engl J Med 1985;313:1191–1200.

15. Barnett HJM, Taylor DW, Eliasziw M, et al. Benefit of carotid endarterectomy in patients with symptomatic moderate or severe stenosis. N Engl J Med 1998;339:1415–25.

16. North American Symptomatic Carotid Endarterectomy Trial collaborators. Beneficial effect of carotid endarterectomy in symptomatic patients with high-grade carotid stenosis. N Engl J Med 1991;325:445–53.

17. Brem H, Langer R. Polymer-based drug delivery to the brain. Scientific American: Science and Medicine 1996; 3:52–61.

18. Brem H, Tamargo RJ, Olivi A, et al. Biodegradable polymers for controlled delivery of chemotherapy with and without radiation therapy in the monkey brain. J Neurosurg 1994;80:283–90.

19. Brem H, Mahaley MS, Vick NA, et al. Interstitial chemotherapy with drug polymer implants for the treatment of recurrent gliomas. J Neurosurg 1991;74:441–6.

20. Brem H, Piantadosi S, Burger PC, et al, for the Polymer-Brain Tumor Treatment Group. Placebo-controlled trial of safety and efficacy of intraoperative controlled delivery by biodegradable polymers of chemotherapy for recurrent gliomas. Lancet 1995;345:1008–12.

21. Brem H, Ewend MG, Piantadosi S, et al. The safety of interstitial chemotherapy with BCNU-loaded polymer followed by radiation therapy in the treatment of newly diagnosed malignant gliomas: phase I trial. J Neurooncol 1995;26:111–23.

22. Valtonen S, Timonen U, Toivanen P, et al. Interstitial chemotherapy with carmustine-loaded polymers for high-grade gliomas: a randomized double-blind study. Neurosurgery 1997; 41:44–8.

23. Ackerman SJ, Steinberg EP, Bryan RN, et al. Persistent low back pain in patients suspected of having herniated nucleus pulposus: radiologic predictors of functional outcome—implications for treatment selection. Radiology 1997 Jun;203(3):815–22.

24. Ackerman SJ, Steinberg EP, Bryan RN, et al. Trends in diagnostic imaging for low back pain: has MR imaging been a substitute or add-on? Radiology 1997 May;203(2):533–8.

25. BenDebba M, Torgerson WS, Long DM. Personality traits, pain duration and severity, functional impairment, and psychological distress in patients with persistent low back pain. Pain 1997; 72:115–25.

26. Long DM, BenDebba M, Torgerson WS, et al. Persistent back pain and sciatica in the United States: patient characteristics. J Spinal Disord 1996;9(1):40–58.

27. Long DM, Zeidman SM. Outcome of low back pain therapy. In: Hadley MN, editor. Perspectives in neurological surgery Vol. 5(1). St. Louis (MO): Quality Medical Publishing; 1994.p. 41–51.

28. Long DM, Gordon T, Bowman H, et al. Evaluation of outcome and cost of craniotomy for tumor performed in regional academic referral centers [forthcoming]. JAMA

29. Solomon RA, Mayer SA, Tarmey JJ. Relationship between the volume of craniotomies for cerebral aneurysm performed at New York state hospitals and in-hospital mortality. Stroke 1996;27(1):13–17.

30. Quick reference guide for clinicians, number 14: acute low back pain problems in adults: assessment and treatment. U.S. Department of Health and Human Services; 1994 Dec. AHCPR Publication No. 95-0643.

31. Walker MD, Green SB, Byar DP, et al. Randomized comparisons of radiotherapy and nitosoureas for the treatment of malignant glioma after surgery. N Engl J Med 1980;303:1323–9.

32. Tamargo RJ, Sills AK, Reinhard CS, et al. Interstitial delivery of dexamethasone in the brain for the reduction of peritumoral edema. J Neurosurg 1991;74:956–61.

33. Long DM. Expanding clinical research is mandatory for future of medicine. Academic Physician and Scientist 1997 Sep/Oct;2-3.

34. Luft HS. The relation between surgical volume and mortality: an explanation of causal factors and alternative models. Med Care 1980;18(9):940–59.

35. Begg CB, Cramer LD, Hoskins WJ, Brennan MF. Impact of hospital volume on operative mortality for major cancer surgery. JAMA 1998;280(20):1747–51.

36. Gordon TA, Burleyson GP, Tielsch JM, Cameron JL. The effects of regionalization on cost and outcome for one general high-risk procedure. Ann Surg 1995;221(1):43–9.

37. Jollis JG, Pertson ED, DeLong ER, et al. The relation between the volume of coronary angioplasty procedures at hospitals treating Medicare beneficiaries and short-term mortality. N Engl J Med 1994;331:1625–9.

38. McArdle CS, Hole D. Impact of variability among surgeons on postoperative morbidity and mortality and ultimate survival. BMJ 1991;302:1501–5.

39. Gillis CR, Hole DJ. Survival outcome of care by specialist surgeons in breast cancer: a study of 3786 patients in the west of Scotland. BMJ 1996;312:145–53.

40. Hannan EL, O'Donnell JF, Kilburn H, et al. Investigation of the relationship between volume and mortality for surgical procedures performed in New York state hospitals. JAMA 1989;262(4):503–10.

41. Hillner BE, Smith TJ (editorial). Hospital volume and patient outcomes in major cancer surgery: a catalyst for quality assessment and concentration of cancer services. JAMA 1998;280(20):1783–4.

42. Luft HS, Bunker JP, Enthoven AC. Should operations be regionalized? The empirical relation between surgical volume and mortality. N Engl J Med 1979;301(25):1364–9.

43. Nguyen HN, Averette HE, Hoskins W, et al. National Survey of Ovarian Carcinoma. Part V: the impact of physician's specialty on patients' survival. Cancer 1993;72:3663–70.

44. Hunt J, Hill D, Besser M, et al. Outcome of patients with neurotrauma: the effect of a regionalized trauma system. Aust N Z J Surg 1995;65(2):83–6.

45. Executive Committee for the Asymptomatic Carotid Atherosclerosis Study. Endarterectomy for asymptomatic carotid artery stenosis. JAMA 1995;273:1421–8.

CHAPTER 44

Evidence-Based Anesthesiology

Elizabeth Martinez, MD, and Peter Pronovost, MD, PhD

The Need for Evidence-Based Anesthesiology

Evidence based medicine (EBM) is an approach to caring for patients that involves the explicit and judicious use of the clinical research literature combined with an understanding of pathophysiology, clinical experience, and patient preferences to aid in clinical decision making. While many may argue that this definition describes what physicians have always done, this approach may in fact improve clinical decision making by incorporating the best available scientific literature, by reducing bias that occurs when medical decision making is based on recent patients, by explicitly weighing the risks and benefits of a clinical decision, and by incorporating patient preferences into a risk-benefit assessment.[1]

While EBM has been championed in internal medicine, there is a great need to extend the evidence-based approach to other disciplines, including anesthesiology and surgery. In the operating room, for example, house staff and fellows may believe that a patient is "volume overloaded," based on either physical examination or pulmonary artery catheter data, without knowledge of the sensitivity, specificity, or likelihood ratio of each particular test. Since the links between the pretest probability, the likelihood ratio of a test, the resultant post-test probability, and the treatment threshold may not be explicitly stated, encouraging physicians to explain consciously and explicitly their medical decision making may improve clinical decision making. Often, this may mean stating that there is no evidence for a particular decision and that one must employ pathophysiologic reasoning to guide clinical decision making.

Indeed, many decisions in the operating room are based on pathophysiologic data obtained from studies of animals or healthy volunteers. Such decisions, however, require consideration of patient preferences and knowledge of risk and benefits, including the risk of a false-positive (ie, extubating somebody who will fail extubation) or a false-negative (ie, leaving somebody intubated who could be extubated). Dispersed literature sources, insufficient clinical research data, and the need to make decisions rapidly all support the need for evidence-based anesthesiology.

This chapter discusses why an evidence-based methodology is needed in anesthesiology and presents two examples of evidence-based anesthesiology. These examples follow a standard approach inclusive of a clinical scenario, literature search, completion of evidence-based medicine worksheets, and summarized findings in a critically appraised topic (CAT), a one-page summary regarding a specific clinical question.

Literature Review and Resources

The literature pertaining to anesthesiology is dispersed across journals of numerous specialized areas, including journals in general medicine, medical subspecialties, critical care, anesthesiology, pediatrics, and surgery. The presence of diverse sources of clinical research information in anesthesiology increases the need for efficient methods to access and search relevant literature. Many clinicians rely on alternative strategies for accessing relevant clinical literature, such as evidence summaries (eg, Intensive Care Monitor) that screen journals relevant to their particular field and summarize the information to facilitate critical appraisal. Both the breadth of knowledge required for anesthesiology and the diverse sources of clinical literature demand efficient access and evaluation of relevant literature.

Potential Limitations of Applying Results of Clinical Trials

Many clinicians view the randomized double blind controlled clinical trial as the "seal of approval" of a high-quality trial and accept without question that the inferences from the study are true. A valid randomized clinical trial is the most powerful tool to evaluate a therapy, but the quality of the trial can significantly impact the validity of the study inferences. In addition, nonrandomized study designs are also acceptable, especially since (a) the results of clinical trials may not be generalizable to the entire population, (b) some clinical questions are more appropriately addressed by observational studies, and (c) clinical trials in critically ill patients can be difficult to perform for ethical or logistic reasons (especially clinical trials of surgical procedures).

This chapter describes how to determine whether the results of a clinical trial apply to an individual patient or whether the patient is so different that the study results would not apply. In most cases, the results may be applied with a quantitative difference (one of degree) rather than a qualitative difference (ie, a different conclusion would be reached for the applicability to the individual patient). Nevertheless, physicians must be cautious about assuming the replicability of the results of a clinical trial on a population of patients when creating a practice guideline or performing a decision analysis or cost-effectiveness analysis. Most clinical trials are efficacy studies in that they evaluate how something works in an artificial world with control over multiple variables. While this control is necessary to maintain the internal validity of the study, it may limit the application of the results of the clinical trial in a population of patients outside the trial. On the other hand, effectiveness studies evaluate how a treatment works in the "real world" and have less internal validity (ie, ability to determine cause and effect) but increased generalizability or external validity.

This difference between efficacy studies and effectiveness studies and the potential problem of assuming applicability of results of a randomized clinical trial to a population of patients is illustrated in the carotid endarterectomy story. The Asymptomatic Carotid Atherosclerosis Study (ACAS) found that the 30-day mortality rate for asymptomatic patients having carotid endarterectomy was 1 in 1,000 cases.[2] Indeed, there was a significant increase in the mortality rate for this operation between 1989 and 1995. However, an effectiveness study of Medicare patients revealed that the mortality rate was 1 in 100 cases, 10 times greater than in the clinical trial.[3] This difference in mortality is likely due to the strict entry criteria for the clinical trial, as patients with comorbid diseases and patients over 79 years of age were excluded from the clinical trial.

The carotid endarterectomy story demonstrates the need for observational studies in addition to randomized trials when creating practice guidelines or performing decision or cost-effectiveness analyses. If it is assumed that the results of a randomized clinical trial on a population of patients can be replicated, then whether the same results are indeed being achieved must be evaluated.[4] This difference in findings between efficacy and effectiveness studies may be particularly large in studies of critically ill surgical patients because there is wide variability in the organization of intensive care units (ICUs), and this variability is associated with in-hospital mortality.[5] Additionally, as the way in which health care is organized, financed, and delivered changes, it is important to evaluate the impact of these changes on patient care, yet it is difficult to evaluate them with a randomized clinical trial. For example, one may wish to evaluate the impact of adding intensive care physicians to an ICU on in-hospital mortality and complication rates. While a randomized clinical trial of this organizational change may be difficult, an observational study can be performed. Moreover, the impact of these changes on long-term patient outcomes needs to be evaluated, and this would be difficult to do with a randomized clinical trial. For example, critical care researchers have largely failed to explore the long-term outcomes associated with ICU care. Without explicit knowledge of what is occurring in a real-world setting, it may be difficult to make optimal clinical decisions that best meet the needs of the patient, the family, and society.

The Need for Rapid Decisions

The need to make rapid clinical decisions may complicate the application of EBM in the operating room. Recently, Sackett and colleagues explored the ability of an "evidence cart" (ie, readily accessible texts and literature, etc) to enhance clinical decision making. This work was partly driven by the concern that EBM, though attractive in theory, may be limited in application simply because of the time and effort required to systematically appraise the literature before a decision is made. Although their study showed such a cart may help, the study was conducted on a general medical ward. Decisions about surgical patients may need to be made even faster than in the normal care of hospitalized patients, and there are little data regarding whether evidence-based medicine can be applied practically. There are some data suggesting that evidence-based medicine treatment and diagnostic protocols may be used effectively even in the treatment of acute processes such as acute respiratory distress syndrome,[6] but it is likely that without such protocols, practical applications of EBM in the operating room will be limited to decisions that are not time-critical.

Other Resources

Other resources for the practice of evidence-based medicine include the following:
- The Center for Evidence-Based Medicine Web site www.cebm.jr2.ox.ac.uk is an excellent source of practical information for the practice of evidence-based medicine.
- *Best Evidence.* This is a CD-ROM produced by the American College of Physicians that contains a critical review of randomized clinical trials since the early 1990s. This is a very efficient means to identify a clinical trial in a particular area.
- *Critical Care Medicine: Users' Guide to the Medical Literature.* This series, based on the *Journal of the American Medical Association* publications, presents a unique opportunity for the reader to learn how to critically evaluate the literature by critiquing an article. The series is well done and should be read by all critical care practitioners.
- *Journal of the American Medical Association Rational Clinical Exam Series.* This series critically evaluates clinical decision making and helps make it explicit.
- *Intensive Care Monitor.* This journal scans specialized critical care journals and summarizes, in structured abstracts and commentaries, articles relevant to critical care.
- *Critical Care Clinic*, 1998, issue 14. This entire issue is devoted to evidence-based critical care and provides an evidence-based review of several specific critical care topics.

CASE STUDIES

Two significant issues in the management of patients intraoperatively are intraoperative transfusion practices of packed red blood cells (RBCs) and intraoperative temperature management. For each of these topics, discussion of the clinical issues, presentation of a case scenario, completion of the evidence-based worksheet (available from URL:http://www.cebm.jr2.ox.ac.uk), and preparation of a critically appraised topic (CAT) are carried out to provide a guideline for the evaluation of an article.

Case Study: Intraoperative Transfusion Practices of Packed Red Blood Cells

Red blood cell transfusions are administered with the intent of optimizing oxygen delivery and adequate tissue perfusion. This is based on the premise that oxygen delivery is a function of cardiac output and arterial oxygen content. In turn, arterial oxygen content is a function of the oxygen saturation of blood times the hemoglobin and the partial pressure of oxygen.

These relationships can easily be expressed mathematically as follows:

$$\text{Oxygen delivery (DO}_2) = (\text{Cardiac output}) \times (\text{arterial oxygen content})$$
$$\text{Arterial oxygen content} = (\text{SaO}_2/100 \times \text{Hgb} \times 1.39) + (0.0003 \times \text{PaO}_2)$$
$$\text{Where: SaO}_2 = \text{hemoglobin saturation}$$
$$\text{Hgb} = \text{Hemoglobin in g/dL}$$
$$\text{PaO}_2 = \text{partial pressure of oxygen in arterial blood}$$

However, blood transfusions pose multiple risks to the patient and add to the cost of care.[7,8] Guidelines for transfusion practices can be found in the surgical, anesthetic, critical care, and transfusion medicine literature.[9–18] Nevertheless, there is a lack of adequate studies guiding transfusion practices, and there remains significant variation in transfusion practices. In general, anesthesiologists follow the "10-to-30" rule of maintenance of hemoglobin 10 g/dL and/or hematocrit of 0.30. Two peer-reviewed articles on transfusion practices are reviewed to evaluate the validity of this practice.

Clinical Scenario

A 55-year-old woman presents for abdominal aortic aneurysm repair. She is seen the morning of surgery, and the anesthesiologist explains the risks of the procedure and anesthesia to the patient and her husband. When the risk of blood transfusion intraoperatively and post-operatively is explained, they ask how it would be decided whether the patient was to receive blood. The patient has never received a blood transfusion and would like to avoid this if at all possible. The anesthesiologist explains that he/she will transfuse the patient to maintain a hemoglobin of 10.0 so as to decrease the risk of perioperative morbidity. He/she is then asked what study this is based on.

Using the *Best Evidence CD-ROM*, the keywords "transfusion," "critical illness," and "allogeneic" are entered. The abstract and commentary for a multicenter randomized controlled trial assessing transfusion requirements in critical care settings are located, and the original article[19] can be obtained.

After reviewing this article, these questions are identified:

1. Is the evidence from this randomized trial valid?
2. If valid, is the evidence important?
3. If valid and important, can you apply this evidence in caring for your patient?

Table 44–1 displays a completed therapy worksheet, and Tables 44–2 and 44–3 show a critically appraised topic (CAT) analysis.

Table 44–1 Completed Therapy Worksheet

1. Are the results of this single preventive or therapeutic trial valid?	
Was the assignment of patients to treatments randomized, and was the randomization list concealed?	Yes, Yes
Were all patients who entered the trial accounted for at its conclusion, and were they analyzed in the groups to which they were randomized?	Yes, Yes
Were patients and clinicians kept "blind" to which treatment was being received?	No
Aside from the experimental treatment, were the groups treated equally?	Yes
Were the groups similar at the start of the trial?	Yes

Table 44–1 *(continued)*

2. Are the valid results of this randomized trial important?

Sample Calculations:

Occurrence of Diabetic Neuropathy		Relative Risk Reduction (RRR)	Absolute Risk Reduction (ARR)	Number Needed to Treat (NNT)
Usual Insulin Control Event Rate (CER)	Intensive Insulin Experimental Event Rate (EER)	$\dfrac{\text{CER} - \text{EER}}{\text{CER}}$	CER – EER	1/ARR
9.6%	2.8%	$\dfrac{9.6\% - 2.8\% = 71\%}{9.6\%}$	9.6% – 2.8% = 6.8% (4.3% to 9.3%)	1/6.8% = 15 pts. (11 to 23)

95% confidence interval (CI) on an NNT = 1 / (limits on the CI of its ARR) =

$$+/-1.96 \sqrt{\frac{\text{CER} \times (1\text{-CER})}{\text{\# of control pts.}} + \frac{\text{EER} \times (1\text{-EER})}{\text{\# of exper. pts.}}} = +/-1.96 \sqrt{\frac{0.096 \times 0.904}{730} + \frac{0.028 \times 0.972}{711}} = +/-2.4\%$$

Your Calculations:

		Relative Risk Reduction (RRR)	Absolute Risk Reduction (ARR) (95% CI)	Number Needed to Treat (NNT) (95% CI)
CER	EER	$\dfrac{\text{CER} - \text{EER}}{\text{CER}}$	CER – EER	1/ARR
23.3%	18.7%	$\dfrac{23.3\% - 18.7\% = 19.7\%}{23.3\%}$	4.6% (– 0.8% – 10.2%)	22 (NNT 10 to infinity, NNH 110 to infinity)

3. Can you apply this valid, important evidence about a treatment in caring for your patient?

Do these results apply to your patient?

Is your patient so different from those in the trial that its results cannot help you?	No. Even though the study was done in the critically ill patients in the ICU, the results likely apply to the operating room.

Are your patient's values and preferences satisfied by the regimen and its consequences?

Do you and your patient have a clear assessment of the patient's values and preferences?	Needs to be assessed in each patient
Are they met by this regimen and its consequences?	Needs to be assessed in each patient

Additional Notes:

The study was an equivalency study designed to detect an absolute difference in mortality of 5.5% between the treatment and control groups. Therefore, one can say that liberal transfusion is not associated with a 5.5% difference in mortality but cannot comment on whether there is a smaller treatment effect. Although the study was underpowered to detect treatment effects less than 5.5%, a treatment effect less than 5.5% may be clinically meaningful since the outcome is mortality.

NNH = Number needed to harm.
Adapted from Hebert PC, Wells G, Blajchman MA, et al. A multicenter, randomized, controlled clinical trial of transfusion requirements in critical care. N Engl J Med 1999;340:409-17.

Table 44–2 Critically Appraised Topic (CAT)

Transfusion in Critically Ill Patients May Not Decrease Mortality.

Clinical Bottom Line:
In critically ill patients, the liberal use of blood transfusions (Hgb 10 g/dL) is not associated with a 5.5% difference in mortality between the treatment and control groups.

Three-part question: In a critically ill patient, will restrictive blood transfusion practices be equivalent to liberal transfusion practices?

Search Terms: "transfusion," "critical care," and "death"

The Study
Concealed, unmasked, randomized, controlled clinical trial of equivalency with intention-to-treat analysis. Patients >16 years of age admitted to ICU with < 9.0 g/dL. Powered to detect a 5.5% or greater decrease in 30-day mortality.
Control Group (liberal strategy of transfusion)
(N=420, 416 analyzed) Transfuse to Hgb 10 to 12 g/dL
Experimental Group (restrictive strategy of transfusion)
(N=418, 413 analyzed) Transfuse to Hgb 7 to 9 g/dL

The Evidence

Outcome	Control Event Rate (CER)	Experimental Event Rate (EER)	Relative Risk Reduction (RRR)	Absolute Risk Reduction (ARR) (95% CI)	Number Needed to Treat (NNT) (95% CI)
30-Day Mortality	23%	19%	20%	4.6% (−0.8% – 10.2%)	22 (NNT 10 to infinity NNH 110 to infinity)
60-Day Mortality	26%	23%	14%	3.8% (−2.1% – 9.5%)	33 (NNT 11 to infinity, NNH 35 to infinity)

Comments

1. Study terminated early because of decrease in enrollment to below 20% of predicted values.

2. Study powered to detect a 5.5 % decrease in mortality or greater, so cannot comment on whether transfusion is associated with a smaller decrease in mortality. Since the outcome is mortality, any decrease in mortality may be clinically important.

3. Those patients who were not enrolled were slightly older, had similar APACHE scores and comorbid diagnoses *except* for cardiac disease. possibly limiting the generalizability of the results.

4. Study had inadequate power to state whether these results apply to patients with significant coronary disease.

5. Subgroup analysis suggests that restrictive transfusion may be associated with reduced 30-day mortality in patients less than 55 years of age (5.7% in the restrictive group and 13% in the liberal transfusion group) and in patients with APACHE II scores less than 20 (8.7% in the restrictive group and 16.1% in the liberal group).

Adapted from Hebert PC, Wells G, Blajchman MA, et al. A multicenter, randomized, controlled clinical trial of transfusion requirements in critical care. N Engl J Med 1999;340:409–17.

For further guidance, the recent American Society of Anesthesiology guidelines for transfusion practices were consulted; a CAT is presented in Table 44–3.

The task force recommends that absolute Hgb is not an adequate "trigger" for transfusion nor is the pure utilization of vital signs for patients under anesthesia. They conclude that transfusion is rarely indicated for Hgb > 10 g/dL and almost always indicated for Hgb < 6 g/dL.

Table 44–3 Critically Appraised Topic (CAT)

Transfusion Guidelines: Report of Task Force

Clinical bottom line:
Intraoperative transfusion guidelines are lacking in evidence from randomized trials to help guide transfusion practice.

Three-part question: Intraoperatively, in high risk patients, what is the optimal Hgb?

Search terms: "Blood transfusion," "Transfusion guidelines"

The Study
A systematic review of controlled and uncontrolled observational studies that assesses the perioperative or peripartum use of blood components and measured effectiveness in terms of clinical outcomes.

The Evidence
160 articles.

Comments
The guidelines were completed prior to the publication of the previously reviewed article in the *New England Journal of Medicine* article about blood transfusion and need to be updated to reflect that article. This demonstrates the need for practice guidelines to be "working documents" and to be continuously updated.

1. The practice guidelines are not based on randomized controlled trials. Most other controlled trials of perioperative morbidity support the guidelines for the outlying Hgb values (< 6 g/dL and > 10 g/dL); however, there is a significant range (> 6 g/dL and < 10 g/dL) that remains ill-defined.
2. It is difficult to assess the validity of the contributing articles. This would have been presented better in a format with odds ratios that could be compared to determine how the conclusions of the task force were arrived at.

Adapted from American Society of Anesthesiologists Task Force on Blood Component Therapy. Practice guidelines for blood component therapy. Anesthesiology 1996;84:732–47.

Discussion

The Task Force on Blood Component Therapy was formed to assess the literature and to develop evidence-based indications for transfusion. Their report was presented in *Anesthesiology*.[20] Unfortunately, these guidelines are of limited utility because of the limited number of studies that have been done and are available for review. The guidelines were based on the findings from case reports and controlled and uncontrolled observational studies. Although these guidelines reflect the current practice of blood transfusion, the systematic evaluation of risks and benefits is lacking. The report clearly stated that published evidence was considered relevant if it addressed the perioperative or peripartum use of blood components and measured effectiveness in terms of clinical outcomes. Effectiveness was judged by considering the potential clinical benefits, adverse effects, and costs of blood component therapy.[20] The recommendations of the task force are (1) transfusion is rarely indicated when the hemoglobin concentration is greater than 10 g/dL and is almost always indicated when it is less than 6 g/dL, especially when the anemia is acute; (2) the determination of whether intermediate hemoglobin concentrations (6 to 10 g/dL) justify or require RBC transfusion should be based on the patient's risk for complications of inadequate oxygenation; (3) the use of a single hemoglobin "trigger" for all patients and other approaches that fail to consider all important physiologic and surgical factors affecting oxygenation are not recommended; (4) when appropriate, preoperative autologous blood donation, intraoperative and postoperative blood recovery, acute normovolemic hemodilution, and measures to decrease blood loss (deliberated hypotension and pharmacologic agents) may be beneficial, and; (5) the indications for transfusion of autologous RBCs may be more liberal than for allogeneic RBCs because of the lower (but still significant) risks associated with the former. Unfortunately, the individual studies were not presented (although "available on request"), and the reader cannot effectively or efficiently evaluate their significance and/or validity. The Surgical Red Blood Cell Transfusion Policies[21] delineate similar guidelines for transfusion practices. These are also limited by the quality of studies evaluating these practices and the absence of studies evaluating the lower limit of acceptability.

As guidelines for transfusion of blood products were greatly scrutinized because of potential infectious complications and improving testing capabilities, the practice of transfusion medicine is continually faced with changing challenges, given the introduction of hemoglobin substitutes. There is inadequate data on the evaluation of the point at which transfusion of packed cells or increase in oxygen-carrying capacity (transfusion of hemoglobin substitutes) improves clinical outcomes, rather than increases complications. Also, the guidelines contain conditional probabilities and are not explicit enough to help in caring for a specific patient such as the one in this clinical scenario. Therefore, physiologic reasoning remains to influence clinical practice.

Summary

Based on these two articles, the issue of allogeneic transfusion guidelines is not completely resolved. Nevertheless, patients without coronary artery disease appear to do as well or better with an Hgb of 7 to 9 g/dL versus 10 to 12 g/dL. For patients with known or suspected coronary artery disease, clinical trials do not provide guidance, and physiologic reasoning only must be employed. However, the decision to transfuse or not to transfuse requires an evaluation of the patient's preferences for receiving transfusion, the patient's risk factors for complications, the nature of the procedure, and the likelihood and the rapidity of significant ongoing blood loss.

Case Study: Intraoperative Temperature Management

Perioperative hypothermia has been associated with multiple complications, including increased postoperative discomfort and shivering, increased surgical bleeding, increased incidence of wound infection, and longer duration of hospital stay.[22–26] It has also been shown that hypothermia can trigger multiple neuroendocrine and metabolic responses as part of the perioperative stress response. These responses in turn have been associated with increased perioperative morbidity and mortality, most commonly cardiac in nature. To guide intraoperative management of temperature, a peer-reviewed article is reviewed.

Clinical Scenario

A 65-year-old male presents for exploratory laparotomy and possible resection of pancreatic mass. The patient is anesthetized, and the surgical exploration is under way. The surgeon and nurse state that the upper body forced-air warming device is making them extremely warm, and they request that the anesthesiologist turn this off to make the room more comfortable. The anesthesiologist discourages this, explaining that a patient's thermoregulation is altered during anesthesia and that hypothermia has been associated with significant perioperative cardiac morbidity. The surgeon and nurse ask what exactly is defined as hypothermia, what complications would result, and what temperature or maneuvers could help to prevent these.

Table 44–4 Completed Thereapy Worksheet

1. Are the results of this single preventive or therapeutic trial valid?

Was the assignment of patients to treatments randomized, and was the randomization list concealed?	Yes, Yes
Were all patients who entered the trial accounted for at its conclusion, and were they analyzed in the groups to which they were randomized?	Yes, Yes
Were patients and clinicians kept "blind" to which treatment was being received?	No (The reviewer of events remained blinded)
Aside from the experimental treatment, were the groups treated equally?	Yes
Were the groups similar at the start of the trial?	Yes

2. Are the valid results of this randomized trial important?

Sample Calculations:

Occurrence of Diabetic Neuropathy		Relative Risk Reduction (RRR)	Absolute Risk Reduction (ARR)	Number Needed to Treat (NNT)
Usual Insulin Control Event Rate (CER)	Intensive Insulin Experimental Event Rate (EER)	$\dfrac{CER - EER}{CER}$	CER – EER	1/ARR
9.6%	2.8%	$\dfrac{9.6\% - 2.8\%}{9.6\%} = 71\%$	9.6% – 2.8% = 6.8% (4.3% to 9.3%)	1/6.8% = 15 pts. (11 to 23)

95% confidence interval (CI) on an NNT = 1 / (limits on the CI of its ARR) =

$$+/-1.96 \sqrt{\frac{CER \times (1\text{-}CER)}{\text{\# of control pts.}} + \frac{EER \times (1\text{-}EER)}{\text{\# of exper. pts.}}} = +/-1.96 \sqrt{\frac{0.096 \times 0.904}{730} + \frac{0.028 \times 0.972}{711}} = +/-2.4\%$$

Your Calculations:

Incidence of Electrocardiographic or Morbid Cardiac Event		Relative Risk Reduction (RRR)	Absolute Risk Reduction (ARR)	Number Needed to Treat (NNT)
CER Hypothermia	EER Normothermia	$\dfrac{CER - EER}{CER}$	CER – EER	1/ARR
21%	8%	$\dfrac{21\% - 8\%}{21\%} = 62\%$	21% – 8% = 13% (95% CI 5% to 21%)	1/13% = 8 pts. (95% CI 20 to 5)

Table 44–4 *(continued)*

3. Can you apply this valid, important evidence about a treatment in caring for your patient?

Do these results apply to your patient?

Is your patient so different from those in the trial that its results cannot help you?	No. This trial included thoracic, abdominal, and lower extremity procedures.

Are your patient's values and preferences satisfied by the regimen and its consequences?

Do you and your patient have a clear assessment of the patient's values and preferences?	Needs to be assessed in each patient
Are they met by this regimen and its consequences?	Needs to be assessed in each patient

Additional Notes:

This study also found that normothermic patients had a lower incidence of early postoperative ventricular tachycardia.

Adapted from Frank SM, Fleischer LA, Beattie C, et al. Perioperative maintenance of normothermia reduces the incidence of morbid cardiac events: a randomized clinical trial. JAMA 1997;277:1127–34.

By searching MEDLINE, a related reference is located. In this article,[27] it is shown that avoiding hypothermia (hypothermia defined as core temperature less than 36°C) during surgery reduces the risk of postoperative myocardial ischemia.

Again, the following questions are to be answered from review of the article:

1. Is the evidence from this randomized trial valid?
2. If valid, is the evidence important?
3. If valid and important, can you apply this evidence in caring for your patient?

Summary

Table 44–4 displays the completed worksheet, and Table 44–5 displays the critically appraised topic (CAT) for normothermia.

CONCLUSION

Evidence-based medicine is an approach to caring for patients that involves the explicit and judicious use of the clinical research literature combined with an understanding of pathophysiology, clinical experience, and patient preferences to aid in clinical decision making. The examples provided in this chapter demonstrate how evidence-based medicine can be applied to common clinical problems and how it can improve patient care. The worksheet format provided in this chapter and on the Center for Evidence-Based Medicine Web site (www.cebm.jr2.ox.ac.uk) can help critically appraise the literature and promote informed clinical decision making.

Anesthesiology continues to evolve, and evidence-based medicine can enable/help anesthesiologists to optimize their management of a diverse patient population. Issues that need to be addressed include the identification of patients requiring preoperative cardiac testing, intraoperative and postoperative monitoring for myocardial ischemia, and the need for postoperative ICU care. Anesthesiologists need to generate new knowledge about these practices through valid clinical studies and also to apply evidence-based methodology to existing knowledge to continue to improve patient care.

Table 44–5 Critically Appraised Topic (CAT)

Northermia Reduces Risk of Perioperative Cardiac Morbidity

Clinical bottom line: In patients who have risk factors for coronary disease, maintenance of intraoperative normothermia (> 36°C) reduces risk of early postoperative cardiac morbidity.

Three-part question: In high-risk patients, does maintenance of normothermia reduce the risk of cardiac morbidity?

Search terms: myocardial ischemia, temperature

The Study
Double blind, concealed, randomized controlled trial with intention-to-treat analysis. Patients scheduled for surgery (peripheral vascular, abdominal, or thoracic) and postoperative admission to the ICU, were over 60 years of age, and either had documented coronary artery disease (CAD) or were at high risk for CAD.

Control Group (hypothermia: N= 158, 143 analyzed, 15 withdrawn for secondary outcome because of missing Holter monitor data). Control group received no active warming.

Experimental Group (normothermia: N= 142, 127 analyzed, 15 withdrawn for secondary outcome because of missing Holter monitor data). Experimental group received an upper or lower body forced-air warming cover.

The Evidence

Outcome within 24 Hours of Surgery	CER	EER	RRR	ARR (95% CI)	NNT
Myocardial Ischemia	9%	5%	44%	4% (−2% to 10%)	25 (10 to infinity)
Ventricular Tachycardia	8%	2%	75% increase	6% (1% to 11%) increase	16 (9 to 100) additional

Comments
1. Morbid cardiac events: cardiac arrest, myocardial infarction, or unstable angina/ischemia occurring in the first 24 hours postoperatively. The 95% CI for ARR of myocardial ischemia crosses 0, so not statistically significant.
2. Study population included diverse surgical groups of high-risk patients.

Conclusion
Maintaining normothermia during surgery may be associated with a reduced risk of postoperative myocardial ischemia and ventricular tachycardia. Nevertheless, the number of events were few, so the confidence intervals around the ARR estimates are wide. Attempts should be made to maintain normothermia in patients during surgery.

Adapted from Frank SM, Fleischer LA, Beattie C, et al. Perioperative maintenance of normothermia reduces the incidence of morbid cardiac events: a randomized clinical trial. JAMA 1997;277:1127–34.

REFERENCES

1. Sackett DL, Richardson WS, Rosenberg W, Haynes RB. Evidence-based medicine: how to practice and teach. Edinburgh: Churchill-Livingstone; 1999. [In press]

2. Executive Committee for the Asymptomatic Carotid Atherosclerosis Study. Endarterectomy for asymptomatic carotid artery stenosis. JAMA 1995;273:1421–8.

3. Wennberg DE, Lucas FL, Birkmeyer JD, et al. Variation in carotid endarterectomy mortality in the Medicare population: trial hospitals, volume and patient characteristics. JAMA 1998;279:1279–81.

4. Groeger JS, Strosberg MA, Halpern NA, et al. Descriptive analysis of critical care units in the United States. Crit Care Med 1992;20:846–63.

5. Pronovost PJ, Jenckes MW, Dorman T, et al. Organizational characteristics of intensive care units related to outcomes of abdominal aortic surgery. JAMA 1999;281:1310–17.

6. East TD, Bohm SH, Wallace CJ, et al. A successful computerized protocol for clinical management of pressure control inverse ratio ventilation in ARDS patients. Chest 1998;101:697–710.

7. Goodnough LT, Brecher ME, Kanter MH, AuBuchon JP. Transfusion medicine: first of two parts: blood transfusion. N Engl J Med 1999;340:438–47.

8. Goodnough LT, Brecher ME, Kanter MH, AuBuchon JP. Transfusion medicine: second of two parts: blood transfusion. N Engl J Med 1999;340:525–33.

9. Allain J, Williamson LM. How can we best achieve optimal transfusion practice? Med J Aust 1997;167:462–3.

10. Audet A, Goodnough LT, Parvin CA. Evaluating the appropriateness of red blood cell transfusions: the limitations of retrospective medical record reviews. Int J Qual Health Care 1996;8:41–9.

11. Carson JL. Morbidity risk assessment in the surgically anemic patient. Am J Surg 1995;170 Suppl:32S–36S.

12. D'Ambra MN, Kaplan DK. Alternatives to allogeneic blood use in surgery: acute normovolemic hemodilution and preoperative autologous donation. Am J Surg 1995;170 Suppl:49S–59S.

13. Goldberg MA. Erythropoiesis, erythropoietin, and iron metabolism in elective surgery: preoperative strategies for avoiding allogeneic blood exposure. Am J Surg 1995;170 Suppl:37S–43S.

14. Goldman EB. Legal considerations for allogeneic blood transfusion. Am J Surg 1995;170 Suppl:27S–31S.

15. Goodnough LT, Despotis GJ. Establishing practice guidelines for surgical blood management. Am J Surg 1995;170 Suppl:16S–20S.

16. Greenburg AG. A physiologic basis for red blood cell transfusion decisions. Am J Surg 1995;170 Suppl:44S–48S.

17. Klein HG. Allogeneic transfusion risks in the surgical patient. Am J Surg 1995;170 Suppl:21S–26S.

18. Straus RG, Schaeffler H. The transfusion alliance: an interdisciplinary approach to improving transfusion medicine. Transfusion 1998;38:887–90.

19. Hebert PC, Wells G, Blajchman MA, et al. A multicenter, randomized, controlled clinical trial of transfusion requirements in critical care. Transfusion Requirements in Critical Care Investigators. Canadian Critical Care Trials Group. N Engl J Med 1999;340:409–17.

20. The American Society of Anesthesiologists Task Force on Blood Component Therapy. Practice guidelines for blood component therapy. Anesthesiology 1996;84:732–47.

21. Spence RK and Blood Management Practice Guidelines Conference. Surgical red blood cell transfusion practice policies. J Surg 1995;170:3S–15S.

22. Schmied H, Kurz A, Sessler DI, et al. Mild hypothermia increases blood flow and transfusion requirements during total hip arthroplasty. Lancet 1996;347:289–92.

23. Kurz A, Sessler DI, Lenhardt R. Perioperative normothermia to reduce the incidence of surgical-wound infection and shorten hospitalization. Study of Wound Infection and Temperature Group. N Engl J Med 1996;334:1209–15.

24. Frank SM, Higgins MS, Breslow MJ, et al. The catecholamine, cortisol, and hemodynamic responses to mild perioperative hypothermia: a randomized clinical trial. Anesthesiology 1995;82:83–93.

25. Frank SM, Raja SN, Fleischer LA, et al. Cardiovascular and adrenergic manifestations of cold stress. In: Zeisberger E, Schonbaum E, Lomax P, editors. Thermal balance in health and disease: recent basis research and clinical progress. Basel: Birkhauser Verlag; 1994. p. 325–31.

26. Frank SM, Higgins MS, Fleischer LA, et al. The adrenergic, respiratory, and cardiovascular effects of core cooling in humans. Am J Physiol 1997;272:R557–R562.

27. Frank SM, Fleischer LA, Breslow MJ, et al. Perioperative maintenance of normothermia reduces the incidence of morbid cardiac events. JAMA 1997;227:1127–34.

CHAPTER 45

Surgical Pathology

Jonathan I. Epstein, MD, and Joseph D. Kronz, MD

Large-scale mandatory second-opinion programs in medicine have their origins in the surgical fields. The intention of these programs was to prevent unnecessary elective surgical procedures by obtaining a second surgical opinion prior to surgery. These programs demonstrated that the need for elective surgery could not be confirmed following a second surgical opinion in 11 to 19 percent of cases.[1–4] Most of these programs also showed a financial benefit for obtaining a second surgical opinion, averaging two to four dollars saved for every dollar spent to obtain the second opinion.[1,2,4]

Compared to the surgical field, the experience of second opinions in diagnostic pathology is more limited. The most common reason for obtaining a second opinion in surgical pathology or cytopathology is to help clarify the diagnosis of a difficult case, with significant discrepancies in diagnoses following expert review being reported in several retrospective, organ-specific studies.[5–13] It is uncommon for patients to seek a second opinion on their pathology. Patients have little contact with pathologists and generally do not understand the process by which a diagnosis is made. Many patients are under the misconception that their clinician (surgeon) renders the diagnosis since he conveys the diagnosis to the patient. Most patients are also unaware that there is a potential for their pathology to be misinterpreted. Although still a small percent of cases, in the past few years we have noted an increase in the number of cases in which patients have initiated the review process. This appears to reflect more informed patients, who have gathered information from other sources (such as the Internet) and have identified experts in the field of pathology whom they would like to review their material.

Second opinions (either on difficult cases or patient initiated) differ from mandatory second-opinion programs to confirm all outside pathologic diagnoses. An increasingly common occurrence in today's medicine is for the diagnostic biopsy to be sent for analysis to one institution or laboratory and for the definitive procedure to be performed at another institution. The question arises of whether pathologists at the institution where the patient will be treated need to review the outside pathologic material to confirm the diagnosis or whether the treating physicians trust the accuracy of the outside pathology report.

Although some hospitals require their own staff pathologists to review the outside pathology prior to surgery, many hospitals have no such policies. Even in hospitals where they exist, such policies may be disregarded. In some cases, surgeons resist having outside slides reviewed prior to surgery; they feel the patient should not be billed for a second diagnosis when nothing suggests that the initial diagnosis was incorrect. Having the outside diagnostic biopsy slides reviewed also becomes an administrative burden to the surgeon. Surgeons may also feel that based on the clinical history, they can detect cases where the pathology may be in error. However, with biopsy of earlier lesions detected by screening techniques, clinical findings are often nonspecific. As a result, clinicians may not recognize a misdiagnosis as being discordant with the clinical findings. For example, with prostate cancer serum prostate-specific antigen (PSA) levels, findings on rectal exam and transrectal ultrasonographic results are all nonspecific.[14] A similar situation is seen with the breast, where mammographic abnormalities are also nonspecific. Consequently, a misdiagnosis on the pathology of a breast or prostate biopsy may not appear at odds with the clinician's preoperative diagnosis. Surgeons may also believe that diagnoses rendered at larger institutions or teaching institutions can be trusted in comparison to diagnoses rendered at smaller institutions. Third-party payers also resist having outside slides reviewed prior to surgery. Capitated payment may also provide a disincentive for the additional cost of pathology review.

There are both differences and similarities between second-opinion surgical programs and second-opinion pathology programs. The major difference is the relative objectivity in a second-opinion pathology program. Fifty percent of patients for whom the initial recommendation for surgery is not confirmed eventually have the operation.[15] In contrast, if pathology review of a patient biopsy fails to confirm the diagnosis of carcinoma, none of the patients would be expected to undergo surgery unless subsequent biopsies or expert consultation prove the diagnosis of cancer.

LITERATURE REVIEW

Single-Organ Surgical Pathology System Review

Second-opinion studies in surgical pathology typically consist of single-organ system review by expert pathologists. The Pathology Panel and Repository Centers for Lymphoma Clinical Studies reviewed 8,915 lymphomas and found that in 16.7 percent of Hodgkin's lymphomas and 27.3 percent of non-Hodgkin's lymphomas there were major disagreements in the diagnoses provided by the panel pathologists with those provided by the submitting pathologists.[6] McGowan and Norris reviewed 339 cases of carcinoma of the ovary and found 43 incorrect diagnoses; in 15 cases, an entirely benign diagnosis was rendered on review.[7] A retrospective study of sarcomas in a northwest England regional cancer registry found that 22 percent of submitted sarcomas were found not to be sarcomas after expert panel review.[8] A review of 500 neuropathology cases received in consultation at the M.D. Anderson Cancer Center revealed serious disagreements in 8.8 percent of outside diagnoses; however, many of these cases were true consults in which the outside pathologist was unsure of the diagnosis.[9] A review limited to the gynecologic system at a tertiary care hospital found a major change in diagnosis in 15 (2%) of 720 cases.[16] Other second-opinion surgical pathology studies include a report in the primary care literature that evaluated the reliability of diagnoses of skin lesions provided by community pathologists as opposed to dermatopathologists[11] and a mandatory review of prostate needle biopsy specimens prior to radical prostatectomy, to be discussed in greater detail as the Case Study.

Other studies have shown that review of surgical pathology can have an impact on the results of clinical studies. Scott and colleagues found that 44 percent of anaplastic astrocytomas were reclassified as glioblastoma multiforme upon expert review and that this change in diagnosis profoundly impacted the comparative survival of the anaplastic astrocytoma and glioblastoma multiforme groups.[10] In an attempt to decrease the number of incomplete or incorrect diagnoses leaving a laboratory, some studies have suggested that a second pathologist should review all surgical pathology material prior to release of the final diagnosis.[12,13,17]

Multiple-Organ System Cytopathology Review

From January 1996 to December 1997, 862 cases were reviewed at The Johns Hopkins Hospital Division of Cytopathology. The submitted diagnoses and second-opinion diagnoses were assigned values according to this scale: (1) insufficient for diagnosis; (2) no tumor; (3) atypical; (4) suspicious for tumor; and (5) tumor.[18] A major change in diagnosis constituted a change of 2 or more grades between diagnoses. A major change in diagnosis occurred in 41 cases (4.8%). Compared to the whole group, one organ system was more likely to have a major change in diagnosis: thyroid (9%, $p > .04$). Mandatory second-opinion cytopathology review uncovered a high rate of discrepant diagnoses. While a few organ systems had a higher rate of change of diagnosis than others did, most organ systems had a sufficiently higher risk to warrant review of all cases.

Multiple-Organ Combined Surgical and Cytopathology System Review

Abt and colleagues found that 45 (5.8%) of 777 interinstitutional cases reviewed resulted in a clinically significant change in pathologic diagnosis.[19] This study included surgical and cytopathologic material and found a significantly increased change in diagnosis rate for the cytopathology cases (21%) versus surgical pathology cases (7.8%). As a result of mandatory slide review, six surgeries were canceled and five patients did not receive adjuvant chemotherapy who would have received it with the original outside diagnosis. The authors of this study noted that there was a tendency to overcall invasion on in situ or borderline lesions by the outside pathologist.

Multiple-Organ Surgical Pathology System Review

The largest review of a mandatory surgical pathology review was recently performed at The Johns Hopkins Hospital.[20] All surgical pathology material and clinical information on patients referred to our hospital for therapy over a 21-month period (April 1995 to December 1996) were prospectively reviewed. This study includes only cases in which the patient was coming to The Johns Hopkins Hospital for therapy based on a definitive diagnosis previously made by an outside pathologist. The material reviewed encompassed the full spectrum of general surgical pathology specimens, with the exception of medical liver and medical kidney cases. In these latter cases, due to the inherent complexity of these diagnoses, it was often difficult to assess whether outside and second-opinion reports differed significantly.

Cases were selected for study analysis only when the change in pathologic diagnosis resulted in a significant change in therapy or prognosis. Subspecialty experts reviewed cases to confirm that the change in pathologic diagnosis would significantly alter therapy or prognosis. Changes that solely modified the grade were not considered significant because it could be argued that assignment of a grade is often subjective and that the consequences of a changed grade on therapy are frequently ambiguous. We also did not regard differences in the interpretation of stage as necessarily being significant since it was often difficult to determine the stage from the slides and paperwork submitted. However, consequential changes in the diagnosis that incidentally changed stage were considered significant changes. For example, recognition of a lymph node metastasis that was not detected until review at our hospital was considered a significant change in diagnosis.

Over the 21-month period, we reviewed, as part of our mandatory second opinion in surgical pathology, 6,171 outside cases from patients scheduled to be treated at The Johns Hopkins Hospital. In 86 cases (1.4%), the second-opinion diagnosis differed significantly from the submitted diagnosis. The mean age of patients with a change in diagnosis was 54.9 years (range 3–80 years). Of the 86 patients, 47 (54.6%) were female.

Two organ systems were more likely to have a change in diagnosis after review at our institution: serosal pathology (9.5%, $p < .0001$) and gynecologic pathology (5.1%, $p < .0001$). Changes in the central nervous system (2.8%) approached statistical significance ($p = .06$). Specimens from the skin (2.9%), breast (1.4%), genitourinary system (1.2%), gastrointestinal tract (1.2%), hematologic system (1.1%), ear, nose and throat (1.0%), bone and soft tissue (0.9%), and lungs (0.6%) all averaged a 1 to 3 percent rate of change in diagnosis and were not significantly more likely to be changed than the group as a whole (Table 45–1).

In 80 (93%) of the 86 cases, treatment was altered due to the change in diagnosis. The second-opinion change in diagnosis was associated with a better prognosis in 70.9 percent of cases, a worse prognosis in 23.3 percent, and unchanged prognosis in 5.8 percent. In 20 (23%) of the 86 cases with a change in diagnosis, the change was from an overtly malignant to an

Table 45–1 Second-Opinion Review Of Surgical Pathology*

Organ System	Changed Diagnoses (number)	Number of Total Cases	Percent of Change
Serosal surfaces	4	42	9.5
Gynecologic	8	158	5.1
Skin	3	104	2.9
Central nervous system	7	252	2.8
Breast	10	720	1.4
Genitourinary	26	2,167	1.2
Gastrointestinal	13	1,108	1.2
Hematopathology	9	812	1.1
Ear/nose/throat	2	196	1.0
Bone and soft tissue	2	223	0.9
Pulmonary	2	347	0.6
Endocrine	0	48	0
Mediastinal	0	32	0
Cardiovascular	0	9	0
Total	86	6,171	1.4

*at Johns Hopkins May 1995 to December 1996.

overtly benign diagnosis (Figures 45–1 and 45–2). In only 5 (5.8%) of the 86 cases did the diagnosis change from overtly benign to overtly malignant (Figure 45–3). Six of the 86 cases involved a change in diagnostic category (carcinoma, sarcoma, lymphoma, and melanoma, Figure 45–4). These cases included: a change from malignant fibrous histiocytoma to lymphoma or vice versa (2 cases); melanoma being mistaken for poorly differentiated carcinoma (2 cases); glioblastoma multiforme being mistaken for metastatic carcinoma (1 case); and a misdiagnosis of primitive neuroepithelial tumor for a case of malignant ependymoma. No diagnoses were changed in the endocrine (N = 48), mediastinal (N = 32), and cardiovascular (N = 9) pathology groups, but this is likely related to the small number of cases reviewed in these systems.

Follow-up data were available in 52 (60%) of the 86 cases. In 44 cases, additional information supported the second-opinion diagnosis rendered at The Johns Hopkins Hospital. In 7 cases, the follow-up information seemed to support the outside diagnosis over the diagnosis rendered at our institution.

Comparison of Studies

It is difficult to compare the percentages of nonconfirming diagnoses among different studies. As details on the changed diagnoses were not provided in the study by Abt and colleagues, it is impossible to compare the Johns Hopkins study with theirs.[19,20] Possible explanations of variations in the incidence of significant changes include different patient populations and differing ideas of what constitutes a "significant" change in diagnosis.

The question arises of whether certain cases need not be reviewed. Abt and colleagues have suggested that some types of specimen with little or no risk of diagnostic error could be

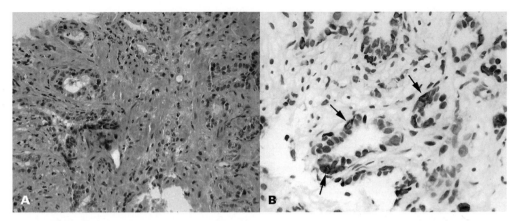

Figure 45–1 Sections of this prostate needle biopsy showed a small focus of crowded "infiltrative" glands with atrophic cytoplasm and benign cytology (A) (Original magnification 100X). The outside diagnosis was adenocarcinoma. Gleason grade 2+1= 3. The Johns Hopkins Hospital diagnosis of atrophy was supported by immunohistochemical staining for high molecular weight cytokeratin demonstrating the presence of basal cells in the glands of concern (B) (Original magnification 200X).

excluded from a mandatory second-opinion program.[19] Our study found that the overall rate of change in diagnosis for all major organ systems was 1 to 3 percent, suggesting that all organ systems are at risk.[20] The three organ systems that had no changes in diagnoses had a limited number of cases for review (48, 32, and 9 cases); if these organ systems had the same 1 to 3 percent change in diagnosis rate seen in the other organ systems, the absence of misdiagnosed cases could be a matter of chance.

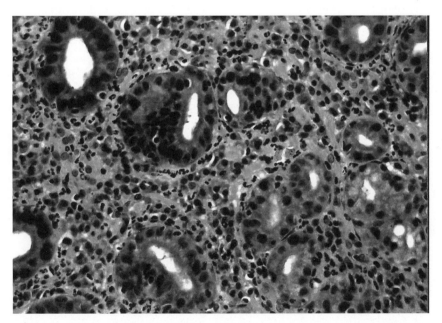

Figure 45–2 Sections taken from an antral biopsy revealed a normal crypt pattern with focal crypts containing enlarged hyperchromatic nuclei and crypt inflammation (compare crypts in the upper left to more normal crypts in the lower right). The outside diagnosis was well-differentiated adenocarcinoma. The Johns Hopkins Hospital diagnosis was active chronic helicobacter gastritis and reactive epithelial atypia. This was confirmed on further tissue studies (Original magnification 400X).

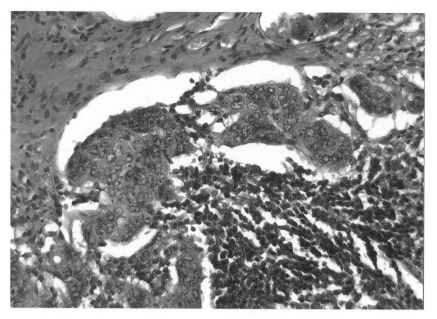

Figure 45–3 Sections taken from axillary lymph nodes in this patient with mammary carcinoma demonstrated a small metastasis in the subcapsular sinus that was not detected on initial outside diagnosis (Original magnification 400X).

Are certain organ systems more likely to have a change in diagnosis? In the Johns Hopkins study, 4 of 42 cases involving serosal membranes (9.5%, $p < .0001$) had changed diagnoses on review.[20] All of the changed cases involved the pleura, and review resulted in a malignant diagnosis being changed to a benign or atypical diagnosis. The diagnostic difficulties with serosal pathology are well documented in the literature.[21–24] Particularly difficult issues include differentiating the desmoplastic variant of mesothelioma from metastatic carcinoma with desmoplasia or from benign reactive processes. The other organ system we found more likely to have a change in diagnosis was the female reproductive tract, with 8 of 158 cases (5.1%, $p < .0001$) reviewed having changes in diagnosis. The rate of change in diagnosis was a little over double that seen in the study by Santoso and colleagues (2%).[16] Whereas 20 percent of

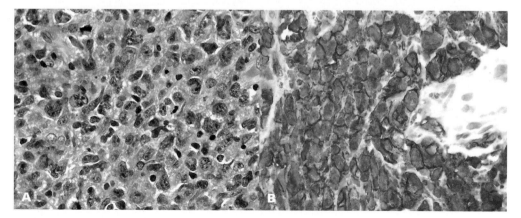

Figure 45–4 Peritoneal mass with sheets of large pleomorphic cells where a minority has spindle features (A) (Original magnification 200X). The outside diagnosis was malignant fibrous histiocytoma. The Johns Hopkins Hospital diagnosis was large B-cell lymphoma that was supported with the immunohistochemical marker for B-cells (B) (Original magnification 200X).

their changed cases involved the endometrium, 50 percent of our changed diagnoses involved the endometrium. Two abstracts by Jacques and colleagues also have noted the significant value of reviewing pathology of the endometrium when a patient is referred to another institution for therapy.[25,26]

Follow-up was obtained in 60 percent of changed cases in the work from Johns Hopkins.[20] In 7 of the 86 cases, follow-up seemed to support the original outside diagnosis over the second-opinion diagnosis provided at The Johns Hopkins Hospital. For instance, two patients with an outside diagnoses of adenocarcinoma on prostate needle biopsy had second-opinion diagnoses of atypia, but eventually each patient was shown to have adenocarcinoma. It is now established that approximately 50 percent of patients with an atypical diagnosis on prostate biopsy will have adenocarcinoma on repeat biopsy due to sampling error on the initial biopsy.[27,28] Consequently, the eventual diagnosis of prostate carcinoma in the two cases cited above does not prove that the second-opinion diagnosis was incorrect. However, occasionally the second opinion is wrong. Abt and colleagues found five cases in which follow-up revealed that the second opinion was incorrect.[19] These data indicate that when two pathologic opinions are at odds, further work-up including rebiopsy or a third expert opinion may be necessary to clarify the diagnosis.

The study performed at The Johns Hopkins Hospital did not address the cost-benefit ratio for reviewing all cases to detect the 1.4 percent of cases that were not confirmed. In part, this would not be feasible. For example, how does one place a dollar figure on the diagnosis of a lesion as oligodendroglioma versus the outside diagnosis of anaplastic astrocytoma even though the distinction has prognostic and therapeutic repercussions? In addition to the direct costs, in cases where second opinion reversed a malignant diagnosis and obviated the need for therapy, there are the indirect costs associated with work-related loss of productivity, therapy-associated morbidity, and potential litigation. The 1 to 3 percent false-positive rate in outside pathology diagnoses seen in the Johns Hopkins study may not seem high compared to the nonconformity rate in second-opinion surgical programs. However, the incidence of pathology misdiagnoses is high when considering total cost and unnecessary patient morbidity. Our data indicate that at The Johns Hopkins Hospital, approximately one patient per week would receive inappropriate treatment and/or inaccurate prognostication if we did not have a policy of mandatory second opinions in surgical pathology.

The current study also evaluated the straightforward issues of cases with major changes in diagnosis and did not factor in changes associated with stage and grade. However, these changes can influence patient management although their assessment may be more subjective. For example, some men with nonpalpable prostate cancers diagnosed by needle biopsy (stage T1c) have relatively "insignificant" tumor and may be candidates for watchful waiting.[29] Preoperative identification of these men requires accurate grading and quantification of cancer on needle biopsy. At the other end of the clinical spectrum, accurate grading of poorly differentiated tumor is necessary since these men are likely to fail systemically and may not benefit from surgery. Only one study has addressed the cost-benefit ratio of mandatory review of surgical pathology, the topic of the case study discussed below.

CASE STUDY

The potential impact of improving the accuracy of diagnosis in prostate carcinoma is substantial. Early diagnosis of prostate cancer has risen in recent years as the result of heightened awareness and screening with serum PSA tests.[30] Concomitantly, the incidence of radical prostatectomy has increased. It is estimated that between 85,000 and 125,000 radical prostatectomies were performed in 1993.[31] Compared to 1987, the number of radical prostatectomies performed in 1992 under the Medicare program increased 460 percent. We sought to determine the impact on cost and treatment of a second opinion on the pathology of needle biopsy prior to radical prostatectomy.[32]

Methodology

From October 1, 1993 to October 1, 1994, 535 patients with a prostate needle biopsy diagnosis of adenocarcinoma were referred to The Johns Hopkins Hospital for radical prostatectomy. As part of a mandatory review program, all outside biopsies were reviewed prior to radical prostatectomy. The outside slides were initially reviewed by any one of six general surgical pathologists. If review of the slides resulted in a discordant diagnosis from that of the outside institution, the case was shown in consultation to the expert uropathologist at our institution.

All efforts were made to ensure that the discordant diagnoses were not attributable to differences in material reviewed. Direct communication with the outside pathologist who rendered the original malignant diagnosis was established. Initially, if only representative slides were sent, all remaining slides from the case were sent to The Johns Hopkins Hospital.

Results

Of the 535 needle biopsies initially diagnosed on the outside as adenocarcinoma of the prostate, 528 cases were confirmed both on biopsy and on subsequent radical prostatectomy. Seven (1.3%) of the 535 biopsies were diagnosed as benign upon review (Table 45–2). Four had been diagnosed as moderately differentiated adenocarcinoma, 2 as well-differentiated adenocarcinoma, and 1 as moderately poorly differentiated adenocarcinoma. The most common lesion misinterpreted as adenocarcinoma was adenosis or less-pronounced examples of adenosis consisting of foci of crowded glands (5 cases). Adenosis mimics cancer but has not been shown to be associated with an increased risk of prostate cancer.[33] Foci of atrophy in the remaining 2 cases were misdiagnosed as adenocarcinoma of the prostate.

In 6 of the 7 patients, the biopsy had been performed to evaluate an elevated serum PSA level. PSA was elevated to 4 to 10 ng per mL in 5 cases; the 6th case had a PSA of 11.6 ng per mL. All the serum PSA levels have been stable over time. One man with a PSA level of 2.1 ng per mL was biopsied because of a nodule on rectal examination. In all other patients, the rectal exam was not suspicious for carcinoma. Transrectal ultrasonography was performed in 5 patients and was normal in all.

Six of the 7 patients, representing 1.1 percent of the total number of men scheduled for radical prostatectomy, were subsequently felt not to have adenocarcinoma of the prostate. As a result of the review, 3 patients had repeat biopsies with widespread sampling of the prostate, all of which were negative for tumor; one of these patients, who had the highest serum PSA level, also had a third needle biopsy and a transurethral resection, both of which were again benign. A 4th patient had two sets of needle biopsies diagnosed as benign prior to the misdiagnosis of adenocarcinoma. There were 2 patients who did not have multiple biopsies of the prostate. One patient did not desire additional procedures and the other has deferred additional biopsy. A 7th case, initially referred with a diagnosis of bilateral adenocarcinoma but classified as bilateral benign atrophy on review, was found on repeat biopsy to have adenocarcinoma.

In six cases the initial biopsy diagnoses originated in a hospital setting; the seventh was from a large national commercial pathology laboratory. Of the six hospitals where the initial biopsy diagnosis was changed from malignant to benign, five were teaching hospitals with residency training programs in pathology. In general, the referring hospitals were sizable, with two having over 1,200 beds and another two having more than 500 beds. The remaining two hospitals were somewhat smaller, with 445 and 150 beds.

An assessment of potential cost savings was compiled from a review of the last 512 discharges for radical prostatectomy performed at The Johns Hopkins Hospital. The average length of stay was 6.1 days. Had these six men undergone radical prostatectomy, the average charges for all patients would have been $8,542 for hospital costs, $768 for anesthesia, and $1,172 for pathology. Surgery charges would have been $1,997 for each Medicare patient and $4,700 for each non-Medicare patient. The total cost of radical prostatectomy for the two

Table 45-2 Second-Opinion Review of Prostate Needle Biopsies (Johns Hopkins)

Case	Date Received	Outside Diagnosis	JHH Diagnosis	Prior Bx.	Repeat Bx.	PSA	DRE	TRUS	Age (Years)
1	10/1/93	well diff. ca.	Atrophy	—	benign	5.2	WNL	—	64
2	10/22/93	mod. diff. ca.	Adenosis	benign x2	benign x2	2.1	nodule	WNL	67
3	11/19/93	well diff. ca.	Crowded glands	—	—	4.5	WNL	—	60
4	2/4/94	mod. diff. ca.	Adenosis	—	—	5.4	WNL	WNL	59
5	2/10/94	mod.-poor diff. ca.	Crowded glands	—	benign	5.7	WNL	WNL	57
6	7/25/94	mod. diff. ca.	Adenosis	—	benign x2; TUR benign	11.6	WNL	WNL	66
7	8/2/94	mod. diff. ca.	Atrophy	—	mod. diff. ca.	7.6	WNL	WNL	68

JHH=The Johns Hopkins Hospital; Bx=needle biopsy; PSA=prostate-specific antigen; DRE=digital rectal examination; TRUS=transrectal ultrasonography; TUR = transurethral resection; WNL=within normal limits; well diff. ca.=well-differentiated cancer (Gleason sum 2–4); mod. diff. ca.=moderately differentiated cancer (Gleason sum 5–6); mod.-poor diff. ca.=moderately to poorly differentiated cancer (Gleason sum 7).

Table 45–3 Medical Cost Impact of Second-Opinion Pathology on Prostate Needle Biopsies

All Men			Projected Cost of Radical Prostatectomy	
		Charges	Non-Medicare (4 patients)	Medicare (2 patients)
Slide review	$42,800	Hospital	$34,168	$17,084
Immunohistochemistry	$ 783	Surgery	$18,800	$ 3,994
Repeat TRUS and biopsy	$ 1,300	Anesthesia	$ 3,072	$ 1,536
		Pathology	$ 4,688	$ 2,344
		Subtotal	$60,728	$24,958
Total	$44,883	Total Charges (6 patients) = $85,686		

TRUS = transrectal ultrasonography.

Medicare and four non-Medicare patients would have been $85,686 (Table 45–3). The charge for pathologic review of each needle biopsy prior to surgery was $80, for a cost of $42,800 for the 535 cases seen during the study period. The cost of six repeat transrectal ultrasonography exams and biopsies in four men whose diagnoses of cancer were not confirmed was $1,300. An additional $783 was spent on immunohistochemical studies with high molecular weight cytokeratin (a marker which is positive in benign prostate glands and negative in cancer)[34] on another seven of the 535 needle biopsies to confirm the diagnosis of cancer, for a total cost of $44,883 (see Table 45–3). Immunohistochemical stains for high molecular weight cytokeratin were performed on only one of the seven cases not confirmed as cancer (case 4). This study was done at the outside institution after review of the biopsy failed to confirm their original diagnosis of malignancy.

Conclusion

This study demonstrated that a second opinion on the diagnostic needle biopsies of the prostate prior to radical prostatectomy saved $1.91 for each dollar spent. This is a gross underestimate of the total costs saved since we have only analyzed the direct costs. We have not analyzed the indirect costs saved by this second-opinion program since these figures vary significantly from case to case. On average, patients undergoing radical prostatectomy at The Johns Hopkins Hospital miss approximately 6 weeks of work and wages. The major complications associated with radical prostatectomy include incontinence and impotence. Approximately 8 percent of men who undergo radical prostatectomy will have some form of stress incontinence, and 32 percent will be impotent.[35] Another cost that was not tabulated in the current study is that of litigation if any of these cases had gone on to inappropriate radical prostatectomy. In a recent case at another hospital in Baltimore, an inappropriate radical prostatectomy resulting from the mislabeling of two patients' prostate needle biopsies was settled for $550,000.[36] We also did not factor in the cost of radiology studies that were performed following the misdiagnosis of cancer. Whether the costs of these studies can be saved depends on the timing of the review process relative to the initiation of the metastatic work-up. The six men in our study who are currently felt not to have cancer had a total of five bone scans, four computerized tomography scans, and one routine bone radiograph prior to their biopsy review.

The rate of change in diagnosis for review of prostate pathology (1.3%) is comparable with another study at our institution which found a 1.2 percent rate of change in diagnosis for genitourinary pathology.[20] This study from a different time period suggests that, at least for the prostate, the rate of change in diagnosis in our department is relatively constant over time.

The 1 percent false-positive rate in outside pathology diagnoses seen in this Johns Hopkins study may not seem high compared to the nonconformity rate in second-opinion surgical programs. However, the incidence of pathology misdiagnoses is high when total cost and unnecessary patient morbidity are considered. Because a discordant diagnosis was initially recognized by general surgical pathologists, we feel our findings are generalized and do not reflect a second opinion by an "expert."

The current study also evaluated the straightforward issue of a case diagnosed on the outside as malignant that was reviewed and changed to a benign diagnosis. Other advantages of a second-opinion pathology program for prostate needle biopsies include potential changes in the diagnosis as regards the extent and grade of tumor as discussed above in the Literature Review.

In summary, we found that the second-opinion pathology review of prostate biopsy prior to radical prostatectomy resulted in a significant change in treatment for 6 of the 535 consecutive cases studied. In the current study, the majority of misdiagnoses were rendered at teaching institutions of varying sizes, such that one cannot use the size or nature of the institution which rendered the outside diagnosis to decide whether a review of the outside diagnosis is necessary. The cost of re-reviewing was more than offset by the actual savings from reduced surgery and by the avoidance of lost wages and potential litigation. Our findings thus indicate that a second review of prostate biopsy prior to surgery is a cost-effective way to improve the quality of clinical treatment of prostate cancer.

FUTURE DIRECTIONS

Although a policy of mandatory second-opinion surgical pathology and cytopathology for referred patients makes good clinical and risk management sense and has been recommended by the Association of Directors of Anatomic and Surgical Pathology, current trends in medical economics has placed this and other quality assurance practices at possible risk.[37–39] Mandatory second-opinion pathology uncovers a significant number of discrepant diagnoses, and pathologic review should be undertaken prior to a major therapeutic endeavor. Although only one study[32] has demonstrated the cost-effectiveness of second-opinion pathology, it can be assumed that such programs, when applied to all organ systems, would most certainly pay for themselves especially considering the high individual and litigation costs associated with unnecessary surgery. In the future, the use of telepathology may expedite the review of diagnostic materials. Because of cost considerations, slow transmission times, and the potential problems with image selection, this technique is not yet ready for clinical practice. Disseminating information on the value of mandatory second opinions in pathology to physicians and medical administrators should increase the use of this practice, resulting in better and more cost-effective patient care.

REFERENCES

1. McCarthy EG, Finkel ML, Ruchlin HS. Second opinions on elective surgery: the Cornell/New York Hospital study. Lancet 1981;1:1352–4.

2. Ruchlin HS, Finkel ML, McCarthy EG. The efficiency of second-opinion consultation programs: a cost-benefit perspective. Med Care 1982;20:3–19.

3. Gertman PM, Stackpole DA, Levenson DK, et al. Second opinions for elective surgery: the mandatory Medicaid program in Massachusetts. N Engl J Med 1980;302:1169–74.

4. Martin SG, Shwartz M, Whalen BJ, et al. Impact of a mandatory second-opinion program on Medicaid surgery rates. Med Care 1982;20:21–45.

5. Leslie KO, Fechner RE, Kempson RL. Second opinions in surgical pathology. Am J Clin Pathol 1996;106:58–64.

6. Kim H, Zelman RJ, Fox MA, et al. Pathology panel for lymphoma clinical studies: a comprehensive analysis of cases accumulated since its inception. J Natl Cancer Inst 1982;68:43–67.

7. McGowan L, Norris HJ. The mistaken diagnosis of carcinoma of the ovary. Surg Gynecol Obstet 1991;173:211–15.

8. Harris M, Hartley AL, Blair V, et al. Sarcomas in North West England: I. Histopathological peer review. Br J Cancer 1991;64:315–20.

9. Bruner JM, Inouye L, Fuller GN, Langford LA. Diagnostic discrepancies and their clinical impact in a neuropathology referral practice. Cancer 1997;79:796–803.

10. Scott CB, Nelson JS, Farnan NC, et al. Central pathology review in clinical trials for patients with malignant glioma. Cancer 1995;76:307–13.

11. Boiko PE, Piepkorn MW. Reliability of skin biopsy pathology. J Am Fam Prac 1994;7:371–4.

12. Safrin RE, Bark CJ. Surgical pathology signout: routine review of every case by a second pathologist. Am J Surg Pathol 1993;17:1190–2.

13. Lind AC, Bewtra C, Healy JC, Sims KL. Prospective peer review in surgical pathology. Am J Clin Pathol 1995;104:560–6.

14. Catalona WJ, Richie JP, Ahmann FR, et al. Comparison of digital rectal examination and serum prostate specific antigen in the early detection of prostate cancer: results of a multicenter clinical trial of 6,630 men. J Urol 1994;151:1283–90.

15. Finkel ML, McCarthy EG, Ruchlin HS. The current status of surgical second opinion programs. Surg Clin North Am 1982;62:705–19.

16. Santoso JT, Coleman RL, Voet RL, et al. Pathology slide review in gynecologic oncology. Obstet Gynecol 1998;91:730–4.

17. Whitehead ME, Fitzwater JE, Lindley SK, et al. Quality assurance of histopathologic diagnosis: a prospective audit of three thousand cases. Am J Clin Pathol 1984;81:487–91.

18. Allen EA, Kronz JD, Rosenthal DL. Second opinion cytopathology at a large referral center. Mod Pathol 1999;12:39A.

19. Abt AB, Abt LG, Olt GJ. The effect of interinstitution anatomic pathology consultation on patient care. Arch Pathol Lab Med 1995;119:514–17.

20. Kronz JD, Westra WH, Epstein JI. Mandatory second opinion surgical pathology at a large referral hospital. Cancer 1999. [In press]

21. Colby TV. Malignancies in the lung and pleura mimicking benign processes. Semin Diagn Pathol 1995;12:30–44.

22. Carter D. Histologic classification and differential diagnosis of mesothelioma. Yale J Biol Med 1981;54:173–80.

23. Whitaker D, Shilkin KB. Diagnosis of pleural malignant mesothelioma in life—a practical approach. J Pathol 1984;143:147–75.

24. Epstein JI, Budin RE. Keratin and epithelial membrane antigen immunoreactivity in nonneoplastic fibrous pleural lesions. Hum Pathol 1986;17:514–19.

25. Jacques SM, Qufeshi F, Munkarah A, Lawrence WD. Value of second opinion pathology review for post-hysterectomy women with endometrial cancer. Mod Pathol 1997;10:103A.

26. Jacques SM, Qufeshi F, Munkarah A, Lawrence WD. Value of second opinion pathology review of endometrial cancer diagnosed on uterine curettings and biopsies. Mod Pathol 1997;10:103A.

27. Iczkowski KA, Bassler TJ, Schwob VS, et al. Diagnosis of "suspicious for malignancy" in prostate biopsies: predictive value for cancer. Urology 1998;51:749–58.

28. Chan TY, Epstein JI. Follow up of atypical prostate needle biopsies. Urology 1999;53:351–5.

29. Epstein JI, Walsh PC, CarMichael M, Brendler CB. Pathologic and clinical findings to predict tumor extent of nonpalpable (stage T1c) prostate cancer. JAMA 1994;271:368–74.

30. Boring CC, Squires TS, Tong T. Cancer statistics. CA Cancer J Clin 1993;43:7.

31. Olsson CA, Goluboff ET. Detection and treatment of prostate cancer: perspective of the urologist. J Urol 1994; 152:1695–9.

32. Epstein JI, Walsh PC, Sanfilippo F. Clinical and cost impact of second-opinion pathology: review of prostate biopsies prior to radical prostatectomy. Am J Surg Pathol 1996;20:851–7.

33. Gaudin PB, Epstein JI. Adenosis of the prostate: histologic features in needle biopsy specimens. Am J Surg Pathol 1995;19:737–47.

34. Wojno KJ, Epstein JI. The utility of basal cell specific anti-cytokeratin antibody (34 beta E12) in the diagnosis of prostate cancer: a review of 228 cases. Am J Surg Pathol 1995;19:251–60.

35. Walsh PC, Partin AW, Epstein JI. Cancer control and quality of life following anatomical radical retropubic prostatectomy: results at 10 years. J Urol 1994;152:1831–6.

36. Prostate cancer lost to an error: patient will get $550,000. The Baltimore Sun 1995 Mar 11; Sect B:1b–2b.

37. Association of Directors of Anatomic and Surgical Pathology. Consultations in surgical pathology. Am J Surg Pathol 1993;17:743–5.

38. Monaco GP, Goldschmidt P. What is proper cancer care in the era of managed care? Oncology 1997;11:65–71.

39. Eisenberg JM. Economics. JAMA 1995;273:1670–1.

Index